ENCYCLOPEDIA OF
MULTIMEDIA

ENCYCLOPEDIA OF MULTIMEDIA

Editor-in-Chief

Borko Furht

Florida Atlantic University
USA

 Springer

Borko Furht, Department Chair
Dept. of Computer Science and Engineering
Florida Atlantic University
Boca Raton, FL 33431

Library of Congress Control Number: 2005935085

ENCYCLOPEDIA OF MULTIMEDIA
Edited by Borko Furht

ISBN-13: 978-0-387-24395-5
ISBN-10: 0-387-24395-X
e-ISBN-13: 978-0-387-30038-2
e-ISBN-10: 0-387-30038-4

Printed on acid-free paper.

Printed in the United States of America.

9 8 7 6 5 4 3 2

springer.com

Encyclopedia of Multimedia

Editor: Borko Furht

Editorial Board

Marios Angelides
Brunel University, UK

Abhaya Asthana
Lucent Technologies, USA

Alan Bovik
University of Texas at Austin, USA

Alberto Del Bimbo
University of Florence, Italy

Nevenka Dimitrova
Philips Research, Briarcliff Manor,
NY, USA

Chabane Djeraba
University of Sciences and
Technologies of Lille, France

Schahram Dustdar
Vienna University of Technology,
Austria

Ahmet Eskicioglu
Brooklyn College, USA

Benjamin Falchuk
Telcordia Technologies, USA

Shahram Ghandeharizadeh
University of Southern California,
USA

David Gibbon
AT&T Labs Research, Middletown,
USA

Forouzan Golshani
Wright State University, USA

Yihong Gong
NEC Laboratories America,
Cupertino, CA, USA

William Grosky
University of Michigan – Dearborn,
USA

Horace Ip
City University of Hong Kong,
Hong Kong

Hari Kalva
Florida Atlantic University, USA

Shunsuke Kamijo
University of Tokyo, Japan

Kwok-Tung Lo
The Hong Kong Polytechnic
University, Hong Kong, China

Wei-Ying Ma
Microsoft Research, Beijing, China

TABLE OF CONTENTS

Contributors

Mohamed Abdel-Mottaleb
University of Miami, Coral Gables, Florida, USA

Harry Agius
Brunel University, Uxbridge, UK

M. Albanese
University of Napoli, Italy

Patrick Alleaume
OuestAudiovisuel, France

Marcelo Dias de Amorim
National Center for Scientific Research, Paris, France

Marios Angelides
Brunel University, Uxbridge, UK

Abhaya Asthana
Lucent Technologies, Westford, MA, USA

Yannis Avrithis
National Technical University of Athens, Greece

Bruno Bachimont
UTC-Heudiasyc, France

Francois Bar
University of Southern California, Los Angeles, CA, USA

Fatima Belkouch
University of Lille, France

Marco Bertini
University of Florence, Italy

Ioan Marius Bilasco
Laboratoire LSR-IMAG, Grenoble, France

Jean de Bissy
Sylis, France

Fatma Bouali
University of Lille, France

Alan Bovik
University of Texas at Austin, USA

Paul Dr Bra
Eindhoven University of Technology, The Netherlands

Stefano Cacciaguerra
University of Bologna, Italy

C. Cesarano
University of Napoli, Italy

Rong-Chi Chang
Tamkang University, Taiwan

Chang Wen Chen
Florida Institute of Technology, Melbourne, USA

Longbin Chen
University of Miami, Coral Gables, Florida, USA

Yu-Ping Chen
Tamkang University, Taiwan

Su-Mei Chou
Tamkang University, Taiwan

Chris Crockford
Brunel University, Uxbridge, UK

Alberto Del Bimbo
University of Florence, Italy

Nevenka Dimitrova
Philips Research, Briarcliff Manor,
NY, USA

Jana Dittmann
Otto-von-Gerick University,
Magdeburg, Germany

Chabane Djeraba
University of Sciences and
Technologies of Lille, France

Alen Docef
Virginia Commonwealth University,
Richmond, Virginia, USA

Schahram Dustdar
Technical University of Vienna,
Austria

Abdulmotaleb El Saddik
University of Ottawa, Canada

Ahmet M. Eskicioglu
Brooklyn College, USA

Benjamin Falchuk
Telcordia Technologies, Piscataway,
NJ, USA

Jun Fan
Philips Research, Briarcliff Manor,
NY, USA

M. Fayzullin
University of Maryland, College
Park, MD, USA

J. Feng
City University of Hong Kong,
Hong Kong, China

Stefano Ferretti
University of Bologna, Italy

Apple W.P. Fok
City University of Hong Kong,
Hong Kong

Jerome Gensel
Laboratoire LSR-IMAG, Grenoble,
France

Edouard Gerard
Sylis, France

Shahram Ghandeharizadeh
University of Southern California,
Los Angeles, CA, USA

David Gibbon
AT&T Labs Research, Middletown,
NJ, USA

Athanasisos Gkoritsas
Brunel University, Uxbridge, UK

Forouzan Golshani
Wright State University, Dayton,
Ohio, USA

Yihong Gong
NEC Laboratories America,
Cupertino, CA, USA

N. Grammalidis
Informatics and Telematics Institute,
Thessaloniki, Greece

William Grosky
University of Michigan – Dearborn,
USA

Zhihai He
University of Missouri-Columbia,
USA

Ahmed Helmy
University of Southern California,
Los Angeles, CA, USA

Nicola Henze
University of Hannover, Germany

K.M. Ho
The Hong Kong Polytechnic
University, Hong Kong, China

Md. Shamim Hossain
University of Ottawa, Canada

Huan-Chi Huang
Tamkang University, Taiwan

Horace Ip
City University of Hong Kong,
Hong Kong

Ebroul Izquierdo
Queen Mary, University of London,
UK

Vinod Jayaraman
NTT Multimedia Labs, Palo Alto,
California, USA

Hari Kalva
Florida Atlantic University, Boca
Raton, FL, USA

Shunsuke Kamijo
University of Tokyo, Japan

Kostas Karpouzis
National Technical University of
Athens, Athens, Greece

Moinul H. Khan
Intel Corporation, Austin, Texas,
USA

Seon Ho Kim
University of Denver, Colorado,
USA

Ross King
Research Studio Digital Memory
Engineering, Vienna, Austria

Wolfgang Klas
University of Vienna, Vienna,
Austria

Stefanos Kollias
National Technical University of
Athens, Greece

Ioannis Kompatsiaris
Informatics and Telematics Institute,
Thessaloniki, Greece

Faouzi Kossentini
UB Video, Vancouver, Canada

Bhaskar Krishnamachari
University of Southern California,
Los Angeles, CA, USA

Deepa Kundur
Texas A&M University, College
Station, USA

Junqiang Lan
Harmonic, New York, USA

Jae-Beom Lee
Intel Corporation, Portland, USA

Hui Li
University of Texas at Dallas, USA

Mingjing Li
Microsoft Research Asia, Beijing,
China

Joo-Hwee Lim
Institute for Infocomm Research,
Singapore

Leslie S. Liu
University of Southern California,
Los Angeles, California, USA

Kwok-Tung Lo
The Hong Kong Polytechnic
University, Hong Kong, China

Oliver Lombard
OuestAudiovisuel, France

William Luh
Texas A&M University, College
Station, USA

Rastislav Lukac
University of Toronto, Toronto,
Canada

Wei-Ying Ma
Microsoft Research Asia, Beijing,
China

Lambros Makris
Informatics and Telemetics Institute,
Thessaloniki, Greece

Sotiris Malassiotis
Informatics and Telemetics Institute,
Thessaloniki, Greece

Hong Man
Stevens Institute of Technology,
Hoboken, New Jersey, USA

Oge Marques
Florida Atlantic University, Boca
Raton, FL, USA

Herve Martin
Laboratoire LSR-IMAG, Grenoble,
France

Vasileios Mezaris
Aristotle University of Thessaloniki,
Greece

Arthur G. Money
Brunel University, Uxbridge, UK

Sylvain Mongy
University of Lille, France

Marta Mrak
Queen Mary, University of London,
UK

Erich Neuhold
Fraunhofer Institute IPSI,
Darmstadt, Germany

Claundia Niederee
Fraunhofer Institute IPSI,
Darmstadt, Germany

Jauvane C. de Oliveira
National Laboratory for Scientific Computation, Petropolis, Brazil

Sharon Oviatt
Oregon Health and Sciences University, USA

Minaz Parmar
Brunel University, Uxbridge, UK

Nigel C. Paver
Intel Corporation, Austin, Texas, USA

Vasanth Philomin
Philips Research, Aachen, Germany

A. Picariello
University of Napoli, Italy

Konstantions N. Plataniotis
University of Toronto, Toronto, Canada

W.F. Poon
The Hong Kong Polytechnic University, Hong Kong, China

Balakrishnan Prabhakaran
University of Texas at Dallas, USA

Min Qin
University of Southern California, Los Angeles, California, USA

Roope Raismo
University of Tampere, Finland

Todd Richmond
University of Southern California, Los Angeles, CA, USA

Wayne Robbins
Defense R&D Canada, Ottawa, Canada

Marco Roccetti
University of Bologna, Italy

Thanassis Rikakis
Arizona State University, Tempe, AZ, USA

Paola Salomoni
University of Bologna, Italy

Simone Santini
University of California, San Diego, USA and Universidad Autonoma de Madrid, Spain

Shin'ichi Satoh
National Institute of Informatics, Tokyo, Japan

Markus W. Schranz
Pressetext GmbH, Austria

Kalpana Seshandrinathan
University of Texas at Austin, USA

Pallavi Shah
Hewlett Packard, USA

Nalin Sharda
Victoria University of Technology, Melbourne, Australia

Xiaojun Shen
University of Ottawa, Canada

Timothy K. Shih
Tamkang University, Taiwan

Shervin Shirmohammadi
University of Ottawa, Canada

Anastasis Sofokleous
Brunel University, Uxbridge, UK

Martin Steinebach
Fraunhofer IPSI, Darmstadt,
Germany

Giorgod Stamou
National Technical University of
Athens, Greece

Michael Stritntzis
Aristotle University of Thessaloniki,
Greece

V.S. Subhramanian
University of Maryland, College
Park, MD, USA

Hari Sundaram
Arizona State University, Tempe,
AZ, USA

Johan W.H. Tangelder
Centre for Mathematics and
Computer Science, Amsterdam,
The Netherlands

G. Triantafyllidis
Informatics and Telematics Institute,
Thessaloniki, Greece

Filareti Tsalakanidou
Aristotle University of Thessalonki,
Thessaloniki, Greece

Robert Turetsky
Columbia University, New York,
USA

Matthew Turk
University of California, Santa
Barbara, USA

Rainer Typke
Utrecht University, The Netherlands

Thierry Urruty
University of Lille, France

Vladimir Uskov
Bradley University, USA

Bharadwaj Veeravalli
National University of Singapore,
Singapore

Remco Veltkamp
Utrecht University, The Netherlands

Anastasios N. Venetsanopoulos
University of Toronto, Toronto,
Canada

Claus Villager
Otto-von-Gerick University,
Magdeburg, Germany

Marlene Villanova-Oliver
Laboratoire LSR-IMAG, Grenoble,
France

Manolis Wallace
National Technical University of
Athens, Greece

Frans Wiering
Utrecht University, The Netherlands

Hau San Wong
City University of Hong Kong,
Hong Kong

Ching-Nung Yang
National Dong Hwa University,
Shou-Feng, Taiwan

Heather Yu
Panasonic Technologies, Princeton,
New Jersey, USA

Wenjun Zeng
University of Missouri, Colombia,
MO, USA

Qian Zhang
Microsoft Research Asia, Beijing,
China

Jiying Zhao
University of Ottawa, Canada

Roger Zimmermann
University of Southern California,
Los Angeles, California, USA

Artur Ziviani
National Laboratory for Scientific
Computing, Petropolis, Brazil

PREFACE

Only a decade ago, multimedia seemed like a brand new research field and an emerging new industry. Today, at the beginning of the new millennium, multimedia has come of age and the multimedia industry has significantly grown. Another aspect of the digital media revolution is the formation of the new media industry comprised of computer, communication, entertainment, and consumer electronic companies.

The *Encyclopedia of Multimedia* provides in-depth coverage of the important concepts, issues and technology trends in the field of multimedia technologies, systems, techniques, and applications. It is a comprehensive collection of entries that present perspectives and future trends in the field from hundreds of leading researchers and experts in the field. The entries in the book describe a number of topics in multimedia systems and applications – from multimedia servers, to multimedia databases and multimedia networks and communications, to emerging multimedia applications.

The editor, working with the Encyclopedia's Editorial Board and a large number of contributors, surveyed and divided the field of multimedia into specific topics that collectively encompass the foundations, technologies, applications, and emerging elements of this exciting field. The members of the Editorial Board and the contributors are world experts in the field of multimedia from both academia and industry. The total number of contributors is 145, who have written total of 265 entries - 85 long and 180 short entries.

The Encyclopedia's intended audience is technically diverse and wide; it includes anyone concerned with multimedia systems and their applications. Specifically, the Encyclopedia can serve as a valuable reference for researchers and scientists, system designers, engineers, programmers, and managers who are involved in multimedia system design and their applications.

I would like to thank the members of the Editorial Board for their help in creating this Encyclopedia, as well as the authors for their individual contributions. The members of the Editorial Board assisted in selecting the entries, they wrote one or more long and short entries, and they solicited the other contributors. Without the expertise and effort of the contributors, this Encyclopedia would never have come to fruition. I would also like to thank Tami Sorgente, Instructor in the Department of Computer Science and Engineering at Florida Atlantic University, for her great help in formatting and styling the Encyclopedia. Special thanks go to Springer's editors and staff, including Jennifer Evans, Susan Langerstrom-Fife, Oona Schmid, and Sharon Palleschi. They deserve my sincere recognition for their support throughout the project.

Editor

Borko Furht
Boca Raton, Florida

Editor-in-Chief

 Borko Furht is a professor and chairman of the Department of Computer Science and Engineering at Florida Atlantic University (FAU) in Boca Raton, Florida. Before joining FAU, he was a vice president of research and a senior director of development at Modcomp (Ft. Lauderdale), a computer company of Daimler Benz, Germany, a professor at University of Miami in Coral Gables, Florida, and a senior researcher in the Institute Boris Kidric-Vinca, Yugoslavia. Professor Furht received Ph.D. degree in electrical and computer engineering from the University of Belgrade. His current research is in multimedia systems, video coding and compression, 3D video and image systems, video databases, wireless multimedia, and Internet computing. He is presently Principal Investigator and Co-PI of two multiyear, multimillion dollar projects – on Coastline Security Technologies, funded by the Department of Navy, and One Pass to Production, funded by Motorola. He is the author of numerous books and articles in the areas of multimedia, computer architecture, real-time computing, and operating systems. He is a founder and editor-in-chief of *the Journal of Multimedia Tools and Applications* (Springer). He has received several technical and publishing awards, and has consulted for many high-tech companies including IBM, Hewlett-Packard, Xerox, General Electric, JPL, NASA, Honeywell, and RCA. He has also served as a consultant to various colleges and universities. He has given many invited talks, keynote lectures, seminars, and tutorials. He served on the Board of Directors of several high-tech companies.

A

ACTIVE BUFFER MANAGEMENT FOR PROVISION OF VCR FUNCTIONALITIES

Definition: *Active buffer management is used to adjust the contents of the buffer after execution of VCR functions in VoD systems.*

The problem of providing VCR functions with the traditional buffering schemes is that the effects of VCR actions in the same direction are cumulative. When consecutive VCR actions in the same direction are performed, the play point will ultimately move to a boundary of the buffer. Thus, the active buffer management (ABM) scheme [1] was developed to use a buffer manager to adjust the contents of the buffer after the VCR functions such that the relative position of the play point can stay in the middle of the buffer. Figure 1 shows the basic operational principle of ABM in a staggered VoD system with no VCR actions. Assuming the buffer can hold 3 segments. At some point, the buffer downloads segments z, z+1, z+2 and the play point is in segment z+1. If there is no VCR action, after a period of time, the play point will be at the start of segment z+2. At this moment, in order to keep the play point in the middle, the client will download segment z+3 and segment z will be discarded.

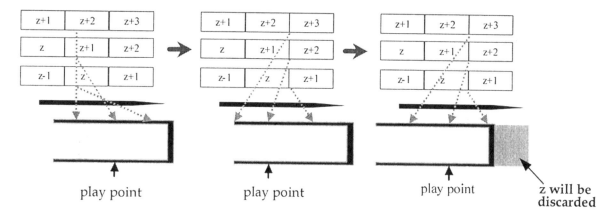

Figure 1. Active buffer management scheme without VCR action.

For the scenario with an interactive function, it is assumed that the buffer now holds segment *z*, *z+1* and *z+2*. If a FF action as illustrated in Figure 2 is issued and the play point moves to the end of segment *z+2*, the buffer manager will select segment *z+3* and

$z+4$ to download. The play point will thus be moved back to the middle segment after one segment time. This is segment $z+3$ in this case.

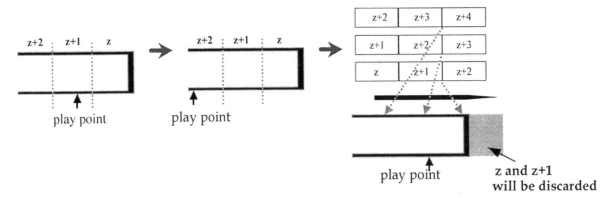

Figure 2. Active buffer management scheme with FF action.

See: Large-Scale Video-on-Demand System

References

1. Z. Fei, M.H. Ammar, I. Kamel, and S. Mukherjee, "Providing interactive functions for staggered multicast near video-on-demand," *Proceedings of IEEE International Conference on Multimedia Computing and Systems '99*, 1999, pp. 949-953.

ADAPTIVE EDUCATIONAL HYPERMEDIA SYSTEMS

Definition: Adaptive educational hypermedia systems include adaptive functionality based on three components: the document space, observations, and the user model.

To support re-usability and comparability of adaptive educational hypermedia systems, we give a component-based definition of adaptive educational hypermedia systems (AEHS), extending the functionality-oriented definition of adaptive hypermedia given by Brusilovsky in 1996 [1]. AEHS have been developed and tested in various disciplines and have proven their usefulness for improved and goal-oriented learning and teaching. However, these systems normally come along as stand-alone systems - proprietary solutions have been investigated, tested and improved to fulfill specific, often domain-dependent requirements. This phenomenon is known in the literature as the *open corpus problem in AEHS* [2] which states that normally, adaptive applications work on a fixed set of documents which is defined at the design time of the system, and directly influences the way adaptation is implemented.

The logical definition of adaptive educational hypermedia given here focuses on the components of these systems, and describes which kind of processing information is needed from the underlying hypermedia system (*the document space*), the runtime information which is required (*observations*), and the user model characteristics (*user model). Adaptive functionality* is then described by means of these three components, or more precisely: how the information from these three components, the static data from the document space, the runtime-data from the observations, and the processing-data from the user model, is used to provide adaptive functionality. The given logical definition of adaptive educational hypermedia provides a language for describing adaptive functionality, and allows for the comparison of adaptive functionality in a well-grounded way, enabling the re-use of adaptive functionality in different contexts and systems. The applicability of this formal description has been demonstrated in [3].

An Adaptive Educational Hypermedia System (AEHS) is a Quadruple (DOCS, UM, OBS, AC) with:

DOCS: *Document Space: A finite set of first order logic (FOL) sentences with constants for describing documents (and knowledge topics), and predicates for defining relations between these constants.*

UM: *User Model: A finite set of FOL sentences with constants for describing individual users (user groups), and user characteristics, as well as predicates and rules for expressing whether a characteristic applies to a user.*

OBS: *Observations: A finite set of FOL sentences with constants for describing observations and predicates for relating users, documents / topics, and observations.*

AC: *Adaptation Component: A finite set of FOL sentences with rules for describing adaptive functionality.*

With the emerging Semantic Web, there is even more the need for comparable, re-usable adaptive functionality. If we consider adaptive functionality as a service on the Semantic Web, we need re-usable adaptive functionality, able to operate on an open corpus, which the Web is.

See: Personalized Educational Hypermedia

References

1. P. Brusilovsky, "Methods and techniques of adaptive hypermedia," User Modeling and User Adapted Interaction, Vol. 6, No. 2-3, 1996, pp. 87-129.
2. P. Brusilovsky, "Adaptive Hypermedia," User Modeling and User-Adapted Interaction, Vol. 11, 2001, pp. 87-110.
3. N. Henze and W. Nejdl, "A Logical Characterization of Adaptive Educational Hypermedia,",New Review of Hypermedia, Vol. 10, No. 1, 2004.

ANALYZING PERSON INFORMATION IN NEWS VIDEO

Shin'ichi Satoh
National Institute of Informatics, Tokyo, Japan

Definition: *Analyzing person information in news video includes the identification of various attributes of a person, such as face detection and recognition, face-name association, and others.*

4 A

Introduction

Person information analysis for news videos, including face detection and recognition, face-name association, etc., has attracted many researchers in the video indexing field. One reason for this is the importance of person information. In our social interactions, we use face as symbolic information to identify each other. This strengthens the importance of face among many types of visual information, and thus face image processing has been intensively studied for decades by image processing and computer vision researchers. As an outcome, robust face detection and recognition techniques have been proposed. Therefore, face information in news videos is rather more easily accessible compared to the other types of visual information.

In addition, especially in news, person information is the most important; for instance, "*who* said this?", "*who* went there?", "*who* did this?", etc., could be the major information which news provides. Among all such types of person information, "*who* is this?" information, i.e., face-name association, is the most basic as well as the most important information. Despite its basic nature, face-name association is not an easy task for computers; in some cases, it requires in-depth semantic analysis of videos, which is never achieved yet even by the most advanced technologies. This is another reason why face-name association still attracts many researchers: face-name association is a good touchstone of video analysis technologies.

This article describes about face-name association in news videos. In doing this, we take one of the earliest attempts as an example: Name-It. We briefly describe its mechanism. Then we compare it with corpus-based natural language processing and information retrieval techniques, and show the effectiveness of corpus-based video analysis.

Face-Name Association: Name-It Approach

Typical processing of face-name association is as follows:

- Extracts faces from images (videos)
- Extracts names from speech (closed-caption (CC) text)
- Associates faces and names

This looks very simple. Let's assume that we have a segment of news video as shown in Figure 1. We don't feel any difficulty in associating the face and name when we watch this news video segment, i.e., the face corresponds to "Bill Clinton" even though we don't know the person beforehand. Video information is composed mainly of two streams: visual stream and speech (or CC) stream. Usually each one of these is not direct explanation of another. For instance, if visual information is shown as Figure 1, the corresponding speech will not be: "The person shown here is Mr. Clinton. He is making speech on...," which is the direct explanation of the visual information. If so the news video could be too redundant and tedious to viewers. Instead they are complementary each other, and thus concise and easy to understand for people. However, it is very hard for computers to analyze news video segments. In order to associate the face and name shown in Figure 1, computers need to understand visual stream so that a person shown is making speech, and to understand text stream that the news is about a speech by Mr.

Clinton, and thus to realize the person corresponds to Mr. Clinton. This correspondence is shown only implicitly, which makes the analysis difficult for computers. This requires image/video understanding as well as speech/text understanding, which themselves are still very difficult tasks.

```
6902 >>> PRESIDENT CLINTON MET
6963 WITH FRENCH PRESIDENT
6993 JACQUES CHIRAC TODAY
7023 AT THE WHITE HOUSE.
7083 MR. CLINTON SAID HE WELCOMED
7113 FRANCE'S DECISION TO END
7143 ITS NUCLEAR TEST PROGRAM
7204 IN THE PACIFIC AND PLEDGED
7234 TO WORK WITH FRANCE TO BAN
7264 FUTURE TESTS.
```

Figure 1. Example of news video segment.

Name-It [3] is one of the earliest systems tackling the problem of face-name association in news videos. Name-It assumes that image stream processing, i.e., face extraction, as well as text stream processing, i.e., name extraction, are not necessarily perfect. Thus the proper face-name association cannot be realized only from each segment. For example, from the segment shown in Figure 1, it is possible for computers that the face shown here can be associated with "Clinton" or "Chirac," but the ambiguity between these cannot be resolved. To handle this situation, Name-It takes a corpus-based video analysis approach to obtain sufficiently reliable face-name association from imperfect image/text stream understanding results.

The architecture of Name-It is shown in Figure 2. Since closed-captioned CNN Headline News is used as news video corpus, given news videos are composed of a video portion along with a transcript (closed-caption text) portion. From video images, the system extracts faces of persons who might be mentioned in transcripts. Meanwhile, from transcripts, the system extracts words corresponding to persons who might appear in videos. Since names and faces are both extracted from videos, they furnish additional timing information, i.e., at what time in videos they appear. The association of names and faces is evaluated with a "co-occurrence" factor using their timing information. Co-occurrence of a name and a face expresses how often and how well the name coincides

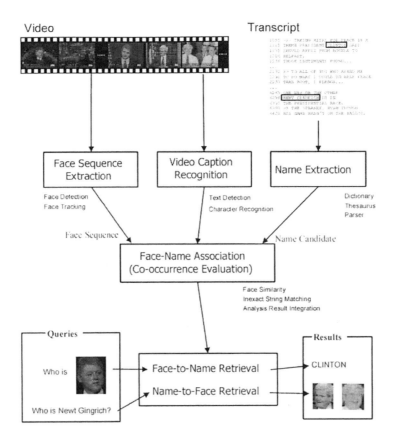

Figure 2. The architecture of Name-It.

with the face in given news video archives. In addition, the system also extracts video captions from video images. Extracted video captions are recognized to obtain text information, and then used to enhance the quality of face-name association. By the co-occurrence, the system collects ambiguous face-name association cues, each of which is obtained from each news video segment, over the entire news video corpus, to obtain sufficiently reliable face-name association results. Figure 3 shows the results of face-name association by using five hours of CNN Headline News videos as corpus.

A key idea of Name-It is to evaluate co-occurrence between a face and name by comparing the occurrence patterns of the face and name in news video corpus. To do so, it is obviously required to locate a face and name in video corpus. It is rather straight forward to locate names in closed-captioned video corpus, since closed-caption text is symbol information. In order to locate faces, a face matching technique is used. In other words, by face matching, face information in news video corpus is symbolized. This enables co-occurrence evaluation between faces and names. Similar techniques can be found in the natural language processing and information retrieval fields. For instance, the vector space model [5] regards that documents are similar when they share similar terms, i.e., have similar occurrence patterns of terms. In Latent Semantic Indexing [6], terms having similar occurrence patterns in documents within corpus compose a latent concept. Similar to these, Name-It finds face-name pairs having similar occurrence patterns in news video corpus as associated face-name pairs. Figure 4 shows occurrence patterns of faces and names. Co-occurrence of a face and name is realized by correlation between occurrence patterns of the face and name. In this example, "MILLER" and F_1, "CLINTON" and F_2, respectively, will be associated because corresponding occurrence patters are similar.

Figure 3. Face and name association results.

Conclusions and Future Directions

This article describes about face-name association in videos, especially Name-It, in order to demonstrate the effectiveness of corpus-based video analysis. There are potential directions to enhance and extend corpus-based face-name association. One possible direction is to elaborate component technologies such as name extraction, face extraction, and face matching. Recent advanced information extraction and natural language processing techniques enable almost perfect name extraction from text. In addition, they can provide further information such as roles of names in sentences and documents, which surely enhances the face-name association performance.

Advanced image processing or computer vision techniques will enhance the quality of symbolization of faces in video corpus. Robust face detection and tracking in videos is still challenging task (such as [7]. In [8] a comprehensive survey of face detection is presented). Robust and accurate face matching will rectify the occurrence patterns of faces (Figure 4), which enhances face-name association. Many research efforts have been made in face recognition, especially for surveillance and biometrics. Face recognition for videos could be the next frontier. In [10] a comprehensive survey for face recognition is presented. In addition to face detection and recognition, behavior analysis is also helpful, especially to associate the behavior with person's activity described in text.

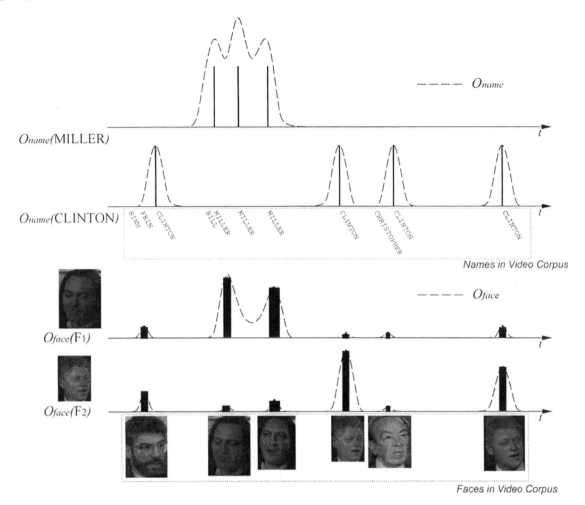

Figure 4. Face and name occurrence patterns.

Usage of the other modalities is also promising. In addition to images, closed-caption text, and video captions, speaker identification provides a powerful cue for face-name association for monologue shots [0, 1].

In integrating face and name detection results, Name-It uses co-occurrence, which is based on coincidence. However, as mentioned before, since news videos are concise and easy to understand for people, relationship between corresponding faces and names is not so simple as coincidence, but may yield a kind of video grammar. In order to handle this, the system ultimately needs to "understand" videos as people do. In [2] an attempt to model this relationship as temporal probability distribution is presented. In order to enhance the integration, we need much elaborated video grammar, which intelligently integrate text processing results and image processing results.

It could be beneficial if corpus-based video analysis approach is applied to general objects in addition to faces. However, obviously it is not feasible to realize detection and recognition of many types of objects. Instead, in [9] one of the promising approaches is presented. The method extracts interest points from videos, and then visual features are calculated for each point. These points are then clustered by features into "words," and then a text retrieval technique is applied for object retrieval for videos. By this, the method symbolizes objects shown in videos as "words," which could be useful to extend corpus-based video analysis to general objects.

References

1. M. Li, D. Li, N. Dimitrova, and I. Sethi, "Audio-Visual Talking Face Detection," Proceedings of the International Conference on Multimedia and Expo (ICME2003), 2003.
2. C. G. M. Snoek and A. G. Haptmann, "Learning to Identify TV News Monologues by Style and Context," CMU Technical Report, CMU-CS-03-193, 2003.
3. J. Yang, M. Chen, and A. Hauptmann, "Finding Person X: Correlating Names with Visual Appearances," Proceedings of the International Conference on Image and Video Retrieval (CIVR'04), 2004.
4. S. Satoh, Y. Nakamura, and T. Kanade, "Name-It: Naming and Detecting Faces in News Videos," IEEE MultiMedia, Vol. 6, No. 1, January-March (Spring), 1999, pp. 22-35.
5. R. Baeza-Yates and B. Ribeiro-Neto, "Modern Information Retrieval," Addison Wesley, 1999.
6. S. Deerwester, S. T. Dumais, G. W. Furnas, T. K. Landauer and R. Harshman, "Indexing by Latent Semantic Analysis," Journal of the American Society for Information Science, Vol. 41, 1990, pp. 391-407.
7. R. C. Verma, C. Schmid, and K. Mikolajcayk, "Face Detection and Tracking in a Video by Propagating Detection Probabilities", IEEE Transactions on Pattern Analysis and Machine Intelligence, Vol. 25, No. 10, 2003, pp. 1216-1228.
8. M.-H. Yang, D. J. Kriegman, and N. Ahuja, "Detecting Faces in Images: A Survey," IEEE Transactions on Pattern Analysis and Machine Intelligence, Vol. 24, No. 1, 2002, pp. 34-58.
9. J. Sivic and A. Zisserman, "Video Google: A Text Retrieval Approach to Object Matching in Videos," Proceedings of the International Conference on Computer Vision (ICCV2003), 2003.
10. W. Zhao, R. Chellappa, P. J. Phillips, and A. Rosenfeld, "Face recognition: A literature survey," ACM Computing Surveys, Vol. 35, No. 4, 2003, pp. 399-458.

APPLICATIONS OF FACE RECOGNITION AND NOVEL TRENDS

Definition: A number of contemporary civilian and law enforcement applications require reliable recognition of human faces.

Nowadays, machine recognition of human faces is used in a variety of civilian and law enforcement applications that require reliable recognition of humans. Identity verification for physical access control in buildings or security areas is one of the most common face recognition applications. At the access point, an image of someone's face is captured by a camera and is matched against pre-stored images of the same person. Only if there is a match, access is permitted, e.g. the door opens. For high security areas, a combination with card terminals is possible, so that a double check is performed. Such face recognition systems are installed for example in airports to facilitate the crew and airport staff to pass through different control levels without having to show an ID or passport [1].

To allow secure transactions through the Internet, face verification may be used instead of electronic means like passwords or PIN numbers, which can be easily stolen or forgotten. Such applications include secure transactions in e- & m-commerce and banking, computer network access, and personalized applications like e-health and e-learning. Face identification has also been used in forensic applications for criminal identification (mug-shot matching) and surveillance of public places to detect the presence of criminals or terrorists (for example in airports or in border control). It is also used for government applications like national ID, driver's license, passport and border control, immigration, etc.

Face recognition is also a crucial component of ubiquitous and pervasive computing, which aims at incorporating intelligence in our living environment and allowing humans to interact with machines in a natural way, just like people interact with each other. For example, a smart home should be able to recognize the owners, their family, friends and guests, remember their preferences (from favorite food and TV program to room temperature), understand what they are saying, where are they looking at, what each gesture, movement or expression means, and according to all these cues to be able to facilitate every-day life. The fact that face recognition is an essential tool for interpreting human actions, human emotions, facial expressions, human behavior and intentions, and is also an extremely natural and non-intrusive technique, makes it an excellent choice for ambient intelligence applications [2].

During the last decade wearable devices were developed to help users in their daily activities. Face recognition is an integral part of wearable systems like memory aids or context-aware systems [2]. A real-world application example is the use of mini-cameras and face recognition software, which are embedded into an Alzheimer's patient's glasses, to help her remember the person she is looking at [2].

See: Face Recognition

References

1. A. Jain, A. Ross, and S. Prabhakar, "An introduction to biometric recognition," IEEE Transactions on Circuits and Systems for Video Technology, Vol. 14, No. 1, January 2004, pp. 4-20.
2. A. Pentland and T. Choudhury, "Personalizing smart environments: face recognition for human interaction," IEEE Computer Magazine, Vol. 33, No. 2, February 2000, pp. 50-55.

ARCHITECTURE OF COMMERCIAL NEWS SYSTEMS

Definition: *The architecture of commercial news systems is based on a layered approach consisting of the following layers: data layer, content manipulation layer, news services layer, and end user layer.*

Multimedia news is presented as content of commercial services by national and international agencies and organizations all over the world. The news community is researching for solutions in different application areas, such as high level semantic analysis, provisioning and management of mixed information, and distribution and presentation of media data to satisfy requirements dictated by business scenarios.

Modern news networks, news syndication services, media observation and international news exchange networks are following the customer needs and provide specific services within the multimedia news application domain. The most-used presentation platform for multimedia news herein is the World Wide Web, providing all facets of news aggregation, manipulation, and dissemination as discussed in "Multimedia news systems". Appropriate Web applications integrate multimedia services in complex environments [1] and modern web-based content management systems (WCMS) handle all assets of multimedia news data for personalized user-oriented news presentation.

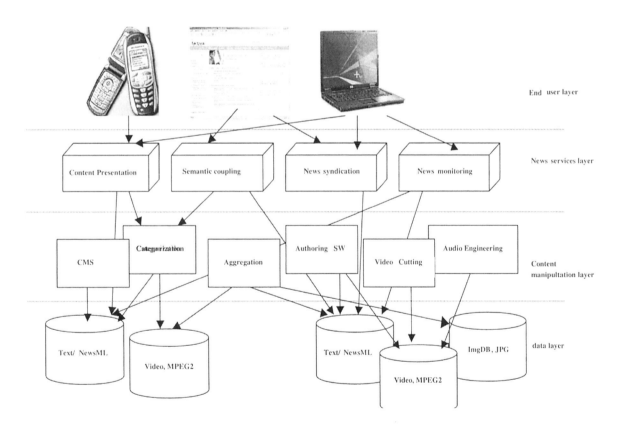

Figure 1. Multimedia news systems layering.

Multimedia news systems typically follow a layered architecture approach as shown in Figure 1. The data layer contains multimedia data that are stored in modern appropriate formats like NewsML for texts, modern image formats such as JPG, PNG, etc. and current versions of multimedia encoding (e.g. MPEG versions) for audio- and video files.

The content manipulation layer provides access to the multimedia data via specific tools that provide methods to control and access news contents along the various transitions in the content lifecycle. The news services layer includes gateways that provide structured and standardized access to the contents by end user applications. Within this layer, tools and services of content provider networks take care of the presentation and distribution of multimedia contents. Most providers run multimedia gateways such as streaming servers or web services and sites to present the multimedia contents.

The top layer presents the end user environment, providing access to multimedia news services based on direct access to multimedia gateways or special services of the news services layer such as multi-agency full-text search engines, semantically coupling services or commercially related gateways like billing servers or subscription access gateways.

See: Multimedia News Systems

References

1. E. Kirda, M. Jazayeri, C.Kerer, and M. Schranz, "Experiences in Engineering Flexible Web Services," IEEE Multimedia, Vol. 8, No. 1, January-March 2001, pp. 58-65.

AUDIO COMPRESSION AND CODING TECHNIQUES

Jauvane C. de Oliveira
National Laboratory for Scientific Computation, Petropolis, RJ, Brazil

Definition: Audio compression and coding techniques are used to compress audio signals and can be based on sampling or on signal processing of audio sequences.

Audio is the most important medium to be transmitted in a conference-like application. In order to be able to successfully transmit audio through a low bandwidth network, however, one needs to compress it, so that its required bandwidth is manageable.

Introduction – Audio Properties

Sound is a phenomenon that happens due to the vibration of material. Sound is transmitted through the air, or some other elastic medium, as pressure waves that are formed around the vibrating material. We can consider the example of strings of a guitar, which vibrate when stroked upon. The pressure waves follow a pattern named *wave form* and occur repeatedly at regular intervals of time. Such intervals are called a *period*. The amount of periods per second denotes what is known as the *frequency* of sound, which is measured in Hertz (Hz) or cycles per second (cps) and is denoted by *f*. *Wavelength* is the space the wave form travels in one period. It may also be understood as the distance between two crests of the wave. The waveform is denoted by λ. Yet with regard to the wave form, the intensity of the deviation from its mean value denotes the *amplitude* of the sound. Figure 1 shows an example of an audio signal, where we can observe both its amplitude and period. The velocity of sound is given by $c=f\lambda$. At sea level and 208 C (688 F), c=343m/s.

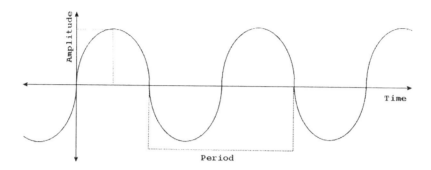

Figure 1. Sound wave form with its amplitude and period.

A sound wave is an analog signal, as it assumes continuous values throughout the time. Using a mathematical technique called Fourier Analysis one can prove that any analog signal can be decomposed as a, possibly infinite, summation of single-frequency sinusoidal signals (See Figure 2). The range of frequencies which build up a given signal, i.e. the difference between the highest and lowest frequency components, is called *signal bandwidth*. For a proper transmission of an analog signal in a given medium that must have a bandwidth equal or greater than the signal bandwidth. If the medium bandwidth is lower than the signal bandwidth some of the low and/or high frequency components of the signal will be lost, which degrades its quality of the signal. Such loss of quality is said to be caused by the *bandlimiting channel*. So, in order to successfully transmit audio in a given medium we need to either select a medium whose bandwidth is at least equal to the audio signal bandwidth or reduce the signal bandwidth so that it *fits* in the bandwidth of the medium.

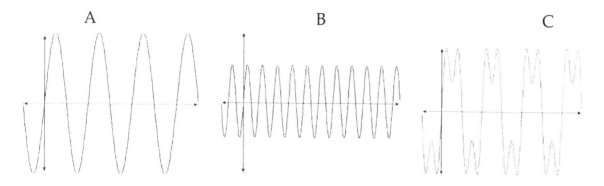

Figure 2. Two sinusoidal components (A, B) and its resulting summation (C)

Audio Digitization Codec

In order to process audio in a computer, the analog signal needs to be converted into a digital representation. One common digitization technique used is the Pulse Code Modulation (PCM). Basically we'll set a number of valid values in the amplitude axis and later we will measure the amplitude of the wave a given number of times per second. The measurement at a given rate is often referred to as *sampling*. The sampled values are later rounded up or down to the closest valid value in the amplitude axis. The rounding of samples is called *quantization*, and the distance from one value to the next refers to as a *quantization interval*. Each quantization value has a well-defined digital bitword to represent it. The analog signal is then represented digitally by the sequence of bitwords which are the result of the sampling + quantization. Figure 3 shows this procedure, whose digital representation of the signal is 10100 00000 00010 00010 10010 10101 10101 10011 00011 01000 01001 00111 00010 10011 10011 00001 00100 00101 00101 00110.

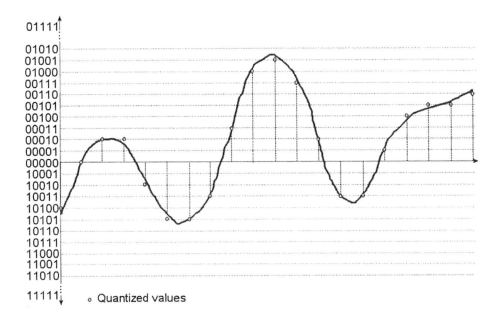

Figure 3. Digitization: samples (vertical dashed), quantized values (dots) and bitwords (left).

Harry Nyquist, a physicist who worked at AT&T and Bell Labs, developed in 1927 a study with regard to the optimum sampling rate for a successful digitization of an analog signal. The *Nyquist Sampling Theorem* states that the sampling frequency must be greater than twice the bandwidth of the input signal in order to allow a successful reconstruction of the original signal out of the sampled version. If the sampling is performed at a frequency lower than the *Nyquist Frequency* then the number of samples may be insufficient to reconstruct the original signal, leading to a distorted reconstructed signal. This phenomenon is called *Aliasing*.

One should notice that for each sample we need to round it up or down to the next quantization level, which leads to what is called *quantization error*. Such procedure actually distorts the original signal. *Quantization noise* is the analog signal which can be built out of the randomly generated quantization errors.

In order to reconstruct the analog signal using its digital representation we need to interpolate the values of the samples into a continuous time-varying signal. A bandlimiting filter is often employed to perform such procedure.

Figure 4 shows a typical audio encoder. Basically we have a bandlimiting filter followed by an Analog-to-Digital Converter (ADC). Such converter is composed of a circuit which samples the original signal as indicated by a sampling clock and holds the sampled value so that the next component, a quantizer, can receive it. The quantized, in its turn, receives the sampled value and outputs the equivalent bitword for it. The bandlimiting filter is employed to ensure that the ADC filter won't receive any component whose Nyquist rate could be higher than the sampling clock of the encoder. That is, the bandlimiting filter cuts off frequencies which are higher than half of the sampling clock frequency.

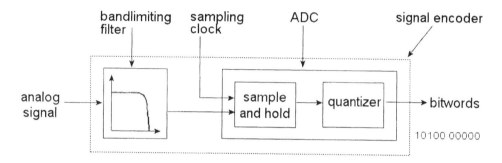

Figure 4. Signal encoder.

The audio decoder is a simpler device that is composed of a Digital-to-Analog Converter (DAC), which receives the bitwords and generates a signal that maintains the sample value during one sampling interval until the next value gets decoded. Such "square" signal then goes through a low-pass filter, also known as *reconstruction filter*, which smoothens it out to what would be equivalent to a continuous-time interpolation of the sample values.

The Human Hearing/Vocal Systems and Audio Coding

The human hearing system is capable of detecting by sounds whose components are in the 20 Hz to 20 kHz range. The human voice, in the other hand, can be characterized in the 50 Hz to 10 kHz range. For that reason, when we need to digitize human voice, a 20 ksps (samples per second) sampling rate is sufficient according to the Nyquist Sampling Theorem. More generally, since we can't hear beyond 20 kHz sinusoidal components, a generic sound such as music can be properly digitized using a 40 ksps sampling rate.

The above-mentioned characteristics of the human audio-oriented senses can be used to classify sound processes as follows:

a) Infrasonic: 0 to 20 Hz;
b) Audiosonic: 20 Hz to 20 kHz;
c) Ultrasonic: 20 kHz to 1 GHz; and
d) Hypersonic: 1 GHz to 10 THz.

The human hearing system is not linearly sensible to all frequencies in the audiosonic range. In fact the curve shown in Figure 5 shows the typical hearing sensibility to the various frequencies.

With regard to the quantization levels, using linear quantization intervals, it is usual to use 12 bits per sample for voice encoding and 16 bits per sample for music. For multi-channel music we'd use 16 bits for each channel. We can then find that we would use respectively 240 kbps, 640 kbps and 1280 kbps for digitally encoded voice, mono and stereo music. In practice, however, since we have much lower network bitrate available than those mentioned herein, we'll most often use a lower sampling rate and number of quantization levels. For telephone-quality audio encoding, for instance, it is common to sample at 8 ksps, obviously cutting off sinusoidal components with frequencies over 4 KHz in order to comply with the Nyquist sampling theorem.

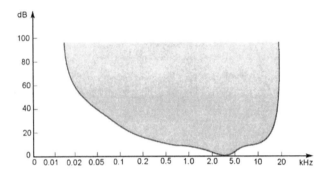

Figure 5. Human hearing sensibility.

Sampling Based Audio Compression Schemes

There are a number of standard compression schemes, which are based on the samples and that are not specific for any type of audio, being hence useable for both voice and music, with the appropriated adaptations with regard to the frequency range considered.

Pulse Code Modulation (PCM): Pulse Code Modulation, defined in the ITU-T Recommendation G.711 [5], is a standard coding technique defined for voice encoding for transmission over telephone lines. A typical telephone line has a bandwidth limited to the range from 200 Hz to 3.4 KHz. For this rate a 6.8ksps sampling frequency would suffice, but in order to accommodate low quality bandlimiting filters, an 8 ksps sampling frequency is employed. PCM uses 8 bits per sample rather than 12, with a compression/expansion circuit being used to achieve a sound quality equivalent to a normal 12 bits per sample encoding. Basically what the compression/expansion circuit does is to indirectly implement non-linear quantization levels, i.e. the levels are closer together for smaller samples and farther apart for larger ones. That minimizes quantization error for smaller samples, which leads to a better overall audio quality. Instead of really using logarithmic quantization levels, the signal is compressed and later linear quantized. The result is nevertheless equivalent to quantizing with logarithmic distributed quantization levels. There are two standard compression/expansion circuits: u-Law, which is used in the North America and Japan; and A-law, which is used in

Europe and other countries. With that a telephone-like audio coded with PCM reaches a total of 64 kbps.

<u>Compact Disc Digital Audio (CD-DA)</u>: Music has sinusoidal components with frequencies in the 20 Hz to 20 kHz range. That requires at least a 40 ksps sampling rate. In practice a 44.1ksps is used to accommodate filter discrepancies. Each sample is then ended with 16 bits using linear quantization levels. For stereo recordings there shall be 16 bits for each channel. Such coding scheme reaches a total of 705.6 kbps for mono and 1.411 Mbps for stereo music.

<u>Differential Pulse Code Modulation (DPCM)</u>: Further compression is possible in an audio signal through the analysis of typical audio samples. If we analyze a sound wave form, we can see that at the Nyquist sampling rate the wave change from one sample to the next is not very abrupt, i.e. the difference between two consecutive samples is much smaller than the samples themselves. That allows one to naturally use a sample as a prediction to the next one, having to code just the difference to the previous rather than the each sample separately. The difference between two samples can be coded with a smaller number of bits, as its maximum value is smaller than the sample itself. That's the motto behind Differential PCM, or DPCM. Typical savings are of about 1 bit per sample; hence a 64 kbps voice stream gets compressed to 56 kbps. The problem with this coding scheme is that quantization errors can accumulate if the differences are always positive (or negative). More elaborated schemes may use various previous samples that are mixed together using *predictor coefficients*, which consists of proportions of each previous sample that is to be used to build the final prediction. Figure 6 shows both the DPCM encoder with a single and three previous values used for prediction.

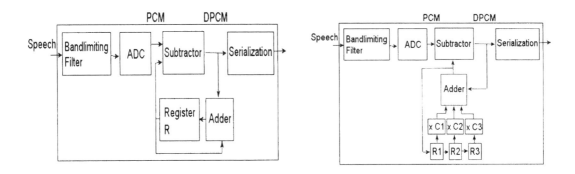

Figure 6. DPCM encoders with single (left) and third order predictions (right).

<u>Adaptive Differential Pulse Code Modulation (ADPCM)</u>. Extra compression can be achieved by varying the number of bits used to encode different signal components, depending on their maximum amplitude. The former ITU-T G.721 Recommendation, now part of the ITU-T G.726 Recommendation [8], uses the same principle as DPCM, but using a eight-order prediction scheme, with either 6 or 5 bits per sample for a total of 32 kbps or 16 kbps. The ITU-T G722 Recommendation [6] adds another technique called *subband coding*. Such technique consists of extending the speech bandwidth to 50 Hz to 7 kHz (rather than cutting off at 3.4 kHz like in PCM) and passing the signal through two

filters: the first allows only frequencies from 50 Hz to 3.5 kHz while the second allows only frequencies from 3.5 kHz to 7 kHz. The two signals are named *lower subband* and *upper subband* signals. Each subband signal is then sampled independently, respectively at 8 ksps and 16 ksps, and quantized using specific tables. The bitstreams are finally merged together in a last stage. This standard leads to 64 kbps, 56 kbps or 48 kbps. We should notice that this standard reaches higher voice quality encoding as it also considers higher frequencies in the 3.4 kHz to 7 kHz range. Yet another ADPCM-based standard, ITU-T G.726 Recommendation [8], also uses the subband coding technique described above, but considering only 50 Hz to 3.4 kHz components, with bitstreams at 40, 32, 24 or 16 kbps.

Adaptive Predictive Coding (APC): Further compression can be achieved if we use adaptive coefficient predictors, which is the basis for a compression technique called Adaptive Predictive Coding, where such coefficients change continuously based on characteristics of the audio signal being encoded. An audio sequence is split into small audio segments, each of which is then analyzed aiming at selecting optimum predictive coefficients. Such compression scheme can reach 8kbps with reasonable quality.

Digital Signal Processing Based Audio Compression Schemes

We call psycho-acoustic system what comprises those two systems. The first consists of all electrical/nervous systems linked to the communication from the senses to the brain and vice-versa and the latter comprises the generation/capture of sound which is transmitted through a given medium, such as the air, to/from the other party of the communication. The human speech is generated by components that come from the diaphragm all the way up to the human lips and nose. Through analysis of the human voice and the psycho-acoustic model of the human being, there is a class of compression schemes which makes use of digital signal processing circuits that are inexpensive as of today inexpensive. In this section, we describe a number of those compression schemes.

Linear Predictive Coding (LPC): The Linear Predictive Coding is based on signal processing performed in the source audio aiming at extracting a number of its perceptual features. Those are later quantized and transmitted. At the destination such perceptual features feed a voice synthesizer which generates a sound that can be perceived as the original source audio. Although the sound does sound synthetic, this algorithm reaches very high compression rates, leading to a low resulting bitstream. Typical output bitstreams reach as low as 1.2 kbps.

The perceptual features that are commonly extracted from voice signals are pitch, period, loudness as well as voice tract excitation parameters. *Pitch* is related to the frequency of the signal, *period* is the duration of the signal and *loudness* relates to the power of the signal. The *voice tract excitation parameters* indicated if a sound is voice or unvoiced. *Voiced* sounds involve vibrations of the human vocal cords while *unvoiced* sounds do not. Lastly *vocal tract model coefficients* are also extracted. Such coefficients indicate probable vocal tract configuration to pronounce a given sound. Such coefficients later feed a basic vocal tract model which is used to synthesize audio at the destination.

Code-excited LPC (CELP): A group of standards which are based on a more elaborate model of the vocal tract is also used. Such model is known as Code Excited Linear Prediction (CELP) model and is one of various models known as enhanced excitation LPC models. This compression scheme achieves better sound quality than LPC. Standards such as ITU-T G.728 [9], G.729 [10], G.723.1 [6] are based in CELP. Those standards achieve respectively 16 kbps, 8 kbps and 5.3 or 6.3 kbps. The price paid for such low final bitrate is the time it takes for the encoding to be performed. Respectively 0.625 ms, 23 ms and 67.5 ms

Perceptual Coding: If we expect to compress generic audio such as music, the previous LPC and CELP are not useable, as those are based on a vocal tract model for audio synthesis. Perceptual Coding is a technique which exploits the human hearing system limitations to achieve compression with not perceived quality loss. Such compression scheme also requires digital signal processing, to analyze the source audio, before it gets compressed. Features explored include: 1) the human hearing sensibility, as shown in Figure 5, where we can cut off signal components whose frequencies have an amplitude which is below the minimum shown, i.e. if a signal component at 100Hz is under 20dB it is not inaudible, 2) frequency masking, which consists of the fact that when we hear a sound that is composed of several waves, if a loud wave is close (frequency-wise) to a low wave, the low wave is not heard because of the sensitivity curve for the human ear, as shown in Figure 5, that gets distorted for frequencies around a given loud wave, much like if the sensitivity levels were pushed up a bit, 3) temporal masking, which consists of the fact that when we hear a loud sound we get deaf for quieter sounds for a short period. When we hear an explosion, for instance, we can't hear quieter noises for a while. All those inaudible sounds can be fully discarded and go unnoticed.

MPEG-Audio: The Motion Picture Expert Group (MPEG), set by ISO to define a number of standards related to multimedia applications that use video and sound, defined a number of MPEG audio coders based on Perceptual Coding. Basically a source audio is sampled and quantized using PCM with a sampling rate and number of pixels per sample determined by the application. In a next step the bandwidth is split in 32 frequency subbands using analysis filters. Such subbands go through a Discrete Fourier Transform (DFT) filter to convert the samples to the frequency domain. In a further step, using the human hearing limitations some frequencies are cut off. For the remaining audible components, quantization accuracy is selected along with the equivalent number of bits to be used. That way, less quantization (and more bits) can be used for the frequencies for which we are most sensible to, such as the range from 2 kHz to 5 kHz. In the decoder, after dequantizing each of the 32 subband channels, the subbands go through the synthesis filter bank. That component generates PCM samples which are later decoded to generate an analog audio. The ISO Standard 11172-3 [11] defines three levels of processing through layers 1, 2 and 3; the first being the basic mode and the other 2 with increasing level of processing associated, respectively with higher compression or better sound quality if bitrate is kept constant.

Dolby AC-1, AC-2 and AC-3: Other coding schemes based on Perceptual Coding are the Dolby AC-1, AC-2 and AC-3. AC stands for *acoustic coder*. Dolby AC-1 is basically a standard for satellite FM relays and consists of a compression scheme based in a low-complexity psychoacoustic model where 40 subbands are used at a 32 ksps sampling rate and fixed bit allocation. The fix bit allocation avoids the need to submit the bit allocation information along with the data. Dolby AC-2 is used by various PC sound cards, producing hi-fi audio at 256 kbps. Even tough the encoder uses variable bit allocations, there is no need to send that information along with the data because the decoder also contain the same psychoacoustic model used by the encoder, being able to compute the same bit allocations. In the negative side, if any change is to be made in the model used by the encoder all decoders need to be changed as well. The decoder needs to have the subband samples to feed the psychoacoustic model for its own computation of bit allocations, reason why each frame contains the quantized samples as well as the encoded frequency coefficients from the sampled waveform. That information is known as the *encoded spectral envelope* and that mode of operation is known as *backward adaptive bit allocation mode*. Dolby AC-3 uses both backward and forward bit allocation principles, which is known as *hybrid backward/forward adaptive bit allocation mode*. AC-3 has defined sampling rates at 32 ksps, 44.1 ksps and 48 ksps and uses 512 subband samples per block, of which only 256 subsamples are updated in each new block, since the last 256 subbands of the previous block become the first 256 subbands of the new block.

See: Human Vocal System, Human Hearing System

References

1. T. F. Quartieri, "Speech Signal Processing – Principles and Practice," Prentice Hall, 2001.
2. B. Gold and N. Morgan, "Speech and Audio Signal Processing – Processing and Perception of Speech and Music," John Wiley & Sons, Inc. 2000, ISBN: 0471351547.
3. F. Halsall, "Multimedia Communications – Applications, Networks, Protocols and Standards," Addison Wesley, 2001. ISBN: 0201398194.
4. R. Steinmetz and K. Nahrstedt, "Multimedia Fundamentals Volume I – Media Coding and Content Processing," Prentice Hall, 2002, ISBN: 0130313998.
5. ITU-T G.711 Recommendation, "Pulse Code Modulation (PCM) of Voice Frequencies," International Telecommunication Union, Telecommunication Standardization Sector.
6. ITU-T G.722 Recommendation, "7kHz Audio-coding Within 64 kbits/s," International Telecommunication Union, Telecommunication Standardization Sector.
7. ITU-T G.723.1 Recommendation, "Dual rate speech coder for multimedia communications transmitting at 5.3 and 6.3 kbit/s," International Telecommunication Union, Telecommunication Standardization Sector.
8. ITU-T G.726 Recommendation, "40, 32, 24, 16 kbit/s adaptive differential pulse code modulation (ADPCM)," International Telecommunication Union, Telecommunication Standardization Sector.
9. ITU-T G.728 Recommendation, "Coding of speech at 16 kbit/s using low-delay code excited linear prediction," International Telecommunication Union, Telecommunication Standardization Sector.
10. ITU-T G.729 Recommendation, "Coding of speech at 8 kbit/s using conjugate-structure algebraic-code-excited linear-prediction (CS-ACELP)", International Telecommunication Union, Telecommunication Standardization Sector.

11. ISO/IEC 11172-3 "Information technology – Coding of moving pictures and associated audio for digital storage media at up to about 1,5 Mbit/s – Part 3: Audio," International Organization for Standardization.

AUDIO CONFERENCING

Definition: Audio conferencing allows participants in a live session to hear each other.

The audio is transmitted over the network between users, live and in real-time. Audio conferencing is one component of teleconferencing; the others are video conferencing, and data conferencing. Since the audio must be encoded, transmitted, and decoded in real-time, special compression and transmission techniques are typically used. In a teleconferencing system that is ITU-T H.323 [1] compliant, the G.711 [2] audio codec, which is basically uncompressed 8-bit PCM signal at 8KHz in either A-Law or μ-Law format, must be supported. This leads to bitrates of 56 or 64kbps, which are relatively high for audio but supported by today's networks.

Support for other ITU-T audio recommendations and compression is optional, and its implementation specifics depend on the required speech quality, bit rate, computational power, and delay. Provisions for asymmetric operation of audio codecs have also been made; i.e., it is possible to send audio using one codec but receive audio using another codec. If the G.723.1 [3] audio compression standard is provided, the terminal must be able to encode and decode at both the 5.3 kbps and the 6.3 kbps modes. If a terminal is audio only, it should also support the ITU-T G.729 recommendation [4]. Note that if a terminals is known to be on a low-bandwidth network (<64kbps), it does not need to disclose capability to receive G.711 audio since it won't practically be able to do so.

To transfer the live audio over the network, a protocol such as the RTP (Real-time Transport Protocol) [5], or simple UDP (User Datagram Protocol) is used.

See: Teleconferencing

References

1. International Telecommunication Union, Telecommunication Standardization Sector H.323 Recommendation – Packet-based multimedia communications systems, July 2003.
2. International Telecommunication Union, Telecommunication Standardization Sector G.711 Recommendation – Pulse code modulation (PCM) of voice frequencies, November 1988.
3. International Telecommunication Union, Telecommunication Standardization Sector G.723.1 Recommendation – Dual rate speech coder for multimedia communications transmitting at 5.3 and 6.3 kbit/s, March 1996.
4. International Telecommunication Union, Telecommunication Standardization Sector G.729 Recommendation – Coding of speech at 8 kbit/s using conjugate-structure algebraic-code-excited linear-prediction (CS-ACELP), March 1996.

5. H. Schulzrinne, S. Casner, R. Frederick, and V. Jacobson, "RTP: A Transport Protocol for Real-Time Applications," IETF RFC 1889, January 1996.

AUDIO STREAMING

Shervin Shirmohammadi
University of Ottawa, Canada

Jauvane C. de Oliveira
National Laboratory for Scientific Computation, Petropolis, RJ, Brazil

Definition: *Audio streaming refers to the transfer of audio across the network such that the audio can be played by the receiver(s) in real-time as it is being transferred.*

Introduction

Audio streaming can be for various live media, such as the Internet broadcast of a concert, or for stored media, such as listening to an online jukebox. Real-time transfer and playback are the keys in audio streaming. As such, other approaches, such as downloading an entire file before playing it, are not considered to be streaming. From a high-level perspective, an audio streaming system needs to address three issues: audio compression, dissemination over the network, and playback at the receiver.

Audio Compression

Whether the audio is coming from a pre-stored file, or is captured live, it needs to be compressed to make streaming practical over a network. Uncompressed audio is bulky and most of the time not appropriate for transmission over the network. For example, even a low-quality 8Khz 8-bit speech in the PCM format can take from 56 to 64 kbps; anything with higher quality takes even more bandwidth. Compression is therefore necessary for audio streaming. Table 1 shows a list of several streaming standards, with the typical target bitrate, relative delay and usual target applications.

It should be noted that the delays disclosed in table 1 are based on the algorithm. For example, for PCM at 8 KHz sampling, we have one sample at every 0.125 milliseconds. Sample based compression schemes, such as PCM and ADPCM, are usually much faster than those that achieve compression based on the human vocal system or psychoacoustic human model like MP3, LPC and CELP. So, for delay-conscious applications such as audio streaming, which needs to be in real-time, one may select a sample-based encoding scheme, bandwidth permitting; otherwise one of the latter would be a better choice as they achieve higher compression. For a detailed discussion about the audio compression schemes please see the "Compression and Coding Techniques, Audio" article. In the streaming context, the Real Audio (ra) and Windows Media Audio (wma) formats, from Real Networks and Microsoft Corp. respectively, are also used quite often.

Table 1. Characteristics of Compression Schemes

Standard	Compression	Target Bitrate	Audio Quality	Relative Delay	Application
G.711 [5]	PCM + compansion	64 kbps	Good Voice	0.125ms	PSTN/ISDN telephony
G.722 [6]	ADPCM w/ subband coding	64 kbps 56/48 kbps	Excellent Voice Good Voice	Slightly higher than PCM	Audio conferencing
G.723.1 [6]	CELP	6.3 kbps 5.3 kbps	Good Voice Fair Voice	67.5ms	Video and Internet telephony Videoconferencing
G.726 [8]	ADPCM w/ subband coding	40/32 24/16 kbps	Good Voice Fair Voice		Telephony at reduced bitrates Conferencing
G.728 [9]	CELP	16 kbps	Good Voice	0.625ms	Low delay/low bitrate telephony
G.729 [10]	CELP	8 kbps	Good Voice	25ms	Telephony in celular networks; Simultaneous telephony & data fax
LPC-10	LPC	2.4/1.2 kbps	Poor Voice		Telephony in military networks
MP3 [11]	Perceptual Coding	32kbps to 320kbps	Music FM to CD Quality		Music Streaming

Dissemination over the Network

Unlike elastic traffic such as email or file transfer, which are not severely affected by delays or irregularities in transmission speed, continuous multimedia data such as audio and video are inelastic. These media have a "natural" flow and are not very flexible. Interruptions in audio while streaming it is undesirable and creates a major problem for the end user because it distorts its real-time nature. It should be pointed out that delay is not always detrimental for audio, as long as the flow is continuous. For example, consider a presentational application where the audio is played back to the user with limited interaction capabilities such as play/pause/open/close. In such a scenario, if the entire audio is delayed by a few seconds, the user's perception of it is not affected due to lack of a reference point, as long as there are no interruptions. However, for a conversational application such as audio conferencing, where users interact with each other, audio delay must not violate certain thresholds because of the interaction and the existence of reference points between the users.

The transport protocol used for audio streaming must be able to handle the real-time nature of it. One of the most commonly-used real-time protocols for audio streaming is the Real-time Transport protocol (RTP), which is typically used with the Real Time

Streaming Protocol (RTSP) for exchanging commands between the player and media server, and sometimes used with the Real -time Transport Control Protocol (RTCP) for Quality of Service (QoS) monitoring and other things. These protocols are briefly discussed next.

Real-time Transport Protocol (RTP)

To accommodate the inelasticity of audio streaming, there is a need for special networking protocols. The most common such protocol is the Real-time Transport Protocol (RTP) [1]. It is usually implemented as an application-level framing protocol on top of UDP, as shown in Figure 1. It should be noted that RTP is named as such because it is used to carry real-time data; RTP itself does not guarantee real-time delivery of data. Real-time delivery depends on the underlying network; therefore, a transport-layer or an application-layer protocol cannot guaranty real-time delivery because it can't control the network. What makes RTP suitable for multimedia data, compared to other protocols, are two of its header fields: Payload Type, which indicates what type of data is being transported (Real Audio, MPEG Video, etc.), and Timestamp, which provides the temporal information for the data. Together with the Sequence Number field of the RTP header, these fields enable real-time playing of the audio at the receiver, network permitting. RTP supports multi-point to multi-point communications, including UDP multicasting.

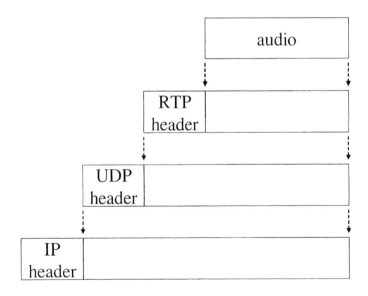

Figure 1. RTP in the TCP/IP protocol suite.

Real-time Transport Control Protocol (RTCP)

RTP is only responsible for transferring the data. For more capabilities, RTP's companion protocol the Real-time Transport Control Protocol (RTCP) can be used [1]. RTCP is typically used in conjunction with RTP, and it also uses UDP as its delivery mechanism. RTCP provides many capabilities; the most used ones are:

- **QoS feedback**: the receiver can report the quality of their reception to the sender. This can include number of lost packets or the round-trip delay, among other things. This information can be used by the sender to adapt the source, if possible. Note that RTCP does not specify how the media should be adapted - that functionality is outside of its scope. RTCP's job is to inform the sender about the QoS conditions currently experienced in the transmission. It is up to the sender to decide what actions to take for a given QoS condition.
- **Intermedia synchronization**: information that is necessary for the synchronization of sources, such as between audio and video can be provided by RTCP.
- **Identification**: information such as the e-mail address, phone number, and full name of the participants can also be provided.
- **Session Control**: participants can send small notes to each other, such as "stepping out of the office", or indicate they are leaving using the BYE message, for example.

Real Time Streaming Protocol (RTSP)

Unlike RTP which transfers real-time data, the Real Time Streaming Protocol (RTSP) [2] is only concerned with sending commands between a receiver's audio player and the audio source. These commands include *methods* such as SETUP, PLAY, PAUSE, and TEARDOWN. Using RTSP, an audio player can setup a session between itself and the audio source. The audio is then transmitted over some other protocol, such as RTP, from the source to the player. Similar to RTP, RTSP is not real-time by itself. Real-time delivery depends on the underlying network.

A Typical Scenario

Figure 2 demonstrates a typical scenario of audio streaming.

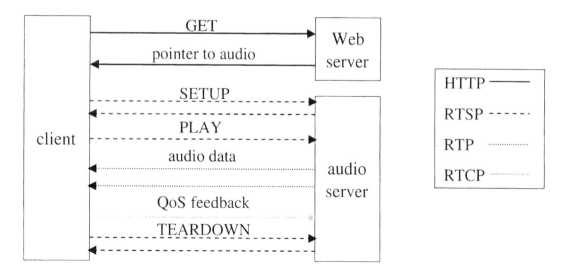

Figure 2. A typical sequence of events when streaming audio from a Web site.

Here, the client first goes to a web site, where there is a link to the audio. Upon clicking on that link, the webs server sends to the receiver the URL of where the audio can be found. In the case of an RTSP session, the link looks something like rtsp://www.audioserver.com/audio.mp3. Note that the Web server and the audio server do not have to be the same entity; it is quite possible to separate them for better maintenance. After receiving the above link, the client's player established an RTSP link with the audio server through the SETUP command. The client can then interact with the server by sending PLAY, STOP, PAUSE, and other commands. Once the audio is requested for playing, RTP is used to carry the actual audio data. At the same time, RTCP can be used to send control commands between the client and the server. Finally, the session is finished with the TEARDOWN command of RTSP.

HTTP Streaming

HTTP streaming is an alternative to using RTP. The idea here is that the player simply requests the audio from the web server over HTTP, and plays it as the audio data comes in from the Web server. The disadvantages of this approach are the lack of RTP/RTCP features discussed above, and the fact that HTTP uses TCP which is not considered a real time protocol, especially under less-than ideal network conditions. As such, there can be more interruptions and delay associated with HTTP streaming compared to RTP streaming. However, HTTP streaming is used quite commonly for cases where the receiver has a high-speed Internet connection such as DSL and the audio bandwidth is not very high. In these cases, using HTTP streaming can be justified by its advantages; namely, the fact that HTTP is always allowed to go through firewalls, and that HTTP streaming is easier to implement as one can simply use an existing Web server.

Playback at the Receiver

Although the coding and transmission techniques described above significantly contribute to the audio steaming process, the ultimate factor determining the real-time delivery of audio is the network condition. As mentioned above, delay severely affects audio in conversational applications. But for presentational applications, delay is less detrimental as long as it has a reasonable amount for a given application and is relatively constant. However, even for presentational applications, the variance of delay, known as jitter, has an adverse effect on the presentation. In order to smoothen out the delay, the player at the receiver's end usually buffers the audio for a certain duration before playing it. This provides a "safety margin" in case the transmission is interrupted for short durations. Note that the buffer cannot be too large, since it makes the user wait for too long before actually hearing the audio, and it cannot be too short since it won't really mitigate the effect of jitter in that case.

An extension to the above buffering technique is the faster-than-natural transmission of audio data. Depending on the buffer size of the receiver, the sender can transmit the audio faster than its normal playing speed so that if there are transmission interruptions, the player has enough data to playback for the user. This technique would work for stored audio, but it does not apply to live applications where the source produces audio at a natural speed.

Interleaved Audio

Interleaved audio transmission is a technique that is sometimes used to alleviate network loss and act as a packet loss resilience mechanism [3] [4]. The idea is to send alternate audio samples in different packets, as opposed to sending consecutive samples in the same packet. The difference between the two approaches is shown in figure 3. In 3a we see 24 consecutive samples being transmitted in one packet. If this packet is lost, there will be a gap in the audio equal to the duration of the samples. In 3b we see the interleaved approach for the same audio sample in 3a, where alternate samples are being sent in separate packets. This way if one of the packets is lost, we only lose every other sample and the receiver will hear a somewhat distorted audio as opposed to hearing a complete gap for that duration. In case of stereo audio, we can adapt this technique to send the left channel and the right channel in separate packets, so that if the packet for one of the channels is lost, the receiver still hears the other channel.

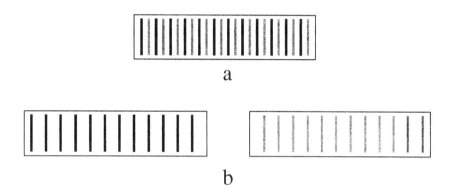

Figure 3. a) Transmission of consecutive samples, b) Transmission of alternate samples.

See: Audio Streaming, Networking Protocols for Audio Streaming, Interleaved Audio, Streaming Audio Player

References

1. H. Schulzrinne, S. Casner, R. Frederick, and V. Jacobson, "RTP: A Transport Protocol for Real-Time Applications," IETF RFC 1889, January 1996.
2. H. Schulzrinne, A. Rao, and R. Lanphier, "Real Time Streaming Protocol (RTSP)", IETF RFC 2326, April 1998.
3. D. Hoffman, G. Fernando, V. Goyal, M. Civanlar, "RTP Payload Format for MPEG1/MPEG2 Video," IETF RFC 2250, January 1998.
4. R. Finlayson, "A More Loss-Tolerant RTP Payload Format for MP3 Audio," IETF RFC 3119, June 2001.
5. ITU-T G.711 Recommendation, "Pulse Code Modulation (PCM) of Voice Frequencies", International Telecommunication Union, Telecommunication Standardization Sector.
6. ITU-T G.722 Recommendation, "7kHz Audio-coding Within 64 kbits/s," International Telecommunication Union, Telecommunication Standardization Sector.

7. ITU-T G.723.1 Recommendation, "Dual rate speech coder for multimedia communications transmitting at 5.3 and 6.3 kbit/s," International Telecommunication Union, Telecommunication Standardization Sector.
8. ITU-T G.726 Recommendation, "40, 32, 24, 16 kbit/s adaptive differential pulse code modulation (ADPCM)," International Telecommunication Union, Telecommunication Standardization Sector.
9. ITU-T G.728 Recommendation, "Coding of speech at 16 kbit/s using low-delay code excited linear prediction," International Telecommunication Union, Telecommunication Standardization Sector.
10. ITU-T G.729 Recommendation, "Coding of speech at 8 kbit/s using conjugate-structure algebraic-code-excited linear-prediction (CS-ACELP)," International Telecommunication Union, Telecommunication Standardization Sector.
11. ISO/IEC 11172-3 "Information technology – Coding of moving pictures and associated audio for digital storage media at up to about 1,5 Mbit/s – Part 3: Audio," International Organization for Standardization.

AUDIO AND VIDEO INFORMATION IN MULTIMEDIA NEWS SYSTEMS

Definition: *Contemporary news systems contain today visual media including audio and video information.*

Historically most relevant information concerning progress in sciences and the growth of general information within human knowledge and accessible to mankind has been documented in written text and occasionally described in images and maps. The technological developments of the 20th century has brought tools and communication channels that increased the ways of communicating and distributing news concerning all facets of human live in various ways. Multimedia news services involve now besides enormous amounts of digitized textual information also images, audio and video material, supported by multiple technical tools for seamless integration and modern distribution.

Image captures people's thrills, emotions, and concerns. Art can shock or inspire, and news images cover most relevant events over the entire globe. Most readers depend on visual and multimedia contents to understand the world around them and as a basis for further creative activities. The popularity of visual media such as photos, videos, and animations attests to their mainstream acceptance.

Technically, multimedia integration has been adopted to middleware software and content management applications to allow a seamless integration with current news management and distribution applications. XML standards like SMIL provide synchronization and integration frameworks and document description standards that cope with traditional and future text information and multimedia data that support modern user's needs.

Modern multimedia services integrate content types of text, images, audio data and streams and current video formats such as MPEG2, MPEG4, MPEG7 and multimedia broadcasting technologies and initiatives like MHP and DVB for providing future interactive digital news access via television, internet and mobile devices.

General purpose news editing systems integrate easy-to-use textual interfaces, mostly based on Web architectures, with modern multimedia features like video studios, composing for example MPEG-4 audio-visual scenes (cf. MPEG-4 STUDIO in [1]).

Modern Internet protocols like HTTP for web-based presentation of text and images, and streaming protocols such as RTSP for audio and video streaming cover the distribution and presentation services of multimedia news systems. Besides the technical enabling of news presentation and distribution, multimedia news services have to face legal and commercial constraints. Recent misuse by illegal file sharing or copyright violence has introduced security topics to multimedia news services. Besides customer oriented access restrictions and modern billing systems, multimedia news have been enriched with up-to-date encrypting mechanisms. Especially for audio and video formats, the time constraints in encoding and decoding live streams have introduced challenges which are met by modern approaches such as encryption and watermarking for copyrighted MPEG [2]. Multimedia data security is vital for multimedia commerce. Early cryptography have focused and solved text data security. For multimedia applications, light weight encryption algorithms as discussed in [3] are attractive and appropriate.

See: Multimedia News Systems

References

1. K. Cha and S. Kim, "MPEG-4 STUDIO: An Object-Based Authoring System for MPEG-4 Contents," Multimedia Tools and Applications, Vol. 25, No. 1, January 2005, pp. 111-131.
2. D. Simitopoulos, N. Zissis, P. Georgiadids, V. Emmanouilidis, and M. Strintzis, "Encryption and watermarking for the secure distribution of copyrighted MPEG video on DVD," Multimedia Systems, Vol. 9, No. 3, September 2003, pp. 217-227.
3. B. Bhargava, C. Shi, and S. Wang, "MPEG Video Encryption Algorithms," Multimedia Tools and Applications, Vol. 24, No. 1, September 2004, pp. 57-79.

AUGMENTED REALITY

Definition: Augmented reality is a system that enhances the real world by superimposing computer-generated information on top of it.

Virtual Reality (VR) is the technology that provides almost real and/or believable experiences in a synthetic or virtual way. Augmented Reality (AR) can be thought of as a variation of VR. In the original publication [1] which coined the term, (Computer-) Augmented Reality was introduced as the opposite of VR: instead of driving the user into a purely-synthesized informational environment, the goal of AR is to augment the real world with synthetic information such as visualizations and audio. In other words, AR is a system that enhances the real world by superimposing computer-generated information on top of it. VR technologies completely immerse a user inside a synthetic environment. While immersed, the user can not see the real world around him/her. In contrast, AR allows the user to see the real world, but superimposes computer-generated information upon or composed with the real world. Therefore, AR supplements reality, rather than completely replacing it. Combining 3D graphics with the real world in a 3D space is useful in that it enhances a user's perception of and interaction with the real world. In addition, the augmented information, such as annotations, speech instructions, images, videos, and 3D models, helps the user perform real world tasks. Figure 1 shows a wearable computer used for the implementation of AR of an industry training application.

See: Virtual and Augmented Reality

References

1.   P. Wellner, W. Mackay, and R. Gold, Eds. "Special issue on computer augmented environments: back to the real world," Communications of the ACM, Vol. 36, Issue 7, July 1993.

Figure 7. Augmented reality.

AUTHORING AND SPECIFICATION

Definition: *Authoring and specification tools provide development environment for multimedia applications and presentations.*

Numerous multimedia authoring tools and specification techniques have been produced across both commercial and research domains. While many articles focus on particular niche, ranging from specific media (e.g., image editing) to complex multimedia scenarios, this article specifically overviews those that have addressed various aspects of multimedia synchronization.

Early efforts in the specification of multimedia synchronization were based on temporal intervals [1] and a broad array of Petri net based techniques, such as [2]. Language-based constructs started with HyTime [3], a SGML-based (Standardized General Markup Language) document language which offered inter-object hyperlinking, scheduling and synchronization. The evolution of such techniques broadened to support the various classes of media synchronization (content, space and time) and included efforts such as MHEG [4] and PREMO (Presentation Environment for Multimedia Objects) [5]. MHEG offered a platform independent, "final" non-editable specification for real-time multimedia presentation, synchronization and interactivity, while PREMO provided a framework/middleware-approach to facilitate a standardized development environment for multimedia applications. Based on a conceptual framework, the latter's major goal was to provide a standard way to integrate emerging technologies from different media and presentation techniques to graphics packages and networks. Another series of research efforts addressed authoring of interactive multimedia presentations through a trio of projects which focused on the expression, specification and provision of media synchronization (DEMAIS, FLIPS and N-Sync [6]).

Recently, the SMIL (Synchronized Multimedia Integration Language) [7] markup language was developed by the World Wide Web Consortium (W3C) based on the eXtensible Markup Language (XML). It does not define any specific media format, but defines how various multimedia components should be played together or in sequence (including position, visibility, scheduling and duration). Complex multimedia scenario content is distributed amongst different servers, sent as independent streams (e.g., audio, video, text and images) and rendered together as a single unified presentation according to the SMIL specification.

See: Multimedia Synchronization – Area Overview

References

1. J. F. Allen, "Maintaining Knowledge About Temporal Intervals," Communications of the ACM, Vol. 26, No. 11, 1983, pp. 832 – 843.
2. M. Diaz and P. Sénac, "Time Stream Petri Nets: A Model for Multimedia Streams Synchronization," Proceedings of International Conference on Multimedia Modeling, Singapore, 1993, pp. 257 – 273.
3. ISO, "Hypermedia/Time-Based Structure Language: HyTime (ISO 10744)," 1992.

4. T. Meyer-Boudnik and W. Effelsberg, "MHEG Explained," IEEE Multimedia, Vol. 2, No. 1, 1995, pp. 26 – 38.
5. I. Herman, N. Correia, D. A. Duce, D. J. Duke, G. J. Reynolds, and J. Van Loo, "A Standard Model for Multimedia Synchronization: PREMO Synchronization Objects," Multimedia Systems, Vol. 6, No. 2, 1998, pp. 88 – 101.
6. B. P. Bailey, J. A. Konstan, and J. V. Carlis, "DEMAIS: Designing Multimedia Applications with Interactive Storyboards," Proceedings of the 9th ACM International Conference on Multimedia, Ottawa, Canada, 2001, pp. 241 – 250.
7. W3C, http://www.w3.org/AudioVideo, 2005.

B

BEHAVIORAL FACILITATION

Definition: *Behavioral facilitation deals with a multi-disciplinary effort to help people work together.*

By its very nature, collaboration is fundamentally behavioral in focus: people interact with other people using technologies and tools to achieve some (set of) goal(s)[1]. How well a tool is used and the caliber of interaction between collaborators, both affect the success of a collaborative effort. As such, these aspects are naturally influenced by the underlying technological environment. That is, the behavior of the collaborators and the collaborative artifacts are affected by the ability of the infrastructure to facilitate desired and appropriate behaviors.

The significance of behavioral issues can be seen in relation to coordination theory [1], a multi-disciplinary effort which aimed at developing "coordination technology" to help people work together more effectively and efficiently, via an integrated theory based on how coordination occurs in a variety of systems.

When working together, the ability to "behave naturally" is the key to encouraging participation and getting value from the effort. Therefore, support for "natural behaviors" is the key to any collaboration "making sense". Consider how a technical issue, such as the frame rate in a video conferencing system, can impact usage. An infrastructure that more accurately meets users' common expectations (30 fps) rather than one which induces artificial and stilted behavior (5 fps) will be more easily adopted and ultimately be more effective. Also consider two routine collaborative activities (co-editing a document and participating in a multi-stage workflow), both of which require that individual actions (be it changing the same text segment or updating entries in a database) be facilitated and managed with respect to others participating in the same activity. That is, the ability to coordinate and synchronize behaviors at a variety of levels, often simultaneously, is important. In a complex collaborative session in which participants are engaged in multiple activities (an audio/video conference in support of document co-editing combined with a related workflow), should the workflow be appropriately managed but the document be corrupted because of improper editing controls, or the conference audio/video be "out-of-sync" (at a "lip sync" level),

---

[1] While espoused in a people-centric manner, an analogous perspective can be applied to virtually any collaborative system.

collaborators will ultimately not be able to work together in an effective manner and the collaborative effort will not be successful.

To more appropriately facilitate potential diversity within a collaborative effort, the ability to adapt to the broad range of collaborator and collaborative artifact needs is fundamental.   In fact, behavioral norms (e.g., who is participating, how applications/tools are used, and whether activities done in an "ad hoc" or "directed" manner) often change over time and relate to many different organizational, personal/societal and technical considerations.   This lack of uniformity therefore suggests the need to address variable and dynamic behavioral patterns while considering the resultant effects on traditional system issues (e.g., application/tool functionality, resource availability, network issues, the user interface and so forth).

Unfortunately, conventional collaborative computing efforts (including many multimedia systems) have focused on the above issues with little attention to facilitating "successful" collaborative behavior.   Conversely, most studies which address usage and/or behavioral issues have been in the social sciences domain.   However, as collaborative technology becomes more widespread, complex in its constituent technologies, and cohesively integrated with other day-to-day systems, increased emphasis on behavioral issues is needed within the architectural, technical and engineering aspects of collaborative computing.

In this light, Robbins [2] proposes an approach to realize behaviors as "first class" instantiable entities within collaborative systems.   Based on the notion of a reflective meta-level architecture, system entities (including behaviors) are constructed using the concept of "open-implementation," allowing the system to monitor (examine) and adapt (modify) its elements in real-time.

As an example, consider two different situations: (1) provision of low-level media synchronization (such as lip synchronization); and (2) facilitation of a large-grain, multi-purpose, multi-participant scenario (such as an on-line meeting or distributed multimedia classroom).   In each case, the various collaborators and collaborative artifacts would need to have their behaviors coordinated appropriately.   In the proposed approach, the various behaviors would be realized as a tangible, and therefore manageable, entity within the collaborative environment.   Consequently, actions such provisioning the appropriate network QoS resources and regulating synchronization parameters, based on dynamic monitoring and adjustment of system resources, could be done to meet the current functional and behavioral needs of the collaboration.

Analogously, such an approach could dynamically guide and delimit group behaviors via the potential to recognize (typical) collaborative behavioral patterns and make appropriate changes in the behavioral and functional relationships between collaborators and collaborative artifacts.   Such a topic area has the potential for significant growth in future collaborative multimedia systems, resulting in the provision of intelligent support for agile, real-time, self-adaptive collaborative environments.   An important benefit to such an approach would be to support collaborators through the lessening of the cognitive load associated with how to use collaborative systems and the corresponding difficulty of interacting with other participants. That is, by providing behavioral facilitation and management in an orthogonal manner to addressing collaborative functionality, collaborators will be able to focus on the intent of their interactions and not all the idiosyncrasies of the technologies being applied.

See: Collaborative Computing – Area Overview

References

1. T. W. Malone and K. Crowston, "The Interdisciplinary Study of Coordination," ACM Computing Surveys, Vol. 26, No. 1, 1994, pp. 87 – 119.
2. R. W. Robbins, "Facilitating Intelligent Media Space Collaboration via RASCAL: The Reflectively Adaptive Synchronous Coordination Architectural Framework," PhD Thesis, School of Information Technology and Engineering, University of Ottawa, 2001.

BIOMETRICS FOR USER AUTHENTICATION

Claus Villager and Jana Dittmann
Otto-von-Gerick University
Magdeburg, Germany

Definition: *User authentication can be viewed at as the problem of binding identities to subjects. Authentication can be based on biometrics information, which uses physiological or behavioral traits.*

Biometrics in Context of Security Goals

Recently security has become one of the most significant and challenging problems for spreading new information technology. As summarized in [1] the following security requirements are essential for multimedia systems: confidentiality, data integrity, data origin authenticity, entity authenticity, non-repudiation and availability. The goal of entity authenticity is to ensure that an entity is the one it claims to be and is useful, for example, to implement further access restrictions or monitor the usage of a service. Entities taking part in a communication can be proven by user authentication protocols. In the following we introduce to a general information flow model for a generic user authentication system, describe the overall components of such a system and give two examples for the information flow protocol based on password and biometrics. In some applications, user authentication require a declaration of intention and therefore we discuss the overall impact of physiological and behavioral biometrics on that matter, stress the psychological impact of identification and observe ascertainability problems with respect to the overall environmental conditions. To enhance the security of biometric user authentication systems, fusion strategies for biometrics, knowledge and possessions play an important role for future applications. On the example of two protocols, multi-factor authentication approaches are summarized: the fusion of passphrase recognition and handwriting biometrics and an approach to combining knowledge and fingerprints.

A General Model for Biometric User Authentication

User authentication can be viewed at as the problem of binding of identities to subjects [2]. Such binding is always based on information available to a decision-making entity, which will either confirm the authenticity (authenticate) a subject or decline the authenticity. With respect to the different types of information for user authentication, the following categories can be found today:

1. Information based on knowledge of the subject (e.g. passwords and personal identification numbers (PIN),

2. Information based on possession (e.g. keys, chip cards),

3. Information based on physiological or behavioral traits, called biometrics. Here, a variety of different modalities such as fingerprints, iris images or signature analysis are available today.

Although these modalities are of quite different nature, the underlying processes in authentication systems can be described uniformly based on a formal nomenclature introduced by Bishop [2]. Here, any authentication requires two types of information, Authentication Information A and Complementary Information C, as well as three categories of functions (Complementary Functions F, Authentication Functions L and Select Functions S). Table 1 summarizes the algebra of Bishop's model, where the actual user authentication process is represented by the authentication method as a function l of some actual Authentication Information A and Complementary Information C: $l(a,c) ==$ $\{true, false\}$, for all $a \in A$ and $c \in C$.

Table 1. Five Components of Bishop's Authentication System [2]

Information Component	Designator	Description
Authentication Information	A	Set of specific information with which entities prove their identities
Complementary Information	C	Set of information that the system stores and uses to validate the authentication information
Complementary Functions	F	Set of functions that generate the complementary information from the authentication information, i.e. $f \in F, f{:}A \to C$, also used in functional notation: $c=f(a)$, for all $a \in A$ and $c \in C$
Authentication Functions	L	Set of functions that verify identity, i.e. $l \in L, l{:}A \times C \to \{true, false\}$, also used in functional notation: $l(a,c) == \{true, false\}$, for all $a \in A$ and $c \in C$
Selection Functions	S	Set of functions that enable an entity to create or alter A and C

For the description of a general model of an authentication system, entities that perform functions, as well as communication channels between those entities have to be defined besides the functional description. Figure 1 presents such a model introduced in [3]. It consists of three entities: Human Subject H (the user), Authentication System U and Reference Storage R. This model further considers two channels for information flow from H to U (Synchronization Forward Channel SFC and Authentication Submission Channel ASC). Further, one reverse channel from U to H (Synchronization Reverse Channel SRC), as well as one channel from U to R and reverse, Reference Information Control Channel (RCC) and Reference Information Submission Channel (RSC) respectively. Finally, the result of an authentication process is communicated to the external via the Authentication Result Channel (ARC).

While further details of the model and the implemented protocols can be found in [3], in this article two examples of information flow in this model shall be given to demonstrate how the process of user authentication by different modalities can be represented. To do so, the information flow protocol between the model's components is shown in Table 2, along with the channel used for knowledge (second column from right) and biometric user authentication (rightmost column).

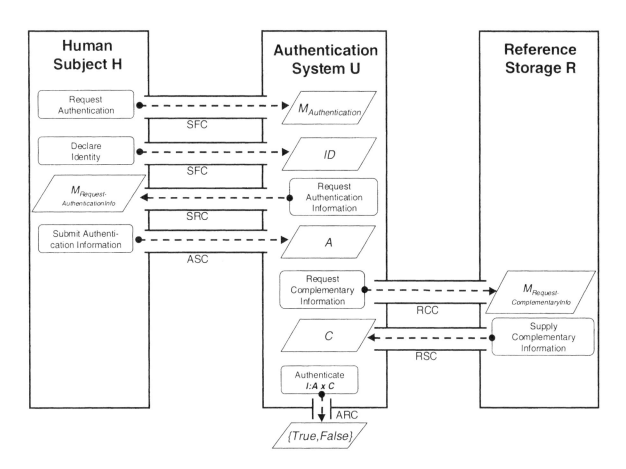

Figure 1. Information flow model for a general authentication system ([3]).

With respect to the example of password based user authentication in the third column of Table 2, the crypt() password authentication mechanism is referred to, as it is widely used in UNIX operating systems [4]. Here, the password of subject H is used as an encryption key for a Data Encryption Standard (DES) encryption of 64-bit runs of zeros, leading to non-reversible, complementary information *C*. Consequently, *C* in this case represents a mathematical digest of the original information, which should not allow any conclusions with respect to the original data. In this scheme, at time of authentication, the same encryption is applied to the actual authentication information *A*. For a decision, the resulting ciphers are compared and in case of equality the authentication yields a positive result. This approach avoids storage of plain-text passwords in *R*, which may be compromised.

The example for biometric authentication fingerprint considers a general image based user verification as authentication scheme, where the particular recognition technique or algorithm is not relevant for understanding the general process. Rather than referencing a particular algorithm, an abstract comparison function *Similarity (Image1, Image2)*, resulting in some numeric similarity score shall be used for the sake of clearness. For protection of reference images, we find recently several approaches such as Biometric Hashes ([4]) or biometric cryptosystems ([6]).

Table 2. Two Examples of the Information Flow Protocol for Password-based (second column from right) and Fingerprint-based (rightmost column) User Authentication

Step	Information Flow	Password based Authentication	Biometric Authentication: Fingerprint
1. (Optional)	$H \xrightarrow{M_{Authentica\_tion}} U \big|_{SFC}$	User requests authentication	User requests authentication
2 (Optional)	$H \xrightarrow{ID} U \big|_{SFC}$	User provides his claimed identity *ID* to *U*, i.e. name of user account	User provides his claimed identity *ID* to *U*, i.e. name of user account
3 (Optional)	$H \xleftarrow{M_{RequestAuthenticationInfo}} U \big|_{SRC}$	*U* prompts for Authentication information *A* (i.e. password)	*U* prompts for Authentication information *A* (i.e. fingerprint image)
4.	$H \xrightarrow{A} U \big|_{ASC}$	*H* provides password (*A*) to *U*	*H* provides fingerprint image (*A*) to *U*
5.	$U \xrightarrow{M_{RequestComplementaryInfo}} R \big|_{RCC}$	*U* requests the digest of the reference password from *R*	*U* requests a reference image *C* from *R*
6.	$U \xleftarrow{C} R \big|_{RSC}$	*R* supplies *U* with digest *C*	*R* supplies *U* with Reference Image *C*
7.	$U \xrightarrow{l:A \times C \rightarrow \{True,False\}} External\,World \big|_{ARC}$	*U* presents the result of an authentication function *l*: *l = TRUE*, if *crypt(A) == C*, *FALSE* otherwise	*U* presents the result of an authentication function *l*: *l = TRUE*, if *Similarity(A,C) <=Threshold T*, *FALSE* otherwise

Physiological vs. Behavioral Biometrics

Research and development in the past decades have suggested a wide variety of different modalities to be used for biometric user authentication. Today, a large number of products are available on the market, based on different recognition techniques. In another article of this book, fingerprints, iris scans, 3D scans of faces and other modalities have been introduced.

Looking at the nature of the underlying modalities, two basic categories can be identified: Behavioral (or active) and Physiological (or: passive) features. Acquisition of biometric information in the first category requires users to be active, i.e. to perform some activity in front of a sensor, whereas data acquisition in biometric systems of the second category, a bodily measurement is taken from subjects, which does not necessarily require an action by the user. From the user's point-of-view, it can be stated that in the first category some *co-operation* is required, whereas biometrics of the second category can be acquired even *without explicit consent* of subjects. Figure 2 illustrates this classification and provides some examples of modalities in each category.

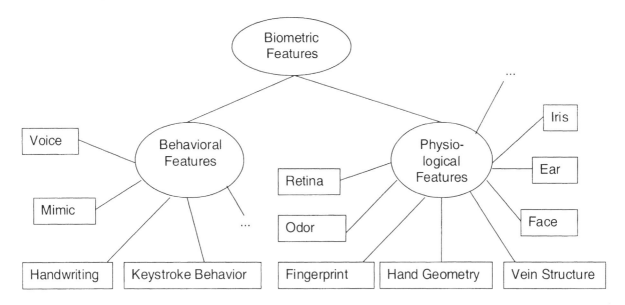

Figure 2. Examples for behavioral and physiological biometrics ([3]).

With respect to potential applications, the differentiation between behavioral and physiological biometrics can be of great importance for many reasons. Among this variety, three aspects shall be mentioned to demonstrate the differences in suitability of single biometric modalities.

Declaration of Intention: In scenarios, where user authentication is linked to an explicit consent to the authentication process, behavioral schemes appear more adequate than physiological. For example signature verification constitutes a socially well-accepted and widely used process and has been in application for many centuries. Besides the possibility for a (manual) user authentication based on the visible and physical traces of the writing process, signatures also serve for at least two additional goals: Declaration of Intention and Warning functions. The first aspect (Authentication) can be confirmed to due to the fact that the result of the signature process represents individual properties of the writing style, intrinsic to the writer. For the second aspect (Declaration of Intention), it can be assumed that if the signature is linked to some document, the signer has produced the signature in an agreeable attitude. The third function (Warning) assumes that subjects are aware that signing documents can have severe consequences and thus should be well considered.

Apparently, behavioral biometrics, particularly signature verification as sub-discipline of handwriting biometrics, are more adequate to reproduce these functions than physiological modalities. This particularly is the case in environments, which are not continuously observed by trusted persons, where no witnesses of voluntariness exist. I needs to be mentioned however that behavioral methods have the tendency towards higher error rates as compared to physiological biometrics.

Identification: As can be seen in another article of this book (See **Digital Biometrics**), biometric authentication can be achieved in two different modes: verification and identification. Applications, where the automated identification of persons is intended have quite different demands. While behavioral features can easily be repudiated (e.g. by disguise of a particular writing style), this is not the case for physiological features. For example in crime prevention, biometric recognition and automated search of suspects can support observation of public areas. Obviously in this scenario, disguise of biometric features is undesired and consequently, physiological traits such as face recognition appear more practical.

Ascertainability: Another important criterion for the use of particular biometric modalities is ascertainability, i.e. the question, if the biometric information can be acquired under different operational, environmental and geographical conditions in sufficient quality and quantities. For example, it appears difficult to implement speaker recognition in scenarios such as factory halls, where noisy machinery is in use. On the other hand, signature verification used for access control to buildings appear infeasible, when biometrics are to be verified frequently and at numerous locations to and inside a building. Further, the later modalities is not appropriate, if it can be foreseen that subjects will not be able to use their hands while transiting access control gates.

Another distinction between behavioral and physiological biometrics is the possibility of including semantic information in behavior. A speaker for example can articulate a specific message in her or his biometric trait as well as a writer in a handwriting trace. This characteristic implies some advantages of behavioral biometrics, when combining them with knowledge and possession-based authentication schemes, as will be discussed in the following section.

Fusion Strategies for Biometrics, Knowledge and Possession

The combination of information from at least two of the categories biometrics, knowledge and possession, sometimes also called multi-factor authentication, can be advantageous mainly due to two reasons: Firstly, it can achieve higher recognition accuracy, i.e. a tendency towards lower error rates. Secondly, it may compensate for those cases, where one or more types of authentication information A is unavailable at time or place of the authentication attempt. Looking at large distributed systems with a great number of workstations, for example, it is quite possible that these workstations have numerous different devices for user authentication. Some of them might be equipped with smart card readers, other with (different types) of biometric sensors and some simply with a keyboard for textual input. Further, combinations of these types of devices can be considered.

In this scenario, multi-factor fusion may allow to ensure a specific security level for those cases, where users move between workstations. If for example, in a scenario where some computers are equipped with an iris recognition system, which is believed to be extremely accurate ([7]), but others only with keyboards and smart card readers, one exemplary access control strategy could be formulated as follows. On those workstations equipped with an iris scanner, (unimodal) biometric authentication is sufficient to grant access by users. For the remaining computers, a dual-factor authentication is required, based on possession (smart card) *and* knowledge (password). Obviously, such an approach of multi-factor authentication can be arbitrarily extended by any other combination of biometric authentication methods. Figure 3 illustrates the fusion concept and the resulting four constellations (Knowledge & Biometrics, Knowledge and Possession, Biometrics and Possession and all three factors) are shown as the respective intersecting planes in the figure.

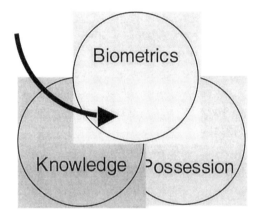

Figure 3. Illustration of multi-factor authentication by fusion of biometrics, knowledge and possession.

In this subsection, two selected approaches for combining knowledge and biometrics shall be introduced. One approach focuses on the biometric modality of handwriting, whereas the second scheme targets at using fingerprints recognition.

Passphrase-based User Authentication based on Handwriting

Modern digitizer tablets such as those integrated in Tablet PCs or PDAs open many new possibilities for recognition tasks. Two main disciplines in this area are user authentication based on dynamic features of writing process (e.g. for signatures) and the recognition of textual content of handwriting. The first category, also denoted as online signature verification, has been researched over the past two decades. A wide variety of methods can be found today, which attempt to utilize dynamic characteristics such as pen tip acceleration velocity or pressure applied to the writing surface to recognize writers by their writing behavior ([8], [9]). Similarly to online signature verification, online handwriting recognition utilizes dynamic features of the writing process as well and has also been a research topic over the past two decades ([10]). Just like in biometrics, error rates are intrinsic to handwriting recognition and can be described for example in terms of correctly recognized letters from an original's ground truth.

The complementary goals of these two categories of handwriting applications allow for the design of a fusion strategy, whereby subjects use passwords or passphrases as authentication information A. For the part of the authentication system U, the complementary (reference) information $C=C_{biometric}$ || $C_{groundtruth}$ is composed of a concatenation (denoted by | |) of the biometric features $C_{biometric}$ and the ground truth (i.e. textual content) $C_{groundtruth}$ of the passphrase.

Authentication is performed by two independent experts: one biometric expert determines a similarity between A and C with respect to biometric features, as known for example from signature verification. The second expert performs a textual recognition to A and compares the resulting text to the ground truth, which is stored as part of C. In the first case, the result can be a biometric matching score, denoting the degree of similarity between the two information. In the second case, since recognition errors have to be considered, string edit distances, for example the Levensthein distance ([11]) can be used in order to find a measure of string similarity. Finally, based on these two similarity measures, various fusion strategies, as known from multimodal biometrics ([12]), can be applied to implement an authentication decision. This can be achieved for example by weighted addition of matching scores and comparison to a given decision threshold.

Combining Knowledge and Fingerprints

The combination of knowledge and fingerprint biometrics has been an area of research followed by science and industry. One consequence of this is that a number of approaches have been registered as patents for example [13]. In a general description, the fusion of knowledge and fingerprint biometrics can be achieved in the following way: Assuming that for each of the $i \in [1..n_{Users}]$ users H_i of an authentication system U, features of images of k_i different fingers are registered with the system, where $k_i>1$. Assuming that:

i)   at least one feature description of each of the k_i fingers exists and

ii)   additionally at least one sequence $R_{i,n}$ ($n >= 1$) exists for authentication of user H_i , whereby a set of $m_{i,n}$ fingerprint assignments exists ($m_{i,n} <= k_i$) referencing the registered k_i fingerprint features,

then, an authentication function l can be designed in a way, that only fingerprints provided in a certain, user specific sequence to the biometric sensor, leads to a successful authentication. With this simple method, for example biometric passwords or personal identification numbers (PIN) can be implemented, as explained by the following example.

Assuming each of the users has registered all $k_i=10$ fingerprints with U, she or he can virtually associate a digit number scheme with the fingers. For example increasing assignment of digits from left to right: 0 for the little finger of the left hand, 1 for the ring finger and so forth, reaching 9 for the little finger of the right hand. Such a virtual assignment is illustrated in Figure 4.

Given such an assignment of fingers to digits, each user is enabled to reproduce a PIN by sequences of fingerprints and consequently, combine knowledge and biometrics for authentication. Naturally with this scheme, alternative assignments of fingers to codes can be found, for example alphabet letters allowing implementation of biometric passwords. Furthermore, the coding suggested here allows to utilize challenge-response protocols, whereby the computer challenges specific sequences of code words as authentication information A, which can only be produced by individuals having both knowledge about the individual coding as well as the biometric characteristics.

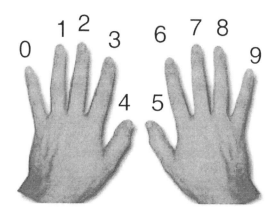

Figure 4. Example: Digit assignment to fingerprints for implementation of a virtual PIN.

Apparently, with strategies for combining knowledge and biometrics as described in this subsection, user authentication can be designed in such way that:

- Authentication information A becomes substitutable. Even if one or more fingerprints do get compromised, by changing for example the virtual key, fingerprints may still be used for recognition of users.

- Context-specific authentication information A: users may choose different fingerprint sequences for different applications and contexts.

- Increase in security level: by logical conjunction of each individual fingerprint verification process, it is possible to reduce the False-Acceptance rates drastically, as we can expect that error probabilities multiply, assuming statistical independence of each of the verification processes. However, future experimental evaluations will have to demonstrate how this will affect the other error classes such as False Rejection Rates in practice.

See: Digital Biometrics

References

1. J. Dittmann, P. Wohlmacher, and K. Nahrstedt, "Multimedia and Security – Using Cryptographic and Watermarking Algorithms," IEEE MultiMedia, October-December 2001, Vol. 8, No. 4, 2001, pp. 54-65.

2. M. Bishop, "Computer Security," Addison-Wesley, Boston, U.S.A, 2003.

3. C. Villager, "Biometric User Authentication For IT Security: From Fundamentals to Handwriting," Springer, New York, U.S.A., to appear in 2006.

4. S. Garfinkel and G. Spafford, "Practical Unix & Internet Security," O'Reilly & Associates, 1996, pp. 247 – 250.

5. C. Villager, R. Steinmetz, and A. Mayerhöfer, "Biometric Hash based on Statistical Features of Online Signatures," In: Proceedings of the IEEE International Conference on Pattern Recognition (ICPR), Quebec City, Canada, Vol. 1, 2002, pp. 123 – 126.

6. Uludag, S. Pankanti, S. Prabhakar, and A. K. Jain, "Biometric Cryptosystems: Issues and Challenges," Proceedings of the IEEE, Special Issue on Multimedia Security for Digital Rights Management, Vol. 92, No. 6, 2004, pp. 948-960.

7. J. Daugman, "The importance of being random: Statistical principles of iris recognition," Pattern Recognition, Vol. 36, No. 2, 2003, pp. 279-291.

8. R. Plamandon and G. Lorette, "Automatic Signature Verification and Writer Identification - the State of the Art," Pergamon Press plc., Pattern Recognition, 22, Vol. 2, 1989, pp. 107 – 131.

9. F. Leclerc and R. Plamondon, "Automatic Verification and Writer Identification: The State of the Art 1989-1993," International Journal of Pattern Recognition and Artificial Intelligence, Vol. 8, 1994, pp. 643 – 660.

10. C. C. Tappert, C. Y. Suen, and T. Wakahara, "The State of the Art in Online Handwriting Recognition," IEEE Transactions on Pattern Analysis and Machine Intelligence, Vol. 12, No. 8, 1990, pp. 787-808.

11. V. I. Levenshtein, "Binary codes capable of correcting deletions, insertions, and reversals," Soviet Physics, Vol. 10, 1966, pp. 707 – 710.

12. A. K. Jain and A. Ross, "Multibiometric Systems," Communications of the ACM, Special Issue on Multimodal Interfaces, Vol. 47, No. 1, 2004, pp. 34-40.

13. WIPO Patent Registration WO 97/04375, Electronic Data-Processing System, 1997.

BLOCK MATCHING

Definition: *Block matching is the most widely used method for disparity estimation in stereo coding algorithms.*

Disparity/depth estimation is an important key step in many stereo coding algorithms, since it can be used to de-correlate information obtained from a stereo pair. In the predictive coding framework (consisting of disparity estimation/compensation, transform/quantization, and entropy coding), the redundancy is reduced by compensating the target image from the reference image with the disparity vectors.

Block matching is the most widely used method for disparity estimation and is simple and effective to implement. The basic idea of block matching is to segment the target image into fixed size blocks and find for each block the corresponding block that provides the best match from the reference image. In general, the block minimizing the estimation error is usually selected as the matching block. However, block matching with a simple error measure may not yield smooth disparity fields, and thus may result in increased entropy of the disparity field and therefore increased bit rate of the disparity field. The proposed schemes to improve the estimation efficiency include: genetic algorithms, subspace projection methods, extended windows, balanced filtering, RD-based estimation and dynamic programming algorithm.

Another approach to improve the estimation efficiency is relaxing the one-vector-per-block assumption, e.g. the annoying blocking artifacts in the reconstructed image. In fixed size block matching, the higher prediction errors occur because the block boundaries do not coincide with the object boundaries. By reducing the block size, the estimation error can be reduced, but as the block size becomes smaller the associated overhead (bit rate) required to transmit the disparity field becomes too large. In addition, smaller blocks frequently fail to provide good matching results because the estimation is subject to various noise effects and thus a less homogeneous disparity field is generated. Note that pixel-based estimation is the best way to reduce the entropy of the disparity compensated difference frame. However, this comes at the cost of an expensive increase in the overhead necessary to represent the resulting disparity field. Meanwhile, increasing the block size increases the robustness against noise in the disparity estimation, but it also increases the magnitude of the estimation error. A good solution to this dilemma is hierarchical (or sequential) block segmentation. Segmenting a block with higher prediction error into smaller subblocks can further reduce the rate. Another approach is region matching, instead of block matching, which allows more efficient estimation by considering complex displacement. Obviously, region or object-based schemes are attractive because they have many advantages and allow the addition of various object-based functionalities, which are well supported by the MPEG-4 standard.

See: Coding of stereoscopic and 3D images and video

References

1. D. Tzovaras and M.G. Strintzis, "Motion and disparity _eld estimation using Rate-Distortion optimization," IEEE Trans. on CSVT, Vol. 8, No. 2, pp. 171-180, Apr. 1998.
2. N.Grammalidis and M.G.Strintzis: "Disparity and Occlusion Estimation in Multiocular Systems and their Coding for the Communication of Multiview Image Sequences", IEEE Transactions on Circuits and Systems for Video Technology, Vol. 8, No. 3, pp. 327-344, June 1998.
3. M.B. Slima, J. Konrad, and A. Barwicz, "Improvement of stereo disparity estimation through balanced filtering: The sliding-block approach," IEEE Transactions on Circuits and Systems for Video Technology, Vol. 7, No. 6, pp. 913-920, December 1997.

BROADCAST ENCRYPTION

Definition: In one-way communication system, broadcast encryption is intended to provide a means for two parties not known to each other, to communicate a cryptographic key for content protection and other applications.

Broadcast encryption was first proposed by Fiat, et. al, of IBM [1]. The initial goal was to allow a central broadcast site to broadcast secure transmissions to an arbitrary set of recipients while minimizing key management related transmissions. If we use a naïve approach where each client device is given its own key and an individually encrypted message is transmitted to all legitimate client devices, a very long transmission (the number of legitimate devices times the length of the message) is required. On the other hand, if we group legitimate devices into groups and each legitimate device is given all the keys corresponding to the group it belongs, every legitimate device needs to store a lot of keys. Motivated to create practical solutions, Fiat, et al, invented Broadcast encryption where efficiency are achieved at both transmission and client device storage. For example, one of the schemes they proposed requires the server to broadcast $O(k^2log^2klogn)$ messages and every client device to store $O(klogklogn)$ keys with a universe of size n and a resilient capability to any coalition of k users.

In recent years, Broadcast encryption found its value not only in broadcast applications but also packaged media content applications. This is because packaged media, from manufacture to consumers possesses the same one-way nature as broadcasting.

One key difference between traditional cryptography and Broadcast encryption [2] is that 'classic security uses a cryptographic handshake at the link level to prevent eavesdropping on the communication between two secure boxes while Broadcast encryption hides device keys deeper in the software, near the point of content consumption'. Several Broadcast encryption schemes have been proposed. They use simple symmetric encryptions instead of public key encryptions, which significantly reduce the computational complexity at both the server and client devices. The basic idea of all proposed schemes is similar. They employ key management block that is available in the one-way communication to communicate a management key for message/content decryption. At the server side, all protected content is encrypted with keys based on the management key. At the client side, the key management block is processed by the client device to generate the management key for content decryption. For instance, in a device key matrix based approach, the key management block, maybe generated by encrypting the management key multiple times using each different device key, is communicated to the client device in the one-way communication. A legitimate client device that knows a device key's position in the matrix can decrypt the value found at that position.

Readers can reference the article listed in the References section for more details on Broadcast encryption.

See: Multimedia Encryption

References

1. A. Fiat and M. Naor, "Broadcast Encryption", Advances in Cryptology (Crypto 93), Lecture Notes in Computer Science 773, Springer-Verlag, New York, 1994, pp. 480-491.
2. J. Lotspiech, S. Nusser, and F. Pestoni, "Broadcast Encryption's Bright Future", IEEE Computer, Vol. 35, No. 8, August 2002

C

CASCADING STYLE SHEETS

Definition: *Cascading Style Sheets (CSS) was introduced within the HTML 4.0 specification to separate content from formatting, and to provide precise document layout and format control.*

The Hypertext Markup Language allows authors to intersperse tags for controlling the display or formatting of a document within the content itself. HTML is designed to be flexible, with the tags acting as directives and being subject to some level of interpretation by the user agent which does the final document rendering. While this practice results in concise documents and provides some measure of adaptability for different devices, it lacks specificity and promotes redundancy since different versions of each document may be required for different device types. To address these concerns, the widely used W3C recommendation know as Cascading Style Sheets (CSS) was introduced within the HTML 4.0 specification to separate content from formatting, and to provide precise document layout and format control. CSS is designed to be hierarchal, wherein base styles are inherited and authors need only specify changes in particular style attributes. This minimizes redundancy, not only in terms of content, but in terms of style specification.

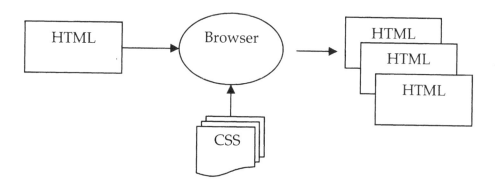

Figure 1. Transforming an HTML document using CSS to create alternative HTML representations.

Style sheets not only support separation of content from presentation, but when combined with dynamic HTML and ECMAScript (JavaScript,) CSS can be used to create interactive user interfaces. Attributes such as element position and visibility can be manipulated under program control to perform a variety of tasks in response to user input.

See: Multimedia Content Adaptation

References

1. H. Lie and B. Bos, "Cascading Style Sheets, Designing for the Web," 2nd edition, Addison Wesley, 1999.

CELL PHONES AND E-COMMERCE

Definition: With advances in handsets, wireless network infrastructure, and improvements in software development platform, mobile multimedia content for cell phones now includes digital music, games, videos, and TV.

NTT DoCoMo pioneered the mobile music market by introducing polyphonic ringtones (Chaku-Melody or Chaku-Melo) on i-Mode in 1999. With advances in handsets, wireless network infrastructure, and improvements in software development platform, mobile multimedia content for cell phones now includes digital music, games, videos, and TV.

Mobile Music

According to the Yankee group research firm, the mobile music market is expected to grow from around $200 million in revenue in 2004 to $1.2 billion by 2008 (IFPI, Jupiter Research, and other firms cite similarly optimistic numbers). Subscribers that tap into the mobile music market are projected to go up from 250, 000 in 2004 to 12 million in 2008.

Newer handset models from Nokia, Motorola, Ericsson and Handspring to name a few support a media player, provide storage of 6 to 10 CDs of songs encoded in MP3 or AAC format and come equipped with 3D stereo sounds through dual speakers. In parallel, wireless carriers are migrating towards Third Generation (3G) wireless infrastructure, as a case in point, Verizon wireless announced in September 2004 availability of its 3G network which now covers around 30 US markets and offers download speeds of 300 Kbps to 500 Kbps and bursts up to 2 Mbps. Revenues from online music are split between the wireless carriers, handset manufacturers, media platform vendors, and online music stores such as Loudeye, I-tunes, and Sony Direct.

Mobile Video and TV

Analysts predict that revenue from mobile video will grow from practically nothing in 2004 to $5.4 billion in 2009, with 22.3 million Americans becoming viewers of mobile video content [1]. In addition to streaming video content comprising of primarily news, sports, adult videos, music video clips, and movie trailers from the web, there is a drive to develop chipsets to decode and display digital TV receptions using new mobile versions of digital television broadcast standards. Supporting digital TV for the cell phone are two emerging digital TV standards for mobile devices: DVB-H (European standard from Digital Video Broadcasting Project) and a competing Japanese standard ISDB-T (Integrated Services Digital Broadcasting–Terrestrial). Wireless carriers such as Cingular and Sprint PCS, deliver live television feeds to subscribers in real-time over existing cellular networks using software from MobiTV (see http://www.mobitv.com). Other innovative ventures include a product from Sling Media (see http://www.slingmedia.com) that connects to a set-top box and redirects the TV signal to a mobile device over broadband Internet connections.

In addition to technical hurdles to support video content for cell phones, there are concerns over Digital Rights Management (DRM) as well as concerns to protect minors from mobile phone content. In particular, the Federal Communications Commission (FCC) aims to enforce a rating system as well as filtering software on phones.

See: Online Multimedia E-Commerce

References

1. Mobile Video Revenue Strategies, available at http://www.iqpc.co.uk/.

CFA IMAGE ZOOMING

Definition: A zooming solution operating on a gray-scale CFA sensor image generates an enlarged gray-scale, mosaic-like, image.

Since the cost of a digital camera rapidly increases based on its optical zooming capabilities, to keep it at a reasonable level, camera manufacturers produce cameras capable of performing digital zooming [1]-[3]. This is especially important for cost-effective, imaging-enabled, consumer electronic devices, such as mobiles phones and wireless personal digital assistants (PDAs). In such a single-sensor device, camera image zooming can be performed before or after the demosaicking step [3]. Unlike color (demosaicked) image zooming by zooming on the CFA image directly the designers avoid processing recovered RGB vectors where imperfections or noise introduced during demosaicking may create visual impairments [1]-[3]. A zooming solution operating on a gray-scale CFA sensor image generates an enlarged gray-scale, mosaic-like, image (Figures 1-2).

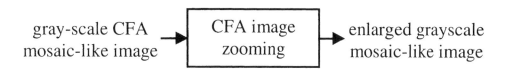

Figure 1. Demonstration of a CFA image zooming concept.

An image zooming technique performs spatial interpolation since it [3]: i) enlarges the spatial resolution of the input image, ii) completes the missing data from the spatially adjacent data using some type of the interpolation operations, and iii) preserves the spectral representation of the input image. The characteristics of the CFA zooming procedure are essentially determined by the edge-sensing mechanism and the spectral model used in the procedure [3]. The edge-sensing mechanism is utilized to preserve the sharpness and structural information of the enlarged image. The spectral model for CFA image processing is employed to preserve the spectral correlation between the spatially shifted color components. Since a CFA image zooming technique produces a gray-scale, mosaic-like, image (Figure 2), it should be succeeded by a demosaicking solution in order for a color output to be produced [3].

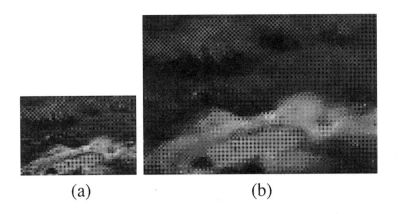

(a)   (b)

Figure 2. CFA image zooming: (a) captured gray-scale CFA sensor image, (b) enlarged gray-scale mosaic-like image.

See: Digital camera image processing, Spectral model, Edge-sensing mechanism, Demosaicking, Demosaicked image postprocessing, Color image zooming.

References

1. R. Lukac and K.-N. Plataniotis, "Digital Camera Zooming on the Colour Filter Array," IEE Electronics Letters, Vol. 39, No. 25, December 2003, pp. 1806-1807.
2. R. Lukac and K.-N. Plataniotis, "Digital Zooming for Color Filter Array Based Image Sensors," Real-Time Imaging, Special Issue on Spectral Imaging II, Vol. 11, 2005.
3. R. Lukac, K.-N. Plataniotis, and D. Hatzinakos: "Color Image Zooming on the Bayer Pattern," IEEE Transactions on Circuit and Systems for Video Technology, Vol. 15, 2005.

CLIENT-SERVER ARCHITECTURE

Definition: The term client-server denotes a class of architectures for distributed systems, that is, a way of structuring and organizing the work of several computers that communicate through a network.

In a client-server system there is usually some kind of resource that that a number of other computers need to use. These resources can be of various kinds: from data that a number of computers need to have, to algorithms that they must execute. These resources are placed on a computer, the server, and the other computers that need to use them—the clients—send opportune requests to the server.

In multimedia, the problems that one has to deal with are usually connected to the size of multimedia data, so client-server systems for data distribution tend to be somewhat more common than those to access to computational resources. This tendency is complemented by the fact that typically in multimedia the computationally intensive applications have to do with the display of data, so that they have to be placed on the computer of the final user, which is typically a client. Computationally services that are provided in client server multimedia system are usually ancillary to data access, such as search services.

Many internet applications are organized in a client-server structure. A typical example is the world-wide web: browsers act as clients, sending requests for pages to the Web servers, who either retrieve the pages from their file system or perform the opportune operations to generate them, and send them to the client, which displays them to the user. (Quite ironically, in the software architecture sense, the world-wide web is not a web at all.)

See: Multimedia File Sharing

CLIENT-SERVER MULTIMEDIA STREAMING

Definition: In the client-server multimedia streaming, each client requests and obtains what it wants directly from the streaming server.

Client-server based multimedia streaming [1] has been widely deployed over the Internet. With this approach, each client requests and obtains what it wants directly from the streaming server. The server is responsible for managing and allocating resources for streaming desired multimedia data for the requests from clients.

Delivery of multimedia data can be achieved by either unicast or multicast. For unicast delivery, each client (C) has a dedicated channel established between the server (S) and itself for data delivery (see Figure 1). The client first issues requests for service to the streaming server. When this request is received, the server decides whether this request will be accepted or not based on the network conditions and the availability of system resources. If all of them are got ready, the request is accepted and the server will allocate resources to handle the request. Otherwise, the server rejects the request and the clients may en-queue for service in the system until the resources are available. This approach is simple to manage, however, it is inefficient in terms of bandwidth utilization when most of the clients request for the same media content. So, another approach, multicast, is used for removing this flaw of replication.

For multicast delivery, no dedicated channel is needed to establish between the client and the server (see Figure 2). The streaming server sends one copy of each media contents to the multicast network. The client simply listens on the multicast channel(s) for desired media content. The beauty of this approach is that the bandwidth requirement is still kept constant compared with the increasing number of clients. The disadvantage of this approach is that the clients have to wait for about half of media duration on average before the next start of the media content. In order to reduce the startup latency, many different broadcast protocols have been developed, such as staggered broadcasting and pyramid broadcasting. These protocols require extra bandwidth consumption which is indirect proportional to the startup latency requirement. On the other hand, lack of flexibility to meet a wide range of QoS requirements from the users also poses a great challenge for streaming media content using multicast.

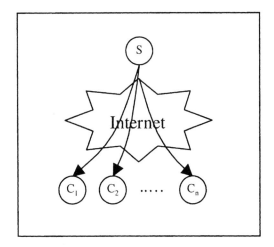

Figure 1. Unicast transmission.   Figure 2. Multicast transmission.

Both unicast and multicast approaches cannot totally adapt the heterogeneous environment such as the Internet. Moreover, multiple channels allocation aggravate bottleneck on the server side. Hierarchical network architecture has exploited to provide scalable system with lower cost. An intermediate device, called proxy, is deployed between the central server and the client. In such framework, part of the multimedia data can be temporarily stored in a proxy so that the workload of the server can be greatly alleviated.

See: Multimedia Streaming on the Internet

References

1.   D.P. Wu, Y.W. Hou, W. Zhu, Y.Q. Zhang, and J.M. Peha, "Streaming video over the Internet: approaches and directions," *IEEE Transactions on Circuits and Systems for Video Technology*, Vol. 11, No. 1, pp. 282-300, February 2001.

CODING OF STEREOSCOPIC AND 3D IMAGES AND VIDEO

G. Triantafyllidis, N. Grammalidis, and M.G. Strintzis
Informatics and Telematics Institute, Thessaloniki, Greece

Definition: *Since the bandwidth required to transmit stereoscopic and 3D image streams is large, efficient coding techniques should be employed to reduce the data rate.*

Introduction

Stereo vision provides a direct way of inferring the depth information by using two images (stereo pair) destined for the left and right eye respectively. The stereo image pair consists by two frames labeled as left frame and right frame.

A stereoscopic pair of image sequences, recorded with a difference in the view angle, allows the three-dimensional (3D) perception of the scene by the human observer, by exposing to each eye the respective image sequence. This creates an enhanced 3D feeling and increased ``tele-presence" in teleconferencing and several other applications (medical, entertainment, etc.) [2].

Since the bandwidth required to transmit both stereoscopic image streams is large, efficient coding techniques should be employed to reduce the data rate. Similar to other coding scenarios, compression for stereo images can be achieved by taking advantage of redundancies in the source data, e.g. spatial and temporal redundancies for monocular images and video. The simplest solution for compressing the two channels is by using independent coding for each image/video with existing compression standards such as JPEG or MPEG. However, in the case of stereo images/video, an additional source of redundancy stems from the similarity, i.e. the strong "binocular redundancy" between two images in a stereo pair, due to stereo camera geometry. Exploiting this binocular dependency allows achieving higher compression ratios.

The subjective quality of the reconstructed image sequence produced by such algorithms should be sufficiently high. Subjective tests have shown that image artifacts are more visible and annoying in a stereoscopic display than in standard (monoscopic) video displays.

One of the most important parameters in the study of stereo coding is *disparity*. Because of the different perspective, the same point in the object will be mapped to different coordinates in the left and right images. The disparity is the difference between these coordinates.

Compression of the right channel can be done by either being compatible with the monoscopic coding techniques such as assuming independent channels and using standard video coding techniques or by being incompatible, such as joint coding of both channels. Figure 1(a) shows a coding technique where each view is coded independently.

A simple modification to exploit the correlation between the two views would be to encode one (the left) view and the difference between the two views. However, this method is not so efficient because each object in the scene has different disparity. Therefore, further improvement can be achieved by adopting predictive coding, where a disparity vector field and the disparity compensated difference frame are encoded. Figure 1(b) illustrates this approach that attempts to exploit crossview redundancy, by coding the right image using the estimated disparity map to predict it from the left image. The corresponding residual image is also encoded to improve the reconstruction of the right image.

Three major approaches are used for coding of stereo sequences: block-based, object-based and hybrid. The block-based approach has the advantage of simplicity and robustness allowing more straight-forward hardware implementations, but the subjective quality of reconstructed images may be unacceptable at low bit-rates. Object-based schemes alleviate the problem of annoying coding errors, providing a more natural representation of the scene, but require a complex analysis phase to segment the scene into objects and estimate their motion and structure. Finally, hybrid methods, combining block-based and object-based methods, are usually preferred since they can combine the merits of both approaches.

Due to the similarity between stereo images and video, many of the concepts and techniques used for video coding are applicable to stereo image coding. Predictive coding with motion estimation increases the coding gain by exploiting the temporal dependency. This is possible because consecutive images in a video sequence tend to be similar. In general, disparity estimation is similar to motion estimation in the sense that they both are used to exploit the similarity between two (or more) images in order to reduce the bit rate. However, the motion estimation schemes developed in video coding may not be efficient unless geometrical constraints for stereo imaging are taken into account.

A predictive coding system of stereoscopic images includes displacement (disparity) estimation / compensation, transform / quantization and entropy coding. Therefore, the overall encoding performance can be controlled by various factors. Especially, for the stereo image coding case, an efficient prediction reduces the "binocular redundancy" between two images in a stereo pair. In addition, optimal quantization that takes into account the "binocular dependency" can further improve the overall encoding performance.

Occlusion regions mark disparity discontinuity jumps which can be used to improve stereo image encoding and transmission, segmentation, motion analysis and object identification processes which must preserve object boundaries [1].

Disparity estimation

To better understand the meaning of disparity, let us imagine overlaying the left and right pictures of a stereo pair by placing the left picture on the top of the right. Given a specific point A in the left picture, its matching point B in the right picture does not in general lie directly underneath point A. Therefore, we define the stereo (or binocular) disparity of the point pair (A,B) as the vector connecting B and A.

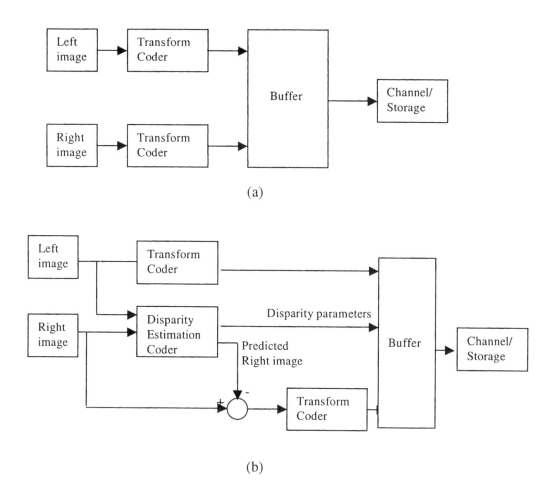

Figure 1. Stereo image coding approaches (a) Independent coding of the two channels (b) Coding of the right image using disparity compensation from the left image.

In the case of parallel axes camera configuration, the disparity reduces to the signed magnitude of the horizontal component of the displacement vector since the vertical component is always zero. Furthermore, the use of the parallel axes camera geometry leads to a simple mathematical relationship between the disparity of a point pair and the distance (depth) to the object it represents; specifically the disparity is inversely proportional to the depth [4].

Disparity estimation is one of the key steps in the stereo coding, because it helps to exploit the similarity along the disparity in the process of disparity estimation/compensation. In the predictive coding framework, the redundancy is reduced by compensating the target (right) image from the reference (left) image using the disparity vectors [7].

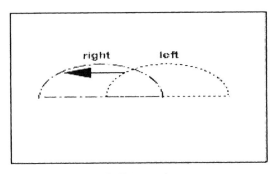

Figure 2. Disparity vector.

Various techniques have been proposed to determine stereo disparities [3][9]. All of these methods attempt to match pixels in one image with their corresponding pixels in the other image. Some basic methods are summarized in Table 1 [11]:

Table 1. Stereo Matching Approaches

METHODS	DESCRIPTION
Block matching	Search for maximum match score or minimum error over small region, typically using variants of cross-correlation or robust rank metrics
Gradient based optimization	Minimize a functional, typically the sum of squared differences over a small region
Feature matching	Match dependable features rather than intensities themselves
Dynamic programming	Determine the disparity surface for a scanline as the best path between two sequences of ordered primitives. Typically order is defined by the epipolar ordering constraint
Intrinsic curves	Map epipolar scanlines to intrinsic curve space to convert the search problem to a nearest-neighbors lookup problem. Ambiguities are resolved using dynamic programming.
Graph cuts	Determine the disparity surface as the minimum cut of the maximum flow in a graph
Nonlinear diffusion	Aggregate support by applying a local diffusion process
Belief propagation	Solve for disparities via message passing in a belief network
Correspondence-less methods	Deform a model of the scene based on an objective function

Stereo video coding

Stereo video coding algorithms can be classified in: Extensions of single view video coding, rate distortion optimized coding, coding based on semantic relevance, object based coding and other techniques.

In traditional MPEG-2 compression, the video includes I-frames which are completely transmitted, P-frames which are predicted from previous I-frames and B-frames which are predicted from both P and I-frames. A method to extend this coding technique to stereo has been proposed. In this method the left channel is coded independently, exactly as in the single-view coding case (MPEG-2). Each frame of the other channel is then predicted from the corresponding frame of the left view, using disparity compensation, or the previously coded frame of the right view, using motion compensation [5].

A predictive video encoding system contains several stages such as motion estimation and compensation, disparity estimation and compensation in the case of stereo coding, transform, quantization and, finally, entropy coding. Therefore, the overall performance of the system can be optimized by adjusting a limited number of variables used in the above mentioned stages. It is observed that, especially in stereo video coding, the better the disparity prediction is, the more efficient the overall compression rate becomes. Rate distortion optimized coding schemes estimate the block-based motion/disparity field under the constraint of a target bitrate for the coding of the vector information [10]. The entropy of the displacement vectors is employed as a measure of the bit rate needed for their lossless transmission.

If the relevancy of the content is considered while encoding, the definition of a semantic relevance measure for video content is crucial. These semantic relevance measures can be performed by the user or the content author can assign common relevancy measures for all users. It is also possible to divide the input video into segments by considering various statistics along temporal segments (coding difficulty hints, motion hints etc.) that affect the ease of coding without taking into account any relevance issues.

Object based coding has long attracted considerable attention as a promising alternative to block-based encoding, achieving excellent performance, and producing fewer annoying effects such as blocking artifacts and mosquito effects than those commonly occurring in block-based hybrid DCT coders at moderate and low bit rates [6]. Furthermore, important image areas such as facial details in face-to-face communications can be reconstructed with a higher image quality than with block-oriented hybrid coding. In addition, the ability of object-based coding techniques to describe a scene in a structural way, in contrast to traditional waveform-based coding techniques, opens new areas of applications [8]. The encoder consists of an analysis part and a synthesis part. The analysis part aims to subdivide the scene into a set of objects representing each one by a set of parameters: shape or boundary, motion, structure or depth and texture or colour. These parameters are encoded and transmitted to the decoder where the decoded parameters are then used to synthesize an approximation of the original images. The analysis phase is the most sophisticated one, consisting of image segmentation and motion/structure estimation.

Standardization Efforts

Stereo video coding is already supported by the MPEG-2 technology, where a corresponding multi-view profile, defined in 1996, is available to transmit two video signals. The main application area of MPEG-2 multiview profile (MVP) is stereoscopic TV. The MVP extends the well-known hybrid coding towards exploitation of inter-view channel redundancies by implicitly defining disparity-compensated prediction. However, there are important disadvantages: disparity vectors fields are sparse and thus the disparity-compensation is not efficient so motion-compensation is usually preferred. Furthermore, the technology is outdated and interactive applications that involve view interpolation cannot be supported. To provide support for interactive applications, enhanced depth and/or disparity information about the scene has to be included in the bitstream, which can also be used for synthesizing virtual views from intermediate viewpoints. A new MPEG activity, namely of 3DAV (for 3D Audio-Visual) explores the need for standardization in this area to support these new applications [12]. Experiments for encoding depth data using different video codecs by putting the depth data into the luminance channel, and simply changing the semantics of its description have been conducted by MPEG and the ATTEST IST project. Results show that this approach makes it possible to achieve extreme compression of depth data while still maintaining a good quality level for both decoded depth and any generated novel views. Furthermore, additional disparity and occlusion information can be included in the form of additional MPEG-4 Video Object Planes (VOPs), Multiple Auxiliary Components (MAC) (defined by MPEG-4), or, preferably, Layered Depth Images, which are defined in a new part of MPEG-4 called Animation Framework eXtension (AFX).

Conclusions

Stereoscopic coding techniques pose an important problem due to the existence of additional correlation between the two views. The most common approach is the predictive coding of the one channel with respect to the other channel and includes displacement (disparity) estimation / compensation, transform / quantization and entropy coding. Depending on the basic elements used approaches can be classified as block-based, object-based and hybrid. Extensions of single view video coding, rate distortion optimized coding, coding based on semantic relevance, object based coding and other techniques have been proposed for efficient stereoscopic coding.

Although both MPEG-2 and MPEG-4 have already standardized specific extensions for stereoscopic and multiview signals, new interactive applications require new coding approaches which are currently under development within a new MPEG activity to support such new applications, under the name of 3DAV (for 3D Audio-Visual).

See: Mesh, 3D, Block matching, Object based video coding, Occlusions, Multi-view video coding, Stereoscopic and multi-view video coding standards

References

1. G.A. Triantafyllidis, D. Tzovaras, and M.G. Strintzis: "Occlusion and Visible Background and Foreground Areas in Stereo: A Bayesian Approach," IEEE

Transactions on Circuits and Systems for Video Technology, Special Issue on 3D Video Technology, Vol. 10, No. 4, pp. 563-576, June 2000.

2. M. Perkins, "Data compression of stereo pairs," IEEE Transactions on Communications, Vol. 40, pp. 684–696, April 1992.
3. N. Grammalidis and M. G. Strintzis, "Disparity and occlusion estimation on multiocular systems and their coding for the communication of multiview image sequences," IEEE Transactions on Circuits and Systems for Video Technology, Vol. 8, pp. 328–344, June 1998.
4. H. Aydinoglu and M. Hayes III, "Stereo image coding: A projection approach," IEEE Transactions on Image Processing, Vol. 7, pp. 506–516, April 1998.
5. N. Grammalidis, S. Malassiotis, D. Tzovaras, and M. G. Strintzis, "Stereo image sequence coding based on 3-D motion estimation and compensation," Signal Processing, Vol. 7, No. 2, pp. 129–145, August 1995.
6. D. Tzovaras, N. Grammalidis, and M. G. Strintzis, "Object-based coding of stereo image sequences using joint 3-D motion/disparity compensation," IEEE Transactions on Circuits and Systems for Video Technology, Vol. 7, pp. 312–328, April 1997.
7. M.B. Slima, J. Konrad, and A. Barwicz, "Improvement of stereo disparity estimation through balanced filtering: The sliding-block approach," IEEE Transactions on Circuits and Systems for Video Technology, Vol. 7, No. 6, pp. 913-920, December 1997.
8. M.G. Strintzis and S. Malassiotis, "Object-Based Coding of Stereoscopic and 3D Image Sequences: A Review", IEEE Signal Processing Magazine, Special Issue on Stereo and 3D Imaging, Vol. 16, No. 3, pp. 14-28, May 1999.
9. D. Scharstein and R. Szeliski, "A Taxonomy and Evaluation of Dense Two-Frame Stereo Correspondence Algorithms", IJCV 47(1/2/3), pp. 7-42, April-June 2002.
10. D. Tzovaras and M.G.Strintzis: "Motion and Disparity Field Estimation Using Rate Distortion Optimization," IEEE Transactions on Circuits and Systems for Video Technology, Vol. 8, No. 2, pp. 171-181, April 1998.
11. M.Z Brown, D. Burschka, and G.D. Hager, "Advances in computational stereo," IEEE Transactions on Pattern Analysis and Machine Intelligence, Vol. 25, No. 8, pp. 993-1008, August 2003.
12. A. Smolic, C. Fehn, K. Müller, and D. McCutchen, "MPEG 3DAV – Video-Based Rendering for Interactive TV Applications," Proceedings of 10th Dortmunder Fernsehseminar, Dortmund, Germany, September 2003.

COLLABORATIVE COMPUTING – AREA OVERVIEW

Wayne Robbins[†] and Schahram Dustdar[‡]
[†]Defence R&D Canada (DRDC), Future Forces Synthetic Environments, DRDC Ottawa; Ottawa, Ontario, Canada
[‡]Distributed Systems Group, Institute of Information Systems Vienna University of Technology, Austria

Definition: *Collaborative computing is a fertile mélange of technologies and techniques which facilitate people working together via computer-assisted means.*

The area offers a plethora of research and development opportunities across a number of disciplines while also constituting an increasingly common part of daily business practice within industry and government.

By its very definition, collaboration implies working in a joint fashion with those not immediately connected. Consequently, it has long been the "cornerstone of group activity" regardless of setting [1]; and in many situations, collaboration has been and continues to address ways to better cooperate in a co-located setting. In most cases, however, the disconnectedness implied by (tele-)collaboration entails the use of modern communications mechanisms as part of working in a distributed manner. Additionally, given the traditional limitation of shared physical spaces, the many subtle and assumed details of how the collaborative process is actually achieved become more pronounced in distributed, computer-assisted systems. The specific and often significant demands on the technology along with the efforts required by collaborators often require special consideration. For example, the social convention and human judgment often tacitly perceived and applied in a physical encounter must be strictly accounted for in computer-assisted collaborative environments.

Now consider the role of media within collaboration. In real-world collaboration, people see each other, talk to each other, point at shared props, sketch ideas on shared surfaces and can view other media (such as text documents, animations, video clips, etc.) in a mutually common environment. In short, as part of the collaborative effort, the participants and the objects they use form a physically shared (i.e., co-located) "media space" in which users interact with each other through the experience and manipulation of media, such as books, papers, overheads, writing instruments, whiteboards and so forth (see [2] for discussion of the actual media space concept). The collaborative process utilizes and benefits from the breadth of media and interaction styles used by the participants. In particular, by combining presentation (of material), conversation (between participants) and interaction (between participants with respect to objects in the shared space), the appropriate medium for the task at hand can be experienced in a shared and globally aware manner. Activities naturally occur in a timely and orderly manner and in relation to the overall goal and state of the collaboration; that is, the activities are coordinated [3] and synchronized enabling a *semantically coherent environment* in which individual collaborators know what is going on (i.e., they are situationally aware) and can interact in a legitimate and sensible fashion. Similarly, the issue of awareness is fundamentally important to enabling real-time interactive exchanges between distributed participants [4]. In such *logical* environments, participants do not implicitly have such simultaneous awareness; therefore, it must be provided so that they can relate to activities at the same time and interact in an equitable manner. Consequently, participants must appropriately (and explicitly) be notified of actions which affect them in non-obtrusive, up-to-date and timely group context [1].

Therefore, in moving towards increased promulgation of collaborative environments, the basics of collaboration, including relevant processes, tools and technologies must first be understood. These considerations, including the role of multimedia and the various types of systems that constitute collaborative computing, are the focus of this article.

Media and Collaboration

Analogous to the handling of material elements within a shared physical space, multimedia systems have also traditionally fallen into the same three categories. *Presentational* multimedia refers to those systems that render multimedia scenarios to a passive audience, typified by the traditional lecture style of delivery. The architecture of presentational systems typically utilizes the retrieval of pre-stored media from remote servers which are then displayed to the viewer. *Conversational* multimedia systems are those which allow people to engage in a dialogue using voice and/or video in a real-time synchronous manner. Such systems can range from text-based instant messaging and audio-enabled "phone" programs to full-fledged audio/video teleconferencing systems. *Interactive* multimedia augments these classifications by enabling their participants to manipulate and interact with their environment, such as being able to control a presentation's progress by rewinding, fast-forwarding or hyper-linking to other parts of the presentation. In a conversational system, interactivity is provided by using a separate teleconference in parallel with the use of shared application (e.g., a drawing tool). While such a combination illustrates the notion of collaborative computing, a key disadvantage is the user-centric setup and coordination required in order to collaborate. That is, while the two streams of communication are occurring in parallel, the lack of integration does not readily facilitate, and sometimes even inhibits, using them together.

To address this issue, the notion of *collaborative multimedia* combines presentational, conversational and interactive multimedia into a single, unified and integrated approach. Thus, rather than relying on disjoint parallel technologies, collaborative multimedia supports participants freely moving between the types of expression, information and interaction as desired and appropriate for the collaborative effort. Providing such an environment necessitates providing interoperable tools and technologies that "fit well" together not only technologically (such as in terms of data formats, communication mechanisms and programming interfaces) but also in terms of comprehensive and complementary functionality, appropriate usability and fluidity relative to the participants and processes (e.g., workflow). Through an integrated environment, support for participant awareness of each other and the overall collaborative effort can be increased through more comprehensive and coordinated interaction. The natural communication styles required within the collaborative process can be supported in an integrated manner that is useful, flexible, comprehensible and meaningful to those involved. Therefore, a various kinds of collaborative practices, processes and behaviours, both at individual and group levels, can be more easily supported.

Characterizing Collaboration

In terms of conduct, collaboration has been characterized in terms of three main types: ad hoc, guided and structured. Ad hoc collaboration is typically informal, often spontaneous and usually short-term in nature. Classic examples of ad hoc collaboration include brainstorming sessions, instant messaging and conference calls. Guided and structured collaboration are ostensibly more formal in that they regulate interactions between collaborators in a organized and continuous (on-going) manner. Guided and structured collaboration offer varying degrees of organization in terms of how much they implement and/or follow prescribed (business) processes. Examples include workflow computing and on-line meetings. However, both conference calls and on-line meetings can range from ad hoc to structured, depending on the rules governing the particular collaborative effort. Similarly, large-scale collaborative efforts such as scientific computing initiatives [5] can range in their degree of formality, in large part based on their particular technological and/or methodological focus. Consequently, this diversity in what it means to collaborate highlights the fact that the true characterization of collaboration is multifaceted, including not only the technologies used but also the people and the processes they employ.

Ultimately, the key drivers affecting the reality of collaborative computing include the cultural, communication and behavioral styles of the individuals and organizations participating in the collaborative process and utilizing the various technologies. In addressing these areas, human-computer interaction (HCI), computer supported cooperative work (CSCW), groupware and computer mediated communications (CMC) have traditionally constituted the predominant R&D areas within collaborative computing. Amongst them, significant effort has been put towards the development of various computer and communication technologies as well as emphasis on user-centric issues.

While such efforts are fundamentally important to the creation of collaborative systems, collaborating in an intelligible manner is ultimately impacted by the often subtle and implicit *coordination* of activities that is part of the collaborative process [3]. Consequently, coordination must be facilitated by all aspects of a collaborative effort (be it technical, process or people) in order to achieve an environment in which the actions performed upon objects and the interactions between participants make sense; that is, meaning must be maintained through synchronizing the participants and their actions relative to the overall behavior and role of the system. Doing so requires knowing the context and type of work being done as well as the informational aspects associated with it [6]. Maintaining knowledge of these aspects as well as facilitating the actual collaborative functionality can be derived from four basic requirements for a collaborative system:

- Connectedness: Ensure necessary connectivity between participants.
- Awareness: Facilitate awareness (and discovery) of other participants.
- Sharing: Facilitate sharing and exchange of information between participants.
- Communication: Facilitate dialogue and interaction between participants (above and beyond information exchange).

Subsequently, these four elements can be seen as being axiomatic enablers for collaboration: given that participants are linked and aware of each other in a way that allows them to share information and communicate (at a metalevel) about the information and the processes/activities they wish to utilize, complex and coordinated collaborative efforts are then a matter of exercising control over these aspects and utilizing the necessary functionality in the correct behavioral contexts (see [7] and the companion article on "Behavioral Facilitation").

Traditional Collaboration – Groupware & Computer-Supported Cooperative Work

The long-standing history of office automation has lead to the classification of collaborative computing into two broad categories: (1) *groupware*; and (2) *computer-supported collaborative work (CSCW)*. Defined as "computer-based systems that support groups of people engaged in a common task (or goal) and that provide an interface to a shared environment" [1], the primary focus of groupware is to provide a group interface for a shared task. In a similar vein, computer-supported cooperative work systems deal with how technology (specifically computer systems) can assist in the work process. These two areas are often combined into a single focus which addresses how groups of people can work together in a (logically) shared environment with the assistance of computer support.

Table 1. Collaborative Time/Place Matrix

Time Place	Same	Different
Same	Synchronous Interaction e.g., face-to-face	Asynchronous Interaction e.g., note left on chair
Different	Synchronous Distributed Interaction e.g., telephone conversation	Asynchronous Distributed Interaction e.g., postal mail

As illustrated in Table 1, groupware systems span a spectrum of usage patterns and the illustrated time/place matrix is a well-known taxonomy. Systems which support synchronous activity are known as *real-time groupware* while those that support asynchronous activity (such as electronic mail) are non-real-time. Synchronous systems therefore offer a concurrent shared environment in which multiple users can interact simultaneously while asynchronous systems provide for serial non-shared interaction. As a rule, most groupware systems primarily support interaction along only one such dimension.

Groupware systems have also been classified based on application functionality, including the categories of message systems, multi-user editors, computer conferencing, intelligent agents, (group) decision support and coordination systems. An overview and discussion can be found in [1]. Systems often span multiple categories in this taxonomy and can be used in an overlapping manner by a group to accomplish its goal. Consequently, collaboration can be seen as a blend of activities used in varying ways across multiple participants. Therefore, the utility of a collaborative environment is directly influenced by its openness and flexibility such that it can support the integration of different technologies to support various collaborative tasks [8].

To support this diversity within collaboration, several different perspectives exist in the application of groupware technologies; these include: distributed systems, communications, human-computer interaction, artificial intelligence and social theory [1]. For practical purposes, many systems (with some exceptions, such as [7, 9]) support group work according to a particular approach and with their own unique focus. Such an example would be *workflow management systems (WfMS)*, which generally aim at assisting business or government groups in communicating, coordinating and collaborating with a special emphasis on the facilitation (i.e., automation and/or augmentation) of business processes. To do so, WfMS deal with temporal aspects such as activity sequencing, deadlines, routing conditions and schedules. They are typically "organizationally aware," containing an explicit representation of organizational processes and often provide a rigid work environment consisting of roles, associated activities and applications. Such systems are usually highly valuable in their organizational context but are either built-for-purpose or require significant customization to meet the needs of a particular group.

Contemporary Trends in Collaboration

The broad character and often ambiguous nature of collaboration have long made the area a difficult one for which to provide satisfactory implementations. Additionally, because the very essence of collaborative systems is as an enabler to other activities, the reality and culture (be it technical, scientific, corporate or otherwise) play a substantial and often dominant role in what can be or should be done in terms of collaboration. Hence, the trends in what collaboration needs to address and how to provide for them in real systems have evolved substantially with the increased integration of information technology into people's daily routine, both at work and at leisure.

Similar to the evolution in the traditional computing world, collaborative systems started out being specialized, purpose-built systems (be it software, hardware and/or facilities). Examples include the use of dedicated video teleconferencing (VTC) rooms (often only by businesses with significant budgets and infrastructure) through to the evolution of various research prototypes over the past decades. A smattering of such efforts includes RAPPORT [10], MERMAID [11], SHASTRA [12], collaboratories [5] and media spaces [2]. While many of the original efforts necessitated special systems that were different from a person's normal work environment, such an approach today would not achieve much success. The desire for commonality and interoperability in work environments has also been made more important by the fact that the boundary between individual and collaborative work is increasingly porous, such that many tasks carried out with single-user tools can really be considered collaborative in nature. For example, the creation of a document or a software module may be done in isolation, but they can also be considered collaborative products via their use of (or use within) other efforts.

This reality is fundamental to modern business, government and scientific organizations, and is the basis for two key trends in how collaboration is facilitated in contemporary systems: (1) integration and interoperability with commonplace IT (information technology) environments, both in form and function; and (2) flexibility in the ability to combine different functionality at different scales and levels of granularity, ranging from workflow and decision support, knowledge management and visualization [13] through to support for enhanced multimedia-based communication and group interaction [14].

An overarching trend is to enable the "single-user experience" to be reconfigured to support the collaborative tasks. The Co-Word project [15] and related work illustrate this idea of "transparently re-purposing" the currently ubiquitous (single-user) word processing tool from Microsoft into a distributed writing tool. Such an effort represents an attempt to deal with the problematic issue of specialized multi-user collaborative tools vs. the use of standard single-user tools in a collaborative manner. In many cases, however, the standard tools are not modified to address the issues that arise in a distributed collaborative environment; rather they rely on the use of application and desktop sharing technologies. The use of such "application containers" effectively attempts to "fake out" a single user application by multiplexing its input and output across a number of users at different physical locations. Such an approach is in contrast to the creation of native, multi-user collaborative tools and does not focus on the group activity that must be coordinated to accomplish the collaborative goal. Therefore, simply using desktop sharing addresses only a portion of difficult issues related to working in a distributed environment.

Additionally, a number of general trends in modern collaborative computing can be illustrated by the typical requirements listed below:

- Support a range of collaborative uses – from ad hoc through to structured
- Integrate workflow and business process support, including daily tasks, scheduling, audit trails and so forth
- Ensure ease and familiarity of use
- Utilize extensible component-based architectures
- Leverage existing infrastructural services
- Utilize commercial off-the-shelf (COTS) and standards-based products
- Promote platform neutrality – availability and consistency across multiple platforms

These requirements are typically aimed at increasing user acceptance, increasing flexibility, reducing costs and benefiting from existing knowledge and systems. Classic means of addressing them include the use of web-based interfaces which promote both ease and familiarity of use, while consequently relying on component-based architectures and the utilization of well-known standards. Additional benefits typically include easier software management and integration into existing systems.

As an example, consider the evolution from the earlier work on collaboratories [5] to the subsequent effort known as the Pervasive Collaborative Computing Environment (PCCE) [16]. The initial collaboratory project was designed to support distributed scientific research initiatives by providing information, control, and a sense of presence to remote researchers. Emphasis was on the tools and infrastructure to provide remote experiment monitoring and control, multimedia conferencing (telepresence) and conference management/coordination. Issues included platform independence as well as ensuring usability in order to promote acceptance amongst its target audience (a highly specialized, technical workforce).   Subsequently, the Pervasive Collaborative Computing Environment (or PCCE) was developed as a persistent collaborative space to support continuous and ad hoc collaboration. Its focus is daily tasks such as document sharing and provides basic connectivity for communication, including an XMPP (Extensible Messaging and Presence Protocol) text-based messaging component and BPEL (Business Process Execution Language) workflow tool that allow visual composition and tracking of the workflow of scientific computations.   Based on a combination of web and grid technologies, the PCCE allows collaborators to:

- Find and contact other participants [thus supporting awareness and discovery]
- Send instant messages synchronously and asynchronously [thus supporting awareness, communication and information sharing]
- Hold private and group conversations [thus supporting communication, information sharing and "community" definition]
- Participate in multiple conversations simultaneously [thus supporting the reality of a multitasking workplace]
- Archive interactions [thus supporting workflow/business processes]
- Submit and track current workflow [thus supporting awareness, coordination and workflow/business processes]
- Dynamic application sharing and audio/video conferencing sessions [thus supporting awareness, communication, information sharing and the reality of a multitasking workplace]

These types of functionality are common to many collaborative environments; however, the kind of work environment they focus on (e.g., a computing infrastructure vs. a repository-oriented workspace) and the style of user (e.g., scientists vs. generalists) can result in different an emphasis being placed on different tools (e.g., experimental control vs. workflow/process). The different efforts also illustrate the trend towards a broader and more integrationist approach to collaborative functionality (i.e., consideration of conferencing as a feature not a focus). The tendency to augment and blend functionalities was also illustrated by the introduction of audio to the (originally text-only) instant messaging component.   This illustrated how an original intention to provide for a balanced communication medium (more immediate than email but less intrusive than telephone) grew to be a richer but also more invasive communications channel.

Despite the merit of some of these trends and the opportunities afforded by the resulting systems, many of them are incongruent with conservative approach to collaborative computing often taken by the very same organizations which wish to mandate them. This dichotomy is illustrated next.

Corporate Collaboration: The Conservative Reality

Despite the wealth of topics that comprise collaborative computing, current practices within government and industry can best be described as somewhat conservative. While many potential benefits are known, the investment in existing infrastructure combined with the comfort of familiar practices offer challenges to those who hope to push the boundary of collaborative computing forward.

Many organizations have a limited scope in terms of what they consider collaborative computing. Specifically, organizational inertia often limits a broader deployment of collaborative computing, further burdened by policy, traditional operating procedures, fear of change and concern over ancillary and support costs [17]. The result is that many organizations' collaborative computing environment consists of four elements:

- Video teleconferencing (VTC)
- Audio conferencing (conference call)
- Electronic mail (e-mail)
- Shared directories (file shares and network file systems)

This standard audio and video conferencing still typically utilize dedicated equipment and facilities (e.g., specially-equipped meeting rooms) based primarily on ISDN (Integrated Services Digital Network) and PSTN (Public Switched Telephone Network). Such designs largely stem from significant legacy investment and interoperability requirements as well as the need to ensure quality and availability via circuit-switched technology. Unfortunately, these traditional VTC systems are typically "video" oriented, usually with an independent, self-contained control system and any support for data display/transfer being limited. Conversely, e-mail and shared directories facilitate collaboration though conventional IT means; thus they represent a trend towards personal computer-based collaboration and a desktop focus. Combined with the current movement towards convergence with conventional computer and network infrastructure, this approach is forcing a re-evaluation of the conventional ISDN/PSTN conferencing approach and a (slow) migration away from ISDN towards systems based on IP. Currently, many current VTC codecs provide support for both protocols (ISDN/IP) and indeed the use of IP telephony, including IP-based handsets is increasing.

As part of the increasing collaborative desktop focus, use of web-based collaboration is proliferating. Browsing now often forms the interface for a large number of organizations' information and knowledge management systems. Other current practices include the use of portal technology (both open source and commercial systems), on-line meeting facilitation (both as externally-provided "pay-as-you-go" and dedicated services), as well as content management and configuration management systems. On-line meeting systems are typically accessed through portals and offer a number of popular business-oriented collaborative services such as agenda management, distributed presentations, workflow support, task management, calendaring, decision support – including voting/polling, desktop sharing and the like. Example systems include MeetingZone and LiveMeeting (based on NetMeeting). Such functionality is often tied to content management systems which are used to provide increased knowledge management services (such as meta-tagging, categorization and classification services) to information traditionally communicated through email and/or shared file systems. Similarly, collaborative and distributed software developments often make the use of configuration management systems (including source control systems). While often treated as a given, the importance of "trivial" features such as version control and baselining cannot be underestimated in any collaborative effort.

While groupware has typically been regarded as the essence of collaborative computing, it is necessary to realize that despite the increased web-based collaborative focus, a sole spotlight on groupware is not a realistic view of collaborative computing – especially in the current business climate. In particular, two areas that can have a significant impact on the acceptance of collaborative computing need to be considered throughout the research, architecting, design, development, selection, deployment and management phases of collaborating computing systems. These are: (1) security and (2) source.

In terms of security, issues range from system and network architectures to software and data management. For example, the current preference for many organizations is to use "thin" vs. "thick" clients in order to lessen management and security concerns surrounding software installation and upgrades. Similarly, the use of the "service" industry to provide remotely hosted collaborative functionality (e.g., data storage, on-line meeting and user presence/awareness servers) are not readily accepted by many organizations. Additionally, the provision of network security often requires far more than firewall and anti-virus solutions; encryption is often hardware-based, and in some cases, a complete physical separation of systems may be required. The idyllic "one big network" often euphemized in collaborative computing and multimedia research can oft times be a major issue in government arenas. Therefore, realizing a "network service" can sometimes prove difficult simply due to the need to demarcate where functionality resides in terms of organizational control and responsibility. This is further complicated by the notion of mobile and ad hoc functionality that moves around the network (e.g., downloadable "applets" that cannot be validated to the organization's satisfaction). While such issues may seem annoying to many, they play a pivotal role in the potential acceptance and growth of collaborative computing in many domains.

The second issue of "source" refers to the contemporary aversion to custom system (software and hardware) solutions. Most large organizations today are (economically) risk-adverse and rely on the "comfort and safety" of using known technologies, benefiting from recognized reliability and user familiarity (with user interfaces, terminology, workflow, etc). Thus the use of the traditional approach to groupware and collaborative computing (via custom shared, multi-user applications) is not generally accepted. Organizations typically wish to use COTS products from well-known, reliable vendors that are shared via desktop sharing (when and as required). While not necessarily the best method to achieve collaboration, it is a reality with a large number of businesses and government agencies. Typically only select institutions, such as pure research organizations, may be willing to utilize speculative and research-level collaborative approaches in their "business practices". While a broader spectrum of organizations are increasingly using collaborative technologies and practices, including ad hoc brainstorming systems, chat/instant messaging and even blogging, such diversity is still typically a microcosm of progressive collaborative computing that serves as a motivational example for others to follow.

See: Behavioral Facilitation; Integration with Modeling and Simulation; Multimedia Conferencing; Portals; Workflow Computing

References

1. C. Ellis, S. Gibbs, and G. Rein, "Groupware: Some Issues and Experiences," Communications of the ACM, 1991, pp. 38-58.
2. W. E. Mackay, "Media Spaces: Environments for Informal Multimedia Interaction," Computer Supported Cooperative Work (M. Beaudouin-Lafon, Ed.), John Wiley and Sons: Chichester, 1999, pp. 55-82.
3. T. W. Malone and K. Crowston, "The Interdisciplinary Study of Coordination," ACM Computing Surveys, Vol. 16, No. 1, 1994, pp. 87-119.
4. P. Dourish and V. Bellotti, "Awareness and Coordination in Shared Work Space," Proceedings of the ACM Conference on Computer-Supported Cooperative Work (CSCW'92), ACM Press, Toronto, Canada, pp. 107-114.
5. D. A. Agarwal, S. R. Sachs and W. E. Johnston, "The Reality of Collaboratories," Computer Physics Communications, Vol. 110, No. 1-3, 1998, pp. 134-141.
6. J. C. Grundy, W. B. Mugridge, J. G. Hosking and M. D. Apperley, "Coordinating, Capturing and Presenting Work Contexts in CSCW Systems," Proceedings of OZCHI'95, Wollongon, Australia, 1995, pp 146-151.
7. R. W. Robbins, "Facilitating Intelligent Media Space Collaboration via RASCAL: The Reflectively Adaptive Synchronous Coordination Architectural Framework," PhD Thesis, School of Information Technology and Engineering, University of Ottawa, 2001.
8. Cockburn and S. Jones, "Four Principles for Groupware Design," Interacting with Computers, Vol. 7, No. 2, 1995, pp. 195-210.
9. W. J. Tolone, "Introspect: A Meta-Level Specification Framework for Dynamic, Evolvable Collaboration Support," Ph.D. Thesis, Department of Computer Science, University Of Illinois at Urbana-Champaign, 1996.
10. S. R. Ahuja, J. R. Ensor, and D. N. Horn, "The Rapport Multimedia Conferencing System," Proceedings of the ACM Conference on Office Information Systems, 1988, pp. 1-8.
11. K. Watabe, S. Sakata, K. Maeno, H. Fukuoka, and K. Maebara, "A Distributed Multiparty Desktop Conferencing System and its Architecture," Proceedings of the IEEE Phoenix Conference on Computers and Communications, IEEE, Phoenix, AZ, 1990, pp. 386 – 393.
12. V. Anupam and C. L. Bajaj, "Shastra: Multimedia Collaborative Design Environment," IEEE Multimedia, Vol. 1, No. 2, 1994, pp. 39-49.
13. H. Chen, J. Nunamaker Jr., R. Orwig and O. Titkova, "Information Visualization for Collaborative Computing," Computer, Vol. 31, No. 8, 1998, pp. 75-82.
14. D. N. Snowdon, E. F. Churchill, and E. Frécon (eds.), "Inhabited Information Spaces: Living with your Data," New York: Springer, 2004.
15. S. Xia, D. Sun, C. Sun, D. Chen, and H. Shen, "Leveraging Single-User Applications for Multi-User Collaboration: The Co-Word Approach," Proceedings of the 2004 ACM Conference on Computer Supported Cooperative Work (CSCW'04), Chicago, Illinois: ACM Press, 2004, pp. 162-171.
16. M. Perry and D. Agarwal, "Collaborative Editing within the Pervasive Collaborative Computing Environment," Proceedings of the 5th International Workshop on Collaborative Editing (ECSCW 2003), Helsinki, Finland, 2003.

17. W. Robbins, S. Lam, and C. Lalancette, "Towards a Collaborative Engineering Environment to Support Capability Engineering," Proceedings of the 2005 INCOSE International Symposium – Systems Engineering: Bridging Industry, Government and Academia, Rochester, New York: International Council on Systems Engineering, 2005.

COLLABORATIVE VIRTUAL ENVIRONMENTS

Definition: A collaborative virtual environment is a shared virtual world that allows its users to collaborate in the synthetic world, performing shared object manipulation and other collaborative tasks.

Virtual Reality (VR) is the technology that provides almost real and/or believable experiences in a synthetic or virtual way. Collaborative Virtual Environments (CVE) are currently one of the most challenging VR research areas. A CVE is a shared virtual world that allows its users to collaborate in the synthetic world, performing shared object manipulation and other collaborative tasks. This adds new dimensions to the needs of human-factors, networking, synchronization, middleware, object model acquisition and representation. Collaborative manipulation requires the consideration of how participants should interact with each other in a shared space, in addition to how to co-manipulated objects should behave and work together. The main issue in a CVE, in addition to the other issues in VR, is how distributed entities share and maintain the same resources. CVE systems must address many important issues, including:

Consistency: The fundamental model presented by a CVE platform is a shared 3D space. Since all clients accessing or updating the data share the 3D graphics database, the issue of distributed consistency must be solved by any CVE to ensure the same view is presented to all participants [1].

Scalability: The number of possible interactions between n simultaneous users in a multi-user system is of order $O(n2)$ at any moment. Ideally network traffic should be almost constant or grow near-linearly with the number of users. Usually, not all the data in the CVE environment would be relevant to a particular user at a given time. This suggests the idea of partitioning the environment into regions (or zones, locales, auras) that may either be fixed or bound to moving avatars.

Ownership: A multi-user CVE world is subject to conflicts. Conflicts occur when collaborating users perform opposing actions, for example, a conflict may arise if one user tries to open a window while another user is trying to close it. These conflicts must be avoided or solved.

Persistence: Some of these applications that involve a large number of users need a large-scale, persistent collaborative virtual environment (PCVE) system that is "never-ending" or "always on". This is either because its users require that it is always running, or because it is so large or distributed that stopping the entire simulation to make changes is just not possible.

<u>Dynamic Configuration:</u> This property allows a PCVE system to dynamically configure itself without user interaction, enabling applications to take on new functionalities after their execution. CVEs should be modifiable at run-time by accepting the contributions of new objects and new behaviors.

See: Virtual and Augmented Reality

References

1. S. Shirmohammadi and N.D. Georganas, "An End-to-End Communication Architecture for Collaborative Virtual Environments," Computer Networks Journal, Vol. 35, No. 2-3, February 2001, pp. 351-367.

COLOR IMAGE FILTERING AND ENHANCEMENT

Rastislav Lukac, Konstantinos N. Plataniotis, and Anastasios N. Venetsanopoulos
University of Toronto, Toronto, Canada

Definition: *Color image filtering and enhancement refer to the process of noise reduction in the color image and enhancement of the visual quality of the image input.*

Noise encountered into the image data reduces the perceptual quality of an image and thus limits the performance of the imaging system. The generation of high quality color images which are visually pleasing is of great importance in a variety of application areas. That pre supposes image filtering, since images captured with sensing devices and transmitted through communication networks are often corrupted by noise (Figure 1) [1],[2],[3]. Therefore, both filtering and enhancement constitute an important part of any image processing pipeline where the final image is utilized for visual inspection or for automatic analysis.

image acquisition and transmission

image filtering and enhancement

Figure 1. A block scheme of the common image acquisition/transmission/processing pipeline.

The filtering operators applied to color images are required to preserve color information and structural content (edges and fine details), and to remove noise [4],[5]. The choice of these criteria follows the well-known fact that the human visual system is sensitive to changes in color appearance and fine details. Further to that, a good filtering/enhancement method should maintain the edge information while it removes image noise. Edges are important features since they indicate the presence, and the shape, of various objects in the image. From this viewpoint it is evident that the noise removal task in digital color imaging may be viewed as compromise between the noise suppression and color/structural content preservation.

Fundamentals of Color Imaging

Following the tristimulus theory of color representation [6], each pixel in a color Red-Green-Blue image (Figure 2) can be viewed as a three-component vector $\mathbf{x}_i = [x_{i1}, x_{i2}, x_{i3}]$ in the color RGB space (Figure 3). Thus, the color image is a vector array or a two-dimensional matrix of three-component samples $\mathbf{x}_i$ with x_{ik} denoting the R ($k=1$), G ($k=2$) or B ($k=3$) component (Figure 2) [1]. The chromaticity properties of color vector $\mathbf{x}_i$ relate to its magnitude and direction (orientation in the vector space) which respectively relate to the luminance and chromaticity characteristics of the color pixel. Since both these measures are essential for human perception, color image processing techniques should preserve the color vectors' characteristics during processing. The processing operations can be performed in the magnitude domain, directional domain, or ideally both magnitude and directional information should be taken into consideration in outputting the color image with enhanced visual quality [1].

| (a) | (b) | (c) | (d) |

Figure 2. Digital color imaging: (a) color RGB image, (b-d) decomposed image channels; (b) R channel, (c) G channel, (d) B channel.

Noise Modeling

Noise in digital images can be introduced by numerous sources, with the most common of them listed in Figure 4, and is present in almost any image processing system. Based on the difference between the observation (noisy) color vector $\mathbf{x}_i = [x_{i1}, x_{i2}, x_{i3}]$ and the original (desired) sample $\mathbf{o}_i = [o_{i1}, o_{i2}, o_{i3}]$, the noise corruption is modeled via the additive noise model $\mathbf{x}_i = \mathbf{o}_i + \mathbf{v}_i$ with $\mathbf{v}_i = [v_{i1}, v_{i2}, v_{i3}]$ denoting the vector which describes the noise process [1],[2]. The noise contribution $\mathbf{v}_i$ can describe either signal-dependent or independent noise.

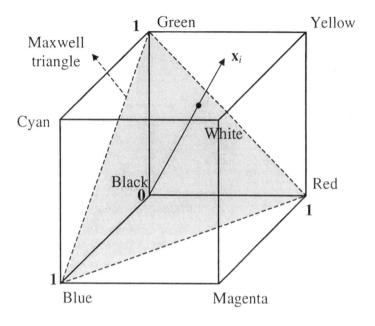

Figure 3. A color RGB space.

Given the definition above, color noise is the amount of color fluctuation given a certain color signal. As such the color noise signal should be considered as a three-channel perturbation vector in the RGB color space, affecting the spread of the actual color vectors in the space [1].

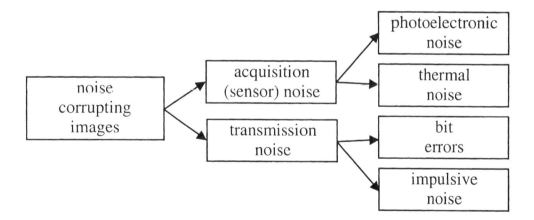

Figure 4. Most frequently sources of noise in digital images.

Image Filtering Basics

Noise reduction techniques are most often divided into two classes [5],[7]: i) linear techniques, and ii) nonlinear techniques. Linear processing techniques have been widely used in digital signal processing applications, since their mathematical simplicity and the availability of a unifying linear system theory make these techniques relatively easy to analyze and implement. However, most of the linear techniques tend to blur structural elements such as lines, edges and other fine image details. Since image signals are nonlinear in nature due to the presence of structural information and are perceived via the human visual system which has strong nonlinear characteristics, nonlinear filters can potentially preserve important multichannel structural elements, such as color edges and eliminate degradations occurring during signal formation or transmission through nonlinear channel.

Since natural images should be considered non-stationary signals due to presence of edges, varying color information and noise, filtering schemes operate on the premise that an image can be subdivided into small regions, each of which can be treated as stationary [1],[8]. Most color filtering techniques operate on some type of sliding window placing the pixel $\mathbf{x}_{(N+1)/2}$ under consideration at the center of the processing window (Figure 5). This pixel's value is changed as a result of a filtering operation on the vectors $\mathbf{x}_1, \mathbf{x}_2, ..., \mathbf{x}_N$ included in a local neighborhood. This window operator slides over the entire image successively placing each image pixel at its center (Figure 5).

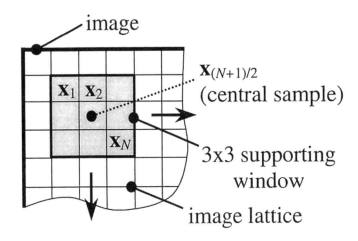

Figure 5. A concept of a 3×3 running filtering window.

The performance of a filtering scheme is generally influenced by the size of the local area inside the processing window [1]. Some applications may require larger support to read local image features and complete the task appropriately. On the other hand, a filter operating on a smaller spatial neighborhood can better match image details. The most commonly used window is a 3×3 square shape (Figure 5) due to its versatility and performance, however, a particular window, such as those presented in [1] can be designed to preserve specifically oriented image edges.

Component-wise vs. Vector Color Image Filtering

Since each individual channel of a color image can be considered a monochrome (gray-scale) image (Figure 2), traditional image filtering techniques such as well-known (scalar) median filters [8],[9] often involved the application of scalar filters on each channel separately (Figure 6a). However, this disrupts the correlation that exists between the color components of natural images represented in a correlated color space, such as RGB or its standardized variants. Given the fact that each processing step is usually accompanied by a certain inaccuracy, the formation of the output color vector from the separately processed color components usually produces color artifacts [1].

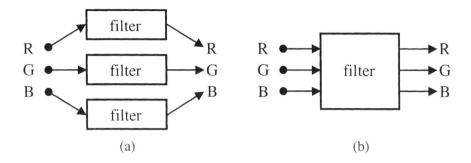

(a)   (b)

Figure 6. Demonstration of: (a) component-wise and (b) vector processing of color RGB images.

It is believed that vector filtering techniques that treat the color image as a vector field (Figure 6b) are more appropriate for color image processing. With such an approach, the filter output is a function of the vectorial inputs $\mathbf{x}_1, \mathbf{x}_2, ..., \mathbf{x}_N$ located within the supporting window (Figure 5). The two basic classes of vector filters are constituted by [1]: i) vector median related filters [10],[11], and ii) vector directional filters [5],[12]-[14].

The vector median filter (VMF) [10] is a vector processing operator which has been introduced as an extension of the scalar median filter. The VMF output is the sample (lowest ranked vector or lowest order statistics) $\mathbf{x}_{(1)} \in \{\mathbf{x}_1, \mathbf{x}_2, ..., \mathbf{x}_N\}$ that minimizes the distance to the other samples inside the processing window as follows [1],[10]:

$$\mathbf{x}_{(1)} = \arg \min_{\mathbf{x}_i \in \{\mathbf{x}_1, \mathbf{x}_2, ..., \mathbf{x}_N\}} \sum_{j=1}^{N} \| \mathbf{x}_i - \mathbf{x}_j \|_L$$

where $\| \cdot \|_L$ is the Minkowski metric used to quantify the distance between two color pixels $\mathbf{x}_i$ and $\mathbf{x}_j$ in the magnitude domain. Since the above concept can be used to determine the positions of the different input vectors without any a priori information regarding the signal distributions, VMF-related filters are robust estimators.

Vector directional filters operate on the directions of image vectors, aiming at eliminating vectors with atypical directions in the color space. The output of the basic vector directional filter (BVDF) [12] is the sample (lowest ranked vector or lowest order statistics) $\mathbf{x}_{(1)} \in \{\mathbf{x}_1, \mathbf{x}_2, ..., \mathbf{x}_N\}$ which minimizes the angular ordering criteria to other samples inside the sliding filtering window:

$$\mathbf{x}_{(1)} = \arg \min_{\mathbf{x}_i \in \{\mathbf{x}_1, \mathbf{x}_2, ..., \mathbf{x}_N\}} \sum_{j=1}^{N} A(\mathbf{x}_i, \mathbf{x}_j)$$

where $A(\cdot,\cdot)$ denotes the angle (angular distance) between two color vectors. Thus, the VDF filters do not take into account the brightness of color vectors. To utilize both features in color image filtering, the generalized vector directional filters (GVDF) and double window GVDF first eliminate the color vectors with atypical directions in the vector space and subsequently process the vectors with the most similar orientation according to their magnitude. In this way, the GVDF splits the color image processing into directional processing and magnitude processing [1],[2].

The traditional VMF and VDF filters do not take into account neither the importance of the specific samples in the filter window or structural contents of the image. Better performance can be obtained when distances are appropriately modified by weighting coefficients representing the degree to which each input vector contributes to the output of the filter [1],[5] or of which the specific distances between multichannel inputs contribute to the aggregated measure serving as an ordering criterion [7]. Such an idea is behind the weighted vector filters such as weighted VMFs [11], weighted VDFs [13],[14] and fuzzy-weighted VDFs [1],[2],[5]. The selection weighted vector filters in [7] allow for the simultaneous utilization of both the magnitude and directional characteristics of the color vectors, and generalize a number of previous filtering techniques including VMF, BVDF and their weighted modifications.

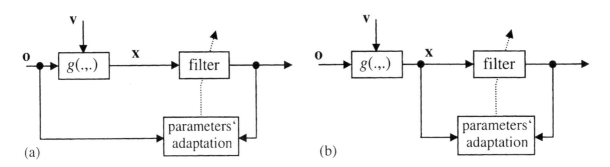

Figure 7. Demonstration of the adaptive filtering concept: (a) filter's adaptation using original image, (b) filter's adaptation using noisy image.

To adapt the filter weights (or parameters in general) to varying signal and noise statistics, different multichannel adaptation algorithms can be utilized (Figure 7) [1],[7]. The achieved weights should be sufficiently robust and their utilization should lead to the essential trade-off between noise smoothing and signal-detail preservation (Figure 8).

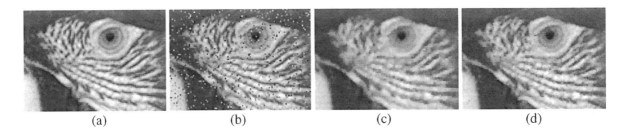

Figure 8. Demonstration of filtering performance: (a) original image, (b) noisy image, (c) VMF output, (d) adaptive vector filter output [7].

Switching Vector Filters

Traditional filtering schemes such as VMF and BVDF which operate on a fixed supporting window introduce excessive smoothing, blur edges and eliminate fine image details [4],[13],[15]. This effect should be attributed to the low-pass filtering characteristics of these color image filters. To prevent excessive smoothing and preserve fine image details, one of the most popular and computationally efficient solutions switch between a robust nonlinear smoothing mode and an identity processing mode which leaves input samples unchanged during the filtering operation (Figure 9) [4],[16],[17]. Such an approach allows for the fast adaptation of the filter behavior to the statistics of the input image and it usually leads to an excellent performance in the environments with impulsive-type noise.

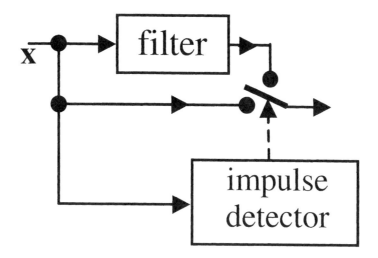

Figure 9. Switching filtering concept.

Emerging Applications

Robust performance characteristics and a trade-off between noise suppression and color/structural information preservation are often required in real-life imaging applications where inputs are often corrupted by noise or other visual impairments. Emerging applications include [1], but not limited to, virtual restoration of artworks and enhancement of the digitized images in digital artwork libraries, reconstruction of television images and old movies, microarray image processing and many others. The appearance of the noise as well as useful color/structural image information differs between the applications and thus, the designer should take into consideration the specifics of each application.

For example, strong color/structural preserving characteristics are required in the virtual restoration of artworks (Figure 10) [4]. In this application, noise is introduced by scanning the granulated, dirty, or damaged surface of the original artworks. To produce visually pleasing enhanced image with removed outliers and sharply looking fine details, adaptive vector filters should be used [1],[4]. On the other hand, cDNA microarray image processing (Figure 11) may require the utilization of robust processing techniques such as the vector order-statistics filters [18],[20] or the vector fuzzy filters [19], which are capable to preserve the spot information and eliminate substantial noise floor in the two-channel cDNA image data.

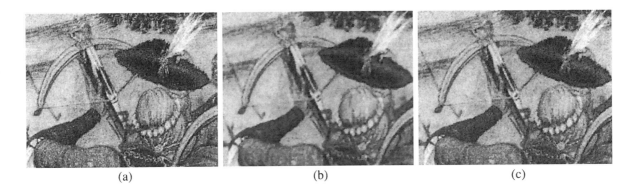

(a)   (b)   (c)

Figure 10. Virtual restoration of artworks: (a) digitized artwork image, (b) image enhanced using the VMF, (c) image enhanced using adaptive switching vector filter in [4].

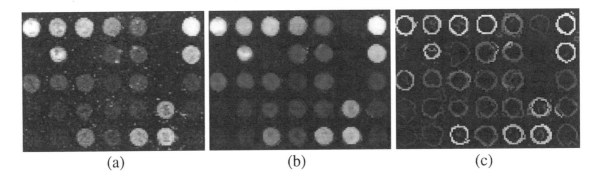

(a)   (b)   (c)

Figure 11. cDNA microarray image processing: (a) acquired cDNA microarray image, (b) image enhanced using the technique in [18], and (c) its corresponding edge-map with localized microarray spots [18],[20].

See: Edge detection, Scalar edge detectors, Vector edge detectors, Color image zooming, Multichannel data ordering schemes, Distance and similarity measures, Digital camera image processing, Image inpainting, Inpainting in virtual restoration of artworks, Video inpainting.

References

1. R. Lukac, B. Smolka, K. Martin, K.-N. Plataniotis, and A.-N. Venetsanopulos, "Vector Filtering for Color Imaging," IEEE Signal Processing Magazine; Special Issue on Color Image Processing, Vol. 22, No. 1, January 2005, pp. 74-86.

2. K.-N. Plataniotis and A.-N. Venetsanopoulos, Color Image Processing and Applications, Springer Verlag, Berlin, 2000.

3. B. Smolka, K.-N. Plataniotis, and A.-N. Venetsanopoulos, "Nonlinear Techniques for Color Image Processing," in Nonlinear Signal and Image Processing: Theory,

Methods, and Applications, K.-E. Barner and G.-R. Arce (Eds.), CRC Press, Boca Raton, 2004, pp. 445-505.

4. R. Lukac, B. Smolka, and K.-N. Plataniotis, "Adaptive Color Image Filter for Application in Virtual Restoration of Artworks," IEEE Trans. Multimedia, submitted.

5. K.-N. Plataniotis, D. Androutsos, and A.-N. Venetsanopoulos, "Adaptive Fuzzy Systems for Multichannel Signal Processing," Proceedings of the IEEE, Vol. 87, No. 9, Sept. 1999, pp. 1601-1622.

6. G. Wyszecki and W. S. Stiles, "Color Science, Concepts and Methods, Quantitative Data and Formulas," John Wiley, N.Y., 2nd Edition, 1982.

7. R. Lukac, K.-N. Plataniotis, B. Smolka, and A.-N. Venetsanopoulos, "Generalized Selection Weighted Vector Filters," EURASIP Journal on Applied Signal Processing: Special Issue on Nonlinear Signal and Image Processing - Part I, Vol. 2004, No. 12, October 2004, pp. 1870-1885.

8. I. Pitas and A.N. Venetsanopoulos, Nonlinear Digital Filters, Principles and Applications. Norwell, MA: Kluwer, 1990.

9. J. Zheng, K.-P. Valavanis, and J.-M. Gauch, "Noise Removal from Color Images," Journal of Intelligent and Robotic Systems, Vol. 7, 1993, pp. 257-285.

10. J. Astola, P. Haavisto, and Y. Neuvo, "Vector Median Filters," Proceedings of the IEEE, Vol. 78, No. 4, April 1990, pp. 678-689.

11. T. Viero, K. Oistamo, and Y. Neuvo, Three-Dimensional Median Related Filters for Color Image Sequence Filtering," IEEE Trans. Circuits and Systems for Video Technology, Vol. 4, No. 2, April 1994, pp. 129-142.

12. P. Trahanias, D. Karakos, and A.-N. Venetsanopoulos, "Directional Processing of Color Images: Theory and Experimental Results," IEEE Trans. Image Processing, Vol. 5, No. 6, June 1996, pp. 868-881.

13. R. Lukac, "Adaptive Color Image Filtering Based on Center-Weighted Vector Directional Filters," Multidimensional Systems and Signal Processing, Vol. 15, No. 2, April 2004, pp. 169-196.

14. R. Lukac, B. Smolka, K.-N. Plataniotis, and A.-N. Venetsanopoulos, "Selection Weighted Vector Directional Filters," Computer Vision and Image Understanding, Special Issue on Colour for Image Indexing and Retrieval, Vol. 94, No. 1-3, April-June 2004, pp. 140-167.

15. B. Smolka, R. Lukac, A. Chydzinski, K.-N. Plataniotis, and K. Wojciechowski, "Fast Adaptive Similarity Based Impulsive Noise Reduction Filter," Real-Time Imaging, Special Issue on Spectral Imaging, Vol. 9, No. 4, August 2003, pp. 261-276.

16. R. Lukac, "Adaptive Vector Median Filtering," Pattern Recognition Letters, Vol. 24, No. 12, August 2003, pp. 1889-1899.

17. R. Lukac, B. Smolka, K.-N. Plataniotis, and A.-N. Venetsanopoulos, "A Statistically-Switched Adaptive Vector Median Filter," Journal of Intelligent and Robotic Systems, Vol. 43, 2005.

18. R. Lukac, K.-N. Plataniotis, B. Smolka, and A.-N. Venetsanopoulos, "A Multichannel Order-Statistic Technique for cDNA Microarray Image Processing," IEEE Transactions on Nanobioscience, Vol. 3, No. 4, December 2004, pp. 272-285.

19. R. Lukac, K.-N. Plataniotis, B. Smolka, and A.-N. Venetsanopoulos, "cDNA Microarray Image Processing Using Fuzzy Vector Filtering Framework," Journal of Fuzzy Sets and Systems: Special Issue on Fuzzy Sets and Systems in Bioinformatics, Vol. 152, No. 1, May 2005, pp. 17-35.

20. R. Lukac and K.-N. Plataniotis, "Vector Edge Operators for cDNA Microarray Spot Localization," IEEE Transactions on Nanobioscience, submitted.

COLOR IMAGE NOISE

Definition: *In real-world scenarios, noise in color images may result from many sources, such as the underlying physics of the imaging sensor itself, sensor malfunction, flaws in the data transmission procedure, and electronic interference.*

Although many sources of sensor noise can be significantly reduced, images are mainly affected by the corruption caused by photon shot noise and dark current shot noise resulting from the photo-electric process. Due to the complex nature of the noise process, the overall acquisition noise is usually modeled as a zero mean white Gaussian noise. Aside from this type of noise, image imperfections resulting from impulsive noise are generated during transmission through a communication channel, with sources ranging from human-made to natural. Thus, noise corruption process in simulated scenarios is usually modeled (Figure 1) [1, 2] using additive Gaussian noise, impulsive noise, or mixed noise.

(a)   (b)   (c)   (d)

Figure 1. Simulated color image noise: (a) original image, (b) additive Gaussian noise, (c) impulsive noise, (d) mixed noise (additive Gaussian noise followed by impulsive noise).

Real images (Figure 2) are corrupted by real, non-approximated noise which may be different in characteristics and statistical properties depending on application [1, 2]. For example, television images are corrupted by noise caused by atmospheric interference and imperfections of the transmission channel. Noise is introduced into the digitized artworks by scanning damaged and granulated surfaces of the original artworks. The noise floor present in the cDNA microarray image data can be attributed to both source and detector noise introduced due to the nature of microarray technology. In secure imaging applications, the introduction of noise-like information is essential to protect the content of digital visual materials.

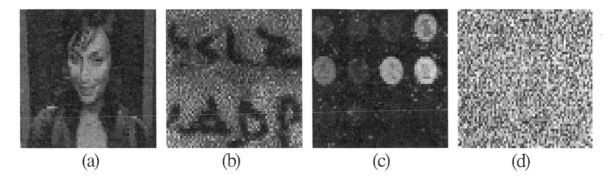

(a)   (b)   (c)   (d)

Figure 2. Examples of color image noise present in: (a) television image, (b) digitized artwork image, (a) cDNA microarray image, (d) encrypted color image.

See: Color image filtering and enhancement, Digital camera image processing, Image secret sharing.

References

1. R. Lukac, B. Smolka, K. Martin, K.-N. Plataniotis, and A.-N. Venetsanopulos, "Vector Filtering for Color Imaging," IEEE Signal Processing Magazine; Vol. 22, No. 1, January 2005, pp. 74-86.
2. K.-N. Plataniotis and A.-N. Venetsanopoulos, Color Image Processing and Applications, Springer Verlag, Berlin, 2000.

COLOR IMAGE ZOOMING

Definition: Image zooming or spatial interpolation of a digital image is the process of increasing the number of pixels representing the natural scene.

Image zooming is frequently used in high resolution display devices [1] and consumer-grade digital cameras [2],[3]. Unlike spectral interpolation, spatial interpolation preserves the spectral representation of the input. Operating on the spatial domain of a digital image, spatial interpolation transforms a gray-scale or color image into an enlarged gray-scale or color image (Figure 1), respectively.

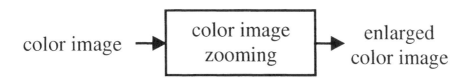

Figure 1. Demonstration of a color image zooming concept.

In the single-sensor imaging pipeline [3], color image zooming operates on the recorded demosaicked image. Such a pipeline typically employs a demosaicking scheme at the first processing stage to produce a full color image. The spatial resolution of the demosaicked image is then increased using a color image zooming technique operating on the RGB color vectors (Figure 2).

It should be noted that since natural color images exhibit strong spectral correlation [2], traditional image zooming methods, which separately process each color channel, often introduce color artifacts. To alleviate the problem and preserve the spectral correlation of the enlarged image's color channels, vector processing is recommended [1],[2]. Vector techniques process the available color pixels as set of vectors and are able to reduce the presence of most color artifacts and eliminate shifted color edges [1],[2].

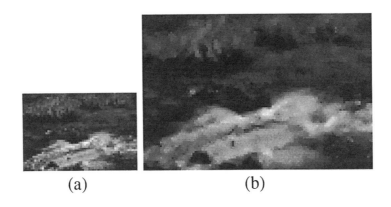

(a)   (b)

Figure 2. Color image zooming: (a) input color image, (b) enlarged color image.

See: Digital camera image processing, Demosaicking, Demosaicked image postprocessing, CFA image zooming, Color image filtering and enhancement.

References

1. N. Herodotou and A.-N. Venetsanopoulos, "Colour Image Interpolation for High Resolution Acquisition and Display Devices," IEEE Transactions on Consumer Electronics, Vol. 41, No. 4, November 1995, pp. 1118-1126.
2. R. Lukac, B. Smolka, K. Martin, K.-N. Plataniotis, and A.-N. Venetsanopulos, "Vector Filtering for Color Imaging," IEEE Signal Processing Magazine; Special Issue on Color Image Processing, Vol. 22, No. 1, January 2005, pp. 74-86.
3. R. Lukac, K.-N. Plataniotis, and D. Hatzinakos: "Color Image Zooming on the Bayer Pattern," IEEE Transactions on Circuit and Systems for Video Technology, Vol. 15, 2005.

COMBINING INTRA-IMAGE AND INTER-CLASS SEMANTICS FOR IMAGE MATCHING

Definition: Both local (intra-image) and global (inter-class) similarities play complementary roles in image matching and ranking, so a simple linear combination scheme has been experimented with significant performance improvement over single image matching schemes.

Given an image retrieval system, the information need of a user can be modeled as the posterior probability of the set of relevant images R given an expression of the information need in the form of query specification q and an image x in the current database, $P(R|q,x)$. The objective of the system is to return images with high probabilities of relevance to the user.

In Query By Example, $P(R|q,x)$ depends on the similarity between query q and image x. On the other hand, we note that the set of relevant images R does not exist until a query has been specified. However we can construct prior categories of images C_k, $k = 1, 2, ...,$ M as some prototypical instances of R and compute the memberships of q and x to these prior categories for contextual similarity (see an article on **Semantic Class-Based Image Indexing**).

Both local (intra-image) and global (inter-class) similarities play complementary roles in image matching and ranking. Using a Bayesian formulation, we have:

$$P(R \mid q, x) = \frac{P(q, x \mid R)\, P(R)}{P(q, x)} \qquad (1)$$

We observe that $P(q,x)$ tends to be small if q and x are similar (i.e. less likely to find similar images than dissimilar pair in a large database). On the other hand, $P(q,x|R)$ tends to be large if q and x are similar with respect to R (i.e. q and x are more likely to co-occur in R if they belong to R). And $P(R)$ is constant for a given query session. Hence $P(R|q,x)$ is proportional to the similarity between q and x given R (denoted as $\mu(q,x)$) and the similarity between q and x in terms of their image contents (denoted as $\lambda(q,x)$) i.e.:

$$P(R \mid q, x) \propto \mu(q, x) \circ \lambda(q, x) \qquad (2)$$

For the purpose of retrieval, Equation (2) provides a principled way to rank images x by their probabilities of relevance to the user's information need as represented by the query example q. When the similarities $\mu(q,x)$ and $\lambda(q,x)$ are expressed in the form of probabilistic distance (i.e. inverse of similarity) such as the Kullback-Leibler distance, ordering images from the smallest distance to the largest distance is the manifestation of the minimum cross-entropy principle ([1],p.13). This echoes the *Probability Ranking Principle* in text information retrieval [2].

To realize local and global semantics, a good choice for $\lambda(q, x)$ and $\mu(q,x)$ are Semantic Support Regions (see an article on **Semantic Image Representation and Indexing**) and Semantic Support Classes (see an article on **Semantic Class-Based Image Indexing**) respectively. Since only ranking matters for practical image retrieval, a simple linear combination scheme has been experimented with significant performance improvement over single image matching schemes [3]. That is, with $\omega \in [0,1]$ and integrated similarity $\rho(q,x)$ replacing $P(R|q, x)$:

$$\rho(q, x) = \omega \cdot \mu(q, x) + (1 - \omega) \cdot \lambda(q, x) \qquad (3)$$

See: Semantic Image Representation and Indexing and Semantic Class-Based Image Indexing

References

1. J.N. Kapur and H.K. Kesava, "Entropy Optimization Principles with Applications," Academic Press, 1992.
2. S.E. Robertson and K. Sparck Jones, "Relevance weighting of search terms," Journal of the American Society for Information Sciences, Vol. 27, 1976, pp. 129-146.
3. J.H. Lim, and J.S. Jin, "Combining intra-image and inter-class semantics for consumer image retrieval," *Pattern Recognition*, Vol. 38, No. 6, 2005, pp. 847-864.

COMPRESSED PROGRESSIVE MESHES

Definition: The decimation method in CPM (Compressed Progressive Meshes) [1] is "edge collapsing", which collapses the two ending points of the selected edge to the midpoint.

CPM collects "edge collapsing" into batches to achieve a high compression rate. The connectivity information of the removed vertex is encoded with the identifiers of the two cut-edges. CPM applies Butterfly subdivision scheme to predict the displacement of the new vertex. The error between the predicted and the original positions is stored as the geometric data in each batch. The amortized connectivity encoding takes 7.2 bits, while the geometry encoding takes 15.4 bits per vertex. Figure 1 shows the base mesh M0 and the mesh M1 constructed with CPM. From M1 to M0, two edges A'A" and F'F" are collapsed to the midpoints A and F, respectively.

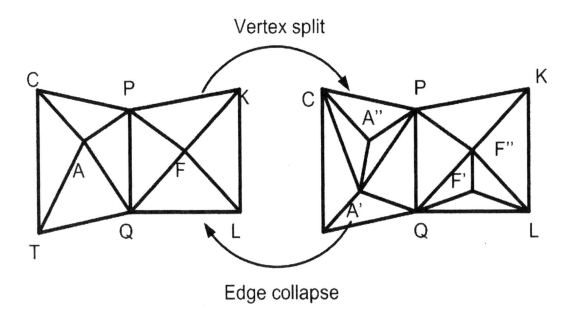

Figure 1. CPM vertex split and edge collapse.

See: Middleware for streaming 3D meshes.

References

1. R. Pajarola and J. Rossignac, "Compressed progressive meshes", IEEE Transactions on Visualization and Computer Graphics, Vol. 6, pp. 79-93.

COMPRESSED VIDEO SPATIO-TEMPORAL SEGMENTATION

Definition: Video spatial-temporal segmentation is used to detect and track moving objects and can be performed on uncompressed or compressed video sequences.

Most spatio-temporal segmentation approaches proposed in the literature operate in the uncompressed pixel domain. This provides them with the potential to estimate object boundaries with pixel accuracy but requires that the processed sequence be fully decoded before segmentation can be performed. Often the need also arises for motion feature extraction using block matching algorithms. As a result, the usefulness of such approaches is usually restricted to non-real-time applications. Real-time pixel-domain methods are usually applicable only on head-and-shoulder sequences (e.g. video-conference applications) or are based on restrictive assumptions (e.g. that the background is uniformly colored).

To counter these drawbacks, compressed domain methods have been proposed for spatio-temporal segmentation. In their majority, they consider the prevalent MPEG-2 standard as compression scheme, and they examine only I- and P-frames of the compressed sequence, since these contain all information that is necessary for the detection and tracking of moving (and non-moving) objects. In [1], translational motion vectors, which are contained in the MPEG-2 stream for P-frame macroblocks, are accumulated over a number of frames and the magnitude of the displacement is calculated. Uniform quantization of the latter is used for assigning macroblocks to regions. In [2], the motion vectors are again accumulated over a few frames and are subsequently spatially interpolated to get a dense motion vector field. The expectation maximization (EM) algorithm is applied to the dense motion vectors of each frame; the resulting foreground regions are then temporally tracked. In [3], a real-time algorithm is proposed; this uses the bilinear motion model to model the motion of both the camera and the identified moving objects. An iterative rejection scheme and temporal consistency constraints are employed to deal with the fact that motion vectors extracted from the compressed stream may not represent accurately the actual object motion. Coarse color information (DC coefficients) is used for the generation of background spatio-temporal objects, whereas additional color information is used to effect pixel-accuracy segmentation mask refinement, if required.

86   C

Figure 1. Exemplary spatio-temporal segmentation result (foreground objects only) before and after pixel-accuracy refinement for a frame of the *table tennis* sequence, using the methods of [3].

See: Segmentation of images and video

References

1. M.L. Jamrozik and M.H. Hayes, "A compressed domain video object segmentation system," Proceedings of the IEEE International Conference on Image Processing, 2002, Vol. 1, pp. 113-116.
2. R.V. Babu, K.R. Ramakrishnan, and S.H. Srinivasan, "Video object segmentation: a compressed domain approach," IEEE Transactions on Circuits and Systems for Video Technology, Vol. 14, No. 4, April 2004, pp. 462-474.
3. V. Mezaris, I. Kompatsiaris, N.V. Boulgouris, and M.G. Strintzis, "Real-time compressed-domain spatiotemporal segmentation and ontologies for video indexing and retrieval," IEEE Transactions on Circuits and Systems for Video Technology, Vol. 14, No. 5, May 2004, pp. 606-621.

COMPRESSION IN IMAGE SECRET SHARING

Definition: Simultaneous coding and encryption of visual material in image secret sharing, which are used for secure transmission over communication channels.

Image secret sharing (ISS) techniques can be used for secure transmission/distribution of private visual material over untrusted communication channels [1]. However, a different kind of cryptographic solutions may be required when still images and video are to be transmitted via public wireless and mobile networks. In this case, the large volume of input data necessitates the use of complex compression algorithms [2]. Following recent advances in digital imaging, coding and encryption technologies, simultaneous coding and encryption of the visual inputs can be achieved [2],[3].

Figure 1. JPEG compression-based image secret sharing concept.

To allow for secure distribution/sharing of large digital images in wireless or mobile networks, the encryption scheme recently introduced in [3] integrates the pixel-based ISS cryptographic operations [1] and the Joint Photographic Experts Group (JPEG) compression pipeline (Figure 1). Using the discrete-cosine transform (DTC) followed by the zig-zag and quantization operations, the $(2,2)$-ISS encryption process encrypts the quantized DCT coefficients into two shares which encounter the entropy coder to produce noise-like shares stored in JPEG format. It should be noted that alternative solutions may use different coders [3], e.g. an arithmetic coder or a Huffman coder, instead of the entropy coder in the scheme depicted in Figure 1.

Figure 2. JPEG decoding/ISS decryption procedure.

As it is shown in Figure 2, the decryption procedure requires both shares in the input of the entropy decoder to generate decoded shares of zig-zagged, quantized DCT coefficients. After ISS decryption, and inverse quantization, zig-zag and DCT operations, the scheme produces the decoded (decompressed) image. It should be noted that although the employed ISS concept of [1] satisfies the perfect reconstruction property, due to the lossy JPEG quantization process used in the encoding procedure, the output, decoded image in Figure 2 is not identical to the input secret image in Figure 1.

See: Image secret sharing, Visual cryptography, Private-key cryptosystem.

References

1. R. Lukac, and K.-N. Plataniotis, "A New Encryption Scheme for Color Images," Computing and Informatics, submitted.
2. K. Martin, R. Lukac, and K.-N. Plataniotis, "Efficient Encryption of Wavelet-Based Coded Color Images," Pattern Recognition, Vol. 38, 2005.
3. S. Sudharsanan, "Visual Cryptography for JPEG Color Images," Proceedings of the SPIE, Vol. 5601, pp. 171-178, October 2004.

CONTENT BASED 3D SHAPE RETRIEVAL

Remco C. Veltkamp
Department of Information and Computing Sciences, Utrecht University,
The Netherlands

Johan W.H. Tangelder
Centre for Mathematics and Computer Science, Amsterdam,
The Netherlands

Definition: *Content based 3D shape retrieval systems retrieve similar 3D objects based on a given query object.*

Recent developments in techniques for modeling, digitizing and visualizing 3D shapes has led to an explosion in the number of available 3D models on the Internet and in domain-specific databases. Currently, large archives recording cultural heritage models like the David of Michelangelo [11], and the Minerva of Arezzo [7] are obtained by laser scanning projects. Also archives containing domain-specific shape models are now accessible on the Internet. Examples are the National Design Repository, an online repository of CAD models, and the Protein Data Bank, an online archive of structural data of biological macromolecules. These developments have led to the design of 3D shape retrieval systems that, given a query object, retrieve similar 3D objects. In visualization, 3D shapes are often represented as a surface, in particular polygonal meshes, for example in VRML format. Often these models contain holes, intersecting polygons, are not manifold, and do not enclose a volume unambiguously. By contrast, 3D volume models, such as solid models produced by CAD systems, or voxels models, enclose a volume properly.

Unlike text documents, 3D models are not easily retrieved. Attempting to find a 3D model using textual annotation and a conventional text-based search engine would not work in many cases. The annotations added by human beings depend on language, culture, age, sex, and other factors. They may be too limited or ambiguous. In contrast, content based 3D shape retrieval methods, which use shape properties of the 3D models to search for similar models, work better than text based methods [14].

In content based shape retrieval, the following terminology is often used. Shape matching is the process of determining how similar two shapes are. This is often done by computing a distance. A complementary process is indexing. Here, indexing is understood to be the process of building a data structure to speed up the search. Note that also "indexing" is also used as a term for the identification of features in models, or multimedia documents in general. Retrieval is the process of searching and delivering the query results. Matching and indexing are often part of the retrieval process.

Recently, a lot of researchers have investigated the specific problem of content based 3D shape retrieval. Also, an extensive amount of literature can be found in the related fields of computer vision, object recognition, geometric modeling, computer-aided design and engineering. Survey papers to this literature have been provided by Besl and Jain [1], Loncaric [12], Campbell and Flynn [3] and Mamic and Bennamoun [13]. Iyer et al. [8] provide an extensive overview of 3D shape searching techniques especially relevant for CAD and engineering. The survey by Cardone et al. [4] primarily focuses on shape similarity methods that are suitable to compare CAD models in the context of product design and manufacturing applications. Shilane et al. [18] compare 12 shape matching methods with respect to processing time, storage requirements and discriminative power.

In addition to these surveys, this chapter evaluates 3D shape retrieval methods with respect to the following requirements: (1) shape representation requirements, (2) properties of dissimilarity measures, (3) efficiency, (4) discrimination abilities, (5) ability to perform partial matching, (6) robustness, and (7) necessity of pose normalization.

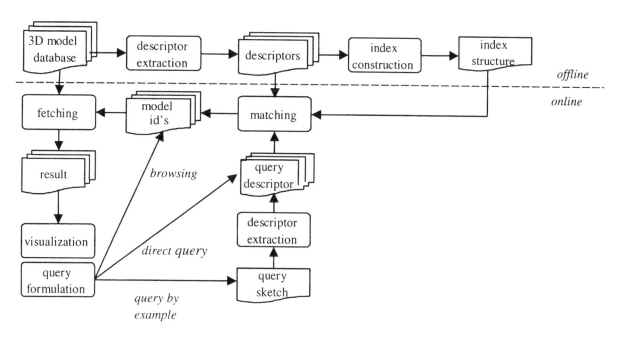

Figure 1. Conceptual framework for shape retrieval.

3D shape retrieval aspects

At a conceptual level, a typical 3D shape retrieval framework as illustrated by fig. 1 consists of a database with an index structure created offline, and an online query engine. Each 3D model has to be identified with a shape descriptor, providing a compact overall description of the shape. To efficiently search a large collection online, an indexing data structure and searching algorithm should be available. The online query engine computes the query descriptor, and models similar to the query model are retrieved by matching descriptors to the query descriptor from the index structure of the database. The similarity between two descriptors is quantified by a dissimilarity measure. Three approaches can be distinguished for providing a query object: (1) browsing to select a new query object from the obtained results, (2) a direct query by providing a query descriptor, (3) query by example by providing an existing 3D model, by creating a 3D shape query from scratch using a 3D tool, or by sketching 2D projections of the 3D model. Finally, the retrieved models can be visualized.

Shape representations: An important issue is the type of shape representation(s) that a shape retrieval system accepts. Most of the 3D models found on the World Wide Web are meshes defined in a file format supporting visual appearance. Currently, the most common format used for this purpose is the Virtual Reality Modeling Language (VRML) format. Since these models have been designed for visualization, they often contain only geometry and appearance attributes. Often, they are represented by "polygon soups", consisting of unorganized sets of polygons. Also, in general these models are not "watertight" meshes, i.e. they do not enclose a volume. By contrast, for volume models retrieval methods depending on a properly defined volume can be applied.

Measuring similarity: In order to measure how similar two objects are, it is necessary to compute distances between pairs of descriptors using a dissimilarity measure. Although the term similarity is often used, dissimilarity better corresponds to the notion of distance: small distance means small dissimilarity, and large similarity. A dissimilarity measure can be formalized by a function defined on pairs of descriptors indicating the degree of their resemblance. Formally speaking, a dissimilarity measure d on a set S is a non-negative valued function $d: S \times S \rightarrow \mathbf{R}^+ \cup \{0\}$. Function d may have metric properties: identity, positivity, symmetry, and triangle inequality. Additionally, transformation invariance is often a useful property.

The identity property says that a shape is completely similar to itself, while the positivity property claims that different shapes are never completely similar. This property is very strong for a high-level shape descriptor, and is often not satisfied. However, this is not a severe drawback, if the loss of uniqueness depends on negligible details. Symmetry is not always wanted. Indeed, human perception does not always find that shape x is equally similar to shape y, as y is to x. In particular, a variant x of prototype y, is often found to be more similar to y than vice versa. The triangle inequality can be applied to make retrieval more efficient [21]. However, dissimilarity measures for partial matching, giving a small distance if a part of one matches a part of the other, do not obey the triangle inequality. Transformation invariance has to be satisfied, if the comparison and the extraction process of shape descriptors have to be independent of the location, orientation and/or scale of the object in its Cartesian coordinate system.

Efficiency: For large shape collections, it is inefficient to sequentially match all objects in the database with the query object. Because retrieval should be fast, efficient indexing search structures are needed to support efficient retrieval. Since for "query by example" the shape descriptor is computed online, it is reasonable to require that the shape descriptor computation is fast enough for interactive querying.

Discriminative power: A shape descriptor should capture properties that discriminate objects well. However, the judgment of the similarity of the shapes of two 3D objects is somewhat subjective, depending on the user preference or the application at hand. E.g. for CAD models often topological properties such as the numbers of holes in a model are more important than minor differences in shape. On the contrary, if a user searches for models looking roughly similar, then the existence of a small hole in the model may be of no importance to the user.

Partial matching: In contrast to global shape matching, partial matching finds a shape of which a part is similar to a part of another shape. Partial matching can be applied if 3D shape models are not complete, e.g. for objects obtained by laser scanning from one or two directions only. Another application is the search inside "3D scenes'" containing an instance of the query object. Also, this feature can potentially give the user flexibility towards the matching problem, if parts of interest of an object can be selected or weighted by the user.

Robustness and sensitivity: It is often desirable that a shape descriptor is insensitive to noise and small extra features, and robust against arbitrary topological degeneracies, e.g. if it is obtained by laser scanning. Therefore, small changes in a shape should result in small changes in the shape descriptor. On the other hand, if large changes in the shape of the object result in very small changes in the shape descriptor, then the shape descriptor is considered not sensitive. Poor sensitivity will lead to poor discriminative abilities. Also, if a model is given in multiple levels-of-detail, representations of different levels should not differ significantly from the original model.

Pose normalization: In the absence of prior knowledge, 3D models have arbitrary scale, orientation, and position in the 3D space. Because not all dissimilarity measures are invariant under scale, translation, or rotation, one or more of the normalization procedures described below may be necessary. The normalization procedure depends on the center of mass, which is defined as the center of its surface points. To normalize a 3D model for scale, the average distance of the points on its surface to the center of mass should be scaled to a constant. Note that normalizing a 3D model by scaling its bounding box is sensitive to outliers. To normalize for translation the center of mass is translated to the origin.

To normalize a 3D model for rotation usually the principal component analysis (PCA) method is applied. It aligns the principal axes to the x-, y-, and z-axes of a canonical coordinate system by an affine transformation based on a set of surface points, e.g. the set of vertices of a 3D model. After translation of the center of mass to the origin, a rotation is applied so that the largest variance of the transformed points is along the x-axis. Then a rotation around the x-axis is carried out such that the maximal spread in the yz-plane occurs along the y-axis.

A problem is that differing sizes of triangles are not taken into account which may cause very different results for models that are identical except for finer triangle resolution in some parts of the model. To address this issue, one may use appropriately chosen vertex weights. The PCA has been generalized to the continuous PCA (CPCA) such that all of the (infinitely many) points on the mesh surface are equally relevant to compute the transformation aligning the principal axes to a canonical coordinate system [22].

Another problem with the PCA algorithm is that due to the lack of information about the direction of the principal axes, either the positive or the negative axes are moved to the x, y- and z-axes. This results in four valid configurations that align the principal axes (four configurations are not valid because they do not define a proper coordinate system).

The PCA algorithm and its variants for pose estimation are fairly simple and efficient. However, if the eigenvalues are equal, principal axes may still switch, without affecting the eigenvalues. Similar eigenvalues may imply an almost symmetrical mass distribution around an axis (e.g. nearly cylindrical shapes) or around the center of mass (e.g. nearly spherical shapes).

Shape matching methods

Based on the representation of the shape descriptor we divide shape matching methods in three broad categories: (1) feature based methods, (2) graph based methods and (3) geometry based methods. Fig. 2 shows a more detailed categorization of shape matching methods. Note that the classes of these methods are not completely disjoint. For instance, a graph-based shape descriptor may be extended to describe shape properties not related to topology. In these cases we categorized the method by the most characteristic aspect of its representation. Recently, a number of approaches to combine multiple shape matching methods have been introduced. Also, a number of techniques have been introduced that improve shape matching in general.

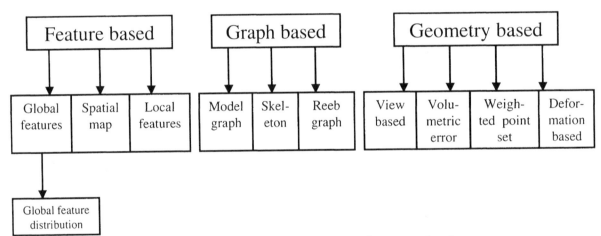

Figure 2. Taxonomy of shape matching methods.

Feature based methods: In the context of 3D shape matching, features denote geometric and topological properties of 3D shapes. So, 3D shapes can be discriminated by measuring and comparing their features. Feature based methods can be divided into four categories according to the type of shape features used: (1) global features, (2) global feature distributions, (3) spatial maps, and (4) local features. Feature based methods from the first three categories represent features of a shape using a single descriptor consisting of a d-dimensional vector of values, where the dimension d is fixed for all shapes. The value of d can easily be a few hundred.

The descriptor of a shape is a point in a high dimensional space, and two shapes are considered to be similar if they are close in this space. Retrieving the k best matches for a 3D query model is equivalent to solving the k-nearest neighbors problem in a high-dimensional space. Although this problem is known to be hard in the worst case, matching feature descriptors can be done efficiently in practice by searching to solve the "approximate k-nearest neighbor" problem.

Global features characterize the global shape of a 3D model. Examples of these features are the extended Gaussian image, statistical moments of the boundary or the volume of the model, volume-to-surface ratio, or the Fourier transform of the volume or the boundary of the shape.

Global feature distributions are a refinement of the concept of global feature based similarity. These methods compare global distributions of features, so-called shape distributions. Examples include distance, angle, area and volume measurements between random surface points [17]. The similarity between two objects is then some distances between distributions.

Spatial maps are representations that capture the spatial location of an object. The map entries correspond to physical locations or sections of the object, and are arranged in a manner that preserves the relative positions of the features in an object. Spatial maps are in general not invariant to rotations, except for specially designed maps. Therefore, typically pose normalization is done first. A general approach to transform rotation dependent shape descriptors into rotation independent ones is based on spherical harmonics, often as a function on a voxel grid [10, 22]. From a collection of spherical functions on a grid, a rotation invariant descriptor is computed by (1) decomposing the function into its spherical harmonics, (2) summing the harmonics within each frequency, and computing the distance for each frequency component. The resulting shape descriptor is a 2D histogram indexed by radius and frequency values. *Local feature* based methods describe the 3D shape around a number of surface points. For this purpose, a descriptor for each surface point is used instead of a single descriptor. For example, 'spin images' are 2D histograms of the surface locations around a point [9]. Typically, local methods are suitable for recognizing models in a cluttered and occluded 3D scene.

Graph-based methods: In general, the feature based methods discussed in the previous section take into account only the pure geometry of the shape. In contrast, graph based methods attempt to extract a geometric meaning from a 3D shape using a graph showing how shape components are linked together. Graph based methods can be divided into three broad categories according to the type of graph used: (1) model graphs, (2) Reeb graphs, and (3) skeletons. Model graphs are extracted from solid model representations [6] used by most CAD systems, while skeletal graph and Reeb graph approaches [2] are applicable to volume models including models of natural shapes.

Efficient computation of existing graph metrics for general graphs is not trivial: computing the edit distance is NP-hard and computing the maximal common subgraph is even NP-complete.

<u>Geometry based methods</u>: The main idea of view based similarity methods is that two 3D models are similar, if they look similar from all viewing angles. A natural application of this paradigm is the implementation of query interfaces based on defining a query by one or more sketches showing the query from different views. The so-called lightfield descriptor [5] compares ten silhouettes of the 3D shape obtained from ten viewing angles distributed evenly on the viewing sphere. Each silhouette is a 2D image, encoded by its Zernike moments and Fourier descriptors. The dissimilarity of two shapes is found as the minimal dissimilarity obtained by rotating the viewing sphere of one lightfield descriptor relative to the other lightfield descriptor. Similar methods use depth buffers from various viewing directions.

Several other methods describe a geometry similarity approach to 3D shape matching based on calculating a volumetric error between two objects, e.g. [16]. To compute that efficiently, they are typically voxelized. Another approach is based on shape descriptors consisting of weighted 3D points. The points are typically samples, and the weights are the amount of local volume or curvature, see e.g. [19]. Shape deformation or evolution based similarity is mostly applied to 2D shapes. Because they often depend on a parameterization, they are difficult to generalize to 3D.

Comparison

Twelve different shape descriptors have been compared using the Princeton Shape Benchmark [18]. The results show that shape matching algorithms do not perform equally well on all object types. For instance, extended Gaussian images are good at discriminating between man-made and natural objects, but not that good at making detailed class distinctions. They also find that the lightfield descriptor [5] is the most discriminating between the 12 shape descriptors tested, but at higher storage and computational costs than most other descriptors. In [22], authors compared a number of shape matching methods using the Princeton shape benchmark, the publicly-available database at the University of Konstanz, and the MPEG-7 test set [15]. These experimental tests show that from the descriptors proposed by others, the spherical harmonics approach [10] significantly outperforms all other approaches. However, the light field descriptor was not included in these experiments. Furthermore, [22] investigates a number of hybrid shape matching methods obtained by combining shape matching methods. In this framework, similarity is measured using a weighted combination of the similarity of the separate methods, where the weight of each separate method is proportional to the dimension of its feature vector. Experiments show that for comparing overall performance, a combination of the depth buffer-based descriptor, a silhouette-based descriptor, and a spherical descriptor performs best. For a more complete survey, see [20].

References

1. P.J. Besl and R. C. Jain, "Three-dimensional object recognition," Computing Surveys Vol. 17, No. 1, 1985, pp. 75-145.
2. S. Biasotti, S. Marini, M. Mortara, and G. Patané, "An overview of properties and efficacy of topological skeletons in shape modeling," Proceedings of Shape Modeling International, 2003, pp. 245-254.

3. R.J. Campbell and P. J. Flynn, "A Survey of Free-Form Object Representation and Recognition Techniques," Computer Vision and Image Understanding 81(2), 2001, pp. 166-210.
4. A. Cardone, S. K. Gupta, and M. Karnik, "A Survey of Shape Similarity Assessment Algorithms for Product Design and Manufacturing Applications," Journal of Computing and Information Science in Engineering, Vol. 3, 2003, pp. 109-118.
5. D.-Y.Chen, X.-P. Tian, Y.-T. Shen, and M. Ouhyoung, "On Visual Similarity Based 3D Model Retrieval," Computer Graphics Forum (EG 2003 Proceedings) 22(3), 2003.
6. V. Cicirello and W. C. Regli, "Machining Feature-based Comparisons of Mechanical Parts," Proceedins of Solid Modeling 2001, pp. 176-185.
7. R. Fontana, M. Greco, M. Materazzi, E. Pampaloni, L. Pezzati, C. Rocchini, and R. Scopigno, "Three-dimensional modeling of statues: the Minerva of Arezzo," Cultural Heritage Journal, 3(4), 2002, pp. 325-331.
8. N. Iyer, K. Lou, S. Janyanti, Y. Kalyanaraman, and K. Ramani, "Three Dimensional Shape Searching: State-of-the-art Review and Future Trends," Accepted for publication in Computer Aided Design.
9. A.E. Johnson and M. Hebert, "Using spin images for efficient object recognition in cluttered 3D scenes," IEEE Transactions on Pattern Analysis and Machine Intelligence, 21(5), 1999, pp. 635-651.
10. M. Kazhdan, T. Funkhouser, and S. Rusinkiewicz, "Rotation invariant spherical harmonic representation of 3D shape descriptors," Proceedings of Symposium on Geometry Processing, 2003.
11. M. Levoy, K. Pulli, B. Curless, S. Rusinkiewicz, D. Koller, L. Pereira, M. Ginzton, S. Anderson, J. Davis, J. Ginsberg, J. Shade, and D. Fulk, "The Digital Michelangelo Project: 3D Scanning of Large Statues," Proceedings of SIGGRAPH 2000, pp. 131-144.
12. S. Loncaric, "A Survey of Shape Analysis Techniques," Pattern Recognition 31(8), 1998, pp. 983-1001.
13. G. Mamic and M. Bennamoun, "Representation and Recognition of 3D Free-Form Objects," Digital Signal Processing Vol. 12, 2002, pp. 47-67.
14. P. Min, M. Kazhdan, and T. Funkhouser, "A Comparison of Text and Shape Matching for Retrieval of Online 3D Models," Proceedings of European Conference on Digital Libraries, 2004, pp. 209-220.
15. MPEG-7 Video Group. Description of Core Experiments for Motion and Shape. Technical report, ISO/IEC N3397, 2000.
16. M. Novotni and R. Klein, "A Geometric Approach to 3{D} Object Comparison," Proceedings of Shape Modeling International, 2001, 154-166.
17. R. Osada, T. Funkhouser, B. Chazelle, and D. Dobkin, "Shape distributions," ACM Transactions on Graphics, 21(4), 2002, 807-832.
18. P. Shilane, M. Kazhdan, P. Min, and T. Funkhouser, "The Princeton Shape Benchmark," Proceedings of Shape Modeling International, 2004. pp. 157-166.
19. J.W.H. Tangelder and R. C. Veltkamp, "Polyhedral Model Retrieval Using Weighted Point Sets," International Journal of Image and Graphics, 3(1), 2003, pp. 209-229.
20. J.W.H. Tangelder and R. C. Veltkamp, "A Survey of Content Based 3D Shape Retrieval Methods," Submitted to Multimedia Tools and Applications, 2005.
21. J. Vleugels and R. C. Veltkamp, "Efficient Image Retrieval through Vantage Objects," Pattern Recognition 35(1), 2002, pp. 69-80.

22. D.V. Vranić, "3D Model Retrieval.," Ph.D. Thesis, University of Leipzig, 2004.

CONTENT BASED MUSIC RETRIEVAL

Remco C. Veltkamp, Frans Wiering, and Rainer Typke
Department of Information and Computing Sciences, Utrecht University,
The Netherlands

Definition: Content-based music retrieval systems search audio data and notated music based on content.

Two main groups of Music Information Retrieval (MIR) systems for content-based searching can be distinguished, systems for searching audio data and systems for searching notated music. There are also hybrid systems that first transcribe audio signal into a symbolic description of notes and then search a database of notated music. An example of such music transcription is the work of Klapuri [10], which in particular is concerned with multiple fundamental frequency estimation, and musical metre estimation, which has to do with ordering the rhythmic aspects of music. Part of the work is based on known properties of the human auditory system.

Content-based music search systems can be useful for a variety of purposes and audiences:

- In record stores, customers may only know a tune from a record they would like to buy, but not the title of the work, composer, or performers. Salespeople with a vast knowledge of music who are willing and able to identify tunes hummed by customers are scarce, and it could be interesting to have a computer do the task of identifying melodies and suggesting records.

- A search engine that finds musical scores (notations of musical works) similar to a given query can help musicologists find out how composers influenced one another or how their works are related to earlier works of their own or by other composers. This task has been done manually by musicologists over the past centuries. If computers could perform this task reasonably well, more interesting insights could be gained faster and with less effort.

- Copyright infringement could be resolved, avoided or raised more easily if composers could find out if someone is plagiarizing them or if a new work exposes them to the risk of being accused of plagiarism. Content-based music retrieval could facilitate such searches.

Content-based search mechanisms that work specifically for audio recordings can be useful for the following purposes:

- It is possible to identify music played, for example, on the radio or in a bar by pointing a cellular phone at the speakers for a few seconds and using an audio fingerprinting system for identifying the exact recording that is being played.

- Recordings made by surveillance equipment can be searched for suspicious sounds.

- Content-based video retrieval can be made more powerful by analyzing audio content, including music.

- Theatres, film makers, and radio or television stations might find a search engine useful that can find sound effects similar to a given query or according to a given description in a vast library of audio recordings.

Although MIR is a rather young field, there are already commercial applications of MIR systems. The automatic identification of recordings via cellular phones using audio fingerprinting, for example, is already offered by several companies that charge customers for identifying tunes and also offers matching ring tones and CDs.

Music Formats

We consider three basic representations of music: music notation, time-stamped events, and audio. Most music retrieval research is concerned with mainstream Western music, based on noted that have a definite pitch. See Byrd and Crawford [1] for a more elaborate overview of the challenges of music information retrieval for these formats.

Western music is notated in so-called Common Music Notation (CMN), which traces its origins to the Middle Ages. Basically, music scores in CMN represent time information horizontally and pitch vertically. Each musical event is rendered as a note that is placed on a staff consisting of 5 horizontal lines; the shape of the note indicates its relative duration (therefore they have names such as whole, half and quarter notes). Many additional symbols may be used: the primary purpose of CMN is to facilitate the performance of a musical composition, by giving as detailed instructions as necessary for creating an adequate performance.

Musical Instrument Digital Interface, or MIDI, is a time stamped industry-standard protocol that defines musical events, allowing electronic musical instruments and computers to talk to each other [14]. Each pitch is stored as a time-stamped note-on and a note-off event. The format also allows saving information about tempo, key signatures, the names of tracks and instruments, and other information.

Digital audio comes in many different file and representation formats. Typically, audio files contain information about the resolution, sampling rate and type of compression. Groups like MPEG have created open standards for compression, for example MP3, the MPEG Audio Layer 3. PCM (Pulse Code Modulation) is a common method of storing and transmitting uncompressed digital audio. Since it is a generic format, it can be read by most audio applications. PCM is the format used on audio CDs, and also a very common format for WAV files, the default file format for digital audio on Windows.

Figure 1 shows a comparison of music formats. The columns 'Convert to lower format' and 'Convert to higher format' indicate how difficult it is to convert one format into the next lower or higher level automatically.

Music format	Example	Compared to image retrieval	Compared to text retrieval	Structure	Convert to lower format	Convert to higher format
music notation (Finale, Sibelius, MusicXML)	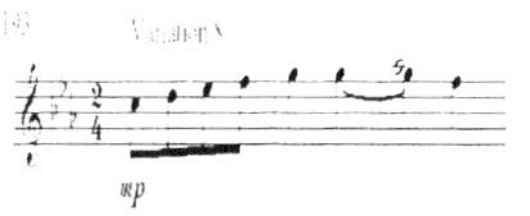	compound objects	text + markup	much	easy (OK job)	--
time-stamped events (MIDI)	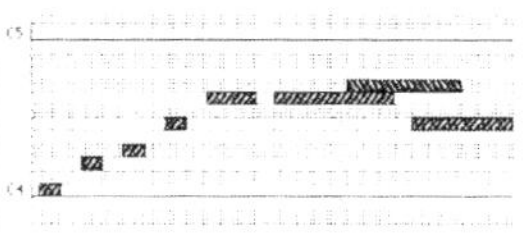	objects, scenes	text	little	easy	fairly hard (OK job)
digital audio (MP3, Wav)	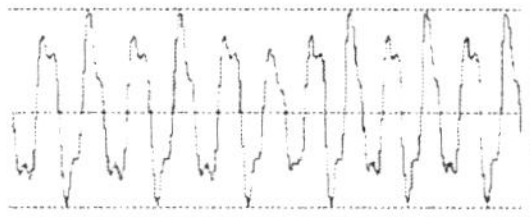	primitive features	speech	none	--	hard

Figure 1. Music format comparison adopted from [1].

Retrieval tasks

Several user groups exist for content-based music retrieval. Three main audiences can be distinguished that can benefit from MIR: (i) industry: e.g. recording, broadcasting, performance (ii) consumers (iii) professionals: performers, teachers, musicologists. The level at which retrieval is needed may differ considerably:

1. Work instance level: the individual score or sound object.
2. Work level: a set of instances that are considered to be essentially the same.
3. Artist level: creator or performer of work.
4. Genre level: music that is similar at a very generic level, e. g. classical, jazz, pop, and world music.

This is not a strict hierarchy. Artists perform in different genres, and one work can be performed, even created, by multiple artists. Also, this classification is a continuum rather than a nominal categorization. Genres can be divided into subgenres, artists grouped in schools. Even the "work" concept is not a fixed given. If a work is primarily determined by the composer's definitive score, changing even a single note may be a violation of the work. On the other hand, different performances of "I did it my way" are usually considered the same work even though the musical content may be rather different. MIR retrieval tasks can be characterised by audience and level of retrieval.

Often, tasks connect a subrange of the continuum (see Figure 1). A non-comprehensive overview of tasks includes:

- Copyright and royalties: receive payments for broadcast or publication of music.
- Detection of plagiarism: the use of musical ideas or stylistic traits of another artist under one's own name.
- Recommendation: find music that suits a personal profile.
- Sounds as: find music that sounds like a given recording.
- Mood: find music that suits a certain atmosphere.
- Emotion: find music that reflects or contradicts an emotional state.
- Style: find music that belongs to a generic category, however defined.
- Performer: find music by (type of) performer.
- Feature: employ technical features to retrieve works in a genre or by an artist.
- Composer: find works by one composer.
- Intertextuality: finding works that employ the same material or refer to each other by allusion.
- Identification: ascribing a work or work instance to an artist or finding works containing a given theme, query by humming.
- Source: identifying the work to which an instance belongs, for example because metadata are missing.

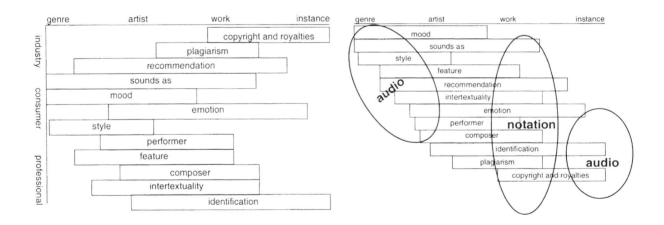

Figure 2. Music retrieval tasks. At the left the tasks are ordered by the type of users, at the right the tasks are ordered by the level of music retrieval.

For typical search tasks and their frequencies of occurrence, see also Lee and Downie [13]. Figure 2 shows which tasks are typical for the different user classes and level of music retrieval. Audio fingerprinting systems are particularly good at identifying recordings, that is, instances of works. This task must be based on audio information because in two different audio renditions, the same musical content might be performed, and therefore only the audio information is different. Audio data is also a good basis for very general identification tasks such as genre and artist [19].

Query-by-humming systems make identification tasks easier for consumers who might lack the expertise that is needed for entering a sequence of intervals or a contour in textual form. These systems focus on identifying works or finding works that are similar to a query.

Audio and symbolic methods are useful for different tasks. For instance, identification of instances of recordings must be based on audio data, while works are best identified based on a symbolic representation. For determining the genre of a given piece of music, approaches based on audio look promising, but symbolic methods might work as well. By offering the possibility of entering more complex queries, systems such as Themefinder [12] cover a wider range of tasks, but they still can only be used on the work level. Since they work with sets of notes or representations that are based on sets of notes, they cannot be used for more specific tasks such as identifying instances, and their algorithms are not meant to do tasks on the more general artist and genre levels. How to address these levels is a research problem that is only beginning to be investigated. Music cognition and perception may have an important role in this.

Searching symbolic music

String-based methods for monophonic melodies: Monophonic music can be represented by one-dimensional strings of characters, where each character describes one note or one pair of consecutive notes. Strings can represent interval sequences, gross contour, sequences of pitches and the like, and well-known string matching algorithms such as algorithms for calculating editing distances, finding the longest common subsequence, or finding occurrences of one string in another have been applied, sometimes with certain adaptations to make them suitable for matching melodies.

Some MIR systems only check for exact matches or cases where the search string is a substring of database entries. For such tasks, standard string searching algorithms like Knuth-Morris-Pratt and Boyer-Moore can be used. Themefinder [12] searches the database for entries matching regular expressions. In this case, there is still no notion of distance, but different strings can match the same regular expression. For approximate matching, it can be useful to compute an editing distance with dynamic programming. Musipedia is an example of a system that does this [16]. Simply computing an editing distance between query strings and the data in the database is not good enough, however, because these strings might represent pieces of music with different lengths. Therefore, it can be necessary to choose suitable substrings before calculating an editing distance.

More recently Cilibrasi et al. [3] have suggested using an approximation to Kolmogorov distance between two musical pieces as a means to compute clusters of music. They first process MIDI representation of a music piece to turn it into a string from a finite alphabet. Then they compute the distance between two music pieces using their Normalized Compression Distance (NCD). NCD uses the compressed length of a string as an approximation to its Kolmogorov complexity. The Kolmogorov complexity of a string is not computable, but the compressed length approximation gives good results for musical genre and composer clustering.

For finding substrings that match exactly, the standard methods for indexing text can be used (for example, inverted files, B-trees, etc.). The lack of the equivalent of words in music can be overcome by just cutting melodies into N-grams [6], where each N-gram is a sequence of N pitch intervals. For most editing distances that are actually useful, the triangle inequality holds. Therefore, indexing methods that rely on the triangle inequality property of the distance measure can be used, for example metric trees, vantage point trees, or the vantage indexing method described in [18].

Geometry-based methods for polyphonic melodies: Unlike string-based methods, set-based methods do not assume that the notes are ordered. Music is viewed as a set of events with properties like onset time, pitch, and duration. Clausen et al. [4] propose a search method that views scores and queries as sets of notes. Notes are defined by note onset time, pitch, and duration. Exact matches are supersets of queries, and approximate matching is done by finding supersets of subsets of the query or by allowing alternative sets. By quantizing onset times and by segmenting the music into measures, they make it possible to use inverted files.

Typke et al. [18] also view scores and queries as sets of notes, but instead of finding supersets, they use transportation distances such as the Earth Mover's Distance for comparing sets. They exploit the triangle inequality for indexing, which avoids the need for quantizing. Distances to a fixed set of vantage objects are pre-calculated for each database entry. Queries then only need to be compared to entries with similar distances to the vantage objects.

Ukkonen et al. [20] propose a number of algorithms for searching notated music. One method find translations of the query pattern such that all onset times and pitches of notes in the query match with some onset times and pitches of notes in the database documents. Another method finds translations of the query pattern such that some onset times and pitches of the query match with some onset times and pitches of database documents. A third one finds translations of the query pattern that give longest common shared time (i.e., maximize the times at which query notes sound at the same time and with the same pitch as notes from the database documents). This algorithm does not take into consideration whether onset times match.

Probabilistic Matching: The aim of probabilistic matching methods is to determine probabilistic properties of candidate pieces and compare them with corresponding properties of queries. For example, the GUIDO system [9] calculates Markov models describing the probabilities of state transitions in pieces and then compares matrices which describe transition probabilities. Features of melodies such as interval sequences, pitch sequences, or rhythm can be used to calculate Markov chains. In these Markov chains, states can correspond with features like a certain pitch, interval, or note duration, and the transition probabilities reflect the numbers of occurrences of different subsequent states. The similarity between a query and a candidate piece in the database can be determined by calculating the product of the transition probabilities, based on the transition matrix of the candidate piece, for each pair of consecutive states in the query. Transition matrices can be organized as a tree. The leaves are the transition matrices of the pieces in the database, while inner nodes are the transition matrices describing the concatenation of the pieces in the subtree.

Searching musical audio

Most audio retrieval overviews (e.g. [8]) are focused on speech-oriented systems. In this chapter we will focus on musical audio. Clausen and Kurth [5] have used their geometry-based method (see above) also for musical audio data. They use a feature extractor for converting PCM3 signals into sets that can be treated the same way as sets of notes. Self-Organizing Map (SOM), have been used for clustering similar pieces of music and classifying pieces. For example [17] describes a system that extracts feature vectors that describe rhythm patterns from audio, and clusters them with a SOM.

Feature extraction

A natural way of comparing audio recordings is to extract an abstract description of the audio signal which reflects the perceptionally relevant aspects of the recording, followed by the application of a distance function to the extracted information. An audio recording is usually segmented into short, possibly overlapping frames which last short enough such that there are no multiple distinguishable events covered by one frame. Wold et al. [21] list some features that are commonly extracted from audio frames with duration between 25 and 40 milliseconds:

- Loudness: can be approximated by the square root of the energy of the signal computed from the shorttime Fourier transform in decibels.

- Pitch: the Fourier transformation of a frame delivers a spectrum, from which a fundamental frequency can be computed with an approximate greatest common divisor algorithm.

- Tone (brightness and bandwidth): Brightness is a measure of the higher-frequency content of the signal. Bandwidth can be computed as the magnitude weighted average of the differences between the spectral components and the centroid of the shorttime Fourier transform. It is zero for a single sine wave, while ideal white noise has an infinite bandwidth.

- Mel-filtered Cepstral Coefficients (often abbreviated as MFCCs) can be computed by applying a mel-spaced set of triangular filters to the short-time Fourier transform, followed by a discrete cosine transform.[1] It transforms the spectrum into perception-based sound characteristics. A mel is a unit of measure for the perceived pitch of a tone. The human ear is sensitive to linear changes in frequency below 1000 Hz and logarithmic changes above. Mel-filtering is a scaling of frequency that takes this fact into account.
- Derivatives: Since the dynamic behaviour of sound is important, it can be helpful to calculate the instantaneous derivative (time differences) for all of the features above.

---

[1] "Cepstrum" is a contraction of "perception" and "spectrum".

Other features include frequencies, attack (the duration from a zero to a maximum amplitude), decay (the duration from the initial maximum amplitude to a stable state amplitude), sustain (the level of the steady state amplitude), release (the duration from the steady state to its final zero amplitude), zero crossing rate, and spectral centroid (the average frequency, weighted by amplitude, of a spectrum). Many audio retrieval systems compare vectors of such features in order to find audio recordings that sound similar to a given query.

It is also possible to directly use coefficients used in the compression scheme. For example, [11] use the coefficients extracted from MP3 coded audio, representing the output of the polyphase filters used in MP3 compression. The polyphase filter bank divides the audio signal into 32 equal-width frequency subbands. Based on the human auditory system, the psychoacoustic model is designed for determining whether the coefficient of a subband should be coded.

Audio Fingerprinting

If the aim is not necessarily to identify a work, but a recording, audio fingerprinting techniques perform quite well. An audio fingerprint is a content-based compact signature that summarizes an audio recording [2]. All phone-based systems for identifying popular music use some form of audio fingerprinting. A feature extractor is used to describe short segments of recordings in a way that is as robust as possible against the typical distortions caused by poor speakers, cheap microphones, and a cellular phone connection, as well as background noise like people chatting in a bar. Such features do not need to have anything to do with human perception or the music on the recording; they just need to be unique for different recordings and robust against distortions. These audio fingerprints, usually just a few bytes per recording segment, are then stored in a database index, along with pointers to the recordings where they occur. The same feature extractor is used on the query, and with the audio fingerprints that were extracted from the query, candidates for matching recordings can be quickly retrieved. The number of these candidates can be reduced by checking whether the fingerprints occur in the right order and with the same local timing. Common fingerprint requirements include [2]:

- Discriminative power over huge collections of fingerprints, so as to keep the number of false positives limited.
- Robustness to distortions such as additive noise and microphone distortions.
- Compactness for ease of processing.
- Computational simplicity for speed of processing.

Concluding Remarks

As can be seen from figure 2, there is a gap between the retrieval tasks and levels that musical audio and notated music are covering. It is a research challenge to fill this gap; a seminal project in this direction is the OMRAS project, http://www.omras.org. Further developments in this direction can be expected by integrating notation and audio based approaches into a high level symbolic approach, for example by audio transcription or harmonic matching [15].

For both audio and notated music, it is believed that retrieval performance may be greatly improved by using human-centered features, rather than technology-based features. Indeed, music is not so much perceived or remembered as a sequence of individual notes or frequencies. Music cognition and perception theory may play an important role in future retrieval systems.

Finally, a primary forum for music retrieval is the International Conference on Music Information Retrieval (ISMIR) series, http://www.ismir.net, and the Music Information Retrieval mailing list, http://listes.ircam.fr, but other music and multimedia related conference are also concerned with related issues.

References

1. D. Byrd and T. Crawford, "Problems of music information retrieval in the real world," *Information Processing and Management*, Vol. 38, 2002, pp. 249–272.
2. P. Cano, E. Batlle, T. Kalker, and J. Haitsma, "A Review of Algorithms for Audio Fingerprinting," Proceedings of the International Workshop on Multimedia Signal Processing 2002.
3. R. Cilibrasi, P. Vitanyi, and R. de Wolf, "Algorithmic clustering of music based on string compression," Computer Music Journal, Vol. 28, No. 4, 2004, pp. 49-67.
4. M. Clausen, R. Engelbrecht, D. Meyer, and J. Schmitz, "PROMS: a web-based tool for searching in polyphonic music," In ISMIR Proceedings, 2000.
5. M. Clausen and F. Kurth, "A unified approach to content based and fault tolerant music identification," Proceedings of International Conference on Web Delivering of Music, 2002.
6. J. S. Downie, "Evaluating a simple approach to music information retrieval: Conceiving melodic n-grams as text," PhD Thesis, University of Western Ontario, London, Ontario, Canada, 1999.
7. A. Ghias et al., "Query by Humming: Musical Information Retrieval in an Audio Database," In Proc. of Third ACM International Conference on Multimedia, 1995, pp. 231-236.
8. J. Foote, "An overview of audio information retrieval," Multimedia Systems, 7(1), 1999, pp. 2-10.
9. H. Hoos, K. Renz, and M. Görg, "GUIDO/MIR - an experimental musical information retrieval system based on GUIDO music notation," In ISMIR Proceedings, pp. 41–50, 2001.
10. A. Klapuri, "Signal Processing Methods for the Automatic Transcription of Music," PhD thesis, Tampere University of Technology, 2004.
11. C.-C. Liu and P.-J. Tsai, "Content-based retrieval of MP3 music objects," Proceedings of the 10th International Conference on Information and Knowledge Management, 2001, pp. 506-511.
12. A. Kornstädt, "Themefinder: A web-based melodic search tool," In W. Hewlett and E. Selfridge-Field, Editors, Melodic Similarity: Concepts, Procedures, and Applications, Computing in Musicology, Volume 11. MIT Press, Cambridge, 1998.
13. J. H. Lee and J. S. Downie, "Survey of music information needs, uses, and seeking behaviours: Preliminary findings," In ISMIR Proceedings, pp. 441–446, 2004.
14. MIDI, Musical Instrument Digital Interface, www.midi.org.

15. J. Pickens, J. P. Bello, G. Monti, T. Crawford, M. Dovey, M. Sandler, and D. Byrd, "Polyphonic Score Retrieval Using Polyphonic Audio Queries: A Harmonic Modelling Approach," Proceedings ISMIR 2002, 3rd International Conference on Music Information Retrieval.

16. L. Prechelt and R. Typke, "An interface for melody input," ACM Transactions on Computer-Human Interaction, 8 (2), pp. 133–149, 2001.

17. A. Rauber, E. Pampalk, and D. Merkl, "The SOMenhanced jukebox: Organization and visualization of music collections based on perceptual models," Journal of New Music Research (JNMR), 32(2), pp. 193–210, 2003.

18. R. Typke, P. Giannopoulos, R. C. Veltkamp, F. Wiering, and R. van Oostrum, "Using transportation distances for measuring melodic similarity," In ISMIR Proceedings, pp. 107–114, 2003.

19. G. Tzanetakis and P. Cook, "Musical Genre Classification of Audio Signals," *IEEE* Transactions on Speech and Audio Processing, 10(5), July 2002.

20. E. Ukkonen, K. Lemström, and V. Mäkinen, "Geometric Algorithms for Transposition Invariant Content-Based Music Retrieval," ISMIR 2003 Proceedings of the Fourth International Conference on Music Information Retrieval, pp. 193–199.

21. E. Wold, T. Blum, D. Keislar, and J. Wheaton, "Content-based classification, search, and retrieval of audio," IEEE Multimedia, 3(3), pp. 27–36, 1996.

CONTENT-BASED PHOTO ALBUM MANAGEMENT USING FACES

Mohamed Abdel-Mottaleb   and   Longbin Chen
University of Miami, ECE Department, Coral Gables, Florida, USA

Definition: The system automatically detects and stores information about the locations of faces in the photos.

Abstract

Photo album management, an application of content-based image browsing/retrieval, has attracted attention in recent years. Identities of individuals appearing in the photos are the most important aspect for photo browsing. However, face recognition generally does not work effectively in this case due to the large variations in pose, illumination and sometimes poor quality of images. In this paper, we present a system for browsing photo albums. A similarity function based on face arrangement is defined. Photos are then clustered based on the similarity function using a clustering algorithm proposed in this paper. The system also represents photos of an event using a composite image. The composite image is built from representative faces and an image that represents the event. Experiments indicate that the face arrangement features are effective in representing the semantic content of the photos and are appropriate for photo albums.

Introduction

Various systems were developed for content-based image retrieval, among them are QBIC [7], CONIVAS Visualseek [8], and Netra [9]. These systems represent image content using a set of low-level attributes, such as color, texture, shape, layout, and motion. Retrieval is performed by comparing features of a query image with corresponding features of images stored in a database and presenting the user with the images in the database that have the most similar features. However, low-level features generally could not properly represent image content. Limiting the application domain enables the use of domain knowledge in building sophisticated tools for the specific application. Recently, there has been some work on family photo album management [1]. In case of photo albums, there are some metadata that are readily available, such as date-time. In addition, faces of individuals play an important role in case of family photos, and can be used in building semantic photo album browsing and retrieval tools.

Users usually remember photos by date, scene type and the individuals in the photos [1]. Date and other metadata could be obtained from the photos. Therefore, to automate photo album management, the "who is in the photo" needs to be automatically obtained. However, automatic face recognition usually does not work well in this case because of the large variations in pose, illumination and sometimes poor photo qualities. Therefore, other individual-related features, instead of identity, should be used for representation. In [1], a semi-automatic face annotation mechanism is proposed. "Cloth features" are used for photos of the same scene or event as a replacement for facial features to identify individuals appearing in multiple photos. In [6], the idea is extended by using a Bayesian framework to identify people from image to image in photo albums, where features such as image date and other face features are used.

In this paper, we present a system for image browsing. The system represents the photos in each event by a synthesized composite image. The composite image is built from an image that represents the event as well as faces of people who appear in the event. In fact, the individuals involved in an event could be a very discriminating feature to recognize the event. If combined with the representative image that shows the background, the user can easily recognize the event. The system also clusters the images within a single event based on face arrangement, which includes the locations of the faces, their sizes and identities. The goal of this clustering is to allow for the user to browse through the photos of the event.

The system described in this article has the following features:

1) Automatic Face Detection with probabilistic output;
2) An effective similarity measurement function based on face arrangement;
3) Event representation using composite images that include faces which appear in the event;
4) Clustering based on the similarity metric to facilitate browsing; each cluster contains photos that could be displayed in one screen.

The digital photo album

During the archiving phase, a fast and robust face detector, based on the algorithms in [5], is applied to the images. This face detector could a) detect faces with large yaw-rotation and in-plane rotation b) produce face detection results with probabilistic measures that indicate the confidence in the detection accuracy. The system allows the user to modify the results of the face detection if there are any false positives or false negatives, which are usually rare. The face detection results are then archived in the database. The results are also used to create composite images that represent the folders of images in the database. These composite images are used for browsing. In this paper, we assume that each folder contains images from the same event.

Figure 1 shows the browsing interface of our system. The interface is composed of three panels. The left panel is the folder browsing section, where folders are listed using the folder representative images. The middle panel is the image browsing section, where all images in one folder are listed by cluster. The photos in the same folder are clustered based on face arrangement similarity, so that each cluster contains exactly the number of photos that can be shown in one screen. Using the scroll bar, the user can browse photos of different clusters in the folder. These clusters are sorted by average number of faces. The right panel is where images could be viewed in more detail.

Figure 1. The user interface for photo album browsing.

Building composite images to represent the folders

Users tend to remember an event by WHEN and WHERE it happened and WHO participated in that event. The Date and Time of an event could be extracted from digital photos' metadata and represented as text. The place of the event could be reasonably represented by a photo of the scene. However, it is not easy to automatically select such a representative photo for the event.

In this paper, we propose to build a composite image to represent the photos in a folder. The composite image is built from an image from the folder that has the largest number of important faces as well as a set of representative faces from the folder (Figure 2). This criterion is natural and usually effective, especially when the user is searching for photos of someone. If the photo's orientation is landscape, the left frame in Figure 2 is used; otherwise, the right one is used.

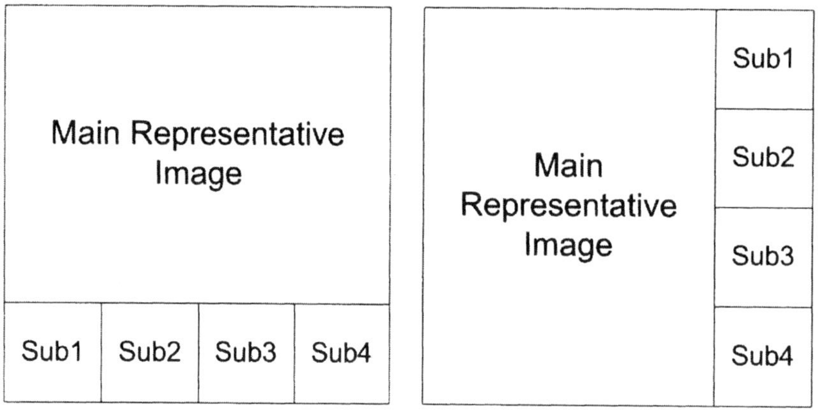

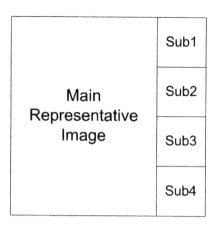

Figure 2. Folder representative images.

The representative faces should be selected according to the following criteria. The faces must be the important ones in that folder in the sense that they should carry as much information as possible because the number of representative faces is limited to a certain number (in our system, the number is four). The choice of important faces depends on the definition of "important". In fact, "important" is a semantic definition which has to be measured quantitatively. In our system, three factors are considered together to evaluate the importance of every face: the size of the face, the position of the face in the photo and the confidence of face detection result. Since faces are detected from all the images in a folder, the face of a person is usually detected multiple times. Therefore, we need to identify these cases in order to represent the folder with faces of different people.

It is usually the case that each individual wears the same cloth in a single event; therefore the color and texture features of the cloth can be an effective feature to roughly identify individuals [1]. The faces of these individuals are then used in creating a composite image that represents the event. Figure 3 is the algorithm for generating a representative image for a folder. In order to extract the texture feature of the cloth, we used the auto-correlogram [2]. It provides good features to describe the texture in color images. Compared with other color texture features, it 1) describes the spatial correlation of colors, 2) easy to compute and 3) the feature size is relatively small. The correlogram features are built using matrices similar to co-occurrence matrices used for describing texture. The difference is that the matrices here are built based on the absolute distance between the pixel values without considering the direction.

1. Detect the faces in photos starting with faces that have larger sizes until a specified number of faces are found or the minimum size of face is reached.
2. Select the body regions based on the results of face detection, extract color-texture features from the body regions;
3. Cluster the body features using 4-center clustering algorithm; then select the faces that are nearest to the cluster centers as sub-photos. These faces are, with great possibility, for different persons.
4. Select the photo with the maximum number of faces as the main representative photo;
5. Combine the main representative photo and sub-photos of the faces to build square images as the representative images of the folder, Figure 2.

Figure 3. Algorithm for generating folder representative image.

Browsing folders by Face Arrangement

We describe our measure of distance/similarity between images based on face arrangement. This measure is used in clustering the images of a folder for browsing as explained later in the article.

Similarity Function Based on Face Arrangements

There are several approaches for representing spatial relations between objects in images. In this paper our goal is to establish similarity between images based on the number of faces, their sizes and locations. Each face is represented by its bounding rectangle. To calculate the distance between two images, correspondence between the faces in the images has to be established as shown in Fig. 5. The distance between two images is defined as the weighted sum of four measures, T_N, T_D, T_A, T_{ov}:

$$dist(i,q) = \alpha * T_D + \beta * (1 - T_{OV}) + \gamma * (1 - T_A) + (1 - \alpha - \beta - \gamma) * T_N$$

T_D measures the relative spatial location:

$$T_D = \frac{1}{M} \left(\frac{\sum_{j=1}^{M} |L_i^j - L_q^j|}{W} + \frac{\sum_{j=1}^{M} |W_i^j - W_q^j|}{W} + \frac{\sum_{j=1}^{M} |T_i^j - T_q^j|}{H} + \frac{\sum_{j=1}^{M} |H_i^j - H_q^j|}{H} \right)$$

T_A measures the average ratio of the area of corresponding faces:

$$T_A = \frac{1}{M} \left[\sum_{j=1}^{M} \frac{\min(A_i^j, A_q^j)}{\max(A_i^j, A_q^j)} \right]$$

T_{ov} measures the average of the ratios of overlapped areas between corresponding faces:

$$T_{OV} = \frac{1}{M} \left[\sum_{j=1}^{M} \frac{Overlapped\ Size(A_i^j, A_q^j)}{\max(A_i^j, A_q^j)} \right]$$

T_N is a measure that captures the difference in the number of faces between the query and a test image:

$$T_N = \frac{|I_N - Q_N|}{M}$$

where I represents an image in the database and Q represents the query image, I_N and Q_N are the numbers of faces in images I and Q, M is $\min(I_N, Q_N)$, $(_i^j, _i^j)$

normalized). In the experiments we used $\alpha = 0.2, \beta = 0.1$ and $\gamma = 0.1$ and the similarity is obtained by the following equation:

$$Similarity(I,Q) = \lceil (1 - dist(I,Q)) \times 100 \rceil$$

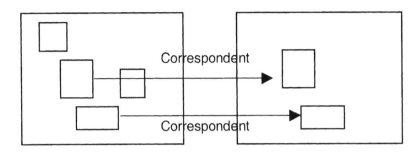

Figure 4. Correspondence between objects in two images.

Correspondence between objects (Figure 4) is accomplished by minimizing T_D for every object in one image with all other objects in the other image.

Clustering the Photo Images According to Face Arrangement

When the number of photos in a single folder is larger than the maximum number of images that can be displayed in one screen, the photos should be arranged in some order to facilitate browsing. This is achieved by clustering the photos based on the arrangement of the faces such that each cluster contains photos that could be displayed in one screen. Clustering images in a database was used before [4], however, in this article the clustering is based on the face arrangement similarity. Each cluster contains a set of images that can be displayed in one screen.

Our distance/similarity measure of face arrangement is a non-metric measure. Therefore, general metric-based clustering algorithms (e.g. k-means), could not be applied in our system. In order to cluster the photos in a folder based on this measure we propose the clustering algorithm in Figure 5.

---

1. Given a set of m photos, and the number of photos, n, which each cluster should contain
2. Calculate the number of cluster centers k

$$k = \left\lfloor \frac{m-1}{n} \right\rfloor + 1$$

3. Sort the photos based on the number of faces and divide them into k clusters; each of the first k-1 clusters contains n photos and the last one contains $m - n * (k-1)$ photos
4. For each pair of photos (x_i, x_j) from different clusters, check whether their exchange could reduce the sum of with-in distance of clusters, if so, exchange them. The with-in distance of clusters is defined as:

$$S_w = \frac{1}{n} \sum_i^n \sum_j^n Similarity\,(x_i, x_j)$$

5. Repeat step 4 until there are no such pairs.

Figure 5. Cluster algorithm for photo album browsing.

After the clusters of photos are built, they are sorted by the average number of faces in each cluster so that they can be browsed in this order.

Representative Images of Folder

After the faces are detected, the system extracts the body patches from the photos. Using the correlogram features, these features for the body patches are clustered (see Figure 6). Although patches in Figure 6.a and Figure 6.d are from the same individual, she changed cloth and clustering produces two clusters for that person. Although this is not desired, it does not affect the system too much.

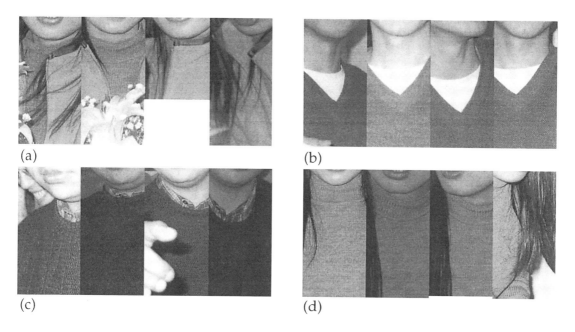

(a)

(b)

(c)

(d)

Figure 6. Body patches extracted from the photo album. Patches of each row are from the some individual. While row *a* and row *d* are of the same individual who changed her clothes.

Ideally, the selected sub-representative faces should be for as many different individuals as possible. This is achieved by assuming that the individuals would wear the same cloth during the time when all these photos are taken. This happens quite often, although it is not always true as in Figure 6. In our experiments, we used folders of photos that are taken in the same daty and the individuals did not change their cloth.

Figure 7 shows two representative folder images generated by our system. The results are compared with the "Thumbnail-views" used in *Windows XP explorer*. The first folder contains 78 photos from a party. Our algorithm selected a representative photo that has the largest number of faces and selected four faces as sub-photos (see algorithm in Figure 3) to build the composite image, while the Windows explorer selected some photos that have furniture and are not good representatives for the event. The second folder contains photos from a trip that contains an outdoor event with gathering in a cabin. Our algorithm selected a representative photo that contains faces of most individuals in that event and attached to it four different faces from the event.

Figure 7. Two examples of folder representative images. Left are auto-generated folder representative images, right are randomly selected photos from that folder, (similar to Thumbnail-views of folders in Windows XP Explorer).

Face Arrangement Similarity and Clustering

We conducted a subjective evaluation of the face arrangement similarity function described in a previous section. The database contained about 3500 images that were archived based on the locations and sizes of the faces. Queries were either images or sketches that contain bounding rectangles at the possible positions of the faces. The retrieved images were judged as either relevant or irrelevant by a subject who is not familiar with the system. Then, a performance measure was calculated. First we explain the performance measure and then present the results.

We used the performance measure used in [3], which is defined to reflect the rank position (Rp) of the relevant images:

$$R_p = \frac{1}{NN_R}\left[\sum_{i=1}^{NLR} R_i - \frac{N_R(N_R+1)}{2}\right],$$

where N is the number of images retrieved for browsing (in our experiment we looked at the top 50 images), N_R is the number of the relevant images for the query, R_i is the rank at which the ith relevant image is retrieved. This measure is 0 for perfect performance and approaches 1 as performance decreases.

The query images contained up to four faces in different positions. The average R_p values are shown in Table 1 for queries with different number of faces. As shown in the table the average R_p values are small, which indicate the good performance of the retrieval.

Table 1. Average rank position for different face number

# faces in query image	Average R_p
1	0.0590
2	0.1275
3	0.1299
4	0.0092

The average time to retrieve a photo by our system depends on the size of the photo albums. For a typical photo album containing 50 folders and each folder containing 256 photos, the number of photos that should be initially viewed is the 50 representative images of the folders. Then, the user could select the right photo clusters and then look for the right photos in the selected cluster.

Conclusions

We presented a system for archiving and browsing photos in a digital photo album. The system allows for browsing based on faces and their arrangements and represents events with a set of composite images. As was demonstrated in the experiments, the results are intuitive and make sense from user's point of view. The archiving process is fully automated.

See article: Multiple Source Alignment for Video Analysis

References

1. L. Chen, B. Hu, L. Zhang, M. Li, and H. Zhang, "Face Annotation for Family Photo Album Management," International Journal of Image and Graphics, Vol. 3, No. 1, pp. 81-94, 2003.
2. J. Huang, S. R. Kumar, M. Mitra, W. J. Zhu, and R. Zabih, "Image indexing using color correlograms," Proceedings of IEEE Conference on Computer Vision and Pattern Recognition pp. 762, 1997.
3. H. Muller, W. Muller, D. Squire, S. Marchand-Maillet, and T. Pun, "Automated Benchmarking in Content-based Image Retrieval," Proceedings of the IEEE International Conference on Multimedia and Expo (ICME2001), Tokyo, Japan, August 2001.
4. S. Krishnamachari and M. Abdel-Mottaleb, "Hierarchical Clustering Algorithm for Fast Image Retrieval," Storage and Retrieval for Image and Video Databases VII, SPIE Symposium on Electronic Imaging: Science & Technology, San Jose, CA, 1999.
5. R. Xiao, L. Zhu, and H.J. Zhang, "Boosting Chain Learning for Object Detection," Proceeding of the International Conference on Computer Vision, pp. 709-715, 2003.
6. L. Zhang, L. Chen, M. Li, and H. Zhang, "Automatic Face Annotation for Family Album," Proceedings of the Eleventh ACM International Conference on Multimedia, pp. 355-358, Berkeley, CA, 2003.
7. M. Flickner et al., "Query by Image and Video Content: The QBIC System," IEEE Computer, Vol. 28, No. 9, pp. 23-32, September 1996.

8. J. R. Smith and S. F. Chang, "Visualseek: A Fully Automated Content-based Image Query System," Proceedings of ACM Multimedia, (Boston, MA), pp. 87-98, November 1996.
9. W. Y. Ma and B. S. Manjunath, "Netra: A toolbox for navigating large image databases," Proceedings of IEEE International Conference on Image Processing, Vol. 1, Santa Barbara, CA, pp. 568-571, October 1997.

CONTENT DISTRIBUTION NETWORK

Definition: Content Distribution Network is designed to minimize the network delays when viewing or downloading a multimedia content over the network.

The HTTP client server model does not scale well as the number of clients and the network bandwidth utilization increase. The server is a choke point, and a single point of failure. Adding redundancy and load balancing can help, but this does not deal with overall network load. Content Distribution Networks (CDN) are designed to minimize the delay that the end user experiences when requesting to view or download content such as HTML pages, images, data files, and streaming media. CDNs achieve this goal by deploying and managing a network of *edge caches* (or *proxy caches*) which maintain content replicas that emanate from an *origin server*. These edge caches are closer to the end user in terms of lower response latency (e.g. smaller number of router hops, higher bandwidth connections) as shown in Figure 1. Algorithms for cache management are employed to optimize resource utilization based on user content consumption patterns. CDNs may also support content management features such as content preloading, prioritization, publication and expiration dates, and digital rights management. Many other CDN architectures are possible including the use of multicast distribution and peer-to-peer caching.

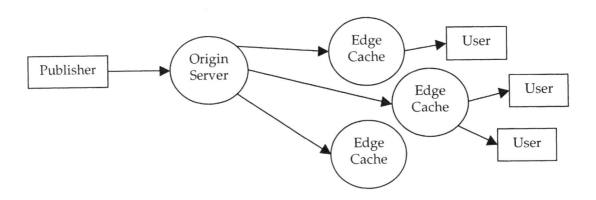

Figure 1. Content flows from an origin server to a set of edge caches in a content distribution network.

See: **Multimedia Content Adaptation**

CONTENT EXTRACTION AND METADATA

Oge Marques
Department of Computer Science and Engineering
Florida Atlantic University, Boca Raton, Florida, USA

Definition: *Context extraction deals with extracting relevant data (metadata) from complex multimedia files.*

Multimedia files contain complex and expensive audiovisual representations. Extracting relevant contents from these files – preferably in a (semi-)automatic manner – in a way that facilitates future indexing, search, and retrieval is a challenging task. The ever growing amount of digitally encoded multimedia content produced, stored, and distributed worldwide [2] makes it an even harder and more relevant job.

Even though creation, storage, and dissemination of multimedia contents have become easier and cheaper than ever before, the resulting content has value only if it can be discovered and used. The most popular way to discover contents on the Internet is to use a text-based search engine. General-purpose text-based search engines usually do a poor job when searching for multimedia contents, primarily due to the fact that they often must rely on potentially subjective, incomplete, and/or ambiguous keyword and free text annotations, describing the multimedia contents. In other words, even though the multimedia data may be relevant, its accompanying description (metadata) does not do justice to it. There is an urgent need to overcome these limitations and find ways to "automatically and objectively describe, index and annotate multimedia information, notably audiovisual data, using tools that automatically extract (possibly complex) audiovisual features from the content to substitute or complement manual, text-based descriptions" [3].

A lot of the research in multimedia over the past 10 years has somehow addressed these issues, mostly through creation of algorithms for specific subtasks, often integrated into research prototypes or commercial products. We will review some of the technical aspects involved in content extraction and description of multimedia data, as well as some of the most relevant attempts to standardize representation of associated metadata.

MPEG-7

In 1996, the Moving Pictures Expert Group recognized the need to address the problem of standardized metadata representation, and work on the MPEG-7 Multimedia Content Description Interface (ISO/IEC 15938) started.

MPEG-7 goals are:
- Create standardized multimedia description framework
- Enable content-based access to and processing of multimedia information on the basis of descriptions of multimedia content and structure (metadata)

- Support range of abstraction levels for metadata from low-level signal characteristics to high-level semantic information

The guiding principles behind MPEG-7 include [3]:

- Wide application base: MPEG-7 shall be applicable to content associated with any application, real-time or not, irrespective of whether it is made available online, off-line, or streamed.
- Wide array of data types: MPEG-7 shall consider a large variety of data types (e.g., speech, audio, image, graphics, video, etc.). No new description tool should be developed for textual data; existing solutions such as Extensible Markup Language (XML) or Resource Description Framework (RDF) should be used instead.
- Media independence: MPEG-7 shall be applicable independently of the medium that carries the content.
- Object-based: MPEG-7 shall support object-based description of content. Since the MPEG-4 standard is built around an object-based data model, the two standards complement each other very well.
- Format independence: MPEG-7 shall be applicable independently of the content representation format, whether analog or digital, compressed or not.
- Abstraction level: MPEG-7 shall support description capabilities with different levels of abstraction, from low-level features (which most likely will be extracted automatically using algorithms beyond the scope of the standard) to high-level features conveying semantic meaning.

For more details on the MPEG-7 standard, please refer to [4]. For the latest updates on the MPEG-7 program of work, check [5].

Content extraction and description

Automatic extraction of contents from multimedia files is a challenging topic that has been extensively investigated over the past decade, often in connection with image and video indexing and retrieval systems, digital libraries, video databases, and related systems. We will look at content extraction from the perspective of the associated MPEG-7-compatible descriptors. Consequently, we will also adopt the MPEG-7 division of the extraction and description steps into two main categories: visual and audio.

Visual descriptors

Visual descriptors, as the name suggests, provide standardized descriptions of the visual aspects of a multimedia file (e.g., a video clip). They can be of two main types: general or domain-specific. The main types of general visual descriptors are:

- **Color descriptors [8]:**
  - *Color space descriptor*: allows a selection of a color space – RGB, HSV, YCbCr, or HMMD (Hue-Max-Min-Diff) – to be used in the description. The associated *color quantization descriptor* specifies how the selected color space is partitioned into discrete bins.

o *Dominant color descriptor* (DCD): allows specification of a small number of dominant color values as well as their statistical properties, such as distribution and variance. The extraction procedure for the DCD is described in [7].

o *Scalable color descriptor* (SCD): is obtained by employing a Haar transform-based encoding scheme across values of a color histogram in the HSV color space.

o *Group-of-frame* (GoF), or *group-of-picture* (GoP) *descriptor*: is an extension of the SCD to a group of frames in a video sequence.

o *Color structure descriptor* (CSD): aims at identifying localized color distributions using a small structuring window.

o *Color layout descriptor* (CLD): captures the spatial layout of the representative colors on a grid superimposed on a region or image.

- **Texture descriptors [8]:**
  o *Homogeneous texture descriptor* (HTD): provides a quantitative representation of the region texture using the mean energy and energy deviation from a set of frequency channels.

  o *Texture browsing descriptor* (TBD): compact descriptor that specifies the perceptual characterization of a texture in terms of regularity, coarseness, and directionality.

  o *Edge histogram descriptor* (EHD): represents local edge distribution in an image.

- **Shape descriptors:**
  o *Region-based shape descriptor*: expresses pixel distribution within a 2-D object or region. It is based on both boundary and internal pixels and can describe complex objects consisting of multiple disconnected regions as well as simple objects with or without holes.

  o *Contour-based shape descriptor*: is based on the Curvature Scale-Space (CSS) representation of the contour of an object and is said to emulate well the shape similarity perception of the human visual system.

  o *3-D shape descriptor*: is based on the histogram of local geometrical properties of the 3-D surfaces of the object.

- **Motion descriptors:**
  o *Motion activity*: captures the intuitive notion of 'intensity (or pace) of action' in a video segment, by encoding the intensity, direction, spatial distribution, and temporal distribution of activity.

  o *Camera motion*: encodes all camera operations such as translations, rotations, and changes of focal length, as well as all possible combinations of these.

  o *Motion trajectory*: describes the displacements of objects in time, whereas an object is any (set of) spatiotemporal region(s) whose trajectory is relevant in the context in which is used.

o *Parametric motion*: represents the motion and/or deformation of a region or image, using one of the following classical parametric models: translational, rotational, affine, perspective, or quadratic.

An example of domain-specific visual descriptor is the face descriptor, which uses Principal Component Analysis (PCA) to represent the projection of a face vector onto a set of 48 basis vectors that span the space of all possible face vectors. These basis vectors are derived from eigenvectors of a set of training faces and are reasonably robust to view-angle and illumination changes [6].

Audio descriptors

- **Low-level audio descriptors:**
  o Basic descriptors: *AudioWaveformType* (describes the minimum and maximum sampled amplitude values reached by the audio signal within the sample period) and *AudioPowerType* (describes the instantaneous power of the samples in the frame).
  o Basic spectral descriptors: provide a very compact description of the signal's spectral content.
  o Basic signal parameters: include the computation of the fundamental frequency of the audio signal and two measures of the harmonic nature of the signal's spectrum.
  o Temporal timbre descriptors: used within an audio segment and intended to compute parameters of the signal envelope.
  o Spectral timbre descriptors
  o Spectral basis representations
  o Silence segment: attaches the semantic of 'silence' (i.e., no significant sound) to an audio segment.

- **High-level audio descriptors:** lower-level audio descriptors can be used as building blocks of higher-level description tools, specialized in tasks such as: general sound recognition, spoken content description, musical instrument timbre description, or melody description.

The role of metadata

"Metadata is the value-added information which documents the administrative, descriptive, preservation, technical and usage history and characteristics associated with resources [1]." It provides the foundation upon which digital asset management systems (such as digital libraries or video databases) rely to provide fast, precise access to relevant resources across networks and between organizations [1]. Some of the main challenges associated with metadata are its cost, its unreliability, its subjectivity, its lack of authentication and its lack of interoperability with respect to syntax, semantics, vocabularies, languages and underlying models [1]. In this section we look at ongoing activity and relevant standards for representation of metadata associated with multimedia contents.

XML Technologies

XML and its associated technologies, such as XML Namespaces, XML Schema Language, and XML Query languages, have become the key to enabling automated computer-processing, integration and exchange of information over the Internet.

Extensible Markup Language (XML)

XML [9] is a simple and flexible (meta-)language that makes it possible to exchange data in a standard format among heterogeneous machines and networks. It has become the *de facto* standard for representing metadata descriptions of resources on the Internet.

XML Schema Language

XML Schema Language [10] provides a means for defining the structure, content and semantics of XML documents. It provides an inventory of XML markup constructs which can constrain and document the meaning, usage and relationships of the constituents of a class of XML documents: data types, elements and their content, attributes and their values, entities and their contents and notations [1]. Thus, the XML Schema language can be used to define, describe and catalogue XML vocabularies for classes of XML documents, such as metadata descriptions of web resources or digital objects [1]. XML Schemas have been used to define metadata schemas in the MPEG-7 standard.

XML Query (XQuery)

XML Query [11] provides flexible query facilities to extract data from real and virtual documents and collections both locally and on the World Wide Web.

Semantic Web-related technologies

The Semantic Web vision of "bringing structure to the meaningful content of Web pages, creating an environment where software agents roaming from page to page can readily carry out sophisticated tasks for users" [12] will only be fully realized when programs and applications are created that collect Web content from diverse sources, process the information and exchange the results with other programs.

Two of the key technological building blocks for the Semantic Web are [1]:

- Formal languages for expressing semantics, such as the Resource Description Framework (RDF) and OWL (Web Ontology Language).
- The ontologies which are being constructed from such languages.

RDF

The Resource Description Framework (RDF) [13] uses triples to makes assertions that particular *things* (people, Web pages or whatever) have *properties* (such as "is a sister of," "is the author of") with certain *values* (another person, another Web page). The triples of RDF form webs of information about related things. Because RDF uses URIs to encode this information in a document, the URIs ensure that concepts are not just words in a document but are tied to a unique definition that everyone can find on the Web [1].

120   C

OWL

The OWL Web Ontology Language is designed for use by applications that need to process the content of information instead of just presenting information to humans. OWL facilitates greater machine interpretability of Web content than that supported by XML, RDF, and RDF Schema (RDF-S) by providing additional vocabulary along with a formal semantics [14].

Integration between multimedia standards, such as MPEG-7, and Semantic Web standards, such as RDF and OWL, is a current research topic. See [15], [16], and [17] for recent examples of activity in this direction.

See: Context and Current Metadata Standards

References

1. J. Hunter, "Working Towards MetaUtopia - A Survey of Current Metadata Research," Library Trends, Organizing the Internet, Edited by Andrew Torok, 52(2), Fall 2003.
2. How much information? 2003. http://www.sims.berkeley.edu/research/projects/how-much-info-2003.
3. F. Pereira and R. Koene, "Context, Goals, and Procedures," a chapter in: B. S. Manjunath, P. Salembier, and T. Sikora (Eds.), Introduction to MPEG 7: Multimedia Content Description Language, Wiley, 2002.
4. B. S. Manjunath, Philippe Salembier, and Thomas Sikora (Eds.), Introduction to MPEG 7: Multimedia Content Description Language, Wiley, 2002.
5. MPEG-7 Standard, http://www.itscj.ipsj.or.jp/sc29/29w42911.htm#MPEG-7 Accessed July 23, 2005.
6. M.A. Turk and A. Pentland, "Eigenfaces for recognition," *Journal of Cognitive Neuroscience*, 3, 72-86, 1991.
7. Y. Deng *et al.*, "An efficient color representation for image retrieval", IEEE Transactions on Image Processing, 10(1), 140-147, 2001.
8. B. S. Manjunath, J.-R. Ohm, V. V. Vasudevan, and A. Yamada, "Color and Texture Descriptors," *IEEE Transactions on Circuits and Systems for Video Technology*, 11(6), June 2001.
9. Extensible Markup Language (XML). http://www.w3.org/XML/ Accessed July 20, 2005.
10. XLM Schema. http://www.w3.org/XML/Schema Accessed July 20, 2005.
11. XML Query (XQuery). http://www.w3.org/XML/Query Accessed July 20, 2005.
12. T. Berners-Lee, J. Hendler, and O. Lassil, "The Semantic Web, Scientific American," May 2001.
13. RDF. http://www.w3.org/RDF/ Accessed July 20, 2005.
14. OWL. http://www.w3.org/2004/OWL/ Accessed July 20, 2005.
15. J. Hunter, "Adding Multimedia to the Semantic Web - Building an MPEG-7 Ontology," International Semantic Web Working Symposium (SWWS), Stanford, 2001.
16. C. Tsinaraki, P. Polydoros, N. Moumoutzis, and S. Christodoulakis, "Coupling OWL with MPEG-7 and TV-Anytime for Domain-specific Multimedia Information Integration and Retrieval," Proceedings of RIAO 2004, Avignon/France, April 2004.

17. G. Tummarello, C. Morbidoni, P. Puliti, A.F. Dragoni, and F. Piazza, "From multimedia to the semantic Web using MPEG-7 and computational intelligence," Proceedings of the Fourth International Conference on Web Delivering of Music (WEDELMUSIC), 2004.

CONTENT MANAGEMENT IN MULTIMEDIA NEWS SYSTEMS

Definition: Content management news systems represent modern tools to author, categorize, control, revise, and publish multimedia content for the news presentation and distribution services.

Recent developments in the scalability and performance of the Internet have brought myriads of information to the average user's fingertips. Information commercialization has reached information society and news networks are sending their contents all over the globe. Based on the typical news sources provided by individual journalists, national and international news agencies and worldwide broadcast networks, contents have been handled with appropriate multimedia management systems. Since content assets are typically out of academic and technical administration, specific user-oriented software has emerged and has become widely popular within the last five years: Content Management Systems.

Based on research oriented Web engineering methodologies [1] the news market has started to adopt management features and high volume capabilities for developing and utilizing commercial and open source systems. Market leaders like Stellent™, Microsoft™, Vignette™, IBM™, Tridion™, OpenText™ and others are offering customer oriented features in their commercial services, thus competing with open source CMS leaders like Zope, OpenCMS, Typo3, Mambo, or Bricolage. All systems manage multimedia news based on specific content repositories and with increasing usability for their target market, the content administrators. Content management systems strictly separate three classes of user services: the service design, the content organization and structuring, and the content manipulation. Obeying the non-technical background of most of the content creators such as journalists and editors, all CMS provide an easy-to-use interface for multimedia content creation and further management in the content asset's lifecycle.

Multimedia news services now involve besides enormous amounts of digitized textual information also images, audio and video material, supported by multiple technical tools for seamless integration and modern distribution. The popularity of visual media such as photos, videos, and animations attests to their mainstream acceptance. Technically multimedia integration has been adapted to middleware software and content management applications [2] to allow a seamless integration with current news management and distribution applications

Research and industry developments in the news management and distribution domain have lead to hundreds of modern and appropriate products to handle multimedia news contents. The market leaders (both commercial and open source frameworks and solutions) cover the most relevant aspects of the news content lifecycle discussed in "Multimedia News Systems".

Content management systems generally distinguish application design from information organization and content manipulation. Most emphasis in the news application domain is given to the content manipulation section, thus providing journalists and editors with appropriate modern tools to author, categorize, control, revise, and publish multimedia contents for the news presentation and distribution services.

See: Multimedia News Systems

References

1. K.M. Göschka and M.W. Schranz, "Client and Legacy Integration in Object-Oriented Web Engineering," IEEE Multimedia, Vol. 8, No. 1, Jan-Mar 2001, pp. 32-41.
2. P. Mulhem and H. Martin, "From Database to Web Multimedia Documents," Multimedia Tools and Applications, Vol. 20, No. 3, August 2003, pp. 263-282.

CONTENT PROTECTION SOLUTIONS FOR DIGITAL HOME NETWORKS

Definition: Content protection solutions include techniques and standards used to protect multimedia content in home networks and devices.

Each of the solutions for digital home networks defines a means of associating the Copy Control Information (CCI) with the digital content it protects. The CCI communicates the conditions under which a consumer is authorized to make a copy. An important subset of CCI is the two Copy Generation Management System (CGMS) bits for digital copy control: "11" (copy-never), "10" (copy-once), "01" (no-more-copies), and "00" (copy-free). The integrity of the CCI should be ensured to prevent unauthorized modification. The CCI can be associated with the content in two ways: (1) the CCI is included in a designated field in the A/V stream, and (2) the CCI is embedded as a watermark into the A/V stream.

The Content Scramble System (CSS) was the first of its kind for protecting multimedia content on DVD players. CSS has a hierarchy of keys: master key, disk key, and title key. DVD Copy Control Association (CCA) has assigned each manufacturer a distinct master key that is embedded in all DVD players. The unique disk key belonging to each disk is encrypted by all the master keys, and this information is stored on every disk. The player decrypts the disk key with its own master key. The disk key decrypts the title key, and the title key decrypts the movie on the DVD. If a particular master is key compromised, it is replaced by a key used in the subsequent manufacturing of DVD players. With the new key assignment, future releases of DVDs cannot be played on the cloned players manufactured with the compromised key. A software implementation of CSS for a DVD drive was hacked in 1999. The software called DeCSS can be used to break the CSS encryption, allowing the decryption of protected DVDs. CSS-protected video is decrypted during playback on the compliant DVD player or drive.

Content Protection for Pre-Recorded Media (CPPM) Specification is designed for protecting audio on DVD-ROM. CPPM-protected audio is decrypted during playback on the compliant DVD player or drive. Content Protection for Recordable Media (CPRM) Specification is designed for protecting audio-visual (A/V) content on recordable DVDs. The A/V stream coming from a source device is re-encrypted before recording on a DVD recordable disc. During playback, the compliant player derives the decryption key.

The 4C/Verance watermark technology embeds inaudible digital data into audio content. The compliant playback or recording device detects the CCI represented by the watermark, and responds accordingly.

The content providers are interested in watermarking DVD content as a second line of defense. In this scheme, invisible watermarks are embedded into video content. The compliant playback or recording device detects the CCI represented by the watermark and responds accordingly. If a copy is authorized, the compliant recorder creates and embeds a new watermark to represent "no-more-copies."

The Digital Transmission Content Protection (DTCP) Specification defines a cryptographic protocol for protecting audio/video entertainment content from unauthorized copying, intercepting, and tampering as it traverses digital transmission mechanisms such as a high-performance serial bus that conforms to the IEEE 1394-1995 standard. The source and sink devices authenticate each other, and establish shared secrets. The A/V content is encrypted across the interface using a content key derived from several parameters. The encryption key is renewed periodically.

High-bandwidth Digital Content Protection (HDCP) is a specification developed by Intel Corporation to protect digital entertainment content across the Digital Visual Interface (DVI) and High Definition Multimedia Interface (HDMI). DVI and HDMI are two of the interfaces protected by HDCP. Video transmitter authenticates the receiver, and establishes shared secrets with it. A/V content is encrypted across the interface with a key based on shared secrets. The encryption key is renewed frequently.

See: Protection of Multimedia Data in Distribution and Storage

CONTEXT AND CURRENT METADATA STANDARDS

Definition: *Standards that define human readable and machine understandable metadata of media content.*

Maintaining human readable and machine understandable metadata descriptions of media content is essential for retrieving, using, and managing non-textual media items. Such descriptions usually contain low-level features (e.g. color histograms) extracted automatically from the underlying media object as well as high-level semantic concepts, annotated by human users. Since semantic content descriptions are always bound to human interpretation, which itself is time- and context-bound, metadata might be misattributed and not very helpful for other users in another context. Assuming that we want to facilitate the user's ability to formulate contextual queries, it is necessary to maintain context-sensitive metadata. One of the key issues for realizing that goal is the use of context-aware data models and metadata standards [1]. Currently there are two promising, standardized metadata frameworks that address the need for machine-processable and context-aware content descriptions: the Multimedia Content Description Interface (MPEG-7) developed by ISO/IEC and the standards developed within the W3C Semantic Web Activity.

The MPEG-7 framework is an attempt to standardize descriptions of audio-visual content by providing Description Schemes (DS) to describe different aspects of multimedia at different levels of abstraction. In MPEG-7 contextual aspects of multimedia are modeled in terms of narrative worlds. A narrative world consists of objects, agents, events, places, time, states, concepts and the relationships among those entities. MPEG-7 descriptions can contain multiple (interrelated) narrative worlds; thus content can be characterized in several contexts. The MPEG-7 Semantic DS is defined to embed descriptions of narrative worlds into standardized metadata descriptions. This approach to model context is rather closed, because the syntax and semantics of the Semantics DS is defined only within the framework and is bound to the domain of audio-visual data [2].

Another attempt to model context in metadata descriptions is the framework provided by the Semantic Web. The Resource Description Framework (RDF) allows for encoding complex metadata descriptions as graphs without associating any specific semantics. On top of the RDF data model, which is a directed label graph, ontology languages like RDFS and OWL were defined. Those languages have a well-defined, logic-based semantics and allow for the definition of arbitrary domain- and context-specific ontologies. In contrast to MPEG-7, which models context within a hard-wired scheme, the Semantic Web is open for any contextual model as long as it is expressed in a semantic language. Furthermore, the logical foundations of those languages are the basic requirement for reasoning services. Such services could infer additional semantics in order to add contextual metadata automatically. A first attempt into this direction is presented in [3] – a camera phone image system that captures the media's context. It relies on reasoning services to infer additional media semantics in order to add contextual metadata automatically.

See: Context-aware Multimedia, Content Extraction and Metadata

References

1. F. Nack, "The Future in Digital Media Computing is Meta," IEEE Multimedia, Vol. 11, No. 2, 2004, pp. 10-13.

2. F. Nack, J.van Ossenbruggen, and L. Hardmann, "The obscure object of desire: multimedia metadata on the Web, part 2," IEEE Multimedia, Vol. 12, No. 1, 2005, pp. 54-63.

3. M. Davis, S. King, N. Good, and R. Savas, "From context to content: leveraging context to infer media metadata," Proceedings of the 12th annual ACM international conference on Multimedia, 2004, pp. 188-195.

CONTEXT-AWARE MODELING OF MULTIMEDIA CONTENT

Multimedia content can have multiple semantics varying over time, i.e. the relevance of metadata used for describing the meaning of the multimedia content depends on the underlying context. Herein, context is defined as a set of concepts from a particular domain that is supposed to encode a view of a party. In comparison to ontologies that stand for themselves and are built to be shared, the context is kept with the content (and often sharing makes only sense together with the content). However, the technical requirements for describing and managing ontology knowledge or context knowledge are the same.   Context-aware modeling of multimedia content means allowing incorporating domain knowledge into the document model for multimedia content.

Context-aware multimedia content needs to be authored, exchanged, and traded between different applications. Therefore one important prerequisite for the realization of context-aware multimedia applications is to establish an exchangeable container unit that aggregates and interrelates the described media objects. The classification of media objects and interrelations between media objects should allow to reflect the particular context. This can be realized by labeling them with concepts originating from the context domain. Finally, as the multimedia content and the associated context information possibly changes over time, the container units and their components should provide some versioning support.

Existing standards for multimedia document models, such as HTML, SMIL, or SVG, have all in common that they merely focus on the encoding of the content, but neglect the information the content conveys. As they are limited to the modeling of presentation-related issues of multimedia content, only inflexible hard-wired, multimedia presentations can be realized. Although, current semantic approaches to multimedia content modeling, such as RDF, Topic Maps, or MPEG-7, establish a starting point for the integration of the required meta knowledge within the management of multimedia content, they do not provide an exchangeable and versionable container unit aggregating both, the multimedia content's media objects and semantic descriptions.

EMMOs, Enhanced Multimedia Meta Objects, [1] are a good example for a modeling approach providing a basis for the context-aware modeling of multimedia content. An EMMO constitutes a versionable and tradable unit that combines media, semantic relationships between media, as well as functionality on the media. The semantic aspect of the EMMO model allows to integrate context information; the unit-character and exchangeable feature of an EMMO allows to share and circulate pieces of context-aware multimedia content within communities or application domains.

See: Context-aware Multimedia

References

1.   K. Schellner, U. Westermann, S. Zillner and W. Klas, "CULTOS: Towards a World-Wide Digital Collection of Exchangeable Units of Multimedia Content for Intertextual Studies," Proceedings of the Conference on Distributed Multimedia Systems, 2003.

CONTEXT-AWARE MULTIMEDIA

Wolfgang Klas
University of Vienna, Vienna, Austria and
Research Studio Digital Memory Engineering, Vienna, Austria

Ross King
Research Studio Digital Memory Engineering, Vienna, Austria

Definition: *Context-aware multimedia refers to a specific subset of context-aware applications related to multiple media types.*

Introduction

Multimedia applications face a variety of media types, from single media types like audio, video, images, text to compositions of these single media forming new *multimedia objects*. Furthermore, single media as well as composed media very often are to be constructed, retrieved, and interpreted according to a particular context given in an application setting.

In this article, we will first establish the meaning of the concept *context-aware multimedia*, first defining the terms *context* and *context-awareness*. We will then explore four key research aspects of context-aware multimedia, namely: modeling, retrieval, authoring, and presentation.

Context

A survey of the literature reveals several variations in the definition of *context*. We infer from the common thread of these definitions that context is a very broad concept including more or less anything that can directly or indirectly affect an application, and consider the following to be the most comprehensive:

"Context is any information that can be used to characterize the situation of an entity. An entity is a person, place, or object that is considered relevant to the interaction between a user and an application, including the user and applications themselves." [7]

In other words, any information that depicts the situation of a user can be entitled context. This would include the number of people in the area, the time of day, and any devices the user may employ [5]. One can however distinguish between those contextual characteristics that are critical to the application versus those that may be relevant but are not critical.

Within computing applications, there are three major context categories of interest: user context, computing resources, and environmental aspects. Orthogonal to this view, context can be explicit (that is, information provided directly by the user) or implicit (derived from on one hand sensors, on the other hand from an analysis of user behavior). As we learn more about human-computer interaction, it is becoming clear that the user is not prepared to deliver a large volume of explicit information and, as a result, information gathered implicitly (from for example sensor networks) is becoming more and more relevant.

In previous decades, a narrow aspect of user context – the user preferences in terms of search and retrieval of data – was denoted in the database community with the concept of *views*. Today, user context is considered far more broadly and includes user interests, goals, social situation, prior knowledge and history of interaction with the system. Thus, the dimension of time may also be included in the user's context. "Context information may be utilized in an immediate, just in time, way or may be processed from a historical perspective "[5].

Computer resources include characteristics of the client, server, and network, as well as additional available resources such as printers, displays, and storage systems. This type of context has become particularly relevant for the mobile computing community, in which the range of client capabilities is enormous and to a great extent limited in comparison with standard computer workstations.

Environmental contextual aspects include (but are not limited to) location, time, temperature, lighting conditions, and other persons present. Note that there is some ambiguity in the literature in the use of the term environment, which can refer to the computing environment as well as the actual physical environment of the user. Here of course we refer to the latter.

The assessment of environmental context faces a number of research challenges, as described in [18]. Context information is often acquired from unconventional heterogeneous sources, such as motion detectors or GPS receivers. Such sources are likely to be distributed and inhomogeneous. The information from these sensors must often be abstracted in order to be used by an application; for example, GPS data may need to be converted to street addresses. Finally, environmental context information must be detected in real time and applications must adapt to changes dynamically.

It should be noted that an enormous amount of research is presently being dedicated to the location context, which is most frequently referred to as location-based services, as this is considered to be one of the potential "killer-applications" of the next generation wireless networks. However, one should not overlook the fact that the question "what are you doing" can be equally or more important than "where you are". It is all well and good to know that a professor is in a lecture hall, but it is even more important to know whether she is attending a lecture or giving it herself. This point leads us from the concept of context in itself to the concept of context-awareness.

Context-Awareness

The phrase *context-aware* begins to appear with regularity in relatively recent literature, although its introduction is largely attributed to a paper from 1994 by Shilit & Theimer, in which they define context-aware computing as any system that "adapts according to its location of use, the collection of nearby people and objects, as well as changes to those over time." [20].

However, given the extended considerations of context reviewed in the previous section, it is clear that the concept of context-awareness has also evolved to meet these considerations, for example: "A system is context-aware if it uses context to provide relevant information and/or services to the user, where relevancy depends on the user's task." [7]

Implicit in the concept of context-awareness is that something must be context-aware, for example, the "system" quoted above. We will follow the literature and assume that this system in question is a context-aware (computing) application.

"Context-aware applications" is a phrase that appears most often in the literature of ubiquitous computing and pervasive computing environments. Context-aware environments refer to fixed locations, either in the workplace or at home, with ubiquitous sensors that can determine the location, actions, and intent of the location inhabitants (be they employees or family members).

Other examples of context-aware applications include the so-called Tour Guide applications (the canonical example of location-based services), or the personalized online shopping services exemplified by Amazon.com, where the analysis of user behavior over time as well as the aggregate behavior of users play a major role.

Context-Aware Multimedia

The term *multimedia* often simply refers to media content other than text; however, more properly, the term multimedia should be applied in situations involving the combination of two or more media types, including text, images, video, audio, animations, three-dimensional models, and so on. We can therefore conclude that *context-aware multimedia* refers to a specific subset of context-aware applications related to multiple media types.

It is interesting to observe that the term context-aware multimedia is most often employed within the mobile computing and applications community – exactly those for whom multimedia content is least suitable, given the constraints on bandwidth and display properties. However, although significant research effort is dedicated towards adaptive multimedia delivery to end devices such as PDAs and mobile telephones, user mobility need not necessarily equate to mobile devices and can instead concentrate on the mobility of the user; see for example [14], [21].

The line between multimedia content and multimedia applications is gradually becoming blurred. Take for example Flash™ presentations, which can be considered traditional multimedia content in the form of graphical animations of images and text, but can also be seen as applications when methods for user interaction and response are packaged and delivered with the presentation. In our opinion, multimedia of the future will continue to blur this distinction, as more and more functionality, including context-awareness, is encapsulated within the medium itself. With this in mind, we will continue by using the terms *context-aware multimedia* with and context-aware multimedia *applications* interchangeably.

Given this definition, and following the analysis of [7], we infer that there are at least two features that a context-aware multimedia application should provide:

- assimilation of new context information within the media metadata in order to support later retrieval
- presentation of multimedia information and services to a user, taking at least some of the discussed aspects of context (user preferences, location, etc.) in to account

In order to support the first feature, methods for modeling and querying are required. In order to support the second, tools for authoring and presentation are required. We now briefly discuss the research challenges in these areas:

Modeling

For the sake of completeness, we note one obvious fact: most multimedia content is not inherently self-describing, and therefore metadata must play a central role in any context-aware multimedia applications. Of course metadata is also required in order to describe other aspects of context, including the computing environment and user preferences (e.g. device and user profiles). In addition to such requirements, context-aware modeling should also include the incorporation of domain knowledge into the document model; that is, not only must one describe the media, but also the relationships between media, in order to create documents and/or presentations that are valuable to the user.

Currently there are a few promising standardized metadata frameworks that address the need for machine-processable and context-aware content descriptions: for example, the Multimedia Content Description Interface MPEG-7 [ISO/IEC TR 15938], and the Resource Description Framework (RDF) and Web Ontology Language (OWL), both standards developed within the W3C Semantic Web Activity [http://www.w3c.org/2001/sw].

Another important W3C recommendation, Composite Capability/Preference Profiles (CC/PP) [4] proposes a standard for modeling the computer resource context. Research is already underway to extend this work in the direction of more general context modeling, for example the universal profiling schema (UPS) model [13], which is built on top of CC/PP and RDF.

Models based on the standards described above tend to only include concrete measurable quantities; however, it is far from clear that these are sufficient to optimally model context. More complex models, allowing the application of fuzzy logic and Bayesian reasoning e.g. [12], are likely to drive future research efforts. The problem of context modeling may also be approached at a more abstract level, see for example [10].

Retrieval

Multimedia content, consisting principally of unstructured data, is clearly a case for the established methods of information retrieval (IR) and information filtering (IF). The concept of retrieval has also evolved to include not only active retrieval or searching, but also passive retrieval, or notification. Multimedia retrieval and filtering are broad research topics and various specific aspects are covered in separate entries of this encyclopedia. We note that most work tends to concentrate on retrieval of a single type of media, be they images or videos or others, due to the divergent spectrum of techniques required by those types.

Owing to its status as a standard, a number of proposed retrieval frameworks are based on MPEG-7. Recent research is directed towards extensions of such systems in order to allow for reasoning, semantic, and context-based searches, for example [9].

Adding context-awareness to the concept of multimedia retrieval results in *context-aware retrieval*, or CAR, a term proposed by Brown and Jones [1]. They categorize CAR methods as either user-driven, which is essentially equivalent to traditional IR where the query is automatically derived or modified by context information, or author-driven, which is nearly identical to information filtering, with the exception that the filters are attached to the media themselves rather than to the user profiles.

Authoring and Presentation

The main question regarding context-aware multimedia presentation is how content can be flexibly delivered to users, while at the same time accounting for the various types of context information discussed above. There are three possible approaches: 1) provide different documents for different contexts; 2) store single media elements and allow the application to select and merge them into a coherent presentation adapted to the context; or 3) employ a flexible document model that inherently includes context information with the multimedia. Even if the number of possible end devices could be enumerated, the first approach is clearly insufficiently dynamic to account for more rapidly changing contextual characteristics such as user activity or environmental factors, leaving the second and third approaches as viable strategies.

Bulterman and Hardman [3] provide a recent (as of this writing) overview of multimedia presentation authoring paradigms and tools, a rich topic that is beyond the scope of this article. They conclude that the future of multimedia authoring lies in two non-exclusive possibilities: first, advances in the authoring interfaces that will enable more efficient and elegant authoring of multimedia presentations, and second, the development of methods for automatic presentation creation, based on user requests. These possibilities correspond to the second (presentation-based) and third (application-based) approaches mentioned in the previous paragraph.

In the first case, the transformation of content to a context-sensitive presentation is often referred to as *adaptation*. Adaptation occurs in at least two phases; first, in the selection multimedia material based on the user preferences, and second in the further adjustment of the selected material based on the computing environment context. Consideration of which display device is currently being used and the available network bandwidth are primary filters for determining what media will be sent and in what format. The groundwork for much of today's research in this area was established in the field of *adaptive hypermedia* (see [2] and references therein). More recent work in this area, taking a very general approach that integrates the consideration of bandwidth, latency, rendering time, quality of service, and utility-cost ratios, is exemplified by [8].

In the case of multimedia applications, the question of presentation authoring is eliminated. Instead of tools for authoring multimedia presentations, one requires tools for authoring context-aware applications. A number of frameworks and middleware systems have been reported in the literature over the past decade:

One of the earlier approaches was the Context Toolkit [14], [18], provides "context widgets" – encapsulated software components that provide applications with access to context information from their operating environment. The QoSDREAM [15] middleware integrates distributed sensor location data with a service to configure and manage real-time multimedia streams with an emphasis, as the name suggests, on quality of service. The M-Studio authoring tool was produced in order to help mobile story creators to design, simulate and adjust mobile narratives [16]. The CAPNET architecture [6] provides a similar tool, combining aspects of both mobile and ubiquitous computing, including a context-based storage system (CBS) [11] as the underlying persistence mechanism.

And as previously mentioned the unnamed framework discussed in [12] takes context-aware multimedia frameworks to the next level by integrating inference mechanisms and Bayesian reasoning.

A final area of research related to authoring is the idea of contextual-metadata capture, which aids the process of including as much metadata as possible during the media production process. As much metadata and semantic information as possible should be captured in the earliest phases of media production, when the producers who can best describe and disambiguate the content are still available. Without this early integration, valuable contextual information can be lost [19]. Given the ever-growing importance of metadata, which is presently hindered by the expense (human and computational) of producing it, it is clear that this concept of "conservation of meta-information" will play an essential role in the future of multimedia content production.

Summary

This article introduces the concept of context-aware multimedia by first defining the terms *context* and *context-awareness*. Based on these definitions four key aspects are addressed: modeling, retrieval, authoring, and presentation. Providing for context-awareness in multimedia applications requires reconsidering the approaches on modeling, retrieving, authoring and presenting multimedia content due to the interdependencies with the concepts of context and context-awareness.

Acknowledgment

We would like to acknowledge contributions for the series of articles linked to this article from our group members (in alphabetical order): Bernhard Haslhofer, Wolfgang Jochum, Bernhard Schandl, Karin Schellner, Maia Zaharieva, and Sonja Zillner.

See: Fuzzy Techniques for Context Representation, Context and Current Metadata Standards, Context-Aware Modeling of Multimedia Content, Context-Aware Musical Audio, Device-Driven Presentation of Multimedia Content, Context Aware Video Production

References

1. P.J. Brown and G.J.F. Jones, "Context-aware retrieval: exploring a new environment for information retrieval and information filtering," Personal and Ubiquitous Computing, Vol. 5, No. 4, 2001, pp. 253-263.
2. P. Brusilovsky, "Methods and techniques of adaptive hypermedia," User Modeling and User-Adapted Interaction, Vol. 6, No. 2-3, 1996, pp. 87-129.
3. D. C. A. Bulterman and L. Hardman, "Structured multimedia authoring," ACM Trans. Multimedia Computing, Communication, and Applications, Vol. 1, No. 1, 2005, pp. 89-109.
4. Composite Capability/Preference Profiles (CC/PP): Structure and Vocabularies 1.0, W3C Recommendation, 15 January 2004, http://www.w3.org/TR/CCPP-struct-vocab.
5. O. Conlan, R. Power, S. Higel, D. O'Sullivan, and K. Barrett, "Next generation context aware adaptive services," Proceedings of the 1st international symposium on Information and communication technologies (ISICT 03), 2003, pp. 205-212.
6. O. Davidyuk, J. Riekki, V.-M. Rautio, and J. Sun, "Context-aware middleware for mobile multimedia applications," Proceedings of the 3rd international conference on Mobile and ubiquitous multimedia (MUM 04), 2004, pp. 213-220.
7. A. K. Dey, "Understanding and using context," Personal Ubiquitous Computing, Vol. 5, No. 1, 2001, pp. 4-7.
8. D. Gotz and K. Mayer-Patel, "A general framework for multidimensional adaptation," Proceedings of the 12th annual ACM international conference on Multimedia (MULTIMEDIA 04), 2004, pp. 612-619.
9. S. Hammiche, S. Benbernou, M.-S. Hacid, and A. Vakali, "Semantic retrieval of multimedia data," Proceedings of the 2nd ACM international workshop on Multimedia databases (MMDB 04), 2004, pp. 36-44.
10. A. Jameson, "Modeling both the context and the user," Personal Ubiquitous Computing, Vol. 5, No. 1, 2001, pp. 29-33.

11. S. Khungar and J. Riekki, "A context based storage for ubiquitous computing applications," Proceedings of the 2nd European Union symposium on Ambient intelligence (EUSAI 04), 2004, pp. 55-58.

12. P. Korpipää, J. Mantyjarvi, J. Kela, H. Keranen, and E.J. Malm, "Managing context information in mobile devices," IEEE of Pervasive Computing, Vol. 2, Issue 3, July-September 2003, pp. 42-51.

13. T. Lemlouma and N. Layada, "Adapted content delivery for different contexts," Proceedings of the 2003 Symposium on Applications and the Internet (SAINT 03), 2003, pp. 190.

14. S. Mitchell, M. D. Spiteri, J. Bates, and G. Coulouris, "Context-aware multimedia computing in the intelligent hospital," Proceedings of the 9th Workshop on ACM SIGOPS European Workshop (EW 9), 2000, pp. 13-18.

15. H. Naguib, G. Coulouris, and S. Mitchell, "Middleware support for context-aware multimedia applications," Proceedings of the 3rd IFIP WG 6.1. International Working Conference on Distributed Applications and Interoperable Systems (DAIS 2001), 2001.

16. P. Pan, C. Kastner, D. Crow, and G. Davenport, "M-studio: an authoring application for context-aware multimedia," Proceedings of the Tenth ACM International Conference on Multimedia (MULTIMEDIA 02), 2002, pp. 351-354.

17. D. Petrelli, E. Not, M. Zancanaro, C. Strapparava, and O. Stock, "Modeling and adapting to context," Personal Ubiquitous Computing, Vol. 5, No. 1, 2001, pp. 20-24.

18. D. Salber, A. K. Dey, and G. D. Abowd, "The context toolkit: aiding the development of context-enabled applications," Proceedings of the conference on Human factors in computing systems (SIGCHI), 1999, pp. 434-441.

19. R. Sarvas, E. Herrarte, A. Wilhelm, and M. Davis, "Metadata creation system for mobile images," Proceedings of the 2nd international conference on Mobile systems, applications, and services (MobiSYS 04), 2004, pp. 36-48.

20. B. Schilit and M. Theimer, "Disseminating active map information to mobile hosts," IEEE Network, Vol. 8, No. 5, 1994, pp. 22-32.

21. B. Schilit, N. Adams, and R. Want, "Context-aware computing applications," In IEEE Workshop on Mobile Computing Systems and Applications, 1994, pp. 85-90.

CONTEXT-AWARE MUSICAL AUDIO

Definition: Context-aware musical audio is the association of any information related to the piece of music.

The phrase *context-aware multimedia*, in the case of audio documents in the music domain, can be defined as the association of any information related to the piece of music extending the information required for or supporting playback. Furthermore, it could be understood as the usage of this information in application scenarios by Music Information Retrieval (MIR) systems, in order to create context-aware multimedia applications.

Such information can either be found implicitly in the content of a piece of music (often referred to as content-based or low-level features) or is associated with the audio instances as external metadata (high-level features). Content-based information is extracted via feature extraction algorithms. Those algorithms are often complex and computational intensive, and one must consider the different formats in which a piece of music can be digitally stored. On the other hand, the symbolic representation of musical works allows easier access to various feature parameters such as pitch or rhythm-related attributes – even for polyphonic music. Musical pieces represented by samples, which will be encountered in most cases, raise the need to compute the symbolic representation out of the audio signal via signal processing techniques [1], [2] or to compute attributes that are not based upon symbolic music representation.

External metadata, understood as information which cannot be extracted out of the audio content of a musical piece itself, is the enabler for the next step in building context-awareness through interpreting or processing this metadata with the intention to retrieve or compute further information describing the piece of music. Such information is generally annotated manually and would be for example the artist, year of production, or music label. These attributes can be processed further to achieve results similar to those obtained when using implicit characteristics [3] or used in combination with low-level features to improve search results, which can be a more efficient and faster method, depending on the application scenario.

Making use of the feature parameters mentioned above leads to context-aware multimedia applications. One example would be an audio player providing additional information related to the actual playback position in a piece of music, such as references to the score or lyrics. Another would be the recommendation of similar tracks related to a user's favorite, based upon various feature parameters. Research related to this topic is very active, because the music industry is beginning to abandon the attitude of restricting digital distribution channels and is attempting instead to make use of them for their own profit. Research results will improve over time and one can expect increasing performance of feature-extraction algorithms, which will in turn provide a solid basis for context-aware multimedia applications in the music domain.

See: Context-aware Multimedia

References

1. G. Tzanetakis and P. Cook "Musical Genre Classification of Audio Signals", IEEE Transactions on Speech and Audio Processing, 10(5), July.
2. A. Rauber, E. Pampalk, D. Merkl "The SOM-enhanced JukeBox: Organization and Visualization of Music Collections based on Perceptual Models", Journal of New Music Research (JNMR), 32(2), pp. 193-210, June 2003.
3. P. Knees, E. Pampalk, and G. Widmer, "Artist Classification with Web-based Data," Proceedings of the 5th International Conference on Music Information Retrieval (ISMIR'2004), 2004.

CONTEXT-AWARE VIDEO PRODUCTION

Definition: *Context-aware video production allows using context to describe and store information about the involved physical or computational entities.*

Context Awareness

There are several ways applications can utilize information about their context [1]. When considering what context can serve for video at least two types of context are well known and supported by international standards: delivery and presentation [MPEG Coding Standards, Scalable Video Coding]. But these are mostly standards that include little support for context aware video production. When focusing on the production of video, context can be used to describe and store information about the situation of involved physical or computational entities. By using standards as MPEG-7, it is possible to store this information in a reusable manner, but the lack of standards to seamlessly integrate different sensors into a recording environment limits a broad utilization of contextual information.

Context Enhanced Retrieval of Video

In terms of context-aware multimedia video is a very complex medium. Its continuous character and large amount of data compared to other media types demand highly sophisticated management tools, including semantic information to support the user while searching or browsing large video files or archives. To fulfill this demand many current video retrieval systems prefer manual annotations compared to automatic technologies.

If context information is used to tag video data while recording, the data can be used to improve the process of information retrieval for the user. A very general example of a context aware video recording system is Life Log [2]. It combines the ideas of wearable and ubiquitous computing to a system that records a person's diary by using camera, microphone and various sensors. The collected context information is used to automatically mark key scenes of the video. While browsing or searching in the recorded data the generated keys improve the retrieval experience. Another interesting, recent development in movie production considering the users context is reported in [3].

Vision

While e.g. Life Log has little previous knowledge about the recorded situation, the results should be even more promising when the scenario has defined structures or even a planned timeline. Applying this information in a context-aware recording system, to automatically link the recorded video and its already existing related production artifacts, would create cheap semantic annotations. Additional information about the context that was stored with the video and the attained semantic links to pre-produced information could make manual annotation obsolete.

See: Context-Aware Multimedia

References

1. A. K. Dey and G. D. Abowd. Towards a Better Understanding of context and context-awareness. Technical Report GIT-GVU-99-22, Georgia Institute of Technology, College of Computing, June 1999.
2. T. Hori and K. Aizawa, Context-based video retrieval system for the life-log applications, Proceedings of the 5th ACM SIGMM international workshop on Multimedia information retrieval, November 2003.
3. S. Tokuhisa, T. Kotabe, and M. Inakage, "atMOS: self expression movie generating system for 3G mobile communication," Proceedings of the 3rd international Conference on Mobile and Ubiquitous Multimedia. MUM '04. ACM Press, New York, NY, pp. 199-206, 2004.

CREATING ADAPTIVE COURSE TEXTS WITH AHA!

Definition: AHA! is an adaptive hypermedia architecture used to create and manage the course content.

The Adaptive Hypermedia Architecture or AHA! [2, 4] was initially developed to create an adaptive version of a course on Hypermedia, taught at the Eindhoven University of Technology, and offered on-line to students of several Dutch and Belgian universities. Through a grant of the NLnet Foundation the *adaptation engine* has been extended to make it very general-purpose, and *authoring tools* have been developed to help course developers in the design of the *conceptual structure* of a course and in the management of the course content. Key characteristics of AHA! are:

- The structure of every course consists of *concepts, concept relationships* and *pages.* For every page there is a corresponding concept. When a student reads a page the system will register *knowledge* about the concept corresponding to that page. Through *knowledge propagation* relationships the page access also leads to knowledge about higher level concepts (e.g. corresponding to a section and/or chapter). AHA! can give students advice on which concepts to study now and which to leave for later through the use of *prerequisite relationships.* The AHA! engine has many more possibilities but the ones mentioned here are sufficient for most adaptive course texts.

- Concepts and concept relationships are created using a graphical tool: the *graph author.* It makes authoring as easy as clicking and drawing, and it translates the conceptual structure into *event-condition-action rules* used by the AHA! engine. Through a second tool, the *concept editor* these rules can be inspected, and modified if desired.

- Special tools exist to create *multiple choice tests* and also to create arbitrary *forms* to allow students to inspect (and perhaps modify) their student model.

- An *application management tool* is available for authors to up- and download pages and to activate the different authoring tools. All the tools have a user interface that consists of Java Applets, so an author need not install any software (other than a Java-enabled Web browser) in order to create a course.

- *inclusion of information* and of *link annotation* or *link hiding*. Through conditional fragments on a page or the conditional inclusion of objects an author can add extra explanations or details that are only shown to students when they have (or lack) some specific knowledge. The link adaptation consists of changes in the link color. There are three colors: *good, neutral* and *bad*. To indicate the status of a link. The defaults (which can be changed) for these colors are blue, purple and black, and result in *hiding* of the *bad* links.

- The presentation of a course is highly customizable, through a *layout model*. As a result different courses served by AHA! can have a very different look and feel.

- The AHA! runtime environment consists of Java Servlets. The AHA! distribution contains these servlets, the authoring applets and all the source code as well. AHA! is an Open Source project, and works with other freely available tools like the Tomcat Web server, and optionally also the mySQL database system. It runs on Windows and Linux.

Examples of AHA! applications, and AHA! documentation and tutorials are all available from the project's website, aha.win.tue.nl. Stable releases are also available through SourceForge. The authoring and delivery platforms can also be used independently. An author can for instance use the annotated MS Word format used for Interbook, and a compiler translates the course to the AHA! authoring format in order for AHA! to serve the course [3]. AHA! can also emulate the Interbook layout completely, making the on-line course virtually indistinguishable from a course served through the Interbook server. Likewise we have been working on compilers for other authoring formats and tools, including MOT (My Online Teacher) [1].

See: Personalized Educational Hypermedia

References

1. A. Cristea, D. Floes, N. Stash, and P. De Bra, "MOT meets AHA!," Proceedings of the PEG Conference, June 2003, (http://www.peg2003.net/peg2003docs/cristea.doc).
2. P. De Bra, A. Aerts, B. Berden, B. De Lange, B. Rousseau, T. Santic, D. Smits, and N. Stash, "AHA! The Adaptive Hypermedia Architecture," Proceedings of the ACM Hypertext Conference, August 2003, pp. 81-84.
3. P. De Bra, T. Santic, and P. Brusilovsky, "AHA! meets Interbook, and more...," Proceedings of the AACE Elearn'2003 Conference, November 2003, pp. 57-64.
4. P. De Bra, N. Stash, and D. Smits, "Creating Adaptive Textbooks with AHA!," Proceedings of the AACE Elearn'2004 Conference, November 2004, pp. 2588-2593.

D

DATA CONFERENCING

Definition: *Data conferencing allows participants in a live session to transfer data and to share applications.*

Information between the users' applications is transmitted over the network, live and in real-time. Data conferencing is one component of teleconferencing; the others are audio conferencing, and video conferencing. For a teleconferencing system that is ITU-T H.323 [1] compliant, the ITU-T T.120 set of standards [2] are recommended for data conferencing and application sharing, providing real-time communication between two or more entities in a conference. Applications specified as part of the T.120 family include application sharing, electronic whiteboarding, file exchange, and chat. Data conferencing is typically an optional capability in multimedia conferences. The shared data is usually transmitted between the users across the network using a reliable network protocol, such as the TCP (Transmission Control Protocol).

See: Teleconferencing

References

1. International Telecommunication Union, Telecommunication Standardization Sector H.323 Recommendation – Packet-based multimedia communications systems, July 2003.
2. International Telecommunication Union, Telecommunication Standardization Sector T.120 Recommendation – Data protocols for multimedia conferencing, July 1996.

DATA DISCOVERY, ROUTING AND TRAFFIC PATTERNS

Definition: *Resource discovery and rendezvous mechanisms are necessary to dynamically locate media servers (e.g., the nearest or best servers), data storages, membership servers (for multicast sessions), or peers (e.g., other users) for direct connections.*

In general, the resource discovery module of CHaMeLeoN can be categorized as either `location-aware' or `location-free'. Location-aware architectures require availability of location information. They typically use geographic or trajectory routing to forward the updates or queries and include geographic rendezvous mechanisms (such as GLS [1],

Rendezvous Regions [2], and GHT [3]) and trajectory advertisement schemes (such as TBF [4]). In location-aware networks, geographic-based distributed hash tables [2, 3] are utilized to efficiently establish content based routing schemes.

In earlier work [2], we designed a geographic rendezvous mechanism based on rendezvous regions. In this architecture, the network is divided into regions, and the resource key space (e.g., file space) is divided into prefixes. Each resource prefixes maps into a region. The mapping can be discovered dynamically using a bootstrap mechanism. We have shown that using regions (instead of locations as in GHT [3]) is robust to mobility and location inaccuracy effects. Furthermore, the performance of the rendezvous architecture depends on the data semantics and access pattern. For example, for media servers, where there is a high lookup-to-insertion ratio (meaning the media is accessed many times per storage), the Rendezvous Regions scheme produces far fewer messages (over 80% less) when compared with GHT, and achieves near perfect success rate. Hence, it is important to tailor the rendezvous mechanism to the application characteristics (e.g., lookup-to-insertion ratio). Characterizing applications, data semantics and access patterns is of key interest. Matching rendezvous architectures to application classes, and designing new (adaptive) rendezvous mechanisms are additional challenges that need to be addressed in future work.

Location-free discovery architectures do not use location information [5]. Some of the main approaches include flooding-based techniques, on-demand routing with caching, hierarchical and hybrid routing. Flooding techniques include simple flooding (or expanding ring search), scoped flooding, and efficient reduced broadcast. Hierarchical routing includes cluster-based, landmark, and dominating set approaches. Hybrid routing includes zone routing and contact-based architectures. We have extensively studied these techniques. Our studies show that a loose hierarchy (using zones) coupled with `contacts' achieves the best performance in terms of bandwidth and energy efficiency for the same success rates. The advantage of this scheme is most prominent for high-activity networks, where the query-to-mobility ratio is high since the cost of establishing and maintaining the hierarchy is amortized across savings in query cost. While route caching schemes are also useful in some scenarios, our studies have shown that the overhead of maintaining the cache up to date may outweigh its benefits for small transfers and high mobility show that for small transfers and high mobility caching validity may limit the efficacy of caching. Resource discovery may also be coupled with routing. For example, ZRP and the contact-based mechanisms are easily combined into one architecture, in which ZRP is used for route discovery while contact-based mechanisms are used for resource discovery (possibly over sub-optimal routes but with very high efficiency).

Routing Protocols

In order to sustain data delivery with least disruption, routing protocols must adapt seamlessly to mobility [5]. Pure proactive approaches (e.g., DSDV) may incur high overhead and may not be able to cope with high mobility scenarios. On the other hand reactive protocols (e.g., DSR and AODV) incur much less overhead and are suitable for small/medium networks (<100 nodes), but also incur delivery disruption due to link failures and route maintenance. Hybrid protocols (e.g., ZRP) uses proactive routing within for nearby nodes (within the zone) and reactive routing discovery for nodes beyond the zone. ZRP is suitable for larger networks (>100 nodes) but also suffers packet loss with link failures. We intend to investigate the use of reactive route discovery with proactive route maintenance in CHaMeLeoN. Such schemes are bandwidth efficient and able to proactively discover new routes before the existing ones break. This investigation borrows from existing work in this area in addition to designing new mechanisms.

Dynamic content, generated by real-time communications, will often be delivered to a group of participants in a session. The mode of communication depends on the definition of the `group'. For dynamically created logical groups, multicast [6] may be used for efficient communication. For ad hoc networks, in general, mesh-based multicast routing is more robust to network dynamics than tree-based routing. This is at the expense of increased overhead. For geographically defined groups, geocast [7] may be used. For locating either any or nearest participant, anycast [6] may be used. Finally, manycast [8] may be used for locating k out of n participants. Hence, routing and transport protocols are needed to support such applications. Dynamics of the multicast group membership (whether in terms of senders/producers or receivers/consumers) would have a great impact on the performance of the various protocols and hence on the quality of data delivery. Dealing with dynamics of membership, traffic patterns, and mobility are issues we address in the routing and protocol design and evaluation phases of CHaMeLeoN.

Storage-Retrieval of Dynamic Content

When dynamic content is to be stored for future retrieval, issues of dynamic storage, indexing, querying and retrieval must be addressed. Resource and data discovery architectures are needed to facilitate server (or file) location by the interested parties without having to flood the request throughout the network. Such storage-retrieval architecture should be self-configuring, scalable and robust to network dynamics (including mobility). They impact the data placement issues discussed previously.

In the design of the above protocols, including resource discovery and multicast protocols, modeling and analysis of user and information association are essential. Association analysis captures traffic and access patterns within groups of nodes. Associations and traffic patterns depend on the nature of the application. The network nodes can be either dedicated to users or can be autonomous (e.g., as in sensor networks). With CHaMeLeoN, we are interested in two types of associations: (a) small world friend associations in user-centric networks (such as wireless classrooms or collaboration using ad hoc networks), and (b) data correlation in data-centric sensor networks.

This analysis will facilitate the design of traffic prediction (and subsequently data placement) schemes to improve the performance and availability of data. In addition, mobility prediction schemes will facilitate seamless delivery of data. We shall address mobility based schemes in research in the following section.

Traffic Patterns and Information Associations

CHaMeLeoN may utilize traditional address-centric (or user-centric) paradigms to associate devices with information. A data-centric approach may also be feasible and must be investigated further. We describe each in turn.

With a user-centric approach, users establish communities that manifest association of conversation, file sharing, trust, correlated mobility or common interests. We have been investigating these social behaviors and the concept of friends in wireless networks using the small world's models [9]. Small worlds refer to classes of graphs that exhibit high clustering similar to that of regular graphs, but a low average path length (i.e., degree of separation) similar to that of random graphs. Small world graphs have been observed in many contexts of human behavior, in security (PGP) associations, web links, and interest groups, among others. By understanding such social underpinnings, we shall develop a better and deeper understanding of correlated access patterns, mobility, security and other network associations. This will result in efficient networking protocols. Moreover, we aim to achieve desirable characteristics of small worlds by constructing carefully chosen short cuts to bridge the gap between otherwise distant clusters of users or information. One example of such structure is building a small world of trust to establish security associations efficiently in large-scale wireless networks. We shall focus on understanding information associations in wireless classrooms as one of our target applications.

Data-centric paradigms apply to sensor networks where the physical phenomena monitored produces data that is observed/recorded by multiple sensors. Hence sensor readings may be correlated. Sometimes the physical phenomenon propagates according to well-known diffusion laws, creating natural spatio-temporal gradients of information in the sensor network. This may relate to protocol design and in-network processing with CHaMeLeoN, e.g., using data aggregation or gradient based routing [10].

See: Data Management Techniques for Continuous Media in Ad-hoc Networks of Wireless Devices

References

1. J. Li, J. Jannotti, D. Couto, D. Karger, and R. Morris, "A Scalable Location Service for Geographic Ad Hoc Routing (GLS/Grid)", Proceedings of the ACM MobiCom, 2000.
2. K. Seada and A. Helmy, "*Rendezvous Regions*: A Scalable Architecture for Service Location and Data-Centric Storage in Large-Scale Wireless Networks," Proceedings of the *IEEE/ACM IPDPS Int'l Workshop on Algorithms for Wireless, Mobile, Ad Hoc and Sensor Networks (WMAN)*, April 2004, pp. 218 – 225.
3. S. Ratnasamy, B. Karp, L. Yin, F. Yu, D. Estrin, R. Govindan, and S. Shenker, "GHT: A Geographic Hash Table for Data-Centric Storage," Proceedings of the ACM WSNA, September 2002.
4. D. Niculescu and B. Nath, "Trajectory-based forwarding and its applications," Proceedings of the ACM Mobicom, September 2003.
5. A. Helmy, "Efficient Resource Discovery in Wireless AdHoc Networks: Contacts Do Help," Book Chapter in "Resource Management in Wireless Networking," Springer,

Series: Network Theory and Applications, Vol. 16, 2005, (Eds. M. Cardei, I. Cardei, and D. Zhu).

6. A. Helmy, "Architectural Framework for Large-Scale Multicast in Mobile Ad Hoc Networks," Proceedings of the IEEE International Conference on Communications (ICC 2002), April, 2002.
7. K. Seada and A. Helmy, "Efficient and Robust Geocasting Protocols for Sensor Networks," Journal *of Computer Communications – Elsevier, Special Issue on Dependable Wireless Sensor Networks*, Fall 2005.
8. C. Carter, S. Yi, P. Ratanchandani, and R. Kravets, "Manycast: Exploring the Space Between Anycast and Multicast in Ad Hoc Networks," Proceedings of the ACM Mobicom, September 2003.
9. A. Helmy, "Small Worlds in Wireless Networks," IEEE Communications Letters, Vol. 7, No. 10, October 2003, pp. 490-492.
10. J. Faruque, K. Psounis, and A. Helmy, "Analysis of Gradient-based Routing Protocols in Sensor Networks," *Proceedings of the IEEE/ACM Int. Conference on Distributed Computing in Sensor Systems (DCOSS)*, June 2005, pp. 258 - 275.

DATA ENCRYPTION STANDARD (DES) AND ADVANCED ENCRYPTION STANDARD (AES)

Definition: *Data Encryption Standard (DES) and Advanced Encryption Standard (AES) are designed to encrypt a sequence of data elements.*

The DES algorithm is designed to encipher and decipher 64-bit blocks of data under control of a 64-bit key, of which 56 bits are randomly generated and used directly by the algorithm. Deciphering must be accomplished by using the same key as for enciphering. The deciphering process is the reverse of the enciphering process. A 64-bit block to be enciphered is subject to an initial permutation to form L_0 and R_0 (32 bits each, respectively the left and right half of the 64-bit block generated by the initial permutation), then to 16-iteration key-dependent computation, and the final result of the computation (L_{16} and R_{16}) is subject to a permutation that is the inverse of the initial permutation. The 16 key-dependent computations can be simply defined as [1]:

$$L_n = R_{n-1}$$
$$R_n = L_{n-1} \oplus f(R_{n-1}, K_n)$$

where n is in the range of 1 to 16; f is the cipher function; L_n and R_n are 32-bits each and respectively the left and right half of the 64-bit iteration result; and K_n is the 48-bit sub key generated by the following key schedule function KS [1]:

$$K_n = KS(n, KEY)$$

where KEY is the 56-bit main key.

With the advance of computation power, a 56-bit key is no longer considered as secure. Triple DES (3DES) is a straightforward way of enhancing the security of DES. 3DES involves repeating the basic DES algorithm three times, using either two or thee unique keys, for a key size of 112 or 168 bits [1].

Both DES and 3DES are not efficient because they operate on a 64-bit block. As a replacement, the Advanced Encryption Standard (AES) specifies the Rijndael algorithm, a symmetric block cipher that can process data blocks of 128 bits, using cipher keys with lengths of 128, 192, and 256 bits [2].

See: Multimedia Authentication

References

1. National Institute of Standards and Technology, "Specification for the Data Encryption Standard (DES)," Technical Report NIST FIPS PUB 46-3, Department of Commerce, October 1999.
2. National Institute of Standards and Technology, "Specification for the Advanced Encryption Standard (AES)," Technical Report NIST FIPS PUB 197, Department of Commerce, November 2001.

DATA MANAGEMENT TECHNIQUES FOR CONTINUOUS MEDIA IN AD-HOC NETWORKS OF WIRELESS DEVICES

Shahram Ghandeharizadeh, Ahmed Helmy, Bhaskar Krishnamachari, Francois Bar, and Todd Richmond
University of Southern California, Los Angeles, USA

Definition: *This article introduces CHaMeLeoN as a large scale software effort to facilitate exchange of both traditional (text, image) and continuous media (audio and video clips).*

CHaMeLeoN is designed to support both delayed and immediate modes of communication. It is targeted toward mobile devices configured with a heterogeneous mix of wired and wireless components. Our primary focus is on the limited radio-range of wireless connections (such as 802.11) and exchange of data among those devices that are in close geographical vicinity of one another to participate in an ad-hoc network. We outline the objectives of CHaMeLeoN, and in short articles summarize our research findings to date.

Introduction

Rapid advances in wireless technology, computational, mass storage, and sensor devices are realizing new paradigms of communication in wireless mobile environments. They offer a compelling vision of the future Internet as a seamlessly integrated heterogeneous system. Continuous media (video and audio) services are of particular interest because they are necessary for many classes of important and interesting applications, ranging from entertainment to scientific collaboration. These applications can be broadly categorized into those that manage content pertaining to either immediate, delayed, or both modes of communication. Delayed communication is when a user records and stores data in anticipation of its future retrieval, e.g., display of a recordings from a recent meeting or seminar. Immediate communication is when a user generates data for display at a client in real-time, e.g., scientists communicating and collaborating across different laboratories. The boundary between these two modes of communication is defined by the delay from when data is produced to the time it is displayed. As this delay increases, immediate mode of communication becomes delayed. A good example is when the collaborating scientists record their real-time communication for future display and analysis.

A number of visionary systems such as Memex [1] and MyLifeBits [4] depend on devices that capture and retrieve data pertaining to both communication modes. The computer and communication industry has started to develop such devices. For example, today's cellular phones facilitate phone conversations between multiple parties, capture photos and record videos of their surroundings, and transmit the recorded information to other cellular phones and devices with Internet Protocol (IP) connectivity. Similarly, cable set-top boxes, termed Digital Video Recorders (DVRs), support telephone conversations (Voice over IP, VoIP), provide time-shifted viewing of broadcasted programs, and store personal audio and still image libraries. (TiVo terms these additional features ``home media" in its Series2 offerings.) It is not far fetched to envision DVR extensions to store personal video libraries along with meta-data associated with the different data items. It might be extended with either one or multiple wireless networking cards to facilitate (1) an in-home network for uploading of content from devices that capture data such as a camcorder, and (2) an ad-hoc network consisting of other DVRs in the neighboring households. Such a device can be implemented using today's wireless technology such as 802.11a/g which offers limited radio-range with bandwidths in the order of tens of Mbps [2]. We term such a device a Home-to-Home Online (H2O) [6] device.

Current technological trends point towards multi-purpose Personal Digital Assistants (PDAs) that are small, inexpensive, weigh less than a pound, and have long lasting battery lives. To facilitate efficient retrieval of data, these PDAs might be equipped with sensors that capture a variety of metadata about their surroundings. An example sensor might be a global positioning system to record the geographical location of different recordings and communications [5]. This would enable a user to retrieve all those photos captured from a specific location, e.g., India. This PDA will communicate with diverse networks. For example, it might interface with a vehicle's multimedia network to enable a passenger to share his or her personal recordings with other passengers using the vehicle's fold-down screen. The same PDA will communicate with any H2O device for sharing of photos and video clips. Mobility of PDAs and their potential intermittent [11] network connectivity differentiates them from H2O devices.

This article provides an overview of the ChaMeLeoN framework and its design decisions. CHaMeLeoN is designed to support both delayed and immediate mode of communication in a wireless, heterogeneous network of multihop, mobile devices. This framework touches upon a wide range of issues such as security and privacy [3], economic fairness, user interfaces, strategies to satisfy the requirements of diverse applications sharing the same infrastructure, and many others. A study of all topics in depth is beyond the scope of this paper. Instead, we focus on the core infrastructure of the network, namely, techniques to deliver continuous media in a manner that meets the application requirements and challenges of a mobile wireless environment.

Overview of CHaMeLeoN

A unique feature of CHaMeLeoN is its awareness of (and adaptation to) the application requirements and environmental constraints. These are shown as the top and bottom layers of Figure 1. CHaMeLeoN, the mid layer, consumes input from these two layers: First, communication mode of the application (immediate, delayed, or both) and its requirements (QoS, efficiency, and availability of data; see below for details). Second, environment and network characterization in the form of: (a) mobility models - including synthetic or trace based mobility models, (b) traffic patterns and information association (e.g., due to users' social behavior or correlation of sensed data), (c) constraints of limited power, computation or communication capabilities, and (d) model of the wireless channel. The core of the framework consists of parameterized adaptive algorithms and protocols for data placement, scheduling and merging, admission control, data and resource discovery, data delivery and routing protocols. In addition, protocol design for mobility is a component that may span multiple other core components to include mobility prediction, mobility-resilient and mobility-assisted protocols. For example, data placement may be based on mobility prediction, and resource discovery may be mobility-assisted.

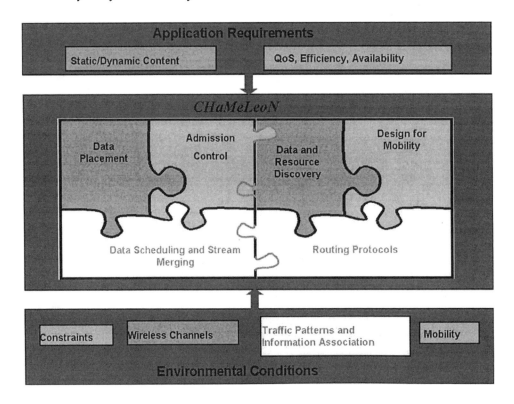

Figure 1. The CHaMeLeoN Framework.

Application Requirements

CHaMeLeoN characterizes an application's requirement using Quality of Service (QoS), efficiency, and data availability. We describe these in turn.

QoS is a qualitative requirement, characterizing the perception of end users. It can be quantified using different metrics. One is the delay observed from when a user references content to the onset of its display, termed startup latency. A second might be the frequency and duration of disruptions observed when displaying audio and video clips, termed hiccups. Audio and video clips are continuous media, consisting of a sequence of quanta, either audio samples or video frames, which convey meaning when presented at a pre-specified rate [8]. Once the display is initiated, if the data is delivered below this rate (without special precautions) then the display might suffer from hiccups. Third, while the displayed data might be hiccup-free, it might have been encoded with significant loss. Scalable compression techniques [9] control the quality of streamed data based on the available amount of network bandwidth.

Efficiency describes how intelligently resources are utilized when streaming content. A key metric is how many devices may display their referenced content simultaneously. With a network of N devices, ideally all N devices should be able to have an active display. Typically, the available wireless network bandwidth between devices must be managed intelligently to accomplish this objective.

Availability of data quantifies what fraction of accessible content is available to a client at a given instance in time. It is impacted by both the discovery and retrieval of content. The system must be able to deliver discovered content to the requesting device in order for that content to be advertised as available. As detailed below, streaming of data between a producing and a consuming device requires reservation of bandwidth. This may exhaust certain paths in the network, isolating a candidate client device from those devices that contain relevant data. This data remains unavailable until the reserved paths are released. Another important factor is the characteristics of the wireless network. Both the bandwidth and loss rate of an 802.11 connection between two devices is dependent on its deployed environment and might vary from one minute to the next due to factors such as exposed node [2, 10]. Finally, mobility of devices poses both challenges and opportunities. It is a challenge when it renders relevant content undeliverable or leads to degradation in quality of service. It is an opportunity when it provides relevant content to a potential consumer directly instead of a multihop transmission.

Design Objectives

Techniques that constitute CHaMeLeoN are designed to be adaptable, facilitate physical data independence, and support streaming of continuous media. Below, we detail these in turn.

By adaptable, we mean employed techniques must support diverse applications with different and potentially conflicting requirements. We categorize these requirements along three dimensions consisting of Quality of Service (QoS), efficiency, and data availability; see below for details. One application may demand the highest QoS while another may emphasize availability of data and services. Proposed techniques are parameterized whose settings navigate the three dimensional optimization space. The challenge here is to identify the parameters of a technique, quantify how their settings navigate the optimization space, and design of algorithms to navigate this space given the physical realities of an environment.

Physical data independence means the organization of data can be modified without causing application programs to be rewritten. Physical organization of data might be manipulated either at its storage or delivery time. To illustrate, CHaMeLeoN must manage physical organization of clips when storing them. In certain environments, participating devices may collaborate by contributing some of their storage to a common pool in order to enhance QoS and efficiency metrics. With a video clip, the data placement component of CHaMeLeoN may aggressively replicate the first few blocks of a clip across many devices to enable a client to display the clip immediately while it discovers and retrieves the remaining blocks of the clip [7]. An application may not want to use this placement strategy because its participating devices are expected to be disconnected from the network for long durations of time. This should not mean that one re-writes the data placement component. Instead, either (a) this component's parameter settings must enable a system designer to deploy it in a manner that meets this application's requirement or (b) metadata associated with a clip provides sufficient context for the data placement strategy to meet this application's requirement. While both approaches realize physical data independence, the first is at system deployment time while the second is at run-time using meta-data provided either by an application or its clips. The challenge here is design, implementation, and testing of flexible software.

Streaming of continuous media facilitates overlapped display of a clip at a client with its delivery from a network of one or several servers. This is essential for immediate mode of communication because participants require real-time data exchange. Even with delayed mode of communication, streaming is useful because it minimizes the amount of time a user waits for the system to initiate display of a clip. To illustrate, a 30 minute DVD quality video is typically 900 Megabytes in size. If the system downloads the clip prior to initiating its display then the client must wait for the duration of time to download 900 Megabytes of data. Even if the network provides a bandwidth of 100 Megabits per second, the client must wait for more than a minute. With streaming, the display starts once sufficient data is prefetched at the client to hide the time required to deliver the remainder of a clip. A challenge here is how to determine the size of prefetch portion. This is a challenge because network bandwidth might fluctuate dramatically during delivery of a clip, causing one or more clients to starve for data. This causes the display to suffer from frequent disruptions and delays, termed hiccups. A related challenge is how to recover from these scenarios. The obvious solution is to free up bandwidth by terminating one or more clients. The key question is how to determine the identity of victim clients in a decentralized manner while respecting the application's overall requirements.

See: Placement of Continuous Media in Ad-Hoc Networks of Devices

References

1. V. Bush. "As We May Think," The Atlantic Monthly, Vol. 176, No. 1, July 1945, pp. 101-108.
2. S. Bararia, S. Ghandeharizadeh, and S. Kapadia, "Evaluation of 802.11a for Streaming Data in Ad-hoc Networks," Proceedings of the Fourth Workshop on Applications and Services in Wireless Networks, August 2004.
3. W. Cheng, L. Golubchik, and D. Kay, "Total Recall: Are Privacy Changes Inevitable?" Proceedings of the First ACM Workshop on Continuous Archival and Retrieval of Personal Experiences, New York, NY, October 2004.
4. J. Gemmell, B. Gordon, R. Lueder, S. Drucker, and C. Wong. "MyLifeBits: Fulfilling the Memex Vision," ACM Multimedia, December 2002.
5. J. Gemmell, L. Williams, K. Wood, G. Bell, and R. Lueder, "Efficient Retrieval of Life Log Based on Context and Content," Proceedings of the First ACM Workshop on Continuous Archival and Retrieval of Personal Experiences, New York, NY, October 2004.
6. S. Ghandeharizadeh and T. Helmi, "An Evaluation of Alternative Continuous Media Replication Techniques in Wireless Peer-to-Peer Networks," In Proceedings of Third International ACM Workshop on Data Engineering for Wireless and Mobile Access (MobiDE, in conjunction with MobiCom'03), September 2003.
7. S. Ghandeharizadeh, B. Krishnamachari, and S. Song, "Placement of Continuous Media in Wireless Peer-to-Peer Networks," IEEE Transactions on Multimedia, April 2004.
8. S. Ghandeharizadeh and R. Muntz, "Design and Implementation of Scalable Continuous Media Servers," Parallel Computing, 24(1):91--122, May 1998.
9. R. Rejaie and A. Ortega, "PALS: Peer to Peer Adaptive Layered Streaming," Proceedings of NOSSDAV, June 2003.
10. D. Shukla, L. Chandran-Wadia, and S. Iyer, "Mitigating the Exposed Node Problem in IEEE 802.11 Ad Hoc Networks," Proceedings of IEEE International Conference on Computer and Communication Networks (ICCN), Oct 2003.
11. A. Spyropoulos, K. Psounis, and C. Raghavendra, "Spray and Wait: An Efficient Routing Scheme for Intermittently Connected Networks," Proceedings of the ACM SIGCOMM Workshop on Delay Tolerant Networking (WDTN-05), August 2005.

DATA MODELING, MULTIMEDIA

Simone Santini
University of California, San Diego, USA and Universidad Autónoma de Madrid, Spain

Definition: *Multimedia data modeling refers to creating the relationship between data in a multimedia application.*

Data modeling (*sans* multimedia), mush like requirement engineering, is in a sense a hybrid discipline that operates as a bridge between, on one side, some branch of the computing profession and, on the other, the problems from other disciplines to which the computing profession applies its solutions. In the general acceptance of the term, data modeling has the purpose of creating a formal data structure that captures as well as possible the (often informal) data of the application, and the relations between them. Standard data modeling is often done using semi-formal methods such as the *entity-relationship diagrams* [1]. These methods, in general, put the emphasis on the relationship between the data, rather than on the data themselves: the data are often represented as simple data types (integers, strings, etc.) connected by the relations of the model.

A greater emphasis on the data themselves is placed by so-called *object-oriented* approaches [2,3], most of which make use of graphic formats such as UML [4]. (Object oriented methods in general, and UML in particular, are designed as notations to specify the structure of programs and, as such, are not quite suitable for data modeling. To name but one problem, in UML design it is necessary to decide immediately which entities are objects and which are attributes, a decision that should properly be left to a later stage of the design process.) It is worth noticing that an object in the typical object oriented modeling formalism is not an object at all, since it is not a truly abstract data type, in that its internal structure is always explicit and part of the model: in this sense, an object in a data model is closer to Pascal's records or C' structures than to objects.

Multimedia data are often complex and have a rich structure and, at least in their static aspects, are often modeled using object oriented modeling formalisms, possibly with a higher level of abstraction since the extreme complexity of certain multimedia structure pushes the designer to place the emphasis of a design on the *behavior* of multimedia data rather than on their *structure*. But, apart from some adjustment to allow a higher degree of abstraction, multimedia data would probably have little to add to the general area of data modeling were it not for the issue of *time*.

Many multimedia data have a time component, and the existence of this component creates issues, such as data flow or synchronization, that are quite alien to traditional modeling techniques. The timing problems of multimedia data are, in fact, quite independent of those of areas such as historical data bases, temporal queries, or real time data bases, *vis à vis* which data modeling has developed its time modeling techniques. Multimedia data are often retrieved and processed in order to be presented, and the technical or psychophysical differences in the perception of different types of data imposes, in the multimedia arena, considerations unknown in the case of other data modeling problems.

To make but an example, in a multimedia presentation the synchronization between the presentation material (typically: transparencies) and the audio-video content is relatively coarse—a mismatch of the order of seconds can be tolerated—while the synchronization between the audio and the video of the speaker must be considerably finer: a mismatch of a single frame (1/30th sec.) is already noticeable. (The means to achieve synchronization also depend on the characteristics of the medium and of its perception: video frames, for example, can be dropped more readily than audio packets, as the human sensory system discerns gaps in audio as more prominent and disruptive than comparative gaps in video; this kind of problems, however, belong to a level different than that of data modeling, and will not be considered here.)

Many of these problems are solved by suitable querying, access, or indexing techniques. The purpose of data modeling is, for multimedia as for other types of data, to provide a suitably formalized view of the relevant data structures, so that a suitable solution can be designed. In the specific area of multimedia, next to the traditional aspects of data modeling, this entails the specification of the temporal relations between the data, as a prolegomenon, e.g., to the temporal schema design of the data bases involved in a system.

An important representation often used in multimedia data modeling is that of *intervals* (in time) [5]. Given a set of instants T, a partial order on T, and two elements $a, b \in T$ with $a \leq b$, the interval [a,b] is the set $\{t \mid t \in T, a \leq t \leq b\}$. Note that, contrary to the common intuition, time is represented here as a *partially* ordered set. This stipulation is useful, e.g. for modeling situations of time uncertainty when, given two events $e_1 \neq e_2$, at instants t_1, t_2, the uncertainty in the measurement of time doesn't allow one to determine which of the two events came first.

Many multimedia modeling problems have to do with synchronization, that is, with the temporal relation between pieces of multimedia data, each one considered as an interval. The simplest case of such relation is that between *two* intervals, in which case there are 13 topologically distinct relations in which they can be, represented, using the graphical notation of Allen [6] by the seven relations in Figure 1 and by the inverses of the first six (the inverse of the seventh is clearly equal to the relation itself).

Here, $\square_a$, $\square_a$ (resp. $\square_b$, $\square_b$) are the start time and duration of event a (resp. b), $\square$ their relative position ($\tau_\delta = |\pi_b - \pi_a|$) and $\square_T$ the duration of the composition of intervals. The relations between intervals can be expressed in terms of conditions on these parameters. For instance:

$$\text{a before b} \equiv \left(\pi_a + \tau_a < \pi_b\right)$$

and so on. Binary relations can be extended to lists of intervals by assuming that each pair of contiguous intervals stands in the same binary relation. In this case, for instance, the n-meets relation would be represented as

I_1	I_2	I_3	⋯⋯⋯⋯⋯	I_n

Several partial order relations can be defined for intervals. Intervals being sets, the most obvious one is probably the set inclusion relation which, in terms of the time parameters of the intervals, translates to

$$a \leq b \Leftrightarrow \left(\pi_a \leq \pi_b\right) \wedge \left(\pi_a + \tau_a \geq \pi_b + \tau_b\right)$$

but this order doesn't capture the temporal semantics, so to speak, of the interval relation: one would like, at least, a partial order that, in the limit when the length of the intervals tends to zero, becomes isomorphic to the total order of time instants (without uncertainty).

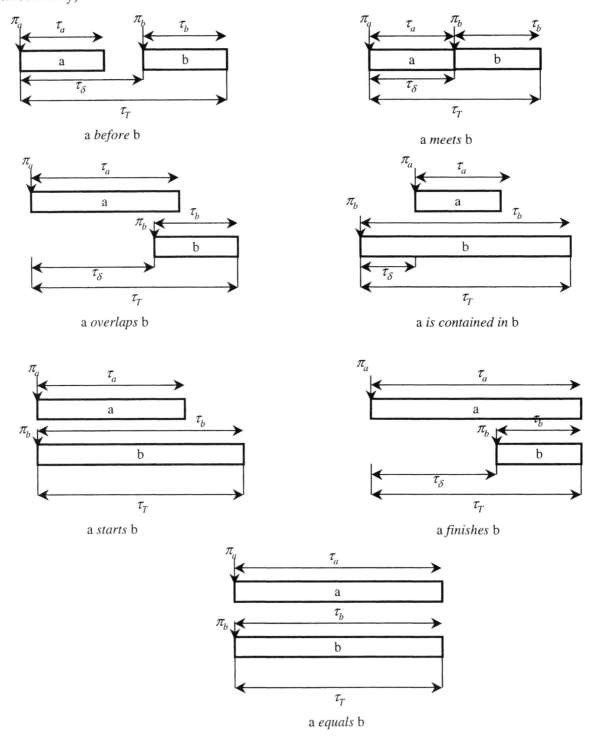

Figure 1. Temporal relations between pieces of multimedia.

A partial ordering such as

$$a \le b \Leftrightarrow (\pi_a \le \pi_b) \wedge (\pi_a + \tau_a \le \pi_b + \tau_b)$$

would do the job. This partial ordering is related somewhat to the qualitative interval relations since, for instance,

a before b $\Rightarrow a \le b$

a meets b $\Rightarrow a \le b$

and so on.

Unrestricted intervals generate unrestricted partial orders, that is, by creating—somewhat artificially—an initial and a final events, every lattice corresponds to a feasible set of temporal intervals. This modeling formalism is therefore very expressive, but it also creates considerable problems in the translation of the model into a data base schema or an algorithm. For instance, not only do some query expressions yield a result exponential in the size of the input but, given a query expression e, whether there is an input p such that $e(p)$ is exponential in $|p|$ is undecidable [7].

Models of reduced expressivity have been proposed. For example, if intervals are used only to model time uncertainty, and such uncertainty can be bounded, then one can use a model in which all intervals have the same length (namely, the bound on the uncertainty). In this case, it can be shown that the resulting lattice will not contain any sub-lattice isomorphic to the following lattices:

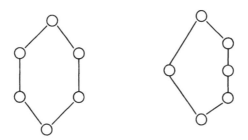

The partial order is then a *semiorder*, for which more efficient algorithms are available [8].

An important, if often imprecise, notion in multimedia modeling is that of *stream*. The intuitive notion here is that, although multimedia presentations are, perforce, finite in time, in many applications one hasn't got access to the whole presentation instantaneously: since processing typically takes place while the presentation is being displayed, at any time only the data up to the time of presentation—or shortly thereafter, if the presentation can be buffered and displayed with a certain delay—are available for processing. Even if buffering is permissible, so that data up to a certain time in the future are available, it is in general unfeasible, both on timing and on storage grounds, to buffer the whole presentation and process it as a whole. Rather, it is assumed that at time t the processing algorithm only has access to data in a suitable time window $[t - t_w, t]$. Because the processing is, so to speak, oblivious of the boundaries of the presentation, it is often convenient to model the presentation itself as an infinite set.

More formally, given a set M of media types (any form of data representing the possible instantaneous values of a given medium), and the lattice I of intervals, a (discrete) stream is a pair of functions $u : N \rightarrow M$, $v : N \rightarrow I$ such that $\pi_a(v(i)) < \pi_a(v(i+1))$ for all i. The number i identifies a sample in the stream, $v(i)$ defines the temporal placement of that sample, and $u(i)$ its contents in terms of data. At time t, only the values of the function such that $\pi_a(v(i)) < t$ are computable.

Many applications of multimedia, towards which these models are oriented, involve either the synchronization of streams (which, at the level of data modeling, is specified using the interval relations seen above) or some form of stream query, not dissimilar to what is done in temporal data bases [9]. In these cases, typically, a feature extraction function is applied to the data function u to yield one or more feature streams, on which the query can be executed.

References

1.   C. Batini, S. Ceri, S. B. Navathe, and S. Navathe, *"Conceptual Database Design: An Entity-Relationship Approach,"* Reading:Addison Wesley, 1991.

2.   W. Klas, E. J. Neuhold, and M. Schrefl, "Using an object-oriented approach to model multimedia data," *Computer Communications*, Vol. 3, No. 4, pp. 204—16, 1990.

3.   D. Woelk, W, Kim, W. Luther, "An object-oriented approach to multimedia databases," *Proceedings of the ACM-SIGMOD 1986 Conference on Management of Data*, pp. 311—25, 1986.

4.   A. Dennis, B. H. Wixom, and D. Tegarden, *"Systems Analysis and Design : An Object-Oriented Approach with UML"*, Wiley, 2001.

5.   T.D.C. Little and A. Ghafoor, "Interval-based conceptual models for time-dependent multimedia data," *IEEE Transactions on Knowledge and Data Engineering*, Vol. 5, No. 4, pp. 551—63, August 1993.

6.   J. F. Allen, "Maintaining knowledge about temporal intervals," *Communications of the ACM*, Vol. 26, No. 11, pp. 832—43, November 1983.

7.   S. Grumbach and T. Milo, "An algebra for pomsets," *Proceedings of the International Conference on Database Theory*, pp. 191—207, Heidelberg:Springer-Verlag, 1995.

8.   S. Bhonsle, A. Gupta, S. Santini, M. Worring, and R. Jain, "Complex visual activity recognition using a temporally ordered database," *Proceedings of Visual 99: International conference on Visual Information Management Systems*, Amsterdam, June 1999.

9.   O. Etzion, S. Jajodia, and S. Sripada (Eds.), *"Temporal databases: research and practice,"* Heidelberg:Springer-Verlag, 1998.

DEAD RECKONING

Definition: *Dead reckoning is commonly used to compensate for packet losses and delays in online gaming.*

With the aim of providing users with high levels of interactivity in the course of frenetic fast paced games, a large number of *latency hiding* techniques have been devised that aim at compensating transmission delays and packet losses. In essence, much of the focus on improving real-time interactions within online multi-player game sessions is on how to reduce response times experienced by players. For timely game state updates at player consoles, *dead reckoning* is commonly used to compensate for packet losses and delays. In this specific context, prominent works are those presented in [1, 2, 3].

In particular, dead reckoning schemes typically aim at predicting the actual positions of moving entities during the game evolution. These schemes are based on the idea of updating entities' trajectories rather than static positions. Thus, for each entity, the position estimation is calculated based on previous moves of the entity.

Different schemes are possible for the prediction of a future event or position. As an example, the most common approach is that of considering entities moving at a constant speed. In this case, the position of a moving entity is predicted by resorting to a first order equation: $x(t_i) = x_0 + v(t_i - t_0)$, where t_i and t_0 represent, respectively, the actual local time and the time of the last received event, while $x(t_i)$, x_0 and v are vectors in a 2D or 3D space. In particular, v represents the constant speed that identifies also the trajectory of the moving entity, and x_0 represents the known position of the entity at time t_0. It is clear that such an approach may be fully exploited to predict the position of moving entities provided that events and correlated movements may be described based on a first order equation. Otherwise, alternative prediction schemes may be exploited such as, for example, second order equations. These assume that entities move with a constant acceleration i.e., $x(t_i) = x_0 + v(t_i - t_0) + \frac{1}{2} a(t_i - t_0)^2$. Finally, different prediction schemes could include methods that exploit constant speed circular motion [1].

It is quite obvious that these dead reckoning schemes work well for game entities that perform simple (and slow) trajectories such as, for example, tank movements in a (game) military simulation. However, the problem of dead reckoning is that moves may be incorrectly predicted, especially in case of (fast moving) complex trajectories. In this case, in fact, inconsistencies may occur. In such situation, dead reckoning schemes must be devised that adopt control techniques that allow identifying possible inconsistencies between the predicted entity's position and the actual real position of the entity.

Finally, due to the fact that dead reckoning algorithms typically encode continuous move actions within game events, it results that synchronized clocks and game event timestamps must be exploited to process such game events at their exact points in time. In fact, network latencies could introduce inaccuracies in the entities trajectories if game events would be roughly processed as soon as they are received without any control on their specific time of generation.

See: Online Gaming

References

1. S. Aggarwal, H. Banavar, A. Khandelwal, S. Mukherjee, and S. Rangarajan, "Accuracy in dead-reckoning based distributed multi-player games," Proceedings of ACM SIGCOMM 2004 Workshop on NetGames '04: Network and System Support for Games, Portland, Oregon, USA, pp. 161-165, 2004.
2. K. Alex and S. Taylor, "Using determinism to improve the accuracy of dead reckoning algorithms," Proceedings of Simulation Technologies and Training Conference, Sydney, 2000.
3. L. Pantel and L.C. Wolf, "On the suitability of dead reckoning schemes for games," Proceedings of the 1st Workshop on Network and System Support for Games, pp. 79–84, ACM Press, 2002.

DEMOSAICKED IMAGE POSTPROCESSING

Definition: *Demosaicked image postprocessing is used after a demosaicking module in a processing pipeline to enhance the quality of demosaicked, full-color, camera images.*

The most essential step in a single-sensor imaging pipeline is the demosaicking process. However, demosaicking solutions usually introduce visual impairments, such as blurred edges and color shifts. Therefore, demosaicked image postprocessing should be used after a demosaicking module in a processing pipeline to enhance the quality of demosaicked, full-color, camera images (Figure 1) [1]-[3].

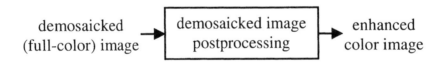

Figure 1. Demonstration of a demosaicked image postprocessing/enhancement concept.

Unlike demosaicking, which is considered a stand-alone procedure, demosaicked image postprocessing is an optional step which complements (without replacing) the available demosaicking solutions [2],[3]. It performs full color image enhancement (Figure 2), as the input to the postprocessor is a demosaicked, full-color, Red-Green-Blue (RGB) image and the output is an enhanced RGB color image. Since the CFA image values are not affected by the demosaicking step and thus, they are included in a demosaicked output image, the postprocessing process should improve the color appearance and sharpness, as well as eliminate false colors by utilizing the information from both its demosaicked components and the original CFA data. The objective can be achieved by employing, in a fully automated manner, both an edge-sensing mechanism and a spectral model to track the varying spatial and spectral characteristics of the demosaicked image.

Such enhancement operations can be treated as either a postprocessing procedure incorporated as the last step in a demosaicking pipeline or as an independent postprocessing operation. Unlike demosaicking, postprocessing can be applied iteratively until certain quality criteria are met [3]. The postprocessor can be implemented either in hardware or software on the camera itself. Alternatively, the postprocessing of the demosaicked image can be performed in a personal computer using software distributed by the camera manufacturer or by utilizing conventional, public image processing tools. Thus, the proposed postprocessing concept can complement the existing CFA based processing pipelines [1]-[3].

(a)   (b)

Figure 2. Visually contrasted: (a) demosaicked image obtained using a cost-effective processing solution, and (b) postprocessed demosaicked image with an enhanced visual quality.

See: Digital camera image processing, Demosaicking, Spectral model, Edge-sensing mechanism, Color image filtering and enhancement.

References

1. R. Lukac, K. Martin, and K.-N. Plataniotis, "Color-Difference Based Demosaicked Image Postprocessing," IEE Electronics Letters, Vol. 39, No. 25, December 2003, pp. 1805-1806.
2. R. Lukac, K. Martin, and K.-N. Plataniotis, "Demosaicked Image Postprocessing Using Local Colour Ratios," IEEE Transactions on Circuits and Systems for Video Technology, Vol. 14, No. 6, June 2004, pp. 914-920.
3. R. Lukac and K.-N. Plataniotis, "A Robust, Cost-Effective Postprocessor for Enhancing Demosaicked Camera Images," Real-Time Imaging, Special Issue on Spectral Imaging II, Vol. 11, No. 2, April 2005, pp. 139-150.

DEMOSAICKING

Definition: Demosaicking is the process of recovering the color information in the systems, which use only a single image sensor.

Cost-effective consumer electronic devices use only a single image sensor to capture the visual scene. The monochromatic nature of the sensor necessitates covering its surface by a color filter array (CFA) which is used to capture all the three, Red-Green-Blue (RGB) primary colors at the same time. Since the single-sensor allows only one color to be measured at each spatial location, the acquired CFA image data constitute a mosaic-like gray-scale image. To recover the color information (Figure 1), the two missing color

158 D

components must be determined from the adjacent pixels. This estimation process is commonly termed demosaicking, but it is also known as CFA interpolation or color interpolation [1]-[3].

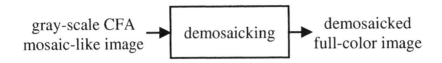

Figure 1. Demonstration of a demosaicking concept.

Demosaicking is an integral, and probably the most common processing step, used in digital cameras. Demosaicking (Figure 2) performs spectral interpolation [2] as it transforms a gray-scale (scalar) image to a three-channel, full color output. Namely, it re-arranges the acquired gray-scale sensor data to an RGB vectorial field, and estimates missing color components from the adjacent sensor data using an interpolator operating in the spectral (color) domain.

The demosaicking solution [3] can be implemented in i) a conventional digital camera which stores the demosaicked (RGB) output, or in ii) a companion personal (PC) computer which interfaces with the digital camera which stores the images in the raw CFA format. Both processing pipelines can use the same demosaicking solution, however, the PC based approach allows for the utilization of sophisticated demosaicking schemes which cannot, due to their complexity, be embedded in the conventional camera image processing solution due to its power and real-time constraints. Finally, it should be noted that a high-quality imaging pipeline should utilize both the spatial and spectral characteristics of the acquired input during the demosaicking process and that such a solution may be complemented by a postprocessing step to produce a naturally colored, sharp image [1],[3]

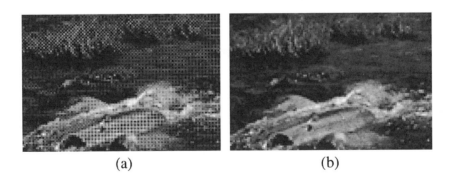

(a)　　　　　(b)

Figure 2. Single-sensor basics: (a) captured gray-scale CFA sensor image, (b) demosaicked, full-color, image.

See: Digital camera image processing, Spectral model, Edge-sensing mechanism, CFA image zooming, Demosaicked image postprocessing, Color image zooming, Color image filtering and enhancement.

References

1. R. Lukac, K.-N. Plataniotis, D. Hatzinakos, and M. Aleksic, "A Novel Cost Effective Demosaicing Approach," IEEE Trans. Consumer Electronics, Vol. 50, No. 1, February 2004, pp. 256-261.
2. R. Lukac, B. Smolka, K. Martin, K.-N. Plataniotis, and A.-N. Venetsanopulos, "Vector Filtering for Color Imaging," IEEE Signal Processing Magazine; Special Issue on Color Image Processing, Vol. 22, No. 1, January 2005, pp. 74-86.
3. R. Lukac and K.-N. Plataniotis, "Data-Adaptive Filters for Demosaicking: A Framework," IEEE Transactions of Consumer Electronics, submitted for publication.

DESKTOP VIRTUAL REALITY

Definition: Desktop virtual reality uses a computer monitor for virtual reality applications.

Virtual Reality (VR) is the technology that provides almost real and/or believable experiences in a synthetic or virtual way. Desktop VR uses a computer monitor as display to provide graphical interface for users. It is cost-effective when compared to the immersive VR as it does not require any expensive hardware and software and is also relatively easy to develop. Although they lack the immersion quality, they consist of computer-generated environments which exist in 3 dimensions (even if they are shown on a 2-D display). Figure 1 below shows an example of a Desktop VR system used for industrial training [1]. It is possible to enhance the user experience by using stereoscopic 3D view, on a regular monitor, through the use of special software and 3D goggles. Because the worlds exist in 3 dimensions, users can freely navigate in 3 dimensions around in the worlds. It is generally believed that the graduate deployment of desktop 3D monitors [2] will increase the applicability of desktop VR in the near future.

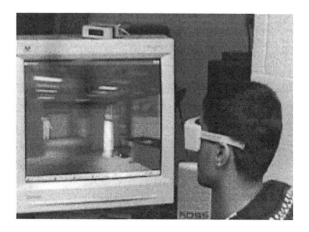

Figure 1. A desktop virtual reality environment.

See: **Virtual and Augmented Reality**

References

1. J.C. Oliveira, S. Shirmohammadi, M. Cordea, E. Petriu, D. Petriu, and N.D. Georganas, "Virtual Theater for Industrial Training: A Collaborative Virtual Environment," Proceedings of the 4th World Multiconference on Circuits, Systems, Communications and Computers (CSCC 2000), Athens, Greece, July 2000, Vol. IV, pp. 294-299.
2. A. Sullivan, "3-Deep," IEEE Spectrum, Vol. 42, No. 4, 2005, pp. 22-27.

DEVICE-DRIVEN PRESENTATION OF MULTIMEDIA CONTENT

Definition: *Device-driven presentation of multimedia content deals with the issue how can multimedia content be made available to end users considering the devices, display characteristics, processing capabilities, and connectivity.*

For some time the only way to access and work with digital content was the personal computer or workstation. Not only is the volume of digital content (including text, pictures, audio, video, or other multimedia content) growing, but in particular the variety of devices that are available for presentation of digital content. Thus there is the need to deliver content that is adapted to the different characteristics and capabilities, i.e., delivery context, of the devices. Delivery context as described in [1] is "a set of attributes that characterizes the capabilities of the access mechanism, the preferences of the user and other aspects of the context into which a web page is to be delivered." Generalizing this definition for any kind of presentation, the main question to be addressed is: how can multimedia content be made available to end users considering the devices, display characteristics, processing capabilities, and connectivity. There are mainly three solutions to this problem: 1) composition of different documents dedicated for presentation on different devices; 2) provision of single media elements and system-driven dynamic selection and merging of these elements into a coherent document/presentation adapted to the delivery context; or 3) use of a highly flexible document model that supports the presentation of the digital content on different devices.

Considering the wide variety of different capabilities and different characteristics of devices composing a separate document for each class of devices is just unacceptable. Provisioning single media elements and developing algorithms that select and merge them into a single document relevant to the delivery context is the first real opportunity to provide context-driven presentation of multimedia content. Projects of this kind are very often single media centered (e.g., delivering text or photos) but there are some novel research approaches aiming at the development of a generic modular framework, e.g. [2, 3] that supports the composition of personalized (i.e., context sensitive) multimedia presentations for multiple devices. The third approach – using a flexible document model that allows to create content once and use it everywhere – has attracted significant research interest: e.g., W3C specifications of document models aiming at support for different devices are SVG Mobile (a model that brings the 2D vector graphics to the mobile web using two profiles: SVG Tiny, suitable for highly restricted devices, and SVG Basic for higher level mobile devices), SMIL 2.1 Mobile Profile (provides support for SMIL presentation within the context of a mobile device), or (X)HTML, which is very often supported by mobile devices as well. The advantages of using the latter type of models are, among others, the easy content development and maintenance using popular authoring tools and well- established support by different devices. Very often the document models are XML-based, which allows XML-based processing techniques. A major drawback of this approach is the resulting complexity for the author since manual authoring of such documents adaptable to different delivery contexts is not feasible without appropriate (WYSIWYG) authoring tools.

See: Context-Aware Multimedia

References

1. W3C, "Delivery Context Overview for Device Independence," W3C Working Group Note, January 2005.
2. A. Scherp and S. Boll, "Generic support for personalized mobile multimedia tourist applications," Proceedings of the 12th Annual ACM International Conference on Multimedia, New York, 2004, pp. 178-179.
3. K. Nahrstedt and W. Balke, "A taxonomy for multimedia service composition," Proceedings of the 12th Annual ACM International Conference on Multimedia, New York, 2004, pp. 88-95.

DIAMOND SEARCH FOR BLOCK MOTION ESTIMATION

Definition: Diamond search technique for block motion estimation is based on diamond search patterns.

The process of block matching motion estimation is to find out a candidate block, within a search area in the previous frame, which is most similar to the current block in the present frame. To speed up the search process, a number of fast search algorithms have been developed in the past two decades. It is shown that the diamond search (DS) algorithm [1] [2] can achieve a better compromise between the complexity and prediction performance among different methods.

Diamond search makes use of the center-biased motion characteristics of video sequences and uses diamond search patterns (Figure 1) instead of rectangular as most of other search methods. It also uses the halfway stop criterion to allow early termination of the search. The detailed steps of DS are shown below. Figure 2 shows an example how DS locates the motion vector.

Step 1   The initial large diamond search pattern is centered at the search origin, the (0,0) position, and nine search location are checked. If the minimum MAD point is located at the center, go to Step 3; otherwise, go to Step 2.

Step 2   Use the minimum MAD point found in the previous step as the center of the large diamond search pattern. Calculate the MAD values for those new search points in the search pattern. If the minimum MAD point is located at the center, go to Step 3; otherwise, recursively repeat this step.

Step 3   Use the small diamond search pattern. Four more search points are checked. The minimum MAD point found in this step is the final solution of the motion vector which points to the best matching block.

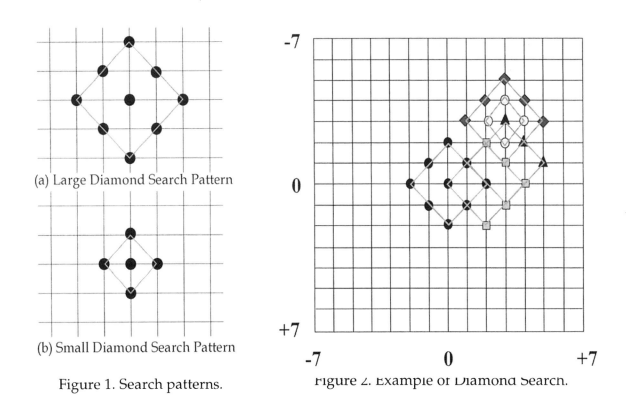

(a) Large Diamond Search Pattern

(b) Small Diamond Search Pattern

Figure 1. Search patterns.

Figure 2. Example of Diamond Search.

See: Motion Compensation for Video Compression

References.

1.   J. Y. Tham, S. Ranganath, M. Ranganath, and A. A. Kassim, "A novel unrestricted center-biased diamond search algorithm for block motion estimation," *IEEE Transactions of Circuits and Systems for Video Technology*, Vol. 8, pp. 369–377, August 1998.
2.   S. Zhu and K. K. Ma, "A new diamond search algorithm for fast block matching motion estimation," *IEEE Transactions of Image Processing*, Vol. 9, pp. 287–290, February 2000.

DIGITAL BIOMETRICS

Forouzan Golshani
Department of Computer Science & Engineering
Wright State University, Dayton, OH, USA

Definition: *Digital biometrics refers to measurements on physiological or behavioral characteristics of a person for determining or verifying the identity of a person.*

Biometrics deals with the science of identification (or verification) of a person based on some physiological, behavioral, or genetic characteristics. Digital biometrics refers to measurements on physiological or behavioral characteristics of a person, generally obtained through automated technological means, for determining or verifying the identity of a person. Physiological biometrics is the data gathered from direct measurement of the human body, obtained by means of various procedures and algorithms that can uniquely identify the individual. Examples include: fingerprint, hand geometry, iris, retinal, vein, voice, and facial imaging. Behavioral biometrics, however, is measured by analyzing a specific set of actions of a person. These may include how a person talks, signs their name, walks, writes, or types on a keyboard. Work in the field of multimedia directly contributes to computational biometrics, both physiological and behavioral. Face recognition techniques and retina scan analysis are examples of contributions to the physiological biometrics. Gait analysis, where the person recognized by their activities, for instance manner of walking, is an example of where multimedia techniques play a crucial role.

From another perspective, biometric technologies can be categorized into active and passive techniques. Active biometrics include: fingerprint, hand geometry, retina scanning, and signature recognition technologies. Examples of passive biometrics procedures are: voice recognition, iris recognition, and facial recognition. The first two are somewhat limited but the last, facial imaging, can be truly passive.

Biometric technologies are becoming the foundation of a large number of highly secure identification and human verification solutions. In the identification mode (one to many), the biometric system compares the given individual to all individuals in the database and ranks the top possible matches. In a verification mode (one to one), the system compares the given individual with who that individual says they are and provides a yes/no answer. Identification is generally associated with surveillance, whereas a clear application of verification is access control.

The need for biometrics-based systems can be found in the government sector (federal, state and local), the military, and commercial applications. Many enterprise-wide network security infrastructures are already benefiting immensely from multimedia-based biometric technologies, including secure electronic banking and other financial transactions, retail sales, law enforcement, and government IDs. Biometric-based authentication applications include access control for workstation, network, and domain, data protection, application logon, and remote access to resources.

The performance of a monomodal biometric system depends greatly on the ability of the sensor to capture data and also on the features of the biometric trait captured. Any irregularity in the capture phase reflects on the performance metrics of the system and might greatly increase the error rates. There are several issues regarding the biometrics being used. Not all of the biometric traits (physiological or behavioral) are universal or unique-enough. Some are variant with time (aging), cannot be quantified well, are not acceptable by all people (intrusive), can be faked to fool the system, and some are not robust enough. Noisy data also creates a variance in matching correctly. The success of any biometric verification system relies on the properties of the trait on which the system is based. Usually these peculiarities result in compromised success.

Incorporating multiple biometric traits for authentication can alleviate most of these problems. Multimodal systems are expected to be more reliable and that is due to the fact that multiple sensors are used to catch different biometric traits. The system thus has multiple pieces of evidence of identity (or lack of it). These systems can be configured to match levels of security based on application. Due to the requirement of several biometrics, it will be difficult for intruders to fake all traits and violate the integrity of the system. *Information fusion,* i.e., how to integrate the information received from individual modalities, is the key to success of these systems. We will review several techniques used in various systems.

Computational Biometrics

Some common sources of biometrics data are: fingerprints, face images, voice patterns, retinal or iris scanning, hand geometry, signatures, key strokes, gait features, and 3D scans. These have the common characteristics of being identifiers that are intrinsically associated with the individual in question, can be reproduced anytime, and cannot easily be lost or stolen.

Fingerprints: This is the oldest and best known biometric parameter for identification and authentication. Each finger on a person's hand has a unique pattern which can distinguish the person from all other members of the universe.
Formed in the embryonic stages of life, the ridges and their flows and patterns do not change over time, other than enlargement due to the natural growth of the body over time. Because of their use in forensics and a number of other applications, fingerprints have been studied more extensively over much longer period of time as compared to other biometrics.

Digital fingerprints are obtained by means of a variety of sensors in the form of an electronic image, to which a series of image enhancement algorithms are applied to remove undesirable artifacts and to improve contrast. Next, local ridge orientations are estimated, followed by local thresholding. The next step, feature extraction from fingerprints leads to extraction of minutiae. A variety of features (up to 50 or more) are extracted from ridges such as ridge bifurcations, patterns created by ridge flow characteristics, highest point of the innermost ridge, and delta points separating pattern areas and non-pattern areas. The feature set, collectively, defines the minutia. Steps leading to minutia extraction are: Calculation of flow orientations; Localization of pattern areas; Extraction of ridges; Thinning of the ridges, and Minutia representation. A common technique for fingerprint matching is based on minutiae comparison. Given two fingerprints with two sets of minutiae points, the matching algorithm creates a mapping between pairs of minutiae based on their relative placement on the finger, as illustrated in Figure 1.

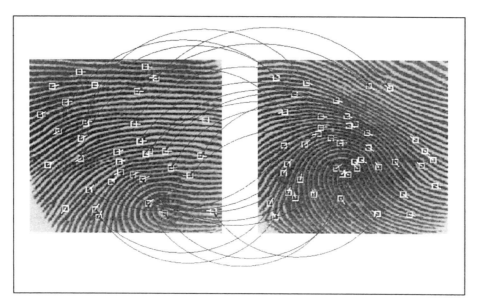

Figure 1. Matching minutiae of two fingerprints.

Iris Scans: Eye scans in general, and retina in particular, are considered to be intrusive forms of biometric authentication. Iris is the colored (green, blue, brown,...) ring around the dark pupil of the eye. Formed at the embryonic stages, the iris does not change throughout the lifetime of a person. An average iris may have more than 200 spots connected together with very complex patterns. These patterns are different even between the left eye and the right eye of each person. As such iris provides a very robust parameter for identification. Fortunately even when the participant is wearing contact lenses or even glasses, the detailed patterns can be captured.

The process begins by a special camera capturing an image of the iris. The camera, typically an infrared imager, must be fairly close to the subject and the participant should preferably look at the lens. Infrared imaging causes this close up, high resolution image to have proper illumination. The detailed patterns extracted from the iris scan are then converted into a set of indecies for more economical representation and faster processing. The process begins with the localization of the iris by determining its inner and outer edges. By applying a series of transforms such as Gabor wavelets, the image is then digitized into a much smaller representation (512 bytes) which is used for generating what is known as the "iriscode". The matching process measures the differences between the query scan and the stored templates using a distance algorithm such as the Hamming algorithm. The template with the lowest distance score is selected as the winner.

Among all biometrics systems, False Accept Rate of iris scan systems is very low. In addition, iris-scan technology is highly resistant to false matching and fraud. For example, by checking for the normal continuous fluctuation in pupil size, many iris scanning products fake eyes from the real live ones.

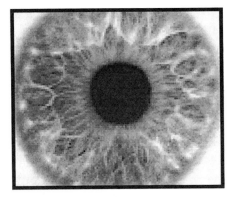

Figure 2. Iris: the colored ring of tissue that surrounds the pupil.

3D Scans: A 3D capture of a body part, say face, contains far more information than any 2D image ever can. Extracting the 3D shape of a face can solve many problems that frustrate users of the conventional imaging systems. 3D scans may be obtained from any body part, but more commonly from face, head and hand. Whole body scans are also common, but they are mostly used for accurate measurement, in such applications as fashion and medicine. 3D imaging technologies vary in accuracy, speed and versatility. The most common technology is range imaging, with two flavors, active and passive. Whereas the ordinary cameras produce images that depict intensity, range cameras produce images that denote distance from camera. Basically, points that are further away from the camera appear differently, and thus depth information is captured and represented. Range images are commonly used in manufacturing inspections, road surface surveying, and industrial robots.

Active range imaging consists of a dedicated and well defined light source, used in conjunction with a sensor. In passive range imaging, on the other hand, no special light, except ambient light, is required. Usually multiple images (at least 2, preferably more) are shot, and 3D image is produced by a common computer graphics technique called triangulation.

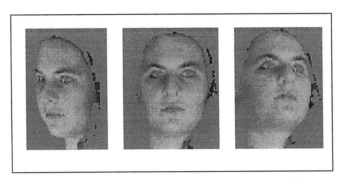

Figure 3. A 3D scan is much richer than a 2D image.

Capturing, processing, and matching 3D images involve the following major steps: triangulation, generation of pointcloud data, application of transforms such as 3D wavelets, generation of polygon and polygon sets, feature analyses for extraction of 3D feature sets, indexing and classification of features, surfaces and surface orientations, topology of objects, production of facial component graphs, and mutli-resolution rendering with multiple layers of detail.

Other Biometrics: Many other biometrics such as voice-Print, keystroke-scan, and hand-writing/signature-scans, are commonly in use. The methodology used for these techniques are in many ways similar to the three representative methods discussed above.

DNA is a yet another biometric but with some major differences. For DNA testing, an actual sample is needed instead of an impression (say a picture or a recording). This makes DNA processing to be an invasive procedure. Since a controlled lab environment is essential, DNA matching cannot be done in real-time. Another major difference is that it does not employ feature extraction and template matching, which are common to the techniques used in biometrics discussed above. Instead it represents the comparison of an actual sample with those in the database.

Biometrics Systems

Conventional identity verification techniques based on the use of passwords or Smart cards rely on the fact that the user possesses information known solely to him or her (*verification of identity by knowledge*: password, PIN) or holds a personal authorization key (*verification of identity by possession*). But such means of identification can be easily lost or stolen. There is also no guarantee that the legitimate owner is using these identification tokens and not an imposter. There is also the added inconvenience of managing an increasing number of PINs. This is where biometrics steps in, by offering solutions that analyze a person's *physiological* or *behavioral* characteristics, guaranteeing legitimacy of user.

The choice of the specific technology depends on factors such as the targeted application scenario, general cost and integration expenses, and most importantly, on the degree of user acceptance and in the future potentially also on the seamless integration into innovative human machine communication.

Two main security usages of biometrics are verification and identification. Operating in verification mode, given an identity for an individual, the system compares the biometrics of the query object with the contents of its database, resulting in a match or no match according to some predefined parameters. Thus a simple one to one match is performed to generate a binary yes/no result. Biometric based identification, on the other hand, allows the user to submit a live sample and the system attempts to identify the subject by examining the population that is stored within the participating databases. The result may be a set of possible matches, ranked with respect to closeness to the given query.

All biometric authentication systems employ pattern recognition and matching techniques and use these to compare the traits of an individual claiming identity against the ones acquired before and stored in a database. The system must be able to differentiate between a 'slightly varying' original from a 'very convincing' fake. There are two modes of operation for biometric system:

Enrollment Mode
    a.   Capture the necessary Biometric from the new subject
    b.   Enrollment process: extract all the necessary measurement and populate the template
    c.   Store the template in a database or on a portable token, e.g., a smart card

Authentication Mode
    a.   Live scan the biometric from the subject
    b.   Process the sampled data and extract the biometric template
    c.   Match the scanned Biometric template against the database
    d.   Produce a matching score, possibly in the form of accept/ reject decision.

Figure 4 illustrates these operations. Unlike password verification and some other traditional authentication methods, where the match/no-match decision is strictly binary, the decision making process in biometric systems is more complicated. The system may return: 'match', 'no-match' or 'inconclusive', by generating a *score* representing the degree of similarity between the submitted sample template and the stored enrollment templates, and comparing the score with a predefined *threshold* (determined by system administrator and set according to required security level). If the sore is above the threshold, a 'match' is declared, otherwise the result is a 'non-match'. With an additional threshold, we can define the range for 'inconclusive', which may also be given in cases where the biometric sample is too noisy.

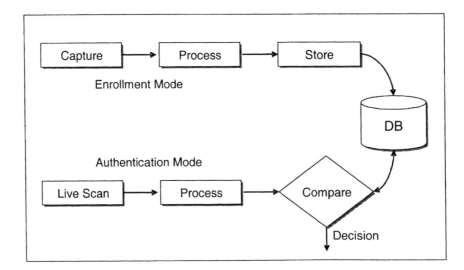

Figure 4. Operations in a biometrics system.

Performance Indicators

The effectiveness of a biometrics system is measured by its accuracy for identifying authorized individuals and rejecting unauthorized ones. Key performance indicators include the following:

1. The **False Rejection Rate** is measured by the number of instances where an authorized individual is falsely rejected by the system. This indicates the likelihood that a genuine person may be rejected by the system.
2. The **False Acceptance Rate** is based on the number of instances where a non-authorized individual is falsely accepted by the system. This indicates the likelihood of an imposter being falsely accepted by the system.
3. The **Failure to Enroll Rate** is the probability that an individual fails to enroll properly because sample was not sufficiently distinctive.

In practice, there are many different ways (i.e., formulas) for measuring each of the above indicators. The False Rejection Rate and the False Acceptance Rate for a system are optimized by adjusting the thresholds. A system may be tuned so that it may be optimized with respect to one or both of these two indicators. In general, False Accept and False Reject rates should be fairly close, yielding an **Equal Error Rate**, which is another common performance indicator. The above list of indicators is not exhaustive and there are several other performance indicators.

Table 1 presents a comparative assessment of various biometrics based systems with respect to a number of relevant parameters.

Table 1. A simple comparison of biometrics from the point of identification/authentication

	Finger prints	Voice	Hand	Signature	Retina scans	Iris scans	Facial imaging	3D scans
Accuracy	High	Medium	Medium	High	Very high	Very high	High	Very high
Longevity	High	Medium	Medium	Medium	High	High	High	High
User acceptability	Medium	High	Medium	High	Medium	Medium	Medium	Low
Possible sources of error	Nonexistence, dirt, age, dryness	Illness, ambient noise,	Injuries, aging	Natural digression	Corrective lenses	Non-cooperation	Lighting, pose, orientation	Motion
Ease of use	High	High	Medium	High	Medium	High	High	Medium
Portability	High	High	Medium	High	Medium	High	High	Low

170 D

Multimodal Biometric Systems

Systems working with a single biometrics have varying degrees of failure. For example, a large portion of the population does not legible fingerprints, voice can be altered by a cold so significantly that voice pattern matching may be impossible, and face recognition systems are susceptible to changes in ambient light and the pose of the subject. For these reasons, often multiple biometrics are used for more robust applications. A Multimodal Biometric System, also known as a Layered Biometric System utilizes more than one technology for user authentication/identification. Each subsystem contributes to the final decision making process. There are several types of multi-modality that can be implemented in a system:

1. Either/Or multimodality describes systems that comprise of more than one biometric subsystems, but verification is done using only one. This way, individuals decide the biometric trait they are most comfortable in using. The user is required to enroll for all participating biometric subsystems, so that fallback options are also available. The biggest drawback is that user will have to familiarize himself to sample submission method for each one of the participating subsystems.

2. Asynchronous multimodality or Sequential multimodality describes systems that need a user to be verified by all biometric subsystems, but this verification is done in sequential order. As the user clears one authentication step, he is subjected to another one. The user must be 'matched' by all biometric subsystems, one after the other before being declared as successfully matched. The plus point is that it's highly improbable that an imposter might be able to clear all authentication steps. This culminates in added security. Along with the problem of familiarizing oneself with each one of the submission processes, the time overhead for each authentication step is an added inconvenience.

3. Synchronous multimodality makes up for the above stated problems. It comprises of more than one biometric technology, which require only one authentication process. The time needed for verification is reduced as compared to asynchronous systems. Special techniques have to be employed to integrate the multiple identifier verification steps.

However, when a Synchronous system is designed, special techniques are needed to combine the subsystems so that they work together smoothly. These techniques deal with *Information fusion* and are engaged to effectively integrate the information received from the experts for making the matching decision accurate to the highest degree.

Flexibility is very important in any authentication system. Modeling an adaptive synchronous multimodal system that accommodates compounded degrees of security necessitates more work due to number of participating systems. Most of the current multimodal biometric systems are of the synchronous type.

Figure 1 is used courtesy of, and with permission from Dr. Anil Jain.

References

1. R. Frischholz and U. Dieckmann, "BioID: A Multimodal Biometric Identification System," IEEE Computer, Vol. 33, No. 2, pp. 64-68, February 2000.
2. K. Jain and A. Ross, "Multibiometric Systems," *Communications of the ACM, Special Issue on Multimodal Interfaces* , Vol. 47, No. 1, pp. 34-40, January 2004.
3. D. Maltoni, D. Maio, A. Jain, and S. Prabhakar, "Handbook of Fingerprint Recognition," Springer Verlag, 2003.
4. S. Narkhede and F. Golshani, "Stereoscopic Imaging: a real time, in depth look," IEEE Potentials, Vol. 23, No. 1, February/March 2004, pp. 38-42.
5. J. Wayman, A. Jain, D. Maltoni, and D. Maio, (Eds.), "Biometric Systems," Technology, Design and Performance Evaluation, Springer Verlag, 2005.
6. D. Zhang, "Automated Biometrics," Technologies and Systems, Kluwer Academic Publishers, Boston, 2000.

DIGITAL CAMERA IMAGE PROCESSING

Rastislav Lukac and Konstantinos N. Plataniotis
University of Toronto, Toronto, Canada

Definition: Digital imaging devices, such as digital camera, contain built-in image processing systems for applications such as computer vision, and multimedia and surveillance.

Digital imaging solutions are becoming increasingly important due to the development and proliferation of imaging-enabled consumer electronic devices, such as digital cameras, mobile phones, and personal digital assistants [1]-[3]. Because its performance, flexibility, and reasonable expenses digital imaging devices are used extensively in applications ranging from computer vision, multimedia, sensor networks, surveillance, automotive apparatus, to astronomy.

Information about the visual scene is acquired by the camera by first focusing and transmitting the light through the optical system, and then sampling the visual information using an image sensor and an analog-to-digital (A/D) converter. Typically, zoom and focus motors control the focal position of the lens. Optical aliasing filter and an infrared blocking filter to eliminate infrared light are also included in apparatus [4][5] Interacting with the sensor, there are other control mechanisms which are used to determine the exposure based on the scene content. Depending on the measured energy in the sensor, the exposure control system changes the aperture size and the shutter speed, by interacting with the gain controller to capture the sensor values using a charge coupled device (CCD) [6] or complementary metal oxide semiconductor (CMOS) [7] sensor. Based on the number of sensors used in camera hardware, conventional digital cameras can be differentiated as three-sensor and single-sensor devices.

The design of a three-sensor device (Figure 1) follows the trichromatic theory of color vision. Since an arbitrary color is matched by superimposing appropriate amounts of three-primary colors [8], and the sensor in the pipeline considered here has a monochromatic nature, professional digital cameras acquire color information using three sensors with Red (R), Green (G) and Blue (B) color filters having different spectral transmittances [1]-[3].

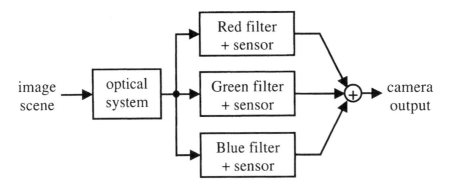

Figure 1. A three-sensor imaging device.

The sensor is usually the most expensive component of the digital camera. To reduce cost and complexity, digital camera manufacturers often use a single CCD or CMOS sensor covered by a color filter array (CFA) [1][2][4][5]. The acquired image is a gray-scale image and thus, digital image processing solutions should be used (Figure 2) to generate a camera output comparable to the one obtained using a three-sensor device (Figure 1).

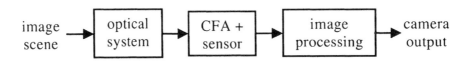

Figure 2. A single-sensor imaging device.

After an A/D conversion, the acquired image data undergo various preprocessing operations [4][5], such as linearization, dark current compensation, flare compensation and white balance. The order of the operations differs from manufacturer to manufacturer. The objective of preprocessing is to remove noise and artifacts, eliminate defective pixels, and produce an accurate representation of the captured scene. After the sensor image data are preprocessed, the image processing is used to perform estimation/interpolation operations on the sensor values in order to reconstruct full color representation of an image and/or modify its spatial resolution. Note that the order, complexity and actual form of image processing operations depend on the form of the CFA employed in an imaging pipeline.

CFA Basics

In the single-sensor imaging pipeline depicted in Figure 2, each pixel of the raw, CFA sensor image has its own spectrally selective filter (Figure 3). The specific arrangements of color filters in the CFA vary between the camera manufacturers which commonly use

RGB CFAs. Alternative solutions include arrays constructed using Cyan-Magenta-Yellow (CMY) complementary colors, color systems with mixed primary/complementary colors, and arrays with more than three colors with spectrally shifted color [2][4].

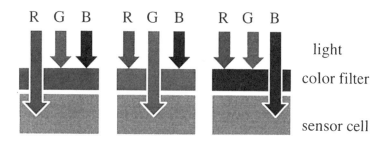

Figure 3. CFA based image acquisition.

Among these, the Bayer pattern (Figure 4) [9] is commonly used due to simplicity of the subsequent processing steps. This pattern contains twice as many G components compared to R or B components reflecting the fact that the spectral response of Green filters is close to the luminance response of human visual system [8].

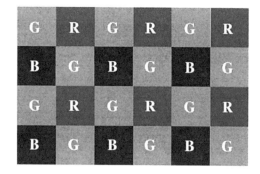

Figure 4. Bayer CFA pattern [9] with a GRGR phase in the first row.

Image Processing for Color Estimation

After the CFA image is captured, numerous image processing operations can be implemented in the camera pipeline (Figure 5). The most critical step in a single-sensor imaging pipeline is a process called demosaicking or CFA interpolation [1][2][10][11]. Demosaicking is used to estimate the two missing components in each spatial location of a CFA sensor image and convert a gray-scale, mosaic-like, CFA image to a full-color image. It performs spectral interpolation operations [12]. Since demosaicking solutions usually introduce various visual impairments, such as blurred edges and color shifts, the quality of demosaicked camera images should be enhanced using demosaicked image postprocessing [13],[14]. By operating on a demosaicked, full-color, image input the postprocessor performs full color image enhancement [14]. Apart from demosaicking and demosaicked image postprocessing, zooming operations are probably the most commonly performed processing operations in digital cameras. Digital image zooming can be performed either on the CFA domain [15][16] or the demosaicked full-color domain [12][16]. By increasing the spatial resolution of the captured image, image zooming techniques perform spatial interpolation operations [12][16]. Finally, it should be noted that while demosaicking constitutes a mandatory step, both CFA and color image zooming as well as demosaicked image postprocessing can be viewed as the optional steps.

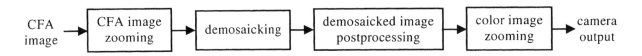

Figure 5. Image processing operations based on similar signal processing concepts.

From the above listing is evident that the demosaicking, postprocessing/enhancement and zooming steps are fundamentally different, although they employ similar, if not identical, image processing concepts. It should be also mentioned that the research in the area of demosaicking has recently culminated due to the commercial proliferation of digital still cameras, which are the most popular acquisition devices in use today. However, both demosaicked image postprocessing and CFA image zooming constitute a novel application of great importance to both the end-users and the camera manufacturers. The similarity of the camera image processing steps listed in Figure 5, along with the limited resources in single-sensor imaging devices suggests that the target is to unify these processing steps in order to provide an integrated, cost-effective, imaging solution to the end-user [17].

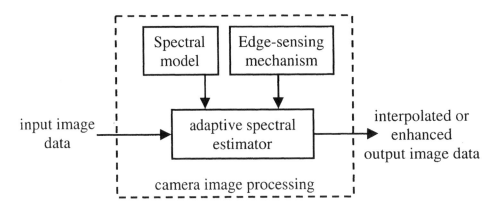

Figure 6. Block scheme of a generalized camera image processing solution.

The visual impairments often observed in processed camera images can be attributed not only to procedural limitations but to the spatial and spectral constraints imposed during processing [2][16][18]. Spatial constraints relate to the size of the supporting area and the form of the shape-mask used in camera image processing as well as the ability of the solution to follow the structural content of the captured image [11][12]. Spectral constraints relate to the utilization of the essential spectral characteristics of the captured image during the estimation process [10][12][18]. As it is shown in Figure 6, to eliminate both the spatial and spectral constraints, a camera image processing solution should employ both an edge-sensing mechanism [2][11][16] and a spectral model [10][13][18], respectively. Such a solution can produce an image which faithfully represents the structural and spectral characteristics of the input scene.

The required performance is obtained using the so-called unbiased, data-adaptive spectral estimator, which can be defined as follows [2][16][18]:

$$\mathbf{y}_{(p,q)} = \sum_{(i,j)\in\zeta} \{w_{(i,j)} f(\mathbf{x}_{(i,j)}, \mathbf{x}_{(p,q)})\} / \sum_{(i,j)\in\zeta} w_{(i,j)}$$

where $w_{(i,j)}$ is an edge-sensing weight, and $f(\cdot)$ is a function implementing the spectral model's concept. Such an estimator operates over the color components available in both the estimation location (p,q) and the neighboring locations $(i,j)\in\zeta$ with ζ denoting the area of support. It also generalizes numerous processing solutions, which may be constructed by changing the form of the spectral model, as well as the way the edge-sensing weights are calculated. The choice of these two construction elements essentially determines the characteristics and the performance of the single-sensor imaging solution [2][10][12][16][18].

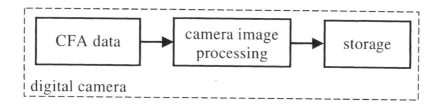

Figure 7. Conventional implementation of the imaging pipeline.

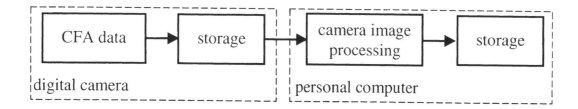

Figure 8. Imaging pipeline constructed using a digital camera interfaced with the companion personal computer.

Depending on the application requirements and implementation constraints, an imaging solution can be implemented either in a digital camera or in a companion personal computer (PC). The architecture shown in Figure 7 is suitable for a computationally efficient method useful for practical, cost-effective camera solutions operating in the real-time constraints. Potentially demanding solutions may be included in the architecture shown in Figure 8. Unlike the conventional solution, using the PC-based pipeline the end-user can control the processing operation, change the parameter setting of the processing solution, and re-run the procedure if the output image does not satisfy the quality requirements.

Camera Image Compression

The outputted camera images (Figures 7 and 8) are usually stored either in a CFA format or as full-color images [4][5][19]. Most professional digital cameras follow the so-called tagged image file format for electronic photography (TIFF-EP) for image storage. In this format, the raw CFA image is stored along with additional information, such as the details about camera setting, spectral sensitivities, and illuminant used. Consumer digital cameras store the full-color image in a compressed format using the Joint Photographic Experts Group (JPEG) standard. However, exchangeable image file (EXIF) format has been popularized due to its easy implementation and possibilities to store additional (metadata) information about the camera and the environment.

Current research in camera image compression indicates that the use of JPEG compression on the CFA image data may lead to new and promising imaging solutions which can be of great interest in wireless imaging-enabled devices since it allows for the transmission of significantly less information compared to the full-color image compression solutions [19]. Further improvements may be expected using JPEG2000 which is a new standard for digital still image compression.

Video-Demosaicking

Recent advances in hardware and digital image/signal processing have allowed to record motion video or image sequences using digital still image or digital video single sensor cameras. Such a visual input can be viewed as a three-dimensional image signal or a time sequence of two-dimensional still images, and it usually exhibits significant correlation in both the spatial and temporal sense [20]. Single-sensor camera image processing solutions devised for still images can also be used in single-sensor video cameras, however by omitting the essential temporal characteristics, conventional camera image processing methods, viewed as spatial solution which process separately the individual frames, produce an output video sequence with motion artifacts. Therefore, a well designed video processing technique should follow the representation of the signal, and utilize all the available information during operation. Such a spatiotemporal solution (Figure 9) should use the spatial, temporal, spectral and structural characteristics of the captured CFA video to produce a full-color, demosaicked, image sequence at the output [20].

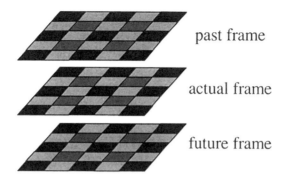

Figure 9. Spatiotemporal video-demosaicking concept defined over three subsequent CFA frames.

CFA Image Indexing

CFA image indexing (Figure 10) constitutes one of the most novel developments in imaging enabled consumer electronics [21]. A single-sensor captured image is connected to digital databases using embedded metadata. Depending on the application, the metadata can vary in the type and amount of the information to be processed. For example, images captured by common digital cameras can be automatically indexed using the camera's identification number, ownership information and a time stamp. In imaging enabled phones, the advanced, satellite tracking based solutions can be used to

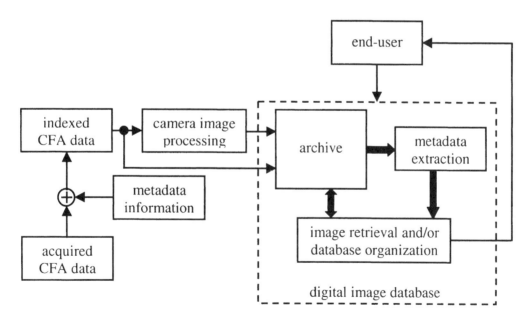

Figure 10. Block scheme of the CFA image indexing and retrieval solution.

provide location stamps. Furthermore, metadata can be completed by adding semantic content through the mobile phone's or pocket device's keyboard. To unify the approach for imaging solutions shown in Figures 7 and 8, the acquired images should be indexed directly in the capturing device by embedding metadata information in the CFA domain using the available data hiding solution. It should be mentioned that the CFA indexing approach can also be used to embed the metadata information which is achieved in EXIF format. Since such information is currently written in the header of the stored file only, it can easily lost by changing the file format or modifying the captured image using any conventional graphic software.

The metadata information should be extracted from either the CFA images or the demosaicked images in personal image databases using PC software commonly available by camera manufacturers (Figure 10). Alternatively, conventional public image database tools such as the well-known World Wide Media eXchange (WWMX) database can be used instead. Thus, the CFA image indexing approach helps to authenticate, organize and retrieve images in digital databases [21].

See: Demosaicking, CFA image zooming, Demosaicked image postprocessing, Color image zooming, Edge-sensing mechanism, Spectral model, Color image filtering and enhancement, Image secret sharing.

References

1. R. Lukac, K.-N. Plataniotis, D. Hatzinakos, and M. Aleksic, "A Novel Cost Effective Demosaicing Approach," IEEE Transactions of Consumer Electronics, Vol. 50, No. 1, February 2004, pp. 256-261.
2. R. Lukac and K.-N. Plataniotis, "Data-Adaptive Filters for Demosaicking: A Framework," IEEE Transactions of Consumer Electronics, submitted.
3. M. Vrhel, E. Saber, and H.-J. Trusell, "Color Image Generation and Display Technologies," IEEE Signal Processing Magazine, Vol. 22, No. 1, January 2005, pp. 23-33.
4. K. Parulski and K.-E. Spaulding, "Color Image Processing for Digital Cameras," in Digital Color Imaging Handbook, (Eds.) G. Sharma, CRC Press, Boca Raton, FL, 2002, pp. 728-757.
5. R. Ramanath, W.-E. Snyder, Y. Yoo, and M.-S. Drew, "Color Image Processing Pipeline," IEEE Signal Processing Magazine, Vol. 22, No. 1, January 2005, pp. 34-43.
6. P.-L.-P. Dillon, D.-M. Lewis, and F.-G. Kaspar, "Color Imaging System Using a Single CCD Area Array," IEEE Journal of Solid-State Circuits, Vol. 13, No. 1, February 1978, pp. 28-33.
7. T. Lule, S. Benthien, H. Keller, F. Mutze, P. Rieve, K. Seibel, M. Sommer, and M. Bohm, "Sensitivity of CMOS Based Imagers and Scaling Perspectives," IEEE Transactions of Electronic Devices, Vol. 47, No. 11, November 2000, pp. 2110-2122.
8. G. Wyszecki and W. S. Stiles, "Color Science, Concepts and Methods, Quantitative Data and Formulas," John Wiley, N.Y., 2nd Edition, 1982.
9. B. E. Bayer, "Color imaging array," U.S. Patent 3 971 065, July 1976.
10. R. Lukac and K.-N. Plataniotis, "Normalized Color-Ratio Modeling for CFA Interpolation," IEEE Transactions of Consumer Electronics, Vol. 50, No. 2, May 2004, pp. 737-745.
11. B.-K. Gunturk, J. Glotzbach, Y. Altunbasak, R.-W. Schaffer, and R.-M. Murserau, "Demosaicking: Color Filter Array Interpolation," IEEE Signal Processing Magazine, Vol. 22, No. 1, pp. 44-54, January 2005.

12. R. Lukac, B. Smolka, K. Martin, K.-N. Plataniotis, and A.-N. Venetsanopulos, "Vector Filtering for Color Imaging," IEEE Signal Processing Magazine, Vol. 22, No. 1, January 2005, pp. 74-86.

13. R. Lukac, K. Martin, and K.-N. Plataniotis, "Demosaicked Image Postprocessing Using Local Color Ratios," IEEE Transactions of Circuits and Systems for Video Technology, Vol. 14, No. 6, June 2004, pp. 914-920.

14. R. Lukac and K.-N. Plataniotis, "A Robust, Cost-Effective Postprocessor for Enhancing Demosaicked Camera Images," Real-Time Imaging, Special Issue on Spectral Imaging II, Vol. 11, 2005.

15. R. Lukac and K.-N. Plataniotis, "Digital Zooming for Color Filter Array Based Image Sensors," Real-Time Imaging, Special Issue on Spectral Imaging II, Vol. 11, 2005.

16. R. Lukac, K.-N. Plataniotis, and D. Hatzinakos: "Color Image Zooming on the Bayer Pattern," IEEE Transactions on Circuit and Systems for Video Technology, Vol. 15, 2005.

17. R. Lukac, K. Martin, and K.-N. Plataniotis, "Digital Camera Zooming Based on Unified CFA Image Processing Steps," IEEE Transactions of Consumer Electronics, Vol. 50, No. 1, February 2004, pp. 15-24.

18. R. Lukac and K.-N. Plataniotis, "A Vector Spectral Model for Digital Camera Image Processing," IEEE Trans. Circuit and Systems for Video Technology, submitted.

19. C.-C. Koh, J. Mukherjee, and S.-K. Mitra, "New Efficient Methods of Image Compression in Digital Cameras with Color Filter Array," IEEE Trans. Consumer Electronics, Vol. 49, No. 4, November 2003, pp. 1448-1456.

20. R. Lukac and K.-N. Plataniotis, "Fast Video Demosaicking Solution for Mobile Phone Imaging Applications," IEEE Transactions of Consumer Electronics, submitted.

21. R. Lukac and K.-N. Plataniotis, "Digital Image Indexing Using Secret Sharing Schemes: A Unified Framework for Single-Sensor Consumer Electronics," IEEE Transactions of Consumer Electronics, submitted.

DIGITAL CINEMA

Definition: Digital cinema includes new computer technologies including the creation of synthetic images, to produce action movies.

While traditional way to make, distribute and consume cinema is becoming obsolete, the IT is promoting the emergence of technologies of digital cinema [1]. Rendering engines can now produce synthetic images in a so realistic way that they can be integrated in a high quality live action movie. Results obtained with digital cinema technologies range from post production effects, such as removing an actor's blemish or fixing a light, to digital animations, such as creating scene where real actors live together with synthetic characters (think Gollum in the Lord of the Rings). Since then, Hollywood has begun a technological revolution creating movies previously impossible to display convincingly, such as, for example, Jurassic Park, Terminator 2, Star Wars, Shrek, Toy Story and Monster Inc. To create this kind of movies a great computational power is needed based on modern hardware (GPUs) and software (Linux OS) equipments. GPUs work as coprocessors to CPUs, adopting a fast AGP bus [2]. Intense competition has driven this field to produce a new GPU generation every six months. The most innovative companies such as Nvidia and ATI, make their GPUs programmable in assembly providing spectacular computer graphical facilities up to the limit threshold of a new art form.

The open source nature and the no license cost of Linux made it one of the best candidates for supporting graphic workstations. For example, super computer like the Cray X-MP (used in the 1985's "The Last Starfighter"), have been abandoned in favor of now cheaper dual-processor Pentium SGI 1100 Linux OS-based servers exploited for realizing the special effects of "the Lord of the Rings" movies. Generally speaking, producing a digital movie eliminates different disadvantages: the celluloid film quality deteriorate through the duplication process, further analogical projectors make the film prone to harmful intermittent mechanical movement. Moreover, the advent of the Internet era, digital distribution could be offered on demand. Studios equipped with digital cinema equipments and broadband Internet access can download the film on the flight thus scheduling faster the coming soon. Moreover, the digital cinema eliminates different disadvantages, and it facilitates the duplication from piracy. While the cost offers resistance to digital cinema yet, innovations in home entertainment push the development of this technology. As of today, the of-the-shelf home theater market offers large televisions, digital projectors, Dolby 5.1 sound systems at a reasonable prize. In practice, it is possible to re-create a small-scale cinema with a high quality at home. Some people claim that the underlying social issues keep attractive the old celluloid cinema for a long time. Obviously, this is a topic to be investigated in the social field. Still, one of the major technological challenges is how to improve the sensorial experiences of the consumers. Possible solutions are exploring 3D stereographic, IMAX, surround sound systems and haptic technologies [3].

See: Multimedia Entertainment Applications

References
1. J. Korris and M. Macedonia, "The End of Celluloid: Digital Cinema Emerges," IEEE Computer, Vol. 34, No. 4, April 2002, pp. 96-98.
2. M. Macedonia, "The GPU Enter Computing Mainstream," IEEE Computer, Vol. 36, No. 10, October 2003, pp. 106-108.
3. M.Ollis and T. Williamson, "The Future of 3D Video," IEEE Computer, Vol. 34, No. 6, June 2001, pp.97-99.

DIGITAL INPAINTING

Timothy K. Shih, Rong-Chi Chang, Su-Mei Chou, Yu-Ping Chen, and Huan-Chi Huang
Tamkang University, Taiwan

Definition: *Digital inpainting is a technique to automatically restore partially damaged photos, repair aged movies, or fill holes on 3D surfaces.*

Digital inpainting requires fundamental knowledge in image processing, video coding, and 3D geometric. Certainly, these topics are important issues in multimedia computing. This article summarizes a few challenge issues in digital inpainting and presents some solutions in the literature. We divide the article into three short sections for each problem (i. e., image, video, and 3D surface). Several short articles (included in this book) related to this article further explain additional issues on image and video inpainting.

Image Inpainting

Aged photos and paintings can be damaged either by scratch, dirt, or other reasons. Even though it is not possible to restore a painting to its original, to repair damaged artifacts with a visually pleasant result is useful, especially for examples in digital museum projects. One of the simplest but efficient mechanisms was presented in [4]. The diffusion kernel is able to repair damages of small area with a barrier to deal with high contrast edges. The computation presented in [4] is proved to be very fast. By using a similar interpolation concept, with an extension to allow different thresholds on different interpolated pixels [8], the mechanism discussed in [8] allows an adaptive computation scheme. Thus, inpainted pixels far away from inpainting boundary can be calculated to achieve a better visual result. Considering inpainting from another perspective, the concept of isophote lines arriving at the boundary of an inpainted area is introduced in [1]. By preventing crossed isophote lines, the mechanism can partially preserve structural information in a damaged image. Other works [2, 3] uses concepts on fluid-dynamics and curvature-driven diffusions for image inpainting. Basically, an image with continuous color and intensity levels can be treated as a two dimensional fluid object. The mathematical model derived in [2, 3] achieve a reasonable result of image inpainting.

On the other hand, a multiple resolution approach is used in [12]. The damaged picture is decomposed into several levels, depending on the color variations of the picture. Interpolated pixels are calculated according to its coordination relation with respect to useful surrounding information (see Figure 1). The algorithm is summarized in the article entitled "Multi-Resolution Image Inpainting" in this book.

Figure 1. A damaged photo and its restored image in [12].

The algorithm is further extended for painting [14]. A painting can be separated into several layers according to color distributions. Each layer is inpainted separately. The results are merged to obtain a reconstructed image (see Figure 2). The inpainting strategy use in [14] is similar to the algorithm used in [12]. However, to merge inpainted results from different layers, a layer fusion algorithm is necessary. The fusion algorithm follows a strategy. For each damaged pixel to be inpainted, two consecutive layers are compared. A window with pixels in a distance with respect to an inpainted pixel is used. A function computes percentages of useful pixels within the distance is applied to each inpainted pixel. Depending on the percentages, a layer is selected. Useful pixels are non-inpainted pixels from the original image, with respect to a layer. The far ground is firstly placed in a blank paper. The picture is restored with a darker layer step-by-step. In Chinese painting, light far grounds are drawn first, followed by darker grounds. The restoring strategy achieves a similar effect.

Figure 2. A Chine painting is repaired according to algorithms in [14].

The work discussed in [12] and [14] also points out an issue of what type of images that can be restored easily. In general, pixel interpolation is suitable for images with continuous color and intensity, for instance, photos. Images with concrete boundaries, such as cartoon drawing, are hard to appreciate pixel interpolation. To restore cartoon pictures one need to use line detection and heuristics.

The above works are computations on special domain of an image via pixel interpolation or extrapolation. With proper heuristics, structural information can be reconstructed to achieve a reasonable effect. However, sometimes, the resulting image is blurred. One drawback of the spatial domain approach is that textural information is hard to restore. The work discussed in [6] uses a multi-resolution texture synthesis mechanism to combine both spatial and frequency information, which can achieve a better result to restore textures. Another example combining spatial and frequency information for restoration is also found in [7].

Algorithms discussed above are effective and efficient in restoring damages of small and discontinue areas. To restore damages of larger area, for instance, to remove a person from a picture, it is necessary to take another approach. Simple pixel interpolation or texture synthesis is not able to produce a visually pleasant result. One useful approach is to copy background information from the same picture to replace the selected area (e.g., a person). The exemplar-based synthesis approach [9] computes a priority for each patch to be selected to inpaint the removed area. After a target area is inpainted, a confidence value is assigned or re-computed. The confidence values are them used for computing the next inpainting area. The following briefly summarizes the approach discussed in [9]:

Let Φ be the source region, Let Ω be a manually selected target region and $\delta\Omega$ be the contour of Ω,
Repeat until region Ω is empty
        Compute boundary $\delta\Omega$ and priorities P(**p**)
        Propagate texture and structure information
                Find patch Ψ**p** on $\delta\Omega$ with highest priority P(**p**)
                Find patch Ψ**q** in Φ which minimizes Sum_of_Square_Difference(Ψ**p**, Ψ**q**)
                Copy Ψ**q** to Ψ**p**
        Update confidence values

Essentially, Ω is an area to be inpainted, with its contour $\delta\Omega$. Patches on this contour are associated with priorities (representing order to be inpainted). Useful patches Ψ**q** from the source region Φ are compared to partial patch on the contour. Best match is selected and copied to the candidate patch. In a few iterations, all candidate patches in the contour are inpainted. This concludes an inpainting step on the contour. The confidence values on inpainted patches are re-computed. And, the same inpainting procedure on the next contour continues, until the target region is empty.

The work discussed in [13] also uses a confidence map (values) and adaptive neighborhood search (finding useful patch of the highest priority). In addition, the picture is refined from coarse level to fine level, which will take several iterations on the same inpainted area. The initial inpainted information relies on a fast estimation scheme known as the push-pull filtering method, to down-sample and up-sample the image in a multi-resolution hierarchically. The algorithm presented in [13] is summarized below:

Let α' be an inverse matte, with a conference value between 0 and 1 for each pixel
For each scale from coarse to fine
    Approximate image from color and coarser scale
    Compute confidence map from α' and coarser scale
    Compute level set from confidence map
    While mean confidence $< 1 - \varepsilon$
        For next target position p
            Compute adaptive neighborhood $N(p)$
            Search for most similar and frequent source match $N(q)$
            Composite $N(p)$ and $N(q)$ at p, updating color and α'
            Compute approximation, confidence map and update level set

Considering image inpainting form another perspective, inpainting technique can be used to attack visible watermarks [5]. Even the mechanism can not completely remove the watermark, since the visible watermark is half transparent (i.e., watermark pixels are interpolated with underlying pixels), it is possible to extend this mechanism to recover aged photos with pasted Scotch taps (half transparent).

Next, an important issue related to image inpainting should be discussed. Most image inpainting algorithms rely on the user to explicitly select a region for repairing or object removal. This is due to the fact that detection of damaged area is hard to achieve automatically, especially on a single image (i.e., compared to motion picture with several images for cross reference). Damaged areas by ink or scratch are created naturally. It is not easy to separate these areas from a scene taken by a camera, which is created naturally as well. It is almost impossible to precisely distinguish the damages by a mathematical function precisely. However, a naïve mechanism developed at Tamkang University is able to detect ink and scratch damages manually created (see Figures 3 and 4). The mechanism uses image processing techniques to find variation of color segments in the picture. With some heuristic rules, the mechanism is able to tell the type of damages (i.e., by ink or by scratch). The black/blue ink traces and scratch in Figures 3 and 4 (as well as other 100 pictures) are created on real photos and scanned for testing. Detected damaged areas are shown in red/yellow. However, there are limitations of the detection mechanism. Extra thin lines and small dots produced from scratch and ink are hard to detect. Ink damages of irregular shape can be mixed with natural objects of dark colors. We are taking a multi-resolution approach to solve the problem. With an improved detection mechanism, a fully automatic system can be implemented for repairing damaged photos in a digital library project.

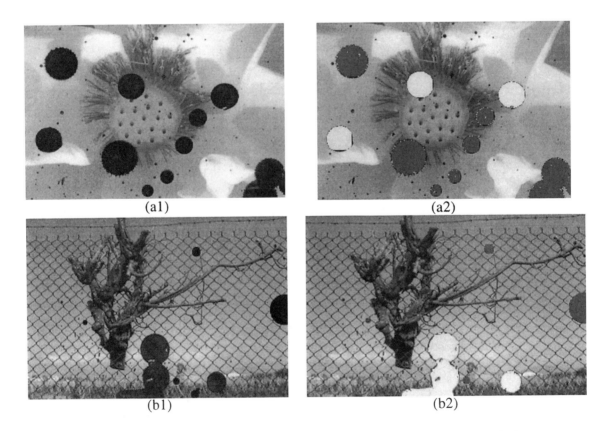

(a1)   (a2)

(b1)   (b2)

Figure 3. Different color of ink traces (a1, b1) are detected (a2, b2).

Figure 4. Scratch (on the left) are detected (on the right).

Video Inpainting

Compared to image inpainting, video inpainting articles are rare to find in the literature. On the detection issue, video inpainting, however, focuses on detection of two types of noises: spikes of brightness and long vertical line of bright or dark intensity. These noises are generated in the process of film development or due to dirt (especially for aged video). The work discussed in [10] estimates movements of small blocks using a reliable displacement map and detect spikes of small regions. Both temporal and spatial strategies are used in inpainting the spike region. Long vertical lines are detected and removed in [11]. The mechanism is an improvement based on the Kokaram's model.

Video inpainting can also be used to remove logos in a film [15]. The mechanism assumes that video logos are small and in a fixed position in general. The location of logo is detected based on distribution of histogram energy. With logo position allocated, image inpainting mechanism can be used to remove the logo. The algorithm presented in [15] is summarized as the following:

- Select a logo region, and find the best logo frame using the following 4 steps:
    - Compute the grey-scale histogram of the selected region for all frames
    - Normalize the histogram
    - Calculate the histogram energy of every frame
    - Choose the frame with the maximum energy

- Enhance and binarize the best logo frame to delineate the extract logo region

- Inpaint on the logo region for all frames in the video sequence

Another video inpainting project is implemented at Tamkang University. The algorithm detects spikes of brightness based on intensity variation in the temporal domain. Spikes occur randomly with a typical duration of a few frames. Usually, spikes of brightness have color values very close to white color. The detected spikes are removed (inpainted) using information from both spatial and temporal domains. Best results, if any, are used from temporal domains since it is possible to recover the lost using the same object property (assuming that the moving object is inpainted). Otherwise, interpolation of pixels is applied using information in the same frame. Figure 5 show an example of spikes in an aged movie by Jacky Chen. The spikes, detected regions, and a restored frame are all shown in Figure 5. Most spikes are detected. However, the ratio of miss detection is increased if a threshold of spike size is set to very small. But, for incorrect detection, the detected small areas are inpainted as well. In general, the visual result, even with miss detections, is pleasant in the inpainted video as compared to seeing lots of spikes.

Figure 5. Video inpainting results – the damaged frame (left), the detected spikes shown in red (middle), and the repaired frame (right).

Holes Removal on 3-D Surfaces

Three dimensional scanners are important for creating avatars or models in virtual reality and augmented reality. However, due to many reasons, such as occlusions, low reflectance, scanner placement, lack of sufficient coverage, etc, 3-D surfaces produced from scanner may have holes. In most situations, watertight surfaces are required. Algorithms to overcome this problem in most scanners use triangulating boundaries calculation. However, it is possible to produce self-intersecting surfaces. A solution using volumetric diffusion was proposed in [16, 17]. The algorithms proposed always produces closed, manifold triangle mesh without self-intersections.

Summary

Digital inpainting is part of multimedia computing research. This article summarizes inpainting techniques used in image, video, and 3D surfaces. Some techniques can be found in image processing literature (i.e., pixel interpolation). Others such as motion estimation algorithms can be found in video coding standard specifications. Digital inpainting techniques are useful and can be used in restoration of aged pictures and films. The approach is different from some signal processing mechanisms which eliminates noises by sacrificing quality of the original multimedia resource.

This interesting research area still has some issues that can be further investigated. For instance, it is possible that different categories of images (e.g., painting, photo, and cartoon drawing) require different inpainting strategies. Also, the assessment strategy needs to be investigated since PSNR values do not always reveal correct visual results. Human evaluation is necessary. For inpainting large blocks on images, it is not possible to inpaint properly unless semantics are considered. Also, exemplar-based technique can consider searching on patches from another picture instead of on the same picture. Thus, an image repository classified according to some semantic criteria is necessary. Most image inpainting tools allow users to select a solid region for inpainting. A fuzzy mask can be added to the region such that partial information from the damaged area can be used. Finally, there is no article of "audio inpainting" found in the literature. It will be interesting if audio inpainting can be used in radio signal transmission.

See: Multi-Resolution Image Inpainting, Motion Picture Inpainting on Aged Films, Photo Defect Detection

References

1. M. Bertalmio, G. Sapiro, V. Caselles, and C. Ballester, "Image Inpainting," Proceedings of the ACM SIGGRAPH Conference on Computer Graphics, SIGGRAPH 2000, pp.417-424.
2. M. Bertalmio, A. Bertozzi, and G. Sapiro, "Navier-Stokes, Fluid-Dynamics and Image and Video Inpainting," Proceedings of the 2001 IEEE Computer Society Conference on Computer Vision and Pattern Recognition, 2001, pp. I355-I362.
3. T.-F. Chan and J. Shen, "Nontexture Inpainting by Curvature-Driven Diffusions," Journal of Visual Communication and Image Representation, Vol. 12, No. 4, 2001, pp. 436-449.
4. M. M. Oliveira, B. Bowen, R. McKenna, and Y.-S. Chang, "Fast Digital Image Inpainting," Proceedings of the International Conference on Visualization, Imaging and Image Processing (VIIP 2001), 2001, pp. 261-266.
5. C.-H. Huang and J.-L. Wu, "Inpainting Attacks against Visible Watermarking Schemes," Proceedings of the SPIE, International Society for Optical Engineering, 2001, No. 4314, pp. 376-384.
6. H. Yamauchi, J. Haber, and H.-P. Seidel, "Image Restoration Using Multiresolution Texture Synthesis and Image Inpainting," Computer Graphics International, 2003, pp. 108-113.
7. M. Bertalmio, L. Vese, G. Sapiro, and S. Osher, "Simultaneous Structure and Texture Image Inpainting," IEEE Transactions on Image Processing, Vol. 12, No. 8, 2003 pp. 882 -889.
8. R. Bornard, E. Lecan, L. Laborelli, and J.-H. Chenot, "Missing Data Correction in Still Images and Image Sequences," ACM Multimedia, 2002, pp. 355 – 361.

9. A. Criminisi, P. Perez, and K. Toyama, "Region Filling and Object Removal by Exemplar-Based Image Inpainting," IEEE Transactions Image Processing, Vol. 13, 2004, pp. 1200-1212.

10. A. Machi and F. Collura, "Accurate spatio-temporal restoration of compact single frame defects in aged motion picture," Proceedings of 12th International Conference on Image Analysis and Processing, September 2003, pp. 454 – 459.

11. L. Joyeux, O. Buisson, B. Besserer, and S. Boukir, "Detection and removal of line scratches in motion picture films," IEEE Conference on Computer Vision and Pattern Recognition, June 23-25, 1999 pp. 548 – 553.

12. T. K. Shih., L.-C. Lu, and R.-C. Chang, "Multi-Resolution Image Inpainting," Proceedings of IEEE International Conference on Multimedia & Expo (ICME'03), July 2003, pp. 485-488.

13. I. Drori, D. Cohen-Or, and H. Yeshurun, "Fragment-Based Image Completion," Proceedings of ACM SIGGRAPH 2003, pp. 303–312.

14. T. K. Shih, R.-C. Chang, and L.-C. Lu, "Multi-Layer Inpainting on Chinese Artwork," Proceedings of IEEE International Conference on Multimedia & Expo (ICME'04), June 2004, pp. 33-36.

15. W.-Q. Yan and M. S. Kankanhalli, "Erasing Video Logos Based on Image Inpainting," Proceedings of IEEE International Conference in Multimedia and Expo (ICME 2002), Vol. 2, 2002, pp. 521-524.

16. J. Verdera, V. Caselles, M. Bertalmio, and G. Sapiro, "Inpainting Surface Holes," Proceedings of IEEE International Conference on Image Processing, Vol. 2, 2003, pp. 903-906.

17. J. Davis S. R. Marschner, M. Garr, and M. Levoy, "Filling Holes in Complex Surfaces Using Volumetric Diffusion", Proceedings of First International Symposium on 3D Data Processing, Visualization, Transmission, (3DPVT'02), 2002, pp. 858-862.

DIGITAL RIGHTS MANAGEMENT

Pallavi Shah
Hewlett Packard

Definition: Digital Rights Management technology offers the ability to control the distribution and use of the intellectual property (including media/content) and thereby protect the associated revenue or investment for the digital content businesses.

What is Digital Rights Management?

Digital Rights management is a key enabler of end to end digital content business models. Historically, Digital Rights Management is viewed primarily as the security technology used for protection of digital media copyright. However, what differentiates DRM from traditional security technologies is its ability to control content dynamically and persistently by setting policy. Policy provides regulations on the types of actions (like record, copy, play, print, view x number of times, etc.) that can be performed on the content along with the timeframe in which the content is accessible. The policy is set by the IP or content owners.

Why DRM?

Everything a person buys has legal restrictions that determine what can and cannot be done with the media assets. If an individual consumer buys a traditional printed book at a bookstore, he or she is given some rights to the content of the book as an owner of the book. The consumer can read the book, lend it to someone, or give it away.

But by law, the purchaser cannot make copies of the book and sell them. As an institutional consumer (public or private company, or educational facility), the rights to copyright reuse with a printed book or physical piece of media (CD, DVD, audio tape, microfiche, etc.) are the same as the individual consumer, but the notion of "fair use" is instituted when it comes to copyright protection. Institutions can invoke "fair use" of copying copyrighted materials for internal distribution for educational or research purposes without breaking copyright laws.

The traditional media world (publishing, music, movies, etc.) is very simple and limited to basic contractual rights. The objectives for managing content rights in the traditional media world include deterring piracy and protecting the content, enabling revenue through outright purchase or licensing, bolstering traditional media brands, and learning more about a company's audience. It is because there is a tangible asset related to each piece of data that is recorded (as a whole or in pieces) that "fair use" can be managed more appropriately in the printed or physical media world. It is much more complex in the digital world. Content conversion, digitization, compression, and storage technologies have created new opportunities and efficiencies for media and information to be archived, repackaged, and redistributed through electronic channels (e.g., the Internet, extranets, cable, terrestrial broadcasts, or satellites). As content becomes more widely available in digital form, it becomes even easier to distribute, share, copy, and alter if it is improperly "meta-tagged" (unique identifying tags related to media format, creator, usage, and distribution rules) and encrypted throughout the digital distribution value chain.

This brings an exponential increase in the threat of piracy and the loss of revenue for original content owners and producers.

Now that electronic content can be copied much more easily, content owners have a greater need for content control. IP authentication and password access are not able to protect the content from being duplicated or shared, thus creating a need for greater rights management controls. At the same time, digital media distribution can bring a variety of new business opportunities for owners or generators of content who incorporate the right technologies to control their digital media distribution value chain.

Technology / Architecture Overview:

There are 2 entities in the content business: the publisher and the consumer.

The publisher creates the content, tags it appropriately for search and retrieval, seals the content with encryption and policy and finally distributes the protected and encrypted sealed copy widely. The consumer then acquires encrypted content, acquires rights (license) after identification or payment, and finally unseals the content and uses according to the policy set by the publisher.

DRM architecture typically consists of the following components:

- **Content Server**: Content Server consists of four blocks:
  1. Content Repository: A content repository contains a meta-data management environment to uniquely identify the digital assets. Some of the more efficient DRM software applications can integrate with asset management and content management systems.
  2. Meta-Data: Product information, consisting of rights and product meta-data
  3. Packager: A packager that encrypts the content with the appropriate mechanisms to unlock the content upon delivery to an end user.
  4. Delivery Mechanism

- **License Server**: License Server Consists of three components:
  1. An encryption key repository
  2. A user identity database which ties back to the content
  3. A DRM license generator that binds the content and the encryption key to the end user's device and registers the user with the appropriate parties involved in the digital distribution value chain.

- **Client**: Client resides on the end-user device that displays the encrypted content, communicating the appropriate rights and permissions to the end user and back to the license server.

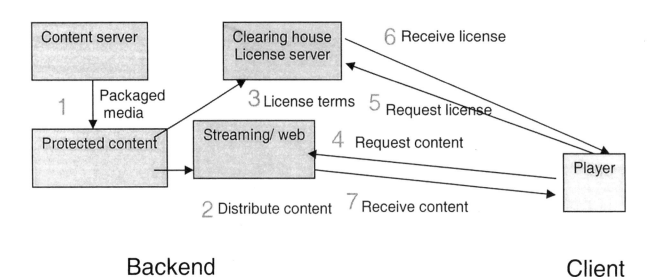

Figure 1. DRM example workflow: How DRM works.

The basic DRM process workflow is as follows:

1. **Packaging:**   The first step in providing a deployable and expandable DRM technology strategy involves the appropriate meta-tagging of the assets that are created and stored within databases and media asset management technologies. Within most of the commonly used DRM applications for text, audio, video, and software, a set of rules is created to determine the rights and policies for use. These rules are defined separately for each party accessing the information, including methodology to check the users' rights to access the content. Access rules may address the price of the content, the frequency and duration of access, and whether the user is authorized to save, print, or transfer the content to other users. Associating the DRM tools back to the original meta-data rights and permissions is critical for the entire digital distribution value chain to ensure that content-creator royalties are tracked. After the assets are meta-tagged, the information is encrypted to ensure the security of the content and locked with a "key." For example, to generate a key, a license key seed and a key ID may be used: The license key seed is a value that is known only to the content owner and license clearing house. The key ID is created by the content owner for each file. This value is included in the packaged file. When the license clearing house needs to issue a license for a packaged file, a key can be recreated by retrieving the key ID from the packaged file. The License Service may use the license key seed (which the clearing house provides) and the key ID from the packaged file to create a key. This key is stored in an encrypted license, which is distributed separately to the client. Other information can be added to the media file, such as the URL where the license can be acquired. Using the key included in the license, the player can play the protected file.

2. **Distribution:** The packaged file can be placed on a web site for download, placed on a media server for streaming, distributed on a CD, or e-mailed to consumers. This enables consumers to send copy-protected digital media files to their friends, as well.

3. **Establishing a License Server/ License Management**: The content provider chooses a license clearing house that stores the specific rights or rules of the license and implements license services. The role of the clearing house is to authenticate the consumer's request for a license. Digital content files and licenses are distributed and stored separately, making it easier to manage the entire system.   Each license contains the key to unlock the protected file. The license also contains the rights, or rules, that govern the use of the digital media file. The content owner sets these rights to determine which actions are allowed from minimal control over playback to more restrictive licenses. The licenses can support a wide range of different business rules, including:

   o   How many times can a file be played.
   o   Which devices a file can be played or transferred on. For example, rights can specify if consumers can transfer the file to portable devices.
   o   When the user can start playing the file and what is the expiration date.
   o   If the file can be transferred to a CD recorder (burner).

    o   If the user can back up and restore the license.

    o   What security level is required on the client to play the file, etc.

Licenses can be delivered in different ways and at different times, depending on the business model. The content owner might want licenses pre-delivered, or they might want the license delivered after a consumer has downloaded and attempted to play a packaged file for the first time. Licenses can be delivered with or without the consumer being aware of the process.

4.   **Request Content:** The consumer requests the content and attempts to play encrypted file. Since the file is protected, the consumer must have a license that contains the key to unlock the content.

5.   **Receive the license:** If the valid license exists on the client, it plays the content. If not, license request is made.

6.   **License Acquisition**: To play a packaged digital media file, the consumer must first acquire a license key to unlock the file. The process of acquiring a license begins automatically when the consumer attempts to acquire the protected content, acquires a pre-delivered license, or plays the file for the first time.

7.   **Playing the Media File:** To play the digital media file, the consumer needs a secure media player that supports the DRM. The consumer can then play the digital media file according to the rules or rights that are included in the license. Licenses can have different rights, such as start times and dates, duration, and counted operations. For instance, default rights may allow the consumer to play the digital media file on a specific computer and copy the file to a portable device. Licenses, however, are not transferable. If a consumer sends a packaged digital media file to a friend, this friend must acquire his or her own license to play the file. Such licensing scheme ensures that the packaged digital media file can only be played by the computer that has been granted the license key for that file.

Selection Guidelines

Companies should consider the selection of DRM product within a whole spectrum of managing and protecting digital rights. They need to know the value of their assets, understand the risks and look for cost effective solutions. Key question is- what content is worth the cost of protecting? Once the DRM needs are established, the following guidelines apply:

- Platforms and services should be able to support multiple DRM technologies and insulate content owners from having to develop customized software applications to accommodate underlying DRM technology, the need for DRM expertise, and the need to build out new infrastructure for content sales and fulfillment.
- Platforms and services should provide support for multiple content types and interoperability, including documents (pdf, HTML), images, audio (streaming and file-based), video (streaming and file-based), games, software, and email.

- Solutions should adhere to open standards and provide interoperability and provide open APIs to content owners and publisher's existing infrastructure environments such as content management, digital asset management, billing, customer care, etc.
- Flexible Business Models: DRM systems should allow companies to pursue multiple business models for different markets, channels or products.

DRM vs. Contracts Rights Management

Contracts rights are the legal agreements between the content creator and publisher or between publishers. Previously, the rights addressed by contracts rights management were inherent in the physical media itself. Examples of rights addressed by contracts rights are related to how the content is licensed: how many times it can be played, how much royalty goes to the content owner, release windows, etc. DRM is about protecting, enforcing, and managing media rights and revenues for the Internet and multi-channel digital delivery world. In the digital world, DRM has the potential to create fundamentally new business models that were not feasible with physical, off-line content. It takes into account many opportunities unthinkable in the past, including micro-payment, pay per listen, dynamic bundling of content, etc.

DRM vs. Conditional Access

Conditional access technology is the media protection technology used for broadcast networks such as satellite, cable, or terrestrial. Video, audio, and data are encrypted during transmission of the uplink site and distributed over an open broadcast network. To block unauthorized users from access, only authorized subscribers receive keys to decrypt content. Typically, the keys are protected using smart card technology to prevent illegal distribution of keys. Typical conditional access systems do not have wide range of policies like DRM systems.

DRM vs. Security

DRM is not synonymous with security. Most security components do not involve rights management in any way. Similarly, DRM includes functions (like reporting or financial interaction) that fall completely outside the scope of security. Nonetheless, security is necessary for DRM to exist. Not only does the content have to be secure from unauthorized access, but also the rights themselves must be secure from tampering. Therefore it is very important that the best security options be available for DRM. An open, standards-based DRM infrastructure makes it possible for solutions providers to use their choice of security.

DRM vs. VPN (Virtual Private Network)

VPN (Virtual Private Network) secures the network only; therefore it is very useful for downloads. However, once the content is downloaded, it is can be freely distributed. It does not address the security of the content itself, nor does it address the rights of the stakeholders. VPN could be a component of DRM. Secured managed networks work ok within or between enterprises. It restricts users to online access only, but it does not necessarily stop them from copying or saving the content on the hard drive.

Applications vs. Services

Building the applications to address the Internet is the first step towards extending the traditional rights models. DRM can be extended as Rights Management Services on Demand that enable companies to market their core competencies over the Internet to provide new broadband-enabled revenue streams. This will result in profit models tied to subscriptions, term licenses, royalties, and transaction-based fees.

Download vs. Streaming

When used with audio and video files, DRM can provide access to a self-contained media file or initiate streaming. Streaming audio and video on the Internet has likewise enjoyed early popularity among consumers. Unfortunately, advertising revenues for these businesses have disappointed expectations. DRM might offer the solution to this revenue problem by enabling the sale of subscriptions or single viewings easily, cheaply, and instantly over the Internet or other networks. The actual broadcast content could vary widely. A few examples include past or current television offerings, radio broadcasts, news, sports, movies, and new offerings created specifically for the online broadcast market.

Tethered vs. Untethered Use

DRM solutions can force the reading device to be connected to the Internet in order to be used (tethered) or can allow the content to be accessed whether or not the device is attached at the moment (untethered).

DRM for Books vs. Music vs. Video

The key differentiator is size of the content and the end device. Books are generally downloaded, whereas music and video are streamed or downloaded. Video requires a more complex infrastructure. Each DRM solution will implement these variables differently depending on the specifics of what it must accomplish. An open DRM infrastructure makes it possible for the industry to fill all these needs. While analysts and industry players generally agree on the need for format-independent DRM solutions, much of today's development effort is geared toward solving these three specific categories of problem.

Encryption vs. Watermarking

Encryption is used for protecting content. It requires the exchange of keys—used for encrypting content, encrypting licenses, or encrypting digital certificates. Watermarking is a way of binding meta-data to content. It is not used for protecting content. Watermarking is also called information hiding, data embedding, or steganography. Unlike encryption, watermarking does not require special application to render content. Watermarking also does not detract from user's experience. It is relatively faster to insert or extract and can hold lot of data. Watermarking is generally used for source identification (visible – deters pirates but degrades images, or invisible – catches pirates in the act). They are convenient as meta-data conveyance—like barcodes on products.

Watermark plus Encryption

Watermarks are sometimes encrypted to protect metadata against alteration. Also, generally files are encrypted and then watermarked to protect AND bind metadata to it. This technique is sometimes used in music DRM.

Super-distribution

Super-distribution refers to the circulation of DRM-protected content files freely on the Internet and through any other pass-along mechanism. Since the content is protected, access must be purchased to fully utilize it. And since DRM offers persistent protection, even after purchase by any given individual, there is no opportunity to pass along the content to friends, co-workers, communities, or pirate boards. However, the protected version of the content can be shared as easily as any other files. Therefore, it is still trivial for consumers to hand this content off to others they feel might also enjoy it. In an effective super-distribution scheme, the file might contain a description of the content and perhaps a sample of that content (part of a song, a clip from a movie, and a chapter from a book) available for free, enhancing the pass-along value of the file and making it more likely that consumers will open it.

Super-distributed content can be passed along from consumer to consumer any number of times. Any recipient can retain it, store it anywhere, and access it at any time in the future. Consumers can pass it along before or after unlocking access for their own use and the passed-along version is still safe from unauthorized viewing by subsequent recipients. Those subsequent recipients enjoy the same rights to access as earlier recipients did. Super-distributed content has the potential to experience viral growth similar to other Internet phenomena. Unlike most viral mechanisms, this one yields revenues directly to the owner of the content. Super-distribution also makes it possible to run legally viable peer-to-peer content exchange services that will benefit their users a great deal without turning into centers for the unauthorized sharing of copyrighted content.

References

1. P. Shah, "Digital Rights Management: Managing the digital distribution value chain," Sun Microsystems, March 2002.
2. "Digital Rights Management Software: Perspective," Gartner Technology Overview.
3. Architecture of Windows Media Rights Manager, Microsoft Whitepaper.
4. R. Iannella, "Introduction to the Resource Description Framework," Proceedings of the Asia Pacific XML Conference, Sydney, October 1998.
5. R. Iannella, "Online Trading of Rights-Enabled Learning Objects," International Journal of Electronic Commerce, Summer 2004, Vol. 8, No. 4.
6. Open Mobile Alliance: www.openmobilealliance.org.

DIGITAL WATERMARKING

Martin Steinebach, Fraunhofer IPSI, Darmstadt, Germany
Jana Dittmann, Otto-von-Guericke University Magdeburg, Germany
Erich Neuhold, TU Vienna, Austria

Definition: *Digital watermarking techniques are based on information hiding techniques similar to steganographic approaches with the overall goal to embed information into a cover signal, usually multi media data.*

The term digital watermarking was used for the first time by Tirkel et al in [8], actually written in two words: "water mark". Instead of a confidential or hidden communication, watermarking addresses the security aspects of data and user authentication or data integrity protection, where a digital watermark is a perceptually transparent pattern inserted in digital data using an embedding algorithm and an embedding key. A detection algorithm using the appropriate detection key can retrieve the watermark information. In most approaches the embedding and detection keys are secret, see more details in [1] or [10].

| Cover | Marked cover | Amplified difference |

Figure 1. Difference between cover and marked cover.

Common watermarking techniques

Watermarking files or streams often requires access to different storage and transmission formats. There are raw data formats based on PCM or bitmaps and lossless or lossy compression formats like MPEG. For some applications, it is sufficient to embed the watermark into format-specific information without direct access to the actual cover signal. The watermark can either be embedded in the format representation, like header or stream information or into the format-specific representation of the media, like for example mp3 scale factors or facial animation parameter of MPEG-4 . This is on the one hand very efficient, as no transformations are necessary and often ensured a high transparency. On the other hand these approaches are not robust against format changes or decoding/re-encoding processes and are easy to attack.

Watermarking methods based on modifying the least significant bit(s) of a cover signal can be applied to every media type robust to bit modifications. Usually the LSB of a media (e.g. sample or pixel) can be changed without degrading the perceived quality. Additional gate functions can be applied to ensure a high transparency by allowing the usage of least significant bits only in those parts of the cover signal where the overall energy is high. This operation can be repeated for each sample or pixel, enabling a very high capacity. As an example one could in theory embed more then 88.000 bits in one second of CD PCM audio. The major drawback of his approach is its usually very low robustness as the least significant bits are often modified by all types of media operations.

The spread spectrum technique is one of the most often used watermark embedding methods for both audio and visual data. It combines high robustness and good transparency at the cost of complexity due to transformation operations. Here a narrow band watermarking signal is transmitted over the cover which features a much larger bandwidth. The amount of energy spread in each frequency component of the spectrum is minimal. The frequency bands are often varied during the embedding process to increase embedding security. The watermarking signal is undetectable, unless one knows the exact location where the information was embedded. The cover can be first submitted to a perceptual analysis process to guarantee invisibility of the watermark. The result of this perceptual analysis is a mask that regulates the strength of the watermark to be embedded.

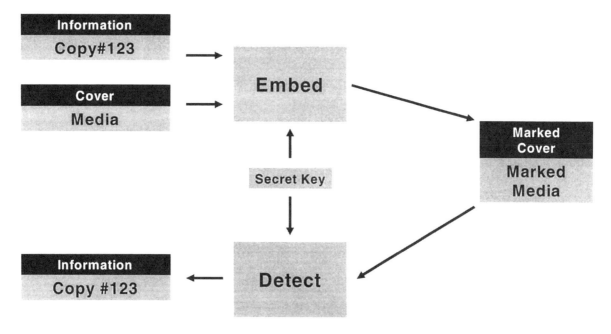

Figure 2. General watermarking concept.

Important Parameters

The most important properties of digital watermarking techniques are transparency, robustness, security, capacity, invertibility (reversibility) and complexity and possibility of verification. Based on these parameters the algorithms can be evaluated if a specific algorithm has adequate properties and can be used for a certain application area.

From [2] we define the parameter as follows

- **Transparency** relates to the properties of the human sensory. A transparent watermark causes no artifacts or quality loss.

- **Robustness** describes whether the watermark can be reliably detected after media operations. It is important to note that robustness does not include attacks on the embedding scheme that are based on the knowledge of the embedding algorithm or on the availability of the detector function. Robustness means resistance to "blind", non-targeted modifications, or common media operations. For example the Stirmark or 2Mosaik tools attack the robustness of watermarking algorithms with geometrical distortions. For manipulation recognition the watermark has to be fragile to detect altered media.

- **Security** describes whether the embedded watermarking information cannot be removed beyond reliable detection by targeted attacks based on a full knowledge of the embedding algorithm and the detector, except the key, and the knowledge of at least one watermarked data. The concept of security includes procedural attacks, such as the IBM attack, or attacks based on a partial knowledge of the carrier modifications due to message embedding [7] or embedding of templates [13]. The security aspect also includes the false positive detection rates.

- **Capacity** describes how many information bits can be embedded. It addresses also the possibility of embedding multiple watermarks in one document in parallel.

- **Invertibility** describes the possibility to produce the original data during the watermark retrieval.

- **Complexity** describes the effort and time we need to embed and retrieve a watermark. This parameter is essential if we have real time applications. Another aspect addresses whether the original data in the retrieval process or not. We need to distinguish between non-blind and blind watermarking schemes.

- The **verification** procedure describes if we have a private verification like private key functions or a public verification possibility like the public key algorithms in cryptography.

The optimization of the parameters is mutually competitive and cannot be clearly done at the same time. If we want to embed a large message, we cannot require large robustness simultaneously. A reasonable compromise is always a necessity. On the other hand, if robustness to strong distortion is an issue, the message that can be reliably hidden must not be too long.

There are algorithms which need the original cover signal to retrieve the watermark from the marked cover and also those which can retrieve the watermark without the original cover. The latter are called blind or oblivious watermarking algorithms, the first are called non-blind or non-oblivious. If the need for the original is acceptable usually depends on the application. In forensic cases the original may be available for comparison. In contrast copy-control environments will not allow access to the original due to the vast overhead and delay caused by such demands. In general blind watermarking algorithms are preferred but more challenging to design and implement. In some applications non-blind algorithms are used due to their potential greater robustness.

Almost all watermarking algorithms use the same secret key for embedding and retrieval. In analogy to cryptography this is called symmetric watermarking. In some algorithms or applications the key is known to the public, which is called public watermarking. The need for the embedding key in the retrieval process induces a serious security challenge in watermarking: Everyone who can retrieve a watermark can also embed a new watermark with the same key as the originator of the first watermark. There are also approaches for asymmetric watermarking, where different keys are used for embedding and retrieval, but a security level comparable with asymmetric watermarking has not been achieved yet and further research is required.

Furthermore, during verification we differ between invertible (reversible) and non-invertible (non-reversible) techniques, where the first one allows the reproduction of the original and the last one provides no possibility to extract the watermark without alterations of the original. Usually robust watermarks should be non-invertible while fragile watermarking has the most interest in invertible schemes to detect bit changes and to allow reproduction of the original.

Applied mechanisms

Digital watermarking algorithms use a number of assisting technologies for embedding information into media files. Common examples are perceptual models, signal transformations and error correction codes. Perceptual models are used for ensuring the resulting quality of the marked cover by identifying areas in the cover where information can be hidden without degrading the perceived quality of the cover. Usage of a perceptual enables a high embedding for most covers, but may lead to a disability of embedding watermarks in certain material with problematic characteristics.

Signal transformations like Fourier Transformation or Wavelet transformation are applied if the cover signal is not provided in a domain suitable for watermark embedding. Many algorithms embed information into the spectrum of the cover, while many media covers are stored in the time or pixel domain. Therefore a transformation is needed to calculate the spectrum of the cover. This spectrum is then modified by the watermarking algorithm and re-transformed to the original domain. Signal transformations often cause the highest computational cost of watermarking algorithms.
Error correction codes are applied to improve the reliability of watermarking retrieval. Especially after attacks individual watermarking bits may flip or are not interpreted correctly. Without error correction, this would lead to a false retrieval result. Using an error correction mechanism therefore improves robustness of a watermarking algorithm, while at the same time capacity is reduced as the error correction codes usually increase

the length of the watermarking information by factor two or more. Furthermore to achieve the required security in most application scenarios cryptographic techniques becomes important and are combined with digital watermarking to so called hybrid systems. For example the watermark information is encrypted before embedding, hashed or signed with a digital signature.

Transparency is based on the properties of the human visual system or the human auditory system. A transparent watermark causes no artifacts or quality loss. Here for image watermarking in most cases visual models determine the watermark strength and adoptive calculated for every mark position individually. Additionally for video, we use the same mark position for each mark frame. The visual quality loss can be evaluated with subjective tests or objective methods, like for example by measuring the signal to noise ratio (SNR) in db.

Applications

Digital watermarking is a flexible technology used in a broad range of applications. The first watermarking approaches were directed at owner authentication or copyright protection, where an owner or producer identification is embedded to prove ownership or source of the cover. Important challenges in this application are a high transparency demand as sold or distributed material of low quality will not be accepted and at the same time high robustness of the watermark to stay in the marked content as long as the quality of the cover is high enough to be of any value.

A more recent approach to copyright protection is to use digital watermarking to identify single copies of an original media file by e.g. embedding a transaction code, a customer ID or a simple continuous number into each copy. Whenever a copy is found, the watermark can be retrieved and the source can be identified by the embedded individual information. With digital watermarking restrictive protection solutions are not necessary to secure digital media. The customer is free to use and consume the media data he bought in any way and on any device he likes. But if he passes the content into illegal environments and copies are found, he can be identified. Therefore this application is called customer identification or customer tracing watermarking. Requirements are similar to copyright watermarking, but in addition a high security to prevent false accusations and often a high capacity due to long transactions codes are required.

The embedding of additional information into a cover or a set of covers is called annotation watermarking. An annotation watermark only needs to be robust against a specified set of transformations which are known to occur in the application scenario. Security usually is not important as it usually makes no sense to forge or change an embedded watermark as long as these are only used for information transmission. One of the most important issues is transparency: An additional service should not reduce the quality of the media or it will not be accepted. Blind methods are necessary as the end user will not have both versions of the media to compare. The capacity should be as high as possible and is very important. The more information can be embedded, the more additional services can be provided.

Watermarking can also be used to identify specific content in a broadcast monitoring system. The watermark is embedded to identify a cover in a broadcast channel to monitor its usage, for example for the automatic generation of song tracking lists. The requirements are similar to copyright protection watermarking with respect to transparency and robustness. But in addition, a low complexity at watermarking detection is necessary to enable real-time monitoring on multiple channels.

Integrity protection is an application domain where the watermark enables to verify the integrity of the cover, to recognize manipulations and sometimes even to recover the original information after manipulations without the need to access the original cover. This can be achieved with or without knowledge of the content. In the knowledge independent approaches a watermark is embedded in the media which is not robust against media manipulations.

If it can be detected later, the integrity of the media has not been attacked. This is called fragile watermarking and can be compared to adding a sigil into the media data which breaks as soon as the content is modified. The sensitivity of fragile watermarks enables their usage in multi media data authentication. Various approaches with differing fragility to attacks exist, which are generally classified as fragile, semi-fragile, content-fragile and self-embedding.

Invertible watermarking

Common watermarking algorithms always cause a certain reduction or modification of the cover. In some scenarios this is not acceptable. To address this, Friedrich et al. presented the concept of invertible watermarking. [3]. Here the original cover can be reproduced from the marked cover if the marked cover has not been modified by attacks. This is achieved by embedding a lossless compressed copy of the cover parts modified by the watermarking algorithm into the cover. The modified parts which carry the watermark can later be replaced by the retrieved copy. In combination with cryptographic mechanisms, this enables advanced and convenient high security media protection, where for example in [4] we find an evaluation of the impact of the chosen cryptographic means to potential attack on invertible authentication schemes.

Content-fragile watermarking

Content-fragile watermarking is the most advanced concept for integrity protection based on digital watermarking. A description of the media content is extracted and embedded with a robust watermarking algorithm. Later, this information can be retrieved and compared with the actual content. Thereby exact positions or detailed information regarding the difference between original and changed copy can be given, enabling an analysis of the nature of occurred attacks.

The syntax or bit stream of multimedia data can be modified without influencing their semantics, as it is the case with scaling, compression or transmission errors. Common security mechanisms like hash functions cannot distinguish between modifications of the representing format and content changes changing the semantics of the media. But usually it is more important to protect the semantics instead of their syntax to vouch for their integrity. Content-based watermarks can be used to verify illegal manipulations and to allow several content-preserving operations. Therefore the main research challenge is to differ from content-preserving and content-changing manipulations. Most existing techniques use threshold-based techniques to decide the content integrity. The main problem is to face the wide variety of allowed content-preserving operations like compression, scaling, format conversion or filtering.

Evaluation and Benchmarking of Watermarking Algorithms

Successful attacks on watermarks can be divided into four large categories. Kutter et al. (see in [5]) distinguishes between removal attacks, geometrical attacks, cryptographic attacks and protocol attacks. If somebody tries to eliminate the watermark from the data we speak from removal attack. The approaches employed most frequently are filter models taken from statistical signal theory. Denoising the marked watermarked data through median or high pass filtering as well as non-linear truncation or spatial watermark prediction are methods considered very likely to succeed. Contrary to this, geometrical attacks are not directly aimed to remove the watermark, but try to either weaken it or disable its detection. This can be done using programs like Unzign or Stirmark, see in [7] [9], or in the short articles on Image, Video and Audio Watermarking for media specific aspects. These introduce either local jittering or local geometrical bending in addition to a global geometrical transformation. As a consequence, most watermark detector looses synchronization with the embedded information and therefore today these attacks are also referred to as synchronization attacks.

Both the removal and the geometrical attack are mostly aimed at the robustness of the watermark. The embedded information is robust if it can be extracted reliably, even if the data material has been modified (but not destroyed completely). Robustness thus signifies the resilience of the watermark-information embedded in the data material to incidental changes or media operations.

In particular, if the watermarking algorithm is known, an attacker can further try to perform modifications to render the watermark invalid or to estimate and modify the watermark. In this case, we talk about an attack on security. The watermarking algorithm is considered secure if the embedded information cannot be destroyed, detected or forged, given that the attacker has full knowledge of the watermarking technique, has access to at least one piece of marked data material, but does not know the secret key. In opposition to robustness, the predicate security signifies resilience to intentional (non-blind) attacks on the watermark itself. Further examples are steganographic attacks, which are referred to as cryptographic attacks in Kutter et al.. As the attacker will try to find the secret key, it is crucial to use keys with a secure length. Other attacks in this category take advantage of the free watermark detector devices available for almost every watermarking technique. Others again try to perform coalition attacks.

The attacks in the last group, the protocol attacks, do neither aim at destroying the embedded information nor at disabling the detection of the embedded information (deactivation of the watermark). Rather than that, they take advantage of semantic deficits of the watermark's implementation. Consequently, a robust watermark must not be invertible or to be copied. A copy attack, for example, would aim at copying a watermark from one media into another without knowledge of the secret key.

See: Audio Watermarking, Image Watermarking, Video Watermarking

References

1. M. Cox and B. Miller, "Digital Watermarking," Academic Press, San Diego, USA, ISBN 1-55860-714-5, 2002.
2. J. Dittmann, P. Wohlmacher, and K. Nahrstedt, "Multimedia and Security – Using Cryptographic and Watermarking Algorithms", IEEE Multimedia, Vol. 8, No. 4, 2001, pp. 54-65.
3. G. Fridrich et al, "Invertile Authentication," In: Security and Watermarking of Multimedia Contents III, P. W. Wong and E. J. Delp III, Editors, Proceedings of SPIE, Vol. 4314, pp. 197 - 208, 2001.
4. S. Katzenbeisser and J. Dittmann, "Malicious attacks on media authentication schemes based on invertible watermarks," Proceedings of E. J. Delp III, P. W. Wong (Eds.): Security, Steganography, and Watermarking of Multimedia Contents VI, SPIE, Vol. 5306, pp. 838-847, Electronic Imaging Science and Technologies, January 2004, San Jose, California, 2004.
5. M. Kutter, S. Voloshynovskiy, and A. Herrigel, "Watermark Copy Attack," Proceedings of SPIE: Security and Watermarking of Multimedia Contents II, San Jose, California, USA, Vol. 3971, pp. 371 - 381, January 2000.
6. A. Lang, J. Dittmann, E. Lin, E.J. Delp III, "Application-oriented audio watermark benchmark service," Proceedings of E. J. Delp III, P. W. Wong (Eds.): Security, Steganography, and Watermarking of Multimedia Contents VII, SPIE, Vol. 5681, pp. 275 - 286, Electronic Imaging Science and Technologies, San Jose, California, USA, January 2005.
7. A. Macq, J. Dittmann, and E.J. Delp, "Benchmarking of Image Watermarking Algorithms for Digital Rights Management," Proceedings of the IEEE, Special Issue on: Enabling Security Technology for Digital Rights Management, Vol. 92, No. 6, pp. 971-984, June 2004.
8. C.F. Osborne R.G. van Schyndel, and A.Z. Tirkel, "A Digital Watermark," IEEE International Conference on Image Processing, Austin, Texas, pp. 86-90, November 1994.
9. F.A.P. Petitcolas, M. Steinebach, J. Dittmann, C. Fontaine, F. Raynal, and N. Fatès, "A public automated web-based evaluation service for watermarking schemes: StirMark Benchmark," In Security and Watermarking of Multimedia Contents III, P. W. Wong, E. J. Delp III, Editors, Proceedings of SPIE, Vol. 4314, pp. 575-584, 2001.
10. F.A.P. Petticolas and S. Katzenbeisser, "Information Hiding Techniques for Steganography and Digital Watermarking," Artech House Computer Security Series, ISBN: 1580530354, 2000.

DISCRETE COSINE TRANSFORM (DCT)

Definition: Discrete Cosine Transform is a technique applied to image pixels in spatial domain in order to transform them into a frequency domain in which redundancy can be identified.

In JPEG compression [1], image is divided into 8×8 blocks, then the two-dimensional Discrete Cosine Transform (DCT) is applied to each of these 8×8 blocks. In JPEG decompression, the Inverse Discrete Cosine Transform (IDCT) is applied to the 8×8 DCT coefficient blocks. DCT and IDCT are defined as follows:

$$\text{DCT:} \quad F(u,v) = \frac{1}{4}C(u)C(v)\sum_{i=0}^{7}\sum_{j=0}^{7} f(i,j)\cos((2i+1)u\pi/16)\cos((2j+1)v\pi/16)$$

$$\text{IDCT:} \quad f(i,j) = \frac{1}{4}\sum_{u=0}^{7}\sum_{v=0}^{7} C(u)C(v)F(u,v)\cos((2i+1)u\pi/16)\cos((2j+1)v\pi/16)$$

where $f(i,j)$ and $F(u,v)$ are respectively the pixel value and the DCT coefficient, and

$$C(\omega) = \begin{cases} \frac{1}{\sqrt{2}}, & \omega = 0 \\ 1, & \omega = 1,2,\cdots,7 \end{cases}$$

As shown in Figure 1, in an 8×8 DCT coefficient block, $F(0,0)$ is called DC coefficient, while other 63 DCT coefficients are called AC coefficients. The coefficients at the bottom-right corner are of high frequencies, and they are sensitive to distortions such as compression. The coefficients at the upper-left corner are of low frequencies, and they are robust to distortions. Human eyes are less sensitive to the high frequencies, while more sensitive to the low frequencies.

F(0,0)	F(0,1)	F(0,2)	F(0,3)	F(0,4)	F(0,5)	F(0,6)	F(0,7)
F(1,0)	F(1,1)	F(1,2)	F(1,3)	F(1,4)	F(1,5)	F(1,6)	F(1,7)
F(2,0)	F(2,1)	F(2,2)	F(2,3)	F(2,4)	F(2,5)	F(2,6)	F(2,7)
F(3,0)	F(3,1)	F(3,2)	F(3,3)	F(3,4)	F(3,5)	F(3,6)	F(3,7)
F(4,0)	F(4,1)	F(4,2)	F(4,3)	F(4,4)	F(4,5)	F(4,6)	F(4,7)
F(5,0)	F(5,1)	F(5,2)	F(5,3)	F(5,4)	F(5,5)	F(5,6)	F(5,7)
F(6,0)	F(6,1)	F(6,2)	F(6,3)	F(6,4)	F(6,5)	F(6,6)	F(6,7)
F(7,0)	F(7,1)	F(7,2)	F(7,3)	F(7,4)	F(7,5)	F(7,6)	F(7,7)

Figure 1. DCT coefficients [1].

For still images, most of the energy is located in the low frequency area (upper-left corner). That means, there are bigger values on the upper-left corner and smaller values on the bottom-right corner. Together with human visual system, this feature can be used for image and video compression.

Compression algorithms are so designed that try to preserve the low frequency components and to depress the high frequency components.

See: Multimedia Authentication

References

1. ISO/IEC 10918-1, Information Technology – Digital Compression and Coding of Continuous-Tone Still Images: Requirements and Guidelines, 1994.

DISCRETE WAVELET TRANSFORM (DWT)

Definition: *Discrete Wavelet Transform is a technique to transform image pixels into wavelets, which are then used for wavelet-based compression and coding.*

The DWT is defined as [1]:

$$W_\varphi(j_0, k) = \frac{1}{\sqrt{M}} \sum_x f(x) \varphi_{j_0, k}(x) \qquad (1)$$

$$W_\psi(j, k) = \frac{1}{\sqrt{M}} \sum_x f(x) \psi_{j, k}(x) \qquad (2)$$

for $j \geq j_0$ and the Inverse DWT (IDWT) is defined as:

$$f(x) = \frac{1}{\sqrt{M}} \sum_k W_\varphi(j_0, k) \varphi_{j_0, k}(x) + \frac{1}{\sqrt{M}} \sum_{j=j_0}^{\infty} \sum_k W_\psi(j, k) \psi_{j, k}(x). \qquad (3)$$

where $f(x)$, $\varphi_{j_0, k}(x)$, and $\psi_{j, k}(x)$ are functions of the discrete variable $x = 0, 1, 2, \cdots, M-1$. Normally we let $j_0 = 0$ and select M to be a power of 2 (i.e., $M = 2^J$) so that the summations in Equations (1), (2) and (3) are performed over $x = 0, 1, 2, \cdots, M-1$, $j = 0, 1, 2, \cdots, J-1$, and $k = 0, 1, 2, \cdots, 2^j - 1$. The coefficients defined in Equations (1) and (2) are usually called *approximation* and *detail coefficients*, respectively.

$\varphi_{j_0, k}(x)$ is a member of the set of expansion functions derived from a *scaling function* $\varphi(x)$, by translation and scaling using:

$$\varphi_{j,k}(x) = 2^{j/2}\varphi(2^j x - k). \qquad (4)$$

$\psi_{j,k}(x)$ is a member of the set of wavelets derived from a *wavelet function* $\psi(x)$, by translation and scaling using:

$$\psi_{j,k}(x) = 2^{j/2}\psi(2^j x - k). \qquad (5)$$

The DWT can be formulated as a filtering operation with two related FIR filters, *low-pass* filter h_φ and *high-pass* filter h_ψ. Both $W_\varphi(j,k)$ and $W_\psi(j,k)$, the scale j approximation and the detail coefficients, can be computed by convolving $W_\varphi(j+1,k)$, the scale $j+1$ approximation coefficients, with the time-reversed *scaling* and *wavelet* vectors, $h_\varphi(-n)$ and $h_\psi(-n)$, and sub-sampling the results by 2, as expressed in Equations (6) and (7) and illustrated in Figure 1.

$$W_\psi(j,k) = h_\psi(-n) * W_\varphi(j+1,n)\Big|_{n=2k, k\geq 0} \qquad (6)$$

$$W_\varphi(j,k) = h_\varphi(-n) * W_\varphi(j+1,n)\Big|_{n=2k, k\geq 0} \qquad (7)$$

The filter bank in Figure 1 can be iterated to implement multi-resolution analysis. The IDWT can be implemented by up-sampling and synthesis filtering. The one-dimensional DWT and IDWT can be extended to two-dimensional.

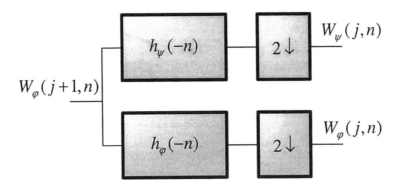

Figure 1. A DWT analysis bank.

See: Multimedia Authentication

References
1. R. Gonzalez and R. Woods, "Digital Image Processing," Prentice Hall, 2002, ISBN: 0-20-118075-8.

DISTANCE AND SIMILARITY MEASURES

Definition: *The notion of distance or similarity between two color vectors is of paramount importance for the development of the vector processing techniques such as noise removal filters, edge detectors and image zoomers.*

Since each color vector is uniquely determined via its magnitude (length) and direction (orientation), the evaluation of the color vectors can be realized in the magnitude domain, the directional domain, or it can utilize both vectors' magnitude and direction [1]-[3].

The most commonly used measure to quantify the distance between two color vectors $\mathbf{x}_i = [x_{i1}, x_{i2}, x_{i3}]$ and $\mathbf{x}_j = [x_{j1}, x_{j2}, x_{j3}]$, in the magnitude domain, is the generalized weighted Minkowski metric:

$$d(\mathbf{x}_i, \mathbf{x}_j) = \| \mathbf{x}_i - \mathbf{x}_j \|_L = c\left(\sum_{k=1}^{3} \xi_k \mid x_{ik} - x_{jk} \mid^L \right)^{1/L}$$

where c is the non-negative scaling parameter denoting the measure of the overall discrimination power and the exponent L, with $L=1$ for the city-block distance, $L=2$ for the Euclidean distance and $L \to \infty$ for the chess-board distance, defines the nature of the distance metric [1]-[3]. The parameter ξ_k, for $\sum_k \xi_k = 1$, measures the proportion of attention allocated to the dimensional component k. Vectors having a range of values greater than a desirable threshold can be scaled down by the use of the weighting function ξ. Alternative measures to the Minkowski metric include, but not limited to, the Canberra distance and the Czekanowski coefficient [1]-[3].

Apart form the distance measures, various similarity measures can be used in support of vector image processing operations. A similarity measure $s(\mathbf{x}_i, \mathbf{x}_j)$ is a symmetric function whose value is large when the vectorial inputs $\mathbf{x}_i$ and $\mathbf{x}_j$ are similar. Similarity in orientation is expressed through the normalized inner product $s(\mathbf{x}_i, \mathbf{x}_j) = (\mathbf{x}_i \mathbf{x}_j / (\| \mathbf{x}_i \| \| \mathbf{x}_j \|))$ which corresponds to the cosine of the angle between the two vectors $\mathbf{x}_i$ and $\mathbf{x}_j$. Since similar colors have almost parallel orientations while significantly different colors point in different directions in a 3-D color space, such as the RGB space, the normalized inner product, or equivalently the angular distance

$d(\mathbf{x}_i, \mathbf{x}_j) = \arccos(\mathbf{x}_i \mathbf{x}_j / (|\mathbf{x}_i| \|\mathbf{x}_j|))$ can be used to quantify orientation difference (angular distance) between the two vectors [1]-[3].

It is obvious that a generalized similarity measure model which can effectively quantify differences among color signals should take into consideration both the magnitude and orientation of the color vectors [1]-[3]. Thus, a generalized measure based on both the magnitude and orientation of vectors should provide a robust solution to the problem of similarity quantification between two vectors. Such an idea is used in constructing the generalized content model family of measures $s(\mathbf{x}_i, \mathbf{x}_j) = C_{ij} / T_{ij}$ which treat similarity between two vectors as the degree of common content, so-called commonality C_{ij}, in relation to the total content, so-called totality T_{ij}, of the two vectors $\mathbf{x}_i$ and $\mathbf{x}_j$. Based on this general framework, different similarity measures can be obtained by utilizing different commonality and totality concepts [1]-[3].

See: Color image filtering and enhancement, Edge detection, Vector edge detectors.

References

1. R. Lukac, B. Smolka, K. Martin, K.-N. Plataniotis, and A.-N. Venetsanopulos, "Vector Filtering for Color Imaging," IEEE Signal Processing Magazine, Vol. 22, No. 1, January 2005, pp. 74-86.
2. K.-N. Plataniotis and A.-N. Venetsanopoulos, Color Image Processing and Applications, Springer Verlag, Berlin, 2000.
3. K.-N. Plataniotis, D. Androutsos, and A.-N. Venetsanopoulos, "Adaptive Fuzzy Systems for Multichannel Signal Processing," Proceedings of the IEEE, Vol. 87, No. 9, September 1999, pp. 1601-1622.

DISTRIBUTED MULTIMEDIA SYSTEMS

Bharadwaj Veeravalli
National University of Singapore, Singapore

Definition: *Distributed multimedia systems consist of multimedia databases, proxy and information servers, and clients, and are intended to for the distribution of multimedia content over the networks.*

In this article, we identify most imperative issues in the design of DMMS architecture. The article is by no means is a survey of DMMS; however it is expected to bring out the key issues and challenges in this domain. We present comprehensive discussions pointing to several key papers published in the literature and highlight existing solutions for small and large-scale DMMS.

Overview

Distributed Multimedia System (DMMS) architecture with all its essential components (Multimedia Databases (MMD), Proxy servers, information services, etc.) is shown in Figure 1.

In a large scale network infrastructure, it is wiser if the control is distributed in the sense that service providers (SPs) choose vantage sites to exercise control to regulate the traffic which in a way assures a respectable quality of service (QoS). This is facilitated via agent-driven approaches. Thus a central dogma in modern days is in adopting agent-driven support [1] within a DMMS to handle overwhelming client population on the network. A

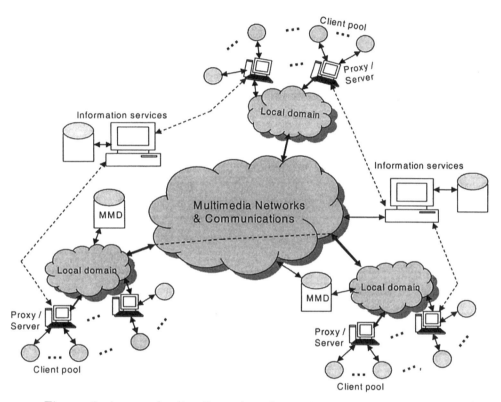

Figure 1. A sample distributed multimedia service architecture.

decade ago, networked multimedia systems were capable of supporting mostly devices like Personal computers and/or a small LAN set-up. However, with the advent of modern day wireless technology, devices such as mobile-technology enabled laptops, handheld devices such as palm-tops, PDAs, etc also fall under active interactive devices. This means that in the volume of traffic ranges from simple short media clips, images, and text messages to long duration media data [2], which is a multi-fold increase. Further, when compared to service architectures conceived from late 80's to mid-90's, modern day services need to account radically different issues in addition to the existing issues in the design of a DMMS architecture. To appreciate this point, one can quickly imagine the issues related to a mobile technology playing crucial roles such as ensuring continuous network connectivity, graceful degradation of service quality under unavoidable circumstances, replication of media data[1] and maintaining consistency for editable data, if any, to quote a few. In addition to such media-rendering service facilities, the purview of modern day DMMS extends to entertainment in the form of games and casinos on networks.

From client' perspective the demands are very simple - design of DMMS must be completely flexible. One would expect different kinds of service facilities ranging from simple pay-per-view shows to an interactive mode of movie viewing for Video/Movie-On-Demand (VoD/MoD)[3]. In each of the above expectations, design of DMMS must account a wide variety of issues. Finally, by resources, one would mean the following: adequate number of copies of movies at the multimedia databases(MMDs), memory capacity at intermediate nodes to buffer data on its transit to destination, adequate bandwidth of the network to support media streams (inclusive of both time-continuous and non-continuous data), and any plug-and-play facilitating software modules. The last component is meaningful under agent-driven systems wherein need for an agent migration and number of agents to be generated at any instance are critical issues.

Key Technologies and Solutions in the Design of a DMMS

In the previous section, we have highlighted some differences between conventional DMMS architectures and expectations of modern day DMMS architecture in providing a wide range of services. In a nut-shell, owing to high-bandwidth availability, several applications become plausible for users that will enforce a continuous work pressure on the media servers on the network. Thus managing resources is indeed a key challenge. In Table 1, we shall present a list of issues which may be considered as either primary or secondary depending on the context and module under consideration. This list, by no means exhaustive, however attempts to capture significant issues that are in practice.

Major Service Categories: Video-On-Demand (VoD) versus Video-On-Reservation(VoR):
VoD and VoR are most commonly used services by network users. VoD is certainly an attractive technology in rendering digital video libraries, distance learning, electronic commerce, etc, as (i) users can request the service any time and from anywhere and, (ii) service allows users to have a complete control of the presentation. Despite continuous research efforts in rendering quality VoD service, the requirement on network resources, such as server bandwidth, cache space, number of copies, etc., are still considered overwhelming owing to an exponential growth in client population. When such fully interactive service demands are met we say that the service is of type *True-VoD*[3]. While small movie clips rendering, learning and video-conferencing kind of applications are almost now delivering a high-quality service, for long-duration movie viewing(say 110mins standard movie) with a presentation control still seems to exhibit annoying experiences for users. Article on long-duration movie retrievals can be found in [2]. Contrary to this, when users reserve for a movie presentation in advance, VoD manifests in the form of VoR[1]. Under VoR service, system is shown to utilize resources in an optimal manner as user viewing times are known in advance. VoD and VoR are completely orthogonal in their service style. Perhaps VoR is better suited for pay-per-view by SPs for digital TV subscribers. Another type of VoD service is called as Near-

---

[1] This is one way of maximizing the availability.

VoD services (NVoD) [4], and it distributes videos over multicast or broadcast channels to serve the requests which demand the same videos and arrive close in time. These technologies have been successful to provide video services in local area networks, say in hotels.

Table 1. Key Issues in the Design of DMMS

Key Issues	Remarks
Networking infrastructure planning; Number of nodes(service and storage) + local proxies; policies on service portfolio; user interface; agent driven service or not;	Networking related issues at the time of implementation; the rest are based on SPs business policies- type of services that are supported and storage of media; number of copies; acquiring popularity profile, etc
Disk and Memory Scheduling and Caching (Block/Interval) Strategies	Within a node level this is extremely an important issue
Designing Distributed object Replacement Algorithms	Primary concern both at node and system level to seek optimum performance; global replacement algorithms can be in place for improving the overall service quality
Placement of Media data	Primary concern to improve the overall service quality; Both at disk and network levels are considered; Could be dynamic in the sense that vantage sites can be decided for maximizing the availability
Admission control algorithms	At the scheduling nodes; For centralized architectures, this is a single node issue; Retrieval mechanisms become an influencing part of this category
Source to Destination delivery path planning	This is from SP's perspective
Type of communications : Broadcasting, multicasting or unicasting; advanced techniques- pyramid, batching, etc	Systems perspective; Sometimes left to the application to decide depending on service portfolio; Objectives such as maximizing the number of customers, media distribution, etc are of primary concern here
Mode of delivery: Single or multiple server usage for servicing clients	Systems perspective and service category
Synchronization/Object oriented design of media Objects	At the system level and important at presentation layer
Multimedia Databases	Primary concern from system's perspective; Includes data organization(lower level issue) and retrieval mechanisms;
Quality-of-Service (QoS)	Manifests at all levels and influences the performance in a complex way; serves as one of the invaluable performance metrics

Media Streaming as a solution to handle large client pool: Fundamentals on media types and concepts pertaining to what media streaming is can be found in [5]. A straightforward technology to realize streaming is to *unicast* streams is by allocating dedicated resources for each individual client session. As this is never a cost effective solution and non-scalable, IP-based multicast approaches were proposed. Techniques such as Batching, Patching, Merging, Periodical and Pyramid broadcasting, etc fall into this category. These can be found in [4,11]. Several variants also exist in the literature to these fundamental schemes. Here, multiple requests share a video stream via the network; thereby the required server network I/O bandwidth can be reduced.

Various types of Media Distribution: There exist several practical approaches to media distribution, ranging from distributing small sized clips to long movies. The solution attempts include: *proxy-based approach* [6], *parallel or clustered servers approach* [7], and *co-operative server scheduling* [8]. In proxy-based approach, a cluster of proxies are placed at vantage sites which can intercept the client requests or client requests can be redirected to these proxies for balancing the overall load and also to minimize access delays. However, in parallel or clustered servers approach, the system sends each request to all the servers and all the servers participate equally to serve the request. This mechanism is shown to enable to improve the system throughput and balance the load of each server. In the case of co-operative type, servers cooperate in a joint caching and scheduling of streams and the typical problem is in deciding when, where, and how long to cache a stream before it can be delivered to the clients and this caching on-the-fly is done for serving several requests demanding the same stream.

Caching in DMMS: Caching is one of the inevitable and powerful solution approaches that influence almost every performance metric under consideration. "Cache-or-not-to-Cache" is often a most common dilemma of the algorithms in place as the decision is based on a combined influence of several parameters. Caching allows nodes to quickly fetch the required documents without incurring annoying delays by circumventing the need to contact the original host. Caching can be at memory/disk level or at node level. Again, performance of a DMMS system can also be quantified in terms of local as well in global terms. In memory caching, the high-speed main memory is referred to as the cache of the relatively slow-speed disk [6,9], while in disk caching, a near-distance disk (e.g., a proxy) is used as the cache of the far-distance disk (e.g., in original server), or the disk is used as the cache of tertiary storage, e.g., CD, tape. For modern day applications, even acquiring a small amount of an intermediate storage seems a critical issue to account for. Day-to-day storage devices have capacities ranging from 18GBytes cache space (Seagate cheetah) to 250Mbytes (Toshiba Flash memories) and bandwidths in MB/sec in the range of 63.2 to 10, respectively. To improve the cache space of storage devices, Redundant Arrays of Inexpensive Disks (RAID) was proposed in [9] to combine multiple small, inexpensive disk drives into an array of disk drives. This disk array can yield performance exceeding that of a single large disk drive related to space, speed and data protection. Apart from these technology oriented advantages, caching schemes such as *Interval Caching, Block caching, Resource-based caching, Multi-policy integrated caching*, etc, attempts to maximize the throughput of the system by cleverly caching streams of media either on-the-fly or on demand. Compilation in [11] gives details on some of these techniques.

Miscellaneous Issues: Other issues at a higher level (system design level) that influence the performance critically include, multimedia databases (access and retrieval), object oriented development of such multimedia information systems, monetary cost optimization, movie placement at vantage sites. Some peripheral issues concerned include, building a distributed multimedia archive, an efficient search engine with or without agent-driven characteristics, an information repository (similar to yellow-page e-directory services), a flexible GUI to user and tracking user behavior. At the lower levels, issues concerned range from data organization, disk scheduling, and retrieving of data to memory management at node and system levels.

Some Key Performance Metrics and Useful Results

Three main key performance metrics that are akin to DMMS are discussed below.

Quality of Service (QoS): Meeting a high-quality QoS demands is often a conflicting issue. From user's perspective it is the timely delivery, full presentation control without any jitters and minimum access delays, while from SPs perspective optimal use of resources for maximizing the number of clients and meeting their demands. With Internet's modern day best effort point-to-point services, quality can be assured. However, for multimedia traffic[2] QoS management is much more challenging. In the literature, there exist several models to capture statistical behavior and nature of multimedia traffic. These include, Markov modulated process models, Fractional Brownian motion model, Hybrid Bounding Interval Dependent (H-BIND) model, M/Pareto distribution model, Self-similar traffic model, and MPEG coded video traffic models, etc. The kind of parameters that a QoS management system must consider on the whole can be classified based on, (i) Network level QoS and, (ii) Application level QoS. Typical to the first category are transmission bit rates, delay, jitters, packet-loss, error rates, etc. IETF (Internet Engineering Task Force) has proposed several promising models such as *Intserv* (Integrated Service model) and *Diffserv* (Differentiated Service model) [12], for supporting multimedia traffic over IP network. The essence of IntServ is to reserve resources (link bandwidth and buffer space) for each individual session so that the QoS can be guaranteed. Details on Diffserve and Intserv can be found in the above literature. A variety of QoS management architectures and technologies have been investigated to provide the desired QoS for the applications having divergent needs. The mechanism of QoS management includes connection acceptance, negotiation of the QoS, congestion control, traffic enforcement, and resource allocation. Several other possible QoS parameters are presented in [13]. QoS aware techniques also exist and these belong to Network-layer and Application-layer multicasting categories.

Access Time: This is one of the key considerations for most of the services offered on networks [2,8]. This is the time duration for which a subscribed user has to wait to avail the service. In VoD case, this is the difference in time between the instant when a user places a request and when the video is available for viewing at the client end. This is more of an issue that is usually from user's perspective and even SPs may use this as their "service promise" in rendering high quality services. Several techniques are in place to minimize this access time. These include, pyramid broadcasting, multiple servers retrieval, careful placement of copies of movies at vantage sites for quick access,

---

[2] Constant bit-rate(CBR) or variable bit-rate (VBR), bursty are a few to quote.

replication of copies of movies, etc, are a few to quote[11]. For large-scale networks this is an important metric to be considered by a SP.

<u>Acceptance Ratio/Blocking Probability and Throughput</u>: This metric is particularly meaningful when requests are for small clips and do not require significant amount of resources to consume. For instance, for VoD or pay-per-view kind of applications, as clients are primarily subscribed with the SP, it will not be meaningful if SP declines a client's request. However, when requests arrive in a time-continuous fashion demanding shorter service requirements, depending on the current loading some requests may be dropped, which leads to these metrics. Also, quantifying the amount of throughput or equivalently the fraction of accepted or rejected requests usually considers a fairly large amount of observation over time by any algorithm/SP. These metrics work in conjunction with caching and cache replacement algorithms that are in place. Hence, most of the literature presenting cache performance also considers these metrics.

Conclusions

In this article we presented an overview of modern day DMMS and summarized all the primary issues leading to the design of DMMS. The literature cited here is by no means exhaustive as DMMS is an ever challenging and growing domain and subsumes several issues in a complex way. A good design of DMMS must attempt to satisfy the common three-letter rule "F-A-S" (can also be referred to as *performability*) – i.e., it must consider Flexibility (in terms of adapting to client's needs and accommodating other applications), Availability of service, and Scalability (in terms of providing a quality service when client population and size of the network grows). As a final remark, a modern day DMMS also considers wireless networks as a connection medium for small scale multimedia applications. However, supporting continuous streaming and interactive multimedia applications is still a major challenge ahead for wireless systems.

See: Long Duration Continuous Media Retrieval on Large-Scale Networked Systems.

References
1. C.H. Papadimitriou, S. Randmanathan, P. Venkat Rangan, and S. Sampathkumar, "Multimedia Information Caching for Personalized Video-on-Demand," Computer Communications, Vol. 18, No. 3, March 1995, pp. 204-216.
2. B. Veeravalli and G. D. Barlas, "Access Time Minimization for Distributed Multimedia Applications," Multimedia Tools and Applications, Kluwer Academic Publishers, Vol. 12, 2000, pp. 235-256.
3. J.B.K. Won and H.Y. Yoem, "Providing VCR Functionality in Staggered Video Broadcasting," IEEE Transactions on Consumer Electronics, Vol. 48, No. 1, 2002, pp. 41-48.
4. L. H. Chang and K.-C. Lai, "Near video-on-demand systems with combining multicasting and unicasting batching," Proceedings of the IEEE International Conference on Electrical and Electronic Technology, 2001, TENCON, Vol. 1, August 2001, pp. 198-201.
5. B. Furht, "Multimedia Technologies and Applications for the 21st Century", Kluwer Academic Publishers, 1998.

6. S. Sen, J. Rexford, and D. Towsley, "Proxy prefix caching for multimedia streams," Proceedings of IEEE INFOCOM, March 1999, pp. 1310-1319.
7. J. Y. B. Lee, "Buffer Management and Dimensioning for a Pull-Based Parallel Video Server," IEEE Transactions on Circuits and Systems for Video Technology, Vol. 11, No. 4, 2001, pp. 485-496.
8. D. Ligang, V. Bharadwaj, and C.C. Ko, "Efficient Movie Retrieval Strategies for Movie-On-Demand Multimedia Services on Distributed Networks," Multimedia Tools and Applications, Kluwer Academic, Vol. 20, No. 2, 2003, pp. 99-133.
9. S.-H. G. Chanand and F.Tobagi, "Distributed Servers Architecture for Networked Video Services," IEEE/ACM Transactions on Networking, Vol. 9, No. 2, April 2001, pp. 125-136.
10. S.M. Chung, "Multimedia Information Storage and Management," Kluwer Academic Publishers, 1996.
11. D. Sitaram and A. Dan, "Multimedia Servers: Design, Environments, and Applications," Morgan Kaufman Publishers, San Francisco, USA, 1999.
12. RFC 1633, RFC 2212, RFC 2215, RFC 2474, and RFC 2475, http://www.ietf.org/rfc.html, Internet Engineering Task Force (IETF).
13. A. Vogel, B. Kerherve, G. von Bochmann, and J. Gecsei, "Distributed Multimedia and QOS: A Survey," IEEE Multimedia, Vol. 2, No. 2, 1995, pp. 10-19.
14. J. Y. B. Lee, "On a Unified Architecture for Video-on-Demand Services," IEEE Transactions on Multimedia, Vol. 4, No. 1, March 2002, pp. 38-47.

DOCUMENT STANDARDS IN MULTIMEDIA NEWS SYSTEMS

Definition: *The International Press and Telecommunication Council (IPTC) has been developing news formats and standards to capture data and meta-information on news, following the specific needs and requirements of the multimedia news industry.*

Although most significant information in the news area is stored in traditional text files, the information management in the news context has been modernized and adopted towards a unique set of contents within international cooperation work. The International Press and Telecommunication Council (IPTC), has been developing news formats and standards to capture data and meta-information on news, following the specific needs and requirements of the multimedia news industry. The IPTC was established in 1965 by a group of news organizations including the Alliance Européenne des Agences de Presse, ANPA (now NAA), FIEJ (now WAN) and the North American News Agencies (a joint committee of Associated Press, Canadian Press and United Press International) to safeguard the telecommunications interests of the World's Press. Lately IPTC's activities have primarily focused on developing and publishing Industry Standards for the interchange of news data.

Since the development of XML the work on meta data management has been seriously improved and the IPTC has developed two specific formats for online news management: NITF (News Industry Text Format, current Version 3.2), and NewsML.

NITF uses the eXtensible Markup Language to define the content and structure of news articles. Because metadata is applied throughout the news content, NITF documents are far more searchable and useful than HTML pages.

The IPTC started to work on an XML-based standard to represent and manage news throughout its entire lifecycle, including production, interchange, and consumer use in 1999. Following requirements definitions, specifications and development, NewsML 1.0 was approved by IPTC in October 2000. The latest work of IPTC experts focuses on version 2 of NewsML, which provides metadata management for any type of news contents. NewsML can be applied at all stages in the (electronic) news lifecycle. It would be used in and between editorial systems, between news agencies and their customers, between publishers and news aggregators, and between news service providers and end users. Because it is intended for use in electronic production, delivery and archiving it does not include specific provision for traditional paper-based publishing, though formats intended for this purpose - such as the News Industry Text Format (NITF) can be accommodated. Similarly it is not primarily intended for use in editing news content, though it may be used as a basis for systems doing this.

Multimedia content types such as image formats, audio- and video files are integrated with appropriate markup and description elements in the NewsML language. The need for NewsML came from the continuing growth in production, use and re-use of news throughout the world, with rapid expansion of the Internet being a strong driving force. The IPTC not only provides news exchange formats to the news industry but also creates and maintains sets of topics to be assigned as metadata values to news objects in NewsML or NITF, like text, photographs, graphics, audio- and video files and streams. This allows for a consistent coding of news metadata over the course of time – thus making these sets the IPTC NewsCodes.

Modern multimedia services integrate content types of text, images, audio data and streams and current video formats such as MPEG2, MPEG4, MPEG7 and multimedia broadcasting technologies and initiatives like MHP and DVB for providing future interactive digital news access via television, internet and mobile devices.

See: Multimedia News Systems

References

1.   IPTC Internet description, http://www.iptc.org, status of April 2005.

E

EDGE DETECTION

Definition: *Edge detection is a process of transforming an input digital image into an edge map which can be viewed as a line drawing image.*

More specifically, edge detection is a process of transforming an input digital image, color or otherwise, into an edge map which can be viewed as a line drawing image with a spatial resolution identical to that of the input (Figure 1) [1]-[3]. An intensity edge map corresponds to sudden changes in brightness which tends to occur at object boundaries. The locations of these changes reflect the shapes of objects. The most popular edge operators generate the edge maps by processing information contained in a local image neighborhood as it is determined by an element of support. These operators i) do not use any prior information about the image structure, ii) are image content agnostic, and iii) are localized, in the sense that the detector output is solely determined by the features obtained through the element of support [1]-[3].

(a)   (b)

Figure 1. Color edge detection: (a) color image, (b) corresponding edge map.

The development of an efficient edge detector, which properly detects the objects' edges, is a rather demanding task. Assuming scalar signals, such as gray-scale images, edges are commonly defined as physical, photometric and geometrical discontinuities in the image function, as physical edges often coincide with places of strong illumination and reflection changes [1] [2]. Since very often the image contrast is proportional to the scene illumination, identified edges are located in that part of the image where rapid image intensity changes take place. It is therefore reasonable to conclude that edges are the boundaries of distinct, in intensity, image regions. However, the definition of an edge in multichannel images is more complex. Compared to gray-scale images, multichannel images carry additional information contained in the various spectral channels. This information can be used to identify and detect edges in multichannel images such as the conventional color images (three channels) [1] [2] or cDNA microarray images (two channels) [3]. In this case, the boundary between two surfaces with different properties can be determined in more than one way.

See: Color image filtering and enhancement, Scalar edge detectors, Vector edge detectors.

References

1. R. Lukac, K.-N. Plataniotis, A.-N. Venetsanopoulos, R. Bieda, and B. Smolka, "Color Edge Detection Techniques," In "Signaltheorie und Signalverarbeitung, Akustik und Sprachakustik, Informationstechnik," W.E.B. Universität Verlag, Dresden, Vol. 29, 2003, pp.21-47.
2. K.-N. Plataniotis and A.-N. Venetsanopoulos, "Color Image Processing and Applications," Springer Verlag, Berlin, 2000.
3. R. Lukac and K.-N. Plataniotis, "Vector Edge Operators for cDNA Microarray Spot Localization," IEEE Transactions on Nanobioscience, submitted for publication.

EDGE-SENSING MECHANISM

Definition: *An edge-sensitive mechanism provides a camera with a capability of maintaining edge information while performing the processing operations.*

A well-designed camera image processing solution should maintain the edge information while performing the processing operations [1]-[3]. Edges are important features since they indicate the presence and the shape of various objects in the image. To preserve edges and details in the captured image, an edge-sensing mechanism should be employed in the processing pipeline.

Both an adaptive behavior of the processing solution and tracking of the structural content of the image data are obtained using the so called edge-sensing weights. Weights are used to regulate the contribution of the available samples inside the spatial arrangements under consideration, emphasize inputs which are not positioned across an edge, and to direct the demosaicking process along the natural edges in the true image. This ensures a sharply formed output camera image.

In most available designs the edge-sensing coefficients use some form of inverse gradient [1]-[3]. Since large image gradients usually indicate that the corresponding inputs are located across edges, weights, defined inversely proportional to gradient values, are used to penalize the associated inputs.

See: Digital camera image processing, Demosaicking, CFA image zooming, Demosaicked image postprocessing, Color image zooming, Spectral model, Color image processing and enhancement.

References
1. R. Lukac, K.-N. Plataniotis, D. Hatzinakos, and M. Aleksic, "A Novel Cost Effective Demosaicing Approach," IEEE Trans. Consumer Electronics, Vol. 50, No. 1, February 2004, pp. 256-261.
2. B.-K. Gunturk, J. Glotzbach, Y. Altunbasak, R.-W. Schaffer, and R.-M. Murserau, "Demosaicking: Color Filter Array Interpolation," IEEE Signal Processing Magazine, Vol. 22, No. 1, pp. 44-54, January 2005.
3. R. Lukac, K.-N. Plataniotis, and D. Hatzinakos, "Color Image Zooming on the Bayer Pattern," IEEE Transactions on Circuit and Systems for Video Technology, Vol. 15, 2005.

ELEMENTS OF MULTIMEDIA IN EDUCATION

Definition: Elements of multimedia used in education include text, video, sound, graphics, and animation.

The growth in use of multimedia within the education sector has accelerated in recent years, and looks set for continued expansion in the future. The elements used in multimedia have all existed before. Multimedia simply combines these elements into a powerful new tool, especially in the hands of teachers and students. Interactive multimedia weaves five basic types of media into the learning environment: text, video, sound, graphics and animation. Since the mode of learning is interactive and not linear, a student or teacher can choose what to investigate next. When is sound more meaningful than a picture? How much text is too much? Does the graphic overwhelm the screen? For a student, this allows them to test all of their skills gained in every subject area. Interactive multimedia learning mode is more like constructing a spider's web, with one idea linked to another, allowing choices in the learner's path.

Out of all of the elements, **text** has the most impact on the quality of the multimedia interaction. Generally, text provides the important information. Text acts as the keystone tying all of the other media elements together.

Sound is used to provide emphasis or highlight a transition from one page to another. Sound synchronized to screen display, enables teachers to present lots of information at once. Sound used creatively, becomes a stimulus to the imagination; used inappropriately it becomes a hindrance or an annoyance.

The representation of information by using the visualization capabilities of **video** can be immediate and powerful. While this is not in doubt, it is the ability to choose how we view, and interact, with the content of digital video that provides new and exciting possibilities for the use of digital video in education. Video can stimulate interest if it is relevant to the rest of the information on the page, and is not 'overdone'. One of the most compelling justifications for video may be its dramatic ability to elicit an emotional response from an individual.

Animation is used to show changes in state over time, or to present information slowly to students so they have time to assimilate it in smaller chunks. Animations, when combined with user input, enable students to view different versions of change over time depending on different variables. Animations are primarily used to demonstrate an idea or illustrate a concept. Video is usually taken from life, whereas animations are based on drawings.

Graphics provide the most creative possibilities for a learning session. They can be photographs, drawings, graphs from a spreadsheet, pictures from CD-ROM, or something pulled from the Internet. With a scanner, hand-drawn work can be included. Standing commented that, "the capacity of recognition memory for pictures is almost limitless". The reason for this is that images make use of a massive range of cortical skills: color, form, line, dimension, texture, visual rhythm, and especially imagination.

See: Multimedia in Education

EMBEDDING MULTIPLE WATERMARKS IN A TRANSFORM DOMAIN

Definition: Multiple watermarks can be embedded in an image by using different subbands.

In a recent non-blind watermarking paper [1], two visual watermarks are embedded in the DWT domain through modification of both low and high values of DWT coefficients. Since the advantages and disadvantages of lower and higher subband watermarks are complementary, embedding multiple watermarks in an image would result in a scheme that is highly robust with respect to a large spectrum of image processing operations. After performing a two level decomposition of the cover image, the authors embed the first watermark in the LL2 band, and the second watermark in the HH2 band. According to their experimental results, embedding in the LL2 band is more resistant to JPEG compression, wiener filtering, Gaussian noise, scaling, and cropping while embedding in the HH2 band is more resistant to histogram equalization, intensity adjustment, and gamma correction. Nevertheless, the implementation of the idea is seriously flawed. Without taking into consideration the difference in magnitudes of lower and higher DWT coefficients, the scheme is implemented with a scaling factor of 0.1 for both bands. This leads to highly visible degradation in all parts of the image, especially in low frequency areas such as the wall, causing two major detriments: the commercial value of the image is reduced, and a clue is provided to the hacker for unauthorized removal of the watermark.

In [2], the idea is generalized by embedding the same watermark in all four bands using first and second level decompositions. The watermark embedded in the largest DWT coefficients is robust against JPEG compression, low pass filtering, Gaussian noise, rescaling, rotation, cropping, pixelation, and sharpening, and the watermark embedded in the smallest DWT coefficients is robust against histogram equalization, intensity adjustment, and gamma correction. In the implementation of the scheme, the scaling factor is larger for the lower frequency band, not causing any visible distortion in the watermarked image.

In a semi-blind watermarking scheme [3], a binary logo is embedded in color images in the DFT domain. After computing the DFT of the cover image, the magnitudes of DFT coefficients are compared, and modified. The given watermark is embedded in three frequency bands: low, middle, and high. The experiments show that the watermarks extracted from the lower frequencies have the best visual quality for low pass filtering, Gaussian noise, JPEG compression, resizing, rotation, and scaling, and the watermarks extracted from the higher frequencies have the best visual quality for cropping, intensity adjustment, histogram equalization, and gamma correction. Extractions from the fragmented and translated image are identical to extractions from the unattacked watermarked image. The collusion and rewatermarking attacks do not provide the hacker with useful tools.

See: Protection of Multimedia Data in Distribution and Storage

References

1. R. Mehul and R. Priti, "Discrete Wavelet Transform Based Multiple Watermarking Scheme," Proceedings of IEEE Region 10 Technical Conference on Convergent Technologies for the Asia-Pacific, Bangalore, India, October 14-17, 2003.
2. P. Tao and A. M. Eskicioglu, "A Robust Multiple Watermarking Scheme in the Discrete Wavelet Transform Domain," Optics East 2004 Symposium, Internet Multimedia Management Systems V Conference, Philadelphia, PA, October 25-28, 2004.
3. J. Kusyk, "A Semi-Blind Logo Watermarking Scheme for Color Images through Comparison and Modification of DFT Coefficients," M.S. Dissertation, Department of CIS, CUNY Brooklyn College.

EMERGENT SEMANTICS

Definition: Emergent semantics deals with discovering and managing a media object's set of context and high-level descriptor pairs.

In the past, multimedia documents were described to users via various sorts of textual descriptors. Librarians described these documents using various structured languages, hoping to convey their contents accurately to users. Over time, more and more researchers became of the opinion that there were more to images (and, by extension, to other forms of media), than could be described by short descriptors in some formal text-based language. They believed that by extracting various content-based descriptors, they could somehow convey automatically the complete nature of media contents in an objective fashion. They lost sight of the fact that media objects may not have a unique, objective nature, and that, even if they did possess such a nature, discovering it would be very difficult. Media objects, after all, also evoke emotions in people and this goes a long way in explaining their differential effects for different people.

It was soon realized that rather than trying to discover a media object's hidden meaning, researchers should try to invent ways of managing media objects so as to help people make more intelligent use of them. They should initiate studies on the *relationship* between users and media objects. Media objects should be interpreted relative to the particular goal or point-of-view of a particular user at a particular time. Media objects that would satisfy a user at one time may not satisfy him at other times. And, of course, media objects that would satisfy one user may not satisfy other users, even at the same time.

Of course, content-based descriptors are necessary to this process, but they are definitely not sufficient. This was soon realized and another far-sighted group of researchers studied measured interactions between users and media objects, with the ultimate goal of trying to satisfy the user community by providing them with the media objects they required individually, based on their previous media interactions. Thus, the field of *emergent media semantics* was born. So, the multimedia community has finally learned that *context* cannot be ignored, but should, and can, be managed. And, that discovering and managing a media object's set of context, high-level descriptor pairs is an important problem.

See: Image Retrieval

References

1. S. Santini, A. Gupta, and R. Jain, "Emergent Semantics Through Interaction in Image Databases," IEEE Transactions on Knowledge and Data Engineering, Vol. 13, No. 3, May/June 2001, pp. 337-351.
2. S. Staab (Ed.), "Emergent Semantics," IEEE Intelligent Systems, Vol. 17, No. 1, January/February 2002, pp. 78-86.

EMOTION AND MULTIMEDIA CONTENT

Definition: Multimedia content can today include the representation, measurements and prediction of emotions.

Representing, measuring, and predicting the emotion related to multimedia content is now accepted as being able to add significant value to multimedia systems; for example, to add an additional querying dimension to multimedia content-based retrieval systems, to enable personalized multimedia content filtering based on emotional intensity, and so on. Emotions are governed by our appraisal of environmental stimuli and our motivation to approach or avoid them. Using subjects' various facial expressions and physiological and behavioral responses to various stimuli, it is possible to infer many emotions, such as happiness, surprise, fear, and so forth. These emotions have been shown to correlate with a two-dimensional space, often termed an *affect space*, made up of two independent dimensions: *valence* or pleasantness (negative to positive) and *arousal* (low to high). For example, fear would invoke negative valence and high arousal. The affect space provides a straightforward but effective means of representing both primary (primitive) and secondary (compound) emotions, which in turn presents a tangible baseline with which to categorize, measure, assess, and predict emotional response.

Approaches to the utilization of emotion in multimedia content research have thus far varied. For example, Colombo and Del Bimbo [1] enable the retrieval of video commercials by emotion based on conformance to semantic indices and similarity to videos held within the database. They abstract emotional content by using a rule-based mapping of perceptual features, such as motion and color, on to the emotional categories of action, excitement, suspense, quietness, relaxation, and happiness. Hanjalic [2] has focused specifically on measuring excitement in video from low-level features, including motion activity, energy in the audio track, and the density of cuts. Results are presented in the form of excitement time curves, modeling temporal frame indices and corresponding excitement levels. The approach has proved successful with various types of content, including that from movies and sports footage. Conversely, Kang [3] has proposed a method to identify fear, sadness and joy from video by analyzing color, motion and shot cut rate, coupled with user relevance feedback to train and improve system performance.

MPEG-7 serves as a first attempt to standardize how multimedia systems may represent emotional metadata. Within its Multimedia Description Schemes, the Affective Description Scheme enables description of a user's emotional response to various types of multimedia content, such as video segments, semantic entities (e.g. events and objects), and so on. Numeric scores on a scale of -1.0 to 1.0 are used to represent the relative intensity of the affective response with respect to a specified affect type. While any set of affect types can be applied, a set of typical types is provided by the AffectType Classification Scheme: *interested, excited, bored, surprised, sad, hateful, angry, expectant, happy, scared, storyComplication* and *storyShape*.

See: Multimedia content modeling and personalization

References

1. C. Colombo and A. Del Bimbo, "Retrieval of Commercials by Video Semantics," Proceedings of the IEEE International Conference on Computer Vision and Pattern Recognition, 1998, pp. 572-577.
2. A. Hanjalic, "Multimodal Approach to Measuring Excitement in Video," Proceedings of the IEEE International Conference on Multimedia and Expo (ICME '03), Vol. 2, 2003, pp. 289-292.
3. H.-B. Kang, "Emotional Event Detection using Relevance Feedback," Proceedings of the International Conference on Image Processing, Vol. 1, 2003, pp. 721-724.

ENCRYPTION IN RTP

Definition: Encryption in Real-time Transport Protocol is used to ensure the confidentiality of the media content.

To transport multimedia over the Internet, appropriate protocol is needed. For instance, RTP, Real-time Transport Protocol [1], are created as a standard protocol for the end-to-end network transport of real-time data, including audio and video. Today, RTP is often used through Internet that can not be considered secure. To ensure the confidentiality of the media content, encryption has to be used. To support on-demand and live streaming media services, a streaming media system needs to support pre-encryption and live-encryption respectively. Further, the system must be capable of delivering the decryption key to the authorized clients securely.

In RTP, when encryption is desired, all the octets that will be encapsulated for transmission in a single lower-layer packet are encrypted as a unit. The presence of encryption and the use of the correct key are confirmed by the receiver through header or payload validity checks. The default encryption algorithm in RTP is specified to be Data Encryption Standard (DES) algorithm in cipher block chaining (CBC) mode [2].

Strong encryption algorithms, such as Triple-DES, can be used in place of the default algorithm for better security. In addition, profiles may define additional payload types for encrypted encodings. RTP consists of a data and a control part. The latter is called RTCP. A framework for encryption of RTP and RTCP streams is provided in SRTP, the Secure Real-time Transport Protocol [3]. SRTP is a profile of RTP that defines a set of default cryptographic transforms. It allows new transforms to be introduced in the future. With appropriate key management, SRTP is secure for unicast and multicast RTP applications.

In RTP, mixer is used to perform remixing of RTP streams, including encrypted streams. They are able to decrypt and re-encrypt streams. Translators are another type of application level devices in RTP. They perform payload format conversions, tunnel the packets through firewalls, and add or remove encryption and enable the coexistence of the different networking technologies. Since in many applications, not all information should be confidential, the use of mixer and translator can help to optimize network usage. As RTP is often used for transferring huge amounts of time critical data, for example video, it is essential that all security features are implemented with minimal delay and jitter. It should be evident that with huge transmission rates even a small timing overhead easily amounts to huge loss of bandwidth[12]. RTP, implemented on an application bases, provides the flexibility to allow splitting of packets into encrypted and unencrypted parts.

Interested readers are directed to IETF's Real-time Transport Protocol [1] and The Secure Real-time Transport Protocol Internet draft [3] documents for more details about the protocols.

See: Multimedia Encryption

References

1. H. Schulzrinne, S. Casner, R. Frederick, and V. Jacobson, "RTP: A Transport Protocol for Real-Time Applications," IETF Internet Draft, RFC-1889, January 1996.
2. B. Schneier, "Applied Cryptography," 2nd edition, John Wiley & Sons, Inc, 1996.

3. M. Baugher, D. McGrew, E. Carrara, M. Naslund, and K. Norrman, "The Secure Real-time Transport Protocol," <draft-ietf-avt-srtp-09.txt>, IETF Internet Draft, December 2003.

EXPERIENTIAL MEDIA SYSTEMS

Hari Sundaram and Thanassis Rikakis
Arts Media and Engineering Program
Arizona State University, Tempe, AZ, USA

Definition: *Experiential media systems refer to new, complementary model of media computing, which allows us to develop a rich contextual understanding of human activity, at different scales of time and space, as well as affect human activity in a radically new way.*

Our civilization is currently undergoing major changes. Traditionally, human beings acquired knowledge through experiential interactions with the physical world. That knowledge allowed them to better adapt to their reality and evolve. Today our interactions with almost every element of our lives (health, weather, economic and social policy, communication) involve computation and mediated information. However, we still lack effective ways of connecting our computational approaches with our physical experience. To achieve knowledge of our new world and significantly improve our condition we need unified experiences of the physical and computational forces that are shaping our reality.

Experiential media systems refer to new, complementary model of media computing. In the traditional multimedia computing model (e.g. the creation / consumption of a video), capture, analysis, and media consumption are not co-located, synchronous or integrated. We are, however, witnessing a rapid decline in cost of sensing, storage [10], computing and display. Thus, sensors (audio, video, pressure, tangible), computing, ambient visual and sound displays and other feedback devices (vibration, light, heat) can now be co-located in the same physical environment, creating a real-time feedback loop. This allows us to develop a rich contextual understanding of human activity, at different scales of time and space, as well as affect human activity in a radically new way. The goal is to achieve enhanced, user-oriented, unified physical-digital experiences. These media systems will give rise to a new set of multimedia applications grounded in human activity in the physical world.

Experiential media applications

We now briefly discuss on three application areas of societal significance – health, education and everyday living as the driving force for the development of these new media systems. In the health domain these systems can reveal new frameworks for successful interactive biofeedback for rehabilitation. In education, examples include hybrid physical digital environments that enable children to acquire complex concepts in science through natural interfaces and social interaction. In social communication and everyday living, experiential media can summarize human activity and present it as part of the physical environment to reveal the situated context in which it has occurred. We have been working on developing initial prototypes of experiential media systems [14,17]. Our efforts in our application areas include (see Figure 1):

- Biofeedback: We have been working on developing an experiential media system that integrates task dependent physical therapy and cognitive stimuli within an interactive, multimodal environment. The environment provides a purposeful, engaging, visual and auditory scene in which patients can practice functional therapeutic reaching tasks, while receiving different types of simultaneous feedback indicating measures of both performance and results.

- Systems for Everyday Living: We are investigating novel forms of media interaction frameworks (incorporating gestures, tangible interfaces), that use media from everyday user activities [3]. In our current work, we have built a real-time, mediated environment that uses tangible interfaces for facilitating social communication [17].

- Experiential education: We are currently investigating the creation of experiential frameworks for pattern awareness in movement and in shape, for children. In our current work, fused vision and audio sensing is coupled to a system modeling gravity. This helps drive a generative model for audio-visual immersion that is cognitively consistent with the underlying physics concepts.

Figure 1. Top: biofeedback, Middle: tangible interfaces, Bottom: experiential education.

We note that these applications are example starting points for research in experiential media. In due course a number of new and exciting applications will emerge within these areas. They include novel interfaces for real time monitoring of patient performance by clinicians and therapists, interactive multimedia for math and teacher education, assisted home living for the elderly, and robotic assistance in navigation. Research and education activities will result in generic frameworks that can also be applied to other problem areas such as intuitive navigation of large scale data sets and new classes of interfaces for fast solutions to complex science problems (i.e. electromagnetic interference in integrated circuits). Figure 2 illustrates tangible interfaces for shared media browsing.

Figure 2. Tangible interfaces for shared media browsing.

Motivating ideas

Experiential media analysis has been motivated by research in artificial intelligence, distributed cognition, human computer interaction / ubiquitous computing as they relate to the physical world.

Artificial Intelligence

There are two research areas in AI that are particularly relevant – robotics [4,5] and bounded rationality [21]. Rodney Brooks' robots essentially contained a set of loosely interacting behaviors (move left leg, avoid obstacles etc.), that were implemented in hardware with short paths from sensors to actuators. The behaviors were all simultaneously active, but there was a hardwired arbitration amongst them. They had no centralized reasoning unit or stored abstract representation of the world. The resulting robots seemed to be "intelligent" to human observers and were capable of complex behavior in the real world spaces. There are three crucial ideas here – situatedness, embodiment and intelligence. Situatedness is the idea that rather using an abstract stored representation of the world, "the world is its own best model" [5] – the current state of the world is responded to by the robot (via the behaviors). Embodiment is the idea that physical grounding is crucial to intelligence and finally the last idea is that intelligence emerges though the dynamics of interaction with the world. Reactivity is another important idea [5] – the ability of the robot to be able to respond to the world in a timely manner is an important aspect of intelligence. Russell's work on bounded rationality [21] deals with finding programs that maximize the expected utility given the machine and the environment – i.e. the ability to generate maximally successful behavior given available information and computing resources. However, Russell's work deals with abstract dis-embodied agents.

Distributed Cognition

There are three important ideas here [11,13] – (a) cognition may be distributed across members of a social network, (b) cognition results as a consequence of coordination between external and internal structures (c) processes may be distributed over time to affect later events. Hutchins [13] provides the example of a ship navigation to illustrate that different sailors have very specialized tasks that must be carefully coordinated for the ship to navigate safely. An example of how cognition is distributed in space (external) as well as internally – we will often rearrange objects on our desk until an arrangement solves a task like a search – indeed our "messy" work environments are often best suited to finding our belongings. In general, we will *adapt the environment* to solve the cognitive task, rather than solve it entirely in our heads [20].

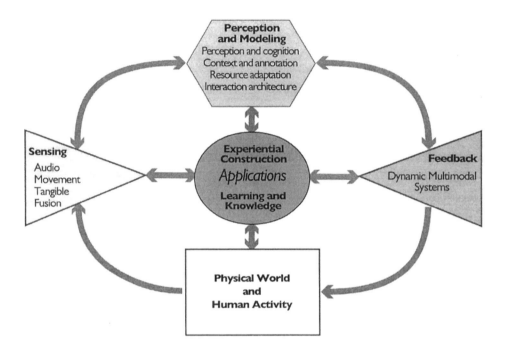

Figure 3. The functional description of an experiential media system.

Human Computer Interaction

Tangible interfaces [15] are an emerging area of interest in the HCI community. They deal with using physical artifacts for both representation and control of media. These interfaces allow us to leverage our extant understanding of the physical world (ability to pick up objects, move objects etc.) to manipulate media. Dourish [9] suggests that in an embodied system – meaning and action are tightly bound together – meaning is an emergent process and achieved through action. Lucy Suchman's work [22] showed that everyday human activities did not have the detailed level of planning found in AI based approaches – indeed they revealed that while human beings may have long term goals such as "I'm going to work" etc. the details of the action are highly improvisatory in nature. For example, you decide to walk to work instead of using the car, then stop by at the coffee shop to pick up some coffee, and then stop to chat with a colleague before heading off to your physical office. She concluded situational resources rather than detailed plans, play an important role in determining human action.

Ubiquitous computing

Marc Weiser's vision [2,23,24] has resulted is many parallel research efforts primarily centered around paradigms of human computer interaction in moving computing away from the desktop [12,19] and context awareness [6,7,8] (limited to location and activity). Importantly, ubiquitous computing has not dealt with research issues concerned with multi-sensory analysis to help us understand the semantics of the interaction.

Summary

A central idea that emerges from these different disciplines is that human activity in the physical world is highly contextualized on the current situational resources. Embodiment allows us to distribute cognitive loads to the environment and also manipulate it to simplify tasks. Meaning can be distributed within a social network, and emerges through dynamic interaction with the environment. Finally, interactions with the environment must be reactive – they must occur in real-time.

The creation of experiential media; challenges and proposed solutions

The development of experiential media systems requires highly integrated research across five areas (see Figure 3).

1. Sensing: multiple types of electronic sensors must be used for sensing and recording the physical world and most importantly human activity. Movement and audio sensing through sensor arrays, pressure and tangible sensors/control devices and multisensory integration and sensor fusion constitute the focal points of our work in this area.

2. Perception and Modeling: The computational modeling of human functioning and sensing allows cognitive and perceptual principles to be incorporated into the design and analysis of control and feedback systems. A clear understanding of cognitive and perceptual capabilities and tendencies, as well as limitations and biases, will be achieved through mathematical modeling and validity testing in the design of new hybrid multimedia systems and interfaces. This will be coupled with research on context representation, annotation, resource adaptation, interaction architectures and computational modeling to optimize the ecological coupling between users and systems. The impact will be to facilitate a cognitively consistent real-time coupling between human action and media perception.

3. Feedback: Appropriate devices and modes of communication must be developed for optimally connecting user(s) into the experiential media environment. The development of dynamic, multimodal feedback systems will allow for content and choice of devices that can adapt and change continuously in congruence with information derived from sensing and modeling areas and the evolving human activity.

4. Experiential construction: The work of the above three areas must be integrally combined with the physical world to produce an enhanced, user-oriented,

physical-digital experience that naturally couples human activity and that can produce new horizons of knowledge and human experience.

5.   Learning and knowledge: The knowledge produced by the resulting physical-digital experience must be evaluated. Weaknesses per component or in the integration of the components must be identified and solutions for improvement and optimization must be developed collaborative with all members of the team creating the system.   Avenues for further evolution of the system and its functioning and learning potential must be identified and tested.

<u>What is the Expertise Needed?</u> The knowledge required to create experiential media systems is fragmented across disciplines. Technological sensing and modeling expertise traditionally lies primarily within engineering. Media communication and experiential construction and design expertise traditionally lies within the arts. Perception, cognition, and learning modeling expertise traditionally lies within psychology and education. Therefore experts from these disciplines will comprise the core of a large interconnected network of experts necessary for experiential media research. Other disciplinary experts are vital to the development of specific applications and thus the network needs to embrace a range of additional specialty members on those projects. For example, in biofeedback for rehabilitation medical doctors, and physical therapists are included as integral contributors.

<u>Current Media Development:</u> The traditional media computing model has led to the development of tools and content within disciplinary silos. Media tools are mostly created by engineers who focus on data and information processing often without considering user behavior and meaningful communication. Perceptual and cognitive optimization modeling often remains theoretical and incorporation and real-world usability testing of developed principles varies widely. Much of the media content is created by artists and designers with limited training in computation, perception and learning. Psychologists and educators are increasingly using media in their work but their relationship to media development is often one of a client rather than a contributor. Marc Weiser's vision [2,23] addressed many parallel research efforts primarily centered around paradigms of HCI / computing away from the desktop [12] and context awareness [8] (limited to location and activity). While there are wonderful examples of interaction design [15,16], we do not have a principled research framework that integrates knowledge from across disciplines to create experiential media systems.

Interdisciplinary efforts have played a significant role in media development. There have been a number of significant efforts in the past 30 years to bring engineering, arts and sciences together for the creation of new media tools and content. Among them are the MIT Media Lab, the CMU Entertainment Technologies Lab, IRCAM at Centre Pompidou and the CCRMA at Stanford. Projects produced there by a collaboration of traditional artists with traditional engineers resulted only in re-working of existing knowledge. Importantly however, there are a small number of researchers with interdisciplinary engineering-science-arts training, from these institutions, who spearheaded collaborations with a major impact. Miller Puckette, a Professor of Music and Computer Science (UCSD), is a scientist also trained in music who lead the development of the

MAX/MSP [1] software tools for interactive audio/visual creation and manipulation while at IRCAM. Psychologist Steven McAdams, who headed many successful collaborative psychology-engineering-arts projects at IRCAM [18], has a PhD in psychology with specialization in music cognition and has working knowledge of digital signal processing and electronic music composition. The "Beyond Productivity" report of the NRC committee on information technology and creativity suggests that hybrid training across engineering, science and art can produce important innovations in information technology.

The development of experiential media systems must be achieved through the training of a new generation of hybrid media engineers-scientists-artists who approach the issue of media development as an integrated multidisciplinary process. These new media scientists need to: (a) combine discipline specific training in one of the key contributing research areas (sensing, perception, modeling, feedback, experiential construction, learning), with broad understanding of the other research areas; (b) have working knowledge of the connections that exist between the constituting areas; and (c) be able to apply their knowledge to the collaborative creation of physical-digital media systems. The proposed training and development requires a large interdisciplinary network of faculty and students covering all areas of necessary expertise as well as a common integrative research and education agenda for this network. The Arts, Media and Engineering Program at Arizona State University has a research and educational mission that integrates the required expertise for development of experiential media.

Experiential media can provide a space for imagination and reflection in new and insightful ways. They will allow us to better understand, express and communicate our current experiences and gradually develop into skillful mediated communicators and storytellers. The dynamic, customizable nature of experiential media will increase diversity in expression and communication and encourage personalized active learning. Experiential media in medical rehabilitation will allow for easier, faster, customizable, substantial training of patients and for increased recapturing of lost functions. Enhanced individual expressive and communication abilities will improve psychotherapy and social work. Mediated art forms will be able to holistically investigate and represent today's experiences rather than those of the past. Experiential media can greatly facilitate communication, increase knowledge in all facets of our lives and improve understanding across our global communities.

References

1. *Max/MS*, http://www.cycling74.com.
2. G. D. ABOWD, E. D. MYNATT, and T. RODDEN, "*The human experience [of ubiquitous computing,*"]ournal of IEEE Pervasive Computing Vol. 1, No. 1, pp. 48-57, 2002.
3. P. APPAN, H. SUNDARAM, and D. BIRCHFIELD, "*Communicating everyday experiences,*" Proceedings of the ACM Multimedia Workshop on Story Representation, Mechanism and Context, also AME-TR-2004-07, pp. 17-24, October 2004, New York, New York.
4. R. BROOKS, "*A robust layered control system for a mobile robot,*" IEEE Journal of Robotics and Automation, Vol. 2, No. 1, pp. 14-23, 1986.
5. R. A. BROOKS, "*Intelligence Without Reason,*" International Joint Conference on Artificial Intelligence," pp. 569-595, August 1991, Sydney, Australia, 1991.

6. A. K. DEY, *"Providing Architectural Support for Building Context-Aware Applications,"* College of Computing, Atlanta, Georgia Institute of Technology, PhD Dissertation, 2000.

7. A. K. DEY, *"Understanding and Using Context,"* Personal and Ubiquitous Computing Journal, Vol. 5, No. 1, pp. 4-7, 2001.

8. A. K. DEY and G. D. ABOWD, *"Towards a Better Understanding of Context and Context-Awareness,"* Proceedings of the 3rd International Symposium on Wearable Computers, pp. 21-28, October 1999, San Francisco, CA.

9. P. DOURISH, :Where the action is : the foundations of embodied interaction," MIT Press Cambridge, Mass., 2001.

10. J. GRAY, *"What next?: A dozen information-technology research goals,"* Journal of the ACM, Vol. 50, No. 1, pp. 41-57, 2003.

11. J. HOLLAN, E. HUTCHINS, D. KIRSH, and A. SUTCLIFFE, *"Distributed cognition: toward a new foundation for human-computer interaction research: On the effective use and reuse of HCI knowledge,"* ACM Transactions on Computer-Human Interactions, Vol. 7, No. 2, pp. 174-196, 2000.

12. E. M. HUANG and E. D. MYNATT, *"Semi-public displays for small, co-located groups,"* Proceedings of the SIGCHI conference on Human factors in computing systems, ACM Press, pp. 49-56, Ft. Lauderdale, Florida, USA, 2003.

13. E. HUTCHINS, "Cognition in the wild," MIT Press Cambridge, Mass., 1995.

14. T. INGALLS, T. RIKAKIS, J. JAMES, G. QIAN, F. GUO, et al., *"A Gesture Recognition Engine for the Development of Interactive Multimedia Works,"* Proceedings of the ConGAS Symposium on Gesture Interfaces for Multimedia Systems, March 2004.

15. H. ISHII and B. ULLMER, *"Tangible bits: towards seamless interfaces between people, bits and atoms,"* Proceedings of the SIGCHI conference on Human factors in computing systems, ACM Press, pp 234--241, 1997.

16. H. ISHII, C. WISNESKI, S. BRAVE, A. DAHLEY, M. GORBET, et al., *"AmbientROOM: integrating ambient media with architectural space,"* Proceedings of the CHI 98 conference summary on Human factors in computing systems, ACM Press, pp. 173--174, 1998.

17. S. KELKAR, H. SRIDHARAN, N. MATTAR, H. SUNDARAM, D. BIRCHFIELD, et al., *"Tangible Interfaces For Concept-Based Web Browsing,"* Technical Report, AME-TR-2005-06, January 2005.

18. S. MCADAMS and E. BIGAND, "Thinking in Sound: The Cognitive Psychology of Human Audition," Clarendon, 1993.

19. E. MYNATT, M. BACK, R. WANT, M. BAER and J. B. ELLIS, *"Designing Audio Aura,"* Proceedings of the SIGCHI conference on Human factors in computing systems, April 1998, Los Angeles, CA, 1998.

20. D. A. NORMAN, "The design of everyday things," Basic Books, New York, 2002.

21. S. J. RUSSELL, *"Rationality and intelligence,"* Artificial Intelligence Vol. 94, No. 1-1, pp. 57-77, 1997.

22. L. A. SUCHMAN, "Plans and situated actions: the problem of human-machine communication," Cambridge University Press Cambridge Cambridgeshire, New York, 1987.

23. M. WEISER, *"Some computer science issues in ubiquitous computing,"* Communications of the ACM, Vol. 36, No. 7, pp. 75--84, 1993.

24. M. WEISER and J. S. BROWN, "*The Coming Age of Calm Technology*. Beyond Calculation: The Next Fifty Years of Computing," P. J. DENNING and R. M. METCALFE (Eds.) Copernicus, 1998.

EXTENSIBLE STYLESHEET LANGUAGE

Definition: *The Extensible Stylesheet Language or XSL is a W3C recommendation used for formatting Extensible Markup Language (XML) documents for displaying or reformatting the XML, perhaps using a different schema.*

Since XML is gaining wide acceptance for data interchange, in particular on the Internet, XSL is of great value for translating documents from one XML dialect to another. Highly optimized XSL transformation (XSLT) engines are available on a wide range of platforms (e.g. Java, .Net, Perl) for this purpose.

The XSL syntax is itself XML compliant, and many development tools are available for authoring and debugging XSL transformations. The language is template based as opposed to procedural, and relies heavily on XPATH to select relevant segments of XML documents upon which to perform operations. The resulting output format for XSL can be XML, HTML, or plain text with a range of character encoding and formatting options (see Figure 1.)

For any application that uses XML for data input and output, XSL is the most efficient and platform-independent tool available to enable interoperability with other such applications. The other main benefit of XSL is to separate content from presentation. The source XML data can be transformed through one of several styles to create suitable renderings or user interfaces for a wide range of devices.

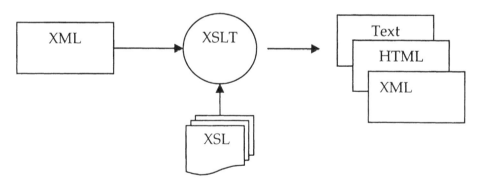

Figure 1. Transforming an XML document using XSL to create alternative representations.

See: Multimedia Content Adaptation

References
1. L. Quin, "The Extensible Stylesheet Language Family (XSL)," W3C. http://www.w3.org/Style/XSL.

F

FACE RECOGNITION

Filareti Tsalakanidou[1,2], Sotiris Malassiotis[2] and Michael G. Strintzis[1,2]
[1] Aristotle University of Thessaloniki, Thessaloniki, Greece
[2] Informatics and Telematics Institute, Centre for Research and Technology Hellas, Thessaloniki, Greece

Definition: *A face recognition system recognizes an individual by matching the input image against images of all users in a database and finding the best match.*

Face recognition has received significant attention in the last 15 years, due to the increasing number of commercial and law enforcement applications requiring reliable personal authentication (e.g. access control, surveillance of people in public places, security of transactions, mug shot matching, and human-computer interaction) and the availability of low-cost recording devices.

Despite the fact that there are more reliable biometric recognition techniques such as fingerprint and iris recognition, these techniques are intrusive and their success depends highly on user cooperation, since the user must position her eye in front of the iris scanner or put her finger in the fingerprint device. On the other hand, face recognition is non-intrusive since it is based on images recorded by a distant camera, and can be very effective even if the user is not aware of the existence of the face recognition system. The human face is undoubtedly the most common characteristic used by humans to recognize other people and this is why personal identification based on facial images is considered the friendliest among all biometrics.

Depending on the application, a face recognition system can be working either on identification or verification mode [1]. In a face identification application, the system recognizes an individual by matching the input image against images of all users in a database and finding the best match. In a face verification application the user claims an identity and the system accepts or rejects her claim by matching the input image against the image that corresponds to this specific identity, which can be stored either in a database or an identification card (e.g. smart card). In other words, face identification is a one-to-many comparison that answers the question "Who is the person in the input image? Is she someone in the database?", while face verification is a one-to-one comparison that answers the question "Is the person in the input image who she claims to be?" In the sequel the term face recognition will be used for both identification and verification unless a distinction needs to be made (see Figure 1).

Image matching usually involves three steps: 1. detection of the face in a complex background and localization of its exact position, 2. extraction of facial features such as eyes, nose, etc, followed by normalization to align the face with the stored face images, and 3. face classification or matching.

In addition, a face recognition system usually consists of the following four modules [1]:

1. Sensor module, which captures face images of an individual. Depending on the sensor modality, the acquisition device maybe a black and white or color camera, a 3D sensor capturing range (depth) data, or an infrared camera capturing infrared images.

2. Face detection and feature extraction module. The acquired face images are first scanned to detect the presence of faces and find their exact location and size. The output of face detection is an image window containing only the face area. Irrelevant information, such as background, hair, neck and shoulders, ears, etc are discarded. The resulting face image is then further processed to extract a set of salient or discriminatory, local or global features, which will be used by the face classifier to identify or verify the identity of an unknown face. Such features maybe the measurements of local facial features (such as eyes, nose, mouth, etc) characteristics or global features such as transformation coefficients of global image decomposition (PCA, LDA, wavelets, etc). These features constitute the template or signature uniquely associated with the image.

3. Classification module, in which the template extracted during step 2 is compared against the stored templates in the database to generate matching scores, which reveal how identical the faces in the probe and gallery images are. Then, a decision-making module either confirms (verification) or establishes (identification) the user's identity based on the matching score. In case of face verification, the matching score is compared to a predefined threshold and based on the result of this comparison, the user is either accepted or rejected. In case of face identification, a set of matching scores between the extracted template and the templates of enrolled users is calculated. If the template of user X produces the best score, then the unknown face is more similar to X, than any other person in the database. To ensure that the unknown face is actually X and not an impostor, the matching score is compared to a predefined threshold.

4. System database module, which is used to extract and store the templates of enrolled users. This module is also responsible for enrolling users in the face recognition system database. During the enrolment of an individual, the sensor module records images of her face. These images are called gallery images and they are used for training the classifier that will perform face recognition. Most commonly, several frontal neutral views of an individual are recorded, but often face images depicting different facial expressions (neutral, smile, laugh, anger, etc) and presence (or non-) of glasses are also acquired. Sometimes gallery images are recorded in more than one session. The time interval between different sessions may result in variations due to

hairstyle, beard, make-up, etc being present in gallery images. The presence of such variations ensures a more robust face recognition performance. Given a user's set of acquired images, a set of features is extracted similarly to step 3 above, and a template that provides a compact and expressive representation of the user based on her images is generated. This is called training. The training algorithm depends on the face recognition method employed by the face recognition system. The aim of the training is to encode the most discriminative characteristics of a user based on the classifier chosen, and to determine the values of the different thresholds. Sometimes, more than one template per enrolled user is stored in the gallery database to account for different variations. Templates may also be updated over time, mainly to cope with variations due to aging.

The different steps of face recognition and a brief description of the most representative face detection and face recognition techniques are presented in the following.

Face Detection

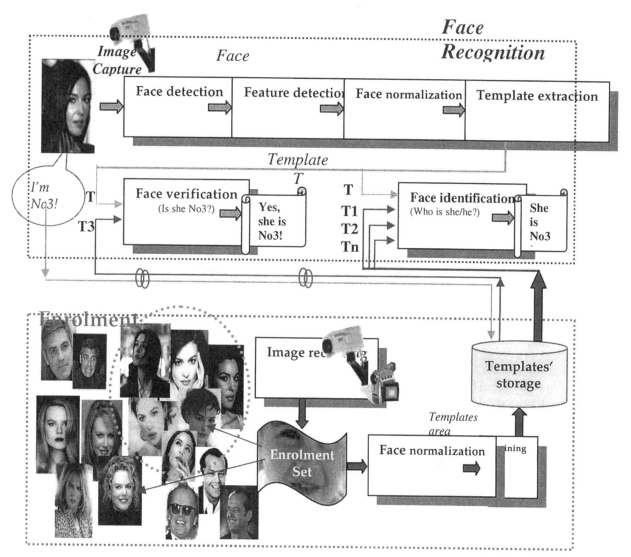

Figure 1. Block diagram of enrolment, face identification and face verification.

Face detection is the first stage of an automatic face recognition system, since a face has to be located in the input image before it is recognized. A definition of face detection could be: given an image, detect all faces in it (if any) and locate their exact positions and size. Usually, face detection is a two-step procedure: first the whole image is examined to find regions that are identified as "face". After the rough position and size of a face are estimated, a localization procedure follows which provides a more accurate estimation of the exact position and scale of the face. So while face detection is most concerned with roughly finding all the faces in large, complex images, which include many faces and much clutter, localization emphasizes spatial accuracy, usually achieved by accurate detection of facial features.

Face detection algorithms can be divided into four categories according to [2]:

1. Knowledge-based methods are based on human knowledge of the typical human face geometry and facial features arrangement. Taking advantage of natural face symmetry and the natural top-to-bottom and left-to-right order in which features appear in the human face, these methods find rules to describe the shape, size, texture and other characteristics of facial features (such as eyes, nose, chin, eyebrows) and relationships between them (relative positions and distances). A hierarchical approach may be used, which examines the face at different resolution levels. At higher levels, possible face candidates are found using a rough description of face geometry. At lower levels, facial features are extracted and an image region is identified as face or non-face based on predefined rules about facial characteristics and their arrangement. The main issue in such techniques is to find a successful way to translate human knowledge about face geometry into meaningful and well-defined rules. Another problem of such techniques is that they do not work very well under varying pose or head orientations [4].

2. Feature invariant approaches aim to find structural features that exist even when the viewpoint or lighting conditions vary and then use these to locate faces. Different structural features are being used: facial local features, texture, and shape and skin color. Local features such as eyes, eyebrows, nose, and mouth are extracted using multi-resolution or derivative filters, edge detectors, morphological operations or thresholding [5]. Statistical models are then built to describe their relationships and verify the existence of a face. Neural networks, graph matching, and decision trees were also proposed to verify face candidates. Skin color is another powerful cue for detection, because color scene segmentation is computationally fast, while being robust to changes in viewpoint, scale, shading, to partial occlusion and complex backgrounds. The color-based approach labels each pixel according to its similarity to skin color, and subsequently labels each sub-region as a face if it contains a large blob of skin color pixels [6]. It is sensitive to illumination, existence of skin color regions, occlusion, and adjacent faces. There are also techniques that combine several features to improve the detection accuracy. Usually, they use features such as texture, shape and skin color to find face candidates and then use local facial features such as eyes, nose and mouth to verify the existence of a face. Feature invariant approaches can be problematic if image features are severely corrupted or deformed due to illumination, noise, and occlusion [2].

3. Template-based methods. To detect a face in a new image, first the head outline, which is fairly consistently roughly elliptical is detected using filters, edge detectors, or silhouettes. Then the contours of local facial features are extracted in the same way, exploiting knowledge of face and feature geometry. Finally, the correlation between features extracted from the input image and predefined stored templates of face and facial features is computed to determine whether there is face present in the image. Template matching methods based on predefined templates are sensitive to scale, shape and pose variations. To cope with such variations, deformable template methods have been proposed, which model face geometry using elastic models that are allowed to translate, scale and rotate [14]. Model parameters may include not only shape, but intensity information of facial features as well.

4. Appearance-based methods. While template-matching methods rely on a predefined template or model, appearance-based methods use large numbers of examples (images of faces and\or facial features) depicting different variations (face shape, skin color, eye color, open\closed mouth, etc). Face detection can be viewed as a pattern classification problem with two classes: "face" and "non-face". The "non-face" class contains images that may depict anything that is not a face, while the "face" class contains all face images. Statistical analysis and machine learning techniques are employed to discover the statistical properties or probability distribution function of the pixel brightness patterns of images belonging in the two classes. To detect a face in an input image, the whole image is scanned and image regions are identified as "face" or "non face" based on these probability functions. Well-known appearance-based methods used for face detection are eigenfaces [7], LDA [7], neural networks, support vector machines and hidden Markov models [9].

Face Recognition

Face recognition techniques can be roughly divided into two main categories: global approaches and feature based techniques [3]. In global approaches the whole image serves as a feature vector, while in local feature approaches a number of fiducial or control points are extracted and used for classification.

Global Approaches for Face Recognition

Global approaches model the variability of the face by analyzing its statistical properties based on a large set of training images. Representative global techniques are eigenfaces [7], Linear Discriminant Analysis (LDA), Support Vector Machines (SVM) and neural networks [3].

The first really successful face recognition method (and a reference point in face recognition literature) is a holistic approach based on principal component analysis (PCA) applied on a set of images in order to extract a set of eigen-images, known as eigenfaces [7]. Every face is modeled as a linear combination of a small subset of these eigenfaces and the weights of this representation are used for recognition. The identification of a test image is done by locating the image in the database, whose weights are the closest to the weights of the test image. The concept of eigenfaces can be extended to eigenfeatures, such as eigeneyes, eigenmouth, etc.

Using a probabilistic measure of similarity instead of the Euclidean distance between weights, the eigenface approach was extended to a Bayesian approach based on image differences [10]. Face recognition is viewed as a two-class classification problem. The first class contains intensity differences between images of the same individual (depicting variations in expression, illumination, head orientation, use of cosmetics, etc) and represents the intrapersonal facial variations. The second class contains intensity differences between images belonging to different people and represents the extrapersonal facial variations due to differences in identity. The distribution probabilities of the two excluding classes are estimated using a large training set. The MAP (Maximum a Posteriori) rule is used for face recognition.

Face recognition techniques using Linear/Fisher Discriminant Analysis (LDA) [7] were also developed. LDA determines a subspace in which the between-class scatter (extrapersonal variability) is as large as possible, while the within-class scatter (intrapersonal variability) is kept constant. In this sense, the subspace obtained by LDA optimally discriminates the classes- faces. A combination of PCA and LDA was also proposed. Other global techniques include Support Vector Machines (SVM) and neural networks (NN) [3].

Feature Based Face Recognition Techniques

The main idea behind feature-based techniques is to discriminate among different faces based on measurements of structural attributes of the face. Most recent approaches are the Embedded Hidden Markov Models (EHMMs) [9], the Elastic Graph Matching [11] and Dynamic Link Architecture [12].

For frontal views the significant facial features appear in a natural order from top to bottom (forehead, eyes, nose, and mouth) and from left to right (e.g. left eye, right eye). EHMMs model the face as a sequence of states roughly corresponding to facial features regions [9]. The probability distribution functions of EHMM states are approximated using observations extracted by scanning training images from left-to-right and top-to-bottom. To verify a face, first the observations are extracted from the input image and then their probability given the stored EHM model is calculated.

One of the most successful feature-based techniques is the Elastic Bunch Graph Matching [11], which is based on the Dynamic Link Architecture (DLA) [12]. The basic idea of EGM is the representation of the face using a set of local image features extracted from the intensity images over fiducial image points and the exploitation of their spatial coherence using a connected graph. Each node in the graph is assigned a set of Gabor wavelet coefficients, over different scales and orientations, extracted from the image function. The graph is adapted to each face in the face database by the minimization of a cost function that locally deforms the graph.

Approaches that use both global and local features have also been proposed. For example, the modular eigenspace approach uses both eigenfaces and eigenfeatures, while the Local Feature Analysis (LFA) extracts topographic local features from the global PCA modes and uses them for recognition.

Problems and Considerations

Automatic face recognition is a particularly complex task that involves detection and location of faces in a cluttered background followed by normalization and recognition. The human face is a very challenging pattern to detect and recognize, because while its anatomy is rigid enough so that all faces have the same structure, at the same time there are a lot of environmental and personal factors affecting facial appearance. The main problem of face recognition is large variability of the recorded images due to pose, illumination conditions, facial expressions, use of cosmetics, different hairstyle, presence of glasses, beard, etc. Images of the same individual taken at different times, may sometimes exhibit more variability due to the aforementioned factors (intrapersonal variability), than images of different individuals due to gender, race, age and individual variations (extrapersonal variability) [3]. One way of coping with intrapersonal variations is including in the training set images with such variations. And while this is a good practice for variations such as facial expressions, use of cosmetics and presence of glasses or beard, it may not be successful in case of illumination or pose variations. Another crucial parameter in face recognition is aging. A robust recognition system should be able to recognize an individual even after some years, especially in mug-shot matching forensic applications. This is a very challenging task, which has not been successfully addressed yet.

Recent public facial recognition benchmarks have shown that in general, the identification performance decreases linearly in the logarithm of number of people in the gallery database [13]. Also, in a demographic point of view, it was found that the recognition rates for males were higher than for females, and that the recognition rates for older people were higher than for younger people. These tests also revealed that while the best recognition techniques were successful on large face databases recorded in well-controlled environments, their performance was seriously deteriorated in uncontrolled environments, mainly due to variations in illumination and head rotations. Such variations have proven to be one of the biggest problems of face recognition systems [3][13].

Several techniques have been proposed to recognize faces under varying pose. One approach is the automatic generation of novel views resembling the pose in the probe image. This is achieved either by using a face model (an active appearance model (AAM)[14] or a deformable 3D model [15]) or by warping frontal images using the estimated optical flow between probe and gallery. Classification is subsequently based on the similarity between the probe image and the generated view. A different approach is based on building a pose varying eigenspace by recording several images of each person under varying pose [16]. Representative techniques are the view-based subspace and the predictive characterized subspace. More recently, techniques that rely on 3D shape data have been proposed [17].

The problem of coping with illumination variations is increasingly appreciated by the scientific community and several techniques have been proposed that may be roughly classified into two main categories [17]. The first category contains techniques seeking illumination insensitive representations of face images. Several representations were seen to be relatively insensitive to illumination variability, e.g. the direction of the image gradient or the sum of gradient of ratios between probe and gallery images [3][18].

The second approach relies on the development of generative appearance models, able to reconstruct novel gallery images resembling the illumination in the probe images. Some of these techniques utilize a large number of example images of the same person under different illumination conditions to reconstruct novel images [19]. Other approaches utilize a 3D range image and albedo map of the person's face to render novel images under arbitrary illumination, while others are based on a combination of the above [17]. Finally, a third more recent approach is based on computer graphics techniques for relighting the probe image so that it resembles the illumination in gallery images [17].

Conclusions and Future Developments

The problem of machine face recognition has been an ongoing subject of research for more than 20 years. Although a large number of approaches have been proposed in the literature and have been implemented successfully for real-world applications, robust face recognition is still a challenging subject, mainly because of large facial variability, pose variations and uncontrolled environmental conditions. The use of novel sensors, such as 3D, can help overcome limitations due to viewpoint and lighting variations [19]. On the other hand, it has been acknowledged that there is no perfect biometric and thus the combination of different modalities, e.g. face combined with speaker, fingerprint and/or hand recognition, is required to achieve the desired level of performance.

See: 3D Face Recognition, Infrared Face Recognition, Video-based Face Recognition, Applications of Face Recognition & Novel Trends, Face Recognition Evaluation and Pilots

References

1. A. Jain, A. Ross, and S. Prabhakar, "An introduction to biometric recognition," IEEE Transactions on Circuits and Systems for Video Technology, Vol. 14, No. 1, January 2004, pp. 4-20.
2. M. -H. Yang, D. J. Kriegman, and N. Ahuja, "Detecting faces in images: a survey," IEEE Transactions on Pattern Analysis and Machine Intelligence, Vol. 24, No. 1, January 2002, pp. 34-58.
3. W. Zhao, R. Chellappa, A. Rosenfeld, and P. J. Phillips, "Face recognition: a literature survey," ACM Computing Surveys, Vol. 35, No. 4, December 2003, pp. 399-459.
4. C. Kotropoulos and I. Pitas, "Rule-Based Face Detection in Frontal Views," Proceedings of the IEEE International Conference on Acoustics, Speech and Signal Processing, 1997, pp. 2537-2540.
5. K. C. Yow and R. Cipolla, "Feature-based human face detection," Image and Vision Computing, Vol. 15, No. 9, September 1997, pp. 713-735.
6. S. McKenna, S. Gong, and Y. Raja, "Modeling facial colour and identity with Gaussian mixtures," Elsevier Pattern Recognition, Vol. 31, No. 12, December 1998, pp. 1883-1892.
7. M. Turk and A. Pentland, "Eigenfaces for recognition," Journal of Cognitive Neuroscience, Vol. 3, No. 1, pp. 71-86, 1991.

8. W. Zhao, R. Chellappa, and A. Krishnaswamy, "Discriminant analysis of principal components for face recognition," Proceedings of the IEEE International Conference on Automatic Face and Gesture Recognition, 1998, pp. 336-341.

9. A. V. Nefian and M. H. Hayes III, "An embedded hmm - based approach for face detection and recognition," Proceedings of the IEEE International Conference on Acoustics, Speech, and Signal Processing, 1999, pp. 3553–3556.

10. B. Moghaddam and A. Pentland, "Probabilistic visual learning for object representation," IEEE Transactions on Pattern Analysis and Machine Intelligence, Vol. 19, No. 7, July 1997, pp. 696 – 710.

11. L. Wiskott, J. M. Fellous, and C. von der Malsburg, "Face recognition by elastic bunch graph matching," IEEE Transactions on Pattern Analysis and Machine Intelligence, Vol. 19, No. 7, July 1997, pp. 775-779.

12. M. Lades, J. Vorbruggen, J. Buhmann, J, Lange, C. V. D. Malburg, and R. Wurtz, "Distortion invariant object recognition in the dynamic link architecture," IEEE Transactions on Computers, Vol. 42, No. 3, March 1993, pp. 300-311.

13. The Face Recognition Vendor Test (FRVT) Homepage: http://www.frvt.org.

14. T. F. Cootes, G. J. Edwards, and C. J. Taylor, "Active appearance models," IEEE Transactions on Pattern Analysis and Machine Intelligence, Vol. 23, No. 6, June 2001, pp. 681–685.

15. V. Blanz, S. Romdhami, and T. Vetter, "Face identification across different poses and illuminations with a 3d morphable model," Proceedings of the IEEE International Conference on Automatic Face and Gesture Recognition, 2002, pp. 192–197.

16. A. Pentland, B. Moghaddam, and T. Starner, "View-based and modular eigenspaces for face recognition," Proceedings of the IEEE International Conference on Computer Vision and Pattern Recognition, 1994, pp. 84–91.

17. S. Malassiotis and M. G. Strintzis, "Robust face recognition using 2D and 3D data: pose and illumination compensation," Elsevier Pattern Recognition, in press.

18. H. F. Chen, P. N. Belhumeur, and D. W. Jacobs, "In search of illumination invariants," Proceedings of International Conference on Computer Vision and Pattern Recognition, 2000, pp. 254–261.

19. A. S. Georghiades, P. N. Belhumeur, and D. J. Kriegman, "From few to many: Illumination cone models for face recognition under variable lighting and pose," IEEE Transactions on Pattern Analysis and Machine Intelligence, Vol. 23, No 6, 2001, pp. 643–660.

20. F. Tsalakanidou, S. Malassiotis, and M. G. Strintzis, "Face Localization and Authentication Using Color and Depth Images," IEEE Transactions on Image Processing, Vol. 14, No. 2, February 2005, pp. 152-168.

FACE RECOGNITION EVALUATION AND PILOTS

Definition: Standard evaluation protocols are used to evaluate various face recognition algorithms and examine their limitations.

The growing number of face recognition (FR) methods has imposed the development of standard evaluation protocols and the creation of large evaluation databases. Based on that, a series of public tests evaluating face recognition algorithms and examining their limitations have been performed. The most recent one is the Facial Recognition Vendor Test of 2002 (FRVT2002), in which several state-of the art commercial FR systems were tested using a database of 121,589 images of 37,437 Mexican VISA applicants collected by the US Department of State [1]. The verification performance was measured using the false acceptance (FAR) and false rejection (FRR) rates. FAR is defined as the percentage of instances that a non-authorized individual is falsely accepted by the system, while FRR is defined as the percentage of instances an authorized individual is falsely rejected by the system. In an indoor environment the best systems had an 18% FRR for a FAR of 0.1% (user unfriendly, high-security application), a 10% FRR for a FAR of 1% and a 4% FRR for a FAR of 10% (user friendly application). For test images taken outdoors the FRR increased by 42% (from 4% to 46%) at FAR=10%, showing that FR under illumination variations is still an open issue [1].

The identification performance was measured in terms of the percentage of images that are correctly identified as the best match. The best performance was 85% on a database of 800 people, 83% on a database of 1,600 and 73% on a database of 37,437, and showed that identification performance decreases linearly in the logarithm of the database size [1]. The identification rates for males were 6%-9% higher than for females. Moreover, it was found that for every 10 years decrease in age the identification performance decreased by approximately 5% (old people are easier to recognize). A reduction of 5% per year of elapsed time between enrolled and new images was also observed. Finally, it was shown that the use of deformable face models could significantly improve recognition under varying pose: for non-frontal images the identification performance of the best system was as low as 26%. When such models were employed for pose compensation, the performance increased impressively to 84% [1].

During the last years, FR systems have been employed by government agencies in several pilot applications [2]. For example, a network of 250 CCTV cameras for surveillance was installed in the London Borough of Newham and has succeeded to reduce local crime. The cameras scan the faces within their view and compare them against a database of criminals. If a match is found, an alert is sent to the Police; otherwise the images are automatically discarded to ensure privacy. A FR system performing a face-to-passport check has been installed in Sydney's Airport to verify the identity of passengers and automate airport controls. If there is a successful match, immigration and customs checks are made by the computer to ensure that border crossing is legitimate, and if so, an electronic gate opens for the passenger to pass. Another example of a FR application with an extremely important social impact is the ChildBase System, which organizes and classifies millions of Internet images of sexually abused children. FR technology is used to identify victims of abuse and their offenders by crosschecking un-indexed images with the world's largest database of child abuse imagery, in order to quickly determine whether a seized computer contains images of known or new abuse victims.

See: Face Recognition, Biometrics

References

1.   The Face Recognition Vendor Test (FRVT) Homepage: http://www.frvt.org.

2. M. Rejman-Greene, "BioVision: Roadmap for Biometrics in Europe to 2010," European Biometric Forum (EBF) Homepage: http://www.eubiometricforum.com/.

FACE RECOGNITION, 3D

Definition: *Three-dimensional (3D) face recognition techniques exploit information about the 3D shape of the human face.*

The majority of existing face recognition algorithms use 2D intensity images of the face. Although such systems have advanced to be fairly accurate under controlled conditions, extrinsic imaging parameters such as pose and illumination are still responsible for serious deterioration of their performance. To improve performance under these conditions, three-dimensional (3D) face recognition techniques have been proposed, that exploit information about the 3D shape of the human face. The use of 3D images for personal identification is based on the intuitive notion that the shape of faces can be highly discriminatory and is not affected by changes in lighting or by facial pigment.

The 3D geometry of the human face may be acquired by means of special sensors, including laser scanners, 3D cameras based on structured light or stereo vision techniques (see Figure 1). Although significant advances have been made in 3D sensor technology, there are still several factors that limit their wide application, such as acquisition time, cost, spatial and depth accuracy, depth of field, existence of artifacts and missing points [1].

The earliest approach adopted towards 3D face recognition is based on the extraction of 3D facial features by means of differential geometry techniques. Commonly, surface properties such as curvature are used to localize facial features invariant to rigid transformations of the face, which are subsequently used to match face images. More sophisticated techniques, such as the Point Signatures [2], have been proposed for 3D face matching. Point Signatures describe the local structure of face points and are used to find correspondences between 3D faces. Recognition is based on the similarity of signature vectors in respective facial points.

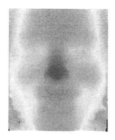

Figure 1. Examples of 3D face representations: a) 2D intensity image, b) 3D as range image, c) 3D as shaded model and d) 3D as wire frame mesh.

Appearance based methods like PCA simplify 3D data processing by using 2D depth images (see Fig. 1b), where pixel values represent the distance of corresponding points from the camera [1]. The main problem of such techniques is alignment of 3D images and pose variations, but it can be overcome, since 3D data can be exploited for accurate pose estimation and compensation. The combination of 2D and 3D images for multimodal face recognition using PCA has also been proposed, and significant performance improvement has been achieved [2].

See: Face Recognition

References

1. K. W. Bowyer, K. Chang, and P. J. Flynn, "A Survey of Approaches to Three-Dimensional Face Recognition," Proceedings of International Conference on Pattern Recognition, 2004, pp. 358-361.
2. C.-S. Chua, F. Han, and Y.-K. Ho, "3D Human Face Recognition Using Point Signature," Proceedings International Conference on Automatic Face and Gesture Recognition, 2000, pp. 233-238.
3. F. Tsalakanidou, S. Malassiotis, and M. G. Strintzis, "Face Localization and Authentication Using Color and Depth Images," IEEE Transactions on Image Processing, Vol. 14, No. 2, February 2005, pp. 152-168.

FACIAL ANIMATION AND AFFECTIVE HUMAN-COMPUTER INTERACTION

Kostas Karpouzis and Stefanos Kollias
Image, Video and Multimedia Systems Laboratory, National Technical University of Athens, Athens, Greece

Definition: *Affective Human-Computer Interaction (HCI) systems utilize multimodal information about the emotional state of users.*

Affective Human-Computer Interaction

Even though everyday human-to-human communication is thought to be based on vocal and lexical content, people seem to base both expressive and cognitive capabilities on facial expressions and body gestures. Related research in both the analysis and synthesis fields is based on trying to recreate the way the human mind works while making an effort to recognize such emotion. This inherently multimodal process means that in order to achieve robust results, one should take into account features like speech, face and hand gestures or body pose, as well as the interaction between them. In the case of speech, features can come from both linguistic and paralinguistic analysis; in the case of facial and body gestures, messages are conveyed in a much more expressive and definite manner than wording, which can be misleading or ambiguous, especially when users are not visible to each other. While a lot of effort has been invested in examining individually these aspects of human expression, recent research has shown that even this approach can benefit from taking into account multimodal information [15].

In general, Human-Computer Interaction (HCI) systems that utilize multimodal information about the emotional state of users are presently at the forefront of interest of the computer vision and artificial intelligence community. Such interfaces give the opportunity to less technology-aware individuals, as well as handicapped people, to use computers more efficiently. In this process, real world actions of a human are transferred in the virtual environment through a representative (ECA – Embodied Conversational Agent), while the virtual environment recognizes these actions and responds via system ECAs. An example of this enhanced HCI scheme is virtual malls. Business-to-client communication via the web is still poor and mostly based on the exchange of textual information. What most clients actually look for is a human, or human-like salesman who would smile at them and adapt to their personal needs, thus enhancing the humane aspects of e–commerce, interactive TV or online advertising applications. ECAs can also be used more extensively in real-time, peer-to-peer multimedia communication, providing enhanced means of expression missing from text-based communication; ECAs can express their emotions using human-like expressions and gestures not only during a chat via the web or a teleconference but also during broadcasting news, making them more attractive since they would be pronounced in a human-like way.

Expressing Emotion

Facial and hand gestures, as well as body pose constitute a powerful way of non-verbal human communication. Analyzing such multimodal information is a complex task involving low-level image processing tasks, as well as pattern recognition, machine learning and psychological studies. Research in facial expression analysis and synthesis has mainly concentrated on primary or universal emotions [14][7]. In particular, sadness, anger, joy, fear, disgust and surprise are categories of emotions that usually attract most of the interest in human computer interaction environments. Very few studies explore non-primary emotions; this trend may be due to the great influence of the works of Ekman and Friesen [14] and Izard [2] who proposed that the universal emotions correspond to distinct facial expressions universally recognizable across cultures. More recent psychological studies [15] have investigated a broader variety of intermediate or blended emotions.

Although the exploitation of the results obtained by the psychologists is far from straightforward, computer scientists can use some hints to their research. The MPEG-4 standard indicates an alternative, measurable way of modeling facial expressions, strongly influenced from neurophysiological and psychological studies. For example, FAPs that are utilized in the framework of MPEG-4 for facial animation purposes, are strongly related to the Action Units (AUs), which consist of the core of the Facial Action Coding System (FACS) [14].

One of the studies carried out by psychologists and which can be useful to researchers of the area of computer graphics and machine vision is the one of Whissel's [3], who suggested that emotions are points in a space with a relatively small number of dimensions, which with a first approximation are only two: activation and evaluation (see Figure 1). In this framework, evaluation seems to express internal feelings of the subject, while, activation is related to the magnitude of facial muscles movement and can be more easily estimated based on facial characteristics.

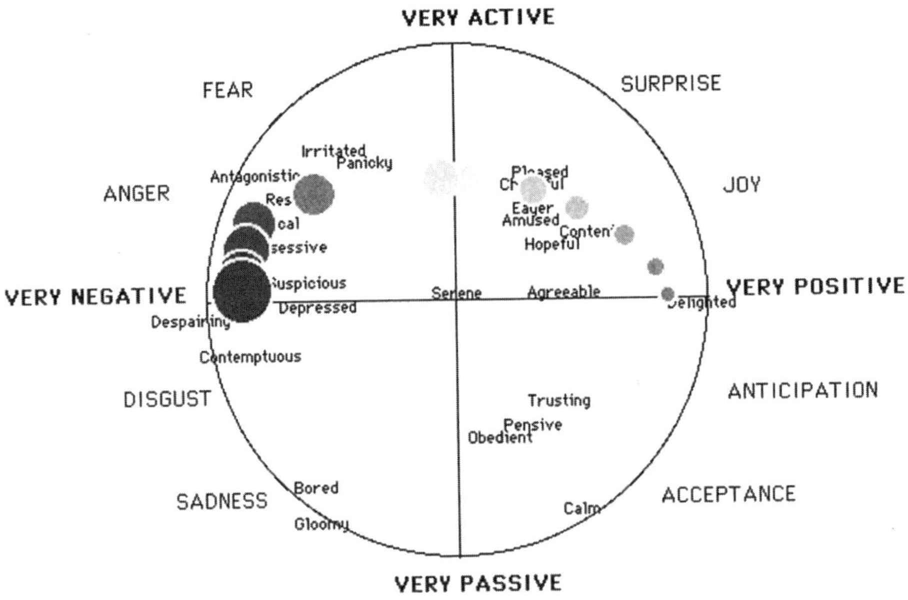

Figure 1. The activation-evaluation space [3].

Facial Animation in MPEG-4

Already early in life, people are instinctively able to recognize and interpret human faces, as well as distinguish subtle expressive differences. Therefore, it is imperative that synthetic face images [5] are as faithful to the original and expressive as possible, in order to achieve the desired effect. Once a generic 3-D head model is available, new views can be generated by adapting it to a real one [9] and then transforming it. Regarding animation, two different approaches are proposed [13], namely the clip-and-paste method [16][17], where prominent facial feature templates are extracted from actual frames and mapped onto the 3-D shape model and algorithms based on the deformation of 3-D surfaces [4].

In order to meet the demands of structured multimedia information, the MPEG-4 standard introduces the fundamental concept of media objects such as audio, visual, 2D/3D, natural and synthetic objects, along with content-based access and behavioral modeling, to make up a multimedia scene [6]. The main aspects of the standard deal with hybrid coding and compression of media objects, universal content accessibility over various networks and provisions of interactivity for the end-user. The spatial and temporal relationships between scene objects are defined in a dedicated representation called BIFS — Binary Format for Scenes, which inherits the scene graph concept, as well as animation procedures from VRML. In terms of functionalities related to ECAs (Embodied Conversational Agents), both standards define a specific set of nodes in the scene graph to allow for a representation of an instance. However, only the MPEG-4 specifications deal with streamed ECA animations. In addition to this, MPEG-4 makes special provisions for the semantic representation of information pertinent to facial animation. The face object specified by MPEG-4 is structured in a way that visemes, i.e. the visual manifestations of speech, are intelligible, facial expressions allow the recognition of the speaker's mood, and reproduction of a real speaker is as faithful and portable as possible. To fulfill these objectives, MPEG-4 specifies three types of facial data [11], namely Facial Definition Parameters (FDPs) used to adapt a generic 3D facial model available at the receiver side, Facial Animation Parameters (FAPs), which allow for animating the 3D facial model and FAP Interpolation Table, which allow the definition of interpolation rules for the FAPs to be interpolated at the decoder. The 3D model is then animated using the transmitted FAPs and the FAPs interpolated according to the FIT.

Table 1. Profiles for the Archetypal Expression *Fear*

Profiles	FAPs and Range of Variation
Fear $(P_F^{(0)})$	$F_3 \in [102,480], F_5 \in [83,353], F_{19} \in [118,370],$ $F_{20} \in [121,377], F_{21} \in [118,370],$ $F_{22} \in [121,377],$ $F_{31} \in [35,173], F_{32} \in [39,183], F_{33} \in [14,130], F_{34} \in [15,135]$
$P_F^{(1)}$	$F_3 \in [400,560], F_5 \in [333,373], F_{19} \in [-400,-340], F_{20} \in [-407,-347], F_{21} \in [-400,-340], F_{22} \in [-407,-347]$
$P_F^{(2)}$	$F_3 \in [400,560], F_5 \in [-240,-160], F_{19} \in [-630,-570], F_{20} \in [-630,-570], F_{21} \in [-630,-570], F_{22} \in [-630,-570], F_{31} \in [260,340], F_{32} \in [260,340], F_{33} \in [160,240], F_{34} \in [160,240], F_{35} \in [60,140], F_{36} \in [60,140]$

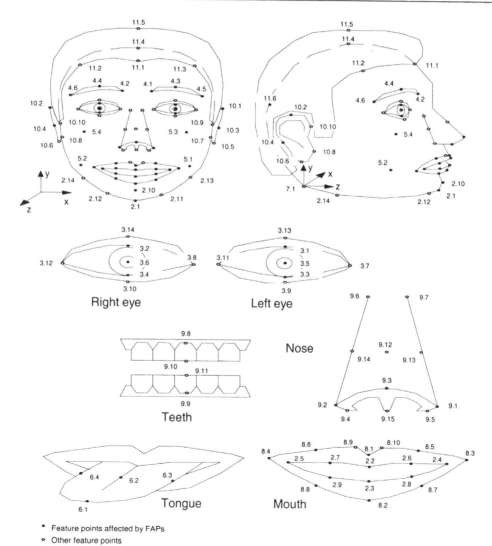

Figure 2. Feature points grouping [12].

FAPs are closely related to face muscle actions and were designed to allow the animation of faces, reproducing movements, expressions and speech-related deformation. The chosen set of FAPs represents a complete set of basic facial movements, allowing terminals to represent most natural facial actions as well as, by exaggeration, some non-human like actions, e.g. useful for cartoon-like animations. The complete FAP set [11] consists of 68 FAPs, 66 low-level parameters associated with the lips, jaw, eyes, mouth, cheek, nose, etc. and two high-level parameters (FAPs 1 and 2) associated with expressions and visemes, respectively. While low-level FAPs are associated with movements and rotations of key facial features and the relevant areas (see Figure 2), expressions and visemes represent more complex actions, typically associated with a set of FAPs. Although the encoder knows the reference feature point for each low-level FAP, it does not precisely know how the decoder will move the model vertices around that feature point, i.e. the FAP interpretation model. The expression FAP enables the animation of a universal expression (joy, sadness, anger, fear, disgust and surprise), while visemes provide the visual analog to phonemes and allow the efficient rendering of visemes for better speech pronunciation, as an alternative to having them represented using a set of low-level FAPs.

Figure 3 shows some examples of animated profiles. Figure 3(a) shows a particular profile for the archetypal expression anger, while Figure 3(b) and (c) show alternative profiles of the same expression. The difference between them is due to FAP intensities. Difference in FAP intensities is also shown in Figures 3(d) and (e), both illustrating the same profile of expression surprise. Finally, Figure 3(f) shows an example of a profile of the expression joy. In the case of intermediate or blended expressions, one may utilize the above mentioned representations, along with their position in the activation-evaluation space to come up with relevant profiles. Details and results of this approach are shown in [1].

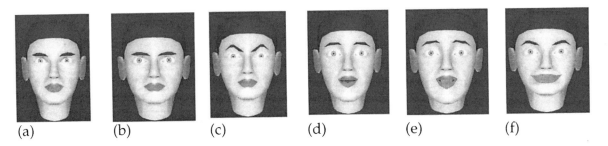

(a)   (b)   (c)   (d)   (e)   (f)

Figure 3. Examples of animated profile: (a)-(c) Anger, (d)-(e) Surprise, (f) Joy.

Conclusions

A straightforward and portable facial animation representation is a crucial factor when catering for affect-aware systems. In this framework, the MPEG-4 standard proposes a set of tools for designing and animating human face models, which enables accurate renderings on a variety of devices and network conditions; in order for these tools to be effective, they must be coupled with a relevant emotion representation in both the analysis and synthesis elements, so as to avoid cartoon-like, unrealistic results. Synthetic facial animation is expected to enhance the usability of a wide variety of applications, especially in the light of powerful dedicated hardware and the presence of structured information standards.

See: Human-Computer Interaction, Embodied Conversational Agents, Universal expressions, Facial Action Coding System (FACS), MPEG-4, Binary Format for Scenes – BIFS, Facial Definition Parameters, Facial Animation Parameters

References

1. A. Raouzaiou, N. Tsapatsoulis, K. Karpouzis, and S. Kollias, "Parameterized facial expression synthesis based on MPEG-4," EURASIP Journal on Applied Signal Processing, Vol. 2002, No. 10, pp. 1021-1038.
2. C. Izard, L. Dougherty, and E.A. Hembree, "A System for Identifying Affect Expressions by Holistic Judgments," Technical Report, University of Delaware, 1983.
3. C. M. Whissel, "The dictionary of affect in language," in R. Plutchnik and H. Kellerman (Eds.) Emotion: Theory, research and experience: Vol. 4, The measurement of emotions, Academic Press, New York, 1989.
4. D. Terzopoulos and K. Waters, "Analysis and synthesis of facial image sequences using physical and anatomical models," IEEE Transactions on Pattern Analysis and Machine Intelligence, pp. 569–579, June 1993.
5. F. Parke and K. Waters, "Computer Facial Animation," A. K. Peters, 1996.
6. F. Pereira and T. Ebrahimi, "The MPEG-4 Book," Prentice Hall, 2002.
7. G. Faigin, "The Artist's Complete Guide to Facial Expressions," Watson-Guptill, New York, 1990.
8. K. Aizawa and T.S. Huang, "Model-based image coding: Advanced video coding techniques for very low bit-rate applications," Proceedings of the IEEE, Vol. 83, No. 2, pp. 259-271, 1995.
9. K. Karpouzis, G. Votsis, N. Tsapatsoulis, and S. Kollias, "Compact 3D Model Generation based on 2D Views of Human Faces: Application to Face Recognition," Machine Graphics & Vision, Vol. 7, No. 1/2, pp. 75–85, 1998.
10. M. Hoch, G. Fleischmann, and B. Girod, "Modeling and animation of facial expressions based on B-splines," Visual Computer, Vol. 11, pp. 87-95, 1994.
11. M. Tekalp and J. Ostermann, "Face and 2-D mesh animation in MPEG-4," Signal Processing: Image Communication, Elsevier, Vol. 15, No. 4-5, pp. 387-421, 2000.
12. MPEG Video & SNHC, "Text of ISO/IEC FDIS 14496-2: Visual," Doc. ISO/MPEG N2502, Atlantic City MPEG Meeting, October 1998.
13. P. Eisert, "Analysis and Synthesis of Facial Expressions," in Sarris and Strintzis (Eds.), 3D Modeling and Animation: Synthesis and Analysis Techniques for the Human Body, pp. 235-265, Idea Group Publishing, 2004.
14. P. Ekman and W. V. Friesen, "Facial Action Coding System," Consulting Psychologists Press, Palo Alto, CA, 1978.
15. R. Cowie, E. Douglas-Cowie, N. Tsapatsoulis, G. Votsis, S. Kollias, W. Fellenz, and J. Taylor, "Emotion Recognition in Human-Computer Interaction," IEEE Signal Processing Magazine, pp. 32-80, January 2001.
16. S. Chao and J. Robinson, "Model-based analysis/synthesis image coding with eye and mouth patch codebooks," Proceedings of Vision Interface, pp. 104-109, 1994.
17. W. J. Welsh, S. Searsby, and J.B. Waite, "Model-based image coding," British Telecom Technology Journal, Vol. 8, No. 3, pp. 94-106, 1990.

FAIRNESS IN ONLINE GAMES

Definition: *Fairness in online games is concerned with the problem of ensuring that players perceive the game evolution in the same moment, despite different network latencies.*

Most players dislike being killed in a game, especially if it is not their fault but network latencies have affected their perception of the game evolution, thus giving advantage to their adversaries. Due to the best-effort nature of the Internet, in fact, players can experience erratic game progresses which often prevent them from appropriately responding to the stimuli generated during the game session [2]. This may obviously lead to frustrating gaming experiences to players. While past classic offline multiplayer games offered reliable and safe real-time interactions among players, which connected to the game through the same local PC or game console, the use of the net as a link for players' game interactions clearly complicates one of the primary game assumptions i.e., each player must have the same chance to win the game.

Focusing on online multiplayer games, the problem above arises regardless of the adopted architectural solutions. When resorting to client/server architectures, for example, as the network delay from the game server to different players is typically different, players may receive the same state update at different times and, similarly, game events generated by players can reach the game server at different times. Thus, if the server processes game events according to the order they arrive, then players that suffer from higher latencies result disadvantaged in the game session. Similar issues arise also in P2P-based or distributed approaches, where links that connect different game nodes may result highly diverse.

Within such context, *fairness* in online games is concerned with the problem of ensuring that players perceive the game evolution in the same moment, despite different network latencies. In other words, to ensure fairness identical movements of game entities must be performed with the same speed on the different end-systems [3]. Fairness schemes avoid imbalanced game sessions when no mechanisms for mitigating the QoS differences are exploited within the online game system.

To accomplish this task, different solutions may be devised. For instance, one approach consists in resorting to a lockstep scheme which prevents that any player will process any given game event until such an event is received by all the players.

Similarly, bucket synchronization mechanisms are based on the idea of imposing a worst case delay d for the transmission of game events, and ensuring that game participants process each game event only after the timeout identified by d [1, 3]. In other words, once the longest packet transmission time among all the players has been determined, each game event is appropriately delayed in queue before being presented on the screen. This permits to have a simultaneous game evolution for all participants.

Instead, a different approach has been devised in [2] that rests upon the idea of exploiting several proxies, distributed at the edge of the network. In particular, a fair delivery of game events is achieved by resorting to the notion of "reaction time", which is the time between the reception of a game event at a client and the sending of another game event (at the same client) in response to the first one. This scheme avoids the need for time buckets, thus eliminating the problem of delaying the processing of all events by a fixed amount of time.

See: Online Gaming.

References

1. L. Gautier and C. Diot, "Design and Evaluation of MiMaze, a Multiplayer Game on the Internet," Proceedings of IEEE Multimedia (ICMCS'98), 1998.
2. K. Guo, S. Mukherjee, S. Rangarajan, and S. Paul, "A fair message exchange framework for distributed multi-player games," Proceedings of the 2nd Workshop on Network and System Support for Games, ACM Press, pp. 29–41, 2003.
3. L. Pantel, L.C. Wolf, "On the impact of delay on real-time multiplayer games," Proceedings of the 12th International Workshop on Network and Operating Systems Support for Digital Audio and Video, ACM Press, pp. 23–29, 2002.

FUZZY TECHNIQUES FOR CONTEXT REPRESENTATION

Definition: Fuzzy techniques for context modeling allow the representation of uncertainty.

Context Representation Formalisms

Context-awareness in the field of multimedia applications means that the user's situation wherein he or she consumes multimedia documents is known to the system. Adaptation to context means to exploit the potentials, meet the restrictions, and fulfill the requirements so that the user stands to benefit from the multimedia presentation to the best. However, the exhaustive, accurate description of a user's actual situation is extremely complex due to two reasons: (1) No context model is able to fully cover all aspects of the "real world" because of complexity restrictions, and (2) not every aspect of the user's context can be defined and measured exactly. Thus, context attributes may remain unknown, unsure, or are afflicted with uncertainty, or *fuzziness*. To solve issue (1), the user context description model must be reduced to a trade-off between expressiveness and complexity, which is often done automatically by omitting less relevant attributes. To solve issue (2), the context model may be designed in a way that allows the representation of uncertainty, i.e. the context model may be extended by elements from fuzzy theory [1].

Fuzzy Context: Formalized Reality

It is the goal of fuzzy theory to formalize the *approximate reasoning* that is used by humans in everyday life. It follows the human functioning of representing values as *terms* instead of *numeric values*: For example, the maximal brightness of a TFT display could be expressed in candela per square meter (cd/m^2), or in natural language terms like *gaunt, dark, bright,* or *luminous*. There exist non-technical context attributes that can not adequately be represented as numeric values, like *tiredness* or *affection*. Using fuzzy techniques, such aspects can be modeled similar to tangible attributes, e.g. [2]. Thus, fuzzy logic provides a well-defined, commonly accepted, sound basis for context modeling in adaptive, multimedia presentation systems.

Fuzzy Ontologies

In the Semantic Web initiative (see http://www.w3.org/2001/sw/), *ontologies* are seen as a well-established approach for the representation of metadata about multimedia content. Fuzzy ontologies definitely have the potential to be employed in many application areas. However, to achieve interoperability, existing Semantic Web standards (e.g. RDF, OWL) will be enriched with elements enabling fuzzy modeling and fuzzy reasoning. It is crucial for these features to be incorporated into open, widely-accepted and established standards to provide a sound, application-independent basis for ontology developers and users.

See: Context-aware Multimedia

References

1. L.A. Zadeh, "Fuzzy Logic and Approximate Reasoning," Syntheses, No. 30, 1965, pp. 407-428.
2. P. Korpipää, J. Mantyjarvi, J. Kela, H. Keranen, and E.J. Malm, "Managing context information in mobile devices," Pervasive Computing, IEEE, Vol. 2, Issue 3, July-September 2003, pp. 42-51.

G

GAME ACCESSIBILITY

Definition: *A new generation of accessible games is emerging, designed to offer multimodal interfaces that allow people with disability to play as equals with all the other players.*

On-line entertainment improves the quality of human life and represents a relevant aspect of human culture and communication. Playing games is a basis for discovery, learning and, finally, growing. Playing is a way to observe, try and manipulate things or ideas, to make experiments, understand and invent. Moreover, playing with others consistently involves people in mutual communication. Inaccessible technology interferes with an individual's ability to be an active part of the society, including when it mainly supports entertainment activities. These considerations encouraged designers to make on-line gaming an inclusive technology that supports access for anyone, regardless of disability. The development of accessible games is fully supported by the International Game Developers Association (IGDA), through a specific workgroup, the Game Accessibility Special Interest Group [1].

Currently, on-line games are mainly based on inaccessible interfaces and people with disabilities have difficulties or are totally left out of the game. As an example, people who are totally blind or visually impaired cannot play most of the available on-line games, which are exclusively based on visual cues. More generally, there are a variety of different conditions that could limit a user in playing a game. There is a vast range of difficulties that arise from limitations in vision, hearing, mobility, or cognitive issues that a disabled user could suffer from.

To overcome these limits, there exist several games designed to meet special requirements of a particular group of disabled users. A significant example is offered by audio games [2} that are based only on an auditive output and are typically played by blind users. This approach is now becoming obsolete because it fails the purpose to be inclusive, creating new forms virtual barriers. A new generation of accessible games is emerging, designed to offer multimodal interfaces that allow people with disability to play as equals with all the other players. Commercial examples of inclusive 3D games are now available including, for example, those games that offer visual/audio hybrid interface and could be played by both sighted and blind players.

Accessibility is also a key issue for *serious games* i.e., video games designed for non-entertainment purposes (e.g., military, education or healthcare). Digital Game Based

Learning (DGBL) [3] represents one of the newest trends in e-learning and combines content provision with computer games to obtain a more effective way to learn. When games are used in support to teaching/learning activities and can be considered as edutainment applications, accessibility could become a legal requirement. Different countries have laws regarding minimum accessibility constraints for didactical materials that have to be applied also to DGBL applications. Finally, similarly to what happens with Web Contents Accessibility, an accessible design could effectively improve the game experience also to mobile players that use portable devices with low bandwidth, slow CPUs or small displays.

See: Online Gaming

References

1. International Game Developers Association (IGDA), "Accessibility in Games: Motivations and Approaches,"
   http://www.igda.org/accessibility/IGDA_Accessibility _WhitePaper.pdf.
2. Audio Games Network home page, http://www.audiogames.net/.
3. M. de Aguilera and A. Mendiz, "Video games and education: (education in the face of a "parallel school")," Computers in Entertainment (CIE), Vol. 1, No. 1, October 2003.

GAME EVENT SYNCHRONIZATION

Definition: Event synchronization in online games deals with the maintenance of game state consistency across several nodes.

Many gaming architectural solutions devised for the support of Massively Multiplayer Online Games are based on the idea of resorting to different nodes, distributed throughout the network, that manage a redundant game state. Indeed, it is well known that these approaches, which replicate the game state across multiple hosts, may ensure high levels of game availability and fault-tolerance. It is also widely accepted that the maintenance of game state consistency across several nodes results as a crucial issue to be addressed. According to this approach, in fact, game events generated by players during a gaming session must be locally processed by all nodes to guarantee that the game computation is kept consistent with those of all other nodes in the game system. This ensures that all game participants will perceive the same game evolution. Several studies have been performed on synchronization models for online games [1, 2, 3]. The most common approach to keep synchronized and consistent the state of an event-based distributed game is based on the idea of guaranteeing that all nodes receive the same information needed to correctly update the replicated game state (reliable event delivery) as well as process this information according to a unique order (typically a timestamp-based order). This, in fact, ensures the consistency of the replicated game state. Unfortunately, it is well known that the use of globally ordered, reliable transmission strategies may result in performance degradation if smart synchronization solutions are not utilized [2].

Along this line, there exist novel mechanisms that adopt a "time bucket"-based approach [3]. In essence, these schemes delay and order events (before being processed) for a time that should be long enough to prevent disordering. In other words, the responsiveness of the application is voluntarily decreased with the aim of eliminating inconsistencies. The problem with all these schemes is mainly concerned with the size of the time bucket, which should be large enough to permit the reception of all game events generated by players within their related bucket without jeopardizing the interactivity degree. Thus, alternative solutions are needed for the support of online games deployed over very dynamic and mutable networks.

There is an emerging need for mechanisms that try to speed up the game event processing activity with the aim of guaranteeing an acceptable interactivity degree among players while maintaining game consistency.
In line with this, several synchronization schemes have been recently presented which adopt optimistic approaches that process game events as soon as they are received and adopt "detect-and-correct" strategies able to rollback the computation when incorrect and inconsistent game states are computed [1, 3].

As an additional alternative, schemes exist that exploit the semantics of the game to relax reliability and ordering delivery requirements in order to speed up the event delivery and the event processing activities, thus guaranteeing an augmented interactivity degree to users without loosing game consistency [2].

See: Online Gaming.

References

1. E. Cronin, B. Filstrup, S. Jamin, and A.R. Kurc, "An efficient synchronization mechanism for mirrored game architectures," *Multimedia Tools and Applications*, Vol. 23, No. 1, pp. 7–30, May 2004.
2. S. Ferretti and M. Roccetti, "A novel obsolescence-based approach to event delivery synchronization in multiplayer games," *International Journal of Intelligent Games and Simulation*, Vol. 3, No. 1, pp. 7–19, March/April 2004.
3. M. Mauve, J. Vogel, V. Hilt, and W. Effelsberg, "Local-lag and timewarp: Providing consistency for replicated continuous applications," *IEEE Transactions on Multimedia*, Vol. 6, No. 1, pp. 47–57, February 2004.

GEOGRAPHIC VIDEO CONTENT

Definition: Geographic video content includes both spatial and temporal geographic characteristics acquired through ground-based or non-ground-based cameras.

Geographic Information Systems (GIS) incorporate three key types of geographic information: *spatial information*, representing areas and entities on a map, *tabular information*, representing related information about these areas and entities, and *image information* of these areas and entities, such as satellite images, aerial photographs, and the like. This information is combined into progressive layers or slices to provide the user with better understanding of a location for various purposes, such as finding the best physical location for a new road or calculating crop rotation patterns to prevent cross-contamination of genetically-modified crops. However, whereas the capture and use of this information within GIS is now well understood, exploiting both the spatial and temporal geographic characteristics of video footage proves more challenging. Geographic video footage can be acquired through *ground-based* or *non-ground-based* cameras, which may have a *fixed target* or be *roving*, e.g. CCTV (closed-circuit television) systems, low earth orbit spy satellites, police helicopter cameras, underwater cameras, electronic news gathering video systems, and so forth. Non-ground-based cameras enable the acquisition of video footage that shares similar geographic ground coordinates but has differing height information, e.g. a spy satellite compared with an underwater camera mounted on a remotely-operated vehicle, both observing an area of seawater. Roving cameras enable further possibilities. For example, whereas a fixed CCTV camera will always capture imagery from the same geographic area, cameras mounted to aircraft can track a subject in motion or follow stationary objects that extend over large areas, such as railway or power lines.

Advanced use of geographic video content requires complex georeferencing and visualization techniques. *Strip maps* have proved popular for visualizing footage from *aerial videography*, which yields reconnaissance video of a particular geographic area. The strip map is created by placing video images adjacently to create a map of the entire area. This approach has been used in a wide range of applications, from automated road determination [1] to the construction of panoramic video sequences [2]. Comprehensively georeferencing this video footage enables strip-map-like constructs to be implemented within four-dimensional virtual environments that the user can then interactively explore. Such georeferencing requires the following [3]: *longitude*, *latitude* and *height* to provide a position in three-dimensional space, the camera's *pitch*, *roll*, and *yaw* to specify how it is mounted at this position, and *focal length*, *target height* and *target width* to accurately specify the field of view. With this information, any camera in any situation capturing any imagery as its target can be fully georeferenced. Furthermore, combining this metadata with conventional multimedia content metadata enables advanced multimedia environments, which have both geographic and semantic knowledge of their content. The MPEG-7 standard is one positive step in this direction since it enables geographic metadata to be represented alongside, and cross-referenced with, multimedia content metadata.

See: Multimedia content modeling and personalization

References

1. R. Pless and D. Jurgens, "Road Extraction from Motion Clues in Aerial Video," Proceedings of the 12th ACM International Workshop on Geographic Information Systems (GIS '04), 2004, pp. 31-38.
2. D. Kimber, J. Foote, and S. Lertsithichai, "FlyAbout: Spatially Indexed Panoramic Video," Proceedings of the 9th ACM International Conference on Multimedia (MM '01), 2001, pp. 339-347.

3. J. Raper, T. McCarthy, and N. Williams, "Georeferenced Four-Dimensional Virtual Environments: Principles and Applications," Computers, Environment and Urban Systems, Vol. 22, No. 6, 1999, pp. 529-539.

H

H.263 VIDEO COMPRESSION

Definition: *H.263 is a teleconferencing video compression standard developed by the ITU, which was designed for low bit rate conversational video services.*

H.263 technology became a basis for later MPEG-4 Part 2 since MPEG-4 community intended to develop a technology optimized for very low bit rate applications at the first stage. As a result, wireless phone standards such as 3GPP include H.263 as a video subsystem compression standard. In addition, MPEG-4 Part 2 requires any compliant decoders to be able to decode H.263B (Base).

Key Compression Tools for H.263 Video

The basic configuration of the video compression algorithm in H.263 is based on H.261 developed by ITU. H.263 is a hybrid coder that is based on 8x8 block DCT and 16x16/8x8 motion compensation with half-pel resolution. In H.263, the source video formats are fixed as the following 5 – SubQCIF/QCIF/CIF/4CIF/16CIF. There are 3 frame types – I, P and PB. MBs in I are all Intra-coded, while MBs in P are either Intra- or Inter-coded. Inter-coded MBs are either 1 MV predicted or 4 MV OBMC (overlapped block motion compensation) predicted. In PB frames, MBs in the P frame and corresponding MBs in the B frame are jointed-coded with a common MB header. A MB in the P can take on either Intra-coded MB or Inter-coded MB. However, any MBs in corresponding B frame are not allowed to be Intra-coded. The QS ranges from 2 to 62 (Qp ranges from 1 to 31). Within a MB, the same QS is used for all coefficients except Intra DC. Intra DC is specially handled with a step size 8 of uniform quantizer.

After zig-zag scanning, 3D RLD (zero-run, level, Last) triplets are formed. And, binary pattern for each triplet is looked up from pre-designed Huffman table. Note that 2D RLD duplets are used for MPEG-1 and MPEG-2. PQAUN, GUANT and DQUANT are used to represent Qp more efficiently. PQUANT data is represented in the Picture layer and it indicates the quantizer QUANT to be used for the picture until updated by any subsequent GQUANT or DQUANT. GQUANT is present in the GOB layer and it indicates the quantizer QUANT to be used for the GOB until updated by any subsequent DQUANT. Only differential DQUANT is described in each MB header when necessary. If no DQUANT data is necessary, MCBPC basically declares the situation. There are four optional coding modes in H.263 – Unrestricted MV mode, Syntax-based Arithmetic Coding (SAC) mode, Advanced Prediction mode and PB-frame mode. In the default prediction mode of H.263, MVs are restricted such that all pixels referenced by them are within the coded picture area. In unrestricted MV mode, MVs are allowed to point outside the picture. When a pixel referenced by a MV is outside the coded area, an edge pixel (a.k.a., extended padded pixel) is used instead. In SAC mode, all VLC/VLD operations are replaced with arithmetic coding. As in VLC table mode of H.263, the syntax of the symbols is partitioned into 4 layers: Picture, GOB, MB and Block. Based on the syntax, probability model changes for arithmetic encoding/decoding. The syntax of the top three layers remains exactly the same. The syntax of the Block layer also remains quite similar, but slightly re-defined. SAC applies mostly to syntax elements of MB and Block levels. The first 3 RLD triplets in Block level are based on different probability models, while the rest of RLD triplets are with a same probability model. Advanced Prediction mode includes OBMC and the possibility of 4 MVs per MB. The use of this mode is indicated in PTYPE. The Advanced Prediction mode is only used in combination with the unrestricted MV mode. If MCBPC indicates 4MV mode, the 1st MV is described in MVD and the other 3 MVs are put into MVD2-4. If MVs are in half-pel resolution, half-pel values are found using bilinear interpolation. Each 8x8 block undergoes OBMC to reduce blocky effect. 5 MVs (4 neighborhood 8x8 block MVs and 1 current 8x8 block MV) centered around the current 8x8 block are used to extract 5 8x8 predictors. And, 5 predictors are used to obtain weighted average as an 8x8 predictor, where each pixel has different weights for each of 5 predictors. Note that application point of neighborhood MVs is at current location of 8x8 block, not at the location of neighborhood blocks. A PB-frame is of two pictures being coded as one unit. The PB-frame consists of one P-picture which is predicted from the previous decoded P-picture and one B-picture which is predicted both from the decoded P-picture and the P-picture currently being decoded. Note that MVD is additionally used for B-block. In a PB-frame, a MB comprises 12 blocks. First the data for the 6 P-blocks is described as in the default H.263 mode, and then the data for the 6 B-blocks is added. MV computation in the B frame part (a.k.a., direct mode) of PB-frame relies on geometrical division of MV of co-located MB in the P frame part of PB-frame. H.263 standard provides a way to derive forward and backward MVs in half-pel units. The prediction of the B-block has 2 modes that are used for different parts of the block. For pixels where the MVb points inside the reconstructed P MB, bi-directional prediction is used for B block predictor. Note that average of forward and backward predictors is used for the predictor. For all other pixels, forward prediction is used for B block predictor. This is almost the same as the direct mode in MPEG-4 Part2 except forward prediction area – the difference comes from the fact that P-MB and B-MB are combined together to represent a single data unit. The story would be different if data were composed with separate frame-based units such as P frame or B frame.

H.263 Video Specific Semantics and Syntax

There are 4 levels of headers in H.263 video bitstream syntax –Picture, GOB, MB and Block. Note that there is no Sequence header. Some extra information needed is signaled by external means. Picture header contains PSC, TR, PTYPE, PQUANT, CPM, PLCI, TRb, DBQAUNT, PEI, PSPARE, EOS, etc. PSC is Picture startcode that is a word of 22 bits. All picture startcodes are byte aligned. TR is temporal reference of 8 bits. In the optional PB-frames, TR only addresses P-pictures. PTYPE is unified information to specify Source Format/ Split/ Freeze Picture Release/ Picture-Intra or Inter/ Optional modes status, etc. CPM is Continuous Presence Multipoint flag. PLCI (Picture Logical Channel

Indicator) is present if CPM is 1, and it is information about the logical channel number for the picture header and all following information until the next Picture or GOB startcode. TRb is present if PTYPE indicates "PB-frame," and indicates the number of non-transmitted pictures since the last P- or I-picture and before the B-picture. Note that H.263 supports for variable-frame rate coding, thus making TRb necessary. DBQUANT is present if PTYPE indicates "PB-frame." QUANT for each P-MB is mapped to BQUANT for the B-MB based on this parameter. GOB header contains GBSC, GN, GLCI, GFID, and GQUANT. GBSC is Group of Block startcode. GN is Group Number with 5 bits. GLCI (GOB Logical Channel Indicator) is only present if CPM is set to 1. GFID (GOB Frame ID) has the same value in every GOB header of a given picture. Moreover, if PTYPE in a picture header is the same as for the previous picture, GFID has the same value as in that previous picture. MB header contains COD, MCBPC, MODB, CBPB, CBPY, DQUANT, MVD1-4, MVDB, etc. COD indicates as INTER block with 0 MV and 0 coefficients. MCBPC is for MB type and coded block pattern for chrominance. MODB/CBPB are for MB mode and coded block pattern for B-blocks, respectively. CBPY is coded block pattern for Chrominance. MVD1-4 are differential MV data for at most 4MVs. MVDB is present if indicated by MODB. MODB is differential MV data that corrects bi-directional MVs. Block layer is composed of IntraDC and Tcoefs like other standards.

See: Video Coding Techniques and Standards

References

1. J. L. Mitchell, W. B. Pennebaker, C. E. Fogg, and D. J. LeGall, "MPEG video compression standard," Digital Multimedia Standards Series, Chapman and Hall, 1996, pp. 135-169

HALFTONING BASED VISUAL SECRET SHARING (VSS)

Definition: In Visual Secret Sharing based on halftoning, the continuous-tone image is first transformed into a halftone image, and then the VSS is applied.

Since VSS-schemes require binary inputs [1][2], the continuous-tone image is first transformed into a halftone image using the density of the net dots to simulate the intensity levels [3]. In the sequence, the halftone version of the secret image is encryptedinto the n shares using the conventional (k,n) visual cryptography based encryption process. The secret image is visually revealed if at least k shares are available for decryption and stacked together on an overhead projector or specialized display.

Due to the nature of visual cryptography, and the expansion and contrast properties of (k,n)-VSS schemes, both binary (conventional) and halftoning-based VSS schemes usually produce shares and decrypted images with expanded dimensions compared to those of the original input (secret) image. In addition, VSS schemes introduce various visual impairments to the output image. Typically, a visually decrypted image is darker compared to the secret (input) image and has a halftone-like appearance (Figure 1).

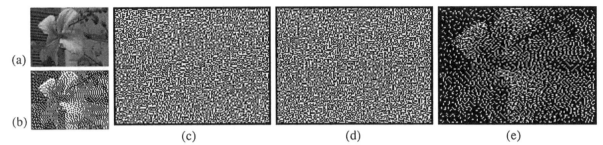

Figure 1. A $(2,2)$ halftoning based VSS scheme constructed using 2×4 basis matrices with $m_1 = 2$ and $m_2 = 2$: (a) secret input image, (b) halftone image produced using Floyd-Stenberg filter, (c,d) binary shares, (e) output image visually decrypted by stacking the share images shown in (c,d).

To avoid the requirement for external hardware (overhead projector, display) or manual intervention, and obtain the decrypted output in digital form, VSS decryption can be realized using logical operations by a personal computer. The decrypted pixel visually appears as transparent (or white) if and only if all share pixels with the identical coordinates are transparent. If any pixel corresponding to the same spatial location of stacked shares has frosted (black) representation, then the decrypted pixel is visually revealed as black. To recover the continuous image from the decrypted halftone-like image, expensive inverse halftoning operations are needed. This feature in conjunction with impairments introduced by the VSS-decryption process make the approach disadvantageous for real-time multimedia applications.

See: Image secret sharing, Visual cryptography, Threshold schemes with minimum pixel expansion.

References

1. C.-C. Lin and T.-H. Tsai, "Visual Cryptography for Gray-Level Images by Dithering Techniques," Pattern Recognition Letters, Vol. 24, No. 1-3, January 2003, pp. 349-358.
2. J.-C. Hou, "Visual Cryptography for Color Images," Pattern Recognition, Vol. 36, No. 7, July 2003, pp. 1619-1629.
3. P.-W. Wong and N.-S. Memon "Image Processing for Halftones," IEEE Signal Processing Magazine, Vol. 20, No. 4, July 2003, pp. 59-70.

HAPTIC DEVICES

Definition: Haptic devices provide sense of sensing the temperature and pressure, grasping, and feeling the surface textures of an object.

Haptics is a new media that deals with the sense of "touch". It provides an interface for the user to interact with objects through synthesized touch. Haptic devices provide sense of sensing the temperature and pressure, grasping, and feeling the surface textures in details of an object, while force haptic devices provide users with the sense of general shape, coarse texture and the position of an object. Apparently, tactile haptic device is more difficult to create than that of kinesthetic. Due to technical problems, currently there is no single haptic device that could combine these two sensations together. Figure 1 below shows some example haptic devices.

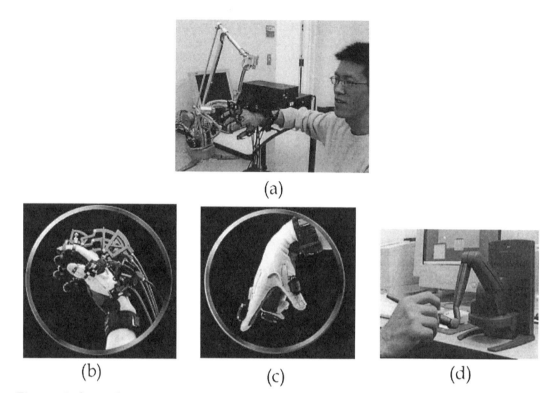

Figure 1. Some haptic devices: a) Immersion's CyberForce™ b) Immersion's CyberGrasp™ c) Immersion's CyberTouch™ d) SensAble's PHANToM® Desktop.

See: Tele-Haptics

HAPTIC FEEDBACK IN USER INTERFACES

Definition: Haptics is a new media that deals with the sense of touch; haptic feedback is currently possible in desktop computers and mobile devices.

The use of desktop computers has traditionally been heavily based on graphical displays and manual input. Sound and speech have been widely integrated in the operating systems, but the auditory modality is still underused. When we consider how the sense of touch is presently used in user interfaces, there is a great difference in the utilization and in the level of sophistication compared to sight and vision.

Haptic Feedback in Desktop Computers

Until recently, sense of touch has mostly been used as a static property of input devices. For example, different materials and tactile markers have been used in keyboards and mice to help to use them without looking. Once a user has got experience in using a certain keyboard, it is not necessary to look at the fingers or keys any more. They can be found using tactile memory and tactile cues present in the device. However, this is only a limited use for sense of touch.

There are several high-end and low-end devices that produce dynamic haptic feedback to stimulate sense of touch. The high-end devices, such as SensAble PHANTOM, are able to produce very realistic tactile and force feedback sensations. These devices are often so large that they are only usable in desktop environments.

Haptics in desktop interfaces has several uses where the sense of touch can really benefit many people. Existing applications include teaching of medical operations, tele-operated remote surgery, sculpting of three-dimensional forms and inclusive applications for visually impaired people [1]. In addition, tactile cues can be used as another information channel to the user when visual or auditory feedback is not preferred. Dividing different feedbacks for different senses helps to manage the problem of information overload.

Haptic Feedback in Mobile Devices

In mobile context haptics has a great potential for being able to mediate information without sound or visual display. Presently tactile information is only used in a very rough way as a replacement for a ring-tone in mobile devices with a vibration motor, such as mobile phones. It is, however, possible to use tactile icons [2] that can present different classes of information. It is also possible to encode certain content in some properties of the haptic feedback, such as magnitude, frequency, duration and wave form. Many of these possibilities have not been realized in the present devices.

See: Human Computer Interactions

References

1. S. Patomäki, R. Raisamo, J. Salo, V. Pasto, and A. Hippula, "Experiences on haptic interfaces for visually impaired young children," Proceedings of ICMI 2004, The Sixth International Conference on Multimodal Interfaces, ACM Press, 2004, 281-288.
2. S. Brewster and L.M. Brown, "Tactons: structured tactile messages for non-visual information display," Proceedings of the Fifth Conference on Australasian User Interface, Vol. 28, ACM Press, 2004, pp. 15-23.

HAPTICS

Definition: Haptics is a new media that deals with the sense of "touch" and provides an interface for the user to interact with objects through synthesized touch.

Traditional media such as audio, video, text and image deal with the hearing and vision human senses. *Haptics* is a new media that deals with the sense of "touch". It provides an interface for the user to interact with objects through synthesized touch. When performed over the network, this is known as *tele-haptics*. Haptics, a term which was derived from the Greek verb "haptesthai" meaning "to touch", introduces the sense of touch and force in human-computer interaction. Haptics enable the operator to manipulate objects in the environment in a natural and effective way, enhance the sensation of "presence", and provide information such as stiffness and texture of objects, which cannot be described completely with only visual or audio feedback. The technology has already been explored in contexts as diverse as modeling & animation, geophysical analysis, dentistry training, virtual museums, assembly planning, mine design, surgical simulation, design evaluation, control of scientific instruments, and robotic simulation. In the haptic device world, tactile haptic devices provide sense of sensing the temperature and pressure, grasping, and feeling the surface textures in details of an object, while force haptic devices provide users with the sense of general shape, coarse texture and the position of an object. Figure 1. shows an example of a haptic device.

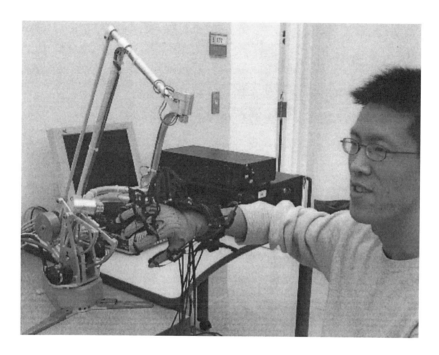

Figure 1. Immersion's CyberForce™.

See: Tele-Haptics

HARMINIC BROADCASTING PROTOCOL

Definition: *Harmonic broadcasting divides a video into equal-size segments.*

Harmonic broadcasting (HB) [1] was initiated to divide the video into N equal-size segments and transmit them into logical channels of decreasing bandwidth. As illustrated in Figure 1, the ith video segment is put on the ith channel with a bandwidth of C/i. Client starts receiving data from each segment stream after it begins to download the first segment of the video.

Thus, the total bandwidth allocated for the video is given by

$$B_{HB} = \sum_{i=1}^{N} \frac{C}{i}. \qquad (1)$$

When the client is ready to consume S_i, it will have received $i-1$ slots of data from that segment and the last slot of that segment can be received during the segment playout time. If L is the length of the video, the start-up time T_{HB} is equal to

$$T_{HB} = \frac{L}{N} \qquad (2)$$

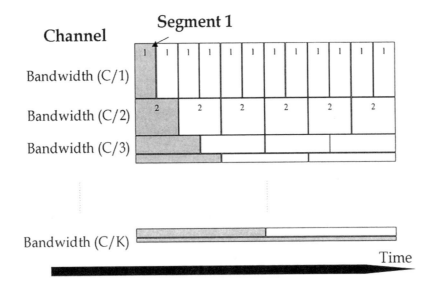

Figure 1. Harmonic broadcasting protocol.

The buffer requirement Buf_{HB} can be calculated by eqn. (3):

$$Buf_{HB} = \max\{Z_i \mid i = 1, \cdots, N-1\} \qquad (3)$$

where

$$Z_1 = I_1$$
$$Z_i = Z_{i-1} + I_i - O_i$$
$$I_i = \frac{L}{N} \sum_{j=i+1}^{N} \frac{1}{j} \qquad [1 \le i < N \ ]$$
$$O_i = \frac{L}{N}\left(\frac{i-1}{i}\right) \qquad [1 \le i \le N \ ]$$

However, it was found that HB could not always deliver all the data on time. Thus, the modified versions of HB called cautious harmonic broadcasting (CHB) and quasi-harmonic broadcasting (QHB) were proposed in [2] to solve the problems.

See: Large-Scale Video-on-Demand System

References

1. L. Juhn and L. Tseng, "Harmonic broadcasting protocols for video-on-demand service," *IEEE Transaction on Broadcasting*, Vol. 43, No. 3, pp. 268-271, September 1997.
2. J.-F. Paris, S. W. Carter, and D. D. E. Long, "Efficient broadcasting protocols for video on demand," *Proceedings of MASCOTS 98*, pp. 127-132, 1998.

HIERARCHICAL VOD SYSTEM

Definition: A hierarchical Video-on-Demand system consists of the central server and several layers of proxy servers.

Hierarchical network architecture is one of the solutions for building a cost effective VoD system. Figure 1 shows the architecture of a hierarchical VoD system [1]. The central server has a large storage to store all available videos for the customers. The central server is connected to several proxy servers, which are physically located closer to the customers. Also the proxy servers are able to store a small portion of videos compared with the capacity of the central server. In a heterogeneous environment like Internet, layered encoded videos can be used to provide different quality of video streams. To serve the low bandwidth environment, the system simply transmits the base layer of the videos to provide the basic video quality. The quality can be increased with the enhancement layers of the videos if the customers subscribe the broadband service.

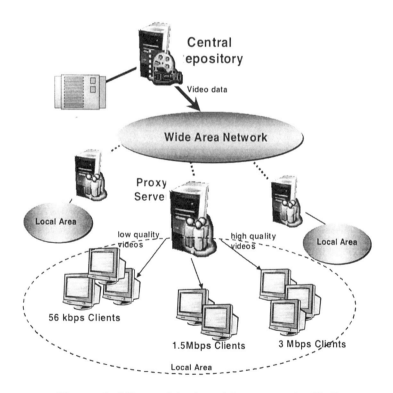

Figure 1. Hierarchical architecture of a VoD system.

In a layered caching strategy, it is assumed that the mth video is encoded into l_m layers. Denote p_m be the popularity of video m. Upon the arrival of the customer's request, the proxy will serve the video request from its cache if the requested layers have been already cached. Otherwise, it will bypass the request to the higher level and the missing video layers will then be retrieved from the central server. By the layered video concept, the number of layers requested is determined by the available bandwidth between the server and the customer. The number of layers in the request is independent of the video being requested. Assume that r_j is the probability of the customers requesting the jth quality of the videos and, hence we have $\sum_{j=1}^{l_m} r_j = 1$. In order to consider the property of the layered video, i.e. all the lower quality layers must be stored before caching the enhancement layer, we define q_{mj} as the fraction of the customers requesting the jth layer of video m such that $q_{mj} = \sum_{k=j}^{l_m} r_k$ .The popularity of each layer can used to determine which layers of the videos should be stored in the proxy. The proxy stores the most popular layers to maximize the cache hits. Defining b_{mj} is used to describe the subsets of the video layers in the proxy. b_{mj} is set to 1 if layer j of video m is in the proxy. Otherwise, it is set as 0. The optimization problem is formally stated as follows.

$$\text{Maximize} \quad \sum_{m=1}^{M}\sum_{j=1}^{l_m} p_m q_{mj} b_{mj} \qquad \text{Subject to} \quad \sum_{m=1}^{M}\sum_{j=1}^{l_m} s_{mj} b_{mj} \leq K$$

where s_{mj} is the size of layer j of video m, K is the proxy size and M is the total number of videos.

See: Large-Scale Video-on-Demand System

References

1. W.F. Poon, K.T. Lo, and J. Feng, "Hierarchical network architecture for layered video streaming," Proceedings of 24th International Conference on Distributed Computing Systems Workshop , Tokyo, Japan, pp. 164-169, March 2004.

HIGH DEFINITION LIVE STREAMING

Min Qin and Roger Zimmermann
Computer Science Department
University of Southern California, Los Angeles, USA

The high-definition (HD) video standard has been developed as the successor to the analog, standard definition (SD) video, which (in the United States) dates back to the first proposal by the National Television System Committee (NTSC) in 1941. The HD standard has been developed by the Advanced Television Systems Committee (ATSC) and was approved in 1995. The ATSC standard encompasses an all-digital system and was developed by a Grand Alliance of several companies. Even though the ATSC standard supports eight-teen different formats, we are restricting our discussion here to the ones that provide the most improvement in picture quality over NTSC. The two best-known HD formats are 1080i (1920 × 1080, 60 fields per second interlaced) and 720p (1280 × 720, 60 frames per second progressive), compared with 480i for SD.

Only after the year 2000 has digital HD equipment become somewhat common and affordable. High-definition displays can be found in many living rooms. The United States Congress has now mandated that all US broadcasters must fully switch to digital and cease analog transmissions by 2009 [1]. On the acquisition side, HD has started to migrate from professional equipment to consumer devices. In 2003 JVC introduced the first affordable camcorder with 720 lines of resolution. A consortium of companies has since announced an augmented standard for consumer equipment under the name HDV. The HDV standard calls for the video sensor streams to be MPEG-2 compressed at a rate that is suitable for storage on MiniDV tapes (i.e., less than 25 Mb/s). On the networking side, significant bandwidth is now available, and therefore high-quality live video streaming over the Internet has become feasible. As HD streaming is graduating from research environments to commercial settings, existing applications — such as video conferencing, CSCW (computer supported cooperative work) and distributed immersive performances — are taking advantage of HD live streaming to achieve enhanced user experiences. Early tests were performed by the University of Washington and the Research Channel in 1999 at the Internet2 member meeting in Seattle. Another example is the UltraGrid project [2], which focuses on uncompressed stream transmissions. Early commercial implementations have been announced by companies such as LifeSize, Polycom, and others.

Because most traditional store-and-forward HD-quality streaming systems use elaborate buffering techniques that introduce significant latencies, there techniques and algorithms are not well suited for real-time environments. Three of the main design parameters for HD live streaming are: (1) the video quality (mostly determined by the resolution of each video frame, the number of bits allocated for each of the three transmitted colors, the number of frames per second, and the compression technique used); (2) the transmission bandwidth; and (3) the end-to-end delay. Due to the massive amount of data required to transmit such streams simultaneously achieving low latency and keeping the bandwidth low are contradictory requirements. Packet losses and transmission errors are other problems in streaming HD live video. Because errors in one video frame may propagate to subsequent frames when certain compression algorithms are used, small transmission errors may result in significant picture quality degradation over a period of time. Also, many live streaming systems do not recover packet losses in order to reduce end-to-end delay.

Figure 1 shows an experimental HD live video streaming system called HYDRA [3]. The source streams captured by a JVC JY-HD10U camera are packetized by a Linux machine and sent through the network. On the receiving side, a similar setting is employed. A Linux machine will recover the stream and perform video decompression and rendering in real time.

Figure 1. The HYDRA live-streaming architecture. Live HD video and
audio streams captured from a camera are transmitted to the stream
transmitter, which is connected to the receiver node via an IP network;
the audio and video streams are then decoded and rendered.

Video Acquisition and Compression

Two commonly used high definition video formats are 1080i and 720p. There is also an
Ultra High Definition Video format proposed by NHK, which has a resolution of 7,680 ×
4,320 pixels. Without any compression algorithms, the required bandwidth to transmit
the raw HD video may rise to as high as 1.485 Gb/s (e.g., the SMPTE[1] 292 standard).
Many existing IP-based networks do not provide such capacity to the end-user.
However, with compression algorithms, the bandwidth can be significantly reduced and
a typical rate is approximately 20Mb/s. Table 1 lists the bandwidth requirements for
some MPEG-2 compressed HD video formats.

Table 1. Commonly used HD video stream formats and their bandwidth requirement
for the H.262 codec[2] (MPEG-2).

Video Format	ATSC 1080i	ATSC 720p	HDV 720p
Frame resolution	1920 x 1080	1280 x 720	1280 x 720
Frames per second	30 (60 interlaced)	60 progressive	30 progressive
Compressed bandwidth	20 Mb/s	20 Mb/s	20 Mb/s

---

[1] Society of Motion Picture Television Engineers, http://www.smpte.org.
[2] Codec is short for compressor-decompressor.

Video cameras provide the sensor media stream in either uncompressed or compressed format. A common uncompressed output format is HD-SDI, which must be either captured with a compatible interface board in a computer or sent through an HD compressor. Some cameras directly produce a compressed stream, often delivered via an IEEE 1394 bus (i.e., FireWire) connection. Although video compression algorithms can reduce the bandwidth requirement, they often introduce additional delays. Commonly used encoding methods for HD video are H.262 (MPEG-2) or H.264 (MPEG-4 part 10). A number of proprietary formats suitable for production and editing environments (e.g., HDCAM) also exist. There are three ways to encode a frame in an MPEG-2 video bitstream: intra-coded (I), forward predicted (P) and bidirectional predicted (B). *I*-frames contain independent image data, which is passed through a series of transformations, including DCT, run-length and Huffman encoding. On the other hand, *P* and *B* frames only encode the difference between previous and/or subsequent images. As a result, *P* and *B* pictures are much smaller than *I* frames. A typical MPEG-2 video stream looks like this:

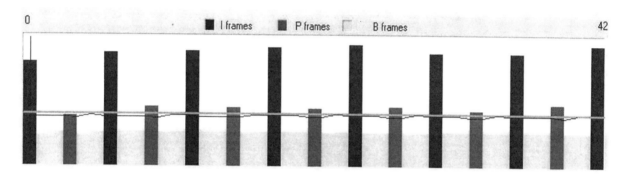

Figure 2. MPEG-2 stream structure with a GOP size of 6 (e.g., the JVC JY-HD10U camera). The y-axis represents the relative frame sizes.

A sequence of frames starting with an *I*-frame and including all subsequent non-*I* frames is called a group of pictures (GOP, see Figure 2). The fact that *P* and *B* frames depend on other frames has two important implications. First, a codec must keep several frames in memory to compute the differences across multiple frames. This increases the latency from the time the video sensor acquires an image until the compressed bitstream can be transmitted. Second, transmission errors in a previous frame may propagate to the current frame. For real-time and networked applications, transmission errors are common, especially when the bit rate is high. Therefore, different strategies may be employed to reliably transmit HD video over a network. We will cover some of them in the next section.

Compared to the H.262 codec, the newer H.264 codec allows a higher compression ratio. The H.264 codec supports multi-frame motion compensation, which allows a frame to compute motion vectors by referencing multiple previous pictures. However, due to its complexity, the H.264 codec may introduce a longer delay.

HD Video Transmission

To send the captured HD video to the remote destination, the source devices must interface with a network. Data streams are digitized and transmitted in discrete packets. The Real-time Transport Protocol (RTP) is often used to transmit video streams over a network. Since the purpose of many live streaming systems is to enable video conferencing among multiple sites, the H.323 protocol is often incorporated. To host a conference among multiple participants, H.323 introduces the concept of a multipoint control unit (MCU), which serves as a bridge to connect participants. Popular H.323 clients (non-HD) include GnomeMeeting and Microsoft NetMeeting.

To transmit HD video from a source to a destination, two factors need to be considered: (1) the actual bandwidth limitation of the link, and (2) its packet loss characteristics. Due to the high bandwidth requirement of HD video, the network may experience temporary congestions if the link is shared with other traffic. Moreover, adapting to these congestions is not instantaneous. As a result, packet losses may occur. For raw HD video, packet losses in one frame only affect that frame. However, for most codecs that use inter-frame compression, the error caused by packet loss in one frame may propagate to later frames. To recover packet losses, there exist three commonly used techniques: 1) forward error correction (FEC); 2) concealment; and 3) retransmission. FEC adds redundant data to the original video stream. As a result, the receiver can reconstruct the original data if packet losses occur. However, FEC adds a fixed bandwidth overhead to a transmission, irrespective of whether data loss occurs or not. Unlike FEC, the concealment solution does not recover packets. The receiver substitutes lost packets with the interpolated data calculated from previous frames. The goal is to keep the residual errors below a perceptual threshold. The receiver must be powerful enough to carry the workload of both rendering and data recovery. Finally, retransmission is a bandwidth-efficient solution to packet loss. Here, the receiver will detect lost data and request it again from the source. Hence, this approach introduces at least one round-trip delay, and therefore it may not be suitable for networks with long round-trip delays. The HYDRA live streaming system, for example, uses a single retransmission strategy to recover packet losses. Buffering is kept to a minimum to maintain a low end-to-end latency.

Rendering of HD Video Streams

When a media stream is transmitted over a network, the receiver side requires a low-delay rendering component to display the HD video stream. Various hardware and software options for decoding HD video streams are currently available. We classify them into the following two categories.

1. Hardware-based: When improved quality and picture stability are of paramount importance, hardware-based video rendering systems are often preferred. Commercial systems include, for example, the CineCast HD decoding board from Vela Research. It can communicate with the host computer through the SCSI (Small Computer Systems Interface) protocol. Other stand-alone decompressors require the input stream to be provided in the professional DVB-ASI format. The hardware solution has the advantage of usually providing a digital HD-SDI (uncompressed) output for very high picture quality and a genlock input for external synchronization. However, this type of solution may

be costly and some of the hardware decoders include significant buffers which increase the rendering delay.

2. <u>Software-based:</u> A cost-effective alternative to hardware-based rendering is using software tools. Recall that rendering HD video streams is computationally expensive. An example software rendering tool is the libmpeg2 library (a highly optimized rendering code that provides hardware-assisted MPEG decoding on current generation graphics adapters). Through the XvMC extensions of the Linux' X11 graphical user interface, libmpeg2 utilizes the motion compensation and iDCT hardware capabilities on modern graphics GPUs. This can be a very cost-effective solution since suitable graphics boards can be obtained for less than one hundred dollars. In terms of performance, this setup can easily achieve real-time performance with a modern CPU/GPU combination. Table 2 illustrates the measurements we recorded from the libmpeg2 library in decoding HD MPEG-2 streams with an Nvidia FX5200 GPU. Two sub-algorithms in the MPEG decoding process — motion compensation (MC) and inverse discreet cosine transform (iDCT) — can be performed either in software on the host CPU or on the graphics processing unit GPU. The tests were performed with dual Xeon 2.6 GHz CPUs. Without hardware support, the machine can only merely satisfy the requirement of HDV 720p.

Table 2. Two sub-algorithms in the MPEG decoding process — motion compensation (MC) and inverse discreet cosine transform (iDCT) — can be performed either in software on the host CPU or on the graphics processing unit (GPU)

Video Format	ATSC 1080i	ATSC 720p	HDV 720p
Rendering performance: Host CPU: MC & iDCT Graphics GPU: MC & iDCT	17.90 fps 33.48 fps	30.37 fps 63.28 fps	31.35 fps 67.76 fps

Delay Measurements

When transmitting live, interactive-media streams, one of the most critical aspects is the end-to-end latency experienced by the participants. The ideal transmission system would achieve very high quality while requiring minimal bandwidth and producing low latency. However, in a real-world design, a system must find a good compromise among all these requirements. Delays may result from many factors, including video encoding, decoding and network latency. Even monitors may introduce certain latency, for example plasma displays contain video scalers that can introduce several frames of latency. Because many rendering tools demultiplex video and audio streams, it is important to measure both the video and audio latency to understand whether the audio and video streams are synchronized.

Figure 3. The latency of the complete video chain: camera; acquisition computer; transmission; rendering computer; and display, with audio rendering disabled. A stop-watch application running on a computer (left). Camera rendering is shown on the right. As can be seen, the stop-watch reads 20:43:01, while the transmitted time shows 20:42:70. The difference of 0.31 seconds represents end-to-end video latency. Some blurring occurs because the monitor refresh rate is less than the 100 Hz required by the stop-watch application.

Many available devices constrain some of the design space and therefore parameters cannot be arbitrarily chosen. Let us consider the JVC JY-HD10U camera as an example video source. The built-in MPEG compressor is very effective, considering that the camcorder is designed to run on battery power for several hours. The unit produces a reasonable output bandwidth of 20 Mb/s. The high compression ratio is achieved by removing temporal redundancies across groups of six video frames (also called inter-frame coding in the MPEG standard with a group-of-picture (GOP) size of 6). Therefore, video-frame data must be kept in the camera memory for up to six frames, resulting in a (6 f)/(30 fps) = 0.2 second camera latency. Figure 3 shows the complete end-to-end delay across the following chain: camera (sensor and encoder); acquisition; computer transmission; and a rendering computer (decoder) display. The camera was directed at a stop-watch application running on a computer screen. Then a still picture is taken to show both the stop-watch application and its rendered video. The latency for video only was approximately 310 milliseconds, which, considering the complex computations in coding and decoding HD MPEG-2, is surprisingly good.

Audio delay can be measured with the set-up shown in Figure 4. An audio source produces a sound signal, which is then split with a Y-cable into two paths. The signal on the test path is sent to the microphone inputs of the camera and then passed through the HD live-streaming system. The audio signal is then converted back to its analog form in the rendering computer via a regular sound card. The measuring device records two audio signals arriving via the path directly from the source and the test path.

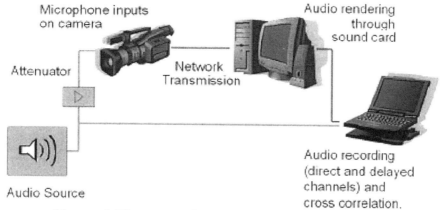

Figure 4. The set-up for audio delay measurements.

Figure 5 shows the original (top) and delayed (bottom) audio signals acquired by the measuring recorder. Due to effects of compression/decompression, the delayed audio signal looks different (i.e., with added noise) from the original waveform. Cross-correlation can be used to compare the two audio files and calculate the estimated delay.

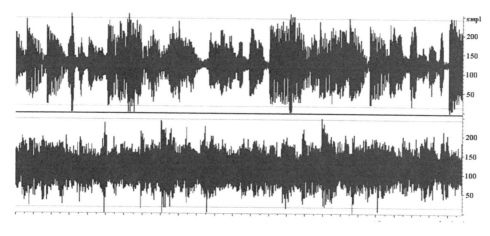

Figure 5. The original signal (top) and the transmitted (delayed) audio signal.

Application Areas

Many applications can benefit from HD live video streaming technology. Here we list several examples.

Video conferencing has become a common business tool, often replacing traditional face-to-face meetings. The user experience is very much dependent on the quality of the video and audio presented. Ideally, the technology should "disappear" and give way to natural interactions. HD video conferencing can aid in this goal in several ways. For example, users can be portrayed in life-size which helps to create the effect of a "window" between the conferencing locations [4]. In addition, non-verbal cues, which are important to human interactions, can be communicated via these high-resolution environments.

The **AccessGrid** is a collection of resources that support video and audio collaborations among a large number of groups. The resources include large display systems, powerful dedicated machines, high quality presentation and visualization environments, and high network bandwidth. AccessGrid can involve more than 100 sites in collaboration and each site is able to see all others. Unlike conventional H.323-based video conferencing systems, AccessGrid does not incorporate any MCU in its design. It uses IP-multicast to transmit the data from one site to all the others. An example AccessGrid system that delivers HD video was implemented at the Gwangju Institute of Science & Technology (GIST) Networked Media Laboratory. It uses the VideoLAN client (VLC) and DVTS (Digital Video Transport System) for high-quality video delivery.

The **Distributed Immersive Performance (DIP)** concept envisions the ultimate collaboration environment: a virtual space that enables live musical performances among multiple musicians and enjoyed by different audiences, all distributed around the globe. The participants, including subsets of musicians, the conductor and the audience, are in different physical locations. Immersive audio and high quality video, along with low latency networks are three major components that are required to bring DIP to reality. Early versions of the DIP concept have been successful demonstrated by a number of research groups. An example is a June 2003 networked duo, where two musicians played a tango together while physically being present in two different locations [5].

References

1. A. Pham and C. Hoffman, "Broadcasters Agree to Go All Digital," Los Angeles Times, Business Section, Page C1, July 13, 2005.
2. C. Perkins, L. Gharai, T. Lehman, and A. Mankin, "Experiments with Delivery of HDTV over IP Networks," Proceedings of the 12th International Packet Video Workshop, Pittsburgh, PA, USA, April 2002.
3. R. Zimmermann, M. Pawar, D. A. Desai, M. Qin, and H. Zhu, "High Resolution Live Streaming with the HYDRA Architecture," ACM Computers in Entertainment journal, Vol. 2, Issue 4, October/December 2004.
4. G. Mark and P. DeFlorio, "An Experiment Using Life-size HDTV," IEEE Workshop on Advanced Collaborative Environments, San Francisco, 2001.
5. A. A. Sawchuk, E. Chew, R. Zimmermann, C. Papadopoulos, and C. Kyriakakis, "From Remote Media Immersion to Distributed Immersive Performance," ACM Multimedia Workshop on Experiential Telepresence (ETP 2003), Berkeley, California, November 7, 2003.

HUFFMAN CODING

The most popular entropy-based encoding technique is the Huffman code [1]. It provides the least amount of information units (bits) per source symbol. This short article describes how it works.

The first step in the Huffman algorithm consists in creating a series of source reductions, by sorting the probabilities of each symbol and combining the (two) least probable symbols into a single symbol, which will then be used in the next source reduction stage.

Figure 1 shows an example of consecutive source reductions. The original source symbols appear on the left-hand side, sorted in decreasing order by their probability of occurrence. In the first reduction, the two least probable symbols (a_3 with prob. = 0.06 and a_5 with prob. = 0.04) are combined into a composite symbol, whose probability is 0.06 + 0.04 = 0.1. This composite symbol and its probability are copied onto the first source reduction column at the proper slot (so as to enforce the requirement that the probabilities are sorted in decreasing order at any reduction stage). The process continues until we reach a 2-symbol reduced source (which happens after four steps in this example).

Original source		Source reductions			
Symbol	Probability	1	2	3	4
a_2	0.4	0.4	0.4	0.4	0.6
a_6	0.3	0.3	0.3	0.3	0.4
a_1	0.1	0.1	0.2	0.3	
a_4	0.1	0.1	0.1		
a_3	0.06	0.1			
a_5	0.04				

Figure 1. Source reductions in Huffman's encoding algorithm.

The first step in the Huffman algorithm consists in encoding each reduced source, starting from the right hand side and moving towards the original source. The most compact binary code for a binary source is, obviously, formed by the symbols 0 and 1. These values are assigned to the two rightmost symbols (in this example, following a convention that states that 'the least probable symbol gets a bit 0'). Since the symbol whose probability is 0.6 was obtained as a combination of two other symbols during the source reduction steps, the 0 used to encode it is now assigned to both symbols from which it originated, appending a 0 or 1 to the right of each symbol (following the same convention) to tell them apart. The process is repeated for each reduced source until we return to the original source (Figure 2). The resulting code appears on the third column of Figure 2. The average codeword length can be calculated as:

$$L_{avg} = (0.4)(1) + (0.3)(2) + (0.1)(3) + (0.1)(4) + (0.06)(5) + (0.04)(5)$$
$$= 2.2 \text{ bits/symbol.}$$

The source entropy (calculated using eq. (1) under the **Image compression and coding** entry) in this case is 2.14 bits/symbol. The efficiency of the Huffman code is, therefore, equal to 2.14 / 2.2 = 0.973.

	Original source		Source reductions							
Symbol	Prob.	Code	1		2		3		4	
a_2	0.4	1	0.4	1	0.4	1	0.4	1	0.6	0
a_6	0.3	00	0.3	00	0.3	00	0.3	00	0.4	1
a_1	0.1	011	0.1	011	0.2	010	0.3	01		
a_4	0.1	0100	0.1	0100	0.1	011				
a_3	0.06	01010	0.1	0101						
a_5	0.04	01011								

Figure 2. Assigning codewords using Huffman algorithm.

The Huffman algorithm is optimal, in the sense that it generates the shortest possible average codeword length for a certain source. It is often referred to as 'instantaneous, uniquely decodable block coding', because each source symbol is encoded into a fixed sequence (block) of bits, each codeword can be decoded instantaneously, i.e., without the need to make reference to past or subsequent symbols, and there is only one way of decoding a certain string of 0s and 1s (i.e., no codeword is the prefix of another valid codeword).

When a large number of source symbols needs to be encoded, however, the original source reduction algorithm becomes impractical and computationally inefficient. This practical constraint has motivated the design of alternatives to the original Huffman coding algorithm in which the optimality of the code is partially sacrificed in name of implementation efficiency. Many variants of the original Huffman coding algorithm have been proposed in the literature. They are usually referred by names such as modified, truncated, or adaptive Huffman coding. Detailed descriptions of some of these variants, as well as many other relevant resources can be accessed from [2].

The optimality of the Huffman coding algorithm was also challenged by the arrival of arithmetic coding [3], a technique that encodes the entire message into a single number, n ($0.0 \leq n < 1.0$), overcoming the integer number of bits per symbol limitation of the original Huffman coding scheme.

References

1. D.A. Huffman, "A Method for the Construction of Minimum Redundancy Codes," Proceedings of the IRE, Vol. 40, No. 10, pp. 1098-1101, 1952.
2. Huffman Coding, http://datacompression.info/Huffman.shtml. Accessed July 13, 2005.
3. Arithmetic Coding, http://datacompression.info/ArithmeticCoding.shtml. Accessed July 13, 2005.

HUMAN COMPUTER INTERACTION

Hau San Wong and Horace H. S. Ip
Centre for Innovative Applications of Internet and Multimedia
*Technologies (**AIM**tech Centre)*
Image Computing Group, Department of Computer Science
City University of Hong Kong, Hong Kong

Introduction

Recent advances in human-computer interaction techniques have resulted in significant enhancement of user experience in different domains. Rather than being restricted to the use of keyboard and mouse for interactive purpose, which requires the learning of unnatural actions such as typing and clicking, and are particularly awkward to use in a 3D interactive environment, current HCI techniques make use of our natural capabilities such as speaking, gesturing, head turning and walking to facilitate the user-machine communication process. For example, speech recognition, which directly transforms spoken commands or dialogs into their textual forms, will minimize the required amount of learning for novice users and will also allow us to bypass the restriction of operating a miniature keyboard in mobile devices. The possibility of speech input will also be invaluable to users with different levels of dexterity impairments. On the other hand, gesture and motion-based interface, which automatically detects and associates various types of spatial movements with different intentions of the users, will be the natural choice for interaction in a 3D virtual environment.

In addition to these interaction modalities, there are recent researches on the possibility of performing automatic facial expression recognition in interfaces, such that the current emotional state of the user can be inferred [1]. The success of these efforts will result in promising new applications such as emotionally responsive virtual agents, and performance evaluation of actors/actresses based on their capabilities of mimicking various facial expressions. There are also recent adoptions of haptic feedback in user interfaces, which conveys important physical cues in a virtual reality interface and allows for effective manipulation of the objects in this environment, thus reinforcing the sense of presence for the users. In addition, the tactile modality is important in providing feedback for visually impaired users in advanced interfaces, as the user can then "feel" and physically "press" the control buttons of the interface through haptic input devices, and the different buttons can be distinguished by associating different levels of tactile feedback with them. Haptic devices are also important for the implementation of interfaces for the training of surgeons by associating the correct level of tactile feedback with particular incisions and suturing actions, and the enhancement of realism in computer games by providing suitable levels of force feedback to match with different scenarios.

To achieve human-computer interaction based on these new modalities, in particular for the case of gesture and motion recognition, will require either the introduction of new devices, or the adoption of advanced pattern classification and computer vision techniques. For example, gesture recognition can be achieved by using a data glove to convey information about the user's finger configuration to the interface, or by using vision-based interaction in which gesture information is directly extracted from a video sequence. The successful adoption of these techniques will thus allow users to freely express their intentions without being required to wear special devices and tethered to particular locations.

While commands issued through special input devices can be efficiently and unambiguously decoded through dedicated circuitries, pattern classification and computer vision techniques are computationally intensive and usually results in a non-zero recognition error. Specifically, pattern classification requires the determination of a set of suitable features for effective characterization of different types of inputs, the design of an optimal classifier based on an underlying feature model for categorizing feature representations into their correct classes, and the evaluation of the model in terms of classification errors. For example, in speech recognition, speech signals are partitioned into segments corresponding to short time frames, and features from the time and frequency domains are extracted and concatenated to form a feature vector. These feature vectors are then modeled as random variable realizations within a probabilistic framework based on the Hidden Markov Model [2], and feature vector sequences associated with different phonemes are modeled using their corresponding HMMs. HMMs are also useful for modeling the space-time trajectories associated with different gestures in gesture recognition [3], and the time-varying motion vector fields associated with different facial expressions in affective computing. As a result, the computational complexity and recognition error will thus highly depend on the selection of suitable features and the design of an optimal model for feature representation and classification. These problems are alleviated to a considerable extent recently by the identification of suitable hardware implementations for the pattern classification algorithms, and the inclusion of feedback mechanisms for users to correct the errors.

In addition, a major challenge is to effectively combine information in different modalities to achieve multimodal interface based on a multiple classifier framework, which can reduce the recognition error level beyond those achievable using a single modality, such that the experience of the users can be considerably enriched. For example, errors in speech recognition in a noisy environment can be compensated to a large extent by the inclusion of the gesture or facial expression modalities to disambiguate the user's intentions.

We next focus on the application of these enhanced interaction modalities to artistic creations. This emphasis is due to our viewpoint that, while the new interaction modalities currently play only a supportive role in conventional applications, since users can resort to keyboards or mice for most operations at the expense of a less enriched interactive process, the expression of artistic intentions cannot be easily supplanted by a set of typed commands or click sequences. As a result, the adoption of these enhanced modalities will be important and even essential for effective artistic expressions. Based on this emphasis, we introduce a number of innovative human-computer interaction environments for visual art creation and music composition.

Novel Body-Gesture Driven Interface for Visual Art Creation

The concept of generating creative work of art through body movement has been an important area explored by a number of artists and researchers in the fields of both arts and technology. These approaches all share the common conceptual ground that the human body movement and gestures are significant human expressions which communicate messages of human inner emotions and intentions when interacting with the outer environment. To further explore this relationship between body movement and users' intentions, the City University of Hong Kong develops a real-time body-driven human-computer interface, the **Body-Brush** [4], which is able to capture human motion and transform the motion data into vibrant visual forms. This interface can preserve the 3-D information of body motion. It enables users to interact intuitively with the machine and control the rich visual simulation in synchronization with the body motion.

With a systematic study of the relations between the human body movement and the visual art language, Body-Brush turns the human body as a whole into a dynamic brush. This is achieved with the development of an immersive computer-vision-based motion analysis system with frontal infrared illumination, and an innovative graphic rendering software that maps the body motion gesture-path-energy to the colour-form-space visual attributes. Since users are not required to wear any specific sensor devices to be recognized by the computer or receive any prior training to use the man-machine interface, Body-Brush enables human to express freely and interact intuitively with the machine. The Body Brush interactive environment is illustrated in Figure 1 (a)

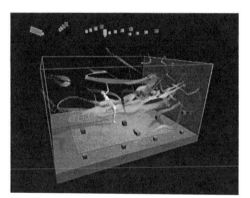 

(a) Illustration of the Body Brush Interface   (b) Setup of the Body Brush Interface

Figure 1. The city University of Hong Kong *Body Brush* system [5].

In this system, human motion is captured by a set of frontal infra-red illumination and a set of infra-red cameras. In this way, the extraction of the body silhouette is not sensitive to the environmental lighting condition, and users are not required to wear specific color clothing or sensor devices. The user can thus move unobstructed and express freely in the space.

The video images of the motion body are taken at orthogonal angles by the two infra-red sensitive cameras mounted outside of the 3-D canvas. From the two streams of video images, the user's position within the 3-D canvas space is calculated and the body gestures of the user are extracted and analyzed at video frame rate. A number of numerical measurements relating to the user's gesture are computed and these measurements are translated into various drawing attributes such as color (hue, value, saturation, and opacity), stroke path and stroke cross-section (for 3D modeling). Finally, these drawing attributes are painted onto a pair of stereo-images and projected back onto the 3-D canvas in synchronization of the user's movement, enabling real-time interaction between the user and the virtual painting and sculpture. The setup of the Body Brush interface is illustrated in Figure 1 (b).

Based on the assumption that uplifted moods are associated with more vibrant color combinations, we design the mapping rules between motion and the color attributes of the virtual brush strokes as follows: Different hues are associated with different points in the 3D space, while the color intensity is related to the motion speed, such that higher speed results in brighter color, and *vice versa*. The color saturation is related to motion acceleration, such that acceleration generates a more saturated color. In addition, the body dimension determines the size of the brushstroke. Examples of virtual paintings created through the Body Brush interface are shown in Figure 2.

Figure 2. Examples of virtual painted created through *Body Brush*.

Hand-Gesture Interface for Music Composition

One of the major functions of music is to express and communicate ones' feelings, emotions and thoughts to the audience. Through an expressive musical piece, the audience could perceive and interpret the emotions and messages delivered by the composer and performer. However, before artists can genuinely express themselves through music, it is usually necessary for them to master music theories or the techniques of using a musical instrument for playing music. As a result, this learning curve is the major barrier that prevents artists from expressing themselves freely through the musical medium. In view of these difficulties, the **AIM**tech Centre at City University of Hong Kong has developed two innovative interfaces, a glove-based system called *Cyber Composer* [6], and a vision-based system known as *Body Baton*, to eliminate this barrier by enabling the users to dynamically control the musical sound generation and variations through their gestures and body motions.

Cyber Composer is designed such that no musical instrument is required in the music generation process. It is composed of the music interface, CyberGlove interface, background music generation module and the melody generation module. Figure 3 shows an overview of the architecture of Cyber Composer.

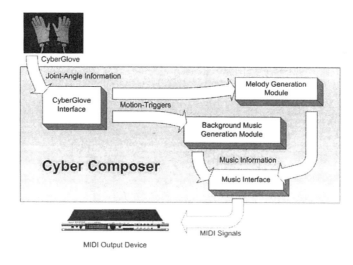

Figure 3. Architecture of the Cyber Composer interface.

The CyberGlove interface sends gesture, in the form of joint angle measurements, and 3D positioning information to the system. These are then translated into parameters for real-time music generation. Background music generation module generates music according to the processed gesture information, constraints imposed by music theories, and user-defined parameters such as tempo and key. The music interface then converts these musical expressions into MIDI signals and output to a MIDI device

Specifically, the height of the user is used to adjust the pitch of the sound. The pitch will change when the user raises his/her hands, jumps up or crouches down. We choose this height-to-pitch mapping because people are used to associating "taller" with note of higher frequency and *vice versa*, so users should be able to learn how to control the pitch easily and intuitively. On the other hand, the body dimension is mapped to the volume control of musical sound generation, given the usual association of a wider body extent to a greater sound amplitude. In addition, the position of the user controls the stereo placement of the musical sound. For example, if the user moves closer to one of the two speakers, that speaker will sound louder. Figure 4 shows a Body Baton user displaying a typical gesture when composing a musical piece.

Figure 4. A Body Baton user displaying a typical gesture.

Conclusion

Human computer interface has moved from communicating with the machines through ways which are natural to them, e.g. textual commands and data via keyboard or the mouse, to ways and means which are natural to the human, e.g. speech, vision, gestures and tactile feedback. We have shown here several examples of applying novel human-computer interaction principles to the realm of artistic creation.

See: Vision-Based Interaction, Haptic Feedback in User Interfaces, Multimodal Interfaces

References

1. R. Picard, "Affective Computing," MIT Press, 1997.
2. L.R. Rabiner, "A tutorial on Hidden Markov Model and selected applications in speech recognition," Proceedings of the IEEE, Vol. 77, No. 2, pp. 257-286, 1989.
3. A.D. Wilson and A. F. Bobick, "Parametric Hidden Markov Models for gesture recognition," IEEE Transactions on Pattern Analysis and Machine Intelligence, Vol. 21, No. 9, pp. 884-900, 1999.
4. H. H S Ip, H. Young, and A. Tang, "Body Brush: A body driven interface for visual aesthetics," ACM Multimedia 2002, Juan-les-Pins, France, December 2002.
5. H. H. S. Ip, H. Young, and A. Tang, "Body Brush: An Interface Where Aesthetic and Technology Meet," SIGGRAPH 2003, Emerging Technologies, San Diego, LA, USA, July 2003.
6. H.H.S. Ip, K. Law, and B. Kwong, "Cyber Composer: Hand Gesture-Driven Intelligent Music Composition and Generation," Proceedings of 11th Multimedia Modeling Conference (MMM2005), Melbourne, Australia, January 2005.

I

IMAGE AND VIDEO CAPTURE

Definition: *Image video capture interface is responsible for acquiring both data and control signals from the CMOS or CCD camera sensor as well as providing the appropriate formatting of the data prior to being routed to memory through DMA.*

The camera sensor may provide either raw or pre-processed image data to the interface through a variety of programmable options. The interface receives the video/image data stream from the camera sensor and provides all control signalling for this operation as either a Master or Slave device. In the Master mode, the line and frame synchronization signals are provided by the CMOS sensor and in Slave mode, the synchronization signals are provided by the interface (see Figure 1). Several reduced pin-count alternatives are supported as subsets of the Master mode of operation. These include allowing the data to be serialized and the elimination of the separate synchronization signals for sensors that utilize the ITU-R BT.656 Start- of-Active-Video (SAV) and End-of-Active-Video (EAV) embedded in the data stream. The width of the data bus is also flexible and may be configured in an 8, 9, or 10- wire parallel mode or in a 4 or 5-wire serialized mode.

The pixel data received may be in several possible formats. These formats include RAW, YCbCr 4:2:2, RGB 8:8:8, RGB 6:6:6, RGB 5:6:5, RGBT 5:5:5, and RGB 4:4:4. When a RAW capture mode is enabled, the data may be in 8, 9, or 10-bit formats. The RAW data is de-serialized if necessary, and then packed as either 8-bit or 16-bit elements prior to transfer to memory. In a similar manner the pre-processed RGB and YCbCr image formats are packed into 16-bit or 32- bit elements.

The YCbCr format has the additional option of being planerized prior to being stored to memory. This planarization facilitates SIMD processing (for example, using Wireless MMX) as well as immediate display using the color space conversion engine available in some advanced the LCD controller. The RGB formats may also be formatted to enable immediate preview using the LCD controller. Programmable options are provided to reduce RGB component precisions and provide the transparency management for use with the LCD overlays. The formatting options offer value in reducing power consumption during the digital viewfinder preview sequence for image and video capture.

For the camera sensors with higher pixel counts, only support raw format in favor of reducing camera complexity. Raw pixel processing (i.e. conversion from bayer pattern, correcting for noise and camera irregularities) can be done on the camera interface. Some advanced camera interfaces support these algorithmic operations.

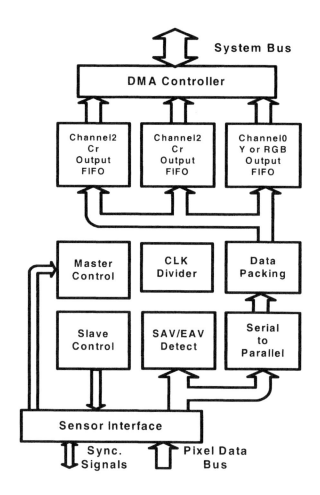

Figure 1. Interface for image and video capture.

See: Multimedia System-on-a-Chip

References

1. Interfaces for Digital Component Video Signals in 525-Line and 625-Line Television Systems operating at the 4:2:2 Level of Recommendation ITU-R BT.601 (Part A), ITU-R Recommendation BT.656-3, 1995.

IMAGE AND VIDEO QUALITY ASSESSMENT

Kalpana Seshadrinathan and Alan C. Bovik
The University of Texas at Austin, USA

Definition: *Image and video quality assessment deals with quantifying the quality of an image or video signal as seen by a human observer using an objective measure.*

Introduction

In this article, we discuss methods to evaluate the quality of digital images and videos, where the final image is intended to be viewed by the human eye. The quality of an image that is meant for human consumption can be evaluated by showing it to a human observer and asking the subject to judge its quality on a pre-defined scale. This is known as *subjective assessment* and is currently the most common way to assess image and video quality. Clearly, this is also the most reliable method as we are interested in evaluating quality *as seen by the human eye*. However, to account for human variability in assessing quality and to have some statistical confidence in the score assigned by the subject, several subjects are required to view the same image. The final score for a particular image can then be computed as a statistical average of the sample scores. Also, in such an experiment, the assessment is dependent on several factors such as the display device, distance of viewing, content of the image, whether or not the subject is a trained observer who is familiar with processing of images etc. Thus, a change in viewing conditions would entail repeating the experiment! Imagine this process being repeated for every image that is encountered and it becomes clear why subjective studies are cumbersome and expensive. It would hence be extremely valuable to formulate some *objective measure* that can predict the quality of an image.

The problem of image and video quality assessment is to quantify the quality of an image or video signal *as seen by a human observer* using an objective measure. The quality assessment techniques that we present in this article are known as *full-reference* techniques, i.e. it is assumed that in addition to the test image whose quality we wish to evaluate, a "perfect" reference image is also available. We are, thus, actually evaluating the fidelity of the image, rather than the quality. Evaluating the quality of an image without a reference image is a much harder problem and is known as *blind* or *no-reference* quality assessment. Blind techniques generally reduce the storage requirements of the algorithm, which could lead to considerable savings, especially in the case of video signals. Also, in certain applications, the original uncorrupted image may not be available. However, blind algorithms are also difficult to develop as the interpretation of the content and quality of an image by the HVS depends on high-level features such as attentive vision, cognitive understanding, and prior experiences of viewing similar patterns, which are not very well understood. *Reduced reference* quality assessment techniques form the middle ground and use some information from the reference signal, without requiring that the entire reference image be available.

Why Do We Need Quality Assessment?

Image and video quality assessment plays a fundamental role in the design and evaluation of imaging and image processing systems. For example, the goal of image and video compression algorithms is to reduce the amount of data required to store an image and at the same time, ensure that the resulting image is of sufficiently high quality. Image enhancement and restoration algorithms attempt to generate an image that is of better visual quality from a degraded image. Quality assessment algorithms are also useful in the design of image acquisition systems and to evaluate display devices etc. Communication networks have developed tremendously over the past decade and images and video are frequently transported over optic fiber, packet switched networks like the Internet, wireless systems etc. Bandwidth efficiency of applications such as video conferencing and Video on Demand (VOD) can be improved using quality assessment systems to evaluate the effects of channel errors on the transported images and video. Finally, quality assessment and the psychophysics of human vision are closely related disciplines. Evaluation of quality requires clear understanding of the sensitivities of the HVS to several features such as luminance, contrast, texture, and masking that are discussed in detail in Section 4.1. Research on image and video quality assessment may lend deep insights into the functioning of the HVS, which would be of great scientific value.

Why is Quality Assessment So Hard?

At first glance, a reasonable candidate for an image quality metric might be the Mean-Squared Error (MSE) between the reference and distorted images. Consider a reference image and test image denoted by $R = R(i, j)$ and $T = T(i, j)$ respectively, where $0 \le i \le N - 1, 0 \le j \le M - 1$. Then, the MSE is defined by:

$$MSE = \frac{1}{NM} \sum_{i=0}^{N-1} \sum_{j=0}^{M-1} [T(i, j) - R(i, j)]^2$$

MSE is a function of the Euclidean distance between the two vectors R and T in an MN-dimensional space. Since the MSE is a monotonic function of the error between corresponding pixels in the reference and distorted images, it is a reasonable metric and is often used as a quality measure. Some of the reasons for the popularity of this metric are its simplicity, ease of computation and analytic tractability. However, it has long been known to correlate very poorly with visual quality [1]. A few simple examples are sufficient to demonstrate that MSE is *completely unacceptable* as a visual quality predictor. This is illustrated in Fig.1 which shows several images whose MSE with respect to the reference are identical, but have very different visual quality. The main reason for the failure of MSE as a quality metric is the absence of any kind of modeling of the sensitivities of the HVS.

The difficulties in developing objective measures of image quality are best illustrated by example. Figure 1(a) and (b) show the original "Caps" and "Buildings" images respectively. Figure 1(c) and (d) show JPEG compressed versions of these images of approximately the same MSE. While the distortion in the "Buildings" image is hardly visible, it is visibly annoying in the "Caps" image. The perception of distortion varies with the actual image at hand and this effect is part of what makes quality assessment difficult. There is enormous diversity in the content of images used in different applications and even within images of a specific category, for example, the class of images obtained from the real world. Consistent performance of a quality assessment algorithm irrespective of the specific image at hand is no easy task. Additionally, different kinds of distortion produce different characteristic artifacts and it is very difficult for a quality assessment algorithm to predict degradation in visual quality *across distortion types*. For example, JPEG produces characteristic blocking artifacts and blurring of fine details (Figure 1(c) and (d)).

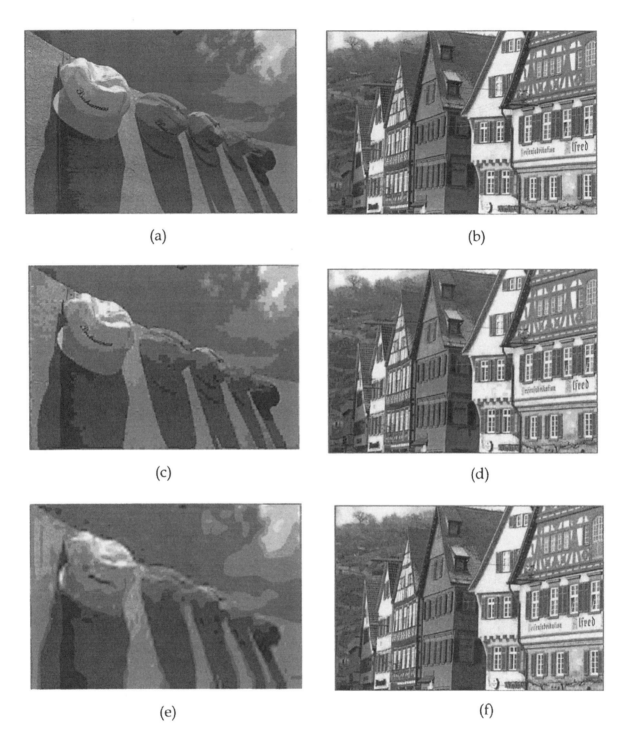

Figure 1. (a) Original "Caps" image (b) Original "Buildings" image (c) JPEG compressed image, MSE = 160 (d) JPEG compressed image, MSE = 165 (e) JPEG 2000 compressed image, MSE = 155 (f) AWGN corrupted image, MSE = 160.

This is due to the fact that it is a block-based algorithm that achieves compression by removing the highest frequency components that the HVS is least sensitive to. JPEG 2000 compression eliminates blocking artifacts, but produces ringing distortions that are visible in areas surrounding edges, such as around the edges of the caps in Figure 1(e). Sub-band decompositions, such as those used in JPEG 2000, attempt to approximate the image using finite-duration basis functions and this causes ringing around discontinuities like edges due to Gibb's phenomenon. Figure 1(f) shows an image that is corrupted by Additive White Gaussian Noise (AWGN) which looks grainy, seen clearly in the smooth background regions of the image. This kind of noise is typically observed in a lot of imaging devices and images transmitted through certain communication channels. A generic image quality measure should predict visual quality in a robust manner across these and several other types of distortions.

Thus, it is not an easy task for a machine to automatically predict quality by computation, although the human eye is very good at evaluating the quality of an image almost instantly. We explore some state-of-the-art techniques for objective quality assessment in the following sections.

Approaches to Quality Assessment

Techniques for image and video quality assessment can broadly be classified as bottom-up and top-down approaches. Bottom-up approaches attempt to model the functioning of the HVS and characterize the sensitivities and limitations of the human eye to predict the quality of a given image. Top-down approaches, on the other hand, usually make some high-level assumption on the technique adopted by the human eye in evaluating quality and use this to develop a quality metric. Top-down methods are gaining popularity due to their low computational complexity, as they don't attempt to model the functioning of the entire HVS, but only try to characterize the features of the HVS that are *most relevant* in evaluating quality. Also, the HVS is a complex entity and even the low-level processing in the human eye that includes the optics, striate cortex and retina are not understood well enough today, which reflects on the accuracy of existing HVS models. In this chapter, we categorize several state-of-the-art quality assessment techniques into three main categories, namely HVS modeling based approaches, structural approaches and information theoretic approaches. Each of these paradigms in perceptual quality assessment is explained in detail in the following sections.

HVS-based Approaches

Most HVS-based approaches can be summarized by the diagram shown in Figure 2. The initial step in the process usually involves the decomposition of the image into different spatial-frequency bands. It is well known that cells in the visual cortex are specialized and tuned to different ranges of spatial frequencies and orientations. Experimental studies indicate that the radial frequency selective mechanisms have constant octave bandwidths and the orientation selectivity is a function of the radial frequencies. Several transforms have been proposed to model the spatial frequency selectivity of the HVS and the initial step in an HVS-based approach is usually a decomposition of the image into different sub-bands using a filter-bank.

The perception of brightness is not a linear function of the luminance and this effect is known as luminance masking. In fact, the threshold of visibility of a brightness pattern is a linear function of the background luminance. In other words, brighter regions in an image can tolerate more noise due to distortions before it becomes visually annoying. The Contrast Sensitivity Function (CSF) provides a description of the frequency response of the HVS, which can be thought of as a band-pass filter. For example, the HVS is less sensitive to higher spatial frequencies and this fact is exploited by most compression algorithms to encode images at low bit rates, with minimal degradation in visual quality. Most HVS-based approaches use some kind of modeling of the luminance masking and contrast sensitivity properties of the HVS as shown in Figure 2.

In Figure 1, the distortions are clearly visible in the "Caps" image, but they are hardly noticeable in the "Buildings" image, despite the MSE being the same. This is a consequence of the contrast masking property of the HVS, wherein the visibility of certain image components is reduced due to the presence of other strong image components with similar spatial frequencies and orientations at neighboring spatial locations. Thus, the strong edges and structure in the "Buildings" image effectively mask the distortion, while it is clearly visible in the smooth "Caps" image. Usually, a HVS-based metric incorporates modeling of the contrast masking property, as shown in Figure 2.

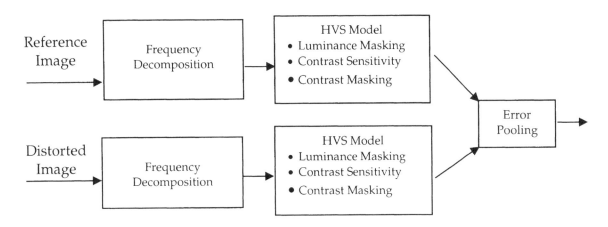

Figure 2. Block diagram of HVS-based quality metrics.

In developing a quality metric, a signal is first decomposed into several frequency bands and the HVS model specifies the maximum possible distortion that can be introduced in each frequency component before the distortion becomes visible. This is known as the Just Noticeable Difference (JND). The final stage in the quality evaluation involves combining the errors in the different frequency components, after normalizing them with the corresponding sensitivity thresholds, using some metric such as the Minkowski error. The final output of the algorithm is either a spatial map showing the image quality at different spatial locations or a single number describing the overall quality of the image.

Different proposed quality metrics differ in the models used for the blocks shown in Figure 2. Notable amongst the HVS-based quality measures are the Visible Difference Predictor [2], the Teo and Heeger model [3], Lubin's model [4] and Sarnoff's JNDMetrix technology [5].

Structural Approaches

Structural approaches to image quality assessment, in contrast to HVS-based approaches, take a top-down view of the problem. Here, it is hypothesized that the HVS has evolved to extract *structural information* from a scene and hence, quantifying the loss in structural information can accurately predict the quality of an image [6]. In Figure 1, the distorted versions of the "Buildings" image and the "Caps" image have the same MSE with respect to the reference image. The bad visual quality of the "Caps" image can be attributed to the structural distortions in both the background and the objects in the image. The structural philosophy can also accurately predict the good visual quality of the "Buildings" image, since the structure of the image remains almost intact in both distorted versions.

Structural information is defined as those aspects of the image that are independent of the luminance and contrast, since the structure of various objects in the scene is independent of the brightness and contrast of the image. The Structural SIMilarity (SSIM) algorithm, also known as the Wang-Bovik Index partitions the quality assessment problem into three components, namely luminance, contrast and structure comparisons.

Let $\vec{x}$ and $\vec{y}$ represent N - dimensional vectors containing pixels from the reference and distorted images respectively. Then, the Wang-Bovik Index between $\vec{x}$ and $\vec{y}$ is defined by:

$$SSIM(\vec{x},\vec{y}) = \left(\frac{2\mu_x\mu_y + C_1}{\mu_x^2 + \mu_y^2 + C_1} \right)^{\alpha} \left(\frac{2\sigma_x\sigma_y + C_2}{\sigma_x^2 + \sigma_y^2 + C_2} \right)^{\beta} \left(\frac{\sigma_{xy} + C_3}{\sigma_x\sigma_y + C_3} \right)^{\gamma} \qquad (1)$$

where:

$$\mu_x = \frac{1}{N}\sum_{i=1}^{N} x_i, \sigma_x = \left(\frac{1}{N-1}\sum_{i=1}^{N}(x_i - \mu_x)^2 \right)^{1/2}, \sigma_{xy} = \frac{1}{N-1}\sum_{i=1}^{N}(x_i - \mu_x)(y_i - \mu_y) \ .$$

C_1, C_2 and C_3 are small constants added to avoid numerical instability when the denominators of the fractions are small. α, β and γ are non-negative constants that control the relative contributions of the three different measurements to the Wang-Bovik Index.

The three terms in the right hand side of Equation (1) are the luminance, contrast and structure comparison measurements respectively. μ_x and μ_y are estimates of the mean luminance of the two images and hence, the first term in Eqn. (1) defines the luminance comparison function. It is easily seen that the luminance comparison function satisfies the desirable properties of being bounded by 1 and attaining the maximum possible value if and only if the means of the two images are equal. Similarly, σ_x and σ_y are estimates of the contrast of the two images and the second term in Eqn. (1) defines the contrast comparison function. Finally, the structural comparison is performed between the luminance and contrast normalized signals, given by $(\vec{x} - \mu_x)/\sigma_x$ and $(\vec{y} - \mu_y)/\sigma_y$. The correlation or inner product between these signals is an effective measure of the structural similarity. The correlation between the normalized vectors is equal to the correlation coefficient between the original signals $\vec{x}$ and $\vec{y}$, which is defined by the third term in Equation (1). Note that the Wang-Bovik Index is also bounded by 1 and attains unity if and only if the two images are equal.

The structural philosophy overcomes certain limitations of HVS-based approaches such as computational complexity and inaccuracy of HVS models. The idea of quantifying structural distortions is not only novel, but also intuitive, and experimental studies show that the algorithm is competitive with several other state-of-the-art quality metrics.

Information Theoretic Approaches

Information theoretic approaches attempt to quantify the *loss in the information* that the HVS can extract from a given test image, as compared to the original reference image [7]. *Mutual information* between two random sources is a statistical measure that quantifies the amount of information one source contains about the other. In other words, assuming the distorted and reference images to be samples obtained from two random sources, mutual information measures the distance between the distributions of these sources. Information theoretic approaches use this measure to quantify the amount of information that the human eye can obtain from a given image, to develop a metric that correlates well with visual quality. The Visual Information Fidelity (VIF) criterion, also known as the Sheikh-Bovik Index, assumes that the distorted image is the output of a communication channel that introduces errors in the image that passes through it. The HVS is also assumed to be a communication channel that limits the amount of information that can pass through it.

Photographic images of natural scenes exhibit striking structures and dependencies and are far from random. A random image generated assuming an independent and identically distributed Gaussian source, for example, will look nothing like a natural image. Characterizing the distributions and statistical dependencies of natural images provides a description of the subspace spanned by natural images, in the space of all possible images. Such probabilistic models have been studied by numerous researchers and one model that has achieved considerable success is known as the Gaussian Scale Mixture (GSM) model [8]. This is the source model used to describe the statistics of the wavelet coefficients of reference images in the Sheikh-Bovik Index. Let $\vec{R}$ represent a collection of wavelet coefficients from neighboring spatial locations of the original image. Then, $\vec{R} \sim z\vec{U}$, where z represents a scalar random variable known as the mixing density and $\vec{U}$ represents a zero-mean, white Gaussian random vector. Instead of explicitly characterizing the mixing density, the maximum likelihood estimate of the scalar z is derived from the given image in the development of the Sheikh-Bovik Index.

Let $\vec{D}$ denote the corresponding coefficients from the distorted image. The distortion channel that the reference image passes through to produce the distorted image is modeled using:

$$\vec{D} = g\vec{R} + \vec{v}$$

This is a simple signal attenuation plus additive noise model, where g represents a scalar attenuation and $\vec{V}$ is additive Gaussian noise. Most commonly occurring distortions such as compression and blurring can be approximated by this model reasonably well. This model has some nice properties such as analytic tractability, ability to characterize a wide variety of distortions and computational simplicity. Additionally, both reference and distorted images pass through a communication channel that models the HVS. The HVS model is given by:

$$\vec{R}_{out} = \vec{R} + \vec{N}_1, \vec{D}_{out} = \vec{D} + \vec{N}_2$$

where $\vec{N}_1$ and $\vec{N}_2$ represent additive Gaussian noise, that is independent of the input image. The entire system is illustrated in Figure 3.

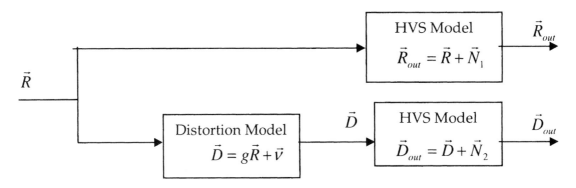

Figure 3. Block diagram of the Sheikh-Bovik quality assessment system.

The VIF criterion is then defined for these coefficients using:

$$VIF = \frac{I(\vec{D}; \vec{D}_{out} / z)}{I(\vec{R}; \vec{R}_{out} / z)} \qquad (2)$$

$I(\vec{D}; \vec{D}_{out} / z)$ represents the mutual information between $\vec{D}$ and $\vec{D}_{out}$, conditioned on the estimated value of z. The denominator of Equation (2) represents the amount of information that the HVS can extract from the original image. The numerator represents the amount of information that the HVS can extract from the distorted image. The ratio of these two quantities hence is a measure of the amount of information in the distorted image relative to the reference image and has been shown to correlate very well with visual quality. Closed form expressions to compute this quantity have been derived and further details can be found in [7]. Note that wavelet coefficients corresponding to the same spatial location can be grouped separately, for example, coefficients in each sub-band of the wavelet decomposition can be collected into a separate vector. In this case, these different quality indices for the same spatial location have to be appropriately combined. This results in a spatial map containing the Sheikh-Bovik quality Index of the image, which can then be combined to produce an overall index of goodness for the image.

The success of the information theoretic paradigm lies primarily in the use of accurate statistical models for the natural images and the distortion channel. Natural scene modeling is in some sense a dual of HVS modeling, as the HVS has evolved in response to the natural images it perceives. The equivalence of this approach to certain HVS-based approaches has also been established. The idea of quantifying information loss and the deviation of a given image from certain expected statistics provides an altogether new and promising perspective on the problem of image quality assessment.

Figure 4 illustrates the power of the Wang-Bovik and Sheikh-Bovik indices in predicting image quality. Notice that the relative quality of the images, as predicted by both indices, is the same and agrees reasonably well with human perception of quality. In the Video Quality Experts Group (VQEG) Phase I FR-TV tests [9], which provides performance evaluation procedures for quality metrics, logistic functions are used in a fitting procedure to obtain a non-linear mapping between objective/subjective scores first. Hence, the differences in the absolute values of quality predicted by the two algorithms are not important.

Conclusions

In this chapter, we have attempted to present a short survey of image quality assessment techniques. Researchers in this field have primarily focused on techniques for images as this is easier and usually the first step in developing a video quality metric. Although insights from image quality metrics play a huge role in the design of metrics for video, it is not always a straight forward extension of a two-dimensional problem into three dimensions. The fundamental change in moving from images to video is the motion of various objects in a scene. From the perspective of quality assessment, video metrics require modeling of the human perception of motion and quality of motion in the distorted image. Most of the algorithms discussed here have been extended to evaluate the quality of video signals and further details can be found in the references.

Considerable progress has been made in the field of quality assessment over the years, especially in the context of specific applications like compression and halftoning. Most of the initial work dealt with the threshold of perceived distortion in images, as opposed to supra-threshold distortion which refers to artifacts that are perceptible. Recent work in the field has concentrated on generic, robust quality measures in a full reference framework for supra-threshold distortions. No-reference quality assessment is still in its infancy and is likely to be the thrust of future research in this area.

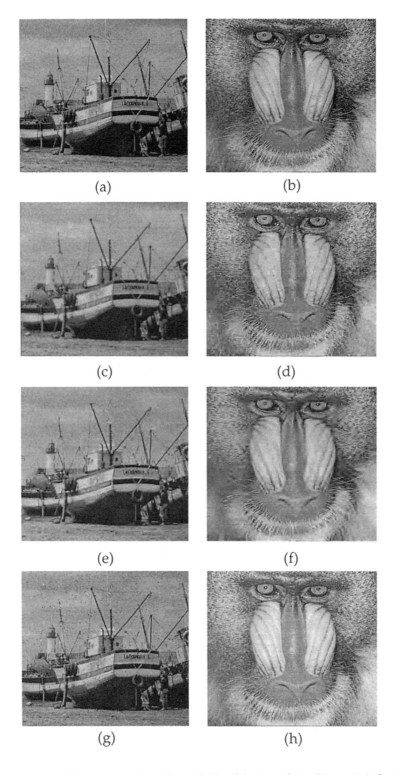

Figure 4. Illustration of the Wang-Bovik and Sheikh-Bovik indices. (a) Original 'Boats' image (b) Original 'Mandrill' image (c) Gaussian Blurring, SSIM = 0.85, VIF = 0.25 (d) JPEG compression, SSIM = 0.54, VIF = 0.07 (e) JPEG2000 compression, SSIM = 0.78, VIF = 0.11 (f) JPEG2000 compression, SSIM = 0.48, VIF = 0.05 (g) Salt and Pepper noise, SSIM = 0.87, VIF = 0.38 (h) Mean shifted, SSIM = 0.99, VIF = 1

References

1. B. Girod, "What's wrong with mean-squared error," Digital Images and Human Vision, A. B. Watson Ed., MIT Press, 1993, pp. 207-220.
2. S. Daly, "The Visible Difference Predictor: An algorithm for the assessment of image fidelity," Proceedings of the SPIE, Vol. 1616, 1992, pp. 2-15.
3. P.C. Teo and D.J. Heeger, "Perceptual image distortion," Proceedings of the SPIE, Vol. 2179, 1994, pp. 127-141.
4. J. Lubin, "The use of psychophysical data and models in the analysis of display system performance," Digital Images and Human Vision, A. B. Watson Ed., MIT Press, 1993, pp. 163-178.
5. Sarnoff Corporation, "JNDMetrix Technology," 2003, evaluation version available: http://www.sarnoff.com/products_services/video_vision/jndmetrix/downloads.asp.
6. Z. Wang, A.C. Bovik, H.R. Sheikh, and E.P. Simoncelli, "Image quality assessment: From error visibility to structural similarity," IEEE Transactions on Image Processing, Vol. 13, No. 4, April 2004, pp. 1-14.
7. H.R. Sheikh and A.C. Bovik, "Image information and visual quality," IEEE Transactions on Image Processing, Accepted for publication, September 2004.
8. M.J. Wainwright and E.P. Simoncelli, "Scale mixtures of Gaussians and the statistics of natural images," Advances in Neural Information Processing Systems, S.A. Solla, T.K. Leen, and K.R. Mueller Eds., Cambridge, MA: MIT Press, May 2000, Vol. 12, pp. 855-861.
9. VQEG, "Final report from the video quality experts group on the validation of objective models of video quality assessment," March 2000. http://www.vqeg.org.

IMAGE COMPRESSION AND CODING

Oge Marques
Department of Computer Science and Engineering
Florida Atlantic University, Boca Raton, FL, USA

Definition: Image compression deals with reducing the amount of data required to represent a digital image by removing of redundant data.

Images can be represented in digital format in many ways. Encoding the contents of a 2-D image in a raw bitmap (raster) format is usually not economical and may result in very large files. Since raw image representations usually require a large amount of storage space (and proportionally long transmission times in the case of file uploads/downloads), most image file formats employ some type of compression. The need to save storage space and shorten transmission time, as well as the human visual system tolerance to a modest amount of loss, have been the driving factors behind image compression techniques.

Compression methods can be *lossy*, when a tolerable degree of deterioration in the visual quality of the resulting image is acceptable, or *lossless*, when the image is encoded in its full quality. The overall results of the compression process, both in terms of storage savings – usually expressed numerically in terms of compression ratio (CR) or bits per pixel (bpp) – as well as resulting quality loss (for the case of lossy techniques) may vary depending on the technique, format, options (such as the quality setting for JPEG), and the image contents. As a general guideline, lossy compression should be used for general purpose photographic images, whereas lossless compression should be preferred when dealing with line art, technical drawings, cartoons, etc. or images in which no loss of detail may be tolerable (most notably, space images and medical images).

We will review the most important concepts behind image compression and coding techniques and survey some of the most popular algorithms and standards.

Fundamentals of visual data compression

The general problem of image compression is to reduce the amount of data required to represent a digital image or video and the underlying basis of the reduction process is the removal of redundant data. Mathematically, visual data compression typically involves transforming (encoding) a 2-D pixel array into a statistically uncorrelated data set. This transformation is applied prior to storage or transmission. At some later time, the compressed image is decompressed to reconstruct the original image information (preserving or lossless techniques) or an approximation of it (lossy techniques).

Redundancy

Data compression is the process of reducing the amount of data required to represent a given quantity of information. Different amounts of data might be used to communicate the same amount of information. If the same information can be represented using different amounts of data, it is reasonable to believe that the representation that requires more data contains what is technically called *data redundancy*.

Image compression and coding techniques explore three types of redundancies: *coding* redundancy, *interpixel* (spatial) redundancy, and *psychovisual* redundancy. The way each of them is explored is briefly described below.

- **Coding redundancy**: consists in using variable-length codewords selected as to match the statistics of the original source, in this case, the image itself or a processed version of its pixel values. This type of coding is always reversible and usually implemented using look-up tables (LUTs). Examples of image coding schemes that explore coding redundancy are the Huffman codes and the arithmetic coding technique.

- **Interpixel redundancy**: this type of redundancy – sometimes called spatial redundancy, interframe redundancy, or geometric redundancy – exploits the fact that an image very often contains strongly correlated pixels, in other words, large regions whose pixel values are the same or almost the same. This redundancy can be explored in several ways, one of which is by predicting a pixel value based on the values of its neighboring pixels. In order to do so, the original 2-D array of pixels is usually mapped into a different format, e.g., an array of differences between adjacent pixels. If the original image pixels can be reconstructed from the transformed data set the mapping is said to be reversible. Examples of compression techniques that explore the interpixel redundancy include: Constant Area Coding (CAC), (1-D or 2-D) Run-Length Encoding (RLE) techniques, and many predictive coding algorithms such as Differential Pulse Code Modulation (DPCM).

- **Psychovisual redundancy**: many experiments on the psychophysical aspects of human vision have proven that the human eye does not respond with equal sensitivity to all incoming visual information; some pieces of information are more important than others. The knowledge of which particular types of information are more or less relevant to the final human user have led to image and video compression techniques that aim at eliminating or reducing any amount of data that is psychovisually redundant. The end result of applying these techniques is a compressed image file, whose size and quality are smaller than the original information, but whose resulting quality is still acceptable for the application at hand. The loss of quality that ensues as a byproduct of such techniques is frequently called *quantization*, as to indicate that a wider range of input values is normally mapped into a narrower range of output values thorough an irreversible process. In order to establish the nature and extent of information loss, different fidelity criteria (some objective such as root mean square (RMS) error, some subjective, such as pairwise comparison of two images encoded with different quality settings) can be used. Most of the image coding algorithms in use today exploit this type of redundancy, such as the Discrete Cosine Transform (DCT)-based algorithm at the heart of the JPEG encoding standard.

Image compression and coding models

Figure 1 shows a general image compression model. It consists of a source encoder, a channel encoder, the storage or transmission media (also referred to as *channel*), a channel decoder, and a source decoder. The source encoder reduces or eliminates any redundancies in the input image, which usually leads to bit savings. Source encoding techniques are the primary focus of this discussion. The channel encoder increase noise immunity of source encoder's output, usually adding extra bits to achieve its goals. If the channel is noise-free, the channel encoder and decoder may be omitted. At the receiver's side, the channel and source decoder perform the opposite functions and ultimately recover (an approximation of) the original image.

Figure 2 shows the source encoder in further detail. Its main components are:

- **Mapper**: transforms the input data into a (usually nonvisual) format designed to reduce interpixel redundancies in the input image. This operation is generally reversible and may or may not directly reduce the amount of data required to represent the image.

- **Quantizer**: reduces the accuracy of the mapper's output in accordance with some pre-established fidelity criterion. Reduces the psychovisual redundancies of the input image. This operation is not reversible and must be omitted if lossless compression is desired.

- **Symbol (entropy) encoder**: creates a fixed- or variable-length code to represent the quantizer's output and maps the output in accordance with the code. In most cases, a variable-length code is used. This operation is reversible.

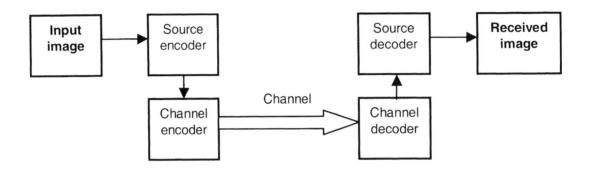

Figure 1. A general image compression model.

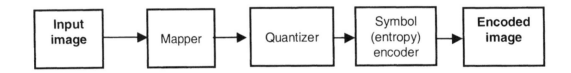

Figure 2. Source encoder.

Error-free compression

Error-free compression techniques usually rely on entropy-based encoding algorithms. The concept of entropy is mathematically described in equation (1):

$$H(\mathbf{z}) = -\sum_{j=1}^{J} P(a_j) \log P(a_j) \qquad (1)$$

where:

    a_j is a symbol produced by the information source
    $P(a_j)$ is the probability of that symbol
    J is the total number of different symbols
    $H(\mathbf{z})$ is the entropy of the source.

The concept of entropy provides an upper bound on how much compression can be achieved, given the probability distribution of the source. In other words, it establishes a theoretical limit on the amount of lossless compression that can be achieved using entropy encoding techniques alone.

Variable Length Coding (VLC)

Most entropy-based encoding techniques rely on assigning variable-length codewords to each symbol, whereas the most likely symbols are assigned shorter codewords. In the case of image coding, the symbols may be raw pixel values or the numerical values obtained at the output of the mapper stage (e.g., differences between consecutive pixels, run-lengths, etc.). The most popular entropy-based encoding technique is the Huffman code [1]. It provides the least amount of information units (bits) per source symbol. It is described in more detail in a separate short article.

Run-length encoding (RLE)

RLE is one of the simplest data compression techniques. It consists of replacing a sequence (run) of identical symbols by a pair containing the symbol and the run length. It is used as the primary compression technique in the 1-D CCITT Group 3 fax standard and in conjunction with other techniques in the JPEG image compression standard (described in a separate short article).

Differential coding

Differential coding techniques explore the interpixel redundancy in digital images. The basic idea consists of applying a simple difference operator to neighboring pixels to calculate a difference image, whose values are likely to follow within a much narrower range than the original gray-level range. As a consequence of this narrower distribution – and consequently reduced entropy – Huffman coding or other VLC schemes will produce shorter codewords for the difference image.

Predictive coding

Predictive coding techniques constitute another example of exploration of interpixel redundancy, in which the basic idea is to encode only the new information in each pixel. This new information is usually defined as the difference between the actual and the predicted value of that pixel.

Figure 3 shows the main blocks of a lossless predictive encoder. The key component is the predictor, whose function is to generate an estimated (predicted) value for each pixel from the input image based on previous pixel values. The predictor's output is rounded to the nearest integer and compared with the actual pixel value: the difference between the two – called *prediction error* – is then encoded by a VLC encoder. Since prediction errors are likely to be smaller than the original pixel values, the VLC encoder will likely generate shorter codewords.

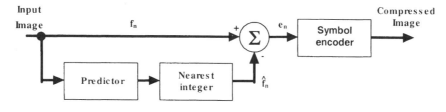

Figure 3. Lossless predictive encoder.

There are several local, global, and adaptive prediction algorithms in the literature. In most cases, the predicted pixel value is a linear combination of previous pixels.

Dictionary-based coding

Dictionary-based coding techniques are based on the idea of incrementally building a dictionary (table) while receiving the data. Unlike VLC techniques, dictionary-based techniques use fixed-length codewords to represent variable-length strings of symbols that commonly occur together. Consequently, there is no need to calculate, store, or transmit the probability distribution of the source, which makes these algorithms extremely convenient and popular. The best-known variant of dictionary-based coding algorithms is the LZW (Lempel-Ziv-Welch) encoding scheme [2], used in popular multimedia file formats such as GIF, TIFF, and PDF.

Lossy compression

Lossy compression techniques deliberately introduce a certain amount of distortion to the encoded image, exploring the psychovisual redundancies of the original image. These techniques must find an appropriate balance between the amount of error (loss) and the resulting bit savings.

Quantization

The quantization stage is at the core of any lossy image encoding algorithm. Quantization, in at the encoder side, means partitioning of the input data range into a smaller set of values. There are two main types of quantizers: scalar quantizers and vector quantizers. A scalar quantizer partitions the domain of input values into a smaller number of intervals. If the output intervals are equally spaced, which is the simplest way to do it, the process is called *uniform scalar quantization*; otherwise, for reasons usually related to minimization of total distortion, it is called *nonuniform scalar quantization*. One of the most popular nonuniform quantizers is the Lloyd-Max quantizer. Vector quantization (VQ) techniques [3] extend the basic principles of scalar quantization to multiple dimensions. Because of its fast lookup capabilities at the decoder side, VQ-based coding schemes are particularly attractive to multimedia applications.

Transform coding

The techniques discussed so far work directly on the pixel values and are usually called *spatial domain techniques*. Transform coding techniques use a reversible, linear mathematical transform to map the pixel values onto a set of coefficients, which are then quantized and encoded. The key factor behind the success of transform-based coding schemes many of the resulting coefficients for most natural images have small magnitudes and can be quantized (or discarded altogether) without causing significant distortion in the decoded image. Different mathematical transforms, such as Fourier (DFT), Walsh-Hadamard (WHT), and Karhunen-Loève (KLT), have been considered for the task. For compression purposes, the higher the capability of compressing information in fewer coefficients, the better the transform; for that reason, the Discrete Cosine Transform (DCT) [4] has become the most widely used transform coding technique.

Transform coding algorithms (Figure 4) usually start by partitioning the original image into subimages (blocks) of small size (usually 8 × 8). For each block the transform coefficients are calculated, effectively converting the original 8 × 8 array of pixel values into an array of coefficients within which the coefficients closer to the top-left corner usually contain most of the information needed to quantize and encode (and eventually perform the reverse process at the decoder's side) the image with little perceptual distortion. The resulting coefficients are then quantized and the output of the quantizer is used by a (combination of) symbol encoding technique(s) to produce the output bitstream representing the encoded image. At the decoder's side, the reverse process takes place, with the obvious difference that the 'dequantization' stage will only generate an approximated version of the original coefficient values; in other words, whatever loss was introduced by the quantizer in the encoder stage is not reversible.

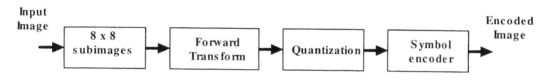

Figure 4. Transform coding.

Wavelet coding

Wavelet coding techniques are also based on the idea that the coefficients of a transform that decorrelates the pixels of an image can be coded more efficiently than the original pixels themselves. The main difference between wavelet coding and DCT-based coding (Figure 4) is the omission of the first stage. Because wavelet transforms are capable of representing an input signal with multiple levels of resolution, and yet maintain the useful compaction properties of the DCT, the subdivision of the input image into smaller subimages is no longer necessary. Wavelet coding has been at the core of the latest image compression standards, most notably JPEG 2000, which is discussed in a separate short article.

Image compression standards

Work on international standards for image compression started in the late 1970s with the CCITT (currently ITU-T) need to standardize binary image compression algorithms for Group 3 facsimile communications. Since then, many other committees and standards have been formed to produce *de jure* standards (such as JPEG), while several commercially successful initiatives have effectively become *de facto* standards (such as GIF). Image compression standards bring about many benefits, such as: (1) easier exchange of image files between different devices and applications; (2) reuse of existing hardware and software for a wider array of products; (3) existence of benchmarks and reference data sets for new and alternative developments.

Binary image compression standards [6]

Work on binary image compression standards was initially motivated by CCITT Group 3 and 4 facsimile standards. The Group 3 standard uses a non-adaptive, 1-D RLE technique in which the last K−1 lines of each group of K lines (for K = 2 or 4) are optionally coded in a 2-D manner, using the *Modified Relative Element Address Designate* (MREAD) algorithm. The Group 4 standard uses only the MREAD coding algorithm. Both classes of algorithms are non-adaptive and were optimized for a set of eight test images, containing a mix of representative documents, which sometimes resulted in data expansion when applied to different types of documents (e.g., half-tone images).. The Joint Bilevel Image Group (JBIG) [5] – a joint committee of the ITU-T and ISO – has addressed these limitations and proposed two new standards (JBIG and JBIG2) which can be used to compress binary and gray-scale images of up to 6 gray-coded bits/pixel.

Continuous tone still image compression standards

For photograph quality images (both grayscale and color), different standards have been proposed, mostly based on lossy compression techniques. The most popular standard in this category, by far, is the JPEG standard [7, 8], a lossy, DCT-based coding algorithm. Despite its great popularity and adoption, ranging from digital cameras to the World Wide Web, certain limitations of the original JPEG algorithm have motivated the recent development of two alternative standards, JPEG 2000 and JPEG-LS (lossless). JPEG, JPEG 2000, and JPEG-LS are described in separate short articles.

See: Huffman coding, JPEG, JPEG 2000, JPEG-LS

References

1. D.A. Huffman, "A Method for the Construction of Minimum Redundancy Codes," Proceedings of IRE, Vol. 40, No. 10, pp. 1098-1101, 1952.
2. T.A. Welch, "A technique for high-performance data compression," IEEE Computer, Vol. 17, pp. 8-19, June 1984.
3. N.M. Nasrabadi and R.A. King, "Image coding using vector quantization: A review," IEEE Transactions on Communications. Vol. 36, No. 8, pp. 957-971, 1988.
4. K.R. Rao and P. Yip, "Discrete Cosine Transform: Algorithms, Advantages, Applications," Academic Press, 1990.
5. JBIG Home page. http://www.jpeg.org/jbig/ Accessed July 13, 2005.
6. R.B. Arps, "Bibliography on Binary Image Compression," Proceedings of the IEEE, Vol. 68, No. 7, July 1980, pp. 922-924.
7. W.B. Pennenbaker and J.L. Mitchell, "JPEG still image data compression standard," Van Nostrand Reinhold, 1993.
8. G. Wallace, "The JPEG still picture compression standard," Communications of the ACM, Vol. 34, pp. 30-44, 1991.

IMAGE DATA REPRESENTATIONS

Oge Marques
Department of Computer Science & Engineering
Florida Atlantic University, Boca Raton, FL, USA

Definition: *At the most basic level, there are two different ways of encoding the contents of a 2-D image in digital format: raster (also known as bitmap) and vector.*

Images are represented in digital format in a wide variety of ways. At the most basic level, there are two different ways of encoding the contents of a 2-D image in digital format: *raster* (also known as bitmap) and *vector*. Bitmap representations use one or more two-dimensional arrays of pixels (picture elements), whereas vector representations use a series of drawing commands to represent an image. Each encoding method has its pros and cons: the greatest advantages of bitmap graphics are their quality and display speed; its main disadvantages include larger memory storage requirements and size dependence (e.g., enlarging a bitmap image may lead to noticeable artifacts). In either case, there is no such a thing as a perfect digital representation of an image. Artifacts due to finite resolution, color mapping, and many others will always be present. The key in selecting an adequate representation is to find a suitable compromise between size (in Bytes), subjective quality, and universality / interoperability of the adopted format or standard. We will review several different image representations used by some of the most common file formats currently available.

Binary (1-bit) images

Binary images are encoded as a 2-D array, using one bit per pixel, where a 0 usually means 'black' and a 1 means 'white' (even though there is no universal agreement on that). The main advantage of this representation (Figure 1(b)) – usually suitable for images containing simple graphics, text or line art – is its small size.

Figure 1. (a) A monochrome image (b) Its binary equivalent.

Gray-level (8-bit) images

Gray-level (also referred to as *monochrome*) images are also encoded as a 2-D array of pixels, using eight bits per pixel, where a pixel value of 0 usually means 'black' and a pixel value of 255 means 'white', with intermediate values corresponding to varying shades of gray. The total number of gray-levels is larger than the human visual system requirements, making this format a good compromise between subjective visual quality and relatively compact representation and storage. An 8-bit monochrome image (Figure

1(a)) can also be thought of as a collection of bit-planes, where each plane contains a 1-bit representation of the image at different levels of detail.

Color images

Representation of color images is significantly more complex and varied. The two most common ways of storing color image contents are: *RGB* representation – in which each pixel is usually represented by a 24-bit number containing the amount of its Red (R), Green (G), and Blue (B) components – and *indexed* representation – where a 2-D array contains indices to a color palette (or look-up table – LUT).

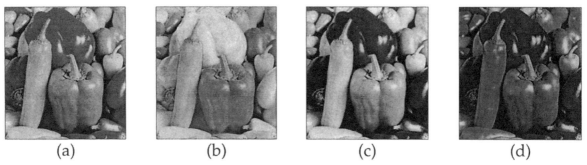

(a)   (b)   (c)   (d)

Figure 2. (a) Color image and its R (b), G (c), and B (d) components.

24-bit (RGB) color images

Color images can be represented using three 2-D arrays of same size, one for each color channel: Red (R), Green (G), and Blue (B) (Figure 2). Each array element contains an 8-bit value indicating the amount of red, green, or blue at that point, in a 0 to 255 scale. The combination of the three 8-bit values into a 24-bit number allows for 2^{24} (16,777,216, usually referred to as 16 million or 16 M) color combinations. An alternative representation uses 32 bits and includes a fourth channel, called the *alpha channel*, which provides a measure of transparency for each pixel and is widely used in image editing effects.

Figure 3. Indexed color image and its color palette.

Indexed color images

A problem with 24-bit color representations is backward compatibility with older hardware which may not be able to display the 16 million colors simultaneously. A solution devised before 24-bit color displays and video cards were widely accessible was to adopt an indexed representation, in which a 2-D array of the same size as the image contains indices (pointers) to a color palette (or look-up table – LUT) of fixed maximum size (usually 256 colors) (see Figure 3).

Other color models

The RGB color model is one of the most popular and straightforward methods for representing the contents of a digital color image, but there are several alternative models, such as: YCbCr – adopted in the JPEG standard – and the CMYK – used to encode color information for printing purposes –, among many others.

Compression

Since raw image representations usually require a large amount of storage space (and proportionally long transmission times in the case of file uploads/downloads), most image file formats employ some type of compression. Compression methods can be *lossy* – when a tolerable degree of deterioration in the visual quality of the resulting image is acceptable – or *lossless* – when the image is encoded in its full quality. The overall results of the compression process, both in terms of storage savings – usually expressed as compression ratio – as well as resulting quality loss (for the case of lossy techniques) may vary depending on the technique, format, options (such as the quality setting for JPEG), and the image contents. As a general guideline, lossy compression should be used for general purpose photographic images, whereas lossless compression should be preferred when dealing with line art, drawings, facsimiles, or images in which no loss of detail may be tolerable (most notably, space images and medical images).

Popular file formats

The selected file formats described below represent some of the most widely used formats at the present time. Research in the field of image compression and encoding remains active and it is possible that other formats may appear and become popular in the future.

Windows BMP

Windows BMP is the native image format in the Windows platform [3]. It is one of the simplest image formats and supports images with 1, 4, 8, 16, 24, and 32 bits per pixel. BMP files are usually uncompressed. Multi-byte integers are stored with the least significant bytes first. The BMP file structure (Figure 4) contains [1]:

- A *file header*, implemented as a BITMAPFILEHEADER structure, serves as the signature that identifies the file format (the first two bytes must contain the ASCII characters 'B' followed by 'M').

- An *image header*, which may come in two different formats: BITMAPCOREHEADER (for the old OS/2 BMP format) and BITMAPINFOHEADER (for the much more popular Windows format). This header stores the images width, height, compression method, and number of bits per pixel, among other things.

- A *color palette*, which contains values for R, G, B, and an additional ('reserved') channel for each pixel.

- The actual *pixel data*, ordered in rows, from bottom to top. The exact format of the pixel data depends on the number of bits per pixel.

The main advantages of the BMP format are its simplicity, widespread distribution (with Windows) and popularity. Moreover, it is a well-documented patent-free format. Because it is usually uncompressed, its main disadvantage is the resulting file size (in Bytes).

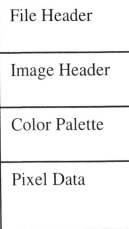

Figure 4. BMP format: file structure.

GIF

Graphic Interchange Format (GIF) was originally devised by CompuServe in 1987. It soon became the most widely used format for image storage [1]. The GIF format became popular because it used LZW (Lempel-Ziv-Welch) data compression, a lossless compression algorithm which was more efficient than the run-length encoding (RLE) compression used by (at that time) competing formats such as PCX and MacPaint. Thanks to its improved compression scheme, reasonably large images could be downloaded in a reasonable amount of time, even with very slow modems. GIF's optional interlacing feature, which allows storing image scan lines out of order in such a fashion that even a partially downloaded image is somewhat recognizable, also helped GIF's popularity, allowing a user to stop the download if it was not what was expected.

The first GIF specification was called GIF87a. In 1989, CompuServe released an enhanced version, called GIF89a, which added support for multiple images in a stream and storage of application-specific metadata. The two versions can be distinguished by looking at the first six bytes of the file, whose ASCII characters are 'GIF87a' and 'GIF89a', respectively.

The LZW compression algorithm on which GIF is based, was covered by U.S. Patent 4,558,302, owned by Unisys, which has led to a legal battle that started when Unisys discovered that GIF used the LZW and announced that they would be seeking royalties on that patent. This led to the development of a patent-free alternative format (PNG, described in a short article) with similar technical characteristics. That patent expired on June 20, 2003, which means that Unisys and CompuServe can no longer collect royalties for use of the GIF format in the United States [2].

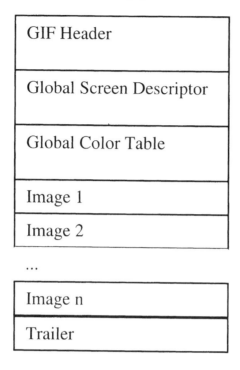

Figure 5. GIF format: file structure.

The GIF file structure in Figure 5 contains [1]:

- A *GIF header*, required, always present at the beginning of the file. It contains a 6-byte signature, either 'GIF87a' or 'GIF89a'.

- A 7-byte *global screen descriptor*, which specifies the dimensions and background color of the logical screen area in which the individual images in the GIF file are displayed.

- A *global color table*, an array of structures containing values for R, G, and B for each pixel.

- One or more *images*, each of which may contain:
  An image header
  An optional local color table
  A collection of data blocks
  A terminator block

- A *trailer*.

The GIF89a feature of storing multiple images in one file, accompanied by control data, is used extensively on the Web to produce simple animations and short, low-resolution films, the so-called *animated GIF*. GIF is palette-based, which limits the maximum number of colors to 256. This limitation is usually not an issue for web page logos and design elements such as buttons or banners. For digital photographs, the JPEG format (described in a short article) is preferred.

PNG

The PNG (Portable Network Graphics) [4-6] format was originally designed to replace the GIF format. It is described in more detail in a separate short article.

JPEG

The JPEG format was originally published as a standard (ISO IS 10918-1) by The Joint Photographic Experts Group in 1994. It has become the most widely used format for storing digital photographs ever since. The JPEG specification defines how an image is transformed into a stream of bytes, but not how those bytes are encapsulated in any particular storage medium. Another standard, created by the Independent JPEG Group, called JFIF (JPEG File Interchange Format) specifies how to produce a file suitable for computer storage and transmission from a JPEG stream. JFIF is described in a separate short article.

Even though the original JPEG specification defined four compression modes (sequential, hierarchical, progressive, and lossless), most JPEG files used today employ the sequential mode. The JPEG encoder (Figure 6) consists of the following main stages:

1. The original RGB color image is converted to an alternative color model (YCbCr) and the color information is subsampled.

2. The image is divided into 8×8 blocks.

3. The 2-D Discrete Cosine Transform (DCT) is applied to each block image; the resulting 64 values are referred to as *DCT coefficients*.

4. DCT coefficients are quantized according to a quantization table; this is the step where acceptable loss is introduced.

5. Quantized DCT coefficients are scanned in a zigzag fashion (from top-left to bottom-right). The resulting sequence is run-length encoded, in preparation for the entropy encoding step.

6. The run-length encoded sequences are converted to variable-length binary codewords using Huffman encoding.

At the decoder side, the process is reversed; it should be noted that the loss introduced at the quantizer stage in the encoder cannot be canceled at the 'dequantizer' stage in the decoder.

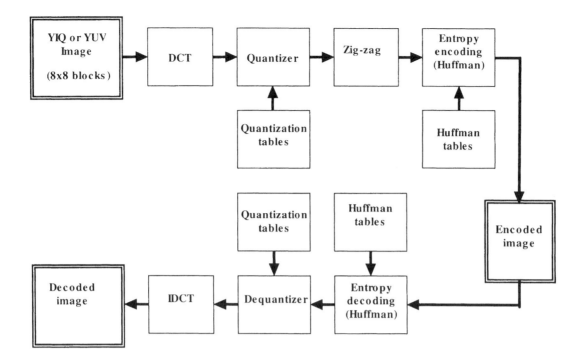

Figure 6. JPEG encoder and decoder: block diagram.

JPEG 2000

The JPEG 2000 format [8] is a wavelet-based image compression standard (ISO/IEC 15444-1:2000), created by the Joint Photographic Experts Group committee with the intention of superseding their original DCT-based JPEG standard. The usual file extension is .jp2. It addresses several well-known limitations of the original JPEG algorithm and prepares the way for next-generation imagery applications. Some of its advertised advantages are:

1. Low bitrate compression

2. Superior lossless and lossy compression in a single bitstream

3. Ability to handle very large images without need for tiling

4. Single decompression architecture

5. Error resilience for transmission in noisy environments, such as wireless and the Internet

6. Region of Interest (ROI) coding

7. Metadata mechanisms for incorporating additional non-image data as part of the file

JPEG 2000 is not yet widely supported in web browsers, and hence is not generally used on the World Wide Web.

TIFF

TIFF (Tagged Image File Format) is another popular image file format, developed in the 1980s by Aldus Corp. The TIFF format includes a number of options that can be used to attach additional information (such as images encoded in another file format); these options can be exercised by including specific "tags" in the header. Many of these tags convey basic image information, such as its size, but others define how the data is arranged and various image compression options. As a result, TIFF can be used as a container for JPEG compressed images, and in this respect is completely universal. However, because of the complexity involved in supporting all of its options, a lowest common denominator variant became "the" TIFF, and even today the vast majority of TIFF files, and the programs that read them, are based on a simple 32-bit uncompressed image.

DNG

Digital Negative Specification (DNG) is a recently announced royalty-free raw image file format introduced by Adobe Systems as a response to demand for a unifying digital camera raw file format [7].

Other formats

It is virtually impossible to cover all image file formats. Other image formats not described here include: ANIM, ART, CGM, CIN, DjVu, DPX, EPS, EXIF, GDF, ILBM, MNG, PCX, PICT, PSD, PSP, XBM, and XPM, among many others. Please refer to [2] for an updated list and useful links.

See: PNG, JFIF

References

1. J. Miano, Compressed Image File Formats, Addison-Wesley, 1999.
2. Wikipedia. http://en.wikipedia.org/wiki/Graphics_file_format. Accessed April 13, 2005.
3. MSDN, http://msdn.microsoft.com/library/default.asp?url=/library/en-us/gdi/bitmaps_99ir.asp. Accessed April 25, 2005.
4. Official PNG home page. http://www.libpng.org/pub/png/ Accessed April 25, 2005.
5. W3C PNG page. http://www.w3.org/Graphics/PNG/ Accessed April 25, 2005.
6. Official PNG specification. http://www.libpng.org/pub/png/spec/iso/ Accessed April 29, 2005.
7. B. Fraser, "Real World Camera Raw with Adobe Photoshop CS2," Peachpit Press, 2005.
8. JPEG 2000. http://www.jpeg.org/jpeg2000/ Accessed April 29, 2005.

IMAGE INPAINTING

Definition: *Image inpainting refers to the process of filling-in missing data in a designated region of the visual input.*

Image inpainting [1]-[3] refers to the process of filling-in missing data in a designated region of the visual input (Figure 1). The object of the process is to reconstruct missing parts or damaged image in such a way that the inpainted region cannot be detected by a causal observer. Applications range from the reconstruction of missing blocks introduced by packet loss during wireless transmission, reversing of impairments, such as cracks, scratches, and dirt, in scanned photographs and digitized artwork images, to removal/introduction of image objects such as logos, stamped dates, text, persons, and special effects on the scene. Typically, after the user selects the region to be restored, the inpainting algorithm automatically repairs the damaged area by means of image interpolation.

To recover the color, structural and textural content in a large damaged area, inpainted (output) pixels are calculated using the available data from the surrounding undamaged areas. The required input can be automatically determined by the inpainting technique or supplied by the user. Since different inpainting techniques focus on pure texture or pure structure restoration, both the quality and cost of the inpainting process differ significantly. For example, exemplar-based techniques effectively generate new texture by sampling and copying color values from an undamaged source [3]. Such an approach produces good results in replicating consistent texture seen in artificially generated imagery, but fails when it comes to reconstruct missing parts in photographs of natural scenes. This is due to the fact that most image areas consist of both texture and structure. Boundaries between image regions constitute structural (edge) information which is a complex, nonlinear phenomenon produced by blending together different textures. Therefore, it is not surprising that the state-of-the-art inpainting methods attempt to simultaneously perform texture and structure filling-in [1]-[3].

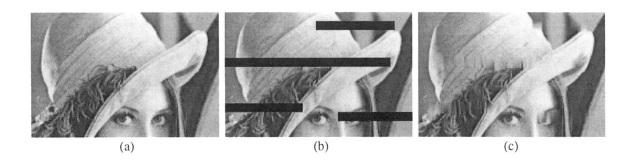

(a)   (b)   (c)

Figure 1. Image inpainting: (a) original image, (b) damaged image with missing rows (blocks) due to wireless transmission, (c) reconstructed image by an inpainting technique.

See: Video inpainting, Inpainting in virtual restoration of artworks, Color image filtering and enhancement.

References

1. S.-D. Rane, G. Sapiro, and M. Bertalmio, "Structure and Texture Filling-In of Missing Image Blocks in Wireless Transmission and Compression Applications," IEEE Transactions on Image Processing, Vol. 12, No. 3, March 2003, pp. 296-303.
2. C.-A.-Z. Barcelos, M.-A. Batista, A.-M. Martins, and A.-C. Nogueira, "Level Lines Continuation Based Digital Inpainting," Proc. XVII Brazilian Symposium on Computer Graphics and Image Processing (SIBGRAPI'04), October 2004, pp. 50-57.
3. A. Criminisi, P. Perez, and K. Toyama, "Region Filling and Object Removal by Exemplar-Based Image Inpainting," IEEE Transactions on Image Processing, Vol. 13, No. 9, September 2004, pp. 1200-1212.

IMAGE RETRIEVAL

William I. Grosky
Department of Computer and Information Science
University of Michigan-Dearborn, Dearborn, MI, USA

Definition: *Image retrieval techniques integrate both low-level visual features, addressing the more detailed perceptual aspects, and high-level semantic features underlying the more general conceptual aspects of visual data.*

The emergence of multimedia technology and the rapid growth in the number and type of multimedia assets controlled by public and private entities, as well as the expanding range of image and video documents appearing on the web, have attracted significant research efforts in providing tools for effective retrieval and management of visual data. Image retrieval is based on the availability of a representation scheme of image content. Image content descriptors may be visual features such as color, texture, shape, and spatial relationships, or semantic primitives.

Conventional information retrieval is based solely on text, and these approaches to textual information retrieval have been transplanted into image retrieval in a variety of ways, including the representation of an image as a vector of feature values. However, "a picture is worth a thousand words." Image contents are much more versatile compared with text, and the amount of visual data is already enormous and still expanding very rapidly. Hoping to cope with these special characteristics of visual data, content-based image retrieval methods have been introduced. It has been widely recognized that the family of image retrieval techniques should become an integration of both low-level visual features, addressing the more detailed perceptual aspects, and high-level semantic features underlying the more general conceptual aspects of visual data. Neither of these two types of features is sufficient to retrieve or manage visual data in an effective or efficient way. Although efforts have been devoted to combining these two aspects of visual data, the gap between them is still a huge barrier in front of researchers. Intuitive and heuristic approaches do not provide us with satisfactory performance. Therefore, there is an urgent need of finding and managing the latent correlation between low-level features and high-level concepts. How to bridge this gap between visual features and semantic features has been a major challenge in this research field.

The different types of information that are normally associated with images are:

- Content-independent metadata: data that is not directly concerned with image content, but related to it. Examples are image format, author's name, date, and location.
- Content-based metadata:
  o Non-information-bearing metadata: data referring to low-level or intermediate-level features, such as color, texture, shape, spatial relationships, and their various combinations. This information can easily be computed from the raw data.
  o Information-bearing metadata: data referring to content semantics, concerned with relationships of image entities to real-world entities. This type of information, such as that a particular building appearing in an image is the *Empire State Building*, cannot usually be derived from the raw data, and must then be supplied by other means, perhaps by inheriting this semantic label from another image, where a similar-appearing building has already been identified.

Low-level visual features such as color, texture, shape and spatial relationships are directly related to perceptual aspects of image content. Since it is usually easy to extract and represent these features and fairly convenient to design similarity measures by using the statistical properties of these features, a variety of content-based image retrieval techniques have been proposed. High-level concepts, however, are not extracted directly from visual contents, but they represent the relatively more important meanings of objects and scenes in the images that are perceived by human beings. These conceptual aspects are more closely related to users' preferences and subjectivity. Concepts may vary significantly in different circumstances. Subtle changes in the semantics may lead to dramatic conceptual differences. Needless to say, it is a very challenging task to extract and manage meaningful semantics and to make use of them to achieve more intelligent and user-friendly retrieval.

High-level conceptual information is normally represented by using text descriptors. Traditional indexing for image retrieval is text-based. In certain content-based retrieval techniques, text descriptors are also used to model perceptual aspects. However, the inadequacy of text description is very obvious:

- It is difficult for text to capture the perceptual saliency of visual features.
- It is rather difficult to characterize certain entities, attributes, roles or events by means of text only.
- Text is not well suited for modeling the correlation between perceptual and conceptual features.
- Text descriptions reflect the subjectivity of the annotator and the annotation process is prone to be inconsistent, incomplete, ambiguous, and very difficult to be automated.

Although it is an obvious fact that image contents are much more complicated than textual data stored in traditional databases, there is an even greater demand for retrieval and management tools for visual data, since visual information is a more capable medium of conveying ideas and is more closely related to human perception of the real world. Image retrieval techniques should provide support for user queries in an effective and efficient way, just as conventional information retrieval does for textual retrieval. In general, image retrieval can be categorized into the following types:

- Exact Matching – This category is applicable only to static environments or environments in which features of the images do not evolve over an extended period of time. Databases containing industrial and architectural drawings or electronics schematics are examples of such environments.

- Low-Level Similarity-Based Searching – In most cases, it is difficult to determine which images best satisfy the query. Different users may have different needs and wants. Even the same user may have different preferences under different circumstances. Thus, it is desirable to return the top several similar images based on the similarity measure, so as to give users a good sampling. The similarity measure is generally based on simple feature matching and it is quite common for the user to interact with the system so as to indicate to it the quality of each of the returned matches, which helps the system adapt to the users' preferences. Figure 1 shows three images which a particular user may find similar to each other. In general, this problem has been well-studied for many years.

Figure 1. Three similar images based on simple feature matching.

- High-Level Semantic-Based Searching – In this case, the notion of similarity is not based on simple feature matching and usually results from extended user interaction with the system. Figure 2 shows two images whose low-level features are quite different, yet could be semantically similar to a particular user as examples of peaceful scenes. Research in this area is quite active, yet still in its infancy. Many important breakthroughs are yet to be made.

For either type of retrieval, the dynamic and versatile characteristics of image content require expensive computations and sophisticated methodologies in the areas of computer vision, image processing, data visualization, indexing, and similarity measurement. In order to manage image data effectively and efficiently, many schemes for data modeling and image representation have been proposed. Typically, each of these schemes builds a symbolic image for each given physical image to provide logical and physical data independence. Symbolic images are then used in conjunction with various index structures as proxies for image comparisons to reduce the searching scope. The high-dimensional visual data is usually reduced into a lower-dimensional subspace so that it is easier to index and manage the visual contents. Once the similarity measure has been determined, indexes of corresponding images are located in the image space and those images are retrieved from the database. Due to the lack of any unified framework for image representation and retrieval, certain methods may perform better than others under differing query situations. Therefore, these schemes and retrieval techniques have to be somehow integrated and adjusted on the fly to facilitate effective and efficient image data management.

Figure 2. Two semantically similar images ("peaceful scenes") with different low-level features.

Existing Techniques

Visual feature extraction is the basis of any content-based image retrieval technique. Widely used features include color, texture, shape and spatial relationships. Because of the subjectivity of perception and the complex composition of visual data, there does not exist a single best representation for any given visual feature. Multiple approaches have been introduced for each of these visual features and each of them characterizes the feature from a different perspective.

Color is one of the most widely used visual features in content-based image retrieval. It is relatively robust and simple to represent. Various studies of color perception and color spaces have been proposed, in order to find color-based techniques that are more closely aligned with the ways that humans perceive color. The color histogram has been the most commonly used representation technique, statistically describing combined probabilistic properties of the various color channels (such as the (R)ed, (G)reen, and (B)lue channels), by capturing the number of pixels having particular properties. For example, a color histogram might describe the number of pixels of each red channel value in the range [0, 255]. Figure 3 shows an image and three of its derived color histograms, where the particular channel values are shown along the x-axis, the numbers of pixels are shown along the y-axis, and the particular color channel used is indicated in each histogram. It is well known that histograms lose information related to the spatial distribution of colors and that two very different images can have very similar histograms. There has been much work done in extending histograms to capture such spatial information. Two of the well-known approaches for this are correlograms and anglograms. Correlograms capture the distribution of colors of pixels in particular areas around pixels of particular colors, while anglograms capture a particular signature of the spatial arrangement of areas (single pixels or blocks of pixels) having common properties, such as similar colors. We note that anglograms also can be used for texture and shape features.

Figure 3. An image and three of its derived color histograms over the red, green, and blue color channels.

Texture refers to the patterns in an image that present the properties of homogeneity that do not result from the presence of a single color or intensity value. It is a powerful discriminating feature, present almost everywhere in nature. However, it is almost impossible to describe texture in words, because it is virtually a statistical and structural

property. There are three major categories of texture-based techniques, namely, *probabilistic/statistical, spectral,* and *structural* approaches. Probabilistic methods treat texture patterns as samples of certain random fields and extract texture features from these properties. Spectral approaches involve the sub-band decomposition of images into different channels, and the analysis of spatial frequency content in each of these sub-bands in order to extract texture features. Structural techniques model texture features based on heuristic rules of spatial placements of primitive image elements that attempt to mimic human perception of textural patterns.

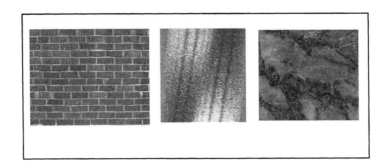

Figure 4. Examples of textures.

The well known *Tamura features* include *coarseness, contrast, directionality, line-likeness, regularity,* and *roughness.* Different researchers have selected different subsets of these heuristic descriptors. It is believed that the combination of *contrast, coarseness,* and *directionality* best represents the textural patterns of color images. Figure 4 illustrates various textures.

Shape representation is normally required to be invariant to *translation, rotation,* and *scaling.* In general, shape representations can be categorized as either *boundary-based* or *region-based.* A boundary-based representation uses only the outer boundary characteristics of the entities, while a region-based representation uses the entire region. Shape features may also be *local* or *global.* A shape feature is local if it is derived from some proper subpart of an object, while it is global if it is derived from the entire object. See Figure 5 for an illustration of these concepts.

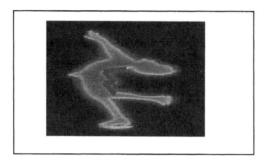

Figure 5. The shape of an object. A local shape feature is the set of angles formed by the red portion of the object's boundary, while a global shape feature is the object's center of mass.

A combination of the above features are extracted from each image and transformed into a point of a high-dimensional vector space. Using this representation, the many techniques developed by the information retrieval community can be used to advantage. As the dimensionality of the underlying space is still quite high, however, the many disadvantages caused by the *curse of dimensionality* also prevail.

Originally devised in the context of estimating probability density functions in high-dimensional spaces, the curse of dimensionality expresses itself in high-dimensional indexing by causing log time complexity indexing approaches to behave no better than linear search as the dimensionality of the search space increases. This is why there has been so much effort spent in the development of efficient high-dimensional indexing techniques, on the one hand, and in dimensional reduction techniques which capture the salient semantics, on the other hand.

As the ultimate goal of image retrieval is to serve the needs and wants of users who may not even know what they are looking for but can recognize it when they see it, there has been much work done in trying to discover what is in the mind of the user. A very common technique for this is *relevance feedback.* Originally advanced in the information retrieval community, it has become a standard in most existing image retrieval systems, although some researchers believe that more involved user interactions are necessary to discover user semantics. This technique helps the system refine its search by asking the user to rank the returned results as to relevance. Based on these results, the system learns how to retrieve results more in line with what the user wants. There have been many new approaches developed in recent years, but the classical techniques are *query refinement* or *feature reweighting*. Query refinement transforms the query so that more of the positive and less of the negative examples will be retrieved. Feature reweighting puts more weight on features which help to retrieve positive examples and less weight on features which aid in retrieving negative examples. This process continues for as many rounds as is necessary to produce results acceptable to the user.

Needless to say, human beings are much better than computers at extracting and making use of semantic information from images. Many researchers believe that complete image understanding should start from interpreting image objects and their relationships. The process of grouping low-level image features into meaningful image objects and then automatically attaching correlated semantic descriptions to image objects is still a challenging problem in image retrieval. One of the earliest examples of such an approach is that used in the ImageMiner system. Their method is structural in nature, using graph grammars, and generates scene descriptions with region labels. Current techniques in this area use Baysian approaches which integrate textual annotations and image features.

Content-Based Image Retrieval (CBIR) Systems

There are several excellent surveys of content-based image retrieval systems. We mention here some of the more notable systems. The first, QBIC (Query-by-Image-Content), was one of the first prototype systems. It was developed at the IBM Almaden Research Center and is currently folded into DB2. It allows queries by color, texture, and shape, and introduced a sophisticated similarity function. As this similarity function has a quadratic time-complexity, the notion of dimensional reduction was discussed in order to reduce the computation time. Another notable property of QBIC was its use of multidimensional indexing to speed-up searches. The Chabot system, developed at the University of California at Berkeley, brought text and images together into the search task, allowed the user to define concepts, such as that of a *sunset*, in terms of various feature values, and used the post-relational database management system Postgres. Finally, the MARS system, developed at the University of Illinois at Urbana-Champaign, allowed for sophisticated relevance feedback from the user.

See: **Emergent Semantics.**

References

1. L.D.F. Costa and R.M. Cesar, Jr., *"Shape Analysis and Classification: Theory and Practice,"* CRC Press, 2000.
2. M. Flickner, H. Sawhney, W. Niblack, et al., "Query by Image and Video Content: The QBIC System," *IEEE Computer,* Vol. 28, No. 9, September 1995, pp. 23-32.
3. W.I. Grosky, "Multimedia Information Systems," *IEEE Multimedia,* Vol. 1, No. 1, Spring 1994, pp. 12-24.

4. M.L. Kherfi and D. Ziou, "Image Retrieval From the World Wide Web: Issues, Techniques, and Systems," *ACM Computing Surveys,* Vol. 36, No. 1, March 2004, pp. 35-67.

5. O. Marques and B. Furht, "Content-Based Image and Video Retrieval," Springer, 2002.

6. V. Ogle and M. Stonebraker, "Chabot: Retrieval from a Relational Database of Images," *IEEE Computer,* Vol. 28, No. 9, September 1995, pp. 40-48.

7. Y. Rui, R.S. Huang, M. Ortega, and S. Mehrotra, "Relevance Feedback: A Power Tool in Interactive Content-Based Image Retrieval," *IEEE Transactions on Circuits and Systems for Video Technology,* Vol. 8, No. 5, September 1998, pp. 644-655.

8. A.W.M. Smeulders, M. Worring, S. Santini, A. Gupta, and R. Jain, "Content-Based Image Retrieval at the End of the Early Years," *IEEE Transactions on Pattern Analysis and Machine Intelligence,* Vol. 22, No. 12, December 2000, pp. 1349-1380.

9. R.C. Veltkamp and M. Tanase, "Content-Based Image Retrieval Systems: A Survey," http://www.aa-lab.cs.uu.nl/cbirsurvey/cbir-survey/index.html.

10. C. Wang and X.S. Wang, "Indexing Very High-Dimensional Sparse and Quasi-Sparse Vectors for Similarity Searches," The VLDB Journal, Vol. 9, No. 4, April 2001, pp. 344-361.

11. I.H. Witten, A. Moffat, and T.C. Bell, "Managing Gigabytes: Compressing and Indexing Documents and Images (2nd Edition)," Morgan Kaufmann, 1999.

IMAGE SEARCH ENGINE

Mingjing Li and Wei-Ying Ma
Microsoft Research Asia, China

Definition: *Image search engines are Web-based services that collect and index images available on the Internet.*

Abstract

Some commercial image search engines have indexed over one billion images so far. Like general web search, image searching is mostly based on text information associated with images, which can be automatically extracted from containing web pages. In addition to text-based image search engines, there are also some content-based image retrieval systems that index images using their visual characteristics. Those systems are mainly developed for research purpose and usually limited to small image collections.

Introduction

Due to improved digital imaging technologies and convenient accessibility facilitated by the Internet, the popularity of digital images is rapidly increasing. As most of those images are not annotated with semantic descriptors, it might be a challenge for general users to find specific images from the Internet.

Image search engines are such systems that are specially designed to help users find their intended images. In general, image search engines may adopt two approaches to achieve this goal. One is text-based; the other is content-based.

Text-based image search engines index images using the words associated with the images. Depending on whether the indexing is done automatically or manually, image search engines adopting this approach may be further classified into two categories: Web image search engine or collection-based search engine. Web image search engines collect images embedded in Web pages from other sites on the Internet, and index them using the text automatically derived from containing Web pages. Most commercial image search engines fall into this category. On the contrary, collection-based search engines index image collections using the keywords annotated by human indexers. Digital libraries and commercial stock photo collection providers are good examples of this kind of search engines.

Content-based image retrieval (CBIR) has been an active research topic since 1990s. Such systems index images using their visual characteristics, such as color, texture and shape, which can be extracted from image itself automatically. They can accept an image example as query, and return a list of images that are similar to the query example in appearance. CBIR systems are mainly experimental and often limited to small image collections.

In the following, we briefly describe how those image search engines work.

Web image search engine

The Word Wide Web (WWW) may be the largest repository of digital images in the world. The number of images available on the Internet is increasing rapidly and will continue to grow in the future. Image search engine is a kind of Web-based services devoted to collect and index those Web images.

There are a number of image search engines commercially available, such as AltaVista [1], Google Image Search [2] and Yahoo! Image Search [3]. AltaVista is the first search engine in the world that launches image search functionalities. It also supports video and music search as well. Yahoo! claims to have indexed over 1.6 billion images in August 2005, while Google claims over 1 billion. Those engines are based on existing search engine technology in the sense that they index images using the text information associated with images.

Such search engines take the text in hosting Web pages as approximate annotation of Web images, assuming that images are embedded into Web pages to complement the text information. Some sources of information might be relevant to the content of embedded images. These include, in the decreasing order of usefulness, image file names, image captions, alternate text, which is an HTML tag used to replace the image when it cannot be displayed, surrounding text, the page tile and others [4, 5]. Surrounding text refers to the words or phrase that are close to the image, such as those in the above, below, left or right areas. However, it is difficult to determine which area is more relevant and how much should be considered. Thus the extraction of surrounding text is somewhat heuristic and subjective. As such information can be extracted automatically from Web pages, the indexing process is automated.

To build a commercial image search engine, a lot of functionalities should be implemented. Among those, at least the following four should be provided.

Image crawler is used to collect Web images, and usually implemented as software robots that run on many machines. Those robots scan the entire Web to identify images and then download images and hosting Web pages. As Web images are usually protected by copyrights, image search engines only keep a thumbnail for each Web image. Original images can be accessed via links in the search result.

Page parser is used to analyze Web pages so as to find informative images and extract associated text for indexing. Not all Web images are useful for search. Some are too small or used for decoration or function only, such as background images, banners and buttons. Some are advertisements that are not relevant to hosting Web pages at all. Those images should be excluded from the indexing. Page parser also tries to determine which parts of the hosting Web page are likely relevant to the contained images and extract corresponding text as for indexing.

Index builder is used to build indexing structure for efficient search of images. The methods adopted are quite similar to general web search, except that each image is treated as a text document rather than a Web page.

Image searching is actually processed in the server side. It accepts users' queries and compares with indexed images. When generating the final search result, it considers a number of factors, e.g. the similarity between the query and an indexed image, the image quality, etc. Google claims to present high-quality images first so as to improve the perceived accuracy.

The search result is organized as a list of thumbnails, typically 20 in one page, along with additional information about the retrieved images, such as the file name, the image resolution, the URL of the host webpage, etc. Some search engines provide advanced search options to limit the search result by size, file type, color or domain, and to exclude adult content.

Image searching service is usually provided via a Web-based user interface. Users may access image search engine in a Web browser, such as Microsoft Internet Explorer.

Collection-based search engine

Unlike Web image search engine, collection-based search engines index image collections using manually annotated keywords. Images in such collections are usually of high-quality, and the indexing is more accurate. Consequently, the search results from collection-based engines are more relevant and much better than those from Web search engines. Large digital libraries and commercial stock photo or clip art providers offer image searching facilities in this way.

Those image collections are often held in databases, and cannot be easily accessed by Web crawlers. Therefore, they are usually not covered by general search engines.

Among those engines, Corbis [6] and Getty [7] are probably the two largest ones that specialize in providing photography and fine art images to consumers. Corbis collection currently contains 25 million images with more than 2.1 million available online. Its search result can be limited by categories and collections, or even by date photographed or created, by number of people in the image. Getty Images offer localized image data and contextual search capabilities in six local languages.

Microsoft Office Online [8] also provides a large collection of clip art and multimedia data with well annotated keywords in multiple languages. The images in this collection can be used in creating documents. Figure 1 shows an example image from this site with its keyword annotations.

Figure 1. A clip art image from Microsoft Office Online and its annotations.

In fact, there are many stock photo or clip art collections available online. A list is provided in TASI's image search engine review [9].

Content-based image retrieval

Content-based image retrieval was initially proposed to overcome the difficulties encountered in keyword-based image search in 1990s. Since then, it has been an active research topic, and a lot of algorithms have been published in the literature. In keyword-based image search, images have to be manually annotated with keywords. As keyword annotation is a tedious process, it is impractical to annotate so many images on the Internet. Furthermore, annotation may be inconsistent. Due to the multiple contents in a single image and the subjectivity of human perception, it is also difficult to make exactly the same annotations by different indexers. In contrast, CBIR systems extract visual features from images and use them to index images, such as color, texture or shape. Color histogram is one of the most widely used features. It is essentially the statistics of the color of pixels in an image. As long as the content of an image does not change, the extracted features are always consistent. Moreover, the feature extraction can be performed automatically. Thus, the human labeling process can be avoided.

In a CBIR system, each image is represented as a vector, which is the feature automatically extracted from the image itself. During the retrieval process, the user may submit an image example as query to the system. After that, the system calculates the similarity between the feature vector of the query and that of each database image, rank images in the descending order of their similarities, and returns images with the highest similarities as the search result.

However, those features often do not match human perception very well. Images with similar concepts may have totally different appearance, while images having similar features may be irrelevant to each other at all. This is the so-called semantic gap, which limits the applicability of CBIR techniques. Figure 2 shows an example. Images A and B should be more semantically similar to each other since both are the image of a butterfly. However, images A and C are closer in the feature space because they contain more similar colors. If A is used as a query, it is more likely to retrieve C as the search result.

A   B   C

Figure 2. The mismatch between low-level features and high-level concepts.

Because the features used in CBIR are usually of high dimensionality and there is no efficient indexing method, current CBIR systems only index small image collections. So far, the largest CBIR system reported in the literature is Cortina [10], which indexes over 3 million images. The overall performance of CBIR systems is not satisfactory.

Conclusion

There are so many images available on the Internet that users do need efficient tools to browse and search for those images. The current image search engines can partially fulfill this need. In the future, a proper combination of textual and visual features may produce better image searching experience.

References

1. AltaVista Image Search, http://www.altavista.com/image.
2. Google Image Search, http://images.google.com/.
3. Yahoo! Image Search, http://search.yahoo.com/images.
4. C. Frankel, M. J. Swain, and V. Athitsos, "WebSeer: An Image Search Engine for the World Wide Web", Technical Report, University of Chicago, July 1966.
5. Z. Chen, W. Liu, F. Zhang, and M. Li, "Web Mining for Web Image Retrieval," Journal of the American Society for Information Science and Technology, Vol. 52, No. 10, August 2001, pp. 831-839.
6. Corbis, http://www.corbis.com/.
7. Getty Images, http://creative.gettyimages.com/.
8. Microsoft Office Online, http://office.microsoft.com/clipart/.

http://www.tasi.ac.uk/resources/searchengines.html, October 2004.
10. T. Quack, U. Monich, L. Thiele, and B. S. Manjunath, "Cortina: A System for Large-scale, Content-based Web," Proceedings of the 12th Annual ACM International Conference on Multimedia, 2004, pp. 508-511.

IMAGE SECRET SHARING

Rastislav Lukac and Konstantinos N. Plataniotis
University of Toronto, Toronto, Canada

Ching-Nung Yang
National Dong Hwa University, Shou-Feng, Taiwan, ROC

Definition: *Among numerous cryptographic solutions proposed in the past few years, secret sharing schemes have been found sufficiently secure to facilitate distributed trust and shared control in various communication applications*

Digital rights management systems are used to protect intellectual property rights of digital media itself or secure its transmission over untrusted communication channels [1]-[3]. The required protection is achieved by employing either cryptography or steganography. Steganography hides the secret message inside a cover signal producing its stego-version with an imperceivable difference from the original cover, whereas cryptography alters the meaningless of the secret message through its encryption necessitating the use of a decryption key to recover the original content.

Among numerous cryptographic solutions proposed in the past few years, secret sharing schemes have been found sufficiently secure to facilitate distributed trust and shared control in various communication applications, such as key management, conditional access, message authentication, and content encryption [4]-[6]. Due to the proliferation of imaging-enabled consumer electronic devices and the extensive use of digital imaging in networked solutions and services, secret sharing concepts have been used to secure transmission and distribution of personal digital photographs and digital document images over public networks [2],[7]-[10].

A (k,n)-threshold scheme

Most of the existing secret sharing schemes are generalized within the so-called (k,n)-threshold framework where $k \leq n$. The framework confidentially divides the content of a secret message into n shares in the way which requires the presence of at least k shares for the secret message reconstruction [11],[12]. If $k = n$, then all the shares are required in the (n,n)-threshold scheme to recover the secret. However, the lost of any of the shares produced using the (n,n)-threshold scheme results in inaccessible secret messages.

Therefore, apart from the simplest $(2,2)$-schemes commonly used as a private key cryptosystem solution [13],[14], general (k,n)-threshold schemes with $k < n$ are often the object of interest due to offer their ability to recover the secret message even if several shares are lost. In this case, any of $[n!/(k!(n-k)!)]$ possible combinations of k shares can be used to recover the secret message. Since protection against cryptoanalytic attacks, including brute force enumeration, should remain unchanged regardless of how many shares are available until the threshold k is reached, the use of $k-1$ shares should not reveal additional information compared to that obtained by a single share.

Basis matrices in visual cryptography

Probably the most well-known (k,n)-secret sharing schemes for encryption of visual data are those based on visual cryptography (VC) [11]-[13],[15]-[19]. Among the numerous VC-based schemes (Figures 1 and 2), such as the (k,n), (k,n,c) and extended VC schemes, the so-called (k,n)-VC framework is the most widely used. The traditional VC schemes (Figure 1) produce meaningless, noise-like, shares as opposed to the meaningful shares obtained using complex, extended VC schemes (Figure 2). Furthermore, compared to (k,n,c)-VC schemes constructed using c colors, the (k,n)-VC framework uses frosted/transparent (or binary) representation of the shares keeping the simplicity of the approach at the level suitable for practical implementation. It should be noted that within the (k,n)-VC framework, the special cases of $(2,2)$, $(2,n)$, and (n,n)-VC schemes can be obtained.

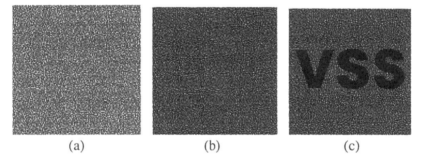

(a)   (b)   (c)

Figure 1. Demonstration of $(3,3)$-VC: (a) one binary share, (b) two binary shares stacked together, (c) three binary shares stacked together.

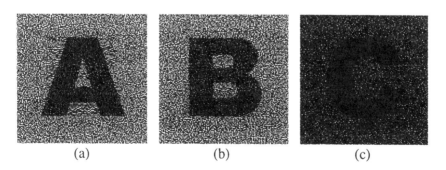

(a)   (b)   (c)

Figure 2. Demonstration of $(2,2)$-extended VC: (a,b) meaningful binary shares, (b) image produced by stacking of the shares shown in (a,b).

Operating on a $K_1 \times K_2$ binary or binarized secret image, a (k,n)-VC scheme encrypts, via an encryption function, each binary pixel into a $m_1 \times m_2$ block of binary pixels in each of the n binary shares. The spatial arrangement of bits in the produced blocks varies depending on the value of secret pixel to be encrypted and the (random) choice of the matrix from the so-called matrices' generation set C_0 or C_1. The sets C_0 and C_1 include all matrices obtained by permuting the columns of the $n \times m_1 m_2$ basis binary matrices A_0 and A_1, respectively [2]. Examples of the basis matrices are listed here for the most widely used (k,n)-VC schemes:

$$(2,2) \quad A_0 = \begin{bmatrix} 0,1,0,1 \\ 1,0,1,0 \end{bmatrix} A_1 = \begin{bmatrix} 0,1,0,1 \\ 0,1,0,1 \end{bmatrix} \qquad (2,3) \quad A_0 = \begin{bmatrix} 1,0,0,0 \\ 0,1,0,0 \\ 0,0,1,0 \end{bmatrix} A_1 = \begin{bmatrix} 1,0,0,0 \\ 1,0,0,0 \\ 1,0,0,0 \end{bmatrix}$$

$$(3,4) \quad A_0 = \begin{bmatrix} 0,1,1,1,1,1,0,0 \\ 0,1,1,1,1,0,0,1,1 \\ 0,1,1,0,0,1,1,1,1 \\ 0,0,0,1,1,1,1,1,1 \end{bmatrix} A_1 = \begin{bmatrix} 1,1,1,1,1,0,0,0 \\ 1,1,1,1,0,0,1,1,0 \\ 1,1,1,0,1,0,1,0,1 \\ 1,1,1,0,0,1,0,1,1 \end{bmatrix}$$

$$(2,6) \quad A_0 = \begin{bmatrix} 0,1,0,1 \\ 1,0,1,0 \\ 1,1,0,0 \\ 0,0,1,1 \\ 1,0,0,1 \\ 0,1,1,0 \end{bmatrix} A_1 = \begin{bmatrix} 0,1,0,1 \\ 0,1,0,1 \\ 0,1,0,1 \\ 0,1,0,1 \\ 0,1,0,1 \\ 0,1,0,1 \end{bmatrix}$$

$$(4,4) \quad A_0 = \begin{bmatrix} 1,0,0,1,0,0,1,0,1 \\ 1,0,1,0,0,0,1,1,0 \\ 1,0,1,0,0,1,0,0,1 \\ 0,1,1,0,0,0,1,0,1 \end{bmatrix} A_1 = \begin{bmatrix} 1,0,0,0,0,0,1,1,1 \\ 1,0,1,0,0,1,1,0,0 \\ 1,1,0,0,0,1,0,1,0 \\ 1,1,1,0,0,0,0,0,1 \end{bmatrix}$$

The value $m_1 m_2$ is the so-called expansion factor and therefore, the basis matrices are constructed in the way to minimize the expansion factor as much as possible [11],[15]. By repeating the encryption operations at each spatial location of the secret image, a $K_1 \times K_2$ secret image is encrypted into n binary shares with dimensions of $m_1 K_1 \times m_2 K_2$ pixels.

VC-based decryption, which has to be performed over the set of $\zeta \leq n$ shares, can be modeled through a decryption function similar to the one proposed in [2]. Following the formulation of a $\{k,n\}$-threshold schemes, the secret image is revealed only if $\zeta \geq k$. Due to the utilization of the transparent/frosted concept: i) the VC decryption process recovers the decrypted pixel as black if any of the share pixels at the same spatial location of the shares stacked for decryption is black, or recover it as white if all the pixels at the same spatial location in the stacked shares are transparent, and ii) do not recover the original secret image.

ISS with perfect reconstruction of the secret image

To recover the original secret image and prevent the introduction of visual impairments, a different decryption strategy should be used. Following the approach introduced in [2],[7], the decryption function should observe the contrast properties of the share blocks when stacked together. Similarly to VC decryption, the difference between the encrypted 'black' and 'white' binary values reveals only if $\zeta \geq k$. In this case, the decryption process recovers the corresponding original binary pixel. By decrypting the binary share blocks over the image domain the procedure recovers the original binary secret image, as it is shown in Figure 3. This suggests that such an approach can be used to construct an image encryption scheme which satisfies the essential perfect reconstruction property [2],[7],[8].

| Encyclopedia of Multimedia | | | Encyclopedia of Multimedia |
(a) (b) (c) (d)

Figure 3. A $(2,2)$-ISS scheme constructed using 2×4 basis matrices with $m_1 = 2$ and $m_2 = 2$: (a) secret binary image, (b,c) binary shares, (d) output image decrypted using the share inputs shown in (b,c).

Built on the framework presented in [2],[20] a number of solutions with different design characteristics and performance can be obtained. For example, instead of the utilization of a halftoning module in processing a $K_1\times K_2$ continuous-tone image as it is suggested by traditional VC, the encryption operations can be performed (Figure 4a) at the decomposed bit-levels of the secret image with B-bits per pixel representation. Each of B bit-levels represents a $K_1\times K_2$ binary image which is commonly required in the input of the VC encryption procedure. By repeating the VC-based encryption operation at each bit-level, the generated share bits are used to obtain the B-bit share pixel and thus, the bit-level processing based encryption process splits the B-bit secret image into n, seemingly random, $m_1K_1\times m_2K_2$ shares. Each of the constructed shares has B-bit representation identical to the bit-level representation of the secret image (Figure 5).

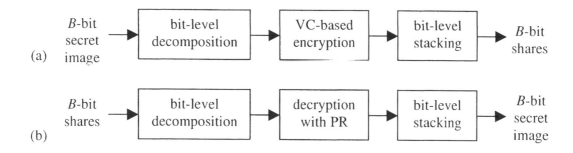

Figure 4. An ISS concept: (a) encryption procedure, (b) decryption procedure satisfying the perfect reconstruction (PR) property.

The decryption process (Figure 4b) decomposes the bit levels of all B-bit shares which are available for decryption. If $\zeta \geq k$, then the procedure recovers the individual bit levels which are then used by to re-construct the original, continuous tone secret image. Thus, the decryption process recovers the original secret image (Figure 5) in a digital form making the framework ideal for modern, digital, multimedia systems.

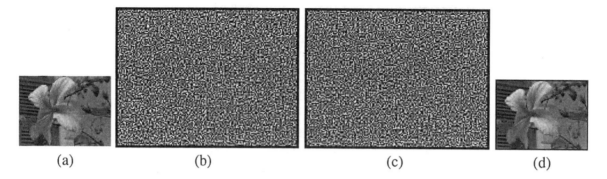

| (a) | (b) | (c) | (d) |

Figure 5. An $(2,2)$ ISS scheme constructed using 2×4 basis matrices with $m_1 = 2$ and $m_2 = 2$: (a) secret grayscale image, (b,c) gray-scale shares, (d) decrypted grayscale image.

The ISS framework allows for the design of both input-agnostic and input-specific solutions [20]. Such solutions: i) differ in their design characteristics and complexity, ii) may introduce different protection levels during the encryption process, and iii) can be used to process the secret image using an arbitrary $\{k, n\}$ configuration and expansion factor $m_1 m_2$.

Input-agnostic ISS solutions

The input-agnostic (IA) ISS solution follows the representation of the input and process sequentially all bit-levels decomposed from the secret image [2],[20]. As it is shown in Figure 6, the IA-ISS solution encrypts: i) the binary secret image into the binary shares, ii) the gray-scale secret image into the gray-scale shares, or iii) the color secret image into the color shares. As the result, the IA-ISS solution always produces shares with the image (bit) representation identical to that of the secret image, and decrypts the original secret image with perfect reconstruction.

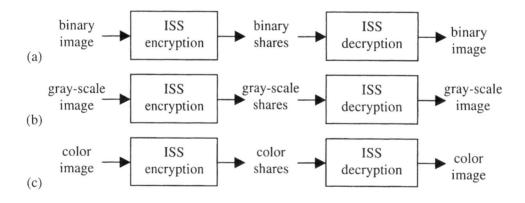

Figure 6. Input-agnostic ISS solution applied to encrypt: (a) binary secret image, (b) gray-scale secret image, (c) color secret image.

Input-specific ISS solutions

The input specific (IS)-ISS solution encrypts the secret image arranged in the specific image format [7],[8],[20]. For example, IS-ISS solution can require to convert: i) the binary or grayscale input image into the color image when the solution is color image specific to produce color shares, ii) the binary or color input image into the gray-scale image when the solution is gray-scale image specific to produce gray-scale shares, and iii) the color or gray-scale input image into the binary image when the solution is binary image specific to produce binary shares. Thus, any IS-ISS solution can be used to process the image with less rich or richer bit-representation than that of the required in the IS input. The approach requires format conversion such as the replication of the input (Figure 7a) or reduction of image representation (Figure 7b) in order to meet the requirements for the input, ii) the procedure requires to transmit Q times more (Figure 7a) or less (Figure 7b) share information compared to the share information produced by the IA-ISS solution, and iii) inverse format conversion is necessary to recover the original (Figure 7a) or due to the loss in input format conversion approximated (Figure 7b) secret image.

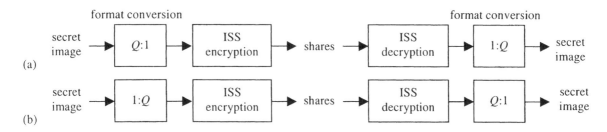

Figure 7. Input-specific ISS solution applied to encrypt: (a) secret image with less rich representation, or (b) richer representation than that of required in the input to the ISS encryption/decryption module.

Security characteristics of the ISS framework

The randomness of the encryption processes in the ISS framework is fortified by the depth of the B-bit representation of the secret image makes the original pixel and the share pixels significantly different [2],[20]. The variety in the share pixels, which can be viewed as the degree of protection, increases with the value of B which denotes the number of bits used to represent the image pixel (Figure 8). Assuming that N denotes the number of unique matrices either in C_0 or C_1, the B-bit pixel is encrypted using one of N^B unique $m_1 \times m_2$ share blocks of B-bit pixels instead of one of only N unique share blocks of binary pixels used in the traditional and halftoning based VC schemes. In this way, the IS-ISS solution in Figure 7a increases the protection by generating 'richer' noise compared to the shares obtained using the IA-ISS solution. Similarly, by reducing the image representation, the IS-ISS solution in Figure 7b reduces protection of the secret image compared to the case when the IA-ISS solution is used. Depending on the application, security requirements, available computational resources, and nature of the secret image, the end-user may select the particular cryptographic solution designed within the proposed framework to process the input (secret) image [20].

334 I

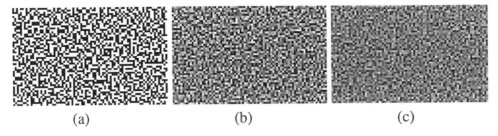

(a) (b) (c)

Figure 8. Examples of the share formats: (a) binary, (b) gray-scale, (c) full-color share.

See: Visual cryptography, Halftoning based VSS, Image watermarking using visual cryptography, Threshold schemes with minimum pixel expansion, Private-key ISS solution, Compression in image secret sharing.

References
1. M. Barni and F. Bartolini, "Data Hiding for Fighting Piracy," IEEE Signal Processing Magazine, Vol. 21, No. 2, March 2004, pp. 28-39.
2. R. Lukac and K.-N. Plataniotis, "Bit-Level Based Secret Sharing for Image Encryption," Pattern Recognition, Vol. 38, No. 5, May 2005, pp. 767-772.
3. E.-T. Lin, A. M. Eskicioglu, R.-L. Lagendijk, and E.-D. Delp, "Advances in Digital Video Content Protection," Proceedings of the IEEE, Vol. 93, No. 1, January 2005, pp. 171-183.
4. A.-M. Eskicioglu, E.-J. Delp, and M.-R. Eskicioglu, "New Channels for Carrying Copyright and Usage Rights Data in Digital Multimedia Distribution," Proc. International Conference on Information Technology: Research and Education (ITRE'03), August 2003, pp. 94-98.
5. E.-D. Karnin, J.-W. Greene, and M.-E. Hellman, "On Secret Sharing Systems," IEEE Transactions on Information Theory, Vol. 29, No. 1, January 1983, pp. 35-41.
6. A. Biemel and B. Chor, "Secret Sharing with Public Reconstruction," IEEE Transactions on Information Theory, Vol. 44, No. 5, September 1998, pp. 1887-1896.
7. R. Lukac and K.-N. Plataniotis, "Colour Image Secret Sharing," IEE Electronics Letters, Vol. 40, No. 9, April 2004, pp. 529-530.
8. R. Lukac, and K.-N. Plataniotis, "A New Encryption Scheme for Color Images," Computing and Informatics, submitted.
9. C.-S. Tsai, C.-C. Chang, and T.-S. Chen, "Sharing Multiple Secrets in Digital Images," Journal of Systems and Software, Vol.64, No.2, 2002, pp. 163-170.
10. C.-C. Chang and J.-C. Chuang, "An Image Intellectual Property Protection Scheme for Gray-Level Images Using Visual Secret Sharing Strategy," Pattern Recognition Letters, Vol. 23, No. 8, June 2002, pp. 931-941.
11. P.-A. Eisen and D.-R. Stinson, "Threshold Visual Cryptography Schemes with Specified Levels of Reconstructed Pixels," Design, Codes and Cryptography, Vol. 25, No.1, January 2002, pp. 15-61.
12. E.-R. Verheul and H.-C.-A. Van Tilborg, "Constructions and Properties of k out of n Visual Secret Sharing Schemes," Designs, Codes and Cryptography, Vol. 11, No. 2, May 1997, pp. 179-196.
13. G. Ateniese, C. Blundo, A. de Santis, and D.-G. Stinson, "Visual Cryptography for General Access Structures," Information and Computation, Vol. 129, No. 2, September 1996, pp. 86-106.

14. R. Lukac and K.-N. Plataniotis, "A Cost-Effective Private-Key Cryptosystem for Color Image Encryption," Lecture Notes in Computer Science, Vol. 3514, May 2005, pp. 679-686.
15. M. Naor and A. Shamir, "Visual Cryptography," Proc. EUROCRYPT'94, Lecture Notes in Computer Science, Vol. 950, 1994, pp. 1-12.
16. C.-N. Yang, "New Visual Secret Sharing Schemes Using Probabilistic Method," Pattern Recognition Letters, Vol. 25, No. 4, March 2004, pp. 481-494.
17. C.-N. Yang and T.-S. Chen, "Aspect Ratio Invariant Visual Secret Sharing Schemes with Minimum Pixel Expansion," Pattern Recognition Letters, Vol. 26, No. 2, January 2005, pp.193-206.
18. C.-N. Yang and T.-S. Chen, "Size-Adjustable Visual Secret Sharing Schemes," IEICE Transactions on Fundamentals, to appear.
19. H. Yamamoto, Y. Hayasaki, and N. Nishida, "Securing Information Display by Use of Visual Cryptography," Optics Letters, Vol. 28, No. 17, September 2003.
20. R. Lukac and K.-N. Plataniotis, "Image Representation Based Secret Sharing," Communications of the CCISA (Chinese Cryptology Information Security Association), Special Issue on Visual Secret Sharing, Vol. 6, April 2005.

IMAGE WATERMARKING

Definition: Image watermarking deals with creating a metadata (a watermark) about the image content and hiding it within the image.

Challenges and benchmarking

Digital images are often printed and scanned again, for example when they are used in magazines and readers want to store digitally. When used as web site illustrations, they are often compressed by lossy compression algorithms like JPEG. Common processing operations include softening, sharpening, denoising, scaling, cropping and colour corrections. A number of benchmarking suits address image watermarking robustness evaluation, Stirmark [1], Checkmark and Certimark are well known examples.

The most challenging attacks on the robustness of image watermarks today are nonlinear transformations, rendering a watermark in an image undetectable for the watermarking algorithm. But even common image processing operations like scaling and rotation can be a serious challenge for the re-synchronisation of an image watermark.

Typical challenges in practical solutions are printing and scanning with low quality devices like customer ink jet printers leading to the additions of noise, colour changes, small rotations and changes in image resolution.

Another important aspect of image watermarking is the broad variety of image types. There are photos, also called natural images in the literature, figures based on line drawings, rendered synthetic images, bitmap representations of textual information, just to give the most common examples. Challenges with respect to transparency and robustness often depend on the characteristics of these images. Many watermarking algorithms address only one image type, like e.g. photographs. Often the dependency can be derived from the embedding principle: An algorithm which needs textures to embed information will not be able to deal with a black and white drawing but performs perfectly with most photographs.

Advanced image watermarking

While all watermarking methods described in this article are known for image watermarking, there are also a number of innovative approaches which are especially suited for image watermarking. They usually could be transferred to video watermarking, but the long computation time caused by high complexity and the stronger compression in digital video are a serious hindrance here. As examples for advanced watermarking methods we describe two innovative algorithms combining existing approaches with new techniques.

Region of interest watermarking

A good example of advanced fragile watermarking for integrity protection is region of interest (ROI) watermarking. The basic idea is distinguish between semantically important and unimportant regions of an image. It is often sufficient to protect the important regions as manipulations changing the meaning of the image will only occur in these. Modifications taking place not in the RIO may be of cosmetic nature or could be simple name tag annotations. An example of ROI watermarking is the face detection approach discussed in [2] protecting only automatically detected faces and the relative positions in an image.

Self-correcting images

While many approaches to identify changes in images are known, some algorithms even allow re-creating the original from the watermark to a certain degree. This enables a comparison of the content of an image before and after an attack. One known approach is based on an algorithm described in [3], using a block-based pseudo-random distribution of pixel information in over the image thereby shuffling and spreading a kind of parity checksum over the whole image. The idea here is to use the spread information about a block of pixels to identify small local changes by identifying parity errors after attacks.

References

1. F. Petitcolas and R. Anderson, "Evaluation of copyright marking systems," Proceedings of IEEE Multimedia Systems, Multimedia Computing and Systems, June 1999, Florence, Italy, Vol. 1, 1999, pp. 574-579.
2. H. Liu, H. Sahbi, L. Croce Ferri, and M. Steinebach, "Image Authentication using automatic detected ROIs," WIAMIS 2004, 5th International Workshop on Image Analysis for Multimedia Interactive Services; April 2004, Instituto Superior Técnico, Lisboa, Portugal.
3. M. Wu and B. Liu, "Digital watermarking using shuffling," ICIP 99, Proceedings of International Conference on Image Processing, 1999, Vol. 1, pp. 291-295.

IMAGE WATERMARKING USING VISUAL CRYPTOGRAPHY

Definition: A new class of digital watermarking techniques is based on visual cryptography.

Recent works have introduced a new class of digital watermarking schemes which employ visual cryptography (VC) concepts to secure watermarked content [1]-[3]. In addition, VC-based watermarking may be used to robustify recognition of an extracted watermark from images which have been subjected to attacks [2],[3]. For example, in the approach shown in Figure 1, instead of embedding a binary logo directly to the host image, a VC-based watermarking scheme first encrypts the binary logo into two noise-like binary shares. One of the two generated shares can be viewed as a private watermark share and is kept by the owner. The other share represents a public watermark share and is being embedded to the host image using a conventional watermarking technique which operates either in the spatial or frequency domain of the host image [2],[3].

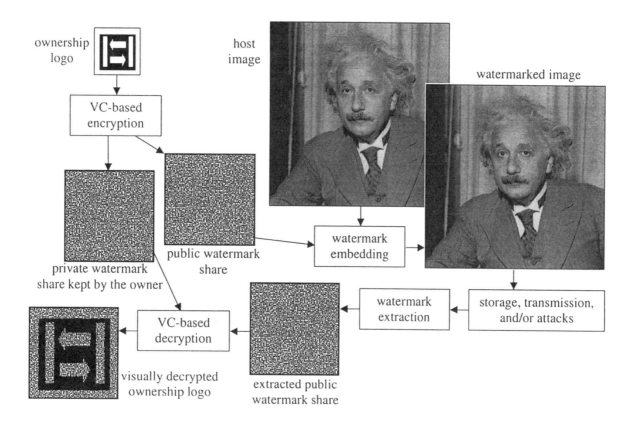

Figure 1. Visual cryptography based digital watermarking.

As it is shown in Figure 1, the resulting watermarked image is to be stored, transmitted via public channel, and thus is vulnerable to various signal processing and cryptoanalysis attacks. After extracting the public watermark share from the attacked watermarked image, a private watermark share is used as a private key and stacked together with a public watermark share to visually reveal a binary logo.

See: Image secret sharing, Visual cryptography, Private-key cryptosystem.

References
1. R. Lukac and K.-N. Plataniotis, "Digital Image Indexing Using Secret Sharing Schemes: A Unified Framework for Single-Sensor Consumer Electronics," IEEE Transactions on Consumer Electronics, submitted.
2. G.-C. Tai and L.-W. Chang, "Visual Cryptography for Digital Watermarking in Still Images," Lecture Notes in Computer Science, Vol. 3332, 2004, pp. 50-57.
3. C.-S. Tsai and C.-C. Chang, "A New Repeating Color Watermarking Scheme Based on Human Visual Model," Eurasip Journal of Applied Signal Processing, Vol. 2004, No. 13, October 2004, pp. 1965-1972.

IMMERSIVE VIRTUAL REALITY

Definition: The goal of Immersive Virtual Reality is to completely immerse the user inside the computer generated world, giving the impression to the user that he/she has "stepped inside" the synthetic world.

Virtual Reality (VR) is the technology that provides almost real and/or believable experience in a synthetic or virtual way. The goal of *Immersive VR* is to completely immerse the user inside the computer generated world, giving the impression to the user that he/she has "stepped inside" the synthetic world. This can be achieved by using either the technologies of *Head-Mounted Display* (HMD) or multiple projections. Immersive VR with HMD uses HMD to project VR just in front of the eyes and allows users to focus on display without distraction. A magnetic sensor inside the HMD detects the users' head motion and feeds that information to the attached processor. Consequently, the user turns his or her head; the displayed graphics can reflect the changing viewpoint. The virtual world appears to respond to head movement in a familiar way.

Immersive VR with multiple projections uses multiple projectors to create VR on a huge screen, which might be a hemispherical surface, in a room where users might ware polarized glasses to maximize the feeling of being present at the scene in standstill. The form of this immersive graphical display is known as the CAVE (stands for Computer-Aided Virtual Environment), where the immersion occurs by surrounding the body on all sides by images, rather than just the eyes. Early versions of these technologies were demonstrated at SIGGRAPH '92 in Chicago by Sun Microsystems and University of Illinois. The CAVE is essentially a five sided cube. The participant stands in the middle of cube, and images are projected onto the walls in front, above, below and on either side of the participant, utilizing full 270-degree peripheral vision. As the user travels through the virtual environment, updated images are projected onto the CAVE's walls to give the sensation of smooth motion. Figure 1 shows a CAVE at the University of Ottawa's DISCOVERLab [1].

Figure 1. Immersive Virtual Reality in a CAVE.

See: Virtual and Augmented Reality

References

1.   DISCOVER Lab, http://www.discover.uottawa.ca.

IN HOME, IN CAR, IN FLIGHT ENTERTAINMENT

Definition: *Entertainment has exited from traditional places and is now an anywhere activity for people at homes, cars, and flights.*

Home entertainment can be considered as a part of a more complex demotic system. *Domestics* is the combination of technologies for improved living in the areas of safety, comfort and security management. New systems can provide consumers with personalized services tailoring to their well-being, communication and entertainment needs. In an entertainment-equipped home, a high-speed, always-on, Internet access combined with WLAN is quite common. At the same time, home theaters, game consoles and other entertainment equipments are widely adopted. The presence of a broadband network and of different entertainment equipments encourage a drastic revolution in future home entertainment promoting the design of a *magic box* where new exciting multimedia applications will be all available for instant enjoyment. According to [1], today, the magic box does not exist yet. While in the computer industry all majors have understood the need to simplify the life for the consumers, the home theater industry has not become aware of this topic. The devices composing a home theater live as fragmented pieces of the same picture, still having many companies fighting to impose their technical choices as standard. Hence, to obtain a fully inclusive system (video, stereo, decoder, console, Web) it is still necessary to acquire a variety of equipments made by different manufacturers. Therefore, many efforts should be devoted should develop a control protocol that permits to configure each device and to build-up a *plug and play* system for new devices.

From home to car, entertainment becomes, usually, an attempt to define a mobile home theatre [2]. For example, Dolby provides an enhanced audio/video experience for all passengers in a car. Other simple multimedia entertainments are based on the use of GPS systems that show the localization of the car on a map, or in alternative, by the use of digital radios that provide dynamically update information. Sophisticated applications exploiting wireless solutions implement *network of cars* that offer multimedia distribution services.

From car to airplane, technical problem becomes more urgent. Entertaining people during an intercontinental flight is really a hard work [3]. Typically, an on-board broadcasting system offers to travelers music and movies. New forms of entertainment are possible, simply equipping the plane with on-board multimedia services and network connections. For example, 757 Boing jet of the Song Airlines is equipped with an in-flight multimedia system that offers GPS tracking, connecting gate, digital shopping, in-seat Internet connectivity, SMS/email messaging, streamed MP3 play lists, 24 channels of live network TV, and interactive networked games for free.

See: Multimedia Entertainment Applications

References

1. D. A. Norman, "Home Theater: Not Ready for Prime Time," IEEE Computer, Vol. 35, No. 6, 2002, pp. 100-102.
2. A. Gilroy, "Car A/V Spotlights iPod Interfaces, MP3 on DVD, mini TFTs," Special Report CES, January 2005, Las Vegas, USA.
3. G. Lui-Kwan, "In-Flight Entertainment: the Sky's the Limit," IEEE Computer, Vol. 33, No. 10, October 2000, pp.98-101.

INDEXING 3D SCENES

Ioan Marius BILASCO, Jérôme GENSEL, Hervé MARTIN, and Marlène VILLANOVA-OLIVER
Laboratoire LSR IMAG, Grenoble, France

Definition: *Semantic queries on indexed objects allow the reuse of the 3D scenes.*

Nowadays, the 3D is a highly expanding media. More particularly with the emergence of dedicated standards such as VRML and X3D, 3D animations are widely used on the Web. The continuous evolution of computing capabilities of desktop computers is also a factor that facilitates the large deployment of 3D information contents. At the same time the demand in term of 3D information is becoming more and more sustained in various domains such as spatial planning, risks management, telecommunications, transports, defense, and tourism. 3D information should represent a real world scene as accurately as possible and should exhibit properties (like, topological relations) to allow complex spatial analysis [12].

The construction of a 3D scene is a complex and time consuming task. Thus, being able to reuse the 3D scenes is a very important issue for the multimedia community. In order to meet this goal, the indexing process is essential. Indexing implies the enrichment of the raw information contained in a multimedia document. In general, indexing is achieved by means of signal analysis or manual or semi-automatic annotations. Signal indexing supposes the automatic extraction of implicit features from the document. For instance, if one analyses a 2D image the signal indexing results in the extraction of the dominant color, the color histogram, etc.

Usually, in a 3D scene, one can model only the geometric features of the scene paying very little attention to semantic information that should guide and help the reuse. Identification of interesting/reusable *objects* in the scene is part of the indexing process. The granularity of a reusable *object* can vary from a simple geometric element (e.g. a cube, etc.) to a full scene (e.g. a casual office scene, a building). Since a 3D scene is built up from different geometric elements, identification of objects is performed by localizing its geometric elements. In order to facilitate the reuse of 3D objects, some semantic information should be added. Semantic queries on indexed objects would yield the most appropriate result according to the intent of reuse.

3D scenes as pure geometric worlds

The 3D community benefits from the support of a highly interactive consortium called the Web3D consortium, involving many companies (NASA, HP, nVIDIA, Sun Microsystem) and academic communities (Communications Research Center of Canada, GIS Research Center at Feng Chia University, and others). The research efforts of the consortium are directed towards the development of a widely adopted standard for deploying 3D information all over the Web.

The Extensible 3D (X3D) [14] standard has emerged in the mid 2002. X3D was proposed as a revised version of the Virtual Reality Modelling Language (VRML97) [2]. In July 2002 the Web3D Consortium made available the final working draft version of X3D. The X3D was accepted by the ISO as an ISO/IEC 19775 standard of communication for 3D real-time scenes in August, 2004. The final specifications were produced by the end of October 2004.

This standard defines a runtime environment and a delivery mechanism for 3D content and applications running over a network. It combines geometry descriptions, runtime behavioral descriptions and control features. It proposes numerous types of encodings including an Extensible Modelling Language (XML) [1] encoding.

X3D is extensible as it is built on a set of components organized in profiles. Each profile contains a set of components. A component introduces a specific collection of nodes. The next extensions of the standard will be made by defining new components and organizing them into new profiles.

An X3D document represents the scene as an n-ary tree. The tree is composed of nodes supported by the selected profile. Among the most important nodes are found: geometric primitives (*Cube, Box, IndexLineSet*, etc), geometric transformations (*Transform* assuring *translations* and *rotations*), composite objects (*Group*), alternate content (*Switch*), multi level representation (*LOD*), etc. The tree also contains ambiental elements: *lights*, *viewpoints*, etc, and a meta-data node (*WorldInfo*).

A view of the scene is shown in Figure 1. The office contains a desk and a chair. On the desk, there are two stacks of books and papers. Hereafter, in Figure 2, we present the tree corresponding to a 3D scene describing a researcher's office. An excerpt of the X3D code corresponding to the materialization of the chair can be found in Figure 3.

Figure 1. A researcher's office modeled using X3D.

The desk is built up using three boxes: one for the desk top and two for the desk legs. The chair is composed of three boxes as well: one for the back side and the back-side legs, one for the front legs and one to sit on. The books are modeled by three boxes: two small ones for the books on the left and a bigger one for the stack of papers.

The resulting model of a 3D scene using the X3D treats exhaustively the geometry, the environmental aspects (lights, etc.), and describes levels of user's interactions. However, the scene is not self-descriptive. The scene does not contain any information on the real-world objects included into the scene. The main scope of an X3D scene model is to ensure the delivery of the scene to the user's rendering device. The semantics aspects are scarcely included.

A 3D scene is a condensed information space (geometric description, spatial organization, etc.). The richness of a 3D scene cannot be fully exploited if information is not explicitly materialized. In our example, the fact that the chair is under the table cannot be directly deduced from the X3D description of the scene. Geometric constructs embed information that it is easily understood by human actors, but raw information, globally, remains unexploitable by means of queries without further analysis. Consequently, some spatial analysis is required.

Even though the structural organization of an X3D file facilitates the retrieval of attributary information (*position*, *color*, *appearance*), a series of spatial or semantic queries still remain unanswered. A complementary description, by means of annotations, should take into account the semantic aspects of information associated with the scene (e.g. the chair is allowing the researcher to sit at the table – semantic relations, the chair cannot support a weight heavier than 200 kg – semantic properties). Firstly, the annotations should allow identifying the geometric elements that correspond to the representation of a real world object. Secondly, semantic properties should be associated with the related real-world object, as well as relations it has with its environment.

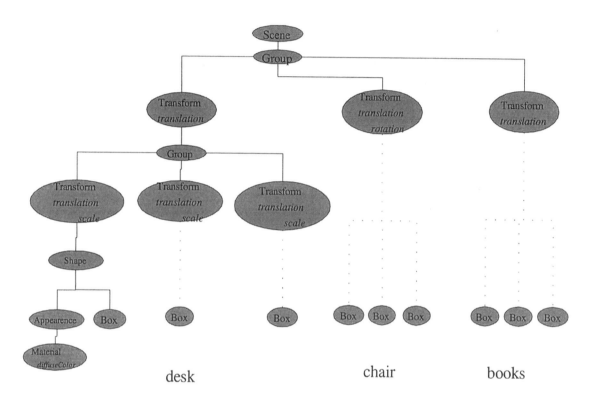

Figure 2. A 3D scene tree.

The boxes are imposed an adequate size using the *scale* attributes of *Transform* nodes as in Figure 3. They are grouped together into *Group* nodes, placed at the right position using the *translation* attribute, and are imposed a fixed orientation using the *rotation* attributes.

Localizing real world objects in a 3D scene

In order to explain the localization of real world objects in a 3D scene one should take also into account the work done in the domain of 2D images. The localization supposes the identification of a set of elements that constitutes the representation of the object. For instance, in the case of a 2D image objects are associated to sub-regions delimited by sets of 2D polygons.

The nature of localized elements can vary from pure geometric elements (*points, lines, surfaces, volumes*) to complex document entries (e.g. a cluster of geometric elements). Hence, we can observe two types of localization, both *geometric* and *structural* localizations.

The Structural Localization uses the structure of a document to indicate the document entries that corresponds to the target element. For instance, if the document is XML-like, then a structural localization would be likely composed of a series of XPATH [4] expressions indicating the parts of the object in the scene.

```
<X3D profile="Core">
  <Scene>
    <Group>
      <Group id ="desk">
        <!--desk top -->
        <Transform translation="0 9 -50"
                          scale="25 0.5 10">
          <Shape>
            <Box />
            <Appearance>
              <Material diffuseColor="0 0 1" />
            </Appearance>
          </Shape>
        </Transform>
        <!--left leg -->
        <Transform translation="-17.5 0 -50"
                          scale="0.5 9 10">
          <Shape>
                  ...
          </Shape>
        </Transform>
        <!--right leg-->
        <Transform translation="17.5 0 -50"
                  scale="0.5 9 10">
          <Shape>
                  ...
          </Shape>
        </Transform>
      </Group>
              ..
      <Transform translation = "50 2 -40"
                          rotation="0 1 0 1.57">
        <Group id="chair">
          ...
        </Group>
      </Transform>
              ...
    </Group>
  </Scene>
</X3D>
```

Figure 3. An excerpt of an X3D scene model.

Let us consider the scene described in Figure 3. The localization of the desk legs can be expressed as the combination of the two following XPATH expressions:

/X3D/Scene/Group/Group[@id='desk']/Transform[position()=2]and
//Group[@id='desk']/ Transform[position()=3].

This localisation contains information about elements that materialize the legs (*Shape*) as well as their position (*Transform*) inside the local cluster (*Group id="desk"*). The structural localisation should target the smallest structural element that offers an adequate description for the object.

Sometimes, this condition cannot be satisfied. It is possible that the structure of the document is not as fine-grained as necessary. In our example, we could imagine that the bottom of the stack of papers contains articles published in the last month while the top of the stack contains articles about the multimedia indexing. The structural localisation does not allow localizing the articles at the bottom of the stack since no structural element corresponds to the respective object. The whole stack is defined as a box, and, hence the same structural element is used to represent two real world objects. The only solution to identify the object is to complete the structural localisation using a geometric localisation. In our example, we can isolate the multimedia indexing related papers with a volume such as, a cube having the same basis as the box and a fixed height. The cube coordinates are defined relatively to the box. In this case, there is a mix between one structural localisation and a geometric one. However, the geometric localisation could be completely separated from the structure of the scene. In this case, the volume should have been defined according to the global reference system. The situation presented above has many similarities with multimedia documents that do not have any internal structure which is often the case in the presence of raw images, simples Digital Terrain Models [8], etc.

When the geometric localisation is used, geometric queries are applied on the scene elements in order to obtain the precise geometric elements composing the object. The granularity of the retrieved geometric elements (pixels, primitives, etc.) - subject of negotiation - is chosen in order to meet specific requirements.

As in the case of 2D images region identification, one can think of three ways of performing localisation:

- manual localisation: the user defines the set of objects and their localisation in the scene.

- semi-automatic localisation: the machine suggests to the user a series of possible objects in the scene. In the case of an X3D structured scene the machine could associate to each Group node a virtual object leaving then the user choose the relevant ones. In the case of an unstructured 3D scene (a Digital Terrain Model), a signal-level analysis could yield interesting regions using algorithmic methods similar to those employed in 2D contour detection for instance [11]. Other propositions suggest the use of specific tools - like intelligent scissoring of 3D meshes [5], etc. - in order to define precise geometric localisation.

- automatic localisation: the system performs all the work. In order to achieve this degree of generality dependant domain knowledge should be implemented in the localisation process.

Indexing multimedia content using MPEG-7

The Moving Picture Experts Group (MPEG) is a working group of the ISO/IEC in charge of developing standards for coded representation of digital audio and video. Established in 1988, the group has produced MPEG-1, MPEG-2, MPEG-4, MPEG-7 and MPEG-21 "Multimedia Framework". MPEG-1, MPEG-2 and MPEG-4 are basically standards concerning the encoding and the transmission of audio and video streams. MPEG-7 is a standard that addresses the semantic description of media resources. MPEG-21 is much more considered as the description of a multimedia framework (coding, transmission, adaptation, etc.) than a specific standard. Even if the MPEG-7 and MPEG-21 were proposed in the context of digital audio and video data, they are highly extensible and could cover other areas. Due to its high capability of evolution, we consider MPEG-7 as a valuable candidate for fulfilling requirements in terms of semantic annotations inside a 3D scene. Hereafter, we focus on the MPEG-7.

MPEG-7 [6][7] formally named "Multimedia Content Description Interface", was officially approved as a standard in 2001. It provides multimedia content description utilities for the browsing and retrieval of audio and visual contents. This standard provides normative elements, such as, Descriptors (Ds), Descriptors Schemes (DSs) and a Description Definition Language (DDL).

The Ds are indexation units describing the visual, audio and semantic features of media objects.

They allow the description of low-level audio-visual features (color, texture, animation, sound level, etc.) as well as attributes associated with the content (localisation, duration, quality, etc). Moreover, visual and audio features are automatically extracted from the encoding level of the media object as described in [9][13] for visual features and [3][10] for audio. Semantic features are mainly added manually.

The DSs are used to group several Ds and other DSs into structured, semantic units. A DSs models a real life entity and the relations it holds with its environment. DSs are usually employed to express high-level features of media content like: objects, events, and segments, metadata linked to the creation, generation and usage of media objects. As for the semantic features, DSs are scarcely filled in automatically.

In order to offer an important degree of extensibility to the standard the DDL is included as a tool for extending the predefined set of Ds and DSs formerly proposed. The DDL defines the syntax for specifying, expressing and combining DSs and Ds allowing creating new DSs.

The existing DSs cover the following areas: visual description (VDS), audio description (ADS), multimedia content description (MDS) (general attributes and features related to any simple or composed media object). We focus on the MDS as it addresses organization aspects that could serve as a valuable starting point in order to extend the indexing capabilities towards 3D documents. The VDS and the ADS are matched against the physical/logical organizations or semantics of the document.

MDSs propose metadata structures for annotating real world or multimedia entities. MDS is decomposed on the following axis: Content Organization, Navigation and Access, User Interaction, Basic Elements, Content Management, Content Description.

We discuss more in detail the *Content Description* axis as it offers DSs for characterizing the physical and the logical structures of the content. It ensures also the semantic description using real world concepts. The basic structural element is called a *segment*. A *segment* corresponds to a spatial, temporal or spatio-temporal partition of the content. A segment (Audio Segment DS, Visual Segment DS, AudioVisual Segment DS, and Moving Regions DS) is associated with a *section*. It can be decomposed in smaller segments creating a hierarchical segmentation of the media content. Each segment is individually indexed using the available tools (visual DSs, audio DSs, ...).

The conceptual aspects of the media content are formulated using the Semantic DS. Objects (*ObjectDS*), events (*EventDS*), abstract concepts (ConceptDS), places (*SemanticPlaceDS*), moments of time (*SemanticTimeDS*) are all parts of the Semantic DS. As for the segment-based description of the content, the semantics can be organized as trees or graphs. The nodes represent semantic notions/concepts and the links define semantic relations between concepts. A semantic characterization of the office scene (Figure 1) using MPEG-7 tools is illustrated below.

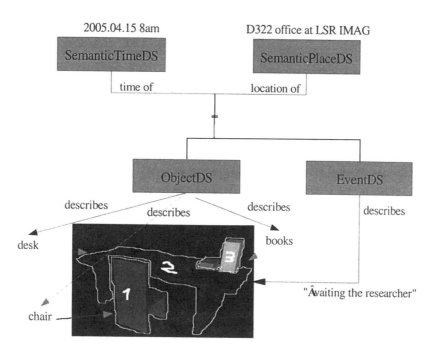

Figure 4. A semantic description of the image issued from the office scene using MPEG-7 tools.

The structural schemas and the semantic ones could be linked to each other. Hence, the content description could be made out of content structure and semantic structure all together.

Conclusions

In this article we presented some problems that are inherent to the process of indexing and reuse of 3D scenes. Widely accepted standards exist for the modeling of 3D scenes (X3D) and multimedia indexing (MPEG-7). They enhance, respectively, the Web deployment of 3D information and the management of multimedia content. However, at our knowledge, no largely accepted research project aims at solving interoperability issues between the two standards in order to support the management – and notably the reuse – of 3D multimedia content.

The interoperability issues concern the capacity of addressing 3D content inside a multimedia document. Specific 3D region/object locators must be designed. A set of specific 3D spatial descriptions schemes have to be provided in order to facilitate the spatial analysis required by most of 3D application domains (spatial planning, transports).

Research efforts will address the interoperability issues between standards in order to improve in flexibility and reuse of 3D scenes. Work is to be performed in order to enhance the capacities of MPEG-7 to address and to characterize 3D content. The semantic added to the pure X3D geometric modeling of the scene enhances the reuse process of 3D objects. Complex geometric, spatial and/or semantic queries could then be formulated in order to extract the most appropriate 3D content according to specific needs of applications or scene designers.

References

1. T. Bray, J. Paoli, C.M. Sperberg-McQueen, and E. Maler, "Extensible Markup Language (XML) 1.0 (Second Edition)," W3C Standard, available on-line *http://www.w3.org/TR/REC-xml*, 1998.
2. R. Carey, G. Bell, and C. Marrin, "Virtual Reality Modelling Language (VRML97) Functional Specification," ISO/IEC 14772-1, 1997, available online http://www.web3d.org/x3d/specifications/vrml/.
3. M. Casey, "MPEG-7 sound-recognition tools", IEEE Transactions on Circuits and Systems for Video Technology, Vol. 11, No. 6, June 2001, pp. 737-747.
4. J. Clark and S. DeRose, "XML Path Language (XPath) Version 1.0," *W3C Recommendation, available on-line http://www.w3.org/TR/xpath*, 1999.
5. T. Funkhouser, M. Kazhdan, P. Shilane, P. Min, W. Kiefer, A. Tal, S. Rusinkiewicz, and David Dobkin, "Modelling by Examples," ACM Transactions on Graphics (SIGGRAPH 2004), Los Angeles, CA, August 2004, pp. 652 - 663
6. J. M. Martinez and R. Koenen, "MPEG-7: The Generic Multimedia Content Description Standard, Part 1," IEEE Multimedia, Vol. 9, Issue 2, April 2002, pp. 78-87.
7. J. M. Martínez, "MPEG-7: Overview of Description Tools, Part 2," *IEEE Multimedia*, Vol. 9, Issue 3, July-September 2002, pp. 83-93.
8. R. Weibel and M. Heller, "Digital terrain modeling," In D.J. Maguire, M.F. Goodchild, and D.W. Rhind, (Eds.) Geographical Information Systems: Principles and Applications, Longman: London, 1991, pp. 269-297.

9. A. Yamada, M. Pickering, S. Jeannin, L. Cieplinski, J.R. Ohm, and M. Kim, "MPEG-7 Visual Part of eXperimentation Model Version 9.0," ISO/IEC JTC1/SC29/WG11 N3914, 2001.
10. A. Zils and F. Pachet, "Automatic Extraction of Music Descriptors from Acoustic Signals using EDS," Proceedings of the 116th AES Convention, May 2004.
11. D. Ziou and S. Tabbone, "Edge Detection Techniques – An Overview," International Journal of Pattern Recognition and Image Analysis, Vol. 8, 1998, pp. 537-559.
12. S. Zlatanova and K. Templi, "Modeling for 3D GIS: Spatial Analysis and Visualisation through the Web," In M. Molennar and K. J. Beek (Eds.), International Archives of Photogrammetry and Remote Sensing, Vol. XXXIII, XIXth Congress ISPRS, Amsterdam, 2000, pp. 1257-1264.
13. MPEG-7 XM Software, Institute for Integrated Circuits, Technische Universität Munchen, Germany, June 2001.
    http://www.lis.e-technik.tu-muenchen.de/research/bv/topics/mmdb/e_mpeg7.html.
14. Web3D Consortium, "Information technology — Computer graphics and image processing — Extensible 3D (X3D) — Part 1: Architecture and base components," ISO/IEC FDIS 19775-1:200x, 2001.

INFRARED FACE RECOGNITION

Definition: *Infrared face recognition systems use infrared sensors to measure the thermal radiation emitted in the infrared spectrum range.*

One of the major problems of traditional face recognition systems is constant performance under uncontrolled environments, and especially under extreme variations in illumination conditions, e.g. operating in total darkness or full daylight in an open area surveillance scenario. Such problems may be alleviated using infrared (IR) images for face recognition. Unlike conventional visual cameras, which measure the electromagnetic energy in the visible spectrum range, infrared sensors measure the thermal radiation emitted in the infrared spectrum range (0.7-0.14 μm) [1]. Thermal images of the human face represent patterns caused from superficial blood vessels up to 4 cm below the skin surface, which transport warm blood throughout the body and heat the skin just above them by an average of 0.1°C [2]. The vein and tissue structure of an individual is unique, even for identical twins [1], and thus ensures that except in case of aging, arterial problems, injury or surgery the vascular patterns acquired by IR cameras can be used for identification. Some examples of infrared face images can be seen in Figure 1.

IR face recognition systems are unaffected by variations in illumination and unlike systems using visual light, they can work without any problem under all lighting conditions, even in complete darkness. They are also unaffected by skin color, suntan, use of cosmetics and colored eye lenses or even plastic surgery. The latter, although it would defeat a visual face recognition system since it would change drastically facial appearance (e.g. facial lift, removal of wrinkles, use of silicon implants, etc), it would not affect IR face recognition, because it does not intervene with the network of blood vessels [2]. IR systems are very robust to impostors using masks or make-up or other means of forgery, because they can readily distinguish between real and artificial skin, hair, etc, based on different values of emissivity. Nevertheless, the extremely high cost of IR sensors, makes the use of IR face recognition systems prohibitive for every day applications.

Like visual face images, thermal images are processed for recognition using appearance-based techniques like PCA, or feature based techniques that locate and use features like the corners of the eye where the upper and lower eyelids meet (canthi), the curves produced by the main facial arteries of the two cheeks, the position and angles of main arteries under the forehead, etc [1]. Contour matching techniques are also suitable for IR recognition. The use of multimodal visual and IR face recognition systems has also been proposed.

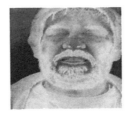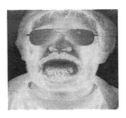

Figure 1. Examples of IR facial images (taken from Equinox IR face database [3]).

See: Face Recognition

References

1. S. G. Kong, J. Heo, B. R. Abidi, J. Paik, and M. A. Abidi, "Recent advances in visual and infrared face recognition - A review," Computer Vision and Image Understanding, Vol. 97, No. 1, January 2005, pp. 103-135.
2. F. J. Prokoski and R. B. Riedel, "Infrared identification of faces and body parts," BIOMETRICS: Personal Identification in Networked Society, Kluwer Academic Publishers, 1999.
3. Equinox public access IR face database: http://www.equinoxsensors.com/products/HID.html.

INFRASTRUCTURE AND ENGINEERING

Wayne Robbins
Defense R&D Canada (DRDC)
Future Forces Synthetic Environments, DRDC Ottawa, Ottawa, Ontario, Canada

Definition: *Multimedia systems rely on a wide variety of infrastructural technologies to enable their communication, processing, and interface/display needs.*

In addition, particular classes of media (e.g., continuous media such as audio and video) often require special computational support to ensure their correct rendering. As such, different categories of infrastructure can be defined as to how systems enable and influence synchronized media playback. These include: operating and real-time systems, middleware and networking, database and data management as well as system and software engineering.

Operating and Real-Time Systems

The operating system (OS) [1-5] is a key element in multimedia synchronization due its fundamental infrastructural role within end-user and network equipment. Specifically, a number of OS issues can cause significant impact in situations where continuous media are utilized. Such time-sensitive data, typically large in volume and isochronous in nature, often require significant computing power to provide a responsive system with predictable behavior. Specific issues which need to be considered include:

- Process Management
- Time Management
- Memory Management
- Inter-Process Communication (IPC)
- Resource and Device Management
- User Interface and Display Management

Process management addresses the area of process (program) execution and processor allocation. For continuous time-based media, predictable processing is required to ensure media readiness for display in accordance with its isochronous nature. Relevant process management issues therefore include scheduling algorithms and priority mechanisms, such that inappropriate scheduling and misuse of priorities can introduce asynchrony into a multimedia application due to inappropriate delays in processing (e.g., other applications "grabbing" the processor).

Time management addresses the issue of whether the OS can both ensure adequate temporal accuracy for application-level synchronization efforts as well as if the OS itself can operate in a timely and synchronized manner. Included in this area are issues of clock management as well the availability of synchronization primitives (for process and resource/device management).

Memory management addresses how the OS controls memory allocation and applications' access to memory spaces. Memory protection, virtual memory (VM), shared vs. non-shared models, dynamic vs. static allocation and automatic garbage collection (in conjunction with certain language/run-time environments) falls in this category. These issues influence media synchronization by affecting data transfer between applications and devices as well as possibly inducing asynchrony into process execution due to automatic system overhead (e.g., use of VM swap files and automatic "cleanup" techniques sometimes associated with dynamic memory/resource allocation).

Inter-Process Communication (IPC) plays a significant role in multimedia synchronization due to the potential to incur delays when transferring large amounts of data between processes. Delays can result from both the data duplication itself but also the incidental (and often hard-to-determine) costs of process management (context switching) and memory management overhead. The result is unexpected and undeterministic delays within the operating system's own execution which (then) ultimately affect the multimedia application.

Resource management refers to how the operating system provides and controls access to any resource (e.g., piece of hardware/software construct). *Device management* specifically refers to the appropriate means to control and facilitate data flow to/from devices; multimedia-oriented examples include capture and rendering devices, hardware codecs, storage and communication equipment and so forth. Because multimedia applications require the timely delivery of data to end-users, devices must enable fine-grain data and control flow in order to ensure asynchrony is not introduced at the final stages just prior to being rendered to the user. Similarly, when media are generated in real-time, any asynchrony resulting from the capture process (i.e., via input devices) can create timing errors which may affect data flow and be difficult to account for in subsequent processing.

User interface and display management issues are also important to multimedia synchronization in much the same way as device management. That is, the display management and user interface subsystems need to provide low-overhead rendering and user interaction with multimedia components. Slow rendering times and unresponsive user interfaces are not viable for time-based media or interactive systems. It is also important to consider the affects of manipulating the visual data (vis-à-vis the aforementioned OS issues) and how synchronization methodologies are compatible with user interaction (e.g., mouse pointer synchronization) [6].

The previous discussion illustrates that multimedia synchronization can be intimately affected by a system's low-level infrastructure. As such, many of these requirements can best addressed in the context a *real-time system* [7] – one whose correct operation depends both on its logical results as well as the temporal properties of its behavior. Such systems are typically characterized as deterministic, with the ability to provide timely responses and flexible scheduling abilities while also providing for security, fault tolerance and robustness. Classic examples include factory robot control and avionic subsystems.

Consequently, the key to real-time systems is highly accurate, temporal predictability; therefore, real-time systems are not necessarily fast but "temporally pedantic," since early event occurrence can be just as damaging as incurring delays. Characterized in Table 1, two classes of real-time systems are defined based on the severity of temporal errors, namely "hard" and "soft" real-time systems. Hard real-time systems are those in which any violation of a timing constraint is considered a system failure. Timely execution is guaranteed through resource allocation based on the worst-case situation, usually resulting in under-utilized resources during normal operation, possibly requiring complete system shutdown when any anomalies occur. Conversely, soft real-time systems are those in which a violation of a temporal constraint does not constitute a system failure.

Table 1. Real-Time System Classification Comparison

Aspect	Traditional Hard Real-Time	Multimedia Soft Real-Time
Data Characterization	Small, often local or with controlled distribution	Large amounts, often heavily distributed
Temporal Accuracy	Strict and static deadlines	Approximate and dynamic timelines
Error Severity	Worst case must be met	Quality of service considerations

Accordingly, multimedia systems are generally classified as soft real-time systems because their temporal performance requirements are usually not so restrictive; for example, asynchrony in a presentation may degrade its quality and annoy its viewers, but no physical damage results. The human-centric character of multimedia systems also facilitates a range of "acceptable" playback quality which varies with the media, the context of their use and ultimately, the individual users. Consequently, human perceptual limitations can be used to relax certain timing constraints, enabling a choice between which playback characteristics are most important and facilitating potential trade-offs between functionality and resource usage. Such an approach maps well to soft real-time systems, in which performance is not guaranteed by worst-case resource allocation. For example, if the "bandwidth" of a video channel is constrained to only 15fps at a specific resolution, the user could decide to accept the provided quality or adjust select parameters more aptly suit his/her needs.

Middleware and Networking

Middleware and networking are also important to multimedia synchronization in that they affect the delivery of media data between end (client) systems.

At a most basic level, the communications infrastructure must ensure data availability to enable synchronized rendering and timely user interaction. Typically, this issue is addressed by providing for a reasonable and ideally predictable quality of service (QoS). Therefore, network QoS can be seen as an enabler for "temporal composition" by which media can be assembled together and playback organized according to individual and group timing constraints. The provision of appropriate network and application level protocols also support synchronized data transfer (in cooperation with any provided QoS). A large body of work on protocols for multimedia synchronization exists [8-13], ranging from lower-level adaptive, feedback-based techniques to those provisioned at the application level, such as RTP (Real-Time Protocol) and RTCP (Real-Time Control Protocol). Additional network-oriented considerations include issues of data buffer management and protocol stack implementation which can impact on synchronization vis-à-vis the OS issues described above (e.g., data copying overhead).

Beyond the basic communications level, middleware [14-16] addresses the need to bridge network and client functionality through the provision of centrally-based services and abstractions. As such, middleware is a "glue" layer of software between the network and applications, intended to ease application programming, application integration and system management tasks while also promoting standardization and interoperability of services by lessening multiple, independently developed implementations. In terms of multimedia synchronization, middleware offers a logically centralized, service-oriented approach to synchronization (orchestration) logic. It also provides support for useful abstractions and constructs for communicating multimedia data, ranging from publish and subscribe models, to streams, flows, sources and sinks.

Database and Data Management

Database and data management [8, 17-19] are relevant to multimedia synchronization in how their design and implementation provide flexible and responsive data access. For aspects of spatial and content synchronization, issues of multimedia querying and multimedia data semantics (e.g., image analysis vs. keyword meta-descriptors) are of interest. For purposes of temporal synchronization, a broad array of other issues includes disk scheduling and storage models for particular classes of data (e.g., continuous media). This last aspect also includes how the fundamental database structure impacts the means by which the actual multimedia data is accessed; that is, do the media reside within the database itself (in which access is constrained to the database management system and query engine) or is the data stored independently on separate systems (and the database only contains references to the external data). Such design considerations must be accounted for due to two primary issues: (1) timing considerations in terms of media data retrieval strictly through the database and its overhead (e.g., the potential effects of multiple, concurrent database queries on the timeliness of continuous media streams); and (2) timing considerations in terms of database efficiency resulting from large data objects (such as video) and/or objects of variable and indeterminate size (e.g., how to represent live instances of media, such as a camera capture).

System and Software Engineering

System and software engineering issues are important to multimedia synchronization in how they can affect the real-time implementation of multimedia systems. To provide an actual real-time environment, systems must be appropriately engineered not only to facilitate the necessary structural and behavioral aspects of a system, but also to ensure inappropriate behavior is not inadvertently introduced and that any such anomalies can be corrected as required.

First, a system should be based on the appropriate hardware and software infrastructure, such as a QoS-enabled communication backbone and a real-time operating system. Systems based on inappropriate infrastructure risk reduced quality in the user experience due to unsuitable substrate behavior [20-21]. Second, system structure (both design and implementation) must provide a flexible and extensible architecture capable of real-time performance. This requirement includes using flexible architectural techniques and technologies, including middleware and component-oriented architectures, along with the appropriate programming interfaces, useful abstractions and developmental paradigms (such as object orientation). Third, the system, application and various software components should have the ability to monitor their behaviors [22-23] (i.e., the actual performance of its various components). This is a necessary step in creating a system which can adapt (i.e., "tune") itself to address structural or behavioral deficiencies. An example is a video system which provides the ability to dynamically change playback frame rate based on monitoring the degree of asynchrony that develops during playback. Doing so illustrates the benefit of building systems that address behaviors as first-class considerations and facilitate adaptive behavior management [24].

As a result of better engineering, the potential exists for more flexible and higher quality systems, based on the increased use of common multimedia infrastructures. The end result would be better interoperability and compatibility across the user community, ultimately aiding in the acceptance and continued growth of multimedia technology across broader audiences.

See: Multimedia Synchronization – Area Overview

References

1. T. M. Burkow, "Operating System Support for Distributed Multimedia Applications: A Survey of Current Research," Technical Report (Pegasus Paper 94-8), Faculty of Computer Science, University of Twente, 1994.
2. R. Steinmetz, "Analyzing the Multimedia Operating System," IEEE Multimedia, Vol. 2, No. 1. 1995, pp. 68 – 84.
3. M. Singhal and N. G. Shivaratri, "Advanced Concepts in Operating Systems: Distributed, Database and Multiprocessor Operating Systems," McGraw-Hill: New York, 1994.
4. R. Govindan and D. P. Anderson, "Scheduling and IPC Mechanisms for Continuous Media," Proceedings of the 13th ACM Symposium on Operating System Principles, ACM, 1991, pp. 68 – 80.
5. V. Baiceanu, C. Cowan, D. McNamee, C. Pu, and J. Walpole, "Multimedia Applications Require Adaptive CPU Scheduling," Technical Report, Department of Computer Science and Engineering, Oregon Graduate Institute of Science and Technology, 1996.
6. S. Greenberg and D. Marwood, "Real-Time Groupware as a Distributed System: Concurrency Control and its Effect on the Interface," Research Report 94/534/03, Department of Computer Science, University of Calgary, 1994.
7. S-T. Levi and A. K. Agrawala, "Real-Time System Design," McGraw-Hill: New York, 1990.
8. D. P. Anderson and G. Homsy, "A Continuous Media I/O Server and Its Synchronization Mechanism," IEEE Computer, Vol. 24, No. 10, 1991, pp. 51 – 57.
9. T. D. C. Little and A. Ghafoor, "Multimedia Synchronization Protocols for Broadband Integrated Services," IEEE Journal on Selected Area in Communications, Vol. 9, No. 12, 1991, pp. 1368 – 1382.
10. S. Ramanathan and P. Rangan, "Feedback Techniques for Intra-Media Continuity and Inter-Media Synchronization in Distributed Multimedia Systems," The Computer Journal, Vol. 36, No. 1, 1993, pp. 19 – 31.

11. I. F. Akyildiz and W. Yen, "Multimedia Group Synchronization Protocols for Integrated Services Networks," IEEE Journal on Selected Areas in Communications, Vol. 14, No. 1, 1996, pp. 162 – 173.

12. J. Escobar, C. Partridge and D. Deutsch, "Flow Synchronization Protocol," IEEE/ACM transactions on Networking, Vol. 2, No. 2, 1994, pp. 111 – 121.

13. H. Schulzrinne, S. Casner, R. Frederick and V. Jacobson, "RTP: A Transport Protocol for Real-Time Applications," Request for Comments rfc1889, 1996.

14. A. Campbell, G. Coulson, F. Garcia and D. Hutchinson, "Orchestration Services for Distributed Multimedia Synchronization," Technical Report MPG-92-52, Distributed Multimedia Research Group, University of Lancaster, 1992.

15. I. Herman, N. Correia, D. A. Duce, D. J. Duke, G. J. Reynolds and J. Van Loo, "A Standard Model for Multimedia Synchronization: PREMO Synchronization Objects," Multimedia Systems, Vol. 6, No. 2, 1998, pp. 88 – 101.

16. S. Didas, "Synchronization in the Network-Integrated Multimedia Middleware (NMM)," Project Report, Universität des Saarlandes, Saarbrücken, 2002.

17. S. Marcus and V. S. Subrahmanian, "Foundations of Multimedia Database Systems," Journal of the ACM, Vol. 43, No. 3, 1990, pp. 474 – 523.

18. B. Özden, R. Rastogi, and A. Silberschatz, "The Storage and Retrieval of Continuous Media Data," Multimedia Database System: Issues and Research Direction (eds., V. S. Subrahmanian and S. Jajodia), New York: Springer-Verlag, 1996, pp. 237 – 261.

19. W. Klas and K. Aberer, "Multimedia and its Impact on Database System Architectures," Multimedia Databases in Perspective (eds., P. M. G. Apers, H. M. Blanken, and M. A. W. Houtsma), Heidelberg, Germany: Springer-Verlag, 1997, pp. 31 – 61.

20. D. C. A. Bulterman and R. van Liere, "Multimedia Synchronization and Unix," Proceedings of the 2nd International Workshop on Network and Operating System Support for Digital Audio and Video (Ed. R. G. Herrtwich), Heidelberg, Germany: Springer-Verlag, 1991, pp. 108 – 119.

21. R. W. Robbins, "A Model for Multimedia Orchestration," M. Sc. Thesis, Department of Computer Science, University of Calgary, 1995.

22. J. A. Boucher and T. D. C. Little, "An Adaptive Real-time Software-Only Player for the MPEG-I Video Stream," Technical Report, Multimedia Communications Lab, Boston University, 1994.

23. F. Jahanian, "Run-Time Monitoring of Real-Time Systems," Advances in Real-Time Systems (ed., Sang H. Son), Prentice-Hall: Englewood Cliffs, 1995, pp. 435 – 460.

24. R. W. Robbins, "Facilitating Intelligent Media Space Collaboration via RASCAL: The Reflectively Adaptive Synchronous Coordination Architectural Framework," PhD Thesis, School of Information Technology and Engineering, University of Ottawa, 2001.

INPAINTING IN VIRTUAL RESTORATION OF ARTWORKS

Definition: Inpainting techniques are used to enhance the quality of the digitized artwork during virtual restoration.

Current trends in this area relate to portal-based access to simulations, collaborative tools and shared work spaces [1] [2], visual development [3], and grid-based computing initiatives [5].

See: Collaborative Computing – An Overview

References

1. S. J. E. Taylor, "Netmeeting: A Tool for Collaborative Simulation Modelling," International Journal of Simulation, Systems, Science and Technology, Vol. 1, No. 1, 2001, pp. 59-68.
2. J. Lee, J. Nunamaker Jr., and C. Albrecht, "Experiences with Collaborative Applications that Support Distributed Modeling", Proceedings of the 34th Hawaii International Conference on System Sciences, 2001.
3. W. A. Filho, C. M. Hirata, and E. T. Yano, "GroupSim: A Collaborative Environment for Discrete Event Simulation Software Development for the World Wide Web," Simulation, Vol. 80, No. 6, 2004, pp. 257-272.
4. R. Maghnouji, G. J. de Vreede, A. Verbraeck, and H. G. Sol, "Collaborative Simulation Modeling: Experiences and Lessons Learned," In Proceedings of the 34th Hawaii International Conference on System Sciences, 2001.
5. M. Bubak, G. D. van Albada, P. M. A. Sloot, and J. J. Dongarra (Eds.), Proceedings of the 4th International Conference on Computational Science (LNCS 3036-3039), 2004.

INTEL® XSCALE® MICRO-ARCHITECTURE

Definition: The Intel XScale micro-architecture is an implementation of the ARM V5TE architecture.

The XScale core supports both dynamic frequency and voltage scaling with a maximum frequency today in handheld devices of 624MHz (and increasing going forward). The design is a scalar, in-order single issue architecture with concurrent execution in 3 pipes that support out-of-order return. To support the frequency targets, a 7-stage integer pipeline is employed with dynamic branch prediction supplied to mitigate the cost of a deeper pipeline (see Figure 1).

In favour of memory access efficiency, the Intel XScale micro-architecture contains instruction and data caches (32KB each). Also, in order to hide memory latency the micro-architecture supports software issued prefetch capability coupled with advanced load and store buffering. Load buffering allows multiple data/cache lines request from the memory concurrently, thus reducing the data loading overhead. Similarly, store buffers combine multiple neighbouring store operations to improve the memory and bus utilization. For virtual memory address translation, the Microarchitecture provides instruction and data translation look-aside buffer with 32-entry for each. Dynamic branch prediction with a target buffer of 32-entries significantly reduces the branch-penalty for deeper pipelines.

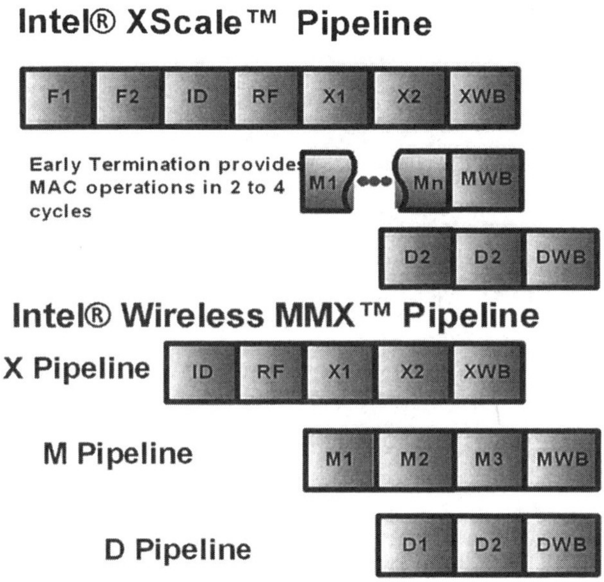

Intel® XScale™ Pipeline

F1	F2	ID	RF	X1	X2	XWB

Early Termination provides
MAC operations in 2 to 4
cycles　M1 ●●● Mn MWB

D2 D2 DWB

Intel® Wireless MMX™ Pipeline

X Pipeline　ID RF X1 X2 XWB

M Pipeline　M1 M2 M3 MWB

D Pipeline　D1 D2 DWB

Figure 1. Pipelines applied in Intel XScale processor.

Intel Xscale Microarchitecture supports standard ARM* coprocessor framework. Intel Wireless MMX™ technology is incorporated as a coprocessor on the Intel XScale® micro-architecture. The ARM architecture specifies that the main core is responsible for fetching instructions and data from memory and delivering them to the coprocessor. An instruction can be issued to the main core pipeline or coprocessor pipeline. For example, an instruction can be issued to the load pipeline while a MAC operation completes in the multiply pipeline.

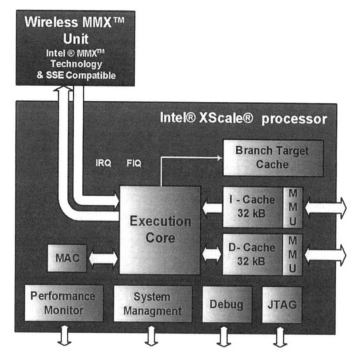

Figure 2. The architecture of Intel XScale processor.

The architecture allows instructions to be retired out of order. The load buffering combined with the out-of-order completion, allows non-dependent load instructions to execute, reducing the impact of memory latency in system on a chip applications.

Figure 2 shows the XScale core supports a debug interface, JTAG and PMU (Performance Monitoring Unit) in addition to a high-speed interface to the Wireless MMX unit.

See: Multimedia System-on-a-Chip, SIMD Data Processing

References

1. Seal, David "Advanced RISC Machines Architecture Reference Manual," Prentice Hall, 1996.

INTERACTIVE STORY TELLING

Definition: Interactive story telling shifts the narrative form from linear to dialectical, creating new stories on the basis of discussions and using dialogue as a method of interactions.

Telling stories is one of the most ancient forms of human communication. Stories allow people to share life experiences through real or imaginary tales. Stories in a book have usually a fixed structure and a specific order. Rather, told stories are more flexible than read ones, while the storyteller can change order and content in response to the audience feedback. The need for playing games pretending to be immersed in fantastic tales has existed for thousand years, with both children and adults subject to this human rite. *Interactive Story Telling* (IST) represents a digital version of this habit [1]. IST shifts the narrative form from linear to dialectical, creating new stories on the basis of discussions and using dialogue as a method of interactions. Integrating new technologies with traditional storytelling is pushing the development of this kind of narrative towards a direction where people may have a role on how the story progresses. Information technologies, ranging from ubiquitous networking to multimodal interfaces, provide support to augment the interactivity degree, thus enhancing user perception. IST has determined a significant change in forms of *collective intelligence*. This means that individuals can share their abilities and generate a more creative final product. Two kinds of IST applications exist, specifically: i) those ISTs that resemble traditional entertainment contents (e.g. movies, fiction, soap, music, etc.) yet give the possibility to users to modify fragments of the multimedia presentation, and ii) applications that involve users in playing a role in a story, composing the final plot through the interaction among them.

In the first category of IST applications, fragments of multimedia contents can be mixed together to create one or more sequences to be used as visual or auditory stories. Fragments are needed to be classified to support users during the composition of sequences composed of multimedia scraps [2]. Further, this form of IST can support cooperative composition and orchestration through collaborative interfaces. As an evolution of this trend, tools exist that permit users to write a story at a virtually unlimited scale and distance. An example of this is Moblogs that creates anthologies of multimedia resources (text, photo, sounds or small videos) directly collected from people's everyday life (by using mobile terminals).

The second class of IST applications involves users in playing a role within a story, a game, and a virtual environment. Also Mixed Reality environments can be merged with IST (MR-IST) with the aim of immersing real actors in virtual settings and deriving the final plot of the story from the interactions among users. As in games, authors have control on the story but its evolution may be influenced by external factors [3]. To this aim, many Mixed Reality based technologies are exploited such as mobile devices, multimodal interfaces, 3D input/output systems and localization tools. Involving people in the story is frequently supported by telling well known stories, such as successful fictions or soaps by using VR artifices to improve sensorial experience.

See: Multimedia Entertainment Applications

References

1. J. Schell, "Understanding entertainment: story and gameplay are one," The human-computer interaction handbook: fundamentals, evolving technologies and emerging applications archive, Lawrence Erlbaum Associates, pp. 835 – 843, 2002.
2. J. Lambert, "Digital Storytelling," Digital Diner Press, 2002.
3. L. Romero, J. Santiago, and N. Correia, "Contextual information access and storytelling in mixed reality using hypermedia," Computers in Entertainment (CIE), Vol. 2, No. 3, July 2004.

INTERLEAVED AUDIO

Definition: *Interleaved audio transmission is a packet loss resilience technique based on sending alternate audio samples in different packets.*

Interleaved audio transmission is a technique that is sometimes used to alleviate network loss and act as a packet loss resilience mechanism [1] [2]. The idea is to send alternate audio samples in different packets, as opposed to sending consecutive samples in the same packet. The difference between the two approaches is shown in Figure 1.

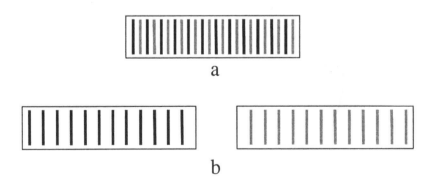

Figure 1. a) Transmission of consecutive samples, b) Transmission of alternate samples.

In Figure 1a we see 24 consecutive samples being transmitted in one packet. If this packet is lost, there will be a gap in the audio equal to the duration of the samples. In Figure 1b we see the interleaved approach for the same audio sample in 1a, where alternate samples are being sent in separate packets. This way if one of the packets is lost, we only lose every other sample and the receiver will hear a somewhat distorted audio as opposed to hearing a complete gap for that duration. In case of stereo audio, we can adapt this technique to send the left channel and the right channel in separate packets, so that if the packet for one of the channels is lost, the receiver still hears the other channel.

See: Audio Conferencing

References

1. D. Hoffman, G. Fernando, V. Goyal, and M. Civanlar, "RTP Payload Format for MPEG1/MPEG2 Video," IETF RFC 2250, January 1998.
2. R. Finlayson, "A More Loss-Tolerant RTP Payload Format for MP3 Audio," IETF RFC 3119, June 2001.

IP TELEPHONY

Abdulmotaleb El Saddik
School of Information Technology and Engineering
University of Ottawa, Ontario, Canada

Definition: Internet telephony is the process of making telephone calls over the Internet.

Internet telephony, also referred to as IP telephony (IPT), is the process of making telephone calls over the Internet, regardless of whether traditional telephones (POTS, GSM, ISDN, etc.), single use appliances, or audio-equipped personal computers are used in the calls. IPT is highly appealing for many reasons, the most important of which is the ease of implementing its services. Internet Telephony Service Providers (ITSP) can use a single IP-based infrastructure for providing traditional Internet, as well as Internet telephony access.

The Session Initiation Protocol (SIP)

The Session Initiation Protocol (SIP) is a signaling protocol for Internet Telephony. It is documented in (RFC3261, 2002) by the Internet Engineering Task Force (IETF), and is ideal for real-time multimedia communication signaling [1]. It is an end-to-end application layer signaling protocol that is used to setup, modify, and teardown multimedia sessions such as audio/videoconferencing, interactive gaming, virtual reality, and call forwarding over IP networks. By providing those services, SIP enables service providers to integrate basic IP telephony services with Web, e-mail, presence notification and instant messaging over the Internet. It is clear that SIP is rapidly changing the way that people make telephone calls and is therefore becoming a real threat to traditional plain old telephone service (PSTN) network [2]. SIP works with many other protocols that were designed to carry the various forms of real time multimedia applications data by enabling endpoints to discover one another and to agree on a characterization of a session that they would like to share. Even though SIP was designed to work with other internet transport protocols such as UDP, TCP when it was developed by the IETF as part of the Internet Multimedia Conferencing Architecture, it is very much a general purpose signaling protocol that works independently of underlying protocol, and regardless of the type of session that is being established [1]. SIP is a text based client server protocol that incorporates elements of two widely used Internet protocols: HTTP and the Simple Mail Transport Protocol (SMTP), used for web browsing and e-mail respectively [1]. HTTP inspired a client server design in SIP, as well as the use of URL's and URI's [1], however, in SIP a host may well act as client and server. From SMTP, SIP borrowed a text –encoding scheme and header style. For example, SIP reuses SMTP headers like To, From, Date and Subject [1].

SIP extensions supports mobility and detects presence to allow users to communicate using different devices, modes, and services, anywhere that they are connected to the Internet. Third-Generation Partnership Project (3GPP) group accepted SIP as the signaling protocol for Multimedia Applications in 3G Mobile Networks.

SIP's Protocol Architecture

As can be seen in Figure 1, SIP does not rely on any particular transport protocol; it can run indifferently over TCP (Transport Control Protocol), UDP (User Datagram Protocol), TLS (Transport Layer Security), SCTP (Stream Control Transport Protocol), and conceptually any other protocol stack, like ATM (Asynchronous Transfer Mode) or Frame Relay. SIP does not dictate the data flow between peers, the Session Description Protocol (SDP) does that and negotiates and determines the format of data exchanged between them. SDP defined in RFC2327 is intended for describing multimedia sessions for the purposes of session announcement, invitation, and other forms of multimedia session initiation.

The benefits of the SIP protocol can be summarized by the following:

- Because it utilizes existing IP architecture, services based on SIP are scalable.
- Since SIP was built as an IP protocol, it integrates seamlessly with other IP protocols and services.
- Global connectivity can be achieved with SIP protocol. Any SIP user can be reached by another SIP user over the Internet, regardless of their location, service provider, and whether they have registered with central services or not.
- Simplicity is hallmark of SIP, due to its text coded, highly readable messages, and its simple transactions models, except for few cases that have special conditions.
- Statelessness: Depicted by the ability of SIP servers to store minimal information about the state or existence of a media session in a network [6]
- Flexibility: Protocols can be used in any host applications that are not restricted to telephony [6].

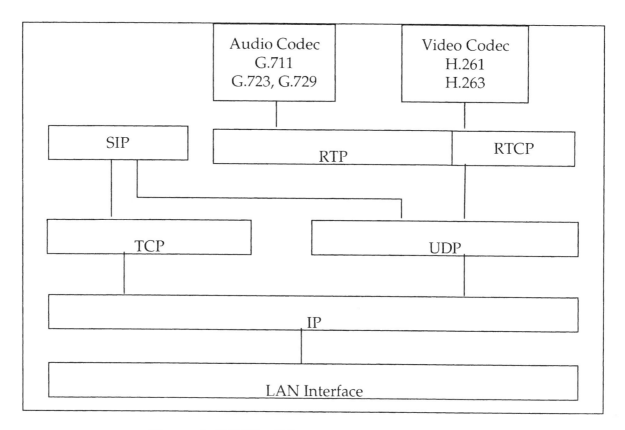

Figure 1. IETF's SIP protocol architecture.

SIP Transport

User Datagram Protocol (UDP): A single UDP datagram or packet carries a SIP request, or response. This implies that a SIP message must be smaller in size than the Message Transport Unit (MTU) of the IP network. Since SIP doesn't support fragmentation at the SIP layer, TCP is used for larger messages. The UDP Source port is chosen from a pool of available port numbers (above 49172) or sometimes the default SIP port, 5060 is used. Lack of a reliable transport mechanism in UDP may cause SIP message to be lost. To tackle this problem, SIP comes with its own reliability mechanism to handle the retransmission, in case a SIP message is lost.

Transport Control Protocol (TCP): Not only does it provide reliable transport, TCP also offers congestion control. It can also transport SIP messages of arbitrary size. As in UDP, TCP uses SIP port number 5060 for the destination port. The source port is chosen from an available pool of port numbers. The main disadvantages of TCP are: the setup delay incurred when establishing a connection, and the need to maintain the connection at the transport layer by the server.

Transport Layer Security Protocol (TLS): SIP employs TLS over TCP for encrypted transport with additional capabilities of authentication. The default SIP port number for TLS is 5061. This use of TLS by SIP takes advantage of the encryption and authentication services. However, encryption and authentication are only useful on a single hop. If a SIP request involves multiple hops, TLS becomes useless for end-to-end authentication.

SIP Network Components

SIP network components include User Agents, Servers and Gateways. The following section discusses these components in detail.

User Agent: A SIP enabled end-device is called a SIP user agent. A User Agent takes directions from a user and acts as an agent on that user's behalf to make or accept and teardown calls with other user agents. The UA terminates the SIP call signaling and acts as the interface to the SIP network. It also maintains the state of calls that it initiates or participates in. UA must support UDP transport, and also TCP if it sends messages that are greater than 1000 octets in size [6]. Also, a SIP user agent must support SDP for media description. A SIP user agent contains both a client application, and a server application. The two parts are designated as User Agent Client (UAC) and User Agent Server (UAS). The UAC initiates requests on behalf of the user and UAS processes incoming requests and generates appropriate responses. During a session, a user agent will usually operate as both a UAC and a UAS [4].

Server: The SIP server assists in call establishment, call teardown, and mobility management. Some SIP servers (proxy and redirect) can be stateless. Usually, logical SIP servers are often co-located within the same physical device. SIP servers must support TCP, TLS and UDP for transport. There is no protocol distinction between these servers, and also a client or proxy server has no way of knowing which it is communicating with. The distinction lies only in function: a proxy or redirect server cannot accept or reject a request, where as a user agent server can. Following are the different types of SIP servers:

- Register Server: The SIP registration server, also known as registrar allows SIP agents to register their current location, retrieve a list of current registrations, and clear all registrations. The registrar accepts a user SIP registration request (REGSITER) message and responds with an acknowledgement message (200 OK) for successful registration, otherwise, it responds with an error message. In a registration request message, the "To" header field contains the name of the resource being registered, and the "Contact" header field contain the alternative addresses or aliases. The registration server creates a temporary binding between the Address of Record (AOR) URI in the "To" and the device URI in the "Contact" fields. Registration servers usually require the registering user agent to be authenticated for security reasons. Thus, registered information will be made available to other SIP servers within the same administrative domain, such as proxies and redirect servers. The registrar is responsible for keeping information up-to-date within the location service by sending updates.

- Proxy Server: The proxy server forwards SIP requests on behalf of SIP User Agents to the next hop server, which may be another proxy server or the final user agent. A proxy does not need to understand a SIP request in order to forward it. After receiving the SIP request, the proxy will contact the location server to determine the next hop to forward the SIP requests to. The proxy may well rewrite the SIP message before forwarding it to its correct location. For incoming calls, it proxy will interrogate the location service to determine how to forward the call. The proxy may use SIP registration, SIP presence, or any other type of information to determine a user's location. The proxy can also be configured to provide authentication control and act as a point of control between the internal private network and an outside public network. A proxy server may be stateful or stateless. A stateless proxy server processes each SIP request or response based solely on the message contents. Once the message has been parsed, processed, and forwarded or responded to, no information about the messages is stored. A stateless proxy server never retransmits a message and doesn't use any SIP timers. A stateful proxy server keeps track of requests and responses that were received in the past, and uses that information in processing future requests and responses. A stateful proxy starts a timer when a request is forwarded. If no response to the request is received within the timer period, the proxy will retransmit the requests, relieving the user agent of this task.

- Redirect Server: The redirect server responds to a UA request with redirection response, indicating the current location of the called party, so that UA can directly contact it. In this case, the UA must establish a new call to the indicated location. A redirect server does not forward a request received by the UA. Redirect server uses a database or location service to look up a user. The user location information is then sent back to caller in a redirection message response [4].

- Location Server: A redirect or proxy server uses a location server to obtain information about a user's whereabouts. The service can be co-located with other SIP servers. The interface between the location service and other servers is not defined by SIP [4].

- Conference Server: Conferencing server is used to aid the multiparty conference call establishment. A conferencing server mixes the media received and sends it out to all the participants using one multicast address or all of the participants' unicast addresses, depending on the mode of conference that was setup.

SIP Gateways: A SIP gateway is an application that provides an interface for a SIP network to another network utilizing another signaling protocol. SIP supports internetworking with PSTN and H.323 via SIP-PSTN gateway and SIP-H.323 gateway respectively. In terms of SIP protocol, a gateway is just a special type of user agent, where the user agent acts on behalf of another protocol rather than a human user. A SIP gateway terminates the SIP signaling path and may sometimes also terminate the media path. SIP Gateway can support hundreds or thousands of users and does not register every user it supports.

- SIP-PSTN gateway terminates both signaling and media paths. SIP can be translated into, or made to inter-work with common Public Switched Telephone Network (PSTN) protocols such as Integrated Service Digital Network (ISDN), ISDN User part (ISUP), and other Circuit Associated Signaling (CAS) protocols. A PSTN gateway also converts RTP media stream in the IP network into a standard telephony trunk or line. The conversion of signaling and media paths allows calling to and from the PSTN using SIP.

- <u>SIP-H.323 gateway</u>: SIP to H.323 terminates the SIP signaling path and converts the signaling to H.323, but the SIP user agent and H.323 terminal can exchange RTP media information directly with each other without going through the gateway.

SIP's Role in Multimedia Services

SIP is heavily involved in today's multimedia services, especially in the following categories:

<u>User Presence Notification and Personalization</u>: SIP Signaling functions request, detect, and deliver presence information and provide presence detection and notification. SIP presence functionality gives the opportunity to know who is online among a given contacts list before the session is established. SUBSCRIBE, NOTIFY messages are used to subscribe and notify users for presence detection and notification in an instant messaging application. A User agent sends a SUBSCRIBE message to another UA with a series of event requests indicating the desire of the sender to be notified by another UA. The NOTIFY message is used to indicate the occurrence of the event to the requested UA [6][4].

<u>Instant Messaging and Collaborative environment</u>: Instant messaging enables User agent to send short messages to another User Agent. It is very useful for short requests and responses. Instant messaging has better real-time characteristics than e-mail. MESSAGE method is used to support instant messaging. Its short messages are sent form UA to UA without establishing a session between them. The messages are sent in multi-part MIME format (similar to e-mail) and can also contain multimedia attachments [6].

<u>Multimedia conference call setup and management</u>: This can be divided into end-to-end call setup and conference setup:

<u>SIP - End to End Call Setup</u>

- (Proxy): After receiving the SIP request from the User agent, the proxy contacts the location server to determine the next hop to forward the SIP requests to. Once it receives the next hop information from the location server, it forwards the UA SIP request message. The proxy then updates the INVITE request message with its host address before forwarding it.
- (Redirect): SIP Redirect Server responds to a UA request with a redirection response, indicating the current location of the called party.

<u>SIP – Conference Setup</u>: Conferencing where many parties can participate in the same call is now a common feature of multimedia communication systems. SIP supports three different multiparty conferencing modes:

- Ad hoc/Full Mesh: In this mode, every participant establishes session with every other participant with a series of INVITE messages and sends an individual copy of the media to the others. This mechanism only scales to small groups [3].

- Meet me/Mixer: In this mode, each participant establishes the point-to-point session to the Conferencing Bridge (or mixer). A mixer or bridge takes each participant's media streams and replicates it to all other participants as a unicast message. This mechanism is idea if all participants are interactive, however, it doesn't scale for a large number of participants [3].

- Interactive Broadcast/Network layer multicast: In this mode, each participant establishes the point-to-point session to the Conferencing Bridge (or mixer). A Conferencing Bridge is used but mixed media is sent to a multicast address, instead of being unicast to each participant. This mechanism can involve active and passive participants. SIP signaling is required for interactive participants only. This mode works well for large-scale conferences [4].

User Mobility: One of the powerful features of SIP is its ability to support terminal mobility, personal mobility, and Service mobility to a SIP user.

- Terminal Mobility (Mobile IP- SIP): **A** SIP user agent will be able to maintain its connections to the Internet as its associated user moves from network to network, and possibly changes its point of connection. The user's generic and location-independent address enables it to access services from both, stationary end devices, or from mobile end-devices [6].

- Personal Mobility (SIP – REGISTER): SIP Personal mobility allows the user to access Internet services from any location by using any end devices. Since SIP URI (similar e-mail address) is device-independent, a user can utilize any end-device to receive and make calls. Participants can also use any end-device to receive and to make calls [6].

- Service Mobility: SIP service mobility provides a feature to a SIP user to keep the same services when mobile as long as the services/tools residing in the user agent can be accessed over Internet (Ex: Call Forwarding etc). Participant can interrupt the session and later on, continue at a different location [6].

Conclusion

SIP is a powerful and flexible application layer signaling protocol for multimedia applications. Its applications are not limited to Internet Telephony, although telephony applications are the main driving forces behind SIP development. Another popular application of SIP is Instant Messaging and Presence (IMP). IETF SIMPLE working Group is working on developing standards for IM and Presence. IP has been adopted by the 3rd Generation Partnership Project (3GPP) for establishing, controlling, and maintaining real-time wireless multimedia sessions using Internet Protocol. SIP is an ASCI text based protocol, and SIP messages are long: up to and exceeding 800 bytes. This is not a problem for fixed networks with a high bandwidth, but it is for wireless cellular networks, where the bandwidth is very limited. For this reason, the SIP messages should be compressed in wireless networks. A number of proposals for SIP message compression have been submitted to the Robust Header Compression (ROHC) working group of the Internet Engineering Task Force (IETF). TCCB (Text Based Compression using Cache and Blank Approach) is a compression technique ideal for the compression of long ASCII text-based messages, such as SIP message bodies. Therefore, SIP message compression using TCCB has the potential to reduce request/response delays [5].

References

1. J. Rosenberg et al., "SIP: Session Initiation Protocol," IETF RFC 3261, June 2002.
2. M. Handley et al, "SIP: Session Initiation Protocol," IETF RFC 2543, March 1999.
3. J. Arkko et al., "Security Mechanism Agreement for the Session Initiation Protocol (SIP)," IETF RFC 3329, January 2003.
4. Jeffrey Bannister et al., "Convergence Technologies for 3G Networks: IP, UMTS, EGPRS and ATM," John Wiley & Sons, Ltd. 2004.
5. John Sweeney, et al, Efficient SIP based Presence and IM Services with SIP message compression in IST OPIUM, http://www.ist-opium.org/bluepapers/CIT%20-%20Blue%20Paper.doc, September 2003.
6. A. B. Johnston, "SIP Understanding the Session Initiation Protocol," Artech House, 2004.

J

JFIF (JPEG FILE INTERCHANGE FORMAT)

Definition: *The JPEG File Exchange Format [1] is a minimal file format that allows the exchange of JPEG bitstreams among different applications and platforms.*

It uses a number of markers to break a JPEG stream down into its component structures. Markers are two bytes in length and the first byte always contains the value 0xFF; the second byte contains a code that specifies the marker type. Table 1 shows some of the most important JFIF markers, whose explanation follows.

Table 1. JFIF markers.

Marker Identifier	Marker Acronym	Marker Name
0xD8	SOI	Start of image
0xE0	APP0	Application use marker
0xE1–0xEF	APPn	Other application segments
0xDB	DQT	Quantization table
0xC0	SOF0	Start of frame 0
0xC4	DHT	Huffman table
0xDA	SOS	Start of scan
0xD9	EOI	End of image
0xFE	COM	Comments field

1. SOI: This marker is found at the start of a JFIF file.
2. APP0: Contains JFIF information, including image thumbnail.
3. APPn: Contains application specific information.
4. DQT: Contains the quantization table for quantization and dequantization operations which are performed after FDCT and before IDCT.
5. SOF0: Contains image bits per pixel, height, and width among other information.
6. DHT: For Huffman encoding after quantization and Huffman decoding before dequantization.
7. SOS: Contains compressed, encoded image data.

8. EOI: Signifies end of image.
9. COM: Contains user defined plaintext comments, often containing image metadata.

The standard also defines the RGB to YCbCr conversion and color subsampling steps.

References

1. E. Hamilton, JPEG File Interchange Format Version 1.02, September 1, 1992, available at http://www.w3.org/Graphics/JPEG/jfif3.pdf. Accessed April 25, 2005.

JPEG

Definition: JPEG is an image compression standard (ISO IS 10918-1) published by The Joint Photographic Experts Group in 1994.

JPEG has become the most widely used format for storing digital photographs ever since. The original JPEG specification defines four compression modes [1, 2]:

- Sequential (baseline): based on the DCT and adequate for most applications;
- Hierarchical: used to encode the image in a hierarchy of several different resolutions;
- Progressive: delivers lower-quality versions of the image quickly, followed by higher-quality passes; enjoyed popularity in the early days of the World Wide Web;
- Lossless: a variant that employs a simple differential coding method instead of DCT followed by quantization.

In this discussion we will limit ourselves to the sequential (default) mode.

The JPEG encoder (Figure 1) consists of the following main stages:

1. The original RGB color image is converted to an alternative color model (YCbCr) and the color information is subsampled.
2. The image is divided into 8×8 blocks.
3. The 2-D Discrete Cosine Transform (DCT) is applied to each block image; the resulting 64 values are referred to as *DCT coefficients*. The first coefficient is usually referred to as DC coefficient and contains the average value of the original 8×8 block; the remaining 63 values are called AC coefficients.
4. DCT coefficients are quantized simply by dividing each value by an integer (stored in a quantization table, see Table 1) and rounding the result; this is the step where acceptable loss is introduced.
5. Quantized DCT coefficients are then scanned in a zigzag fashion (from top-left to bottom-right, see Figure 2). The resulting sequence is run-length encoded, in preparation for the entropy encoding step.

6. The run-length encoded sequences are converted to variable-length binary codewords using Huffman encoding Look-up tables.

At the decoder side, the process is reversed; it should be noted that the loss introduced at the quantizer stage in the encoder cannot be canceled at the 'dequantizer' stage in the decoder.

Table 1. JPEG quantization tables

Luminance

```
16  11  10  16   24   40   51   61
12  12  14  19   26   58   60   55
14  13  16  24   40   57   69   56
14  17  22  29   51   87   80   62
18  22  37  56   68  109  103   77
24  35  55  64   81  104  113   92
49  64  78  87  103  121  120  101
72  92  95  98  112  100  103   99
```

Chrominance

```
17  18  24  47  99  99  99  99
18  21  26  66  99  99  99  99
24  26  56  99  99  99  99  99
47  66  99  99  99  99  99  99
99  99  99  99  99  99  99  99
99  99  99  99  99  99  99  99
99  99  99  99  99  99  99  99
99  99  99  99  99  99  99  99
```

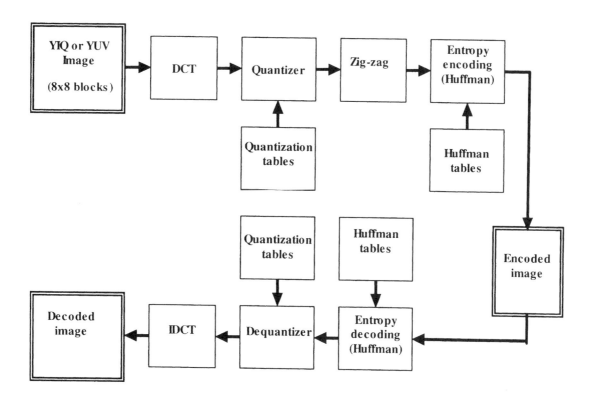

Figure 1. JPEG encoder and decoder: block diagram.

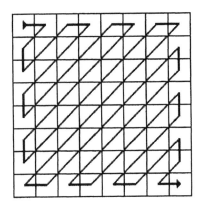

Figure 2. Zigzag scan in JPEG.

References

1. W.B. Pennenbaker and J.L. Mitchell, "JPEG still image data compression standard," Van Nostrand Reinhold, 1993.
2. G. Wallace, "The JPEG still picture compression standard," Communications of the ACM, Vol. 34, pp. 30-44, 1991.

JPEG 2000 IMAGE CODING STANDARD

Hong Man
Stevens Institute of Technology, Hoboken, New Jersey, USA

Alen Docef
Virginia Commonwealth University, Richmond, Virginia, USA

Faouzi Kossentini
UB Video, Vancouver, British Columbia, Canada

Definition: *JPEG 2000 is a wavelet-based image compression standard created by the Joint Photographic Experts Group committee with the intention of superseding their original DCT-based JPEG standard.*

Abstract

Some of the major objectives of the JPEG 2000 still image coding standard were compression and memory efficiency, lossy to lossless coding, support for continuous-tone to bi-level images, error resilience, and random access to regions of interest. This presentation will provide readers with some insight on the basic coding structure of the baseline JPEG 2000 algorithm and various features and functionalities supported by the standard. It can serve as a guideline for users to evaluate the effectiveness of JPEG 2000 for various applications, and to develop JPEG 2000 compliant software.

Introduction

Since the release of the Joint Photographic Experts Group (JPEG) still image coding standard in 1994 [5], it has been widely adopted in applications involving digital communication and storage of still images and graphics. Motivated by the evolution of image coding technology and by an increasing field of applications, the JPEG committee initiated a new project in 1997 to develop the next generation still image coding standard. The joint effort of the International Organization for Standardization (ISO) and the International Telecommunication Union (ITU-T), resulted in the JPEG 2000 International Standard [7], published in December 2000.

The original Call for Contributions for the JPEG 2000 standardization effort [6] identified a set of coding features believed to be vital to many existing and emerging image applications. These were translated into goals for the new standard, as shown below.

- The system should offer excellent compression performance at very low bit rates, typically 0.25 bits-per-pixel (bpp) or less.
- The system should be able to compress both continuous-tone and bi-level images with similar system resources.
- The system should provide lossy to lossless compression by means of a progressive coding process.
- The system should be able to perform progressive coding in terms of both pixel accuracy and spatial resolution.
- The system should produce code streams that are robust to channel errors.
- The system should allow random access to and processing of certain parts of the image such as regions of interest.

Various techniques have been proposed to address these requirements. The standard eventually converged to a baseline coding system that achieves a good balance in supporting the desired features. This became the Part 1 (ISO/IEC 15444-1: 2004) of the standard. Additional parts have been constantly developed and standardized to enhance the functionality of the baseline coding system, or to facilitate development of JPEG 2000 compliant applications. To date, the available parts include:

Part 2: *Extensions* on wavelet decomposition, quantization, region of interest encoding, and new data formats (ISO/IEC 15444-2: 2004).

Part 3: *Motion JPEG 2000* which applies JPEG 2000 image coding algorithm on individual frames of video sequences independently (ISO/IEC 15444-3: 2002).

Part 4: *Test procedures* for both encoding and decoding processes to validate conformance to JPEG 2000 Part 1 (ISO/IEC 15444-4: 2002).

Part 5: *Reference implementations* of JPEG 2000 Part 1, including JasPer (in C) and JJ2000 (in Java) (ISO/IEC 15444-5: 2003).

Part 6: *Compound image format* JPM for document imaging (ISO/IEC 15444-6: 2003).

Part 8: *JPSEC* addressing security aspects of the standard, such as encryption, source and content authentication, authorization, and IP protection (ISO/IEC FCD 15444-8).

Part 9: *JPIP* interactive protocol supporting image delivery over the Internet with feature such as bit stream reordering, random access and incremental decoding (ISO/IEC 15444-9: 2004).

Part 10: *JP3D* supporting volumetric coding of 3D data (ISO/IEC WD 15444-10).

Part 11: *JPWL* introducing mechanisms to protect the codestream from transmission errors, to describe error sensitivities within the codestream, and to indicate possible residual errors within the codestream (ISO/IEC FCD 15444-11).

Part 12: *ISO Base media file format* for timed sequence of media data (ISO/IEC 15444-12: 2005).

Part 13: *An entry level JPEG 2000 encoder* (ISO/IEC CD 15444-13).

The purpose of this presentation is to provide readers with some insight on the coding structure of JPEG 2000, its functional parameters, and their effect on coding performance. It is not our intention to discuss the detailed coding algorithm and its implementations in this presentation. For such information, the reader should refer to a tutorial on the coding engine by Taubman [10], a system level introduction by Christopoulos et al. [3], and the standard text [7].

The JPEG 2000 Coding Algorithm

JPEG 2000 is essentially a transform coder, which consists of three stages: image transform, quantization and entropy coding. An image transform is used to achieve image data decorrelation. An efficient transformation yields a representation of the image data where the energy is concentrated in a small number of transform coefficients. Transform coefficients are then quantized to a finite number of quantization levels. It is during quantization that intentional loss of information occurs and most of the compression gain is achieved. Finally, the quantized coefficients are scanned and encoded into a bit stream using an entropy coder. An image decoder performs the inverse operations to obtain a reconstructed image. The coding engine of the JPEG 2000 standard is a coding algorithm derived from the Embedded Block Coding with Optimal Truncation (EBCOT) technique proposed by Taubman [10]. Detailed descriptions of the codec are given in, among others [1, 9, 12, 13]. Currently there are three publicly available implementations of JPEG 2000: the JasPer implementation [14], the Kakadu implementation [11], and the JJ2000 implementation [4].

The Image Transform

The JPEG 2000 algorithm is based on the Discrete Wavelet Transform (DWT). It is therefore not compatible with the JPEG coding algorithm, which uses the two-dimensional (2-D) Discrete Cosine Transform (DCT). Studies have shown [2] that a well designed DWT may have a moderate gain over DCT in the sense of data decorrelation. More importantly, a significant improvement in performance is achieved by applying the transform to the whole image or large blocks thereof instead of small image blocks (JPEG uses 8×8-pixel blocks). The drawback of this approach is its increased computational complexity. The selection of DWT at the beginning of the JPEG 2000 project essentially determined the coding structure of this new standard.

The 2-D DWT is usually implemented through iterative 2-D subband decomposition, as seen in *Figure 1*. First, the image is decomposed into four subbands, LL_N, LH_N, HL_N, and HH_N. The same 2-D subband decomposition is then applied to the lowest frequency subband (LL_N) to obtain subbands LL_{N-1}, LH_{N-1}, HL_{N-1}, and HH_{N-1}. The process is repeated N times, for an N -level decomposition. Commonly, the number of decomposition levels is around N = 5. This subband decomposition structure is called the Mallat (or dyadic, or pyramid) decomposition. This is the only decomposition structure supported by Part 1 of the standard. The inverse DWT transformation consists in N 2-D subband synthesis operations starting at the lowest resolution.

A one-level 2-D subband decomposition is usually achieved by applying a one-dimensional (1-D) two-band decomposition to all the rows (or columns) of a 2-D array and then to all the columns (or rows) of the resulting array. Therefore, the decomposition generates four subbands, as shown in Figure 1. Each 1-D subband decomposition consists of filtering the input sequence with a low-pass/high-pass filter bank and downsampling the two filtered sequences by a factor of two. JPEG 2000 specifies two sets of 1-D filter banks. The reversible 5/3 filter bank performs a reversible integer-to-integer transformation which can be used to achieve lossless coding. The irreversible 9/7 filter bank performs a real-to-real transformation which is reversible in infinite precision but irreversible in finite precision. The resulting DWT achieves better energy compaction and is used in lossy coding.

In addition to the DWT for spatial decorrelation, the standard also defines two sets of component transforms for multi-component images, such as color images. Again, an irreversible component transformation (ICT) is defined for lossy coding and a reversible component transformation (RCT) is defined for lossless coding.

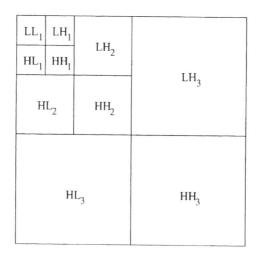

Figure 1. A three-level (*N* = 3) 2-D DWT decomposition.

Quantization

To quantize DWT coefficients, JPEG 2000 uses a uniform scalar quantizer with a dead zone around zero. This quantizer has been chosen mostly because of its simplicity. It can easily be implemented as a rounding operation. Each DWT coefficient $a_b(u,v)$ in subband b is quantized to the integer $q_b(u,v)$ using the formula:

$$q_b(u,v) = sign(a_b(u,v)) \left\lfloor \frac{|a_b(u,v)|}{\Delta_b} \right\rfloor,$$

where Δ_b is the quantization step, which can vary from one subband to another and is encoded into the bit stream. The standard does not specify how the quantization step Δ_b is chosen, and different implementations can use various strategies. The decoder performs inverse quantization, described by the equation:

$$\hat{a}_b(u,v) = \begin{cases} 0, & \text{if } q_b(u,v) = 0 \\ sign(q_b(u,v))(|q_b(u,v)|+0.5)\Delta_b, & \text{if } q_b(u,v) \neq 0 \end{cases}$$

In lossless coding, coefficients of reversible transforms are not quantized, or they can be thought as quantized by a step size of one. In lossy compression, the quantization step sizes control the final size of the compressed data file, and thus the compression ratio. The larger the step sizes are, the smaller the compressed file size will be. Therefore, selecting the step sizes is a rate control issue and will be discussed in a later section.

Entropy coding

The major differences between various wavelet-based image coding algorithms are mostly in the lossless entropy coding stage. This is the step that affects their different coding performances and features to the greatest extent.

Bit-plane coding

To encode quantized DWT coefficients, JPEG 2000 uses a block based bit-plane coding method with multiple passes per bit-plane. Each subband is partitioned into a set of non-overlapping rectangular code blocks with a fixed size. Each block is then encoded independently of other blocks. Within each block, the coding starts from the most significant non-zero bit-plane and proceeds to the least significant bit-plane. In each bit-plane, three coding passes are performed, namely the *significance propagation pass*, the *magnitude refinement pass* and the *cleanup pass*. Each coding pass scans the block according to a scanning pattern, and generates coding symbols using a set of pre-defined rules. The scanning pattern, shown in Figure 2, has been chosen to facilitate efficient software and hardware implementations.

During the *significance propagation pass*, the encoder identifies the block coefficients which have been zero (or insignificant) at higher bit-planes but have non-zero (or significant) neighbors. It is assumed that these coefficients are more likely to become significant in the current bit-plane.
For each tested coefficient, the test result is encoded into the bit stream (1 if significant, 0 if insignificant). If a new significant coefficient is detected, its sign bit is encoded immediately.

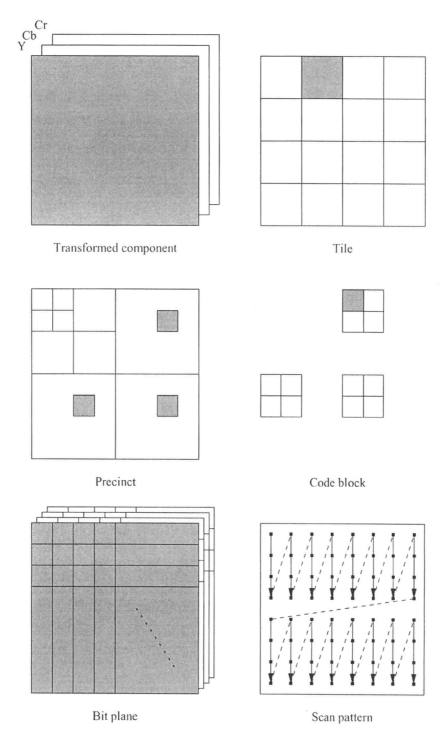

Figure 2. Components of the JPEG 2000 image data structure.

The *magnitude refinement pass* processes coefficients which have been found significant in previous bit-planes. For each such coefficient, the magnitude bit in the current plane is encoded into the bit stream.

The *cleanup pass* tests all the insignificant coefficients which have not already been tested in the significance propagation pass in the current bit-plane. It is expected that these coefficients are less likely to become significant because they do not have any significant neighbor. Therefore, to reduce the number of symbols generated in this pass, test results are run-length encoded when four consecutive coefficients in a scan pattern column are all insignificant. Once a significant coefficient is identified, its sign bit is also encoded immediately.

Each coefficient in a code block will be coded once and only once in each bit-plane. The symbols generated by these three passes are usually passed through a binary adaptive arithmetic coder with context modeling. Specific context models are defined for the coding of each pass and for the coding of sign bits. Each context determines which adaptive probability model will be used in the arithmetic coding of the current symbol. The contexts are selected based on the significance of the eight or four connected neighboring coefficients. To simplify context calculation and achieve reliable probability estimation, the number of contexts is kept small. More specifically, the significance propagation pass uses nine contexts, the magnitude refinement pass uses three contexts, the cleanup pass uses the nine significance propagation contexts plus one extra context for run-length coding, and the sign bit coding uses five contexts. JPEG 2000 uses a binary adaptive arithmetic coder called the MQ coder, designed to reduce computational complexity. It is closely related to the well-known QM and an offspring of the Q coder. Arithmetic coding is always initialized at the beginning of a code block and can be optionally reinitialized at the beginning of a coding pass.

Rate control

One rough method for rate control has been mentioned in the context of quantization. However, the multipass bit-plane coding approach described above allows for rate control with better precision and reliability. A distinguishing feature of JPEG 2000 is its post-compression rate-distortion (PCRD) optimization [12], or optimal bit stream truncation. Its purpose is to determine the optimal bit allocation for each code block under the constraint of a target bit rate.

During quantization, a very fine quantization step size Δ_b is used for all the coefficients inside a subband. Encoding of each code block results in a bit stream which represents all the quantized coefficients to a very fine scale. For most useful compression ratios, it is not possible to send all these streams in their entirety. Therefore, these streams are subject to truncation in order to meet the overall target bit rate. PCRD attempts to choose the truncation points in a way that minimizes the coding distortion for a target bit rate. The possible truncation points in a bit stream are at the end of each coding pass. If a bit stream of a certain block is truncated at a bit-plane that is N bit-planes higher than the least significant bit plane, the effective quantization step of this block is $2^N \Delta_b$.

During the coding process, whenever a coding pass is completed, the bit rate consumption and the reduction in distortion due to this coding pass are calculated and recorded. When the coding of a whole block is completed, the rates and distortions of all the passes are recorded in a rate-distortion (R-D) table. Similar tables are generated for all code blocks. PCRD optimization uses a Lagrangian optimization method to determine which rate-distortion pair is to be used for each code block. Details for the optimization routine are given in [12], pp. 339–348.

An embedded code stream is a code stream that can be decoded as a whole, or it can be truncated and decoded at various bit rates lower than the original bit rate. Therefore, the lower bit rate streams can be seen as embedded in a higher bit rate stream. This scalability feature can be helpful in applications involving multiple bandwidth channels or multiple decoding platforms. In this context, although the complete code stream is optimized in the R-D sense, an arbitrarily truncated stream may not be optimal at its reduced bit rate. To address this problem, EBCOT supports the concept of quality layers. During PCRD optimization, instead of performing one R-D optimization for a single target rate, the coder can perform a series of R-D optimizations from lower rates to higher rates. Each new optimization is built upon the previous optimal bit stream truncations, and each optimization generates a quality layer that will be appended to previous layers to form the final code stream. Therefore, any truncation of the code stream at the end of a quality layer will always be optimal in the R-D sense. The number of bits corresponding to each data block included in a layer is encoded in the code stream as header information.

Regions of interest

Many applications may require that some areas within an image (or *regions of interest*, ROI) be encoded with higher accuracy than the rest of the image. Therefore, at a certain total bit rate, the encoder should allocate more bits for ROI pixels and fewer bits for non-ROI (or background) pixels. This feature usually involves an *ROI mask* and a shift *scale s*. The ROI mask is a binary map defining an arbitrary-shape region of interest. A set of smaller ROI masks are calculated for each subband according to the original mask. The shift scale s specifies how much the ROIs will be emphasized. It is used to shift the quantization indices of all ROI subband coefficients to higher bit-planes, and effectively amplify their magnitude by a factor of 2^s. This shift will be corrected at the decoder. In Part 1 of the standard, the ROI implementation is based on the Maxshift method [12], in which the shift scale is always larger than the largest number of magnitude bit-planes of all the background regions. As a result, after the ROI shift, the least significant bit-plane of the ROIs will still be higher than the most significant bit-plane of the background regions. This shift scale will have to be coded into the code stream and sent to the decoder. Entropy coding of the shifted subband coefficients is performed as usual. Since the decoder is using bit-plane decoding, it will always complete the decoding of all ROI coefficients before it can reach the background coefficients. Therefore the decoder can determine the ROI mask as the set of significant coefficients after s bit planes have been decoded. Thus the ROI mask does not have to be transmitted.

The JPEG 2000 data structure

The JPEG 2000 defines a set of data structures that standardizes the access and reference to all the data involved. One set of structures is related to the processing of image data, the other is related to the formation of the code stream.

The image data structure

A diagram showing the image data structure is shown in Figure 2. An *image* refers to the input of the encoder and the output of the decoder. The associated data structure is described below, the components being listed in decreasing order of their size.

Component: An image is first separated into one or more components. A component can be an arbitrary 2-D rectangular array of samples. The most common image components are the color components representing the three color (R, G, B) planes of an image. The inter-component transform defined in the standard is mainly used with RGB images. However, other decompositions are possible for multi-component images such as radar images (in phase and quadrature) or printer output images (the CMYK color space). Components do not necessarily have the same size, nor the same bit depth.

Tile: Each component is divided into one or several tiles, which are then encoded independently. All tiles are the same size, except tiles at the boundaries. The purpose of tiling is to allow for the coding of very large images by reducing memory consumption and speeding up the coding process. Tiling may cause a slight decrease in compression efficiency, since the ability to exploit spatial redundancy is reduced when small tiles are used. Also, at low bit rates, blocking artifacts may be visible at tile boundaries.

Subband: Each tile in a particular component is encoded using the JPEG 2000 DWT coding algorithm. The tile is input to the wavelet transform, which generates a set of subbands representing different spatial frequency components. Due to subsampling in the wavelet transform, subband sizes decrease by a factor of four at each subband decomposition level.

Precinct: At a particular resolution level except the level 0, a precinct contains a group of code blocks that cover the same rectangular area in all three subbands. At level 0, a precinct is just a group of code blocks in the subband LL_1. Therefore a precinct represents all the information in a particular image region at a certain resolution level. It is then reasonable to suggest that such information should be packed together in the final code stream. In the code stream, bits are organized by precincts, instead of subbands.

Code block: After the quantization of all subband coefficients, each subband is partitioned into non-overlapping rectangular code blocks. These code blocks are confined within a certain subband, and have the same size except at boundaries of the subband. The maximum size of a code block is 64×64. They are input to the EBCOT coding engine. Each code block is encoded independently, and produces a bit stream to be included in the final code stream.

The code stream data structure

The code stream refers to the output of the encoder and the input of the decoder. Its associated data structure, sketched in Figure 3, includes the following components, in increasing order of their size.

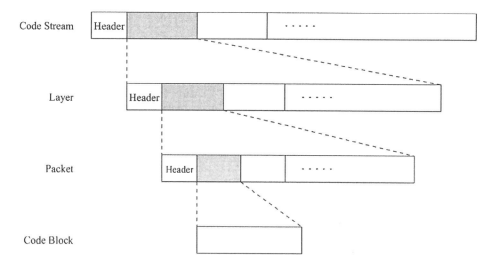

Figure 3. Components of the JPEG 2000 code stream structure.

Encoded code block: After a code block is encoded using the EBCOT coding engine, a bit stream results. This is the smallest independent unit in the JPEG 2000 code stream.

Packet: Packets are the basic data units in the final code stream. A packet contains all the encoded code blocks from a specific precinct in a tile at a quality layer. The length of a packet can be affected by the size of the precinct and the number of layers. Packets may certainly have different lengths, but they are always aligned at 8-bit boundaries in the final code stream. Each packet has a header indicating its content and related parameters.

Layer: We have introduced the concept of quality layer, which provides finer code stream truncation points with R-D optimization. In order to preserve the embedded feature of the layered coding mechanism, the final code stream should be organized by quality layers. The lower layers should be at the front of the code stream and the higher layers should be at the end. When the code stream is truncated at the decoder, the lower quality layers will be used to reconstruct the image.

Resolution level: The resolution level is closely related to the decomposition level in the discrete wavelet transform in *Figure 1*. The four subbands, LL_l, LH_l, HL_l, and HH_l at each decomposition level l represent a particular resolution. For example, LL_1, LH_1, HL_1, and HH_1 can be used to reconstruct the image at its original resolution. Also, LL_2, LH_2, HL_2, and HH_2 can be used to reconstruct LL_1, which is the original image at 1/4 resolution. The four resolution levels are defined as follows: LL_N belongs to resolution 0, LH_N, HL_N and HH_N belong to resolution level 1, LH_{N-1}, HL_{N-1} and HH_{N-1} belong to resolution level $l + 1$, and finally LH_1, HL_1, and HH_1 belong to resolution level N.

Progression order

Because the code stream can be arbitrarily truncated at the decoder, the order of packets in the code stream will affect the decoding performance. The standard defines a set of progression orders, which can be easily implemented through reordering the packets in the code stream. The LRCP progression first encodes all the Precincts in a component, then all Components at the current resolution level, then all the Resolution levels for the current quality layer and finally sequences through all quality Layers. This procedure is implemented using four nested loops, where the precinct loop is the innermost and the quality layer loop is the outermost. Four additional progression orders are defined: RLCP, RPCL, PCRL, and CPRL. Notice that the LRCP order is accuracy progressive, RLCP and RPCL are resolution progressive, while PCRL and CPRL are spatially progressive.

Summary of performance analysis tests

In [8], we conducted a comprehensive performance analysis on JPEG 2000 baseline coding algorithm. Three JPEG 2000 software implementations (Kakadu, JasPer, JJ2000) were compared with several other standard codecs, including JPEG, JBIG, JPEG-LS, MPEG-4 VTC and H.264 intra coding. Some observations and conclusions of these tests are summarized as follows.

Photographic images: For natural images with consistent global structures (e.g. LENA and WOMAN), JPEG 2000 clearly outperforms all other codecs. This is where the DWT coding structure achieves its best efficiency. For natural images with uncorrelated regional structures or detailed textures (e.g. GOLD HILL, BIKE, and CAFE), JPEG 2000's advantage over other codecs becomes less significant.

Synthetic and medical images: For computer graphics, compound images and some medical images (e.g. CHART and ULTRASOUND), the block-based H.264-intra codec appears to be more efficient than JPEG 2000 because of its ability to efficiently encode inter-block correlation within a single frame.

Bi-level images: JBIG and JBIG2 perform significantly better than JPEG 2000 on bi-level images such as scanned documents.

Lossless coding: JPEG 2000 in lossless mode and JPEG-LS achieve similar performance on lossless coding, however JPEG-LS is much faster.

Large images: With conventional implementations (e.g. JasPer), tile partition is an effective tool to balance memory usage with coding performance. It can also facilitate efficient parallel processing, especially for images containing several less correlated regions.

Progressive coding: LRCP progression provides fine scale SNR progressive coding, while RLCP progression provides resolution progressive coding.

Error resilience: Both PRED-TERM/RESTART and SEGMARK are effective error resilient mechanisms in JPEG 2000. However, combinations of these or other settings will not achieve noticeable further protection.

Conclusion

An introduction of the JPEG 2000 image coding standard was presented. The important aspects of the JPEG 2000 coding algorithm, structure specifications, as well as frequently used features were discussed. The description of the coding structure and a performance analysis summary provide an objective view of the advantages and disadvantages of this new standard. It is evident that JPEG 2000 will be adopted in many applications that require high image quality over bandwidth constrained channels and media. However, it is unlikely that it will become the only image coding tool to be used in every still image coding applications.

References

1. M.D. Adams, "The JPEG-2000 still image compression standard," ISO/IEC JTC 1/SC 29/WG 1 N 2412. Available online from http://www.ece.uvic.ca/~mdadams and distributed with the JasPer software, 2001.

2. M. Antonini, M. Barlaud, P. Mathieu, and I. Daubechies, "Image coding using wavelet transform," IEEE Transactions on Image Processing, Vol. 2, No. 1, pp. 205–220, 1992.

3. C. Christopoulos, A. Skodras, and T. Ebrahimi, "The JPEG 2000 still image coding system: An overview," IEEE Transactions on Consumer Electronics, Vol. 46, pp. 1103–1127, 2000.

4. JJ2000: An Implementation of the JPEG 2000 Standard in Java, Version 4.1: http://jj2000.epfl.ch, 2000.

5. JTC1/SC29/WG1: "10918-1: Information technology—Digital compression and coding of continuous-tone still images: Requirements and guidelines," International standard, ISO/IEC, 1994.

6. JTC1/SC29/WG1: "Call for contributions for JPEG 2000 (JTC 1.29.14, 15444): Image Coding System," Approved call for contributions, ISO/IEC, 1997.

7. JTC1/SC29/WG1: "15444-1: Information technology—JPEG 2000 image coding system—Part 1: Core coding system," International Standard, ISO/IEC, 2000.

8. H. Man, A. Docef, and F. Kossentini, "Performance analysis of the JPEG 2000 image coding standard," Multimedia Tools and Applications Journal, 26(1):27-57, May 2005.

9. M. Rabbani and R. Joshi, "An overview of the JPEG2000 still image compression standard," Signal Processing: Image Communication, Vol. 17, No. 1, pp. 3–48, 2002.

10. D. Taubman, "High performance scalable image compression with EBCOT," IEEE Transactions on Image Processing, Vol. 9, pp. 1158–1170, 2000.

11. D. Taubman, "Kakadu: A comprehensive, heavily optimized, fully compliant software toolkit for JPEG2000 developers, version 3.2," 2002, http://maestro.ee.unsw.edu.au/~taubman/kakadusoftware.

12. D. Taubman and M. Marcellin, "JPEG2000: Image Compression Fundamentals, Standards, and Practice," Kluwer Academic Publishers, 2001.

13. D. Taubman and M. Marcellin, "JPEG2000: Standard for Interactive Imaging", Proceedings of the IEEE, Vol. 90, pp. 1336-1357, Aug. 2002.

14. The JasPer project, version 1.500.4. 2000, http://www.ece.uvic.ca/ mdadams/jasper.

JPEG-LS

Definition: JPEG-LS is an image compression standard (ISO/IEC-14495-1 / ITU-T Rec. T.87) designed to provide effective lossless and near lossless compression of continuous-tone, gray scale and color still images.

Near lossless, in this context, means a guaranteed maximum error between the original image data and the reconstructed image data. One of its main potential driving forces is the compression of medical images without any quality loss.

The core algorithm behind JPEG-LS is called *LOw COmplexity LOssless COmpression for Images* (LOCO-I), proposed by Hewlett-Packard [1, 2, 3]. LOCO-I builds upon a concept known as *context modeling*. The main idea behind context modeling is to take advantage of the structure in the input source, modeled in terms of conditional probabilities of what pixel values follow from each other in the image (Figure 1).

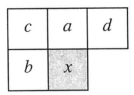

Figure 1. JPEG-LS / LOCO-I context model: pixel value x is predicted based on the values of a, b, c, and d.

LOCO-I has three main components:

- **Predictor**: uses a fixed predictor, whose output will be: a (when there is a vertical edge to the left of the current pixel location); b (when there is a horizontal edge above the current pixel location); or $a + b - c$ when the neighboring pixels have comparable values.

- **Context model**: the context model that conditions the current prediction error (*residual*) is indexed using a three-component context vector whose values represent the local gradients around the reference pixel. These values are quantized and the vector is mapped into an integer in $[0, 364]$.

- **Coder**: the error residuals are coded using adaptively selected codes based on Golomb codes [4], which are optimal for sequences with geometrical distributions.

For more information on JPEG-LS, including code, please refer to [3].

References

1. M. Weinberger, G. Seroussi, and G. Sapiro, "The LOCO-I Lossless Image Compression Algorithm: Principles and Standardization into JPEG-LS," IEEE Transactions on Image Processing, Vol. 9, August 2000, pp.1309-1324.
2. M. Weinberger, G. Seroussi, and G. Sapiro, "LOCO-I: A Low Complexity, Context-Based, Lossless Image Compression Algorithm," Proceedings of IEEE Data Compression Conference, Snowbird, Utah, March-April 1996.
3. HP Labs LOCO-I/JPEG-LS Home Page, http://www.hpl.hp.com/loco/ Accessed July 12, 2005.
4. S. W. Golomb, "Run-length Encodings," IEEE Transactions on Information Theory, Vol. IT-12, pp. 399–401, 1966.

KEY MANAGEMENT

Definition: *Key management refers to an encryption algorithm and deals with the secure generation, distribution, storage, and disposal of keys.*

The security of an encryption algorithm often depends on the strength of the encryption algorithm and the key two factors. In practice, most attacks on public-key systems are targeted at the key management level instead of the cryptographic algorithm itself. When a key is compromised, the entire system maybe compromised. Hence it is extremely important to secure the keys. This is the task of key management.

Key management deals with the secure generation, distribution, storage, and disposal of keys [1]. In other words, one must be able to get the key/s for the targeted application with the targeted security and efficiency requirement; the key/s must be stored securely so that no intruders can get it; legitimate users must be able to acquire the key/s for legitimate uses; and the lost or compromised keys are ready to be replaced and made aware to the legitimate users.

Many key management schemes have been developed. For example, manual key distribution, center-based key distribution, and certificate-based key distribution systems are widely used.

In recent years, multicast (communication that allows multiple receivers to simultaneously receive the same transmission,) key management schemes have been studied extensively. Many multicast key management schemes have been proposed. Interested readers can reference the paper by Eskicioglu [2], RFC2627 by Wallner, et al. [3], and the IETF Internet Draft by Dondeti, et al. [4] for more information.

See: Multimedia Encryption

References

1. RSA Laboratories, "RSA Laboratories' Frequently Asked Questions About Today's Cryptography," Version 4.1, RSA Security Inc., 2000.
2. A. M. Eskicioglu, "Multimedia Security in Group Communications: Recent Progress in Key Management, Authentication, and Watermarking," ACM Multimedia Systems Journal, Special Issue on Multimedia Security, pp. 239-248, September 2003.
3. D. Wallner, E. Harder, and R. Agee, "Key Management for Multicast: Issues and Architectures," The Internet Society RFC 2627, June 1999.

4. L. Dondeti, B. Decleene, S. Griffin, T. Hardjono, J. Kurose, D. Towsley, C. Zhang, and S. Vasudevan, "Group key management in wireless and mobile environment," IETF Internet Draft (draft-dondeti-irtf-smug-gkm-mobility-00.txt), Jan., 2002.

KNOWLEDGE-ASSISTED IMAGE AND VIDEO ANALYSIS

Definition: Knowledge-assisted image and video analysis refers to the use of domain-specific prior knowledge about images or video.

Segmentation of images and video is generally an ill-posed problem, i.e. for a given natural image or image sequence, there exists no unique solution to the segmentation problem. In order for the segmentation problem to be transformed to a well-posed one, restriction of the number of admissible solutions is necessary. To this end, the introduction of prior knowledge to the segmentation procedure, leading to the development of domain-specific knowledge-assisted analysis techniques, has been proposed.

Prior knowledge for a domain (e.g. F1 racing) typically includes the important objects that can be found in any given image or frame belonging to this domain (e.g. car, road, grass, sand, etc.), their characteristics (e.g. corresponding color models) and any relations between them. See example in Figure 1. Given this knowledge, there exists the well-posed problem of deciding, for each pixel, whether it belongs to any of the defined objects (and if so, to which one) or to none of them.

A knowledge-guided segmentation and labeling approach for still images is presented in [1], where an unsupervised fuzzy C-means clustering algorithm along with basic image processing techniques are used under the guidance of a knowledge base. The latter is constructed by automatically processing a set of ground-truth images to extract cluster-labeling rules.

An approach to the knowledge-assisted analysis of MPEG-2 video of the F1 racing domain is presented in [2], where the employed prior knowledge includes three semantic objects and their characteristics in the form of qualitative attributes (e.g. color homogeneity, indicating suitable pre-processing methods), numerical data generated via training and relations among semantic objects. This approach is extended in [3], where more semantic objects are specified and a genetic algorithm is applied to the atom regions initially generated via simple segmentation in order to find the optimal scene interpretation according to the domain conceptualization.

Figure 1. Exemplary results (initial segmentation and final analysis outcome, respectively) using the knowledge-assisted analysis framework of [3].
In the final result mask, only five shades of gray corresponding to the five objects of interest that were defined for the examined domain are used for expressing the membership of each pixel.

See: Segmentation of images and video

References

1. M. Zhang, L.O. Hall, and D.B. Goldgof, "A generic knowledge-guided image segmentation and labeling system using fuzzy clustering algorithms," IEEE Transactions on Systems, Man and Cybernetics, Part B, Vol. 32, No. 5, October 2002, pp. 571-582.
2. V. Mezaris, I. Kompatsiaris, and M. G. Strintzis, "A knowledge-based approach to domain-specific compressed video analysis," Proceedings of the IEEE International Conference on Image Processing, October 2004, Singapore, pp. 341-344.
3. N. Voisine, S. Dasiopoulou, V. Mezaris, E. Spyrou, T. Athanasiadis, I. Kompatsiaris, Y. Avrithis, and M. G. Strintzis, "Knowledge-Assisted Video Analysis Using a Genetic Algorithm," Proceedings of the Workshop on Image Analysis For Multimedia Interactive Services, April 2005, Montreux, Switzerland.

L

LARGE-SCALE VIDEO-ON-DEMAND SYSTEMS

J. Feng
City University of Hong Kong, Hong Kong

W.F. Poon and K.T. Lo
The Hong Kong Polytechnic, Hong Kong

Definition: *Large-scale video-on-demand systems allow distributed users to interactively access video files from remote servers and consist of four components: video server, directory server, proxy server, and clients/set-top-box.*

With the advances in digital video technology and high speed networking, video-on-demand (VoD) services [1][2] have come into practice in recent years. The VoD service allows geographically distributed users to interactively access video files from remote VoD servers. Users can request videos from a server at any time and enjoy the flexible control of video playback with VCR-like functions. Nevertheless, such systems have not yet been commercial success because server and network requirements are the limiting factors in the wide deployment of such services. Engineers have thus tried to minimize the resources requirement as well as increase the system scalability. There are mainly two approaches for building a large scale VoD system in a cost-effective way. The first is to use a proxy server to minimize the backbone network transmission cost. The second is to use multicasting/broadcasting techniques to share the system resources. Currently, caching, broadcasting and patching are the major data sharing techniques to provide a cost-effective VoD service.

Figure 1 shows a general large-scale VoD system architecture that basically consists of four components: video server, directory server, proxy server and clients/set-top-box. The video server is responsible for streaming the videos to the distributed clients. It determines whether there are sufficient resources such as disk bandwidth and available network channels for the clients. The server application is able to support both unicast and broadcast connections depending on the Quality of Service (QoS) requirement of the clients. When the server receives video requests, the video data are retrieved from the repository such as RAID [3] and then transmitted to the clients. For a good design of the VoD system, the server should mostly handle the complexity. The set–top-box is only responsible for sending/receiving signals to/from the VoD server. The buffer is used to store the video data before playback to maintain a continuous and jitters-free display.

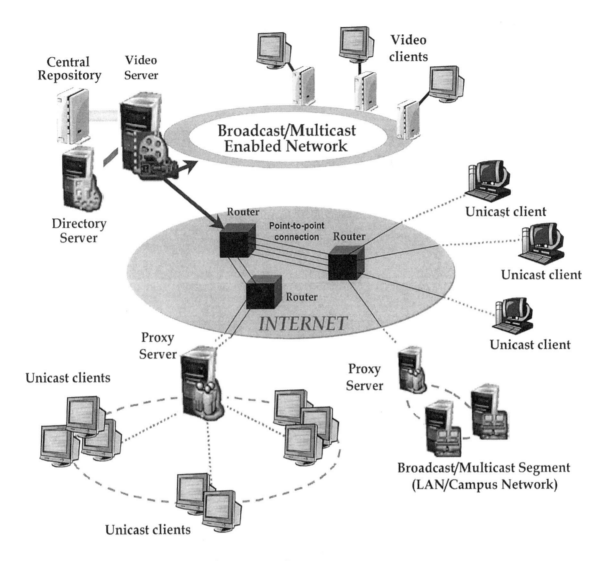

Figure 1. An architecture of a typical large scale VoD system.

Caching

To reduce the backbone network traffic, a proxy server can be installed between the central server and the clients as shown in Figure 1. In this hierarchical VoD system, video data can be temporarily stored in a proxy server. In general, the proxy server caches the most popular videos for users' repeating requests in order to minimize the backbone transmission cost. Upon the user's request received by the proxy server, it will send back the video request if the video have been already cached. Otherwise, it will bypass the request to the higher level and then retrieve the requested video from the central server. One of the challenges in this hierarchical architecture [4] is to decide which video and how many copies have to maintain at each proxy server. On the other hand, instead of storing the videos as entity, the proxy servers can just pre-cache the beginning portion of the video [5] to support the local customers in order to efficiently utilize the limited proxy server capacity.

Apart from updating the video content in the proxy server periodically say 1 or 2 days, dynamic replacement algorithms may also be implemented to maximize the server's utilization. The least frequently used (LFU) algorithm [6] exploits the history of accesses to predict the probability of an object. However, it was originally designed for web caching purpose that does not work well for continuous media data like videos. A resource-based caching (RBC) algorithm [7] for constant bit-rate encoded videos was proposed to employ caching gain and resource requirement of videos to make a decision in a limited cache resource environment. In addition, some people suggested encoding the videos into a number of fixed-sized [8] or variable-sized [9] segments as an atomic unit for a caching policy. For a heterogeneous network environment such as Internet, the system may use layered encoded videos [10][11] to flexibly provide different quality of the videos streams according to the clients' available bandwidth. In this case, some layers of the videos will be stored in the proxy server.

Broadcasting

If the network supports the broadcast/multicast traffic, data broadcasting techniques [12] can further increase the system scalability. For example, if the video server is installed in the broadcast/multicast enabled network (see Figure 1) in which routers/switches support the multicast protocols such as Internet Group Management Protocol (IGMP) [13], all the users in this domain then enjoy the broadcast/multicast transmission technology and the video server can simply use the broadcast/multicast channels to serve a large group of users.

Staggered broadcasting (STB) [14] is the simplest broadcasting protocol proposed in the early days. The approach of STB is to open the video channels at a fixed regular interval. Suppose that the video length is L minutes and the video data rate is C. The protocol allocates K channels each with bandwidth C to transmit the whole video. The video is then broadcast at its transmission rate over the channels at a phase delay and the start-up latency is equal to L/K. Figure 2 illustrates that a video, which is composed of 4 segments, is delivered over 4 broadcasting channels. If the video is 120 minutes long, the maximum start-up delay, i.e. the waiting time of the user, will be as long as 30 minutes.

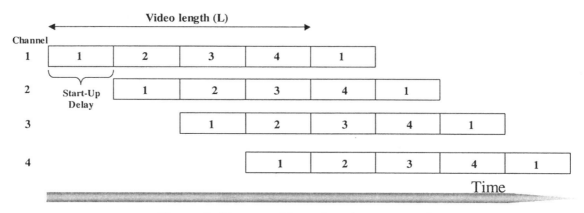

Figure 2. Staggered broadcasting protocol.

To reduce the start-up delay, pyramid broadcasting (PB) [15] was introduced. In this scheme, the access time can be reduced with the cost of a large receiver buffer. The principle behind PB is to divide the physical channel into K logical channels of equal bandwidth B/K, where B is the total bandwidth of the network. Each video is partitioned into K segments of geometrically increasing size so that the ith logical channel will periodically broadcast the ith video segment for M videos in turns. No other segments are transmitted through this channel. With the PB scheme, both client I/O capacity and buffer requirement are very high.

To overcome the problems of PB, skyscraper broadcasting (SB) [16] was developed. In SB, a new video fragmentation function was developed to divide the video into different segments. The system then broadcasts the video segments over K channels. The size of the ith video segment, in the units of the first segment size $D_{1,SB}$, is given by eqn. (1).

$$f(i) = \begin{cases} 1 & i = 1, \\ 2 & i = 2,3, \\ (2 + 2\lfloor \frac{i}{2} \rfloor - i)f(i-1) + (1 + 2\lfloor \frac{i}{2} \rfloor - i)(1 + \lfloor \frac{i - 4\lfloor i/4 \rfloor}{2} \rfloor) & otherwise . \end{cases}$$

(1)

At the client side, reception of segments is done in terms of transmission group, which is defined as consecutive segments having the same sizes. Users need to download data from at most two channels at any time and the receiver buffer requirement is constrained by the size of the last segment. Figure 3 shows the transmission schedule of SB when K is equal to 5 and the shaded area is the receiver reception schedule when the customer arrives at time t.

D_{SBMAX} is defined to restrict the segment from becoming too large. Thus, the start-up latency T_{sb}, that is equal to the size of the first segment, si:

$$T_{SB} = D_{1,SB} = \frac{L}{\sum_{j=i}^{N} \min(f(i), D_{SBMAX})}.$$

(2)

The storage requirement Buf_{SB} can be computed by eqn. (3).

$$Buf_{SB} = D_{1,SB}(D_{SBMAX} - 1)$$

(3)

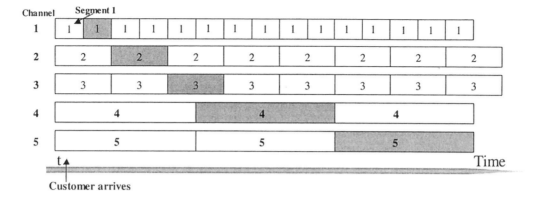

Figure 3. Skyscraper broadcasting protocol.

With similar approach, fast-data broadcasting (FB) [17] can further reduce the start-up latency by dividing a video into a geometrical series of $[1, 2, 4, ..., 2^{K-1}, 2^K]$. This protocol is very efficient in terms of server bandwidth requirement but the receiver is required to download video segments from all K channels simultaneously. Other broadcasting protocols like harmonic broadcasting [18], cautious harmonic broadcasting (CHB) and quasi-harmonic broadcasting (QHB) [19] were also developed. In addition, some hybrid protocols called pagoda-based broadcasting [20] were derived. These protocols tried to partition each video into fixed size segments and map them into video streams of equal bandwidth but use time-division multiplexing to minimize the access latency and bandwidth requirement.

Patching

As described before, all the video broadcasting protocols would introduce start-up latency that is ranged from several ten seconds to several ten minutes. The delay depends on the efficiency of the broadcasting schemes, channel bandwidth requirement as well as receiver buffer size. Thus, the patching scheme [21] was designed to provide a true (zero-delay) VoD system in a broadcast environment. The idea of patching is that clients are able to download data on two channels simultaneously when they request for the videos. They can merge into the broadcasting channels while watching the videos. In this case, the video playback does not have to synchronize with the transmission schedule of the broadcasting channels and the clients can start the video as soon as they make the video requests.

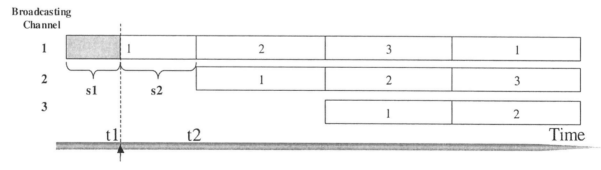

Figure 4. Simple patching scheme.

Figure 4 shows the patching scheme based on the staggered broadcasting protocol. When a client arrives at time t1, instead of waiting for the video data from broadcasting channel 2 at t2, he/she will receive the missing portion of the video, s1, from a unicast channel and at the same time buffer the video data from the broadcasting channel 1. Once s1 has been received, the unicast channel can be disconnected, and the client can be served by the broadcasting channel until the end of the video. Thus, compared to the traditional VoD system in which the individual client is served by the unicast channel, the patching scheme can significantly reduce the resources requirement.

Based on the similar idea, the hierarchical stream merging (HSM) [22] scheme hierarchically merges clients into broadcasting groups such that the bandwidth requirement can be further reduced compared with the simple patching scheme.

VCR Functionality

In a VoD system, clients may request different types of VCR functions such as pause and fast forward. Actually, it is still an open issue for implementation of continuous VCR functions in the above broadcasting systems except for the STB protocol. To implement the pause function in the STB system, we use the receiver buffer and exploit the jumping group property [23]. Figure 5 illustrates how the system provides the pause operation. For example, the client who is being served by broadcasting group i pauses the video at t1. Since the client continues to receive the video data, his/her buffer will be full at t1+W where W is the start-up delay. At this moment, he/she jumps from broadcasting group *i* to succeeding group *i+1*. After the change of the broadcasting group, the duplicated buffer content is removed. The data from group *i+1* can then continue to transmit to the buffer. In general, the customer can jump to group *i+2*, *i+3*, and so on until he/she resumes from the pause operation.

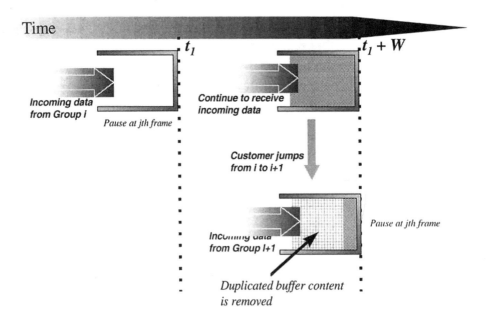

Figure 5. Pause operation in the STB system.

In the STB system, we may apply the Split-And-Merge (SAM) protocol [24] to cover the details for the other interaction types that include Jump Forward/Backward and Fast Forward/Reverse. The basic idea of SAM is to use separated channels called interactive (unicast) channels to support the VCR functions. When the playout resumes, the VoD server attempts to merge the interactive user back into one of the broadcasting channels. Each interactive customer is allocated a buffer of maximum size *SB* located at the access nodes for the synchronization purpose. Instead of using the shared buffer in the access nodes, people suggested that a decentralized non-shared buffer [25] is more suitable for a large-scale VoD system providing the interactive functions. Figure 6 shows the state diagram of interactive user's behavior.

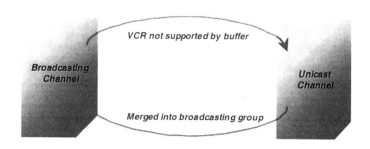

Figure 6. Interactive user's behavior.

Apart from using the contingency channels, a buffer management scheme called Active Buffer Management (ABM) [26] was developed to support the VCR functions using the receiver buffer. With the ABM scheme, it was assumed that the receiver can listen and receive data from several broadcasting channels at the same time. Data loading strategies are used to maintain the play point in the middle of the receiver buffer so as to support more VCR requests. Since the buffer size is limited, the system cannot guarantee to provide the continuous VCR functions.

See: Hierarchical VoD System, Harmonic Broadcasting Protocol, Active Buffer Management for Provision of VCR Functionalities

References

1. W.D. Sincokie, "System architecture for a large scale video on demand service," *Computer Networks and ISDN Systems*, Vol. 22, pp. 155-162, September 1991.
2. W.F. Poon, K.T. Lo, and J. Feng, "Determination of efficient transmission scheme for video-on-demand (VoD) services," *IEEE Transactions on Circuits and Systems for Video Technology*, Vol. 13, No. 2, pp. 188-192, February 2003.
3. D.A. Patterson, G.A. Gibson, and R.H. Katz, "A case for redundant array of inexpensive disks (RAID)," *Proceedings of the ACM Conference Management of Data*, pp. 1009-116, 1988.
4. K Li, W.J. Liao, X. X. Qiu, and W. M. Wong, "Performance Model of Interactive Video-on-Demand Systems," *IEEE Journal on Selected Areas in Communication*, Vol. 14, No. 6, pp. 1099-1109, August 1996.

5. G. S. H. Chan and F. Tobagi, "Distributed servers architecture for networked video services," *IEEE/ACM Transactions on Networking*, Vol. 9, No. 2, pp. 125-136, April 2001.

6. S. Jin and A. Bestavros, "Popularity-aware greedy dual-size web proxy caching algorithms," *Proceedings of the 20th International Conference on Distributed Computing Systems*, pp. 254–261, 2000.

7. R. Tweari, H.M. Vin, A. Dan, and D. Sitaram, "Resource based caching for web server," *Proceedings of the ACM/SPIE Multimedia Computing and Network*, pp. 191-204, 1998.

8. R. Rejaie and J. Kangasharju, "Mocha: A quality adaptive multimedia proxy cache for Internet streaming," *Proceedings of the 11th International Workshop on Network and Operating Systems Support for Digital Audio and Video*, January 2001.

9. K.L. Wu, P.S. Yu, and J. L. Wolf, "Segment-based proxy caching of multimedia streams," *Proceedings of the 10th International WWW Conference (WWW10)*, May 2001.

10. J. Kangasharju, F. Hartanto, M. Reisslein, and K.W. Ross, "Distributing layered encoded video through caches," *IEEE Transactions on Computers*, Vol. 51, No. 6, pp. 622–636, 2002.

11. W.F. Poon, K.T. Lo, and J. Feng, "Hierarchical network architecture for layered video streaming," *Proceedings of the 24th International Conference on Distributed Computing Systems Workshop*, pp. 164-169, March 2004, Tokyo, Japan.

12. W.F. Poon, K.T. Lo, and J. Feng, "First segment partition for video-on-demand broadcasting protocols," *Computer Communications*, Vol. 26, No. 14, pp. 1698-1708, September 2003.

13. W. Fenner, "Internet group management protocol, version 2," RFC2236, November 1997.

14. J.W. Wong, "Broadcast Delivery," *Proceedings of the IEEE*, Vol. 76, No. 12, pp. 1566-1577, December 1998.

15. S. Viswanathan and T. Imielinski, "Metropolitan area video-on-demand service using pyramid broadcasting," *ACM Multimedia Systems*, Vol. 4, No. 4, pp. 197-208, 1996.

16. K.A. Hua and S. Sheu, "Skyscraper broadcasting: A new broadcasting scheme for metropolitan video-on-demand systems," *Proceedings of the SIGCOMM 97*, pp. 98-100, 1997.

17. L. Juhn and L. Tseng, "Fast data broadcasting and receiving scheme for popular video service," *IEEE Transactions on Broadcasting*, Vol. 44, No. 1, pp. 100-105, March 1998.

18. L. Juhn and L. Tseng, "Harmonic broadcasting protocols for video-on-demand service," *IEEE Transactions on Broadcasting*, Vol. 43, No. 3, pp. 268-271, September 1997.

19. J.-F. Paris, S. W. Carter, and D. D. E. Long, "Efficient broadcasting protocols for video on demand," *Proceedings of the MASCOTS 98*, pp. 127-132, 1998.

20. J.-F. Paris, S. W. Carter, and D. D. E. Long, "A hybrid broadcasting protocol for video on demand," *Proceedings of the 1999 Multimedia Computing and Networking Conference (MMCN 99)*, pp. 317-326, 1999.

21. K.A. Hua, Y. Cai, and S. Sheu, "Patching: A multicast technique for true video-on-demand services," *Proceedings of the 6th ACM International Conference on Multimedia*, pp. 191-200, 1998.

22. H. Tan, D. L. Eager, and M. K. Vernon, "Delimiting the range of effectiveness of scalable on-demand streaming," *Proceedings of IFIP International Symposium on*

Computer Performance Modeling, Measurement and Evaluation (Performance 2002), Rome, September 2002.

23. W.F. Poon and K.T. Lo, "Design of multicast delivery for providing VCR functionality in interactive video-on-demand systems," *IEEE Transactions on Broadcasting*, Vol. 45, No. 1, pp. 141-148, March 1999.

24. W.J. Liao and O.K. Li, "The split and merge protocol for interactive video-on-demand," *IEEE Multimedia*, Vol. 4, No. 4, pp. 51-62, 1997.

25. L. Emmanuel, Abram-Profeta, and K.G. Shin, "Providing Unrestricted VCR Functions in Multicast Video-on-Demand Servers," *Proceedings of IEEE International Conference on Multimedia Computing and Systems*, pp. 66-75, 1998.

26. Z. Fei, M.H. Ammar, I. Kamel, and S. Mukherjee, "Providing interactive functions for staggered multicast near video-on-demand," *Proceedings of IEEE International Conference on Multimedia Computing and Systems '99*, pp. 949-953, 1999.

LCD DISPLAY INTERFACES

Definition: The LCD display controller provides an interface between the multimedia processor and a flat-panel display module.

The controller can be integrated as a part of system on chip or can be discrete. The image rendered by the application is displayed on the screen for the user by the LCD controller. The image of the screen on the memory is called the frame buffer. The configuration of the controller is typically established through programmable options for display type, resolution, pixel depth, overlays, hardware cursor, and output data formatting.

LCD panels can be passive (Dual scan STN or regular STN) or active (based on TFT-Thin Film Transistors). Active matrix panels are power efficient and have higher density as well as higher retention capability. There are some panels which incorporate the display buffer with the panel, allowing the controller to refresh the buffer at the content update rate as opposed to refresh rate specified for the panel. Display resolution varies based on the platform. QVGA(320x240) and VGA (640x480) sized panels are becoming common in the hand-held space. Typical controllers today support resolution up to 800x600. Typical panels support 2, 4, 8, 16, 18 19, 24 and 25 bits per pixel (bpp) (referred to as Pixel depth) are used with RGB and RGBT formats. The RGBT format uses the most significant bit to indicate transparency for overlay support. For bit depths less than 8 bpp, there are three separate 256x25-bit palette RAMs that can be used to map the 2,4, or 8bpp values to 16- or 25-bit values. The display buffer is organized as, a base plane and a set of overlays. Overlay represent display content which is superposed (or blended) on the base-plane. Overlays ease the software burden of sharing the display buffer between different system components while displaying multiple display objects simultaneously (e.g. an overlay is used to display camera image or the cursor on the screen where as the base plane displays the desktop).

LCD controllers typically have a set of DMA engines to read data from the display buffer for the base plane and overlays. Logic is provided to ensure overlay and the base planes are superposed in the desired fashion. The controller also has a set of FIFOs to manage the flow rate difference at the display interface and memory interface. Advanced integrated controllers also suport different color formats such as YUV, YCbCr (444, 422, 420) color formats, so that the controller works efficiently with both video playback and video preview from a CMOS or CCD image sensor. Since the display panels accept only RGB format, the controllers support color space conversion (YUV to RGB conversion based on the CCIR 601-2 standard). Display buffer for YCbCr can be organized as planner format (Y, Cb and Cr can occupy different memory regions) or packed (Y, Cb, Cr data values interleave). Also for effective combination of different display planes, dithering engine is introduced. LCD controllers also optionally support double buffering so that application can render next frame while the controller displays the current one. Figure 1 shows a block diagram of a typical LCD controller as used in the PXA27x processor.

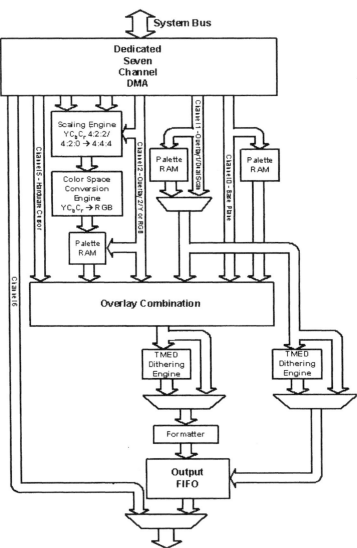

Figure 1. The architecture a LCD controller used in the PXA27x processor.

See: Multimedia System-on-a-Chip

LEGACY AND CURRENT PRACTICE – THE REALITY OF CONTEMPORARY COLLABORATIVE COMPUTING

Definition: Current practices in collaborative computing within government and industry are still conservative consisting of four main elements: video teleconferencing, audio conferencing, electronic mail, and shared directories.

Despite the wealth of research topics that comprise collaborative computing, current practices within government and industry can best be described as somewhat conservative. While many potential benefits of such an approach are known, the investment in existing infrastructure combined with the comfort of familiar practices offer challenges to those who hope to push the boundary of collaborative computing forward.

Many organizations have a limited scope in terms of what they consider collaborative computing. Specifically, organizational inertia often limits a broader deployment of collaborative computing, further burdened by policy, traditional operating procedures, fear of change and concern over ancillary and support costs. The result is that many organizations' collaborative computing environments consist of four elements:

- Video teleconferencing (VTC)
- Audio conferencing (conference call)
- Electronic mail (e-mail)
- Shared directories (file shares and network file systems)

This standard audio and video conferencing typically utilize dedicated equipment and facilities (e.g., specially-equipped meeting rooms) based primarily on ISDN (Integrated Services Digital Network) and PSTN (Public Switched Telephone Network). Such designs largely stem from significant legacy investment and interoperability requirements as well as the need to ensure quality and availability via circuit-switched technology. Unfortunately, these traditional VTC systems are typically "video" oriented, usually with an independent, self-contained control system and any support for data display/transfer being limited. Conversely, e-mail and shared directories facilitate collaboration though conventional IT means; thus they represent a trend towards personal computer-based collaboration and a desktop focus. Combined with the current movement towards convergence with conventional computer and network infrastructure, this approach is forcing a re-evaluation of the conventional ISDN/PSTN conferencing approach and a (slow) migration away from ISDN towards systems based on IP. Currently, many current VTC codecs provide support for both protocols (ISDN/IP) and indeed the use of IP telephony, including IP-based handsets is increasing.

As part of the increasing collaborative desktop focus, use of Web-based collaboration is proliferating. Browsing now often forms the interface for a large number of organizations' information and knowledge management systems. Other current practices include the use of portal technology (both open source and commercial systems), on-line meeting facilitation (both as externally-provided "pay-as-you-go" and dedicated services), as well as content management and configuration management systems. On-line meeting systems are typically accessed through portals and offer a number of popular business-oriented collaborative services such as agenda management, distributed presentations, workflow support, task management, calendaring, voting/polling, desktop sharing and the like. Example systems include MeetingZone and LiveMeeting (based on NetMeeting). Such functionality is often tied to content management systems which are used to provide increased knowledge management services (such as meta-tagging, categorization and classification services) to information traditionally communicated through email and/or shared file systems. Similarly, collaborative and distributed software development often makes the use of configuration management systems (including source control systems). While often treated as a given, the importance of "trivial" features such as version control and baselining cannot be underestimated in any collaborative effort.

While groupware has typically been regarded as the essence of collaborative computing, it is necessary to realize that despite the increased web-based collaborative focus, a sole spotlight on groupware is not a realistic view of collaborative computing – especially in the current business climate. In particular, two areas that can have a significant impact on the acceptance of collaborative computing need to be considered throughout the research, architecting, design, development, selection, deployment and management phases of collaborating computing systems. These are: (1) security and (2) source.

In terms of security, issues range from system and network architectures to software and data management. For example, the current preference for many organizations is to use "thin" vs. "thick" clients in order to lessen management and security concerns surrounding software installation and upgrades. Similarly, the use of the "service" industry to provide remotely hosted collaborative functionality (e.g., data storage, on-line meeting and user presence/awareness servers) are not readily accepted by many organizations. Additionally, the provision of network security often requires far more than firewall and anti-virus solutions; encryption is often hardware-based, and in some cases, a complete physical separation of systems may be required. The idyllic "one big network" often euphemized in collaborative computing and multimedia research can be a major issue in government arenas. Therefore, realizing a "network service" can sometimes prove difficult simply due to the need to demarcate where functionality resides in terms of organizational control and responsibility. This is further complicated by the notion of mobile and ad hoc functionality that moves around the network (e.g., downloadable "applets" that cannot be validated to the organization's satisfaction). While such issues may seem annoying to many, they play a pivotal role in the potential acceptance and growth of collaborative computing in many domains.

The second issue of "source" refers to the contemporary aversion to custom system (software and hardware) solutions. Most large organizations today are (economically) risk-adverse and rely on the "comfort and safety "of using known technologies, benefiting from recognized reliability and user familiarity (with user interfaces, terminology, workflow, etc). Thus the use of the traditional approach to groupware and collaborative computing (via custom shared, multi-user applications) is not generally accepted. Organizations typically wish to use COTS (Commercial Off-The-Shelf) products from well-known, reliable vendors that are shared via desktop sharing (when and as required). While not necessarily the best method to achieve the ultimate in collaboration, it is a reality with a large number of businesses and government agencies. Typically only select institutions, such as pure research organizations, may be willing to utilize speculative and research-level collaborative approaches in their "business practices". While a broader spectrum of organizations are increasingly using collaborative technologies and practices, such as chat/instant messaging and even blogging, such diversity is still typically a microcosm of progressive collaborative computing that serves as a motivational example for others to follow.

See: Collaborative Computing – Area Overview

LONG DURATION CONTINUOUS MEDIA RETRIEVAL

Definition: Pool of servers can be used to retrieve very long duration movies.

A central issue in the design networked/distributed multimedia services or DMMS is in addressing how to *retrieve* and *transmit* compressed-format videos (e.g., movies) from the server sites to the clients using the underlying network without under-utilizing the resources (e.g., storage of disk and memory, bandwidth of disk and network, etc.). Single-server systems fail obviously with an increase in the user access rates and also the network bandwidth becomes a natural bottleneck, especially for a DMMS type. A decentralized (or distributed) approach would rather handle this increased access rates more elegantly, a typical of a requirement on Internet like networks. As opposed to the idea of employing a single server, multiple servers can be employed for retrieval. This strategy is referred to as Multiple Server Retrieval Strategy (MSRS) [1,2]. In MSRS, several servers retrieve disjoint portions of a movie (taking into account the server and link bandwidths) in a particular sequence to form one complete continuous stream for the user. This novel idea of employing a pool of servers to retrieve is more meaningful for very long duration movies (110 to 140 minutes).

Some inherent advantages of MSRS: on a DMMS environment, if a single server system, however sophisticated it may be (in terms of speed and capacity) is used there is a continuous "work pressure" that is enforced on the system. For instance, when there is a continuous demand for a long duration video retrieval by several clients, more than 80% of the time is spent in servicing these requests, while some small number of requests demanding short services may undergo long waiting times. By employing MSRS, the work pressure can be balanced among the servers. Secondly, even low-bandwidth servers, that may not be efficient to utilize, can now be a part of several servers in retrieving the movie. Thirdly, considering fault-tolerance aspects, even under server/link failures, the workload imbalance can be gracefully accounted by the remaining servers. Also, failure of one or more servers, will allow the service to continue without any interruption so long as there is at least one server to cater. In fact, with a clever design of a retrieval strategy, the clients will continue to view the presentation while certain number of servers may "die" and come back to "life" after some time. Also, as shown in some feasible studies [2], scalability and heterogeneity of the system can be easily accounted in the design. Fourthly, the service providers can use a mix of heterogeneous servers to offer this service, as server bandwidths are inherently considered in servicing a request. Finally, from SP's perspective, since each server, on the whole, is engaged only for a short while in retrieving a portion of the media document, the number of clients that can be entertained simultaneously can be maximized. Thus MSRS offers a clear win-win situation for both the customers and the service providers.

See: Distributed Multimedia Systems: Issues and Challenges.

References

1. J. Y. B. Lee, "On a Unified Architecture for Video-on-Demand Services," IEEE Transactions on Multimedia, Vol. 4, No. 1, March 2002, pp. 38-47.
2. D. Ligang, V. Bharadwaj, and C.C. Ko, "Efficient Movie Retrieval Strategies for Movie-On-Demand Multimedia Services on Distributed Networks," Multimedia Tools and Applications, Kluwer Academic, Vol. 20, No. 2, 2003, pp. 99-133.

MEDICAL IMAGE SEGMENTATION

Definition: *Medical image segmentation refers to the segmentation of known anatomic structures from medical images.*

Structures of interest include organs or parts thereof, such as cardiac ventricles or kidneys, abnormalities such as tumors and cysts, as well as other structures such as bones, vessels, brain structures etc. The overall objective of such methods is referred to as computer-aided diagnosis; in other words, they are used for assisting doctors in evaluating medical imagery or in recognizing abnormal findings in a medical image.

In contrast to generic segmentation methods, methods used for medical image segmentation are often application-specific; as such, they can make use of prior knowledge for the particular objects of interest and other expected or possible structures in the image. This has led to the development of a wide range of segmentation methods addressing specific problems in medical applications.

Some methods proposed in the literature are extensions of methods originally proposed for generic image segmentation. In [1], a modification of the watershed transform is proposed for knee cartilage and gray matter/white matter segmentation in magnetic resonance images (MRI). This introduces prior information in the watershed method via the use of a previous probability calculation for the classes present in the image and via the combination of the watershed transform with atlas registration for the automatic generation of markers.

Other methods are more application specific; for example in [2], segmentation tools are developed for use in the study of the function of the brain, i.e. for the classification of brain areas as activating, deactivating, or not activating, using functional magnetic resonance imaging (FMRI) data. The method of [2] performs segmentation based on intensity histogram information, augmented with adaptive spatial regularization using Markov random fields. The latter contributes to improved segmentation as compared to non-spatial mixture models, while not requiring the heuristic fine-tuning that is necessary for non-adaptive spatial regularization previously proposed.

Another important application of segmentation tools is in the study of the function of the heart. In [3], a contour detection algorithm based on a radial edge-detection filter is developed for cardiac echographic images. Objective of this algorithm is to define a region of interest in which measurements (e.g. image intensity) can lead, after appropriate interpretation, to the estimation of important cardiovascular parameters without the need for invasive techniques.

In addition to the aforementioned techniques, numerous other algorithms for applications of segmentation to specialized medical imagery interpretation exist.

See: Segmentation of images and video

References

1. V. Grau, A.U.J. Mewes, M. Alcaniz, R. Kikinis, and S.K. Warfield, "Improved watershed transform for medical image segmentation using prior information," IEEE Transactions on Medical Imaging, Vol. 23, No. 4, April 2004, pp. 447-458.
2. M.W. Woolrich, T.E.J. Behrens, C.F. Beckmann, and S.M. Smith, "Mixture models with adaptive spatial regularization for segmentation with an application to FMRI data," IEEE Transactions on Medical Imaging, Vol. 24, No. 1, January 2005, pp. 1-11.
3. M. Mischi, A.A.C.M. Kalker, and H.H.M. Korsten, "Cardiac image segmentation for contrast agent video densitometry," IEEE Transactions on Biomedical Engineering, Vol. 52, No. 2, February 2005, pp. 277-286.

MESH, 3D

Definition: *Mesh is a 3D object representation consisting of a collection of vertices and polygons.*

The 3D object representation can be a polygon mesh, which consists of a collection of vertices and polygons that define the shape of an object in 3D (Figure 1). To benefit from current 3D graphic cards hardware acceleration polygon meshes usually contain only triangles because the hardware is optimized for triangle mesh computation.

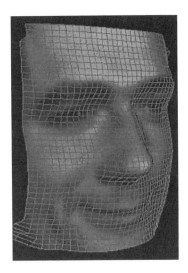

Figure 1. Polygon mesh corresponding to a human face.

Polygon meshes, as a 3D surface representation with 3D points and connectivity, have initially been considered for compression in a static way. The contributions were focused on compression of vertex positions and connectivity. Static mesh coding, exploiting spatial dependencies of adjacent polygons, is also currently part of MPEG-4. The MPEG-4 computer graphics part AFX (Animation Framework eXtension) offers a tool called AFX Interpolator Compression which allows the compression of such a linear keyframe animation.

Animated sequences of 3D objects stem from a number of different applications, starting with pure virtual Computer Graphics objects that deform over time. One of the newer application fields includes mixed-reality object reconstruction, where natural images are captured to reconstruct 3D objects with natural appearance for virtual environments. Those objects are referred to as "3D video objects" or 3DVOs, a term that describes a new representation format for visual media. It allows free navigation around real world dynamic objects by choosing arbitrary viewpoints and viewing directions similar to navigation in virtual-reality environments. 3DVOs are an extension of classical computer graphic objects towards representing motion and appearance of real world moving objects. Similar to animated synthetic objects, there is a 3D geometry, which changes over time. Animation however refers to a 3D geometry that applies a deformation while representing the same object with constant topology. 3DVOs require a more general approach of change over time, as there is not only geometry deformation, but also topology changes. Even new scene content, analogue to scene cuts in 2D films may appear. A coding scheme must therefore consider these general requirements. This can be achieved by coding dynamic meshes as separated groups of meshes (GOMs) with constant connectivity over a certain period of time within each GOM. In this case conventional static mesh coding (e.g. MPEG-4 3DMC) can be used for the Intra-Mesh (I-Mesh) coding and a predictive coding scheme can be applied for the positions of the vertices for all following P-Meshes of each GOM.

See: Coding of stereoscopic and 3D images and video

References

1. J. Rossignac, "Edgebreaker: Connectivity Compression for Triangle Meshes," IEEE Transactions on Visualization and Computer Graphics, Vol. 5, No. 1, pp. 47-61, 1999.

MESSAGE DIGEST (MD5) ALGORITHM AND SECURE HASH ALGORITHM (SHA)

Definition: Message Digest and Secure Cash are the standard algorithms to provide data security for multimedia authentication.

The MD5 algorithm takes as input a message of arbitrary length and produces as output a 128-bit "fingerprint" or "message digest" of the input message [1]. MD5 is currently a standard, Internet Engineering Task Force (IETF) Request for Comments (RFC) 1321. In comparison, MD5 is not quite as fast as the MD4 algorithm, but offers much more assurance of data security.

SHA is considered to be the successor to MD5. The Federal Information Processing Standard (FIPS 180-2) specifies four secure hash algorithms (SHA) – SHA-1, SHA-256, SHA-384, and SHA-512 [2]. As shown in Table 1, all four of the algorithms are iterative, one-way hash functions that can process a message with a maximum length of 2^{64}- to 2^{128}-bits to produce a 160- to 512-bit condensed representation called a *message digest*. The input message is processed in 512- to 1024-bit blocks. The four algorithms differ most significantly in the number of bits of security that are provided for the data being hashed – this is directly related to the message digest length. Different message will, with a very high probability, result in a different message digest.

Table 1. SHA properties [2]

Algorithm	Maximum message size (bits)	Block size (bits)	Message digest size (bits)
SHA-1	2^{64}	512	160
SHA-256	2^{64}	512	256
SHA-384	2^{128}	1024	384
SHA-512	2^{128}	1024	512

Each SHA algorithm processes a message in two stages: preprocessing and hash computation. Preprocessing involves padding a message, parsing the padded message into 512- or 1024-bit blocks, and setting initialization values to be used in the hash computation. The hash computation generates a *message schedule* from the padded message and uses that schedule, along with functions, constants, and word operations to iteratively generate a series of hash values. The final hash value generated by the hash computation is used to determine the message digest [2].

Due to the fact that SHA produces larger message digest size than MD5, SHA is considered more secure than MD5.

See: Multimedia Authentication

References

1. R.L. Rivest, "RFC 1321: The MD5 Message-Digest Algorithm," Internet Activities Board, 1992.
2. National Institute of Standards and Technology, "Specifications for Digital Signature Standard," Technical Report NIST FIPS PUB 180-2, Department of Commerce, August 2002.

MIDDLEWARE FOR STREAMING 3D MESHES

Hui Li and Balakrishnan Prabhakaran
University of Texas at Dallas, TX, USA

Definition: *A 3D middleware between a 3D application layer and the transport layer provides reliable and efficient multimedia streaming.*

Introduction

3D meshes have been widely used in multimedia applications such as 3D video gaming, virtual reality and animation databases. Due to the large data size of 3D meshes, the end user typically experiences long delay waiting for a 3D model to download from networks. For example, it requires 168s to download 42 MB "Happy Buddha" model (Large geometric models archive at Georgia Institute of Technology) over a channel offering an average bandwidth of 2 Mbps. To alleviate this limitation, it is desirable to compress 3D meshes first, and then transmit the compressed data over networks. Single-resolution techniques [1][2][3][4] are not suitable for the network transmission since the global view of the model cannot be rendered until the entire model is downloaded. Progressive compression techniques [5][6][7][8][9][10] address this issue by sending a base mesh first, and following it with a sequence of refinements when needed. The decoded model quality is improved progressively by adding these refinements. There are two categories of information in a refinement: structural data and geometric data. The structural data contains the connectivity information of the removed/added vertices to their neighbors. To improve the encoding efficiency, instead of the absolute position of a new vertex, an estimation scheme is applied to predict the position of the new vertex based on its existing neighbors. The geometric data contains the difference in geometric coordinates between the absolute and the estimated vertex positions.

Progressive compression techniques are scalable with respect to both network bandwidth and user's quality requirement. If the channel has a high bandwidth or the user requires a high quality model, more refinements can be transmitted. However, loss of packets during transmission affects the decoded mesh quality in the progressive representation. To meet this gap, error-control schemes must be applied.

Error-control schemes can be broadly divided into three categories: sender-based, network-based and receiver-based. For sender-based error-control methods such as FEC [11][12], the sender estimates the channel condition (loss ratio) and inserts redundant bits to protect the 3D data. Unfortunately, these methods have to generate different codes for different channel conditions. For receiver-based error-concealment schemes such as [13], the receiver can reconstruct the meshes if some of the 3D data is lost during the transmission. The drawback for this method is that the reconstructed mesh cannot guarantee the same mesh connectivity and thus it is only an approximation of the original mesh. In network-based error-control methods, reliable transport protocols such as TCP are used. However, TCP is not real-time streaming friendly due to its retransmission and congestion control mechanisms. On the other hand, RTP (real-time transport protocol)/UDP are streaming friendly but are not reliable. Therefore, hybrid protocols have been proposed [14][15][16] to take advantages of both TCP/UDP. In these hybrid protocols, the more important 3D data is transmitted over reliable channel and the less important data is transmitted over unreliable channel. However, following issues are not explained in these protocols. 1) How to handle multiple progressively compressed 3D representations such as PM, CPM, PFS and VD. 2) How to identify the relative importance of a given 3D data stream irrespective of its format so that the more important data can be delivered first and reliably. 3) How to consider user's environment. For example, if the end user device is PDA, it is not necessary to transmit the entire mesh that exceeds PDA's display capability. 4) How to select the transport channel for the 3D data so that the delay and distortion experienced at the user can be minimized simultaneously. 5) How to construct packets for transmission so that out of sequence packets can be detected and delivered to the 3D applications.

3D Middleware

We propose a generic 3D middleware between the 3D application layer and the transport layer. First, by observing the fact that the structural data affects the quality of the decoded mesh more than the geometric data does, without any changes to the encoder/decoder, we identify and separate the structural data from the geometric data for a given 3D data stream irrespective of its format. Then the geometric data is further decomposed into sub-layers based on the significant bit, and the distortion of the rendered 3D mesh due to the loss of a sub-layer is calculated. Next, a subset of the 3D data stream is selected for the transmission based on the user's quality requirement. In order to maintain the same mesh connectivity, the base mesh and the selected structural sub-layers are transmitted over reliable channel. For geometric sub-layers, we choose reliable/unreliable channel for the transmission depending on the relative importance to minimize the delay and distortion simultaneously. Finally, we handle packet loss and out of sequence packets by inserting additional fields into packets and synchronize the reliable and unreliable channels by sending an "END" marker on the reliable channel to indicate the end of a refinement. Our simulation results show that the proposed scheme can effectively reduce the delay and distortion experienced at the receiver. Figure 1 depicts the architecture of the proposed middleware.

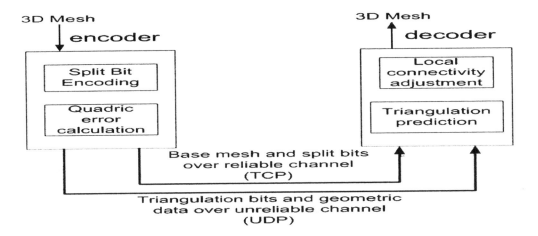

Figure 1. Middleware framework.

The proposed middleware consists of the following four modules:

(1) Pre-processor. We proposed a generic pre-processor that works for multiple progressive compression techniques (CPM, PFS and VD). In the pre-processor, we separate the structural and geometric data, decompose the geometric data into sub-layers and then, calculate a distortion metric. The distortion metric represents the importance of a sub-layer to the quality of the decoded mesh. Then, the geometric data is decomposed into different sub-layers and a distortion metric is calculated for each sub-layer. After pre-processing, the 3D data is stored as structural and geometric sub-layers along with their distortion metrics. Note that the pre-processing needs to be performed only once offline for a given 3D data stream.

(2) Minimum set selector. We represent user's environment diversity by user's display resolution and rendering capabilities. These parameters are converted into the number of triangles required by the client and communicated to the server. The minimum set selector selects the data set with the minimum size for transmission to satisfy user's quality requirement. This is a 0/1 knapsack problem and NP-complete. We propose a greedy heuristic algorithm to solve this problem. The generated subset is passed to the reliable set selector.

(3) Reliable set selector. In order to utilize the underlying reliable/unreliable channels efficiently, we select the data set to be transmitted over reliable channel based on the bandwidth and loss ratio. To evaluate the delay and distortion, we assume that the server can monitor the network conditions such as the reliable/unreliable channel bandwidth (Br, Bur) [17][18][19]. First, to guarantee the same connectivity of the decoded mesh as the original mesh, we transmit the base mesh and all the structural sub-layers over reliable channel. Therefore, approximately one third of the data stream is transmitted over reliable channel. Next, we consider the transmission for the geometric data. Since the loss of the geometric data only affects the quality of the decoded mesh and will not make it crash, we can use unreliable channel for transmission. We define a cost function that computes the total effect of the delay and distortion for a given bandwidth, loss ratio and geometric sub-layers. We generate the delivery list with the minimum cost function and pass it to the packet constructor. In addition, it is necessary to consider the dynamics of the network. If Br, Bur or l changes, the reliable set selector calculates a new delivery list. If the number of the geometric sub-layers between the new delivery list and the old delivery list is greater than the given threshold, the reliable set selector sends a revised set of sub-layers to the packet constructor.

(4) Packet constructor. Packet constructor at the server segments the sub-layers into packets and uses the specified transport channels for delivery so that the stream constructor at the receiver can reconstruct the compressed 3D data stream. In order for the receiver to detect out of order packets and lost packets over unreliable channel, additional information must be added to each packet. Three fields are inserted into each packet by the packet constructor: refinement index, sub-layer index and vertex index. Vertex index is the number of vertices that have been transmitted. The stream constructor uses these three fields to uniquely position a

received packet and detect out of order packets. Since we use reliable channel and unreliable channel alternatively, the stream constructor has to know the end of the transmission of a refinement, and then it can construct the 3D compressed data stream and deliver it to the decoder. Therefore, synchronization between reliable channel and unreliable channel is necessary. Here, we propose to use an "END" marker for each refinement to indicate that the transmission for the refinement is complete and ready to be assembled and delivered. For each refinement, we transmit the data over unreliable channel first, and followed by the data over reliable channel. When the transmission over reliable channel is complete for a refinement, an "END" marker is sent over reliable channel. Upon receiving the "END" marker, the stream constructor begins assembling the received data and then delivers it to the decoder. Once a refinement is delivered to the decoder, the stream constructor discards all the delayed packets that belong to this delivered refinement.

Results

Effectiveness of minimum set selector

To show the effectiveness of the minimum set selector, we compare the proposed selection process with a sequential selection process. The sequential selection process picks sub-layers sequentially in the ordinary order. Tables 1 and 2 show the comparison of the selected data size between the proposed selection and the sequential selection for "bunny" and "horse", respectively. Given a distortion requirement Dr, the data size generated by the proposed selection process is less than or equal to the one generated by the sequential selection scheme. For example, given Dr=10 for "bunny" model, if we choose sub-layers sequentially in the refinement order, the size of the selected data set is 1109 KB. With the proposed selection process, the size of the data set is reduced to 913 KB. The proposed selection process saves 18% of the data size to be transmitted. The reason is that some sub-layers selected by the sequential method do not have the relative importance as much as the ones selected by the proposed selection process.

Table 1. Comparison of the selected data size for
different selection schemes for "bunny" model

Dr	Sequential (KB)	Proposed (KB)	Save (%)
500	113	95	16
230	137	137	0
120	220	213	3
40	293	293	0
20	773	641	17
10	1109	913	18
0	2053	2053	0

Table 2. Comparison of the selected data size for different selection schemes for "horse" model

Dr	Sequential (KB)	Proposed (KB)	Save (%)
553	33	33	0
165	69	48	30
130	201	127	37
34	282	254	10
8	399	359	10
2	798	736	8
0	1091	1091	0

It should be noted that the proposed selection scheme is a "heuristic" algorithm; the generated data set may not be the optimal solution with the constraints. For example, from Table 1, for Dr = 40 and Dr = 230, the data set generated by the proposed selection process is the same as the one generated by the sequential scheme. Similarly, Table 1 shows the data size picked by the proposed selection scheme is less than or equal to the one picked by the sequential scheme.

Effectiveness of reliable set selector

The simulations are performed on wireless networks. Single-hop mode is used for the transmission from the server to the client. We use Qualnet, developed at Scalable Network Technologies, as the wireless network simulator. Wireless users are randomly distributed over a 350 × 350 area and node one is designated as the server. The physical bandwidth is 2 Mbps. We assume that the network drops packets randomly. For each simulation case, we ran 100 times and took the average distortion as the expected distortion.

To show the effectiveness of the proposed reliable set selection scheme ("Proposed"), the performance of following three schemes are compared.

(1) "Reliable all". The base mesh and all the selected sub-layers are transmitted with reliable channel.
(2) "Hybrid". It transmits the base mesh, the selected structural sub-layers with reliable channel and the selected geometric sub-layers with unreliable channel.
(3) "Optimized". The proposed method presented in "Reliable Set Selector".

Figures 2 and 3 show the delay-distortion curves for the above three methods with different loss ratios. We chose to transmit the entire mesh. "Hybrid" has the worst performance. The reason is that the distortion of the geometric sub-layers in the coarse refinements is relatively large. If we transmit such sub-layers over unreliable channel, the users will experience large distortion. As loss ratio decreases, this distortion can be reduced. This indicates that such geometric sub-layers should be transmitted over reliable channel

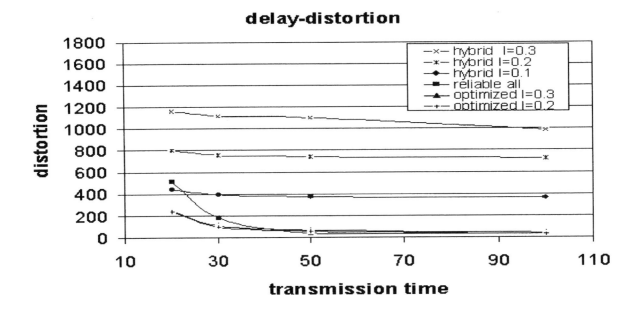

Figure 2. Transmission time-distortion for "bunny" with different scheduling schemes under different loss ratios.

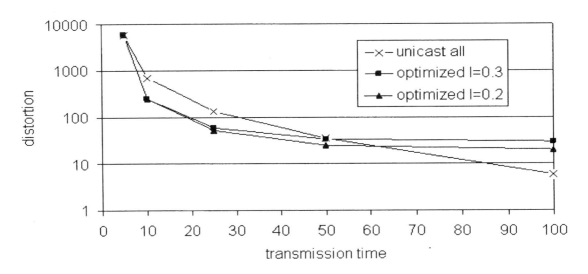

Figure 3. Transmission time-distortion for "horse" with different scheduling schemes under different loss ratios.

"Reliable all" performs better than "Hybrid" but worse than "Optimized" in the range from 0-50s. The reason is that the proposed method uses reliable channel to transmit the geometric sub-layers with large relative importance value to reduce the distortion at the user and the same time, it uses unreliable channel to transmit the geometric sub-layers with small relative importance value to reduce the delay. Moreover, with unreliable channel, the server can transmit more sub-layers than "Reliable all" given the same time frame. Therefore, with the proposed reliable set selector, the 3D compressed data stream can be delivered in such way that both small distortion and low delay can be achieved. Because our scheme obtains both the minimum delay and distortion, if the user prefers distortion to delay, one needs to trade delay for it.

See: Compressed progressive meshes, Progressive forest split and Valence-driven conquest.

References

1. M. Deering, "Geometry compression," Proceedings of the SIGGRAPH 95, 1995, pp. 13–20.
2. J. Rossignac, "Edgebreaker: Connectivity compression for triangle meshes," IEEE Transactions on Visualization and Computer Graphics, 1999, pp. 47–61.
3. G. Taubin and J. Rossignac, "Geometric compression through topological surgery," ACM Transactions on Graphics, 1998, pp. 84–115.
4. M. Isenburg and S. Gumhold, "Out-of-core compression for gigantic polygon meshes," Proceedings of SIGGGRAPH 03, 2003, pp. 935–942.
5. H. Hoppe, "Progressive meshes" Proceedings of SIGGRAPH 96, 1996, pp. 99–108.
6. H. Hoppe, "Efficient implementation of progressive meshes," Technical Report, MSR-TR 98-02, Microsoft, January 1998.
7. G. Taubin, A. Gueziec, W. Horn, and F. Lazarus, "Progressive forest split compression," Proceedings of SIGGRAPH 98, 1998, pp. 123–132.
8. R. Pajarola and J. Rossignac, "Compressed progressive meshes," IEEE Transactions on Visualization and Computer Graphics Vol. 6, 2000, pp. 79–93.
9. P. Alliez and M. Desbrun, "Progressive compression for lossless transmission of triangle Meshes," Proceedings of SIGGRAPH 01, 2001.
10. S. Valette and R. Prost, "A wavelet-based progressive compression scheme for triangle meshes: wavemesh," IEEE Transactions on Visualization and Computer Graphics, Vol. 10, 2004.
11. G. Al-Regib and Y. Altunbasak, "An unequal error protection method for packet loss resilient 3D mesh transmission," Proceeding of INFOCOM, 2002.
12. G. Al-Regib, Y. Altunbasak, and J. Rossignac, "A joint source and channel coding approach for progressively compressed 3D mesh transmission," Proceedings of the International Conference on Image Processing, 2002.
13. S. Bischoff and L. Kobbelt, "Towards robust broadcasting of geometric data," Computers and Graphics, 2002, Vol. 26, pp. 665–675.
14. Z. Chen, B. Bodenheimer, and J. Barnes, "Robust transmission of 3D geometry over lossy Networks," Proceeding of the 8th International Conference on 3D Web Technology, 2003, pp.161–172.
15. G. Al-Regib and Y. Altunbasak, "3TP: An application-layer protocol for streaming 3D Graphics," Proceedings of IEEE International Conference on Multimedia and Expo, 2003.
16. G. Al-Regib, and Y. Altunbasak, "3D models transport protocol," Proceedings of the 9th International Conference on 3D Web Technology, 2004.
17. S. Mark, J. Padhye, and J. Widmer, "Equation-based congestion control for unicast applications," Proceedings of SIGCOMM 2000.

18. M. Kazantzidis, M. Gerla, and S. J. Lee, "Permissible throughput network feedback for adaptive multimedia in AODV MANETs," Proceedings of IEEE International Conference on Communications (ICC01), 2001.

19. S.H. Shah, K. Chen, and K. Nahrstedt, "Dynamic bandwidth management for single-hop ad hoc wireless networks," Special Issue on Algorithmic Solutions for Wireless, Mobile, Ad Hoc and Sensor Networks, 2004.

MIME TYPES

Definition: Mime (Multi-purpose Internet Mail Extensions) is a simple standard prefix that is sent before a file is sent on the World Wide Web or as an e-mail attachment.

Essentially, a MIME type is a string consisting of two words: the first denotes the *general type* of the file that is about to be sent, the second denotes its *format*. A MIME type is specified in a single line, in the format:

```
<mime_type> ::= <type>/<format>:
<type>      ::= text | image | video | application | ...
<format>    ::= <string>
```

The number of general types is, more or less, fixed, if not by a mutually agreed standard, at least by a sort of a gentlemen's agreement deriving from practice. Whenever a web server sends a web page (in html format) to a web browser, for instance, what is actually sent on the internet is the text:

```
text/html:
<html>
  ...
</html>
```

Here the fragment *text/html:* is the *MIME type* of the data, and is followed by the data themselves, that is, by the html code. A JPEG image would be sent as:

```
image/jpeg:
[image data]
```

Note that, in general, the MIME specification is not interested about the nature of the data to be sent: the interpretation of the data is left to the client: the type simply serves the purpose of telling the client what the nature and the format of the data are. In the case of images, there is an additional complication, since the data are binary, and recent internet protocols (unlike older and more efficient ones such as ftp), do not allow sending binary files as they are, since many of the bytes with a value less than 32 (corresponding to the ASCII *control codes*) are interpreted and, possibly, transformed. To make an example, Unix systems use the character 0D (hexadecimal), the ASCII *carriage return* to mark the end of a line, while Windows system, inheriting from DOS, use the pair 0A 0D (*line feed* and *carriage return*) for the same purpose. Many Windows programs, upon observing a 0D in input convert it in a pair 0D 0A. Clearly, if the character 0D was part of a binary file, this will result in an incorrect interpretation of the file. To ovviate to this problem, binary mime types are in general encoded so that only "printable" ASCII characters, that is, only bytes with a code between 32 and 128, are used. In this way, a binary file can be sent as if it were a text message. This is done through a method originally devised for unix systems and generally called, after the program that originally did the encoding, *uuencode*. The idea is to take a group of 3 binary bytes, divide them into four groups of six bytes each, and add a binary "01" in front of each one of them in order to obtain a printable ASCII character. Consider, for instance, the following encoding:

```
      byte 1      byte 2    byte 3
     00000101  01001100  10010011

              groups of 6 bit
    000001    010100      110010      010011

              "augmented" codes

  01000001    01010100  01110010  01010011
     A           T          r          S
```

so, the three bytes are transformed into the string "AtrS", which can be transmitted as a text message. The disadvantage if this encoding is evident: three bytes are encoded using four characters, so the length of the data file to be transmitted is increased by about 35%.

See: Multimedia File Sharing

MOTION COMPENSATION FOR VIDEO COMPRESSION

J. Feng
City University of Hong Kong, Hong Kong

K.T. Lo
The Hong Kong Polytechnic University, Hong Kong

Definition: *Motion compensation has been used widely in video compression, because of its abilities to exploit high temporal correlation between successive frames of an image sequence.*

Video compression [1]-[4] plays an important role in modern multimedia applications. Inside digitized video, there is a considerable amount of redundancy and compression

---

can be achieved by exploiting such redundancies. The redundancy of video data is generally divided into two classes: statistical redundancy and subjective redundancy. For statistical redundancy, it can be derived from the highly correlated video information both spatially and temporally. For example, adjacent picture elements of a television picture are almost alike and successive pictures often have small changes. Thus the differences among these similar elements are small, and hence the average bit-rate of video data can be saved by sending the differences of these similar elements instead of the individual element. On the other hand, video contains information that is not visually obvious to the human eye, and thus it can be removed without noticeable degradation on the picture quality. This kind of information is known as subjective redundancy. Further bit-rate reduction of video data can be achieved by throwing away this subjectively redundant information. For example, humans are less sensitive to the image details of a moving object so it can be reproduced with coarser image resolution than a static object inside a picture.

The aim of video compression is to remove redundancies in both spatial and temporal domains. As illustrated in Figure 1, video compression is normally a two-stage process. Interframe coding techniques are used to reduce the temporary redundancies between successive frames of a video sequence while intraframe coding techniques are used to reduce the spatial redundancies within the difference frame obtained by interframe coding.

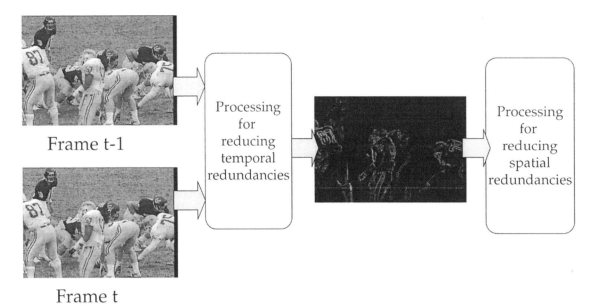

Figure 1. Two-stage video compression.

Motion compensation [5] has been used widely in video compression, because of its abilities to exploit high temporal correlation between successive frames of an image sequence. Motion compensation mainly consists of two parts: motion estimation [6] and prediction error coding. As shown in Figure 2, the displacement of objects between successive frames is first estimated (motion estimation). The resulting motion information is then exploited in efficient interframe predictive coding (motion compensation). Both the motion information and prediction error are required to encode and transmit to the decoder, where the prediction error is the difference between the current frame and the motion-predicted frame.

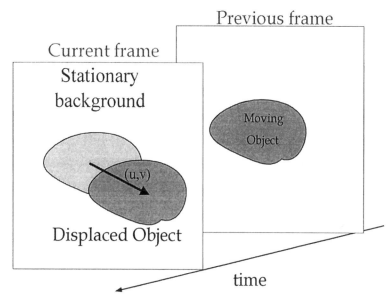

Figure 2. Motion compensated predicted coding.

Motion compensated predictive techniques have been explored by many researchers over the past twenty years. One of the solutions is partitioning images into regular non-overlapped blocks and assuming that the moving objects can be approximated reasonably well by these regular blocks. Then a single displacement vector is determined to represent the movement of the entire image block, as illustrated in Figure 3.

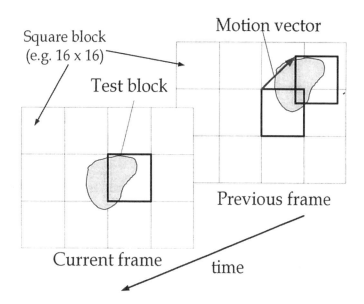

Figure 3. Block based motion compensation.

With both the displacement vector and prediction error, the current video frame can be reconstructed from the reference video frames in the past. This block-based motion compensation method is widely adopted in current video compression systems including MPEG and H.26x.

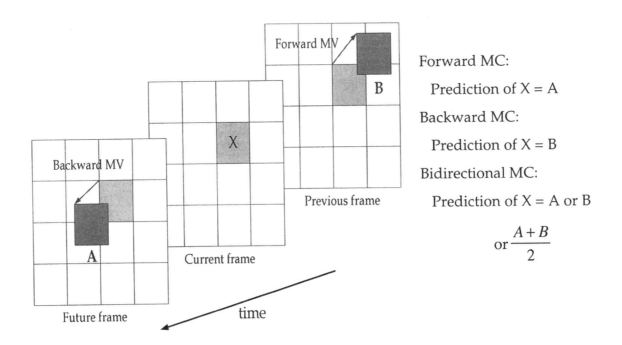

Figure 4. Types of motion compensation.

Depending on the choice of reference frame(s), three types of motion compensation (MC) are defined: forward MC, backward MC and bidirectional MC. As illustrated in Figure 4, forward MC will use the previous frame as the reference frame, hence the prediction for block X is block A and the resultant motion vector (MV) is called forward MV. On the contrast, backward MC uses the future frame as reference.

The resultant motion vector is called backward MV. In the example, block B will be used as the prediction for X. Bidirectional MC uses both the previous and the future frame as references. In this case, there are three candidates for the prediction of X: A, B and the interpolated block by A and B. Two motion vectors, forward MV and backward MV, are required to transmit to the decoder if the interpolated block is selected.

Figure 5 shows the effects of forward MC on a particular video sequence. It is seen that the amplitude of the prediction error is greatly reduced when applying MC for interframe prediction.

(a) Original frame

(b) Prediction error without MC

(c) Motion vector of the frame

(d) Prediction error with MC

Figure 5. Effects of motion compensation on prediction error.

Motion Compensated Discrete Cosine Transform (DCT) Video Coder

Figure 6 shows the block diagram of a typical motion compensated DCT video codec that is currently adopted in various video coding standards like MPEG and H.26x [7]-[12]. In such a coder, motion compensated predictive coding is used for interframe coding to remove the redundancies between successive video frames. The DCT based intraframe coder is then used to exploit the spatial redundancies exists between pixels of the prediction error or the video frame.

Block Matching Motion Estimation

The block matching algorithm is a relatively simple and effective motion vector estimation technique. It assumes that all the pixels within the block have a uniform motion. The process of block matching is to find a candidate block, within a search area in the previous frame, which is most similar to the current block in the present frame.

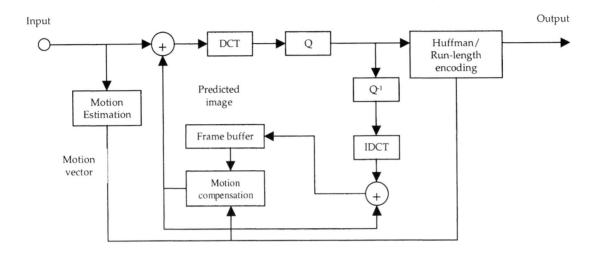

a)   Video encoder

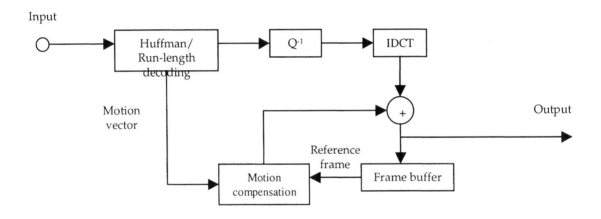

b) Video decoder

Figure 6. Motion compensated DCT video codec.

The full search block matching (FSBM) algorithm exhaustively examines all locations in the search area and provides an optimal solution. The FSBM algorithm is illustrated in Figure 6, in which the present frame of a video sequence is divided into rectangular or square blocks of pixels. For each block ($N{\times}N$) in the current frame, we look for the block of pixels in the previous frame that is the closest to it according to a predetermined criterion. The commonly used criterion is mean absolute difference (MAD). For the present frame n, we denote the intensity of the pixels with coordinates (i, j) by $F_n(i, j)$.

We refer to a block of *N×N* pixels by the coordinate (*k, l*) of its upper left corner. The MAD between the block (*k, l*) of the present frame and the block (*k+x, l+y*) of the previous frame can be written as

$$MAD_{(k,l)}(x,y) = \frac{1}{N*N}\sum_{i=0}^{N-1}\sum_{j=0}^{N-1}\left|F_n(k+i,\ l+j) - F_{n-1}(k+x+i,\ l+y+j)\right| \qquad (1)$$

The motion vector *v(k, l)* of the block (*k, l*) is given by

$$v(k,\ l) = \arg\min MAD_{(k,\ l)}(x,\ y) \qquad (2)$$

where the vectors (*k+x, l+y*) are valid block coordinates.

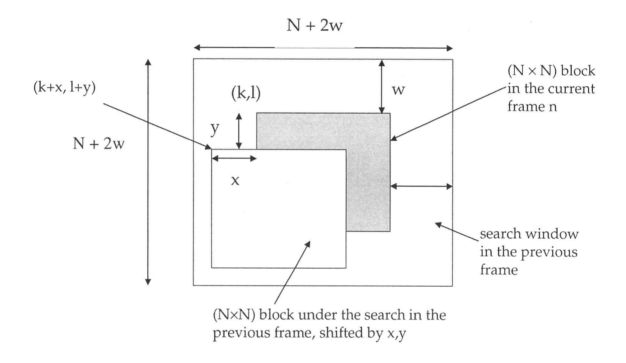

Figure 7. Full search block matching motion estimation algorithm.

The block in the previous frame must be within a search area of size (*N+2w × N+2w*), where w is the maximum displacement that an object can move between two adjacent frames. For each location in the previous frame to be tested, the calculation of the MAD requires ($2N^2-1$) additions. Therefore, the computational requirement for an FSBM algorithm is quite high and becomes one of the bottlenecks in implementing the video encoder. The heavy computational loading of FSBM hence motivates the development of various fast block matching algorithms.

Among different fast searching approaches, many researchers adopted the idea to limit the number of search locations so as to reduce the computations. These algorithms generally assume that the distortion function increases monotonically as the searched point moves away from the direction of the minimum distortion. Based on this assumption, some specific searching patterns are defined for the search to follow along with the decrease of the distortion function until the motion vector is found. Some famous fast search algorithms in this category include two-dimensional logarithmic search [13], three-step search (TSS) [14], cross search [15], new three-step search (NTSS) [16], four-step search (FSS) [17], block-based gradient descent search (BBGDS) [18], diamond search [19] [20] and hexagonal search [21] [22]. Among these fast block matching algorithms, the three-step search (TSS) algorithm is still commonly used in various video codec implementation because of its simplicity and effectiveness. Compared with other methods, TSS has a larger searching pattern in the first step, hence TSS is more efficient to find the globe minimum especially for those sequences with large motion.

Figure 8 shows an example of finding the motion vector using TSS for a maximum displacement of 7 (w=7). TSS is based on a coarse-to-fine approach with logarithmic decreasing in step size. The detailed steps of TSS are listed as follows.

First Step :

- The center point (x, y) and 8 search points in location (x ± w/2, y ± w/2) are tested.
- The location of the minimum point is denoted as $(x^{(1)}, y^{(1)})$.
- The step size is reduced by half.

Second Step:

- Use $(x^{(1)}, y^{(1)})$ as the center and 8 more points in location $(x^{(1)} \pm w/4, y^{(1)} \pm w/4)$ are tested.
- The location of the minimum point is denoted as $(x^{(2)}, y^{(2)})$.
- The step size is reduced by half.

Third Step:

- Use $(x^{(2)}, y^{(2)})$ as the center and 8 more points in location $(x^{(2)} \pm w/8, y^{(2)} \pm w/8)$ are tested.
- The test is completed when the step size becomes 1.

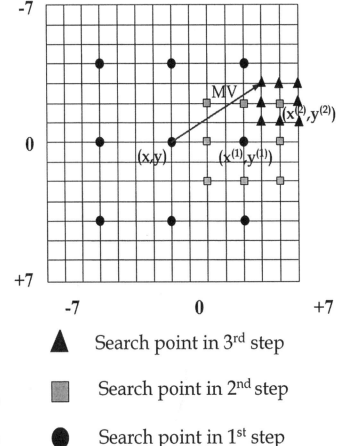

▲ Search point in 3rd step

■ Search point in 2nd step

● Search point in 1st step

Figure 8. Three Step Search (TSS).

The algorithms mentioned above can be easily trapped in the local minimum of the distortion function giving prediction with appreciably higher error than the full search method. Furthermore, the capability of adaptation to local characteristics of those algorithms is always poor since they use the same searching approach for all image blocks. This may limit the efficiency of the fast algorithm since image data are highly non-stationary. As a result, considerable research has been carried out to find alternative approaches [23]-[27] for block matching motion estimation.

See: Diamond Search for Block Motion Estimation, Motion Estimation with Half-Pixel Accuracy, Overlapped Block Motion Compensation

References

1. V. Bhaskaran and K. Konstantinides, "Image and video compression standards: algorithms and architectures," Kluwer Academic Publishers, 1995.
2. K.R. Rao and J.J. Kwang, "Techniques and Standards for Image, Video and Audio Coding," Prentice-Hall, 1996.
3. B. Vasuder, "Image and Video Compression Standard: Algorithms and Architectures," Kluwer Academic Publishers, 1997.
4. T. Ebrahimi and M. Kunt, "Visual data compression for multimedia applications," Proceedings of the IEEE, Vol. 86, No. 6, pp. 1109-1125, June 1998.
5. A. N. Netravali and J. P. Robbins, "Motion compensated television coding - part I," Bell System Technical Journal, Vol. 58, pp. 631-670, 1979.
6. F. Dufaux and F. Moscheini, "Motion estimation techniques for digital TV: a review and a new contribution," *Proceedings of the IEEE*, Vol.83, pp.858-876, 1995.
7. ISO/IEC, "Information Technology - Coding of moving pictures and associated audio for digital storage at up to about 1.5 Mbits/s - Part 2: Video," ISO/IEC 11172-2 (MPEG-1), 1993.
8. ISO/IEC and ITU-T, "Information Technology - Generic coding of moving pictures and associated audio information - Part 2: Video," ISO/IEC 13818-2 (MPEG-2) - ITU-T Recommendation H.262, 1996.
9. ISO/IEC, "Information Technology - Coding of audio-visual object – Part 2: Visual," ISO/IEC 14496-2 (MPEG-4), 1999.
10. ITU-T, "Video codec for audiovisual services at p x 64 kbit/s," *ITU-T Recommendation H.261*, 1993.
11. ITU-T, "Video coding for low bit rate communication," *ITU-T Recommendation H.263*, 1996.
12. T. Wiegand, G. J. Sullivan, G. Bjøntegaard, and A. Luthra, "Overview of the H.264/AVC video coding standard," *IEEE Transactions on Circuits and Systems for Video Technology*, Vol. 13, pp. 560–576, July 2003.
13. J.R. Jain and A.K. Jain, "Displacement measurement and its application in interframe image coding," *IEEE Transactions on Communications*, Vol. COM-29, pp. 1799-1808, December 1981.
14. T. Koga, K. Iinuma, A. Hirano, Y. Iijima, and T. Ishiguro, "Motion compensated interframe coding for video conferencing," *Proceedings of the NTC81*, pp. C.9.6.1-9.6.5, New Orleans, LA, Nov./Dec. 1981.
15. M. Ghanbari, "The cross search algorithm for motion estimation," *IEEE Transactions on Communications*, Vol. 38, pp.950-953, July 1990.

16. R. Li, B. Zeng, and M. Liou, "A new three-step search algorithm for block motion estimation," *IEEE Transactions on Circuits and Systems for Video Technology*, Vol. 4, No. 4, pp. 438-442, August 1994.

17. L. M. Po and W. C. Ma, "A novel four-step algorithm for fast block motion estimation," *IEEE Transactions on Circuits and Systems for Video Technology*, Vol. 6, No. 3, pp. 313-317, June 1996.

18. K.L. Liu and E. Feig, "A block-based gradient descent search algorithm for block motion estimation algorithms in video coding," *IEEE Transactions on Circuits and Systems for Video Technology*, Vol. 6, No. 4, pp. 419-422, August 1996.

19. J. Y. Tham, S. Ranganath, M. Ranganath, and A. A. Kassim, "A novel unrestricted center-biased diamond search algorithm for block motion estimation," *IEEE Transactions on Circuits and Systems for Video Technology*, Vol. 8, pp. 369–377, August 1998.

20. S. Zhu and K. K. Ma, "A new diamond search algorithm for fast block matching motion estimation," *IEEE Transactions on Image Processing*, Vol. 9, pp. 287–290, February 2000.

21. C. Zhu, X. Lin, and L. P. Chau, "Hexagon-based search pattern for fast block motion estimation," *IEEE Transactions on Circuits and Systems for Video Technology*, Vol. 12, pp. 349–355, May 2002.

22. C. Zhu, X. Lin, L. P. Chau, and L.M. Po, "Enhanced hexagonal search for fast block motion estimation," *IEEE Transactions on Circuits and Systems for Video Technology*, Vol. 14, No. 10, pp. 1210–1214, October 2004.

23. B. Liu and A. Zaccarin, "New fast algorithm for the estimation of block motion vectors," *IEEE Transactions on Circuits and Systems for Video Technology*, Vol. 3, pp. 148-157, April 1993.

24. L.C. Chang; K.L. Chung; T.C. Yang, "An improved search algorithm for motion estimation using adaptive search order," IEEE Signal Processing Letters, vol.8, no.5, pp.129-130, May 2001.

25. J.N. Kim, S.C. Byun, Y.H. Kim, and B.H. Ahn, "Fast full search motion estimation algorithm using early detection of impossible candidate vectors," IEEE Transactions on Signal Processing, Vol. 50, No. 9, pp. 2355 – 2365, September 2002.

26. K.R. Namuduri, "Motion estimation using spatio-temporal contextual information," *IEEE Transactions on Circuits and Systems for Video Technology*, Vol. 14, No. 8, pp. 1111-1115, August 2004.

27. C. Zhu, W.S. Qi, and W. Ser, "Predictive fine granularity successive elimination for fast optimal block-matching motion estimation," *IEEE Transactions on Image Processing*, Vol. 14, No. 2, pp. 213–221, February 2005.

MOTION ESTIMATION

Jauvane C. de Oliveira
National Laboratory for Scientific Computation, Petropolis, RJ, Brazil

Definition: *Motion estimation explores the temporal redundancy, which is inherent in video sequences, and it represents a basis for lossy video compression.*

Other than video compression, motion estimation can also be used as the basis for powerful video analysis and video processing.

Introduction

A standard movie, which is also known as *motion picture*, can be defined as a sequence of several scenes. A scene is then defined as a sequence of several seconds of motion recorded without interruption. A scene usually has at least three seconds [2]. A movie in the cinema is shown as a sequence of still pictures, at a rate of 24 frames per second. Similarly, a TV broadcast consists of a transmission of 30 frames per second (NTSC, and some flavors of PAL, such as PAL-M), 25 frames per second (PAL, SECAM) or anything from 5 to 30 frames per second for typical videos in the Internet. The name *motion picture* comes from the fact that a video, once encoded, is nothing but a sequence of still pictures that are shown at a reasonably high frequency. That gives the viewer the illusion that it is in fact a continuous animation. Each frame is shown for one small fraction of a second, more precisely $1/k$ seconds, where k is the number of frames per second. Coming back to the definition of a scene, where the frames are captured without interruption, one can expect consecutive frames to be quite similar to one another, as very little time is allowed until the next frame is to be captured. With all this in mind we can finally conclude that each scene is composed of at least $3 \times k$ frames (since a scene is at least 3 seconds long). In the NTSC case, for example, that means that a movie is composed of a sequence of various segments (scenes) each of which has at least 90 frames similar to one another.

The Figure 1 shows a sequence of five consecutive frames in a 10fps-video stream of the standard "mother and daughter" reference video ([8] presents other reference videos). Changes from frame 1 to frame 2 is almost negligible; only changes in frames 3 through 5 are in fact noticeable due to the hand movement. Do notice, however, that while the hand of the mother moves, the rest of each frame is quite similar to its previous frame. Such similarity between neighbor frames is known as "temporal redundancy", while the similarity of pixels in a given frame (for instance those that render the wall in the frames in Figure 1) is known as "spatial redundancy". Motion estimation is a technique that is often used to exploit the temporal redundancy described above.

Figure 1. Consecutive frames of a typical videoconference-like video stream.

Before going further with details on motion estimation we need to describe briefly how a video sequence is organized. As mentioned earlier a video is composed of a number of pictures. Each picture is composed of a number of pixels or pels (picture elements). A video frame has its pixels grouped in 8×8 *blocks*. The blocks are then grouped in *macroblocks* (MB), which are composed of 4 luminance blocks each (plus equivalent chrominance blocks). Macroblocks are then organized in *"groups of blocks"* (GOBs) which are grouped in pictures (or in layers and then pictures). Pictures are further grouped in scenes, as described above, and we can consider scenes grouped as movies. Motion estimation is often performed in the macroblock domain. For simplicity' sake we'll refer to the macroblocks as blocks, but we shall remember that most often the macroblock domain is the one in use for motion estimation.

For motion estimation the idea is that one block *b* of a current frame *C* is sought for in a previous (or future) frame *R*. If a block of pixels which is similar enough to block *b* is found in *R*, then instead of transmitting the whole block just a "motion vector" is transmitted. The definition of "similar enough" here is detailed in section 3 below.

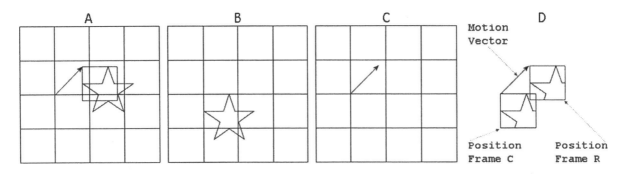

Figure 2. Reference Frame (A); Current Frame (B); Motion Vector for block [3,2] (C); & Motion Detected and Motion Vector for block [3,2] (D).

The Figure 2 shows a couple of neighbor frames (A and B), B being the currently encoded frame while A is a previous reference frame. The block that contains the top-left portion of the star if sought for in frame A can be found shifted as much as denoted by the arrow which represents the motion vector (C). All is summarized in D. So, instead of encoding the pixels of the current blocks of the frame B one can simply send the motion vector which would, in this example, suffice.

Ideally, a given macroblock would be sought for in the whole reference frame; however, due to the computational complexity of the motion estimation stage the search is usually limited to a pre-defined region around the macroblock. Most often such region includes 15 or 7 pixels to all four directions in a given reference frame. The search region is often denoted by the interval [*-p, p*] meaning that it includes *p* pixels in all directions. Figure 3 shows this concept.

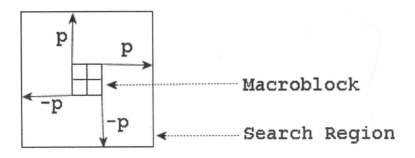

Figure 3. Motion Estimation Search Region

Two-Stage Video Compression Model

The video compression model is a two-stage procedure. The first procedure consists of taking advantage of the temporal redundancy followed by a procedure similar to that used for lossy image compression which aims at exploring the spatial redundancy. The Figure 4 shows the two stages in halves *A* and *B* using the last two consecutive frames from Figure 1. In the temporal redundancy exploitation stage (*A*) we have motion estimation of the current frame (**C**) using the reference frame (**R**). The first stage produces both a set of motion vectors (**i, j**) as well as difference macroblocks (**C-R**). The difference macroblocks then go through the second stage which exploits spatial redundancy. One may notice that the difference frame has usually very high spatial redundancy due to the fact that it only stores information of difference of motion estimated macroblocks as well as macroblocks where a good match is not found in the reference frame(s). The matching criteria are detailed in the next section.

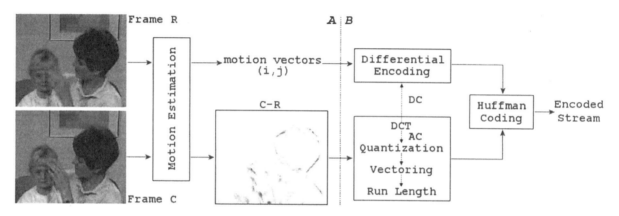

Figure 4. Two-Stage Model: Temporal Redundancy (*A*) and Spatial Redundancy (*B*) Exploitation.

We should notice that in Figure 4 the reference to *C-R* is a didactic reference to what in fact would be each macroblock of *C* minus the equivalent match block in *R*. It is also worth mentioning that in the image shown as *C-R* was applied the *negative* so that pixels whose difference is zero show up white rather than black, which would be tougher to visualize.

Matching Criteria

Let *x*, *y* denote the location of the current macroblock. The pixels of the current macroblock can then be denoted by $C(x+k, y+l)$ while the pixels in the reference frame can be denoted as $R(x+i, y+j)$. We can now define a cost function based on the Mean Absolute Error (MAE) or Mean Absolute Difference (MAD) [1] as:

$$MAE(i, j) = \frac{1}{MN} \sum_{k=0}^{M-1} \sum_{l=0}^{N-1} \left| C(x+k, y+l) - R(x+i+k, y+j+l) \right|, \text{ where } M, N \text{ denotes}$$

the size of the macroblock, $-p \leq i \leq p$ and $-p \leq j \leq p$, with $[-p,p]$ being the search region as described above. The matching block will be $R(x+i,y+j)$ for which $MAE(i,j)$ is minimized, henceforth i, j defines the motion vector.

It is important to notice that the MAE is not the only option for matching criteria, as one can use Mean Square Error and other expressions as well. MAE is, however, often selected due to its computational simplicity. It is also worth mentioning that when the minimum MAE has a value higher than a given threshold the block is said "not found". That means that the motion estimation failed and that block is to be encoded without exploiting temporal redundancy with regard to the R reference frame. We can observe this phenomena when there is a scene change or a new object is inserted in the scene between the reference frame and the current frame, or yet if motion goes beyond the search area $[-p,p]$.

Motion estimation doesn't have to be performed in a single reference frame. In some cases bi-directional motion estimation is performed. That means that other than looking for a macroblock in a previous reference frame R, the block is also sought for in a reference frame F in the future. That is very useful for the case where a new object is inserted into the scene, as it'll be found in a future reference frame F even tough not being present in a previous reference frame R. More generally, multiple frames in the past and future can be used by a motion estimator, but more often we either use a single frame in the past or one in the past and one in the future, as described herein.

Algorithms

The motion estimation is the most computational intensive procedure for standard video compression. To seek a match for a macroblock in a $[-p, p]$ search region leads to $(2p+1)^2$ search locations, each of which requires $M \times N$ pixels to be compared, where M, N give the size of the source macroblock. Considering F the number of reference frames being considered in the matching process, such procedure reaches a total of $(2p+1)^2 \times MN \times F$ executions of the Mean Absolute Error expression:

$$\left| C(x+k, y+l) - R(x+i+k, y+j+l) \right|,$$

which involves 3 operations per pixel. Considering a standard 16×16 macroblock with $p=15$ and $F=1$ in a VGA-sized video stream (640×480 pixels) we have 40×30 = 1200 macroblocks per frame. That leads to a grand total of 778.41M operations for a single frame. In a 30-fps video stream that would entail 23.3523G operations per second for motion estimation alone. If bi-directional motion estimation is in place we'd reach 46.7046G operations per second (Remember that we still have to perform the spatial redundancy exploitation stage which includes a number of steps as shown in Figure 4). The scheme described herein is refereed to as *exhaustive search*. If a video needs not to be processed in real time it may be the best option as the exhaustive search ensures that we'll find the best match for every macroblock. In some cases, however, we won't be able to afford an exhaustive search. Some algorithms have been developed aiming at finding a sub-optimal match in much less time than the exhaustive search.

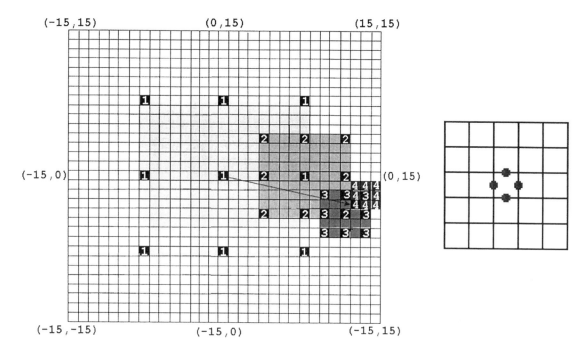

Figure 5. Two-Dimensional Logarithm Search (left) and
Half-Pixel Motion Estimation (right)

One example of algorithm that provides a sub-optimal result in much less operations is the two-dimensional logarithm, which resembles binary search. The basic idea is to divide the search region in two areas at each step: the first is inside of the $[-p/2, p/2]$ area, whilst the latter is outside of such. We select nine positions: (0,0) as well as the four corners and four medium points of the limit area, as shown in Figure 5 (left – marked as 1). The MAE is then calculated for each of the eight perimeter values and the smaller MAE is selected as the starting point for the next pass. We then go on selecting a $[-p/4, p/4]$ region around the selected position (marked as 2 in the Figure 5) and repeat the process until we search in a one-pixel region around the previously selected pixel (marked as 4 in the Figure 5). The last MAE selected will be the ending point of the motion vector.

Sub-pixel Motion Estimation

Some video encoders allow the motion estimation to go one step further than the whole-pixel-domain motion estimation, allowing sub-pixel motion estimation. Half-pixel motion estimation, for instance, is found in video codecs such as H263. Sub-pixel motion estimation consists of creating imaginary pixels between existing pixels as some sort of average of the neighbor pixels. That extra level of pixels would allow for a motion vector which stops in between real pixels. That allows better matching in the event that an object didn't move in the whole-pixel domain. The Figure 5 (right) shows the four extra positions between pixels, which are to be interpolated and also considered in an extra last-step in the motion estimation process.

Detection of Camera Motion, Motion Detection and Object Tracking

Motion Estimation and the resulting motion vectors can be used for a number of scene analysis through which it is possible to detect what happens in the video sequence. For instance, let us consider a video scene where the camera is panning right, such as that shown in Figure 6. If we consider a couple of consecutive frames we can verify that as the camera pans right the objects in the scene move leftwards until they eventually disappear at the left edge of the video frame. Considering macroblocks which compose the frame we can then deduct that most of the motion vectors should be pointing leftwards, as that's where the objects are moving to in the video sequence. If there is no motion in the scene but the camera is moving, the motion vectors will be basically aligned and with similar intensity and direction than neighbor vectors. For some scene where we have both motions in the scene and the camera, we would also have a large number of motion vectors pointing in the opposite direction to where the camera is moving, at least in the macroblocks that compose the background. We can, hence, analyze the orientation of the motion vectors of a given frame (or a given set of consecutive frames) to identify camera movements.

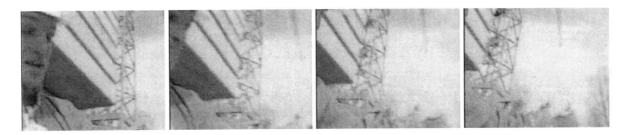

Figure 6. Camera Panning to the Right.

Similarly we can verify other camera movements, as depicted in Figure 7, such as camera panning left (A), panning right (B), tilting down (C), tilting up (D), zooming out (E) or zooming in (F).

Scene change, i.e. an indoor scene change to an outdoor scenario for instance, can be detected through the failure to estimate motion from one frame to the next, as typically no matches should be easily found.

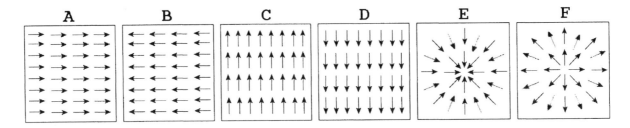

Figure 7. The displacement of motion vectors indicating left panning (A),
right panning (B), tilt down (C), tilt up (D), zoom out (E), and zoom in (F).

When we put all the camera movement/scene change detection together, we can build a comprehensive set of procedures for classification/analysis of video sequences based purely in motion estimation, as well as its resulting motion vectors.

Going one step further, if we have a scene which doesn't change much, for instance consider a surveillance camera which captures a safe lock inside a bank, the motion estimation should overall find excellent matches right at the same position where a given macroblock was located in the previous frames. If someone approaches the safe there will be a group of macroblocks which will have some motion vectors pointing in the opposite direction as that individual moves. That could be used to trigger a security alarm. In order to prevent the alarm from being trigged if a small animal (a rat perhaps) moves around in the room, one can model the system to only trigger the alarm if the amount of macroblocks with movement detected is larger than a given threshold which would be typical of a human being.

Going yet another step further, in the surveillance application described above, the macroblocks which compose the movement of an object in the room delimits the format of such object. Analyzing such format may allow the identification of the object.

Conclusion

Even tough more commonly linked to lossy video compression, motion estimation is in fact a technique that goes beyond and allows for video processing and computational vision algorithms and applications. It allows a computer to detect movement as well as to perform comprehensive video sequence analysis, identifying scenes, and camera and object movements. A video compression standard such as MPEG4, which allows the coding of objects separately, requires such objects to be found in the first place. Motion estimation is one technique that allows for a simple, yet effective, object identification scheme. Since motion estimation is one of the most computer intensive tasks linked to video compression, it is fairly common to find specific hardware which performs at least parts of the motion estimation [6, 7].

See: Compression and Coding Techniques, Video; Compression and Coding Techniques, Images

References

1. V. Bhaskaran and K. Konstantinides, "Image and Video Compression Standards: Algorithms and Architectures," 2nd Edition, Kluwer Academic Publishers, 1997, ISBN: 0792399528.
2. F. Halsall, "Multimedia Communications – Applications, Networks, Protocols and Standards," Addison Wesley, 2001, ISBN: 0201398184.
3. G. Ahanger and T.D.C. Little, "A Survey of Technologies for Parsing and Indexing Digital Video," MCL Technical Report 11-01-95, Multimedia Communication Laboratory, Boston University, 1995.
4. I. Grinias and G. Tziritas, "Robust pan, tilt and zoom estimation," International Conference on Digital Signal Processing, 2002.

5. G. Kühne, S. Richter, and M. Beier, "Motion-based segmentation and contour-based classification of video objects," ACM Multimedia 2001, Ottawa, Ontario.

6. R. Strzodka and C. Garbe, "Real-Time Motion Estimation and Visualization on Graphics Cards," Proceedings of the IEEE Visualization 2004 (VIS'04).

7. C. Sanz, M. J. Garrido, and J. M. Meneses, "VLSI Architecture for Motion Estimation using the Block-Matching Algorithm," Proceedings of the European conference on Design and Test, 1996.

8. http://jStreaming.com [last visit on April 13, 2005].

MOTION ESTIMATION WITH HALF-PIXEL ACCURACY

Definition: *Half-pixel accurate motion vectors can be found by interpolating the current frame and reference frame by a factor of two and then using any of the fast block matching algorithms for motion estimation.*

In real world video sequences, the true frame-to-frame displacements are unrelated to the integer pixel sampling grids. Thus, the motion prediction accuracy is limited to integer-pel accuracy. In fact, the motion prediction accuracy can be improved by half-pel accurate motion estimation. That is to determine motion vectors with half-pel accuracy. Many coding standards [1][2] permit motion vectors to be specified to a half-pixel accuracy.

Half-pixel accurate motion vectors can be found by interpolating the current frame and reference frame by a factor of two and then using any of the fast block matching algorithms for motion estimation. The method in finding the half-pel accurate motion vector is illustrated as follows.

Step 1   Find the motion vector with integer-pixel accuracy using any fast block matching algorithm to obtain a motion vector $v(k, l)$.

Step 2   Refine the motion vector $v(k, l)$ to half-pixel accuracy as follows:

a. Obtain the 8 surrounding half-pel blocks using bilinear interpolation as shown in Figure 1. The method used in this figure is adopted by various coding standards.

b. Compute the MAD of all the 8 half-pel checking points and compared them with the one of $v(k, l)$. The minimum one is the output half-pixel accurate motion vector as illustrated in Figure 2.

See: Motion Compensation for Video Compression

References

1. ISO/IEC and ITU-T, "Information Technology - Generic coding of moving pictures and associated audio information - Part 2: Video," ISO/IEC 13818-2 (MPEG-2) - ITU-T Recommendation H.262, 1996.

2. ISO/IEC, "Information Technology - Coding of audio-visual object – Part 2: Visual," ISO/IEC 14496-2 (MPEG-4), 1999.

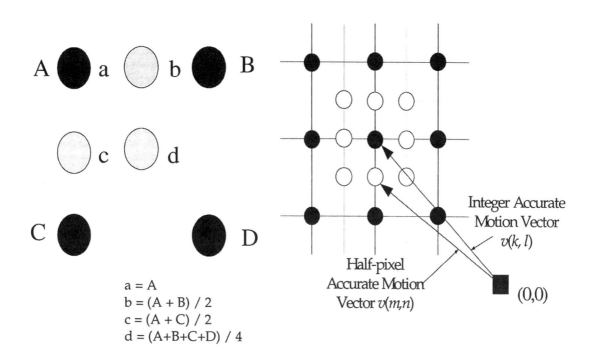

$$a = A$$
$$b = (A + B) / 2$$
$$c = (A + C) / 2$$
$$d = (A+B+C+D) / 4$$

Figure 1. Half-pixel prediction by bilinear interpolation

Figure 2. Half-pixel accurate motion vector estimation

MOTION PICTURE INPAINTING ON AGED FILMS

Definition: *Motion picture inpainting refers to the detection of damages in video frames and repairing them.*

Video inpainting, as we have discussed in the article entitled "Digital Inpainting," has a different challenge issue compared to image inpainting. Most image inpainting methods require the user to select a target area. This requirement is not possible on video due to the large number of video frames. Detection of damages in video frames is a must. Damages in video frames include spikes (usually in a bright intensity) and long vertical lines (usually in bright or dark intensity). The former is due to dust and dirt, which occurs randomly and mostly appears in one frame. The later is accidentally produced in film development and usually occurs in the same position for an unknown duration (from several frames to several minutes). Detections of the two types of damages are different problems. Both problems need to look at the damage from temporal and spatial domains. A video inpainting project at Tamkang University uses the following strategy for video inpainting on spikes, as illustrated below:

Motion Estimation and Defect Block Detection

> *Subdivide each frame in the defect video into a number of 2 by 2 blocks*
> *Compare each block in frame F_i with a block in the same position in frame F_k, where $i-1 \leq k \leq i+3$*
> *If the SAD (Sum of Absolute Differences) is large, the block could be a noise*
> *Compare a noise block to its surrounding, merge adjacent blocks with a small difference*
> Defect Block Inpainting
> *If there exists good candidate source blocks in frame F_{i-1} or frame F_{i+1}*
> *Use the candidate source block to inpaint the damaged block in frame F_i*
> *Otherwise*
> *Use a multi-resolution image inpainting technique on frame F_i*

The results of color and B&W video inpainting are shown in Figure 1 and Figure 2, respectively.

Figure 1. Video inpainting results (Color) – the damaged frame (left), the detected spikes (middle), and the repaired frame (right).

Figure 2. Video inpainting results (B&W) – the damaged frame (left),
the detected spikes (middle), and the repaired frame (right).

See: Digital Inpainting, Multi-Resolution Image Inpainting, Photo Defect Detection

MPEG-1 VIDEO COMPRESSION

Definition: *MPEG-1 video and audio compression standards were mainly devised for CD-ROM applications at 1.5 Mbps.*

The MPEG-1 video compression algorithm was optimized for bitrates of 1.1 Mbps since coded video at about 1.1 Mbps and coded stereo audio at 128kbps together match the CD-ROM data rates of approximately 1.4Mbps [2]. SIF was used for optimal performance in MPEG-1 [2]. SIF corresponding to NTSC and PAL have the size of 352x240 at 29.97 fps and the size of 352x288 at 25 fps, respectively.

Key Compression Tools for MPEG Video

All MPEG standards are based on motion compensated transform coding, where main compression tools are following three: 1. Color conversion to YUV and down sampling in

UV domain, 2. Spatial de-correlation, and 3. Temporal de-correlation. The video is encoded one macro block (MB) at a time. Each MB corresponds to a 16x16 luma component and the corresponding chroma components. First, UV domain down sampling is adopted to minimize domain resolution in color components. Second, a transform (DCT) is adopted to de-correlate spatial redundancy. Note that DCT was chosen in most of MPEG standards as a de-facto transform since it was proven to be an approximation of optimal K-L transform at 1st order Markov model source. The size of 2-D transform is 8x8. Third, motion estimation/compensation is adopted to de-correlate temporal redundancy – we take a difference between current MB and the best match MB (a.k.a., prediction MB) in the reference frame to only send residual data (a.k.a., prediction error). Note that residual data is again spatially-de-correlated with 2D transform after motion predicted temporal de-correlation. The best match MB is described with motion vectors that are actually semantic data, not pixel data, which describes the displacement between current MB and its best match MB in the bitstream. The size of motion estimation/ compensation is 16x16 in Luma resolution. Figure 1 shows the frame structure and prediction modes supported in MPEG-1. For a better temporal de-correlation, bi-directional prediction is used. Bi-directional prediction is very effective when occlusion happens in neighboring shots. B frames, that undergo bi-directional prediction, can choose the better reference frame out of two (past and future) references. Which reference frame is better typically depends on which reference frame is closer to current frame and where occlusion happens in the scene, etc. There are 3 different prediction modes for MBs in B frames. Basically each MB area in a B frame adaptively can declare which of three modes is used for that particular MB: 1. forward, 2. backward, and 3. interpolative. In other words, the direction is chosen based on which reference frame the best match MB comes from. In interpolative mode case, the best match MB is pixel wise average of two MBs in both prediction directions.

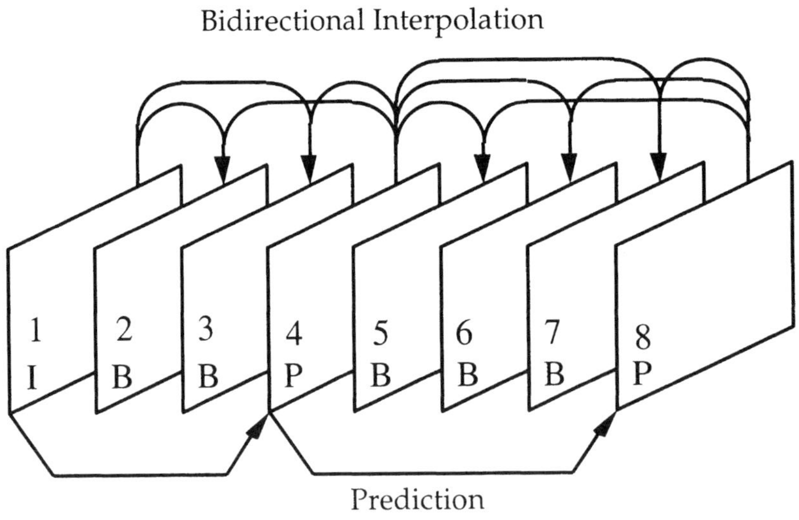

Figure 1. Structure of a Group of Pictures (GOP).

Digitized NTSC resolution video has a bit rate of approximately 100 Mbps. When MPEG compression is applied to get 1.1 Mbps output bit rate, the compression ratio is about 100:1. In other words, almost 99% data are discarded in the compression stage to extract only about 1% of net video information. Accordingly, approximately 99% data are re-created back from about 1% of net information.

MPEG-1 Video Specific Semantics and Syntax

MPEG-1 is a hybrid coder that is based on 8x8 block DCT and 16x16 motion compensation with half-pel resolution. The 8x8 motion compensation is not used in MPEG-1. The purpose of half-pel motion compensation is to further reduce prediction errors. The exact interpolation method used for half-pel data in an encoder is to be applied in any decoder as well. And, the interpolation is performed on reconstructed reference frames even at the encoder to eliminate "drift". Note that the interpolation method adopted for MPEG-1 is simple bilinear interpolation of adjacent integer-pels. MPEG-1 supports the maximum MV range of -512 to +511.5 pixels for half-pel resolution and -1024 to +1023 for integer-pel resolution. Half-pel resolution motion compensation is typically quite effective when the size of video is relatively small as in cell phone videos.

DCT is performed on residual data obtained through motion prediction process for NonIntra MBs, while DCT is applied on original pixel data for Intra MBs [1]. After 2-D DCT is applied to each block, the DCT coefficients are quantized to generate more zero-runs to constitute compact representation of RLC. If we quantize DCT coefficients with a bigger Quantization Scale (QS), more zero-runs are generated. Note that Quantization is the only one place where we artificially introduce errors in entire encoder and decoder systems. The purpose of artificially introducing errors in picture quality is to obtain a demanded compression ratio for specific applications. The level of degradation of quality depends on the value of QS we choose to use for each MB. Therefore, MB header includes QS information. MB header is composed of MB type, QS, MV data and coded block pattern. Note that QS in MB is optional since the mandatory one is in Slice layer. Two different weighting matrices for Intra and NonIntra are, respectively, applied to DCT coefficient quantization. The idea of weighting matrix is to assign different amount of bit-resolution to different frequency components based on sensitivity of human visual systems.

An MB contains 6 block data in the body, and a block consists of quantized DCT coefficients of an 8x8 size block. In Block level, DC value is coded in difference between the DC coefficient of the block and the prediction made from the DC coefficient of the block just coded from the same components. The bits assigned to it ranges from 1 to 8 – represented in variable size bits. For blocks in NonIntra MBs, DC coefficients are treated just like the rest of AC coefficients. The coding of AC coefficients is based on zig-zag scanning to construct RLC. The mapping index of AC RLC Huffman table is (zero-RUN, LEVEL) duplet. The half of AC RLC Huffman table in MPEG-1 is exactly same as that of H.261.

There are 6 levels of headers in MPEG-1 video bitstream syntax – Sequence, GOP, Picture, Slice, MB and Block. Sequence header contains basic parameters such as the size of video pictures, PAR, picture rate, bit rate, VBV buffer size and some other global parameters. GOP header provides support for random access, fast searching due to I pictures. Picture header contains information about type of picture such as I, P, B and D. Note that special D picture, which consists of blocks with only DC coefficient, is allowed in MPEG-1. D frames are rarely used, but were designed for fast search since DC component alone doesn't need IDCT computation at all [3]. In Picture header, there are two important parameters – temporal reference and vbv_delay. Temporal reference indicates the position of picture in display order within the GOP. Vbv_delay tells about how long to wait after a random access to avoid underflow or overflow of the bitstream buffer of the decoder [2].

See: Video Coding Techniques and Standards

References

1. J. L. Mitchell, W. B. Pennebaker, C. E. Fogg, and D. J. LeGall, "MPEG video compression standard," Digital Multimedia Standards Series, Chapman and Hall, 1996, pp. 135-169.
2. A. N. Netravali and B. G. Haskell, "Digital Pictures – Representation, Compression and Standards," 2nd Edition, Plenum, 1995, pp. 613-628.
3. A. Bovik, "Handbook of Image and Video Processing," Academic Press, 2000, pp. 597-610.

MPEG-2 VIDEO COMPRESSION

Definition: Following MPEG-1, MPEG-2 video and audio compression standards were developed to meet the need in entertainment TV for transmission media such as satellite, CATV and digital storage media such as DVD.

The main effort was to compress CCIR-601 4:2:0 interlaced video with high quality since virtually all TV materials archived for last 50 years have been interlaced signals. Since the resolution is approximately 4 times that of CIF, the bit rate chosen for optimizing MPEG-2 was 4 Mbps [1, 2]. For the first time, functionality tools other than compression tools were specified in MPEG-2 -- Scalability tools. MPEG-2 standards' scope was enlarged to cover HD applications in July 1992. Now MPEG-2 handles a range of 4-15 Mbps as a generic coder. By generic, it is meant that the coding is not targeted for a specific application, but that the standard includes many algorithms/tools that can be used for a variety of applications under different operating conditions. To give interoperability between such different MPEG-2 applications, profiles and levels were defined [2].

MPEG-2 Video New Features with respect to MPEG-1

MPEG-2 too is a hybrid coder that is based on 8x8 block DCT and 16x16 motion compensation with half-pel resolution – a straight forward extension of MPEG-1. This is a key factor for the rapid acceptance of MPEG-2 in such a short period of time. However, there are many new features added in MPEG-2. Frame picture and Field picture were defined. Note that a video sequence in MPEG-2 is a collection of Frame pictures and Field pictures. Frame/Field adaptive motion compensation was introduced. Dual prime motion compensation was devised for P-pictures at no B-pictures. Frame/Field/Dual prime adaptive motion compensation was developed for Frame pictures, while Field/16x8MC/Dual prime adaptive motion compensation was devised for Field pictures. In terms of DCT, Frame and Field DCT was defined. And, nonlinear quantization table with increased accuracy for small values was proposed on top of linear quantization table. New coefficient scanning pattern for DCT was added in Intra block scanning – the alternative scan was mainly designed for interlaced data. New VLC table for DCT coefficient for Intra blocks was introduced. In addition, YUV4:2:2 and YUV4:4:4 formats were also considered in input for high quality studio applications.

In MPEG-2, IDCT mismatch control involves adding or subtracting 1 to coefficient[7][7] if all coefficient sum is even. Coefficient VLCs support a larger range of quantized DCT coefficients in 24bits MPEG-2 FLC compared with MPEG-1 FLC due to more efficient representation. Coefficient VLC table escape format is not allowed if shorter VLC can be used. Chrominance samples horizontally co-sited as luminance samples. Slices always start and end at the same horizontal row of MBs. Concealment motion vectors for Intra MBs are possible. Motion vectors always coded in half-pel units, so full-pel flag must be zero in the Picture header. Display aspect ratio is specified in bitstream and pel aspect ratio is derived from it.

MPEG-2 Video Specific Semantics and Syntax

The 8x8 motion compensation is not used in MPEG-2. However, Frame and Field pictures are defined and fully exploited to further reduce prediction errors for the interlaced video. To optimally encode the interlaced video, MPEG-2 can encode a picture either as a Field picture or a Frame picture. In the Field picture mode, the two fields in the frame are encoded separately. If the first field in a picture is an I picture, the second field in the picture can be either I or P pictures. In other words, the second field can use the first field as a reference picture. However, if the first field in a picture is a P- or B-field picture, the second field has to be the same type of picture. In a Frame picture, two fields are interleaved to define a Frame picture and coded together as one picture.

In MPEG-2, Frame-based and Field-based predictions are defined due to which type of reference is used. Frame-based prediction is obtained based on reference frames, while Field-based prediction is obtained based on reference fields. Note that in a Frame picture, either Frame-based prediction (one 16x16) or Field-based prediction (two 16x8) is selected on MB basis. No matter which prediction is used, forward/backward/ interpolative modes are options to choose in each MB. In other words, optimal prediction mode is considered for each MB. For a Field picture, no Frame-based prediction is possible. For Field-based prediction in P Field pictures, the prediction is formed from the two most recent decoded fields. However, for Field-based prediction in B Field pictures, the prediction is formed from the two most recent decoded reference frames. Note that the size of 16x16 in the Field picture covers a size of 16x32 in the Frame picture. It is too big size to assume that behavior inside the block is homogeneous. Therefore, 16x8 size prediction was introduced in Field picture. Two MVs are used for each MB. The first MV is applied to the 16x8 block in the field 1 and the second MV is applied to the 16x8 block in field 2. The idea of Dual prime adaptive motion prediction is to send minimal differential MV information for adjacent field MV data – this looks very similar to direct mode in upcoming standards such as H.263 and MPEG-4. For adjacent two fields, the MV data look very similar in most cases. If two independent MVs were compressed/ sent, it would be just too expensive in this case. The Dual prime motion prediction investigates geometrical similarity between a MV in current field and the MV already sent in the previous field. Given the first MV, the second MV is geometrically derived from the first MV and only differential MV for fine adjustment is sent for the second one. To reduce the noise in the data, the same MV derivation is applied to opposite priority too in order to capture averaged pixel values of the prediction. In other words, the motion-compensated predictions from two reference fields are averaged. Two DCT modes, Frame/ Field DCT, were introduced in MPEG-2. In Frame DCT, luminance MB is broken down to 4 8x8 DCT blocks. On the other hand, in Field DCT, luminance MB is divided to 4 DCT blocks where the pixels from the same field are grouped together.

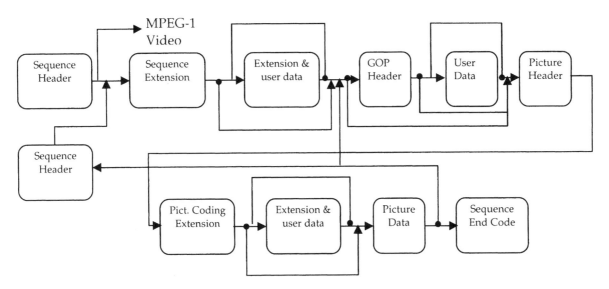

Figure 1. MPEG-2 Video Bitstream Syntax.

The interpolation method adopted for MPEG-2 is simple bilinear interpolation of adjacent integer-pels like MPEG-1. MPEG-2 supports the maximum MV range of -2048 to +2047.5 pixels for half-pel resolution. MB header is composed of MB type, QS, MV data and coded block pattern. Note that QS in MB is optional since it is in Slice layer. Two different weighting matrices for Intra and NonIntra are, respectively, applied to DCT coefficient quantization. An MB contains 6 block data in the body, and a block consists of quantized DCT coefficients of an 8x8 size block. In Block level, DC value is coded differentially between the DC coefficient of the block and the prediction made from the DC coefficient of the block just coded from the same components. The bits assigned to it ranges from 1 to 11 bits. For blocks in NonIntra MBs, DC coefficients are treated just like the rest of AC coefficients. There are 2 VLC tables – one for NonIntra coefficients and the other for Intra AC coefficients. Intra AC coefficient table is only used for Intra AC coefficients when intra_vlc_format=1.The coding of AC coefficients are based on zig-zag scanning or alternative scanning to construct RLC. This scanning order is chosen on picture-by-picture basis. The mapping index of AC RLC Huffman table is (zero-RUN, LEVEL) duplet. The NonIntra RLC Huffman table in MPEG-2 is exactly same as that of MPEG-1. The dct_type is in each MB of Frame pictures to indicate whether MB is Frame DCT coded or Field DCT coded. Note that no Field DCT is needed for Field pictures because each field is captured at one time point.

There are 6 levels of headers in MPEG-2 video bitstream syntax – Sequence, GOP, Picture, Slice, MB and Block. Sequence header contains basic parameters such as the size of video pictures, PAR or IAR, picture rate, bit rate, VBV buffer size, QS type (linear or non-linear) and some other global parameters. GOP header provides support for random access, fast searching due to I pictures. GOP header has SMPTE time code, closed-gop and broken_link information. Picture header contains information about type of picture such as I, P and B. In Picture header, there are parameters like temporal reference and vbv_delay. And importantly full_pel_forward_vector and full_pel_backward_vector flags should be always set to 0 since half-pel resolution is mandatory in MPEG-2.

Scalability

The purpose of scalability video is to achieve video of more than one resolution, quality or implementation complexity simultaneously. MPEG-2 supports four types of scalability modes: SNR, spatial, temporal and data partitioning. These allow a different set of trade-offs in bandwidth, video resolution, or quality and overall implementation complexity. Data partitioning is bitstream scalability, where a single-coded video bitstream is artificially partitioned into two or more layers. In the SNR scalability quality scalability each layer is at different quality but at the same spatial resolution. Spatial scalability is spatial resolution scalability, where each layer has the same or different spatial resolution. Temporal scalability is frame rate scalability, where each layer has the same or different temporal resolution but is at the same spatial resolution.

In a basic MPEG-2 scalability mode, there can be two layers of video: base and enhancement layers. Data partitioning splits the block of 64 quantized transform coefficients into two partitions. Base partition has low frequency DCT coefficients that are usually of importance. By doing so, important bitstream and moderate bitstream are obtained. SNR scalability is to transmit coarse DCT coefficients with base layer. The difference between the non-quantized DCT coefficients and the base layer DCT coefficients is encoded with finer quantization step size in the enhancement layer. By doing so, two quality videos are obtained. Note that spatial resolution is not changed in enhancement layer in SNR scalability. Spatial scalability down-samples video/ transmits it in base layer bitstream. To generate a prediction in enhancement layer, spatial scalability upsamples based layer video signal and weights/ combines with the motion compensated prediction from the enhancement layer. Note that the weighting factor producing smallest prediction error is selected and identified on MB basis and the information is put into enhancement layer bitstream. By doing so, two spatial resolution videos are obtained. Temporal scalability skips/ transmits frames to generate lower frame rate in base layer bitstream. To generate prediction in enhancement layer, Temporal scalability uses base layer pictures as references for motion compensated prediction. By doing so, two temporal resolution (different frame rate) videos are obtained [3].

Two different scalability modes can be combined to generate 3 layers – base layer, enhancement layer 1 and enhancement layer 2. Note that enhancement layer 1 is the lower layer for enhancement layer 2. Such an extended scalability is defined as Hybrid scalability.

See: Video Coding Techniques and Standards

References
1. J. L. Mitchell, W. B. Pennebaker, C. E. Fogg, and D. J. LeGall, "MPEG video compression standard," Digital Multimedia Standards Series, Chapman and Hall, 1996, pp. 135-169.
2. B. Haskell, A. Puri and A. N. Netravali, "Digital Video – An Introduction to MPEG-2," Chapman and Hall, 1997, pp. 258-279.
3. A. Bovik, "Handbook of Image and Video Processing," Academic Press, 2000, pp. 597-610.

MPEG-4 ADVANCED VIDEO COMPRESSION (MPEG-4 AVC)/H.264

Definition: MPEG-4 AVC or H.264 video compression standard was developed to enhance compression performance over current de facto standard MPEG-2 that was developed about 10 years ago primarily for digital TV systems with interlaced video coding.

H.264 is known to achieve a significant improvement in rate-distortion efficiency compared with existing standards, and is designed for broadcast TV over cable/DSL/satellite, IP set-tops and high-definition DVD recorders.

Network Adaptation Layer (NAL) and Video Coding Layer (VCL)

VCL is designed to efficiently represent the video content, while NAL encapsulates the VCL representation of video with header information in such a way that a variety of transport layers and storage media can easily adopt compressed contents. To this end, a NAL unit specifies both byte-stream and packet-based formats. NAL units are classified into VCL and non-VCL NAL units. The VCL NAL units contain the data that represents the values of the samples in the video pictures, and the non-VCL NAL units contain additional information such as timing information.

Key Compression Tools for H.264 Video

H.264 is based on motion compensated transform coding. Originally YUV4:2:0 was defined as input format for H.264. However, FRExt (Fidelity Range Extension) provides new profiles where YUV4:2:2 and YUV4:4:4 are handled as input formats. Even lossless coding is specified in High 4:4:4 Profile of FRExt. The key concept in H.264 is Slice. The information of two higher layers over Slice is Sequence parameters set and Picture parameters set. Note that those are parameters set to be pointed either directly or indirectly by each Slice. Sequence parameter ID ranges from 0 to 31 while Picture parameter ID does so from 0 to 255. There is no GOP structure since referencing order is decoupled from display order in H.264. But there is an imaginary Picture structure that is composed of one or more Slices. Here, the term "imaginary" means to be that there is no Picture layer in the bitstream structure, but a picture is generated through decoding process of Slices. The characteristic of the picture is declared with primary_pic_type, where the value indicates what kind of slices are in the primary coded picture. Note that many different types of Slices can constitute a single picture. For example, a primary coded picture can be composed of I, P and B Slices. There are 5 Slice types -- I (Intra), P (Predicted), B (Bi-predictive), SP (Switching P) and SI (Switching I).

In H.264, geometrical structure of Slices is very generic. There are 6 pre-defined Slice geometrical structures—Interleaved, Dispersed, Fore&Background, Box-out, Raster scan and Wipe. The last one is such an option to define any kind of Slice shape explicitly. Note that the geometrical structure of Slice can help visual recovery of lost data. For example, Interleaved 2 Slices improve visual perception when one of them is lost. Multiple reference pictures can be used in motion compensation. The syntax element, num_ref_frames, specifies the maximum total number of short-term and long-term reference frames, and it ranges from 0 to 16. In addition, a B frame can be used as a reference in H.264. References are stored in a DPB (Decoded Picture Buffer) in both the encoder and the decoder. The encoder and the decoder maintain a list of previously coded pictures -- reference picture list0 for P Slices and reference picture list0 and list1 for B Slices. These two lists can contain short- and long-term pictures. Especially, list0 is about past and list1 is about future coded pictures. There is pre-defined index management for list0 and list1. For example, an encoded picture is reconstructed by the encoder and marked as a short-term picture that is identified with its PicNum. However, the reference list0 and list1 can be entirely controlled by an encoder itself. For example, if a certain pattern is continuously used as a background during 10 minutes in a video, an encoder may want to keep it as a long-term picture reference.

That kind of encoder decision about list management can be written in the bitstreams with two syntax elements – reference picture list reordering syntax and decoded reference picture marking syntax. These could be thought of as memory control commands on the fly in the bitstreams. And, an encoder can send an IDR (Instantaneous Decoder Refresh) coded picture made up of I- or SI-Slices to clear all DPB contents. This means that all subsequent transmitted slices can be decoded without reference to any frame decoded prior to the IDR picture [1].

A key compression tool in H.264 is adaptive size MC (motion compensation) with a small fixed size transform. The size of MC is described in two levels – MB partition and MB sub-partition. The MB partition size can be broken down into sizes of 16x16, 16x8, 8x16 and 8x8. If 8x8 size broken down happens in MB partition, each MB sub-partition (8x8 Block) can be broken into sizes of 8x8, 8x4, 4x8 and 4x4. The color components, Cr and Cb, have half the size of luma components, but each chroma block is partitioned in the same way as the luma component. Note that resolution of MVs in luma is quarter-pel while that of derived MVs in chroma is 1/8-pel where 6 tap-FIR filter and bi-linear filter are used for interpolation. And, MVs can point over picture boundaries with extended padding. The 4x4 transform is an approximation of DCT with the following two aspects: 1. It is an integer transform, where all operations can be carried out with integer arithmetic. 2. Mismatch between encoders and decoders doesn't occur. The 4x4 transform captures quite good locality. As a fact, small size transform performs well in random-looking area such as residual data. Consequently, it reduces "ringing" artifact. Note that directional spatial prediction for Intra coding is introduced in H.264 to eliminate redundancy resulting in random-looking area even at I Slices.

Directional spatial prediction has a couple of options to best de-correlate intra block data based on previously-decoded parts of the current pictures. Hierarchical transform is applied on DC values of 4x4 transforms in 16x16 Intra mode MB and chroma blocks since R-D characteristics with longer basis transform is better over smooth area. There are improvements in skipped mode and direct mode in motion compensation over existing standards in syntax representation to suppress space for MV data. In addition, weighted prediction is extended to contain fading scene situations by providing weights and offsets. The direct mode uses bi-directional prediction with derived MVs based on the MV of co-located MB in the subsequent picture RL1. Note that a default weight based on geometrical division can be overridden with explicit weights to improve prediction performance.

One important difference between H.264 andVC-1 in terms of direct mode technique is that actual blending for a predictor happens based on weights in H.264, while pixel-wise average for a predictor is obtained in VC-1 with weights only being considered for MV computation. Multi-hypothesis mode is worthwhile noting since a joint estimation for a predictor is possible. While bi-directional prediction type only allows a linear combination of a forward/ backward prediction pair, any possible combination of references is possible such as (backward/ backward) and (forward/ forward) cases. In-loop deblocking filter (ILF) is used to reduce blocking artifacts. H.264 ILF is to dynamically adapt the length of FIR filter tap. The decision of filter type and taps is dependent on how serious the blocky effect is. And, the standard provides ways to measure it. Based on measurement, 5/4/3 tap filters are applied on horizontal and vertical block boundaries. The handling of 4x4 transform block coefficients is quite different compared with other standards. 3D RLC or 2D RLC is not used, but Token, Sign, Level, run_before groups are described in the other way around of scanning order (the last to the first coefficient). H.264 standard suggests two different types of entropy coding – CA-VLC (Context-based Adaptive Variable Length Coding) and CA-BAC (Context-based Adaptive Binary Arithmetic Coding). In CA-VLC, Huffman (VLC) tables are chosen based neighboring contexts or historical contexts. Examples are following: the choice of Token VLC tables is dependent on the number of non-zero coefficients in upper and left-hand previously coded blocks.

The choice of Level VLC tables is triggered by the present Level value. If a present Level value is over a certain threshold, new VLC tables for Level are used to compress Level symbols. When CA-BAC is selected for entropy coding, following 4 consecutive stages follow: 1. Binarization, 2. Context-model selection, 3. Arithmetic encoding, 4. Probability update. Generally speaking, CA-BAC over-performs CA-VLC. The reason for this is that arithmetic coding is block entropy coding (the block size is the size of overall input bits), while Huffman (VLC) coding is scalar entropy coding. An additional benefit for using arithmetic coding is to dynamically adapt probability model as probability of symbols change w. r. t. time. There can be many adaptation methods. One is to use accumulation of Symbols up to present for the model probability. However, this method doesn't capture local statistics, but only considers long-term average. An excellent method is to use neighboring contexts to capture local statistics as is in CA-BAC. Note that the context models are initialized depending on the initial value of the Qp. And, the Binarization method and Context-model selection for each Syntactic element are specified in the standard. A multiplication-free method for the arithmetic coding is used in H.264 based on a small set of representative values of range and probability of symbols. The range is quantized into 4 distinct values and the probability of symbols is quantized into 64 distinct values. This allows pre-computed table approach in the arithmetic coding, thus making it multiplication-free.

H.264 Video Specific Semantics and Syntax

There are 5 levels of headers in H..264 video bitstream syntax – Sequence parameter set, Picture parameter set, Slice level, MB, and Block. Sequence parameter set contains basic parameters such as profile and level data, seq_parameter_set_id (identifies sequence parameter set that is referred to), MaxFrameNum, display order related parameters, num_ref_frames (maximum total number of short-term and long-term reference frames), frame_mbs_only_flag, direct_8x8_inference_flag (specifies the method used in the derivation process of luma MVs for B_Skip, B_Direct_16x16, B_Direct_8x8), etc. Picture parameter set contains information about pic_paramter_set_id (identifies the picture parameter set that is referred to in the Slice header), seq_parameter_set_id, entropy_coding_mode_flag (either CA-BAC or CA-VLC), slice definition related parameters, maximum reference index data for reference list0 or list1, weighted_pred_flag (whether weighted prediction is applied to P and SP Slices), weighted_bipred_idc (weighted bi-prediction mode applied to B Slices), Qp related data, deblocking_filter_control_present_flag (syntax element controlling the characteristics of the deblocking filter is present in the Slice header), etc.

In Slice header, there is information about slice attributes, extra display order related parameters, direct_spatial_mv_pred_flag, override information about reference index for list0 and list1, deblocking filter related data, etc. Slice data contains mb_skip related data and MB layer information. MB layer contains mb_type, coded_block_pattern, mb_qp_delta. Based on mb_type information, mb_pred or sub_mb_pred data are put into the bitstream. And then residual data are appended. The mb_pred and sub_mb_pred information contain reference picture indices and MV data. Note that each 8x8 block area refer to a same reference picture even though different MVs can be used for different 4x4 blocks in a single 8x8 block. There are two residual data syntax order defined – one for CA-VLC and the other for CA- BAC.

See: Video Coding Techniques and Standards

References

1. D. Marpe, H. Schwartz, and T. Weigand, "Overview of the H.264/ AVC Video Coding Standard," IEEE Transactions on Circuits and Systems for Video Technology, Vol. 13, No. 7, July 2003, pp, 560-575.

MPEG-4 VIDEO COMPRESSION

Definition: *MPEG-4 multimedia compression standard was developed to provide technological foundations to deal with multimedia content in object-based, interactive, and non-linear way.*

Consequently, MPEG-4 video (Part 2 of the MPEG-4 standards series) had to meet the need with shape coding for arbitrary shaped video representation. Since MPEG-4 is a generic coder, the standard includes many algorithms/tools that can be used for a variety of applications under different operating conditions. Compared with the MPEG-2 standard, MPEG-4 covers novel profiles and levels with shape coding and low-bit rate tools additionally. As a result, wireless phone standards such as 3GPP include MPEG-4 video as a video subsystem compression standard. This section discusses about MPEG-4 video natural coding tools focusing on shape coding and texture coding.

MPEG-4 Shape Coding

There are two types of shape data in MPEG-4: grey scale and binary shape information. Context-based Arithmetic Encoding (CAE) technique is used to encode both types of shape data. The only difference is that the grey scale shape data needs an additional process for texture data compression on top of binary (i.e., support) compression. To define a coding unit, Binary Alpha Block (BAB) is defined as a set of 16x16 binary pixels.

MPEG-4 Shape Coding is performed in two steps: 1. size conversion process, 2. CAE process. The size conversion process is actually lossy coding where Conversion Ratio (CR) is taken as one of {1, ½, ¼}. A CR is chosen for each BAB by encoder based on targeted rate and distortion characteristics. CAE is applied on size converted blocks for further lossless coding. A size converted block can be encoded in one of 7 modes -- 2 modes (MVDs=0 && No Update, MVDs!=0 && No Update) for copy from a reference, 3 modes (all_255, all_0, IntraCAE) for no-reference-need-coding and 2 modes (MVDs=0 && InterCAE, MVDs!=0 && InterCAE) for reference-need-coding. No-reference-need-coding modes can be used for I/P/B-VOPs, while reference-need-coding modes are used for P/ B-VOPs. Following 3 are worth remembering - 1. MVs are all in pel domain, 2. MC is carried out on 16x16 dimension, and 3. B-VOP chooses only 1 reference based on geometry.

The principal method used on size converted blocks is CAE with block-based motion compensation. Note that 2 modes for copy from reference use motion compensation in binary alpha pixels, but 2 reference-need-coding modes use merely motion vectors to extract spatio-temporal context (i.e., template) to obtain CAE probability from the context-probability mapping table in the standard. The input for CAE is anyway binary alpha bits. The key issue here is how probability table is updated for a better performance in CAE. Probability adaptation comes from spatio-temporal neighborhood's pattern – so Context-based Arithmetic Encoding is named for this technology.

In MPEG-4 Shape Coding, there are two types of contexts defined – spatial for IntraCAE and spatio-temporal for InterCAE. Note that InterCAE is not mandatory for BABs in P/B-VOPs – IntraCAE can be used for P/B-VOPs as well as I-VOPs. Mode decision is based on rate distortion policy – in other words, additional sending of MV data might not be preferred.

The motion vectors are compressed in differential form. MPEG-4 video standard suggests using two different VLC tables based on whether x-axis differential MV is 0. In addition, there are two options to choose MV predictor (MVP). If binary_only flag is on or B-VOP is encoded, independent shape vectors are kept in MV history buffers. Otherwise, MVs from corresponding texture data are used to define the MVP.

MPEG-4 Texture Coding

MPEG-4 natural video coding tools comprise a whole tool-set for different applications and user cases. These tools can be combined to code different source of natural video. Not all of the tools are required for every application.

Originally MPEG-4 video standardization was initiated to cover low bit rate applications that were missing in the development of MPEG-2. H.263 technology, which was optimized for low bit rate applications, became a basis for further MPEG-4 development at that time. Some interesting technology coming from H.263 includes 1MV/4MV, unrestricted MV, overlap motion compensation, 3D RLD (zero-run, level, Last) triplets, direct mode motion compensation (PB frame), hybrid 8x8 DCT with half-pel resolution, PQAUNT/DQUANT, DBQUANT (PB frame), etc.

On top of these tools, there were a couple of techniques put into MPEG-4 Texture Coding: Intra DC/AC adaptive prediction (DC coefficient, the first row and the first column), Intra DC non-linear quantization (luminance and chrominance were separately optimized), alternative scan modes, weighting matrices (this was not used in H.263, while it was used in other MPEG standards) option, SA-DCT (Instead of SA-DCT, boundary padding method can be used, too. – some visual object support both algorithms), generalized direct mode (multiple B frames between two reference frames), quarter-pel motion compensation, global motion compensation, etc. Note that MPEG-4 natural video coding supports the use of 4 to 12 bits per pixel for luminance and chrominance values. This is called N-bit tool [1,2].

Scalability Coding Tool

In MPEG-4 video, object-based scalability can be achieved, where multiple objects have different level of basic scalabilities. Basic scalabilities are as follows: 1. Spatial scalability, 2. Temporal scalability, and 3. SNR fine granularity scalability. Fine granularity scalability was designed to provide a very accurate bandwidth adaptation for streaming applications. To do so, enhancement layer was further bit-plane-by-bit-plane partitioned to obtain many small granularity of a bitstream.

Other MPEG-4 Coding Tools

MPEG-4 video was intended for applications such as delivery over best-effort and lossy networks. As a result, several tools were included to improve the error resiliency of the video. The supported error resilience tools are: Video Packet based resynchronization,

Data Partitioning, Reversible VLC, Header Extension Code, New Prediction. The MPEG-4 standard also includes such as interlaced coding and sprite coding.

Visual Texture Coding Tool

Visual Texture is a still image most likely used for a base material for 2D/3D graphics rendering. VTC technique is to achieve high-quality, coding efficiency and scalable textures. MPEG-4 VTC is based on the discrete wavelet transform (DWT) and zero-tree coding. Due to the nature of wavelet transform coding for still images, the following characteristics are obtained: 1. Efficient compression over a wide range of qualities, 2. Easy Spatial and SNR scalability coding, 3. Robust transmission in error-prone environments, 4. Random access, and 5. Complexity scalability levels. VTC compression tool was adopted in MPEG-4 Visual version1, while error-resilience, tiling, and shape-adaptive tools were adopted in MPEG-4 Visual version 2 [1, 2].

See: Video Coding Techniques and Standards

References

1.   F. Pereira and T. Ebrahimi, "The MPEG-4 Book," IMSC Press Series, Prentice Hall PTR, 2002, pp. 293-381.
2.   I. Richardson, "H.264 and MPEG-4 Video Compression," John Wiley & Sons, 2003, pp. 258-279.

MULTICAST TRUE VoD SERVICE

Definition: The conventional true VoD system uses one dedicated channel for each service request, which offers the client the best QoS and interactive services, while multicast true VoD offers more efficient data transmission.

Video-on-Demand (VoD) service allows remote clients to play back any video from a large collection of videos stored at one or more video servers in any mode at any time. VoD service is usually long-lived and real-time, and requires high storage-I/O and network bandwidths and needs to support VCR-like interactivity. A VoD system is usually designed with a focus on system cost and client-perceived Quality-of-Service (QoS). Key cost components are the video server capacity, storage-I/O bandwidth, network bandwidth and throughput, and customer premise equipment (CPE). VoD clients' QoS is related to service latency, interactivity, and playback effects. Usually, there is a trade-off between clients' QoS and system costs. The True VoD (TVoD) service supports all of the control functions, and is an ideal service for customers [1]. The conventional TVoD system uses one dedicated channel for each service request, which offers the client the best QoS and interactive services. However, it incurs high system costs, especially in terms of storage-I/O and network bandwidth. Moreover, the conventional VoD service has poor scalability and low cost/performance efficiency. Efficient solution to improve VoD systems is to use multicast [2].

Multicast offers efficient one-to-many data transmission and thus provides the foundation for various applications that need to distribute data to many receivers in a scalable manner. It reduces both the server-side overhead and the overall network load. A survey of multicast VoD services is given in [3].

(This short article has been adapted from [2]).

See: Large-Scale Video-on-Demand Systems

References

1. T.D.C. Little and D. Vankatesh, "Prospects for Interactive Video-on-Demand," IEEE Multimedia, Vol. 1, No. 3, 1994, pp. 14-24.
2. H. Ma, K.G. Shin, and W. Wu, "Best-Effort Patching for Multicast True VoD Service," Multimedia Tools and Applications, Vol. 26, 2005, pp. 101-122.
3. H. Ma and K.G. Shin, "Multicast Video-on-Demand Services," ACM Computer Communication Review, ACM Press, Vol. 32, No. 1, 2002, pp. 31-43.

MULTICHANNEL DATA ORDERING SCHEMES

Definition: Multichannel data ordering schemes are used for color image filtering and enhancements in order to produce better and more efficient results.

Probably the most popular family of nonlinear filters is the one based on the concept of robust order-statistics [1]-[3]. In univariate (scalar) data analysis, it is sufficient to detect any outliers in the data in terms of their extremeness relative to an assumed basic model and then employ a robust accommodation method of inference. For multivariate data however, an additional step in the process is required, namely the adoption of the appropriate sub-ordering principle, such as marginal, conditional, partial, and reduced ordering as the basis for expressing extremeness of observations [1],[2].

Using marginal ordering the vector's components are ordered along each dimension independently. Since the marginal ordering approach often produces output vectors which differ from the set of vectorial inputs, application of marginal ordering to natural color images often results in color artifacts. In conditional ordering the vector samples are ordered based on the marginal ordering of one component. Similarly to marginal ordering, conditional ordering fails to take into consideration the true vectorial nature of the color input. Using partial ordering the samples are partitioned into smaller groups which are then ordered. Since partial ordering is difficult to perform in more than two dimensions, it is not appropriate for three-component signals such as RGB color images. Finally, in reduced (or aggregated) ordering each vector is reduced to a scalar representative and then the vectorial inputs are ordered in coincidence with the ranked scalars. The reduced ordering scheme is the most attractive and widely used in color image processing since it relies an overall ranking of the original set of input samples and the output is selected from the same set [1],[2].

To order the color vectors $\mathbf{x}_1, \mathbf{x}_2, \ldots, \mathbf{x}_N$ located inside the supporting window, the reduced ordering based vector filters use the aggregated distances or the aggregated similarities

$$D_i = \sum_{j=1}^{N} d(\mathbf{x}_i, \mathbf{x}_j) \text{ or } D_i = \sum_{j=1}^{N} s(\mathbf{x}_i, \mathbf{x}_j)$$

associated with the vectorial input $\mathbf{x}_i$, for $i = 1, 2, \ldots, N$. By ordering the scalar values $D_1, D_2, \ldots, D_N$, the ordered sequence of scalar values $D_{(1)} \leq D_{(2)} \leq \ldots \leq D_{(i)} \leq \ldots \leq D_{(N)}$, for $D_{(i)} \in \{D_1, D_2, \ldots, D_N\}$ and $i = 1, 2, \ldots, N$, implies the same ordering of the corresponding vectors $\mathbf{x}_i$ as follows: $\mathbf{x}_{(1)} \leq \mathbf{x}_{(2)} \leq \ldots \leq \mathbf{x}_{(i)} \leq \ldots \leq \mathbf{x}_{(N)}$.

Many noise removal techniques utilize the lowest ranked sample $\mathbf{x}_{(1)}$, referred to lowest vector order-statistics, as the output [1],[2]. This selection is due to the fact that: i) the lowest ranked vector $\mathbf{x}_{(1)}$ which is associated with the minimum aggregated distances $D_{(1)}$ is the most typical sample for the vectorial set $\mathbf{x}_1, \mathbf{x}_2, \ldots, \mathbf{x}_N$, and that ii) vectors that diverge greatly from the data population usually appear in higher ranks of the ordered sequence. Therefore, the lowest ranked vector $\mathbf{x}_{(1)}$ can also be used in vector color image zoomers to minimize the processing error and produce sharply looking images [1]. On the other hand, vector edge detectors often utilize the lowest and the uppermost ranked vectors to determine edge discontinuities in color images [1],[2].

See: Color image filtering and enhancement, Color image zooming, Vector edge detectors, Distance and similarity measures.

References

1. R. Lukac, B. Smolka, K. Martin, K.-N. Plataniotis, and A.-N. Venetsanopulos, "Vector Filtering for Color Imaging," IEEE Signal Processing Magazine, Vol. 22, No. 1, January 2005, pp. 74-86.
2. K.-N. Plataniotis and A.-N. Venetsanopoulos, "Color Image Processing and Applications," Springer Verlag, Berlin, 2000.
3. I. Pitas and A.N. Venetsanopoulos, "Nonlinear Digital Filters, Principles and Applications," Kluwer Academic Publishers, Norwell, MA, 1990.

MULTIMEDIA ARCHIVES AND MEDIATORS

Manolis Wallace, Yannis Avrithis and Stefanos Kollias
National Technical University of Athens, Greece

Definition: *The integration of multimedia archives through a common, unified access point for end users, always considering their particular copyright and access policies, emerges as a necessary step for the preservation of their content and their financial viability.*

During the last decade, the cost of storage and wide area communication services has decreased, while their capacity increased dramatically. This fact, along with the increasing penetration of e-commerce applications, has made digital storage, annotation and access of multimedia information a mature and viable choice for content holding organizations and individuals. Numerous multimedia archives have, either totally or incrementally, turned to the utilization of digitized archive technologies. The content of these archives can be made accessible, depending upon copyright, policy and security decisions, over the Internet in a cost efficient, time efficient, anyplace, anytime fashion.

However, one of the main problems of multimedia archiving has been inherited to their digital descendants. For traditional archives, where raw media were stored in the form of analog hard copies, search was not an easy task as a human had to either go through a separate annotation archive, or, ideally, search using keywords in a custom, proprietary, metadata database. Much similarly to the case of books in a library that have not been indexed, information stored in a multimedia archive that cannot be searched, identified and accessed easily is practically unavailable.

Trends in research and standardization

In order to provide for more efficient search services in the always augmenting space of available digital multimedia content, several systems have been proposed and several research projects and initiatives have been funded, making important contributions to theoretical fields ranging from multimedia signal processing, computer vision, multimedia database and knowledge management to artificial intelligence, human computer interaction and information retrieval. Still, considering the number and diversity of multimedia archives existing worldwide, being able to search in each one of them independently but not in all of them at the same time through a common interface is much like having independent indices for each corridor in a library. When the library becomes larger, data is once again as good as non existing.

Current and evolving international standardization activities, such as MPEG-4 [1] for video, JPEG-2000 [2] for still images, and MPEG-7 [3], MPEG-21 [4], SMIL [5] for generic multimedia, deal with aspects related to audiovisual (a/v) content and metadata coding and representation, aiming to provide a framework for uniformity and interoperability between developed systems. Still, mainly due to the fact that digital archives have pre-existed the developed standards, very few of them fully comply with them. In most cases, multimedia archives operate using proprietary data structures as well as administrator and end user software. Thus, the integration of multimedia archives through a common, unified access point for end users, always considering their particular copyright and access policies, emerges as a necessary step for the preservation of their content and their financial viability.

In order to achieve this goal, several research activities are currently active in the direction of knowledge acquisition and modeling, capturing knowledge from raw information and multimedia content in distributed repositories to turn poorly structured information into machine-processable knowledge [6][7]. A second future direction is knowledge sharing and use, combining semantically enriched information with context to provide infrencing for decision support and collaborative use of trusted knowledge between organizations [8]. Finally, in the intelligent content vision, multimedia objects integrate content with metadata and intelligence and learn to interact with devices and networks [9].

It is becoming apparent in all the above research fields that integration of diverse, heterogeneous and distributed – pre-existing – multimedia content will only be feasible through the design of mediator systems. In [10] for instance, a multimedia mediator is designed to provide a well-structured and controlled gateway to multimedia systems, focusing on schemas for semi-structured multimedia items and object-oriented concepts, while [11] focuses on security requirements of such mediated information systems. On the other hand, [12] deals with media abstraction and heterogeneous reasoning through the use of a unified query language for manually generated annotation, again without dealing with content or annotation semantics. A semantically rich retrieval model is suggested in [13], based on fuzzy set theory with domain-specific methods for document analysis and allowing natural language queries. Finally, [14] focuses on the design of a single intuitive interface supporting visual query languages to access distributed multimedia databases.

Mediator systems

A mediator is "one who resolves or settles differences by acting as an intermediary between two conflicting parties", "an impartial observer who listens to both sides separately and suggests how each side could adjust its position to resolve differences", "a negotiator who acts as a link between parties" and so on, depending on which dictionary one consults. In information systems, a mediator is a independent system residing between the end user and an information system. Its role is to provide a kind of translation between the two ends, by setting up a user friendly interface towards the user which serves information acquired from the typically more rigid information system [15][16].

In the case of multimedia archives, the main hurdle to overcome is not the rigidness of the end systems, but rather the fact that numerous representation standards have been developed up to date. Even if the MPEG series seem to be gaining momentum and setting themselves up as the definitive choice for the future, numerous existing archives follow other standards, or even totally proprietary representation and storage models. As a result, unified access is not feasible. The role of a mediator in this framework is to provide a single interface to the end user, while at the same time making sure that the user query is properly translated in order to be communicated to all sorts of different multimedia archives, thus offering unified multimedia access services. The typical mediator follows a 3-tier architecture such as the one depicted in Figure 1. The central idea in its design is the strict and formal definition of the interface points between the three components.

From the *developer's* point of view (*presentation-tier*) this allows for the design of multiple, customized user interfaces that are all able to connect and interact with the central system. This way, for example, the same mediator can be used by uses in different countries, by simply providing user interfaces with different languages. This can also allow for the generation of different user interfaces for first time users and experts, as well as for customized user interfaces for users with different access rights.

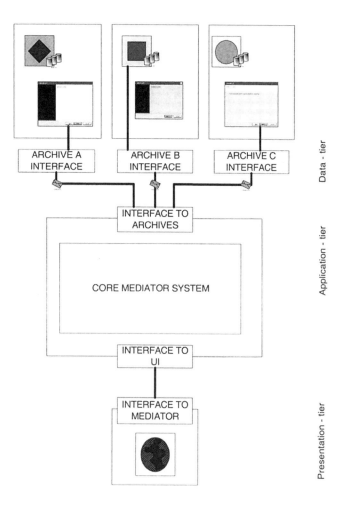

Figure 1. A typical 3-tier architecture for a multimedia mediator.

From the *researcher*'s point of view (*application-tier*) this allows for the constant update and extension of the core system with the inclusion of knowledge and intelligent processing modules. The application-tier is the processing heart of the mediator where all intelligence is included. The definition of formal and strict interfaces to the other tiers allows for the standardization of the data accepted as input and data provided at the output. By choosing a flexible and descriptive data model for the application-tier we allow for maximum extensibility though the integration of emerging and future technologies in the processing stages, as, for example, contextual and ontological reasoning.

Finally, from the *archivist*'s point of view (*data-tier*) this allows for the easy inclusion of more archives. Having a strictly defined interface between the application-tier and the data-tier allows for

i) The participation in the same system of archives that are diverse in storage structure,

ii) The inclusion of more archives at a time later than the design and development of the overall system, with minimal cost and effort, and

iii) The development of new archives that are able to be connected directly to the mediator system

Unified access: mediators vs. integration

A good way for one to fully grasp the importance of mediator technology is to consider its predecessor. In the case of a business take over, or in strategic alliances, archives had the need to have and/or to offer unified access to their data. Prior to mediator systems this need for unified access was satisfied through data integration. In this approach, existing data from two, or more, existing systems had to be ported to a single system.

The storage structure of this system would ideally be flexible enough to support all annotation features existing in either of the participating archives. Then, in the merging phase, all existing data had to be processed, manually to the greatest part, in order for the existing annotation to be transformed into the supported structure. In practice, due to the fact that this manual processing is strenuous, time consuming and expensive, the structure chosen was typically that of the largest – in amount of contained data – archive, thus minimizing the size of the manually processed data.

The data integration approach to data unification has important drawbacks, most of which are rather obvious:

i) The cost of data integration is often prohibitive, so unified access is only provided in the limited cases that the foreseen financial benefits are important,

ii) The storage structure chosen for the integrated system is not the optimal one, so there is limited descriptive power and limited support for future extension,

iii) The integration of more archives at a later time is not straight forward and

iv) The integration of large-scale archival systems, or equivalently of large numbers of archival systems, is not practically and financially feasible.

What is most important is that archives are required to either abandon their existing systems, thus loosing the ability to serve a part of their existing clientele, or maintain duplicated data in both systems, thus having to suffer the burden of manually assuring that the two versions remain identical trough all future updates and insertions of new data. Mediator technology provides an answer to all these issues, by separating the notions of data and access integration; mediators allow for unified access while at the same time avoiding the costly and problematic procedure of integrating archived data into a single system.

Syntactic vs. semantic integration

The role of a mediator system is to allow for unified access, though a single user interface, to multiple data storage locations. In a multimedia environment, the typical role of a mediator system to date has been to allow for unified access to archives that are possibly diverse in storage structure; this is often referred to as structural or syntactic integration. With the development of larger, international and multicultural multimedia markets, syntactic integration is no longer sufficient. Emerging multimedia mediator systems take a step further and also aim for semantic integration [17]; this refers to the integration of systems that are not only diverse in structure, but also in nature – and possibly even in annotation language.

The desired goal is to be able to provide a system that is able to connect to any type of multimedia archive, be it a movie archive, news archive, audio archive, multimedia library etc. and allow end users to uniformly query all available data, much like Google for web pages. The difference from Google is that considered data is available in structured annotated forms and the annotation needs to be exploited to the greatest possible extent in order to be able provide optimal access services to end users.

Of course, the uniform exploitation of annotation information that is not available in a uniform format is not trivial. As a result, a main difference of this new breed of mediator systems is in the way they process available information. Most existing mediators rely on methodologies borrowed from textual and multimedia retrieval systems for their retrieval and indexing procedures, respectively. Emerging multimedia mediators rely on methodologies from knowledge engineering and ontologies for retrieval, and multimedia ontologies for indexing purposes, on order to be able to consider this diverse annotation information.

The *Faethon* multimedia mediator system is a characteristic example of semantic oriented multimedia mediators [18]. The abstract architecture of the system is depicted in Figure 2. The *interface to archives* (data-tier) is at the top and the user interface (presentation-tier) is at the bottom – the interaction components are in charge of accepting data and forwarding to the core system while the presentation components are in charge of accumulating data from the core system (application-tier), formatting it and forwarding to the communications component.

The system operates in two distinct and parallel modes: query and update. In *query mode*, the end user is offered the ability through the UI to specify a *syntactic query* – a query based on strict annotation details of the desired documents specified through the MPEG-7 descriptors, e.g. creation information like title or production date – as well as a *semantic query* – a free text query that the mediator will have to process, interpret semantically and match to document semantics. The syntactic query is forwarded to the search engine and handled with traditional multimedia retrieval techniques. Specifically, the search engine forwards the query to the participating archives and merges the responses of those archives that respond in a timely fashion. The semantic query is received, interpreted, analyzed and expanded by the query analysis module. Matching to documents is again performed by the search engine, relying on indexing information already stored in the

DBMS of the core system during update mode. The overall response – considering both the semantic and metadata part of the user query – is then personalized and re-ranked based on the user profile and returned to the user.

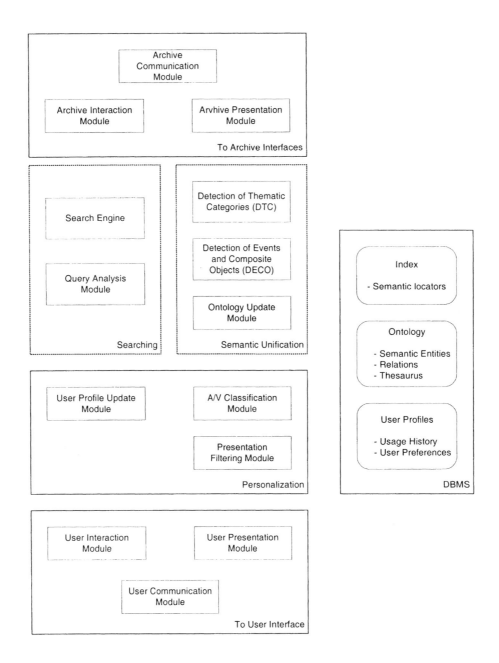

Figure 2. Abstract architecture of the Faethon multimedia mediator system.

Of course, in order for the query analysis module to be able to provide a response, an appropriate indexing of documents needs to have already been performed. This is performed in the offline, *update mode* of operation by the DTC (Detection of Thematic Categories) and DECO (Detection of Events and Composite Objects) modules. It is worth mentioning that the offline mode is not a mode of operation that requires the system to be unavailable; the "offline" term simply refers to the fact that there is no strict time frame within which it is imperative for the participating processes to have provided their output, and thus more sophisticated algorithms may be utilized. In fact the DTC and DECO modules are always active, indexing new documents or refreshing indexing information based on newly acquired knowledge, much like web crawlers of internet search engines that continuously crawl the web indexing new pages or refreshing the indexing information for known ones. In the same mode, accumulated usage information can be processed for the update of the user profiles for personalization purposes.

All of the processes of the core system, both online and offline, are heavily dependent on the knowledge stored in the ontology which allows for intelligent, semantic treatment of data that is independent of the annotation style and language. Other system components include the index, ontology update module, and the personalization subsystem along with the user profiles. These are discussed in [19], [20] and [21].

References

1. S. Battista, F. Casalino, and C. Lande, "MPEG-4: A Multimedia Standard for the Third Millennium," Part 2. IEEE Multimedia Vol. 7, No. 1, pp. 76-84, 2000.
2. ISO/IEC JTC1/SC29/WG1 N1646R: JPEG 2000 Part I Final Committee Draft Version 1.0, 2000.
3. T. Sikora, "The MPEG-7 Visual standard for content description - an overview," IEEE Transactions on Circuits and Systems for Video Technology, Special Issue on MPEG-7, Vol. 11, No. 6, pp. 696-702, June 2001.
4. MPEG-21 Overview v.3, ISO/IEC JTC1/SC29/WG11 N4511, December 2001
5. Synchronized Multimedia Integration Language (SMIL). Recommendation REC-smil-1998 0615, World Wide Web Consortium (W3D), 1998.
   http://www.w3.org/TR/REC-smil.
6. M. R. Naphade, I.V. Kozintsev, and T.S. Huang, "A factor graph framework for semantic video indexing," IEEE Transactions on Circuits and Systems for Video Technology, Vol. 12, No. 1, January 2002, pp. 40-52.
7. O. Mich R. Brunelli, and C.M. Modena, "A survey on video indexing," Journal of Visual Communications and Image Representation, Vol. 10, 1999, pp. 78-112.
8. J. Euzenat, D. Fensel, R. Lara, and A. Gómez-Pérez, "Knowledge Web: Realising The Semantic Web, all The Way to Knowledge Enhanced Multimedia Documents," Proceedings of European Workshop on the Integration of Knowledge, Semantics and Digital Media Technology (EWIMT), London, U.K., November 2004.
9. I. Kompatsiaris, Y. Avrithis, P. Hobson, and M.G. Strinzis, "Integrating Knowledge, Semantics and Content for User-Centred Intelligent Media Services: the aceMedia Project," Proceedings of Workshop on Image Analysis for Multimedia Interactive Services (WIAMIS), Lisboa, Portugal, April 2004.
10. J. Biskup, J. Freitag, Y. Karabulut, and B. Sprick, "A mediator for multimedia systems," Proceedings of 3rd International Workshop on Multimedia Information Systems, Como, Italy, September 1997.
11. C. Altenschmidt, J. Biskup, U. Flegel, and Y. Karabulut, "Secure mediation: requirements, design, and architecture," Journal of Computer Security, Vol. 11, No. 3, March 2003, pp. 365 – 398.

12. A. Brink, S. Marcus, and V. Subrahmanian, "Heterogeneous Multimedia Reasoning," IEEE Computer, Vol. 28 , No. 9, September 1995, pp. 33-39.

13. I. Glöckner and A. Knoll, "Natural Language Navigation in Multimedia Archives: An Integrated Approach," Proceedings of the 7th ACM International Conference on Multimedia, Orlando, FL, pp. 313-322.

14. I. Cruz and K. James, "A user-centered interface for querying distributed multimedia databases," Proceedings of the 1999 ACM SIGMOD International Conference on Management of Data, Philadelphia, PA, 1999, pp. 590-592.

15. B.R. Rao, "Making the Most of Middleware," Data Communications International, Vol. 24, No. 12, September 1995, pp. 89-96.

16. S. Steinke, "Middleware Meets the Network," LAN: The Network Solutions Magazine, Vol. 10, December 1995, pp. 56.

17. M. Wallace, T. Athanasiadis, Y. Avrithis, A. Delopoulos, and S. Kollias, "Integrating Multimedia Archives: The Architecture and the Content Layer," Systems Man and Cybernetics, 2005.

18. Y. Avrithis, G. Stamou, M. Wallace, F. Marques, P. Salembier, X. Giro, W. Haas, H. Vallant, and M. Zufferey, "Unified Access to Heterogeneous Audiovisual Archives," Journal of Universal Computer Science, Vol. 9, No. 6, pp. 510-519, 2003.

19. M. Wallace and G. Stamou, "Towards a Context Aware Mining of User Interests for Consumption of Multimedia Documents," Proceedings of the IEEE International Conference on Multimedia (ICME), Lausanne, Switzerland, August 2002.

20. M. Wallace, G. Akrivas, G. Stamou, and S. Kollias, "Representation of user preferences and adaptation to context in multimedia content -- based retrieval," Proceedings of the Workshop on Multimedia Semantics, SOFSEM 2002: Theory and Practice of Informatics, Milovy, Czech Republic, November 2002.

21. S. Bloehdorn, N. Simou, V. Tzouvaras, K. Petridis, S. Handschuh, Y. Avrithis, I. Kompatsiaris, S. Staab, and M. G. Strintzis, "Knowledge Representation for Semantic Multimedia Content Analysis and Reasoning," Proceedings of European Workshop on the Integration of Knowledge, Semantics and Digital Media Technology (EWIMT 04), London, U.K., November 2004.

MULTIMEDIA AUTHENTICATION

Jiying Zhao and Abdulmotaleb El Saddik
School of Information Technology and Engineering
University of Ottawa, Ontario, Canada

Definition: *Multimedia authentication deals with confirming the genuineness or truth of the structure and/or content of multimedia.*

Multimedia signal can be easily reproduced and manipulated. Although we cannot perceive the change, what we are seeing or listening to may have been changed maliciously for whatever reasons. Multimedia authentication is to confirm the genuineness or truth of the structure and/or content of multimedia. Multimedia authentication answers the following questions: 1) is the multimedia signal from its alleged source? 2) has it been changed in any way? 3) where and to what degree has it been changed if changed? There are mainly two approaches that can answer these questions. The first approach to multimedia authentication is cryptograph; while the second approach is the digital watermarking. In addition, cryptograph can be integrated into digital watermarking to provide more desirable authentication. It is worth mentioning that multimedia authentication is different from user authentication.

Authentication using cryptography

Treating multimedia signal as normal text (sequence of bytes), cryptographic techniques and hash functions can be used to authenticate multimedia content. There are three common authentication modes:

1) The sender uses a secure one-way hash function to generate a hash value $H(m)$ and appends to the plain message m without further encryption to form $m + H(m)$ to send; the receiver calculates hash value $H(m')$ of the received possibly-attacked message m', and compare $H(m')$ with the received possibly-damaged hash value $(H(m))'$. If $H(m')$ and $(H(m))'$ are same, the received message m' is authentic ($m' = m$); otherwise is not.

2) The sender uses a one-way hash function (secure or not) to generate a hash value $H(m)$, encrypts the hash value and appends to the plain message to form $m + E(H(m))$ to send; the receiver decrypts the received encrypted hash value to obtain the possibly-damaged hash value $(H(m))'$, calculates the hash value $H(m')$ of the received possibly-attacked message m', and compares the calculated hash value $H(m')$ with the decrypted hash value $(H(m))'$. If $H(m')$ and $(H(m))'$ are same, the received message m' is authentic ($m' = m$); otherwise is not.

3) The sender uses a one-way hash function (secure or not) to generate a hash value $H(m)$, appends to the plain message, encrypts the resulting combination of the plain message and the hash value to form $E(m + H(m))$ to send; the receiver decrypts the received combination of the plain message and hash value to obtain the possibly attacked or damaged combination $m' + (H(m))'$, calculates hash value $H(m')$, and compares the calculated hash value $H(m')$ with the received hash value $(H(m))'$. If $H(m')$ and $(H(m))'$ are same, the received message m' is authentic ($m' = m$); otherwise is not.

In the above three modes, + stands for appending (concatenation) operation, m' stands for the possibly attacked version of the transmitted message m, and $(H(m))'$ stands for the possibly-damaged version of $H(m)$.

In the above authentication modes, both cryptography and hash function are indispensable. In the following, we introduce symmetric-key cryptography (sometimes called private-key cryptography), asymmetric-key cryptography (sometimes called public-key cryptography), and secure one-way hash functions.

Symmetric-key cryptography

In symmetric-key cryptography, two parties share a single cipher key, K. There are an encryption function, $E(\bullet)$, and a decryption function $D(\bullet)$. A plaintext, m, is converted to encrypted ciphertext, m_c, by $m_c = E(m, K)$. Similarly, the ciphertext, m_c, is decrypted back to the plaintext m by $m = D(m_c, K)$. The two most important symmetric algorithms are the Data Encryption Standard (DES) [15] and the Advanced Encryption Standard (AES) [16]. See the short article: Data Encryption Standard (DES) and Advanced Encryption Standard (AES).

In addition to encryption, a symmetric-key cryptographic algorithm can be used for the abovementioned three authentication modes. It can authenticate the multimedia content and the source. Assuming that only the sender and receiver share a secret key K, then only the genuine sender would be able to successfully to encrypt a message for the receiver. If the message includes a hash value, $H(m)$, the receiver is assured that no alternations have been made if the re-calculated hash value is equal to the sent hash value.

Symmetric cryptography is more efficient than asymmetric cryptography when used on peer-to-peer session, but does not work well when there are more parties involved.

Hash functions

A hash function maps a variable-length string into a fixed-length hash value [2]. The simplest hash functions can be error detection codes such as parity check, checksum, or Cyclic Redundancy Code (CRC). However, these error detection codes cannot check out malicious alternations, since an attacker can try to change the content in a way that does not change the error detection result. For example, the attacker can make the alternation divisible by the used CRC polynomial in order to defeat CRC. Therefore, these insecure error detection codes should be used together with a symmetric-key or asymmetric-key cryptographic algorithm to authenticate multimedia content. Without using cryptography, a secure hash function is needed to defeat malicious attacks.

A secure hash function accepts a variable-size message m as input and produces a fixed-size message digest $H(m)$ as output. A secret key can be appended to the end of message to generate a more secure hash value. A one-way hash function is a hash function that is reasonably cheap to calculate, but is prohibitively expensive to invert [2]. Common one-way secure hash functions are MD5 Message-Digest Algorithm [13] and the Secure Hash Algorithm (SHA) [17]. MD5 produces a 120-bit digest. SHA is considered to be the successor to MD5. SHA has four members, SHA-1, SHA-256, SHA-384, and SHA-512. They produce respectively a 160-, 256-, 384-, and 512-bit digest. The longer the digest size a hash function produces, the more difficult to beak, therefore the more secure it is. SHA is considered more secure than MD5 because it can produce longer digest size. See the short article: MD5 Message-Digest Algorithm and Secure Hash Algorithm (SHA).

Hash functions are indispensable in cryptograph-based multimedia content authentication, and it is also used in watermarking-based authentication algorithms.

Asymmetric-key cryptography

Asymmetric-key cryptography uses a different key for encryption than is used for decryption. The most widely used public-key algorithm is RSA [14]. In RSA's encryption, a pair of keys are used, the receiver's public key K_{RE} and the receiver's private key K_{RD}. The message is encrypted using the receiver's public key K_{RE}, in $m_c = E(m, K_{RE})$; and is decrypted using the receiver's private key K_{RD}, in $m = D(m_c, K_{RD})$. See the short article: the RSA Public-Key Encryption Algorithm.

Asymmetric-key cryptography can be used for authentication in terms of source and data integrity. To do this, the sender's private key K_{SD} and sender's public key K_{SE} are used. For authentication, the message is encrypted using the sender's private key K_{SD}, in $m_c = E(m, K_{SD})$; and is decrypted using the sender's public key K_{SE}, in $m = D(m_c, K_{SE})$. No one else except for the sender can encrypt a message that can be decrypted by using the sender's public key. This feature can be used to ensure that the message is from the right sender and has not been altered. Sometimes, it is difficult to judge whether the message is altered by using only the encryption. Therefore a secure hash function is indispensable no mater whether it is symmetric cryptograph or asymmetric cryptograph.

Asymmetric cryptography scales better than symmetric cryptography, but it is slower.

The cryptography and hash function based authentication gives a binary judgment, as to whether the message has been changed or not. A message with even 1-bit change will be judged as inauthentic. This is not always desirable for multimedia content authentication, since for some applications a multimedia signal with imperceptible changes may be considered as authentic. Digital watermarking is a good candidate for authenticating multimedia content. Cryptograph and digital watermarking can work together to provide better solutions.

Authentication using digital watermarking

Digital watermarking can be used to authenticate the multimedia content. The basic idea is that the embedded watermark will become undetectable if the multimedia content is changed. Depending on the robustness of the watermark, the watermarking based authentication can be classified into exact authentication, selective authentication, and localization [2]. It is worth pointing out that the classification is fuzzy since some watermarking algorithms belong to more than one class.

Exact authentication

Exact authentication is to check whether the multimedia content has undergone any change at all. If even a single bit, pixel, or sample has been changed, the multimedia content will be declared as inauthentic. Exact authentication can be fulfilled by using fragile watermarking.

A fragile watermark becomes undetectable after multimedia content is modified in any way. A simple example of a fragile watermark is the least-significant-bit (LSB) watermark, in which the LSB of each signal sample is replaced (over written) by a payload data bit embedding one bit of data per input sample. If a predefined bit sequence embedded in the least-significant-bit can be detected, it is implied that the content has not undergone changes. The least significant bit is the most vulnerable and will be changed by the lightest global processing. However, malicious attacks can defeat this approach if the watermark is independent from the multimedia content. Attackers can simply replace the LSB of a multimedia content by the LSB of the authentic one. In addition the method cannot detect the changes in the significant bits.

Yeung and Mintzer [7] proposed a pixel-wise image authentication system. The extraction process employs a pseudo-random mapping, $m(\bullet)$, from pixel intensities into binary values [2]. To embed a binary bit at pixel $X(i, j)$, the embedder enforces the equation $W(i, j) = m(X_w(i, j))$, where $W(i, j)$ is the watermark bit, and $X_w(i, j)$ is the watermark pixel. The embedder compares the mapped binary value $m(X(i, j))$ to the watermark bit $W(i, j)$. If $W(i, j) = m(X(i, j))$ no action is needed ($X_w(i, j) = X(i, j)$). If $W(i, j) \neq m(X(i, j))$, $X(i, j)$ is replaced by $X_w(i, j)$ that the closest to $X(i, j)$ and $W(i, j) = m(X_w(i, j))$. The detector extracts the watermark from pixel $X'_w(i, j)$ of the possibly attacked watermarked image using mapping $W'(i, j) = m(X'_w(i, j))$. If the watermarked image has not been modified, this extracted value $W'(x, j)$ exactly matches the watermark bit $W(i, j)$. However, if a region has been modified, $W'(x, j)$ will not match $W(i, j)$.

The LSB based algorithms and Yeung and Mintzer's algorithm are not secure. An authentication signature can be created to solve the problem. Friedman [6] described a "trustworthy digital camera" in which a digital camera image is passed through a hash function and then is encrypted using the photographer's private key to produce a piece of authentication data separated from the image. These data are used in conjunction with the image to ensure that no tampering has occurred. Specifically, the photographer's public key is used to decrypt the hashed original image and the result is compared to the hashed version of the received image to ensure authentication. The resulting signature can be embedded into the least significant bits of the image to enhance the security. The authentication signature can guarantee the integrity of the content, therefore exact authentication. Walton [11] proposed a technique in which a separate piece of data is not required for authentication. The method requires the calculation of the checksums of the seven most significant bits of the image, so that they may be embedded into randomly selected least significant bits. These two techniques are focused on detecting whether an image was tampered with or not. However, they do not clearly specify how and where the image has been changed.

A well-known block-based algorithm is the Wong's scheme [10], where the hash value from a block with LSB zeroed out is XORed with the corresponding block of the binary logo image, encrypted, and inserted to the LSB of the block [9]. To verify an image, the LSBs are extracted, decrypted, and XORed with the hash value calculated from the possibly attacked image. If the result is the original binary logo, then the image is authentic. Any tamper to a block will generate a very different binary output for the block due to the property of the hash function.

Selective authentication

Image, video, or audio is different from text message. A small change may not be noticeable to human's eyes or ears. That is also the reason why they can be compressed lossy. Some distortions are acceptable such as light compression and noise addition. Some attacks are considered as malicious such as modification and cropping. This can be implemented via semi-fragile watermarking. A semi-fragile watermark is robust to light changes and fragile to significant changes. The watermark should be embedded in such as way that when the distortion is light the watermark should be detectable; when the distortion is significant the watermark should become undetectable.

Most semi-fragile watermarking algorithms are designed based on quantization. Here only a few typical algorithms are discussed. Wu and Liu [3] proposed a watermarking scheme for image authentication which was based on a look-up table in frequency domain. The table maps every possible value of JPEG DCT coefficient randomly to 1 or 0 with the constraint that runs of 1 and 0 are limited in length to minimize the distortion to the watermarked image. To embed a 1 in a coefficient, the coefficient is unchanged if the entry of the table corresponding to that coefficient is also a 1. If the entry of the table is a 0, then the coefficient is changed to its nearest neighboring values for which the entry is 1. To embed a 0 is similar to embedding a 1.

Lin and Chang [8] proposed a semi-fragile watermarking algorithm to survive light distortions. Signature is extracted from the low-frequency coefficients of the pairs of DCTs of an image and is embedded into high frequency coefficients in the DCT domain. The authentication signature is based on the invariance of the relationship between DCT coefficients of the same position in separate blocks of an image. According to a property of quantization, if two values are quantized by the same step size, the resulting values maintain the same relation to one another [2]. That is, if $a > b$, then $a \lozenge q \geq b \lozenge q$ [2], where $\lozenge$ is the quantization operator defined in the short article: Quantization. The relationship will be preserved when these coefficients are quantized in a JPEG compression by a quantization step size that is smaller or equal to the quantization step size used for watermark embedding [8]. Other distortions such as cropping will destroy the relationship between DCT blocks, therefore destroy the authentication watermark. See the short articles: Discrete Cosine Transform (DCT) and Quantization.

Kundur and Hatzinakos [4] presented a fragile watermarking approach that embeds a watermark in the discrete wavelet domain of an image. In this approach, the discrete wavelet decomposition of a host image is first computed. A user-defined coefficient selection key is then employed. The binary watermark bit is embedded into the selected coefficient through an appropriate quantization procedure. Finally, the corresponding inverse wavelet transform is computed to form the tamper-proved image. In the extraction procedure, a quantization function is applied to each of the selected coefficients to extract the watermark values. For authentication, if it fails, then a tamper assessment is employed to determine the credibility of the modified content. The quantization technique used is similar to the one used in [3]. This approach is also referred to as "tell-tale" watermarking. Watermark in the different wavelet level can give different authentication precision. For discrete wavelet transform, see the short article: Discrete Wavelet Transform (DWT).

It is desirable to know not only whether the content has been changed, but also where has been changed, even how has been changed. This can be fulfilled by using tell-tale watermark.

Localization

Some authentication algorithms can identify whether the content has been changed, where has not been changed (therefore still usable). This is referred to as localization. Watermarking algorithms that have localization function must be able to provide temporal or spatial information. Block-wise and sample-wise authentication can locate the change to the content [2]. The algorithm of Wu and Liu [3] embeds 1 bit to each DCT block, and the block position provides spatial information of an image. If the embedded bit cannot be detected, then it is clear that the corresponding 8×8 block has been changed. The algorithm of Kundur and Hatzinakos [4] embeds watermark into wavelet coefficients. Discrete wavelet transform carries both frequency and spatial (or temporal) information. Embedding watermark in the discrete wavelet domain allows the detection of changes in the image in localized spatial and frequency domain regions [4].

Audio, video, and image all allow lossy compression, that is, slight changes will not be noticeable. Therefore, watermarking based authentication methods can be used. In addition, most ideas used for image authentication normally can be extended to audio or video authentication. For example, discrete wavelet transform based watermarking algorithms are applicable to audio, video and image.

In addition to multimedia content authentication, some research is on authentication of multimedia structure. Sakr and Georganas [18] first proposed an algorithm for authentication and protection of MPEG-4 XMT structured scenes. They generate a unique data signature about the XMT-A structured scene using MPEG-4 BIFS and pseudo-random encoding sequence. By doing so, the algorithm can detect the structure change of an MPEG-4 stream.

Related to multimedia authentication, digital watermarking can be used for quality evaluation. The basis for this is that a carefully embedded watermark will suffer the same distortions as the host signal does. Cai and Zhao proposed an algorithm that can evaluate the speech quality under the effect of MP3 compression, noise addition, low-pass filtering, and packet loss [19]. Watermarking also can be used for the quality evaluation of image and video [20]. For example, a watermark can be designed to evaluate the effect of JPEG or MPEG compression, i.e., what quantization factor has been used for the compression.

In conclusion, there are currently two approaches to multimedia authentication. One is cryptograph, and the other is digital watermarking. Cryptograph is a relatively well-studied topic, while the digital watermarking is still in its infancy. A strong and seamless integration between cryptograph and digital watermarking will provide us with advanced means of authenticating multimedia content.

See: Data Encryption Standard (DES) and Advanced Encryption Standard (AES), MD5 Message Digest Algorithm and Secure Hash Algorithm (SHA), RSA Public-Key Encryption Algorithm, Discrete Cosine Transform (DCT), Discrete Wavelet Transform (DWT), Quantization

References

1. W. Stallings, "Data and Computer Communications," 7th edition, Prentice Hall, 2004. ISBN: 0-13-100681-9.
2. I. Cox, M. Miller, and J. Bloom, "Digital Watermarking," Morgan Kaufmann Publishers, 2002, ISBN: 1-55860-714-5.
3. M. Wu and B. Liu, "Watermarking for Image Authentication," Proceedings of IEEE International Conference on Image Processing, Vol. 2, pp. 437-441, 1998.
4. D. Kundur and D. Hatzinakos, "Digital Watermarking for Tell-tale Tamper Proofing and Authentication," Proceedings of IEEE, Vol. 87, No. 7, pp. 1167-1180, 1999.
5. C. Lu and H. Liao, "Multipurpose Watermarking for Image Authentication and Protection," IEEE Transactions on Image Processing, Vol. 10, No. 10, pp. 1579-1592, 2001.
6. G.L. Friedman, "The Trustworthy Digital Camera: Restoring Credibility to the Photographic Image," IEEE Transaction on Consumer Electronics, Vol. 39, No. 4, pp. 905-910, 1993.
7. M. Yeung and F. Minzer, "An Invisible Watermarking Technique for Image Verification," Proceedings of the International Conference on Image Processing, Vol. 1, pp. 680-683, 1997.
8. C.Y. Lin and S.F. Chang, "A Robust Image Authentication Algorithm Surviving JPEG Lossy Compression," Proceedings of Storage and Retrieval of Image/Video Databases, SPIE-3312, pp. 296-307, 1998.
9. B.B. Zhu, M.D. Swanson, and A.H. Tewfik, "When Seeing Isn't Believing," IEEE Signal Processing Magazine, Vol. 21, No. 2, pp. 40-49, 2004.
10. P.W. Wong and N. Memon, "Secret and Public Key Image Watermarking Schemes for Image Authentication and Ownership Verification," IEEE Transactions on Image Processing, Vol. 10, No. 10, pp. 1593-1601, 2001.

11. S. Walton, "Information Authentication for a Slippery New Age," *Dr. Dobbs* Journal, Vol. 20, No. 4, pp. 18-26, 1995.
12. C.Y. Lin and S.F. Chang, "Issues and Solutions for Authenticating MPEG Video," Proceedings op Security and Watermarking of Multimedia Contents, SPIE-3657, pp. 54-65, 1999.
13. R.L. Rivest, "RFC 1321: The MD5 Message-Digest Algorithm," Internet Activities Board, 1992.
14. R.L. Rivest, A. Shamir, and L.M. Adleman, "A Method for Obtaining Digital Signature and Public-key Cryptosystems," Communications of the ACM, Vol. 21, No. 2, pp. 120-126, 1978.
15. National Institute of Standards and Technology, "Specification for the Data Encryption Standard (DES)," Technical Report NIST FIPS PUB 46-3, Department of Commerce, October 1999.
16. National Institute of Standards and Technology, "Specification for the Advanced Encryption Standard (AES)," Technical Report NIST FIPS PUB 197, Department of Commerce, November 2001.
17. National Institute of Standards and Technology, "Specifications for Digital Signature Standard," Technical Report NIST FIPS PUB 180-2, Department of Commerce, August 2002.
18. Z. Sakr and N.D. Georganas, "An MPEG-4 XMT Scene Structure Algorithm for Authentication and Copyright Protection," Proceedings of 14th International Workshop on Research Issues on Data Engineering: Web Services for e-Commerce and e-Government Applications, pp. 48-55, 2004.
19. L. Cai and J. Zhao, "Evaluation of Speech Quality Using Digital Watermarking," IEICE Electronics Express, Vol. 1, No. 13, pp. 380-385, October 2004.
20. S. Wang, D. Zheng, J. Zhao, W.J. Tam, and F. Speranza, "Video Quality Measurement Using Digital Watermarking," Proceedings of HAVE2004, IEEE International Workshop on Haptic, Audio and Visual Environments and their Applications, Ottawa, Ontario, Canada, pp. 183-188, 2004.

MULTIMEDIA AUTHORING

Nalin Sharda
Victoria University, Melbourne, Australia.

Definition: *Multimedia authoring involves collating, structuring and presenting information in the form of a digital multimedia, which can incorporate text, audio, and still and moving images.*

Introduction

Authoring involves collating, structuring and presenting information in the form of a document created in some medium or media (Csinger, 1995). Traditionally this has been applied to the production of static text documents. With the advent of digital multimedia systems – that can incorporate text, audio, and still and moving images – authoring process has become much more complex. Interactive multimedia systems allow the user to change the presented content, and therefore, add another level of complexity to the authoring process.

The driving force behind all authoring is the human need to communicate. Verbal, pictorial, sign and written languages have provided the means to communicate meaning since time immemorial (Elam, 1994). Today we can employ multimedia systems to combine text, audio, still and moving images to communicate. Computer-based digital multimedia systems not only provide the means to combine these multiple media elements seamlessly, but also offer multiple modalities for interacting with these elements (Elin, 2001). The cross-product of these multiple elements and modalities gives rise to a very large number of ways in which these can be combined (Lemke, 1998).
To handle the complexity of multimedia authoring we need to combine theories, models, tools, and processes from the domains of the arts, sciences and technology for creating meaningful content (Sharda, 2004a). Movies have a much longer history than digital multimedia, and their authoring processes can be used to inform the development of multimedia authoring processes.

Who is the Author?

Digital multimedia systems provide much greater flexibility than the traditional textual documents; this predicates the need for redefining the meaning of authoring. We can get some insight into this new meaning of authoring by exploring the question, "Who is the author of a movie"?

As shown in table 1, a movie is created by a series of transformations. The inspiration and ideas for a story come from life. The Writer uses life experiences to create a story plot; at this stage the Writer is a user, while Life is the author. The Writer then writes a film script, or screenplay, which is used by the Director. Then the Director becomes the author of the raw footage based on the script. Often people consider the Director as the ultimate author of a movie; if this was true, then we should all be happy watching the raw footage. It is the Editor who puts this raw footage together to make the complete movie that can be watched as a meaningful presentation. Therefore, we can say that the Editor is the final author of the movie. However, with a videocassette or a DVD, the Borrower can use the remote control and change the order in which the various scenes are viewed. Now the Borrower is the author, and the other home viewers (deprived of the remote control) are the Users.

Table 1. Transforming life into a movie on the screen

Step	Author	Story transformation stage	User
1	Life	Creates story ideas used by the:	Writer
2	Writer	Writes a script or screenplay used by the:	Director
3	Director	Directs the shooting of raw footage used by the:	Editor
4	Editor	Produces a finished movie, videocassette or DVD for the:	Borrower
5	Borrowers	Can play the movie scenes in any order with a remote control for:	Viewers

Interactive multimedia systems provide the users with the ability to change the presented content, making them the final Authors of the presentation. However, with the ability to easily manipulate multimedia content, new collaborative authoring paradigms are constantly being invented, based on the ideas of remixing and Open Source software (Manovich, 2001b).

Authoring Dimensions

This highly complex process of authoring multimedia content can be viewed as a three dimensional activity, as shown in Figure 1.

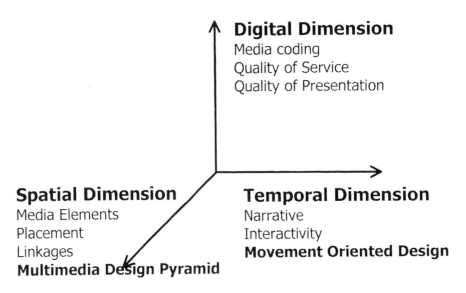

Figure 1. Three authoring dimensions – temporal, spatial and digital.

These three dimensions, namely, temporal, spatial and digital dimensions are not entirely orthogonal. Therefore, changes in one dimension can effect the composition in the other dimensions.

The temporal dimension relates to the composition of the multimedia presentation in time. The main aspect of the temporal composition is the narrative, which is akin to the plot of a story. In traditional media – such as a novel or a movie – the narrative is fixed, and the user is expected to traverse the narrative as per the predetermined plot. In interactive multimedia systems, the user is given the ability to vary the order in which the content is presented; in other words, the user can change the narrative. The Movement Oriented Design (MOD) paradigm (Sharda, 2004b) provides a model for the creation of temporal composition of multimedia systems.

The spatial dimension deals with the placement and linking of the various multimedia elements on each 'screen'. This is similar to the concept of *mis e scéne* used by the film theorists (Cook and Ernink, 1999). In a time varying presentation – such as a movie or an animation – the spatial composition changes continuously: most of the time the change is smooth, and at other times the change is abrupt, i.e. a change of scene. The spatial composition at any point in time must relate to the narrative, or the plot of the temporal composition, while fulfilling the aims and objects of the system. The Multimedia Design and Planning Pyramid (MUDPY) model (Sharda, 2004c) provides a framework for developing the content starting with a concept.

The digital dimension relates to coding of multimedia content, its meta-data, and related issues. Temporal and spatial composition was part of pre-digital multimedia designs as well, e.g. for films, slide shows, and even the very early multimedia projection systems called the Magic Lantern. The digital computer era, particularly over the last two decades has provided much greater freedom in coding, manipulating, and composing digitized multimedia content (Manovich, 2001a). This freedom brings with it the responsibility of providing meaningful content that does not perform fancy 'bells and whistles' (e.g. bouncing letter, or dancing eyeballs) just for the sake of it. The author must make sure that any digital artifact relates to the aims and objectives of the presentation.

Authoring Processes

Authors aim to convey some ideas or new meanings to their audience (Sharda, 2004a). All authoring systems require a process that the author needs to follow, to effectively convey their ideas to the consumers of the content. Novels, movies, plays are all 'Cultural Interfaces' that try to tell a story (Manovich, 2001). Models of processes for creating good stories have been articulated for thousands of years. Nonetheless, some scholars stand out, such as Aristotle, who over 2300 years ago wrote Poetics, a seminal work on authoring (Aristotle, 1996). Robert McKee details story authoring processes as applied to screenplay writing (McKee, 1998). Michael Tierno shows how Aristotle's ideas for writing tragedies can be applied to creating good screenplays (Tierno, 2002). Dramatica is a new theory of authoring, based on the problem solving metaphor (Phillips and Huntley, 2001).

Processes involved in creating a meaningful digital multimedia presentation have evolved from the processes used in other media authoring systems; and some of these are used as metaphors for underpinning the process of creating multimedia. For example, PowerPoint uses the slideshow metaphor, as it relates to lecture presentations based on the (optical) slide projector. Multimedia authoring is one of the most complex authoring processes, and to some extent not as well grounded as those for the more traditional media (England, 1999). The following sections present two authoring models developed for supporting the process of authoring multimedia systems (Sharda, 2004 b, c).

Movement Oriented Design (MOD)

Movement Oriented Design uses story-telling concepts for multimedia authoring. Some of these concepts come from screenplay writing principles. It provides a framework for creating multimedia experience by focusing on three facets: motivation, need and structure, which form the why, what and how of multimedia authoring.

Why / Motivation: The motivation facet directs a project by formulating the project concept as a series of questions, because, only when we ask the right questions, can we get the right answers. We start with a problem statement, break it down into sub-problems and look for solutions by telling a story that solves these problems. This concept is similar to the idea used by Phillips and Huntley in developing the Dramatica authoring paradigm and software.

<u>What / Need:</u> The need facet explores what the user wants. The generic answer is: to get emotional movement. Users crave emotional engagement and stimulation. Consequently, systems that manage to achieve this emotional movement succeed; and the best way to achieve emotional movement is through story telling.

Let us first explore emotional movement from a humanistic story perspective. As viewers come out of a good movie crying or laughing, they often say, "That was so moving". They are talking of emotional movement. Students coming out of a good lecture may not say that it was moving, however, they have gone through a similar experience. Their experience probably began with anticipation, was followed by discoveries, and ended in a new understanding; making it a moving experience. A good multimedia presentation must achieve emotional movement.

<u>How / Structure:</u> To facilitate the creation of a moving story we view each story as an ensemble of story units. In addition, each story unit has three parts: Begin, Middle, and End (BME). This follows the axiom given by Aristotle in his Poetics, that every story must have a beginning, middle and an ending. The beginning (termed Begin) of a story unit lays the groundwork. A good Begin should hook the user, and arouse desire to find out more. Middle should convey the main story message. The End should provide a natural termination; it should conclude the current story unit, and / or link to the next story unit. Any story unit that does not have exactly these three parts is incomplete. Finding effective Begins and Ends is always more challenging than creating the Middles.

<u>Screenplays</u> consist of three acts, which form the BME of the overall story. Each act comprises a number of sequences; each sequence is made-up of scenes. In the current screenplay writing practice, the scene is used as the atomic story element and it changes whenever there is a sudden change in location or time. With Movement Oriented Design, we can further divide scenes into story Movements. The word Movement is used to signify that each of these sub-scenes must move the story. In music, the term movement refers to "a principle self-contained section of a symphony, sonata etc." (Penguin, 1982). A Story Movement must be self-contained; i.e. it must be a micro-story with BME components.

A story works if its Movements work. And a Movement works if its BME components fulfill their function: Begin creates a sense of anticipation, Middle reveals the main message, and the End gives a sense of closure. In addition, the End, wherever possible, should link to the Begin of the next Movement. By linking these Movements in a cause and effect relationship we can create stories that keep the users interested in the narrative. Just as we can create a moving humanistic story, we can create a moving story of any other type, including a multimedia story.

<u>Story Development:</u> To develop a multimedia story, we start by stating its story problem, and propose a solution by identifying, in broad terms, its BME components. Next, we can take each component, and break it down into sub-components, each having its own BME

structure. We follow this process until we arrive at the story Movements. Finding suitable navigation path(s) through these Movements give us either a single story or a collection of alterative stories.

Navigation: Interactive multimedia design presents a level of complexity much higher than that of a linear multimedia presentation. By breaking the entire story into Movements it becomes possible to create a structure where the Movements are linked non-linearly. Different navigation paths provide different solutions to the various story problems. Movement Oriented Design helps in managing the complexity of creating non-linear interactive multimedia system.

Thus, succinctly, the Movement Oriented Design methodology predicates that we can create emotional movement by taking a story problem and developing it into a sequence of connected Movements; where each Movement is a complete story unit with BME components. These Movements can be linked linearly or non-linearly for interactive systems.

Multimedia Design and Planning Pyramid (MUDPY)

Multimedia Design and Planning Pyramid (MUDPY) is a model that supports systematic planning, design, and production of multimedia projects. Designing multimedia is an iterative process that involves ideas taken from a wide range of fields, including marketing, pedagogy, digital technology, aesthetics, graphics, intellectual property law, and management (Elin, 2001). Most projects are team-based, and the development responsibilities are shared amongst the core members of the team: producer, writer, and director. Other personnel involved in the production, such as programmer, photographer, videographer, and voiceover artists may contribute to the design, especially if some aspect proposed in the original design is not feasible, and the system needs to be redesigned. Thus, it is essential to have a framework for clear communications between the members of the design and the production teams. Providing this communications framework is one of the main objectives of the Multimedia Design and Planning Pyramid (MUDPY) model, shown in Figure 2.

Most multimedia creation models and tools are disjoint entities (England and Finney, 1999). It remains the multimedia author's responsibility to integrate the functionality of these models and tools. MUDPY model facilitates the creation of meaningful multimedia (stand-alone or online) by exposing the semantic connections between the various aspects of multimedia authoring.

Multimedia provides a wide range of symbols from the domains of text, audio, still and moving images for creating meaning. These symbols can link in many complex patterns on a page (or screen), and different pages (or screens) can be hyperlinked in multiple ways, each creating a new meaning or a new shade of the same meaning. This makes multimedia-authoring much more complex then traditional authoring in a single medium.

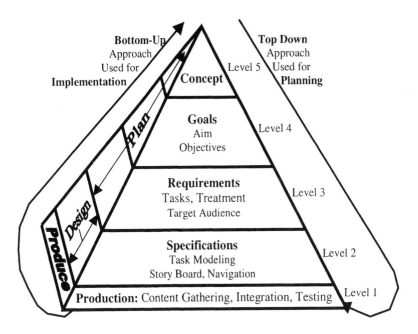

Figure 2. Multimedia Design and Planning Pyramid (MUDPY) model
and its components.

MUDPY provides a conceptual framework for understating multimedia authoring process, and managing their complexity by partitioning the entire process into five levels. To design a multimedia system, we work top-down from level-5 to level-1, expanding higher-level design components into lower-level components; and for implementation we take the bottom-up approach, where the lower-levels aim to fulfill the dictum of the levels above them. Clear understandings of the function of various design components that comprise the MUDPY model helps in creating meaningful multimedia.

Concept statement should give an overview of the entire project in two or three sentences, similar to an "elevator-pitch". All decisions at the lower levels of the project must relate to the Concept statement. The lower levels must do their best to fulfill the intent of the Concept statement, and refer to the same, to resolve any implementation conflicts.

Goals are specified as the Aim and Objectives. Aim should be a short statement that embodies the intention and the purpose of the project. Objectives should be presented as a list of outcomes, or deliverables that need to be attained.

Requirements include the tasks that the system must perform. The dictionary meaning of requirement is, "a compelling need". Thus, in deriving the requirements one has to filter out the needs that are not compelling. This is never an easy task. The system designers need all the help that they can get for this filtering process. More importantly, it is incumbent upon them to make sure that any compelling need is not left out.

<u>Target Audience</u> must be known to the designer to create the most appropriate system. Stating, "anyone can use the system" is not good enough, even if anyone can access it. One can specify the target audience based on age group, profession, interests, special needs etc., as these influence the treatment.

<u>Treatment</u> refers to the look and feel of a multimedia presentation, and that of its various sections. The first level of treatment specificity comes in terms of the percentage of each content type used, that is, text, audio, still images, animation, and video. In selecting the content type one must be aware of the space and bandwidth requirement for each.

<u>Specifications</u> often become the main form of documentation articulating the contractual obligations for all the players in a project. These include the lowest hardware specifications and the communication bandwidth required for delivering the required Quality of Service in online or networked multimedia (Sharda, 1999). Detailed specification of the content can be derived from the Storyboard.

<u>Storyboard</u> is a representative sketch of each page's spatial composition. It helps in developing ideas into screens. It is one of the best means of expanding Objectives and Tasks into screens. It gives the option of visualizing the entire system as a whole, or focusing on one section at a time. It is important to understand that the storyboard should contain meta-information, i.e. information about the content, and not the actual content. A storyboard should then be augmented with navigation links.

<u>Navigation</u> refers to the way various pages and their components link together. The level of interactivity offered by a multimedia system comes primarily from its navigation structure. A well-designed navigation structure links all the components into a cohesive system. Widely used navigation structures include: linear, circular, network and tree structures.

<u>Task Modeling</u> techniques provide the means to specify goal-oriented tasks (Paternò, 2002). Over and above this, Task Modeling provides a window into the required user interface, which has significant influence on the spatial composition and the navigation structure.

<u>Production</u> begins with content gathering, i.e. selecting text, photos, audio and video elements that fulfill the purpose of higher layer design components, followed by integration of these elements using authoring tools such as Authorware, PowerPoint and Flash. Testing of the individual sections as well as the systems a whole must take place under various operating conditions.

Conclusion

Authoring multimedia is much more complex than authoring traditional media. Collaboration between various parties is necessary for authoring any significant multimedia system. There are three multimedia-authoring dimensions: temporal, spatial and digital. These dimensions interact with each other in complex ways. The Movement Oriented Design (MOD) methodology uses story-telling concepts to develop the narrative of a multimedia system in the temporal dimension. Multimedia Design and

Planning Pyramid (MUDPY) is model that supports systematic planning, design and production of multimedia projects. Multimedia project planning and design components include: Concept statement, Goals, Requirements, Target Audience, Treatment, Specifications, Storyboard, Navigation, Task Modeling, Content Gathering, Integration, and Testing. The MUDPY model exposes the relationship between these multimedia authoring aspects, suggests the order in which these should be tackled, and thus, supports cooperation between the members of a multimedia authoring team.

See: Multimedia Project Planning, Multimedia Design, and Multimedia Production

References

1. Aristotle (Translated with an introduction and notes by Malcom Heath), *"Poetics,"* Penguin Books, 1996.
2. P. Cook and M. Ernink, Editors, *"The Cinema Book,"* British Film Institute, 1999.
3. A. Csinger, K.S. Booth, and D, Poole, *"AI Meets Authoring: User Models for Intelligent Multimedia,"* Artificial Intelligence Review, Special issue on user modelling, Vol. 8, pp. 447-468, 1995.
4. L. Elin, *"Designing and Developing Multimedia A Practical Guide for the Producer, Director, and Writer,"* Allyn and Bacon, 2001.
5. K. Elam, *"The Semiotics of Theater and Drama,"* Routledge, 1994.
6. E. England and A. Finney, *"Managing Multimedia,"* Addison Wesley, 1999.
7. J.L. Lemke, *"Multiplying Meaning: Visual and Verbal Semiotics in Scientific Text,"* in J. R. Martin & R. Veel (Eds.), Reading Science, London: Routledge, 1998, pp. 87-113.
8. L. Manovich, *"The Language of New Media,"* The MIT Press, 2001. (a)
9. L. Manovich, *"Who is the Author? Sampling / Remixing / Open Source,"* Retrieved April 2005 from http://www.manovich.net/DOCS/models_of_authorship.doc.
10. R. McKee, *"Story: Substance, Structure, Style and the Principles of Screenwriting,"* Methuen, 1998.
11. F. Paterno, *"Tools for Task Modeling: Where we are, Where we are headed,"* Proceedings of TAMODIA 2002, INFOREC, Bucharest, July 2002, pp. 10-17.
12. The Penguin English Dictionary, Penguin Books Ltd., Harmondsworth, Middlesex, England, 1982.
13. M.A. Phillips and C. Huntley, *"Dramatica: A New Theory of Story,"* 2001, Screenplay Systems Incorporated, California.
14. N.K. Sharda, *"Multimedia Information Networking,"* Prentice Hall, New Jersey, 1999.
15. N. Sharda, *"Multimedia: The Art, Science and Technology of Creating Meaning, Readers' Remarks,"* IEEE MultiMedia, April-June 2004. (a)
16. N. Sharda, *"Movement Oriented Design: A New Paradigm for Multimedia Design,"* Keynote address at the First World Congress on Lateral Computing, Bangalore, India, December 2004. (b)
17. N. Sharda, *"Creating Meaningful Multimedia with The Multimedia Design and Planning Pyramid,"* 10th International Multimedia Modeling Conference, January 2004, Brisbane, Australia. (c)
18. M. Tierno, *"Aristotle's Poetics for Screenwriters: Storytelling Secrets from the Greatest Mind in Western Civilization,"* Hyperion, 2002.

MULTIMEDIA CONFERENCING

Definition: Multimedia Conferencing [1] is one of the main building blocks of collaborative multimedia computing today.

It has been repeatedly hailed as on the brink of ubiquity and as a panacea for communications in distributed teams. In this article, we use the term "multimedia conferencing" instead of videoconferencing because the systems discussed in this section integrate multiple media formats into one system, not just video. The multimedia conferencing market is believed to be one of the key markets within the multimedia market segment. Recent developments in multimedia systems and networking technology show that using desktop multimedia conferencing for group decision-making on WANs such as the Internet is feasible. Researchers have often discussed the failure of video to support interpersonal communication.

The merging of workstation technology and real-time computer conferencing has had a significant impact on CSCW and group decision-making and lead to the term "desktop conferencing". Research on early multimedia conferencing systems such as those developed at AT&T Bell Laboratories, Bellcore, and NEC had as their aim the provision of the facilities found at face-to-face meetings with remote groups. It is generally accepted that computer-supported decision-making and communication results in many changes in communication patterns, greater task orientation and shorter meetings. The main obstacle, we argue in this chapter, is that group problem solving and task accomplishments as well as organizational structure and - process support have never been addressed adequately. Research in communications studies showed that voice is only a little slower than face-to-face communications. This might imply that video is not relevant for effective and efficient communications. Hence, studies provided evidence that the final outcome of any given task is not influenced positively by multimedia conferencing support, although people were happy to use it.

Another promising area in multimedia conferencing research deals with so called "gaze-awareness" support. This research deals with the question of how to provide eye contact between conferencing participants. From a social perspective people who use frequent eye contact are perceived as more attentive, friendly, cooperative, confident, mature, and sincere than those who avoid it. The loss of gaze-awareness is one important contributing factor to the failure of multimedia conferencing as a mass tool. Today, systems supporting gaze-awareness are still in their infancy and mostly first research prototypes.

See: Collaborative Computing – Area Overview

References

1. S. Dustdar, "Cooperative Multimedia Information Systems: Systems, Architectures, and Management Issues," In Multimedia Information Retrieval and Management, D. Feng, W. C. Siu, and Hong-Jiang Zhang (Eds.), Springer Verlag, 2003.

MULTIMEDIA CONTENT ADAPTION

David C. Gibbon
AT&T Labs Research, Middletown, NJ, USA

Definition: *Multimedia content adaptation allows the ever increasing variety of IP enabled devices such as personal digital assistants (PDA), Smartphones, and set-top boxes, to access existing rich media resources available on the Internet.*

Broadly, it is the process of transforming a logical set of video, images, text, and other media from a source representation to one or more target representations. These new forms of content not only accommodate restricted device input and output capabilities, but they also support content delivery over bandwidth constrained connections such as wireless links. Content adaptation techniques can be applied in multimedia indexing and browsing systems and can be used to help maintain quality of service (QoS) for multimedia network services. Note that aspects of content adaptation are often referred to as *content repurposing*, and sometimes as *content reuse* or *re-authoring*.

Purpose: Multimedia content authoring is a time-consuming and expensive process, often involving a production staff. Content owners maintain collections of their assets, eventually building large multimedia archives. Usually the content is designed to be consumed on a specific class of devices, such as desktop PCs. Recently however, the availability of new wireless network services has spurred dramatic growth in numbers of mobile device users. Also, broadband IP services are coming to the set-top through technologies such as ADSL2+ and IPTV. Although these emerging devices may attempt to support access to legacy content, for example by including an HTTP client, often the resulting user experience is unworkable due to device limitations.

Multimedia content adaptation maximizes the return on the authoring investment by increasing the diversity of the content consumption options thereby allowing the content to reach a wider audience. It frees authors from the tasks of creating a specific version for each possible user device. In fact, for legacy content, the devices may not have existed or been widely available at the time of that the content was produced and without content adaptation, existing archives of multimedia content would not be accessible from these emerging devices.

Additional Applications: Since multimedia content adaptation reduces the required bandwidth or bit rate to deliver the content, it can be used for maintaining quality of service by reducing the resource utilization of servers and networks in a more elegant manner than strict admission control [7]. Additionally, it increases flexibility for end-users, reducing costs in cases where the data connection is billed per kilobyte as in some GSM services. While normally intended for rendering content for end users, content adaptation is also useful as a systems preprocessing operation, e.g. feeding video input to a still image retrieval system. The distilled representations that are formed as a result of content adaptation are also relevant to content summarization or indexing. The combination of these benefits allows content adaptation techniques to be used in systems designed for searching and quickly browsing content.

In addition to device/bandwidth adaptation, other types of content adaptation are related to internationalization of content which may involve language translation and localization issues such as character encodings. Persons with hearing impairments or other disabilities can also benefit from content adaptation techniques because adaptation can involve media conversion to a form that is more easily interpreted.

Techniques: When designing and creating multimedia content, authors assume a particular target *user context* which is a specification of device capabilities, connection bandwidth, and usage environment (e.g. whether the user is in a private office or on public transportation.) In some cases, authors may plan for content adaptation by adding semantic tags, specifying allowable substitution sets, prioritizing data, or using scalable codecs. They may even design multiple versions of the presentation for a number of target devices. However, given the sheer number of possible user contexts, it is not practical to build customized versions for each device. Therefore, automatic or semi-automatic methods must be employed, and they should leverage as much knowledge as possible that has been captured from the content author through metadata annotation.

Figure 1 is a conceptual diagram showing how content adaptation occupies a central role in the process of content creation and delivery to end users. The main components of multimedia content adaptation include content analysis to extract semantics, content conversion (transcoding, modality conversion, etc.), decision-making based on user preferences or device capabilities, and view rendering or marshalling multimedia components for delivery.

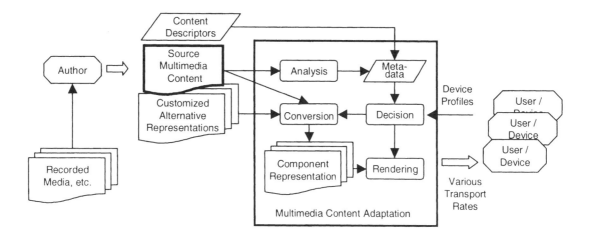

Figure 1. Content adaptation as part of the multimedia delivery process.

As authors generate source multimedia content they may assemble and edit existing recorded media to enhance the presentation. They may produce alternative representations designed for multiple end user devices and differing bandwidth connections. Authors create some level of content description as well; this may range from a minimal set of bibliographic attributes such as title, author name, and creation date, to a very detailed description in a markup language such as HTML or XML. For example, with HTML, document outline level can be expressed using header tags and image descriptors may be included via the "alt" attribute. The authors may use HTML styles encoded in CSS format or, for XML use XSL transformations to help separate content from presentation. For video and audio content, MPEG-7 specifies an XML schema for representing content descriptors [8]. Multimedia Metamodels have also been proposed to formally model the content adaptation process taking human factors into account and using the Unified Modeling Language (UML) for model representation [6]. Since creating detailed content descriptors is tedious, automated media analysis techniques are often used to provide additional metadata to be used for content adaptation. Analysis may include segmentation, such as identifying topic boundaries in long-form content to create smaller, more manageable segments. Pagination techniques compensate for the lack of device spatial resolution by segmenting HTML content into multiple pages to be consumed sequentially, or as a hierarchal outline-like structure [1]. Finally, note that analysis and conversion often are implemented as a joint process rather than as separate modules as shown in the figure.

Device Capabilities: As indicated in Figure 1, when users consume content, they first specify their device capabilities and presentation preferences either explicitly through a profile or active selection of content, or implicitly by virtue of the device that they choose to use to access the content. The device itself may inform the service of its capabilities, or it may simply identify itself and rely upon the server to be aware of its capabilities. There are several standards efforts that address these issues including: HTTP content negation for HTML content, MPEG-7 user preference descriptors, MPEG-21 usage environment descriptors, and SIP feature negotiation.

Table 1 provides a general indication of the range of input and output capabilities (shown as the number of display picture elements) for a typical computer, television, digital assistant, and mobile phone. The last row indicates a rough measure of input capability as the number of keys in the device's keyboard or remote control. Of course this is just one metric, and each device has its own UI strengths, e.g. the TV may display video at higher quality than the PC, PDAs typically include stylus input with touch screens, etc.

Table 1. General indication of input and output capabilities of some common devices.

Device Class	PC	TV	PDA	Phone
Display Capacity (Pixels)	1000K	300K	70K	15K
Input Capacity (Keys)	130	40	10	20

There are many other metrics for quantifying device capabilities including display bandwidth and number of degrees of freedom for input devices. In addition to I/O capabilities, device profiles may also indicate computational capabilities, locale information, or maximum network interface bandwidth. For mobile devices, power consumption is a fundamental concern and users may indicate preferences that will specify scaled down content to conserver power during content rendering and display.

Conversion: Adaptation of time-based media such as audio and video poses different challenges than adapting documents using styles or pagination techniques mentioned above. Many types of devices cannot render video due to the computing and system resource requirements associated with decoding and displaying 15 or 30 frames per second. Other devices may not have audio playback capability. To address these issues, media *modality conversion* attempts to deliver the best possible representation of multimedia content to resource constrained devices [10]. The idea is to convey the content author's message, be it informative or for entertainment, with as much fidelity as possible. Obviously there are limits to the applicability of modality conversion, due not only to the device in question, but also as a function of the type of multimedia content. Since modality conversion involves extracting a concise representation of the author's message, highly structured or annotated content will be more readily processed than unstructured content. For example, modality conversion has been successfully applied for broadcast television news using key-frame extraction and exploiting the closed caption text [5][3]. Another motivation for modality conversion is that it provides for bandwidth reduction beyond what is possible with traditional transcoding.

Figure 2 gives an indication of the order of magnitude of the bandwidth necessary to transmit individual streaming media components.

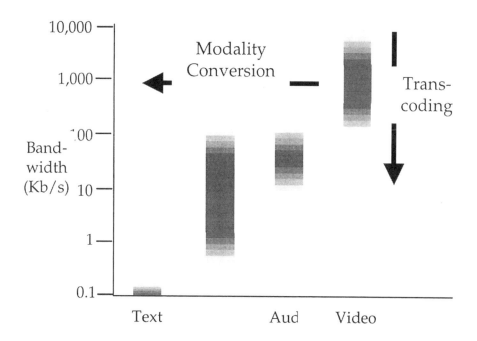

Figure 2. The range of bandwidth requirements for different media types provides motivation for modality conversion and transcoding.

As can be seen, transcoding reduces the bit rate within a media component, while modality conversion achieves this goal by switching among components. Note that while the primary goal of transcoding is bandwidth reduction, it also reduces the client (decoder) computational load if the frame rate or frame size is reduced, thus enabling delivery to a wider range of devices. Similarly, modality conversion not only expands the range of target device types, it also reduces communication bandwidth. The figure suggests a hierarchical priority scheme, where smaller, more critical information is retained, while larger components may be degraded or omitted if necessary [5]. Ideally, authors will provide versions of content in several modalities and indicate allowable substitutions, otherwise automated analysis and conversion methods must be relied upon to generate surrogates.

Transcoding: Media components are compressed using general purpose signal processing techniques to reduce bandwidth requirements while minimizing distortion. Transcoding involves conversion from one encoding to another, reducing the bitrate a second time (*transrating*) or performing format conversion, which may be necessary if the target device is not capable of decoding the content in its native format (e.g. an MP3 player that cannot decode AAC format audio.)

If *scalable encoding* is used for the media components, then transcoding is not necessary; lower bit rate representations can be efficiently derived or extracted from the source material. JPEG 2000's use of wavelet encoding for still frames intrinsically encodes multiple spatial resolutions. MPEG-4 supports spatial, temporal, and even object scalability, where a chroma-keyed layer of video may be independently transmitted.

Content-based Transcoding: Transcoding is largely content-independent and is applicable to a much broader range of content types than modality conversion methods. The limitations of encoding algorithms are related to the basic nature of the content, e.g. natural scenes vs. graphics, or audio vs. speech. However, in some cases specialized content-based processing can be used to reduce bit rates within the same modality. Motion analysis or face detection can be used to extract regions of interest from videos and still frames to dynamically crop source material rather than simply scaling down to a smaller frame size [9]. Along the same lines, video summarization or text summarization can be used to reduce the overall volume of data within a particular modality [10].

Modality Conversion: Common examples of modality conversion include video to image conversion using shot boundary detection and audio to text conversion. Content based video sampling goes beyond shot boundary detection in that intra-shot representative samples are collected via monitoring camera operations such as panning and zooming to more accurately convey the visual contents of a scene. The resulting set of representative images can be played back in a slide-show mode with accompanying audio or displayed as a series of web pages. This latter mode is particularly effective when combined with text from closed captioning or other transcription.

Most modality conversion algorithms assume a particular content domain, e.g. shot boundary detection is only useful for edited or post-production video. Obviously these techniques are not suitable for stationary camera input such as from web cams, and instead, motion based event detection methods are more applicable. Also, speech to text modality conversion using speech recognition cannot be applied directly to arbitrary audio streams that may contain music or multiple languages.

Streaming content and proxy servers: Although Figure 1 suggests an on-demand usage paradigm, content adaptation can also be used on live input streams. In the on-demand case, the content analysis, conversion, and even perhaps rendering can take place before the content is published. Then as users request the content, the decision module can simply select the appropriate rendering, or perhaps marshal some components from sets of renderings and deliver this to the user. However, for real-time communications such as live television or distance learning, these functions must be performed dynamically as the data flows from the producer to the consumer. In these cases, a proxy server architecture can be employed. [10] Dynamic adaptation can also be useful for reducing the storage requirements for large multimedia collections, albeit at the cost of increased computational load. In addition to taking place at production time or distribution time via proxies, content adaptation can take place on the client device in cases where bandwidth and device computational capabilities are not a limiting factor, e.g. as with a set-top box. Clearly the design of content distribution networks (CDN) will be influenced by these alternative architectural design decisions which determine where adaptation takes place.

Content Personalization: Having the ability to convert a particular rich media presentation in to a form that is consumable on a user's device may not be sufficient to build truly useable systems and services. Devices such as mobile phones or IP connected televisions have severely restricted user input modalities which make interacting with multimedia content, or even selecting content for viewing extremely difficult. For these situations, content personalization can be employed to assist in content selection, or to go further and automatically assemble presentations based on user's interests. Users can express their interests beforehand (perhaps using a conventional PC with keyboard) in the form of keywords, categories, news feeds, channels, etc. and this information can be stored by the service provider. Then, when accessing content from input-constrained devices, the system can apply the profile to select appropriate content, and extract relevant segments if necessary [3] [8].

Depending on the task, multimedia content adaptation may involve using a combination of techniques including content personalization, modality conversion, transcoding, and incorporating style sheets. With these tools, the goal of delivering multimedia content to a wide range of user devices can be largely achieved.

See: Cascading Style Sheets (CSS), Content Distribution Network, Video Transcoding, Scalable Coding, Extensible Stylesheet Language (XSL)

References

1. T.W. Bickmore and B.N. Schilit, "Digestor: Device-independent Access to WWW," Proceedings of the 6th WWW Conf., Santa Clara, CA, USA 1997.

2. S. Buchholz and T. Buchholz, "Adaptive content networking," Proceedings of the 1st international symposium on Information and communication technologies, September 2003, Dublin, Ireland.

3. D. Gibbon, L. Begeja, Z. Liu, B. Renger, and B. Shahraray, "Creating Personalized Video Presentations using Multimodal Processing," *Handbook of Multimedia Databases*, Edited by B. Furht and O. Marques, CRC Press, June 2003, pp. 1107-1131.

4. M. Metso, M. Löytynoja, J. Korva, P. Määttä, and J. Sauvola, "Mobile Multimedia Services – Content Adaptation," Proceedings of 3rd International Conference on Information, Communications and Signal Processing, Singapore, 2001.

5. R. Mohan, J. Smith, and C.-S. Li, "Adapting Multimedia Internet Content For Universal Access," *IEEE Transactions on Multimedia*, March 1999, pp. 104-114.

6. Z. Obrenovic, D. Starcevic, and B. Selic, "A Model-Driven Approach to Content Repurposing," *IEEE Multimedia*, Vol. 11, No. 1, January-March 2004, pp. 62-71.

7. N. Shaha, A. Desai, and M. Parashar, "Multimedia Content Adaptation for QoS Management over Heterogeneous Networks," Proceedings of the International Conference on Internet Computing, 2001.

8. B. L. Tseng, C.-Y. Lin, and J.R. Smith, "Using MPEG-7 and MPEG-21 for Personalizing Video," *IEEE Multimedia*, Vol. 11, No. 1, January-March 2004, pp. 42-52.

9. X. Xie, W.-Y. Ma, and H.-J. Zhang, "Maximizing Information Throughput for Multimedia Browsing on Small Displays," 2004 IEEE International Conference on Multimedia and Expo, Taipei, June 2004.

10. H.-J. Zhang, Keynote Speech, "Adaptive Content Delivery: A New Research Area in Media Computing," Proceedings of the International Workshop on Multimedia Data Storage, Retrieval, Integration and Applications, Hong Kong, January 2000.

MULTIMEDIA CONTENT ADAPTATION IN MPEG-21

Definition: MPEG-21 enables the use of multimedia resources across a wide range of networks and devices, and provides multiple adaptation operations such as transcoding, video summarization, replacement, and synthesis.

Content adaptation aims to make content universally accessible (Universal Multimedia Access) depending on terminal capabilities, network, usage and natural environment characteristics. Different networks and terminals imply different quality of service, bit rate, computing and presentation capabilities. MPEG-7, MPEG-21 and a number of adaptation operations aid the development of mechanisms for providing universal multimedia access. While MPEG-7 concentrates on the description of multimedia content and enables quick and efficient searching, identification, processing and filtering of multimedia material, MPEG-21 enables the use of multimedia resources across a wide range of networks and devices [1]. According to their functionality and use for Digital Item Adaptation, the Digital Item Adaptation tools are clustered into three major categories: (i) Usage Environment Description Tools, (ii) Digital Item Resource Adaptation Tools and (iii) Digital Item Declaration Adaptation Tools [2].

The adaptation space comprises of multiple adaptation operations such as transcoding, video summarization, replacement, and synthesis. Similarly, the resource and utility spaces comprise of multiple adaptation operations; the former with transmission, display capabilities, processor speed, power, and memory and the latter with quality or users' satisfaction of the video content, e.g. PSNR, subjective scores, comprehension level. Adapting content for universal access requires selection of either a single or a combination of operations from all three spaces in order to have the generated content, both best optimized for the network and the target device' capabilities and for the user [3]. During adaptation the objective is to find a set of adaptation operations that will maximize the utility of the presentation whilst satisfying various constrains, such as terminal and network limitations, always subject to the user's diversity of preferences.

Using MPEG-21, a user can specify the relative order of each conversion of an original modality and the numeric weight of each conversion. The weights of conversions may help the selection process to determine when conversion should be made. A set MPEG-21 tools [2] namely Terminal and Network QoS describe the relationship between QoS constraints (e.g. on network bandwidth or a terminal's computational capabilities), feasible adaptation operations that may satisfy these constraints and associated media resource qualities that result from adaptation. The Adaptation QoS descriptor provides the means to trade-off these parameters with respect to quality so that an adaptation strategy can be formulated and optimal adaptation decisions can be made in constrained environments.

See: Multimedia Content Modeling and Personalization

References

1. I. Burnett, R. Van de Walle, and K. Hill, J. Bormans, and F. Pereira, "MPEG-21: Goals and Achievements," IEEE Multimedia, Vol. 10, No. 4, October 2003, pp. 60-70.
2. ISO/IEC, "MPEG-21 Digital Item Adaptation," N5845, 2003.
3. S. F. Chang and A. Vetro, "Video Adaptation: Concepts, Technologies, and Open Issues," Proceedings of the IEEE, Vol. 93, No. 1, January 2005, pp. 148-158.

MULTIMEDIA CONTENT MODELING AND PERSONALIZATION

Marios C Angelides
Brunel University, Uxbridge, UK

Definition: *Personalization of information requires content interpretation and modeling, suitable content retrieval and filtering, and filtered-content adaptation to the usage environment.*

Introduction

Increasingly, users want to view multimedia content created specifically or at least tailored to cater for their needs and preferences. When people watch videos, they are likely to be interested only in content that matches their request and they often expect the content to be of certain duration. In addition, achieving interoperability across platforms dictates that content either original or modified adheres to certain standards. While some image tracking techniques create or tailor content by working directly with raw multimedia content, matching the user content needs and preferences becomes harder as the complexity of the user requirements increases.

Personalization of information requires content interpretation and modeling, suitable content retrieval and filtering and filtered-content adaptation to the usage environment. Content interpretation and modeling can be done by extracting semantic and structural information about the content and by examining content meta-data. Once a content model has been built, filtering information from it assumes a user profile or at least expression by the users of their needs or preferences. Whilst the simplest form of information filtering requires users to create their own profile manually or with limited assistance, advanced information filtering may build a profile through the application of learning techniques by direct observation of user behavior during interaction. The content may also be adapted to fit current usage conditions and user preferences. Both filtering and adaptation of multimedia content throughout use requires that the user's needs, preferences, interests, and usage environment are understood and modeled.

Content Modeling

The MPEG-7 Multimedia Description Scheme (MDS) provides the necessary tools for building multimedia content models. At the core of the MDS are the content description and content meta-data tools (see Figure 1).

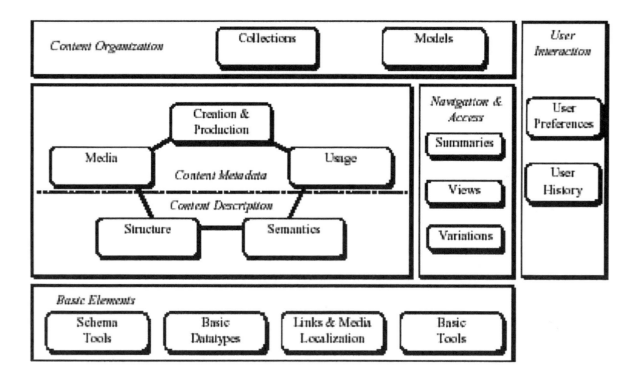

Figure 1. The Multimedia Description Scheme (MDS).

The former (Structure DS and Semantic DS) can be used to describe the structural and semantic information of multimedia content. The latter (Creation & Production, Media and Usage) can be used to describe any meta-information that is available with the content. MDS also includes description schemes that model the user's preferences in relation to video content and which can be stored under the user's control. These schemes support personalized navigation and browsing, by allowing the user to indicate the preferred type of view or browsing, and automatic filtering of preferred content based on the user's needs and preferences. Literature reports various tools that work with MPEG-7.

The approach one normally follows to build the content model is not as essential in achieving the interoperability across platforms as the compliance of the model with a standard is. As a consequence, approaches vary but most authors agree that the basic ingredients of a content model are (not in order of importance or modeling): *objects* depicted in the media stream and their visible and known properties, *spatial relationships* between those objects, *video segments* that describe events involving one or more objects and the *temporal order* between segments.

Video segmentation is traditionally the first step toward multimedia content interpretation and modeling. Segmentation is usually driven by often competing factors such as visual similarity, time locality, coherence, color, motion, etc. Some authors adopt cinematic definitions and rules, such as the 180^0, montage and continuity rules. Often video segments with similar low-level features or frame-level static features such as key frames are grouped together. Over the years, a plethora of different schemes have been suggested to describe the segments: scenes with shots, events with actions, events with sub-events, sequences with sub-sequences, to name just a few. The segments are then mapped into some kind of structure; from the time before MPEG-7, a hierarchical structure or decomposition with incremental top to bottom semantic granularity was the most dominant. What is not unusual, is to have parts of the original stream appearing in more than one segment. This is not necessarily a fault in boundary detection techniques; it may be the case that a video sequence serves multiple interpretations or perspectives of multimedia content, thereby, adding multiple perspectives to a content model.

Once the video has been segmented according to one or more perspectives, the original video sequence looses its meaning in the new and often non-sequential structure. It is therefore important to describe the new chronological order of the segments. The MDS has developed a new set of temporal relationships (see Table 1) in addition to those suggested by Allen in 1983. Often it is necessary to describe the temporal relationship of each segment to all other segments.

However, the actual content of the media stream is the *objects* and their absolute and relative locations in a frame, i.e. their *spatial relationships* to other objects (see Table 1). There are two competing camps with respect to modeling objects: those who use automated image tracking tools to identify objects in each segment and then use automated extraction tools to separate them from the background and those who undertake the painstaking task of manual or semi-automated modeling. With the latter, there is no limit as to what can be modeled: what is visible, what is not, what can be derived, what is known, etc. It is very laborious but it usually ends in very rich and multi-faceted content models. The former tracks and extracts quickly what is visible, what may be obscured, but it does not map or derive from what is known unless it is visible in the footage. Hence, some alternative modeling still needs to be done even with the former. Which of the two is the more efficient is currently subject to debate.

Table 1. MPEG-7 spatial and temporal relationships.

Temporal Relationships			Spatial Relationships	
Binary	**Inverse Binary**	**N-ary**	**Relation**	**Inverse relation**
Precedes	Follows	Contiguous	South	North
CoOccurs	CoOccurs	Sequential	West	East
Meets	MetBy	CoBeing	Northwest	Southeast
Overlaps	OverlappedBy	CoEnd	Southwest	Northeast
StrictDuring	StrictContains	Parallel	Left	Right
Starts	StartedBy	Overlapping	Right	Left
Finishes	FinishedBy		Below	Above
Contains	During		Over	Under

Spatial relationships between objects describe the relative location of objects in relation to other objects (rather than their absolute screen co-ordinates) within the segment and will differ over time. Spatial representations are not an alternative to screen co-ordinates but they complement them. Sometimes when it is difficult to derive screen co-ordinates, a spatial relationship may be the only way to model the object presence.

Content Filtering

The multimodal form of multimedia as well as the heterogeneity of digital media formats makes filtering an intricate problem due to the disparity between the internal structural representations of content elements and the external user requirements for content consumption. Continuous media (Video and audio) requires different filtering techniques from non-continuous media (still images and text) and these can be compartmentalized even further. Filtering techniques analyze content information and prepare presentation of content recommendations using either one or a combination of: rule-based, content-based and collaborative filtering agents.

Rule-based filtering works with rules that have been derived from statistics, such as user demographics and initial user profiles. The rules determine the content that is to be presented to a user. Both the accuracy and the complexity of this type of filtering increase proportionally with the number of rules and the richness of the user profiles. Hence, a major drawback is that it depends on users knowing in advance what content might interest them. Consequently, with this type of filtering, the accuracy and comprehensiveness of both the decision rules and the user modeling are critical success factors.

Content-based filtering chooses content with a high degree of similarity to the content requirements expressed either explicitly or implicitly by the user. Content recommendations relies heavily on previous recommendations, hence, a user profile delimits a region of the content model from which all recommendations will be made. This type of filtering is simple and direct but it lacks serendipity; content that falls outside this region (and the user profile) and might be relevant to a user will never be recommended. Like with rule-based filtering, a major drawback is that the user requirements drive the content filtering process. Hence, this type of filtering is a combined challenge of knowledge engineering and user modeling.

With **collaborative filtering** every user is assigned to a peer-group whose members' content ratings in their user profiles correlate to the content ratings in his own user profile and content is then retrieved on the basis of user similarity rather than matching user requirements to content. The peer group's members act as "recommendation partners" as content retrieved for them but not for a target user can be recommended. With this type of filtering, the quality of filtered content increases proportionally to the size of the user population, and since the matching of content to user requirements does not drive filtering, collaborative recommendations will not restrict a user to a region of the content model. Major drawbacks are the inclusion of new non-rated content in the model as it may take time before it is seen and get rated and the inclusion of users who do not fit into any group because of unusual requirements.

Hybrid filtering techniques are being developed on an *ad hoc* basis, with the aim being to combine strengths and solve weaknesses. For example, a collaborative content-based hybrid eradicates the problems of new non-rated content with collaborative filtering and content diversity with content-based filtering.

Content Adaptation

Adaptation may require that communication of filtered multimedia content take place via different interconnected networks, servers and clients that assume different Quality of Service (QoS), media modality and content scalability (spatial and temporal). Consequently, this will either require real-time content transcoding, if what is required is changing on the fly a multimedia object's format into another, or pre-stored multi-modal scalable content with variable QoS (or a hybrid).

This can be achieved through a combination of MPEG-7 and MPEG-21 capabilities. MPEG-7's *Variation Description Scheme (Variation DS)* enables standardized scalable variations of multimedia content and meta-data for both summarization and transcoding. While transcoding may transform the spatial and temporal relationships, code, color and properties of an object or even remove completely non-essential objects, it seeks to preserve the content model semantics because it is semantic content sensitive. With *intramedia transcoding* content semantics are usually preserved as no media transformation takes place. However, with *intermedia transcoding* content semantics preservation guides the process because media are being transformed from one form to another, e.g. video to text. In this case, while the visual perception of an object may have changed as a result, the semantics of the object should be preserved in the new medium.

MPEG-21's *Digital Item Adaptation (DIA)* (see Figure 2) enables standardized description of a digital object, including meta-data, as a structured digital item independently of media nature, type or granularity. Consequently, the object can be transformed into, and communicated as, any medium. MPEG-21 supports standardized communication of digital items across servers and clients with varying QoS. In order to achieve this, the digital item undergoes adaptation through a resource adaptation engine and/or a descriptor adaptation engine.

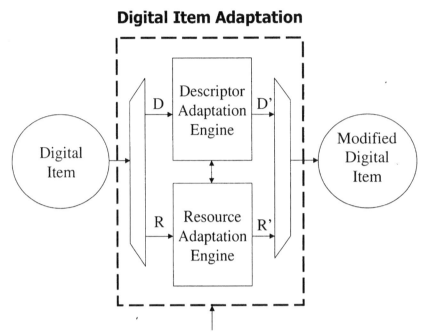

Figure 2. Digital item adaptation.

It is also necessary to describe the usage environment in order to provide the user with the best content experience for the content requested. The usage environment description tools enable description of the terminal capabilities (Codec capabilities, input-output capabilities, device properties) as well as characteristics of the network (network capabilities, network conditions), User (user info, usage preferences, and usage history, presentation preferences, accessibility characteristics, location characteristics), and natural environment (location and time, audiovisual environment).

User Modeling

Personalizing content to the needs of users requires recognizing patterns in users' behavior. In turn this requires a user model which stores past behavior as this is valuable in predicting a user's future interactive behavior. However, basing decisions merely on the past does not fully exploit the user potential, it merely stereotypes a user. Furthermore, the model needs to include personal information about the user. MPEG-7's UserPreferencesDS allows users to specify their preferences for a certain type of content, desired content, ways of browsing, etc. Personal (i.e. demographic) information including prior knowledge and skills, current needs, preferences, interests, goals and plans are acquired directly from the user.

Peer group information is acquired when the user is assigned to a user group. A new member of a peer group may initially be stereotyped often by assuming one of many stereotyped user models. Usage information is acquired by observation during interaction. Filtering shows that is equally important to link content to user needs and preferences as it is to link user needs and preferences to a peer user group in order to acquire a collective user experience.

Concluding discussion

Modeling the semantic content of multimedia enables both the user and the application to engage in intelligent interaction over content and creates the impression that interaction is with the content. Furthermore, semantic content models bestow the ability on the applications that use them to make just-in-time intelligent decisions regarding personalization of multimedia content based on the man-machine interaction and the user expectations. Having the right content filtered through and then adapting it makes interaction with the multimedia content an individual if not an individually rewarding experience. With such applications, multimedia content to be interacted with is not a static commodity but it evolves dynamically.

Unfortunately, neither standard specifies how meta-data are to be used nor filtered according to user requirements. The accuracy and reliability of filtered meta-data to user requirements relies largely on two factors: the richness and depth of detail used in the creation of the meta-data model and the level of content-dependency of the filtering techniques employed. Furthermore, the interoperability of user-driven information retrieval, especially across platforms, is greatly enhanced if the underlying process is standardized and consumption of multimedia content is adapted to suit each user individually. Consequently, whilst it has become necessary to work with standards when modeling, filtering and adapting multimedia content, the entire process of doing so still remains relatively open to individual interpretation and exploitation.

See: Multimedia Content Modeling in COSMOS-7, User Modeling in MPEG-7, Multimedia Content Adaptation in MPEG-21, Geographic Video Content, Emotional Multimedia

References

1. J. F. Allen, "Maintaining knowledge about temporal intervals," Communications of the ACM, Vol. 26, No. 11, November 1983, pp. 832-843.
2. J. Assfalg, M. Bertini, C. Colombo, and A. Del Bimbo, "Semantic annotation of sports videos," IEEE Multimedia, Vol. 9, No. 2, April 2002, pp. 52-60.
3. J. Bekaert, L. Balakireva, P. Hochstenbach, and H. Van de Sompel, "Using MPEG-21 DIP and NISO OpenURL for the Dynamic Dissemination of Complex Digital Objects in the Los Alamos National Laboratory Digital Library," D-Lib Magazine, Vol. 10, No. 2, February 2004.

4. J. Bormans, J. Gelissen, and A. Perkis, "MPEG-21: The 21st century multimedia framework," IEEE Signal Processing, Vol. 20, No. 1, March 2003, pp. 53-62.
5. N. Bryan-Kinns, "VCMF: A Framework for Video Content Modeling," Multimedia Tools and Applications, Vol. 10, No. 1, January 2000, pp. 23-45.
6. I. Burnett, R. Van de Walle, K. Hill, J. Bormans, and F. Pereira, "MPEG-21: Goals and Achievements," IEEE Multimedia, Vol. 10, No. 4 , October 2003, pp. 60-70.
7. S. F. Chang and A. Vetro, "Video Adaptation: Concepts, Technologies, and Open Issues," Proceedings of the IEEE, Vol. 93, No. 1, January 2005, pp. 148-158
8. Cingil, A. Dogac, and A. Azgin, "A Broader Approach to Personalization," Communications of the ACM, Vol. 43, No. 8, August 2000, pp. 136-141.
9. S. H. Ha, "Helping Online Customers Decide through Web Personalization," IEEE Intelligent Systems, Vol. 17, No. 6, December 2002, pp. 34-43.
10. S. Hammiche, S. Benbernou, M. S. Hacid, and A. Vakali, "Semantic Retrieval of Multimedia Data," Proceedings of the 2nd ACM workshop on Multimedia Databases 2004 (ACM MMDB'04), 2004, pp. 36-44.
11. H. Hirsh, C. Basu, and B. D. Davison, "Learning to Personalize," Communications of the ACM, Vol. 43, No. 8, August 2000, pp. 102-106.
12. ISO/IEC, "Information Technology - Multimedia Content Description Interface – Part 5: Multimedia Description Schemes," FDIS 15938-5, 2002.
13. ISO/IEC, "MPEG-21 Digital Item Adaptation," N5845, 2003.
14. H. Kosch, "Distributed multimedia database technologies supported by MPEG-7 and MPEG-21," CRC Press, Boca Raton, Florida, 2003.
15. J. Kramer, S. Noronha, and J. Vergo, "A User-Centred Design Approach to Personalization," Communications of the ACM, Vol. 43, No. 8, August 2000, pp. 45-48.
16. P. Maglio and R. Barrett, "Intermediaries personalize information streams," Communications of the ACM, Vol. 43, No. 8, August 2000, pp. 96-101.
17. M. R. Naphande and T. S. Huang, "A probabilistic framework for semantic video indexing, filtering, and retrieval," IEEE Transactions on Multimedia, Vol. 3, No.1, March 2001, pp. 141-151.
18. F. Pereira and I. Burnett, "Universal multimedia experiences for tomorrow," IEEE Signal Processing, Vol. 20, No. 2, June 2003, pp. 63-73.
19. I. E. G. Richardson, "H.264 and MPEG-4 Video Compression: Video Coding for Next-generation Multimedia," John Wiley, New York, 2005.
20. B. Smyth and P. Cotter, "A personalized television listings service," Communications of the ACM, Vol. 43, No. 8, August 2000, pp. 107-111.
21. B.L. Tseng, C.-Y. Lin, and J.R. Smith, "Using MPEG-7 and MPEG-21 for Personalizing Video," IEEE Multimedia, Vol. 11, No. 4, October 2004, pp. 42-53.

MULTIMEDIA CONTENT MODELING IN COSMOS-7

Definition: *The COSMOS-7 is a content modeling scheme that uses the MPEG-7 standard to describe high and low level features.*

Content modeling is the cornerstone for describing multimedia semantics and accessing content based on user criteria [1]. The COSMOS-7 is a content modeling scheme that uses the MPEG-7 standard to describe all sorts of high and low level features. It is also an interface for creating multimedia semantics that also allows querying of the content.

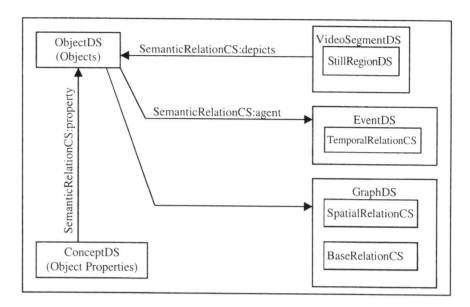

Figure 1. Overview of the COSMOS-7 model.

Figure 1 shows the semantic aspects that COSMOS-7 is modeling, using MPEG-7 [2]. It is assumed that a video is already segmented into smaller and meaningful parts. The media stream contains objects with their absolute position. Objects and their properties are described with the ObjectDS and ConceptDS respectively. The absolute location of an object at a given snapshot is outlined with the StillRegionDS, which is linked with the object it depicts. The objects layout in the video shot defines the spatial relationships between them. These can be either in 2D space, i.e. left, above, or in 3D, i.e. before, inside. The MPEG-7 provides two classification schemes for this; the SpatialRelationCS is used for 2D relationships, while the BaseRelationCS is used for 3D. Finally, events that occur are described with the EventDS. They appear at a given order in a video shot and last for a certain period of time. Their relation in time defines the temporality, and to model this the TemporalRelationCS is used.

A wide range of applications, starting from Video summarization and personalization requires a content modeling scheme as the first step [3], but to benefit the most out of it, all the aspects described have to be present.

See: Multimedia Content Modeling and Personalization

References

1. S. Hammiche, S. Benbernou, M. S. Hacid, and A. Vakali, "Semantic Retrieval of Multimedia Data," Proceedings of the 2nd ACM workshop on Multimedia Databases 2004 (ACM MMDB'04), 2004, pp. 36-44.

2. ISO/IEC, "Information Technology - Multimedia Content Description Interface – Part 5: Multimedia Description Schemes," FDIS 15938-5, 2002.
3. B.L. Tseng, C.-Y. Lin, and J.R. Smith, "Using MPEG-7 and MPEG-21 for Personalizing Video," IEEE Multimedia, Vol. 11, No. 4, October 2004, pp. 42-53.

MULTIMEDIA CONTENT REPURPOSING

Abdulmotaleb El Saddik and Md. Shamim Hossain
School of Information Technology and Engineering
University of Ottawa, Ontario, Canada

Definition: *Content repurposing is the process of converting multimedia content from one format to another, and then representing it to handcraft the device, network and user characteristics.*

The recent advancements in multimedia technology have enabled content providers and consumers alike to gain access to multimedia content over any type of network, via any device, from almost any where, at any time. However, with this rapid growth of pervasive devices, their associated ubiquitous network connections, and their imposed user preferences, new problems, related to distributing multimedia content have emerged:

- Heterogeneity of pervasive client devices and their ubiquitous connections: Heterogeneous clients range from desktop to ubiquitous information appliances, such as DTV, HTV, Laptop, PDA, Cell phone, smart phone etc. They vary greatly in their processing powers, storage and display capabilities. Their connection speeds and methods which range from slow speed wireless networks to high speed wired networks.
- Mobility of clients: Clients may very likely move frequently while accessing multimedia content. Most of the time, there is no QoS guarantee and satisfaction is not even a priority. As network traffic may change with time from high speed to congested. Access networks include a wide range of technologies that vary from Ethernet, Bluetooth, and 3G Mobile, to ISDN, xDSL, and GPRS.

One may, and rightly so, deem the task of developing and handcrafting appropriate multimedia content for some, let alone all of the pervasive devices mentioned above, to be a difficult and expensive one. Considering the ubiquitous network connections and their preferences, as well as each of their combinations, the task becomes even unfathomable. A solution to the problem is content repurposing which refers to the conversion process by which multimedia content that is originally designed for a particular device, platform, or user, is transformed to fit other devices, platforms, or users. By doing so, a single copy of the content is preserved in its original form and is easily separable from its corresponding presentation format. Content repurposing uses existing content to enable its use and reuse in different context depending on the various devices, and user profiles. Hundreds of different device profiles are available for accessing online multimedia content. However, the large variety of existing formats, their proprietary access protocol standards, and the lack of general agreement on how to universalize these multimedia contents make it very difficult to use and reuse content.

Content Repurposing

As mentioned above, content repurposing is the process of converting multimedia content from one format to another, then representing it to handcraft the device, network and user characteristics. This transformation can take place in different ways; some of which are:

- Conversion of different modes (e.g. Speech to text, voice to image, image to text)
- Conversion of video coding format (e.g. MPEG1 to MPEG4)
- Conversion of coding parameter
  - Frame rate (e.g. 30fps to 10 fps)
  - Bit rate (e.g. 6 Mbps TV broadcast to 56 kbps cell phone)
  - Spatial resolution (e.g. CIF to QCIF or 4QCIF)
- Conversion of Spatio-temporal resolution (e.g. VGA to QVGA)
- Content Summarization (e.g. 2 hours news in 15 minutes by highlighting some of the news)
- Visualization of Content (e.g. key fame visualization and browsing for a video).
- Selection of best variation based on MPEG21 part 7 [10] standards:
  - Network Capabilities (e.g. bandwidth, delay and error characteristics).
  - Terminal Capabilities (coding and decoding capabilities, device profiles, and I/O capabilities).
  - User Preferences (e.g. content preferences, presentation preferences, accessibility, mobility and destination).
  - Natural Enviroments (e.g. location, noise level etc.).

Multimedia content repurposing essentially customizes multimedia content and thereby promotes their reuse. Designing and developing multimedia content in a manner that allows the customization, editing, and adaptability to the user's needs is vital to providing high quality content that is cost effective and sustainable [1].

The abstract view of content repurposing is shown in Figure 1.

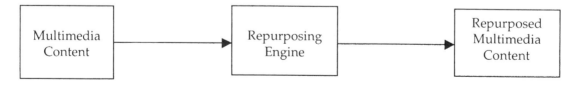

Figure 1. Block diagram of multimedia content repurposing.

Approaches to content repurposing

According to content variation, multimedia content repurposing is divided into the following approaches:

Static repurposing: In this approach, a server pre-processes and stores multiple versions of the multimedia content. A version is 'shaped' by capabilities of network and client and by user preferences, i.e. these factors determine how the content varies. When a client makes a request, the appropriate version is selected from among the existing versions of multimedia content, without any alteration. Most current websites use this approach to avoid extra processing. The advantage of this approach is that there is no processing required since the desired version is already available. This allows for quick delivering and optimal utilization of bandwidth. On the other hand, there is the need for large storage capacities to house the different formats of the multimedia content. Also, every time new formats/versions are invented, content on the server needs to be converted to the new version, rendering the task of maintaining the content a costly one.

Dynamic repurposing: In this approach, after reading multimedia content from the server, it is repurposed on the fly in order to match the client's capabilities. While this approach requires obviously low storage space because server keeps single version of original multimedia content, it requires significant computing power, as there are many operations involved other than repurposing, such as accepting and dynamically classifying user requests, providing transcoding and personalization, and holding and constantly updating user preference profiles [2]. This problem could be solved by content summarization, as the repurposing could be referred to as text summarization, format/version changes, reduction of image or audio quality, cutting down number of key frames, audio to text transcoding etc. Due to the heterogeneity and mobility of devices and their ubiquitous networks connections, dynamic content repurposing is critical.

Hybrid Repurposing: This approach, which was introduced by Shin and Koh [2], uses both the static and the dynamic repurposing approaches selectively in order to preserve bandwidth and storage space. The Static approach is used for the frequently accessed multimedia content, while dynamic approach is used when multimedia content is accessed infrequently. For example, cellular phone accesses multimedia content frequently. In this situation, static repurposing is more appropriate than dynamic, as for each request, the server sends the appropriate version or format to match the client's capabilities. When the content to be accessed is large and infrequently required, network bandwidth requirements are kept at a low priority. Thus, the hybrid approach, in this case, selects the dynamic repurposing scheme.

Multimedia Content Repurposing Architectures

Repurposing may occur at some point between the creation of the initial content and the final rendering on the client device. This can take place at the client's end, at the server's, or at an intermediate proxy between server and client. Based on the architecture, repurposing can be classified into: client-based, server-based, or proxy-based. Each of the mentioned architectures possesses strengths and weaknesses. The main issue is to consider the effectiveness of content repurposing and the efficiency of utilization of the client capabilities in terms of processing power, bandwidth, and storage capacity.

Client Based Repurposing Architecture: This is a raw form of repurposing which is performed mainly on the client devices, without affecting the communication protocol.

This approach helps to avoid transporting large volumes of device and user metadata to the server or the intermediate proxy for repurposing. The repurposing approach is performed on the client device without changing its characteristics, by transferring the entire application from the server to the client. For example, multimedia content and its corresponding style sheets are delivered to the client. Then conversion is performed. Here, multimedia content may include text, images, audio, and video. Another way to client-based repurposing is to deliver the entire multimedia content to the client for the appropriate navigation and selection, based on the client capabilities.

The W3C consortium proposed a client-based repurposing approach [3] including some techniques such as: image resizing, font substitution, transcoding, dedicated rendering and contextual selection.

Used with thin clients such as mobile computing and cellular phones, client-side architecture has significant limitations including restrictions of network bandwidth, device memory, and processing power. However, there are some advantages such as incurring the adaptation overheads at the client site, rather than server end. This architecture is also advantageous when the server is unable to determine device capabilities from the request. Windows CE [4], e.g., version 3.0 is an example for client-side repurposing. It provides a client-side repurposing for some rich multimedia content by using a color reduction feature which is useful when presenting high quality images on low-color displays of mobile and handheld devices. Client-based repurposing architecture does not depend on the employed communication protocol. The approach helps to avoid the sending of large extents of device and user profile information to the server or intermediate proxies for repurposing. Opera Software is another example for client side architecture. It introduces small screen rendering (SSR) and medium screen rendering (MSR) [5]. SSR repurposes contents and generates a user-friendly version of the contents for small mobile browsers, like smartphone, therefore eliminating the need for horizontal scrolling. MSR identifies the Web page's content and adapts these different elements individually to fit medium-sized screens, ranging from PDAs to low resolution TVs. Original fonts, colors, design and style are left virtually untouched.

Server-based repurposing: In this architecture, repurposing is performed at the server by determining client's capabilities in terms of storage, network bandwidth, processing power, screen size, media format (e.g. HTML, XML, WML etc), and user preferences (e.g. language, fonts etc.). Both static (off-line) and dynamic (on the fly) repurposing are supported by this architecture. The Static approach generates pre-repurposed variants of the same content off-line in order to match client and user capabilities, while the dynamic approach repurposes content on the fly when a request is received. For example, due to the lack of proper translation engines, multimedia content with different languages is appropriately repurposed by the static approach; the dynamic approach is not useful here. Language preferences can be accepted via content negotiation, using the HTTP requester header field. The server can discover the appropriate content version by parsing the HTTP header as the case in using MPEG-21 digital item adaptation.

In the server-side architecture, authors can control the repurposed result under different client characteristics and user preferences with a lower cost, but in reality, it cannot repurpose the content to complex dynamic context. This architecture may depend on the communication protocol used in the content delivery. For example, in Stateful protocols, such as RTP, the server requires the client's response to perform efficient repurposing. However, in a stateless protocol such as HTTP, it does not happen. In that case, repurposing depends on the client or server interaction. Existing Server-side repurposing solutions include *IBM WebSphere Tarnscoding Publisher, BEA Weblogic* and *AvantGo*. All of these solutions are suitable for wired and wireless clients. An example of server-side repurposing is what is used by some news providers such as CNN or Canadian Broadcasting Corporation (CBC). They provide several different media formats on the server representing the original media content. This media content can be selected by the client, based on its preferences and capabilities. For example, three different formats: QuickTime, Real Player, and Windows Media Player, are offered by CBC or CNN, employing three different network connections: Dial-up (56 kbps), GPRS (144 Kbps) and DSL Basic (256 kbps). When a user wants to watch a streaming video from CBC or CNN, he or she should select the format supported by his hardware or software and the network connection that he or she is using.

The advantages of using Server-side adaptation architecture are:

- Content creators have more control on how the content is presented to the clients.
- The server offers more processing power than the client devices, this is very important in the case of Video transcoding.
- In the event of the existence of multimedia content in XML. XSLT is used to transform this content to another appropriate markup language in order to match the browser's capabilitiespresentation such as using Scalable Vector Graphics (SVG), and filtering HTML documents to WML.

As for the weakness of using server-based content adaptation architecture, they can be summed up by the following:

- Not all browsers support content negotiation, or the server may not have control over all browsers. So, the server must make assumptions or use default parameters based on the browser's ability to present the content.
- Heavy server-side applications may slow down the server.

Proxy-based architecture: In this architecture, the proxy server is located on the network between server and client. The proxy, which makes request to the server on behalf of the client, receives content response from the server, analyzes and repurposes the requested content on the fly, and finally sends the repurposed content back to the client, based on its capabilities. The repurposing performed by the proxy is transparent to the clients and server. The proxy can cache the repurposed results for future use, thus reducing the need for re-repurposing and maintaining multiple variants of the same content. This architecture which supports hybrid repurposing, addresses the heterogeneity and mobility problem of the devices, and reduces the overall end to end response time. It also reduces the size of the multimedia content object while maintaining its semantic value. Existing proxy-based repurposing include IBM's Web Intermediaries (WBI) [6], UC Berkeley's Ninja project [7], RabbiT proxy server [8] etc.

In proxy-based architecture, the proxy can control the delivery by applying appropriate QoS algorithm. Some multimedia content repurposing such as audio and video requires transcoding. There may be one or more transcoders in one proxy. Figure 2 depicts a simple architecture of a proxy based repurposing that uses only one transcoder with different transcoding capabilities to deliver to different devices. The content on the server which requires 256 kbps bandwidth is transcoded into four different formats, for four different clients, over four different connections. The transcoded streams are trafficked over lower bandwidths than the original one; they require 128 kbps, 64 kbps, 32 kbps and 16 kbps respectively. Furthermore, the UMTS, GPRS, DVI, and GSM require less computing power than MPEG-1. The audio/video quality of the transcoded streams is lower than that of the original. However, the clients would probably opt for lower, yet acceptable quality, rather than discontinuous video clip or news due to the lack of bandwidths.

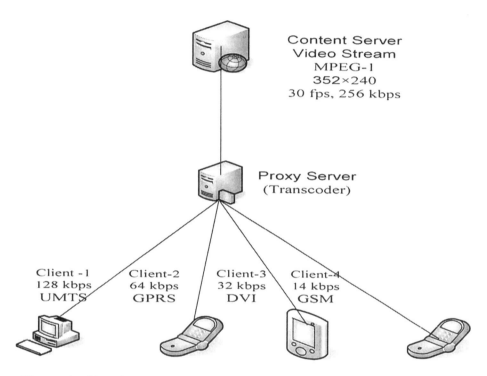

Figure 2. Simple architecture of a simple proxy-based repurposing.

Transcoding also can be defined as a combinatorial process [9], where multiple transcoders can be chained together in order to obtain a larger transcoding sequence. For example, for the task of transcoding MPEG-2 video to Quicktime, the video could first be transcoded from MPEG-2 to MPEG-1 using one transcoder, then the output could be passed on to another transcoder in order to obtain Quicktime. The result would be exactly the same as if transcoding had been performed in one step. This approach, first of all, ensures that even with a limited number of transcoders, more complicated transcodings can be done, and second of all, allows for the computations to be distributed.

Conclusion

Content Repurposing, or adaptation, has the potential to play a key role in the successful distribution and access of multimedia content. The rapid increase in diversity of multimedia content types and formats, and the ubiquitous nature of accessing them from heterogeneous pervasive limited capability devices and networks are currently major challenges. In order to meet these challenges, the multimedia community proposed MPEG-21, which is an open standard multimedia based framework for multimedia content delivery, adaptation, personalization consumption, and presentation.

See: MPEG 1, MPEG 4 and MPEG

References

1. http://www.edusource.ca/english/What_content_eng.html.
2. I. Shin and K. Koh, "Hybrid Transcoding for QoS Adaptive Video-on-Demand Services," IEEE Transactions on Consumer Electronics, Vol. 50, No. 2, May 2004.
3. http://www.w3.org/TR/di-atdi/ [Accessed March 30, 2005].
4. http://msdn.microsoft.com/embedded/windowsce/default.aspx [Accesed April1, 2005].
5. http://www.opera.com/pressreleases/en/2004/01/20/ [Accessed March 29, 2005].
6. http://www.almaden.ibm.com/cs/wbi/, [Accessed April 15, 2005].
7. http://ninja.cs.berkeley.edu/ [Accessed April 15, 2005].
8. http://www.khelekore.org/rabbit/ [Accessed April 15, 2005].
9. J. R. Smith, R. Mohan, and C.-S. Li, "Scalable Multimedia Delivery for Pervasive Computing," Proceedings of ACM Multimedia '99, Oct. 30 - Nov. 1999.
10. ISO/IEC FDIS 21000-7:2004(E): Multimedia Framework (MPEG-21) - Part 7: Digital Item Adaptation.

MULTIMEDIA DESIGN

Definition: In designing multimedia systems, a designer combines knowledge of art, science, and technology.

Any design entails creating conceptual models of artifacts that fulfill some user needs. To design good multimedia systems a designer must combine knowledge of art, science and technology of creating multimedia (Elin, 2001). The Multimedia Design and Planning Pyramid (MUDPY) is a five-level model (Figure 1), in which the level-2 comprises the project design phase (Sharda, 2004). Task Modeling and Storyboarding techniques, in conjunction with a Navigation structure, can be used to compile a multimedia design specification document.

Specifications can include the lowest hardware and communication bandwidth required for delivering the required Quality of Service in online or networked multimedia systems. However, the main specifications relate to the task the system must perform and the type and quality of the content.

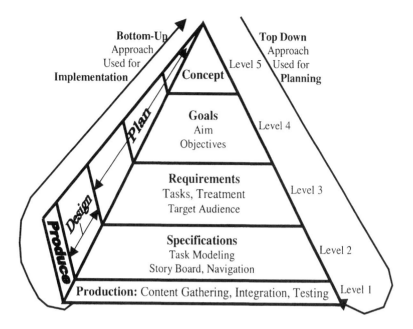

Figure 1. Multimedia design and planning pyramid.

Task Modeling techniques provide the means to specify goal-oriented tasks (Paternò, 2002), and a window into the required user interface. The user interface has significant influence on the spatial composition of various screens, and the navigation structure.

Storyboard represents each page's spatial composition with a sketch. It helps in developing ideas into screens. It is one of the best means of expanding Objectives and Tasks into screens. It gives the option of visualizing the entire system as a whole, or focusing on one section at a time. The storyboard should contain meta-information, and not the actual content.

Navigation refers to the way various pages and their components link. The level of interactivity offered by a multimedia system comes primarily from its navigation structure. A well-designed navigation structure links all the components into a cohesive system.

Issues confirmed in the planning phase should guide the design phase, which in turn should guide the production phase.

See: Multimedia Authoring, Multimedia Project Planning, Multimedia Production

References

1. L. Elin, *"Designing and Developing Multimedia: A Practical Guide for the Producer, Director, and Writer,"* Allyn and Bacon, 2001.
2. F. Paterno, *"Tools for Task Modeling: Where we are, Where we are headed,"* Proceedings of TAMODIA 2002, INFOREC, Bucharest, July 2002, pp. 10-17.
3. N. Sharda, *"Creating Meaningful Multimedia with The Multimedia Design and Planning Pyramid,"* 10th International Multi-Media Modeling Conference, January 2004, Brisbane, Australia.

MULTIMEDIA ENCRYPTION

Heather Yu
Panasonic Digital Networking Laboratory, New Jersey, USA

Definition: *Multimedia data encryption attempts to prevent unauthorized disclosure of confidential multimedia information in transit or storage.*

If we call a multimedia data stream (message) *plaintext*, the process of transforming the plaintext into unintelligible data stream is referred to as *MultiMedia Encryption (MME)* where the encrypted message (data stream) is often named *ciphertext*. The process of transforming the ciphertext back into plaintext is termed *decryption* (see Figure 1.)

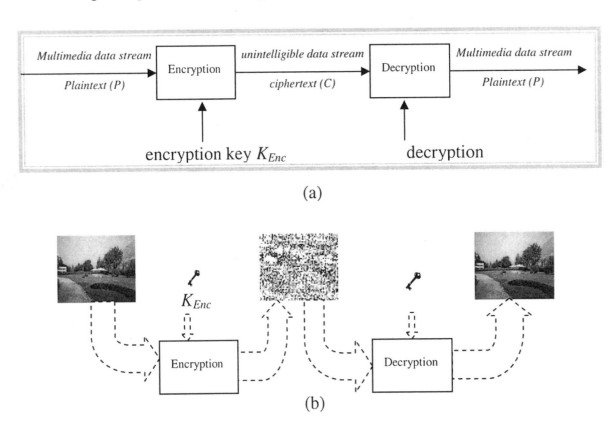

(a)

(b)

Figure 1. Illustration of multimedia encryption and decryption.

<u>Naïve approach:</u> The most straightforward technique for multimedia encryption is to treat the multimedia signal to be protected as a traditional digital data stream, such as text, and select an application appropriate classical encryption scheme and key management scheme to encrypt the entire data stream. Upon reception, the entire ciphertext data stream would be decrypted and playback can be performed at the client device. The key factors to consider when choosing an application appropriate encryption scheme include:

1. It should provide suitable security for the target application
2. It should be cost effective for the specific application and the end user device capability

Which determine, for example, whether a lightweight encryption algorithm is sufficient, if an asymmetric key encryption algorithm is more proper than a symmetric key algorithm, the key length, and the key management approach.

Today, many recognize the importance of selecting an application adequate encryption. For instance, in the Real-Time Transport Protocol (RTP) standard, the default encryption algorithm is specified to be Data Encryption Standard (DES) algorithm in cipher block chaining (CBC) mode where strong encryption algorithms, such as Triple-DES, can be used in place of the default algorithm for better security. This allows different multimedia streaming applications to choose a corresponding encryption algorithm that best fits its application requirements.
The successful attack [10] on DVD CSS (Content Scramble System) [18]using DeCSS [19], a small piece of software that breaks the CSS encryption and allows the reading of encrypted DVDs, is a good example that shows the importance of selecting a suitable cipher scheme to satisfy the application security requirement.

Assume E and D denote the encryption function and the decryption function respectively, we have:

$$E_{K_{Enc}}(P) = C$$

$$D_{K_{Dec}}(C) = D_{K_{Dec}}(E_{K_{Enc}}(P)) = P$$

where P denotes the plaintext multimedia data stream and C designates the ciphertext.

Challenges: However, life is not always that simple. Multimedia data stream has different characteristics from traditional digital data stream. They are often larger in size (which is especially true for video data stream), compressed for transmission and storage, structured in different ways for different applications, with transcoding and other requirements at times. For average consumer multimedia applications, low decryption and re-encryption cost overhead is critical for many applications and end user devices. Using streaming multimedia application as an example, because content is being viewed while streaming, the client player must be able to perform reassembling, decoding, decryption, error control, (and reencrption if specified by usage rules) prior to displaying the next segment. Computational overhead and/or additional hardware requirement at the client device is entailed. This processor-intensive routine can significantly deter the end-user experience if the computational overhead caused by the decryption and re-encryption processes is more than the client device can handle. (That is, it is critical to satisfy the 2nd requirement above. Obviously, the larger the data stream is, the more data need to be encrypted and decrypted, the more processing power is required at both the server and the client, and hence the higher the cost is.) The essence of complexity trades security, i.e., the difficulty to satisfy both the 1st and the 2nd requirements simultaneously, makes it harder to design a secure multimedia system with minimum additional client device cost. Consequently, large computational overhead due to the large size of multimedia data stream became the most commonly known challenge of multimedia encryption [15]. Classical encryption schemes, for instance, the traditional online encryption model for credit card information which has no need to address the computation intensity problem caused by large data set, were rarely designed to serve large amounts of data, and hence may not satisfy the requirement for many today's multimedia applications. These imply the need for new ways to handle multimedia, especially video encryption.

Furthermore, VCR-like or audio player-like function, end-to-end system security, interoperability, upgradeability, and renewability impose additional challenges for MME in various applications.

Design requirements: To maintain a user-friendly, yet secure, end-user experience, there are a number of reasonable requirements, which include a secure multimedia system:

- Should be secure but low cost in implementation to appeal to more content creators and providers
- Should provide end-to-end system security throughout the entire distribution chain

- Should sustain current and new heterogeneous environment to attract more applications and more customers

- Should be scalable from distributed caches and storage device to heterogeneous client devices

- Should be extendable from PCs to mobile devices and still remain secure, for flexible new business models

- Should be easily renewable

- Should not reduce the playback quality of the streaming media, i.e., it should not impact continuous playback, loss resilient capability, and scalability of the system in real-time streaming applications

- Should be able to preserve entertainment like experience – users should be able to fast-forward or rewind content without any degradation on the viewing or playback experience

Among various types of applications, streaming video encryption perhaps is the most challenging one due to its time constraint for continuous playback at client device. In the following, we use streaming video encryption as an example to study the design requirement.

Streaming Video Encryption

Traditional cryptography systems are not intended for large continuous media, especially video, and are not designed for streaming media services in heterogeneous environment. The design of a secure streaming media system is non-trivia. The real-time constraint of streaming video, the potential cost increase introduced by complex encryption algorithms, possible bit rate increase due to intermediate data structure change caused by data scrambling, the dynamic network along with the heterogeneous communication channel capacity and end user device capability, and VCR-like function requirement are just some of the challenges need to be considered when designing a streaming video encryption system.

To deal with some of the streaming video encryption challenges, for instance, the real time constraint and the cost challenge, the bitrate preservation challenge, and the heterogeneous environment challenge, several techniques, such as selective encryption (or called partial encryption) and light weighted encryption [1, 3, 4, 5, 6, 9, 13], format compliant encryption [16], and scalable encryption [12, 15, 17], maybe employed.

Preserve real time playback and decrease cost via partial encryption

Selective encryption intends to encrypt only some parts of the entire bitstream to reduce the overall computational requirement, and hence the cost, introduced by encrypting large volumes of video data stream in a limited period of time. That is the multimedia data stream to protect P is partitioned into subsets: P_A and P_B, $P = P_A \bigcup P_B$, where P_A is the subset to be encrypted while P_B is left in the clear.

$$C = E_{select\ K_{Enc}}(P) = E_{K_{Enc}}(P_A)$$

For instance, the I-frames [1, 5] or I-frames plus the I-blocks in P and B frames [1] of a MPEG video are encrypted. Another simple light weighted algorithm is to encrypt only the sign bits and leave the rest in the clear [9].

Security considerations: It's not too difficult to notice, partial encryption does not strive for maximum security. It trades off security for computational complexity. One key for crafting a suitable partial encryption scheme for a particular application is to exploit the application specific data structures, partition the data stream in a way that the most critical information will be hidden (encrypted) and only the critical information is contained in P_A; and therefore creating a most efficient encryption system. An empirical study on the security of some selective video encryption schemes was reported in [1]. It suggests that partial encryption may cause information leakage if care is not taken. For instance, they found for MPEG video, encrypting I-frames alone may not be sufficiently secure for some types of video. When playback such encrypted MPEG video, they found patterns of movement and sometimes even large chunks of plaintext video. Instead, encrypting the I-blocks improves security. Hence, identify the most important part of a multimedia data stream for encryption and further partition the data stream in a most efficient and effective way based on the specific application requirements is an important step for MME to warrant both adequate security and computational cost.

[2] and [4] both presented comprehensive surveys of partial encryption algorithms in the literature. Interested readers can reference these two articles for different partial encryption algorithms and their strength.

Avoid bitrate increase via format compliant encryption

When a bitstream is scrambled, the original format of the bitstream maybe compromised if care is not taken. This is especially serious for compressed multimedia data stream. If scrambling destroys certain inherent structure, compression efficiency can be compromised. For streaming video applications, user experience could be noticeably worsened due to quality reduction or playback delay at the client machine caused by bitrate increase. Let's look at a simple example. Assume we encrypt only the I-frames of MPEG video using intra-block DCT coefficient shuffling. That is we shuffle the DCT coefficients within each DCT block. Assume a low bit rate video transmission over wireless network. As a result of shuffling, some clustered zero coefficients maybe shuffled apart that results in considerable bit rate increase.

To guarantee a full compatibility with any decoder, the bitstream should only be altered (encrypted) in ways that do not compromise the compliance to the original format. This principle is referred to as *format compliance* [16]. [16] Suggests a framework under which encryption of compressed content can be achieved in the compressed domain securely while still maintaining compliance to the compression format. For instance, bits from the fields chosen to encrypt are extracted, concatenated in an appropriate way, encrypted, and then put back into their original positions to achieve format compliance.

Scalable streaming video encryption to cope with heterogeneous environment

Several scalable streaming video encryption schemes were proposed. Here we look at a couple of examples.

A scalable streaming media encryption scheme that enables transcoding without decryption was proposed in [12]. It utilizes Cipher Block Chaining (CBC) or Stream Cipher (SC) to achieve progressive decryption ability. First, the input video frame is segmented into regions. Then, each region is coded into scalable video data and header data. Next, the scalable video data is encrypted with CBC or SC based progressive encryption, which allows truncation of the scalable video data stream and quality adaptation in accordance. Finally, secure scalable packets are created by combining the unencrypted header data with the progressively encrypted scalable video data. The unencrypted header contains information, such as recommended truncation points or hints, for subsequent transcoding and decoding operations. The transcoders simply read the unencrypted header data at the beginning of each packet, then use that information to discard packets or truncate packets at the appropriate locations. The decoders then decrypt and decode the received packets; the resolution and quality of the reconstructed video will depend on the transcoding operation.

A fine-grained scalable (FGS) steaming media encryption scheme compliant to FGS coded video is presented in [15]. The algorithm provides a lightweight encryption that preserves the full fine grained scalability and the error resilience performance of MPEG-4 FGS after encryption. It applies different encryption schemes to the base layer and the enhancement layer. The base layer is encrypted in either a selective or a full encryption mode. Different encryption algorithms can be selected based on the application requirement. A lightweight selective encryption is applied to the enhancement layer to make the encryption transparent to intermediate processing stages. In this way, the FGS fine granularity scalability is fully preserved in an encrypted FGS stream. It ensures the same fine granularity scalability and error resilience performance as an unencrypted FGS video stream.

In [17] Zhu et al proposed two encryption algorithms for MPEG-4 that preserve MPEG-4's adaptation capability to varying network bandwidths and different application needs and enable intermediate stages to process encrypted data directly without decryption. Both schemes fully sustain the original fine-grained scalability of MPEG-4 FGS in the encrypted stream. The second algorithm, called SMLFE, supports both full and partial encryption that preserves the compression format of the video. It encrypts a single FGS stream into multiple quality layers partitioned according to either PSNR or bit rates to enable multiple access control of the MPEG-4 data stream. Notice that streaming applications also require that the changing network conditions will not result in streaming interruption but only quality adaptation to the changing network conditions. That is, encryption should preserve the loss resilient capability of the streaming media system. Using SMLFE, there is no adverse effect to the error resilience performance of MPEG-4 FGS when packet losses occur. In other words, the algorithm is format compliant, scalable, and robust to packet losses.

Overall, the ultimate goal in designing a suitable streaming video encryption scheme is to offer user with none interrupted continuous playback, random access capability, and loss resilient user experiences while providing adequate security. Evidently, the above described sample algorithms all offer scalability for video streaming applications to cope with the heterogeneous environment we are facing today. From consumer's perspective, the provided scalability to various multimedia content, different network topologies, changing bandwidth, and diverse device capabilities is valuable in offering satisfactory end user experiences.

The above discussed approaches, partial, format compliant, and scalable encryption; all take advantage of signal processing tools to achieve multimedia encryption for some applications. Another set of approaches in the literature deals with joint design of multimedia encryption schemes and proxy for secure and efficient multimedia communication in an end-to-end system.

Secure Multimedia Proxy

To provide quality of service, video proxies may be used to cache some part of a video data stream, so that client can access the cached video from their nearby proxy to minimize delays and converse bandwidth. For protected video, care has to be taken to reduce the risk of revealing the original data stream or critical visual information to unauthorized parties at the proxy. If the cached part of the video is decrypted at the proxy (method 1 in Figure 2), this part of the video shall be vulnerable to attacks since it is in the clear at the proxy and from the proxy to the client. If the cached part of the video is kept encrypted and transferred to the clients at a later time (method 2 in Figure 2), the video is subject to attacks when the key is compromised at any client since all clients share the same decryption key. If this part of the video is decrypted and reencrypted at the proxy before sending to the clients (method 3 in Figure 2), assuming the proxy is secure, the drawback is the computational overhead at the proxy caused by constant decryption and reencryption with frequent client access requests. To solve the problem and improve the security, a multi-key encryption scheme (method 4 in Figure 2) is proposed in [14]. By means of multi-key encryption at the proxy with a single key decryption at the client, the system adds lesser computational overhead (compared with previous approaches) at proxy without compromising the security of the system.

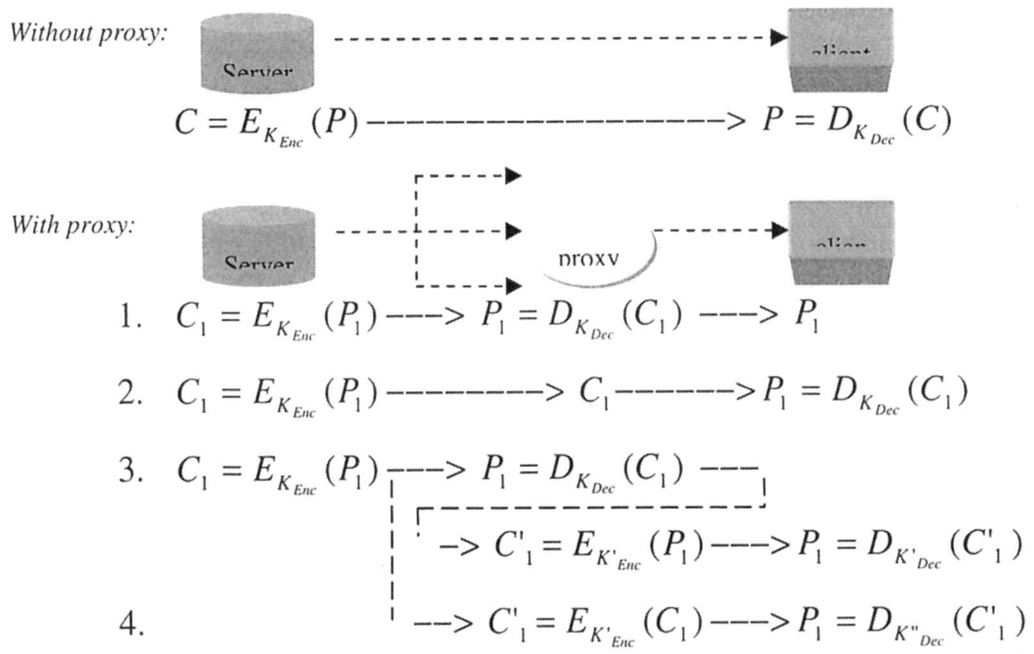

Without proxy:

$$C = E_{K_{Enc}}(P) \text{ -----------------> } P = D_{K_{Dec}}(C)$$

With proxy:

1. $C_1 = E_{K_{Enc}}(P_1) \text{ ---> } P_1 = D_{K_{Dec}}(C_1) \text{ ---> } P_1$

2. $C_1 = E_{K_{Enc}}(P_1) \text{ ---------> } C_1 \text{ -------> } P_1 = D_{K_{Dec}}(C_1)$

3. $C_1 = E_{K_{Enc}}(P_1) \text{ ---> } P_1 = D_{K_{Dec}}(C_1) \text{ ---}$
   $\text{-> } C'_1 = E_{K'_{Enc}}(P_1) \text{ ---> } P_1 = D_{K'_{Dec}}(C'_1)$

4. $\text{---> } C'_1 = E_{K'_{Enc}}(C_1) \text{ ---> } P_1 = D_{K''_{Dec}}(C'_1)$

Figure 2. Video proxy and video encryption schemes.

Interestingly, in a heterogeneous environment where streaming media are transmitted through time-varying communication channels, transcoders are often used at intermediate network nodes to perform transcoding operations on compressed bitstreams to provide proper QoS for different clients. If a transcoder requires decryption and re-encryption of the encrypted streaming media for all transcoding operations, extra computational overhead and additional security threat at the intermediate network node are imposed.

Scalable encryption together with a secure proxy design perhaps can provide more adequate solutions for these sets of applications.

Some other related interesting readings

Since streaming video encryption is one of the most challenging ones to handle, we used that as an example to study MME requirements and design in this chapter. For those interested in other types of media encryption and applications, the following are some interesting references to read. In [11], several selective image encryption algorithms were described. A partial-encryption scheme for MPEG audio is discussed in [8], a low-complexity, perception-based partial encryption scheme for compressed telephone-bandwidth speech is presented in [7], and [20] provides some general information about voice encryption. For those interested in a comprehensive survey, [2] summarizes many multimedia encryption algorithms, especially image, video, and audio selective encryption algorithms available in the literature.

See: Public Key vs. Secret Key Encryption, Key management, Multimedia Proxy Caching, Broadcast Encryption, and Encryption in RTP

References

1. I. Agi and L. Gong, "An empirical study of MPEG video transmissions," *Proceedings of Internet Society Symposium on Network and Distributed System Security*, February 1996, pp. 137-144.
2. B. Furht, D. Socek, and A. Eskicioglu, "Fundamentals of multimedia encryption techniques," *Multimedia Security Handbook*, CRC Press, 2005.
3. Y. Li, Z. Chen, S. Tan, R. Campbell, "Security enhanced MPEG player," *Proceedings of IEEE First Int. Workshop on Multimedia Software Development*, March 1996.
4. X. Liu and A. M. Eskicioglu, "Selective Encryption of Multimedia Content in Distribution Networks: Challenges and New Directions," *Proceedings of the 2nd IASTED International Conference on Communications, Internet, and Information Technology (CIIT 2003)*, 2003, pp. 527-533.
5. T. B. Maples and G. A. Spanos, "Performance Study of selective encryption scheme for the security of networked real-time video," *Proceedings of the 4th International Conference on Computer and Communications*, Las Vegas, NV, 1995.
6. L. Qiao and K. Nahrstedt, "A new algorithm for MPEG video encryption," *Proceedings of the First International Conference on Imaging Science, Systems and Technology*, July 1997, pp. 21-29.
7. A. Servetti and J.C. De Martin, "Perception-based selective encryption of G.729 speech," Proceedings of the IEEE Int. Conference on Acoustics, Speech, and Signal Processing, May 2002.
8. A. Servetti, C. Testa, and J.C. De Martin, "Frequency-selective partial encryption of compressed audio," Proceedings of the IEEE International Conferences on Acoustics, Speech, and Signal Processing, April 2003.
9. C. Shi and B. Bhargava, "A fast MPEG video encryption algorithm," Proceedings of the 6th International Multimedia Conference, 1998.
10. F. A. Stevenson, "Cryptanalysis of Contents Scrambling System", http://www.insecure.org/news/cryptanalysis_of_contents_scrambling_system.htm November 1999.
11. M. Van Droogenbroeck and R. Benedett, "Techniques for a selective encryption of uncompressed and compressed images," Proceedings of Advanced Concepts for Intelligent Vision Systems, Ghent, 2002.
12. S. J. Wee and J.G. Apostolopoulos, "Secure scalable streaming enabling transcoding without decryption," Proceedings of IEEE Int. Conference on Image Processing, October 2001.
13. C.-P. Wu and C.-C.J. Kuo, "Fast encryption methods for audiovisual data confidentiality," Proceedings of the SPIE Multimedia Systems and Applications III, V 4209, November 2000.

14. S. F. Yeung, J. C. S. Lui, and D. K. Y. Yau, "A case for a multi-key secure video proxy: theory, design, and implementation," Proceedings of the tenth ACM International Conference on Multimedia, December 2002.
15. H. Yu, "Streaming media encryption," Multimedia Security Handbook, CRC, 2005.
16. J. Wen, M. Severa, W. Zeng, M. Luttrell, and W. Jin, "A format-compliant configurable encryption framework for access control of video," IEEE Transactions on Circuits and System for Video Technologies, Vol. 12, No. 6, 2002.
17. B. B. Zhu, C. Yuan, Y. Wang, and S. Li, "Scalable Protection for MPEG-4 Fine Granularity Scalability," IEEE Transactions on Multimedia, Vol. 7, No. 2, April 2005.
18. DVD CCA, "Content Scramble System CSS," http://www.dvdcca.org/css/.
19. "DeCSS", http://web.lemuria.org/DeCSS/decss.html.
20. Technical Communications Corporation, "Technical discussion on voice encryption methods," http://www.tccsecure.com/voicetx.htm, 2003.

MULTIMEDIA ENTERTAINMENT APPLICATIONS

Stefano Cacciaguerra, Marco Roccetti, and Paola Salomoni
Department of Computer Science, University of Bologna, Bologna, Italy

Definition: *Multimedia entertainment applications aim at diverting users, engaging them in amazing experiences such as reading a book, listening to music, enjoying videos, and playing a game.*

Concepts

To understand modern multimedia entertainment applications a definition of both entertainment and multimedia notions is needed. *Entertainment* is something diverting or engaging, i.e. a public performance, a usually light comic or an adventure novel. *Multimedia* means using, involving, or encompassing several media. Classic media are hypertexts, sound, image, video and animation. From these standpoints, multimedia entertainment applications aim at diverting users, engaging them in amazing experiences such as reading a book, listening to music, enjoying videos, and playing a game. While in the past, traditional multimedia entertainment technology offered predominantly passive experiences, such as, video on demand for example, advances in ICT are promoting a greater interactivity as well as allowing more exciting immersive experiences to consumers, such as interactive virtual environments, interactive storytelling and online games [1, 2, 3]. In fact, with the coming of the Internet era, the network communications have been fueled in a way not available on any other medium. This fact improved the chance to interact in real-time with remote applications rather than to sit passively, bringing online the multimedia entertainment.

Further, multimedia entertainment was historically not considered as a topic deserving of serious study. Yet, two main reasons attract, today, an increasing number of researchers and practitioners. The former is the explosive growth of the multimedia entertainment market, from its niche position to a multi-billion dollar industry with an ever-increasing trend. Analysts report the following. In February 2004, 51 million people were using Microsoft's Windows Media Player, Apple sold over 2,016,000 iPods during the 4th quarter of 2004 as compared to 336,000 one year ago, Jupiter Research estimates in 1.7 billion $ the 2009 online music market in the US, the gaming industry surpasses even the cinematography industry expecting to increase the sales up to 31.6 billion $ in 2009. The latter reason is represented by the correlation between problems that emerge while developing innovative multimedia entertainment applications and those typical of more serious settings in the Computer Science fields.

The reminder of this article is organized as follows. Section 2 presents surveys for enabling technologies in multimedia entertainment. Further, Section 3 discusses on the main trends of modern multimedia entertainment applications. Finally, Section 4 provides some final considerations about multimedia entertainment applications of the future.

Enabling Technologies

Multimedia technologies provide an important support to entertainment services with a myriad of coding, access and distribution alternatives. Anywhere and anytime communication technologies facilitate entertainment services, while final devices enhance the user experience. Unfortunately, a global end-to-end solution "from the producer to the consumer" involving several media to provide entertainment contents to the final user does not exist. Yet, the main streams for passing from the entertainment producer to the final consumer step through the four following phases shown in Figure 1 and discussed below in isolation.

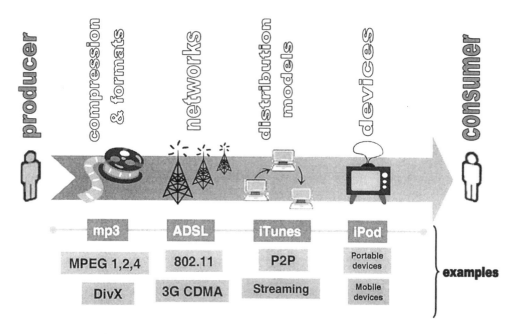

Figure 1. Pipeline of multimedia entertainment.

Enabling Technologies: Formats and Compression

Nowadays, different standard compression formats exist that are at the basis of several multimedia entertainment services (MPEG-1, MPEG-2, MPEG-4, MP3, DivX) [4]. MPEG-1, 2 and 4 represent the standard for the efficient bandwidth transmission of digital audio/video. Historically, MPEG-1 targets a bandwidth of 1-1.5 Mbps providing a final user with a VHS quality that works well for VCR activities with a CD-ROM. MPEG-2 improved MPEG-1 supporting higher resolution video, increasing audio capabilities and extending the bit rate at 4-15Mbits/s. Based on these features, MPEG-2 enables for satellite broadcast applications by encoding up to 5 digital channels in the same bandwidth used by a single analog channel. Unfortunately with the Web revolution, MPEG-2 results to be too expensive for Internet infrastructures, as it requires a large amount of bandwidth. MPEG-4, instead, promotes a data rate from 64Kbits/s to higher ones that enable high quality video distributions. MPEG-4 represents units of aural, visual or audiovisual content, as *media objects*. Media objects can be recorded with a camera, a microphone, or generated with a computer as a synthetic scene.

MP3 is defined as the MPEG Layer III audio compression scheme. MP3 revolutionized the entire music world due to its perfect tradeoff between size and quality. It is possible to transport on a CD support hundreds of MP3 songs, ready to be exchanged at a good sound quality. Finally, few words should be spent on the large diffusion of the DivX format. DivX employs the most advanced video compression technology to creating high-quality video files, up to one tenth the size of MPEG-2: that is small enough to be delivered over the Internet or burned to single CDs.

Enabling Technologies: Networks

Multimedia entertainments, such as, DivX downloads, digital TV, video on demand, online games require tens of megabits per second to work in a suitable way. The main obstacle, until now, has been the inadequate access to the network infrastructure and the huge cost of the installations. Further, users ask for mobile technologies which permit to enjoy with multimedia entertainment contents from anywhere. Figure 2 shows the most important network technologies and correlate them with both bandwidth and mobility requirements. Emerging network technologies range from the wired copper enhancements (e.g. ADSL, Ethernet to the home, VDSL) to mobile cellular systems (e.g. 3G CDMA) and Wi-Fi (e.g. WLAN). It is reported that more than the 50% of American households (up to the 70% of Korean ones) has a high-speed *always-on* broadband access to the Internet [5]. In particular, ADSL became the milestone of broadband Internet access speeding up to 40 times faster than the traditional 56Kbps dial-up connection. This technology allows a *downstream* rate from 1.5 to 9 Mbps and an *upstream* rate from 16 to 640 Kbps over existing copper telephone lines. Wired post-ADSL network technologies, such as Ethernet to the home or VDSL, has further increased the downstream rate up to 50 Mbps.

On the other side, the invasion of mobile post-ADSL technologies has fueled the demand for multimedia entertainment on portable devices. 3G CDMA cellular systems are able to carry out, simultaneously, voice, video and data at a data rate of: i) 144 Kbps for fast-moving mobile users in vehicles, ii) 384 Kbps for slower moving pedestrian users, and iii) 2 Mbps from fixed locations. Unfortunately, the cost of the 3G spectrum and the build-out of 3G network infrastructures are very high. Alternatively, WLAN solutions are cheaper thanks to their low-cost transceivers and to the use of shared unlicensed spectrum. WLANs offer higher bandwidth (2.4 Ghz 802.11 b offers as many as 11 Mbps) supporting a direct access to the Internet, working only within a short range. As consequence, there exists a trade off. Wireless technologies suffer either from low data rates (3G CDMA) or from a short coverage (WLAN). Instead, wired technologies offer high data rates without any mobility support. From these heterogeneous scenarios emerges the need for networking integration aimed at guaranteeing seamless connectivity, transparent vertical handoff and service continuity.

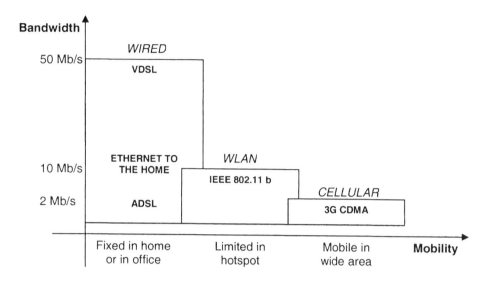

Figure 2. Networks: bandwidth vs. mobility.

Enabling Technologies: Distribution Models

Multimedia distribution played a key role in driving digital entertainment. There exist two basic modes: online streaming and P2P file sharing. Online streaming allows consumers to enjoy radio or TV on the desktop. Streaming enables playback of audiovisual content in real time through the use of the Real-Time Streaming Protocol (RTSP). This allows consumers to start, stop, and pause digital audio/video. RTSP relies on the Real-Time Transfer Protocol (RTP) that enables Web casting of live events, supports multiple consumers and uses the bandwidth efficiently. In particular, broadband American users have consumed in 2003 music video (33% of the view share), news (28%) and sports (17%) [6]. On the content owners' side, the audio/video stream is discarded by clients after play, thus preventing unauthorized duplication.

However, it is worth mentioning that many consumers prefer to play MP3s or DivXs on their devices where digital contents had been previously downloaded sharing them with their friends without resorting to an online connection. This preference promoted the planetary success of P2P file sharing [7, 8]. The evolution of multimedia download systems has passed through different P2P generations (Table 1). The success of Napster was based on the high costs of the other traditional distribution systems and on easily downloadable MP3s. Napster implemented a centralized global list for the discovery of files (available on the network at any time) for P2P exchange. To overcome the vulnerability of the centralized global list, 2nd generation peers act as server or client to perform both searching and downloading activities. Still, servers are used to provide authentication-type activities and general support to other peers. Multiple peers ensure service availability but make the exchange protocol overhead an issue to be solved. The development of 3rd generation P2P networks are completely server less and peers are responsible for both client and server duties. Each peer should maintain and distribute available-file lists. Unfortunately, performance may be jeopardized by network dimensions: a wide network may be rich of resources, yet difficult to be discovered. The P2P networks have appeared in the music/video community for unauthorized file distribution. Hence, the industry has attacked P2P networks because it thinks of it as a method to circumvent the authority instead of a mean to boost the music/video distribution. Undoubtedly, a way to exploit the P2P distribution without violating the copyright laws is to adopt specific payment models, such as, pay per download, per play, per subscription, or an all-inclusive flat rate.

Table 1. P2P generations

	1st Generation	2nd Generation	3rd Generation
P2P Networks	• Napster	• E-donkey • Freenet • Gnutella • Kazaa • …	• Bittorrent • kadMule • Overnet • WinMX • …

Enabling Technologies: Final Devices

Consuming multimedia entertainment applications is possible through a multitude of portable devices (e.g. iPod, DVD-player), mobile devices (e.g. smart phone, PDA) and pervasive devices (e.g. head-mounted displays, datagloves). These devices are quickly evolving to simplify user activities and to enhance its experience. Portable devices offer a simple way to play multimedia data, collected by means of an Internet distribution service or bought in a shop, from anywhere. New generations of DVD/CD player devices support also DivX and MP3 formats. In line with this, iPod represents the archetypical music player device (portable) [9]. An iPod can carry personal music collections anywhere, can play up to 12 hours straight, and can even store up to 5000 songs. FireWire and USB 2.0 technologies support the transfer of music from an entire CD to an iPod in a few of seconds.

Mobile devices, such as smart phone, combine computing, phone, Internet and networking features. Smart phones improve the capabilities of typical mobile phones, by running a complete operating system that provides a standardized interface and platform for application developers. Compared to standard phones, they have larger displays and more powerful processors. Typically, they mount software for media exchanging, simple multiplayer games and chats.

Pervasive devices serve as portals into virtual reality to augment the sensorial experience of the user. Head-mounted displays adopted to obtain a stereoscopic vision and a stereo sound effect of a Virtual Environment (VE) build up a physical connection between the user and the computer promoting an immersive audio/visual experience. Further, data gloves enable immersive haptic experience allowing users to interact in the VE by touching objects inside it.

Entertainment Applications

It is possible to identify different ways with which people have fun: i) listening to music, ii) watching videos, iii) playing games, iv) participating in an interactive story, v) meeting people in virtual environments. Nowadays, innovation in entertainment applications emerges as a response to different requirements to be met: high interactivity, mobility, context awareness. Older computer-mediated digital technologies offer predominantly passive experiences (e.g., audio/video on demand). Modern entertainment, instead, is taking advantage from high interactivity and offers new applications that consumers can control. Interesting examples are represented by applications that involve participating in virtual environments, interactive story telling and online gaming. Along this line, consumers can enjoy the accuracy of an environment, the immediateness of an interface, the interactivity of their avatars and the fascination in a given story. Radical innovations (in both user devices and network technologies) have fueled the development of mobile forms of entertainment. Further, new entertainment applications use context information (e.g. location, time, temperature, and other people nearby) in interactions thus adapting to specific situations. In the reminder of this article, we will discuss first on same examples of applications aimed at offering passive experiences. Then, we will report on more interactive ways of enjoying computer based entertainment experiences.

Digital Music/Video

Listening to music and Watching videos have existed in known digital versions for tens of years as a much appreciated way of entertaining. As of today, modern forms of multimedia entertainment allow users to consume a digital song or a video comfortably seated in their armchair exploiting online connections or wandering about a city with a portable device. Today's market for music/video players is currently dominated by Microsoft's Windows Media Player (WMP) [10] and RealNetworks' RealOne Player (ROP) [11]. Microsoft has benefited from its dominant position of desktop software integrating WMP in all versions of Windows OS. The WMP 10 series shows interesting features such as surround sound, variable speed playback, cross-fading, auto-volume leveling and sophisticated video smoothing technology for content encoding along low-bandwidth connections. Rather, the latest version of RealOne lets users rewind and fast-forward live video during play, and adjust brightness, contrast, and sharpness. Microsoft and Real are competing for streaming music/video data, moving from the Web to the mobile devices. Earlier in the 2004, Microsoft bought the exclusive Web casting right for Major League Baseball and it is trying to enter in the smart phone market, where Real leads Microsoft. The mobile version of Real's player is preinstalled on Symbian OS mounted by Nokia, Siemens, Sony-Ericsson, and other smart phones. Further, Real and Microsoft are competing with US-based PacketVideo, also if the mobile streaming is at the beginning of it era, and consumers would be disappointed by low quality streams showing grainy choppy video in small windows. Today's music market on portable device is currently dominated by Apples' iPod + iTunes [9, 12]. iPod + iTunes is offering a complete pipeline of multimedia entertainment allowing users to buy more than one million of different songs and to play them anywhere. iTunes has been one of the first successful initiatives that legally offer pay-per-download music in massively distributed contexts. The perfect marriage between iPod and iTunes provides users the opportunities for managing a digital music collection. iTunes Music Store offers to users the possibility to browse through more than 9,000 audio books. iTunes application makes also easier to quickly transfer songs, just popping a CD into a PC and clicking a button.

As a consequence of this success, modern radio stations offer to consumer an eclectic selection of music in iPod-style [13]. Traditional way to schedule programs picks from a library of 300-400 titles with the same 30-40 songs, repeating them several time in a day. Modern radio stations, such as U.S. "Jack", for example, offer broadband diffusion of serendipitous playlists obtained by more than 1200 songs get played only once every few days. The Jack format claims that users want to hear a large selection and a variety of familiar music. Hence, Jack implements this idea in line with iPodders podcatching the last podcast [14]. Finally, advances in the video technologies are also fueling the emergence of digital cinema.

Virtual Environment, Interactive Storytelling, Online Games

A more recent phenomenon in the Internet is to create VEs into which humans are embedded [15]. This approach implements realistic and entertaining environments where humans can participate by controlling the behavior of software agents within a synthetic world. Take a virtual café, where each user can be represented by an avatar playing the role of a costumer or of a barman engaged in the typical activities of a bar, such as ordering/serving a cup of tea or speaking about the last football match. One of the main goals of virtual reality is to achieve an immersive sensorial representation of the imagined system, realistic enough to be perceived by the participants. To implement such virtual reality it is necessary to build VEs that allows embedded humans to develop skills applicable in similar real cases. One of the prominent examples is represented by Second Life [16]: a new online virtual society, shaped entirely by its residents. Participants join a world full of people, activities, and fun. Second Life is an evolutional shared reality where people can explore, build on virtual land, socialize, or vie for status. In particular, if people play specific roles according to a fantasy scenario, it is possible to compose a dynamic story whose final plot is obtained by interactions of all participants. Hence, the integration of interactive virtual environments with fascinating story drives the development of dynamic narrative structure called Interactive StoryTelling (IST). An interesting example is Supafly [17]: a virtual soap opera where the goal is to become a virtual celebrity. To reach this goal, a user should create as much gossip around him/her-self as possible, while maintaining relations and status in him/her group. In particular, the participation in Supafly can take place, anytime and anywhere, in the real world through SMS commands, voice services and Web interfaces.

Indeed, it is not important that VE reproduces exactly a real system, but rather that the sensorial perception should be acceptable. Hence, if two independent events occur close enough in time that the human being is not able to perceive which has been generated first, VE can process them in its preferred order. On the other side, VE should correctly reproduce the ordering of the events if there is a causal relationship among them. These considerations are at the basis of several interactive games Real Tournament [18] and the NeverWinter Nights (NWN) [19]. In the former, each player uses a customized handset integrating GPS, sensors, Wi-Fi, GPRS, and a PDA to competitively capture monsters in a virtual arena mapped onto a park in Lancaster. The latter is a role-playing game based on Dungeons and Dragons, where a player chooses the skills of a character and develops it during a synthetic life in a fantasy world. NWN allows to create virtual worlds giving to each player the tools needed to construct lands of adventure for a cooperative group of friends.

Conclusions

Multimedia entertainment is at the same time a great technological challenge and a wide still-increasing market. New scenarios arise considering multimedia entertainment applications lining in anytime, anywhere, any device dimensions, further fueled by the advent of mobile terminals. These applications start new technological challenges, offer new services and open new markets. Participations in virtual environment, interactive storytelling and online games are near to offer users "virtual life" experiences. In spite of this phenomenon, multimedia distribution is not ready to leave the role of killer application and new services are still under development to better fit users needs, including mobility. New forms of entertainment based on network availability and new amazing devices are arising. In the near future, pervasion of multimedia entertainment will still increase and humans will be soon immersed in online devices that follow us: during all day, in many different places, inside a wide part of our daily activities. While we hail the arrival of the digital revolution and the information era, the average citizen continues to wait for the realities of these promises to materialize in their daily lives. To maintain this promise, technology experts should provide the consumers with simplicity of use (plug and play devices, simple commands, no need of manuals), simplicity of integration (interoperability of devices), seamless mobility of users and applications.

See: In Home, in Car, in Flight Entertainment; Interactive Story Telling; Digital Cinema

References

1. A. Weiss, "Trends for 2005," ACM Press, Vol. 8, No. 4, December 2004, pp. 20-27.
2. M. Roccetti and P. Salomoni "Concepts, Technologies, Systems and Applications for Online Entertainment," Tutorial 4 at the Consumer Communication and Networking Conference 2005, January 2005, Las Vegas, USA.
3. B. Kozbe, M. Roccetti, and M. Ulema, "Entertainment Everywhere: System and Networking Issues in Emerging Network-Centric Entertainment Systems," Special Feature Topic of the IEEE Communications Magazine, May 2005.
4. S. M. Tran, K. Lajos, E. Balazs, K. Fazekas, and S. Csaba, "A Survey on the Interactivity Feature of MPEG-4," 46th International Symposium Electronics in Marine, June 2004, Zadar, Croatia.
5. Y. K. Lee and D. Lee, "Broadband Access in Korea: Experience and Future Perspective," IEEE Communications Magazine, December 2003.
6. J. Krikke, "Streaming Video Transforms the Media Industry," IEEE Computer Graphics and Applications, Vol. 24, No. 4, July/August 2004, pp. 6-12.

7. S. Androutsellis-Theotokis and D. Spinellis, "A Survey of Peer-to-Peer Content Distribution Technologies," ACM Computing Surveys, Vol. 36, No. 4, December 2004, pp. 335–371.
8. J. Lee, "An End-User Perspective on File-Sharing Systems," ACM Communications, Vol. 46, No. 2, February 2003, pp. 49-53.
9. iPod + iTunes, Home page, www.apple.com/ipod/, 2005.
10. Windows Media Player 10, http://www.microsoft.com/windows/windowsmedia/default.aspx, 2005.
11. RealOne Player 10, Home page, http://www.realnetworks.com/, 2005.
12. S. Cass, "Tools & Toys : IPOD a Go-Go," IEEE Spectrum, Vol. 41, No. 8, August 2004, pp. 49-51.
13. S. McBride, "Hit by iPod, Satellite, Radio Tries New Tune," The Wall Street Journal Europe, 21 March 2005.
14. P. McFedries, "Technically Speaking: The iPod People," IEEE Spectrum, Vol. 42, No. 2, February 2005, pp. 76.
15. M. Cavazza, S. Hartley, J. L. Lugrin, P. Libardi, and M. Le Bras, "New Behavioural Approaches for Virtual Environments," Proceedings of Entertainment Computing ICEC 2004, Eindhoven, September 2004, Netherlands.
16. Second Life, "Your world. Your imagination." Home page, http://secondlife.com/, 2005.
17. A.D. Joseph, "Gaming, Fine Art, and Familiar Strangers," IEEE Pervasive Computing, Vol. 3, No. 1, January-March 2004, pp. 35-37.
18. K. Mitchell, D. McCaffery, G. Metaxas, J. Finney, S. Schmid, and A. Scott, "Six in the city: introducing Real Tournament - a mobile IPv6 based context-aware multiplayer game," Proceedings of the 2nd workshop on Network and system support for games, ACM Press, 2003, pp. 91-100.
19. Neverwinter Nights, Home page, http://nwn.bioware.com/, 2005.

MULTIMEDIA FILE SHARING

Simone Santini
University of California, San Diego, USA

Definition: *In multimedia file sharing we define two, quite separate, modalities: one, which we might call private file sharing, consists in being able to send multimedia files to a well identified person or to a small group of well identified persons; the other, which we might call public file sharing, consists in publishing multimedia files so that an unspecified number of possible unknown people may copy them.*

Background

File sharing, in one form or another, is as old as computer networks. Programs such as *uucp* (unix to unix copy) and, later, ftp (from the *file transfer protocol* that it used) constituted the early means through which files were shared among network users. The birth of open source software, and the creation of communal development projects was facilitated and, to a certain extent, made possible by these programs, which allowed people located even at a great distance from one another to work on the same project, and to other people to enjoy the fruits of their labor without moving any physical data support around. Many open source programs in use today—*gnu emacs*, just to make an example—were at first developed and distributed in such communities.

One of the problems presented by these file sharing programs is that they lacked any function to search for a specific file: in order to retrieve a file using *ftp*, for instance, it is necessary to know the name of the file, that address (or network name) of the computer where it is stored, the directory where the file is, and, depending on the circumstances, a password to gain access to the computer. This information was not available within the system, and had to be distributed using other means. In the 80's, during the first massive distribution of the internet inside universities, these means were mainly *user groups* and *e-mail messages*. In the early 1990's, the first systems for assisting users in locating the diles that they desired to download (the term *download* also made its appearance around the same time) made their appearance. The most diffuse were *archie*, a name based search engine, and *gopher*, a taxonomization of available files that could be visited using menus.

The Web was, in its early years (roughly 1994-1998), relatively uninterested in file sharing: the emphasis was on documents, that is, on *html* files created for the sole purpose of being displayed in a browser and, while more and more people started putting files on the web for downloading, the underlying protocol was ftp, and the file localization services were rather primitive, since the early search services (*lycos, altavista,...*) were meant to search for pages, not for files.

Early multimedia file sharing

During all this time, there were some quite formidable obstacle to the wide diffusion of multimedia file sharing habits and services: for one thing, bandwidth was still a problem for many users, who connected to the internet throughout modems that, although their speed increased quite rapidly from 14Kbps to 28, 33, and 56, were still too slow for a convenient transfer of a relatively large multimedia files; for another thing, most computers didn't have any means of reproducing the content of audio and video files, and the lack of accepted standards for these files made the problems worse.

Just as it had happened two decades before with the VCR, the first market interested in multimedia file sharing was that of pornography. In the early 1990's, a number of bulletin boards, with direct phone line connectivity, offered modem access to collections of pornographic images and, to a lesser extent, video, using proprietary access protocols. These systems survived well into the web era, until a satisfactory and secure way of making payment on the web was devised, and until the increasing bandwidth made acceptable the worse performance of the general-purpose http protocol with respect to the specially designed proprietary protocols (see *mime types*). As with the VCR, pornography was an eager early adopter since the social stigma attached to it makes the search for privacy an overwhelmingly important goal, worth the uncertainties, the costs, and the problems of a new medium. But, while these experiments provided valuable expertise in multimedia file sharing, pornography, by its very nature, was destined to remain a niche market, as large as it may be, or, in any extent, a market with which companies don't like to be publicly associated; a truly massive development of multimedia file sharing required a different market and a great convenience of use in order to appeal to the great public.

Private file sharing

In multimedia file sharing we can talk, in general terms, of two, quite separate, modalities: one, which we might call *private* file sharing, consists in being able to send multimedia files to a well identified person or to a small group of well identified persons; the other, which we might call *public* file sharing, consists in publishing multimedia files so that an unspecified number of possible unknown people may copy them.

The main technical factor behind the success of private file sharing was the agreement on standards for "attaching" binary files to e-mail messages. These standards are in general based on the so-called *mime types*, which are the same types that the browsers use in order to display properly data of different types. The e-mail protocol doesn't allow sending binary files as they are, since many of the bytes with a value less than 32 (corresponding to the ASCII *control codes*) are interpreted and, possibly, transformed. To make an example, Unix systems use the character 0D (hexadecimal), the ASCII *carriage return* to mark the end of a line, while Windows system, inheriting from DOS, use the pair 0A 0D (*line feed* and *carriage return*) for the same purpose. Many Windows programs, upon observing a 0D in input convert it in a pair 0D 0A. Clearly, if the character 0D was part of a binary file, this will result in an incorrect interpretation of the file. To obviate to this problem, binary mime types are in general encoded so that only "printable" ASCII characters, that is, only bytes with a code between 32 and 128, are used.

While this technical standard for attachments is important, one should not underestimate the importance, for the diffusion of private multimedia file sharing, of e-mail programs: the ease with which a file can today be attached to a message through an opportune interface, and the simplicity of "playing back" the attachments that one received are instrumental in the success of private file sharing.

Public file sharing

Public file sharing, especially of audio files, is the form of multimedia file sharing that most readily comes to mind to most people, and has configured itself, at this historical juncture, almost as the epitome of all file sharing, a not entirely fair situation. The first widely known and used audio file sharing system was called *napster* and various factors of different nature contributed to its success in 2000. For one thing, the network infrastructure had reached a level where a significant number of users had the bandwidth necessary to make sending and receiving relatively large files (5-20 Mbytes) reasonable; the choice of napster to concentrated on audio rather than on video, the fact that audio had an obvious market among the many young people that in the three years before had started using the internet, as well as the diffusion of the mp3 compression standard that kept the size of audio files within manageable limits, all these factors were crucial in the success of audio file sharing. To this, napster added a well integrated application, distributed through their Web site, which made it easy to search, download, manage, and play files, and the idea of using a peer-to-peer system rather than a client-server one.

The idea of using an application that the user had to download and install was in itself a minor challenge to the corporate conventional wisdom of the time that insisted that users would not download and install applications, that requiring them to do so would result in dramatic loss of audience, and that, therefore, only interfaces composed of web pages should be used. It turned out, as it is not seldom is the case, that the corporate conventional wisdom was more conventional than wise. Napster's choice to develop an application allowed them to overcome the drastic limitation of the page based web interfaces, to provide an easier way to use the system and, in the end, it was an essential element of its success, helped in this by the fact that the security paranoia was not raging as high in 2000 as it is in 2005.

Technically, the main contribution of napster and other similar services (gnutella, audiogalaxy, kazaa,...) was the introduction in the arena of multimedia file exchange of *peer ro peer* architectures [gnutella]. At the time, and probably today as well, the most common form of distributed system was the *client server* architecture. In a client server data system, all the data are kept in a single computer or in a small group of computers, and the "clients" send their request for data to them. Since all the requests go to the same server (or small group of servers), its performance and that of its network connection are crucial for the whole system, and servers are prone to become the bottleneck of a client server system, a problem that is exacerbated by the large file sizes typical of multimedia. An economic and political consequence of this fact is that setting up a client server multimedia architecture requires a massive up front investment, a situation that makes it relatively hard for a start-up to initiate such a service. By contrast, in a peer to peer system, all the participating computers contain some data: the participant seeking a particular file will broadcast a request for it (an operation whose modalities depend on the specific type of peer to peer system: the problem of *location* is indeed one of the most studied into the peer to peer system literature [Chord,Lv]), and all the participant that possess that file will answer back with some information, such as their network bandwidth or the number of requests that they are serving at the moment, from which the requestor can determine from which is access more convenient. The two computers will then use a standard protocol (e.g. Ftp) to transfer the file. The etiquette of a peer to peer community now requires that the user who just received a file should keep it available, becoming an additional source for it.

The details of the transition may vary from system to system. Napster, for example, was, so to speak, an *impure* peer to peer system, in that the information about the participants was kept in a central server to which all localization requests were made, a technical solution that might have contributed to make Napster vulnerable to the legal attacks of which it was object (see below). The file exchange services that came on the scene after the demise of Napster realized a more peer to peer system which proved more robust technically and legally. These systems use the redundancy of the community—that is, the fact that the same file is present on many participants-- to avoid sending all the requests to all the participants, without having to keep information in a central server. In Kazaa, a typical representative of the post-Napster file exchange services, whenever a new participant enters the system, it is assigned a (rather large) number of *neighbors*. When a file is requested, the search request goes only to the neighbors; if the result of the search is not satisfactory, the user can request to extend it to the neighbors' neighbors, then to the neighbors of the latter, and so on until a number of steps fixed in advance has been reached (2 or 3, typically). In these systems, the role of the central server is limited to the technically peripheral but commercially essential function of distributing advertisement to the users.

Today's multimedia file sharing systems are in general not limited to audio files, but allow their users to exchange videos and images as well. In many cases videos are musical, due both to the relatively slow transition of the users community out of the musical arena, and to the duration of these videos, which is typically that of a song (3~6 min.), leading to more manageable file sizes. The exchange of full-length films is rapidly developing although, due to legal problems with copyright owners, it is still largely an "underground" activity.

Finally, one should give a brief mention to the exchange of open source software that although, *stricti ductu*, does not fit in the area of multimedia as commonly intended, shows some of the same problems and uses some of the same techniques (noticeably, mime types). In the area of software, however, the different characteristics of the user community (which is formed both of developers and of users of software) appears to have steered the interest towards centralized repositories (e.g. sourceforge.org, or gnu.org) that can serve, at one time, as locations for program downloads, and as a meeting point for the developers.

The legal issues

Beyond its technical significance, multimedia file sharing is having important social and legal repercussions, probing and, in all likelihood, changing, the power relations within the music industry between musicians, recording labels, and music listeners. Ever since the legal confrontation that led eventually to the demise of Napster, multimedia file sharing services have been the point of contention between two different and often irreconcilable views of music and the musical profession.

The recording industry association of America (RIAA) considers virtually every form of musical copy and of musical exchange outside of its control as a form of copyright infringement. During the last 300 years (roughly since the Statute of Anne, in 1712 [Author]), the notion of copyright has evolved from that of a natural right of the author, designed to protect the author's interests, to a form of good that, like any other good, can be bought and sold. This has made it possible, together with the possibility of the mechanical reproduction of sound, the creation of copyright holding organizations, such as the recording labels, with great economic strength and (at least in the US) considerable power to steer the political process. At first, in the case of Napster, the legal strategy of the RIAA has been to go after the service provider, facilitated, in this, by Napster's architectural decision to have a centralized indexing server: this helped the RIAA make a credible case that Napster was actively participating in copyright violation, and not merely providing the technical tools through which the violation was perpetrated (which, in itself, would not have been illegal, much like a gun manufacturer is not legally liable for a murder). With the more decentralized systems such as gnutella or kazaa, such strategy couldn't work, and the RIAA moved directly against the users of these systems, obtaining from the courts the authorization to force the internet providers to reveal the names of the possessors of unauthorized copies of copyrighted songs, a decision that has been widely regarded as a violation of the privacy of communication and of the civil rights of the users.

On the side of file sharing, the arguments were essentially two: a softer one, so to speak, held that, much like the repeatability of video tapes has not prevented the creation of a vast, copyright compliant rental market, providing in the end a major source of revenues for the very film studios that, in the beginning, were fighting the introduction of VCR, so, in the end, the file exchange phenomenon will result beneficial to those copyright holders that are willing to embrace it. The problem, in other words, would not be in file sharing, but in the timidity of the music industry, that is not able to see beyond the current business model.

The second, more radical, argument [Santini] sees copyright as a product of the historical circumstances of the industrial revolution, and sees the recording industry as a product of mechanical reproduction on a physical medium: much like the automobile made the horse carriage construction business disappear, so the disappearance of the recording industry based on copyright and of the "star system" in the new musical phase is a natural economic fact, and that the revenues of the vast majority of the world's musicians depend on live performances, not on record sales.

In the meantime, other providers are experimenting with copyright compliant pay-per-song services. An example of this is Apple, with its services connected to its audio player "ipod." In these cases, however, we are typically not in the presence of file sharing systems, but of client-server style downloads.

See: Mime Types, Client Server Systems, Peer to Peer Systems

References

1. M. Ripenau and I. Foster, "Peer-to-peer architecture case study: gnutella network," Proceedings of the *First international conference on peer to peer computing*, Lingköping, Sweden, August, 2001.
2. I. Stoica, R. Morris, D. Karger, M. F. Haashoek, and H. Balakrishnan, "Chord: a scalable peer-to-peer lookup service for internet applications," *Proceedings of SIGCOMM '01*, August 2001, San Diego, CA.
3. Q. Lv, P. Cao, E. Cohen, C. Li, and S. Shenker, "Search and replication in unstructured peer-to-peer networks," *Proceedings of ICS '02*, New York, June 2002.
4. A. Crespo and H. Garcia-Molina, "Routing indices for peer-to-peer systems," *Proceedings of the 22nd International Conference on Distributed Computing Systems*, 2002.
5. J. Lowenstein, *"The Author's due,"* The University of Chicago Press, Chicago, 2002.
6. S. Santini, "Bringing Copyright into the information age," *IEEE Computer*, August 2003.

MULTIMEDIA FINGERPRINTING

William Luh and Deepa Kundur
Texas A&M University, Texas, USA

Definition: *A digital fingerprint is a buyer-dependent serial number that is inconspicuously embedded in the multimedia, such that it is used to trace the original legal buyer of the multimedia.*

The ever-increasing consumption of digital data, such as digital images, video and audio, has lead to a number of security threats on multimedia content. Of these threats, multimedia piracy has dominated the technical, legal and business communities due to its impact on intellectual property protection, its influence on public policy, and its power to adapt business models. Multimedia piracy is defined as the unlawful copying, tampering, distribution, or downloading of multimedia content. The goals of multimedia pirates, who conduct the act of piracy, may include: (1) unrightfully claiming ownership of the intellectual property; (2) altering the multimedia data thus creating a misrepresentation of semantic content; (3) illegally selling or freely distributing the multimedia resulting in a loss of profits for members of the content distribution chain. The first two malicious objectives are popularly countered through the use of multimedia encryption, digital signatures, and robust and fragile watermarking methods. In this article, we present the problem of *multimedia fingerprinting*, a counterattack to the third goal.

Although it is possible to prevent the illegal selling or free distribution of multimedia through copy-protection on hardware consoles, multimedia fingerprinting is a cheaper approach that detects such illegal activities *after* they have taken place, or *passively deters* such illegal acts from taking place. Since detection of piracy occurs after-the-fact and by third parties often representing the content owners, consumers do not bear the burden of purchasing expensive tamper-proof hardware consoles.

Wagner [1] introduced fingerprinting in 1983. In multimedia fingerprinting, a *digital fingerprint* is a buyer-dependent serial number that is inconspicuously embedded in the multimedia, such that it is used to trace the original legal buyer of the multimedia. In this way, the original buyer is deterred from illegally distributing her fingerprinted multimedia. A general weakness of digital fingerprinting occurs when a coalition of pirates compares their uniquely fingerprinted multimedia to exploit the differences amongst their unique fingerprints in hopes of detecting, removing, or altering the fingerprint so as to evade being traced, and at the same time possibly frame an innocent buyer. This attack is known as *collusion*. Successful digital fingerprints will partially survive specific collusion attacks and correctly identify the pirate(s). The method of identifying pirate(s) is also called the *tracing algorithm* as depicted in Figure 1.

buyer. This attack is known as *collusion*. Successful digital fingerprints will partially survive specific collusion attacks and correctly identify the pirate(s). The method of identifying pirate(s) is also called the *tracing algorithm* as depicted in Figure 1.

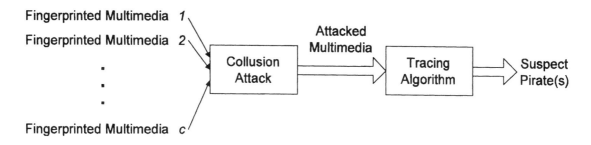

Figure 1. Collusion attack by pirates followed by identification of pirates.

Collusion has been the main research challenge in the realm of fingerprinting, and this article presents trend techniques in curbing this attack. Another area of interest pertaining to fingerprinting is the efficient distribution of fingerprinted multimedia. This article presents various methods of fingerprinting distribution.

Collusion-resistant, *c*-secure, Traitor Tracing Codes

In this paradigm a *codeword*, which is an element of a *codebook*, is used as a watermark; this watermark is embedded into the host media via watermarking techniques. What differentiates this from robust and fragile watermarking is that the codebook is deigned such that its codewords are resistive to specific collusion attacks. Figure 2 depicts the codebook paradigm.

Formally [2, 3, 4], a codebook with N codewords of length L over an alphabet Σ is defined as $\Gamma = \{w_1, w_2, \ldots, w_N\}$, such that for all codewords i, $w_i = x_{i,1} x_{i,2} \ldots x_{i,L}$ and $x_{i,j}$ are in Σ (in this notation the subscript i denotes the ith codeword, while the subscript j denotes the alphabet position in a codeword). In other words, the codewords are strings created by concatenating alphabets from the finite set Σ.

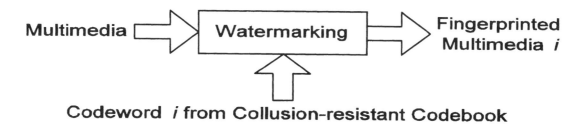

Figure 2. Fingerprinting using the codebook paradigm.

To define *collusion-resistant codebooks*, let the collusion attack be represented by a function C that takes a subset of codewords, and outputs a word of length L. Also define a tracing algorithm A to be a function that takes a word of length L, and outputs another word of length L. The codebook Γ is said to be *c*-collusion-resistant (or *c-secure*) with ε-error, for 0

$< \varepsilon < 1$, if for any subset S of Γ with cardinality no greater than c, $Pr[A(C(S))$ in $P(S)] > 1 - \varepsilon$, where $P(S)$ is the power set of S excluding the null set. The codebook Γ is said to be c-frameproof if $C(S)$ is a codeword then $C(S)$ in S. This formal definition states that the tracing algorithm is capable of identifying at least one member of the malicious coalition given a word created by the coalition's collusion attack function.

To make the problem of deriving a collusion-resistant codebook tractable, restrictions or assumptions are often placed on the collusion function C. A popular restriction known as the *Marking Assumption*, creates a word $C(S) = y_1 y_2 \ldots y_L$, where for fixed position j, $y_j = z$ if $x_{i,j} = z$ (in which case position j is said to be *undetectable*) for all codewords w_i in S, otherwise y_j can be any alphabet in Σ or an alphabet not in Σ, which is denoted *. Codebooks that are resistive to such collusion attacks are termed *fingerprinting codes*. On the other hand, if y_j must be in Σ, then codebooks resistive to this more restrictive collusion attack are termed *traitor tracing codes*. Some common collusion attacks that obey the Marking Assumption are: majority voting ($y_j = MODE(\{x_{i,j} \mid w_i$ in $S\})$, where MODE gives the most common value in the set); random ($y_j = x_{i,j}$ with probability $1/c$ for all w_i in S). It is proven in [2] that ε must be greater than 0, and the codebook design must employ an element of randomness under the Marking Assumption attack.

Some techniques for creating fingerprinting codes and tracing algorithms can be found in [2, 3, 4, 5, 6, 7, 8, 9, 10, 11, 12, 13]. Some techniques for creating traitor tracing codes and tracing algorithms can be found in [14, 15, 16]. Much of the research in fingerprinting and traitor tracing codes has revolved around creating large codebooks with short codeword lengths, robustness against large collation sizes, small probability of error, and fast tracing algorithms. In all these cases, the codebook is designed independently of the multimedia, and only embedded into the multimedia through watermarking.

Random Distortion-Constrained Codes

Another popular design is to randomly choose fingerprints according to some distribution. Some techniques and analysis for designing Gaussian fingerprints under different attack scenarios can be found in [12, 17, 18]. Collusion attacks on Gaussian codebooks include *linear attacks* such as *averaging, weighted averaging,* or *additive multiple access channel* (MAC), and *nonlinear attacks* such as the order statistics: min, max, median, minmax, modified negative, randomized negative in [17]. The only constraint on these collusion attacks is that the multimedia resulting from the attack should be perceptually similar to the pristine multimedia (i.e. the distortion-constraint), and hence the Marking Assumption and its variants do not apply.

Under various scenarios of this problem, information theoretic results on the fingerprinting capacity have also received some interest [18, 19, 20]. In all cases, as the number of pirates increases, the ability to trace the pirates becomes increasing difficult. For example in [20], it is shown that the maximum amount of information pertaining to the fingerprints that survives after a distortion-constrained collusion attack is proportional to $O(1/c)$, where c is the number of pirates.

Joint Source Fingerprinting

The *joint source fingerprinting* (JSF) paradigm describes a method of designing fingerprints by directly using the source multimedia, hence the name joint source. This is in contrast with the two techniques above, in which the fingerprints are designed/chosen independently of the multimedia and then hidden in the multimedia. Another difference between the JSF and the two aforementioned techniques is that popular collusion attacks, such as averaging, result in perceptually degraded multimedia when the JSF is used, but does not when the aforementioned techniques are used. This property forces the pirates to employ more costly attacks to create a perceptually distortionless multimedia.

In [21], images are randomly warped (i.e. rotated) to create fingerprinted images. When these uniquely fingerprinted images are averaged, the result is a blurry image. In this method the original multimedia is directly used to create fingerprinted multimedia and a common collusion attack results in perceptual degradation. In [22] video frames are used as fingerprints. When pirates average or randomly choose pixels between their copies, the resulting video is perceptually degraded.

The JSF methodology begins by decomposing the multimedia into two sets: the semantic set and the feature set. The semantic set is comprised of elements that result in a coarse representation of the original multimedia, and the feature set contains the details/features that when combined with the semantic set, result in the pristine multimedia. Fingerprinting begins by selecting subsets from the feature set such that these subsets when combined with the semantic set result in a perceptually distortionless multimedia. These subsets of the feature set are the fingerprints. The JSF methodology is depicted in Figure 3.

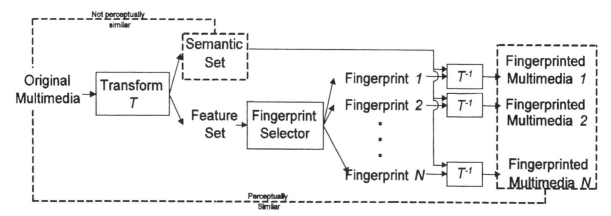

Figure 3. JSF design methodology.

When a coalition of pirates compares their fingerprinted multimedia, the coalition can detect the fingerprints. However, removing all their fingerprints will result in the semantic set, which is a coarse representation of the multimedia, and hence valueless. In contrast, if the pirates include all their fingerprints in the attack on the multimedia, all the pirates will be detected. Finally, if the fingerprints are designed correctly, a common collusion attack such as averaging results in perceptual degradation.

Fingerprinting Distribution

Upon creating N uniquely fingerprinted multimedia, the next task is to deliver these to the end-users over a communications network. The simplest and least efficient method is to send the N copies to the N different users. The ratio of the number of unique copies sent through the network to the number of unique fingerprints is thus equal to 1.

In [2, 23] a more efficient distribution means is proposed. Two distinctly watermarked media are produced where each media is partitioned into q pieces, so that there are a total of 2q pieces between the two watermarked media. These $2q$ pieces are encrypted with $2q$ unique keys, and then transmitted to the end users. Each end user has a unique set of q keys that will only decrypt q pieces, resulting in uniquely fingerprinted multimedia. This distribution scheme is outlined in Figure 4. This technique is well suited for fingerprinting schemes that use a codebook built over the binary alphabet, since the two distinctly watermarked media represent two alphabets. Since two uniquely watermarked media are sent over the network, the ratio of the number of unique copies sent to the number of unique fingerprints is $2/N$, which is more efficient than the previous scheme.

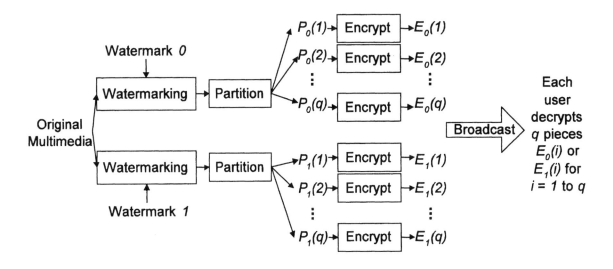

Figure 4. Efficient distribution for binary alphabet codebooks.

The distribution of JSF fingerprinted multimedia differs from the above approach and may be more efficient depending on some parameters. The semantic set is encrypted and broadcast to all users. Since the semantic set is much smaller than the original multimedia, distribution of the semantic set is equivalent to the distribution of less than one copy through the network. The fingerprints are then encrypted for individual end users and either broadcast to all users, upon the receipt of which users can decrypt their own fingerprints, or, privately transmitted to each individual. Since the fingerprints are drawn from the feature set, approximately one copy in total is sent through the network. The ratio of the number of unique copies sent to the number of unique fingerprints is approximately $1/N$ which is more efficient than the previous scheme [22]. A distribution method for Gaussian codewords that is similar in spirit can be found in [24].

Another interesting approach to fingerprinting and efficient distribution relies on tamperproof proprietary players. In [25], a watermark *w* is inserted into multimedia that is required to be purchased legally in order to be played in the proprietary player. On the other hand multimedia that may be distributed freely without purchasing does not have such a watermark and can be played in the proprietary player. Identical copies of the watermarked multimedia are transmitted to all users. To play the protected multimedia, a user must supply the player with a unique key issued to him. If the unique key contains the watermark *w*, then the player is permitted to play the multimedia. Hence the goal of a coalition of pirates is to remove the watermark *w* so that anyone can play the multimedia. In trying to remove the watermark *w*, the pirates leave unique traces of their unique keys in the attacked multimedia, and these unique traces can be used to uniquely identify the pirates. Since only one watermarked multimedia is broadcast to all end users, the ratio of the number of unique copies sent to the number of unique keys is *1/N*. Figure 5 depicts this fingerprinting and distribution method.

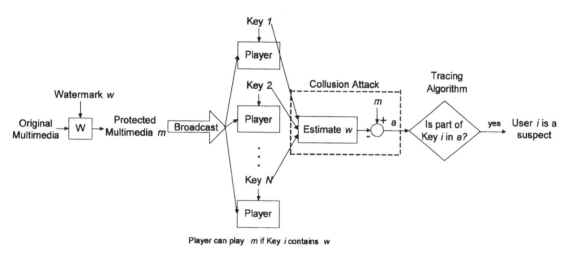

Figure 5. Fingerprinting and distribution with proprietary player. W = watermarking.

Another distribution method involves fingerprinting multimedia at intermediate nodes in a network instead of at the source or the destination in the network. In this scheme the intermediate nodes are trusted and assumed not to be malicious. The desired multimedia is uniquely watermarked several times in proportion to the number of end users. These uniquely watermarked multimedia are then packetized. Hence for each part of the multimedia there exists a set of similar packets corresponding to that part of the multimedia. The entire set of packets corresponding to a part of the multimedia is sent through the network. However at each intermediate node, only some of the packets from that set are chosen to continue their journey to a specific end user. By following this methodology all the way to each destination node, each end user will receive slightly different packets for each part of the multimedia. Thus overall each user receives a uniquely fingerprinted multimedia. These distribution schemes can be found in [26, 27]. Figure 6 captures the spirit of such schemes.

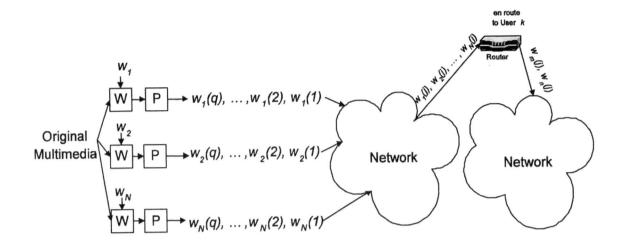

Figure 6. Fingerprinting distribution using intermediary nodes.
W = watermarking, P = packetizing.

Another distribution scheme involves fingerprinting at the user's end through the use of a *joint fingerprinting and decryption* (JFD) device that not only decrypts the encrypted media, but also adds a fingerprint; these cryptographic algorithms are also called *chameleon ciphers* [28]. The advantage of this method is that one encrypted copy of the multimedia is sent to all users, hence saving bandwidth. The fingerprints are encapsulated by each user's private keys. The drawback of these schemes is the tradeoff between bandwidth efficiency and security, with the latter somewhat lowered. Some JFD schemes can be found in [28, 29]. In [29] a lightweight video encryption scheme is used, offering additional computational efficiency. Figure 7 depicts the spirit of the JFD scheme.

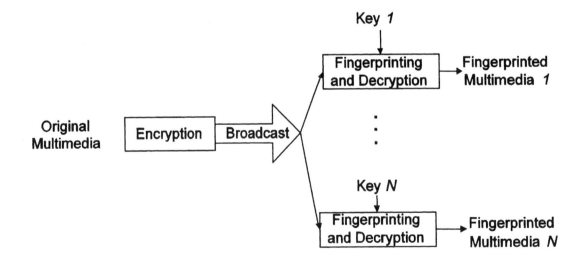

Figure 7. Joint fingerprinting and decryption model.

Buyer Protection

In the aforementioned fingerprinting schemes, the goal is to protect merchants against dishonest buyers who illegally distribute their multimedia. These are known as symmetric fingerprinting schemes. On the other hand, to protect buyers from dishonest merchants, protocols are needed in which buyer information is also incorporated into the fingerprinting scheme. In asymmetric fingerprinting [30], buyer information is disclosed to the merchant and then incorporated into the fingerprinting scheme. In anonymous fingerprinting [31], the buyer's information is not disclosed to the merchant but rather to a third party, thus preserving the anonymity of the buyer.

See: **Media watermarking; Watermarking, image; Watermarking, audio; Watermarking, video; Multimedia encryption**

References

1. N. R. Wagner, "Fingerprinting," Proceedings of IEEE Symposium on Security and Privacy, 1983, pp. 18-22.
2. D. Boneh and J. Shaw, "Collusion-secure fingerprinting for digital data," IEEE Transactions on Information Theory, Vol. 44, September 1998, pp. 1897–1905.
3. A. Barg, G. R. Blakley, and G. A. Kabatiansky, "Digital fingerprinting codes: Problem statements, constructions, identification of traitors," IEEE Transactions on Information Theory, Vol. 49, April 2003, pp. 852–865.
4. W. Luh and D. Kundur, "Digital media fingerprinting: techniques and trends," in Handbook of Multimedia Security, B. Furht and D. Kirovski, Eds. CRC Press, 2004, pp. 567-594.
5. G. Tardos, "Optimal probabilistic fingerprint codes," Proceedings of the 35th Annual ACM Symposium on Theory of Computing, 2003, pp. 116–125.
6. M. Wu, W. Trappe, Z. J. Wang, and K. J. R. Liu, "Collusion-resistant fingerprinting for multimedia," IEEE Signal Processing Magazine, March 2004, pp. 15–27.
7. J. Dittmann, A. Behr, M. Stabenau, P. Schmitt, J. Schwenk, and J. Ueberberg, "Combining digital watermarks and collusion secure fingerprints for digital images," SPIE Journal of Electronic Imaging, Vol. 9, pp. 456–467, 2000.
8. R. Safavi-Naini and Y. Wang, "Collusion secure q-ary fingerprinting for perceptual content," in Security and Privacy in Digital Rights Management, ACM CCS-8 Workshop DRM 2001, pp. 57–75.
9. F. Sebe and J. Domingo-Ferrer, "Scattering codes to implement short 3-secure fingerprinting for copyright protection," Electronics Letters, Vol. 38, No. 17, 2002, pp. 958–959.
10. V. D. To, R. Safavi-Naini, and Y. Wang, "A 2-secure code with efficient tracing algorithm," Proceedings in the Third International Conference on Cryptology, 2002, pp. 149–162.
11. J. Domingo-Ferrer and J. Herrera-Joancomarti, "Simple collusion-secure fingerprinting schemes for images," Proceedings of the International Symposium on Information Technology, March 2000, pp. 128–132.
12. Z. J.Wang, M.Wu, W. Trappe, and K. J. R. Liu, "Group-oriented fingerprinting for multimedia forensics," EURASIP Journal on Applied Signal Processing, Vol. 14, 2004, pp. 2153–2173.

13. G. R. Blakley, C. Meadows, and G. B. Purdy, "Fingerprinting long forgiving messages," in Lecture notes in computer sciences - On Advances in cryptology, 1986, Vol. 218, pp. 180–189.

14. B. Chor, A. Fiat, M. Naor, and B. Pinkas, "Tracing traitors," IEEE Transactions on Information Theory, Vol. 46, No. 5, 2000, pp. 893–910.

15. A. Silverberg, J. Staddon, and J. Walker, "Applications of list decoding to tracing traitors," IEEE Transactions on Information Theory, Vol. 49, No. 5, 2003, pp. 1312–1318.

16. M. Fernandez and M. Soriano, "Soft-decision tracing in fingerprinted multimedia content," IEEE Transactions on Multimedia, Vol. 11, No. 2, 2004, pp. 38–46.

17. H. Zhao, M. Wu, Z. J. Wang, and K. J. R. Liu, "Nonlinear collusion attacks on independent fingerprints for multimedia," Proceedings of the IEEE International Conference on Acoustics, Speech, and Signal Processing, 2003, pp. 613–616.

18. P. Moulin and A. Briassouli, "The Gaussian fingerprinting game," Proceedings of the Conference on Information Sciences and Systems, Princeton, NJ, March 2002.

19. J. K. Su, J. J. Eggers, and B. Girod, "Capacity of digital watermarks subjected to an optimal collusion attack," Proceedings of the European Signal Processing Conference (EUSIPCO 2000), Tampere, Finland, 2000.

20. A. Somekh-Baruch and N. Merhav, "On the capacity game of private fingerprinting systems under collusion attacks," IEEE Transactions on Information Theory, Vol. 51, No. 3, March 2005, pp. 884-889.

21. M. U. Celik, G. Sharma, and A. M. Tekalp, "Collusion-resilient fingerprinting using random pre-warping," IEEE Signal Processing Letters, Vol. 11, pp. 831–835, October 2004.

22. W. Luh and D. Kundur, "New paradigms for effective multicasting and fingerprinting of entertainment media," IEEE Communications Magazine, June 2005, accepted.

23. R. Parviainen and P. Parnes, "Large scale distributed watermarking of multicast media through encryption," in Proc. of the IFIP TC6/TC11 International Conference on Communications and Multimedia Security Issues of the New Century, 2001, Vol. 64, pp. 149–158.

24. H. Zhao and K. J. R. Liu, "Bandwidth efficient fingerprint multicast for video streaming," Proceedings of the IEEE International Conference on Acoustics, Speech, and Signal Processing, May 2004.

25. D. Kirovski, H. S. Malvar, and Y. Yacobi, "Multimedia content screening using a dual watermarking and fingerprinting system," IEEE Multimedia Magazine, Vol. 11, No. 3, pp. 59–73, 2004.

26. I. Brown, C. Perkins, and J. Crowcroft, "Watercasting: Distributed watermarking of multicast media," in Network Group Communications, November 1999, pp. 286–300.

27. P. Q. Judge and M. H. Ammar, "Whim: Watermarking multicast video with a hierarchy of intermediaries," Proceedings of the NOSSDAC, June 2000, pp. 699–712.

28. R. Anderson and C. Manifavas, "Chameleon - a new kind of stream cipher," in Fast Software Encryption, Haifa, Israel, January 1997, pp. 107–113.

29. D. Kundur and K. Karthik, "Digital fingerprinting and encryption principles for digital rights management," Proceedings of the IEEE Special Issue on Enabling Security Technologies for Digital Rights Management, Vol. 92, No. 6, June 2004, pp. 918–932.

30. B. Pfitzmann and M. Schunter, "Asymmetric fingerprinting," Lecture Notes in Computer Science, Vol. 1070, 1996, pp. 84–95.

31. B. Pfitzmann and M. Waidner, "Anonymous fingerprinting," Lecture Notes in Computer Science, Vol. 1233, 1997, pp. 88–102.

MULTIMEDIA IN EDUCATION

Abhaya Asthana
Bell Labs, Lucent Technologies, Westford, MA, USA

Definition: *Multimedia combines five basic types of media into the learning environment: text, video, sound, graphics and animation, thus providing a powerful new tool for education.*

Introduction

The world in which we live is changing rapidly and the field of education is experiencing these changes in particular as it applies to Media Services. The old days of an educational institution having an isolated audio-visual department are long gone! The growth in use of multimedia within the education sector has accelerated in recent years, and looks set for continued expansion in the future [1-6].

Teachers primarily require access to learning resources, which can support concept development by learners in a variety of ways to meet individual learning needs. The development of multimedia technologies for learning offers new ways in which learning can take place in schools and the home. Enabling teachers to have access to multimedia learning resources, which support constructive concept development, allows the teacher to focus more on being a facilitator of learning while working with individual students. Extending the use of multimedia learning resources to the home represents an educational opportunity with the potential to improve student learning [7].

The elements used in multimedia have all existed before. Multimedia simply combines these elements into a powerful new tool, especially in the hands of teachers and students. Interactive multimedia weaves five basic types of media into the learning environment: text, video, sound, graphics and animation. Since the mode of learning is interactive and not linear, a student or teacher can choose what to investigate next. For example, one does not start on the first page of a linear document and read to the end. Interactive multimedia learning mode is more like constructing a spider's web, with one idea linked to another, allowing choices in the learner's path.

The multimedia technologies that have had the greatest impact in education are those that augment the existing curriculum, allowing both immediate enhancement and encouraging further curriculum development. For example, the WWW serves as a storehouse of information that individual learners can search for subject matter content that specifically fits their learning agendas. Multimedia applications for computers have been developed for single computing platforms such as the PC, Apple Mac and games machines.

The Elements of Multimedia in Education

It is very tempting to use the latest computer wizardry to represent information and develop computer enhanced learning materials. However, the instructional design of these systems should be based on a careful examination and analysis of the many factors, both human and technical, relating to visual learning. When is sound more meaningful than a picture? How much text is too much? Does the graphic overwhelm the screen? For a student, this allows them to test all of their skills gained in every subject area. Students must be able to select appropriate multimedia tools and apply them to the learning task within the learning environment in order for effective learning to take place.

A *Multimedia Learning* environment involves a number of components or elements in order to enable learning to take place. Hardware and software are only part of the requirement. As mentioned earlier, multimedia learning integrates five types of media to provide flexibility in expressing the creativity of a student and in exchanging ideas (See Figure 1).

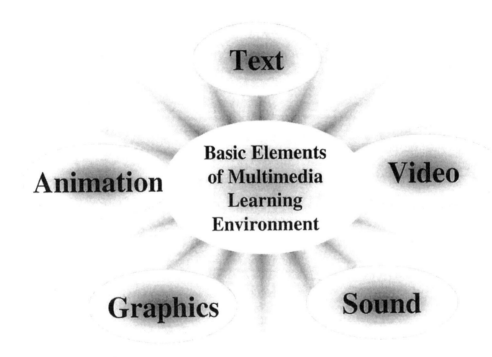

Figure 1. Five basic media elements in a learning environment.

Text
Out of all of the elements, text has the most impact on the quality of the multimedia interaction. Generally, text provides the important information. Text acts as the keystone tying all of the other media elements together. It is well written text that makes a multimedia communication wonderful.

Sound
Sound is used to provide emphasis or highlight a transition from one page to another. Sound synchronized to screen display, enables teachers to present lots of information at once. This approach is used in a variety of ways, all based on visual display of a complex

image paired with a spoken explanation (for example, art – pictures are 'glossed' by the voiceover; or math – a proof fills the screen while the spoken explanation plays in the background). Sound used creatively, becomes a stimulus to the imagination; used inappropriately it becomes a hindrance or an annoyance. For instance, a script, some still images and a sound track, allow students to utilize their own power of imagination without being biased and influenced by the inappropriate use of video footage. A great advantage is that the sound file can be stopped and started very easily.

Video
The representation of information by using the visualization capabilities of video can be immediate and powerful. While this is not in doubt, it is the ability to choose how we view, and interact, with the content of digital video that provides new and exciting possibilities for the use of digital video in education. There are many instances where students, studying particular processes, may find themselves faced with a scenario that seems highly complex when conveyed in purely text form, or by the use of diagrams and images. In such situations the representational qualities of video help in placing a theoretical concept into context [8].

Video can stimulate interest if it is relevant to the rest of the information on the page, and is not 'overdone'. Video can be used to give examples of phenomena or issues referred to in the text. For example, while students are reading notes about a particular issue, a video showing a short clip of the author/teacher emphasizing the key points can be inserted at a key moment; alternatively, the video clips can be used to tell readers what to do next. On the other hand, it is unlikely that video can completely replace the face-to-face lecture: rather, video needs to be used to supplement textual information.

One of the most compelling justifications for video may be its dramatic ability to elicit an emotional response from an individual. Such a reaction can provide a strong motivational incentive to choose and persist in a task.

The use of video is appropriate to convey information about environments that can be either dangerous or too costly to consider, or recreate, in real life. For example: video images used to demonstrate particular chemical reactions without exposing students to highly volatile chemicals, or medical education, where real-life situations can be better understood via video.

Animation
Animation is used to show changes in state over time, or to present information slowly to students so they have time to assimilate it in smaller chunks. Animations, when combined with user input, enable students to view different versions of change over time depending on different variables.

Animations are primarily used to demonstrate an idea or illustrate a concept [9]. Video is usually taken from life, whereas animations are based on drawings. There are two types of animation: Cel based and Object based. Cel based animation consists of multiple drawings, each one a little different from the others. When shown in rapid sequence, for example, the operation of an engine's crankshaft, the drawings appear to move. Object based animation (also called slide or path animation) simply moves an object across a screen. The object itself does not change. Students can use object animation to illustrate a point - imagine a battle map of Gettysburg where troop movement is represented by sliding arrows.

<u>Graphics</u>
Graphics provide the most creative possibilities for a learning session. They can be photographs, drawings, graphs from a spreadsheet, pictures from CD-ROM, or something pulled from the Internet. With a scanner, hand-drawn work can be included. Standing [10] commented that, "the capacity of recognition memory for pictures is almost limitless". The reason for this is that images make use of a massive range of cortical skills: color, form, line, dimension, texture, visual rhythm, and especially imagination [11, 12].

Educational Requirements

Employing multimedia tools into the learning environment is a rewarding, but complex and challenging task. All of the multimedia formats available: text, sound, video, animation and graphics, already exist in one form or another in most libraries. Students can explore an almost infinite variety of information. All these explorations can certainly lead to new discoveries, but unless consumption is followed by production, the story ends. Without a chance to use their new discoveries and demonstrate what they have learned, the knowledge gained soon becomes the knowledge forgotten.

Giving students an opportunity to produce multimedia documents of their own provides several educational advantages. Students work with the same information from four perspectives: 1) as researcher, they must locate and select the information needed to understand the chosen topic; 2) as authors, they must consider their intended audience and decide what amount of information is needed to give their readers an understanding of the topic; 3) as designers, they must select the appropriate media to share the concepts selected; and 4) as writers, they must find a way to fit the information to the container including the manner of linking the information for others to retrieve.

When defining the appropriate medium to use it is vital to 'know' the audience and the technical specification of users' machines. There may be technical reasons for choosing which multimedia element will best communicate certain concepts. Whatever medium is chosen, to apply a principle mentioned above to all digital media elements, visuals must be congruent, relevant, and consistent with other information presented in order to be effective. Whatever the latest technological advance, instructional design principles apply. For example, care needs to be taken when using visuals for aesthetic reasons. The misuse of a single visual element can cause misrepresentation of information and become a barrier to content and impede learning, even if the program overall may, in all other aspects, follow the principles of instructional design. It is important to bear in mind the nature of the audience, especially their age group and culture mix.

<u>Human - Computer Interface</u>
Multimedia applications like any other application, appliance or tool, benefit from being easy to use, with minimal training or self-learning. The need for a well designed human - computer interface, which may be screen or audio based is well accepted. The standards

for computer- based publications are set by the publishers of books, music, Walt Disney cartoons and television producers. With the development of High Definition TV and beyond, it is likely that there will be a continual increase in the demands placed on computer based multimedia systems.

Access, Delivery, Scheduling and Recording
On demand access times to computer information need to be below one second to be usable in real time. Alternatively the delivery of information at a later time is acceptable if it can be scheduled, as in a TV broadcast schedule. Scheduling can have advantages for users over on demand delivery. In open learning situations learners can control their program by requesting a multimedia unit at a convenient time. Computer users will wish to record a film, session, or learning experience for future reference.

Interactivity
Computer based multimedia needs the same degree of interactivity that a school exercise book, or a laboratory experiment has in order to remain credible as a learning medium. Educationists have shown that certain forms of learning becomes easier, and is retained more permanently if the learner participates in some way with the learning material. The generation of computer based virtual reality is an extension of this process. The incorporation of interactivity is really the job of the application designer. The incorporation of interactivity is assisted if the network is capable of two-way communication, and for some applications the sense of interactivity is aided by the ability to deliver a moving picture, or a sound very quickly, so that a sense of two-way human participation can be generated. Real time video conferencing is an example.

Classroom Architecture and Resources

The technology needed to support classroom teaching has increased in complexity [13]. Until only a few years ago all that a lecture room needed were some seats for the students, and a blackboard and a lectern or table for the teacher. Then came the overhead projector, slide projector and the return of TV with video player. Now there is the computer, networks and related display tools. From having a next to zero maintenance cost, the teaching room is becoming not only costly to equip, but costly to run and maintain, including the escalating costs of security. Figure 2 shows a typical multimedia based educational environment. The main teaching spaces are equipped with a standard set of presentation equipment, and full details of what is, and is not, available in each room.

The live lecture in the digital theater is concurrently broadcast to the remote distance-learning site. Even home-based students may join the live session. The ways in which users or participants in multimedia sessions access multimedia or connect with others have important consequences for the storage and transmission systems. For instance multimedia learning material can be accessed directly from a server during a class or downloaded to student machines prior to a session. The demands on a connecting network are very different in each access mode. Students learn to make use of multimedia as an aid to retrieving information from multiple sources such as digital libraries and multimedia servers that could support computer-assisted learning environments. Students learn to develop multimedia materials, especially as a component of project-based learning that is rooted in constructivism and in cooperative learning [14].

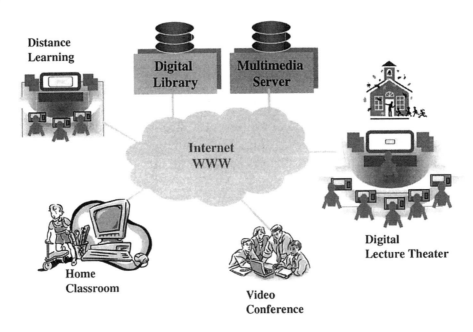

Figure 2. A typical multimedia based educational environment.

Multimedia offers the lecturer many benefits including: satisfying educational objectives, increasing students understanding, demonstrating events, showing places, conducting experiments which would otherwise be impossible. Sharing of multimedia outputs is done carefully such that it will not disturb other learners working in the same classroom! Not only may a number of students be performing similar activities at the same time on a network, the lecturer must decide whether to control the activities via the media of the computer. The use of multi-party desktop conferencing with the lecturer chairing the running of the conferencing session, showing selected parts of a video is a case in point.

Many school reform models focus on a significant restructuring of the classroom. They propose a shift from a teacher-centered didactic model to a learner-centered constructivist model. While details of these constructivist models vary, they typically include an emphasis on cooperative learning and on the use of project-based learning. Most types of school reform models recognize that multimedia brings a new dimension to reading and writing, and the need for students to develop basic skills in information retrieval in multimedia environments [15].

Training and Staff Development
Of course all of these teaching innovations require a new methodology to support the technology. It requires a change of direction in terms of academic planning and lectures need to be carefully structured to maximize the benefits that interactive systems bring to teaching.

The installation of any new technology inevitably brings with it the need for staff development courses, and the costs of such staff development should not be overlooked. With regards to presentation equipment within teaching spaces there are two main groups of people who require training, the lecturers and the support staff, though increasingly students also seek training in presentation skills. The availability of standards for multimedia networking, particularly for inter-working between applications, the development of networked applications, and interworking between networks are essential to reduce the complexity and level of skill required in using multimedia.

<u>Resources – WWW and Virtual Environments</u>
The World-Wide Web was created to support remote collaborative research, but it has developed primarily as a means of providing information that is linked to other information sources. It is an essential medium for accessing, delivering and exchanging information. The WWW provides a number of opportunities for teachers and students. Resources can be accessed which might otherwise have been unavailable. These include virtual libraries and museums. Other resources can be built up and used by students, for example questions and answers that can be searched or routed through to an expert if it is a new query and then the answer logged for future use. Teaching programs can be accessed and used by students as part of their modules.

The Web can be thought of as a digital global multimedia library (See Figure 2). With the steadily increasing classroom use of multimedia resources, students are required to develop the skills needed to locate information contained in this format. Developing skills for locating and evaluating information requires learning to distinguish good multimedia from poor multimedia materials.

Multimedia in education has the potential to go beyond the boundaries of interaction and explorative learning. The actors in the education community could establish a 'Virtual Education Space' (VES). A student can 'create' artifacts that reflect his/her understanding of concepts by combining text, voice and animation utilities. A teacher could customize lesson plans that can be individualized. Literally it is setting up an education lab to innovate and create.

Concerns

The fusion of all types of media in a digital world captures the ethos of the new technological age. Multimedia: a combination of video, text, still images and sound can provide an effective learning aid. But the adage, "Putting computers into schools will directly improve learning," is negated by the reality that, "all this expensive technology will yield little educational return until schools and districts address the need for professional development, technical support, the availability of appropriate software, classroom management, and curriculum integration."

The full potential of using multimedia technologies for learning in primary and secondary schools can only be realized after there has been some re-engineering of the way learning experiences are offered in the traditional schools and colleges. A critical element is for teachers to be familiar with multimedia technologies in order for them to know how to use them within their curriculum areas.

Moreover, the freedom of the Internet has some disadvantages. There is too much information on the Internet. Students must decide what information they need and what they do not need. The quality of the information can also be misleading. Students must be taught how to distinguish between quality and unimportant information. Since no rules exist on the Internet in terms of what can and cannot be disclosed, anyone can put any material on the Internet.

Lastly, "High-Tech Kids: Trailblazers or Guinea Pigs?" introduces the debate over whether computer use by young children is helping or hindering their brain development, social and physical health. Are we using this generation of young people as guinea pigs? It is a thought- provoking question for educators to ponder.

References

1. Center for Highly Interactive Computing in Education.http://hi-ce.eecs.umich.edu/.
2. Educational Resources Info Center Digests: http://www.ed.gov/databases/ERIC_Digests/index/.
3. Federal Resources for Educational Excellence: http://www.ed.gov/free/.
4. International Society for Technology in Education Standards Projects: http://www.iste.org/standards/.
5. D. Moursund, "Ten powerful ideas shaping the present and future of IT in education," Learning and Leading with Technology, Vol. 27 No. 1, 1999.
6. U.S. Department of Education, Secretary's conference on educational technology: "Evaluating the effectiveness of educational technology," July 1999, http://www.ed.gov/Technology/TechConf/1999/.
7. P. Barker, "Multi-Media Computer Assisted Learning." Kogan Page Ltd, London, 1989.
8. L. P. Reiber, "Computers, Graphics, & Learning." Brown & Benchmark, Madison, Wisconsin, Dubuque, Iowa. ISBN 0-697-14894-7, 1994.
9. R. E. Mayer and R. B. Anderson, "Animations need narrations: An experimental test of a dual-coding hypothesis," Journal of Educational Psychology, 19: 1991, pp. 30-42.
10. L. Standing, "Learning 10,000 pictures," Quarterly Journal of Experimental Psychology, Vol. 25, 1973, pp. 207-222.
11. R. N. Haber, "How we remember what we see." Scientific American, 1970, pp.105.
12. J. Levin and A. Lesgold, "On pictures in prose," Educational Communications and Technology Journal, 26: 1978, pp. 233-234.
13. J. Sandholtz, C. Ringstaff, and D. Dwyer, "Teaching with technology: Creating student-centered classroom," New York: Teachers College, Columbia University, 1997.
14. I. Abdal-Haqq, "Constructivism in teacher education: Considerations for those who would link practice to theory," ERIC Digest, 1998. http://www.ed.gov/databases/ERIC_Digests/ed426986.html.
15. P. C. Blumenfeld et al., "Motivating project-based learning: Sustaining the doing, supporting the learning," Educational Psychologist, Vol. 26, No. 3 & 4, 1991, pp. 369-398.

MULTIMEDIA LIBRARIES

Erich Neuhold and Claundia Niederée
Fraunhofer Institute IPSI, Darmstadt, Germany

Definition: *Digital Library is an information system targeted towards a specific community, where content from different sources is collected and managed, content is structured and enriched with metadata, and a set of services is offered that makes the content available to a user community via a communication network, typically the Internet.*

Digital Libraries are the electronic counterparts of traditional paper libraries, where the digital medium opens new opportunities, especially in the area of improved access support, increased content availability, powerful content interlinking, and reduced costs, but also imposes new challenges like long-term preservation in the context of fast changing storage technologies. Further important challenges are issues of copyright and digital rights management and the cost of digitization for not digitally-born content.

Various definitions for Digital Libraries exist (see e.g. [1, 2]). These can be summarized as follows: A Digital Library is an information system targeted towards a specific community, where content from different sources is collected and managed, content is structured and enriched with metadata, and a set of services is offered that makes the content available to a user community via a communication network, typically the Internet.

Multimedia Libraries are Digital Libraries, where the managed content is not restricted to the usually mainly textual documents. Such libraries contain, next to the "textual" contents, media types like music, videos, images, maps, and mixtures of different content types (multimedia objects) as they are, for example used in e-Learning or in the documentation of history [3]. Multimedia libraries may also contain content types that were not supported in traditional libraries at all like 3D objects, executable software (e.g. computer games) or callable services. One of the main challenges for a multimedia library is to provide effective access to these types of context (based on adequate indexing) and to provide support for the "real-time" integration of different content types. Some challenges of multimedia libraries are closely related to those of museums and archives that make multimedia representations of their artifacts available online.

This article starts with a discussion of the role of Digital Libraries in mediating between the individual information needs of the members of a community and the vast amount of globally available content. In this context the services provided by a library play a central role. Therefore, search services and further value adding services within a Digital Library are discussed next in the article with a focus on the special requirements of multimedia content. The article closes with some current trends and open research issues in Digital Library technology.

Role of Digital Libraries in Content-to-Community Mediation

A Digital Library mediates between the information needs of its user community and the globally available content. Contributions in four task areas are essential for supporting this mediation (see figure 1 and [4]):

– *Content preselection:* The library selects high-quality content potentially relevant for the members of its user community;

– *Content structuring:* The library structures the content according to the predominant domain understanding of its user community;

– *Content enrichment:* The library enriches content objects with descriptive and value-adding metadata provided by domain experts, librarians, and community members;

– *Library services:* Support for content retrieval, access, annotation, etc. enable the identification of relevant material and facilitate access of content and its use by community members as a group or as individuals;

These contributions allow a Digital Library to reduce the gap that exists between the wide variety and large amount of globally available content and specific information needs of individuals and small group within its community. Ideally, many of these contributions should be achieved without or with little human inference. However, for technological reasons, but also for reasons of quality control and trust, human involvement and especially involvement of representatives from the library now and in the future will be essential for these tasks.

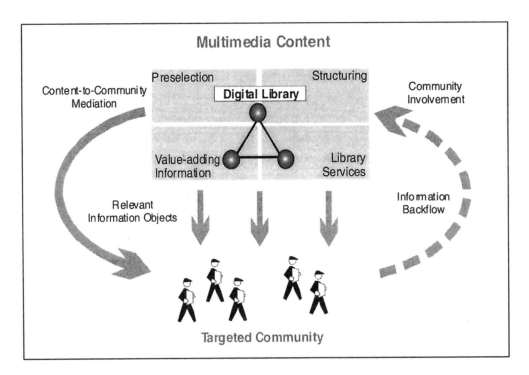

Figure 1. Contribution of a digital library to content to community mediation.

Metadata and Search Services

Search services are required for efficiently and effectively finding relevant content in the content collection(s) managed by a Digital Library. There are two approaches for supporting search in Digital Libraries, which may also be combined with each other: On the one hand, methods of information and multimedia retrieval and on the other hand metadata-based search.

Information retrieval is a search approach which is based on a direct analysis of the content objects of a Digital Library. For efficient information retrieval, retrieval indices are automatically built and updated. For (mainly) textual documents indices are built based on an analysis of word occurrences within documents (with some extra processes like stemming, removing stop words, taking into account term frequency, etc.). For multimedia objects, the task of creating useful indices is more demanding: Features like the color distribution for images, that can easily be extracted automatically, are in most cases not the features the users is interested in. The challenge is in finding adequate associations between low-level features like color distributions and high-level features that represent aspects of content objects a user is interested in like e.g. objects displayed in an image, scenes of a movie or genre of a music title. Such association rules are highly domain dependent and they are still subject of current research in multimedia retrieval and will remain so for some time.

A second method of information access is the use of metadata for retrieving relevant content objects. Metadata is data about data, or more precisely in the Digital Library context, metadata are data for describing information objects and for supporting information processes within the respective domain. Such a described information object may be an individual content object like a scientific paper or an image, but also an entire collection and other metadata. Metadata form an additional information layer on top of the content objects, which are managed by a DL, and can be used in retrieving interesting information, in selecting relevant content objects from a search result list (e.g. selecting a paper based on the author of the paper or the proceeding it was published in) and in supporting an improved understanding of content objects (e.g. by taking into account the historical context a film was produced in). The management of metadata is comparable with the management of library catalogues in traditional (paper) libraries.

There is a wide range of different metadata types that can be classified in multiple ways, e.g. according to their purpose or the depth of description (see e.g. [5]). Standardization of metadata formats plays an important role in Digital Libraries. Metadata standards like Dublin Core [6] and MARC [7] enable the re-use of metadata records in different libraries and the development of re-usable services that operate on such standards, and facilitate search across different collections. Additional types of metadata are required for describing multimedia content objects like images, videos etc. This includes, for example information related to the production of a video or the description of objects in an image. Special multimedia metadata standards have been developed like MPEG-7 or MPEG-21. In addition, there are multimedia metadata standards for specific application domains like SCORM [8] for the area of e-learning.

Of course, the separation between content-based information retrieval and metadata-based search services is not that strict. Retrieval indices may be considered as a special type of metadata, information retrieval methods can be applied on some types of metadata like e.g. abstracts or annotations and information retrieval and metadata-based search can be combined to more powerful access methods.

The dialog with the user has been identified as another starting point for improvements in the efficiency of multimedia retrieval. Going beyond entering text into query forms, approaches exist, where the user may formulate his/her information needs in innovative ways that are adapted to the type of content to be retrieved. This includes humming the tune of the music one wants to access (QBH, see e.g. [9, 10]) as well as painting a sketch of an image or using an example image to retrieve similar pictures.

Mediation between content and community can be further improved by taking into account information about the user in retrieval and information filtering. Such personalization approaches require an adequate model of the user as well as methods for collecting and updating information for the individual user profiles based on this model. User models typically focus on cognitive patterns like interests and skills. Information about the user can be collected explicitly, by asking the user, or implicitly by observing user behavior and by analyzing this data to infer user characteristics like interests. The information in the user profiles is, for example, used to refine queries posed by the user and to give recommendations to the user.

Further retrieval challenges in Digital Libraries are multi- and cross-lingual search, adequate result visualization and structuring as well as federated search that efficiently manages searches over different collections (within one Digital Library or across the boundaries of Digital Libraries). Selection of promising collections, decomposition of queries and combination of query results, which requires duplicate detection and re-ranking of the combined result, are the challenges in federated search.

Digital Library Services beyond Search

In addition to search services, a Digital Library also supports other classes of services. This mainly includes community services, annotation services, and administrative services.

Services for supporting the community beyond search are, for example, services that foster community formation and services for supporting the communication and collaboration between community members (chat, discussion forum etc.). Collaborative filtering services are an option to combine community and search services: Ratings provided by community members and similarities between community members are used to provide recommendations to community members about relevant information objects in the Digital Library. Other community services are services that involve community members into the content collection process by enabling them to include their own content into the Digital Library collection or to build their own private libraries.

Annotation services enable members of the community to add annotations in the form of comments, ratings, etc. to content objects of the Digital Library. In this way, community members may profit from the experiences and expertise of other community members. Advanced annotation services enable the annotation of annotations and support different types of annotations. Annotation can also be used in the retrieval process, since the comments about a document may provide additional information about its content and its reception in the community [11].

The adequateness and the form of the aforementioned services clearly depend on the size of the community supported by the library. In small, well-connected communities, for example, self-organization and quality assurance might work based on social networks and control. In large communities, however, issues like quality control, intellectual property rights, and mutual trust as well as avoiding information overload and spam become more critical issues and have to be taken into account by the services.

In addition to the services provided to the user, Digital Library also supports administrative processes for the management of the Digital Library [12]. Main goal of this process is to keep the collection focused and attractive for the targeted community. Collection management includes deciding upon which new content to acquire and possibly also when to delete content from the collection (based on an adequate collection strategy), and restructuring the collection, when this is implied by changes in the underlying domain (e.g. new trends). Furthermore, necessary administrative Digital Library processes include the management of users and user groups, digitization of content, creation and acquisition of metadata records, just to name the most prominent. In addition, a careful handling of access rights, copyrights, and intellectual property rights contributes to the "trust" of the community members into the services of a Digital Library.

Many Digital Libraries do not only have to provide efficient and effective access to their content, but also have to take actions for achieving long-term accessibility for content objects. Special services and organizational strategies are required to achieve long term preservation in Digital Libraries due to the fast changes in storage technology (see e.g. [13]). Adequate methods for ensuring long-term preservation in the digital age are still subject of research.

Current Trends in Digital Libraries and Multimedia Libraries

The first generation of Digital Libraries has been built from scratch in an experimental fashion. After a certain understanding has been established about the core functionality of a typical Digital Library, so-called Digital Library management systems like DSpace [14] or Greenstone [15] have been developed that offer basic, out-of the box functionality for managing a Digital Library. Such systems are now available and used in various Digital Library projects. The latest trend in Digital Library technology is a more decentralized, service-oriented approach for Digital Library architectures. The overall goal here is to systematically make Digital Library functionality available to a broader audience, reduce the cost of entry for this technology, to improve flexibility and adaptability and to foster shared and synergetic use of content, metadata, services and other resources. In this context current technological developments like Grid Computing, Web and Grid Services and the Peer-to-Peer computing paradigm are exploited. The project DILIGENT (EU IST-004260), for example, works on building a Grid-based Digital Library infrastructure that enables the on-demand creation of tailored Digital Libraries, so called Virtual Digital Libraries on top of the generic infrastructure (see [16]). In general, Digital Libraries migrate from centralized systems to dynamic federations of services.

A second trend that was already addressed in the previous part of the article is the offering of additional services beyond search and collection management that reflects a broadened understanding of the role of a Digital Library within a community. This includes community services that support community formation, awareness of a community for trends in the domain and the role of individual within the community as well as services for fostering collaboration in the community. In addition, these are also services that enable community members to take a more active part in content provision and annotation. In summary, the idea is to support the collaborative information processes of the community in a more comprehensive and participative way, migrating from the information access support provided by Digital Libraries to the idea of tailored virtual information and knowledge environments (see e.g. [17]). For research libraries this trend is reflected by current research activities in the area of e-Science.

A third trend in Digital Libraries is the use of Semantic Web technology for intelligent search services. This includes semantic annotation of content objects based on domain ontologies, the use of concepts and ontological knowledge instead of strings in search, and concept-based clustering of query results. Another area of research and development in intelligent search support is to more systematically take context into account (see e.g. [4]). On the one hand, this refers to user context. More comprehensive, ontology-based models of the user and his current situation (including user tasks and relationships a user is involved in) are used to go beyond existing personalization approach. On the other hand the context of an information object can be used to improve retrieval results like, for example, the information a content object is linked with or the annotations about a content object.

References

1. W. Arms, "Digital Libraries," Digital Libraries and Electronic Publishing, MIT Press Cambridge and London, 2000.
2. M. E. Lesk, "Books, Bytes, and Bucks," Morgan Kaufmann, San Francisco, 1997.
3. The University of Queensland Library, "From Lunchroom to Boardroom - Stories and Images of Women's Achievements in the Labour Movement 1930's - 1970's", http://media.library.uq.edu.au:8080/lunchroom/index.html.
4. E. Neuhold, C. Niederée, A. Stewart, I. Frommholz, and B. Mehta, "The Role of Context for Information Mediation in Digital Libraries," Proceedings of the *7th International Conference on Asian Digital Libraries*, Shanghai, China, 2004.
5. A. Gilliland-Swetland, "Defining Metadata," in M. Baca, Editor: Metadata: Pathways to Digital Information, Getty Information Institute, 1998.
6. M. Dekkers and S. Weibel, "State of the Dublin Core Metadata Initiative," April 2003. D-Lib Magazine, 9(4), http://www.dlib.org/dlib/april03/weibel/04weibel.html.

7. Library of Congress, MARC Standards, http://lcweb.loc.gov/marc/marc.html.
8. Advanced Distributed Learning (ADL) Initiative, Sharable Content Object Reference Model (SCORM), http://www.adlnet.org/scorm/index.cfm, 2004.
9. R. McNab, L. Smith, I. Witten, and C. Henderson, "Towards a Music Library: Tune Retrieval from Acoustic Input," Proceedings of the 1st ACM International Conference on Digital Libraries, March 1996, Bethesda, Maryland, USA.
10. L. Smith, and R. Medina, "Discovering themes by exact pattern matching," Proceedings of the International Symposium on Music Information Retrieval (2001), Bloomington, IN, USA, pp. 31-32.
11. M. Agosti, N. Ferro, I. Frommholz, and U. Thiel, "Annotations in Digital Libraries and Co laboratories – Facets, Models and Usage," In Research and Advanced Technology for Digital Libraries: Proceedings of the 8th European Conference, ECDL 2004, Bath, UK, September 2004.
12. P. S. Graham, "The Digital Research Library: Tasks and Commitments," Proceedings of Digital Libraries '95, The Second Annual Conference on the Theory and Practice of Digital Libraries, June 1995, Austin, Texas, USA
 http://csdl.tamu.edu/DL95/contents.html.
13. J. Hunter and S. Choudhury, "Implementing Preservation Strategies for Complex Multimedia Objects," In Research and Advanced Technology for Digital Libraries, 7th European Conference, ECDL 2003, Trondheim, Norway, August 2003,
14. R. Tansley, M. Bass, and M. Smith, "DSpace as an Open Archival Information System: Current Status and Future Directions," In Research and Advanced Technology for Digital Libraries, 7th European Conference, ECDL 2003, Trondheim, Norway, August 2003.
15. I. H. Witten, D. Bainbridge, and S. J. Boddie, "Greenstone Open-Source Digital Library Software," D-Lib Magazine, 7(10), October 2001.
16. DILIGENT Consortium, "Homepage of the DILIGENT Project",
 http://www.diligentproject.org/.
17. M. Hemmje, C. Niederée, and T. Risse (Eds.), "From Integrated Publication and Information Systems to Virtual Information and Knowledge Environments," Essays Dedicated to Erich J. Neuhold on the Occasion of His 65th Birthday. LNCS 3379, Springer 2005.

MULTIMEDIA NEWS SYSTEMS

Markus W. Schranz
Pressetext GmbH, Austria

Schahram Dustdar
Technical University of Vienna, Austria

Definition: Multimedia news systems deal with architectures to manage complex multimedia news databases, online presentation and distribution services or the integration of several existing services to meta-services using intelligent news retrieval engines.

The full integration of digital media as a commonly available data type for business applications such as multimedia news services causes a major transition in computing infrastructure and solution architectures. While many corporate uses of digital media can be handled with the current infrastructure, in multimedia application domains, as the amount and file size of the digital media grows, more than simple capacity improvements need to be implemented. The business needs for media are concrete; the problems we need to address are real. The media and news operating community needs to find real solutions too, for high-level semantic analysis, provisioning and management of mixed-media information, and distribution and delivery of media data to satisfy requirements dictated by business scenarios. The article describes technical and business backgrounds of the multimedia news application domain, focusing on architectures, standards, network topologies and the variety of offered services. Additionally we describe scenarios that show how corporations are using digital media to enhance their employee and customer communications, improve the effectiveness and efficiency of business processes, and create new business and revenue opportunities.

Introduction

Advertising campaigns and highly popular government programs have for many years emphasized the need to get people connected to the Internet. That meant solving the technological and sociological issues involved in providing network access to the population and turning them into regular users. The message echoes today in a slightly muted form. Except in developing parts of the world, getting people connected is no longer a major challenge. The challenge today is to create and support experiences and contents that users continue to value [1]. In particular, we concentrate on multimedia content that might be the glue that connects, defines, and supports communities on the Internet. Irrespective of views on intellectual property issues or business models, even a cursory reading of recent news and events makes it undeniable that the Web is becoming a remarkably effective-if not yet efficient-multimedia content distribution platform. While this may not have been a design goal earlier, it's now a significant driving force in the evolution of network technology, user services, and access devices. Overlooking the manifold entrepreneurs and business developments in online advertising, marketing, internet services and the publishing industry, the wide acceptance and utilization of current news as reliable and reputable service contents document the success of multimedia news contents in the networked information industry.

As the fastest growing medium in the last decade the Internet has brought unmanageable amounts of information to the average user's fingertips. This especially holds true for the multimedia news application domain with hundreds of thousands of journalists and digital news professionals producing a steadily increasing set of news content day by day. Since this growth will only continue, it is vital that users be supported in channeling this universe of information into improved productivity. Failing to address information overload will be costly for enterprises and individuals, often in ways not easily measured. To really satisfy user needs and restricted budgets, the myriads of news information need to be structured and organized in intelligent and user-oriented ways.

Technically, appropriate architectures to manage complex multimedia news databases, online presentation and distribution services or the integration of several existing services to meta-services using intelligent news retrieval engines have been developed [2]. Appropriate standards such as XML as well as current communication technologies like Web Services are being used for news management and transportation. Modern database and content management features handle text and graphical contents and specific multimedia formats and technologies integrate even audio and video material in complex multimedia news systems.

News services have taken the Internet by storm in the late 90's. The successful use of digital media requires new or transformed genres of digital communication. Not only particular technologies or modes of communication or presentation such as hypertext, email, or the Web, but also complex communicative forms anchored in specific institutions and practices prove the establishment of new and emergent genres of the digital community[3]. Initially news sites were conceived as "electronic newspapers" or "digital newspaper" but have generated a specific genre of their own with special use and design elements. Ihlström[4] documents a move from print to multimedia in the sense that the news is not only presented as text but as audio and video as well at the news sites today.

Technical solutions provide the presentation, management and distribution of multimedia news based on dozens of different business models. Integrated multilingual and multinational services provide amongst others news syndication, online streaming or customer oriented news monitoring and media clipping services.

Multimedia News

Based on the typical news sources provided by individual journalists, national and international news agencies, and worldwide broadcast networks the contents have been handled with appropriate multimedia management systems. Since content assets are typically out of academic and technical administration, specific user-oriented software has emerged and has become widely popular within the last 5 years: Content Management Systems.

Content Management Systems

Based on research oriented web engineering methodologies [5] the news market has started to adopt management features and high volume capabilities for developing and utilizing commercial and open source systems. Market leaders like Stellent™, Microsoft™, Vignette™, IBM™, Tridion™, OpenText™ and others are offering customer-oriented features in their commercial services, thus competing with open source CMS leaders like Zope, OpenCMS, Typo3, Mambo, or Bricolage. All systems manage multimedia news based on specific content repositories and with increasing usability for their target market, the content administrators. Content management systems strictly separate three classes of user services: the service design, the content organization and structuring, and the content manipulation. Obeying the non-technical background of most of the content creators such as journalists and editors, all CMS provide an easy-to-use interface for multimedia content creation and further management in the content asset's lifecycle.

Content Types

Historically most relevant information concerning progress in sciences and the growth of general information within human knowledge and accessible to mankind has been documented in written text and occasionally described in images and maps. The technological developments of the 20th century has brought tools and communication channels that increased the ways of communicating and distributing news concerning all facets of human live in various ways. Multimedia news services involve now besides enormous amounts of digitized textual information also images, audio and video material, supported by multiple technical tools for seamless integration and modern distribution. Schneiderman describes in [6] the emphasis on focusing news technologies around our visual capabilities. Image capture many people's thrills, emotions, and concerns. Art can shock or inspire, and news images cover most relevant events over the entire globe. Most readers depend on visual and multimedia contents to understand the world around them and as a basis for further creative activities. The popularity of visual media such as photos, videos, and animations attests to their mainstream acceptance.

Technically multimedia integration has been adapted to middleware software and content management applications [7] to allow a seamless integration with current news management and distribution applications. XML standards like SMIL [8] provide synchronization and integration frameworks and document description standards that cope with both traditional and future textual base information and multimedia data that support modern user's needs.

News Formats and Standards

Although most significant information in the news area is stored in traditional text files, the information management in the news context has been modernized and adopted towards a unique set of contents within international cooperation work. The international Press and Telecommunication Council IPTC, based in Windsor, UK is a consortium of the world's major news agencies and news industry vendors.

Following the specific needs and requirements of the multimedia news industry the IPTC has been developing news formats and standards to capture data and meta-information on news. Since the development of XML the work on meta data management has been seriously improved and the IPTC has developed two specific formats for online news management: NITF (News Industry Text Format, current Version 3.2), and NewsML. NewsML provides metadata management for any type of news contents. Consequently, the IPTC does not only provide news exchange formats to the news industry but also creates and maintains sets of topics to be assigned as metadata values to news objects in NewsML or NITF, like text, photographs, graphics, audio- and video files and streams. This allows for a consistent coding of news metadata over the course of time – thus making these sets the IPTC NewsCodes (cf. www.iptc.org). The universe of NewsCodes is by 2005 split into 28 individual sets for increased manageability as topics usually relate to a specific area and likely to be used exclusively in a specific metadata element of a news exchange format. Typical NewsCode sets include format, genre, media type, subject code, urgency, etc.

Modern multimedia services integrate content types of text, images, audio data and streams and current video formats such as MPEG2, MPEG4, MPEG7, and multimedia broadcasting technologies and initiatives like MHP and DVB for providing future interactive digital news access via television, internet, and mobile devices.

News Management

As described above research and industry developments in the news management and distribution domain have lead to dozens of modern and appropriate products to handle multimedia news contents. The market leaders (both commercial and open source frameworks and solutions) cover most relevant aspects of the news content lifecycle as shown in Figure 1.

Content management systems generally distinguish application design from information organization and content manipulation. Most emphasis in the news application domain is given to the content manipulation section, thus providing journalists and editors with appropriate modern tools to author, categorize, control, revise, and publish multimedia contents for the news presentation and distribution services.

General purpose news editing systems integrate easy-to-use textual interfaces, mostly based on Web architectures with modern multimedia features like video studios, composing for example MPEG-4 audio-visual scenes (cf. MPEG-4 STUDIO in [9]) . Some content management systems focus on end user personalization, providing a unique and specific experience for the individually guided and supported end user. Based on classification frameworks [10] user modeling provides appropriate input parameters to individually present news services for the subscriber s and readers.

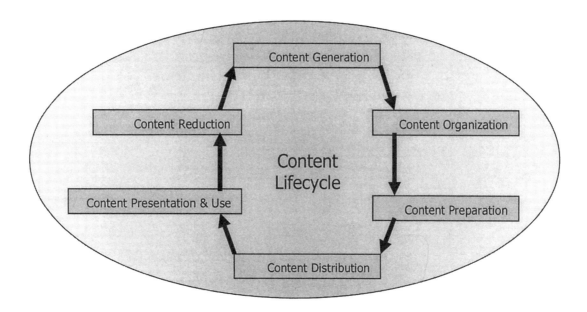

Figure 1. Content Lifecycle in Content Management Systems
for Multimedia News Services.

Multimedia News Distribution and Presentation

Multimedia news are presented as commercial services by national and international agencies and organizations all over the world. Digital media as a commonly available data type for business applications like news presentation and distribution services brings challenges for computing infrastructure and solution architectures [11]. While many corporate uses of digital media can be handled with current infrastructure, multimedia news services, as the amount and file size of the digital media grows, require more than simple capacity improvements. The news community is researching for solutions in multiple areas such as high level semantic analysis, provisioning and management of mixed information, and distribution and presentation of media data to satisfy requirements dictated by business scenarios.

Modern news networks, news syndication services, media observation and international news exchange networks are following the customers' needs and provide specific services within the multimedia news application domain. The leading presentation platform in multimedia news presentation are clearly news networks providing Television services and Internet content distribution. Considering the language and geographical restrictions of TV, Internet-based services are in the main focus of multimedia news systems within this article. The most-used presentation platform for multimedia news herein is the World Wide Web, providing all facets of news aggregation, manipulation, and dissemination discussed in section "news networks". Modern web-based content management systems (WCMS) handle all assets of multimedia news data for personalized user-oriented news presentation.

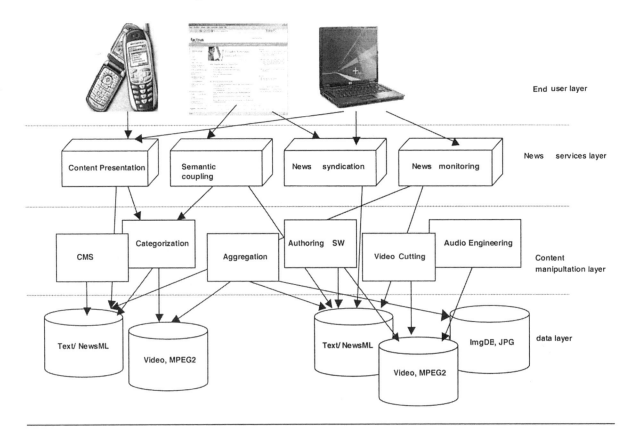

Figure 2. Multimedia news systems layering.

Architectures

Multimedia news systems typically follow a layered architecture approach as shown in Figure 2. The data layer contains multimedia data that are stored in modern appropriate formats like NewsML for texts, modern image formats such as JPG, PNG, etc. and current versions of multimedia encoding (e.g. MPEG versions) for audio- and video files. The content manipulation layer provides access to the multimedia data via specific tools that provide methods to control and access news contents along the various transitions in the content lifecycle (see Figure 1). The news services layer includes gateways that provide structured and standardized access to the contents by end user applications. Within this layer, tools and services of content provider networks take care of the presentation and distribution of multimedia contents. Most providers run multimedia gateways such as streaming servers or web services and sites to present the multimedia contents.

The top layer presents the end user environment, providing access to multimedia news services based on direct access to multimedia gateways or special services of the news services layer such as multi-agency full-text search engines, semantically coupling services or commercially related gateways like billing servers or subscription access gateways.

Infrastructure

Multimedia news services are facing multiple challenges in storing, providing, and distributing high volume data contents. Competing news providers manage voluminous textual databases, image repositories and multimedia databases. Most appropriate server cluster technology and storage networks handle the data and application management for highly available and scalable multimedia systems.

Modern Internet protocols like HTTP for web-based presentation of text and images, and streaming protocols such as RTSP for audio and video streaming cover the distribution and presentation services of multimedia news systems.

Besides the technical enabling of news presentation and distribution, legal and commercial constraints contribute challenges to the news application domain and the main business players within this area. Recent misuse and content theft by illegal file sharing or copyright violence have introduced security topics to multimedia news services. Besides customer oriented access restrictions and modern billing systems, multimedia news are enriched with up-to-date encrypting mechanisms. Especially for audio and video formats, the time constraints in encoding and decoding live streams have brought challenges which are met by modern approaches such as encryption and watermarking for copyrighted MPEG [12]. Multimedia data security is vital for multimedia commerce. Early cryptography have focused and solved text data. For multimedia applications, light weight encryption algorithms as discussed in [13] are attractive and appropriate.

Common network problems and known issues like bandwidth restrictions at end user sites and peak loads at certain times of the day in news distributions are handled via appropriate network topologies (strategically located service caches) and server side caching of frequently retrieved news data. Caching mechanisms in multimedia news systems allow even smaller providers to approach some hundreds of thousands of subscribers of multimedia news with small and cost-efficient server clusters and open source news systems [14].

News Networks

The demand for networked consumer systems such as news presentation and distribution software is growing rapidly. As a result, consumer networking is gaining increasing attention from industry, spawning a range of different solutions in different environments such as wireless, wireline, and satellite communication systems. News networks reach the professional news consumer at every corner of our world at almost any electronic device imaginable [15].

The purpose of news networks is to reach as many targeted consumers as possible to present and distribute multimedia news at the cost of the providing customer.

Since technology has driven the expansion of news networks dramatically in the last decades, this field is attracting researchers and commercial entrepreneurs with a yet unbroken vehemence.

While the industry is optimizing quality of service parameters such as connectivity, data transfer speed, availability and scalability of data exchange and news distribution, research is focusing on qualitative enhancements such as security optimization, semantic coupling of relevant news items, improved multimedia authoring and integration of ubiquitous computing services. The EC-funded project Nedine [16] manages a modern multimedia news distribution network consisting of the integration of international news agency partner systems based on a modern P2P approach. Nedine provides multimedia news content exchange as well as semantic coupling of the most relevant business news based on modern Vector Space methodology [17].

Searching and retrieval optimization is a major issue in news systems, thus research progress is requested and presented in various fields. Multimedia news are currently searched mainly on a textual basis by performance optimized full-text keyword search engines. Alternatives are involving semantics like the weighted vector space model as discussed in [17], the contextual integration of content types and document features [18], the ranking of relationships between news based on multiple data facets [19], or the automated extraction of video highlights in video files that are based on audio, text, and image features [20].

News networks are based on modern Internet communication, but additionally and especially for commercial reason trust in dedicated fixed lines, encrypted satellite networks or specific broadcasting frequencies. Since security and availability in standard Internet communication has evolved, modern multimedia news services are based on standardized protocols such as HTTP for textual and image contents and for example RTSP for video streaming purposes.

<u>Business Branches</u>
The current market for multimedia news systems is enabling various business solutions and marketing concepts in the news application area. General purpose news broadcasting and distribution is provided by Television cable and satellite networks, future encryption standards and activities are targeting towards Video on demand based on Internet technology. Business news networks are using news presentation and distribution platforms on WWW servers and email distribution networks. Multimedia data are offered by streaming servers on Internet protocols, thus allowing full service news providers and such as U.S. Newswire™, Reuters™, Factiva™, Yahoo!News™, MSN™, LexisNexis™, Apdigitalnews™ and many others.

Specific news services such as content brokering for multimedia news syndication, news monitoring services, or multilingual and multinational news search and retrieval services round up the enormous variety of business services in the multimedia news domain.

Conclusion

The management of multimedia data, servicing ubiquitous computing and the fact that every news professional around the globe wants to be first informed on all relevant news occurred in his interest area cause new challenges to business applications, computing infrastructure, and solution architectures. The news application area is researching concrete basic solutions for multimedia news management, presentation, and distribution and additionally tries to satisfy requirements dictated by business scenarios of the news industry world. We have discussed the application area of multimedia news, the specific tasks of news presentation and distribution in multimedia news systems and their industrial and commercial application in current news networks. Especially the growing commercialization of digital information systems in the multimedia news domain is facing new issues. in terms of security, scalability and service quality that attract researchers and entrepreneurs as well as experienced market-players in the news domain.

See: Content Management in Multimedia News Systems, Multimedia News Systems Infrastructure, Architectures of Commercial News Systems, Document Standards in Multimedia News Systems, Audio & Video Information in Multimedia News Systems

References

1. N. Dimitrova and V.M. Bove Jr., "Connected by media [vision and views]," IEEE Multimedia, Vol. 8, No. 4, Oct-Dec 2001, pp. 13-15.
2. M.W. Schranz and B. Paepen, "Architecture Design and Application for an Intelligent Distributed News Archive," Proceedings of the 8th ICCC International Conference of Electronic Publishing (ELPUB 04), 2004, pp. 159-169.
3. L.B. Eriksen and C. Ihlström, "Evolution of the Web News Genre – The Slow Move Beyond the Print Metaphor," Proceedings of the Thirty-Third Annual Hawaii International Conference on System Sciences (HICSS 33), 2000, pp. 61.
4. C. Ihlström, "Online Newspapers," Proceedings of the IADIS International Conference WWW/Internet 2002, ICWI 2002, Lisbon, Portugal, November 2002, pp. 855-858.

5. K.M. Göschka and M.W. Schranz, "Client and Legacy Integration in Object-Oriented Web Engineering," IEEE Multimedia, Vol. 8, No. 1, Jan-Mar 2001, pp. 32-41.

6. B. Schneidermann, "Meeting human needs with new digital imaging technologies," IEEE Multimedia, Vol. 9, No. 4, Oct-Dec 2002, pp. 8-14.

7. P. Mulhem and H. Martin, "From Database to Web Multimedia Documents," Multimedia Tools and Applications, Vol. 20, No. 3, August 2003, pp. 263-282.

8. D.C.A. Bulterman, "SMIL 2.0 Part 1: Overview, Concepts, and Structure," IEEE Multimedia, Vol. 8, No. 4, Oct-Dec 2001, pp. 82-88.

9. K. Cha and S. Kim, "MPEG-4 STUDIO: An Object-Based Authoring System for MPEG-4 Contents," Multimedia Tools and Applications, Vol. 25, No. 1, January 2005, pp. 111-131.

10. P. De Vrieze, P. Van Bommel, T. van Der Weide, and J. Klok, "Adaptation in Multimedia Systems," Multimedia Tools and Applications, Vol. 25, No. 3, March 2005, pp. 333-343.

11. C. Dorai and M. Kienzle, "Challenges of business media," IEEE Multimedia, Vol. 11, No. 4, Oct-Dec 2004, pp. 18-21.

12. D. Simitopoulos, N. Zissis, P. Georgiadids, V. Emmanouilidis, and M. Strintzis, "Encryption and watermarking for the secure distribution of copyrighted MPEG video on DVD," Multimedia Systems, Vol. 9, No. 3, September 2003, pp. 217-227.

13. B. Bhargava, C. Shi, and S. Wang, "MPEG Video Encryption Algorithms," Multimedia Tools and Applications, Vol. 24, No. 1, September 2004, pp. 57-79.

14. M.W. Schranz and A. Cvitokvich, "Applied Middleware: Object-Oriented Content Management Components with Mason," Proceedings of the IADIS Applied Computing Conference AC2005, Algarve, Portugal, February 2005, pp. 147-155.

15. M. Roccetti, P. Salomoni, V. Ghini, and S. Ferretti, "Bringing the Wireless Internet to UMTS Devices: A Case Study with Music Distribution," Multimedia Tools and Applications, Vol. 25, No 2, February 2005, pp. 217-251.

16. M. Schranz, "Employing Web Services and P2P Technology to integrate a Pan-European News Distribution Network," Proceedings of the IEE International Conference on Internet Technologies and Applications, ITA05, Wrexham, North Wales, UK, September 2005.

17. W.Z. Wong and P. Wong, "Generalized vector space model in information retrieval," ACM, 1985.

18. M. Johnson, F. Fotouhi, S. Draghici, M. Dong, and D. Xu, "Discovering Document Semantics QBYS: A System for Querying the WWW by Semantics," Multimedia Tools and Applications, Vol. 24, No. 2, November 2004, pp. 155-188.

19. S. Adali, C. Bufi, and M.-L. Sapino, "Ranked Relations: Query Language and Query Processing Methods for Multimedia," Multimedia Tools and Applications, Vol. 24, No. 3, December 2004, pp. 197-214.

20. S. Dagtas and M. Abdel-Mottaleb, "Multimodal detection of highlights for multimedia content," Multimedia Systems, Vol. 9, No. 6, June 2004, pp. 586-593.

MULTIMEDIA NEWS SYSTEMS INFRASTRUCTURE

Definition: *The leading presentation platform in multimedia news presentation is news networks providing television services and Internet content distribution.*

The demand for networked consumer systems and devices is large and growing rapidly. At home, in a car, at work or at play, Internet users want transparent internetworking and permanent connection to services, providing them entertainment, information, and communication. News professionals like journalists or opinion leaders in leading roles of companies and organizations request news as essential part of their business life. Digital media as a commonly available data type for news applications brings challenges for computing infrastructure and solution architectures [1]. While many corporate uses of digital media can be handled with current infrastructure, multimedia news systems require more than simple capacity improvements for multimedia contents. The news community is researching for solutions like high level semantic analysis, management of mixed-type information, and distribution and presentation of multimedia data to satisfy requirements by business scenarios.

Modern news networks, news syndication services, and media observation and international news exchange networks are following the customers' needs and provide specific services within the multimedia news application domain. The leading presentation platform in multimedia news presentation is clearly news networks providing Television services and Internet content distribution. Considering the language and geographical restrictions of TV, Internet-based services are in the main focus of multimedia news systems at present and in the future. The most-used presentation platform for multimedia news herein is the World Wide Web, providing all facets of news aggregation, manipulation, and dissemination.

Multimedia news services are facing multiple challenges in storing, providing, and distributing high volume data contents. Competing news providers manage voluminous textual databases, image repositories and multimedia databases. Most appropriate server cluster technology and storage networks handle the data and application management for highly available and scalable multimedia systems. Modern Internet protocols like HTTP for web-based presentation of text and images, and streaming protocols such as RTSP for audio and video streaming cover the distribution and presentation services of multimedia news systems.

Besides the technical enabling of news presentation and distribution, legal and commercial constraints contribute challenges to the news application area and the main business players within this area. Recently, besides customer oriented access restrictions and modern billing systems, multimedia news are enriched with up-to-date encrypting mechanisms. Especially for audio and video formats, the time constraints in encoding and decoding live streams have introduced challenges which are met by modern approaches such as encryption and watermarking for copyrighted MPEG [2]. Data security is vital for multimedia commerce and for multimedia applications, light weight encryption algorithms are attractive and appropriate.

Common network problems and known issues like bandwidth restrictions at end user sites and peak loads at certain times of the day in news distributions are handled via appropriate network topologies (strategically located service caches) and server side caching of frequently retrieved news data.

See: Multimedia News Systems

References

1. C. Dorai and M. Kienzle, "Challenges of business media," IEEE Multimedia, Vol. 11, No. 4, October-December 2004, pp. 18-21.
2. D. Simitopoulos, N. Zissis, P. Georgiadids, V. Emmanouilidis, and M. Strintzis, "Encryption and watermarking for the secure distribution of copyrighted MPEG video on DVD," Multimedia Systems, Vol. 9, No. 3, September 2003, pp. 217-227.

MULTIMEDIA PRODUCTION

Definition: Multimedia production begins with gathering content elements that fulfills the purpose of higher layer components, followed by integration of these elements to create a meaningful presentation.

Multimedia production must come after careful planning and design; as depicted in the Multimedia Design and Planning Pyramid (Figure 1) by showing planning as the lowest level. Production begins with gathering content elements that fulfills the purpose of higher layer components, followed by integration of these elements to create a meaningful presentation. This must be accompanied by ongoing testing conducted under various operating conditions (England and Finney, 1999). A bottom-up approach is employed for implementation, where the choices made at the lower-levels follow the dictum of the higher-levels (Sharda, 2004).

Content Gathering refers to collating appropriate multimedia content, such as, text, photos, video etc. that will populate the various screens. Some of this content may already exist; the remaining must be acquired or created. The Storyboard is a key design tool that helps in deciding what content is required. Apart from the Storyboard, the production team must refer to the other design aspects, such as the Target Audience.

Integration combines all elements to create a working system. An integration plan – e.g. allocating tasks to team members – should be developed with the help of the Storyboard. Integration is performed with the help of authoring tools such as Authorware, PowerPoint, and Flash. Each Authoring tool has its underplaying metaphor, and is suitable for specific applications. For example, PowerPoint uses the slideshow metaphor and is widely used for lecture presentations. At times, the content for different sections is authored with the help of different tools and then integrated into a unified system.

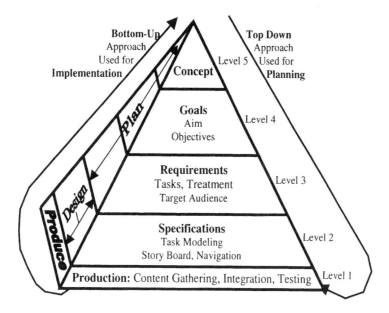

Figure 1. Multimedia design and planning pyramid.

Testing is an integral part of the Production stage. First each section needs to be tested as it is created, and then the system as a whole is tested. This testing must take place under various operating conditions. A well-defined testing plan must be developed, that includes in-house testing (alpha testing), as well as testing with the user in the loop (beta testing).

While, production is the final stage of any multimedia-authoring project, most systems need ongoing maintenance to keep the content current.

See: Multimedia Authoring, Multimedia Project Planning, Multimedia Design

References

1. E. England and A. Finney, *"Managing Multimedia,"* Addison Wesley, 1999.
2. N. Sharda, *"Creating Meaningful Multimedia with The Multimedia Design and Planning Pyramid,"* 10th International MultiMedia Modeling Conference, January 2004, Brisbane, Australia.

MULTIMEDIA PROJECT PLANNING

Definition: Any significant multimedia project involves a core team that includes: producer, writer, and director, who work with other personnel, such as, programmer, photographer, videographer, and voiceover artists.

Multimedia project planning is a complex problem (England and Finney, 1999). Any significant multimedia project involves a core team that includes: producer, writer, and director, who work with other personnel, such as, programmer, photographer, videographer, and voiceover artists (Elin, 2001). Close coordination between these team members is essential. The Multimedia Design and Planning Pyramid (MUDPY) is a five-level model (Figure 1) in which the top three levels comprise the project planning process (Sharda, 2004). The planning process should begin by articulating a clear Concept statement, and then expand it into Goals and Requirements.

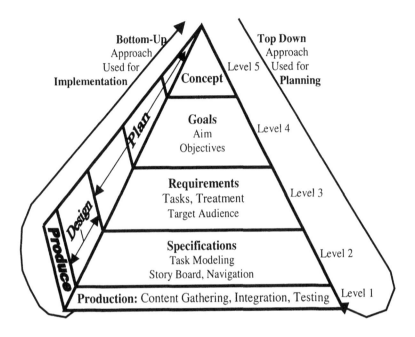

Figure 1. Multimedia design and planning pyramid.

Concept statement should give a succinct overview of the entire project, and become its guiding "mantra".

Goals can be articulated as an Aim and a list of Objectives. *Aim* should be a short statement that embodies the intention and the purpose of the project. *Objectives* should be the list of project outcomes, or deliverables derived from the project Aim; and listed as a series of dot-points.

Requirements refer to the tasks that the system must perform. Involving the users in deriving the requirements is very important. *Target Audience* should be specified based on factors such as age group, profession, interests, special needs etc., as these influence the treatment. *Treatment* refers to the look and feel of a multimedia presentation, and that of its various sections. The first level of treatment specification can be given as the percentage of each content type, that is, text, audio, still images, animation, and video. These can then be elaborated in terms of the quality of presentation of each component that relates to its digital coding aspects.

Planning is followed by design and production of the multimedia system. The relationship between various Planning, Design, and Production aspects is shown in the MUDPY model.

See: **Multimedia Authoring, Multimedia Design, Multimedia Production**

References

1. L. Elin, "Designing and Developing Multimedia: A Practical Guide for the Producer, Director, and Writer," Allyn and Bacon, 2001.
2. E. England and A. Finney, *"Managing Multimedia,"* Addison Wesley, 1999.
3. N. Sharda, *"Creating Meaningful Multimedia with the Multimedia Design and Planning Pyramid,"* Proceedings of the 10th International Multi-Media Modeling Conference, January 2004, Brisbane, Australia.

MULTIMEDIA PROXY CACHING

Definition: Multimedia proxy caching, which is a small proxy server cache that is located close to a group of clients and is administrated by them, caches some popular streams from different servers with appropriate quality, with the goal to improve scalability and quality of service by reducing network traffic and delivery delay.

The high bandwidth requirements and continuous streaming demand of digital video coupled with the best effort service model of IP networks and the heterogeneity of end user devices makes it difficult to provide quality of service for multimedia streaming. Multimedia Proxy caching, a small proxy server cache that is located close to a group of clients and is administrated by them, caches some popular streams from different servers with appropriate quality, wit the goal to improve scalability and quality of service by reducing network traffic and delivery delay. Figure 1 illustrates one example of multimedia proxy caching. One sample approach is segmentation based proxy caching (e.g., reference [1, 2]) where the multimedia objects are segmented and partial segments are cached in the proxy instead of the entire multimedia objects.

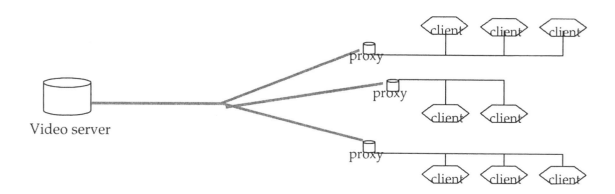

Figure 1. Multimedia proxy caching.

Interested readers can reference the papers by Rejaie [1, 2], et al and Chen, et al [3] or some other technical papers published in the last five years.

See: **Multimedia Encryption**

References

1. R. Rejaie, M. Handley, H. Yu, and D. Estrin, "Proxy caching mechanism for multimedia playback streams in the Internet," Proceedings of the Fourth International WWW Caching Workshop, March 1999.
2. R. Rejaie, M. H. H. Yu, and D. Estrin, "Multimedia proxy caching mechanism for quality adaptive streaming applications in the internet," Proceedings of the IEEE INFOCOM, Tel-Aviv, Israel, March 2000.
3. S. Chen, B. Shen, S. Wee, and X. Zhang. "Designs of High Quality Streaming Proxy Systems," Proceedings of IEEE INFOCOM, Hong Kong, China, March, 2004.

MULTIMEDIA SEMANTICS

Giorgos Stamou and Stefanos Kollias
Institute of Communication and Computer Systems,
National Technical University of Athens, Greece

Definition: *Multimedia semantics deals with the question how to conceptually index, search and retrieve the digital multimedia content, which means how to extract and represent the semantics of the content of the multimedia raw data in a human and machine-understandable way.*

Conceptualization of the multimedia content

The late advances in computer and communication technologies caused a huge increase of digital multimedia information distributed over the web. On the one hand, the production line of digital multimedia content can now be followed by everyone: the production houses shoot high quality video in digital format; organizations that hold multimedia content (TV channels, film archives, museums, libraries, etc.) digitize it and use the different digital formats for preservation, management and distribution; most of people has digital cameras, scanners etc and produces image and video content in MPEG and JPEG formats, ready to be delivered. On the other hand, due to the maturity of storage and data network technologies, *digital formats* provide now the most cheap, safe and easy way to store and deliver multimedia content even in high resolutions. And, of course, a great role in this pace chain has been played by the standardization activities that provided MPEG, JPEG and other digital coding formats.

The amount of multimedia information delivered on the Web is now so huge that the improvement of the coding standards and web technologies is not enough to satisfy the needs of the end user in the searching and retrieving process. Although the standardization activities of the ISO (and other) communities (MPEG-7, MPEG-21, Dublin Core, etc.) ([3], [6], [7], [10], [11], [18]) have provided standards for describing the content, using formal representation languages like XML, these standards have not been widely used mainly for two reasons. The first is that the task of manually annotating the multimedia content in the standard metadata form is difficult and time-consuming, thus very expensive. The second is that the representation languages used by the standards (like XML and XML Schema) do not provide any way to formally represent semantics, thus do not solve the problem. The main question is how to *conceptually* index, search and retrieve the digital multimedia content, which means how to extract and represent the semantics of the content of the multimedia raw data in a human *and* machine-understandable way.

The problem has been pointed out by Tim Berners-Lee [1] some years ago and boosted the research and the standardization in the emerging technology of the Semantic Web. W3C followed the late research in knowledge representation and reasoning and started a standardization process of a new content representation language with formal semantics, the latest result of which is the Web Ontology Language (OWL). Still, the new question is whether the semantic web technology, is mature enough to be used in the multimedia content annotation area. Several approaches have been proposed for facing this problem. Some of them try to transfer all the multimedia standards in the new knowledge representation languages like OWL. Others keep some of the metadata in the structural form of the multimedia standards and represent the rest that needs semantics in RDF or OWL [12-14]. In any case, the clear message is that the multimedia standards have to use the semantic web technology, although it is still "under construction". And not only for the main reason that the representation languages of the semantic web (like OWL) will be the only standard to represent content with formal semantics in the web in the very near future (like HTML and XML for the serialization of unstructured and structured information). But also because they provide a formal framework to represent the knowledge needed for the automatic analysis of raw multimedia content and the extraction of its semantic annotation.

Extraction and representation of multimedia semantics

Multimedia documents are complex spatio-temporal signals providing information in several levels of abstraction [2], [15]. The user conceptualizes and understands the multimedia content by capturing all different cues (audio, video, speech, images, text ...), specifying the sources of semantic information (a scene of a video, a shot, a frame, a specific object, a text box, a narration, a specific sound etc) in various levels of detail and then understanding the semantic information provided by these sources and their interrelations. Following the above syllogism, the information provided by the multimedia document can be formalized, represented, analyzed and processed in three different levels of abstraction: the *subsymbolic*, the *symbolic* and the *logical* (see Figure 1).

The *subsymbolic* level of abstraction covers the raw multimedia information represented in the well known formats of the different cues like video, image, audio, text, metadata etc. At this level, the information is processed by several processing, feature extraction and classification tools and the final result is the extraction, representation and description of the different information sources. The detection of these sources is actually a matter of temporal, spatial and spatio-temporal multi-cue segmentation and feature extraction that provides the *structure* of the multimedia document, i.e. a tree (or more general a graph) representing all the different sources, their characteristics and their interrelations in a symbolic manner. This information forms the *symbolic* level of abstraction. Moreover, at this level information (metadata) covering all the lifecycle of the multimedia document, from pre-production to post-production and use, is stored. All the above information is serialized in descriptive representation languages like XML and processed by feature-based recognition systems that provide the semantics of the multimedia document. The semantics are actually mappings between the symbolic-labeled and structured information sources and a terminology (a higher knowledge), described in a formal knowledge representation language, like OWL. This formal terminology forms the *logical* level of abstraction, in which the implicit knowledge of the multimedia document description can be explicit with the aid of reasoning algorithms. This means that syllogistic processing of the existing and formally represented knowledge, interpreted and instantiated in the world of the multimedia document description would provide further knowledge for this multimedia document, also serialized in formal descriptive languages and semantically interpreted with the aid of the terminology.

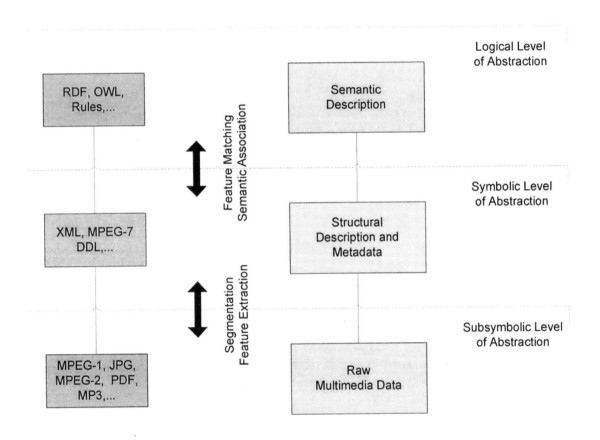

Figure 1. Analysis and representation of multimedia documents.

The analysis of the multimedia document and its automatic annotation is actually a continuous process in all the levels of abstraction that generally performs the followings: detects possible information sources with the aid of processing and clustering; extracts the appropriate features and represents them; tries to recognize the semantic meaning of the information source with the aid of semantic interpretation (assertion through feature matching); reason with the aid of the terminology; checks the consistency of the knowledge. For example, let us suppose, without loss of generality, that the multimedia document is a simple image containing a face (as a small object of the image). With the aid of a spatial color segmentation algorithm, a possible information source is detected. Suppose also that this area is actually the area of the face (of course it is not yet recognized and labeled with the "face" symbol). Then, several predefined features can be extracted and all the above information (possible object and its descriptors) is serialized in MPEG-7 XML. The next step is the feature matching of the represented features and others stored in an existing knowledge of objects. If the matching with the "face" object is done, then a semantic association is defined between the object and the "face" object of the higher knowledge and thus the analysis tool has recognize the object. Continuing this process several objects could be recognized and then using the reasoning additional objects or relations between the existing ones can be also added to the description of the image.

The above situation is very optimistic and there are no real-world systems providing all the steps of the above analysis for general multimedia documents due to several obvious reasons. Unfortunately, this also seems to be the case for the very near future (the next five years). The most important obstacles that the automatic analysis process should overcome are mainly two: the detection of the right possible information sources and the definition of the semantic interpretation through the feature matching process. Nevertheless, in semi-automatic approaches the above two steps are generally obvious for the human and the whole process could be performed in cases where the higher knowledge is there (at least formally providing the terminology, i.e. the names of the objects and their inter-relations in a formal knowledge representation language like OWL). Moreover, in all the steps of the production chain of the multimedia content, from pre-production to post-production, useful information (that is completely impossible to be automatically recognized like for example the name of the color corrector of a video sequence) can be described in the form of metadata again in a formal descriptive language like XML and semantically interpreted with the aid of higher knowledge. Thus, the definition and formal representation of multimedia semantics in all levels of abstraction remains a critical issue for both the short and long term future [15].

Several standards have been proposed and used in the literature for the representation of multimedia document descriptions and their semantic interpretation (Dublin Core, MPEG-7, MPEG-21 etc). The main focus of the above standards is given to the extraction of a set of predefined categories and types of metadata. For example, MPEG-7 provides a very rich set of Descriptors and Description Schemes covering almost all the levels of abstractions. Using this predefined set, it is not difficult to provide the semantics. For the above representation XML is used (with some minor extensions). Moreover, a not so powerful way of defining new descriptors is given (mainly using XML Schema). Although the above approach can be perfectly applied to the structural description of the multimedia documents and to metadata like director, producer etc, it is rather inappropriate for the semantic description of their content. The main reason for this disadvantage is the inability of the above framework to provide formal semantics and inference services in arbitrary structures of descriptions. On the other hand, the work on knowledge representation and reasoning and the standards provided by the W3C community (DAML+OIL, OWL, ...) are ideal for the representation of the content, providing formal semantics and inference services, still it is very difficult to be used for the structural description of the multimedia content. Moreover, since the main focus of the above standardization was not on the representation of multimedia knowledge, some language extensions are needed in order for these standards to be widely used. Consequently, a combination of the above standards seems to be the most promising way for multimedia document description in the near future ([4], [5], [8], [9], [15-17], [19], [20]).

References

1. T. Berners-Lee, "Weaving the Web," Orion Business, 1999.
2. A. Del Bimbo, "Visual Information Retrieval," Morgan Kaufmann Publishers Inc., 1999.
3. Dublin Core Community, Dublin Core Element Set, Version 1.1, 1999, http://www.dublincore.org/documents/dces/.
4. J. Hunter, "Adding Multimedia to the Semantic Web - Building an MPEG-7 Ontology," International Semantic Web Working Symposium (SWWS), Stanford, July-August 2001.
5. J. Hunter, J. Drennan, and S. Little "Realizing the Hydrogen Economy through Semantic Web Technologies," IEEE Intelligent Systems Journal, Special Issue on eScience, January 2004.
6. International Organization for Standardization/International Electrotechnical Commission, Overview of the MEG-7 Standard (Version 8). ISO/IEC JTC1/SC29/WG11/N4980, Klagenfurt, July 2002.
7. ISO/IEC 15938-5 FCD Information Technology - Multimedia Content Description Interface - Part 5: Multimedia Description Schemes, Singapore, March 2001.
8. A. Jaimes and J. R. Smith, "Semi-Automatic, Data-Driven Construction of Multimedia Ontologies," Proceedings of the IEEE Intl. Conference on Multimedia and Expo (ICME), Baltimore, MD, July, 2003.
9. S. Little and Hunter, J., "Rules-B-Example – a Novel Approach to Semantic Indexing and Querying of Images," Proceedings of the 3rd International Semantic Web Conference (ISWC2004), Hiroshima, Japan, November 2004.
10. MPEG-21 Multimedia Framework, http://www.cselt.it/mpeg/public/mpeg-21_pdtr.zip.
11. NewsML http://www.newsml.org/.
12. OWL Language Specification, March 2001 http://www.daml.org/2001/03/daml+oil-index.
13. OWL Web Ontology Language Use Cases and Requirements, W3C Recommendation, 10 February 2004, http://www.w3.org/TR/2004/REC-webont-req-20040210/.
14. RDF Schema Specification 1.0, W3C Candidate Recommendation, 27 March 2000 http://www.w3.org/TR/rdf-schema/.
15. G. Stamou and S. Kollias, Eds., "Multimedia Content and the Semantic Web: Methods, Standards and Tools," John Wiley & Sons Ltd, 2005.
16. R. Troncy, "Integrating Structure and Semantics into Audio-Visual Documents," Proceedings of the Second International Semantic Web Conference, ISWC 2003, LNCS 2870, pp. 566-581, 2003.
17. C. Tsinaraki, P. Polydoros, and S. Christodoulakis, "Interoperability support for Ontology-based Video Retrieval Applications," Proceedings of Third International

Conference on Image and Video Retrieval (CIVR), Dublin, Ireland, July 2004, pp. 582-591.

18. TV-Anytime Forum http://www.tv-anytime.org/.

19. J. van Ossenbrugen, F. Nack, and L. Hardman, "The Obscure Object of Desire: Multimedia Metadata on the Web (Part I)," Technical Report INS-E0308, CWI, December 2003.

20. J. van Ossenbrugen, F. Nack, and L. Hardman, "The Obscure Object of Desire: Multimedia Metadata on the Web (Part II)," Technical Report INS-E0309, CWI, December 2003.

MULTIMEDIA SEMIOTICS

Simone Santini
University of California, San Diego, USA

Definition: *Multimedia signals are artifacts intended to convey messages and, as such, they are a legitimate object of semiotic analysis.*

Some care must be taken in semiotic analysis because, if it is legitimate to consider multimedia as a form of text, the peculiar characteristics of this text, and the intertwined reading modalities that it presents, impose the use of specific analysis instruments.

The first issue that presents itself is about the very nature of the multimedia sign: to put it in Piercean terms: is the multimedia sign an icon, an index, or a symbol? (See *semiotics* for a definition of these and other technical terms.) The complexity of the multimedia sign is revealed by the fact that it participates in all these natures: it is at one time an icon, an index, and a symbol.

The iconic status of the multimedia sign that, at a superficial analysis would appear the most obvious, is in reality quite complex and problematic. It won't do, in fact, to say that a picture of Charles V "stands for" Charles V by virtue of its resemblance with the king. It has long since been recognized in semiotics [1] that similarity is too generic to create a sign relation. With suitably elastic similarity criteria, virtually everything can be found to be similar in some respect to anything else, dissolving signification in a sea of symbols worth of the hermetic tradition. Things are not such, of course: both a red apple and the picture of a Ferrari sports car are similar to a Ferrari sports car by virtue of their color, but only in the case of the picture does the color form an iconic sign. Sonesson [2] distinguishes between an *iconic ground* and an *iconic sign*. The iconic ground is any relation of similarity that, under opportune circumstances, could generate an iconic sign. Color is an iconic ground but, in the example above, it generates an iconic sign only in the case of the picture.

Equally problematic is the indexicality of the multimedia sign, that is, the existence of constitutive causal connections between the signifier and the signified. In some cases such a connection does clearly exist: in photographs there is a causal connection between the subject and its representation, which includes the optical properties of the lens and the chemical properties of the photographic film (or, these days, the properties of the CCD device and of the printer). The problematicity of indexicality comes from the fact that these properties can't, in general, be ascertained. This is especially true in an age of almost unlimited possibilities of digital manipulation, but it is also true at a more fundamental level. There is a fundamental difference between what a picture or a film represents by cultural convention and what they represent as the end point of a causal chain. The famous photograph *l'embrasse de l'Hôtel de Ville* by Doisenau, owes its signification to the historical and social position it has (France after World War II), and not to its causal connection with two lovers in Paris: its meaning—and its place in the history of photography—didn't change after Doisenau revealed that the picture was staged so that the two lovers were not, quite likely, lovers at all. Every studio shot—Humphrey Bogart as Sam Spade, say—works at two different levels: an indexical one—the chain from Humphrey Bogart in a studio—and the one that indexical is not—Sam Spade in his office. Which one is the true signifier depends on what one is doing: whether one is writing a biography of Humphrey Bogart, or telling the story of *The maltese falcon*.

These considerations lead us to the analysis of the multimedia sign as symbolic and culturally mediated. The meaning of, say, an image is often a cultural construction that has little to do with the possible iconic or indexical aspects of the sign: the picture of Charles V mentioned earlier has that representational meaning because of its cultural placement, regardless of whether the man in the portrait resembles Charles V or not—a fact that nobody today is in a position to ascertain.

One particularly clear example of this fact is the iconography of Jesus. The contemporary accepted image of Jesus, with the beard and the long hair, is a creation of the middle ages: until the VII century, the Roman iconography prevailed: Jesus had short hair, no beard, appeared much younger, and was in general represented as a shepherd. Both iconographies co-exist face to face in the magnificent mosaics of the basilic of *Sant'Apollinare in Classe*, near Ravenna (Italy). The iconography of Jesus is clearly symbolic: it signifies because of thirteen hundred of cultural tradition, quite independently of its resemblance to the person the paintings signify, or to the actual existence of such a person.

The symbolic and cultural aspects of the multimedia sign are arguably the most relevant for the problem of signification, in spite of the superficial preponderance of the iconic aspects. The evolution of cinema in the early XX century is exemplar in this respect. At the turn of the century, cinema was little more than a way to register observables in an iconic way (but, even in this case, it is to be noted that the choice of *what* should be registered was a cultural act: cinema was never neutral in the way a security camera is). Less then thirty years later its complex symbolic language, theorized by the likes of Eisenstein and Vertov, was firmly established, to the point that many people regarded the introduction of audio as a useless intrusion that didn't add anything substantial to the language of the medium. Of course, the different aspects of the multimedia sign often interact and are present together in the same semiotic act. A picture of a red Ferrari, for instance, *denotes* the red Ferrari by iconicity, but *connotes* things such as wealth or success through the cultural associations of the Ferrari: the sign, as a denotative sign, is an icon, but as a *myth*[3] is a symbol. The situation is by no means unusual: myth (Althausser calls the mythological phenomenon *ideology* [4]) depends on social relations of power and, although the sign that the myth uses as a signifier may be iconic or indexical, the myth itself is in general symbolic.

The symbolism of the visual sign, especially in video, also takes place according to different modalities. In the case of the Ferrari, the cultural and symbolic aspect of the sign is in the connotations of the *subject* of the multimedia sign: the video *stands for* a Ferrari, which *stands for* wealth and success. The signification that involves multimedia (the first *stands for*) is iconic (with the caveat of the cultural influence in the transition from an iconic ground to an iconic sign), quite independent of the symbolic connotations of its subject, and prior to it: the same iconic relation would have occurred had the video represented a Ford Pinto, with quite different connotations. In this case, the interpretation of the multimedia sign takes place in two distinct phases: the interpretation of the sign itself ("the video represents a Ferrari") and that of its connotation ("therefore it stands for wealth and success"). It is worth noticing that a lot of attention has been given to the standardization of the first of these problems (in standards such as MPEG7, RDF, ...) but not to the second, which, in light of these observations, is the most interesting and relevant of the two.

In a second modality, the symbolism is in the content itself. This modality is often very evident in cartoons: when a character starts running its legs move for a while before it actually starts, and when Wile E. Coyote falls at the bottom of a canyon the whole frame shakes, and we see a cloud of dust coming up from the bottom. These signs are not completely unmotivated, and do have a residue of iconicity in them. The characters beginning to run, for instance, are reminiscent of the way in which a powerful automobile skids its tires before starting at high speed, an obvious signifier of the fast run. Certain exaggerations, however (the shaking of the frame) are part of the language of cartoons that is symbolic and that, associated with certain genre markers, has made its way into films.

A third modality of symbolism has to do not with the content of the video, but with the way in which the content is presented. Film, for example, has a language of its own, a sign system whose elements are editing techniques, containing cultural norms such as the one, observed at least until the 60's, prescribing that a "dissolve" marks the passage of a relatively long time, and always implies a discontinuity in the action, while a "cut" marks the passage of a typically shorter time or no time at all preserving, in this case, the continuity of the action; or the rules about the interest line and the positioning of the dominant character [5]. This language is symbolic, although one sometimes finds surprising and tortuous indexical connections. The American *film noir* of the 1940's was at first shot in black and white for economic reasons: these were low budget films, and color film was very expensive. The cult status of these films in the following decades, however, contributed to give a completely different meaning to black and white: to shoot films in black and white today hasn't the same connotations it would have had the film noir never existed. This symbolic modality is very useful technically because it is prior and, often, independent of the contents of the video, therefore it can provide access to certain meanings of the video without requiring the interpretation of the fames and, sometimes, drive the interpretation process. To this day, the use of this type of language is in general limited to its temporal aspects, such as the identification of cuts and dissolves [6,7].

Syntagm and Paradigm

One of the important semiotic shifts caused by the digital medium and by the computer interface is that from the preponderance of the *syntagmatic* plane to that of the *paradigmatic*. In a text, speech, or video, the semiotic units are linked on the syntagmatic plane: they form a chain connected by relations of contiguity and complementarity. By contrast, a computer interface typically presents a choice of different alternatives, only one of which will be chosen by the user. The choices are all equivalent in the sense that, at the point of the interaction when they appear, each one of them could be made. They are, in Saussurean terms, in a paradigmatic relation. Of course, during each interaction episode, a user will go through a specific sequence of choices, that will therefore constitute a syntagm; the syntagm, however, is a product of the interaction act: the interface in itself is paradigmatic and, in this sense, it resembles more a dictionary from which the textemes that constitute a text come from than the text itself. This semiotic discordance between the paradigm of the interface and the syntagm of the video is at the basis of the difficulties experienced by many researchers of creating a good interface for video that could take advantage of the possibilities of the computer: the vast majority of computer interfaces for video are but glorified VCR interfaces. To the same semiotic discordance one can trace the interest of many researchers in the so-called *video summarization* techniques, which try to transform a video into a series of representative images that can be presented simultaneously on a computer screen, transforming the syntagm into a paradigm.

These problems are compounded by the dichotomy between *opaque* screens and *transparent* ones (the terminology and the concept are due to Lev Manovich [8]). When looking at a video, the screen works as a window through which we observe the world of the video; that is, the screen becomes transparent and disappears from view. By contrast, in an interface, the different elements are placed *on* the screen: the user looks *at* the screen as an opaque support: there is nothing beyond it. Changing between these two modes of operation requires a cognitive shift that disturbs the integration of video and its interface. One interesting possibility in this respect would be—at least for videos produced specifically for the digital medium—to place the manipulation interface *in* the video itself, so that the transparency of the screen can be preserved. The few attempts in this direction (dubbed hyper-linking) have been quite limited in scope, often directed to linking products placed in films to a web page where one can buy the product. One of the limitations of these attempts is that, while the links were placed in the video, they were selected using the mouse, and the mouse's cursor, of course, leads one back to an opaque screen. An even more reductive circumstance is that, so far, digital video has been thought more or less as the digitalization of broadcast video, and the expressive possibilities of the multimedia sign haven't been explored at all. Experimental videos of the 1960's and 70's, with their exploration of non-linear narratives and *pastiche* foreshadowed the future use of video in interactive media [9] but mainstream internet video appears to be tied to a more traditional narrative models, that deal problematically with interaction and interfaces.

A computer interface and a video are both sign systems but, possibly for the first time since computer scientists started to think about interfaces, the interface reveals profound semiotic discrepancies with the sign system that constitutes the data, the interface working on the paradigmatic plane on an opaque screen, the video working on the syntagmatic plane "behind" a transparent screen. The difficulty of reconciliation of these very different sign systems is responsible in no small measure of the difficulty of creating an interface for the effective manipulation of video.

Quite interestingly, things work better for images. The relation between the different parts of an image is syntagmatic: they are associated by juxtaposition to form one image-text. Their stability, however, makes it easy to intervene paradigmatically on an image, that is, to replace some of its parts with other elements that stand in a paradigmatic relation with them. In a picture, say Rembrandt's *Aristotle contemplating the bust of Homer*, the various elements (Aristotle and the and the bust of Homer) stay in a syntagmatic relation about which—as in the case of video—little can be done apart from showing it on the screen. But the stability of the image creates the possibility of an interface that works on the paradigmatic plane, with elements that could be substituted to those in the picture and that would stay in the same syntagmatic relation (Thelonious Monk instead of Aristotle, a picture of the Queen of England instead of the bust of Homer): the interfaces of all image manipulation systems work on the elements that are *not* in the images, but that could be *placed* in the image. In the case of the images, moreover, the screen becomes opaque: we usually look at a picture *on* the screen rather than at a scene *through* a screen.

The formalization of semiotics

One of the difficulties that one has when dealing with the semiotics of multimedia from the point of view of computing science (or, indeed, in any form of study of the communication between computers and people) is the dichotomy between the qualitative nature of semiotic statements and the quantitative and fully formalized form that any computing activity must take. An attempt to a formal theory of the communication of signification in a rather general setting is Joseph Goguen's *algebraic semiotics* [11]. A sign system, in algebraic semiotic, is a *theory*, defined as follows:

A sign system S is a 7-tuple $S=(T,V,\leq_T,\leq_V,F,A)$, where:

1. *T* is a set of data types;
2. *V* is a set of parameter types;
3. $\leq_T$ is a partial order on T, called the *subtype* relation;
4. $\leq_V$ is a partial order on $T \cup V$, called the *level* relation such that for each $v \in V$, and $t \in T$ is it $v \leq_V t$, and there is a unique type t' (called the top) such that for all t, $t \leq_V t'$;
5. *C* is a set of partially ordered sets of constructors, one set of constructors for each level;
6. *F* is the set of functions and relations on signs;
7. *A* is a set of logic sentences called axioms.

The data types describe the "informative" elements of an interface, and their organization allows one to mirror the structure of the data that the interface must deal with; the parameter types are, typically, used to describe interface elements, and contain things such as colors, sizes, and so on. With these systems, one can define *semiotic morphisms*, that is, morphisms that transform a sign system into another one while maintaining as much structure as possible, allowing one to create a hierarchy of expressivity of sign system, and to decide whether an interface, model as a sign system, has sufficient expressive power to deal with a given set of data.

It is not clear, as yet, the extent to which this or other formalizations will help elucidate the nature of the multimedia sign and help users interact with them through suitable interfaces. Algebraic semiotics has been used to study the transformation of the "message" of image interfaces for image data bases [11], but so far, there doesn't seem to be any study of their applicability to other multimedia data.

See: Mime types, Client Server Systems, Peer to Peer Systems

References

1. U. Eco, "*A theory of semiotics,*" Bloomington:Induana University Press, 1985.
2. G. Sonesson, "La iconicidad en un marco ecológico," in *De Signis*, 4, July 2003, pp. 45-60
3. R. Barthes, *Mythologies*, Paris:Seuil, 1970.
4. L. Althausser, "Ideology and ideological state apparatuses (notes towards an investigation)," in *Lenin and philosophy and other essays*, New Left Books, 1971.
5. D. Arijon, *Grammar of the film language*, Silman-James Press, Los Angeles, 1976.
6. B. T. Truong, C. Dorai, and S. Venkatesh, "New enhancements to cut, fade, and dissolve detection processes in video segmentation," Proceedings of the *ACM Multimedia*, 2000.
7. R. Lienhart, "Reliable transition detection in videos: a survey and practitioner's guide," *International Journal of Image and Graphics*, Vol. 3, pp. 469-86, 2001.
8. L. Manovich, "*The language of new media,*" MIT Press, Cambridge, 2001.
9. F. Jameson, *Postmodernism, or: the cultural logic of late capitalism*, Duke University Press, Durham, 1991.
10. J. Goguen, "An introduction to algebraic semiotics, with application to user interface design," in C. Nehaniv (Ed.) *Computation for metaphors, analogy, and agents*, University of Aizu, Aizu-Wakamatsu, Japan.
11. S. Santini, *Exploratory image databases*, Academic Press, 2001.

MULTIMEDIA SENSOR NETWORKS

Deepa Kundur and William Luh
Department of Electrical Engineering
Texas A&M University, College Station, TX, USA

Definition: *In multimedia sensor networks the multimodal sensors collect multimedia information including images, video and audio.*

Sensor networks are comprised of low-cost unattended groups of densely placed sensor "nodes" that locally observe, communicate (often using wireless means), and coordinate to collectively achieve high-level inference and actuation tasks. The nodes are distributed in a physical region, often containing a specific phenomenon of interest, which is to be monitored and possibly controlled. When the sensor nodes collect diverse types of information such as temperature, humidity, acoustic and visual data simultaneously, they are termed "multimodal sensors." Multiples types of sensing can occur within the same node through the use of distinct sensing technologies or across different nodes each having a single, but distinct sensor type. If the multimodal sensors collect multimedia information such as digital images, video and audio, they form a *multimedia sensor network*.

Sensing Nodes and Networks

The 2003 MIT Technology Review listed sensor networks as one of the "Ten Emerging Technologies That Will Change the World." Sensor networks represent a low-cost means to link communications and computer networking to the physical world, and are expected to have profound consequences for the monitoring and control of physical environments such as buildings, cities and ecosystems. Multimedia sensor networks often employ visual data such as video streams for surveillance and safety applications.

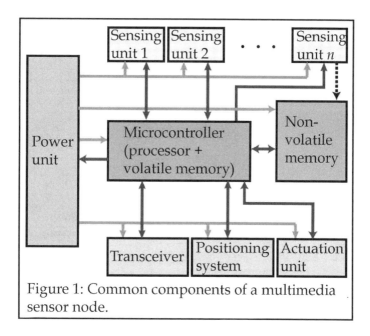

Figure 1: Common components of a multimedia sensor node.

The individual nodes in the network cooperate via localized sensing, processing, communication and actuation to have large-scale effects and influence in a more practical and cost-effective manner. An example of the most common components found in a multimedia sensor node is highlighted in Figure 1. The power unit is responsible for the generation (e.g., through solar cells), conditioning and regulation of energy into the device. The microcontroller, which consists of a low-cost microprocessor and volatile memory, interacts with the power, sensing devices, transceiver, positioning system, and actuation units for effective operation. Longer-term storage of data is placed by the microcontroller in non-volatile memory. The one or more multimodal sensors, normally short-range, are controlled by the microcontroller that may set sensing parameters such as resolution and frame rate for video information and sampling rate for audio. Although it is expected that compression is required of the sensor data prior to storage, direct memory access for some types of sensing may be useful. The dashed arrow from the nth sensing unit to the non-volatile memory block describes this. The transceiver may transmit or receive sensor readings from neighboring nodes to enable localized processing for distributed inference in the network. The positioning system determines the location of the node to aid certain types of collaborative processing for tasks such as data routing, and intruder triangulation. The actuation unit may provide node mobility based on a user-requested query or based on localized detection of an event. Actuation may also be more general including temperature modulation, and common robotics-based interaction with the environment.

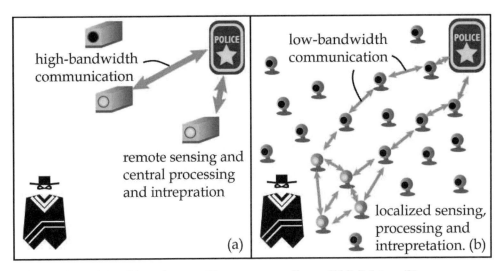

Figure 2: (a) Traditional surveillance network vs. (b) Multimedia sensor network.

A distributed network of such low-cost sensors will collect significantly different information than a system relying on a small number of expensive large-range sensitive sensors with limited processing capabilities, which can often result in more distorted readings. Figure 2 provides a distinction between a standard multimedia surveillance network that has centralized data processing and control with possibly more expensive sensing technology, and a multimedia sensor network, which has distributed and localized behavior. In Figure 2(a), longer-range cameras are used to collect information that is transmitted (after compression) in raw high-bandwidth form to a central station (here, the police station), for processing and interpretation. The distinction in Figure 2(b) is that short-range sensors in the localized region of an event (here, an intruder is present in a physical region to be protected), collect data, process the information using correlated readings from neighboring cameras that are communicated amongst the nodes, and locally interpret the results. Some form of localized fusion or aggregation is necessary to make the necessary decisions and inference. The resulting low-bandwidth interpretation-data is communicated with possible redundancy to the central station. It is expected that distributing "intelligence" throughout the physical environment in this way will promote scalability by massively reducing sensor, communications and processing cost overall.

Applications of Multimedia Sensor Networks

Multimedia sensor networks are effective for a wide range of surveillance applications in which the physical phenomena to be observed have strong perceptual (e.g., visual or acoustic) signatures. Real-time traffic monitoring for more efficient vehicle flow and the identification of accidents, building safety observation to identify intruders, military sensing and tracking for unmanned vehicle operation in hostile terrains, environmental understanding such as nearshore oceanographic monitoring, and robot navigation for civilian and military applications are some examples of applications that greatly benefit from multimedia sensor networks. The successful adoption of such networks ultimately lies in the ability to make these systems practical and cost-effective. For this reason, multimedia sensor networks are designed to have a number of defining characteristics.

Defining Characteristics of Multimedia Sensor Networks

Multimedia sensor networks provide observation capabilities that are practical and cost-effective by exploiting the following distinctive system features.

Multimodal:

Multimedia sensor networks are comprised of multimodal sensor nodes in which the same node observes distinct types of physical parameters, or the sensor nodes collect unigenous readings, but are specialized, so that the overall network collects different types of physical data. A video or imaging sensor, for example, may be considered multimodal because different color, temporal and spatial data is simultaneously collected.

Distributed Nodes:

In order to improve the accuracy and geographical range of practical sensing devices, distributing (often untethered) nodes directly within the physical environment under observation is essential. Although long-range remote sensing devices can be used, they do not often possess the level of range, sensitivity, resolution, and detection speed necessary for emerging applications. For visual sensors, the distributed nature of the nodes is effective against occlusions; the sensing range of cameras is highly dependent on the number of objects that are between the sensor and phenomena of interest. Thus, distributed short-range cameras are more flexible than those that are longer-range and higher-cost. In addition, the dispersed nature of the network nodes provides significant advantages through distributive processing by exploiting a number of characteristics such as redundancy.

Node and Network Redundancy:

The use of many densely deployed sensors in a physical region provides an inherent protection against natural and intentional system faults. The redundancy of information gathered by neighboring nodes can be exploited for more accurate and robust observation results through effective data fusion. In addition, the redundancy can be exploited for networking to avoid single-points of communication failure. For example, critical data can be communicated via multiple routes to guarantee communication of the event with higher probability. The success of this built-in system redundancy is dependent on how effectively redundancy is incorporated into the system. To manage the density of devices and diversity of sensors, hierarchy is used.

<u>Hierarchical Architecture:</u>
Multimedia sensor networks, in particular, exploit multi-level tier architectures for communication and network management. This is because in addition to sensor compression, data aggregation amongst nodes in a common neighborhood is necessary for scalable decision-making and network operation. Figure 3 provides an example in which hierarchical three-tier architecture is used for a video-based sensor network.

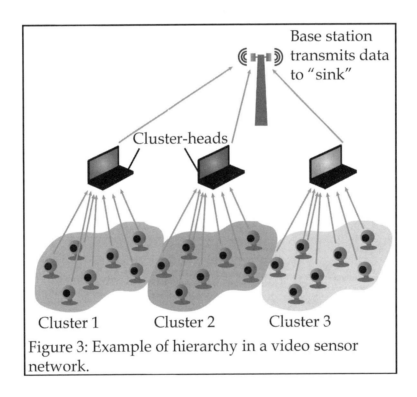

Figure 3: Example of hierarchy in a video sensor network.

Clustered multimedia sensors are managed by a local "cluster-head" that aggregates data and passes it on to a "base station" that takes input from active cluster-heads, makes decisions and sends the final interpretation to a "sink" that consumes the information to achieve a higher level objective. The nodes have video sensing capability as well as limited computational resources effective for compression. The cluster-heads have higher computing power (perhaps at the order of a common laptop) that is necessary for real-time data fusion and image interpretation. The base station has even higher transceiver power and computational resources to collect the intermediate information from the cluster-heads and respond to the often geographically displaced sink. The sink can query the network through the base station that broadcasts information requests. The corresponding cluster heads and sensors will then collaborate and respond appropriately.

Collaboration and Data-Centricity:
The communications in a sensor network is often ad hoc peer-to-peer given the limited range of the low-cost node transceivers. Unlike systems in which the primary objective is communications (such as the Internet), the goal of sensor networks is to provide an application-specific inference to an end-user. Thus, for communications, which is an intermediate process, each node must cooperate to transmit data throughout the network; no fixed communication infrastructure comprised of routers is employed. Multi-hop routing is characteristic of these systems. Communication bandwidth and error rates can be optimized, in part, if nodes collaborate through "in-network processing." In-network processing represents intermediate network computing amongst localized nodes to promote network scalability through energy savings. In-network processing includes sensor data aggregation (i.e., data fusion), passive participation, and the sensor-dependent processing of control data for network operation. For example, in data aggregation two cameras may collectively fuse their information to obtain a lower bandwidth aggregated result, which is then routed peer-to-peer (and possibly fused with other sensor node readings along the way) to the cluster head or base station. Passive participation entails nodes within a geographical neighborhood that monitor each other's transmissions making energy-preserving decisions; for instance, a node may refrain from transmitting sensor readings that are redundant to information collected and communicated by adjacent nodes. In-network processing may also take the form of the creation of data-dependent efficient peer-to-peer routing tables by using local node information. Overall, this characteristic of sensor networks called "data-centricity" directly contrasts traditional networking paradigms in which there is generic addressed-based operation for such tasks as routing.

Application-specific:
The data-centric paradigm easily facilitates application-specific network operation. Because the overall goal of a sensor network is inference, which is an application-dependent objective, the in-network processing can be tailored to efficiently achieve application-based queries. For multimedia sensor networks aggregation can be significantly more complex than for homogenous scalar sensor networks. The volume and diversity of multimedia information necessitates sophisticated processing borrowing from fields such as computer vision, and multimodal fusion.

Autonomous:
Autonomous network behavior is attractive to promote the pervasive use of sensor networks. Because the application-specific requirements are integrated with networking operation, little human interaction is required. Autonomy can imply self-sustained system operation, robustness to incidental faults and malicious attacks, as well as adaptation to changing physical conditions. Self-sustainability is particularly challenging because the sensor nodes are often untethered and must communicate via wireless means and may not have direct sources of power.

Two proposals for wireless communications based on radio frequency (RF) and optical free space (OSF) technologies have been proposed for sensor devices. RF technologies are, for the most part, more technologically developed than OSF and (at this time) are easier to integrate within a sensor device. The latter, however, holds promise for ultra low power wireless communications. OSF can also accommodate bursty traffic and high bandwidth. For this reason, it is expected that OSF, in particular, will enable the early use of high bandwidth multimedia sensor nodes.

In addition, the untethered characteristic of sensor networks makes power consumption and energy scavenging significantly issues in network design. Battery lifetime must be conserved through the use of "energy-aware" algorithms and protocols. Furthermore, communications must be wireless adding to the burden of power management within the network. The energy cost of wireless communications can be orders of magnitude greater than wired.

Resource-constrained:

A distinguishing feature of sensor networks is their severe resource constraints in comparison to other types of ad hoc networking infrastructure. Power management through limited communications, processing and storage is essential to sustain network lifetime. Thus, suboptimal algorithms and protocols may often be favored and the inherent redundancy and diversity in the network may be leveraged for performance. The resource constraints are especially problematic for multimedia sensor networks in which communication bandwidth and processing volume is often high. Here, compression and in-network processing play a significant role in conserving resources. In addition, energy scavenging methods such as the use of solar cells can sustain the network. Power management is one of the most critical design and research issues for sensor systems.

Multimedia Sensor Network Systems

At the time of this writing, several proposals for multimedia sensor networks focusing on video data have been proposed. These include the Distributed Interactive Video Array (DIVA) under development at Spawar Systems Center, the "Smart" Sensor Networks for Visual Context Capture and Interactivity project at the University of California, San Diego, the Collaborative Visual Sensor Networks project at Stanford University, Video Sensor Networks research on managing spatiotemporal objects at Boston University, and network research on Wireless Video Sensor Networks at Virginia Tech. In addition, video sensor networks are being applied to nearshore environment monitoring for oceanographic research at the Coastal Imaging Lab at Oregon State University. A group at Oregon Graduate Institute has developed the Panoptes wireless video sensor network test bed, which shows potential for environmental monitoring, healthcare, robotics applications, and security/surveillance.

For the evolving details of these systems, readers are referred to the References section.

References

1. "Agent-based intelligent reactive environments Project at Massachusetts Institute of Technology," URL: http://www.ai.mit.edu/projects/aire/index.shtml.

2. F. Akyildiz, W. Su, Y. Sankarasubramaniam, and E. Cayirci, "A survey on sensor networks," IEEE Communications Magazine, Vol. 40, No. 8, pp. 102–114, August 2002.

3. "CareMedia: Automated video and sensor analysis for geriatric care Project at Carnegie Mellon University, URL: http://www.informedia.cs.cmu.edu/caremedia/.

4. W. C. Feng, B. Code, E. Kaiser, M. Shea, and W. C. Feng, "Panoptes: A scalable architecture for video sensor networking applications," Proceedings of the ACM International Conference on Multimedia, November 2003, pp. 562–571.

5. W. C. Feng, J. Walpole, W. C. Feng, and C. Pu, "Moving towards massively scalable video-based sensor networks," Proceedings of the Workshop on New Visions for Large-Scale Networks: Research and Applications, March 2001.

6. C.-Y. Chong and S. P. Kumar, "Sensor networks: Evolution, opportunities and challenges," Proceedings of the IEEE, Vol. 91, No. 8, pp. 1247–1256, August 2003.

7. D. Estrin, L. Girod, G. Pottie, and M. Srivastava, "Instrumenting the world with wireless sensor networks," Proceedings of the IEEE International Conference on Acoustics, Speech and Signal Processing, Vol. 4, pp. 2033-2036, May 2001.

8. Dr. Estrin, R. Govindan, J. Heidemann, and S. Kumar, "Next century challenges: Scalable coordination in sensor networks," Proceedings of the ACM/IEEE International Conference on Mobile Computing and Networking, pp. 263—270, August 1999.

9. R. Holman, J. Stanley, and T. ˝Ozkan-Haller, "Applying video sensor networks to nearshore environment monitoring," IEEE Pervasive Computing, Vol. 2, No. 4, pp. 14–21, October-December 2003.

10. J. M. Kahn, R. H. Katz, and K. S. J. Pister, "Next century challenges: Mobile networking for "smart dust", Proceedings of the ACM/IEEE International Conference on Mobile Computing and Networking, Seattle, Washington, August 1999, pp. 271–278.

11. S. Mao, S. Kompella, Y. T. Hou, H. D. Sherali, and S. F. Midkiff, "Optimal routing for multiple concurrent video sessions in wireless ad hoc networks," Technical Report, The Bradley Department of Electrical and Computer Engineering, Virginia Tech, Blacksburg, Virginia, April 2004.

12. G. J. Pottie and W. J. Kaiser, "Wireless integrated network sensors," Communications of the ACM, Vol. 43, No. 5, pp. 51–58, May 2000.

13. M. Rahimi, H. Shah, G. S. Sukhatme, J. Heideman, and D. Estrin, "Studying the feasibility of energy harvesting in a mobile sensor network," Proceedings of the IEEE International Conference on Robotics and Automation, Taipei, Taiwan, September 2003, Vol. 1, pp. 19–24.

14. "Sensorium at Boston University, URL: http://www.cs.bu.edu/groups/sensorium/.

15. "'Smart' sensor networks for visual context capture and interactivity Project at University of California at San Diego," URL: http://cwc.ucsd.edu/rp 03-05 G.html.

16. "SU Media X: Collaborative visual sensor networks Project at Stanford University," URL: http://mediax.stanford.edu/projects/cvsn.html.

MULTIMEDIA SERVERS

Abhaya Asthana
Bell Labs, Lucent Technologies, Westford, MA

Seon Ho Kim
Computer Science Department, University of Denver, Denver, CO

Definition: Multimedia servers store and manage multimedia objects and deliver data streams in real-time, in response to requests from users.

Introduction

The creation, storage and delivery of ubiquitous, high performance multimedia services present a formidable challenge to the underlying telecommunications and computing infrastructure. Nevertheless, recent advances in computing and communication technologies have made it feasible and economically viable to provide on-line access to a variety of information sources such as books, periodicals, images, video clips, and scientific data. With an efficient standardized data compression technology such as MPEG (Moving Picture Experts Group), huge video files become manageable in computer systems and transferable over networks. Computers with faster processors and storage subsystems make it feasible to support multiple simultaneous displays for large-scale multimedia services. Widely implemented residential broadband network with real-time aware streaming protocols such as RTSP (Real Time Streaming Protocol) are another driving force of the multimedia applications. Multimedia communication also suggests a rich sensory interface between humans and computers that gives the user control over the pace and sequence of the information. While the integration of multiple media, e.g., voice, video, image, and data, provides an effective means of communication and delivery, to effectively support the emerging IP Multimedia Services, great care is required to control the multimedia resources, the transport channels, and the transformation engines [1].

The architecture of such systems consists of *multimedia servers* that are connected to client sites via high-speed networks. A generalized environment supporting multimedia applications to homes or to business environments is shown in Figure 1 in which the user at home has access to a service through an access network, while a business user is connected through a local area network.

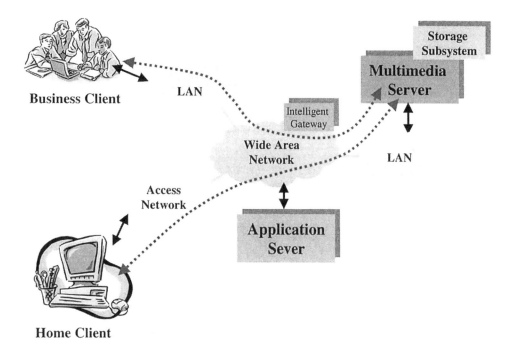

Figure 1. Typical multimedia system.

A multimedia server delivers services over a series of heterogeneous networks to the clients, and the need to provide flawless service to user places significant requirements on a large number of components, which have to work well together. These include:

- Network subsystems with adequate bandwidth to transport, deliver and adapt the data streams isochronously (i.e., at a specified rate, without observable delay) to the clients.

- Client subsystems that receive and/or pre-fetch the data streams and manage the presentation of data.

- Application programs that deal with relationships among data frames and media segments, and manage user navigation and retrieval of this data.

- High performance storage subsystem with data organization, buffering, indexing and retrieval mechanisms to support multimedia applications.

- User satisfaction measured by real-time delivery and adaptability to the environment; Quality-of-service (QoS) management.

- Security, especially management of content rights.

Multimedia applications utilize multiple audio and video streams and time-, user-, and data-dependent behaviors. Multiple applications: operate on the same data, manage information, analyze images, search for appropriate items, and mesh live, pre-recorded, and interactive streams. The multimedia server software framework makes it easy for application developers to create software that satisfies these needs [2].

Multimedia Server Architecture

Multimedia servers store and manage multimedia objects and deliver data streams in real-time, in response to requests from users. Additionally, they process the stored information before delivery to users. The content may range from long, sequentially accessed videos to composite documents consisting of a mixture of small multiple-media segments (e.g., video, audio, image, text). To manipulate these objects, the servers provide computation capabilities encompassing storage, manipulation, construction, distribution and synchronization [3-4]. Multimedia servers may range from low-cost, PC-based simple servers that deliver a few streams, to scalable large (either centralized or distributed) servers that provide thousands of streams. Regardless of the server capacity, with given resources, the objectives of multimedia servers are to maximize the number of clients that can be simultaneously supported (high throughput), to minimize the latency between issuing request and initiation of display (low startup latency), and to support a smooth display without any artifacts, disruptions or jitters (continuous display).

Multimedia servers are similar to their predecessors: network file servers. However, they are faced with several added requirements. Traditional file servers are not designed to support the storage and retrieval of "continuous media" data such as video and audio. In a multimedia application, such data must be stored and retrieved at certain guaranteed rates. Clients of such services are permitted to retrieve multimedia objects from the server for real-time playback at their respective sites. Furthermore, the retrieval may be interactive, i.e. clients may stop, pause, resume, and even record and edit the media information. Sometimes many or all of the clients may play the same material. In such cases, multimedia objects must be played continuously at a constant rate once play begins. Therefore, multimedia servers must be scalable in order to serve very large numbers of clients. These challenges are met in part through the use of high-performance computing resources and efficient data storage system. Figure 2 shows a simplified diagram of a typical multimedia server. Servers can be centralized or distributed [5,15].

Large-scale servers that serve thousands of streams can be quite complex [6]. The multimedia objects that are large and are played back sequentially require relatively large storage space and playback bandwidth. A common implementation of server software can consist of the following layers:

- Data placement and retrieval scheduling: for load balancing, fault-tolerant design, efficient retrieval of data from disks to amortize seek time, and scheduling of system resources to avoid jitters.

- Buffer management: for absorbing variance in data retrieval time and network delays, and for implementing memory-based techniques such as batching.

- Quality of services and admission control: for maintaining the performance criteria of the server such as the maximum number of concurrent displays with a guaranteed smooth display.

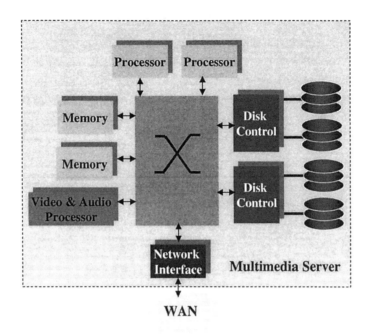

Figure 2. Multimedia server architecture.

Delivery of *time-sensitive* information, such as voice and video, and handling of large volumes of data require special considerations to produce successful applications. Digitization of video yields a sequence of frames and that of audio yields a sequence of samples. Since media quanta, such as video frames or audio samples, convey meaning only when presented continuously in time, a multimedia server must ensure that the recording and playback of each media stream proceeds at its real-time rate. Specifically, during recording, a multimedia server must continuously store the data produced by an input device (e.g., microphone, camera, etc.) so as to prevent buffer overruns at the device as shown in Figure 3. During playback, on the other hand, the server must retrieve data from the disk at a rate that ensures that an output device (e.g., speaker, video display) consuming the data does not starve.

Information retrieved from the disk is buffered prior to playback. Thus, the problem of efficiently servicing a single stream becomes one of preventing starvation while at the same time minimizing buffer space requirement and initiation latency. Since the data transfer rates of disks are significantly higher than the real-time data rate of a single stream, employing modest amount of buffering enables conventional file and operating systems to support continuous storage and retrieval of isolated media streams [7].

Network subsystems create delivery paths from the multimedia servers to the individual clients, and transport the media objects. To avoid long latency and the need for large client buffers, some media objects (e.g., large video and audio files) are streamed isochronously to the clients from the servers.

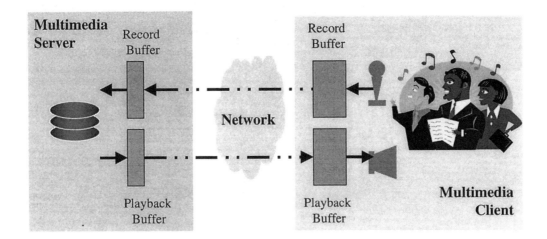

Figure 3. Buffering for real-time record and playback.

Raw bandwidth is not enough for effective delivery of multimedia services, especially when this bandwidth is shared among several systems or applications; it is necessary to provide mechanisms that achieve delivery of voice and video information isochronously, so that the corresponding network connections allow users to enjoy flawless delivery of media information. Special processor and disk scheduling is needed to ensure that disk blocks are read and delivered to the network on time. In addition, they must know the total capacity required to deliver a video stream to ensure that when a new play back is started it can be completed without jitter. Network technology and the communication protocol stack(s) used for multimedia information transmission clearly play an important role in achieving the above goals [8-9].

Data Placement and Retrieval Scheduling

A multimedia server has to process requests from several clients simultaneously. In the best scenario, all the clients will request the retrieval of the same media stream, in which case, the multimedia server needs only to retrieve the stream once from the disk and then multicast it to all the clients [10]. However, more often than not, different clients will request the retrieval of different streams; and even when the same stream is being requested by multiple clients (such as a popular movie), requests may arrive at arbitrary intervals while the stream is already being serviced. Thus, each client may be viewing a different part of the movie at the same time.

A simple mechanism to guarantee that the real-time requirements of all the clients are met is to dedicate a disk head to each stream, and then treat each disk head as a single stream system. This, however, limits the total number of streams to the number of disk heads. In general, since the data transfer rate of disks are significantly higher than the real-time data rate of a single stream, several streams can be serviced simultaneously by multiplexing a disk head among the streams. However, in doing so, the server must ensure that the continuous playback requirements of all the streams are met. To achieve this, the server must carefully schedule disk requests so that no stream starves. Furthermore, it must ensure that it does not admit so many clients as to make such disk scheduling impossible. While simple striping is effective for load balancing across a set of homogeneous storage devices for long sequential accesses, complex *block-allocation* policies that take into account bandwidth and storage capacities of the devices are necessary.

A variety of disk scheduling algorithms (e.g., first come first served (FCFS), shortest seek time first (SSTF), SCAN) have been employed by servers to reduce the seek time and rotational latency, to achieve a high throughput, or to provide fair access to each client. The best, known algorithm for real-time scheduling of tasks with deadlines is the Earliest Deadline First (EDF) algorithm. In this algorithm, after accessing a media block from disk, the media block with the earliest deadline is scheduled for retrieval. Scheduling of the disk head based solely on the EDF policy, however, increase the seek time and rotational latency. This drawback is overcome by SCAN that operates by "scanning" the disk head back and forth across the surface of the disk, retrieving a requested block as the head passes over it.

Disk Configurations

If an entire multimedia file is stored on a single disk, the number of concurrent accesses to that file is limited by the throughput of that disk. One approach to overcome this limitation is to maintain multiple copies of the file on different disks. However, this approach is expensive because it requires additional storage space. A more effective approach to this problem is to scatter the multimedia file across multiple disks. This scattering can be achieved using two techniques: "data striping" and "data interleaving". RAID (redundant array of inexpensive disks) technology has popularized the use of parallel access to an array of disks. Under the RAID scheme, data is "striped" across each disk. A combination of data striping and data interleaving can be used to scatter the media file across a large number of disks attached to a networked cluster of server machines. Moreover, various redundancy techniques using mirroring and parity encoding can be applied to the media file to increase availability and throughput [15].

Storage Hierarchies

Fixed disks are sufficient for providing efficient access to a small number of video streams. However, the high cost per gigabyte of storage makes such magnetic disk-based server architectures ineffective for large-scale servers. In fact, the desire for sharing and providing on-line access to a wide variety of video sequences indicates that large-scale multimedia servers must utilize very large tertiary storage devices (e.g., tape and optical jukeboxes).

These devices are highly cost-effective and provide very large storage capacities by utilizing robotic arms to serve a large number of removable tapes or disks to a small number of reading devices. Because of these long seek and swap times, however, they are poor at performing random access within a video stream. Moreover, they can support only a single playback at a time on each reader. Consequently, they are inappropriate for direct video playback. Thus, a large-scale, cost-effective multimedia server will be required to utilize tertiary storage devices (such as tape jukeboxes) to maintain a large number of video streams, and then achieve high performance and scalability through magnetic disk-based servers.

In the simplest case, such a hierarchical storage manager may utilize fast magnetic disks to cache frequently accessed data. In such a scenario, there are several alternatives for managing the disk system. It may be used as a staging area (cache) for the tertiary storage devices, with entire media streams being moved from the tertiary storage to the disks when they need to be played back.

A distributed hierarchical storage management extends this idea by allowing multiple magnetic disk-based caches to be distributed across a network. In such a scenario, if a high percentage of clients access data stored in a local (or nearby) cache, the perceived performance will be sufficient to meet the demands of continuous media. On the other hand, if the user accesses are unpredictable or have poor reference locality, then most accesses will require retrieval of information from tertiary storage devices, thereby significantly degrading the performance. Fortunately, for many applications such as video-on-demand, user accesses are likely to exhibit high locality of reference.

Buffer Management

Multiplexed data retrieval from storage subsystem inherently introduces variance in retrieval time of a unit of data, which may result in a jitter. To absorb the variance and provide a smooth display, *double buffering* has been widely used. One data unit from a buffer is being transmitted to a client while the next unit is being retrieved into another buffer. As long as the next data unit can be retrieved into a buffer before the starvation of data in the other buffer allocated to the same stream, there would be no jitter. Buffering can be extended to have more than two buffers per stream as a trade-off between memory space and a greater tolerable margin of statistical variance of data retrieval time [14].

In a large-scale service such as a video-on-demand server, multiple requests for the same popular video can arrive within a short time period requiring multiple playback streams from the storage subsystem. The requests arrived within a short duration of time (*window*) can be *batched* for service by a single playback stream, resulting in a higher throughput. A longer batching window allows more users to be serviced concurrently but introduces longer startup latency. Adaptive *piggy-backing* approaches provide a solution for a longer latency by gradually merging multiple streams into one.

Some memory buffer space can also be used as a cache for the underlying storage subsystem. In applications where objects have skewed access frequencies, the server may cache the most frequently accessed objects in memory for an expedited service. The cache performance is determined by the size of cache, the granularity of objects to cache, and the replacement algorithms.

Quality of Service and Admission Control

Given the real-time performance requirements of each client, a multimedia server must employ admission control algorithms to determine whether a new client can be admitted without violating the performance (QoS) requirements of the clients already being serviced. This implies, for example, that a video server has to know in advance the number of streams it can serve without jitter. The admission control relies on finding a delivery path from the storage devices to the selected network interface and reserving appropriate capacities on all components on this path for normal playback. The admission control may also rely on resource-optimization techniques, e.g., batching and caching.

The performance requirement of a multimedia server can be accomplished in two ways: deterministic and statistical guarantee. The performance objectives of an application that doesn't tolerate any jitter are determined using a deterministic quantification with worst-case scenario. When some applications might tolerate some missed deadlines, one can determine the objectives within a tolerable statistical variation. For example, a few lost video frames, or the occasional pop in the audio may be tolerable in some cases - especially if such tolerance is rewarded with a reduced cost of service. Hence, a multimedia server may be able to accommodate additional clients by employing an admission control algorithm that exploits the statistical variation in the access times of media blocks from disk (or statistical variations in compression ratios, where applicable) [11-14].

Client Subsystem

The design of the client subsystem is dominated by cost, functionality, and comfort considerations. The client device could be an upgraded television set (with internal or external "set-top" capability), or a full-fledged personal computer. The restrictions on local capabilities certainly affect which functions are performed well locally and which depend on server or network support. Limiting buffer sizes and local computing affect the load on the network. Classic VCR control operations can be implemented in many different ways. In addition, audio and video inputs (for video conferencing) result in significant implications for upstream bandwidth and control.

Searching image, audio, and video data is far more difficult than doing the same for text. Approaches to finding desired information include creation and analysis of text annotations, examining reduced versions of the video (thumbnails or key frames), and full- scale analysis of high-resolution data. Practical considerations force us to maximize the value received from a small amount of computation. The requirements become particularly onerous in interactive and real-time situations such as push technology, browsing, and interactive navigation in large sets of multimedia data.

Presenting the information is also difficult, especially when system and network capabilities are limited. Managing controlled collaborations and teleconferences with many audio, video, and data streams is even more challenging. In the future, people will want even more complicated composite moving media, with complex constraints on location and timing of the various parts.

The computer industry is providing demand and an expanding market for the key hardware technologies that underlie multimedia. Now that the multimedia server technology has been developed the marketplace will determine future direction. As a result, the application of multimedia, which appears expensive now, will become less expensive and more attractive. Finally, a fundamental understanding about composition and flow of multimedia services will help to define appropriate strategies for the development of next generation mixed mode communication, presence, location, and telephony services.

References

1. D. Sitaram and A. Dan, "Multimedia Servers – Applications, Environments and Design," Morgan Kaufman Publishers, 2000.

2. S. Burkhard, et. al., "A Flexible Middleware for Multimedia Communication: Design, Implementation, and Experience," IEEE Transactions on Selected Areas in Communications, Vol. 17, No. 9, September 1999, pp. 1580-1598.

3. A. Asthana and V. Krishnaswamy, "ATRI: An Advanced Multimedia Worktop - Architecture and Applications," Proceedings of the IEEE COMSOC Workshop, Multimedia'94, Kyoto, Japan May 1994.

4. A. Asthana and M. B. Srivastava, "Kaleido: A System for Dynamic Composition and Processing of Multimedia Flows," *Symposium on Multimedia Communications & Video Coding,* October 1995, New York.

5. D. Serpanos and A. Bouloutas, "Centralized versus Distributed Multimedia Servers," IEEE Transactions on Circuits and Systems for Video Technology, Vol. 10, No 8, December 2000.

6. K. Argy, "Scalable Multimedia Servers," IEEE Concurrency, Vol. 6, Issue 4, Oct-Dec 1998, pp.8-10.

7. A. Asthana, et al. "An Experimental Active Memory Based I/O Subsystem," IEEE Workshop on I/O in Parallel Computer Systems, Cancun, Mexico, April 1994.

8. A. L. N. Reddy and J. C. Wyllie, "I/O Issues in a Multimedia System," IEEE Computer, March 1994, pp. 17-28.

9. H. Schulzrinne, S. Casner, R. Fredrick, and V. Jacobson, "RTP: A Transport Protocol for Real-Time Applications," RFC 1889, January 1996.

10. J. Gemmell et. al., "Multimedia Storage Servers: A Tutorial," IEEE Computer, Vol. 28, No. 5, May 1995, pp. 40-49.

11. J. Y. B. Lee, "Parallel Video Serves: A Tutorial," IEEE Multimedia, Vol. 5 Issue 2, April-June 1998, pp. 20-28.

12. R. Boutaba and A. Hafid, "A Generic Platform for Scalable Access to Multimedia-on-Demand Systems," IEEE Journal on SAC, Vol. 17, No. 9, September 1999.

13. R. Rooholamini and V. Cherkassky, "ATM-Based Multimedia Servers," IEEE Multimedia, Spring 1995, pp. 39-52.

14. S. Kim, "Bulk Prefetching with Deadline-Driven Scheduling to Minimize Startup Latency of Continuous Media Servers," Proceedings of the IEEE International Conference on Multimedia and Expo (ICME2001), Tokyo, Japan, August 2001.

15. A. Dashti, S. Kim, C. Shahabi, and R. Zimmermann, "Streaming Media Server Design", Prentice Hall PTR, April 2003.

MULTIMEDIA STORAGE ORGANIZATIONS

Seon Ho Kim
University of Denver, Denver, USA

Definition: *Magnetic disk drives are typically used as multimedia storage systems due to their high data transfer, large storage capacity, and low price.*

Introduction

Considering the large size of multimedia files, especially streaming media (SM) such as audio and video that require real-time data retrieval, magnetic disk drives have been the choice of multimedia storage systems due to their high data transfer rate, large storage capacity, random access capability, and low price [3]. Therefore, this article also focuses on disk based storage organization for multimedia servers.

As discussed in the article, *Multimedia Servers*, the objectives of multimedia servers are to support a smooth display without any jitters (continuous display), to maximize the number of simultaneous displays (high throughput), and to minimize the latency between issuing request and initiation of display (low startup latency). Thus, the design of storage organization to support such servers should also follow these objectives. Additionally, load balancing and fault tolerance issues should be considered to complete the discussion of multi-disk storage systems.

A basic approach to support continuous display is to divide an SM object into equi-sized blocks. Each block is a unit of retrieval and is contiguously stored in a disk. For example, a SM object X is divided into n equi-sized blocks: $X_0, X_1, X_2, ..., X_{n-1}$. The size of blocks, the display time of a block, and the time to read a block from a disk drive can be calculated as a function of display bandwidth requirement of an object, the number of maximum simultaneous displays that a disk drive can support, and the physical disk characteristics such as the data transfer rate [3]. Upon the request for the SM object X, the system stages the first block of X, i.e., X_0, from the disk into main memory and initiates its display. Prior to the completion of the display of X_0, the system stages the next block X_1 from the disk into main memory to provide for a smooth transition and a hiccup-free display. This process is repeated until all blocks of X are displayed. This process introduces the concept of a *time period* (T_p), or a *round*, which denotes the time to display a block. For example, the display time of one 0.5 MByte block of a SM object encoded with 4 Mb/s is one second $(T_p = 1$ sec). Traditionally, double buffering has been widely used to absorb the variance of block retrieval time. The idea is as follows: while a buffer is being consumed from memory, the system fills up another buffer with data. The system can initiate display after the first buffer is filled and a request for the next one is issued.

In general, the display time of a block is longer than its retrieval time from a disk drive. Thus, the bandwidth of a disk drive can be multiplexed among multiple simultaneous displays accessing the same disk drive. For example, with 4 Mb/s of display bandwidth requirement of MPEG-2 encoded objects, a disk drive with 80 Mb/s of data transfer rate can support up to 20 simultaneous displays. This is the ideal case when there is no overhead in disk operation. However, in reality, a magnetic disk drive is a mechanical device and incurs a delay when required to retrieve data. This delay consists of: 1) *seek time* to reposition the disk head from the current cylinder to the target cylinder, and 2) *rotational latency* to wait until the data block arrives under the disk head. These are wasteful operations that prevent a disk drive from transferring data. Both their number of occurrence and duration of each occurrence must be reduced in order to maximize the number of simultaneous displays supported by a disk drive (throughput). Thus, the performance of SM servers significantly depends on the physical characteristics of magnetic disk drives (such as data transfer rate, seek times, and rotational latency), the data placement of blocks, and the block retrieval scheduling. Moreover, a single disk is not enough for most multimedia applications in both storage capacity and bandwidth. It is critical to manage multiple storage devices in a coordinated manner to support the requirement of a large-scale server, the aggregate storage capacity and bandwidth. With multiple disks, the storage system must meet the contiguous display requirements of all streams through careful data placement and retrieval scheduling. An additional issue in multi-disk system is load imbalance problem. Load to an individual device can vary over time depending on many factors such as the fluctuation of the number of user requests during a day and the popularity of objects. This may make a specific disk a bottleneck of the entire system. Thus, one may need a busy hour analysis to quantify the peak system load. Another important practical issue is the reliability of storage systems.

Data Placement

Assuming SM servers with multiple disk drives, data blocks are assigned to disks in order to distribute the load of a display evenly across the disks. Thus, data placement can affect the continuous display and performance of SM servers in conjunction with scheduling techniques. There are two well-known approaches to assign blocks of an object across multiple disk drives; *constrained* and *unconstrained*. A typical example of constrained data placement is *round-robin* [2]. As suggested by its name, this technique assigns the blocks of an object across disks in a round-robin manner, starting with an arbitrarily chosen disk. Assuming d disks in the system, if the first block of an object X is assigned to disk d_i, j^{th} block of X is assigned to disk $d_{(i+j-1) \mod d}$. An example of unconstrained data placement is *random* [5] that assigns data blocks to disk drives using a random number generator. Figure 1 shows examples of both approaches.

Round-robin data placement can be generalized using the concept of clustering. The system partitions D disks (total number of disks in the system) into k clusters of disks with each cluster consisting of d disks. Then data blocks are assigned across clusters in a round-robin manner as shown in Figure 1. Inside a cluster, a block is further divided into d fragments: X_0 is divided into $X_{0.0} \dots X_{0.d-1}$ and assigned to d disks in a cluster. The fragments of a block are concurrently retrieved in parallel from a cluster while blocks are periodically retrieved across clusters in a round-robin manner. Depending on the degree of striping, wide striping stripes blocks across all disks while narrow striping stripes blocks across a subset of disks. When $d = 1$, each disk is a cluster so it is possible to independently control individual disk. This produces a higher throughput and longer startup latency as throughput and latency scale linearly as a function of the number of disks. When $d = D$, all disks are accessed in a synchronized manner because all fragments of a data block should be retrieved concurrently while incurring a seek in each disk, resulting in a lower throughput. However, this approach provides shorter startup latency. Thus, it is important to determine the optimal striping size and configure the system considering the performance requirements of an application: data transfer rate of disks, display rate of objects, number of disks in the system, amount of main memory, and cost per display [3].

Due to the harmony of round-robin data placement and periodic cycle-based data retrieval, this approach provides a deterministic service guarantee for a hiccup-free display of a SM object once its retrieval is initiated. This approach maximizes the utilization of disk bandwidth by distributing the load of a display across disks evenly. Thus, the system throughput scales linearly as a function of the number of disk drives in the system. The drawback of this approach is that the startup latency also scales because the system might delay the initiation of data retrievals of objects. Thus, this approach is suitable to the applications that require a high throughput and can tolerate a long startup latency such as movie-on-demand systems.

With random data placement, fixed size blocks are randomly assigned across disks. Each block request is tagged with a deadline. By controlling the deadlines for block retrievals, this approach can provide shorter startup latency than the cycle-based and round-robin approach. Hence, this is more appropriate fot the applications requiring a short startup latency such as a digital editing system. However, random may suffer from statistical variation of the number of block retrievals in a disk drive. Due to the nature of random data placement, a disk might receive more than its fair share of requests. A formation of bottleneck on a disk drive may result in the violation of deadlines set forth on requested blocks, causing some displays to incur hiccups. This hiccup probability might be significant depending on the system load. To reduce the hiccup probability, a multiple buffering scheme with prefetching was proposed in [4].

Data placement, combined with the data retrieval scheduling, can significantly impact on the performance of the storage system for multimedia servers. The performance issues, throughput and startup latency, are discussed in the article, *Scheduling, Multimedia*.

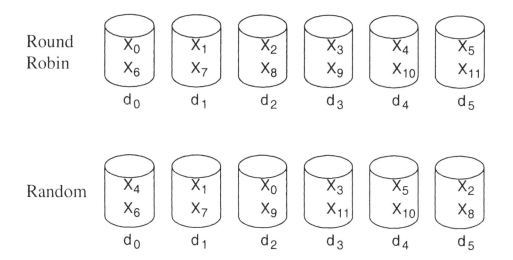

Figure 1. Two typical data placement approaches.

Fault Tolerant Storage Organization

Even though the reliability of an individual disk drive is high, disks can fail in a large system. For example, when the MTBF (Mean Time Between Failures) of a disk is

1,000,000 hours, the MTBF of a system with 1000 such disks can be reduced to 1,000 hours without any consideration. Thus, it is critical to construct a reliable storage system. Fault tolerant design of storage systems commonly use redundant design, *mirroring* (object or block level replication) [1] and *parity encoding* [7]. In order to support multimedia data, especially streaming media data, these basic techniques can be refined into several alternative variations, each with its own specific characteristics. Figure 2 shows a classification of fault tolerant design of storage organization.

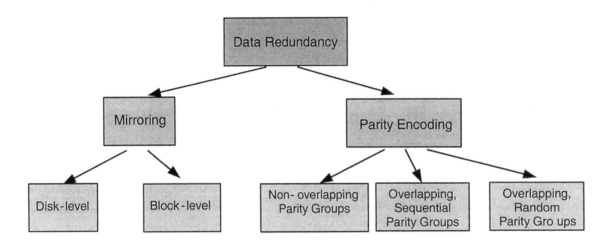

Figure 2. Classification of fault tolerant storage organization.

Mirroring approach maintains at least two identical copies of the same data block in different disk drives so that no two copies are stored in the same disk. Thus, when a disk fails, the system still can service the same block from a different disk. Depending on the location of copies across disks, Mirroring can be implemented at either *disk-level* or at *block-level* (see Figure 3). Disk-level mirroring maintains two identical disks where the complete contents of each disk are duplicated. In general, the bandwidth of only one disk (primary disk) is utilized in normal mode without any disk failure. In the degraded mode when one or more disks fail, the mirrored disk (standby disk) will switch the failed disk to continue the service. It looks wasting the valuable disk bandwidth in normal mode but there will be a seamless continuation of service even in degraded mode. This approach also can survive multiple disk failures unless the system loses two mirrored disks simultaneously. Block-based mirroring also replicate data blocks but copies can be arbitrarily distributed across disks as long as two copies of the same block can be stored in two different disks. With this approach, all disk bandwidth are available in normal mode. In the presence of a disk failure, the load on the failed disk will be evenly distributed across remaining disks increasing load on each disk. The disadvantage of this approach is that it tolerates only one disk failure in the system.

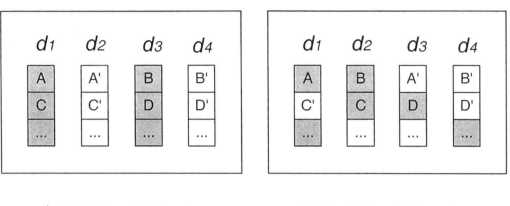

(a) Disk-based Mirroring   (b) Block-based Mirroring

Figure 3. Mirroring.

In parity encoding approach, a data block is stored in a *parity group*. For example, with the parity group size g, the parity information is calculated from $g-1$ participating data blocks and g^{th} block is dedicated to store the parity information. In the first approach, the disks of a storage system are partitioned into multiple *non-overlapping* parity groups, see Figure 4. In a parity group, blocks are distributed in a round-robin manner so that all disk bandwidth are utilized in normal mode. This approach can survive multiple disk failures unless two disks fail in the same parity group, i.e., it can tolerate one disk failure per parity group. However, when a parity group operates in degraded mode, each access to the failed disk triggers the retrieval of blocks from all of the disks within this parity group to reconstruct the lost data. Thus, the load on all operational disks significantly increases under failure, making this parity group a hot spot for the entire system.

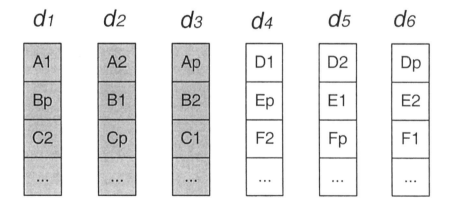

Figure 4. Non-overlapping parity groups.

To distribute the additional load more evenly, parity groups may be rotated such that they overlap [8]. In this scenario, termed *overlapping, sequential* (see Figure 5.a), parity groups are distributed across all disks in a sequential manner. Then, a failure will generate additional load on the $g-1$ disks before and $g-1$ disks after the failed disk drive. Thus, this provides a better load distribution in degraded mode than the non-overlapping. The improved load-balance is traded for a reduced fault tolerance of approximately one failure per two parity groups.

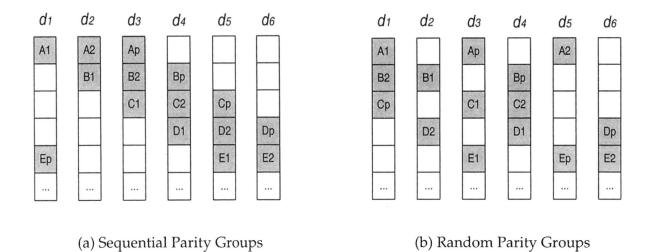

(a) Sequential Parity Groups   (b) Random Parity Groups

Figure 5. Overlapping parity groups.

A third approach alleviates the possibility of bottlenecks even further by assigning blocks randomly to parity groups. By abandoning the requirement for data blocks on sequential disk drives to be placed in the same parity group, the additional load generated by a failed disk can be almost uniformly distributed across all operational disks. Hence, in this *overlapping, random* (see Figure 5.b) approach, very little bandwidth must be reserved on each disk during normal operation. With the pseudo-random placement algorithms described above, some parity data may be placed within the same node and hence node failures cannot be tolerated. By extending the allocation strategy such that parity data is placed only on mutually exclusive nodes this problem can be eliminated. Mappings of parity group members to disks that exhibit the desired property are, for example, a complete combinatorial approach which results in (*d choose g*) different parity groups, or a design devised using the theory of *balanced incomplete block designs* [6]. Such a system is somewhat less reliable because only one disk failure can be tolerated in the whole storage system. Furthermore, additional meta data is needed for each block to associate it with a parity group. However, this provides the best load distribution in degraded mode.

See: Multimedia Servers, Scheduling Multimedia

References

1. D. Bitton and J. Gray, "Disk Shadowing," Proceedings of the International Conference on Very Large Databases (VLDB), September, 1988.
2. S. Berson, S. Ghandeharizadeh, R. Muntz, and X. Ju, "Staggered Striping in Multimedia Information Systems," *Proceedings of the ACM SIGMOD International Conference on Management of Data*, 1994.
3. A. Dashti, S. Kim, C. Shahabi, and R. Zimmermann, "Streaming Media Server Design," Prentice Hall PTR, April 2003.

4. S. Kim, "Bulk Prefetching with Deadline-Driven Scheduling to Minimize Startup Latency of Continuous Media Servers," *Proceedings of the IEEE International Conference on Multimedia and Expo (ICME2001)*, August 2001.

5. R. Muntz, J. Santos, and S. Berson, "RIO: A Real-time Multimedia Object Server," *ACM Sigmetrics Performance Evaluation Review*, Vol. 25, No. 2, September, 1997.

6. B. Ozden, R. Rastogi, P. Shenoy, and A. Silberschatz, "Fault-tolerant Architectures for Continuous Media Servers," *Proceedings of the ACM SIGMOD International Conference on Management of Data*, June 1996.

7. D. Patterson, G. Gibson, and R. Katz, "A Case for Redundant Arrays of Inexpensive Disks (RAID)," *Proceedings of the ACM SIGMOD International Conference on Management of Data*, May 1988.

8. R. Tewari, R. P. King, D. Kandlur, and D. M. Dias, "Placement of Multimedia Blocks on Zoned Disks," *Proceedings of IS&T/SPIE Multimedia Computing and Networking*, January 1996.

MULTIMEDIA STREAMING ON THE INTERNET

K.M. Ho and K.T. Lo
The Hong Kong Polytechnic University, Hong Kong, China

J. Feng
City University of Hong Kong, Hong Kong, China

Definition: Streaming is an enabling technology for providing multimedia data delivery between clients in various multimedia applications on the Internet.

The Internet has seen miraculous growth since its appearance. Web browsing and file transfer are the dominant services provided through the Internet. However, these kinds of service providing information about text, pictures and document exchange are no longer satisfied the demand of clients. With the recent advances in digital technologies, such as high-speed networking, media compression technologies and fast computer processing power, more and more multimedia applications involving digital audio and video are come into practice on the Internet.

Streaming is an enabling technology [1]-[3] for providing multimedia data delivery between (or among) clients in various multimedia applications on the Internet. With this technology, the client can playback the media content without waiting for the entire media file to arrive. Compared with conventional data communication, delivery of multimedia data has more stringent requirements on network bandwidth, delay and loss [3]. However, the current Internet is inherently a packet-switched network that was not designed to handle isochronous (continuous time-based) traffic such as audio and video. The Internet only provides best-effort services and has no guarantee on the quality of service (QoS) for multimedia data transmission. As a result, there are still many open problems in designing protocols and transmission strategies for multimedia streaming.

Figure 1 depicts the architecture for a typical multimedia streaming system on the Internet. Video and audio compression algorithms are first applied to compress the raw audiovisual data to achieve efficiency on storage and transmission. Streaming protocols provide means to the client and the server for services negotiation, data transmission and network addressing. When a request for service is received, the server will decide whether this request will be accepted or not based on the information from the service manager. With the acceptance of the request, resources will be allocated. Media contents retrieved from the storage device are packetized with media information such as timestamp and then delivered to the client. If the server cannot fulfill the request, the client may be blocked or en-queue in the system. The arriving packet at the client is decapsulated into media information and media content. QoS Monitor utilizes these media information to analyze the network condition and feeds back to QoS control in the server for adapting the QoS requirements. On the other hand, the media content is decoded and passed to the application for playback. Audio and video may be transmitted by separated streams. To achieve synchronization among various streams, media synchronization mechanisms are required.

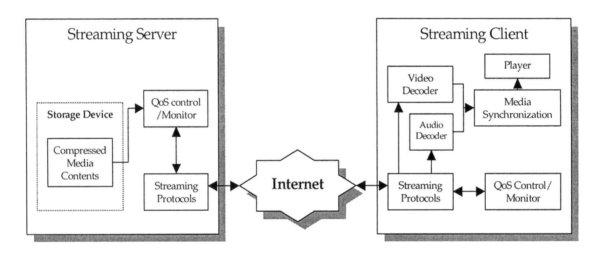

Figure 1. A multimedia streaming system on the Internet.

Compression

As the large volume of raw multimedia data imposes a stringent bandwidth requirement on the network, compression is widely employed to achieve transmission efficiency. Since video has larger bandwidth requirement (56 Kbps-15 Mbps) than audio (8 Kbps-128 Kbps) and loss of audio is more annoying to human than video, audio is given higher priority for transmission in a multimedia streaming system. Hence, only video will be used for adaptation in order to meet the QoS requirements. Therefore, we will focus on the features of video compression that are useful for adaptation in the following.

Video compression schemes can be classified into two types: scalable and non-scalable. With scalable coding, streams of different rates can be extracted from a single stream when required. Hence, a single stream can suit to requirements of different clients in a heterogeneous network environment. As the encoder may not know the network condition, the traditional scalable coding approach providing only a step-like quality

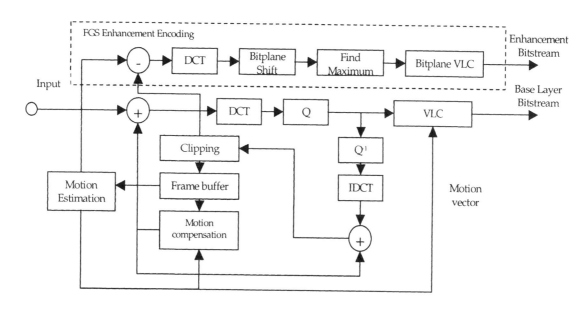

enhancement may not be able to fully utilize the available bit-rate of the channel. On the other hand, the decoder may not be able to decode all the received data fast enough for reconstruction. Therefore, the objective of video coding for multimedia streaming is to optimizing the video quality over a given bit-rate range instead of a given bit-rate. Also the bitstream should be partially decodable at any bit-rate within the bit-rate range to reconstruct with optimized quality [14]. To meet these demands, a new scalable coding mechanism, called fine granularity scalability (FGS) [15] was proposed in MPEG-4.

The block diagram of FGS video encoder is illustrated in Figure 2. An FGS encoder compresses raw video data into two streams, base layer bitstream and enhancement bitstream. Similar to the traditional video encoder, it relies on two basic methods for compression: intra-frame DCT coding for reduction of spatial redundancy and inter-frame motion compensation for reduction of temporal redundancy.

Figure 2. Block diagram of FGS video encoder.

Different from traditional scalable encoder, the FGS encoder produces the enhancement stream using bitplane coding, which is achieved by coding the difference between the DCT coefficients on the reconstructed frame and the original frame and then extracting each bit from 64 DCT coefficients with same significant to form a bitplane (BP). Therefore, all the most significant bits (MSB) from the 64 DCT coefficients form BP-1 and all the second MSB form BP-2, and so on (see Figure 4). With this coding technique, the encoder can truncate the bitstream of the enhancement layer anywhere to achieve continuous rate control. Figure 3 shows the block diagram of FGS video decoder, which operates in the reversed manner to the encoder. Unlike conventional decoder, the FGS decoder can partially decode the received bitstream based on the current available resources (e.g. computational resource) in order to construct the frame before its predicted playback time.

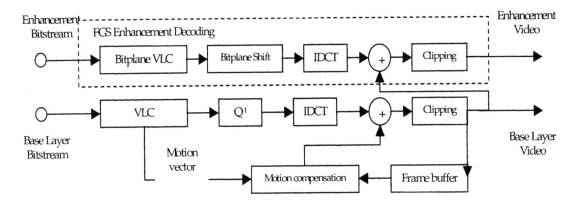

Figure 3. Block diagram of FGS video decoder.

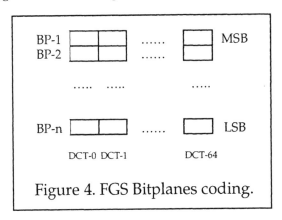

Figure 4. FGS Bitplanes coding.

QoS Control/Monitor

The dynamic nature of the Internet introduces unpredicted delay and packet loss to the media streams during transmission, which may affect the presentation quality. QoS Control/Monitor mechanism aims to avoid congestion and maximize the presentation quality in the presence of packet loss. The techniques, congestion control and error control, are deployed to the end-system without the aid from network to provide certain level of QoS support to the system. Figure 5 summarizes different congestion control and error control techniques.

Each router has a finite storage capacity and all streams flows attached to the router compete for occupying these capacity. If the router has enough resources to serve all its attached flows, its operation runs normally. However, when the data flows reach the capacity of its attached router, the router starts to drop packets. Excessive queuing time and packet drop in the router result in excess delay and bursty loss that have a devastating effect on the presentation quality of media contents. So, congestion control aims at minimizing the possibility of network congestion by matching the rate of the multimedia streams to the available network bandwidth.

Two approaches are widely used for congestion control: rate control and rate shaping [5]. The former is used to determine the transmission rate of media streams based on the estimated network bandwidth while the latter aims at matching the rate of a precompressed media bitstreams to the target rate constraint by using filtering. Based on the place where rate control is taken in the system, rate control can be categorized into three types: source-based, receiver-based and hybrid-based [1].

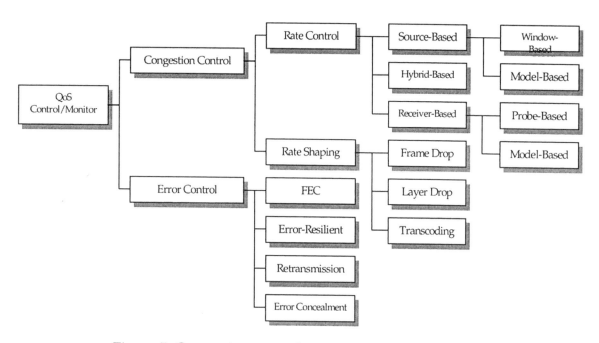

Figure 5. Congestion control and error control techniques.

With the source-based rate control, only the sender (server) is responsible for adapting the transmission rate. In contrast, the receiving rate of the streams is regulated by the client in the receiver-based method. Hybrid-based rate control employs the aforementioned schemes at the same time, i.e. both the server and client are needed to participant in the rate control. Typically, the source-based scheme is used in either unicast or multicast environment while the receiver-based method is deployed in multicast only. Either of these rate-control mechanisms uses the approaches of window-based [16] or model-based [12] for rate adaptation. The window-based approach uses probing experiments to examine the availability of network bandwidth. In case of no packet loss, it increases its sending rate; otherwise, it reduces its sending rate. The model-based approach is based on a throughput model of Transmission Control Protocol (TCP) to determine the sending rate (λ), which is characterized by [13]:

$$\lambda = \frac{c \times MTU}{RTT \times \sqrt{p}} \qquad [1]$$

where *MTU* is maximum transmit unit, *RTT* is round-trip time for the connection and *p* is packet loss ratio. This approach prevents congestion in a similar way to that of TCP. On the other hand, because the stored media contents are pre-compressed at a certain rate, the current network condition may not fulfill this rate requirement. By utilizing frame drop filter, layer drop filter and transcoding filter [17], rate shaping performs a filter-like mechanism for rate adaptation of media contents. Frame drop filter is used to reduce the data rate of the media content by discarding a number of frames. Layer drop filter drops (video) layers according to the network condition. And transcoding filter performs transcoding between different compression schemes to achieve the target sending rate.

Packet misroute, packet drop from the router and packet obsolete due to the miss of its predicted playback time are the reasons of presentation quality degradation. To enhance the quality in presence of packet loss, error control should be deployed. Recovering the packet loss can be achieved by the traditional methods of forward error coding (FEC) and retransmission. The principle of FEC is to add extra information to a compressed bitstream. Media contents are first packetized into a number of packets which then form a group for every k packets. Each group is applied to FEC encoder to generate n packets ($n > k$). To reconstruct the original group of packets, the receiving side only needs to have any k packets in the n packets (see Figure 6).

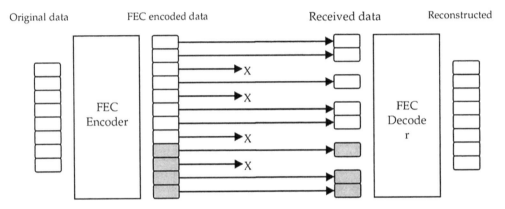

Figure 6. Principle of FEC.

Retransmission is simply to ask for resend the loss packet in case loss has detected. On the other hand, error control mechanisms such as error resilience and error concealment are developed to minimize the level of visual quality degradation when loss is present. Error resilience, being executed by the sender, attempts to prevent error propagation or limit the scope of damage on the compression layer. Re-synchronization marking, data partitioning and data recovery are included in the standardized error-resilient encoding scheme. Error concealment is performed by the receiver when packet loss has already occurred. It tries to conceal the lost data and makes the presentation less annoying to the human. With error concealment, missing information in the receiver is reconstructed using neighboring spatial information from the data in the current frame or temporal information from the data in the previous frames.

Streaming Protocols

Streaming protocols provide means to the client and the server for services negotiation, data transmission and network addressing. Protocols relevance to multimedia streaming can be classified into three categories: network-layer protocol, transport protocol and session control protocol [1]. Network-layer protocol, being served by IP, provides basic network service such as address resolution and network addressing. Transport protocols, such as TCP, UDP and RTP/RTCP, provide end-to-end transport functions for data transmission. Defining the messages and procedures to control the delivery of multimedia data is done by session control protocol, e.g. RTSP or SIP. The whole picture for these protocols in the system is depicted in Figure 7.

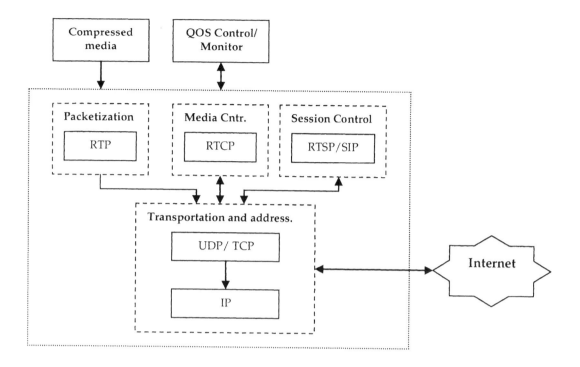

Figure 7. Streaming protocols for multimedia streaming.

Before the multimedia data can be delivered properly, a session should be established between end-points to negotiate the services based on their capabilities and requirements. Depending on the service requirements, different session protocols can be employed. The Real-Time Streaming Protocol (RTSP) [11] is used for controlling the delivery of data with real-time properties in a streaming system. RTSP also provides VCR-like function to control either a single or several time-synchronized streams of continuous media between the server and the client. While RTSP is suitable for media retrieval system, another protocol, Session Initiation Protocol (SIP) [10], is mainly designed for interactive multimedia application, such as Internet phone and video conferencing. Once the session has been established and the required services have negotiated successfully, compressed multimedia data is retrieved and packetized in RTP [7] module which defines a way to format the IP packets carrying multimedia data and provides information on the type of data transported, timestamp for multiple streams synchronization, and sequence numbers for packet sequence reordering and loss detection. RTP itself does not guarantee QoS or reliable delivery, so RTCP [7] is designed to work in conjunction with RTP to provide QoS feedback information such as packet loss ratio and inter-arrival jitter to the system. The system (QoS control/monitor) utilizes this information to evaluate the network condition and react with suitable actions, says, rate adaptation. The packetized packets are then passed to the UDP/IP layer for transmission over the Internet. The media streams are then processed in the reversed manner before playback in the client.

Media Synchronization

Due to different route and incurred unpredictable delay during transmission, media streams may lose synchronization. Therefore, media synchronization mechanism is needed to maintain the original temporal relationships within one media stream or among various media streams such that the media contents can be presented properly. There are three levels of synchronization, namely, intra-stream, inter-stream and inter-object synchronization [8]. Intra-stream synchronization is deployed to maintain the continuity of the stream itself that each received video/audio frame should be played back within its predicted playback time; otherwise, the presentation will be interrupted by pauses or gaps. Inter-stream synchronization aims at maintaining the temporal relationship among various media streams, such as audio frame should be played back with its corresponding video frame in the same way as they were originally captured. Inter-object synchronization is used to synchronize the media streams with time-independent data such as text and still images. For example, each slide should be appeared within the corresponding commenting audio stream in the slide show (see Figure 8).

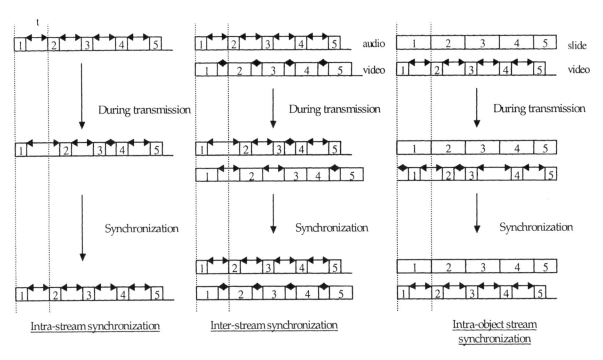

Figure 8. Various media synchronization mechanisms for multimedia streaming.

See: Peer-to-Peer Multimedia Streaming, Client-Server Multimedia Streaming, Real-Time Transport Protocol

References

1. D.P. Wu, Y.W. Hou, and Y.Q. Zhang, "Transporting real-time video over Internet: Challenges and approaches," *Proceeding of the IEEE*, Vol. 88, No. 12, pp. 1855-1877, December 2000.

1. D.P. Wu, Y.W. Hou, W. Zhu, Y.Q. Zhang, and J.M. Peha, "Streaming video over the Internet: approaches and directions," *IEEE Transactions on Circuits and Systems for Video Technology*, Vol. 11, No.1, pp. 282-300, February 2001.

2. G. Lu, "Issues and technologies for supporting multimedia communications over the Internet," *Computer Communications*, Vol.23, pp.1323-1335, August 2000.

3. J.-C. Bolot, T. Turletti, and I. Wakeman, "Scalable feedback control for multicast video distribution in the Internet," *IEEE Journal on Selected Areas in Communications*, Vol. 14, pp. 5-35, January 1996.

4. A. Eleftheriadis and D. Anastassiou, "Meeting arbitrary QoS constraints using dynamic rate shaping of coded digital video," *Proceedings of the 5th Int. Workshop on Network and Operating System Support for Digital Audio and Video (NOSSDAV'95)*, April 1995, pp. 95-106.

5. Information Technology-Coding of Audio-Visual Objects, Part 1: Systems, Part2: Visual, Part 3: Audio, ISO/IEC JTC 1/SC 29/WG11, FCD 14 496, December 1998.

6. H. Schulzrinne, S. Casner, R. Frederick, and V. Jacobson, "RTP: A transport protocol for real-time applications," Internet Engineering Task Force, RFC 1889, January 1996.

7. R. Steinmetz and K. Nahrstedt, *"Multimedia: Computing, Communications and Applications,"* Englewood Cliffs, NJ: Prentice-Hall, 1995.

8. D. Wu, Y.T. Hou, W. Zhu, H.-J. Lee, T. Chiang, Y.-Q. Zhang, and H.J. Chao, "On end-to-end architecture for transporting MPEG-4 video over the Internet," *IEEE Transactions on Circuits and Systems for Video Technology*, Vol. 10, pp. 923-941, September 2000.

9. M. Handley, H. Schulzrinne, E. Schooler and J. Rosenberg, "SIP: Session Initiation Protocol," Internet Engineering Task Force, RFC 2543, March 1999.

10. H. Schulzrinne, A. Rao, and R. Lamphier, "Real-time streaming protocol (RTSP)," Internet Engineering Task Force, RFC 2326, April 1998.

11. T. Turletti and C. Huitema, "Videoconferencing on the Internet," *IEEE Transactions on Networking*, Vol. 4, pp. 340-351, June 1996.

12. S. Floyd and K. Fall, "Promoting the use of end-to-end congestion control in the Internet," *IEEE Transactions on Networking*, Vol. 7, pp. 458-472, August 1999.

13. W.P. Li, "Overview of fine granularity scalability in MPEG-4 video standard," *IEEE Trans. Circuit and System for Video Technology*, Vol. 11, No. 3, pp. 301-317, March 2001.

14. Coding of Audio-Visual Objects, Part-2 Visual, Amendment 4: Streaming Video Profile, ISO/IEC 14 496-2/FPDAM4, July 2000.

15. V. Jacobson, "Congestion avoidance and control," *Proceedings of the ACM SIGCOMM'88*, pp. 314-329, August 1988.

16. N. Yeadon, F. Garcia, D. Hutchison, and D. Shepherd, "Filters: QoS support mechanisms for multipeer communications," *IEEE Journal on Selected Areas in Communications*, Vol. 14, pp. 1245-1262, September 1996.

MULTIMEDIA SYNCHRONIZATION – AREA OVERVIEW

Wayne Robbins
Defense R&D Canada (DRDC), Future Forces Synthetic Environments,
DRDC Ottawa; Ottawa, Ontario, Canada

Definition: *Multimedia synchronization refers to the coordination of multimedia information along three axes: content, space, and time.*

Informally, synchronization has long referred to "being at the right place at the right time." In many ways, this maxim forms the essence of multimedia synchronization, which can be described as the coordination of multimedia information along three orthogonal axes: content, space and time – that is, "the right stuff, the right place, and the right time".

Historical Perspective

The breadth and diversity of the multimedia arena have lead to multimedia synchronization needing to address a broad array of situations and issues [1-7]. An area of avid interest and intense research for well over a decade, multimedia synchronization originated as a necessity to address the convergence of networked and multimedia systems combined with the increased use of continuous, time-based media, such as audio and video. Originally, multimedia systems primarily dealt with "traditional media" such images and text, which were stored, manipulated and rendered locally, on individual workstations. Consequently, issues relating to handling media were related to local computer infrastructure (e.g., storage and retrieval, encoding/decoding, display management and so forth). Timing considerations (i.e., synchronization), however, were not a significant issue because the media did not have a temporal component; therefore, best effort timing was adequate and utilized for simplicity.

Given the introduction of time-based media, however, best effort synchronization became insufficient. Aspects related to workstation processing (such as those associated with general purpose, multitasking operating systems) soon necessitated that more emphasis be placed on synchronization. Combined with the introduction of network technologies, distributed multimedia systems also required that data transfer be considered. Examples included managing latencies to facilitate interactivity and providing synchronization both internally (the actual media, both individually and with respect to each other) and externally (e.g., relative to different distributed endpoints and devices). Increasingly, these aspects needed to be considered in the context of complex multimedia scenarios consisting of multiple time-based media of different temporal characteristics (e.g., frame rates) coming from different sources, each with its own data transfer characteristics (e.g., network QoS).

The evolution of the expectations and execution context for multimedia systems has paralleled its growing pervasiveness and increased integration into wider computational, communication and collaborative systems. Originally, multimedia functionality was realized solely by dedicated applications and multimedia synchronization addressed a variety of fundamental topics, ranging from taxonomies [6-7] and modeling [8-11] to formal specification methods [12-13], algorithms [14-16] and software architectures [17-20]. While such topics still offer challenges and research issues, the contemporary approach to multimedia synchronization is as an infrastructural service, used and configured by applications and other system layers as required [21-22]. As such, synchronization services need to interface with lower-level devices and system layers while also responding to higher-level applications issues. In the context of a networked environment, the source (e.g., server), the receiver (e.g., client application) and the infrastructure (e.g., operating system, storage, network, middleware, etc.) all need to be taken into account, both in terms of classic distributed system issues as well as multimedia-specific considerations.

The Axes of Synchronization

The three axes of content, space and time provide a useful way to categorize the "organization" of multimedia information. Within the literature, the term multimedia synchronization addresses each of these dimensions. In contemporary practice, however, multimedia synchronization typically refers to the temporal axis while issues of space and content are more commonly addressed under the terms "layout" and "content management."

Spatial synchronization [23-25] refers to the physical arrangement (i.e., layout) of multimedia objects and the corresponding relationships between them on a particular output device (e.g., display monitor). Conversely, *content synchronization* [26] refers to the maintenance of a media object's relationship to (dependency on) a particular piece of data. Content synchronization can be seen as part of a larger topic known as *content management*, the managing of electronic content throughout its lifecycle, ranging from creation and storage to dissemination and destruction. The premise is that the media content can exist as independent components within the content management system and then be "assembled" into presentations at "run time."

Temporal synchronization [1, 3, 6-7, 23-25] refers to the maintenance of temporal relationships between media. For example, consider the classic "lip sync" relationship between the audio/video of someone speaking, or the animated "build" of a typical PowerPoint slide. For the audio/video pairing, if the media are not synchronized (i.e., the temporal relation is not maintained), their intended meaning can be degraded to the point of being completely lost. In the case of the animated slide build, the clarity of the presentation is often determined by the appropriate ordering, timing and layout of objects on the slide. Therefore, should any of these aspects (e.g., ordering or timing) be incorrect, the slide can become difficult to understand, or possibly even convey incorrect information. Consequently, the specification, characterization and facilitation of such temporal relationships can be an important but involved effort.

With these issues in mind, the rest of this article will discuss the various facets of temporal synchronization, the de facto reference for multimedia synchronization.

Temporal Synchrony: Basic Constructs

In the nomenclature traditionally associated with multimedia synchronization [6], independent media entities are generally known as *media* (or *multimedia*) *objects*. To more clearly identify media types, classifications are used to identify particular objects (e.g., a video object). By virtue of objects having variable durations, each is divided into a sequence of (one or more) informational units for purposes of synchronization. These subdivisions are usually known as *Logical Data Units* (LDUs). For example, an image would consist of a single LDU while a video object would consist of multiple LDUs, typically known as "frames."

To meet the needs of modern multimedia environments, synchronization between media objects must consider relationships between time-dependent (i.e., time-based) media objects and time-independent (i.e., non-time-based) media objects. Time-dependent media are referred to as *continuous* media while time-independent media objects are known as *discrete*. A discrete medium has a single LDU while a continuous media consists of a series of LDUs which are isochronous (i.e., regularly spaced) in nature. Consequently, continuous media objects are often characterized (and abstracted) as a *media stream*. Playback of a media stream therefore constitutes rendering its LDUs in sequence and at the appropriate time. The terms object and stream are generally used interchangeably, with the choice usually being context (e.g., medium and activity) dependent.

To convey the meaning of a particular medium, its individual temporal requirements must be met. For example, a video object must be played back at the appropriate frame rate. Additionally, those media objects used in combination must also consider the temporal requirements of their composite group. For example, a presentation may specify the concurrent display of a text string with a video clip for n seconds, followed by an image. Enabling such a presentation requires specifying the temporal relationships between the media objects as well as deriving their playback schedule [27-28]. Furthermore, to ensure that playback conforms to the schedule, a synchronization mechanism must be used to enforce it. Large-grain synchrony at an object level must therefore be provided in order to correctly begin playback. Media objects within a presentation, however, may have different temporal dimensions (i.e., continuous vs. discrete). Therefore, the synchronization mechanism must support multiple synchronization granularities so that continuous media can also be rendered correctly. The combination of media objects with differing synchronization characteristics has been characterized as a *multisynchronous space* [29].

To address such a mix of synchronization characteristics, multimedia synchronization is typically classified in relation to the number of media objects within a temporal relationship as well as their temporal dimension:

- intra-stream vs. inter-stream
- event vs. continuous

Intra-stream synchronization (or continuity) refers to synchronization internal to a media stream; i.e., exercising the flow of data within a single stream so that it is played back correctly. Conversely, *inter-stream synchronization* refers to the synchronization between independently running media streams; i.e., aligning the playback of two or more streams. These categories refer to synchronization autonomy, be that within a single stream or between multiple ones.

Event synchronization denotes the alignment of a media object's start to a specific time or event; for example, the display of an image when the background music starts or the execution of an action in response to a hyperlink being navigated (i.e., "clicked"). *Continuous synchronization*, however, refers to the fine-grain synchrony required by continuous media within the duration of the object. For a continuous medium, continuous synchronization is the means by which intra-stream synchronization (continuity) is achieved. The result is the typical isochronous rhythm associated with continuous media. Conversely, the classic "lip sync" problem between audio and video streams is an illustration of continuous inter-stream synchronization. Of course, for continuous inter-stream synchronization to be realized, it is assumed that each stream has also been intra-stream synchronized.

Another classification scheme refers to the artificiality of the temporal relationships within or between streams. Specifically, the categorization of *live* vs. *synthetic* refers to the *mode* [29] of a medium in two distinct but related ways: (1) its stored vs. non-stored source; and (2) how its temporal aspects were determined. In terms of its source, media mode refers to whether the object is being captured "live" in real-time from a real-world sensor (e.g., camera, microphone, etc.). Conversely, synthetic refers to those media which are being retrieved from secondary storage, even though they may have originally been captured "live" and then stored. Such differences directly impact on the approaches (e.g., mechanisms) used to control synchronization within a system, such as buffering techniques and the ability to defer data retrieval. The second interpretation of mode refers to how the temporal aspects of a medium were determined. Specifically, live synchronization attempts to reproduce the temporal relations that (naturally) existed during the capture process. On the contrary, synthetic synchronization utilizes temporal relations that are artificially specified. The combination of synthetic and live synchronization in a single environment has been referred to as *mixed mode synchrony* [29].

Various traditional synchronization issues are also relevant within a multimedia context, such as timeliness, precision, granularity, causality [30-31] and paradigm [32]. For example, timeliness applies to many levels within a multimedia system, including network QoS and the availability of LDUs at display devices. Variations from the appropriate times result in asynchrony and can lower system quality as perceived by the user. Timeliness is also necessary to achieve natural and fluid communication between participants in conversational and interactive environments. However, pin-point precision is not always required in order to preserve semantics; rather, a tolerable degree of asynchrony at the user interface is acceptable. Consider the two well-known and classic cases of lip synchronization (or "lip sync") and pointer synchronization [33]. The first refers the alignment of the audio and video tracks of a human speaking, while the second refers to the placement of the (mouse) pointer over an image relative to accompanying audio data. The importance of lip synchronization is crucial to ensuring people's level of comfort and attention within real-time conferencing, or any system involving vocal accompaniment to "speaking" visuals. In particular, the audio/video tracks in the traditional "lip sync" scenario must render their corresponding LDUs within 80ms in order to appear synchronized; otherwise, user comprehension is degraded. Similarly, "pointer lag" must be bounded in order for the user to relate its action to the audio commentary. Indeed, Steinmetz's seminal work [33] on measuring human tolerances to asynchrony for different media combinations in different visual alignments (e.g., "talking heads") continues to serve as an empirical baseline for system design and performance.

Temporal Synchrony: Basic Mechanics

Beyond the abstractions, constructs and frameworks to describe multimedia synchronization requirements, there is the need to address the mechanisms to implement them. Primarily, this issue involves three questions: (1) what kind of mechanisms are required; (2) where should the mechanisms be placed; and (3) what are their implementation considerations.

Two general techniques (mechanisms) were proposed in [34]: synchronization markers and synchronization channels. Synchronization markers function as tags (akin to timestamps) by which media streams can correlate their temporal position during rendering. These tags effectively mark off sections of the media stream and could be transmitted as part of a raw data stream or generated externally and imposed on the data stream. For example, a video clip could be transmitted as individual frames with inter-frame markers inserted between each frame; the SMPTE (Society of Motion Picture and Television Engineers) code used by high-end video equipment is an example of synchronization markers that are embedded within each video frame itself. The use of synchronization channels is designed to isolate the control to a separate communications channel running in parallel to the data stream. The control information within the synchronization channel contains references to the data transmitted in data-only channels, directing the synchronization mechanism at the receiver as to how to align the data.

Numerous approaches [9, 17, 18, 20, 22, 35, 36] to media synchronization within presentational systems can be found in the literature. In general, the underlying mechanisms can be characterized as follows:

- Layered construction: Synchronization is addressed at multiple stages, using different entities and mechanisms to correct asynchrony as it becomes noticeable (e.g., the network and playback levels, within and between streams, etc.).
- Object abstraction: Media data and system components are modeled as independent but interacting objects.
- Event synchronization enabled through scheduling: Coarse-grain event-level synchronization is facilitated by using scheduled media object playback times. The specification of the scenario's timeline can either mimic a real situation or be completely artificial.

- Continuous synchronization enabled through fine-grain temporal intervals: Fine-grain continuous synchronization is achieved through the division of a media object into a series of small temporal sub-divisions which are individually aligned to their correct playback time.

In contrast, conversational systems tend to rely more on protocol-based techniques [2, 37-41]. Well-known examples include MBONE tools such as *ivs*, *vat* and *rat* [40], which are based on the RTP (Real-Time Protocol) protocol [41]. In these systems, the synchronization mechanism is a protocol engine ensuring that the media data conforms to the protocol. Such an approach is in contrast to presentational systems in which the synchronization mechanism ensures the data conforms to an external specification (i.e., the presentation's timeline). In conjunction with the protocol-oriented approach, conversational systems also tend to use the stream-oriented abstraction and media playback is generally intended to reflect the temporal characteristics of the media as obtained during the capture process.

In tandem with the selection of the kind of synchronization mechanism, there is also the question of where to place the synchronization mechanism. Within a distributed multimedia system, there are basically three possible locations: the media source, the receiving site and the intervening network.

<u>Synchronization at the source</u> (e.g., server) implies that data is synchronized before transmission to the receiving site. Consequently, the temporal relationships imposed prior to transmission must be maintained during transmission and up until playback at the receiving site. A fundamental assumption of this method is that all the media to be synchronized are located at the same source and can be "wrapped up" or multiplexed into a single data stream. However, these assumptions may not always be realistic, desirable or amenable to the system in question. Furthermore, this technique implies an intelligent source that is knowledgeable about the media it is providing and well as its intended use at the receiver. Should source synchronization techniques be employed with multiple sources, there will still be the need to provide an additional coordination layer at the sink(s) to align the separate incoming streams.

<u>Synchronization at the receiving site</u> (i.e., client or sink) enforces the required temporal constraints on each media stream after it is received from its source over the network. This kind of synchronization mechanism allows each media stream to originate from its own source and does not require any inter-stream management by the network. However, it can place a large processing burden on the receiver and provides (as with source-based synchronization) a solitary approach to the synchronization of media and their interactions. For those systems consisting of multiple receiving sites, there is also the need to ensure coordination between the sites as well as synchronization at each one. *Synchronization within the network* was traditionally viewed as a protocol-based approach that formed an elaborate "hand-shaking" mechanism with precisely defined timing [34]. As such, it proved a complex technique that was network-dependent and prohibitively difficult when a large number of media streams became involved. As with source-based synchronization, this technique also assumed an intelligent source and a receiving site

that will do nothing that could somehow induce asynchrony between the streams. The latter assumption is completely unrealistic in terms of contemporary computing reality.

The prime difficulty with the above categorization is the implicit notion that the mechanisms would be used in isolation. An additional problem is that it assumes the "old-style" computer vs. network model: the source and sink are the computational entities while the network is a "dumb" transport agent. However, by employing a combination of mechanisms deployed at various parts of the distributed system (e.g., source, sink and network), the complexity and overhead of synchronization can be amortized throughout the system. It also allows more flexibility in what kinds of synchronization aspects are dealt with at the various locations. The ability to combine these approaches has been augmented by the development of intelligent, service-based networks, allowing synchronization to be transformed into a network service using computationally-enabled "smart" communications systems [29]. These and other implementation considerations need to be addressed in terms of how actual technological choices (ranging from operating system to design practices) can influence the ability to provide synchronization within a multimedia environment. Some of these aspects are addressed in the companion article on infrastructure and engineering.

See: Authoring and Specification; Infrastructure and Engineering

References

1. R. Steinmetz, "Synchronization Properties in Multimedia Systems," IEEE Journal on Selected Areas in Communications, Vol. 8, No. 3, 1990, pp. 401 – 412.
2. L. Ehley, B. Furht, and M. Ilyas, "Evaluation of Multimedia Synchronization Techniques," Proceedings of the IEEE Conference on Multimedia Computing and Systems, Boston, Massachusetts, 1994, pp. 514 – 519.
3. M. Haindl, "Multimedia Synchronization," Technical Report CS-R9538, Department of Computer Science/Interactive Systems, CWI, 1995.
4. N. D. Georganas and R. Steinmetz (Eds.), "IEEE Journal on Selected Areas in Communications – Special Issue: Synchronization Issues in Multimedia Communication", Vol. 14, No. 1, 1996.
5. B. Prabhakaran, "Multimedia Synchronization," Handbook of Multimedia Computing, (Ed., B. Furht), CRC Press, 1999.
6. T. Meyer, W. Effelsberg, and R. Steinmetz, "A Taxonomy on Multimedia Synchronization," Proceedings of the 4th IEEE International Workshop on Future Trends in Distributed Computing Systems, Lisbon, Portugal, 1993, pp. 97 – 103.
7. G. Blakowski and R. Steinmetz, "A Media Synchronization Survey: Reference Model, Specification and Case Studies," IEEE Journal on Selected Areas in Communications, Vol. 14, No. 1, 1996, pp. 5 – 35.
8. J. F. Allen, "Maintaining Knowledge About Temporal Intervals," Communications of the ACM, Vol. 26, No. 11, 1983, pp. 832 – 843.
9. S. Gibbs, C. Breiteneder, and D. Tsichritzis, "Data Modeling of Time-Based Media," Proceedings of the 1994 ACM SIGMOD International Conference on Management of Data, 1994, pp. 91 – 102.

10. B. Prabhakaran and S. V. Raghavan, "Synchronization Models for Multimedia Presentation with User Participation," Multimedia Systems, Vol. 2, No. 2, 1994, pp. 53 – 62.
11. Y. Y. Al-Salqan and C. K. Chang, "Temporal Relations and Synchronization Agents," IEEE Multimedia, Vol. 3, No. 2, 1996, pp. 30 – 39.
12. J.-P. Courtiat, R. C. de Oliveira, and L. F. R C. Carmo, "Towards a New Multimedia Synchronization Mechanism and its Formal Specification," ACM International Conference on Multimedia, 1994.
13. H. Bowman, H. Cameron, P. King, and S. Thompson, "Mexitl: Multimedia in Executable Interval Temporal Logic," Formal Methods in System Design, Vol. 22, No. 1, 2003, pp. 5 – 38.
14. T. V. Johnson and A. Zhang, "Dynamic Playout Scheduling Algorithms for Continuous Multimedia Streams," Multimedia Systems, Vol. 7, No. 4, 1999, pp. 312 – 325.
15. S. Ramanathan and P. Rangan, "Feedback Techniques for Intra-Media Continuity and Inter-Media Synchronization in Distributed Multimedia Systems," The Computer Journal – Special Issue on Distributed Multimedia Systems, Vol. 36, No. 1, 1993, pp. 19 – 31.
16. W. Liao and V. O. K. Li, "Synchronization of Distributed Multimedia Systems with User Interactions," Multimedia Systems, Vol. 6, No. 3, 1998, pp. 196 – 206.
17. D. P. Anderson and G. Homsy, "A Continuous Media I/O Server and Its Synchronization Mechanism," IEEE Computer, Vol. 24, No. 10, 1991, pp. 51 – 57.
18. S. Gibbs, "Composite Multimedia and Active Objects," OOPSLA'91, Phoenix, Arizona: ACM Press, 1991, pp. 97 – 112.
19. T. D. C. Little and A. Ghafoor, "Synchronization and Storage Models for Multimedia Objects," IEEE Journal on Selected Areas in Communications, Vol. 8, No. 3, 1990, pp. 413 – 427.
20. M. Woo, N. U. Qazi, and A. Ghafoor, "A Synchronization Framework for Communication of Pre-orchestrated Multimedia Information," IEEE Network, Vol. 8, No. 1, 1994, pp. 52 – 61.
21. M. Muhlhauser and J. Gecsei, "Services, Frameworks and Paradigms for Distributed Multimedia Applications," IEEE Multimedia, Vol. 3, No. 3, 1996, pp. 48 – 61.
22. A. Campbell, G. Coulson, F. Garcia, and D. Hutchinson, "Orchestration Services for Distributed Multimedia Synchronization, "Technical Report MPG-92-52, Distributed Multimedia Research Group, University of Lancaster, 1992.
23. S. Gibbs, L. Dami and D. Tsichtritzis, "An Object Oriented Framework for Multimedia Composition and Synchronization," Multimedia – Principles, Systems and Applications, (Ed., L. Kjelldahl), Springer, 1991.
24. T. D. C. Little and A. Ghafoor, "Spatio-Temporal Composition of Distributed Multimedia Objects for Value-Added Networks," IEEE Computer, Vol. 24, No. 10, 1991, pp. 42 – 50.
25. M. Iino, Y. F. Day, and A. Ghafoor, "An Object-Oriented Model for Spatial-Temporal Synchronization of Multimedia Information," Proceedings of the IEEE International Conference on Multimedia Computing and Systems, 1994, pp. 110 – 120.
26. C. D. Cranor, R. Ethington, A. Sehgal, D. Shur, C. Sreenan, and J. E. van der Merwe, "Design and Implementation of a Distributed Content Management System," Proceedings of the 13th International Workshop on Network and Operating Systems

Support for Digital Audio and Video, (Eds., C. Papadopoulos and K. Almeroth), Monterey, California: ACM Press, 2003, pp. 4 – 11.

27. K. S. Candan, B. Prabhakaran, and V. S. Subrahmanian, "Retrieval Schedules Based on Resource Availability and Flexible Presentation Specifications," ACM Multimedia Systems Journal, Vol. 6, No. 4. 1996, pp. 232 – 250.

28. A. Karmouch and J. Emery, "A Playback Schedule Model for Multimedia Document," IEEE Multimedia, Vol. 3, No. 1, 1996, pp. 50 – 63.

29. R. W. Robbins, "Facilitating Intelligent Media Space Collaboration via RASCAL: The Reflectively Adaptive Synchronous Coordination Architectural Framework," PhD Thesis, School of Information Technology and Engineering, University of Ottawa, 2001.

30. L. Lamport, "Time, Clocks and the Ordering of Events in a Distributed System," Communications of the ACM, Vol. 21, No. 7, 1978, pp. 558 – 565.

31. J.-P. Courtiat, L.F.R.C. Carmo, and R. C. de Oliveira, "A General-Purpose Multimedia Synchronization Mechanism Based on Causal Relations," IEEE Journal on Selected Areas in Communications, Vol. 14, No. 1, 1996, pp. 185 – 195.

32. S. Greenberg and D. Marwood, "Real-Time Groupware as a Distributed System: Concurrency Control and its Effect on the Interface," Research Report 94/534/03, Department of Computer Science, University of Calgary, 1994.

33. R. Steinmetz, "Human Perception of Jitter and Media Synchronization," IEEE Journal on Selected Areas in Communications, Vol. 14, No. 1, 1996, pp. 61 – 72.

34. P. Leydekkers and B. Teunissen, "Synchronization of Multimedia Data Streams in Open Distributed Environments," Proceedings of the 2nd International Workshop on Network and Operating System Support for Digital Audio and Video, (Ed., R. G. Herrtwich), Heidelberg, Germany: Springer-Verlag, 1991, pp. 94 – 104.

35. T. D. C. Little and F. Kao, "An Intermedia Skew Control System for Multimedia Data Presentation," Proceedings of the 3rd International Workshop on Network and Operating System Support for Digital Audio and Video, (Ed., P. V. Rangan), La Jolla, California: Springer-Verlag, 1992, pp. 130 – 141.

36. R. W. Robbins, "A Model for Multimedia Orchestration," M. Sc. Thesis, Department of Computer Science, University of Calgary, 1995.

37. T.D.C. Little and A. Ghafoor, "Multimedia Synchronization Protocols for Broadband Integrated Services," IEEE Journal on Selected Area in Communications, Vol. 9, No. 12, 1991, pp. 1368 – 1382.

38. I. F. Akyildiz and W. Yen, "Multimedia Group Synchronization Protocols for Integrated Services Networks," IEEE Journal on Selected Areas in Communications, Vol. 14, No. 1, 1996, pp. 162 – 173.

39. C.-M.Huang and R.-Y.Lee, "Achieving Multimedia Synchronization Between Live Video and Live Audio Streams Using QoS Controls," Computer Communications, Vol. 19, No. 5, 1996, pp. 456 – 467.

40. V. Hardman, M. A. Sasse, and I. Kouvelas, "Successful Multi-Party Audio Communication over the Internet," Communications of the ACM, Vol. 41, No. 5, 1998, pp. 74 – 80.

41. H. Schulzrinne, S. Casner, R. Frederick, and V. Jacobson, "RTP: A Transport Protocol for Real-Time Applications," Request for Comments rfc1889, 1996.

MULTIMEDIA SYNCHRONIZATION – INFRASTRUCTURE AND ENGINEERING

Wayne Robbins
Defense R&D Canada (DRDC), Future Forces Synthetic Environments,
DRDC Ottawa; Ottawa, Ontario, Canada

Definition: *Multimedia systems rely on a wide variety of infrastructural technologies to enable their communication, processing, and interface/display needs.*

In addition, particular classes of media (e.g., continuous media such as audio and video) often require special computational support to ensure their correct rendering. As such, different categories of infrastructure can be defined as to how systems enable and influence synchronized media playback. These include: operating and real-time systems, middleware and networking, database and data management as well as system and software engineering.

Operating and Real-Time Systems

The operating system (OS) [1-5] is a key element in multimedia synchronization due its fundamental infrastructural role within end-user and network equipment. Specifically, a number of OS issues can cause significant impact in situations where continuous media are utilized. Such time-sensitive data, typically large in volume and isochronous in nature, often require significant computing power to provide a responsive system with predictable behavior. Specific issues which need to be considered include:

- Process Management
- Time Management
- Memory Management
- Inter-Process Communication (IPC)
- Resource and Device Management
- User Interface and Display Management

Process management addresses the area of process (program) execution and processor allocation. For continuous time-based media, predictable processing is required to ensure media readiness for display in accordance with its isochronous nature. Relevant process management issues therefore include scheduling algorithms and priority mechanisms, such that inappropriate scheduling and misuse of priorities can introduce asynchrony into a multimedia application due to inappropriate delays in processing (e.g., other applications "grabbing" the processor).

Time management addresses the issue of whether the OS can both ensure adequate temporal accuracy for application-level synchronization efforts as well as if the OS itself can operate in a timely and synchronized manner. Included in this area are issues of clock management as well the availability of synchronization primitives (for process and resource/device management).

<u>Memory management</u> addresses how the OS controls memory allocation and applications' access to memory spaces. Memory protection, virtual memory (VM), shared vs. non-shared models, dynamic vs. static allocation and automatic garbage collection (in conjunction with certain language/run-time environments) falls in this category. These issues influence media synchronization by affecting data transfer between applications and devices as well as possibly inducing asynchrony into process execution due to automatic system overhead (e.g., use of VM swap files and automatic "cleanup" techniques sometimes associated with dynamic memory/resource allocation).

<u>Inter-Process Communication (IPC)</u> plays a significant role in multimedia synchronization due to the potential to incur delays when transferring large amounts of data between processes. Delays can result from both the data duplication itself but also the incidental (and often hard-to-determine) costs of process management (context switching) and memory management overhead. The result is unexpected and undeterministic delays within the operating system's own execution which (then) ultimately affect the multimedia application.

<u>Resource management</u> refers to how the operating system provides and controls access to any resource (e.g., piece of hardware/software construct). *Device management* specifically refers to the appropriate means to control and facilitate data flow to/from devices; multimedia-oriented examples include capture and rendering devices, hardware codecs, storage and communication equipment and so forth. Because multimedia applications require the timely delivery of data to end-users, devices must enable fine-grain data and control flow in order to ensure asynchrony is not introduced at the final stages just prior to being rendered to the user. Similarly, when media are generated in real-time, any asynchrony resulting from the capture process (i.e., via input devices) can create timing errors which may affect data flow and be difficult to account for in subsequent processing.

<u>User interface and display management</u> issues are also important to multimedia synchronization in much the same way as device management. That is, the display management and user interface subsystems need to provide low-overhead rendering and user interaction with multimedia components. Slow rendering times and unresponsive user interfaces are not viable for time-based media or interactive systems. It is also important to consider the affects of manipulating the visual data (vis-à-vis the aforementioned OS issues) and how synchronization methodologies are compatible with user interaction (e.g., mouse pointer synchronization) [6].

The previous discussion illustrates that multimedia synchronization can be intimately affected by a system's low-level infrastructure. As such, many of these requirements can best addressed in the context a *real-time system* [7] – one whose correct operation depends both on its logical results as well as the temporal properties of its behavior. Such systems are typically characterized as deterministic, with the ability to provide timely responses and flexible scheduling abilities while also providing for security, fault tolerance and robustness. Classic examples include factory robot control and avionic subsystems.

Consequently, the key to real-time systems is highly accurate, temporal predictability; therefore, real-time systems are not necessarily fast but "temporally pedantic," since early event occurrence can be just as damaging as incurring delays. Characterized in Table 1, two classes of real-time systems are defined based on the severity of temporal errors, namely "hard" and "soft" real-time systems. Hard real-time systems are those in which any violation of a timing constraint is considered a system failure. Timely execution is guaranteed through resource allocation based on the worst-case situation, usually resulting in under-utilized resources during normal operation, possibly requiring complete system shutdown when any anomalies occur. Conversely, soft real-time systems are those in which a violation of a temporal constraint does not constitute a system failure.

Table 1. Real-Time System Classification Comparison

Aspect	Traditional Hard Real-Time	Multimedia Soft Real-Time
Data Characterization	Small, often local or with controlled distribution	Large amounts, often heavily distributed
Temporal Accuracy	Strict and static deadlines	Approximate and dynamic timelines
Error Severity	Worst case must be met	Quality of service considerations

Accordingly, multimedia systems are generally classified as soft real-time systems because their temporal performance requirements are usually not so restrictive; for example, asynchrony in a presentation may degrade its quality and annoy its viewers, but no physical damage results. The human-centric character of multimedia systems also facilitates a range of "acceptable" playback quality which varies with the media, the context of their use and ultimately, the individual users. Consequently, human perceptual limitations can be used to relax certain timing constraints, enabling a choice between which playback characteristics are most important and facilitating potential trade-offs between functionality and resource usage. Such an approach maps well to soft real-time systems, in which performance is not guaranteed by worst-case resource allocation. For example, if the "bandwidth" of a video channel is constrained to only 15fps at a specific resolution, the user could decide to accept the provided quality or adjust select parameters more aptly suit his/her needs.

Middleware and Networking

Middleware and networking are also important to multimedia synchronization in that they affect the delivery of media data between end (client) systems.

At a most basic level, the communications infrastructure must ensure data availability to enable synchronized rendering and timely user interaction. Typically, this issue is addressed by providing for a reasonable and ideally predictable quality of service (QoS). Therefore, network QoS can be seen as an enabler for "temporal composition" by which media can be assembled together and playback organized according to individual and group timing constraints. The provision of appropriate network and application level protocols also support synchronized data transfer (in cooperation with any provided QoS). A large body of work on protocols for multimedia synchronization exists [8-13], ranging from lower-level adaptive, feedback-based techniques to those provisioned at the application level, such as RTP (Real-Time Protocol) and RTCP (Real-Time Control Protocol). Additional network-oriented considerations include issues of data buffer management and protocol stack implementation which can impact on synchronization vis-à-vis the OS issues described above (e.g., data copying overhead).

Beyond the basic communications level, middleware [14-16] addresses the need to bridge network and client functionality through the provision of centrally-based services and abstractions. As such, middleware is a "glue" layer of software between the network and applications, intended to ease application programming, application integration and system management tasks while also promoting standardization and interoperability of services by lessening multiple, independently developed implementations. In terms of multimedia synchronization, middleware offers a logically centralized, service-oriented approach to synchronization (orchestration) logic. It also provides support for useful abstractions and constructs for communicating multimedia data, ranging from publish and subscribe models, to streams, flows, sources and sinks.

Database and Data Management

Database and data management [8, 17-19] are relevant to multimedia synchronization in how their design and implementation provide flexible and responsive data access. For aspects of spatial and content synchronization, issues of multimedia querying and multimedia data semantics (e.g., image analysis vs. keyword meta-descriptors) are of interest. For purposes of temporal synchronization, a broad array of other issues includes disk scheduling and storage models for particular classes of data (e.g., continuous media). This last aspect also includes how the fundamental database structure impacts the means by which the actual multimedia data is accessed; that is, do the media reside within the database itself (in which access is constrained to the database management system and query engine) or is the data stored independently on separate systems (and the database only contains references to the external data). Such design considerations must be accounted for due to two primary issues: (1) timing considerations in terms of media data retrieval strictly through the database and its overhead (e.g., the potential effects of multiple, concurrent database queries on the timeliness of continuous media streams); and (2) timing considerations in terms of database efficiency resulting from large data objects (such as video) and/or objects of variable and indeterminate size (e.g., how to represent live instances of media, such as a camera capture).

System and Software Engineering

System and software engineering issues are important to multimedia synchronization in how they can affect the real-time implementation of multimedia systems. To provide an actual real-time environment, systems must be appropriately engineered not only to facilitate the necessary structural and behavioral aspects of a system, but also to ensure inappropriate behavior is not inadvertently introduced and that any such anomalies can be corrected as required.

First, a system should be based on the appropriate hardware and software infrastructure, such as a QoS-enabled communication backbone and a real-time operating system. Systems based on inappropriate infrastructure risk reduced quality in the user experience due to unsuitable substrate behavior [20-21]. Second, system structure (both design and implementation) must provide a flexible and extensible architecture capable of real-time performance. This requirement includes using flexible architectural techniques and technologies, including middleware and component-oriented architectures, along with the appropriate programming interfaces, useful abstractions and developmental paradigms (such as object orientation). Third, the system, application and various software components should have the ability to monitor their behaviors [22-23] (i.e., the actual performance of its various components). This is a necessary step in creating a system which can adapt (i.e., "tune") itself to address structural or behavioral deficiencies. An example is a video system which provides the ability to dynamically change playback frame rate based on monitoring the degree of asynchrony that develops during playback. Doing so illustrates the benefit of building systems that address behaviors as first-class considerations and facilitate adaptive behavior management [24].

As a result of better engineering, the potential exists for more flexible and higher quality systems, based on the increased use of common multimedia infrastructures. The end result would be better interoperability and compatibility across the user community, ultimately aiding in the acceptance and continued growth of multimedia technology across broader audiences.

See: Multimedia Synchronization – Area Overview

References

1. T. M. Burkow, "Operating System Support for Distributed Multimedia Applications: A Survey of Current Research," Technical Report (Pegasus Paper 94-8), Faculty of Computer Science, University of Twente, 1994.
2. R. Steinmetz, "Analyzing the Multimedia Operating System," IEEE Multimedia, Vol. 2, No. 1. 1995, pp. 68 – 84.
3. M. Singhal and N. G. Shivaratri, "Advanced Concepts in Operating Systems: Distributed, Database and Multiprocessor Operating Systems," McGraw-Hill: New York, 1994.
4. R. Govindan and D. P. Anderson, "Scheduling and IPC Mechanisms for Continuous Media," Proceedings of the 13th ACM Symposium on Operating System Principles, ACM, 1991, pp. 68 – 80.
5. V. Baiceanu, C. Cowan, D. McNamee, C. Pu, and J. Walpole, "Multimedia Applications Require Adaptive CPU Scheduling," Technical Report, Department of Computer Science and Engineering, Oregon Graduate Institute of Science and Technology, 1996.
6. S. Greenberg and D. Marwood, "Real-Time Groupware as a Distributed System: Concurrency Control and its Effect on the Interface," Research Report 94/534/03, Department of Computer Science, University of Calgary, 1994.

7. S-T. Levi and A. K. Agrawala, "Real-Time System Design," McGraw-Hill: New York, 1990.

8. D. P. Anderson and G. Homsy, "A Continuous Media I/O Server and Its Synchronization Mechanism," IEEE Computer, Vol. 24, No. 10, 1991, pp. 51 – 57.

9. T. D. C. Little and A. Ghafoor, "Multimedia Synchronization Protocols for Broadband Integrated Services," IEEE Journal on Selected Area in Communications, Vol. 9, No. 12, 1991, pp. 1368 – 1382.

10. S. Ramanathan and P. Rangan, "Feedback Techniques for Intra-Media Continuity and Inter-Media Synchronization in Distributed Multimedia Systems," The Computer Journal, Vol. 36, No. 1, 1993, pp. 19 – 31.

11. I. F. Akyildiz and W. Yen, "Multimedia Group Synchronization Protocols for Integrated Services Networks," IEEE Journal on Selected Areas in Communications, Vol. 14, No. 1, 1996, pp. 162 – 173.

12. J. Escobar, C. Partridge and D. Deutsch, "Flow Synchronization Protocol," IEEE/ACM transactions on Networking, Vol. 2, No. 2, 1994, pp. 111 – 121.

13. H. Schulzrinne, S. Casner, R. Frederick and V. Jacobson, "RTP: A Transport Protocol for Real-Time Applications," Request for Comments rfc1889, 1996.

14. A. Campbell, G. Coulson, F. Garcia and D. Hutchinson, "Orchestration Services for Distributed Multimedia Synchronization," Technical Report MPG-92-52, Distributed Multimedia Research Group, University of Lancaster, 1992.

15. I. Herman, N. Correia, D. A. Duce, D. J. Duke, G. J. Reynolds, and J. Van Loo, "A Standard Model for Multimedia Synchronization: PREMO Synchronization Objects," Multimedia Systems, Vol. 6, No. 2, 1998, pp. 88 – 101.

16. S. Didas, "Synchronization in the Network-Integrated Multimedia Middleware (NMM)," Project Report, Universität des Saarlandes, Saarbrücken, 2002.

17. S. Marcus and V. S. Subrahmanian, "Foundations of Multimedia Database Systems," Journal of the ACM, Vol. 43, No. 3, 1990, pp. 474 – 523.

18. B. Özden, R. Rastogi, and A. Silberschatz, "The Storage and Retrieval of Continuous Media Data," Multimedia Database System: Issues and Research Direction (eds., V. S. Subrahmanian and S. Jajodia), New York: Springer-Verlag, 1996, pp. 237 – 261.

19. W. Klas and K. Aberer, "Multimedia and its Impact on Database System Architectures," Multimedia Databases in Perspective (Eds., P. M. G. Apers, H. M. Blanken, and M. A. W. Houtsma), Heidelberg, Germany: Springer-Verlag, 1997, pp. 31 – 61.

20. D. C. A. Bulterman and R. van Liere, "Multimedia Synchronization and Unix," Proceedings of the 2nd International Workshop on Network and Operating System Support for Digital Audio and Video (Ed. R. G. Herrtwich), Heidelberg, Germany: Springer-Verlag, 1991, pp. 108 – 119.

21. R. W. Robbins, "A Model for Multimedia Orchestration," M. Sc. Thesis, Department of Computer Science, University of Calgary, 1995.

22. J. A. Boucher and T. D. C. Little, "An Adaptive Real-time Software-Only Player for the MPEG-I Video Stream," Technical Report, Multimedia Communications Lab, Boston University, 1994.

23. F. Jahanian, "Run-Time Monitoring of Real-Time Systems," Advances in Real-Time Systems (ed., Sang H. Son), Prentice-Hall: Englewood Cliffs, 1995, pp. 435 – 460.

24. R. W. Robbins, "Facilitating Intelligent Media Space Collaboration via RASCAL: The Reflectively Adaptive Synchronous Coordination Architectural Framework," PhD

Thesis, School of Information Technology and Engineering, University of Ottawa, 2001.

MULTIMEDIA SYSTEM-ON-A-CHIP

Nigel C. Paver and Moinul H. Khan
Intel Corporation, Austin, Texas, USA

Definition: *Multimedia system-on-a-chip includes all components necessary to run contemporary multimedia applications; these components are a powerful processor, a SIMD coprocessor, SRAM memory, and a variety of interfaces.*

Introduction

Mobile multimedia is growing at a startling rate. This is fueling the trend toward rich multimedia and communications capabilities on mobile devices. End users in the handheld wireless market segment are demanding multimedia and communication experiences similar to those they enjoy on their desktop—but in a mobile setting. Video playback, multi-player gaming, and video conferencing are a few of the key applications driving the path to higher performance multimedia. The availability of more incoming multimedia data via wireless networks, camera sensors, and audio capture is feeding these ever hungry multimedia applications.

One of the biggest challenges for multimedia on mobile devices is to provide high performance with low power consumption. Playing a richly detailed 3D game on a phone or Personal Digital Assistant (PDA) can be highly enjoyable until the phone or PDA runs out of power. Another critical aspect of enabling multimedia on mobile devices is the availability of compelling applications and content. Providing a productive software design flow is the key to making this happen.

This article presents an architectural overview of the PXA27x processor family as a real world example of a multimedia system on a chip and the key components of the related embedded system.

A SoC for handheld Multi-media

In wireless and handheld platforms area, performance, power, and cost are key metrics for product success. The every shrinking form factor of cell phone and PDA devices is driving increasing levels of on-chip integration in state of the art application processors. The Intel® PXA27x processor family is an example of a highly integrated System-on-a-Chip (SoC) targeting wireless and handheld platforms. Figure 1 presents an overall block diagram of the Intel® PXA270 processor, and shows the Intel® XScale® microarchitecture and Intel® Wireless MMX™ SIMD coprocessor as key features. It also includes 256 KB of SRAM memories which is useful in video and graphics applications as a frame buffer. The PXA27x processor also provides multimedia components such as an LCD controller, camera interface, and a extensive set of peripheral interfaces such as UART, USB, AC97, SSP and I2S.

The level of integration provided in such a system on a chip is intended to provide the main elements required to support the application subsystem without unnecessary external components thus reducing the system component count.

The primary source of multimedia content on handheld devices is from onboard interfaces such as camera interfaces, audio devices, and content stored on removable media such as flash memory cards. The resolution of camera sensors in handheld platforms is evolving rapidly from VGA still image capture to megapixel resolutions more typically seen in digital cameras. The resolution and frame rate for video captured from the same sensors is following a similar growth path; today video can be encoded at QCIF (176×144) with QGVA and VGA resolutions on the roadmap for many product lines. The more pixels in an image or image sequence, the more computation power is required to process them.

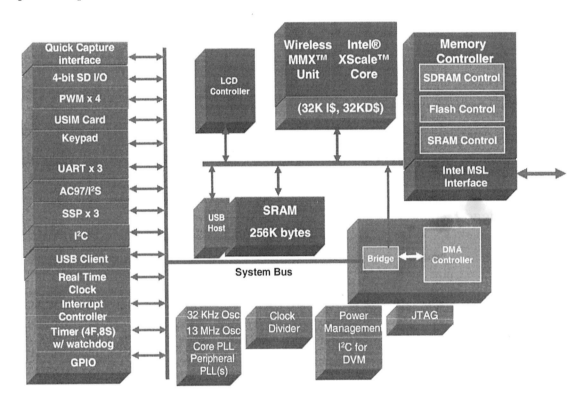

Figure 1. Intel® PXA270 processor block diagram.

The capacity of removable storage media is increasing today. 1-gigabyte cards are available today and 4 gigabyte and beyond are being introduced. With this amount of storage available it becomes possible to store many hours of VGA resolution video content. This is driving the need for an increase in both the computing power to process the VGA content and the power efficiency so that many hours of video can be viewed from a single battery charge. The increased capacity of the storage cards is also being utilized for audio content where many hundred of MP3 tracks may be stored. In this case power efficiency becomes critical to ensure playback time meets user expectations.

For a multi-media SoC it is important that interfaces are provided for the input and output of video data and also that enough critical memory card formats are supported.

Intel® XScale® Micro-architecture

The Intel XScale microarchitecture [27] is an implementation of the ARM[1] V5TE architecture [29,30,31]. The XScale core supports both dynamic frequency and voltage scaling with a maximum frequency today of 624 MHz. The design is a scalar, in-order single issue architecture with concurrent execution in 3 pipes that support out-of-order return. To support the frequency targets a 7-stage integer pipeline is employed with dynamic branch prediction supplied to mitigate the cost of a deeper pipeline. The memory subsystem contains 32 KByte instruction and data caches with corresponding 32 entries I translation look-aside buffer (TLB) and 32 entries D TLB. The memory subsystem also contains an eight entry write buffer that supports write coalescing and a four entry fill buffer to support multiple outstanding load operations.

Intel® Wireless MMX™ Architecture

Significant research effort and desktop processor development has been under-taken related to SIMD processing for media applications[1718,19,20]. Wireless MMX technology [22,23,24,25,26] integrates equivalent functionality to all of Intel® MMX™ technology [21] and the integer functions from SSE 18 to the Intel® XScale® microarchitecture 27[27]. Like MMX technology and SSE, Wireless MMX technology utilizes 64-bit wide SIMD instructions, which allows it to concurrently process up to eight data elements in a single cycle. This style of programming is well known to software developers.

Wireless MMX technology defines three packed data types (8-bit byte, 16-bit half word and 32-bit word) and the 64-bit double word. The elements in these packed data types may be represented as signed or unsigned fixed point integers. Using special SIMD instructions it is possible to operate on data elements in the packed format, where each data element is treated as an independent item.

It should be noted that, for multi-media acceleration other system level solution can be adopted, such as, dedicated HW acceleration solution. Trade-offs between these solutions are in terms of programmablity, cost and efficiency.

Multimedia Interfaces

The growing demand for multimedia processing on the converged platforms is driven by two primary factors. The first is the growing capability and resolution of the display devices. The second factor is the increasing supply of multimedia data arriving over the network and through onboard sensors such as cameras.

Cellular phone handsets in the past had very restricted display capabilities. This was limited to a few lines of monochrome text on a small LCD panel. The recent evolution in both display technology and available computing power is producing more advanced

---

1   Other names and brands may be claimed as the property of others

products with higher resolution displays. Figure 2 shows that the trend towards increasing resolution follows two tracks, depending on the physical size, or form factor of the product. The PDA form factor has historically been physically larger than a phone so has supported bigger display resolutions. Today quarter VGA (QVGA) displays (320×240 pixels) are common with VGA displays (640×480 pixels) emerging.

In the smaller physical form factor of the phone handset the common display resolution is around 176×144 size, with a trend towards QVGA (and ultimately VGA) as the data processing capabilities of the phone increase.

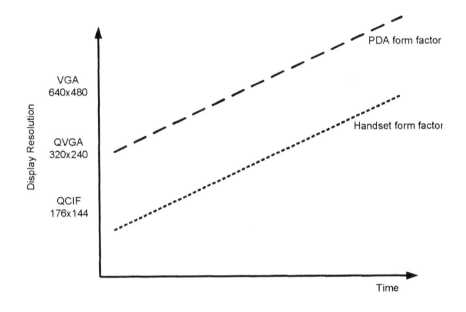

Figure 2. LCD form factor display resolution trends.

As the numbers of pixels in the display increases so does the processing power needed to calculate each pixel value. For example a VGA display typically takes four times the computation that a quarter VGA does to generate the content.

The ability to send, receive, and capture digital images and video has been one of the more important developments in the cell phone and PDA market segment in recent years. Management of data streams to image display and from capture resources becomes a necessary and critical aspect of the system design. Any inefficiency when dealing with video data streams has a direct impact on the user experience. The effect is often manifested with reduction in battery life and decreases in video frame rates and resolution. In order to address these issues, key multimedia features have been introduced with the PXA27x processor family. The features have been integrated with the multimedia interfaces used for image display and image capture.

There are a number of critical flows which target the LCD panel in handheld devices. These include the display of video data following decode for playback mode, the simultaneous display of two streams of video data used in a video conferencing mode, and also the display of a digital viewfinder stream when performing camera or camcorder functions. Figure 3 illustrates some possible multimedia streams.

The PXA27x processor family introduces both flexibility and coherency in the image display and capture peripherals. The quick capture interface provides the flexibility to connect to a wide variety of CMOS sensors using several possible interface options.

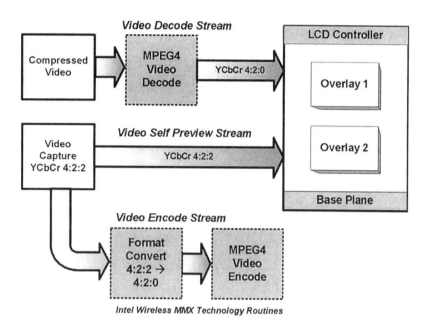

Figure 3. Possible video imaging scenarios.

In addition, image data formatting using Wireless MMX technology facilitates efficient processing and display using the LCD controller. The LCD controller also provides the ability to connect to a wide variety of LCD panels using a number of programmable options. The image data may be received in several different formats including various flavours of RGB and YCbCr.

Power Management

To support extended battery life Multimedia SoCs such as the the Intel® PXA27x processor family provide advanced power management. In the case of the PXA27x processor this power management is known as Wireless Intel® SpeedStep™ Technology. At the hardware level, the technology provides several power domains and modes. A dedicated PMU provides for interaction with the software control components of the system. The software components enable the hardware features to be integrated into embedded operating systems through performance and policy management strategies.

The PXA27x processor family supports six power modes. Three new power modes, Deep Idle, Standby, and Deep Sleep enhance the power management capabilities from previous designs[32].

The power modes are primarily differentiated by available functionality, total power consumption, and the amount of time to enter and exit a mode. As a function of workload and resource utilization, the device can transition between the power modes to minimze power consumption. Each of the six modes provide different levels of power consumption and resource availablity in addition to variation, the detail of each mode is provide in Table 1.

Table 1. Power States if the PXA27x processor family

Instruction	Description
Run	All internal power domains (chip areas powered by separately switched and regulated voltage sources). All clocks are enabled and running.
Idle	The clocks to the CPU core are gated off. Clock frequency (can be the highest available) will be delivered to the CPU upon recovery from Idle Mode. Recovery is triggered by interrupts.
Deep Idle	This mode is similar to Idle Mode except for it is at the lowest (13MHz) frequency.
Standby	All internal power domains are placed in their lowest power mode except the real-time clock and the oscillator. Both PLLs are disabled to save power. Recovery is via external means or internal events such as time delays.
Sleep	Similar to Standby Mode in preserving oscillator and real-time clock functionality, except PXA27x core power is turned off. Remaining domains, such as on-chip memory, are placed in a state-preserving low-power state. Recovery requires reboot.
Deep Sleep	Similar to Sleep Mode, except all clock sources are disabled. High- voltage supplies are disabled. All remaining power domains are powered directly from the backup battery so states are preserved. Recovery is via external means or internal events such as time delays. Recovery requires reboot.

It is not possible to move arbitratily form one state to the next but a number of well defined transtions between power states are supported that correspond to appropriate platform power states. The state transition diagram between the different modes is shown in Figure 4.

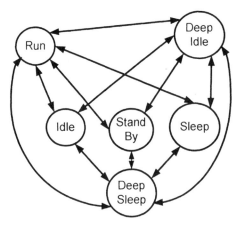

Figure 4. Power mode state transitions.

Effective usage of the Power management hardware can be achieved through a software level management solution. The PXA27x family offers a generic framework to implement the management policy. Information is extracted about the system level activity from the OS, application, user preference and various other sources to decide optimal voltage and frequency settings. The performance management unit (PMU) can be used to monitor different system level activities (i.e. CPI-cycles per instruction, cache- efficiency etc.), providing additional information for dynamic voltage and frequency management. The software power management framework is shown in Figure 5.

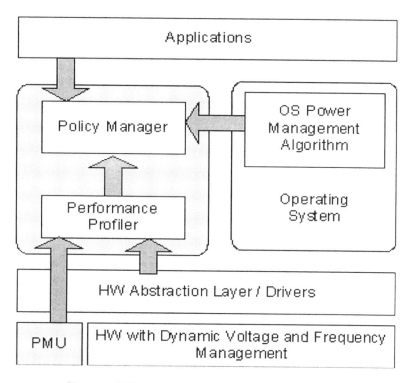

Figure 5. Power management framework.

There are two key components to the power manager software, the policy manager and the performance profiler. The policy manager receives task-level activity information (how many threads are running, or how often the processor is idle) from the OS. In addition, it can receive information from OS's own power manager. The policy manager decides the power mode in the system, such as, when should the system be in sleep or deep- sleep. When the system is in the run mode the policy manager performs dynamic voltage and frequency management based on the inputs from performance profiler. The performance profiler periodically samples performance monitoring event counters and determines frequency for the different components in the system (i.e. core-frequency, memory frequency, system communication fabric frequency). Based on the periodic profile information, if the current mix of application is computation bound, the core-frequency may be raised and similarly, if the application is memory bound, the memory controller frequency may be raised. On the other hand, as the thread-level activity reduces core and memory frequency can also reduced. Based on the chosen operating frequency the voltage is adjusted as well. The performance profiler also communicates with the software-drivers for different peripherals so that peripherals can be turned off/on based on the usage. The policy manager and performance manager co-ordinate these transition acitivies. Depending on the target platform the policy can be optimized in terms of transition thresholds, frequency changing steps and method of profiling. There are many possible algorithms to sue for power management and the best algorithm to use varies from one platform to the next.

System in a Package

As well as providing high levels of integration in the system on a chip there is also an opportunity to increase levels of integration by incorporating multiple silicon die in a single package. In small form factor platforms such as cell phone the multiple die at stacked on top of each other to provide what is known as stacked multi-chip package or MCP for short. The PXA27x processor family supports a number of configurations of stacked MCP with the other die in the package being memory. A key advantage of the stacked packages in phone and PDA applications is the saving in PCB real estate required to implement the platform. This in turn allows smaller form factor products to be created. Figure 6 shows an example of how such multi-chip stacked package may be constructed.

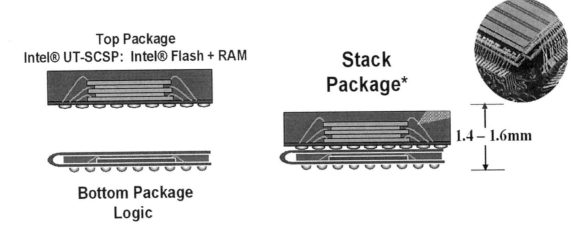

Figure 6. Example stacked MCP configuration.

See: LCD Display Interface, Image and Video Capture, SIMD processing, Intel XScale® Microarchitecture

References

17. A. Peleg and U. Weiser, "MMX Technology Extension to Intel Architecture," IEEE Micro, Vol. 16, No. 4, pp. 42-50, August 1996.

18. K. Diendroff, "Pentium III = Pentium II+ SSE," Micro Processors Report, Vol. 13, No. 3, pp. 6-11, March, 1999.

19. R. Lee, "Subword Parallelism in MAX-2," IEEE Micro, Vol. 16, No. 4, pp. 51- 59, August 1996.

20. M. Tremblay, et al. "VIS Speeds Media Processing," IEEE Micro, Vol. No. 4, pp. 10-20, August 1996.

21. U. Weiser, et al., "The Complete Guide to MMX™ Technology," McGraw-Hill, 1997, ISBN 0-07-006192-0.

22. N.C. Paver, B.A. Aldrich, and M.H. Khan, "Programming with Intel® Wireless MMX™ Technology: A Developer's Guide to Mobile Multimedia Applications," Hillsboro, OR, Intel Press, 2004.

23. M.H. Khan, N.C. Paver, B.A. Aldrich, and A. Hux, "Optimization Techniques for Mobile Graphics and Gaming Applications using Intel® Wireless MMX™ Technology," GSP 2004.

24. N.C. Paver et. al. "Accelerating Mobile Video with Intel® Wireless MMXTM Technology," Proceedings of the IEEE Workshop on Signal Processing Systems (SIPS), Aug 27-29, 2003.

25. N.C. Paver et. al., "Intel® Wireless MMX(TM) Technology: A 64-Bit SIMD Architecture for Mobile Multimedia," Proceedings of the International Conference on Acoustics, Speech, and Signal Processing (ICASSP), 2003.

26. B.A. Aldrich, N.C. Paver, M.H. Khan, and C.D. Emmons, "A Spatial Clustering Approach for Reduced Memory Traffic in Motion Estimation using Intel Wireless MMX™ Technology", Proceedings of the 8th World Multiconference on Systems, Cybernetics and Informatics (SCI 2004), July 2004.

27. Intel XScale(R) Core Developer's Manual, http://www.intel.com/ design/intelxscale/273473.htm

28. P. Kuhn, "Algorithms, Complexity Analysis and VLSI Architectures for MPEG-4 Motion Estimation," Kluwer Academic Press.

29. D. Seal, "Advanced RISC Machines Architecture Reference Manual," Prentice Hall, 1996.

30. S.B. Furber, "ARM System-on-Chip Architecture," Addison Wesley, 2000.

31. http://www.arm.com/aboutarm/55CE4Z/$File/ARM_Architecture.pdf.

32. http://developer.intel.com/design/pca/prodbref/253820.htm.

MULTIMEDIA WEB INFORMATION SYSTEMS

Lambros Makris and Michael G. Strintzis
Informatics and Telematics Institute, Thessaloniki Greece

Definition: *Multimedia Web information systems represent a whole new breed of information systems intended to process, store, retrieve, and disseminate information through the Internet using Web protocols.*

Since its inception the World Wide Web (WWW) has revolutionized the way people interact, learn and communicate. A whole new breed of information systems has been developed to process, store, retrieve, and disseminate information through the Internet using Web protocols. These systems are using hypertext to link documents and present any kind of information, including multimedia, to the end user through a Web browser. Web based information systems are often called Web Information Systems (WIS). A WIS, which uses multimedia as its key component, is a Multimedia Web Information System.

World Wide Web History

The notion of hypertext, small pieces of information interlinked with one another using active words or hotspots, was well defined before the introduction of the WWW. Vannevar Bush in 1945 [1] describes the Memex, a photo-electrical-mechanical device for memory extension which could make and follow links between documents on microfiche. In 1962 Doug Engelbart sets the foundation for an "oNLine System" (NLS) which does browsing and editing of interlinked information [2]. Ted Nelson in 1965 first uses the word "hypertext" in [3] to describe the ideas behind his Xanadu system. But it was not until 1989 when Tim Berners-Lee, while he was consulting for CERN – the European Organization for Nuclear Research located in Geneva, Switzerland – described a system of "linked information systems" [4] which he called the World Wide Web. Berners-Lee made a prototype, the WorldWideWeb browser (Figure 1), together with a special hypertext server to demonstrate the capabilities of his system.

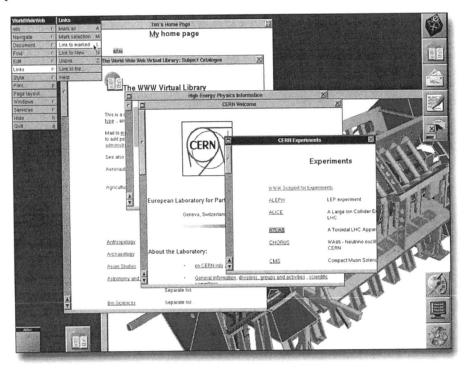

Figure 1. The first Web browser developed by Tim Berners-Lee (www.w3.org)
Copyright © 2005 World Wide Web Consortium, (MIT, ERCIM, Keio). All Rights Reserved.

The wide acceptance of the WWW came with NCSA Mosaic, a Web browser developed by Marc Andreessen and Eric Bina, at the National Center for Supercomputing Applications, University of Illinois, in 1993. NCSA Mosaic was originally written for X-Windows but it was later ported to the Windows and Macintosh platforms, thus making Mosaic the first multi-platform Web browser. The first commercial browsers, e.g. Netscape Communicator and Microsoft Internet Explorer, were mostly based on the source code of NCSA Mosaic but were wildly re-written while they were caught in the "Browser Wars" of mid-1995 to late 1996. By 1998 Netscape's market share, which once was more than 90%, evaporated, leaving Internet Explorer the unchallenged dominator for more than five years.

It was not until recently, when a new round has begun. Mozilla Firefox, the open-source descendant of Netscape Communicator, is offering standards compliance, a better security model and various other tidbits that make life easier for designers and users. Firefox, together with other browsers, such as Opera and Safari, now challenge the lead position of Internet Explorer cutting pieces off its share, and probably starting a new round of technological advancement for the WWW.

World Wide Web Protocols and Standards

The WWW was originally based on three simple ideas, the HyperText Transfer Protocol (HTTP) which is used to transmit information between a server (Web server) and a client (Web browser), the Uniform Resource Locator (URL) which identifies any file or document available on the Internet and the HyperText Markup Language (HTML) which is used to structure and format the hypertext documents. It was this simplicity that made WWW stand out of its competition – Gopher, Hyper-G, and WAIS to name a few – and survive on those early days of the information reform.

HTTP [5] is a simple protocol that allows easy exchange of documents, much like the File Transfer Protocol (FTP). HTTP defines how messages are formatted and transmitted between the server and the client, and what actions should be taken in response to the various commands. HTTP is a stateless protocol, which means that each request is completely independent with no relationship whatsoever to the requests that preceded it. This is not usually a problem for viewing statically generated pages but for applications that generate dynamic content (for example a shopping cart) it is extremely important to know what has happened previously. To the rescue came the cookies mechanism. Cookies allow a Web server to store small pieces of information on a user's machine and later retrieve it. They are embedded in the headers of the HTTP protocol flowing back and forth, identifying each request as coming from the same user.

Information on the WWW can be anything from HTML files to audio and video. Each piece of data is pinpointed by its URL [6]; the global address of documents and other resources on the WWW. URLs are strings that specify how to access network resources, such as HTML documents. A URL has, in general, the following form:

<scheme>://<user>:<password>@<host>:<port>/<url-path>

where <scheme> is the protocol that should be used to access the resource (e.g. ftp, http, file etc.), <user> and <password> is used for resources that need authentication, <host> is the name of the server which hosts the resource, <port> is the port on which the particular server is listening on, and <url-path> is data specific to the scheme (i.e. for http or ftp, url-path may be the complete path and filename to a file).

The URL solved a perpetual problem of information systems in networked environments. After its introduction, each and every file, executable and resource could be accurately addressed thus making possible the development of interlinked documents not necessarily bound to a particular system but rather able to include any widely used protocol. To wrap all that, Berners-Lee introduced HTML [7], a language which could be used to produce and present structured documents, but most of all a language which could include links to other resources – the foundation of the WWW.

HTML was not something new. It was actually an application of SGML (Standard Generalized Markup Language - ISO 8879) which is an international standard for defining structured document types and markup languages. HTML spared the complexity of SGML by defining a small set of rules which were easy to learn and could initially deliver what promised – a true universal way of building hypertext documents. But as in all other sides of the human life people got greedy. They wanted to get more out of its simplicity, and as a result the language was heavily abused. Tables were used to fake document layout, GIF graphics to create white space and typography effects and tags which were only meant to be used to convey the meaning of the document were used according to the way browsers rendered them. On top of that, HTML expanded without a plan, driven by the supply and demand of the market, which consequently leaded to the balkanization of the language. Users are familiar with browser incompatibilities which break document layout and often cause much frustration or even inability to access a particular document or site.

To battle this situation, the World Wide Web Consortium (W3C) was formed in 1994 as an industry consortium dedicated to building consensus around Web technologies [8]. In late 1997 HTML 4.0 was released as a W3C Recommendation bringing an end to vendors' "inventions" and hacks. HTML 4.0 added new features, such as the ability to include Cascading StyleSheets (CSS) for separation of content from structure, and the definition of the Document Object Model (DOM) which enabled more interactive pages through JavaScript. HTML 4.0 also included important features to make content more accessible to some users with disabilities. But standards conformance and accessibility, even now, is suffering from badly written browsers and design tools, "traditional" designers, and the millions of obsolete pages which are already in place.

A step forward is now being prepared as committed researchers are setting the foundations for a Semantic Web, an extension of the current Web, which will better convey information and meaning for both computers and people. XML (Extensible Markup Language) is used throughout this effort since it provides a basic syntax that is extensible and can describe any resource or data structure. The Semantic Web will provide the tools necessary for the development of breakthrough applications which will rely more on automated procedures rather than human interaction.

Multimedia on the World Wide Web

HTTP is built on top of TCP (Transmission Control Protocol) which guarantees correct delivery of data packets using acknowledgements, timeouts and retries. While this behavior may be desirable for documents and images it is not suitable for time-sensitive information such as video and audio. TCP imposes its own flow control and windowing schemes on the data stream, destroying the temporal relations between video frames and audio packets. On the other hand reliable message delivery is not required for video and audio, which can tolerate frame losses. For this reason the Real-time Transport Protocol

(RTP) [9], along with the Real Time Streaming Protocol (RTSP), were designed to stream media over computer networks.

Applications typically run RTP on top of UDP (User Datagram Protocol) to make use of its multiplexing and checksum services; however, RTP may be used with other suitable underlying network or transport protocols. RTP, despite its name, does not in itself provide for real-time delivery of multimedia data or other quality-of-service (QoS) guarantees, but relies on lower-layer services to do so. RTP combines its data transport with a control protocol (RTCP), which makes it possible to monitor data in order for the receiver to detect if there is any packet loss and to compensate for any delay jitter. Except RTP, other implementations also exist, which offer streaming audio and video for both unicast and multicast transmission.

Web Browsers, in general, do not have the inherent ability to play audio and video streams. This can be accomplished through special plug-ins, which establishes their own connections to servers and present multimedia within the flow of the hypertext document or in a separate window. Typically, these plug-ins use some form of the aforementioned RTP family of protocols to control their communication with the server and low-bit rate compression schemes to encode the audio and video streams. As network bandwidth to the end-user increases, applications such as video on demand, multimedia presentations, two-way multimedia communication etc. are becoming common place.

Another area which benefits from the ability of browsers to host third-party plug-ins is that of 3D applications (Figure 2).

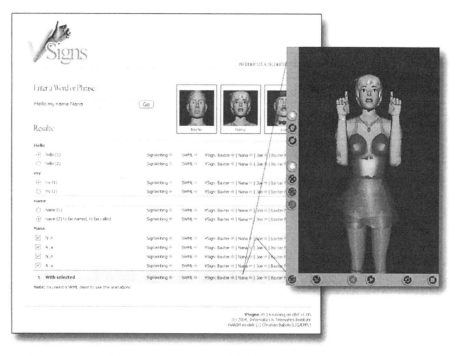

Figure 2. VSigns combines the power of Web and VRML to generate animation sequences from Sign Language notation, based on MPEG-4 Body Animation (vsigns.iti.gr).

Extensible 3D (X3D) [10], the successor to the Virtual Reality Modeling Language (VRML) [11], is an XML-based 3D file format which enables real-time communication of 3D data both for stand-alone and networked applications. X3D builds on top of VRML offering XML conformance and easier integration with other XML-based applications, a componentized approach which allows developers to support subsets of the specification (profiles), and better support for not only 3D data but also text, audio and video which, this way, can participate in complex 3D scenes. VRML and X3D scenes can be combined with web applications to form sophisticated systems that add a new dimension to human-computer interaction.

The Scalable Vector Graphics (SVG) [12] specification, on the other hand, deals with interactive and animated 2D data. Graphics created in SVG can be scaled without loss of quality across various platforms and devices. SVG is XML-based and scriptable through the SVG Document Object Model (DOM). Web applications using SVG can allow programmers to produce personalized graphics on-the-fly for users, which in-turn can modify this data on the client, or input their own data. Since text in SVG graphics is text and not some bitmap information, it can be searched normally, and localized with minimum effort. Finally the combination of SVG with the Synchronized Multimedia Integration Language (SMIL) [13] can produce animations of the SVG objects, with characteristics such as motion paths, fade-in or fade-out effects, and objects that grow, shrink, spin or change color.

Search and Retrieval of Multimedia for the World Wide Web

As the amount of multimedia data stored on the Web, keeps increasing, the problem arises of devising efficient methods for retrieving and employing it in the context of complex activities. The coexistence of information in various formats (i.e. Image, Video, Audio, and Text) and the fact that pieces of data relevant to a user's needs may exist in any of the aforementioned forms, potentially associated with each other, make evident the importance of information systems supporting querying and accessing of multimedia content.

Multimedia content-based access would put fewer burdens on the user, who would not have to repeat the query using a different tool for each of the desired media types, while at the same time would allow for the possible associations between information of various types to be exploited, thus making possible the maximization of the relevance of the returned results. Nevertheless, one should not neglect the possibility that most efficient search for one type of media may require a totally different approach than that required for another type of media, thus an attempt to integrate query methodologies may lead either to poor performance due to compromises being made or, alternatively, to excessive system or graphical user interface complexity, that could make the system hardly usable by the non-expert. Another technical barrier results from the expectations of the user for searching and filtering. Evidence [14] has shown that users consider high-level semantic concepts when looking for specific multimedia content. Typical high-level semantics include objects, people, places, scenes, events, actions and so forth, which are difficult to derive automatically from the multimedia data.

The very first attempts for multimedia retrieval were based on exploiting existing captions and surrounding text to classify visual and aural data to predetermined classes or to create a restricted vocabulary. Although relatively simple and computationally efficient, this approach has several restrictions; it neither allows for unanticipated queries nor can be extended easily. Additionally, such keyword-based approaches assume either the preexistence of textual annotation (e.g. captions) or that annotation using the predetermined vocabulary is performed manually. In the latter case, inconsistency of the keyword assignments among different indexers can also hamper performance.

To overcome the limitations of the keyword-based approach, the use of low-level indexing features has been proposed. Relevant items are retrieved by comparing the low-level features of each item in the database with those of a user-supplied sketch or, more often, a key-item that is either selected from a restricted set or is supplied by the user. This retrieval methodology is known as Query-by-Example. One of the first attempts to realize this scheme is the Query by Image Content (QBIC) [15] system (Figure 3). Other systems also exist [16], which use various proprietary indexing feature-sets.

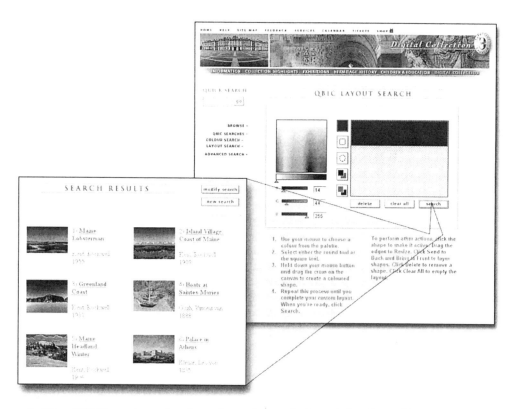

Figure 3. The QBIC system deployed on the website of the State Hermitage Museum (www.hermitagemuseum.org).

MPEG-7 [17], on the other hand, aims to standardize the description of multimedia content by defining a set of binary Descriptors and corresponding Description Schemes (DS), thus supporting a wide range of applications. The MPEG-7 DSs provide a way to describe in XML the important concepts related to audio-visual data in order to facilitate the searching, indexing and filtering of audio-visual data. The MPEG-7 reference software, known as XM (eXperimentation Model) implements a set of general descriptors (i.e. color, texture, shape, motion) which can be readily used to for multimedia search and retrieval. The SCHEMA Reference System [18] is an example of a web based system which uses the MPEG-7 XM for content-based information retrieval.

See: Markup Languages, Streaming Hypermedia, Multimodal Web Interfaces, Web Multimedia Databases

References

1. V. Bush, "As We May Think," The Atlantic Monthly, Vol. 176, No. 1, July 1945, pp. 101-108.
2. D.-C. Engelbart, "A Conceptual Framework for the Augmentation of Man's Intellect," Vistas in Information Handling, Howerton and Weeks (Eds.), Washington, D.C., Spartan Books, 1963, pp. 1-29.
3. T.-H. Nelson, "A File Structure for the Complex, The Changing and the Indeterminate," Proceedings of the 20th ACM National Conference, 1965, pp. 84-100.
4. T.-J. Berners-Lee, R. Cailliau, J.-F. Groff, and B. Pollermann, "World-Wide Web: An Information Infrastructure for High-Energy Physics," Proceedings of the Second International Workshop on Software Engineering, Artificial Intelligence and Expert Systems in High Energy and Nuclear Physics, 1992, pp. 157-164.
5. R. Fielding et al, "Hypertext Transfer Protocol – HTTP/1.1", RFC-2068, January 1997, updated by RFC-2616, June 1999.
6. T. Berners-Lee, L. Masinter, and M. McCahill, "Uniform Resource Locators (URL)," RFC-1738, December 1994.
7. D. Raggett, A. Le Hors, and I. Jacobs, "HTML 4.01 Specification," W3C Recommendation, December 1999.
8. I. Jacobs, "About the World Wide Web Consortium", http://www.w3.org/Consortium/.
9. H. Schulzrinne et al, "RTP: A Transport Protocol for Real-Time Applications," RFC-1889, January 1996.
10. ISO/IEC 19775:200x, "Extensible 3D (X3D)," Final Draft International Standard, 2003.
11. ISO/IEC 14772:1997, "The Virtual Reality Modeling Language (VRML)," 1997.
12. J. Ferraiolo, F. Jun, and D. Jackson (Eds.), "Scalable Vector Graphics (SVG) 1.1 Specification", W3C Recommendation, January 2003.
13. J. Ayars et al (Eds.), "Synchronized Multimedia Integration Language (SMIL 2.0) - [Second Edition]," W3C Recommendation, January 2005.
14. J.R. Smith, "Interoperable Content-based Access of Multimedia in Digital Libraries," DELOS Network of Excellence Workshop on "Information seeking, searching and querying in digital libraries," 2000.
15. M. Flickner, et al, "Query by image and video content: the QBIC system," Computer, Vol. 28, No. 9, pp. 23-32, 1995.
16. Y.A. Aslandogan and C.T Yu, "Techniques and systems for image and video retrieval," IEEE Transactions on Knowledge and Data Engineering, Vol. 11, No. 1, pp. 56-63, 1999.
17. ISO/IEC 15938:2002, "Multimedia Content Description Interface (MPEG-7)," 2002.

18. V. Mezaris, H. Doulaverakis, S. Herrmann, B. Lehane, N. O'Connor, I. Kompatsiaris, and M. G. Strintzis, "The SCHEMA Reference System: An Extensible Modular System for Content-Based Information Retrieval," Proceedings of the Workshop on Image Analysis for Multimedia Interactive Services (WIAMIS), 2005.

MULTIMODAL INTERFACES

Definition: *Multimodal interfaces process two or more combined user input modes, such as speech, pen, touch, manual gestures, and gaze, in a coordinated manner with multimedia system output.*

They are a new class of emerging systems that aim to recognize naturally occurring forms of human language and behavior, with the incorporation of one or more recognition-based technologies (e.g., speech, pen, vision). Multimodal interfaces represent a paradigm shift away from conventional graphical user interfaces. They are being developed largely because they offer a relatively expressive, transparent, efficient, robust, and highly mobile form of human-computer interaction. They represent users' preferred interaction style, and they support users' ability to flexibly combine modalities or to switch from one input mode to another that may be better suited to a particular task or setting.

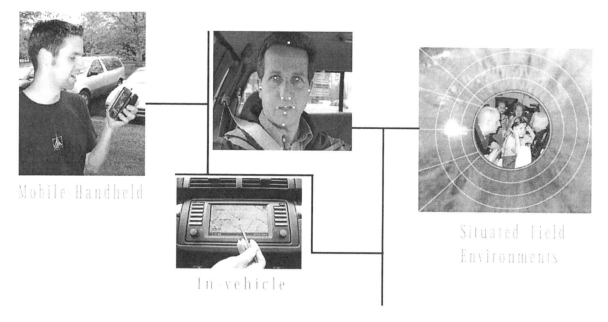

Figure 1. Multimodal interfaces for field and mobile use.

Multimodal systems have evolved rapidly during the past decade, with steady progress toward building more general and robust systems. Major developments have occurred in the hardware and software needed to support key component technologies incorporated in multimodal systems, in techniques for fusing parallel input streams, in natural language processing (e.g., unification-based integration), and in time-sensitive and hybrid architectures. To date, most current multimodal systems are bimodal, with the two most mature types involving speech and pen or touch input (Oviatt et al., 2000), and audio-visual input (e.g., speech and lip movements; Potamianos et al., 2004). However, these systems have been diversified to include new modality combinations such as speech and manual gesturing, and gaze tracking and manual input. Multimodal applications also range from map-based and virtual reality systems for simulation and training, to multi-biometric person identification/verification systems for security purposes, to medical, educational, and web-based transaction systems (Oviatt et al., 2000).

Given the complex nature of users' multimodal interaction, cognitive science has played an essential role in guiding the design of robust multimodal systems. The development of well integrated multimodal systems that blend input modes synergistically depends heavily on accurate knowledge of the properties of different input modes and the information content they carry, how multimodal input is integrated and synchronized, how users' multimodal language is organized, what individual differences exist in users' multimodal communication patterns, and similar issues (Oviatt, 2003). Prototyping of new multimodal systems also has depended heavily on the use of high-fidelity simulation methods.

Commercial activity on multimodal systems has included PDAs, cell phones, in-vehicle systems, and desktop applications for CAD and other application areas. Commercial systems typically do not include parallel processing of two semantically rich input modes delivered together by the user, and those that are not fusion-based systems but instead process just one mode alternative at a time. In contrast, for over a decade research-level multimodal systems have included fusion-based processing of two parallel input streams that each conveys rich semantic information (Oviatt et al., 2000). Such systems can support mutual disambiguation of input signals. Mutual disambiguation involves recovery from unimodal recognition errors within a multimodal architecture, because semantic information from each input mode supplies partial disambiguation of the other mode (Oviatt, 2003).

One particularly advantageous feature of such multimodal systems is their superior error handling. The error suppression achievable with a bimodal system, compared with a unimodal one, can be in excess of 40%. Trimodal multi-biometric systems have also been demonstrated to perform more robustly than bimodal ones. In addition to improving the average system reliability, a multimodal interface can perform in a more stable manner for challenging user groups (e.g., accented speakers) and in real-world settings (e.g., mobile contexts).

Research has begun to design more tangible, adaptive, and collaborative multimodal systems for a variety of application areas (e.g., meetings, education). Recent progress in cognitive science, neuroscience, and biology is also contributing to the theoretical foundations needed to design future multimodal interfaces with greater flexibility, generality and power.

See: **Human Computer Interactions**

References

1. S.L. Oviatt, P.R. Cohen, L. Wu, J. Vergo, L. Duncan, B. Suhm, J. Bers, T. Holzman, T. Winograd, J. Landay, J. Larson, and D. Ferro, "Designing the user interface for multimodal speech and gesture applications: State-of-the-art systems and research directions," *Human Computer Interaction*, 2000, Vol. 15, No. 4, pp. 263-322 (also in *Human-Computer Interaction in the New Millennium*, Ed. by J. Carroll, Reading, MA.: Addison-Wesley, 2001).
2. S.L. Oviatt, "Multimodal interfaces," *Handbook of Human-Computer Interaction*, (Ed. by J. Jacko and A. Sears), Lawrence Erlbaum Assoc: Mahwah, New Jersey, 2003, Chapter 14, pp. 286-304.
3. G. Potamianos, C. Neti, J. Luettin, and I. Matthews, "Audio-visual automatic speech recognition: An overview," in *Issues in Visual and Audio-Visual Speech Processing*, (Eds. G. Bailly, E. Vatikiotis-Bateson, and P. Perrier), MIT Press, 2004.

MULTI-RESOLUTION IMAGE INPAINTING

Definition: Multiple resolution approach can be used in image inpainting (see the article on Digital Inpainting).

We firefly summarize below the mechanism of multi-resolution image painting [1]. The algorithm is further extended and used in a multiple layer approach to repair Chinese paintings [2].

Let **DIB** be a damaged image block, Let α be a threshold of variance, Let β_1, β_2 be a threshold of percentage, $\beta_1 < \beta_2$

```
Algorithm inPaint(block DIB)
 if DIB is a small block then return
 divide DIB into n*n image blocks
 for each image block IB
  let var be the color variance of IB, let Mcolor be the mean color of IB
    if var < α then { /* 1 */
      let PB be an x*y pixel block in IB, let Ncolor be the mean color of PB
      for each PB in the image block { /* 2 */
        if the percentage of damaged pixels in PB > β2
          inpaint the damaged pixels using Mcolor
        else if the percentage of damaged pixels in PB > β1
          inpaint the damaged pixels using Ncolor
        else
          inpaint the damaged pixels using neighbor pixels
      } /* 2 */
    } /* 1 */
    else
      call inPaint(IB)
```

Color variance has a strong indication of the degree of details in an **IB**. The threshold α sets the criterion of whether a multi-resolution inpainting is required. In our implementation, the value of α is a percentage in the range between 0 and 100 (the maximum *var*) of an **IB**. Another criterion is the percentage of potential damaged pixels. We argue that, if the percentage is too high, using surrounding color information to fix a pixel is less realistic as compared to using a global average color. In some severe cases, it is impossible to use neighborhood colors. Note that, both thresholds are adjustable for the sake of analysis. The recursive algorithm iterates through each of the **IBs** in a **DIB**. If the color variance of IB is below the threshold α, there is not much difference of pixels in **IB**. No subdivision is required (i.e., no need of looking at the next level of details). Thus, the algorithm further divides **IB** into several pixel blocks (i.e., **PBs**). If the percentage of damaged pixels in a **PB** is too high (i.e., greater than β_2), the mean color of **IB** is used. One example is that the entire **PB** is damaged (thus we need to use the mean color of **IB**). Alternatively, if the percentage is still high (i.e., greater than β_1), the mean color of **PB** is used. Note that, the computation of mean colors does not take damaged pixels into the account. If the percentage is low, neighbor pixels are used for inpainting. Finally, if the color variance of **IB** is not below the threshold α, the algorithm is called recursively to handle the next level of details. In the article [1], a complete analysis is given to show the inpainted results are satisfiable.

See: Digital Inpainting, Motion Picture Inpainting on Aged Films, Photo Defect Detection

References
1. T. K. Shih., L.-C. Lu, and R.-C. Chang, "Multi-Resolution Image Inpainting," Proceedings of the IEEE International Conference on Multimedia & Expo (ICME'03), July 2003, pp. 485-488.
2. T. K. Shih, R.-C. Chang, and L.-C. Lu, "Multi-Layer Inpainting on Chinese Artwork," Proceedings of the IEEE International Conference on Multimedia & Expo (ICME'04), June 2004, pp. 33-36.

MULTI-VIEW VIDEO CODING

Definition: Multi-view image display systems provide the viewer with the appropriate monoscopic or stereoscopic view of a scene.

Recent advances in multi-view three dimensional (3-D) television may revolutionalize information systems in the near future. Three or more cameras may be used to form a multi-ocular system for the production of several image sequences obtained from slightly different viewpoints. Multi-view image display systems may provide the viewer with the appropriate monoscopic or stereoscopic view of a scene, depending on his position. As an example, an autostereoscopic display system is implemented using several projectors and a lenticular screen.

Another example is integral imaging , which is a technique that is capable of creating and encoding a true volume spatial optical model of the object scene in the form of a planar intensity distribution by using unique optical components (arrays of lenses).

However, the cost for the associated recording and transmission systems increases considerably as the number of views increases. In order to reduce this cost, virtual images from intermediate viewpoints have to be generated, using the existing real views and additional disparity information. Virtual view generation can be either *image-based*, i.e. no explicit 3-D modeling of the scene is made, however disparity estimation may be used to improve the quality of the generated intermediate images or *3-D model based*, where the true shapes and texture of the objects in the scene are determined and computer graphics techniques are used to render other viewpoints of the 3-D scene.

Efficient communication of multi-view image sequences can be achieved by transmitting the encoded image sequences obtained from the real views along with disparity or depth information. Intermediate views are then produced at the receiver using spatial interpolation on the basis of intensity images and transmitted disparity or depth information. By transmitting additional bit rate corresponding to disparity or depth information, the generation of intermediate images is simplified; hence, the complexity of the receiver is significantly reduced. Offsetting this is the cost of transmitting this additional bit rate, which may be considerable.

While MPEG-2 and MPEG-4 provide some support for the coding of standard stereo and multi-view scenes, these techniques have specific limitations and cannot support new applications with significant user interaction. Therefore, MPEG recently started a new activity, namely MPEG 3DAV, with the aim of exploring new applications, such as omni-directional video, interactive stereo and multi-view video and even free viewpoint video, where a user can freely navigate within a 3-D environment captured using a small number of real cameras. Although many of these applications can be realized through the application of existing MPEG tools, especially those for the coding of audio and visual objects contained under MPEG-4, the need for further extensions to existing standards is now being explored.

See: Coding of stereoscopic and 3D images and video

References

1. A. Smolic, C. Fehn, K. Müller, and D. McCutchen, "MPEG 3DAV – Video-Based Rendering for Interactive TV Applications," Proceedings of 10th Dortmunder Fernsehseminar, Dortmund, Germany, September 2003.
2. N. Grammalidis and M.G. Strintzis, "Disparity and Occlusion Estimation in Multiocular Systems and their Coding for the Communication of Multiview Image Sequences," IEEE Transactions on Circuits and Systems for Video Technology, Vol. 8, No. 3, pp. 327-344, June 1998.

MULTIPLE SOURCE ALIGNMENT FOR VIDEO ANALYSIS

Nevenka Dimitrova[1] and Robert Turetsky[1,2]
(1) Philips Research, Briarcliff Manor, NY, USA
(2) Columbia University, New York, NY, USA

Definition: *High-level semantic information, which is otherwise very difficult to derive from the audiovisual content, can be extracted automatically using both audiovisual signal processing as well as screenplay processing and analysis.*

Abstract

Multimedia content analysis of video data so far has relied mostly on the information contained in the raw visual, audio and text signals. In this process the fact that the film production starts with the original screenplay is usually ignored. However, using screenplay information is like using the recipe book for the movie. We demonstrated that high-level semantic information that is otherwise very difficult to derive from the audiovisual content can be extracted automatically using both audiovisual signal processing as well as screenplay processing and analysis.

Here we present the use of screenplay as a source of ground truth for automatic speaker/character identification. Our speaker identification method consists of screenplay parsing, extraction of time-stamped transcript, alignment of the screenplay with the time-stamped transcript, audio segmentation and audio speaker identification. As the screenplay alignment will not be able to identify all dialogue sections within any film, we use the segments found by alignment as labels to train a statistical model in order to identify unaligned pieces of dialogue. Character names from the screenplay are converted to actor names based on fields extracted from imdb.com. We find that on average the screenplay alignment was able to properly identify the speaker in one third of lines of dialogue. However, with additional automatic statistical labeling for audio speaker ID on the soundtrack our recognition rate improves significantly.

Introduction

Current practice in film production relies on screenplay as the crucial element for the overall process. The screenplay provides a unified vision of the story, setting, dialogue and action of a film – and gives the filmmakers, actors and crew a starting point for bringing their creative vision to life. For researchers involved in content-based analysis of movies, the screenplay is a currently unexploited resource for obtaining a textual description of important semantic objects within a film coming straight from the filmmakers. Hundreds of copies of a screenplay are produced for any film production of scale. The screenplay can be reproduced for hobbyist or academic use, and thousands of screenplays are available online.

The difficulty in using the screenplay as a shortcut to content-based analysis is threefold: First, the screenplay follows only a semi-regular formatting standard, and thus needs robust parsing to be a reliable source of data. Second, there is no inherent correlation between text in the screenplay and a time period in the film. Third, lines of dialogue or entire scenes in the movie can be added, deleted, modified or shuffled. We address these difficulties by parsing the screenplay and then aligning it with the time-stamped subtitles of the film. Statistical models can then be generated based on properly aligned segments in order to estimate segments that could not be aligned.

Our test-bed of this framework is in character/speaker identification [7]. Unsupervised (audio) speaker identification on movie dialogue is a difficult problem, as speech characteristics are affected by changes in emotion of the speaker, different acoustic conditions, ambient noise and heavy activity in the background. Patel and Sethi [3] have experimented with speaker identification on film data for use in video indexing/classification, but require that training data be hand-labeled and that all dialogues be hand-segmented. Salway et al. describe the association of temporal information in a movie to collateral texts (audio scripts)[5]. Wachman et al have used script information from situation comedy for labeling and learning by example in interactive sessions [8].

The remainder of this article will proceed as follows. First, we introduce the content and structure of the screenplay. Subsequently, we detail extracting information from the screenplay and the alignment process. We present a quantitative analysis of alignments, and preliminary results of automatically trained audio speaker ID.

Screenplays in movie production practice

The screenplay is the most important part of making a movie. It describes the story, characters, action, setting and dialogue of a film. Additionally, some camera directions and shot boundaries may be included but are generally ignored. The screenplay generally undergoes a number of revisions, with each rewrite looking potentially uncorrelated to prior drafts (see *Minority Report*[2]). After the principal shooting of a film is complete, the editors assemble the different shots together in a way that may or may not respect the screenplay.

The actual content of the screenplay generally follows a (semi) regular format. Figure 1 shows a snippet of a screenplay from the film *Contact*. The first line of any scene or shooting location is called a *slug line*. The slug line indicates whether a scene is to take place inside or outside (INT or EXT), the name of the location (e.g. 'TRANSPORT PLANE'), and can potentially specify the time of day (e.g. DAY or NIGHT). Following the slug line is a description of the location. Additionally, the description will introduce any new characters that appear and any action that takes place without dialogue. Important people or objects are made easier to spot within a page by capitalizing their names.

```
INT.   TRANSPORT PLANE

The Major Domo leads Ellie down a corridor of the plane's
custom interior.  Through one door we can see into a room
where several very beautiful, very young women sit
watching TV with vacant eyes.  Ellie only catches a
glimpse before the Major Domo nods for her to enter the
main room and takes his post outside.

Ellie cautiously enters the interior of what appears to be
a flying Dascha; dark, heavy on the chintz.  Bookshelves,
an exercise machine... and a wall of monitors, filled top
to bottom with scrolling hieroglyphics.  Ellie reaches out
to them --

                    HADDEN (O.S.)
          Dr. Arroway, I presume.

Ellie turns to see S.R. HADDEN.  Thick glasses, wearing a
cardigan, he stands by a silver samovar.

                    ELLIE
          S.R. Hadden...
                    (beat)
          You compromised our security codes.

                    HADDEN
          Once upon a time I was a hell of an
          engineer.  Please, sit, Doctor.  I
          have guests so rarely, it's
          important to me they feel welcome in
          my home.
                    (turns to the
```

Figure 1. Example segment from a screenplay.

The bulk of the screenplay is the dialogue description. Dialogue is indented in the page for ease of reading and to give actors and filmmakers a place for notes. Dialogues begin with a capitalized character name and optionally a (V.O.) or (O.S.) following the name to indicate that the speaker should be off-screen (V.O. stands for "Voice-over"). Finally, the actual text of the dialogue is full-justified to a narrow band in the center of the page.

The continuity script, a shot-by-shot breakdown of a film, is sometimes written after all work on a film is completed. A method for alignment of the continuity script with closed captions was introduced by Ronfard and Thuong [4]. Although continuity scripts from certain films are published and sold, they are generally not available to the public online. This motivates analysis on the screenplay, despite its imperfections.

System Architecture

One reason why the screenplay has not been used more extensively in content-based analysis is because there is no explicit connection between dialogues, actions and scene descriptions present in a screenplay, and the time in the video signal. This hampers our effectiveness in assigning a particular segment of the film to a piece of text. Another source of film transcription, the closed captions, has the text of the dialogue spoken in the film, but it does not contain the identity of characters speaking each line, nor do closed captions possess the scene descriptions, which are so difficult to extract from a video signal. We get the best of both worlds by aligning the dialogues of screenplay with the text of the film's time stamped closed captions.

Second, lines and scenes are often incomplete, cut or shuffled. In order to be robust in the face of scene re-ordering we align the screenplay to the closed captions one scene at a time and filter out potential false positives through median filtering.

Finally, it is not possible to correlate every sentence in the screenplay for every piece of dialogue. Thus, it is important to take information extracted from the time-stamped screenplay, combined with multimodal segments of the film (audio/video stream, closed captions, information from external websites such as imdb.com, other films), to create statistical models of events not captured by the screenplay alignment.

A system overview of our test-bench application, which includes pre-processing, alignment and speaker identification throughout a single film, is shown in Figure 2. First we parse the text of a film's screenplay, so that scene and dialogue boundaries and metadata are entered into a uniform data structure. Next, the closed caption and audio streams are extracted from the film's DVD. In the most important stage, the screenplay and closed caption texts are aligned. The aligned dialogues are now time-stamped and associated with a particular character. These dialogues are used as labeled training examples for generic machine learning methods (in our case we've tested neural networks and GMM's) which can identify the speaker of dialogues which were not labeled by the alignment process.

In our experiments, we were working towards very high speaker identification accuracy, despite the difficult noise conditions. It is important to note that we were able to perform this identification using supervised learning methods, but the ground truth was generated automatically so there is no need for human intervention in the classification process.

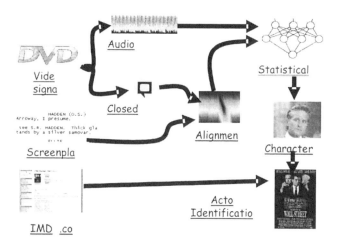

Figure 2. System architecture.

a. Screenplay parsing

From the screenplay, we extract the location and time and description of a scene, the individual lines dialogue and their speaker, and the parenthetical and action direction for the actors, and any transition suggestion (cut, fade, wipe, dissolve, etc) between scenes. We used the following grammar for parsing most screenplays:

SCENE_START:	.* | SCENE_START | DIAL_START | SLUG | TRANSITION
DIAL_START:	\t+ <CHAR NAME> (V.O. | O.S.)? \n \t+ DIALOGUE | PAREN
DIALOGUE:	\t+ .*? \n\n
PAREN:	\t+ (.*?)
TRANSITION:	\t+ <TRANS NAME> :
SLUG:	<SCENE #>?<INT/EXT><ERNAL | .> ? - <LOC> <- TIME>

A similar grammar was generated for two other screenplay formats which are popular on-line.

b. Extracting time-stamped subtitles and metadata

For the alignment and speaker identification tasks, we require the audio and time stamped closed caption stream from the DVD of a film. In our case, four films, *Being John Malkovich*, *Magnolia*, *L.A. Confidential* and *Wall Street*, were chosen from a corpus of DVDs. When available, subtitles were extracted from the User Data Field of the DVD. Otherwise, OCR (Optical Character Recognition) was performed on the subtitle stream of the disc.

Finally, character names from the screenplay are converted to actor names based on fields extracted from imdb.com. If no match from a character's name can be found in IMDB's reporting of the film's credit sequence (e.g. 'Hank' vs. 'Henry'), we match the screenplay name with the credit sequence name by matching quotes from the "memorable quotes" section with dialogues from the screenplay.

c. Dialogue screenplay alignment

The screenplay dialogues and closed caption text are aligned by using dynamic programming to find the "best path" across a similarity matrix. Alignments that properly correspond to scenes are extracted by applying a median filter across the best path. Dialogue segments of reasonable accuracy are broken down into closed caption line sized chunks, which means that we can directly translate dialogue chunks into time-stamped segments. Below, each component is discussed.

The similarity matrix is a way of comparing two different versions of similar media [1,6]. In our similarity matrix, every word i of a scene in the screenplay is compared to every word j in the closed captions of the entire movie. In other words, we populate a matrix:

$$SM(i,j) \leftarrow screenplay(scene\_num, i) == subtitle(j)$$

$SM(i,j)=1$ if word i of the scene is the same as word j of the closed captions, and $SM(i,j)=0$ if they are different. Screen time progresses linearly along the diagonal i=j, so when lines of dialogue from the screenplay line up with lines of text from the closed captions, we expect to see a solid diagonal line of 1's. Figure 3 shows an example similarity matrix segment.

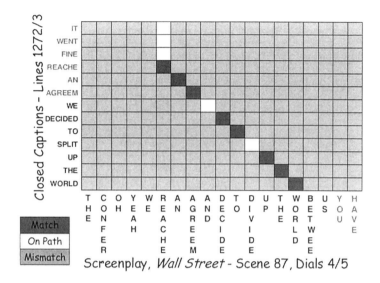

Figure 3. Screenplay vs. closed captions similarity.

In order to find the diagonal line which captures the most likely alignment between the closed captions and the screenplay scene, we perform dynamic programming. Figure 4 visualizes the successful alignment of scene 30 of *Magnolia*. The three diagonal regions indicate that much of this scene is present in the closed captions, but there are a few dialogues which written into the screenplay but were not present in the finished film and vice versa.

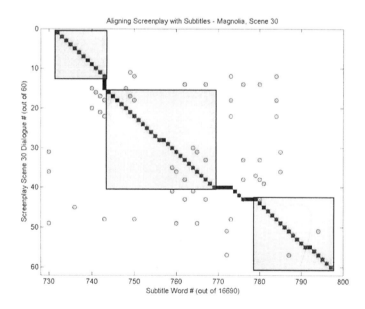

Figure 4. Visualization of the final screenplay – speaker alignment.

The missing dialogues can be removed by searching for diagonal lines across DP's optimal path, as in [4]. We use an m-point median filter on the slope of the optimal path, so that in addition to lining up with the rest of the scene, the dialogue must consistently match at least (m+1)/2 (e.g. 3) out of m (e.g. 5) words to be considered part of a scene. In Figure , proper dialogues are demonstrated in the shaded regions. The bounds of when the alignment is found to be proper are used to segment aligned scenes from omitted ones. We can then warp the words of the screenplay to match the timing of the closed captions.

Performance evaluation

In order to analyze quantitatively the alignment we define the *coverage* of the alignment to be the percentage of lines of dialogue in the film in which the alignment was able to identify the speaker. The *accuracy* of the alignment is the percentage of speaker IDs generated by the alignment which actually correspond to dialogue spoken by the tagged speaker. Accuracy is a measure of the purity of the training data and coverage is a measure of how much data will need to be generated by classification.

Table 1. Confusion Matrix for segment speaker label accuracy, *Being John Malkovich*.

	CRA	LES	LOT	MAL	MAX	?
CRA	82	0	1	1	0	11
LES	0	41	0	0	0	0
LOT	0	0	40	0	0	2
MAL	0	0	0	25	0	2
MAX	0	0	1	0	71	4

Table 1 presents lines of dialogue that were identified as belonging to a main character in *Being John Malkovich*. We were able to achieve a high degree of accuracy in labeling the speaker for each segment.

While the alignment process affords a high level of confidence in terms of the accuracy (approximately 90%) of segment speaker label generation, the liquid nature of the screenplay means we are unable to label most of the film. Table 2 presents a measure of how much dialogue the alignment is able to cover in each of our four films. This motivates creating a speaker-identification system based on statistical models generated from the segment labeling as found by alignment.

Table 2. Accuracy and coverage of alignments

Movie	#CC's	Coverage	Accuracy
Malkovich	1436	334 (23%)	311 (93%)
LA Conf	1666	548 (33%)	522 (95%)
Wall St.	2342	954 (41%)	850 (89%)
Magnolia	2672	843(32%)	747 (89%)

Automatic Speaker ID using Statistical Models

Our speaker identification system examines the behavior of audio features over time. We performed extensive testing with various combinations of audio features reported to have high discriminability (MFCC, LSP, RASTA-PLP), incorporating mean subtraction and deltas. In our case we have a good deal of training data so we can use simple classifiers. The goal of our classifier is to allow for different clusters in feature-space that correspond to the voice characteristics of an actor under different emotional and acoustic conditions.

While our method is under large scale benchmarking, initial results are promising. Table 3 presents frame accuracy on unlabeled data for the main characters of "being John Malkovich.". Here we are using the first 13 MFCC components at 12.5msec intervals stacked across a .5sec time window. We should note here that speech segments in movies have a mean length of .5 seconds, whereas the best performing speaker ID systems use a signal length of 2-5 seconds. Principal Component Analysis was used to reduce the dimensionality of feature-space, and classification was performed using an 8-component Gaussian Mixture Model. Note that the table demonstrates that identification accuracy is highly speaker dependant.

Table 3. Confusion Matrix for percentage of frames labeled
by automatic speaker identification

	CRA	LES	LOT	MAL	MAX
CRA	57 %	17 %	21 %	27 %	28 %
LES	5 %	77 %	4 %	15 %	1 %
LOT	8 %	0 %	49 %	10 %	13 %
MAL	7 %	2 %	8 %	31 %	4 %
MAX	23 %	4 %	19 %	17 %	55 %

Conclusions

High level semantic information can be used to automatically create models for automatic content analysis. The screenplay contains data about the film, that is not extractable at all by audiovisual analysis or if it can be extracted then the reliability is very low. These high level concepts are closer to the human understanding of the film and to the potential methods of searching of audiovisual content. We used screenplay information for speaker ID, which has limited coverage of about 30%. Then we used the same framework for generating labels for a statistical approach to audio speaker ID. There is a limitless number of potential applications for the alignment such as extraction of semantic description of a scene, affective descriptions, mood analysis and others.

References

1. J. Foote, "Methods for the Automatic Analysis of Music and Audio," TR FXPAL-TR-99-038, 1999.

2. S. Frank, "Minority Report," Early and revised Drafts, available from Drew's Script-o-rama, http://www.script-o-rama.com.

3. N. Patel and I. Sethi. "Video Classification Using Speaker Identification," IS&E SPIE Proceedings of Storage and Retrieval for Image and Video Databases V, January 1997, San Jose, California.

4. R. Ronfard and T.T. Thuong, "A Framework for Aligning and Indexing Movies with their Script," Proceedings of ICME 2003, Baltimore, MD, July 2003.

5. A. Salway and E. Tomadaki, "Temporal information in collateral texts for indexing moving images," LREC Workshop on Annotation Standards for Temporal Information in Natural Language, 2002.

6. R. Turetsky and D. P. W. Ellis. "Ground-Truth Transcriptions of Real Music from Force-Aligned MIDI Syntheses," ISMIR 2003.

7. R. Turetsky and N. Dimitrova, "Screenplay Alignment for Closed-System Speaker Identification and Analysis of Feature Films", ICME 2004, Taipei, Taiwan.

8. J. Wachman and R. W. Picard, "Tools for browsing a TV situation comedy based on content specific attributes," Multimedia Tools and Applications, Vol. 13, No. 3, 2001, pp. 255–284.

N

NETWORKING PROTOCOLS FOR AUDIO STREAMING

Definition: Networking protocols for audio streaming are used to provide uninterrupted audio transmission over networks, such as the Internet.

Unlike elastic traffic such as email or file transfer, which are not severely affected by delays or irregularities in transmission speed, continuous multimedia data such as audio and video are inelastic. These media have a "natural" flow and are not very flexible. Interruptions in audio while streaming it is undesirable. Therefore, it creates a major problem for the end user because it distorts its real-time nature. It should be pointed out that delay is not always detrimental for audio, as long as the flow is continuous. For example, consider a presentational application where the audio is played back to the user with limited interaction capabilities such as play/pause/open/close. In such a scenario, if the entire audio is delayed by a few seconds, the user's perception of it is not affected due to lack of a reference point, as long as there are no interruptions. However, for a conversational application such as audio conferencing, where users interact with each other, audio delay must not violate certain thresholds because of the interaction and the existence of reference points between the users.

Due to the above requirements, the transport protocol used for audio streaming must be able to handle the real-time nature of it. One of the most commonly-used real-time protocols for audio streaming is the Real-time Transport protocol (RTP) [1], which is typically used with the Real Time Streaming Protocol (RTSP) for exchanging commands between the player and media server, and sometimes used with the Real -time Transport Control Protocol (RTCP) [2] for Quality of Service (QoS) monitoring and other things. As an easier-to-implement alternative to RTP, HTTP streaming is sometimes used in cases where users have high speed and high bandwidth connection to the network. In HTTP streaming, the player simply requests the audio from the web server over HTTP, and plays it as the audio data comes in from the Web server. The disadvantages of this approach are the lack of RTP/RTCP features such as faster handling of the audio by the receiver and QoS reporting, and the fact that HTTP uses TCP which is not considered a real time protocol, especially under less-than ideal network conditions. As such, there can be more interruptions and delay associated with HTTP streaming compared to RTP streaming.

See: Audio Conferencing

References

1. H. Schulzrinne, S. Casner, R. Frederick, and V. Jacobson, "RTP: A Transport Protocol for Real-Time Applications," IETF RFC 1889, January 1996.
2. H. Schulzrinne, A. Rao, and R. Lanphier, "Real Time Streaming Protocol (RTSP)," IETF RFC 2326, April 1998.

O

OBJECT BASED STEREOSCOPIC VIDEO CODING

Definition: *Object-based coding techniques have the ability to describe a scene in a structural way and to convey depth information that can be computed directly from the images.*

Object based coding has long attracted considerable attention as a promising alternative to block-based encoding, achieving excellent performance and producing fewer annoying effects. Furthermore, important image areas such as facial details in face-to-face communications can be reconstructed with a higher image quality than with block-oriented hybrid coding. In addition, the ability of object-based coding techniques to describe a scene in a structural way, in contrast to traditional waveform-based coding techniques, opens new areas of applications. Video production, realistic computer graphics, multimedia interfaces and medical visualization are some of the applications that may benefit by exploiting the potential of object based schemes. Object-based approaches applied in coding of stereo image sequences have the additional benefit of conveying depth information which may be computed directly from the images. Using the depth information the scene may be separated in layers and depth keying is possible.

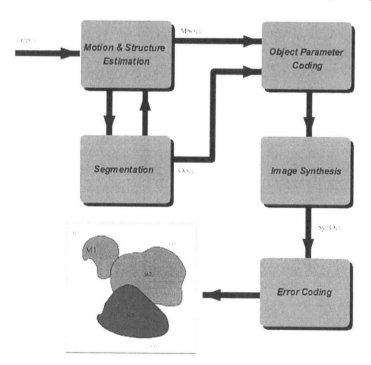

Figure 1. General structure of an object-based stereo coding scheme.

Also, accurate 3D modeling of the scene structure may be achieved. The main problem in object based analysis is the automatic extraction and modeling of objects directly from the image intensities. This task may require complex image analysis techniques to segment the scene into homogeneous regions or even user interaction so that image regions correspond to real objects on the scene.

Figure 1 illustrates the basic structure of an object-based stereoscopic image coding scheme. The encoder consists of an analysis part and a synthesis part. The analysis part aims to subdivide the scene into a set of objects representing each one by a set of parameters: shape or boundary, motion, structure or depth and texture or colour. These parameters are encoded and transmitted to the decoder where the decoded parameters are then used to synthesize an approximation of the original images. The analysis phase is the most sophisticated one, consisting of image segmentation and motion/structure estimation.

See: Coding of stereoscopic and 3D images and video

References

1. M.G. Strintzis and S. Malassiotis: "Object-Based Coding of Stereoscopic and 3D Image Sequences: A Review," IEEE Signal Processing Magazine, Special Issue on Stereo and 3D Imaging (invited paper), Vol. 16, No. 3, pp. 14-28, May 1999.

OCCLUSIONS

Definition: Occlusion regions mark disparity discontinuity jumps, which can be used to improve stereo image encoding and transmission, segmentation, motion analysis, and object identification processes which must preserve object boundaries.

In early stereo image research, the segmentation into visible and occlusion regions is treated as a secondary process, postponed until matching is completed and smoothing is underway. Techniques are also proposed that indirectly address the occlusion problem by minimizing spurious mismatches resulting from occlusion regions and discontinuities. It has been pointed out that occlusion areas must be identified and incorporated into matching process. By using Bayesian reasoning, they derive an energy function based on pixel intensity as the matching feature. Dynamic programming is then used to find a minimal-energy solution.

Techniques based on dynamic programming have been used for the purpose of disparity estimation and simultaneous occlusion detection. A significant advantage of these techniques is that they can provide a global solution for the disparity estimation/occlusion detection problem under local constraints such as constraints related to correlation, smoothness, or disparity gradient limit.

Other methods directly address occlusion regions by defining an a priori probability for the disparity field based upon a smoothness function and an occlusion constraint. For matching two shifted windows are used to avoid errors over discontinuity jumps.

Assuming monotonicity, the matching problem is solved using dynamic programming. The stereo occlusion problem is formulated as a path-finding problem in a left-scanline to right-scanline matching process. It has been also proposed a dynamic programming solution to stereo matching based on matching edge-delimited intervals between corresponding scan lines that does not require the smoothing term. It has been pointed out that several equally good paths can be found through matching space when using only the occlusion and ordering constraints. To provide enough constraints forcing their system to produce a single solution, they optimize a Bayesian maximum likelihood cost function minimizing inter- and intra-scanline disparity discontinuities. A similar strategy uses a dynamic programming algorithm for the detection of significant disparity changes and large occlusion areas in a stereoscopic image pair. In this approach no smoothness or interscan-line compatibility constraints are used. Two additional constraints, namely the extended continuity constraint and the disparity gradient limit, can also be considered. Finally, an algorithm using forms of Bayes decision criteria can be employed for segmenting a stereo pair into occlusion and visible background and foreground regions.

See: Coding of stereoscopic and 3D images and video

References

1. G.A. Triantafyllidis, D. Tzovaras, and M.G. Strintzis: "Occlusion and Visible Background and Foreground areas in Stereo: A Bayesian Approach," IEEE Transactions on Circuits and Systems for Video Technology, Special Issue on 3D Video Technology, Vol. 10, No. 4, pp. 563-576, June 2000.
2. N. Grammalidis and M. G. Strintzis, "Disparity and occlusion estimation on multiocular systems and their coding for the communication of multiview image sequences," IEEE Transactions on Circuits and Systems for Video Technology, Vol. 8, pp. 328–344, June 1998.

ONLINE GAMING

Stefano Ferretti, Marco Roccetti, and Paola Salomoni
University of Bologna, Bologna, Italy

Definition: Online gaming refers to playing the game over the network using a personal computer, a game console, a PDA, or a smart phone.

Concepts

Computer games, whether played on a classic personal computer, on a game console, on a PDA or even on a smart phone, are among the most commercially successful applications. Today, games such as Star Wars Galaxy and Everquest command audiences from 200000 to 400000 clients in US and Europe, while NCSoft's Lineage has approximately 4 million of users in Korea [11]. A new report from DFC Intelligence states that revenues from the game industry will bypass the music industry within the next five years, based on projected rates of expansion for the market [1]. This report forecasts that worldwide sales of traditional PC game, video game and portable game hardware and software are expected to increase from \$23.2 billion in 2003 to \$31.6 billion in 2009. In a separate report, they also estimated that the online game market would reach sales of \$9.8 billion by 2009. This would result in combined interactive entertainment revenues of \$41.4 billion in the same year. Those are not only rumors, as they are confirmed by the following. Informa Media forecasts that in 2010 the game market will be worth of \$40 million, with the new gaming sectors of broadband, mobile and interactive TV contributing 40% of this amount. Datamonitor predicts that in 2006 only wireless gaming will generate revenues of \$17.5 billion worldwide. Finally, Paul Merry at the ARC Group asserts that the overall market for mobile entertainment services will top \$27 billion by 2008.

Parallel to the online game market, the online game research proceeds at a fast pace as well. Indeed, highly interactive networked multiplayer games impose rigorous demands on consistent game world modifications, responsive interaction schemes among players that permit to mitigate delays and jitters in game event transmissions, and fairness of handling players' actions. Thus, advancements on game technologies and most of all, online game technologies, are felt as urgent to provide full support to latest kinds of entertainment services.

With this in view, in the remainder of this article we will overview some aspects of paramount importance for an effective game development to ensure compelling and exciting online game experiences. In particular, first, we present a brief discussion on game typologies and overview a simple games' categorization that helps to identify the main technical requirements needed to ensure exciting game experiences. Then, some game architectural issues are covered, followed by a discussion on commonly exploited gaming communication protocols. Finally, we survey some important open problems that still require deeper investigation.

Games Classification

The game design is primarily affected by the characteristics and properties of the game logic. Indeed, the peculiarities of a game result in different technical needs and requirements that must be guaranteed to effectively deploy such a game over a network. Thus, taxonomy of possible games may be useful to better understand common factors and differences between games.

According to [4], two broad game categories may be identified: *skill-and-action* games (also often called fast-paced games) and *strategy* games. While the former category is mainly characterized on perceptual and motor skills of players (i.e., the more the player is skilled to react to external stimuli in real-time the more is likely to win the game), the latter emphasizes on cognitive efforts (i.e., real-time play is rare in strategy games that mostly require more time to let the user think and then play). Combat, sport, maze and race games are examples of skill-and-action games. Adventures, D&D, Wargames, games of chance and board games are examples of strategic games. It is easy to observe that these two main categories are very diverse and present very different requirements. In fact, the primary concern of skill-and-action game developers is responsiveness, i.e., game events produced within the game must be perceived by players in real-time. Instead, the main requirements of strategic games are reliability and game consistency i.e., the evolution of the game must be described to players in a very precise and correct way, in order to allow users to effectively plain their strategies. Needless to say, due to the best effort nature of the Internet, responsive interactions are tricky requirements in online games. This complicates the development of skill-and-action online games.

Along with this categorization, we claim that today new attention must be paid on Role-Playing Games (RPGs), which in past were typically associated to classic adventure or D&D games.

Figure 1. Role playing game.

Indeed, since the first birth of video games, RPGs have truly evolved in time. Focusing on other game genres, in fact, as years go by new games have been developed characterized by always more advanced graphics, advanced human-computer interfaces and advanced ways of interaction within the game, yet the way to play these games always remains the same. Online RPGs, instead, are truly different. When deployed online, these games allow players to interact within a virtual world with thousands of other players in real-time (see Figure 1). Players form alliances and collaborate to work out complex strategies, thus living a parallel (virtual) life within the virtual game environment. Online RPGs have no ending and players influence the global game plot. Summing up, these new networked games present both skill-and-action and strategic games requirements.

Finally, due to the "never-ending" nature of RPGs, the player could be so interested in following the game evolution that it would continue to play the game while moving in real world. Hence, it is easy to envisage that in a near future new online RPGs will allow players to access the game thanks to different terminals (and with the possibility of dynamically switching among different terminals e.g., from a PC to a PDA) while continuing to play the same game session.

Gaming Architectures

Classic game consoles were typically standalone platforms able to offer incredible graphical (offline) gaming experiences. Sony's Playstation, Microsoft's Xbox, Sega's Dreamcast, Nintendo's GameCube are well known products that had a great commercial success in the game market. They integrate functionalities to perform fast sprite drawing, 3D polygons, and full motion video and pulse code modulation waveform sound. As an example, new Sony Playstation 3 incorporates a Cell Processor, a multicore chip featuring a 64-bit power processor core with multiple synergistic processor cores capable of massive floating point processing. The chip is optimized for intensive gaming applications and also excels in broadband-rich media applications, such as movies. Moreover, these game consoles typically incorporate powerful Graphic Processor Units (GPUs) for sophisticated graphics renderings. For instance, Playstation exploits powerful Nvidia GPUs while ATI GPUs are used by Microsoft and Nintendo.

As of today, the new trend is *connectivity*. Most of all the entertainment commercial companies are equipping their game consoles with network adapters that provide access to the Internet, and more and more online-enabled game titles are released in the gaming market. Famous examples of new online games are Everquest, Half Life II, NeverWinter Nights, Quake, Ultima Online. In this sense, the experience of Korea is a clear demonstration of the possible success of online games. Indeed, Koreans are probably the more avid online game users, thanks to an extremely wide adoption of broadband access but, most of all, thanks to the incredible success of PC Baang, places where people meet and pay to play together online [16].

Looking forward, we claim that wireless terminals may be the games' real future [7]. Thanks to their new computational, graphics, storage and network capabilities, handheld devices will become real game consoles-to-go. However, latency in wireless games has no easy fix, especially when the attention is focused on 3G cellular networks. In fact, while these new wireless technologies guarantee a potentially "always on" connection to the game, the problems due to the possibly limited transmission throughput (caused by bandwidth constraints and possible link outages) make the cellular environment an obscure and ambiguous partner for game developers. On the other hand, the use of Wi-Fi, Bluetooth and HomeRF technologies may provide high bandwidths but only within short ranges. Thus, access points and gateways are needed in the proximity of mobile players to provide an access to large scaled game architectures.

Nevertheless, a new scenario is emerging stating that future online players' equipment will be very heterogeneous. People will play by means of a plethora of diverse network enabled devices (e.g., PC, game consoles, handheld devices) and bandwidth connections (e.g., dialup, DSL, fiber, Wi-Fi, Bluetooth, HomeRF, 3G cellular networks). This promise certainly boosts the popularity of online games, as games and players will appear in many flavors. However, the vast diversity of possible future client configurations gives rise to a number of new issues to address.

First, games must be developed in a portable fashion to deploy them over multiple architectures and platforms. Thus, a middleware game platform, which allows developing a game once and deploys it over multiple mobile systems, is going to become a fundamental tool. Two specific developing platforms must be mentioned. First, the Java 2 platform Micro Edition (J2ME), which represents a natural solution due to the wide diffusion of Java as a developing language. J2ME is actually exploited by many developing companies such as, for example, Motorola, Nokia (see Figure 2) and Samsung. Another solution is represented by Qualcomm's Binary Runtime Environment for Wireless (BREW). This platform provides common APIs that application developers can use to harness hardware capabilities without having to code to the system interface. Currently, BREW is exploited by Alltel, Verizon Communications and KDDI Corp. [8].

Figure 2. Nokia NGage mobile game console.

Another important distribution issue is concerned with the management of nodes that participate to the online game. Diverse architectural solutions may be adopted, ranging from client/server to P2P-based approaches. Needless to say, when the game is deployed over large scaled networks to support a huge number of players distributed solutions must be devised [5]. In other words, focusing on Massively Multiplayer Online Games (MMOGs), emerging approaches follow the idea that the game state should be partitioned, distributed and/or replicated across multiple game servers in order to i) reduce the number of client hosts connected to a single server, ii) eliminate central bottlenecks that typically affect classic client/server solutions, iii) alleviate the problem of network congestion and iv) augment the robustness of the system. However, if portions of the game state are kept replicated across multiple servers, synchronization schemes are required to ensure the global consistency of the redundant distributed game state.

Gaming Protocols

Once game nodes have been organized to manage the distributed game system, a key point is concerned with the protocols employed for the communications among these nodes. Indeed, it is well known that skill-and-action online games suffer from slow communications, changing network conditions and consequent high levels of delay jitters. In particular, the time elapsed since the generation of a game event by a given player and the time when such an event is perceived by all other players characterizes the pace of evolution of the game. Researchers and gamers assert that network delays should not exceed 150 milliseconds when the game advances at a constant rate [12, 17, 18]. Thus, much of the focus in online multi-player games is concerned with the problem of reducing response times experienced by players.

With this in view, the employed communication protocols should not increase latencies and must take care of conveying game messages to other nodes as fast as possible. In point of this fact, it is worth mentioning that a standard game communication protocol has not yet been devised because of the different requirements of developed games.

For sure, classic completely reliable transmission protocols, such as TCP, are not appropriate for fast-paced networked games. The motivation is that much of TCP's behavior such as "congestion control" may damage the speed of the event transmission, thus hampering the achievement of real-time constraints. Moreover, it may be that game events that arrive too late may become useless; thus, a completely reliable approach may sometimes just increase transmission delays [5, 19]. Hence, typically only game start-up messages are sent over TCP. Alternatively, TCP may be adopted in turn-based online games (e.g., chess games) where only a single player is allowed to perform actions in the game at a given time.

Indeed, because of the real-time nature of online multi-player games, the majority of developed game communication protocols are built over unreliable (i.e., UDP) or partially reliable communication schemes [5]. For instance, Quake, a milestone in the online game community, adopts UDP as game events transmission protocol, similarly to MiMaze that also uses RTP to manage the game session.

Obviously, one may add functionalities by developing new protocols over UDP [5]. As an example, new ad-hoc transport protocols may be devised such as, for example, the Game Transport Protocol (GTP) that provides facilities to devise mechanisms for session management and adaptive retransmission [13].

As online games involve multiparty communications (i.e., many senders, multiple receivers), group communications or multicast paradigms could be really of service during the game messages delivery. In this sense, while IP multicast is actually not widely deployed, due to various technical and administrative reasons [20], interesting alternative proposals are represented by multicast protocols developed at the application level. In substance, each node within the game system becomes also a node of the multicast tree. Thus, overlay distribution schemes may be dynamically built that reduce the amount of messages sent throughout the network and augment the scalability of the system.

Finally, an interesting consideration is concerned with the possibility of utilizing communication protocols able to dynamically transcode contents depending on the (possibly heterogeneous) clients' configurations. Indeed, schemes may be devised that allow different players to receive different types of information, depending on the utilized terminal (PC, game console, iTV, PDA, smart phone) and on the user capabilities (is the user on the car? Is the user blind?) Needless to say, tuning the type (and the amount) of the transmitted information opens new ways of gaming, which enable players to connect to the game at any time, from any where, and with any device (ubiquitous gaming) [7].

Open Problems

There are plenty of open problems that still need to be addressed in order to guarantee a full support to online multiplayer games on large scale networked. The aim of this section is to overview some research issues that require investigation and are at the basis of online games.

The need for an effective game management is mainly concerned with the optimization of the resources composing the game architecture. In this context, a typical problem amounts to the fact that the processing of unnecessary game events may cause bandwidth and computational overheads, if techniques able to reduce the amount of information exchanged within the distributed game are not utilized. In other words, in certain MMOGs, players may perceive only a subset of actions produced within the game world, depending on their potential field of sight. To surmount these kinds of problems *event filtering* approaches have been devised that are based on spatial considerations. In substance, the game world is divided into areas of interest and the virtual map over which the game is globally carried out is split into several small pieces. Clients subscribe to one or more areas of interests and receive information sent by all others within that area. This approach has the great benefit of reducing the amount of game events transmitted among nodes of the distributed system and should be taken into serious consideration during the development of a MMOG.

Another important field of investigation is concerned with latency hiding schemes, which aim at providing users with a higher level of interactivity by compensating transmission delays and packet losses. Most of these approaches are based on *dead reckoning* techniques which are typically exploited to reduce the number of game events transmitted through the network. Moreover, due to their prediction schemes, dead reckoning may also compensate game event losses.

Latency often causes another typical problem that affects online games: *fairness*. Simply put, due to the best effort nature of the Internet, different players that connect to the game system may perceive game state updates at different times, as soon as they deliver game events transmitted though the network. In simpler words, as different network latencies and jitters characterize the network connections of different players, it is possible that certain players are treated unfairly. Fairness schemes try to compensate and hide additional latencies perceived by disadvantaged players, thus providing all the players with the same capabilities of winning the game.

Conclusions

The design of novel networked games demands ever increasing technical and interdisciplinary sophistications. Exciting game experiences can be provided to a large number of players connected through diverse terminals only if smart schemes are exploited for the support of online game systems. In this paper, we overviewed some main issues that require to be fully addressed along with typical solutions. Needless to say, as each game presents its own characteristics, the employed approaches must be adapted to the peculiarities of the game so as to tune the trade-off that emerge at the design level. Finally, we claim that only deep experimental assessments may guarantee the success of the devised management schemes for the support of a particular online game.

See: Game Event Synchronization, Fairness in Online Games, Dead Reckoning, Game Accessibility

References

1. DFC Intelligence, "DFC Intelligence Releases New Market Forecasts for Video Game Industry," September 2004, http://www.dfcint.com/news/prsep222004.html.
2. DFC Intelligence, "The Online Game Market 2004," August 2004, http://www.dfcint.com/game_report/Online_Game_toc.html.
3. A.R. Bharambe, S. Rao, and S. Seshan, "Mercury: a scalable publish-subscribe system for internet games," *Proceedings of the 1st Workshop on Network and System Support for Games*, 3–9, ACM Press, 2002.
4. C. Crawford, "The Art of Computer Game Design," http://www.vancouver.wsu.edu/fac/peabody/game-book/Coverpage.html.
5. S. Ferretti and M. Roccetti, "A novel obsolescence-based approach to event delivery synchronization in multiplayer games," *International Journal of Intelligent Games and Simulation*, Vol. 3, No. 1, pp. 7–19, March/April 2004.
6. S. Fiedler, M. Wallner, and M. Weber, "A communication architecture for massive multiplayer games," *Proceedings of the 1st Workshop on Network and System Support for Games*, pp. 14–22, ACM Press, 2002.
7. M. Macedonia, "E3 2001: The Birth of Ubiquitous Gaming?" *IEEE Computer*, August 2001, pp. 90-91.
8. N. Leavitt, "Will Wireless Gaming Be a Winner," IEEE Computer, January 2003, pp. 24-27.
9. K. Lee and D. Lee, "A scalable dynamic load distribution scheme for multiserver distributed virtual environment systems with highly-skewed user distribution," Proceedings of the ACM Symposium on Virtual Reality Software and Technology, pp. 160–168, ACM Press, 2003.
10. J.C.S. Lui and M.F. Chan, "An efficient partitioning algorithm for distributed virtual environment systems," IEEE Transactions on Parallel Distributed Systems, Vol. 13, No. 3, pp. 193–211, 2002.
11. A. Fleming Seay, W.J. Jerome, K.S. Lee, and R.E. Krant, "Project Massive: A Study of Online Gaming Communities," Proceedings of ACM CHI 2004, pp. 1421-1424, April 2004.
12. T. Henderson and S. Bhatti, "Networked Games – a QoS-sensitive application for QoS insensitive users?" Proceedings of the ACM SIGCOMM 2003, pp. 141-147, August 2003.
13. T. Henderson and S. Bhatti "Game transport protocol: Transport protocol for efficient transmission of game event data," Proceedings of JCCI 2002, April 2002.
14. M. Henning, "Massively Multiplayer Middleware," ACM Queue, Vol. 1, No. 10, pp. 38-45, February 2004.

15. S.J. Kim, F. Kuester, and K.H. Kim, "A Global Timestamp-based Scalable Framework for Multi-player Online Games," Proceedings of the IEEE Fourth International Symposium on Multimedia Software Engineering (MSE'02), pp. 2-10, December 2002.
16. J. Krikke, "South Korea Beats the World in Broadband Gaming," IEEE Multimedia, pp. 12-14, April-June 2003.
17. L. Pantel and L.C. Wolf, "On the impact of delay on real-time multiplayer games," Proceedings of the 12th International Workshop on Network and Operating Systems Support for Digital Audio and Video, pp. 23–29, ACM Press, 2002.
18. M.S. Borella, "Source models for network game traffic," Computer Communications, Vol. 23, No. 4, pp. 403–410, February 2000.
19. S. Rooney, D. Bauer, and R. Deydier, "A Federated Peer-to-Peer Network Game Architecture," IEEE Communication Magazine, pp. 114-122, May 2004.
20. J. Vogel, J. Widmer, D. Farin, M. Mauve, and W. Effelsberg, "Priority Based Distribution Trees for Application Level Multicast," Proceedings of NetGames 2003, Redwood City, CA, USA, pp. 148-157, May 2003.

ONLINE MULTIMEDIA AND TELEVISION

Definition: *In a drive to provide premium video services using a pay per view or a subscription service, there is a parallel attempt to deliver on demand multimedia content from the web directly to a regular television set, over broadband Internet connections.*

Ubiquitous presence of broadband home connections and improvements in compression and transmission technology has led to the marriage of the Internet and traditional entertainment devices such as the Television set.

Internet-to-TV

A large number of traditional television channels as well as Internet-only channels offer diverse, free, and legal video content over the Web. In such a system the media server encodes (compresses) the stream using a codec and the end pc-user views the compressed video content using a media player. Common streaming media systems include QuickTime, Windows Media, Real System, and SHOUTcast.

In a drive to provide premium video services using a pay per view or a subscription service, there is a parallel attempt to deliver on demand multimedia content from the web directly to a regular television set, over broadband Internet connections.

In this architecture a set-top box connects to a home entertainment system (typically composite video / S-Video output coupled with optical digital plugs) and to a broadband Internet connection (via Ethernet or 802.11 wireless connection). The set-top box comes equipped with a remote control, search functionality, and Digital Rights Management (DRM) package. A high capacity storage (around 80GB) allows for storage in MPEG-2 format for high quality viewing. Content is not restricted to videos but also includes digital audio and online radio stations, typically stored in MP3 format. In a model popularized by TiVo, viewers use an on-screen program guide to download content to their set-top box, and have the capability to pause/fast-forward/rewind programs on TV. Add-ons to the box allow the user to customize and personalize their digital video and audio content.

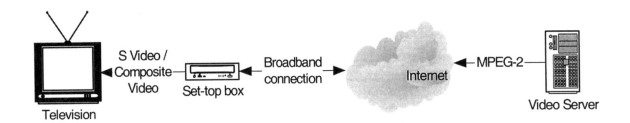

Figure 1. Internet-to-TV.

Players in this field include giants such as SBC Communications, EchoStar, Communications, and Disney, along with revolutionary startups such as Akimbo, Dave TV, Ripe TV, and TiVo [1]. Content providers include cable TV channel providers, aspiring filmmakers and video artists, online video archives, as well as online DVD rental companies such as NetFlix, which announced in 2004, a tie-up with TiVo to allow consumers to directly download their DVDs to their set-top boxes.

See: Online Multimedia E-Commerce

References

1. http://www.akimbo.com.
2. http://www.dave.tv.
3. http://www.ripe.tv.
4. http://www.tivo.com.

ONLINE MULTIMEDIA E-COMMERCE

Ben Falchuk
Telcordia Technologies, Inc., Piscataway, USA

Vinod Jayaraman
NTT Multimedia Labs, Palo Alto, USA

Definition: Online multimedia e-commerce refers to a secure transfer of multimedia data over the Internet.

This article outlines some of the main concepts and use-cases associated with online multimedia e-commerce. By *online multimedia e-commerce*, we mean to imply a transfer of multimedia data achieved securely (or within the requirements of the participants) over the Internet (via wireline or wireless network infrastructure). The transferred data has some intrinsic value to the buyer and so a payment to the seller follows or precedes the data transfer in some secure fashion. Buying and activating a new ringtone from a mobile cellular phone or buying digital audio (a song) from a desktop PC are two quintessential examples, though the concept generalizes.

At the time of writing, digital multimedia e-commerce is on the rise. Digital audio, video, ringtones, and imagery lead the way. The International Federation of the Phonographic Industry (IFPI) and Jupiter Research estimate the digital music market at around $330 million in 2004 (with over 200 million tracks downloaded) and expect that to double in 2005. While this may represent the market peak, it is unlikely; and the industry is serious. Elsewhere, Sony, Matsushita, Samsung and Phillips will attempt to jointly develop common standard Digital Rights Management technologies for their devices. Meanwhile, some say ringtone e-commerce revenue is reaching $2-$3 billion worldwide and the pages of Billboard Magazine now track best-selling ringtones beside best-selling CDs. Online multimedia e-commerce has the following main use-cases:

1. Find multimedia of interest on the network
2. Secure its delivery and payment
3. Display the media on the Device
4. Manipulate the media via other E-Commerce applications

The remainder of this chapter describes aspects of these main use-cases with details and examples from current prevalent technologies. As this topic is very broad and touches many aspects of technology, this chapter is intended to be a non-exhaustive high-level introduction to the concepts – technical and commercial – related to this domain.

Finding Multimedia on the Internet

The volume of online digital multimedia content is expanding at an exponential rate. Users can choose from a variety of mediums such as digital music, video segments, ringtones, and images, to name a few. Availability and use of this information is dependent upon the ease with which this information can be accessed, retrieved, filtered and managed. To this end, search engines and custom software tools such as music/video libraries and peer-to-peer applications play an indispensable role.

While the amount of available content has been increasing by many orders of magnitude, the user's ability to look at content has not [7]. People are still only willing to look at the first few tens of results yielded by a search engine. As a result, with enormous growth of digital audio-visual information on the internet, there is a need for new indexing algorithms that generate high precision results. Most search engines today make use of the structured information present in a hypertext document. Understanding the structure of an HTML document can reveal valuable information about the multimedia content located within the document. As outlined in [8], these include:

1. File names: This includes the name of the file as well as the top-level directory and provides interesting clues for indexing the content of the image.
2. File Captions: this may be thought of as the text located within the same center tag as the file or in the same paragraph. If present file captions can provide accurate information on the associated file.

3. ALT=Text: Image fields may contain a special ALT=section for alternate text that is displayed in the event when the actual media is not displayed.
4. HTML-title – the HTML title of the document
5. Hyperlink: The text of the hyperlink refers to can provide clues to the nature of the content.

Search engines such as Google (http://www.google.com) make use of both link structure and anchor text sections. Google uses the link structure of the web to calculate quality ranking for each page - which it calls PageRank - and uses the anchor text to glean description of the web page that it points to [7].

In a parallel effort, to simplify the design of multimedia capable search engines, there is a drive for the development of content-based metadata standards for audiovisual data on the web. One such standard is MPEG-7 ("Multimedia Content Description Interface") standard whose objective is to specify a standard set of descriptors and description schemes for describing the content of audiovisual information. It aims for standardized representation of multimedia metadata in XML and addresses access and delivery, in addition to indexing, and searching. MPEG-7 Version 1 was released in October 2001 and work is currently in progress on version 2.

To facilitate search of televised content including popular shows, documentaries, sports, and news segments – search engines (e.g. http://video.google.com) use the closed captioning text for searching relevant content. Another innovative search initiative is undertaken by Blinkx TV (http://www.blinkx.tv) which proactively searches for relevant multimedia content based on the content being viewed by the individual user. Blinkx TV captures and stores content from Television and Radio broadcast stations on a continuous basis. Using image and audio analysis techniques such as advanced speech recognition techniques, with intelligent Context Clustering Technology (CCT) and synchronization technologies it analyses and understands the actual content (spoken words) of an audio/video file, which is then used to accurately index the multimedia content.

Metadata for music is provided by online music libraries. The CDDB (CD Database) service provided by Gracenote (http://www.gracenote.com) describes itself as the industry standard for music recognition services. It claims to run the largest online database of music information in the world (about 2.5 million CDs, 32 million songs), and to be used by over 1 million people in over 130 countries every day. Using the ISRC code, CDDB can provide information even on compilations. It provides expanded album and track fields, credits, genres, web-links and segments. In addition Gracenote provides uses waveform recognition technology and matches it against its database of audio footprints to uniquely identify music segments. CDDB is used in the Apple iTunes application.

Regardless of how multimedia content is located on a network, an e-commerce transaction of a secured nature is an important next step.

Securing Multimedia E-Commerce

Secure data transactions over the Internet must generally meet the following requirements: authentication, authorization, confidentiality, integrity, and accounting [1]. *Authentication* is the notion of identifying the buyer and/or seller. *Authorization* refers to the permissions of the participants with respect to the transaction and the data. *Integrity* refers to the process of ensuring that transaction data remains in an untampered-with form, agreed upon by all parties. *Confidentiality* is the notion that the details of both the transaction and the data remain known only to the parties involved. *Accounting* is the process by which trustworthy billing, reporting, and auditing information is reliably created [2][3]. These requirements are not always met in all cases, and note that some technologies (described below) help to meet more than one requirement.

Digital certificates play a key underlying role in securing multimedia e-commerce. Certificates, issued by trusted 3rd parties called Certificate Authorities (CA), verify the holder's identity in an unforgeable way (for example, CREN.net grants "campus" certificates). A certificate is generally either a client certificate (to authenticate in individual's identity, restrict access, etc.), server certificate (to allow visitors to an e-commerce site to authenticate the site's identity), institutional certificates (allowing institutions to grant further certificates), or a root certificates from a CA. Certificates are used in the Secure Sockets Layer (SSL) (see next section) as well as Secure MIME, Internet Protocol Secure Standard (IPSec) and Secure Electronic Transactions (SET) protocols. The combination of certificates, CA's, clients, and servers, together with the related policies and human roles, comprise a Public Key Infrastructure (PKI). Managing PKI's in deployment remains a challenge for many reasons, including costs of ownership [4].

Secure Sockets Layer

Secure Sockets Layer (SSL) is a de facto standard, originally created and implemented by Netscape Corp. It is now very widely used to secure the transport of information between Internet entities, including servers and Web browsers. SSL secures the transport layer – recall in the well known Open System Interconnection 7-layer protocol stack that physical, data link, and network layers are 'below' transport, and session, presentation, and application layers are 'above' it. Therefore SSL and its equivalents are concerned with securing transfer of data between end systems, as well as end-to-end error recovery and flow control. The Transport layer ensures complete data transfer. Transport level security is not concerned with MAC-level issues, encoding packets into bits, or connections between applications themselves, as these are handled at other levels. Since SSL is implemented by Internet Explorer and Netscape browsers, casual Web users see SSL in action daily. Both browsers indicate secure (encrypted) sessions with lock icons on the bottom toolbar (see Figure 1). Note that the IETF stewards the Transport Layer Security (TLS) protocol, which it has worked from SSL, and will attempt to move it through to standardization.

Figure 1. Web Browsers Netscape (left) and Internet Explorer (right) indicating SSL.

First, a brief outline of the basic SSL e-commerce use-case:

1. Web client (e.g. Firefox, Internet Explorer, etc.) connects to an SSL-compliant Website (e.g. to submit a credit card payment)
2. The Web client asks Web server to authenticate itself. This usually involves getting a legitimate CA's declaration that the server has indeed registered. Once this 'handshake' is complete the parties have authenticated themselves (usually only the server) and exchanged 'session keys'.
3. Data sent from the web client during the SSL session is encrypted and cannot be read by interceptors, nor can it be tampered with

SSL works on two main fronts: a) ensuring data integrity and security, and b) coordinating connections. A view of the SSL layers of control is shown in Figure 2.

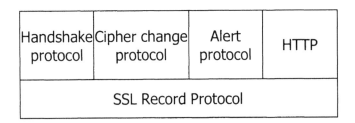

Figure 2. SSL layers of control.

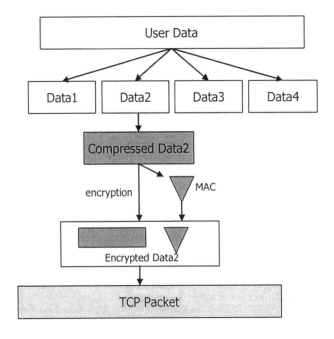

Figure 3. SSL record protocol.

The SSL Record Protocol is used in the encryption of user data for packaging into a TCP packet (e.g. the credit card number above). Figure 3 illustrates this packaging procedure. User data is fragmented into (optionally compressed) small fragments (e.g. *Data2* in the Figure 3). Header information is added to each fragment, including record lengths, and a Message Authentication Code (MAC) value which results from hashing the data in the fragment with a secret key and other information. Then the data and the MAC are encrypted using some agreed upon encryption technique; additional headers (such as SSL version types) are added. Finally, the data is placed into a TCP packet for transmission. Note that past work has shown that the SSL's overhead can incur a significant performance hit on SSL-enabled servers [5].

Single Sign-On

Single Sign-On (SSO) is an increasingly important enabler for online multimedia ecommerce. SSO alleviates the need for online users to have a user name and password for each Service Provider (SP) – that is, the need to be authenticated at *each* e-commerce site. Instead, a user with SSO technology can be authenticated only once for a circle of SP e-commerce sites. For example, once signed-on, the user can go to an airline web site and book tickets, and to a car rental web site for a car. At each site the user's credentials and authorization (e.g. credit card number) are accessible to the SP via SSO technologies. The user is authenticated by a third party Authentication Service Provider (ASP) who has a special relationship with the SP's in the 'circle'. The user may have many identities with the ASP, and one or more may be associated with any of the SP's. The ASP necessarily communicates user updates and identity information to SP's in a secure fashion. At the time of writing, the Liberty Alliance (see projectlibery.org) and Microsoft Passport (see passport.com) are two prevalent SSO technologies. The OASIS[1] Security Assertion Markup Language (SAML) defines an XML schema allowing authentication, authorization, and attribution assertions to be represented, and can serve as representation syntax for SSO-related assertions. In the example above, the SSO provider sends SAML assertions to both the airline and car rental e-commerce sites.

Multimedia E-Commerce Formats

Digital audio and video - movies and music – are two very important multimedia commodities (i.e. types), with respect to e-commerce. Online music and movie downloads comprise a large part of Internet multimedia revenue. For both of these there exist many digital formats, some of which are proprietary, while others are open standards; others still are grass-roots formats gathering community support (or losing it as the case may be). This section informally outlines some of these technologies. Table 1 summarizes some popular Internet file types for multimedia. Due to the lossy nature of the Internet, maintaining quality while delivering these multimedia types across the Internet to users is a challenge. Most audio and video playback tools rely on buffering to help 'smooth out' losses; some utilize a dynamic view of the current application bit rate to maintain quality.

---

[1] Organization for the Advancement of Structured Information Standards, http://www.oasis-open.org

Table 1. A small subset of Internet Multimedia File Formats

	Type	Description	Developer/status
Digital Audio	.mp2	MPEG audio layer 2. Finalized into the MPEG-1 efforts. Excellent quality at 256...384 kbit/sec.	MPEG
	.mp3	MPEG audio layer 3. Performance improvements over mp2. Max bitrate of 320 kbit/sec.	MPEG
	.aac	Advanced Audio Coding; compression ratios and quality superior to .mp3 in most cases.	MPEG, Fraunhofer
	.wma	Windows Media Audio.	Microsoft
	.ra	A proprietary audio format resulting from a Real Networks tools	Real Networks
	.ogg	Open, free, unpatented audio format. The Vorbis compression scheme is mostly used in this format.. Claims to better qualitative results given comparable file sizes with other audio formats.	Open source, public domain, vendor-neutral
	.wav	Wave file; uncompressed audio. Built upon the Microsoft RIFF specification.	Microsoft
	.mpc	Musepack audio files. A lossy format deemed good at medium bitrates 128-256kbit/sec.	Musepack
	.au	8 bit uncompressed audio file format developed by Sun Microsystems for their workstations.	Sun
	.raw (many)	A format in which audio is written (or burned) 'as is' onto media (such as CD's), including errors	--
	Cda	Audio format for audio CD. Personal computers do not store .cda directly; instead, CD tracks are 'ripped' to some other common format (e.g. .mp3)	--
	vox	An audio format used in telephony applications	Dialogic
	.aiff	Apple uncompressed audio interchange file format.	Apple
Digital Video	MPEG	The MPEG-* video standards (e.g. MPEG-2, MPEG-4, MPEG-7). Moving Pictures Experts Group is an ISO/IEC working group charged with studying and creating standards for digital audio and video representation.	MPEG
	.wmv	Windows Media Video, a catch-all for Microsoft video encoding technology. Used in conjunction with Windows Media Player.	Microsoft
	.asf	A Microsoft 'file format' (or 'container format) not a compression technology per se. Encapsulates multimedia payloads of various types.	Microsoft
	.qt, .mov	A format for storing and specifying multimedia information, most notably movies. The movie may be self-contained but in general the .qt file is a data structure identifying 'external' multimedia data.	Apple
	.ram, .rm	A streaming (audio and) video format originally intended to work well over low bandwidth Internet connections.	Real Networks
	.avi	Audio Video Interleave format; a container-type format which can be used with a variety of video compression techniques.	Microsoft

In general, audio and video codecs intended for Internet use should compensate for anticipated packet losses (and subsequent *retransmit*s) to optimize the end-user Quality of Experience (QoE). Codecs sample analog music and create a digital format. The sample length (in bits) and rate (number of samples per sec) essentially determine the resulting quality. As an example, audio CD's are sampled in 16 bits at 44.1 kHz.

The audio encoding formats MP3 (MPEG-1/2 Layer 3) and AAC (MPEG-2 Advanced Audio Coding) are two of a small handful of dominant Internet audio formats. There are several reasons for this, including these standards' open nature, availability of codecs/decoders, and their performance in audio quality tests. AAC is the more recent of the above two technologies and is widely seen as a successor to MP3. Both are lossy perceptual encodings, meaning that the file recovered by uncompressing the audio is not a bit-for-bit replica of the original. However, the algorithms have been designed to get close to the threshold at which these bit losses are inaudible to the human perception system (hence the coding is therefore referred to as *perceptual encoding*).
Some of the differences are pointed out below (see [6] for more detailed explanations, and for block diagrams of MP3 and AAC encoder functionality):

- Compressed file size - Given equal bit rates, AAC-encoded audio's superior compression will yield a smaller file
- Joint Stereo Coding - More flexible mid/side and intensity AAC coding algorithm (yields better compression)
- Huffman Coding – in MP3, the coding of quantized samples occurs mostly in pairs (rarely quadruples). AAC uses quadruples coding more often.
- High Freq. Resolutions – MP3: 576 frequency lines, AAC: 1024 frequency lines
- Perceived Audio quality – AAC encoded audio fares better than MP3 (at the same bit rate). Note that such perceptual tests are difficult to administer and subjective

Multimedia formats enable content to be experienced on various hardware devices.

Consumer Devices

The target destination of online multimedia content, apart from the home computer, is a variety of consumer devices. With declining memory prices, shrinking hard drive sizes, and significant advances in compression technologies, there is wide array of consumer devices available for the public. Consumer devices come packaged with software to directly connect to an online store and allow the user to transfer, store, and catalog content. Content can then be synchronized with a PC over USB/FireWire/Bluetooth links. The end consumer devices fall in various categories:

- Mobile Music players - In this scenario an individual user performs the following step:
  - Uses an application (e.g. iTunes from Apple) on his computer to access an online music store.
  - Browses, samples, and selects the music he wants.
  - Purchases the music through a secure encrypted channel such as SSL.

o   The user can, then, listen to the music on his home computer, burn it to a CD, or transfer it to a mobile device.

Mobile audio players come in various sizes and flavors – the storage capacity ranges from 16MB (flash) to over 60 GB (hard disk – space equivalent to around 15,000 songs). These devices are capable of playing music in various formats including AAC, MP3, WAV, and WMA. Popular vendors include: Apple, Creative Zen Micro, iRiver, and Yepp.

- Cell Phones
    - o   Music - At the time of this writing, newer models of phones come equipped with over two gigabytes of disk space with optional memory. Stereo audio is supported wirelessly over Bluetooth technology. Handsets support MP3, WMA, RealAudio/Video, MIDI, WAV, AAC and a range of others formats – providing wide-ranging industry compatibility.
    - o   Images/ Video / TV – Camera cell phones with photo and video capture capabilities along with media players are increasingly popular. Streaming video along with TV for cell phones (e.g. MobiTV from Idetic: http://www.mobitv.com) is on the rise. Content providers such as sports and news channel tailor their content for display on cell phones. Current configurations support video encoded in 3GPP2 (MPEG-4 and H.263), video can be captured at QCIF (176x144 pixel) or Sub-QCIF (128 x 95 pixel) with resolution of 15 frames per second.

- Home entertainment – With current audio and video compression techniques and streaming technologies there is a drive to integrate multimedia content from the web with home entertainment devices such as television and home stereo. This combines the capabilities of PC software to search, purchase, and catalog content with more sophisticated playback capabilities of home entertainment equipment. Wireless networking is one of the most attractive options to connect home equipment together [9]. Competing technologies are:

    - o   *IEEE802.11* is a family of evolving standards – 802.11b/g operates at 2.4GHz and provides data rates of 11Mbs and 54Mbs respectively. 802.11a operates at 5GHz and provides data rates of up to 54Mbs.
    - o   *Home RF* is specifically designed for connecting home devices operates at 2.4GHz and provides data rates of around 10Mbs.
    - o   *Bluetooth* designed for short range devices operates at 2.4GHz and provides data rates of about 1Mbs.
    - o   *Ultra wideband (UWB)* still under approval process from FCC operates between 3.1GHz and 10.6 GHz and can potentially have higher data rates than IEEE802.11 based networks.

Use of mobile devices for e-commerce is constantly evolving. Standardized in ISO 18092 and operating in the 13.56-MHz range, NFC is an interface technology for exchanging data between consumer electronic devices at a distance of about 10 cm. An example is an NFC-enabled mobile phone that reads a smart tag embedded in a concert poster to download information about the artist and can initiate transactions to purchase songs or order concert tickets from the web.

See: Trends in Multimedia E-Commerce, Online Multimedia and Television, Cell phones and E-Commerce, Peer to Peer Systems and Digital Rights Management

References

1. D. Greer, "Taking steps to Secure Web Services," IEEE Computer, October 2003, pp. 14-16.
2. J. Park and R. Sandhu, "Secure Cookies on the Web," IEEE Internet Computing, July 2000, pp. 36-44.
3. B. Lampson, "Computer Security in the Real World," IEEE Computer, June 2004, pp. 37-46.
4. A. Nash, W. Duane, and C. Joseph, "PKI: Implementing and Managing E-Security," McGraw-Hill, New York.
5. G. Apostolopoulos, V. Peris, and D. Saha "Transport Layer Security: How much does it really cost?," Proceedings of the InfoCom'99, New York, March, 1999.
6. K. Bradenburg, "MP3 and AAC Explained," Proceedings of the Audio Engineering Society (AES) 17th Int'l Conf. on High Quality Audio Encoding, Florence, 1999.
7. S. Brin and L. Page, "The anatomy of a Large-Scale Hypertextual Web Search Engine," available at http://www-db.stanford.edu/pub/papers/google.pdf.
8. C. Frankel, M.J. Swain, and V. Athitsos, "WebSeer: An Image Search Engine for the World Wide Web," Technical Report 96-14, August 1996.
9. S. Teger and D. Waks, "End-User Perspectives on Home Networking," IEEE Communication Magazine, April 2002.

OPEN SYSTEMS FOR ONLINE FACE RECOGNITION

Definition: As opposed to the traditional supervised learning approach, online approaches using unsupervised learning techniques have been explored for online face recognition.

Generic person identification is important for novel applications such as video news library and continuous lifelog video. Face recognition technology has seen significant advances, and the FERET evaluation program has created sound testing methodologies [1]. In spite of these advances, face recognition to date, remains a very hard problem. As opposed to the traditional supervised learning approach, online approaches using unsupervised learning techniques have been explored. In [2], authors investigate such an "open" system based on eigenfaces and clustering techniques that allows a humanoid robot to automatically learn the faces of people it interacts with. In [3], authors describe an algorithm that uses virtual labels created from clustering in the output space (name or gender of a person) to incrementally derive discriminative features in input space (face pictures). Next, in [4] authors present a technique for optimally selecting face exemplars from video with the initial help of an expert for online learning of gender.

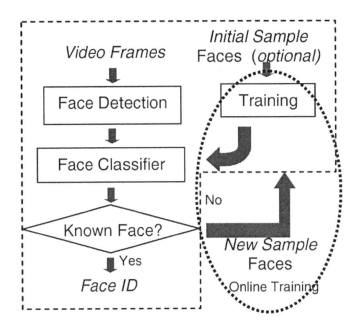

Figure 1. Face recognition system architecture.

Finally, in [5] authors present a method for an online-learning face recognition system for a variety of videos based on Modified Probabilistic Neural Networks (MPNN). This system can automatically detect unknown faces and train new face classifiers such that an "unknown face" can be recognized if it appears again. Figure 1 distinguishes a training phase and classification phase just like any other face recognition system (depicted with a dashed line). The difference with the closed systems is the feedback arrow to the training phase for unknown faces. These unknown persistent faces (assumed to be important) become new sample faces for the online training (dotted ellipse in Figure 1).

See: Face Recognition

References

1. P.J. Phillips, H. Moon, P. Rauss, and S.A. Rizvi, "The FERET Evaluation Methodology for Face-Recognition Algorithms," Proceedings of the Computer Vision and Pattern Recognition, Puerto Rico, pp. 137-143, 1997.

2. L. Aryananda, "Recognizing and Remembering Individuals: Online and Unsupervised Face Recognition for Humanoid Robot," Proceedings of the 2002 IEEE/RSJ International Conference on Intelligent Robots and Systems (IROS 2002), Vol. 2, pp. 1202-1207, 2002.

3. J. Weng, C. Evans, and W. Hwang, "An Incremental Learning Method for Face Recognition under Continuous Video Stream," Proceedings of the IEEE Conference on Automatic Face and Gesture Recognition, pp. 51-256, 2000.

4. M. Castrillon-Santana, O. Deniz-Suarez, J. Lorenzo-Navarro, and M. Hernandez-Tejera, "Face Exemplars Selection from Video Streams for Online Learning,"

Computer and Robot Vision, pp. 314-321, 2005.

5. J. Fan, N. Dimitrova, and V. Philomin, "Online Face Recognition System for Videos based on Modified Probabilistic Neural Networks with Adaptive Threshold," Proceedings of the IEEE ICIP 2004, Singapore, October 2004.

OPTIMIZATION OF VIDEO CONTENT DESCRIPTIONS FOR RETRIEVAL

Thierry Urruty [1], Fatima Belkouch[2], Chabane Djeraba[1], Bruno Bachimont[3], Edouard Gérard[4], Jean de Bissy[4], Olivier Lombard[5], and Patrick Alleaume[5]

[1] *LIFL - UMR CNRS USTL 8022, University of Lille 1, France*
[2] *STID, University of Lille 2, France*
[3] *UTC-Heudiasyc – UMR CNRS 6599, France*
[4] *SYLIS FRANCE*
[5] *OuestAudiovisuel, France*

Definition: XML descriptions need to be optimized to speed up the matching and retrieval processes for video content.

Abstract

The search of audiovisual information becomes today a peremptory necessity for a number of applications (for example: movie production) that require frequent accesses to audiovisual content. The search of information requires audiovisual content descriptions, and preferably content descriptions based on a standard, such as XML. The standard is necessary to share content descriptions by different search tools. XML is suitable to represent the complexity of descriptions; however, it is not suitable to support efficient matching and retrieval. Therefore, XML descriptions need to be optimized to speed up the matching and retrieval processes. And this is the scope of this article: developing a method that deals with this shortcoming of XML descriptions.

The method proceeds in two steps: Firstly, it transforms audiovisual content description from XML space into a multidimensional space, composed of numeric vectors. Secondly, the vectors are organized in a new multidimensional indexing structure, called Kpyr. Kpyr combines a pyramid technique and a clustering method to avoid the disadvantages of the current approaches that are not efficient when data are not uniformly distributed in the multidimensional space. Experiment results confirm our expectations: good quality of answers in a relatively short time.

Introduction

In recent years, the size of digital video archives has grown enormously in many application domains, such as news agencies, TV broadcasters, and advertising agencies that run large digital archives of movies and video footage. The data volume growing and the use of those increasingly turned towards audiovisual professionals made video information retrieval a major problem. Many research efforts and progresses have been deployed by researchers these last years. Although these efforts and progresses, tools available remain insufficient or unsuited, and the need to study and analyze for better managing this mass of information is strongly made feel.

When retrieval process and standard representation are considered, an important mass of content descriptions are generated, using XML standard format. We use also the term of normalized (standardized) content descriptions. Normalized content descriptions are powerful to represent the complexity of descriptors. However, they are not designed for efficient matching and retrieval, when dealing with high number of descriptors and thousands of video hours. And this is the major shortcoming of normalized content descriptions.

This article deals with this major shortcoming of the normalized audiovisual content descriptions, based on XML format. Historically, the use of this standard in content description is partly the result of multimedia content description interface (MPEG-7 [11]) recommendations, actually not really used in audiovisual industry; however, it had the merit to promote XML for multimedia content description.

To deal with this shortcoming, our method transforms the normalized audiovisual content description into vectors of a multidimensional space model. And then, the vectors are organized efficiently using our multidimensional indexing method, Kpyr. In such representation, user queries and video segments are both represented by vectors in the multidimensional space model. The length of dimension is equal to the number of descriptors by video segments.

The paper is organized as follows: Section 2 describes the normalized audiovisual content description. Section 3 describes the vector space model and our indexing method. Section 4 details the implementation of the search engine that includes our method. Section 5 concludes the paper and addresses future works.

Normalized audiovisual content description

We use the term of "normalized" or "standard" to highlight XML format. So, normalized audiovisual content description means audiovisual content description based on XML format. We use also the term of standardized or normalized meta-data. In our point of view, MPEG-7 standard [11] boosted the use of XML for audiovisual content description.

The use of XML to describe audiovisual content is the result of two important properties of XML. Firstly, XML format is able to describe the complexity of audiovisual descriptors. Secondly, XML is a standard, so it is easy to share the standardized representation by different search tools. And more generally, the interest of the standard is to support interoperability of search tools. In other way, we can see audiovisual content description based on MPEG-7, as a particular case, of normalized audiovisual content description.

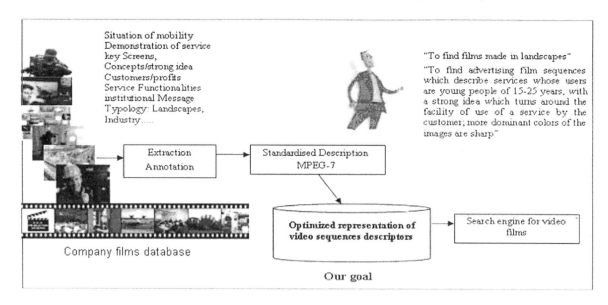

Figure 1. Global Schema of our exploratory project.

Annotating audiovisual content for retrieval requires the generation of masses of descriptions, which must be filtered, indexed and stored efficiently to ensure fast information accesses. Our research objective aims at managing masses of normalized audiovisual content descriptions. More particularly, our research objective is to develop tools around the normalized content description, in order to allow efficient audiovisual content search (Figure 1).

Normalized audiovisual content description is composed of audiovisual descriptors and description schemes. The descriptors define the syntax and the semantics of audiovisual features. The description schemes specify, basically, the structure and semantics of relationships between descriptors. In general, it is composed of descriptors and sub-description schemes.

In the context of our application, we consider about sixty audiovisual descriptors, and description schemes. The majority of descriptors are included in the text annotation description scheme. These audiovisual descriptors are associated to thousands of video segments of audiovisual database. These descriptors and description schemes constitute the normalized audiovisual content description. And, they are generated automatically from professional annotation tools.

The efficiency of audiovisual searches depends mainly of the access method to the normalized audiovisual content description. These accesses include frequent matching and retrieval. We propose a method that optimizes normalized audiovisual content description for efficient matching and retrieval. The optimization consists of transforming normalized descriptions into numeric vectors, and creating of an index structure suitable for frequent matching and retrieval. In this paper, we will focus on these points: creating a suitable index structure in vector space model.

The numeric vectors consider both numeric and semantic descriptors. The numeric descriptors have numeric values, which admit orders (ex. Media time point, Media increment duration). And semantic descriptors represent semantic information such as (Free text annotation: mountain, rivers, and forest). In this step of work, we didn't consider proper noun (ex. Michel, Dupond,…). Each audiovisual segment is a numeric vector (point) in the space model.

Our approach

Our approach proceeds as shown in Figure 2. First, audiovisual content descriptions based on XML are transformed (coded) into numeric vectors of a multidimensional space model. Second, vectors are organized in efficient data structure. In addition, the query processing needs two different algorithms: the first one uses a Boolean search on the whole audiovisual bases in order to consider the proper nouns; the second one consists of transforming the query into a point in the vector space and doing search in the indexing structure. First, we describe the vector space model we use. Then, we present our indexing structure.

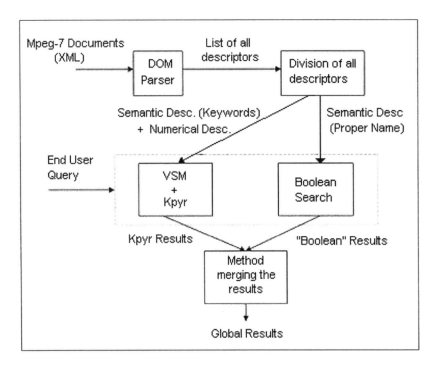

Figure 2. Architectural overview of our method.

Vector Space Model (VSM)

The vector Space Model transforms XML description of audiovisual segments into points P in the space of N dimensions: P ($x0, x1…, xN$). The size of dimensions (N) is equal to the number of audiovisual descriptors, excluding proper nouns. So, each audiovisual descriptor corresponds to a dimension in the space. N dimensions are resulting from numeric semantic descriptors N' < N. N" remaining dimensions corresponds to proper noun descriptors, and determined as following:

- We get all the key words present in MPEG-7 document describing the contents of video sequences.

- The set of all proper nouns is classified by categories, for example Actor, Producer... Those are stored in hash tables and will be used for a Boolean research only on the proper nouns.

- Using a thesaurus, all keywords are classified into several categories e.g. River, mountain, animals belong to Landscape Category.

- Each category corresponds to a dimension. We obtain thus the N" dimensions of the space.

The transformation of a video sequence into a point P (x0, x1,...,xN) in this space is done following these rules:

The set of coordinates is normalized xi € [0, 1], 0<i<N. If dimension corresponds to a numerical descriptor, then xi is equal to the normalized value of this descriptor:

$$xi = \frac{descriptorValue}{MaximumValueOfTheDescriptor}$$

If the dimension corresponds to a category resulting from semantic descriptors, value xi is equal to:

$$xi = \frac{NumberOfKeywordsInTheCategory}{NumberOfKeywordsInTheDocument}$$

Figure 3 gives an example of a vector space model related to normalized audiovisual content description. For semantic descriptors, using a thesaurus, all key words belonging to the FreeTextAnnotantion (FTA) Descriptor are classified into several categories e.g. River, mountain, animals belong to Landscape Category. The method extracts the frequency of key word by category. So, it counts the number of word keys by category. For numerical descriptors, we keep the value. The obtained vector will be then normalized.

Once the transformation of data into Vector Space Model is established, then the treatment will relate only to the multidimensional points corresponding to the video sequences. Below we describe the method we develop to index the set of these points.

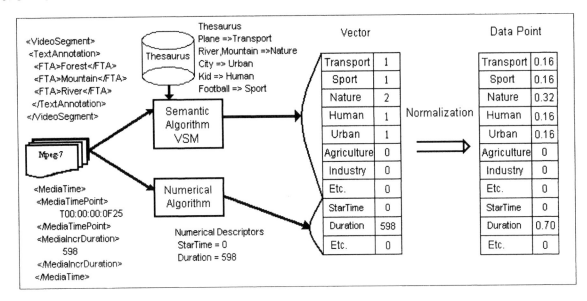

Figure 3. Vector space model.

Kpyr: our indexing structure

In a first time we present briefly some related works of multidimensional indexing method then we give an overview of Kpyr method.

<u>Related Work</u>

Many indexing structures have been proposed in the literature. Among them, we have VA File [7], Pyramid technique [1], IQ-Tree [8], LPC File [6], and Idistance [2]. The known Pyramid Technique, appeared in 1998, deals with the « curse of dimensionality ». Its performances are not affected in high dimensional space. However, its effectiveness depends on the data distribution and the volume of the database. It is also sensitive to the position of the queries in the space. In some cases, a sequential scan over all the data points may be more effective. The Pyramid Technique has been used by other indexing methods appeared more recently, such as P+Tree [3]. However those methods don't offer efficient structures that support both type of queries: KNN and WQ, furthermore they are strongly dependent of the workload (data size, dimensionality and data distribution).

<u>Overview of Kpyr</u>

Kpyr Algorithm follows four main steps:

- For a better clustering technique of data, we use K-means algorithm [5]. We obtain as results K homogenous clusters.

- For each cluster, we transform the corresponding subspace into a hypercube unit so that the Pyramid technique can be applied (transformation base function).

- We apply pyramid technique and obtain one B+Tree [9] by cluster.

- We determine borders delimiting the space regions represented by clusters. "A binary space tree" will be built from these borders. As shown in Figure 8, leaf nodes store pointers to B+Trees corresponding to different clusters. Others nodes represent the borders.

The search is done in two steps. The first one consists in determining the regions concerned with research using the borders. We deduce from them the clusters reached by the request. The second one corresponds to WQ inside the pyramid, associated to clusters.

Window query follows two steps. In the first one, the regions of points (vectors) concerned by the search are extracted, and then clusters, that are target of search, are deduced. The region extraction is based on borders in the binary space tree. In the second one, we search data points in all B+Trees of concerned clusters.

The contribution of our method is to provide the best conditions to apply the Pyramid Technique: The resulting indexing is more effective. Indeed, the space and the number of data to be indexed by Pyramid technique are reduced. The clusters are globally homogeneous; their center is the top of each pyramid, a reference point for the points of the cluster.

The calculation of the borders is achieved on data already clustered, which allows a better division of space than P+Tree using a approximated version of Bisecting K-means [4]. Borders are solely used to determine the clusters concerned by the query, which efficiently reduces the search space and therefore the response time. Algorithms and experiments of our indexing method Kpyr have been presented in [10].

Search Engine

One goal of our project is to build a tool for video sequences retrieval. This search engine has been realized in order to be used on line. The search made by end users is possible through three steps: the first step concerns the search interface where the end user makes his query. The end user can choose a category within a list of categories concerning the application field. Categories are corresponding to company films field. After choosing a category, our interface gives the end user a list of frequent keywords links to this category. For example, « professional sector » category, we have « office », « industrial workshop », « Commerce »… as frequents keywords linked. The end user can choose categories and keywords he likes, before submitting his search. In the figure example, we got three categories and keywords.

Second step of the search send the end user query to the server that contains our database and our indexing structure created off line.

The last step concerns the results of the search. Indeed, as shown in Figure 4, all video sequences resulting from this search appeared in our result interface with some information related to each sequence. We print in screen the pertinence value, the video title, the number of videotape linked to the same project, the beginning of the sequence in the videotape, its duration and a key image of the video sequence. A detail button has been added if the end user needs to see the normalized audiovisual content description.

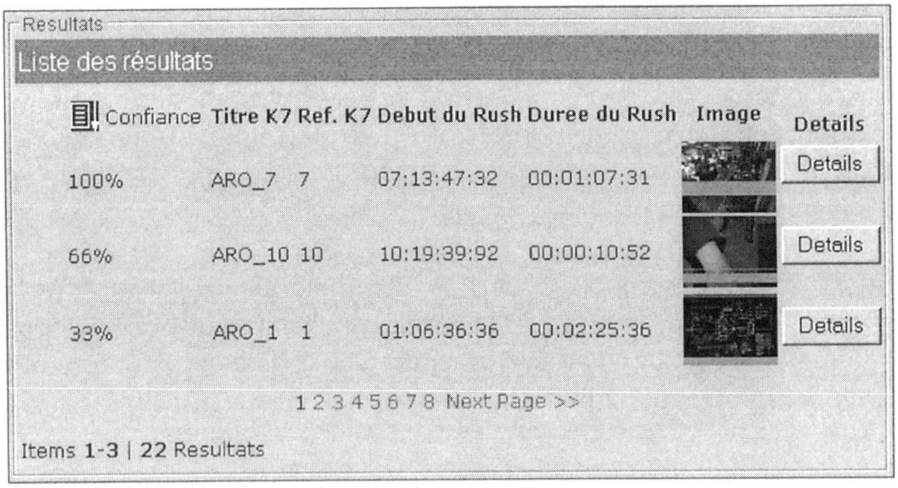

Figure 4. Results display.

Conclusion

More and more experimental search engines are based on normalized audiovisual content descriptions (normalized meta-data). The notion of normalized meta-data is strongly linked to XML standard. The use of the standard for audiovisual content description has become a reality on the basis of multimedia content description interface recommendations, known as MPEG-7. Using XML to describe audiovisual content has several advantages. Firstly, XML is a standard. So, different search tools may access to the same audiovisual content descriptions. Secondly, XML is powerful enough to represent complexity of audiovisual descriptors.

The XML standard, even if suitable to deal with complexities of audiovisual descriptors, is just a model of representation. It was not designed for efficient matching and retrieval processes. This is the role of non-normative methods around the standard necessary to exploit it. This point was particularly underlined during MPEG-7 recommendations. So, there are needs of methods or system mechanisms necessary to make efficient the use of the standard.

This article describes a method necessary to make efficient the use of the audiovisual content description based on XML in matching and retrieval processes. The method proceeds initially by a transformation of XML audiovisual content descriptions into a vector space model. Then, a new indexing technique is designed, implemented and tested, called Kpyr. Kpyr clusters vectors into categories and represents category vectors into pyramid structures. The main idea of the technique is the association of pyramid structures with categories (clusters) of vectors. The best state of art techniques, including pyramid and P+-tree, offer good performances in high dimensional spaces, and propose a powerful indexing method when the data are distributed homogeneously in the representation space. However, when data are not distributed homogeneously in the multidimensional space, these techniques loose their performances. That is why, firstly, our method clusters vectors, and then applies a pyramid technique in clusters. Globally, clusters contain homogeneous vectors. The cluster is considered homogeneous when the distortion of vectors is minimum. It means that the mean distance between the vectors and their center of gravity is minimum, on the basis of partition clustering.

References

1. S. Berchtold, C. Bohm, and H.-P. Kriegel, "The Pyramid Technique: Towards Breaking the Curse of Dimensionality," Proceedings of the ACM SIGMOD Int. Conference on Management of Data, 1998, pp. 142-153.
2. C. Yu, B.C. Ooi, K.-L. Tan, and H.V. Jagadish, "Indexing the distance: An efficient method to knn processing," in VLDB, September 2001, pp. 421-430.
3. R. Zhang, B.-C. Ooi, and K.-L. Tan, "Making the Pyramid Technique Robust to Query Types and Workloads," Proceedings of the IEEE, 20th International Conference on Data Engineering, April 2004.
4. S.M. Savaresi, D.L. Boley, S. Bittanti, and G. Gazzaniga, "Cluster selection in divisive clustering algorithms," Proceedings of SIAM Int. Conference on Data Mining, 2002.
5. J. MacQueen, "Some methods for classification and analysis of multivariate observations," Proceedings of the Fifth Berkeley Symposium, 1966, pp. 281-297.
6. G.-H. Cha, X. Zhu, D. Petrovic, and C.-W.Chang, "An efficient indexing method for nearest neighbors searches in high dimensional image databases," IEEE Transactions on Multimedia, 2002, pp. 76-87.
7. R. Weber, H.-J. Schek, and S. Blott, "A quantitative analysis and performance study for similarity-search methods in high-dimensional spaces," in 24th VLDB, 1998, pp. 194-205.
8. S. Berchtold, C. Böhm, H.V. Jagadish, H.P. Krieger, and J. Sander, "Independent quantization: An index compression technique for high-dimensional data spaces," Proceedings of the 16th International Conference on Data Engineering, 2000, pp. 577-588.
9. D. Comer, "The Ubiquitous B-Tree," ACM Computing Surveys, Vol. 11, No. 4, 1979, pp. 121-137.
10. T. Urruty, F. Belkouch, and C. Djeraba, "Kpyr: an efficient indexing method," Proceedings of the IEEE International Conference on Multimedia & Expo, Amsterdam, July 2005.
11. MPEG: Moving Picture Experts Group, http://www.chiariglione.org/mpeg/.

OVERLAPPED BLOCK MOTION COMPENSATION

Definition: The overlapped block motion compensation (OBMC) [1] aims at reducing the blocking effects by performing a weighted average of overlapped block segments during motion prediction.

In normal motion compensation, the current block is composed of 1) the predicted block from the previous frame (referenced by the motion vectors); and 2) the residual data transmitted in the bit stream for the current block. In OBMC, the prediction is a weighted sum of *three* predictions.

Let *(m, n)* be the column & row indices of an 8×8 pixel block in a frame; *(i, j)* be the column & row indices of a pixel within an 8×8 block; and *(x, y)* be the column & row indices of a pixel within the entire frame so that $(x, y) = (m×8 + i, n×8 + j)$. Then the weighted prediction for the current block is given by [2]:

$$P(x,y) = (q(x,y) H^0(i,j) + r(x,y) H^1(i,j) + s(x,y) H^2(i,j) +4)/8 \qquad (1)$$

where,

$$q(x,y) = (x + MV^0{}_x, y + MV^0{}_y),$$
$$r(x,y) = (x + MV^1{}_x, y + MV^1{}_y),$$
$$s(x,y) = (x + MV^2{}_x, y + MV^2{}_y).$$

$(MV^0{}_x, MV^0{}_y)$ denotes the motion vectors of the current block, $(MV^1{}_x, MV^1{}_y)$ denotes the motion vectors for the block above (below) if the current pixel is in the top (bottom) half of the current block, and $(MV^2{}_x, MV^2{}_y)$ denotes the motion vectors for the block to the left (right) if the current pixel is in the left (right) half of the current block (as illustrated in Figure 1).

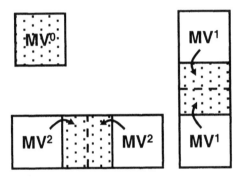

Figure 1. Overlapped blocks arrangement.

$H^0(i, j) =$

4	5	5	5	5	5	5	4
5	5	5	5	5	5	5	5
5	5	6	6	6	6	5	5
5	5	6	6	6	6	5	5
5	5	6	6	6	6	5	5
5	5	6	6	6	6	5	5
5	5	5	5	5	5	5	5
4	5	5	5	5	5	5	4

$H^1(i, j) =$

1	2	2	2	2	2	2	1
1	1	2	2	2	2	1	1
1	1	1	1	1	1	1	1
1	1	1	1	1	1	1	1
1	1	1	1	1	1	1	1
1	1	1	1	1	1	1	1
1	1	2	2	2	2	1	1
1	2	2	2	2	2	2	1

and $H^2(i, j) = (H^1(i, j))^T$

See: Motion Compensation for Video Compression

References

1. S. Nogaki and M. Ohta, "An overlapped block motion compensation for high quality motion picture coding," *Proceedings of the International Symposium on Circuits and Systems (ISCAS'92)*, Vol. 1, pp. 184-187, 1992.
2. ITU-T, "Video coding for low bit rate communication," *ITU-T Recommendation H.263*, 1996.

P

PEER-TO-PEER MULTICAST VIDEO

Definition: *Peer-to-peer multicast video refers to the concept of peer-to-peer communication, where nodes are both clients and servers.*

In the tradition video distribution scheme, a client contacts a server and establishes a unicast session before starting to receive the required content. Although this configuration is enough in many simple scenarios, it presents a number of problems. Indeed, the source's maximum output bandwidth limits the number of parallel clients. Moreover, since this approach follows a centralized configuration, it is vulnerable to attacks. A number of alternative solutions have appeared to overcome these limitations. They generally propose the use of replicated servers to increase both the robustness and the capacity of the system to serve more clients. A more recent approach relies upon the concept of peer-to-peer (p2p) communication, where nodes are both clients and servers. Virtual links associating two IP addresses are established forming an *overlay* network.

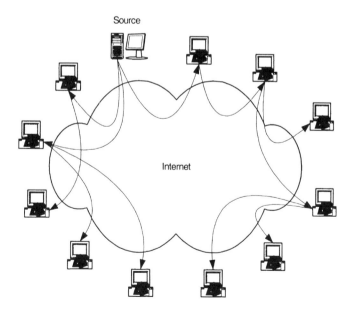

Figure 1. Example of an overlay distribution tree.

In addition to being more resistant to attacks, the inherent distributed nature of p2p is a solution for the problem of multiple clients bottlenecking the source. Peer-to-peer overlays have been rapidly adopted as a promising substrate for video distribution, for both video sharing (in the same way people share general data files) and streaming. In the latter case, a distribution tree is established between the source and the receivers [1]. The particularity here is that intermediate nodes are also end-systems (and in general also a client). In this way, the source sends the video to a number of clients that, in turn, send to other clients, and so on until all clients receive the video. We refer to this approach as *application-layer multicast* (since it forms an overlay distribution tree). Figure 1 shows an example of a video multicast tree using p2p concepts.

Although very attractive, video transmission over p2p networks presents a number of technical challenges. First, the distribution tree cannot grow indefinitely, since nodes closer to the leaves may experience high delays. While in a video on demand service this may not be a real issue, for other applications, such as interactive video communication, delays beyond a certain threshold are unacceptable. Another challenge is inherently related to the dynamic nature of peer-to-peer communications: nodes in an overlay may join/leave whenever they want, without any notice. A third problem concerns the complexity of establishing the distribution tree. Indeed, nodes are extremely heterogeneous in terms of receiving, transmitting, and storage capacities. For a small network, managing such a structure is feasible, but for larger dynamic topologies (even millions of receivers) it is likely that the overlay always operates in a sub-optimum configuration. Different solutions have been (and are being) proposed to overcome such limitations, which include, for instance, advanced algorithms for correctly placing nodes on the overlay. Recent results show that p2p video distribution is a promising solution to contour the limitations of the current Internet architecture [2].

See: Video over IP

References

1. Y.-H. Chu, S.G. Rao, S. Seshan, and H. Zhang, "A case for end system multicast," IEEE Journal on Selected Areas in Communications, Vol. 20, No. 8, pp. 1456-1471, October 2002.
2. D.A. Tran, K.A. Hua, and T.T. Do, "A peer-to-peer architecture for media streaming," IEEE Journal on Selected Areas in Communications, Vol. 22, No. 1, pp. 121-133, January 2004.

PEER-TO-PEER STREAMING

Roger Zimmermann, Leslie S. Liu
Computer Science Department
University of Southern California, Los Angeles, USA

Definition: *Peer-to-Peer (P2P) architecture for multimedia streaming is emerging in recent years which can eliminate the need for costly dedicated video servers in the traditional client-sever approach.*

The basic concept of peer-to-peer (P2P) computing is not new and some techniques date back many years when the Internet was first designed. However, the key phrase "peer-to-peer" has become widely and publicly recognized mostly after the pioneering Napster [1] file sharing network emerged in the late 1990's. Peer-to-peer is a very general term and people associate different concepts with it. Various forms of P2P techniques have been used in the fields of computing, networking, distributed file systems, and others. In this chapter we focus on how P2P techniques are being used for streaming media distribution.

P2P systems have some key characteristics that distinguish them from the traditional and widely used client-server model. The most prominent feature is that a P2P system is composed of a number of member *nodes*, each of which combines the functionality that is traditionally associated with *both* the server and the client. As such, multiple P2P nodes can form a collective that aggregates their resources and functionality into a distributed system. Node *A* may act as a client to node *B*, while at the same time function as a server to Node *C*. Beyond this fundamental characteristic, there are a number of features that are often associated with P2P systems. Note, however, that usually only a subset of the following characteristics holds true for any practical system.

- Reduced central control. Many P2P systems work in a fully decentralized fashion where all the nodes have equal functionality. The members are connected based on a system-specific construction policy and form a distributed topology. Exceptions to this model exist. For example, the original Napster file sharing network used a centralized index to locate files; subsequently the data was exchanged directly between individual peers.

- Heterogeneity. Members of a P2P system are usually heterogeneous in terms of their computing and storage capacity, network bandwidth, etc. A system may include high performance nodes on a university network and computers owned by residential users with broadband or modem connections.

- Flat topology. Members of the P2P network are often treated equally which results in a flat connection topology. However, hierarchical systems exist that introduce the concept of "super-peers."

- Autonomy. The time and resources that a member node can or will contribute to the system are dynamic and unpredictable. Often, nodes are under different administrative control. Hence the enforcement of global policies is a challenge.

- Fault resilience. P2P members may join or leave the topology at any time. Therefore, not only is the formed community very dynamic, but no assumptions should be made about the availability of resources or network paths. A P2P system must be able to recover from the unexpected and ungraceful leave of any of its members at any time.

Members of a P2P system are also referred to as nodes because they are often represented as network nodes in topology graph.

Streaming P2P Architectures

Streaming is a process of generating and delivering a steady, isochronous flow of data packets over networking medium, e.g., the Internet, from a source to a destination. The rendering of the content starts as soon as a small fraction of the data stream has been received. Streaming media usually denotes digital audio and video data, however haptic or other data may be streamed as well. One of the main resource bottlenecks that afflicts large client-server distribution architectures is the massive bandwidth that must be available from the server into the core of the network. This network connection is often very costly (compared to the server and client hardware) and may render a technically feasible solution economically not viable. Peer-to-Peer streaming is an alternative that alleviates the bandwidth cost problem by offering a service to deliver continuous media streams directly between peer nodes. However, the previously listed characteristics of P2P systems influence the design of such decentralized streaming solutions.

Theoretically, P2P architecture can be built over any networking medium and at potentially different layers of the network. However, most of the existing P2P implementations and their associated research have focused on application-level overlay networks. The Internet, as the dominant networking medium for research, business and entertainment, is also the preferred choice for P2P network substrates.

One of the virtues of today's P2P systems is their scalable nature. Peer-to-peer technologies were first widely used and accepted as file-sharing platforms in systems such as Napster, Gnutella and KaZaA. Subsequently, the P2P architecture evolved and was adapted for store-and-forward streaming. Examples of streaming systems that may be used to distribute previously stored content are Narada, HMTP, and Pastry. One distinguishing characteristic among these proposals is the shape of the streaming topology they construct, which will be described later in this chapter. Even though these designs promise good performance in terms of network link stress and control overhead, only a few of them have been implemented in real systems. Next, P2P technology was adapted for live streaming. In this scenario, media streams are generated by live sources (e.g., cameras and microphones) and the data is forwarded to other nodes in real-time. We distinguish two types of live streaming: one-way and two-way. The requirements for the two are quite different and more details follow below.

Streaming Process

A streaming process can be separated into three stages that overlap in time (Figure 1): data acquisition, data delivery and data presentation. Data acquisition is the stage that determines how the streaming content is acquired, packetized and distributed for streaming. The data presentation stage represents the methods on how to buffer, assemble and render the received data. Data delivery is the process of how the stream data is transported from the source to the destination. The source, the destination and all the intermediate nodes in a streaming system participate in a topology that is constructed based on the specific system's protocol. In a P2P streaming system, this network architecture exhibits peer-to-peer characteristics.

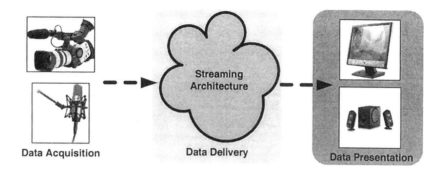

Figure 1. Streaming process.

Data Acquisition and Presentation

At the streaming source, the content is prepared for distribution. If the data was pre-recorded and is available as files, we categorize this as on-demand streaming (Figure 2). On the other hand, if the data is acquired in real time from a device, we term this live streaming (Figure 3). Content for on-demand streaming is pre-recorded and made available at source nodes usually long before the first delivery requests are initiated. This pre-recorded content can be distributed onto a single or multiple source nodes. Compared with a live streaming system, on-demand streaming usually can utilize a more sophisticated distribution process which may mean encoding the content into a processing-intensive, high-quality format and pre-loading it onto multiple source nodes. The efficiency and scalability of on-demand streaming is improved by caching copies of the content at the intermediate peers. With this approach, popular content is automatically replicated many times within the network and a streaming request can often be satisfied by peers in close proximity.

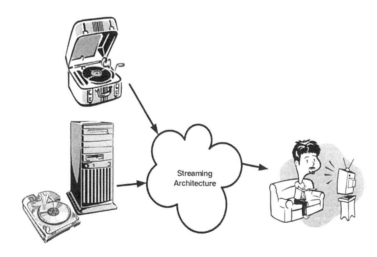

Figure 2. On-demand streaming.

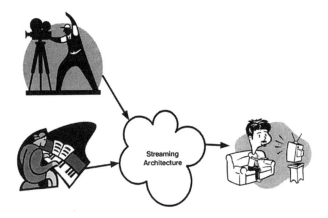

Figure 3. Live streaming.

One-way live applications have similar requirements as their on-demand cousins. One obvious difference is that the source data is generated in real time by a source device such as a camera, a microphone or some other sensor. One application is the broadcasting of live events such as sports games. Data may be cached for later on-demand viewing. Two-way live applications have very different requirements. Here, the end-to-end latency is crucial to enable interactive communications. Note that P2P topologies have a disadvantage in terms of minimizing the latency among participants because application-level processing is often required at every node. Skype [2] was probably the first successful Internet telephony system built on a P2P streaming architecture. It demonstrated that the latency problem can be solved and that P2P technology, with its many advantages, can indeed be used for live streaming purposes. AudioPeer [3], which is built on top of the ACTIVE [5] architecture, is another multi-party audio conferencing tool. It is designed specifically for large user groups. Its design distinguishes active users from passive users and provides low-latency audio service to active users.

Data Delivery
The transition of one or multiple copies of the content from a source node to a destination node is called a *streaming session*. A streaming session starts when a streaming request is made and ends when all associated destination nodes have received the last byte of the content. Depending on the number of source and destination nodes involved in a streaming session, we can distinguish three types of streaming systems: one-to-many, many-to-one and many-to-many (see Figures 4, 5, 6). All of these three types apply to either live or on-demand streaming. One-to-many streaming is also called broadcasting. It delivers content from a single source to multiple destination nodes. Much research has focused on how to make the delivery process fast and efficient for one-to-many streaming. P2P systems naturally produce a multi-cast distribution tree since any peer that receives a stream can forward it to multiple other nodes. Many-to-one streaming delivers data from multiple sources to a single destination. A good example is an on-demand movie viewer who simultaneously downloads fragments of the movie clip from multiple peers. Many-to-many streaming combines the features of the previous two

designs and usually requires a more complicated delivery network, which we will discuss in detail in following sections.

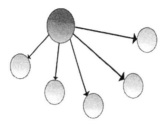

Figure 4. One to Many streaming.

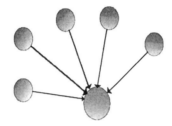

Figure 5. Many to One streaming.

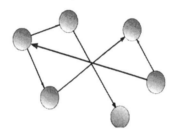

Figure 6. Many to Many streaming.

The P2P *network architecture* represents the topology how the nodes are inter-connected in a P2P system. P2P *streaming architecture* is the data path over which the streaming content is delivered from source to destination nodes. For a P2P streaming system, the network architecture is not necessary the same as the streaming architecture. For example, Scribe is a P2P network protocol constructing a ring-shaped network architecture and Pastry is the streaming architecture built on top of Scribe. But for most P2P systems, these two architectures are identical and can be represented in a single topology graph.

P2P streaming topologies, including the network architecture and the streaming architecture, can be categorized into four types: tree, mesh, ring and hybrid (see Figure 7). Tree structures start with a root node and add new nodes in a parent/children fashion. Many systems are built as tree topologies, e.g., AudioPeer, Yoid [8] and HMTP [9] . A mesh-based topology builds a full interconnect from each node to every other node and constructs a fully-connected map. For example, Narada [10] builds a mesh structure among all the

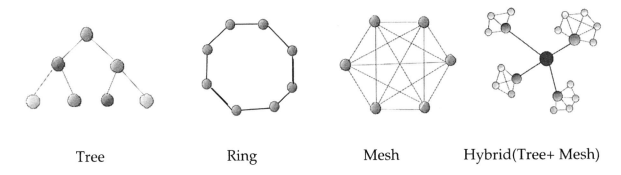

Tree · · · · Ring · · · · Mesh · · · · Hybrid(Tree+ Mesh)

Figure 7. Peer-to-Peer topologies.

peers and then for each peer constructs a single-source multicast tree from the mesh structure. Due to its centralized nature, Narada does not scale well. A ring-shaped topology links every node in the graph sequentially. This is usually done by assigning each node a unique node ID, which is generated by specific algorithms such as a distributed hash table (DHT). Finally, a hybrid approach combines two or more of the previous designs into their topology graph. Hybrid systems are usually divided into multiple hierarchical layers and different topologies are built at each layer. For example, NICE [11] was developed as a hierarchical architecture that combines nodes into clusters. It then selects representative parents among these clusters to form the next higher level of clusters, which then is represented as a tree topology.

Peer-to-Peer System Operation

From the perspective of a peer, the life-cycle of a P2P streaming session can be decomposed into a series of four major processes: finding the service, searching for specific content, joining or leaving the service, and failure recovery when there is an error.

Service Discovery and Content Search

In most P2P systems, service discovery is accomplished through a bootstrap mechanism that allows new nodes to join the P2P substrate. It may be accomplished through some dedicated "super-peers" to act as the well-known servers to help new peers to find other member nodes. These "super-peers" are called Rendezvous Point (RP) servers and are sometimes under the control of the administrator of the P2P system. A new peer finds the existence of the running Rendezvous Point Server from its pre-loaded RP server list. The list can be updated once a peer is connected to one of the RP servers. RP servers can also be used to collect statistic data and in some systems, these "super-peers" are connected to form a backbone streaming platform to make the system more stable.

The next step for a peer, after joining the collective, is to locate a stream or session. The availability of specific content can be discovered in two distinct ways. In an *unstructured* design, streams and files are located by flooding the P2P network with search messages. This technique is obviously wasteful and may result in significant network traffic. The second approach, called *structured*, is to index the content such that search messages can be forwarded efficiently to specific nodes that have a high probability to manage the desired content. To keep with the distributed theme of P2P systems, indexing is often achieved by hashing a content key and assigning that key to nodes with a distributed hash table (DHT) mechanism.

JOIN: After retrieving the necessary information from the RP server, or gaining enough information from the P2P system through some methods such as flood-based search, a new peer can join an existing session by establishing the necessary connections to already joined peers. After the join operation is done, a peer is considered to be a legitimate member.

LEAVE: Every member of a P2P system is usually also serving some other peers as part of the duty to share the load of the whole system. An unexpected departure of a peer can cause disruptions or loss of service for other peers in the system. Ideally a peer should help to reconcile the disconnect in the streaming network caused by its departure. If a system protocol is well designed, this process can be very fast and almost unnoticeable to the end user application.

RECOVERY: In the dynamic environment of a P2P system where peers are under different administrative control, the unexpected departure of peers is unavoidable. A P2P streaming system must cope with these failures and include a robust and efficient recovery mechanism to repair the streaming topology. However, on the positive side, since a robust recovery mechanism is an integral part of the design, this makes P2P systems naturally very tolerant to faults.

Challenges for Peer-to-Peer Streaming

P2P systems are designed to distribute the workload and network traffic among the peers and take advantage of the computing and storage resources of each individual peer. There are two aspects to this approach. One the positive side, a P2P system is very scalable and can potentially serve a very large streaming community where the network and processing load will be a significant challenge for a centralized system. The drawback of P2P systems is that because of the dynamic and unpredictable nature of peers a more complicated, fully distributed protocol is required to constantly maintain the system and recover from errors. A lack of centralized control also introduces difficulties for the administration and security of P2P systems. Below we list a few of the challenges commonly encountered in a P2P streaming system.

Quality of Service (QoS)
The quality of service (QoS) of a streaming system usually refers to the end-users experience. Criteria may include the smoothness of the display, the frequency of visual distortions, and the startup latency from session initiation to the onset of the display. QoS requirements depend on the type of P2P streaming systems. For example, users can tolerate a relatively longer delay in a non-interactive streaming system such as on-demand movie watching. This is in contrast to the requirements of a live, two-way audio conferencing system in which the delay must be bounded at the millisecond scale.

The fact that a P2P system is connected in a distributed topology introduces some challenges that are usually less relevant for a centralized system. For example, in order to accommodate a large number of members, P2P systems usually build an application-level overlay network among all members. The resulting stream forwarding or processing at the application level increases the end-to-end delay through the additional intermediate hops from source to destination and as a result it is difficult to build a low latency streaming platform using a P2P platform. Some existing work has investigated low-latency P2P streaming. One idea is to distinguish active users who require low latency from passive users who can tolerate longer latency. By clustering the active users logically close together the delay among them can be reduced [5]. The remaining challenge is to distinguish active users effectively and automatically.

Dynamics
One of the biggest challenges for all P2P streaming systems is how to provide a reliable service over an unreliable, constantly changing and most likely, heterogeneous streaming architecture. The members of a P2P system are often of different computing power, network bandwidth and network connectivity. Some are connected from behind a firewall and some are connected through a network address translation (NAT) device. Peers may join and leave at any moment, leaving some fraction of the P2P streaming network isolated and disconnected. These dynamics make the construction of a reliable and deterministic streaming service very challenging.

A common solution is to maintain redundant information to recover the lost service. For example, in the AudioPeer system, each peer caches information about a fraction of the other online peers and when there is a disruption, this cached peer list is used to repair the network. Another possibility is to ask the rendezvous point server for help. This approach is easier to implement and the service may be more reliable since the server is usually monitored and maintained professionally. However such a centralized recovery design hinders the scalability of a distributed system and may increase its costs. A hybrid approach that combines the above two designs is often a good compromise.

Security
Starting from the early days when P2P systems were mostly used for file sharing until today's blooming online audio conferencing systems that employ P2P as the streaming architecture, security has always been a big concern that affects the acceptance of P2P applications. Members in a P2P system are usually untrusted entities and service is received through such peers. This cooperative model opens the door to unfair service distribution (i.e., a peer only consumes services but does not provide any) and abuse. Since most peers computers are not maintained and configured by network security professionals, a P2P network provides an opportunity for hackers and malicious attacks (e.g., injection of bogus content).

Aside from worries that the P2P service could open a back door to intruders, many people are also concerned about the possibility that confidential information can be obtained by the intermediate peers who are used to relay the content form source to destination. Unfortunately many of current paradigms for P2P systems are limited to the authentication phase and scant research has been done in terms of how to assure the integrity and confidentiality of content being delivered. It will be helpful to revise some research proposals in multicast areas and find the appropriate implementations for P2P streaming platform.

<u>Profit model</u>

Despite the popularity and promising advantages of P2P streaming systems, finding a viable business model remains elusive. One of the challenges is to measure the usage of each individual in a distributed system and charge fairly for the services received. Since each peer in the P2P streaming system is acting as both a customer and a provider, it would not be fair to charge the user by the volume of content received without considering her contribution to help relay the content to other peers. It is also quite challenging to monitor the activities of peers even when permission is given. Various P2P streaming systems may require different profit models. One possible revenue stream is to display advertising on a companion website or in the content itself. Another possibility is to charge a fee for add-on services. Creating a fair and efficient subscription model for P2P streaming systems is a practical challenge that needs to be resolved before P2P streaming systems become a mature commercial platform.

References

1. Napster, http://www.napster.com.
2. Skype, http://www.skype.com.
3. R. Zimmermann, B. Seo, L. S. Liu, R. S. Hampole, and B. Nash, "AudioPeer: A Collaborative Distributed Audio Chat System," Proceedings of the Tenth International Conference on Distributed Multimedia Systems (DMS 2004), San Francisco, CA, September 2004.
4. M. Castro, P. Druschel, A. Kermarrec, and A. Rowstron, "SCRIBE: A large-scale and decentralized application level multicast infrastructure," IEEE Journal on Selected Areas in Communications (JSAC), 2002.
5. L. S. Liu and R. Zimmermann, "ACTIVE: A Low Latency P2P Live Streaming Architecture," Proceedings of the SPIE Conference on Multimedia Computing and Networking Conference, San Jose, CA, January 2005.
6. M. Steiner, G. Tsudik, and M. Waidner, "Key agreement in dynamic peer groups," IEEE Transactions on Parallel and Distributed Systems, Vol. 11, No. 8, pp. 769--780, August 2000.
7. D. Malkhi, M. Merrit, and O. Rodeh, "Secure reliable multicast protocols in a WAN," Proceedings of the International Conference on Distributed Computing Systems (ICDCS 97), 1997, pp. 87—94.
8. P. Francis, Yoid: Your own internet distribution.
9. B. Zhang, S. Jamin, and L. Zhang, "Host Multicast: A Framework for Delivering Multicast to End Users," Proceedings of IEEE Infocom, New York, June 2002.
10. Y. H. Chu, S. G. Rao, S. Seshan, and H. Zhang, "Enabling conferencing applications on the internet using an overlay multicast architecture," Proceedings of the ACM SIGCOMM 2001, San Diego, CA, August 2001.
11. S. Banerjee, B. Bhattacharjee, and C. Kommareddy, "Scalable application layer multicast," 2002.

12. S. Ratnasamy, M. Handley, R. Karp, and S. Shenker, "Application-level multicast using content-addressable networks," Proceedings of the Third International Workshop Networked Group Communications, November 2001.

PEER-TO-PEER SYSTEMS

Definition: *The term peer to peer denotes a class of distributed system architectures, that is, a way of structuring and organizing the work of several computers that communicate through a network.*

In a peer to peer system, each computer that participates in the system has some kind of resource (data, computing capacity, disk space, algorithms, etc.) that it offers to the other users of the system. In a multimedia peer to peer system, the most common resource is constituted by data files. A computer needing a particular file or algorithm will send a request for it to all or some of the participants of the system. (The details of how this happens depend on the specific architectural details of the systems, and will be debated shortly.) The participants that have that resource available will answer, possibly with some additional information about the computer on which the resource is located, such as its computing power, network bandwidth, work load at the moment, etc. Based on this information, the requester contacts one of the participants that answered, and instaurates with it a one to one communication during which the file is exchanged, or the algorithm is invoked, the disk space is allocated and used, etc...

With respect to client server, peer to peer systems present the advantage of avoiding the concentration of network traffic or the computation on a single computer—or on a small group of computers—, namely the server. On the other hand, knowing where a resource is located is a more complicated affair in a peer to peer system, and subject to more compromises. There are, with respect to the localization of a resource, several solutions possible.

The most immediate possibility is that of complete broadcast: whenever a computer needs a resource, it will send a request to *all* the other computers in the system to verify which ones have the resource. Two are the problems with this solution: firstly, the network traffic that it generates: in a system with N computers, for each request, $N-1$ messages (this problem is not too dramatic, since only short messages are sent); secondly, every computer must contain a list of all other participants that, at a given time, are active. In a large system, in which computers come on-line and go off-line frequently, creating and maintaining such lists might be a considerable problem.

A different architectural solution is what might be called *impure* peer to peer. In this solution, there is a central server that contains the location of all available resources. Whenever a participants comes on-line, it communicates its availability to the central server, and whenever the participants goes off-line, it communicates that it will be no longer available; in this way the server can maintain an updated list of active participants. Whenever a participant needs to access a certain resource (e.g. a file), it will first contact the server to obtain the location(s) of that resource (e.g., given the name of the file, a list of computers and the relative directories where files with that name are located) and then contact one of these computers in order to access the resource (viz. copy the file). This solution relieves the problem of the previous one, since only the server needs to keep a list of available resources, and it also avoids some of the problems of client-server architectures, since the server only deals with short search requests, and not with the actual use of the resources. On the other hand, many simultaneous requests can still result in congestion, and the system is, just as client-server, susceptible to malfunctions in the server.

A third solution involves partial indexing: every computer in the system keeps a list of a certain, usually fixed, number of other computers, called its (first order) *neighbors*. A search request goes from a computer to its neighbors, from these to their neighbors (the second order neighbors of the requester), and so on until a prescribed and fixed order of neighborhood is reached: these are the computers on which the sought resource is searched. The most serious problem of this solution is that a search might fail to find a resource even if it is present in the system, since not the whole system is searched. For peer to peer systems in which resources are duplicated on many computers (e.g. file exchange, in which the number of locations where a given file can be found grows with every copy), and in which absolute reliability is not a requirement, this solution can be usefully applied.

See: Multimedia File Sharing

PEER-TO-PEER SYSTEMS AND DIGITAL RIGHTS MANAGEMENT

Definition: Peer to peer file sharing and the management and enforcement of digital rights remain two very important cogs in online multimedia e-commerce.

Peer to Peer File Sharing and Tools

While large multimedia repositories such iTunes and Download.com store media in an organized and *centralized* fashion, other technologies allow multimedia to be replicated and distributed upon thousands of servers. In this latter case – the peer-to-peer case – only the media index may be centralized; the media themselves are stored on distributed servers. When a client wants a particular media the following main steps occur: 1) a search algorithm yields the best source(s) of the media for this user, 2) the transfer occurs (the media may arrive in chunks from different sources), 3) the media is recovered and validated at the client (e-payments may be made at this point), 4) the media and its new location are registered, allowing subsequent clients to be served the media from its new location. Decentralized media indices are another variation of these frameworks in which case no single server indexes all the media. At any rate, such systems (first popularized by Napster) allow the exchange of copyrighted media (e.g. music in mp3 format and movies in MPEG-4 format) and brought legality issues of file-sharing to the forefront in the late 1990's. In 1999 the RIAA (backed by AOL Time Warner, Bertelsmann, EMI,

Vivendi Universal and Sony) filed suit against Napster; the suit symbolically ended the era of care-free peer-to-peer exchange of copyrighted material.

Current Landscape

The current peer-to-peer file sharing landscape is dynamic. Napster has been reborn into an outlet for legal file exchange. It is joined by many other legal systems. In 2004, more than 200 million music tracks were downloaded and the related revenues increased six-fold from 2003. Some industry experts estimate the online music market at $660 million for 2005.

Digital Rights Management

Despite the systems and tools listed above experts agree that digital piracy of online multimedia will remain a threat. For this reason, Digital Rights Management (DRM) [1] technologies are important. Simply put, DRM allows media rights holders to restrict the usage of media. Such restrictions are implemented by various technologies; for example, a rights database persists usage rights and policies of use, while a cryptographic layer provides the 'lock and key' that the rights holders requires. A common DRM issues is how to restrict content buyers from copying and redistributing media. As a case in point, at the time of writing the Open Mobile Alliance (OMA) – a large and influential forum for mobile service enablers - is the proponent of a DRM standard for mobile wireless content. OMA's DRM specification will consist of 1) a rights expression language, 2) a content format, and 3) a framework for content metadata. For rights holders wishing to allow e-commerce on mobile devices on the basis of their content, efforts like OMA's DRM and others are key stepping stones.

See: Online Multimedia E-Commerce

References

1. R. Ianella, "Digital Rights Management Architectures," D-Lib Magazine, Vol. 7, No. 6, June 2001.

PERSONALIZED EDUCATIONAL HYPERMEDIA

Apple W. P. Fok and Horace H. S. Ip
Sun Centre of Excellence on Pervasive Computing
Centre for Innovative Applications of Internet and Multimedia
Technologies, City University of Hong Kong, Hong Kong

Definition: *Enabling technologies that support the personalization of Web-based applications include technologies for user profiling, intelligent search, filtering and recommendation of hypermedia contents, adaptive hypermedia, tracking and characterization of user browsing behaviors, and adaptive user interface.*

Introduction

The emergence of personalization technologies on the Web allows customized information to be delivered to users according to their pertinent needs and interests as perceived by the system. Enabling technologies that support the personalization of web-based applications include technologies for user profiling, intelligent search, filtering and recommendation of hypermedia contents, adaptive hypermedia, tracking and characterization of user browsing behaviors, and adaptive user interface. In order to boost the commercial advantages and to retain internet-based customers' loyalties, personalization technologies have been adopted and driven predominantly by e-commerce applications and information portals such as MyYahoo, Amazon, Persona [1] etc. Enterprises increase their profits by providing personalization services to their customer on the web, for example, by providing personalized features such as making suggestions based on users' transaction and historical records. The idea of personalization can be summarized into three main themes: "Building a meaningful one-to-one relationship [2], "Delivering appropriate content and services to fulfill user's needs [3], and "Understanding where and when to suggest the 'right' things [4]. The ultimate goal of personalization is "User satisfaction". User satisfaction means getting the right thing at the right time in the right place.

In order to create a personalized experience, a general Personalized Hypermedia System must perform several distinct tasks: i) Identify the user; ii) Store and Update user information; iii) Learn and identify the user preferences, needs and interests; and iv) Provide and recommend specific personalized services. In summary, personalization techniques serve to enable the system to know the user, remember the user, and adjust their personal memory of the user according to the user's changing needs.

With the increasing demand of learning just-in-time and just-in-place, the Web has become a new and effective channel for education and the acquisition of knowledge, particularly in adult education and distant learning. Streaming technology allows the delivery of continuous media such as video and audio content for educational purpose. The process of learning in the cyber space is more complex than conventional class learning for many reasons. From the educational point of views, the educational philosophers and psychologists are interested in the influences of technologies in human's beliefs, knowledge and learning. Research in the learning environment, on the other hand, focused on the changes of traditional classroom settings to computer-based learning and the impacts of web-based learning have on the learning process.

The demand of adaptability in a computer-based educational system is due to the fact that every person possesses distinctive collection of talents, abilities, and limitations. One-size-fits-all approach to education forgets that individuals are different and have different needs. In response to this demand, research interest towards personalized education hypermedia systems has evolved. An emerging approach is the Adaptive Educational Hypermedia Systems, which inherits and combines two earlier paradigms of computer-based educational systems: Intelligent Tutoring Systems (ITSs) and Adaptive Hypermedia Systems (AHSs). Adaptive educational hypermedia systems (AEH) interact with user through a learner model of the goals, preferences and knowledge of each individual learner and adapt the hypermedia to the needs of that user. A challenge to the development of adaptive hypermedia system is the authoring of adaptive hypermedia materials. In additional to hypermedia content, the presentation of the content should also be adaptive to the user needs through mechanisms such as link annotation link hiding, and conditional inclusion of materials. The Adaptive Hypermedia Architecture (AHA!) provides a set of authoring tools and a run-time environment for creating and presenting adaptive hypermedia courseware.

Conceptual Framework and Functionality Layers of Personalized Education System

Instead of focusing on the creation and presentation of adaptive hypermedia materials, a Personalized Educational System (PES) [5] takes advantage of the vast resource of educational hypermedia on the Web and integrates a range of supportive tools for participants to conduct their teaching or learning activities in a personalized manner. These supports range from automatic search of relevant teaching and learning hypermedia materials from the Web, anticipating needs of the participants based on his/her individual descriptive profile and the filtering, matching and sequencing of the retrieved materials based on dynamic monitoring of the student's progress supported by a learner model or based on the teacher's intended pedagogy. Due to the diverse but inter-related functions that need to be provided in a Personalized Educational System (PES), software agent technology has been applied to the design and development of a PES. Particularly, an agent architecture has been proposed [6] that deploys a team of Personalized agents to achieve the goals of a PES. Figure 1 shows the conceptual agent framework of PES.

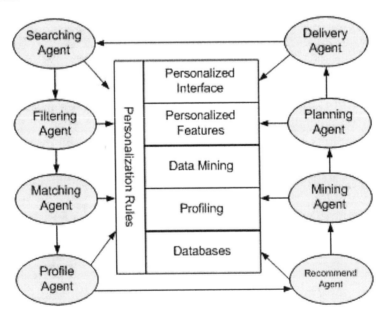

Figure 1. Conceptual framework of a personalized education system.

The functionality of PES can be divided into three functional layers. Action Layer: Within this layer, personal agents positioned between the browser and the Web, capture a complete clickstream history for all hypermedia resources visited by the user, and the complete navigational history of the user.

A user profile is generated together with its schema that is both human readable and machine processable. Web servers use the profile information, obtained from the client to deliver personalized information. Domain-specific Search agents as intelligent searching assistant focus on getting relevant hypermedia or documents in one specific subject domain (i.e. educational websites or teaching/learning resources). These agents can recognize not only the types of information provided, but also automatically classified those retrieved documents and hypermedia into different categories based on the subject ontologies as well as the personalized attributes stored in the personalized knowledge base/libraries. Industrial Layer: this is where collaboration work takes place. The actual process matching retrieved content to the learner's needs is carried out by a Matching Agent. The task of the matching agent is to match document metadata against registered profiles. Also in this layer, intelligent filtering agent transforms static data and information into meaningful and useful information for knowledge construction.

Various filtering and data mining techniques would be used. Demographic filtering technique uses to identify the relationship between a particular resource and the type of users. Content-based filtering technique is used to learn the relationship between the content and a single user. Collaborative filtering technique uses the "like minded" approach, in which the navigational history of each user is kept to determine the learning dependent behaviors to make recommendations based on the user profile groups. Knowledge Layer: Educational psychologies, philosophies and instruction design theories/principles as the cognitive knowledge domain of the decision-theoretic agents, these agents are capable of handling queries from other agents for expert advices or diagnosing learner behaviors. To generate different types of profiles and accurately locate the relevant information, the profiling agents take up the responsibilities of handling different representation of profiles and automatically construct an active profile for the other agents. Each learner has his/her own knowledge status which is constructed throughout his/her own development process (i.e. learning or experience). Various pieces of data form different episodes. The Knowledge Management agent helps to manage and organize the acquired knowledge for personalization processes. Figure 2 illustrates the layer structure of the PES agent functionality.

Semantic Web for Educational Hypermedia and Standards for Interoperability of PES

Learning technologies standardization helps to increase the integration, usability and reusability of heterogeneous systems for education. Many professional organizations and institutions have contributed towards such standardization efforts to strengthen the process of delivering educational services, to define learning data and metadata as well as recommendations for the development of software architectures devoted to computer-based education. One of the main contributors to this effort is the IEEE Learning Technology Standards Committee (LTSC) (http://ltsc.ieee.org/) Learning Objects Metadata (LOM) working group.

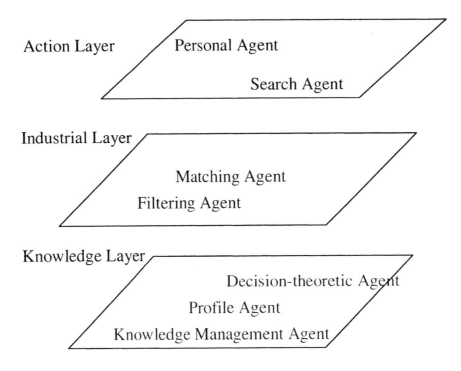

Figure 2. Three functionality layers of PES.

The LOM specification (http://ltsc.ieee.org/doc/wg12/LOM_WD4.PDF) describes learning content cataloguing information. This specification is the result of the effort of many contributors. The European ARIADNE project (http://ariadne.unil.ch) uses LOM for indexing and exploiting its network of interconnected knowledge pools (KPS) and the IMS project (http://www.imsproject.org/metadata) provides the IMS Learning Resources Metadata Specifications which would be incorporated into the IEEE specifications. Apart from the learning metadata definition studies, the description of learner profiles and records (http://edutool.com/papi/), course structure formats, course packaging (http://www.imsproject.org/content), questions and tests interoperability (http://www.imsproject.org/question), learning architectures and run time environments, have also been investigated with a view to provide recommendations and specifications to enhance interoperability between different educational platforms.

In order for PES to effectively search and make use of the vast amount of potential learning resources that exist in the Web, it exploits the Semantic Web (http://www.w3.org/2001/sw/) and the development of appropriate ontology for education hypermedia for various subject domains so that content and its inherent educational values can be understood, shared and used across educational platforms. For hypermedia content description, eXtensible Markup Language (XML) allows users to add arbitrary structure to their documents, the meaning of the structure is expressed by Resource Description Framework (RDF), which encodes it in sets of triples, each triple being rather like the subject, verb and object of an elementary sentence. These triples can be written using XML tags. Subject and object are each identified by a Universal Resource Identifier (URI), just as used in a link on a Web page. (URLs, Uniform Resource Locators, are the most common type of URI.) In order to handle the problem between two different education platforms that use different identifiers for what is in fact the same concept,

Semantic Web provides a basic component – Ontology. Ideally, an ontology helps a system to discover the common meanings in a subject domain. A typical kind of ontology for the Web consists of taxonomy and a set of inference rules. The taxonomy defines classes of objects and relations among them. For example, English may be defined as a type of subjects, and topic codes may be defined to apply only to subject, and so on. Classes, subclasses and relations among entities are a very powerful tool for Web use. A recent development in this area is a set of ontology for high school subjects, e.g. EduOnto (http://web.syr.edu/~jqin/eduonto/eduonto.html). The emergence of ontology for educational content allows educational content available on the Web to be searched and identified effectively for specific subject domains and for meeting specific learning goals.

One of the outcome of a personalized education system is an individualized learning plan that specifies the sequence for which a set of learning materials should be studied by a learner in order to achieve his/her learning goal or objective. The Sharable Content Object Reference Model (SCORM), first proposed by The Advanced Distributed Learning (ADL) initiative (http://www.adlnet.org/) is an emerging standard for sharing and defining learning sequence of educational multimedia content. (Link to SCORM, T Shih). By adhering to such standards and making use of the ontology defined for various subject domains, PES is not only able to search and reuse educational multimedia content generated from desperate sources from the Web, its personalized output such as a plan of individualized learning sequence would also be (re-)used by different educational platforms.

See: Streaming Media and its Applications in Education, Definition of Adaptive Educational Hypermedia Systems, Creating (and Delivering) Adaptive Course Texts with AHA!, The Sharable Content Object Reference Model (SCORM)

References

1. F. Tanudjaja and L Mui, "Persona: A contextualized and Personalized Web Search," Proceedings of the 35 Annual Hawaii International Conference on System Sciences (HICSS'02), Big Island, Hawaii, 2002, Vol. 3, 2002.
2. D. Riecken, "Personalized Views of Personalization," Communications of the ACM, Vol. 43, No. 8., 2000.
3. M. Bonett, "Personalization of Web Services: Opportunities and Challenges," http://www.ariadne.ac.uk/issue28/personalization/.
4. "The Art of Personalization," An Oracle White Paper, August 2003.
5. A. W. P. Fok and H. H S Ip, "Personalized Education (PE) – Opportunities and Challenges in Technology Integration for Individual Learning," Proceedings of IASTED International Conference on Web-Based Education (WBE 2004), pp.48-53, Innsbruck, Austria, February 2004.
6. A. W. P. Fok and H. H. S. Ip, "Personalized Education (PE) – An Exploratory Study of Learning Pedagogies in Relation to Personalization Technologies," in Lecture Notes in Computer Science (LNCS 3143), Advances in Web-Based Learning (ICWL 2004), Eds. W.-Y. Liu, Y.-C. Shi, and Q. Li, pp. 407-415, Springer, 2004.

PHOTO DEFECT DETECTION

Definition: *Image inpainting techniques include photo defect detection, where ink traces, scratch, and damage from ink pens are automatically detected.*

The concept of image inpainting is discussed in the article entitled "Digital Inpainting." Most existing inpainting mechanisms allow users to select a defect area or a mask of object to be removed. To cope with the inconveniency, we developed a naïve photo defect detection mechanism. Ink traces, scratch, and damage from ink pens are automatically detected. We consider the intensity and shape of photo defects. Though, it is almost not possible to discriminate ink regions from objects in photos. The intensity variation of ink regions is usually quite smooth and steady while comparing with objects in photos. Thus, we use the HSI color space and use intensity in the first filter. In the second filter, we record the number of pixels been detected in each intensity variation. We calculate the variance of pixel numbers detected between two different continuous steps. If the variance is low, it means that pixels detected in the last adjustment are not much affected by the present adjustment of intensity. And the pixels been detected are possible to be pixels of ink spray because of its steady intensity. Keeping on the calculation of variance of pixels detected, a collection consists of consecutive adjustments of intensity can be constructed. The collection needs to be analyzed since sometimes the variance of pixels been detected is low only because it has low discrimination in a step of adjustment. If so, the collection been record has no use and we can't detect the ink. Thus, if the collection of adjustment contains too many passes of adjustment, we just leave it and go on to analysis the photo image. After the calculation and analysis, a set of adjustment of intensity can be found out to separate pixels of defects from objects in the photo. Figure 1 and 2 illustrates our results.

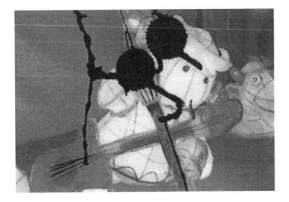 

Figure 1. Damages from black ink are detected and shown in red.

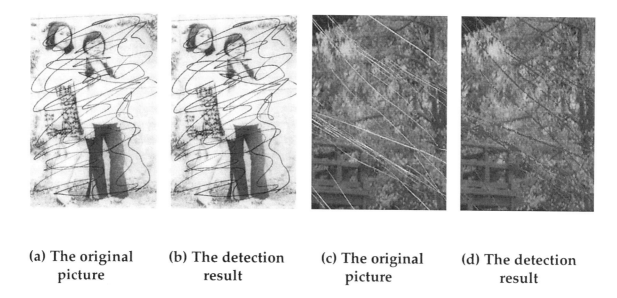

(a) The original picture (b) The detection result (c) The original picture (d) The detection result

Figure 2. Damages from ink pen (a) are detected (b). Scratch (c) is detected (d).

See: Digital Inpainting, Multi-Resolution Image Inpainting, Motion Picture Inpainting on Aged Films

PLACEMENT OF CONTINUOUS MEDIA IN AD-HOC NETWORKS OF DEVICES

Definition: Using the ad-hoc network, we deliver data from the local storage of one or more neighboring devices to reduce the demand for the network infrastructure to remote servers. This mode of delivery requires the devices to collaborate with one another by sharing a fraction of their available storage.

One may enhance availability of a clip by bringing it closer to the device that displays it. To elaborate, in [4], it was noted that the overall bandwidth required to implement an interactive video-on-demand solution based on a naive design that employs one centralized server would be as high as 1.54 Petabits per second for the entire United States. Using the ad-hoc network, we deliver data from the local storage of one or more neighboring devices to reduce the demand for the network infrastructure to remote servers. This mode of delivery requires the devices to collaborate with one another by sharing a fraction of their available storage. In return, the storage manager provides physical data independence which means the physical organization of data can be modified without causing application programs to be rewritten. It empower authenticated users to stream a clip to any device as long as it has either wired or wireless network connectivity to devices containing the referenced clip. This means the system (instead of the user) resolves the identity of the device that delivers the data requested by the user. Moreover, the system may offer each user a larger amount of storage capacity than that offered by one device. The exact capacity is dictated by the total storage of devices connected in the ad-hoc network and the capacity of remote servers. This storage might be shared by service providers that provide households with on-demand entertainment content.

Bringing clips closer to a user means that an individual who employs others' devices to share his or her experiences may have personal content (typically a fraction of it) pre-staged on many devices in anticipation of future access. This may raise a host of privacy, copyright, and legal issues. While there are techniques for some of these challenges, a significant amount of future research is necessary to ensure privacy of users' personal libraries. We believe the advantages of physical data independence will usher-in a new host of techniques to address these challenges.

Placement of data consists of a collection of techniques to: 1) collect statistics about the environment and how the application references data, 2) place data across devices, 3) re-organize placement of data in response to changes in access profiles and the environment.

Each topic is vast and most research to date has focused on topic number 2. Formally, given a repository of C clips with a pre-specified frequency of access (f_i) for each clip i, a data placement strategy addresses the following questions. First, what is the granularity of placement for data (a block or a clip)? Second, how many replicas of a granule should be constructed in the system? Third, how should these replicas be placed across devices? Answers to these questions are a trade-off between (a) the average startup latency and (b) the number of simultaneous H2O devices that can display clips. These two metrics constitute the dimensions of a recent experimental study used to evaluate three data placement strategies for an ad-hoc network of stationary H2O devices: Simple, Halo-Clip, and Halo-Block [1]. Granularity of data placement is a clip with both Simple and Halo-Clip. It is a block with Halo-Block. Simple employs the profile of a device to pack its storage with its most frequently accessed clips. If the demographics of each device is identical then Simple assigns the same collection of clips to each device. Halo-Clip strives to maintain a replica of the clips that constitute the repository across the devices participating in the ad-hoc network. This is possible when the storage capacity of the participating devices exceeds the repository size. Similar to Halo-Clip, Halo-Block also strives to maintain a copy of every clip in the ad-hoc network. When sufficient storage is available, it replicates the first few blocks of each clip aggressively in order to enhance startup latency.

Mobile Devices

In [2], we investigated how many replicas of different clips should be constructed in a mobile environment that provides on-demand access to audio and video clips. This environment consists of vehicles equipped with a Car-to-Car Peer-to-Peer (C2P2) device that might serve as a component of the vehicle's entertainment system. Mobility is the key difference between a C2P2 and a H2O environment. With C2P2 devices, a vehicular entertainment system offers its user a list of available movie titles during the car's journey. A particular title is available only if sufficient replicas of that title are expected to be encountered in the vicinity of the car to enable successful viewing. However, a title may have a certain time delay after which it is available. We define a related QoS metric for content availability, termed availability latency, defined as the earliest time after which the client vehicle encounters a replica of its referenced title. To minimize this metric, the system may replicate popular clips more aggressively than the less popular clips.

A family of replication techniques to compute the number of replicas for a title as a power law function of its popularity, i.e., frequency of access, is presented in [2]. The exponent value (n) identifies a specific technique. Three distinct exponent values are studied in [2]: random (n=0), square root (n=0.5), and linear (n=1). Availability latency is impacted by a large number of system parameters such as density of C2P2 devices in a geographical area, title display time, size of clip repository, trip duration, the mobility model, storage per C2P2 device and the popularity of the titles. We refer the interested reader to [2] for details.

In [3], we explore the use of mobile C2P2s that carry a referenced data item from a mobile C2P2 containing that data item to a client C2P2 that requested it. Such devices are termed zebroids. A device acts as a zebroid when it is in close vicinity of a server C2P2 and travels along a path that rendezvous with the client C2P2. A key finding of [3] is that zebroids enhance the availability latency of a client with a random mobility model. An investigation of this finding with other mobility models is a future research direction.

See: Data Management Techniques for Continuous Media in Ad-hoc Networks of Wireless Devices

References

1. S. Ghandeharizadeh, T. Helmi, T. Jung, and S. Kapadia, "A Comparison of Alternative Data Placement Strategies for Continuous Media in Multi-hop Wireless Networks," Submitted for publication, August 2005.
2. S. Ghandeharizadeh, S. Kapadia, and B. Krishnamachari, "A Comparison of Replication Strategies for Content Availability in C2P2 Networks," Proceedings of the Sixth International Conference on Mobile Data Management (MDM'05), Ayia Napa, Cyprus, May 2005.
3. S. Ghandeharizadeh, S. Kapadia, and B. Krishnamachari, "Zebroids: Carrier-based Replacement Policies to Minimize Availability Latency in Vehicular Ad-hoc Networks," Submitted for publication, August 2005.
4. J. Nussbaumer, B. V. Patel, F. Schaffa, and J. P. G. Sterbenz, "Networking Requirements for Interactive Video on Demand," IEEE Journal of Selected Areas in Communications, Vol. 13, No. 5, pp. 779--787, 1995.

PORTABLE NETWORK GRAPHICS (PNG)

Definition: Portable Network Graphics (PNG) format uses lossless data compression and contains support for device-independent color through gamma correction and the XYZ color model.

The PNG (Portable Network Graphics) [1] format was originally designed to replace the GIF format. PNG, now on version 1.2, is an International Standard (ISO/IEC 15948:2003), also released as a W3C Recommendation on November 10, 2003 [2].

PNG uses lossless data compression and contains support for device-independent color through gamma correction and the XYZ color model. A PNG file consists of an 8-byte signature (89 50 4E 47 0D 0A 1A 0A in hexadecimal) followed by a number of *chunks*, each of which conveys certain information about the image. Chunk types can come from three main sources: the PNG standard, registered public chunk types maintained by the PNG Development Group, and private chunks, defined by some applications. This chunk-based structure is designed to allow the PNG format to be extended while maintaining compatibility with older versions. Chunks follow the format shown in Table 1.

Table 1. PNG chunk fields

Field	Size (in Bytes)	Description
Length	4	Number of bytes in the chunk's *Data* field.
Type	4	Chunk name. Each byte of a chunk type is restricted to the decimal values 65 to 90 and 97 to 122. These correspond to the uppercase and lowercase ISO 646 letters (A-Z and a-z) respectively for convenience in description and examination of PNG datastreams.
Data	*Length*	The data bytes appropriate to the chunk type, if any. This field can be of zero length.
CRC	4	A four-byte CRC (Cyclic Redundancy Code) calculated on the preceding bytes in the chunk, including the chunk type field and chunk data fields, but not including the length field. The CRC can be used to check for corruption of the data. The CRC is always present, even for chunks containing no data.

The MIME media type for PNG is image/png. Most current Web browsers support (most features of) the PNG format, paving the way for the PNG format to finally replace GIF for still images.

An extension of PNG, called APNG (Animated Portable Network Graphics), has been proposed to allow for animated PNG files, similar to their animated graphics interchange format (GIF) counterpart, but compatible with non-animated PNG files.

References

1. Official PNG home page. http://www.libpng.org/pub/png/, Accessed April 25, 2005.
2. W3C PNG page. http://www.w3.org/Graphics/PNG/ Accessed April 25, 2005.

PORTALS

Definition: *Portals serve as entry points to public and private IP-based networks, including the Internet.*

Borrowing from its historical definition as a "grand doorway," the modern technological interpretation of "portal" is as an entry point (or gateway) to a broad array of collaborative network-based resources and services. In the early days of personal computing, portals served as the means of access to bulletin board services (BBS) such as CompuServe, Prodigy and the like. Today, portals have evolved to serve as entry points to public and private IP-based networks, including the Internet. As part of this transition, portals now typically utilize browser technology (rather than proprietary software) to provide a standard Web interface not just to HTML pages, but to various information management, communication and collaborative services. As such, they are an example of the contemporary reality of collaborative computing.

Typical functionality exposed through a portal ranges from accessing information stores (including traditional web sites and databases, as well as document, information and knowledge repositories) to providing wide-ranging search functionality, access to (group) communication tools such as e-mail, chat/instant messaging, audio and video conferencing, discussion and news groups, blogging and so forth. Workflow support, calendaring, voting/polling and on-line meeting systems are also typical functionalities enabled through portal systems. Effectively, they serve as a user-centric access point to the user's "electronic world" – thus necessitating per-user configuration (i.e., profiles supporting custom user interface layout, information service specification, content selection/aggregation, unified logon to the various services, and so forth). Many of the specifics on what functionality is offered and how it is accessed often depends on whether the portal is intended for a private or public audience.

Private, organization-specific portals are typically used to provide a logically centralized access to organizational information, tools and services. Such a common forum provides for increased awareness and faster dissemination of organizational information by providing a common front-end to employees. For example, by providing a familiar interface to the organization through a content management system (vs. shared file systems), issues of scalability and knowledge-management (e.g., search and audit via version control, meta-tagging, classification and categorization) can be addressed. The result is that portals can help stimulate new ways of working, including Communities of Practice.

Conversely, public portals typically offer services of wide-spread interest to large, diverse audiences. These include: Web site directories, access to news, weather, stock quotes, phone and map information, as well as e-mail, chat/instant messaging and community forums according to individual interests. For organizations that provide a public interface to their business process, a portal can supplement traditional means of communicating and interacting with clients; examples include electronic banking, account management for utility companies and e-commerce support for retail outlets.

Scientific and engineering organizations, such as ACM, IEEE and numerous others, also use portals both to facilitate their operation as well as their interaction with members and the wider scientific/engineering communities. Examples of portal technology being used in a wide array of specific scientific research projects, ranging from geo-science and on-line biology labs to astrophysics and grid computing management can be found in [1].

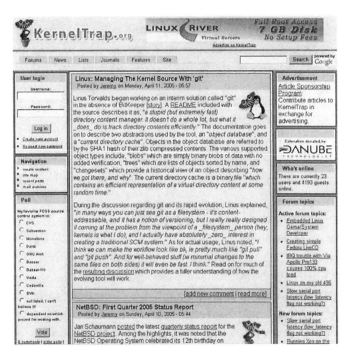

Figure 1. Example portal.

In terms of implementation, the technologies and tools used to build portals range significantly in capability and cost. Some common portal technologies are commercial (Sharepoint, Livelink, WebLogic, WebSphere, 10g, amongst others) while others are open source (e.g., Plone, Nuke/PHP-Nuke, Drupal, XOOPS, eXo). Most are built using a modular approach in which additional or enhanced functionality can be added to the "portal server" via implementation-specific add-on modules. The end-user generally accesses the portal server using a standard browser interface which typically employs any number of common browser technologies. These include XML, HTML/DHTML, CGI, Java, ASP/JSP, PHP, Python and so forth. Recent efforts towards a more interoperable approach for portal development have lead to an container-based architecture for portal and portal extensions (called portlets) via the JSR 168 portlet specification [2] and WSRP (Web Services for Remote Portlets) [3].

In all cases, by employing "thin client" architecture, portals benefit from the ubiquity of browser technology on virtually every computer system as well as user comfort with the browser interface. Such an approach also promotes acceptance through easier software management (less difficult installation and upgrading) along with potentially fewer security considerations (when compared to custom software). Even so, the specifics of implementation technology can have considerable impact on the portal's acceptability within organizations, as some do not allow downloadable technologies (e.g., applets) to be used in certain situations, often based on network topology and inter-organizational connectivity.

See: Collaborative Computing – Area Overview

References

1. GridSphere, "GridSphere Portal Framework," http://www.gridsphere.org, 2005.
2. Sun Microsystems, "Introduction to JSR 168: The Java Portlet Specification," http://developer.sun.com, 2003.
3. T. Schaeck and R. Thompson, "Web Services for Remote Portlets Whitepaper," http://www.oasis-open.org/committees/wsrp, 2003.

POWER-RATE DISTORTION ANALYSIS FOR WIRELESS VIDEO

Definition: Power-rate distortion analysis is important for wireless video communication applications in energy management, resource allocation, and QoS provisioning, especially over wireless video sensor networks.

To design an energy-scalable standard video encoder, we take three major steps:

Step 1) We group the encoding operations into several modules, such as motion prediction, pre-coding (transform and quantization), and entropy coding, and then introduce a set of control parameters $\Gamma = [\gamma_1, \gamma_2, ... \gamma_L]$ to control the power consumption of each module. The encoding power consumption, denoted by P, is then a function of Γ, denoted by $P(\gamma_1, \gamma_2, ... \gamma_L)$. The expression of this function also depends on the power consumption model of the specific micro-processor [1, 2].

Step 2) We analyze the rate-distortion behavior of each control parameter, and integrate these models into a comprehensive parametric rate-distortion model for the video encoder, denoted by $D(R; \gamma_1, \gamma_2, ... \gamma_L)$.

Step 3) We perform optimum configuration of the power control parameters to maximize the video quality (or minimize the video distortion) under the power constraint. This optimization problem can be mathematically formulated as follows:

$$\min_{\{\gamma_1, \gamma_2, ... \gamma_L\}} D = D(R; \gamma_1, \gamma_2, ... \gamma_L) , \text{ s.t. } P(\gamma_1, \gamma_2, ... \gamma_L) \leq P \tag{1}$$

where P is the available power consumption for video encoding. The optimum solution, denoted by $D(R; P)$, describes the P-R-D behavior of the video encoder. To view the P-R-D model in more detail, we plot the D-P curves for different bit rates, ranging from

0.01 bpp to 1.0 bpp in Fig.1-(a). Fig.1-(b) shows the D-P curves at different bit rates R_s, and Fig.1-(c) shows the D-R curves at different power consumption levels P_s (in percentages of the maximum power consumption level). We can see that when the power supply level is low, the $D(R)$ function is almost flat, which means the video processing and encoding efficiency is very low; hence, in this case, more bandwidth does not improve the video presentation quality. The P-R-D model has direct applications in energy management, resource allocation, and QoS provisioning in wireless video communication, especially over wireless video sensor networks. For detailed energy-scalable encoder design and P-R-D analysis, please refer to [2].

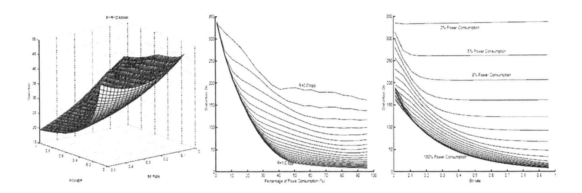

Figure 1. (a) The P-R-D Model; (b) the D-P curves at different bit rates R_s
(c) The D-R curves for different power consumption levels.

See: Wireless Video

References

1. T. Burd and R. Broderson, "Processor Design for Portable Systems," *Journal of VLSI Signal Processing*, Vol. 13, No. 2, pp. 203–222, August 1996.
2. Z. He, Y. Liang, L. Chen, I. Ahmad, and D. Wu, "Power-rate-distortion analysis for wireless video communication under energy constraint," *IEEE Transactions on Circuits and System for Video Technology*, Vol. 15, No. 5, May 2005.

PRIVATE-KEY CRYPTOSYSTEM

Definition: *A private-key cryptosystem can be obtained using the visual cryptography concepts or perfect-reconstruction based image secret sharing.*

A $(2,2)$-scheme is the most popular solution within the (k,n) framework due to its common acceptance as a private-key cryptosystem [1]-[3]. Such a cryptographic solution encrypts the secret image into two noise-like shares. One of the two generated shares can be viewed as a private share or private-key, and is kept by the owner. The other share represents a public share which can be transmitted over an untrusted communication channel. The secret image is reconstructed only if both the public and private shares are used for decryption.

A private-key cryptosystem can be obtained using the visual cryptography concepts [1] or perfect-reconstruction based image secret sharing [2]. Both these solutions encrypt each pixel of the secret image into a block of share pixels and because of their expansion nature, such solutions produce the shares with the enlarged spatial resolution. To reduce the complexity, a cost-effective private-key cryptosystem in [3] uses pixel operations to both encrypt and decrypt the images. As a result, the solution produces the shares with spatial dimensions identical to those of the secret image (Figure 1). In addition, operating on the bit-levels of the processed images, the solution satisfies the essential perfect reconstruction property. Thus, similarly to the (k,n) image secret sharing framework proposed in [2], the private-key cryptosystem in [3] recovers the original secret image (Figure 1).

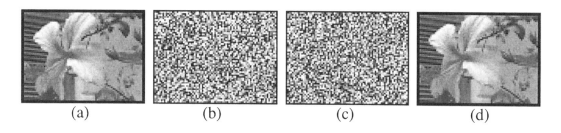

(a)   (b)   (c)   (d)

Figure 1. A cost-effective private-key cryptosystem: (a) secret gray-scale image, (b,c) gray-scale shares, (d) secret image decrypted using the share images shown in (b,c).

The utilization of the bit-level processing operations in [2],[3] allows for selective encryption of image bit-planes. Such an approach offers solutions which differ in their security characteristics. For example, as it is shown in Figure 2, sufficient protection is usually obtained when the two or three most significant bits of the secret image's pixels are encrypted.

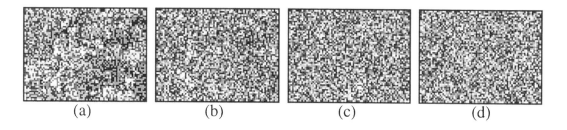

(a)   (b)   (c)   (d)

Figure 2. A public share obtained by encrypting: (a) the most significant bit only, and (b) two, (c) three, (d) four most significant bits of the secret image.

See: Image secret sharing, Visual cryptography, Threshold schemes with minimum pixel expansion, Compression in image secret sharing.

References

1. G. Ateniese, C. Blundo, A. de Santis, and D.-G. Stinson, "Visual Cryptography for General Access Structures," Information and Computation, Vol. 129, No. 2, September 1996, pp. 86-106.
2. R. Lukac and K.-N. Plataniotis, "Bit-Level Based Secret Sharing for Image Encryption," Pattern Recognition, Vol. 38, No. 5, May 2005, pp. 767-772.
3. R. Lukac and K.-N. Plataniotis, "A Cost-Effective Private-Key Cryptosystem for Color Image Encryption," Lecture Notes in Computer Science, Vol. 3514, May 2005, pp. 679-686.

PROGRESSIVE FOREST SPLIT

Definition: Progressive Forest Split is an efficient encoding technique for a simple polygon; it groups the decimations into a batch to achieve a high compression ratio.

PFS (Progressive Forest Split) [1] is much more efficient in encoding at the expense of looser granularity. Similar to CPM [2], it groups the decimations into a batch to achieve a high compression ratio. PFS cuts the mesh through the forest edges, triangulates each tree boundary loop, and displaces vertices to new positions. The geometric data contains the error between the predicted and the real vertex positions. The amortized connectivity encoding takes 10 bits and geometry encoding takes 30 bits per vertex. MPEG-4 accepts PFS as the standard compression scheme. However, PFS is not widely implemented in current 3D players [3].

PFS provides an efficient encoding for a simple polygon (triangulated with no internal vertices). For each refinement, at compression, certain simple polygons are selected for removal. Each simple polygon is simplified to a set of connected edges. All these edge sets form a forest. At decompression, the decoder cuts through the edges in the forest and fills in the hole with the encoded corresponding simple polygon. Figure 1. shows the simplification/triangulation of a simply polygon with four triangles.

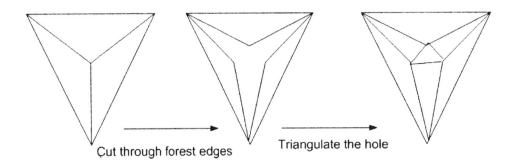

Cut through forest edges   Triangulate the hole

Figure 1. PFS cuts through forest edges and fills in the hole with a simple polygon.

See: Middleware for streaming 3D meshes.

References

1. G. Taubin, A. Gueziec, W. Horn, and F. Lazarus, "Progressive forest split compression", Proceedings of SIGGRAPH 98, pp. 123-132.
2. R. Pajarola and J. Rossignac, "Compressed progressive meshes", IEEE Transactions on Visualization and Computer Graphics, Vol. 6, pp. 79-93.
3. M. Isenburg and J. Snoeylink, "Coding polygon meshes as compressible ASCII", Web 3D, 2002.

PROTECTION OF MULTIMEDIA DATA IN DISTRIBUTION AND STORAGE

Ahmet M. Eskicioglu
Department of Computer and Information Science
Brooklyn College of the City University of New York

Definition: Multimedia data needs to be protected from unauthorized duplication and consumption, from unauthorized disclosure and misuse, and from unauthorized use and exploitation.

Introduction

Multimedia can be defined as a combination of different types of media (e.g., text, images, audio, video, and graphics) to communicate information in a given application.

Recent advances in digital technologies have drastically increased the capacity of both data channels and storage:

- When compare with floppy disks and CDs, the capacity of DVDs, digital tapes, and hard disk is much larger. Personal computers can be configured with a processor speed of 3 GHz, main memory of 2 GB, and a hard disk of 500GB. DVDs manufactured with a double sided format, each side having a dual layer, have a data capacity of 17GB. Digital Linear Tapes (DTLs) come with a storage space above 200GB for compressed data.

- Asymmetric digital subscriber line (ADSL) is a new technology that allows more data to be sent over existing copper telephone lines, supporting data rates up to 9 Mbps when receiving downstream data. Very High Speed Digital Subscriber Line (VDSL) transmits data in the 13 Mbps - 55 Mbps range over short distances, usually between 1000 and 4500 feet.

The transition from analog to digital technologies started in 1990s. With the higher capacity of storage devices and data communication channels, multimedia content has become a part of our daily lives. This type of data is now commonly used in many areas such as education, entertainment, journalism, law enforcement, finance, health services, and national defense. The lowered cost of reproduction, storage, and distribution has added an additional dimension to the complexity of the problem. In a number of applications, multimedia needs to be protected for several reasons. Table 1 includes three applications where the data should be protected.

Table 1. Protection of data in three applications

Application	Provider	Data	What needs to be prevented?
Entertainment	Content owners (e.g., movie studios and recording companies) and service providers (e.g., cable companies and broadcasters)	Copyrighted movies and songs	Unauthorized duplication and consumption
Health services	Hospitals	Medical data for patients (e.g., X-ray pictures and history of illnesses)	Unauthorized disclosure and misuse
Finance	Investment bankers	Financial data (stocks and mutual funds)	Unauthorized use and exploitation

Encryption and watermarking are two groups of complementary technologies that have been identified by content providers to protect multimedia data [1,2,3]. Watermark embedding and detection are sometimes considered to be analogous to encryption and decryption [4].

- Encryption makes the content unintelligible through a reversible mathematical transformation based on a secret key [5,6]. In secure multimedia content distribution, the audio/visual stream is compressed, packetized and encrypted. In symmetric key encryption, which is commonly used for protecting multimedia elements, each encryption transformation E_K is defined by an encryption algorithm E and a key K. Given a plaintext M, the transformation produces the ciphertext $C = E_K(M)$. Each decryption transformation D_K is defined with a decryption algorithm D and K. For a given K, $D_K = E_K^{-1}$ such that $D_K(E_K(M)) = M$. One of the most challenging problems in distribution architectures is the delivery of the decryption key.

- Watermarking (data hiding) [7,8] is the process of embedding data into a multimedia element such as image, audio or video. The embedding transformation E_K is defined by an embedding algorithm E and a key K. In watermarking, the usual approach is to use a symmetric key although there is a recent trend to use asymmetric techniques. Given a cover image I and a watermark W, the transformation produces the watermarked image $I_W = E_K(I,W)$. Each detection (or extraction) transformation D_K is defined with a detection (or extraction) algorithm D and K. For a given K and the watermarked image I_W, the watermark is either detected (or extracted): $W = D_K(I_W)$.

Encryption

Figure 1 shows five primary means of multimedia delivery to consumers: satellite, cable, terrestrial, Internet and prerecorded media (optical and magnetic).

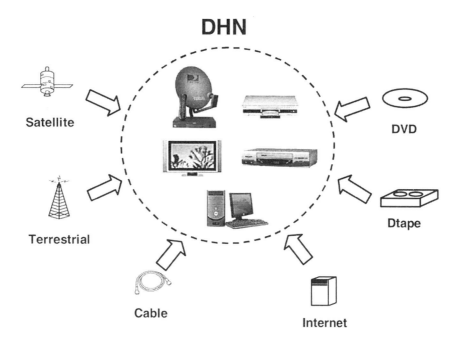

Figure 1. Multimedia distribution systems.

For end-to-end security from the source to the final destination, the most important requirements are:

- Secure distribution of multimedia content
- Secure distribution of access keys
- Authentication of source and sink consumer devices in home networks
- Association of digital rights with content
- Manufacturing of licensed devices that have the protection technology
- Renewability of secure solutions

In the last 10 years, three industries (consumer electronics, information technology, and motion picture) have been working on solutions for protecting copyrighted multimedia content. Some of the key players with interest in developing or implementing secure solutions are ATSC (Advanced Television Systems Committee), CableLabs, CPTWG (Copy Protection Technical Working Group), DVB (Digital Video Broadcasting) Organization, DVD Forum, EIA (Electronics Industries Association), IETF (Internet Engineering Task Force), MPAA (Motion Picture Association of America), MPEG (Moving Pictures Expert Group), North American Broadcasters Association (NABA), RIAA (Recording Industries Association of America), and SCTE (Society of Cable Television Engineers).

In digital distribution networks, copyrighted multimedia content is commonly protected by encryption:

- Cable, satellite, and terrestrial distribution [9,10,11]:   A conditional access (CA) system provides the encryption technology to control access to digital television services.   Digital content ("program") is compressed, packetized, encrypted and multiplexed with the entitlement messages. Two types of entitlement messages are commonly used associated with each program: The Entitlement Control Messages (ECMs) and the Entitlement Management Messages (EMMs).   ECMs carry the decryption keys ("control words") and a short description of the program while EMMs specify the authorization levels related to services. The programs are usually encrypted using a symmetric cipher such as the Data Encryption Standard (DES) or any other public domain or private cipher. The CA providers often protect the ECMs privately although public-key cryptography and one-way functions are useful tools for protecting access keys. Authorized users can use the appropriate decoder to decrypt the programs.   Because of their secure features, smart cards are a good option for set-top boxes.

- Internet distribution [11,12,13]: Digital Rights Management (DRM) refers to the protection, distribution, modification, and enforcement of the rights associated with the use of digital content.   The primary responsibilities of a DRM system include secure delivery of content, prevention of unauthorized access, enforcement of usage rules, and monitoring of the use of content.   A customer obtains an encrypted file from a server on the Internet for viewing purposes. To be able to decrypt the file, a license (that contains the usage rights and the decryption key) needs to be downloaded from a clearing house. A major responsibility of the clearing house is to authenticate the customer based on his credentials.   The client device should have a player that supports the relevant DRM system to play the file according to the rights included in the license. Superdistribution is a process that allows a customer to send the encrypted file to other people. However, as licenses are not transferable, each new customer has to purchase another license for playback. Today, interoperability of DRM systems is a major problem.

- Distribution in digital home networks [11,14]: A digital home networks is a cluster of consumer electronics devices (e.g., DTV, DVD player, DVCR, and STB) that are interconnected.   The multimedia content is encrypted in transmission across each digital interface, and on storage media. The technical solutions developed in recent years are listed in Table 2. In a digital home network, multimedia content moves from one device to another for storage or display. These devices need to authenticate each other to make sure that they are equipped with the licensed protection technology.

Watermarking

A digital watermark is a pattern of bits inserted into a multimedia element such as a digital image, an audio or video file. The name comes from the barely visible text or graphics imprinted on stationery that identifies the manufacturer of the stationery. There are several proposed or actual watermarking applications [4]:   broadcast monitoring, owner identification, proof of ownership, transaction tracking, content authentication, copy control, and device control. In particular, watermarks appear to be useful in plugging the analog hole in consumer electronics devices [22].

Table 2. Content protection solutions for digital home networks

Media	Solution	What is protected?
Optical media	CSS[15]	Video on DVD-ROM
	CPPM [16]	Audio on DVD-ROM
	CPRM [17]	Video or audio on DVD-R/RW/RAM
	4C/Verance Watermark [18]	Audio on DVD-ROM
	To be determined.	Video on DVD-ROM/R/RW/RAM
Magnetic media	High Definition Copy Protection (HDCP) [19]	Video on digital tape
Digital interfaces	DTCP [20]	IEEE 1394 serial bus
	HDCP [21]	Digital Visual Interface (DVI)

The components of a watermark embedding/detection/extraction system are depicted in Figure 1. A watermarking system consists of watermark structure, a marking algorithm that inserts some data into multimedia and an extraction or detection algorithm that extracts the data from, or detects the data in, a multimedia element.

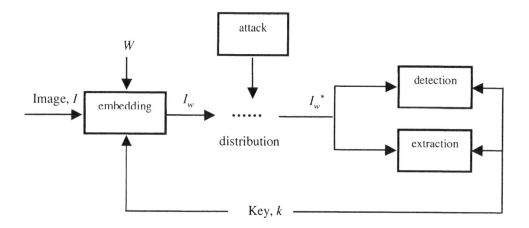

Figure 1. Watermarking system.

In applications such as owner identification, copy control, and device control, the most important properties of a watermarking system are perceptual transparency, robustness, security, high data capacity, and unambiguousness. The relative importance of these properties depends on the requirements of a given application.

- Perceptual transparency: An embedded watermark should not introduce a significant degree of distortion in the cover image. The perceived degradation of the watermarked image should be imperceptible.

- Robustness : Robustness refers to the ability to detect the watermark after normal A/V processes or intentional attacks. A watermark can still be detected or extracted after the image has undergone some common signal processing operations. These operations include special filtering, lossy compression, printing/scanning, and geometric distortions such as rotation, translation, cropping, and scaling.

- Security: Security is the ability to resist unauthorized removal, embedding, or extraction. A hostile attack is any process specifically intended to thwart the watermark's purpose.

- Capacity: Data capacity can be defined as the amount of data that can be embedded. A watermarking system should be able to embed relatively high amount of data without affecting perceptual transparency.

- Unambiguousness: The watermark should unambiguously identify the owner. It is desired that the difference between the extracted and the original watermark is as low as possible. For accuracy of identification, the system should exhibit a graceful degradation irrespective of the type of attack.

Several criteria can be used to classify image watermarking systems. Five of such criteria are the type of watermark, the type of domain, the type of watermarking scheme, type of algorithm, and the type of information needed in the detection or extraction process. The classification according to these criteria is listed in Table 3. In general, systems that embed the watermark in the pixel domain are simpler but are less robust to image manipulations. On the other hand, frequency domain watermarking techniques are more complex and robust.

Embedding multiple watermarks in a transform domain using the coefficients in several frequency bands drastically increases the overall robustness of a watermarking scheme [34,35,36]. For one group of attacks, detection or extraction in lower frequencies is better, and for another group of attacks, detection or extraction in higher frequencies is better. Since the advantages and disadvantages of low and middle-to-high frequency watermarks are complementary, embedding multiple watermarks in an image (namely, one in lower frequencies and the other in higher frequencies) would result in a scheme that is highly robust with respect to a large spectrum of image processing operations.

Table 3. Classification of image watermarking systems.

Criterion	Class	Brief description
Domain type	Pixel [23]	Pixels values are modified to embed the watermark.
	Transform [24]	Transform coefficients are modified to embed the watermark. Recent popular transforms are Discrete Cosine Transform (DCT), Discrete Wavelet Transform (DWT), and Discrete Fourier Transform (DFT).
Watermark type	Pseudo random number (PRN) sequence (having a normal distribution with zero mean and unity variance) [25]	Allows the detector to statistically check the presence or absence of a watermark. A PRN sequence is generated by feeding the generator with a secret seed.
	Visual watermark [26]	The watermark is actually reconstructed, and its visual quality is evaluated.
Scheme type	Reversible [27]	Exact restoration of the original unwatermarked image is possible
	Irreversible[28]	The distortion in the watermarked image is small but irreversible.
Information type	Non-blind [29]	Both the original image and the secret key(s)
	Semi-blind [30]	The watermark and the secret key(s)
	Blind [31]	Only the secret key(s)
Algorithm type	Additive Algorithm [32]	Additive algorithm performs linear modification of the host image and the correlative processing in the detection process.
	Quantization Algorithm [33]	Quantization algorithm performs non-linear modification of the host image and quantizing the received samples to map in the detection process.

References

1. M. Eskicioglu and E. J. Delp, "Overview of Multimedia Content Protection in Consumer Electronics Devices," Signal Processing: Image Communication, Vol. 16, No. 7, pp. 681-699, April 2001.
2. M. Eskicioglu, J. Town, and E. J. Delp, "Security of Digital Entertainment Content from Creation to Consumption," Signal Processing: Image Communication, Special Issue on Image Security, Vol. 18, No. 4, pp. 237-262, April 2003.

3. E. T. Lin, A. M. Eskicioglu, R. L. Lagendijk, and E. J. Delp, "Advances in Digital Video Content Protection," Proceedings of the IEEE, Special Issue on Advances in Video Coding and Delivery, 2004.

4. I. J. Cox, M. L. Miller, and J. A. Bloom, Digital Watermarking, Morgan Kaufmann Publishers, 2002.

5. J. Menezes, P. C. van Oorschot, and S. A. Vanstone, "Handbook of Applied Cryptography," CRC Press, 1997.

6. B. Schneier, "Applied Cryptography," John Wiley and Sons, Inc., 1996.

7. I. J. Cox, M. L. Miller, and J. A. Bloom, "Digital Watermarking," Morgan Kaufmann Publishers, 2001.

8. M. Arnold, M. Schmucker, and S. D. Wolthusen, "Techniques and Applications of Digital Watermarking and Content Protection," Artech House, Inc., 2003.

9. R. de Bruin and J. Smits, "Digital Video Broadcasting: Technology, Standards and Regulations," Artech House, Inc., 1999.

10. W. Mooij, "Advances in Conditional Access Technology," International Broadcasting Convention, IEE Conference Publication, No. 447, September 1997, pp. 461-464.

11. A. M. Eskicioglu, J. Town, and E. J. Delp, "Security of Digital Entertainment Content from Creation to Consumption," Signal Processing: Image Communication, Special Issue on Image Security, Vol. 18, Issue 4, pp. 237-262, April 2003.

12. Microsoft Windows Media DRM, available at http://www.microsoft.com/windows/windowsmedia/drm.aspx.

13. Helix DRM, available at http://www.realnetworks.com/products/drm/index.html.

14. Content Protection System Architecture (CPSA), available at http://www.4Centity.com.

15. Content Scramble System, available at http://www.dvdcca.org.

16. Content Protection for Prerecorded Media, available at http://www.4Centity.com.

17. Content Protection for Recordable Media, available at http://www.4Centity.com.

18. 4C/Verance Watermark, available at http://www.verance.com.

19. High Definition Copy Protection, available at http://www.jvc-victor.co.jp/english/products/vcr/D-security.html.

20. Digital Transmission Content Protection, available at http://www.dtcp.com.

21. High-bandwidth Digital Content Protection, available at http://www.digital-CP.com

22. Content Protection Status Report III, November 7, 2002, available at http://judiciary.senate.gov/special/mpaa110702.pdf.

23. W. Bender, D. Gruhl, and N. Morimoto, "Techniques for Data Hiding," IBM Systems Journal, Vol. 35, No. 3-4, 1996, pp. 313-336.

24. Y. Wang, J. F. Doherty, R. E. Van Dyck, "A Wavelet-based Watermarking Algorithm for Ownership Verification of Digital Images," IEEE Transactions on Image Processing, Vol. 11, No. 2, February 2002.

25. W. Zhu, Z. Xiong, and Y.-Q. Zhang, "Multiresolution Watermarking for Images and Video," IEEE Transactions on Circuits and Systems for Video Technology, Vol. 9, No. 4, June 1999, pp. 545-550.

26. R. Liu and T. Tan, "A SVD-Based Watermarking Scheme for Protecting Rightful Ownership," IEEE Transactions on Multimedia, Vol. 4, No. 1, March 2002, pp.121-128.

27. J. Fridrich, M. Goljan, and R. Du, "Lossless Data Embedding - New Paradigm in Digital Watermarking," EURASIP Journal on Applied Signal Processing, Special Issue on Emerging Applications of Multimedia Data Hiding, Vol. 2002, Issue 2 February 2002, pp. 185-196.

28. D. Kundur and D. Hatzinakos, "Toward Robust Logo Watermarking Using Multiresolution Image Fusion Principles," IEEE Transactions on Multimedia, Vol. 6, No. 1, February 2004.

29. I. J. Cox, J. Kilian, T. Leighton and T. Shamoon, "Secure Spread Spectrum Watermarking for Multimedia," IEEE Transactions on Image Processing, 6(12), December 1997, pp. 1673-1687.

30. R. Dugad, K. Ratakonda, and N. Ahuja, "A New Wavelet-Based Scheme for Watermarking Images," Proceedings of 1998 International Conference on Image Processing (ICIP 1998), Vol. 2, Chicago, IL, October 4-7, 1998, pp. 419-423.

31. S. Pereira and T. Pun, "Robust Template Matching for Affine Resistant Image Watermarks," IEEE Transactions on Image Processing, Vol. 9, No. 6, June 2000, pp. 1123-1129.

32. M. L. Miller, G. J. Doerr, I. J. Cox, "Applying Informed Coding and Embedding to Design a Robust, High Capacity Watermark," IEEE Transactions on Image Processing, Vol. 13, No. 6, June 2004, pp. 792-807.

33. B. Chen and G. W. Wornell, "Quantization index modulation: A class of provably good methods for digital watermarking and information embedding," IEEE Transactions on Information Theory, 1999.

34. R. Mehul and R. Priti, "Discrete Wavelet Transform Based Multiple Watermarking Scheme," Proceedings of IEEE Region 10 Technical Conference on Convergent Technologies for the Asia-Pacific, Bangalore, India, October 2003.

35. P. Tao and A. M. Eskicioglu, "A Robust Multiple Watermarking Scheme in the Discrete Wavelet Transform Domain," Proceedings of Optics East 2004 Symposium, Internet Multimedia Management Systems V Conference, Philadelphia, PA, October 2004.

36. E. Ganic, S. D. Dexter, and A. M. Eskicioglu, "Embedding Multiple Watermarks in the DFT Domain Using Low and High Frequency Bands," IS&T/SPIE's 17th Symposium on Electronic Imaging, Security, Steganography, and Watermarking of Multimedia Contents VII Conference, San Jose, CA, January 2005.

PUBLIC KEY VS. SECRET KEY ENCRYPTION

Definition: *The purpose of a key in encryption systems is to ensure privacy by keeping information hidden from whom it is not intended. There are two types of encryption systems: secret-key and public-key systems.*

Encryption is the transformation of data, the *plaintext*, into a form that is as close to impossible as possible to read, the *ciphetext*, without the appropriate knowledge (a key). Its purpose is to ensure privacy by keeping information hidden from anyone for whom it is not intended, even those who have access to the encrypted data, the *ciphetext* [1].

There are two types of encryption systems: *secret-key* and *public-key* systems (see Figure 1). In secret-key encryption, also referred to as symmetric cryptography, the same key is used for both encryption and decryption. The most popular secret-key cryptosystem in use today is the *Data Encryption Standard* (*DES*, see [1, 2, 3]). In general, the security of a secret-key system depends on the strength of the algorithm and the length of the key. In a brute-force attack, an N bits long key, which implies 2^N possible keys, will take 2^N attempts for the hacker to find the correct key. That is, the longer the key is, the longer it will take for a certain computer to find the correct key among the 2^N possible keys. Besides the key, there is another factor to determine the interval of a successful brute force attack: the speed of each test which relies on the speed of the computer and the computational complexity of the encryption algorithm. Unfortunately in most cases, the longer the key is, the longer it takes to encrypt/decrypt the message, and the more one need to pay for it in terms of cost. To determine the length of a proper key for a certain application, one needs to look at several aspects: the intended security, the current and future computer power, and the speed of the state-of-the-art factoring algorithms. That is, you need a key long enough to be secure but short enough to be computationally feasible and low cost.

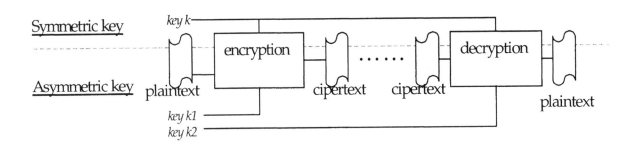

Figure 1. Illustration of symmetric key encryption vs. asymmetric key encryption.

On the other hand, in a public-key system, each user has a *public key* and a *private key*. The public key maybe made public while the private key remains secret. Encryption is performed with the one key while decryption is done with the other. Today's dominant public key encryption algorithms are factorization based [2]. That is, the algorithms are based on the difficulty of factoring large numbers that are the product of two large prime numbers. One of the most popular public-key encryption algorithms, the *RSA public-key cryptosystem*, (see [1, 2, 3],) is a typical factorization based algorithm. To break such systems, one need to factor out the large number. Intuitively, the large the number is, the harder it is for a hacker to factor it.

See: Multimedia Encryption

References

1. RSA Laboratories, RSA Laboratories' Frequently Asked Questions About Today's Cryptography, Version 4.1, RSA Security Inc., 2000.
2. B. Schneier, "Applied Cryptography," 2nd edition, John Wiley & Sons, Inc, 1996.
3. R. K. Nichols, "ICSA guide to cryptography," McGraw-Hill, 1999.

QOS ASSESSMENT OF VIDEO OVER IP

Definition: *At the network level, the QoS offered to a video transmission can be evaluated by monitoring network performance parameters, such as delay, jitter, and packet loss rate.*

The capacity of measuring the Quality of Service (QoS) of a video communication becomes increasingly important because of the growing interest in video delivery over unreliable channels, such as wireless networks and the Internet. A key point for the success of new multimedia applications and video applications in particular, is the network QoS provided to video and audio streams. At the network level, the QoS offered to a video transmission can be evaluated by monitoring network performance parameters, such as delay, jitter, and packet loss rate. Nevertheless, it is challenging to establish how these network-level parameters and the consequent delivered QoS to video streams effectively map onto application QoS, *i.e.* the delivered QoS as perceived by a (human) end user.

At the application level, the quality of a video transmission may be evaluated by subjective and objective metrics [1]. An example of a subjective metric is the Mean Opinion Score (MOS). MOS provides a measure of the quality perceived by a user of a multimedia transmission. The scheme uses subjective controlled tests that are averaged after applied to a number of individuals to obtain a quantitative indicator of the system performance in transmitting a multimedia stream. In the case of video transmission assessment, these individuals rate the perceived quality of test videos after they are sent over simulated or experimental networks. Each video is given a rating as follows: (1) bad; (2) poor; (3) fair; (4) good; (5) excellent. The MOS rate is the mean of all individual scores and can then range from 1 (worst) and 5 (best). This is useful to establish reference scores on video quality transmission, as it is indeed perceived by end users. However, the subjective assessment provided by MOS is expensive and time-consuming, thereby preventing it to be conducted in real-time. As a consequence, it is also hard to embed the MOS metric into a practical video processing system because it cannot be implemented automatically.

Objective techniques offer an alternative to subjective techniques by avoiding human intervention to rate the quality of the video transmission and allowing a means to automatically estimate the quality of a video transmission [2]. Indeed, objective metrics for assessing video performance are useful for the practical specification of performance requirements, comparison of service offerings, automatic network QoS monitoring, and better utilization of limited network resources, such as transmission bandwidth. An example of objective metric for video transmission assessment is the Peak Signal-to-Noise Ratio (PSNR). PSNR measures the error between a reconstructed image and the original one. Prior to transmission, one may then compute a reference PSNR value sequence on the reconstruction of the encoded video as compared to the original raw video. After transmission, the PSNR is computed at the receiver for the reconstructed video of the possibly corrupted video sequence received. The individual PSNR values at the source or receiver do not mean much, but the difference between the quality of the encoded video at the source and the received one can be used as an objective QoS metric to assess the transmission impact on video quality at the application level.

See: Video over IP

References

1. F.A. Shaikh, S. McClellan, M. Singh, and S.K. Chakravarthy, "End-to-end testing of IP QoS mechanisms," IEEE Computer, Vol. 35, No. 5, pp. 80-87, May 2002.
2. S. Olsson, M. Stroppiana, and J. Baina, "Objective methods for assessment of video quality: state of the art," IEEE Transactions on Broadcasting, Vol. 43, No. 4, pp. 487-495, December 1997.

QUALITY OF SERVICE IN MULTIMEDIA NETWORKS

Abdulmotaleb El Saddik
School of Information Technology and Engineering
University of Ottawa, Ontario, Canada

Definition: *Multimedia applications must adjust their QoS according to the heterogeneous terminals with variable QoS requirements and support*

During the last decade, the multitude of advances attained in terminal computers, along with the introduction of mobile hand-held devices, and the deployment of high speed networks have led to a recent surge of interest in Quality of Service (QoS) for multimedia applications. Computer networks able to support multimedia applications with diverse QoS performance requirements are evolving. To ensure that multimedia applications will be guaranteed the required QoS, it is not enough to merely commit resources. It is important that distributed multimedia applications ensure end-to-end QoS of media streams, considering both the networks and the end terminals. The degradation in the contracted QoS is often unavoidable, thus there is a need to provide real-time QoS monitoring that not only is capable of monitoring the QoS support in the network, but that can also take actions in real-time manner to sustain an acceptable multimedia presentation quality when the QoS level degrades. Presently, there are various kinds of networks; wired and wireless that co-exists with each other. These networks have QoS characteristics that are drastically different and whose degree of variability of the different QoS parameters, such as bandwidth, delay and jitter, differ considerably. Furthermore, there are various kinds of terminals, such as desktop computers, laptop computers, personal digital assistants (PDA), and cell phones, each with some multimedia support. Thus, multimedia applications must adjust their QoS according to the heterogeneous terminals with variable QoS requirements and support. ISO defines QoS as a concept for determining the quality of the offered networking services. In this article, we consider the following three issues: a) QoS elements, b) Realization of QoS, and c) Manifesting QoS in appropriate network.

QoS Elements

We can divide Quality of Service into the following three layers:

- *Application level Quality of Service:* specifies those parameters related to user requirements and expectations. Frame size, sample rate, image and audio clarity are some parameters of this level.
- *System level Quality of Service:* includes operating system and CPU requirements, such as processing time, CPU utilization, and media relations like synchronization.
- *Network level Quality of Service:* defines communication requirements, such as throughput, delay, jitter, loss, and reliability.

The main QoS parameters are discussed next.

Bandwidth or throughput is a network QoS parameter that refers to the data rate supported by a network connection or interface. The most common term for bandwidth is bits per second (bps) i.e. effective number of data units transported per unit time. Multimedia applications usually require high bandwidth as compared to other general applications. For example, MPEG2 video requires around 4Mbps, while MPEG1 video requires about 1-2 Mbps. Network technologies that do not support such high bandwidth can not play multimedia contents. For instance, Bluetooth technology version 1 only supports a maximum bandwidth of 746 kbps and thus, devices relying on Bluetooth for connectivity can not play MPEG1 videos. Better throughput means better QoS received by the end-user.

Delay is defined as the time interval elapsed between the departures of data from the source to its arrival at the destination. In the case of a communication system, delay refers to the time lag between the departure of a signal from the source and its arrival at the destination. This can range from a few nanoseconds or microseconds in local area networks (LANs) to about 0.25 s in satellite communications systems. Greater delays can occur as a result of the time required for packets to make their way through land-based cables and nodes of the Internet. Because of the clock synchronization problem, it is difficult to measure one-way delays; therefore, round-trip (i.e. forward and return paths on the Internet) delays are used.

Jitter refers to the variation in time between packets arriving at the destination. It is caused by network congestion, timing drift, or route changes. Depending on the multimedia application type, jitter may or may not be significant. For example, audio or video conference applications are not tolerable to jitter due to the very limited buffering in live presentations, whereas prerecorded multimedia playback is usually tolerable to jitter, as modern players buffer around 5 seconds to alleviate the affect of jitter. In jitter, the deviation can be in terms of amplitude, phase timing or the width of the signal pulse.

Loss mainly denotes the amount of data that did not make it to the destination in a specified time period. Loss is directly proportional to the QoS applicable. Different methods can be used to reduce the chances of loss; either by providing individual channels/guaranteed bandwidth for specific data transmissions, or by retransmission of data for loss recovery.

Reliability: some multimedia applications require real-time processing, which makes packet retransmission impossible. Multimedia applications usually employ recovery mechanisms, such as Forward Error Correction (FEC), to deal with packet loss. Most Multimedia applications are error tolerant to a certain extent. However, few multimedia applications, like distance learning examination or Tele-Surgery are sensitive to packet loss. The successful delivery of all packets of the Multimedia content in such applications is vital. System reliability depends on many factors in the network. Reliability is inversely proportional to failure rate, meaning that reliability will be deteriorating as the failure rate rises.

Frame size defines the size of the video image on the display screen. A bigger frame size requires a higher bandwidth. In QoS adaptation, frame size can be modified according to available QoS support. For example, if a video is transmitted at 800 * 600 pixel size frames, and network congestion is experienced, then the frame size can be reduced to 640 * 480 pixels to lower the bandwidth requirement for the video transmission.

Frame rate defines the number of frames sent to network per unit time. A higher Frame rate requires higher bandwidth. If QoS adaptation is required, the frame rate can be modified to lessen the bandwidth requirements at the cost of video quality.

Image clarity refers to the perceptual quality of the image which a user perceives for a certain delivery of Multimedia content. Human eyes are less sensitive to high frequency components of the image, so the high frequency components can be suppressed without any noticeable loss in image quality.

Audio quality is defined in terms of sampling rate per second. A higher sampling rate renders better audio quality. For example, audio encoded in 128kbps is higher in quality than that is encoded in 16kbps. Usually, for audio conversation, 64kbps audio quality is adequate, however, 128kbps or higher is required for stereo music contents.

Audio Confidentiality and Integrity dictates the security and access right restrictions for an audio stream. Depending on the media contents, this parameter may or may not be of great importance. For example, security is vital for an audio conference between two campuses of a company discussing the new product line, whereas security is not important for a news broadcast over the Internet.

<u>Video Confidentiality and Integrity</u>; Video security defines the security and access right restrictions of video (Sequence of images). Like audio confidentiality, video confidentiality may or may not have importance, depending on the multimedia contents and the used business model.

Realization of QoS

To realize and implement QoS parameters in a network, the following characteristics of network traffic need to be explained: packet classification, congestion management, congestion avoidance, traffic-shaping and policing and Link efficiency management.

<u>Packet or traffic classification</u> identifies and splits traffic into different classes and marks them accordingly. Packet classification allows for different treatments of transmitted data, therefore giving audio packets higher priority if, e.g., the underlying network supports it. Figure1 is an example of classification. Traffic classifications can be determined in several ways, including physical ingress interface, ISO/OSI Layer 2 or Layer 3 address or Layer 4 Port number, or the Universal Resource Locator (URL).

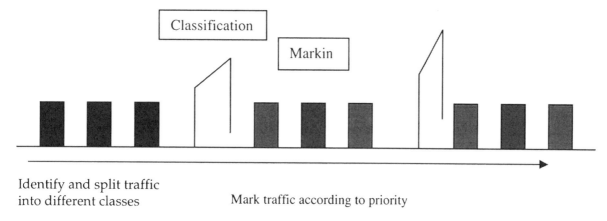

Figure 1. Traffic classification.

<u>Congestion management</u> prioritizes traffic based on markings. It encompasses several mechanisms and algorithms, such as FIFO, PQ, CQ, FBWFQ, CBWFQ, IP RTP and LLQ. First-in first-out (FIFO) is the default algorithm used for congestion management; it forwards packets in order of arrival when the network is not congested. FIFO may drop some important packets because of its limited buffer space. Priority queuing (PQ) places packets into four levels based on assigned priority: high, medium, normal, and low. Custom queuing (CQ) reserves a percentage of an interface's available bandwidth for each selected traffic type for up to 16 queues available. Weighted fair queuing (WFQ) is designed to minimize configuration effort and automatically adapts to changing network traffic conditions. It schedules interactive traffic to the front of the queue to reduce response time, and fairly shares the remaining bandwidth among high-bandwidth flows. Flow-based weighted fair queuing (FBWFQ) allows each queue to be serviced fairly in terms of byte count. Class-based weighted fair queuing (CBWFQ) extends the standard WFQ function by providing support for user-defined traffic classes. IP Real-time protocol queuing (IP RIP), also called PQ-WFQ, provides strict priority to time-sensitive traffic,

such as voice traffic. Low latency queuing (LLQ) is PQ+CBWFQ. It also provides strict priority to time-sensitive traffic.

<u>Congestion avoidance</u> predicts and avoids congestion on network. It is achieved by packet dropping techniques. Random Early Detection (RED), Weight Random Early Detection (WRED), Random Early Detection with In/Out (RIO), Adaptive Random Early Detection (ARED), and Flow Random Early Detection (FRED) are main congestion avoidance algorithms.

The goal of RED is to control the average queue size by alerting end hosts on when to temporarily slow down their transmission rate. RED avoids congestion by monitoring the traffic load at points in the network and stochastically discarding packets before a queue becomes full. WRED combines the RED algorithms with a weight that is decided by the IP Precedence. This effectively assigns higher precedence traffic flows lower drop rates, and thus QoS is guaranteed. RIO uses packet marking to modify RED algorithms based on a packet-by-packet criterion. RIO assumes that packets have already passed through an upstream marker, and a single bit in the packet header signifies the packet to be "In" or "Out" of profile. More specifically, when the packet is within the limits of a specified policy, it is marked as "In" profile; when the packet crosses the limits of specified policy, it is marked as "Out" profile. ARED addresses RED's limitations by modifying the RED parameters based on recent congestion history. FRED provides greater fairness to all flows through an interface with regards to how packets are dropped. With WRED, packets are dropped based on the average queue length. When the packet number of the average queue length exceeds the minimum threshold, it begins to drop packets that arrive to the router interface indiscriminately to the type of flow to which the packets belong. Therefore, WRED applies the same loss rate to all kinds of packet flow.

<u>Traffic Shaping and Policing</u> can also be used within certain types of networks to manage ingress and egress traffic and data flow. The main reasons to using traffic shaping are controlling access to available bandwidth, ensuring that traffic conforms to the policies established for it, regulating the flow of traffic in order to avoid congestion.

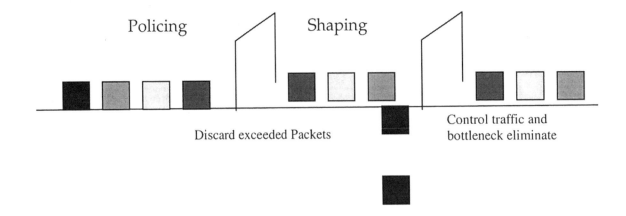

Figure 2. Traffic shaping and policing.

<u>Link efficiency management</u> uses compression technique (see chapter MPEG coding standard) and/or media scaling to increase throughput, and by doing so, improves link efficiency.

Network support and protocols for QoS

Recently, there has been much research conducted on the development of IP QoS (Quality of Service), keeping in mind the goal of allowing network operators to offer diverse levels of treatment to multimedia packets. These efforts have caused several approaches to emerge: the Integrated Services (Intserv) [9] and its accompanying signaling Resource Reservation Protocol (RSVP) [9], the Differentiated Services (Diffserv) [9] desired to accommodate heterogeneous application requirements and user expectations, and the permission of differentiated pricing of Internet services, and Multi Protocol Label Switching (MPLS) [8].

<u>Intserv</u> is basically an extension of the original Internet architecture to support new types of real-time applications, and to improve the network manager's ability to control the network. The IntServ model [9] enables applications to choose from multiple, controlled levels of delivery service for their data packet. Intserv model includes the Control Load (CL) service, Guaranteed (G) service, and Best Effort (BE) service to define QoS along the network. The Guaranteed service is defined for applications with rigid end-to-end constraints, and ensures that packets arrive within the guaranteed delivery time and that they will not be discarded due to buffer overflows. The Controlled-Load service, on the other hand, is defined for applications with looser performance criteria, and offers a commitment to a service similar to that provided to best-effort traffic under lightly loaded conditions. IntServ works in conjunction with a signaling protocol such as Resource Reservation Protocol (RSVP). In this architecture, the sender and the receiver exchange data in order to negotiate specific packet classification and forwarding behavior in the network. Once a path is established, the sender transmits the data knowing that resources have been reserved for its packets all the way to the receiver. The routers in the network need to store state information for every sender-receiver path passing through them, which renders this scheme less scalable in comparison to others. The problems with RSVP architecture is that it does not scale well in the Internet core, since the amount of information increases proportionally with the number of flows, which imposes huge storage requirements and processing overhead on the routers.

<u>DiffServ</u> is an architecture that provides service differentiation. Using DiffServ, applications can mark the first six bits of the type of service (TOS) field in the IP header for requesting a higher level of service. These marked packets are then forwarded through the network by mapping the 6-bit TOS value to a forwarding behavior supported in a Domain router. In this model, the role and importance of edge routers and core routers are more clearly defined compared to the aforementioned approaches. The <u>Diffserv</u> model introduces a mechanism to aggregate micro-flows into a number of predefined set of building blocks from which a variety of aggregate router behaviors may be designed to provide quality of service. IP packets are tagged with distinct labels before entering an IP Diffserv domain and given a particular forwarding treatment at each network node along the path. Currently, the Diffserv model defines three standard Per-

Hop-Behaviors (PHBs): the Expedited Forwarding (EF), the Assured Forwarding (AF), and the Best-Effort PHB. In practice, there existtwo models for implementing Diffserv on networks: the relative Diffserv, and the absolute Diffserv model.

Using Label-switching technique, a forwarding 'label' (link-layer addressing) is attached to the packet that contains the next hop address in the network. This label also determines the forwarding behavior of the packet and the value of the replacement label at the next hop. An example of this approach is MPLS (Multi-protocol Label Switching), which is a technology that integrates the label-swapping paradigm with network-layer routing. Using MPLS is another way of receiving service differentiation [8]. Multi-protocol implies that MPLS supports various protocols at both, Layer-2 (link layer) and Layer-3 (network layer) of the OSI (Open Systems Interconnection) model. Layer 2 protocols supported include ATM, Frame Relay, etc. and some of the Layer-3 protocols supported are IPv4, IPv6 and IPX.

Network Scalability and Application Layer Multicasting

The traditional Internet unicasting service is based on one-to-one data communication. Unicasting is well suited when communications occurs between two specific hosts (e.g. Email, web browsers). However, many applications today require one-to-many and many-to-many communications. Among them are shared virtual space, multimedia distribution service, Video conferencing, etc. For these kinds of applications, which involve transmitting a large amount of data to multiple recipients, the unicast service is no longer efficient. For example, consider a multimedia content provider that uses unicasting to distribute a 2 Mbps streamed video. To support 1,000 viewers, the server needs a 2 Gbps access. Therefore, the server interface capacity can very well be a significant bottleneck, limiting the number of unicast video streams per video server. Replicated unicast transmissions eat up a lot of bandwidth within the network, which is another significant limitation [5]. To overcome this unnecessary consumption of bandwidth, an efficient one-to-many communication scheme – multicasting – has been developed. Multicasting is an efficient way of distributing data from one sender to multiple receivers with minimal data duplication. Traditionally multicasting is implemented at the network layer, analogous to the manner that network routers define the data delivery tree. As packets flow through this tree, they are replicated by routers at different branch points of the tree. This is IP Multicast architecture [1]. IP Multicasting eliminates traffic redundancy and improves bandwidth usage in group data delivery on wide-area networks. However, although IP Multicasting has been available for years, today's Internet service providers are still reluctant to provide a wide-area multicast routing service due to some technical, as well as non-technical reasons [2][3]. The first of these reasons is scalability. IP Multicasting is designed for a hierarchical routing infrastructure. It does not scale well in terms of supporting large number of concurrent groups. Secondly, there are deployment hurdles. Current deployment practices of IP Multicasting require manual configuration at routers to form the MBone, which makes the MBone expensive to set up and maintain. Lastly, there are the marketing reasons. The traditional charging model is that only downstream is charged. But in multicasting, any participant may introduce large amount of upstream (e.g. video conferencing), therefore the charging model needs to be redefined. Therefore an alternative has been proposed to shift multicast support to end systems. This is Application-Layer Multicasting (ALM). In ALM, data packets are replicated at end-hosts, not routers. The end-hosts form an overlay network, and the goal of ALM is to construct and maintain an efficient overlay for data transmission. Application-Layer Multicasting has advantages over IP Multicast. Since the routing information is maintained by application, it is scalable. It supports a large number of concurrent groups; and since it needs no infrastructure support, it is fully deployable on the Internet. By using ALM, it is possible for Content Providers to deliver bandwidth-intensive contents such as TV programs to a vast number of clients in real-time via the Internet. The network layer multicasting and application layer multicasting models are shown in Figure 3. This was impractical before because the bottleneck bandwidth between content providers and consumers is considerably 'narrower' than the natural consumption rate of such media [5].

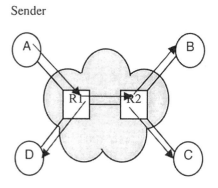
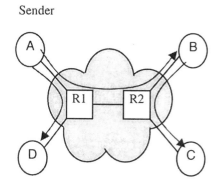

Network layer multicasting   Application layer multicasting

Figure 3. Network layer multicasting and application layer multicasting (Square nodes are routers and circular nodes are end-hosts).

However, ALM does come with a tradeoff: more bandwidth and delay (compared to IP multicasting) for the sake of supporting more users and scalability. But it has been shown that ALM-based algorithms can have "acceptable" performance penalties with respect to IP Multicasting, and when compared to other practical solutions [6].

References

1. R. Steinmetz and K. Nahrstedt, "Multimedia Systems," ISBN 3-540-40867-3, Springer 2004.
2. A. El-Sayed and V. Roca, "A Survey of Proposals for an Alternative Group Communication Service," IEEE Network, Vol. 17, No. 1, pp. 46-51, February 2003.
3. B. Zhang, S. Jamin, and L. Zhang, "Host multicast: A framework for delivering multicast to end users," Proceedings of the IEEE INFOCOM, June 2002.
4. R. Jain and K. Ramarkishman, "Congestion Avoidance in Computer Networks with a Connectionless Network Layer: Concepts, Goals and Methodology," Proceedings of the IEEE Computer Networking Symposium, Washington, D.C., April 1988, pp. 134-143.

5.   J. Jannotti, D. Gifford, K. L. Johnson, and M. F. Kaashoek, "Overcast: Reliable multicasting with an overlay network," Proceedings of the 4th Symposium on Operating System Design Implementation (OSDI), October 2000.
6.   Y. Chu, S.G. Rao, S. Seshan, and H.S. Zhang, "A Case for End System Multicast," IEEE Journal on Selected Areas in Communication, Special issue on networking support for multicast, Vol. 20, No. 8, 2002, pp. 1456-1471.
7.   Y. Zhong, S. Shirmohammadi, and A. El Saddik, "Measurement of the Effectiveness of Application-Layer Multicasting" Proceedings of the 2005 IEEE Instrumentation and Measurement Technology Conference (IMTC/05), Ottawa, Ontario, Canada, May 2005.
8.   http://www.mplsrc.com, last visited April 2005.
9.   RFC 2475 – DiffServ Model.
10. RFC 2990 – QoS Architectures: IntServ and DiffServ.

QUANTIZATION

Definition: *Quantization is a technique used in lossy image and video compression algorithms based on DCT, DFT, or DWT.*

Quantization can be modeled as [1]:

$$x_q = \left\lfloor \frac{x}{q} + 0.5 \right\rfloor, \tag{1}$$

where q is a constant quantization step size, and $\lfloor x + 0.5 \rfloor$ rounds x to the nearest integer x_q.

Dequantization can be modeled as:

$$x' = x_q \times q, \tag{2}$$

where x' is the regenerated integer, which is normally not equal to x. Therefore the quantization process is lossy.

Most common lossy compression algorithms first transform the original signals into a different domain such as Discrete Cosine Transform (DCT), Discrete Fourier Transform (DFT), or Discrete Wavelet Transform (DWT) domain. Then, each of the resulting coefficients is independently quantized.

Quantization is being used by many robust or semi-fragile watermarking algorithms. A robust watermarking algorithm need survive the quantization process, while an ideal semi-fragile watermarking algorithm need provide fragility that is proportional to the quantization step size q.

Quantization has the following property [1]. Let $x \lozenge q$ be the result of quantizing x to an integral multiple of the quantization step size, q:

$$x \lozenge q = q \left\lfloor \frac{x}{q} + 0.5 \right\rfloor \tag{3}$$

If a is a read-valued scalar quantity, and q_1 and q_2 are quantization step sizes, with $q_2 \leq q_1$, then

$$((a \lozenge q_1) \lozenge q_2) \lozenge q_1 = a \lozenge q_1 . \tag{4}$$

The feature represented by Equation (4) guarantees that if a quantization-based watermark is embedded by using quantization step size q_1, it will be detectable even after the host signal is re-compressed by using quantization step size q_2 ($q_2 \leq q_1$).

See: Multimedia Authentication

References

1. I. Cox, M. Miller, and J. Bloom, "Digital Watermarking," Morgan Kaufmann Publishers, 2002, ISBN: 1-55860-714-5.

REAL TIME MULTIMEDIA

Wenjun Zeng
University of Missouri, Columbia, MO, USA

Junqiang Lan
Harmonic, Inc., NY Design Center, NY, USA

Definition: *Real-time multimedia refers to applications in which multimedia data has to be delivered and rendered in real time; it can be broadly classified into interactive multimedia and streaming media.*

Multimedia is a term that describes multiple forms of information, including audio, video, graphics, animation, images, text, etc. The best examples are continuous media such as animation, audio and video that are time-based, i.e., each audio sample or video frame has a timestamp associated with it, representing its presentation time. Multimedia data has to be presented in a continuous fashion, in accordance with their associated timestamp. For example, video is typically rendered at 30 frames per second to give the viewers the illusion of smooth motion. As a result, multimedia applications typically have the real-time constraint, i.e., media data has to be delivered and rendered in real time.

Today, with the advances of digital media and networking technologies, multimedia has become an indispensable feature on the Internet. Animation, audio and video clips become increasingly popular on the Internet. A large number of distributed multimedia applications have been created, including Internet telephony, Internet videoconferencing, Internet collaboration that combines video, audio and whiteboard, Internet TV, on demand streaming or broadcasting, distance learning, distributed simulation, entertainment and gaming, multimedia messaging, etc.

Multimedia data, unlike traditional data, exhibits several unique characteristics. First, multimedia applications usually require much higher bandwidth than traditional textual applications. A typical 25-second movie clip with a resolution of 320x240 could take 2.3 mega-bytes, which is equivalent to about 1000 screens of textual data. Second, most multimedia applications have stringent delay constraints, including real-time delivery. Audio and video data must be played back continuously at the rate they are sampled. If the data does not arrive in time, the playing back process will stop and the artifact can be easily picked up by human ears and eyes. Third, multimedia data stream is usually bursty due to the dynamics of different segments of the media. For most multimedia applications, the receiver has a limited buffer. The bursty data stream, if not smoothed, may overflow or underflow the application buffer. When data arrives too fast, the buffer will overflow and some data packets will be lost, resulting in poor quality. When data arrives too slowly, the buffer will underflow and the application will starve, causing the playing back process to freeze. Other characteristics of multimedia data include power-hungry, synchronous, loss-tolerant, having components of different importance, highly adaptable, etc. Some of the characteristics such as loss-tolerance, prioritized components and adaptability can in fact be exploited in a real-time multimedia communication system.

Contrary to the high bandwidth, real-time and bursty natures of multimedia data, in reality, networks are typically shared by thousands and millions of users, and have limited bandwidth, unpredictable delay and availability. For example, the Internet provides only the best effort service, i.e., data packets can be lost, re-ordered, or delayed for a long time. As a result, advanced networking technologies have been designed specifically for the efficient delivery of multimedia data. There is typically a trade-off between delay and quality. Different applications may require different levels of quality of service (QoS).

Real-Time Networked Multimedia

Real-time multimedia can be broadly classified into interactive multimedia and streaming media. Interactive multimedia applications include Internet telephony, Internet video-conferencing, Internet collaboration, Internet gaming, etc. In interactive multimedia applications, the delay constraint is very stringent in order to achieve interactivity. For example, in Internet telephony, human beings can only tolerate a latency of about 250 milliseconds. This imposes an extremely challenging problem for interactive multimedia applications over the Internet that provides only the best effort service. Over the years, great efforts have been made to facilitate the development of interactive multimedia applications over the Internet. For example, Microsoft Research's ConferenceXP Research Platform 1 supports the development of real-time collaboration and videoconferencing applications by delivering high-quality, low-latency audio and video over broadband connections that support multicast capability.

The second class of networked multimedia technology is streaming media. Streaming media technology enables the real time or on demand distribution of audio, video and multimedia on the Internet. Streaming media is the simultaneous transfer of digital media so that it is received as a continuous real-time stream. Streamed data is transmitted by a server application and received and rendered in real-time by client applications. These client applications can start playing back audio and video as soon as enough data has been received and stored in the receiver's buffer. There could be up to a few seconds of startup delay, i.e., the delay between when the server starts streaming the data and when the client starts the playback. Some of the popular streaming media products are Microsoft's Windows Media Player and RealNetworks's RealPlayer for

Internet streaming, and PacketVideo's embedded media player for wireless streaming to embedded devices such as the next generation multimedia phones.

Standards have been developed to facilitate the inter-operability of the products from different vendors for both interactive multimedia and real-time streaming media applications. These standards are briefly described below.

Multimedia Conferencing Standards

Multimedia conferencing, or video conferencing, is an important application of real time media. In video conferencing, people at different sites are brought together for a meeting by transmitting real time audio, video and collaboration data on communication channels, as illustrated in Figure 1. Video conferencing are widely used in telecommuting, distant collaboration, telemedicine, distant learning, career services and etc. With the fast development of technology, video conferencing will have broader impacts and huge potential market.

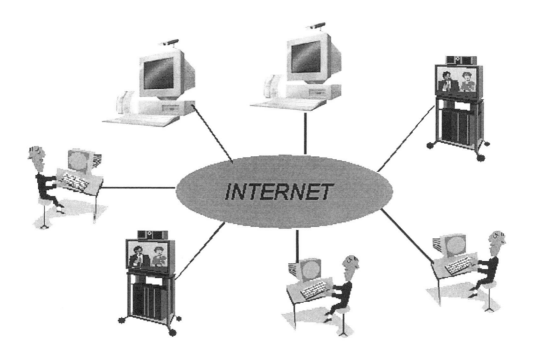

Figure 1. Video conferencing on the Internet.

As an advanced communication tool, inter-connectivity and inter-operability require that the video conferencing devices involved in the same conference can talk to each other, i.e., they comply with some common standard. Video conferencing standard is an umbrella set of standards because it not only has to specify audio and video coding standards, but also needs to address call control, conference management, media packetization and delivery. There are two major categories of video conferencing standards, H.32x series from the telecommunication world, standardized by ITU (International Telecommunications Union), and SIP (Session Initial Protocol) based video conferencing standard from the Internet world, recommended by IETF (Internet Engineering Task Force).

ITU-T H.32x video conferencing standards

H.320 2, the first international standard of video conferencing, was released by ITU in the early 1990s. The standard was designed for narrow band switched ISDN (Integrated Service Digital Networks). Later on its variants for different network infrastructures were standardized in the mid and late 1990s, which include H.321 3 (for broadband ISDN), H.322 4 (for guaranteed bandwidth packet switched networks), H.324 6 (for Public Switched Telephone Network) and H.323 5 (for non-guaranteed bandwidth packet switched networks). Due to the overwhelming of IP networks, H.323 becomes the most popular video conferencing standard in recent years. H.323 standard has been updated to version 5 7 to improve reliability, scalability, flexibility and extensibility. We will use H.323 as an example to illustrate the H.32x video conferencing standards.

H.323 defines four major components for a network-based communication system: Terminals, Gateways, Gatekeepers, and Multipoint Control Units (MCU), as shown in Figure 2. Terminals are the client endpoints that provide real-time, two-way communications. A Gatekeeper is the most important component of an H.323 enabled network. It acts as the central point for all calls within its zone and provides call control services to registered endpoints. Gateways, which are optional in H.323, provide translation function between H.323 conferencing endpoints and other terminal types such as H.324 and H.320. The MCU supports conferences between three or more endpoints.

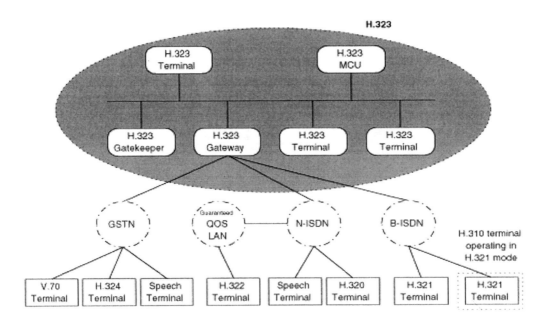

Figure 2. H.323 architecture overview.

Figure 3 describes the protocol stack of H.323 systems. All terminals must support voice communications; video and data are optional. H.323 specifies the modes of operation required for different audio, video, and/or data terminals to work together. All H.323 terminals must also support H.245, which is used to negotiate channel usage and capabilities. Three other components are required: Q.931 for call signaling and call setup, a component called Registration/Admission/Status (RAS), which is a protocol used to communicate with a Gatekeeper, and support for RTP/RTCP for sequencing audio and video packets. Optional components in an H.323 terminal are video codecs, T.120 data conferencing protocols, and MCU capabilities. The real time media data (audio and video) is carried over RTP (Real Time Protocol)/RTCP (Real Time Control Protocol), which will be further discussed in the following section.

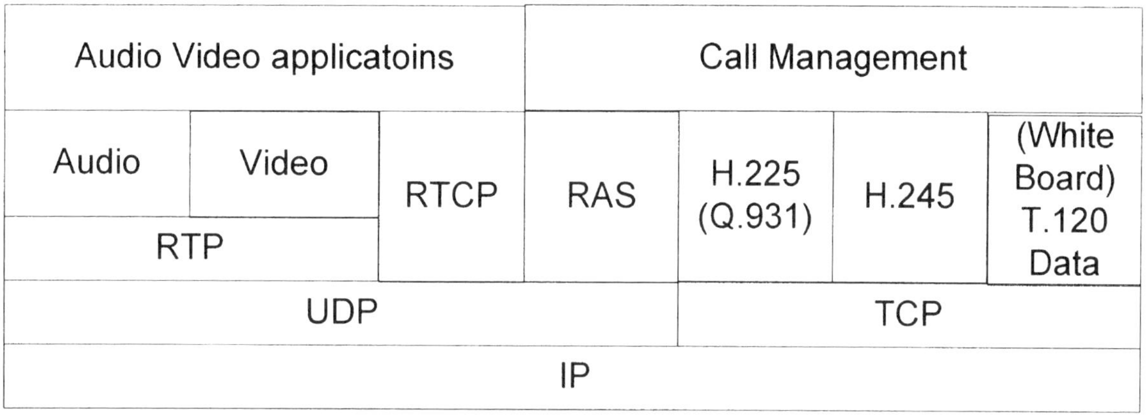

Audio Video applicatoins			Call Management			
Audio	Video	RTCP	RAS	H.225 (Q.931)	H.245	(White Board) T.120 Data
RTP						
UDP			TCP			
IP						

Figure 3. H.323 protocol stack.

SIP based video conferencing standards
In parallel to ITU, IETF has also released standards for multimedia teleconferencing (MMTC) over IP networks, including the Session Initiation Protocol (SIP) 8 and the Session Announcement Protocol (SAP) 10. Developed by the IETF Multiparty Multimedia Session Control Working Group (MMUSIC WG) to support Internet teleconferencing and multimedia communications, SIP is a lightweight, text-based signaling protocol used for establishing sessions in an IP network. SIP deals generically with sessions, which can include audio, video, chat, interactive games, and virtual reality. The sessions are described using a separate protocol called Session Description Protocol (SDP) 9. SDP is transported in the message body of a SIP message. SIP is an application-independent protocol; it simply initiates, terminates and modifies sessions without knowing any details of the sessions. This simplicity means that SIP was designed at the outset to be extremely flexible, scalable and extensible. SIP is a request-response protocol that closely resembles two other Internet protocols, HTTP and SMTP (the protocols that power the World Wide Web and email). Consequently, using SIP, conferencing easily becomes another web application and can be integrated easily into other Internet services. In addition, IP streaming techniques are used for media delivery, and the IP Multicast Protocol is adopted as the foundation for building bandwidth-efficient and scalable multipoint-to-multipoint communication applications over IP. SAP is the protocol to announce MMTC sessions. Figure 4 shows the protocol stack used in

SIP based video conferencing systems. Similar to H.323, audio and video data is carried on RTP/RTCP, but the call management is done using SIP.

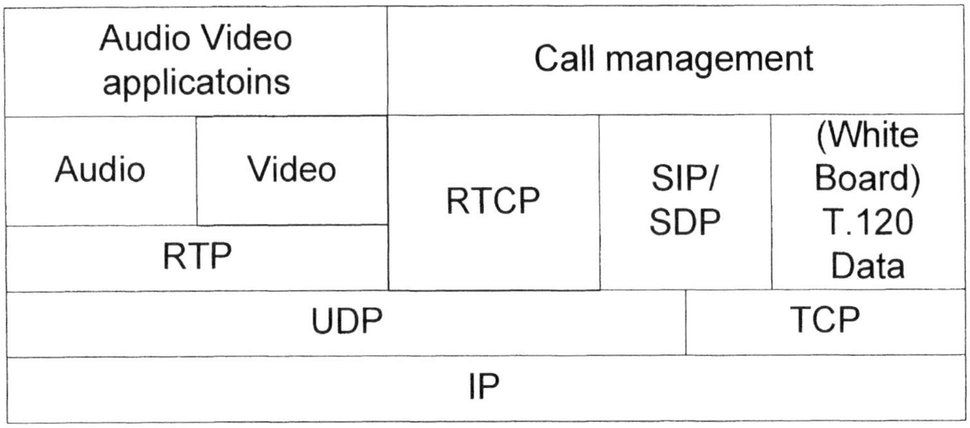

Audio Video applicatoins	Call management		
Audio	Video	RTCP	SIP/ SDP	(White Board) T.120 Data
RTP				
UDP			TCP	
IP				

Figure 4. Protocol stack of SIP based conferencing system.

H.323 vs. SIP

H.323 is originated from telecommunication world; the encoding of H.323 protocols is binary; while SIP is a HTTP like text-based protocol. Based on principles gained from the Internet community, text based protocol is easy to extend, process and debug. SIP has lower complexity, richer extensibility and better scalability, according to the early comparison done by the authors of SIP 11, although this comparison is out dated as H.323 has been updated to version 5. On the other hand, H.323 has a better inter-operability with legacy PSTN networks and other H.32x conferencing systems. H.323 based products have been largely deployed. More than 90 percent of VoIP (Voice over IP) traffic is carried using H.323, and it is supported on 80 percent of new videoconferencing systems, according to the H.323 Forum 12. SIP supports instant messaging and can be easily integrated with other web-based applications. SIP was adopted by 3GPP (the 3rd Generation Partnership Project) and more and more SIP based conferencing products have been released such as Cisco's IP phone and Microsoft's XP messenger. It is really a topic of debate to say which will gain more popularity in the future, but it is worth noting that both H.323 and SIP are improving themselves by learning from the other side, and the differences between them are decreasing with each new version. For example, in version 5 of H.323, SIP is adopted as a supported protocol; H.323 gateways can have the wherewithal to advertise themselves as both an H.323 gateway and a SIP gateway to a Gatekeeper.

Real-time Streaming Media Protocols

Real time media delivery requires a maximum end-to-end delay to guarantee that live audio and video can be received and presented continuously. For this reason, underlying protocols other than TCP are typically used for streaming media, since TCP is targeted for reliable transmission and frequent retransmission may violate the real time delay constraint, and also TCP is not suitable for IP multicast. The most commonly used transport protocol for real time streaming is the User Datagram Protocol (UDP). UDP is an unreliable protocol; it does not guarantee that there is no packet loss or packets are arrived in order. It is the higher layer's responsibility to recover from lost data, duplicated packets, and out of order packets.

RTSP/RTP/RTCP

Since UDP is a general transport-layer protocol, to address some of the specific problems in real time streaming; the Real-Time Transport Protocol (RTP) was designed to transport real time media. As mentioned in the previous section, RTP is both an IETF Proposed Standard (RFC 1889) 13 and an ITU Standard (H.225.0). It is a packet format for multimedia data streams. RTP enables the end system to identify the type of data being transmitted, determine in what order the packets of data should be presented, and synchronize media streams from different sources. While RTP does not provide any mechanism to ensure timely delivery or provide other quality of service guarantees, it is augmented by a control protocol (RTCP, Real time Transport Control Protocol) 14 that enables the system to monitor the quality of the data distribution. As a part of RTP protocol, RTCP also provides control and identification mechanisms for RTP transmissions.

RTSP (Real Time Streaming Protocol, RFC 2326) 15 is a client-server multimedia presentation control protocol, designed to address the needs for efficient delivery of streamed multimedia over IP networks. It leverages existing web infrastructure (for example, inheriting authentication and PICS (Platform for Internet Content Selection)) from HTTP) and works well for both large audiences and single-viewer media-on-demand. RealNetworks, Netscape Communications and Columbia University jointly developed RTSP within the MMUSIC working group of IETF. In April 1998, it was published as a Proposed Standard by IETF. RTSP has mechanisms for time-based access to any part of media. In addition, RTSP is designed to control multicast delivery of streams, and is ideally suited to full multicast solutions.

SMIL

SMIL (pronounced smile) stands for Synchronized Multimedia Integration Language. It is a new markup language being developed by the World Wide Web Consortium (W3C) that would enable Web developers to divide multimedia content into separate files and streams (audio, video, text, and images), send them to a user's computer individually, and then have them displayed together as if they were a single multimedia stream. By using a single time line for all of the media on a page, their display can be properly time-coordinated and synchronized.

References

1. Microsoft Research ConferenceXP platform.
   http://www.conferencexp.net/community/Default.aspx?tabindex=0&tabid=1
2. ITU-T Recommendation H.320, Narrow-band visual telephone systems and terminal equipment.
3. ITU-T Recommendation H.321, ITU-T recommendation for adapting H.320 systems to operation over ATM networks.
4. ITU-T Recommendation H.322, Visual telephone systems and terminal equipment for local area networks which provide a guaranteed quality of service.
5. ITU-T Recommendation H.323, Packet-based multimedia communications systems.

6. ITU-T Recommendation H.324, Terminal for low bit-rate multimedia communication.

7. http://www.itu.int/rec/recommendation.asp?type=folders&lang=e&parent=T-REC-H.323.

8. M. Handley, H. Schulzrinne, E. Schooler, and J. Rosenberg, "SIP: Session Initiation Protocol," Network Working Group, RFC 2543, Category: Standards Track, March 1999.

9. M. Handley and V. Jacobson, "SDP: Session Description Protocol," Network Working, RFC 2327 Category: Standards Track, April 1998.

10. M. Handley, C. Perkins, and E. Whelan, "Session Announcement Protocol (SAP)," Network Working Group, RFC 2974, Category: Experimental, October 2000.

11. H. Schulzrinne and J. Rosenberg, "A Comparison of SIP and H.323 for Internet Telephony," Proceedings of the Network and Operating System Support for Digital Audio and Video (NOSSDAV), Cambridge, England, July 1998.

12. http://www.h323forum.org/.

13. [RFC 3550] RTP: A Transport Protocol for Real-Time Applications.

14. [RFC 3605] Real Time Control Protocol (RTCP) attribute in Session Description Protocol (SDP).

15. [RFC 2326] RTSP: Real Time Streaming Protocol.

REAL TIME TRANSPORT PROTOCOL

Definition: Real-Time Transport Protocol (RTP) is a protocol designed for providing end-to-end network transport functions suitable for applications transmitting real-time data, such as audio and video over multicast or unicast network services.

RTP provides services including payload type identification, sequence numbering, time-stamping and delivery monitoring (with RTCP) [1]. The sequence numbers included in RTP allow the receiver to reconstruct the sender's packet sequence and to detect packet loss. Also, the timestamp contained in the RTP header can be used to maintain the original timing sequence of the media stream and perform synchronization with other media streams. However, RTP itself does not provide any mechanism to ensure timely delivery of data and does not guarantee quality-of-service (QoS) for real-time services.

RTP is implemented at the application level and normally run on the top of UDP/IP. In general, RTP is designed to be independent of the underlying protocols. Hence, RTP may also be used with other suitable underlying network or transport protocols. The data encapsulation process of RTP running on the top of UDP/IP is shown in Figure 1. RTP supports any media format. A complete RTP packet contains a RTP common header and a payload field. Different media has different payload formats for packing data into the RTP packet.

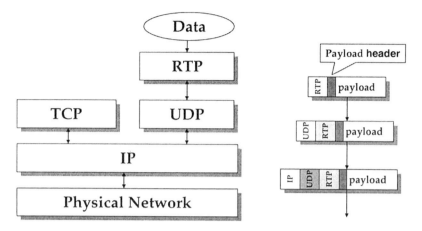

Figure 1. RTP data encapsulation.

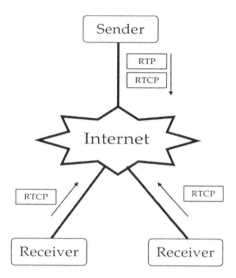

Figure 2. RTP and RTCP.

The RTP control protocol (RTCP) is designed to monitor the quality of service of the RTP data delivery and to convey information about the participants in an on-going session. For each RTP session, RTCP packets are transmitted by each participant to all other participants in the session (as illustrated in Figure 2). RTCP packets are sent periodically and contain sender and/or receiver reports that announce statistics that are useful to the application. The statistics include number of packets sent, number of packets lost and inter-arrival jitter. For bandwidth scaling, RTCP attempts to limit its traffic to 5% of the session bandwidth.

See: Multimedia Streaming on the Internet

References

1. H. Schulzrinne, S. Casner, R. Frederick, and V. Jacobson, "RTP: A Transport Protocol for Real-Time Applications," RFC 1889, January 1996.

REAL-WORLD MULTIMEDIA SYSTEMS

Harry Agius, Chris Crockfor, and Arthur G. Money
Brunel University, Uxbridge, UK

Definition: *Real-world multimedia systems can be defined as systems that utilize real-world data to support the querying and retrieval of multimedia content.*

Multimedia systems have always been at the heart of technical convergence, fusing video and audio with text, images and graphics. However, increased and cheaper processing power combined with other advances such as affordable sensor equipment, has enabled this to take on new dimensions whereby multimedia content and real-world data converge within a *real-world multimedia system*. Real-world multimedia systems can be defined as systems that utilize real-world data to support the querying and retrieval of multimedia content. This retrieval may be either pulled or pushed. Real-world multimedia systems vary substantially, but broadly can be seen to embody the architecture shown in Figure 1.

Various real-world data is captured from the environment and/or human subjects. Sensors may be used to capture the data automatically, or semi-automatically since some sensors require manual adjustment at multiple stages of capture. The use of intelligent sensors enables some analysis to be automatically undertaken on the real-world data at the point of capture. If sensors are not used, the data may be derived from various non-real-time sources and input into the system manually or, for suitable real-world data, derived from real-world multimedia content and noninvasive techniques such as intelligent computer vision during the Analysis component. Real-world data may optionally be complemented by captured real-world multimedia content of the environment or human subjects, such as surveillance video footage, sporting events, consumer digital photographs, reconnaissance video footage, video depicting user's facial expressions, and so on. More conventional, non-real-world multimedia content may also be used by the system, such as movies, TV programs, and news footage. During Analysis, real-world data is analyzed together with the real-world and non-real-world multimedia content to interpret and structure the data and derive further information. During the Association component of the architecture, relationships between the real-world data and the multimedia content within the system are expressed, so that all data and content may be stored in a structured and integrated format to create a real-world multimedia resource. This resource is used in a variety of ways during the Querying and Retrieval components, ranging from direct retrieval based on real-world content-based or contextual data to navigation within interactive, immersive real-world-like environments.

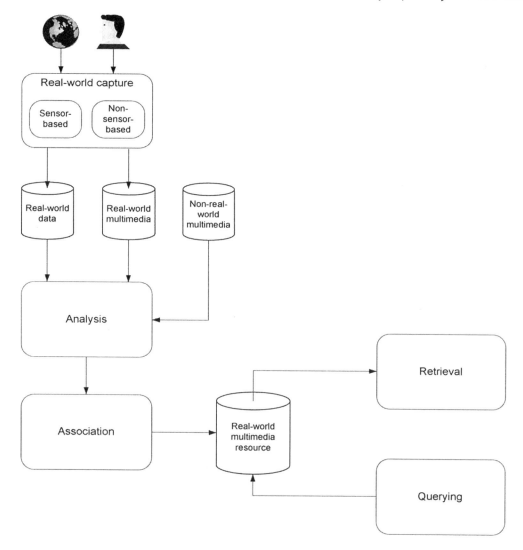

Figure 1. Generic architecture of a real-world multimedia system.

Real World Capture

Environmental data can provide a wealth of information regarding artifacts in the world and properties of the world itself at specific times. This data includes geographic positioning using GPS (Global Positioning System) or differential GPS, camera parameters such as pitch or yaw, weather data such as wind speed, temperature and humidity, detection of smoke, flames and radiation, topological maps depicting shape and elevation, traffic speed and movements, and so on. In the Informedia Experience-on-Demand system [22], GPS units wired into wearable vests are exploited to generate panoramic views from various perspectives for video captured by users wearing the vests. Arbeeny and Silver [4] use a GPS receiver to encode spatial and temporal coordinates of the location of a mobile camera, together with a digital compass sensor to encode direction of travel in relation to magnetic north. In this way, captured video streams depicting real-world images may be suitably geo-referenced. In the situated documentary augmented reality system created at Columbia University [10], a single-sensor inertial/magnetometer orientation tracker is mounted rigidly on a head band attached to a see-through HMD (head mounted display) worn by the user. The tracker enables the position of the user to be determined through a differential GPS system. 3D graphics, imagery and sound are then overlaid via the HMD on top of the real world viewed by the user. Additional material is presented on a hand-held pen computer. The situated documentaries tell the stories of events that took place on the campus. For virtualized architectural heritage systems, which seek to recreate accurate, virtual historic and cultural landmarks, a range of contact (touch) and non-contact (camera-based) capture technologies may be used. Examples of the former include sonic, optical, electromagnetic and satellite triangulation, laser and target-based time-of-flight mass spectrometry (TOF-MS), and stereo photogrammetry. Examples of the latter include stereo video auto-photogrammetry, sonic TOF-MS, and phase-based laser interferometry [1]. Use of RFID-based (radio frequency identification) devices have also proven useful for data capture in real-world multimedia systems. Volgin et al. [21] describe a multimedia retrieval system for images captured by mobile devices where sensor motes are used to capture environment-specific data, such as light intensity, temperature, humidity, location and users in proximity. These sensor motes communicate with gateway motes attached to laptops which collect this data and turn it into metadata for use in the multimedia retrieval system.

Human subject data concerns real-world data about human subjects, typically users of the real-world multimedia system. This data typically concerns their biological properties or their physical or mental behavior, including heart rate, galvanic skin response (GSR), blood volume pulse (BVP), respiration, gestures, facial expressions, motion, and content browsing and usage behavior. In 3D Live [17], an augmented reality video conferencing system, users wear a video see-through HMD connected to a computer. Real name cards contain a black tracking pattern which is used by the system to calculate the user's viewpoint. This is then used to overlay virtual video onto the card which is taken from fourteen video cameras that surround a remote collaborator. The Conductor Jacket [13] is a sensor interface that gathers its wearer's gestures and physiology. It aims to interpret and synthesize music to accompany conducting gestures. Camurri et al. [6] use a range of sensors, some on-body, as well as live audio and video captured from the user, to detect the expressiveness and affection of users as they communicate in various non-traditional ways, such as through gestures, postures, facial expressions, movement or voice. This is used in a range of systems to provide personalized multimedia content which alters according to the expressiveness or affection of the users, e.g. changing how characters are animated or the type or style of music which is played back. The Point At system and the Interactive Blackboard system [3] allow users to communicate with natural hand gestures to indicate which part of a painting interests them so that audio information about the subject or object can be provided (in the former) or to zoom in and out of various zones on a map and select icons to gain further information (in the latter). In both cases, camera capture the gestures which are later analyzed and interpreted. Aizawa et al. [2] capture a range of real-world data to support retrieval of multimedia life logs (which record a user's daily experiences in detail). This includes a brain wave signal acquired from a brain wave analyzer which is used to determine a person's arousal status at the time they captured the real-world video. This can later be used to interpret whether the user was interested in the content of the video at that time. Motion sensors are used to capture information about activities occurring during video capture. These motion sensors include an acceleration sensor and a gyro sensor, which can be used to identify activities such as walking, running, or standing still. Logs of users' video browsing behavior have proven useful to video summarization [19, 23], where they are later subjected to analysis in order to infer user interest.

As an example of how non-real-world multimedia content may be exploited by a real-world multimedia system, GeoPlot [15] relates real-world data to news videos and actual geographic distances are calculated so that patterns in the geospatial relationships of news events may be discovered.

Analysis

Once all data and content have been captured, a real-world multimedia system analyzes it jointly to interpret it as well as consolidating and aggregating to higher levels of abstraction, where each layer adds progressively further useful data. Typically, human subject data requires more detailed analysis than environmental data, although this is not always the case. In the Point At system, mentioned in the previous section, two digital cameras capture the visitors' pointing action and computer vision techniques are used to calculate the screen location that they are pointing at. Similarly, in the Interactive Blackboard system, the user's gesture is captured by a single digital camera which is positioned high above the blackboard and is pointed at the inclined screen. The system computes the zone the user points to in real time, after image processing and interpretation [3]. In Camurri et al.'s approach, also previously mentioned, a layered framework is used to distinguish and map between signal-based descriptions of syntactic features of human movements, descriptions of these movements within a trajectory space, and semantic descriptions relating to meaning, affect, emotion and expressiveness [6]. The 3D Live system, discussed above, processes video from the cameras surrounding the remote collaborator to segment the person out from the background so that a real-time view generation algorithm, based on shape-from-silhouette information, can be used to generate a synthetic view from the user's viewpoint [17]. In virtualized reality systems, view synthesis involves the rendering of a viewpoint perspective to the user. A variety of techniques may be used for analysis here, such as image flow or pixel correspondence, or by densely sampling the viewing space and using interpolation to cater for missing views. Additional knowledge about the scene or the imaging process may also contribute [12]. In surveillance-based real-world multimedia systems, analysis frequently involves identifying and classifying objects from camera video streams. For example, objects may be tracked in time, identified as people, and then analyzed to determine their posture. From this posture, a given event may be identified. For example, a transition from a standing or sitting posture to a lying down posture may indicate a 'falling down' event [8]. In the LucentVision system [16], video streams taken from eight cameras observing a tennis match (two for player tracking and six for ball tracking) are fed into a domain-specific, real-time tracking subsystem. This subsystem analyzes the streams to determine player and ball motion trajectories and to assign a player trajectory to a specific player via domain knowledge. This domain knowledge incorporates tennis rules and the current score to determine which player is on which side of the court and can be seen by which camera. Naaman et al. [14] use captured longitude and latitude data for a given photo to derive the country, province/state, county, as well as further optional location information such as city, park, nearby landmarks, and so on. Together with time, this location data is then used to derive further data such as light status, weather status and temperature, elevation, season, and time zone, using various online Web resources.

Association

Using the output from the Analysis component, the Association component of the architecture structures and integrates the real-world data and multimedia content within the system for storage within a real-world multimedia resource. Metadata schemes are key to this. The LucentVision system just discussed uses a relational database to organize data by the hierarchical structure of events in tennis, that is, a 'match' consisting of 'sets' consisting of 'games' consisting of 'points'. Each event has an associated identifier, temporal extent, and score. Trajectories corresponding to the two players and the ball are associated with every point. Each point also has pointers to video clips from the broadcast production. Because the relational database structure does not support spatiotemporal queries based on analysis of trajectory data, an additional spatiotemporal analysis structure is used on top of the relational structure [16]. In the XML-based VSDL-RW (Real World Video Stream Description Language) [7], a variety of user-defined real-world data, such as location and map route patterns, may be represented in a hierarchical structure. This may be linked to the video streams through a variety of referencing methods, such as matching name labels, map patterns, or texture properties. A number of metadata standards also exist, which permit representation of real-world data. EXIF specifies how digital still cameras represent a variety of data associated with digital photographs, including real-world data such as the make and model of the camera, location and lighting conditions, time that the photograph was taken, and so on [20]. In the Multimedia Description Schemes (MDS) of the MPEG-7 standard [11], a variety of real-world data may be described and integrated with multimedia content. These include data regarding persons, groups, organizations, citizenship, addresses, locations (including geographic position via longitude, latitude and altitude for various geodetic datum systems), relative and absolute times (down to fractions of a second), affective responses to multimedia content by users, usage histories, real-world entities and properties (such as length, height, weight, and temperature) and (for both multimedia content and metadata) creators, creation tools, creation locations and creation times.

Querying and Retrieval

The Querying and Retrieval components of the architecture concern the use of the real-world multimedia resource created in the other parts of the architecture. Querying may be explicit, where a formal query is made by the user, e.g. using a formal query language, or implicit, where the user expresses their requirements indirectly, e.g. through interaction with the system or through filtering processes. In Volgin et al.'s multimedia retrieval system, mentioned earlier, the captured real-world data allows users to query and retrieve images based on real-world contextual properties such as whether it was hot or cold on the day that the user took the picture, or which users where nearby when the picture was taken, and so on [21]. In LucentVision, mentioned previously, the user may query the database through a visualization interface to retrieve various reconstructions of tennis events ranging from high quality video representations to compact summaries, such as a map of players' coverage of the court. Content-based queries are also supported as well as spatiotemporal queries which may be combined with score-based queries [16].

In the MediaConnector framework [5], digital cameras record time, position and heading metadata, even when users are *not* taking pictures but just have their cameras with them. This enables a rather unique perspective on retrieval whereby a user could retrieve pictures taken at the same time as their own but from different viewpoints, or when the user was not using their camera.

Conclusion

Through their use of real-world data, real-world multimedia systems more naturally reflect and behave like ourselves and our real-world environments. This can help to reduce the *semantic* and *sensory gaps*. The sensory gap is the gap between an object in the real world and the data in a computational description derived from multimedia content analysis, whereas the semantic gap is the lack of coincidence between the data that one can extract from multimedia content and the interpretation that that same data has for a user in a given situation [18]. Integrating other sources of information, particularly real-world contextual data [9], provides much data that could not be derived otherwise but is still required by users, thus making the process of multimedia querying and retrieval more effective. However, while many advances have been made in real-world multimedia systems, we are still at the stage of learning and discovering how best we can use much of this real-world data, particularly human subject data where there are no hard and fast rules as to how best it may be interpreted and associated with multimedia content. Consequently, further research is required for each component of the architecture presented in Figure 1 in order to improve both efficiency and effectiveness, as well as to enable new applications in new domains that we cannot yet envisage.

See: Geographic Video, Emotional Multimedia

References

1. A.C. Addison and M. Gaiani, "Virtualized Architectural Heritage: New Tools and Techniques," IEEE MultiMedia, Vol. 7, No. 2, April-June 2000, pp. 26-31.
2. K. Aizawa, D. Tancharoen, S. Kawasaki, and T. Yamasaki, "Efficient Retrieval of Life Log Based on Context and Content," Proceedings of the 1st ACM Workshop on Continuous Archival and Retrieval of Personal Experiences (CARPE '04), 2004, pp. 22-31.
3. T.M. Alisi, A. Del Bimbo, and A. Valli, "Natural Interfaces to Enhance Visitors' Experiences," IEEE MultiMedia, Vol. 12, No. 3, July-September 2005, pp. 80-85.
4. S. Arbeeny and D. Silver, "Spatial Navigation of Media Streams," Proceedings of the Ninth ACM International Conference on Multimedia (MM '01), 2001, pp. 467-470.
5. V.M. Bove Jr., "Connected by Media," IEEE MultiMedia, Vol. 8, No. 4, October-December 2001, pp. 13-15.
6. A. Camurri, G. Volpe, G. De Poli, and M. Leman, "Communicating Expressiveness and Affect in Multimodal Interactive Systems," IEEE MultiMedia, Vol. 12, No. 1, January-March 2005, pp. 43-53.
7. Y. Cao, W. Zhang, Y. Yaginuma, and M. Sakauchi, "Proposal of Real World Video Stream Description Language (VSDL-RW) and its Application," Proceedings of the International Conference on Image Processing (ICIP 2000), Vol. 3, 2000, pp. 218-221.

8. R. Cucchiara, C. Grana, A. Prati, and R. Vezzani, "Probabilistic Posture Classification for Human-Behavior Analysis," IEEE Transactions on Systems, Man, and Cybernetics—Part A: Systems and Humans, Vol. 35, No. 1, January 2005, pp. 42-54.

9. K. Haase, "Context for Semantic Metadata," Proceedings of the 12th Annual ACM International Conference on Multimedia (MM '04), 2004, pp. 204-211.

10. T. Hollerer, S. Feiner, and J. Pavlik, "Situated Documentaries: Embedding Multimedia Presentations in the Real World," Proceedings of the Third International Symposium on Wearable Computers, 1999, pp. 79-86.

11. ISO/IEC, Information Technology □□Multimedia Content Description Interface □□Part 5: Multimedia Description Schemes, International Standard 15938-5, International Organization for Standardization, Geneva, Switzerland, 2003.

12. T. Kanade, P. Rander, and P.J. Narayanan, "Virtualized Reality: Constructing Virtual Worlds from Real Scenes," IEEE MultiMedia, Vol. 4, No. 1, January-March 1997, pp. 34-47.

13. T. Marrin, "Synthesizing Expressive Music Through the Language of Conducting," Journal of New Music Research, Vol. 31, No. 1, March 2002, pp. 11-26.

14. M. Naaman, S. Harada, Q. Wangy, H. Garcia-Molina, and A. Paepcke, "Context Data in Geo-Referenced Digital Photo Collections," Proceedings of the 12th Annual ACM International Conference on Multimedia (MM '04), 2004, pp. 196-203.

15. J.-Y. Pan and C. Faloutsos, ""GeoPlot": Spatial Data Mining on Video Libraries," in Proceedings of the Eleventh International Conference on Information and Knowledge Management (CIKM '02), 2002, pp. 405-412.

16. G.S. Pingali, A. Opalach, Y.D. Jean, and I.B. Carlbom, "Instantly Indexed Multimedia Databases of Real World Events," IEEE Transactions on Multimedia, Vol. 4, No. 2, June 2002, pp. 269-282.

17. S. Prince, A.D. Cheok, F. Farbiz, T. Williamson, N. Johnson, M. Billinghurst, and H. Kato, "3-D Live: Real Time Interaction for Mixed Reality," Proceedings of the ACM Conference on Computer Supported Cooperative Work (CSCW '02), 2002, pp. 364-371.

18. A.W.M. Smeulders, M. Worring, S. Santini, A. Gupta, and R. Jain, "Content-Based Image Retrieval at the End of the Early Years," IEEE Transactions on Pattern Analysis and Machine Intelligence, Vol. 22, No. 12, December 2000, pp. 1349-1380.

19. T. Syeda-Mahmood and D. Ponceleon, "Learning Video Browsing Behavior and its Application in the Generation of Video Previews," Proceedings of the Ninth ACM International Conference on Multimedia (MM '01), 2001, pp. 119-128.

20. J. Tešić, "Metadata Practices for Consumer Photos," IEEE MultiMedia, Vol. 12, No. 3, July–September 2005, pp. 86-92.

21. O. Volgin, W. Hung, C. Vakili, J. Flinn, and K.G. Shin, "Context-Aware Metadata Creation in a Heterogeneous Mobile Environment," Proceedings of the International Workshop on Network and Operating System Support for Digital Audio and Video (NOSSDAV '05), 2005, pp. 75-79.

22. H.D. Wactlar, M.G. Christel, A.G. Hauptmann, and Y. Gong, "Informedia Experience-on-Demand: Capturing, Integrating and Communicating Experiences across People, Time and Space," ACM Computing Surveys, Vol. 31, No. 2, June 1999.

23. B. Yu, W.-Y. Ma, K. Nahrstedt, and H.-J. Zhang, "Video Summarization Based on User Log Enhanced Link Analysis," Proceedings of the Eleventh ACM International Conference on Multimedia (MM '03), 2003, pp. 382-391.

RECORDING TELECONFERENCING SESSIONS

Definition: Recording a teleconferencing session consists of recording everything that transpires in that session, including audio, video, and application sharing.

Temporal relation between events and media must be preserved for the accurate reconstruction of the session. The ability to record a teleconferencing session is an important requirement for many applications. In many cases, it is necessary to play back the events that took place in a session. For example, when a participant misses a teleconferencing meeting, he/she can play back exactly what happened in the meeting, if the session was recorded. This includes conversations and discussions among participants, as well as applications and documents that were shared. Ideally, this recording should be done in a transparent way; i.e., user applications need not be modified for this recording to take place. One approach to achieve this would be for the "recorder" module to join the session as a regular client and observe what is taking place and record it. This is also referred to as non-intrusive recording. The J-VCR system is an example of a non-intrusive teleconferencing recording tool [1].

See: Teleconferencing

References

1. S. Shirmohammadi, L.Ding, and N.D. Georganas, "An Approach for Recording Multimedia Collaborative Sessions: Design and Implementation," Journal of Multimedia Tools and Applications, Vol. 19, No. 2, 2003, pp. 135-154.

ROLE OF SEMANTICS IN MULTIMEDIA APPLICATIONS

Definition: Semantic Web Tools and Standards greatly assist in both description and reasoning stages of computation.

Many types of multimedia applications can - and do - leverage rich information model semantics. Much like textual applications (such as multi-schemata databases) in which ontologies and semantics come into play, multimedia applications constitute a rich proving-ground due to their naturally diverse and disparate properties (i.e. encoding types, temporal attributes, spatial attributes, and so on.)

Multimedia Applications using Semantic Computation

A few of many multimedia domains in which semantics are pivotal include: digital libraries, broadcast media, editing, entertainment, telemedicine, and surveillance. The following list is only partially representative; each entry describes in what sense semantics are exploited or particularly important (not all use the same sense of the term or supporting technologies):

- The Motion Pictures Expert Group – The MPEG-7 standard attempts to provide a content description interface and tools for describing audiovisual information (e.g. audio, speech, video, 3D) independently of how it is stored or coded. Using *Multimedia Description Scheme* (MDS) "visual descriptors" will describe visual features of the media – such features include: color, objects, and events, interactions amongst objects, storage format, lyrics and title. A reference schema with carefully contrived syntax and semantics will support this.

- Classification and Filtering of Image Information – Image classification, searching, and filtering are hard problems that benefit from semantic domain knowledge. For example, it has been shown that when filtering algorithms rely not only on pixel content but also on image semantics then results are superior. That is, the image is first classified and then *filtered,* allowing the filter search only for features relevant to the type (e.g. nature, nudity, etc.). Alternatively, in the automatic segmentation of video into 'shots' separated by camera cuts, it is common to exploit the semantic of video content – e.g. at a high level, news video clips often admit to an almost 'templated' sequence of shots (e.g. intro shot, head shot, etc.)

- Quality of Service – QoS is invariably important in the delivery of multimedia information across a network and when defining service agreements for application performance. QoS can have many dimensions (e.g. jitter, delay, frames per second, etc.). Rich semantic models of QoS requirements and capabilities assist middleware in brokering QoS between clients and providers. Some current applications (particularly Web Service-oriented ones) are beginning to use W3C's RDF and OWL as bases for both describing QoS requirements and performing brokering. This trend will continue and absorb multimedia services as well.

- Pervasive Computing (PC) – The PC paradigm is the state of affairs when multimedia devices, agents, and services all seamlessly support human objectives. For example, a user with a laptop enters a new office and is seamlessly offered services in the new context thanks to interacting software agents and services. Underlying the agents is a rich representation of context, user and device requirements, and service capabilities.

- Multimedia Databases – Multimedia DBMS's benefit from sophisticated semantic models accommodating rich semantics of multimedia data (e.g. spatio-temporal aspects, etc.) [1]

See: Semantic Web

References

1. S. Chen, R. Kashyap, and A. Ghafoor, "Semantic Models for Multimedia Database Searching and Browsing," Springer, New York, 2000.

THE RSA PUBLIC-KEY ENCRYPTION ALGORITHM

Definition: The RSA is one of the popular public-key encryption algorithms.

Rivest et al published a method for obtaining digital signatures and public-key cryptosystems in 1978 [1]. In order to use the method, the encryption and decryption keys must be chosen as follows:

1. Compute n as the product of two primes p and q: $n = p \times q$. These two primes are very large and randomly selected primes.
2. Compute $\phi(n) = (p-1)(q-1)$.
3. Select e such that e is relatively prime to $\phi(n)$.
4. Select d such that $e \times d \equiv 1 \bmod (\phi(n))$, where mod stands for modular operation.
5. Choose (e,n) as the public key.
6. Choose (d,n) as the private key.

In encryption and decryption, receiver's public key (e_R, n_R) and private key (d_R, n_R) are used. Encryption is carried out by using $m_c = m^{e_R} \bmod n_R$, where m is the plaintext and m_c is the ciphertext. Decryption is carried out by using $m = (m_c)^{d_R} \bmod n_R$.

For authentication, sender's public key (e_S, n_S) and private key (d_S, n_S) are used. The signature is generated by using $m_c = m^{d_S} \bmod n_S$. The signature is authenticated by using $m = (m_c)^{e_S} \bmod n_S$.

See: Multimedia Authentication

References

1. R.L. Rivest, A. Shamir, and L.M. Adleman, "A Method for Obtaining Digital Signature and Public-key Cryptosystems," Communications of the ACM, Vol. 21, No. 2, pp. 120-126, 1978.

S

SCALABLE VIDEO CODING

Marta Mrak and Ebroul Izquierdo
Department of Electronic Engineering, Queen Mary, University of London, UK

Definition: *Scalable video coding targets seamless delivery of and access to digital content, enabling optimal, user-centered multi-channel and cross-platform media services, and providing a straightforward solution for universal video delivery to a broad range of applications.*

The recent convergence trend of multimedia technology and telecommunications along with the materialization of the Web as strong competitor of conventional distribution networks have generated an acute need for enrichment in modalities and capabilities of the delivery of digital media. Within this new trend a main challenge relates to the production of easy adaptable content capable of optimally fitting into evolving and heterogeneous networks as well as iterative delivery platforms with specific content requirements. Network supported multimedia applications involve many different transmission capabilities including Web based applications, narrowcasting, conventional terrestrial for interactive broadcasting, wireless channels, high definition television for sensitive remote applications, e.g., remote medical diagnosis, etc. These applications are used to deliver content to a wide range of terminals and users surrounded by different environments and acting under totally different circumstances. Conventional video coding systems encode video content using a fix bit-rate tailored to a specific application. As a consequence conventional video coding does not fulfill the basic requirements of new flexible digital media applications. Contrasting this, scalable video coding (SVC) emerges as a new technology able to satisfy the underlying requirements. SVC targets seamless delivery of and access to digital content, enabling optimal, user centered multi-channel and cross-platform media services, and providing a straightforward solution for universal video delivery to a broad range of applications.

There are several major challenges in the engineering aspects of scalable video coding. The most important relates to the capability of automatically render broadcasting content onto a Web browser or other low-bit rate end-devices such as PDAs, 3G phones and vice-versa. That is, the capability of dynamically perform resolution changes in order to deliver the best quality under a given bandwidth budget. Since this functionality should be provided "on the fly" without using expensive and time consuming transcoders, it requires the production of content in a specific "hierarchically embedded" form. It also enables applications that are both network and terminal aware, i.e., applications that can tailor content quality and size to optimally fit bandwidth and terminal requirements automatically and without expensive or time consuming additional processing.

Scalable image coding is useful for applications where efficient adaptation of compressed images is required. Such adaptations are usually context driven and involve adaptation of the quality, spatial resolution, color components (grey scale or full color) and more importantly, regions of interest (ROI). In this article we discuss the scalability features required in image adaptations and evaluate the current state-of-the-art scalable and non-scalable image coding algorithms.

Requirements

There are several types of scalability which should be supported by an advanced video coding system. The basic scalability types are:

- spatial (resolution) scalability,
- SNR (quality) scalability,
- temporal (frame rate) scalability.

Scalable coding should also support combinations of these three basic scalability functionalities. Moreover, advanced scalable video coders may support

- complexity scalability,
- region of interest scalability,
- object based scalability,

and other features such as:

- support for both progressive and interlaced material,
- support for various color depths (including component scalability),
- robustness to different types of transmission errors.

Scalable video coder provides embedded bit stream, which we refer to as precoded stream. To address specific application or network conditions, a rate allocation mechanism extracts necessary data from the precoded bit-stream, as a part of scalable video transmitter (see Figure 1).

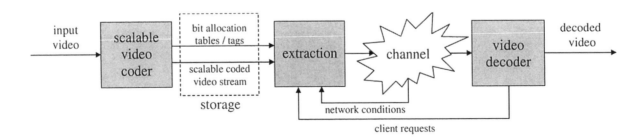

Figure 1. Building blocks of a scalable video coding system.

As the bit allocation tables are provided or appropriate flags are inserted in the bit-stream, the extractor is of a very low-complexity. State-of-the-art scalable video coders feature at least two of the scalability types described before. Figure 2 depicts the most important scalability features in advanced video coders.

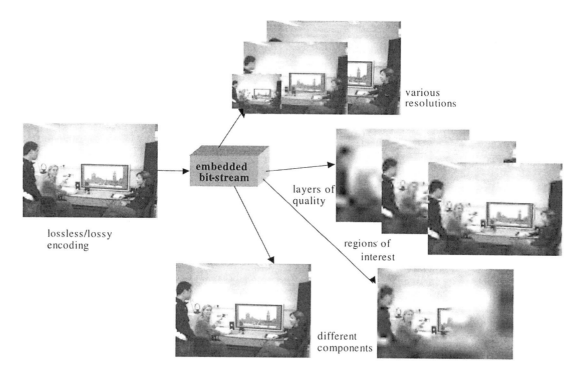

Figure 2. Representation of various scalability types.

Spatial transforms for SVC

There are two categories of transforms commonly used in video and still image coding: discrete cosine transform (DCT) or DCT-like transform and discrete wavelet transform (DWT). DCT is used in the popular JPEG still image coding standard and in a wide variety of video coding standards including MPEG and H264. It is performed on the blocks of original frame or motion-compensated error frames and it is not resolution scalable. However, scalability may be imposed on DCT-based video coding schemes which results in systems with low complexity, but with limited scalable features and significant decrease in the compression efficiency.

The application of the wavelet transform in video coding has been exhaustively examined but is still not regarded as the main decorrelation transform in video coding. However, it is the base for the more advanced JPEG2000 still image coding standard that, beside excellent compression performance, offers broad range of other functionalities including full scalability.

The wavelet transform can be efficiently used in video compression, enabling simple selection of the desired bit allocation, rate optimization and progressive transmission functionalities. The wavelet transform can be applied on single frames, as a 2D transform on image pixels or on motion compensated frames. Alternatively, it can be also used as 3D transform on groups of frames in a video sequence. Accordingly to [1], wavelet-based video coding schemes can be grouped as follows:

a.   **Wavelet in loop**
Both intra coded frames and motion-compensated residual frames are transformed using 2D wavelet transform. Basically, DCT is replaced by DWT. Since the decoder would not perform the same prediction as the coder, the so-called *drift problem* is originated. The blocky edges caused by motion compensation (MC) cannot be efficiently coded using wavelet transform and may introduce unpleasant ringing artifacts. To reduce the blockiness in the prediction error images, overlapped block motion compensation (OBMC) can be used [2]. Moreover, the drift problem can be avoided using motion estimation on the lowest quality and resolution layer. However, if a coder has to meet a wide range of bit-rates, the efficiency becomes very poor.

b.   **In-band prediction**
This approach performs a 2D wavelet transform to remove inter-frame redundancy. Therefore, wavelet coefficients can be coded using temporal prediction and temporal context modeling. Motion compensation is also used but while the drift is avoided for resolution scalability it remains for SNR scalability. MC can be performed for each resolution level individually, thus enabling efficient resolution scalability. The drawback is that in the wavelet domain, spatial shifting results in phase shifting. Thus, motion compensation does not perform well and may cause motion tracking errors in high-frequency bands [2]. To overcome this problem, overcomplete wavelet representations are recommended for MC.

c.   **Interframe Wavelet**
Wavelet filtering is used both in spatial and temporal domain. High degrees of scalability can be achieved without drift problems. Two classes can be distinguished: temporal filtering preceding spatial filtering, i.e., t+2D and vice versa, i.e. 2D+t. To achieve higher degree of temporal decorrelation, motion compensated interframe wavelet techniques are used. This process is called motion-compensated temporal filtering (MCTF).

Motion compensated temporal filtering (MCTF)

MCTF was firstly introduced in 3-D transform coding in [3] and has been used in several scalable coding proposals. MCTF performs the wavelet transform after MC. It enables improved rate-distortion performance. Wavelet filtering can be implemented in a lifting structure where prediction and update steps include MC. A lifting scheme also enables sub-pixel realization and perfect reconstruction.

Subsequent video frames in MCTF based schemes are transformed into temporal low-pass frames L and high-pass frames H. Qualitatively, in the simplest case, H is a motion-compensated difference between two subsequent frames, and L is their mean.

Higher depth of temporal decomposition can be achieved by repeated filtering of L frames. This process is depicted in Figure 3. Usually, temporal decomposition can be non-dyadic, which enables wider implementation possibilities.

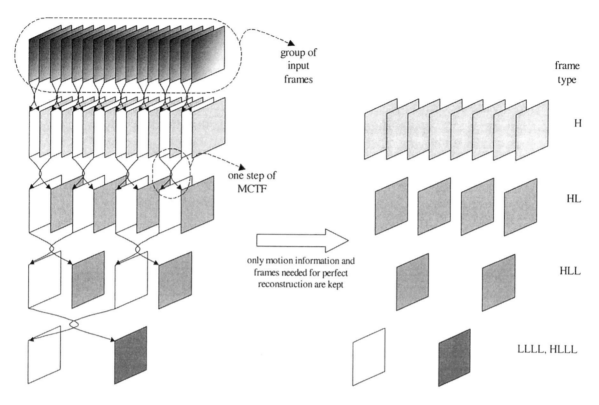

Figure 3. Motion-compensated temporal filtering for the group of 16 frames using Haar transform.

The simplest implementation of MCTF in a lifting filter structure uses Haar filters, but more complex wavelet filter banks can achieve a higher-quality interpolation [4]. Longer filters take better use of the temporal redundancies, but a doubling of the number of motion vectors to be transmitted negatively influences the quality on the lower bit-rates. To improve the prediction performance in MCTF schemes, prediction tools of hybrid video codecs can be used.

A wide variety of spatial-domain MCTF (SD MCTF), also known as t+2D, codecs have been proposed [5], [6]. In these approaches, motion estimation and temporal filtering are the first steps. Since motion estimation is performed in spatial domain on full resolution frames, lower quality, resolution and temporal scale streams, contain complete motion information which do not necessary represent the optimal block-matching decision. This motion information will also be highly redundant for lower resolution applications.

In 3D MC transformations consisting of in-band MCTF (IB MCTF, 2D+t), input frames are firstly spatially transformed. MCTF is performed on these transformed frames. Since a complete wavelet transform is shift-variant, a complete-to-overcomplete wavelet transform (CODWT) may be used.

IB MCTF introduces higher degree of scalability in video coding since different resolutions are separately motion compensated. This allows tuning of the motion information budget depending on desired resolution. The issue of complexity scalability can be easier achieved because MCTF may be different on each resolution level. Moreover, a variable number of temporal levels for each resolution can be included. IB MCTF and SD MCTF coding schemes may be implemented without the update step in MCTF, while the temporal filtering still remains invertible.

Overview of Scalability Features in Current Standards

Currently, no video coding standards provides full scalability. However, available standards feature basic scalability functionality. The following is an overview of scalability features of the most popular video coding standards.

MPEG-2 video coding standard: The MPEG-2 video coding standard incorporates modes to support layered scalability. The signal may be encoded into a base layer and a few enhancement layers. The enhancement layers add spatial, temporal, and/or SNR quality to the reconstructed base layer. Specifically, the enhancement layer in SNR scalability adds refinement data for the DCT coefficients of the base layer. For spatial scalability, the first enhancement layer uses predictions from the base layer without the use of motion vectors. For temporal scalability the enhancement layer uses motion compensated predictions from the base layer.

MPEG-4 Fine-Granular Scalability and hybrid temporal-SNR scalability: Fine-Granular Scalability (FSN) enables progressive SNR coding. FSN is adopted in MPEG-4 in the way that image quality of the base-layer (non-scalable) frames can be enhanced using single enhancement layer. A progression is achieved by embedded compression. MPEG-4 uses embedded DCT which is based on bit-plane by bit-plane coding. Moreover, it uses VLC tables for entropy coding.

SNR FGS in MPEG-4 features temporal scalability. The temporal SNR FGS scalability is achieved by including only B-frames in the enhancement layer. B-frames are called FGST frames. Before texture coding of FGST frames, a complete motion vector set for that frame has to be transmitted. For base-layer frames motion vectors are transmitted before texture information for each macroblock. The granularity of temporal scalability depends on the GOP structure determined by the coder.

MPEG and JVT scalable video coding: The MPEG standardization body has identified applications that require scalable and reliable video coding technologies. It has defined the requirements for scalable video coding [7]. The first Call for Proposals on Scalable Video Coding Technology was issued in October 2003. It proposes the evaluation methodology and respective experimental conditions. The most promising proposals have been considered as the starting point for the development of a scalable video coding standard.

H.264/AVC was the first coding standard achieving high efficiency in the terms of rate-distortion performance. It is a block-based (4x4 DCT-like transform) system using highly efficient motion compensation on variable block sizes and highly efficient context based entropy coding (CABAC). However, the first version of the H.264/AVC does not support scalable coding. However, it is regarded as the base for several scalable video coding approaches.

References

1. Report on Ad hoc Group on Exploration of Interframe Wavelet Technology in Video, ISO/IEC JTC1/SC29/WG11, M8205, 59th MPEG Meeting, Jeju Island, Korea, March 2002.
2. K. Shen and E. J. Delp, "Wavelet Based Rate Scalable Video Compression," IEEE Transactions on Circuits and Systems for Video Technology, Vol. 9, No. 1, pp. 109-122, February 1999.
3. J.-R. Ohm, "Three-dimensional Subband Coding with Motion Compensation," IEEE Transactions on Image Processing, Vol. 3, No. 5, pp. 559-571, September 1994.
4. Complexity and Delay Analysis of MCTF Interframe Wavelet Structures, ISO/IEC JTC1/SC29/WG11, M8520, 61st MPEG Meeting, Klagenfurt, Austria, July 2002
5. B.-J. Kim, Z. Xiong, and W. A. Pearlman, "Low Bit-Rate, Scalable Video Coding with 3D Set Partitioning in Hierarchical Trees (3D SPIHT)," IEEE Transactions on Circuits and Systems for Video Technology, Vol. 10, No. 8, pp. 1374-1387, December 2000.
6. V. Bottreau, M. Benetiere, B. Felts, and B. Pesquet-Popescu, "A Fully Scalable 3D Subband Video Codec," Proceedings of the IEEE Conference on Image Processing (ICIP'01), Greece, Vol. 2, pp. 1017-1020, October 2001.
7. Requirements and Applications for Scalable Video Coding, ISO/IEC JTC1/SC29/WG11, N6025, 66th MPEG Meeting, Brisbane, Australia, October 2003.

SCALAR EDGE DETECTORS

Definition: Since color images are arrays of three-component color vectors, the use of scalar edge detectors requires pixels' dimensionality reduction through the conversion of the color image to its luminance-based equivalent.

Since color images are arrays of three-component color vectors, the use of scalar edge detectors requires pixels' dimensionality reduction through the conversion of the color image to its luminance-based equivalent [1],[2]. Then traditional (scalar) edge operators, such as those used in gray-scale imaging are applied to the luminance image to obtain the corresponding edge map (Figure 1).

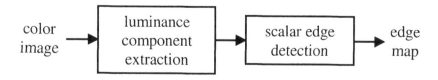

Figure 1. Scalar color edge detection based on dimensionality reduction.

Alternatively, the edge map of the color image can be achieved using component-wise processing [1]-[3]. In this way, each of the three color channels are processed separately (Figure 2). The operator then combines the three distinct edge maps to form the output map. The output edge description corresponds to the dominant indicator of the edge activity noticed in the different color bands.

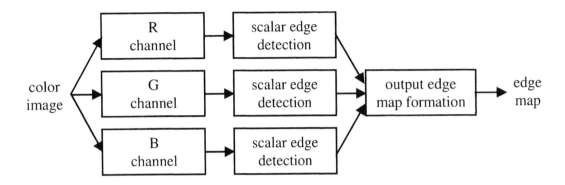

Figure 2. Scalar color edge detection based on component-wise processing.

It is well documented in the literature that edge operators are usually sensitive to noise and small variations in intensity, and therefore the achieved edge map contains noise. To improve performance the edge operator's output in Figures 1 or 2 is often compared with a predefined threshold in order to generate more accurate edge maps. The purpose of the thresholding operation is to increase the accuracy of the edge maps by extracting the structural information which corresponds to the edge discontinuities.

Both scalar edge detection approaches shown in Figures 1-2 can be grouped into two main classes of operators, namely [1]: i) gradient methods (e.g. Canny, Prewitt, Sobel, and isotropic operators), which use the first-order directional derivatives of the image to determine the edge contrast used in edge map formation, and ii) zero-crossing based methods (e.g. Laplacian, LwG, LoG, and DoG operators), which use the second-order directional derivatives to identify locations with zero crossings. The first derivative provides information on the rate of change of the image intensity. Of particular interest is the gradient magnitude denoting the rate of change of the image intensity and the gradient direction denoting the orientation of an edge. Note that when the first derivative achieves a maximum, the second derivative is zero. Thus, operators may localize edges by evaluating the zeros of the second derivatives.

In practice, both gradient and zero-crossing edge operators are approximated through the use of convolution masks. Scalar edge operators do not use the full potential of the spectral image content and thus, they can miss the edges in multichannel images [1]-[3].

See: Color image filtering and enhancement, Edge detection, Vector edge detectors.

References

1. R. Lukac, K.-N. Plataniotis, A.-N. Venetsanopoulos, R. Bieda, and B. Smolka, "Color Edge Detection Techniques," In "Signaltheorie und Signalverarbeitung, Akustik und Sprachakustik, Informationstechnik," W.E.B. Universität Verlag, Dresden, Vol. 29, 2003, pp.21-47.
2. R. Lukac and K.-N. Plataniotis, "Vector Edge Operators for cDNA Microarray Spot Localization," IEEE Transactions on Nanobioscience, submitted.
3. K.-N. Plataniotis and A.-N. Venetsanopoulos, Color Image Processing and Applications, Springer Verlag, Berlin, 2000.

SCHEDULING IN MULTIMEDIA SYSTEMS

Seon Ho Kim
University of Denver, Denver, USA

Definition: *Streaming media servers employ the scheduling of available disk bandwidth to guarantee a continuous display of streaming media and to maximize the throughput by minimizing the wasteful work of disk drives.*

Introduction

A general software structure of a multimedia server supporting continuous displays of streaming media (SM) objects such as audio and video consists of three main components: data placement and scheduling, buffering, and admission control. As shown in Figure 1, SM objects are stored in multiple magnetic disk drives following a specific data placement scheme. Assume that a user requests the display of object X, the server schedules the retrieval of the data blocks of X, while the network ensures the timely delivery of these blocks to the client. The SM server stages a block of X (say X_i) from disk into memory buffer and initiates its delivery to the display station (via the network). The server schedules the retrieval and delivery of the next block X_{i+1} prior to the completion of the display of X_i. This ensures a smooth transition between the two blocks in support of continuous display. This process is repeated until all blocks of X have been retrieved, delivered, and displayed.

Upon an arrival of user request to display an object, admission control estimates a resource requirement of the request and admits it only when the required resource is available. This is to ensure maintaining the required quality of service for a smooth display. Once the request is accepted, the requested object will be retrieved from a disk array in a pre-defined scheme and staged in memory buffer. Various buffering scheme can absorb the variance of block retrieval time and provide a smooth data transmission over the network. Some buffering schemes such as batching can also increase the throughput by grouping requests for the same object that arrive within a short duration of time.

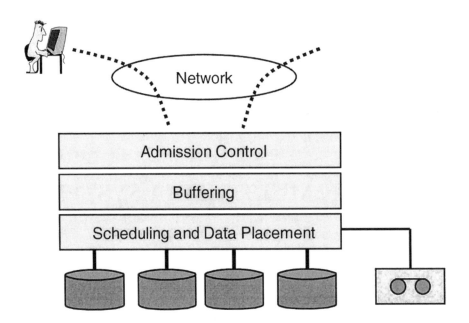

Figure 1. The architecture of a multimedia server.

Data Placement and Scheduling

Traditionally, in conjunction with data placement, SM servers employ the *scheduling* of available disk bandwidth to guarantee a continuous display and to maximize the throughput by minimizing the wasteful work of disk drives. Among various possible disk scheduling algorithms, two scheduling approaches are widely utilized: *deadline-driven* and *cycle-based*. A technique for real-time scheduling of I/O tasks is a deadline-driven approach and it can be applied for the scheduling of SM data retrievals [3]. With this approach, a request for a block is tagged with a *deadline* that ensures a continuous display. Disks are scheduled to service requests with the *Earliest Deadline First* scheme. A limitation of this approach is that seek times may not be optimized because the sequence of block retrievals are determined by deadlines. A cycle-based scheduling technique [1,4,9] is an approach exploiting the periodic nature of SM display. To support continuous display of an object X, it is partitioned into n equi-sized blocks: $X_0, X_1, ..., X_{n-1}$, where n is a function of the block size (B) and the size of X. A block is laid out contiguously on the disk and is the unit of transfer from disk to main memory. The time required to display a block is defined as a *time period* (T_p). A time period is partitioned into a number of time slots such that the duration of a slot is long enough to retrieve a block from a disk. The number of slots denotes the number of simultaneous displays supported by a disk. During a given time period (or a cycle), the system retrieves up to N blocks, only one block for each display. Block requests for the next cycle are not issued until the current cycle ends. During the next cycle, the system retrieves the next blocks for displays in a cyclic manner. For example, assuming that the system can support up to three block retrievals during a time period, suppose that the system retrieves X_i, Y_j, and Z_k for a given time period. During the next time period, it retrieves X_{i+1}, Y_{j+1}, and Z_{k+1}.

In general, the display time of a block is longer than its retrieval time from a disk drive. Thus, the bandwidth of a disk drive can be multiplexed among multiple simultaneous displays accessing the same disk drive. For example, with 4 Mb/s of display bandwidth requirement of MPEG-2 encoded objects, a disk drive with 80 Mb/s of data transfer rate can support up to 20 simultaneous displays. This is the ideal case when there is no overhead in disk operation. However, in reality, a magnetic disk drive is a mechanical device and incurs a delay when required to retrieve data. This delay consists of: 1) *seek time* to reposition the disk head from the current track to the target track, and 2) *rotational latency* to wait until the data block arrives under the disk head. These are wasteful operations that prevent a disk drive from transferring data. Both their number of occurrence and duration of each occurrence must be reduced in order to maximize the number of simultaneous displays supported by a disk drive. Thus, the performance of SM servers significantly depends on the physical characteristics of magnetic disk drives such as data transfer rate, seek times, and rotational latency. For example, it is obvious that we can increase the throughput of a server using disk drives having a higher data transfer rate.

Assuming SM servers with multiple disk drives, data blocks are assigned to disks in order to distribute the load of a display evenly across the disks. Thus, data placement can affect the continuous display and performance of SM servers in conjunction with scheduling techniques. There are two well-known approaches to assign blocks of an object across multiple disk drives; *constrained* and *unconstrained*. A typical example of constrained data placement is *round-robin* [1,4,9]. As suggested by its name, this technique assigns the blocks of an object to disks in a round-robin manner, starting with an arbitrarily chosen disk. Assuming d disks in the system, if the first block of an object X is assigned to disk d_i, j^{th} block of X is assigned to disk $d_{(i+j-1) \mod d}$. An example of unconstrained data placement is *random* [6,7] that assigns data blocks to disk drives using a random number generator.

With the combination of cycle-based scheduling and round-robin data placement, one block is retrieved from each disk drive for each display in every time period. Thus, assuming d disk drives in the system, data retrieval for a display cycles through all d disks in d successive time periods, following the round-robin data placement in a lock-step manner. The system load should be distributed across disk drives to prevent formation of bottlenecks. This load can be balanced by intentionally delaying the retrieval of the first block of requested object whenever a bottleneck is formed on a disk drive. Due to the harmony of round-robin data placement and periodic cycle-based data retrieval, this approach provides a deterministic service guarantee for a hiccup-free display of a SM object once its retrieval is initiated. This approach maximizes the utilization of disk bandwidth by distributing the load of a display across disks evenly. Thus, the system throughput scales linearly as a function of the number of disk drives in the system. The drawback of this approach is that the worst startup latency linearly scales as a function of the number of disks while the average startup latency increases sub-linearly. This is because the system might delay the initiation of data retrievals of objects. Thus, this approach is suitable to the applications that require a high throughput and can tolerate longer startup latency such as movie-on-demand systems. To minimize this limitation, data replication techniques have been proposed to reduce latency while maintaining the same throughput [2].

Deadline-driven scheduling with random data placement controls the deadlines for block retrievals. This approach can provide shorter startup latency than the cycle-based and round-robin approach. Hence, this approach is more appropriate for the applications requiring short startup latency such as a digital editing system. However, this approach may suffer from the statistical variation of the number of block retrievals in a disk drive. Due to the nature of random data placement, a disk might receive more than its fair share of requests. A formation of bottleneck on a disk drive may result in the violation of deadlines set forth on requested blocks, causing some displays to incur hiccups. This hiccup probability might be significant depending on the system load. To address this limitation, a bulk prefetching technique [5] has been proposed to minimize the hiccup probability while maintaining short startup latency.

Cycle-based Scheduling

The system is configured with a fixed amount of memory and a disk array. The transfer rate of a disk drive is denoted as R_D. The objects that constitute the SM server belong to a single media type and require a fixed bandwidth for their display (R_C). Without loss of generality, $R_D > R_C$. Then, in order to support simultaneous displays of several objects, a time period is partitioned into fixed-size slots, with each slot corresponding to the retrieval time of a block from the disk drive. The number of slots in a time period defines the number of simultaneous displays that can be supported by a disk drive. Figure 2 demonstrates the concept of time period and time slots. Each box represents a block reading time. Assuming that each block is stored contiguously on the surface of the disk, the disk incurs a disk head movement every time it switches from one block of an object to another, which is termed as *seek*.

Since the blocks of different objects are scattered across the disk surface, a basic technique (*Basic*) should assume the maximum seek time, i.e., a full stroke that is the time to reposition the disk head from the outermost cylinder to the innermost one, between two adjacent block retrievals. Moreover, it should also assume the maximum rotational latency of the disk drive. Otherwise, a continuous display of each object cannot be guaranteed. Thus, the following equation should be satisfied to support maximum N simultaneous display.

$$N(\frac{B}{R_D} + seek(\#cyl)) \leq T_P \qquad (1)$$

For a fixed block size, N is:

$$N = \left\lfloor \frac{R_D}{R_C} \times \frac{B}{(B + R_D \times seek(\#cyl))} \right\rfloor \qquad (2)$$

The maximum startup latency (l) observed by a request with this technique is one T_p because a request might arrive a little too late to employ the empty slot in the current time period. Note that the average latency is $l/2$ when the number of active users is smaller than N. If the number of active displays exceeds N, then l should be extended with appropriate queuing models.

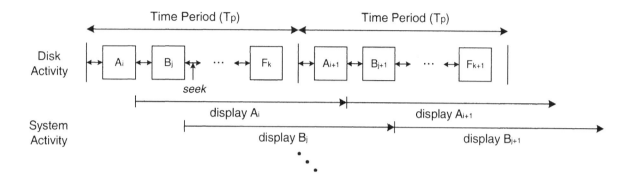

Figure 2. Basic scheduling.

One approach to reduce the worst seek time is scheduling of the disk bandwidth for multiple block retrievals in a time period. One can apply a SCAN algorithm [7] for the block retrievals during a time period. The system sorts the order of block retrievals during a time period based on the location of blocks in a disk. The movement of the disk head to retrieve blocks during a time period abides by the SCAN algorithm, in order to reduce the incurred seek times among retrievals. However, a hiccup may happen if the system initiates the display of a block immediately after its retrieval as in Basic. This is because the time elapsed between two consecutive block retrievals can be greater than a time period. In order to prevent hiccups, the displays of all the blocks retrieved during the current time period must start at the beginning of the next time period. Figure 3 demonstrates a continuous display with SCAN. The blocks A_i, B_j, ..., F_k are retrieved during the first time period. The displays of these blocks are initiated at the beginning of the next time period.

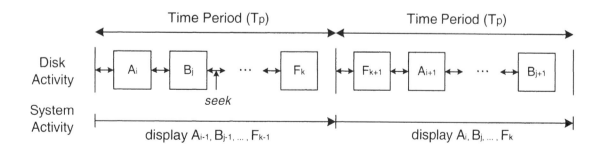

Figure 3. SCAN scheduling.

Eq. (1) and (2) still hold with SCAN but with a reduced seek time, *seek(#cyl/N)*. SCAN requires two buffers for a display because a block is displayed from one buffer while the next block is being retrieved from the disk into the other buffer. The maximum startup latency happens when a request arrives just after a SCAN begins in the current time period and the retrieval of the first block is scheduled at the end of the next time period. Thus, it is $2T_p$.

A more general scheduling technique is *Grouped Sweeping Scheme* [9], GSS. GSS groups N active requests in a T_p into g groups. This divides a T_p into g subcycles, each corresponding to the retrieval of $\lfloor N / g \rfloor$ blocks. The movement of the disk head to retrieve the blocks within a group abides by the SCAN algorithm, in order to reduce the incurred seek time in a group. Across the groups, there is no constraint on the disk head movement. To support the SCAN policy within a group, GSS shuffles the order that the blocks are retrieved. For example, assuming A_i, B_j, C_k, and D_l are retrieved within a time period, the sequence of the block retrieval might be A_i followed by B_j during the first subcycle of T_p and C_k followed by D_l during the second subcycle of the same time period. In the next time period, the retrieval order might change to B_{j+1} followed by A_{i+1} and then D_{l+1} followed by C_{k+1} during the first and second subcycle, respectively. In this case, the display of (say) A might suffer from hiccups because the time elapsed between the retrievals of A_i and A_{i+1} is greater than one time period. Thus, in GSS, the displays of all the blocks retrieved during subcycle *i* start at the beginning of subcycle *i+1*. To illustrate, consider Figure 4 where *g=2* and *N=4*. The blocks A_i and B_j are retrieved during the first subcycle. Their displays are initiated at the beginning of subcycle 2 and last for two subcycles. Therefore, while it is important to preserve the order of groups across the T_p s, it is no longer necessary to maintain the order of block retrievals within a group. Eq. (1) and (2) still hold with a further reduced seek time, $seek(\dfrac{\#cyl}{N / g})$.

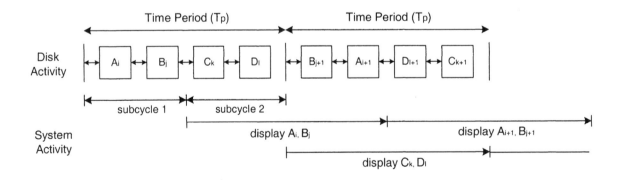

Figure 4. Grouped sweeping scheduling scheme (GSS).

The maximum startup latency observed with this technique is the summation of one time period (if the request arrives when the empty slot is missed) and the duration of a subcycle, i.e.,

$l = T_p + T_p/g$. It may appear that GSS results in a higher latency than *Baisc*. However, this is not necessarily true because the duration of a time period is different with these two techniques due to the choice of different block size. The duration of a time period is a function of the block size. GSS is a generalization of different techniques. Observe that $g=N$ simulates *Basic* and $g=1$ simulates SCAN.

Deadline-driven Scheduling

With random, the system may suffer from a statistical variation of the number of block requests in a disk. Even though all the objects are displayed with a constant rate, the probability that a disk receives a higher number of requests in a given time than other disks might be significant. Thus, the time to retrieve a block might be greater than a time period, resulting in a hiccup. Each disk has its own queue and requests remain in queues until being serviced. For a simple discussion, assume that each block request is tagged with the same deadline, a T_p, and each disk drive can support up to three block retrievals during a T_p. Then, all requests can be serviced in a T_p when there are less than 4 requests in a queue. However, with more than 3 requests, say 5, the deadlines of the 4th and 5th requests are violated and hiccups happen.

We can employ a queueing model to quantify an expected hiccup probability with deadline-driven scheduling. With a Poisson arrival process and a deterministic service process, this is the probability that a request remains in the system more than the duration of a given deadline, T_p (including waiting time in the queue and the service time) [8]. In particular, when a new request finds N or more waiting requests in the queue of a disk, this request cannot be serviced in T_p and will experience a hiccup. Suppose there are d disks in a system and each disk supports a maximum of N requests in a T_p. When there are k active requests in the system, each disk receives k/d requests on the average per T_p. This is because blocks are randomly distributed across disks and a request accesses a specific disk with a probability of $1/d$. Using a M/D/1 queueing model, the probability that a request spends time less than or equal to t in the system can be calculated using the queue length distribution, p_n:

$$P[\omega \le t] = \sum_{n=0}^{j-1} p_n \tag{3}$$

where $js \le t < (j+1)s$, $j=1,2,...$ and ω is the random variable describing the total time a request spends in the queueing system, and s is the average service time of a block request. And the probability that n requests are in the queue, p_n, is:

$$p_0 = 1 - \rho,$$
$$p_1 = (1-\rho)(e^\rho - 1), \tag{4}$$
$$p_n = (1-\rho)\sum_{j=1}^{n} \frac{(-1)^{n-j}(j\rho)^{n-j-1}(j\rho+n-j)e^{j\rho}}{(n-j)!} \quad for\ n = 2,3,...$$

where ρ is the system utilization (load). Then, the probability of hiccups is:

$$P[hiccup] = 1 - P[\omega \leq t] \quad when \; t = T_p = s \times N \tag{5}$$

The average startup latency with deadkine-scheduling and random placement can be defined by the average time in the queueing system (average queueing time plus service time):

$$E[l] = \varpi = \frac{\rho s}{2(1 - \rho)} \tag{6}$$

Other Scheduling Polices

Above mentioned techniques mainly consider retrieval scheduling of data blocks placed across multiple disks without any consideration of the location of blocks within a disk drive. There are some techniques constraining block locations within a disk as well as placing across disks. *Organ-pipe placement* tries to place more frequently accessed blocks near the center of a disk, i.e., cylinders in the middle of the disk. This approach can reduce the average seek time when objects are accessed with a deterministic access frequency. However, it fails when access frequency of objects varies over time. A *region based block allocation (REBECA)* was introduced to reduce seek times between two adjacent block retrievals by dividing a disk space into multiple regions and constraining disk accesses within a region during a certain time period. This technique can significantly reduce seek times by increasing the number of regions in a disk but it increases at the same time the maximum startup latency as a function of the number of regions.

Some techniques have studied scheduling of data blocks in multi-zone disks. Modern hard disks consist of multiple zones where each zone has a different storage capacity and data transfer rate. Disk manufacturers utilize *zoning* technique to store more number of bits in outer cylinders than inner cylinders based on the fact that physically longer outer tracks can provide more space than shorter inner tracks with a constant bit density (bits per inch). However, this zoning technique makes deterministic guarantee difficult in servicing real-time multimedia objects because of a greater variance in block retrieval times. Various techniques to handle multi-zone disks can be found in [2].

See: Multimedia Servers, Multimedia Storage Organization

References

1. S. Berson, S. Ghandeharizadeh, R. Muntz, and X. Ju, "Staggered Striping in Multimedia Information Systems," *Proceedings of the ACM SIGMOD International Conference on Management of Data*, 1994.
2. A. Dashti, S. Kim, C. Shahabi, and R. Zimmermann, "Streaming Media Server Design," Prentice Hall PTR, April 2003.

3. A. L. Reddy and J. C. Wyllie, "I/O Issues in a Multimedia System," *IEEE Computer*, Vol. 27, No. 3., March 1994, pp 69-74.

4. S. Ghandeharizadeh, S.H. Kim, W. Shi, and R. Zimmermann, "On Minimizing Startup Latency in Scalable Continuous Media Servers," *Proceedings of Multimedia Computing and Networking*, Proceedings of SPIE 3020, February 1997, pp 144-155.

5. S. Kim, "Bulk Prefetching with Deadline-Driven Scheduling to Minimize Startup Latency of Continuous Media Servers," *Proceedings of the IEEE International Conference on Multimedia and Expo (ICME2001)*, August 2001.

6. R. Muntz, J. Santos, and S. Berson, "RIO: A Real-time Multimedia Object Server," *ACM Sigmetrics Performance Evaluation Review*, Vol. 25, No. 2, September 1997.

7. T.J. Teorey, "A Comparative Analysis of Disk Scheduling Policies," *Communications of ACM*, Vol. 15, No. 3, 1972.

8. R. Tewari, R. P. King, D. Kandlur, and D. M. Dias, "Placement of Multimedia Blocks on Zoned Disks," *Proceedings of IS&T/SPIE Multimedia Computing and Networking*, January 1996.

9. P. S. Yu, M. S. Chen, and D. D. Kandlur, "Design and Analysis of a Grouped Sweeping Scheme for Multimedia Storage Management," *Proceedings of the Third International Workshop on Network and Operating System Support for Digital Audio and Video*, November 1992.

SECURITY ISSUES IN WIRELESS VIDEO

Definition: Security issues in wireless video systems include viruses, malicious attacks, and denial of service.

Video has been or is expected to be widely used by mobile devices and transmitted over wireless networks such as cellular networks for mobile phones and Wireless Local Area Networks (WLANs) for eHomes. Wireless video services include video downloading, streaming, and conferencing. Users in a wireless network communication with each other through the open air that unauthorized users can intercept content transmissions or attackers can inject malicious content or penetrate the network and impersonate legitimate users. This intrinsic nature of wireless networks has several specific security implications. Sensitive and valuable video content must be encrypted to safeguard confidentiality and integrity of the content and prevent unauthorized consumption. Wireless enables mobility which requires small form factors. Therefore a wireless video device is easily lost or stolen, adding additional security requirement to prevent somebody from gaining access to confidential information in or through the device. A mobile device and its user must be authenticated before a wireless video service. The private information such as what video content is downloaded or viewed, the device's location, etc. should also be protected. Most of the security issues in wired video systems such as viruses, malicious attacks, denial of service, are equally applicable to wireless video systems.

The security implications of wireless video have a great impact on the design of such a system. A wireless device has limited memory and computing power. Battery capacity is also at a premium. Growth in battery capacity has already lagged far behind the increase of energy requirement in a wireless device. The security concerns mentioned above make it even worse since security processing has to take away some of the premium computing resources and battery life. Security processing generally applies asymmetric encryption such as RSA or Elliptic Curve Cryptosystem (ECC) for authentication and key management, symmetric encryption such as Advanced Encryption Standard (AES) for data encryption, and the Secure Hash Algorithm (SHA)-1 for integrity checking, and a random sequence generator to generate random numbers. Some of those operations are expensive. For example, when a Toshiba Satellite 1200 laptop transmits a 5MB file, encryption with AES of 128 bits would increase battery consumption by 75% and time consumption by 65% as compared to the case without encryption [1]. Asymmetric encryption is even worse. To make things worse, a wireless device is often required to execute multiple security protocols at different network layers. Compared to wired networks, a wireless network has certain unique features: wireless communications have poor channel quality and are prone to errors, have limited and fluctuating bandwidths. All those issues have to be carefully considered and balanced in designing a wireless video system.

There are several technologies proposed to address the above issues in wireless video. Typical ones include:

1. Lightweight cryptographic algorithms and encryption schemes. Due to low processing power and premium battery life, low complexity cryptographic algorithms are used for wireless devices. For example, ECC uses much shorter keys than RSA for the same level of security, resulting in more efficient asymmetric encryption. This feature makes ECC highly suitable for small wireless devices. Video encryption can also be lightweight. For example, selective encryption can be used to encrypt only important video data instead of the whole data, dramatically reducing the amount of data to be encrypted or decrypted.

2. Security processing instructions and chips. Security operations can be executed more efficiently if a general purpose processor supports certain security and multimedia related instructions. Many embedded processors used for wireless devices have already extended to include basic cryptographic instructions. For example, SecureCore processors [2] have added cryptographic instructions to speed up secure data processing. An independent security coprocessor or chip completely devoted to security processing is also a viable approach.

3. Scalable protocols. Wireless devices may have a large range of capacities, from powerful laptops to small handset devices. A security protocol designed for wireless systems must be scalable that different wireless devices can apply a subset of the protocol that matches its capability. The Open Mobile Alliance (OMA) has adopted Digital Rights Management (DRM) specifications for portable devices that support three different modes for different devices and applications: forward lock which prevents the content from leaving the destination device; combined delivery which adds digital rights definition to the content; and separate delivery which offers content encryption and supports super distribution.

4. Scalable coding and encryption. The bandwidth of a wireless network fluctuates greatly. Wireless devices have a great variety of display characteristics, from a full screen in a laptop to a tiny screen in a cellular phone. Video content should be in a format that is well adapted to the dynamic nature of wireless networks, and different display characteristics. Scalable coding and encryption have been proposed to serve the purpose. A scalable video coding such as MPEG-4 Fine Granularity Scalability (FGS) encodes video content into a small non-scalable base layer and scalable enhancement layers. Data in the enhancement layer can be dropped during bandwidth fluctuation. Scalable encryption such as the scheme in [3] enables FGS in encrypted codestream so that encrypted video data can be adapted without decryption. No secret key is therefore needed to perform a truncation of encrypted data to fit the current bandwidth.

5. Error resilience. Video data when transmitting over wireless networks must be organized to be error resilience to prevent extensive visual degradation when errors occur. For example, data for wireless networks should be packetized into small packets so that errors in a packet or loss of a packet affect a small amount of data. Error resilience technologies such as placing resynchronization markers periodically are also used to stop error propagation.

See: Wireless Video

References

1. S. Hirani, "Energy Consumption of Encryption Schemes in Wireless Devices," M. S. Thesis, Univ. of Pittsburgh, 2003.
2. ARM SecureCore, http://www.arm.com.
3. B.B. Zhu, C. Yuan, Y. Wang, and S. Li, "Scalable Protection for MPEG-4 Fine Granularity Scalability," IEEE Transactions on Multimedia, Vol. 7, No. 2, pp. 222-233, April 2005.

SEGMENTATION AND CODING

Definition: Various coding schemes employ segmentation for different purposes, such as for extracting image regions in order to subsequently approximate the contours and image characteristics of those regions, or for object-based coding.

Segmentation is an important tool for image and video coding applications. Various coding schemes employ segmentation for different purposes, such as for extracting image regions in order to subsequently approximate the contours and image characteristics of those regions, or for object-based coding. The latter presents a framework for achieving improved coding efficiency without compromising the quality of at least the important parts of the image or video, such as a person's face in a videoconference image sequence, particularly in very low bit-rate communications. One way of achieving this goal is by coding with lower quality the least significant parts of the sequence. Taking advantage of coding schemes like the aforementioned ones requires the use of a segmentation algorithm for partitioning the visual medium to spatial or spatio-temporal objects.

With respect to standards, the MPEG-4 International Standard supports the representation of video as a collection of objects, enabling object-based video coding; however, no International Standard (including MPEG-4) defines a set of segmentation tools that can be used for this or any other application. Thus, numerous segmentation approaches for efficient image and video coding have been proposed, considering various coding techniques.

In [1] an object-based video compression scheme based on the derivation and efficient coding of motion boundaries is developed. It is based on initially identifying a small number of global movement classes. Then, regions of a spatial segmentation are assigned to each movement class and spatial regions are merged using various similarity metrics. Eventually, the boundaries of different motion classes are coded using an efficient asymmetric binary tree coding scheme.

In [2], two approaches to object-based content representation for coding are developed: a foreground/background segmentation method for stereo sequences and a face segmentation method for monoscopic video. Using these segmentation approaches, a constant-quality variable bit-rate (CQ-VBR) control algorithm is developed. It is shown that in low bit-rate applications, a significant reduction in the overall bit-rate can be achieved while maintaining the same visual quality of the region of interest (the foreground and face object, respectively), as compared to conventional frame-based coding.

A different approach is followed in [3], where the problem of efficient coding of still images overcoming the need for defining regions of interest is considered. A coding scheme based on quad-tree segmentation (i.e. a split and merge approach) is proposed, that can jointly encode similar neighboring segments. In doing so, this scheme achieves the optimal rate-distortion behavior for piecewise polynomial signals and is shown to be superior to conventional schemes not making use of a segmentation method.

See: Segmentation of images and video

References

1. A. Shamim and J.A. Robinson, "Object-based video coding by global-to-local motion segmentation," IEEE Transactions on Circuits and Systems for Video Technology, Vol. 12, No. 12, December 2002, pp. 1106-1116.
2. K. Challapali, T. Brodsky, Y.-T. Lin, Y. Yan, and R.Y. Chen, "Real-time object segmentation and coding for selective-quality video communications," IEEE Transactions on Circuits and Systems for Video Technology, Vol. 14, No. 6, June 2004, pp. 813-824.
3. R. Shukla, P.L. Dragotti, M.N. Do, and M. Vetterli, "Rate-Distortion Optimized Tree-Structured Compression Algorithms for Piecewise Polynomial Images," IEEE Transactions on Image Processing, Vol. 14, No. 3, March 2005, pp. 343-359.

SEGMENTATION EVALUATION

Definition: *Objective segmentation evaluation includes both standalone evaluation methods, which do not make use of reference segmentation, and relative evaluation methods employing ground truth.*

The plethora of image and video segmentation techniques in the literature and their wide use in a variety of applications makes increasingly important the need for the objective evaluation of segmentation results. Objective segmentation evaluation can be a valuable tool for supporting the selection of suitable segmentation tools for a given application. It could also serve in joint segmentation/evaluation schemes, to allow for iterative improvement of segmentation accuracy.

Work on objective segmentation evaluation includes both standalone evaluation methods, which do not make use of reference segmentation, and relative evaluation methods employing ground truth. Standalone evaluation methods rely on the calculation of statistical properties of a given segmentation, such as intra-object homogeneity and inter-object disparity with respect to the given features (typically, color information). This alleviates the need for using reference segmentation. In [1], this fact is exploited in the development of a combined segmentation and evaluation scheme for domain-specific images, utilizing the confidence of region classification results for evaluating segmentation accuracy and forcing the repetition of segmentation using different parameter values until a classification of regions with desired confidence is achieved.

Although standalone evaluation methods can be very useful in such constrained applications, the findings of standalone evaluation methods are likely to deviate from the human perception of the goodness of segmentation, since the latter is largely dependent upon prior knowledge rather that statistical properties alone. Relative evaluation methods overcome this problem by using some form of a reference segmentation result (e.g. a segmentation mask, a binary edge mask etc.) generated by a human observer; evaluation of any segmentation result is performed by comparison with the reference one and calculation of a suitable discrepancy measure. This approach is followed in [2], where a relative evaluation method using an area-based approach is proposed for the evaluation of still image segmentation results. This method takes into account the accuracy of the region boundary localization as well as under-segmentation and over-segmentation effects, and is shown to be appropriate for comparing segmentation algorithms on the basis of their performance. A related approach to spatio-temporal video segmentation evaluation is developed in [3], where perceptually weighted evaluation criteria are developed to quantify the spatial and temporal accuracy of segmentation masks.

See: Segmentation of images and video

References

1. Y. Ding, G.J. Vachtsevanos, A.J. Yezzi Jr., Y. Zhang, and Y. Wardi, "A recursive segmentation and classification scheme for improving segmentation accuracy and

detection rate in real-time machine vision applications," Proceedings of the 14th International Conference on Digital Signal Processing (DSP02), Vol. 2, July 2002.

2. V. Mezaris, I. Kompatsiaris, and M. G. Strintzis, "Still image objective segmentation evaluation using ground truth," Proceedings of the Fifth COST 276 Workshop on Information and Knowledge Management for Integrated Media Communication, October 2003, Prague, Czech Republic, pp. 9-14.

3. P. Villegas and X. Marichal, "Perceptually-weighted evaluation criteria for segmentation masks in video sequences," IEEE Transactions on Image Processing, Vol. 13, No. 8, August 2004, pp. 1092- 1103.

SEGMENTATION OF IMAGES AND VIDEO

Vasileios Mezaris[1,2], Ioannis Kompatsiaris[2] and Michael G. Strintzis[1,2]
[1] Aristotle University of Thessaloniki, Thessaloniki, Greece
[2] Informatics and Telematics Institute, Centre for Research and Technology Hellas, Thessaloniki, Greece

Definition: *Segmentation is the process of partitioning a piece of information into meaningful elementary parts termed segments.*

Considering still images, *(spatial)* segmentation means partitioning the image to a number of arbitrarily shaped regions, each of them typically being assumed to constitute a meaningful part of the image, i.e. to correspond to one of the objects depicted in it or to a part of one such object. Considering moving images, i.e. video, the term segmentation is used to describe a range of different processes for partitioning the video to meaningful parts at different granularities. Segmentation of video can thus be *temporal*, aiming to break down the video to *scenes* or *shots, spatial*, addressing the problem of independently segmenting each video frame to arbitrarily shaped regions, or *spatio-temporal*, extending the previous case to the generation of temporal sequences of arbitrarily shaped spatial regions. The term segmentation is also frequently used to describe foreground/background separation in video, which can be seen as a special case of spatio-temporal segmentation. Regardless of the employed decision space, i.e. 1D, 2D or 3D for temporal, spatial and spatio-temporal segmentation, respectively, the application of any segmentation method is often preceded by a simplification step for discarding unnecessary information (e.g. low-pass filtering) and a feature extraction step for modifying or estimating features not readily available in the visual medium (e.g. texture, motion features etc., but also color features in a different color space etc.), as illustrated in [1] for a variety a segmentation algorithms (Figure 1).

Segmentation of images and video is generally an ill-posed problem, i.e. for a given natural image or image sequence, there exists no unique solution to the segmentation problem; the spatial, temporal or spatio-temporal segments that should ideally be formed as a result of segmentation largely depend on the application under consideration and most frequently on the subjective view of each human observer.

Commonly considered applications of segmentation include region-based image and video description, indexing and retrieval, video summarization, interactive region-based annotation schemes, detection of objects that can serve as cues for event recognition, region-based coding, etc. Particularly image and video description, indexing and retrieval has been on the focus of attention of many researchers working on segmentation, since the benefits of introducing segmentation to this application have recently been documented well and significant progress has been made on related topics such as region-based description for indexing, most notably with the introduction of the MPEG-7 Standard.

Most segmentation methods serving all aforementioned applications are *generic*, i.e. make no restrictive assumptions regarding the semantics of the visual content, such as that the content belongs to a specific domain; however, *domain-specific* methods for applications like medical image segmentation also exist.

Spatial segmentation

Segmentation methods for 2D images may be divided primarily into region-based and boundary-based methods. Region-based approaches rely on the homogeneity of spatially localized features such as intensity, texture, and position. On the other hand, boundary-based methods use primarily gradient information to locate object boundaries. Hybrid techniques that integrate the results of boundary detection and homogeneity-based clustering (e.g. region growing), as well as techniques exploiting additional information such as structural properties (e.g. inclusion), have also been proposed.

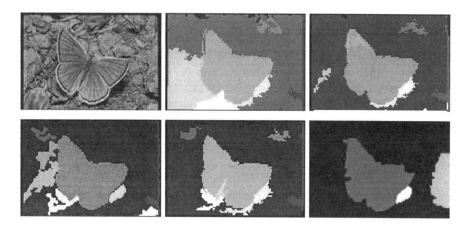

Figure 1. Exemplary spatial segmentation results for a natural image of the Corel gallery, using the different segmentation methods outlined in [1].

Traditional region-based approaches include region growing and split and merge techniques. Starting from an initial region represented by an arbitrarily chosen single pixel, region growing is the process of adding neighboring pixels to this region by examining their similarity to the ones already added; when no further additions are possible according to the defined similarity criteria, a new region is created and grows accordingly. The opposite of this approach is split and merge. Starting from a single initial region spanning the entire image, region homogeneity is evaluated; if the homogeneity criterion is not satisfied, the region is split according to a pre-defined pattern and neighboring regions are subsequently merged, providing this does not violate the homogeneity criterion. The interchange of split and merge steps continues until the latter is satisfied for all regions.

Region-based approaches also include the Recursive Shortest Spanning Tree (RSST) algorithm [2], which starts from a very fine partitioning of the image and performs merging of neighboring nodes while considering the minimum of a cost function; the latter preserves the homogeneity of the generated regions. In order to avoid a possible premature termination of the merging process, resulting to over-segmentation, in the case that the desired final number of regions is not explicitly defined, the introduction of syntactic visual features to RSST has been proposed [3]. The K-means algorithm, an iterative classification method, has also been used as the basis of several region-based approaches. In [4], the K-Means-with-Connectivity-Constraint variant of K-means is used to effect segmentation by means of pixel clustering in the combined intensity-texture-position feature space (Fig. 2). Another approach to pixel clustering is based on the Expectation-Maximization (EM) algorithm, which is a method for finding maximum likelihood estimates when there is missing or incomplete data. For the application of EM to segmentation, the cluster membership for each pixel can be seen as such [5]. In [6], image segmentation is treated as a graph partitioning problem and the normalized cut, a global criterion measuring both the total dissimilarity between the different groups as well as the total similarity within the groups, is employed for segmenting the graph.

In contrast to the aforementioned methods, boundary-based methods rely on detecting the discontinuities present in the feature space. The Canny edge detector is a popular such scheme, based on the convolution of the image, over a small window, with the directional derivatives of a Gaussian function. Another approach to boundary detection is anisotropic diffusion, which can be seen as a robust procedure for estimating a piecewise smooth image from a noisy input image [7]. Anisotropic diffusion employs an edge-stopping function that allows the preservation of edges while diffusing the rest of the image.

Mathematical morphology methods, including in particular the watershed algorithm [8], have also received considerable attention for use in image segmentation. The watershed algorithm determines the minima of the gradients of the image to be segmented, and associates a segment to each minimum. Conventional gradient operators generally produce many local minima, which are caused by noise or quantization errors, and hence, the watershed transformation with a conventional gradient operator usually results in over-segmentation. To alleviate this problem, the use of multiscale morphological gradient operators has been proposed. More recently, the use of the watershed algorithm to generate an initial over-segmentation and the subsequent representation of this result as a graph, to which partitioning via the weighted mean cut criterion is applied, was proposed to combat the over-segmentation effect [9].

Finally, global energy minimization schemes, also known as snakes or active contour models, involve the evolution of a curve from an initial position toward the boundary of an object in such a way that a properly defined energy functional is minimized. Depending on the definition of the energy functional, the resulting scheme may be edge-based, region-based or based on a combination of boundary detection and homogeneity-preserving criteria [10].

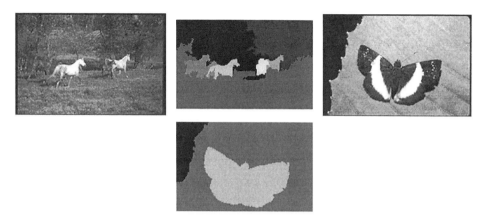

Figure 2. Exemplary spatial segmentation results for two natural images of the Corel gallery, using the method of [4].

Temporal segmentation

Temporal video segmentation aims to partition the video to elementary image sequences termed *scenes* and *shots*. A shot is defined as a set of consecutive frames taken without interruption by a single camera. A scene, on the other hand, is usually defined as the basic story-telling unit of the video, i.e. as a temporal segment that is elementary in terms of semantic content and may consist of one or more shots.

Temporal segmentation to shots is performed by detecting the transition from one shot to the next. Transitions between shots, which are effects generated at the video editing stage, may be *abrupt* or *gradual*, the former being detectible by examining two consecutive frames, the latter spanning more than two frames (Fig. 3) and being usually more difficult to detect, depending among others on the actual transition type (e.g. fade, dissolve, wipe, etc.). Temporal segmentation to shots in uncompressed video is often performed by means of pair-wise pixel comparisons between successive or distant frames or by comparing the color histograms corresponding to different frames. Methods for histogram comparison include the comparison of absolute differences between corresponding bins and histogram intersection [11]. Other approaches to temporal segmentation include block-wise comparisons, where the statistics of corresponding blocks in different frames are compared and the number of "changed" blocks is evaluated by means of thresholding, and edge-based methods. The latter involve the detection of edges by application of an edge detector (e.g. Canny) and the subsequent comparison of edges in different frames to calculate values such as the edge change ratio. Other methods, involving the comparison of motion features at different time instances have also been proposed. In [12], a method for foveated shot detection is proposed. This is based on the generation of patterns of visuomotor behavior (traces) for the sequence and their subsequent use for inferring shot boundary presence.

Other recent efforts on shot detection have focused on avoiding the prior decompression of the video stream, resulting to significant gains in terms of efficiency. Such methods consider mostly MPEG video, but also other compression schemes such as wavelet-based ones. These exploit compression-specific cues such as macroblock-type ratios to detect points in the 1D decision space where temporal redundancy, which is inherent in video and greatly exploited by compression schemes, is reduced.

Temporal segmentation to scenes involves grouping of shots to semantically coherent clusters. Several methods have been proposed for this, including clustering algorithms also used to effect homogeneity-based spatial segmentation. One approach is, starting from one shot, to progressively group similar shots with it until no similar shots can be found within a chosen temporal distance; this is a simple application of the previously discussed region-growing algorithm to the 1D segmentation case. Another approach, also used for 2D segmentation as well, involves treating shots as nodes of a graph and using the normalized cut to segment the graph, this forming shot clusters corresponding to the scenes [13]. The aforementioned approaches make use of visual features to describe the different shots and to estimate the similarity between any two. The use of audio and linguistic information extracted via speech recognition, although possibly not applicable to any kind of video, has also been proposed to assist the detection of semantically similar shots.

Figure 3. Sample gradual transition (dissolve).

Spatio-temporal segmentation

Several approaches have been proposed for spatio-temporal video segmentation (i.e. segmentation in a 3D decision space), both unsupervised, as is almost always the case in 1D and 2D decision spaces, and supervised. The latter require human interaction for defining the number of objects present in the sequence, for defining an initial contour of the objects to be tracked or more often for grouping homogeneous regions to semantic objects, while the former require no such interaction. In both types of approaches, however, it is frequently assumed that the video comprises a single shot; this assumption dictates that spatio-temporal segmentation is preceded by temporal segmentation to shots.

Some spatio-temporal segmentation approaches rely on initially applying spatial segmentation methods to each frame independently. Spatio-temporal objects are subsequently formed by associating the spatial regions formed in successive frames using their low-level features. In [14], this general approach is realized by adopting a seeded region-growing scheme for performing spatial segmentation; the temporal correspondence of spatial regions between adjacent frames is established by examining the overlapping of seeds, which in the case of the selected region growing technique may be quite large, ranging from 1/3 to 2/3 of the final region size.

A different approach is to use motion information to perform motion projection, i.e. to estimate the position of a region at a future frame, based on its current position and its estimated motion features. In this case, a spatial segmentation method need only be applied to the first frame of the sequence, whereas in subsequent frames only refinement of the motion projection result is required. In [15], a homogeneity-based spatial segmentation method, namely the watershed algorithm, is applied to the first frame of the sequence; then, motion projection is used to estimate a segmentation of the following frame, which is eventually refined by applying a marker-controlled watershed algorithm. Final results are obtained by merging those of the resulting 3D watershed volumes that have similar motion characteristics. A similar in nature approach is followed in [16], where the need for motion projection is substituted by a Bayes-based approach to color-homogeneous region-tracking using color information. Color- and motion-homogeneous spatio-temporal regions generated by means of spatial segmentation at the first frame of the sequence and tracking at subsequent frames are eventually clustered to different objects using again the region long-term motion trajectories (Figure 4).

Region tracking is an important part of 3D segmentation. This is true both for approaches of the previous category, where tracking of regions generated via 2D segmentation at previous frames may be required, as well as for interactive schemes supporting the manual initialization of the tracked region. Noisy data and illumination conditions that change with time are two key factors limiting the efficiency of temporal tracking algorithms. To address these issues, a color-based deformable model that is robust against noisy data and changing illumination is developed in [17]. Measuring color constant gradients and estimating the corresponding amount of sensor noise, this approach uses a weighting term in the deformation process to force noisy and unstable gradient information to contribute less to the deformation process than reliable gradient information yielding robust tracking. In [18] a geometric prior is introduced to the active contour framework in order to improve the temporal coherency of the tracking result, and the application of this approach to interactive segmentation is considered.

Alternatively to the above techniques, one could restrict the problem of video segmentation to foreground/background separation. The latter can be achieved either by using primarily motion information, or by performing in parallel segmentation using other feature spaces as well (e.g. intensity information) and employing rule-based processing to enhance the motion segmentation result. In [19], where a number of different methods are presented, a method for foreground/background separation using intensity information, based on the assumption that the background comprises large uniform regions, is developed. In [20] a fast moving object segmentation algorithm is developed, based upon change detection and background registration techniques; this algorithm also incorporates a shadow cancellation technique for dealing with light changing and shadow effects.

Finally, as in temporal segmentation, the spatio-temporal segmentation of compressed video has recently attracted considerable attention. Algorithms of this category generally employ coarse motion and color information that can be extracted from the video stream without full decompression, such as macroblock motion vectors and DC coefficients of DCT-coded image blocks.

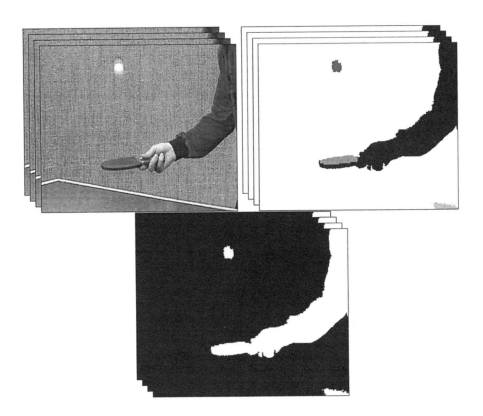

Figure 4. Exemplary spatio-temporal segmentation result (5 final objects) and corresponding foreground/background mask for a frame of the *table tennis* sequence, using the method of [16].

Future directions

Segmentation methods for generic visual content have significantly improved over the last few years. While the further improvement of generic segmentation techniques will continue to attract attention, particularly techniques considering the segmentation of compressed data, an important future direction is the introduction of prior knowledge to the segmentation procedure, leading to the development of knowledge-assisted analysis techniques. Although the applicability of the latter is by definition limited to specific domains, the introduction of prior knowledge to the segmentation process is the key to transforming the ill-posed segmentation problem to a well-posed one by restricting the number of admissible solutions.

See: Compressed video spatio-temporal segmentation, Segmentation evaluation, Medical image segmentation, Segmentation and coding, Knowledge-assisted image and video analysis

References

1. N. O'Connor, S. Sav, T. Adamek, V. Mezaris, I. Kompatsiaris, T. Y. Lui, E. Izquierdo, C. Bennström, and J. Casas, "Region and object segmentation algorithms in the Qimera segmentation platform," Proceedings of the Third International Workshop on Content-Based Multimedia Indexing (CBMI03), Rennes, France, September 2003, pp. 381-388.

2. S.H. Kwok and A.G. Constantinides, "A fast recursive shortest spanning tree for image segmentation and edge detection," IEEE Transactions on Image Processing, Vol. 6, No. 2, February 1997, pp. 328-332.

3. T. Adamek, N. O'Connor, and N. Murphy, "Region-based segmentation of images using syntactic visual features," Proceedings of the Workshop on Image Analysis For Multimedia Interactive Services (WIAMIS), Montreux, Switzerland, April 2005.

4. V. Mezaris, I. Kompatsiaris, and M. G. Strintzis, "Still Image Segmentation Tools for Object-based Multimedia Applications," International Journal of Pattern Recognition and Artificial Intelligence, Vol. 18, No. 4, June 2004, pp. 701-725.

5. C. Carson, S. Belongie, H. Greenspan, and J. Malik, "Blobworld: image segmentation using expectation-maximization and its application to image querying," IEEE Transactions on Pattern Analysis and Machine Intelligence, Vol. 24, No. 8, August 2002, pp. 1026-1038.

6. J. Shi and J. Malik, "Normalized cuts and image segmentation," IEEE Transactions on Pattern Analysis and Machine Intelligence, Vol. 22, No. 8, Aug. 2000, pp. 888-905.

7. P. Perona and J. Malik, "Scale-space and edge detection using anisotropic diffusion," IEEE Transactions on Pattern Analysis and Machine Intelligence, Vol. 12, No. 7, July 1990, pp. 629-639.

8. H. Gao, W.-C. Siu, and C.-H. Hou, "Improved techniques for automatic image segmentation," IEEE Transactions on Circuits and Systems for Video Technology, Vol. 11, No. 12, December 2001, pp. 1273-1280.

9. R.J. O'Callaghan and D.R. Bull, "Combined morphological-spectral unsupervised image segmentation," IEEE Transactions on Image Processing, Vol. 14, No. 1, January 2005, pp. 49-62.

10. M. Jacob, T. Blu, and M. Unser, "Efficient energies and algorithms for parametric snakes," IEEE Transactions on Image Processing, Vol. 13, No. 9, September 2004, pp. 1231-1244.

11. U. Gargi, R. Kasturi, and S.H. Strayer, "Performance Characterization of Video-Shot-Change Detection Methods," IEEE Transactions on Circuits and Systems for Video Technology, Vol. 10, No. 1, February 2000, pp. 1-13.

12. G. Boccignone, A. Chianese, V. Moscato, and A. Picariello, "Foveated Shot Detection for Video Segmentation," IEEE Transactions on Circuits and Systems for Video Technology, Vol. 15, No. 3, March 2005, pp. 365-377.

13. C.-W. Ngo, Y.-F. Ma, and H.-J. Zhang, "Video summarization and scene detection by graph modeling," IEEE Transaction on Circuits and Systems for Video Technology, Vol. 15, No. 2, February 2005, pp. 296-305.

14. Y. Deng and B.S. Manjunath, "Unsupervised segmentation of color-texture regions in images and video," IEEE Transactions on Pattern Analysis and Machine Intelligence, Vol. 23, No. 8, August 2001, pp. 800-810.

15. Y.-P. Tsai, C.-C. Lai, Y.-P. Hunga, and Z.-C. Shih, "A Bayesian approach to video object segmentation via merging 3-D watershed volumes," IEEE Transactions on Circuits and Systems for Video Technology, Vol. 15, No. 1, January 2005, pp. 175-180.

16. V. Mezaris, I. Kompatsiaris, and M. G. Strintzis, "Video Object Segmentation using Bayes-based Temporal Tracking and Trajectory-based Region Merging," IEEE Transactions on Circuits and Systems for Video Technology, Vol. 14, No. 6, June 2004, pp. 782-795.

17. T. Gevers, "Robust segmentation and tracking of colored objects in video," IEEE Transactions on Circuits and Systems for Video Technology, Vol. 14, No. 6, June 2004, pp. 776-781.

18. M. Gastaud, M. Barlaud, and G. Aubert, "Combining shape prior and statistical features for active contour segmentation," IEEE Transactions on Circuits and Systems for Video Technology, Vol. 14, No. 5, May 2004, pp. 726-734.

19. E. Izquierdo and M. Ghanbari, "Key components for an advanced segmentation system," IEEE Transactions on Multimedia, Vol. 4, No. 1, Jan.-March 2002, pp. 97-113.

20. S.-Y. Chien, Y.-W. Huang, B.-Y. Hsieh, S.-Y. Ma, and L.-G. Chen, "Fast video segmentation algorithm with shadow cancellation, global motion compensation, and adaptive threshold techniques," IEEE Transactions on Multimedia, Vol. 6, No. 5, October 2004, pp. 732-748.

SEMANTIC AGENTS ON THE INTERNET

Definition: Semantic agents belong to intelligent agents, which is a software program that exhibits a goal oriented behavior, interacts with distributed entities – including media and other agents – and attempts to satisfy user-specified requirements.

Agent-oriented programming and Agent Communication Languages (ACL) are now relatively well understood and documented [1]. Key to all ACL's - and all agent interactions - is a shared syntax and semantic of the domain of discourse and the interaction protocols. An *ontology* is an artifact that can provide such a shared model. Naturally, on the Internet, no single ontology describes all information from every attitude. In fact, the vast majority of Internet information is unstructured, informally interlinked at best, and lacking formal semantic. These facts hinder agent-based internet activities and as a result, semantic agents on the Internet tend to be specialized for particular domains; i.e. those domains providing well-structured well-specified ontologies.

Ontologies for Internet Agents

Many technologies are now beginning to play major roles in facilitating the development of global-scale Internet agent applications. One example is the *OpenCyc.org* project which aims to create a very large open-source general knowledge base (about 6,000 concepts, 60,000 assertions). More 'vertically' oriented, the OASIS *Electronic Business using XML* (ebXML) is a large specification of XML-encoded business collaborations, specifications, taxonomies, and structures, and has wide industry consensus. ebXML allows e-commerce software agents to programmatically understand and engage in e-commerce. Many researchers are currently examining how the rich semantics of OWL and RDF can make e-commerce registries such as *ebXML* and *Universal Description, Discovery and Integration* (UDDI) (e.g. which hold descriptions of services) more descriptive, capturing the semantics of the business and operational semantics [2]. Regardless, such ontologies allow Internet agents to programmatically interact, to more easily adapt to exception cases, and to make ad hoc decisions during goal processing.

Search Agents

Almost all Internet search Web sites (e.g. Google, Yahoo!, etc.) ask the user to enter keyword constraints. There are several problems with this approach: a) search engine invariably fails to filter out the unintended intentions of terms (e.g. to the user, does *Apple* mean the fruit or the company?), b) certain documents may not actually use the terms entered by the user but may nonetheless be highly relevant (e.g. they may use other terms, synonyms, etc.) These same issues are relevant to intelligent agents in the Internet, who may be tasked by their users to find information. In general, a strong notion of semantics (e.g. as in W3C's OWL) together with ontologies and rule-bases (or other means for making inference) partially solve these problems. Various related techniques are currently in use including: Google.com's *link structure* semantics, Bayesian networks, clustering, and latent semantic indexing.

See: Semantic Web

References

1. G. Weiss (Ed.), "Multiagent Systems: A Modern Approach to Distributed Artificial Intelligence," MIT Press, Cambridge, 2000.
2. N. Srinivasan, M. Paolucci, and K. Sycara, "Adding OWL-S to UDDI, implementation and throughput," Proceedings of the ICWS'04, San Diego, July 2004, pp. 75-86.

SEMANTIC CLASS-BASED IMAGE INDEXING

Definition: In a unique Class Relative Indexing (CRI) scheme, image classification is a means to compute inter-class semantic image indexes for similarity-based matching and retrieval.

A natural and useful insight is to formulate image retrieval as a classification problem. In very general terms, the goal of image retrieval is to return images of a class C that the user has in mind based on a set of features computed for each image x in the database. In probabilistic sense, the system should return images ranked in the descending return status value of $P(C \mid x)$, whatever C may be defined as desirable. For example, a Bayesian formulation to minimize the probability of retrieval error (i.e. the probability of wrong classification) had been proposed [1] to drive the selection of color and texture features and to unify similarity measures with the maximum likelihood criteria.

Image classification or class-based retrieval approaches are adequate for query by *predefined* image class. However, the set of relevant images R may not correspond to any predefined class C in general. In a unique *Class Relative Indexing* (CRI) scheme [2], image classification is not the end but a means to compute inter-class semantic image indexes for similarity-based matching and retrieval.

When we are dealing with Query By Example (QBE), the set of relevant images R is obscure and a query example q only provides a glimpse into it. In fact, the set of relevant images R does not exist until a query has been specified. However, to anchor the query context, we can define Semantic Support Classes (SSCs) C_k, $k = 1, 2, ..., M$ as prototypical instances of the relevance class R and compute the relative memberships to these classes of query q. Similarly we can compute the inter-class index for any database image x. These inter-class memberships allow us to compute a form of categorical similarity between q and x.

Using the softmax function, the image classification output R_k given an image x is computed as

$$R_k(x) = \frac{\exp^{C_k(x)}}{\sum_j \exp^{Cj(x)}} \tag{1}$$

The similarity $\lambda(q,x)$ between a query q and an image x is then computed as

$$\lambda(q,x) = 1 - \frac{1}{2}\sum_k | R_k(q) - R_k(x) | \tag{2}$$

This semantic class-based image indexing scheme has been tested on 2400 consumer images using taxonomy of seven predefined classes (i.e. M = 7), aggregated local semantic regions as image features and support vector machines as image classifiers with good precision and recall performance [2].

See: Semantic Image Representation and Indexing

References

1. N. Vasconcelos and A. Lippman, "A probabilistic architecture for content-based image retrieval," Proceedings of IEEE Computer Vision and Pattern Recognition, 2000, pp. 1216-1221.
2. J.H. Lim and J.S. Jin, "From classification to retrieval: exploiting pattern classifiers in semantic indexing and retrieval," in U. Srinivasan and S. Nepal (Eds.), Managing Multimedia Semantics, Idea Group Publishing, 2005.

SEMANTIC CONSUMER IMAGE INDEXING

Definition: Using Semantic Support Regions, the indexing process automatically detects the layout and applies the right tessellation template.

As a structured learning approach to represent and index consumer images with Semantic Support Regions (SSRs) (see article on **Semantic Image Representation and Indexing**), 26 SSRs have been designed and organized into 8 super-classes (Figure 1) from a collection of 2400 unconstrained consumer images, taken over 5 years in several countries with indoor/outdoor settings, portrait/landscape layouts, and bad quality images (faded, over-/under-exposed, blurred etc). After removing noisy marginal pixels, the images are resized to 240 × 360. The indexing process automatically detects the layout and applies the right tessellation template.

People: Face, Figure, Crowd, Skin

Sky: Clear, Cloudy, Blue

Ground: Floor, Sand, Grass

Water: Pool, Pond, River

Foliage: Green, Floral, Branch

Mountain: Far, Rocky

Building: Old, City, Far

Interior: Wall, Wooden, China, Fabric, Light

Figure 1. Examples of 26 semantic support regions.

A total of 554 image regions from 138 images are cropped and 375 of them are used as training data for Support Vector Machines (SVMs) and the remaining one-third (179) for validation. Among all the kernels evaluated, those with better generalization result on the validation set are used for the indexing and retrieval tasks.

Table 1. Training statistics of the 26 SSR classes

	minimum	maximum	average
Number of positive training examples	5	26	14.4
Number of support vectors computed	9	66	33.3
Number of positive test examples	3	13	6.9
Number of classification errors	0	14	5.7
Classification error (%)	0	7.8	3.2

Table 1 lists the training statistics of the 26 SSR classes. The negative training (test) examples for a SSR class are the union of positive training (test) examples of the other 25 classes. After learning, the SSR detectors are used to index the 2400 consumer images. Both Query By Example and Query by Spatial Icons (see article on **Semantic Visual Query and Retrieval**) experiments have produced promising results [1].

References

1. J.H. Lim and J.S. Jin, "A structured learning framework for content-based image indexing and visual query," Multimedia Systems Journal, 2005.

SEMANTIC IMAGE REPRESENTATION AND INDEXING

Joo-Hwee Lim
Institute for Infocomm Research, Singapore

Definition: *Besides low-level visual features, such as color, texture, and shapes, high-level semantic information is useful and effective in image retrieval and indexing.*

Low-level visual features such as color, texture, and shapes can be easily extracted from images to represent and index image content [1-3]. However, they are not completely descriptive for meaningful retrieval. High-level semantic information is useful and effective in retrieval. But it depends heavily on semantic regions, which are difficult to obtain themselves. Between low-level features and high-level semantic information, there is an unsolved "semantic gap" [4].

The semantic gap is due to two inherent problems. One problem is that the extraction of complete semantics from image data is extremely hard as it demands general object recognition and scene understanding. Despite encouraging recent progress in object detection and recognition [5,6], unconstrained broad image domain still remains a challenge for computer vision. For instance, consumer photographs exhibit highly varied contents and imperfect image quality due to spontaneous and casual nature of image capturing. The objects in consumer images are usually ill-posed, occluded, and cluttered with poor lighting, focus, and exposure. There is usually large number of object classes in this type of polysemic images. Robust object segmentation for such noisy images is still an open problem [4].

The other problem causing the semantic gap is the complexity, ambiguity and subjectivity in user interpretation. Relevance feedback is regarded as a promising technique to solicit user's interpretation at post-query interaction [7,8]. However the correctness of user's feedback may not be statistically reflected due to the small sampling problem.

Pre-query annotation enables textual search but the tedious manual process is usually incomplete, inconsistent, and context sensitive. Moreover there are situations when image semantics cannot be captured by labeling alone [9].

Query By Example (QBE) [1,2] requires a relevant image to be visible or available as an example during query to start with. The semantics of the query is implicit in the content of the query image. Query By Canvas (QBC) [1,3] let user compose a visual query using geometrical shapes, colors and textures and leave the system to interpret the semantics of the composed query. It is desirable to have the user communicate his or her query expectation to the system using some unambiguous vocabulary. A new query formulation method that allows user to specify visual semantics explicitly is described in the article on **Semantic Visual Query and Retrieval.**

In order to build semantic image retrieval systems for various application domains such as consumer photographs, medical images etc, it is important to have a structured framework to represent and index images with respect to domain-specific visual semantics. To reduce the human effort in annotating images with visual semantics, a systematic and modular approach to construct visual semantics detectors from statistical learning is essential. These are the subject of this article.

A Detection-Based Image Representation and Indexing Scheme

In essence, the objective of the structured framework [10] is to represent an image in an application domain as a distribution of meaningful visual objects relevant to the application domain, rather than low-level features such as colors, texture, and shapes. In a systematic manner, an application developer designs a visual vocabulary with intuitive meanings (e.g. faces, buildings, foliage, etc in consumer images; cerebrum, teeth, skeletal joints, etc in medical images) called Semantic Support Regions (SSRs), based on typical images of the application domain. Training samples of the visual vocabulary cropped from typical images are then used to construct modular visual detectors of these SSRs using statistical learning based on visual features suitable to characterize the visual vocabulary.

To index an image from the same application domain as a distribution of SSRs, the learned visual detectors are first applied to the image in a multi-scale manner. The detection results are reconciled across multiple resolutions and aggregated spatially to form local semantic histograms, suitable for efficient semantic query and retrieval. The key in image representation and indexing here is not to record the primitive feature vectors themselves but to project them into a classification space spanned by semantic labels (instead of a low-level feature space) and uses the soft classification decisions as the local indexes for further aggregation.

To compute the SSRs from training instances, we could use Support Vector Machines (SVMs) [11] on suitable features for a local image patch. The feature vectors depend on the application domain. Suppose we denote a feature vector as z. A support vector classifier S_i is a detector for SSR i on a region with feature vector z. The classification vector T for region z can be computed via the softmax function [12] as:

$$T_i(z) = \frac{\exp^{S_i(z)}}{\sum_j \exp^{Sj(z)}} \qquad (1)$$

For illustration, we assume both color and texture are important as in the case of consumer images. That is, a feature vector z has two parts, namely, a color feature vector z^c and a texture feature vector z^t. As a working example, for the color feature, we can compute the mean and standard deviation of each color channel (i.e. z^c has 6 dimensions). As another example, for the texture feature, we can compute the Gabor coefficients [13]. Similarly, the means and standard deviations of the Gabor coefficients (e.g. 5 scales and 6 orientations) in an image block are computed as z^t (60 dimensions). Zero-mean normalization [14] is applied to both the color and texture features.

The distance or similarity measure depends on the kernel adopted for the SVMs. Based on past experimentation and for illustration, the polynomial kernels are used here. In order to balance the contributions of the color and texture features, the similarity measure $sim(y,z)$ between feature vector y and z is defined as:

$$sim(y,z) = \frac{1}{2}\left(\frac{y^c \cdot z^c}{|y^c|\,\|z^c|} + \frac{y^t \cdot z^t}{|y^t|\,\|z^t|}\right) \qquad (2)$$

where y•z denotes dot product operation.

The Mercer's condition for the kernel $K(y,z)$ ensures the convergence of the SVM algorithm towards a unique optimum because the SVM problem will be convex whenever a Mercer kernel is used [11]. The Mercer's condition requires that if and only if, for any g(z) such that $\int g(y)^2\, dy$ is finite, then $\int K(y,z)\, g(y)\, g(z)\, dy\, dz \geq 0$. However defining or proving a kernel that satisfies the Mercer's condition is non-trivial. This difficulty has not stopped researchers from experimenting with non-Mercer kernels with practical values (e.g. [15]).

To detect SSRs with translation and scale invariance in an image to be indexed, the image is scanned with windows of different scales. More precisely, given an image I with resolution $M \times N$, the middle layer (Figure 1), Reconciled Detection Map (RDM), has a lower resolution of $P \times Q$, $P \leq M$, $Q \leq N$. Each pixel (p,q) in RDM corresponds to a two-dimensional region of size $r_x \times r_y$ in I. We further allow tessellation displacements $d_x, d_y > 0$ in X, Y directions respectively such that adjacent pixels in RDM along X direction (along Y direction) have receptive fields in I which are displaced by d_x pixels along X direction (d_y pixels along Y direction) in I. At the end of scanning an image, each pixel (p,q) that covers a region z in the pixel-feature layer will consolidate the SSR classification vector $T_i(z)$ (Equation (1)).

As an empirical guideline, we can progressively increase the window size $r_x \times r_y$ from 20 × 20 to 60 × 60 at a displacement (d_x, d_y) of (10, 10) pixels, on a 240 × 360 size-normalized image. That is, after the detection step, we have 5 maps of detection of dimensions 23 × 35 to 19 × 31.

To reconcile the detection maps across different resolutions onto a common basis, we adopt the following principle: If the most confident classification of a region at resolution r is less than that of a larger region (at resolution $r + 1$) that subsumes the region, then the classification output of the region should be replaced by those of the larger region at resolution $r + 1$. For instance, if the detection of a face is more confident than that of a building at the nose region (assuming nose is not in the SSR vocabulary), then the entire region covered by the face, which subsumes the nose region, should be labeled as face.

Using this principle, we start the reconciliation from detection map based on the largest scan window (60 × 60) to the detection map based on next-to-smallest scan window (30 × 30). After 4 cycles of reconciliation, the detection map that is based on the smallest scan window (20 × 20) would have consolidated the detection decisions obtained at other resolutions.

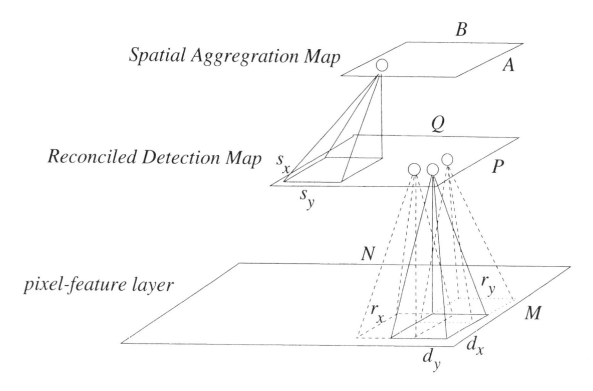

Figure 1. A 3-layer architecture for semantic image indexing.

The purpose of spatial aggregation is to summarize the reconciled detection outcome in a larger spatial region. Suppose a region Z comprises of n small equal regions with feature vectors $z_1, z_2, ..., z_n$ respectively. To account for the size of detected SSRs in the spatial area Z, the SSR classification vectors of the RDM is aggregated as

$$T_i(Z) = \frac{1}{n} \sum_k T_i(z_k)$$

(3)

This is illustrated in Figure 1 where a Spatial Aggregation Map (SAM) further tessellates over RDM with $A \times B$, $A \leq P$, $B \leq Q$ pixels. This form of spatial aggregation does not encode spatial relation explicitly. But the design flexibility of s_x, s_y allows us to specify the location and extent in the image to be focused and indexed. We can choose to ignore unimportant areas (e.g. margins) and emphasize certain areas with overlapping tessellation. We can even have different weights attached to the areas during similarity matching.

That is, for Query by Examples (QBE), the content-based similarity λ between a query q and an image x can be computed in terms of the similarity between their corresponding local tessellated blocks as:

$$\lambda(q,x) = \frac{\sum_j \omega_j \cdot \lambda(Z_j, X_j)}{\sum_k \omega_k} \tag{4}$$

where ω_j are weights, and $\lambda(Z_j, X_j)$ is the similarity between two image blocks. As an important example, the image block similarity based on L_1 distance measure (city block distance) is defined as:

$$\lambda(Z_j, X_j) = 1 - \frac{1}{2}\sum_i |T_i(Z_j) - T_i(X_j)| \tag{5}$$

This is equivalent to histogram intersection [16] except that the bins have semantic interpretation as SSRs. Indeed the SAM has similar representation scheme as local color histograms and hence enjoys similar invariant properties such as translation and rotation invariant about the viewing axis and change only slowly under change of angle of view, change of scale, and occlusion [16].

There is a trade-off between content symmetry and spatial specificity. If we want images of similar semantics with different spatial arrangement (e.g. mirror images) to be treated as similar, we can have larger tessellated blocks (i.e. similar to global histogram). However in applications where spatial locations are considered differentiating, local histograms will provide good sensitivity to spatial specificity.

The effect of averaging in Equation (3) will not dilute $T_i(Z)$ into a flat histogram. As an illustration, we show the $T_i(Z) \geq 0.1$ of SSRs (related to consumer images, see **Semantic Consumer Image Indexing**) in Table 1 for the 3 tessellated blocks (outlined in red) in Figure 2. We observe that the dominant $T_i(Z)$ shown capture the content essence in each block with small values distributed in other bins.

Figure 2. A consumer image example to illustrate SSR-based image index.

Table 1. Key SSRs recorded as index for image shown in Figure 2

Image Block	Key SSRs Aggregated	$T_i(Z)$
Top	Foliage:Green	0.78
Top	Foliage:Branch	0.11
Center	People:Crowd	0.52
Center	Foliage:Green	0.20
Right	People:Crowd	0.36
Right	Building:Old	0.32

Note that we have presented the features, distance measures, kernel functions, and window sizes of SSR-based indexing in concrete forms to facilitate understanding. The SSR-based indexing scheme is indeed generic and flexible to adapt to application domains.

The SSR-based representation and indexing scheme supports visual concept hierarchy. For instance, a two-level IS-A hierarchy has been designed and implemented for consumer images (see **Semantic Consumer Image Indexing**). The learning and detection of SSR classes are based on the more specific SSR classes S_i such as People:Face, Sky:Clear, and Building:City etc and the detection value A_k of a more general concept C_k (e.g. People, Sky, Building) within an image region Z can be derived from the detection values $T_i(Z)$ of those SSR classes S_i that are subclasses of C_k. Since the subclasses S_i under C_k are assumed to be disjoint, $A_k(Z)$ can be computed as:

$$A_k(Z) = \max_i T_i(Z) \qquad (6)$$

On the other hand, a complex visual object can be represented in terms of its parts, i.e. a Part-Whole hierarchy. For instance, a human figure can be represented and detected by the presence of a face and a body. Indeed interesting approaches to recognize objects by their components have been proposed and applied to people detection based on adaptive combination of classifiers (e.g. [17]). This approach is especially useful when a 3D object has no consistent shape representation in a 2D image. The detection of multiple parts of a complex object can help to enhance the detection accuracy although not every part of an object is good candidate for detection (e.g. besides the wheels, the other parts of a car may not possess consistent color, texture, or shape feature for reliable detection).

Similar to the detection in IS-A hierarchy, the detection value B_k of a multi-part object C_k within an image region Z can be inferred from the detection values $T_i(Z)$ of those SSR classes S_i that correspond to the parts of C_k. Since the parts S_i of C_k can co-occur and they occupy spatial areas, $B_k(Z)$ can be derived as:

$$B_k(Z) = \sum_i T_i(Z) \tag{7}$$

This article has focused on local semantic regions learned and extracted from images. The local semantic regions illustrated are based on consumer images (also see article on **Semantic Consumer Image Indexing**). For another illustration on medical images, please refer to article on **Semantic Medical Image Indexing**.

The supervised learning approach described here allows the design of visual semantics with statistical learning. To alleviate the load of labeling image regions as training samples, alternative approach based on semi-supervised learning to discover local image semantics has been explored [19][20].

When the semantics is associated with entire image, image categorization is another approach to bridge the semantic gap and has received more attention lately. For example, a progressive approach to classify vacation photographs based on low-level features such as color, edge directions etc has been attempted [18]. For semantic image indexing related to class information, please see article on **Semantic Class-Based Image Indexing**. Both local and global image semantics can also be combined in image matching to achieve better retrieval performance (see article on **Combining Intra-Image and Inter-Class Semantics for Image Matching**).

References

1. M. Flickner et al., "Query by image and video content: the QBIC system," IEEE Computer, Vol. 28, No. 9, 1995, pp. 23-30.
2. A. Pentland, R.W. Picard, and S. Sclaroff, "Photobook: content-based manipulation of image databases," International Journal of Computer Vision, Vol. 18, No. 3, 1995, pp. 233-254.
3. J.R. Bach et al. "Virage image search engine: an open framework for image management," Proceedings of SPIE 2670, Storage and Retrieval for Image and Video Databases IV, 1996, pp. 76-87.

4. A.W.M. Smeulders et al., "Content-based image retrieval at the end of the early years," IEEE Transactions on Pattern Analysis and Machine Intelligence, Vol. 22, No. 12, 2000, pp. 1349-1380.

5. R. Fergus, P. Perona, and A. Zisserman, "Object class recognition by scale-invariant learning," Proceedings of IEEE CVPR 2003, Vol. 2, 2003, pp. 264-271.

6. V. Ferrari, T. Tuvtelaars, and L.J. van Gool, "Simultaneous object recognition and segmentation by image exploration," Proceedings of the ECCV 2004, 2004, pp. 40-54.

7. I. Cox et al, "The Bayesian image retrieval system, PicHunter: theory, implementation and psychophysical experiments," IEEE Transactions on Image Processing, Vol. 9, No. 1, 2000, pp. 20-37.

8. Y.L. Lu et al., "A unified framework for semantics and feature based relevance feedback in image retrieval systems," Proceedings of ACM Multimedia 2000, 2000, pp. 31-37.

9. L. Armitage and P. Enser, "Analysis of user need in image archives," Journal of Information Science, Vol. 23, No. 4, 1997, pp. 287-299.

10. J.H. Lim and J.S. Jin, "A structured learning framework for content-based image indexing and visual query," Multimedia Systems Journal, 2005.

11. V.N. Vapnik, Statistical Learning Theory, Wiley, New York, 1998.

12. C.M. Bishop, Neural Networks for Pattern Recognition, Clarendon Press, Oxford, 1995.

13. B.S. Manjunath and W.Y. Ma, "Texture features for browsing and retrieval of image data," IEEE Transactions on Pattern Analysis and Machine Intelligence, Vol. 18, No. 8, 1996, pp. 837-842.

14. M. Ortega et al., Supporting similarity queries in MARS, Proceedings of ACM Multimedia 1997, 1997, pp. 403-413.

15. S. Boughorbel, J.-P. Tarel, and F. Fleuret, "Non-Mercer kernel for SVM object recognition," Proceedings of British Machine Vision Conference, London, UK, 2004.

16. M.J. Swain and D.N. Ballard, "Color indexing," International Journal of Computer Vision, Vol. 7, No. 1, 1991, pp. 11-32.

17. A. Mohan, C. Papageorgiou, and T. Poggio, "Example-based object detection in images by components," IEEE Transactions on Pattern Analysis and Machine Intelligence, Vol. 23, No. 4, 2001, pp. 349-361.

18. A. Vailaya et al. "Bayesian framework for hierarchical semantic classification of vacation images," IEEE Transactions on Image Processing, Vol. 10, No. 1, 2001, pp. 117-130.

19. J.H. Lim and J.S. Jin, "Semantics discovery for image indexing," in Tomas Pajdla & Jiri Matas (Eds.), Proceedings of European Conference on Computer Vision, Prague, Czech Republic, May 11-14, 2004, Springer-Verlag, Germany, LNCS 3021, 2004, pp. 270-281.

20. J.H. Lim and J.S. Jin, "Discovering recurrent image semantics from class discrimination," EURASIP Journal of Applied Signal Processing, 2005.

SEMANTIC MEDICAL IMAGE INDEXING

Definition: Semantic information is useful and effective in medical image retrieval and indexing.

Medical images are an integral part in medical diagnosis, research, and teaching. Medical image analysis research has focused on image registration, measurement, and visualization. Besides being valuable for medical research and training, medical image retrieval systems can assist doctors in diagnosis by retrieving images with known pathologies that are similar to a patient's image(s). In reality, pathology bearing regions tend to be highly localized [1]. However, it has been recognized that pathology bearing regions cannot be segmented out automatically for many medical domains [2]. Hence the detection-based Semantic Support Regions (SSRs) representation and indexing scheme described in the article **Semantic Image Representation and Indexing** provides a promising alternative for semantic medical image indexing and retrieval.

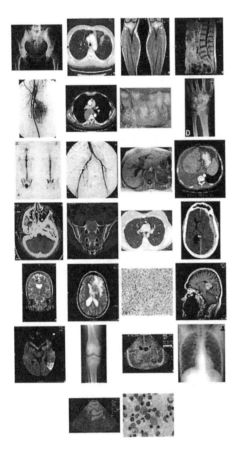

Semantic Support Regions	#	Semantic Support Regions	#
arteriography-agent	40	xray-face	40
xray-neck-spine	30	xray-lung	40
xray-pelvis	40	xray-bone	40
xray-finger	30	xray-joint	40
xray-implant	30	ct-head-brain	20
ct-head-bones	20	ct-thorax-lung	30
ct-abdomen-mediastin	30	ct-abdomen-liver	30
ct-abdomen-intestine	20	ct-abdomen-sacrum	30
mri-head-brain	40	mri-head-bones	20
mri-head-face	30	mri-head-diffusion	30
mri-abdomen-spine	40	mri-abdomen-liver	30
mri-pelvis-tissue	40	mri-legs-coronal	40
ultrasound-grey	30	print-scintigraph	40
print-sketch	30	print-slide	20
print-blank	20	print-dark	20
pathology-pink	20	pathology-blue	20
pathology-purple-big	20	pathology-purple	40
pathology-brown	20	pathology-dark	20
ultrasound-color	20	mouth-teeth	20
mouth-tissue	20	mouth-lesion	30

Figure 1. Example of semantic medical image indexing and retrieval.

Based on 172 images (2%) of the 8725 CasImage collection used in the medical retrieval task of the ImageCLEF 2004 benchmark (http://ir.shef.ac.uk/imageclef2004/), 1170 image regions are cropped to train and validate 40 SSRs (names and numbers of cropped samples as listed in Figure 1) using support vector machines. The Mean Average Precision over 26 query topics (as represented by the query images shown above) is 0.4156, an improvement over all the automatic runs submitted to ImageCLEF 2004. The average precisions at top 10, 20, and 30 retrieved images are 0.70, 0.65, and 0.60 respectively.

References

1. J.G. Dy et al., "Unsupervised feature selection applied to content-based retrieval of lung images," IEEE Transactions on Pattern Analysis and Machine Intelligence, Vol. 25, No. 3, 2003, pp. 373-378.
2. C.R. Shyn et al., "Using human perceptual categories for content-based retrieval from a medical image database," Computer Vision and Image Understanding, Vol. 88, 2002, pp. 119-151.

SEMANTIC VISUAL QUERY AND RETRIEVAL

Definition: *As an alternative to content based queries, semantic visual queries, such as Query by Spatial Icons, allow user to specify visual semantics explicitly based on a predefined visual vocabulary used to index the images.*

Searching images by text queries is effective if the images are associated with comprehensive keywords. Query By Example (QBE) and Query By Canvas (QBC) [1] allow image retrieval based on image contents. However QBE and QBC are implicit as they expect the image retrieval systems to understand the visual semantics embedded in the image or drawn respectively. As an alternative, Query by Spatial Icons (QBSI) [2] allows user to specify visual semantics explicitly based on a predefined visual vocabulary used to index the images (see example in Figure 1).

A QBSI query is composed as a spatial arrangement of visual semantics. A Visual Query Term (VQT) q specifies a region R where a Semantic Support Region (SSR) S_i should appear and a query formulas chains these terms up via logical operators. The truth value $\lambda(q,x)$ of a VQT q for any image x is simply defined as

$$\lambda(q,x) = T_i(R) \tag{1}$$

where $T_i(R)$ is as defined in Equation (3) in the article on **Semantic Image Representation and Indexing**.

A QBSI query Q is a disjunctive normal form of VQTs (with or without negation):

$$Q = (q_{11} \wedge q_{12} \wedge \ldots) \vee \ldots \vee (q_{c1} \wedge q_{c2} \wedge \ldots) \tag{2}$$

The query processing of query Q for any image x is to compute the truth value $\lambda(Q,x)$ using appropriate logical operators. As uncertainty values are involved in SSR detection and indexing, we adopt fuzzy operations [3] as follows (for efficient approximation and other details, please refer to [2]),

$$\lambda(\overline{q},x)=1-\lambda(q,x) \tag{3}$$

$$\lambda(q_i \wedge q_j,x)=min(\lambda(q_i,x),\lambda(q_j,x)) \tag{4}$$

$$\lambda(q_i \vee q_j,x)=max(\lambda(q_i,x),\lambda(q_j,x)) \tag{5}$$

A typical QBSI interface allows a user to specify a VQT by clicking on a SSR icon from a palette of icons associated with the SSRs and dragging it as a rectangle into a canvas. To apply negation, the user can click on the `NOT' button and then the rectangle (a yellow cross will be shown on the selected rectangle). The user can continue to specify more VQT in a conjunct by repeating the above steps. To start a new conjunct in the disjunctive normal form (Equation (2)), the user can click on the `OR' button to start a new canvas with SSR icons.

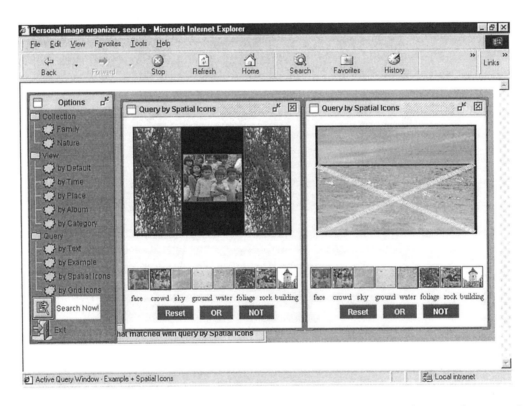

Figure 1. Query by Spatial Icons (QBSI) [2] allows user to specify visual semantics explicitly based on a predefined visual vocabulary used to index the images.

References

1. M. Flickner et al., "Query by image and video content: the QBIC system," IEEE Computer, Vol. 28, No. 9, 1995, pp. 23-30.
2. J.H. Lim and J.S. Jin, "A structured learning framework for content-based image indexing and visual query," Multimedia Systems Journal, 2005.
3. G.J. Klir and T.A. Folger, "Fuzzy Sets, Uncertainty, and Information," Prentice Hall, 1992.

SEMANTIC WEB

Schahram Dustdar
Technical University of Vienna, Austria

Ben Falchuk
Telcordia Technologies, NJ, USA

Definition: *The Semantic Web, in particular the W3C Ontology Web Language (OWL) Recommendation, provides powerful new use-cases for information retrieval, searching, and manipulation.*

Introduction

For the most part, today's World-Wide Web provides the mechanisms for interactions between human users, web servers, and the content stored on servers. The HTML standard, while nicely render-able on Web browsers, is concerned almost exclusively with content *presentation* (as opposed to the meaning). This leads to problems when trying to enable software agent-based interaction with the web server content because HTML may not be easily machine-processable due to under-specified information semantics. Why is agent-based interpretation of the Web important? Consider the following use-cases (some from W3C specifications) which, for various reasons, are difficult to achieve based solely on the first generation Web (see [3] for more details):

- Corporate Web-site management of disparate but related documents such as briefings, research, white papers, and processes
- Automated agent-based search for information; two examples are consumer applications which search for specific travel information, and business agents which search for and automatically inter-work with Internet business partners

The Semantic Web is one solution arc to the above problems; *Description Logics* (DL) combined with description languages such as XML, is another. DL is a family of knowledge representation languages with a formal logic-based semantics and can be an underpinning of domain representation and exploitation.

The remainder of this chapter presents both a review and some current research streams in the area of Semantic Web and Semantic Web Services. The former is concerned mainly with the techniques involved in adding semantics to World-Wide Web content, whereas the latter is focused on adding semantics to the area of Web Services and in describing, finding, and binding to Web Services.

Semantic Web Benefits and Detailed Example

The Semantic Web, in particular the W3C Ontology Web Language (OWL) Recommendation, provides powerful new use-cases for information retrieval, searching, and manipulation. This section provides a high level overview of the arguments that support the above statement. We present a running example (incorporated a W3C example found at www.w3c.org) and describe some of the ways in which OWL facilitates the powerful new use-cases. Where possible, we point out the limitations of the technologies that OWL supersedes (such as HTML, and RDF).

Figure 1 (left) shows the Web Services 'stack', as presented by Tim Berners-Lee in 2003. In comparison to the "current Web" we note that today's Web technology stack (mostly HTML) would mostly sit above XML and below RDF. Related specifications such as Java Server Pages (JSP) (together with Java Server Faces), and Java Script add a layer of sorts above HTML, but with nowhere near the semantic richness of RDF and OWL. Note that Web Services (see www.w3c.org/2002/ws) have a complex 'stack' of syntax protocols themselves. Figure 1 (right) shows a 'join' between 3 disparate 'tables'.

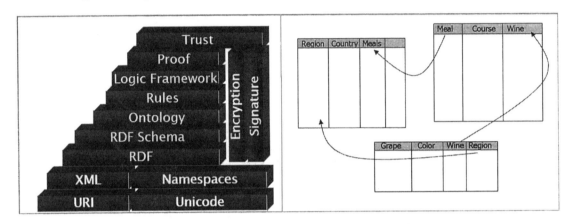

Figure 1. Semantic Web 'stack' (left),
and Semantic Web as Internet 'join' tool (right) (see [1]).

One table stores regions and their traditional meals, another stores meals, courses and wines, while a third stores grapes and their characteristics. In a Relational Database scenario a single company might store all 3 tables using identical technology; a join between them would therefore be simple. On the Internet, we cannot count on information having the format or meaning that we assume. Therefore, an Internet analogy to the Database join would not be easily possible with the current Web. For example, if the three tables were now three Websites with HTML information, one might see an HTML table of meals:

```
<table border="1" cellpadding="0" cellspacing="0" >
  <tr><td>Country</td><td>Region</td><td>Meal</td></tr>
  <tr><td>France</td><td>Bordeaux</td><td>Steak Frites</td></tr>
  <tr><td>France</td><td>Normandy</td><td>Magret de Canard</td></tr>
</table>
```

While the above HTML will render appealingly in most Web browsers and create a meaningful table for human users, the information therein is not easily interpreted by a software agent wishing to 'join' this table with other information. This is because the HTML mixes presentation with semantic tags, cannot not make it explicitly clear what the table semantics are, and does not differentiate instances from labels, from examples, and so on (e.g .all the things that are easy for human readers to do). The HTML <meta> tag can be used to document a limited, but insufficient, amount of page metadata.

The *Web Ontology Language* (OWL), a W3C Recommendation and a Semantic Web building block, supports the kind of machine interpretability described above. W3C's OWL Lite, OWL DL, and OWL Full are the three increasingly powerful variants of the OWL specification. The language is built on formalisms that admit to *Description Logic* (DL) forms and therefore allows reasoning and inference. Reasoning is the act of making implicit knowledge explicit. For example, an OWL knowledge base containing descriptions of students and their parents could infer that two students exhibited the 'brother' relationship if there were both male and shared one or more parent. No explicit markup indicating the 'brotherhood' relationship need ever have been declared. A *Reasoning Engine* is computational machinery that uses facts found in the knowledge base and rules known a priori to determine Subsumption, Classification, Equivalence, and so on. F-OWL, FaCT, and Racer [2] are examples of such engines. OWL Full is so expressive that there are no computational guarantees that inferences can be made effectively and it is unlikely that any such engine will be able to support all its features soon. However, OWL Lite and subsets of OWL DL can be supported.

OWL Syntax and Description of Selected Key Aspects[1]

Suppose, as in the full example found in [3], that one wishes to create an ontology describing the domain of 'wines' (e.g. wine characteristics, wineries, grapes, regions, etc.), or, for example, people, drivers, pets, and animals as in [4]. HTML, XHTML, and XML Schema, while ubiquitous, are not appropriate syntaxes because their semantics are simply not rich enough (and, to be fair, not *designed* to support reasoning).

Classes and Subclasses

OWL classes are groups of individuals that belong together. For example, the set of all 'wheeled vehicles' or the set of all 'wineries'. A class is a key building block in the ontology as it can be subclassed (creating specialization hierarchy), and properties can be defined upon it. Instances of classes (sometimes called individuals) can also be created. The following code shows creation of a simple OWL class called 'vehicle' and subclass called 'bicycle':

```
<owl:Class rdf:about="http://myNS#vehicle">
   <rdfs:label>vehicle</rdfs:label>
</owl:Class>
<owl:Class rdf:about="http://myNS#bicycle">
   <rdfs:label>bicycle</rdfs:label>
   <rdfs:subClassOf><owl:Class
rdf:about="http://myNS#vehicle"/></rdfs:subClassOf>
</owl:Class>
```

---

[1] OWL code snippets are illustrative only. For detailed explanation of the syntax, please see [3]

Class Intersection, Disjointedness and Individual Equivalency

Classes can be defined by logical intersections of other named classes. This is a powerful feature not found in other formats (esp HTML and XML Schema). An example below shows a class called 'grownup' whose members are those that exist as members of both 'person' and 'adult' (i.e. *a grownup is any adult person*):

```
<owl:Class rdf:about="http://myNS#grownup">
<owl:equivalentClass>
<owl:Class><owl:intersectionOf rdf:parseType="Collection">
  <owl:Class rdf:about="http://myNS#adult" />
  <owl:Class rdf:about="http://myNS#person" />
</owl:intersectionOf></owl:Class>
```

It is often useful to model artifacts as disjoint. For example if we want our reasoner to 'catch' the inconsistency of an artifact marked as both 'pasta' and 'fowl', the model can explicitly capture this disjointedness as follows:

```
<owl:Class rdf:ID="pasta">
<owl:disjointWith rdf:resource="#meat"/>
<owl:disjointWith rdf:resource="#fowl"/>
</owl:Class>
```

It is also often useful to allow ontology makers naming flexibility, in particular to allow different names for the same individual. OWL allows such a mechanism - for example, the code below an ontology creator declares Mike's favorite wine as the same individual as 'Texas White':

```
<Wine rdf:ID="MikesFavoriteWine"><owl:sameAs
rdf:resource="#TexasWhite"/></Wine>
```

Properties

Modeling OWL Classes is a key step in ontology creation, but without OWL Properties there is little that ties the classes together beyond subsumption. OWL *Properties* relate classes and individuals to other classes, and also to data values. Each Property has a domain (the individuals to which the property applies) and range (the values the property may have). Properties may also form a hierarchy. For example, the snippet below defines a Property called 'has_pet' which associates 'person's to 'animal' individuals. In addition, the Property is a type of another Property called 'likes', and therefore inherits its characteristics.

```
<owl:ObjectProperty rdf:about="http://myNS#has_pet">
    <rdfs:subPropertyOf rdf:resource="http://myNS#likes" />
<rdfs:domain><owl:Class rdf:about="http://myNS#person" /></rdfs:domain>
<rdfs:range><owl:Class rdf:about="http://myNS#animal" /></rdfs:range>
</owl:ObjectProperty>
```

OWL Properties can also be defined as inverse to each other. For example OWL can capture the notion, "if an animal is 'eaten_by' another, then a 2nd Property 'eats' is the inverse of 'eaten_by' because for any animal X *eaten by* Y the relation Y *eats* X also holds". OWL also supports the modeling of transitive properties.

```
<owl:ObjectProperty rdf:about="http://myNS#eats">
  <rdfs:label>eats</rdfs:label>
  <owl:inverseOf rdf:resource="http://myNS#eaten_by" />
  <rdfs:domain><owl:Class rdf:about="http://myNS#animal" /></rdfs:domain>
</owl:ObjectProperty>
```

It should be becoming clear now how reasoning engines, executing upon large KB's in which inverse and transitive Properties are defined, can exploit the benefits of these rich semantic linkages. Finally, Individuals are instances of Classes and are identified uniquely by the namespace and an rdf:ID identifier. The following OWL denotes that 'CentralCoastRegion' is an individual of the Class 'Region'.

```
<Region rdf:ID="CentralCoastRegion" />
```

This section has outlined only a small subset of the OWL syntax and artifacts. Readers should see [3] and other definitive sources for more details.

OWL Reasoning Examples

In [4] several illustrative examples of inference upon an OWL Knowledge Base (ontology plus its defined individuals) are presented. In general, one can talk about several types of inference which are demonstrable in Description Logics-based systems [5], including those systems captured in OWL:

- Consistency – determine if the model is consistent. For example, [4] presents an OWL model containing the facts: (a) cows are vegetarian, (b) sheep are animals, and (c) a 'mad cow' is one that has eaten sheep brain. From these facts a computational reasoning engine can infer that 'mad cows' are *inconsistent* since any cow eating sheep violates (a). The following (incomplete, but informative) OWL snippets help illustrate some salient issues. Informally, note the description of mad_cow (line 1). Note that mad_cow is an intersection class (line 4) defined as any cow (line 5) that has a property 'eats' (line 6) such that the range of that property (i.e. *what* it eats) is a part_of a sheep (lines 11, 13) and that part is a 'brain' (line 16). Below note that the 'sheep' class is defined as subclass of 'animal' while 'cow' is a subclass of 'vegetarian'.

- Subsumption – infer knowledge structure, mostly hierarchy; the notion of one artifact being more general than another. For example, [4] presents a model incorporating the notions (a) 'drivers drive vehicles', (b) 'bus drivers drive buses', and (b) a bus is a vehicle, and subsumption reasoning allows the inference that 'bus drivers are drivers' (since 'vehicle' is more general than 'bus').

808 S

- <u>Equivalence</u> – determine if classes in the model denote the same set of instances

- <u>Instantiation</u> – determine if an individual is an instance of a given Class. This is also known as 'classification' – that is, determine the instance of a given Class.

- <u>Retrieval</u> – determine the set of individuals that instantiate a given Class

```
<owl:Class rdf:about="http://myNS#mad_cow">
<owl:equivalentClass>
  <owl:Class>
    <owl:intersectionOf rdf:parseType="Collection">
      <owl:Class rdf:about="http://myNS#cow" />
        <owl:Restriction><owl:onProperty
rdf:resource="http://myNS#eats" />
            <owl:someValuesFrom>
              <owl:Class>
                  <owl:intersectionOf rdf:parseType="Collection">
                    <owl:Restriction>
                      <owl:onProperty
rdf:resource="http://myNS#part_of" />
                        <owl:someValuesFrom>
                            <owl:Class rdf:about="http://myNS#sheep" />
                        </owl:someValuesFrom>
                    </owl:Restriction>
                    <owl:Class rdf:about="http://myNS#brain" />
                  </owl:intersectionOf>
              </owl:Class>
            </owl:someValuesFrom>
        </owl:Restriction>
    </owl:intersectionOf>
  </owl:Class>
</owl:equivalentClass>
</owl:Class>

<owl:Class rdf:about="http://myNS#sheep">
  <rdfs:subClassOf>
    <owl:Class rdf:about="http://myNS#animal" />
  </rdfs:subClassOf>
</owl:Class>
<owl:Class rdf:about="http://myNS#cow">
  <rdfs:subClassOf>
    <owl:Class rdf:about="http://myNS#vegetarian" />
  </rdfs:subClassOf>
</owl:Class>
```

OWL's use of formal semantics as well as a language feature-set that is richer than that of RDF and RDF-S, affords OWL models complex reasoning. One tradeoff of such reasoning is efficiency [6]. Table 1 contrasts OWL, and RDF, vis a vis reasoning [5].

Needless to say, XHTML is not designed to provide, and does not provide, any of the mechanisms in Table 1.

Semantic Web Services

Service-Oriented Computing (SoC) and Service-Oriented Architectures have been receiving considerable attention recently and many view them as the emerging distributed computing model for the Internet applications. The Service-Oriented Architecture is manifested by Web Services, which are self-contained, self-describing, modular applications built from components and which may be instantiated on the Internet. The Web Services model develops a componentized view of web applications and is becoming the emerging platform for distributed computing. The standardization process is driven by the growing need to enable dynamic Business-to-Business (B2B) interactions on the Web. Those interactions require smooth choreography (or coordination, orchestration) of Web Services. The Service-Oriented Architecture considers a loosely coupled component model, where a Web Service interface (component) encapsulating any type of business logic is described in a standardized interface definition language, the Web Services Description Language (WSDL). Web Service components interact over an XML messaging protocol and interoperate with other components using the Simple Object Access Protocol (SOAP).

Table 1. Comparison of RDF and OWL
(*Simplified reasoning examples. See [2][5][6] for further details)

Feature	RDF	OWL	Reasoning Example*
Class specification	Classes cannot be built via Boolean combinations.	A Class X *can* be defined, for example, as the intersection between classes Y and Z.	If instance I is belongs to Y and Z it also belongs to X.
Class disjoints	Class disjointed-ness cannot be expressed.	Classes may be fully disjoint from each other (e.g. 'flying vehicles' disjoint from 'land vehicles')	Inconsistency if instance I belongs to 'flying vehicle' *and* 'land vehicle'
Property scope	Property ranges apply to all classes in which it is used.	Property range *restrictions* allow their flexible assignment to only *some* classes only.	More sophisticated models.
Property characteristics	Properties cannot be defined, for example, as transitive or inverse.	Property P, for example, *can* be declared as the inverse of Property Q. e.g. 'X eats Z' is the inverse of 'Z eaten by X'	If P (with range C) holds true on an instance I then Q holds true on C

At the same time, Semantic Web Services combine Web Service standards, briefly outlined above, with semantic techniques, methods, and tools. The research domain of semantic Web Services is fairly new and, therefore, research has yielded many forms of prototypes, proposals and test-beds. The overall goal of initiatives under the semantic Web Services umbrella are to semantically enrich all activities carried out with Web Services, i.e., publishing, finding, and binding Web Services. This enrichment can be basically achieved by allowing for the attachment of semantic information to Web Services artifacts (documents). In related articles in this book we provide a brief overview of some research initiatives in the area of semantic Web Services.

See: Semantic Standards and Recommendations, Agents on the Internet, Role of Semantics in Multimedia, Ontology Design and Languages for Applications, Semantic Web Tools and Technologies, Semantic Web Services

References

1. T. Berners-Lee, "Standards, Semantics, and Survival," a talk given to the *Software and Information Industry Association*, New York, January 2003.
2. V. Haarslev and R. Moller, "Racer: A Core Inference Engine for the Semantic Web," *Proceedings of the 2nd International Workshop on Evaluation of Ontology-based Tools* (EON2003) at 2nd Int'l Semantic Web Conference ISWC 2003, Sanibel Island, pp. 27-36, 2003.
3. World Wide Web Consortium (W3C), "OWL Web Ontology Language Guide," available at http://www.w3.org/TR/owl-guide/.
4. S. Bechhofer, "OWL Reasoning," available at http://owl.man.ac.uk/2003/why/latest/.
5. I. Horrocks, "Logical Foundations for the Semantic Web", a talk given at the University of Glasgow, March 10th, 2003, available at http://www.cs.man.ac.uk/~horrocks.
6. G. Anoniou and F.V.Harmelen, "Semantic Web Primer," MIT Press, Cambridge, 2004

SEMANTIC WEB SERVICES

Definition: The W3C Semantic Web initiative introduces new Web Services which include appropriate service description mechanisms.

Web Services promise a new level of service on top of the current web. However, in order to employ their full potential, appropriate service description mechanisms need to be developed. The W3C Semantic Web initiative intends to overcome these problems by introducing new Web Service methodologies and standards.

Intelligent Web Services

Before the Web Service infrastructure can realize the vision of automated service composition, more work needs to be done. Current technology around UDDI, WSDL, and SOAP provide limited support in mechanizing service recognition, service configuration and combination (i.e., realizing complex workflows and business logics with Web Services), service comparison and automated negotiation. In a business environment the vision of flexible and autonomous Web Service translates into automatic cooperation between enterprise services. Any enterprise requiring a business interaction with another enterprise can automatically discover and select the appropriate optimal Web Services relying on selection policies. Services can be invoked automatically and payment processes can be initiated. Any necessary mediation would be applied based on data and process ontologies and the automatic translation and semantic interoperation. Supply chain relationships where an enterprise who manufactures short-lived goods must frequently and dynamically seek suppliers and buyers, is one example. Therefore, instead of employees constantly searching for suppliers and buyers, the Web Service infrastructure does it automatically within the defined constraints. Other applications areas for this technology are *Enterprise-Application Integration, eWork,* and *Knowledge Management.*

Web Service Technology

The current Web is mainly a collection of information but does not yet provide support in processing this information, i.e. in using the computer as a computational device. Recent efforts around UDDI, WSDL, and SOAP try to lift the Web to a new level of service. Software applications can be accessed and executed via the Web based on the idea of Web Services. Web Services can significantly increase the Web architecture's potential, by providing a way of automated program communication, discovery of services, etc. Therefore, they are the focus of much interest from various software development companies. Web Services connect computers and devices with each other using the Internet to exchange data and combine data in new ways.

The key to Web Services is on-the-fly software composition through the use of loosely coupled, reusable software components. This has fundamental implications for technical and business terms. Software can be delivered and paid for in fluid streams as opposed to packaged products. It is possible to achieve automatic ad hoc interoperability between systems to accomplish organizational tasks: Examples include business applications, such as automated procurement and supply chain management, and military applications. Web Services can be completely decentralized and distributed over the Internet and accessed by a wide variety of communications devices.

Organizations are liberated from complex and expensive software integration to focus instead on the value of their offerings and mission critical tasks. In the Semantic Web Services scenario, dynamic enterprises and value chains become achievable; those enterprises, without such technologies, may lose competitive advantage.

See: Semantic Web

References

1. Additional pointers to literature available at http://www.deri.org.

SEMANTICS STANDARDS AND RECOMMENDATIONS

Definition: *The World Wide Web Consortium (W3C) began their semantic web activities in 2001 by introducing several semantic standards and recommendations, including Resource Description Framework (RDF) and Web Ontology Language (OWL) recommendations.*

Beginning mostly in the late 1990's, researchers began to focus on making their semantic tools' syntaxes and semantics compatible with Internet technologies (e.g. XML, Uniform Resource Identifiers). This was necessary as data sources came online on a global scale, and were open for searching and retrieval by application programs. It was also the result of a challenge from Web visionary Tim Berners-Lee to create the Web's next incarnation. The World Wide Web Consortium (W3C) began their semantic web activities in 2001. In parallel, other research influenced W3C's directions, including: the *Simple Hypertext Ontology Extensions* (SHOE) and the *DARPA Agent Markup Language* (DAML). W3C's work resulted in the *Resource Description Framework* (RDF) and *Web Ontology Language* (OWL) recommendations [1][2].

RDF is "intended to provide a simple way to make statements about Web resources (objects)" [2]. With RDF, objects have properties which in turn have values. RDF uses the URI concept throughout, and while it admits to several concrete syntaxes, XML is the most prevalent. RDF *statements* are triples consisting of a resource, a property and a value (an English analogy: "John Smith edits the web page http://smith.com"). *The RDF Schema* (RDFS), a semantic extension of RDF, allows users to create rich vocabularies (for application domains) that can be used to describe properties of other RDF resources. Together, RDF and RDFS provide a previously unsupported semantics layer to XML and allow collaboration on a global scale (from previously closed-world approaches).

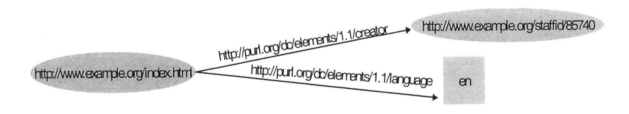

Figure 1. RDF graph representing an object with two properties and their values.

Built upon RDF, the W3C OWL Language was designed to provide more expressive power than RDF, to admit to a formal semantic, to enable reasoning, and to be widely distributed and scalable. Expressivity improvements resulted from OWL's features beyond RDF's fairly rudimentary ones (class, subclass, property, domain, range, etc.); these included concepts of class disjointedness, class union, cardinality restrictions and transitivity among others. OWL formal semantics and reasoning arose from the ability to map the language onto description logics. Already, OWL has interworked with various reasoning engines to provide compelling civilian and military applications (in line with

Berners-Lee's vision). Like RDF, OWL supports distribution via the ability to include and reference resources via URI and scalability through language constructs that allow metadata about classes and ontologies themselves (e.g. naming instances A and B from different ontologies as the "sameAs" each other). The following snippet of the OWL XML syntax illustrates a subclass definition (violin as a type of stringed instrument):

```
<owl:class rdf:ID="violin">
      <rdfs:subclassOf rdf:resource="#stringedInstrument"/>
</owl:class>
```

To satisfy a wide range of application requirements, W3C has proposed OWL in three progressively more powerful sublanguages named: OWL Lite, OWL DL, and OWL Full.

See: Semantic Web

References

1. World Wide Web Consortium, Web-Ontology Working Group, http://www.w3c.org/2001/sw/WebOnt.
2. World Wide Web Consortium, Resource Description Format, http://www.w3c.org/RDF.

SEMANTICS WEB TOOLS AND TECHNOLOGIES

Definition: To realize potential of the Semantic Web, scientists and information technologists must forge new models of cooperation and new thinking must go into the funding and dissemination of this next generation of scientific tools on the Web.

As modern science grows in complexity and scope, the need for more collaboration between scientists at different institutions, in different areas, and across scientific disciplines becomes increasingly important. An emerging generation of World Wide Web technology known as the Semantic Web offers tremendous potential for collaborative and interdisciplinary science. However, to realize this potential, scientists and information technologists must forge new models of cooperation and new thinking must go into the funding and dissemination of this next generation of scientific tools on the Web. This article outlines several such tools.

Sesame

Sesame is an open source RDF [3] database with support for RDF Schema inferencing and querying. Originally, it was developed by Aduna (then known as Administrator) as a research prototype for the EU research project *On-To-Knowledge*. It is now more mature and maintained by Aduna in cooperation with *NLnet Foundation*, developers from *OntoText*, and a number of volunteer developers who contribute ideas, bug reports and fixes. Sesame has been designed with flexibility in mind. It can be deployed on top of a variety of storage systems (relational databases, in-memory, file systems, keyword indexers, etc.), and offers a large scala of tools to developers to leverage the power of RDF and RDF Schema, such as a flexible access API, which supports both local and remote (through HTTP, SOAP or RMI) access, and several query languages of which *SeRQL* is the most powerful [1].

ICS-FORTH RDFSuite

ICS-FORTH R&D activities focus on high-level and scalable software tools enabling the realization of the full potential of the Semantic Web:

- The *Validating RDF Parser* (VRP): The First RDF Parser supporting semantic validation of both resource descriptions and schemas
- The *RDF Schema Specific DataBase* (RSSDB): The First RDF Store using schema knowledge to automatically generate an Object-Relational (SQL3) representation of RDF metadata and load resource descriptions.
- The *RDF Query Language* (RQL): The First Declarative Language for uniformly querying RDF schemas and resource descriptions.

Jena

Jena [2] is a popular Java-based Semantic Web framework. Some of its features are:

- Statement centric methods for manipulating an RDF model as a set of RDF triples
- Resource centric methods for manipulating an RDF model as a set of resources with properties
- Cascading method calls for more convenient programming
- Built in support for RDF containers - bag, alt and seq
- Extensible resources - the application can extend the behaviour of resources
- Integrated parsers and writers for RDF/XML (ARP), N3 and N-TRIPLES
- Support for typed literals

See: Semantic Web

References

1. Aduna BV, OpenRDF, http://www.openrdf.org/about.jsp, 2005.
2. Jena Framework, http://jena.sourceforge.net/, 2005.
3. World Wide Web Consortium, Resource Description Format, http://www.w3c.org/RDF.

SEMIOTICS

Definition: Semiotics, or semiology, is the discipline that studies systems of signs.

One of the precursors of semiotic was a debate, around 300BC, between the Stoics and the Epicureans about the difference between "natural signs" (freely occurring in nature, such as the signs of a disease that were, for the Stoics, the quintessential signs), and "conventional" signs (those designed for the purpose of communication). The interest in signs resounded well with the philosophical interests of the late classic era and the middle ages; St. Augustine was maybe the first to see signs as a proper subject of philosophical investigation, and narrowed it to the study of *signa data*, conventional signs, an emphasis that was to be retaken and exacerbated in the late middle ages by William of Ockam and, in the early modern age, by John Locke.

The birth of modern semiotics is traditionally found in the work of Charles Saunders Pierce, and in Ferdinand de Saussurre's *Cours the linguistique générale.*

Saussurre considers signs as composed of two elements: the *signifier* (more or less the phenomenological impression of the sign, such as the sound of a word), and the *signified* (roughly the mental object associated to the sign), and starts from the consideration that the relation between the two, that is, the signification relation, is *arbitrary*. There is nothing that makes the sequence of three letters /d/, /o/, and /g/ stand for the mental concept *dog*; as a matter of fact, different languages use different signifiers for the same signified (perro, chien, cane, hund, etc.). If the relation is arbitrary, then the only characteristic that allows us to identify "dog" is its difference from other signs of the language: "dog" is what it is because it is not *bog*, or *dot* or, for that matter, *cat*. This leads Saussurre to formulate the structuralist basis of his linguistics: *in a sign system there are only differences, without positive terms.*

Saussurre divides the field of semiotics along two main axes: one is the difference between *la langue* and *la parole*. La langue refers, more or less, to the linguistic system in which the speech acts are possible, while la parole is the study of the individual speech acts. Saussurre claims that the proper goal of linguistics (and, by extension, of semiotics) is the study of la langue. The other distinction is between the *diacronic* study of language—the study of the changes and evolution of language in time—and its *synchronic* study—the study of the linguistic system "frozen" at an instant in time. In this case, Saussurre claims the synchronic study as the proper object of linguistics.

Saussurre recognizes two important classes of relations between signs, which he calls *syntagmatic* and *paradigmatic*. In a phrase such as "the cat is on the mat," the signs "cat," "is," or "mat," stand in a syntagmatic relation: they are related by juxtaposition and their relation contributes to the meaning of the phrase. On the other hand, one could, in the same syntagmatic structure, replace "cat" with "dog" or "mat" with "couch." Replaceability constitutes a paradigmatic relation. This can be represented in a schema

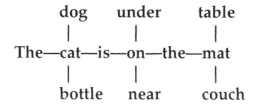

where the horizontal relations are syntagms, while the vertical are paradigms.

Charles Saunders Peirce developed his "semeiotic" independently of Saussurre and with a less linguistic perspective. He considers a sign as composed by three elements: a *representamen* (the material component of the sign), an *object* (more or less corresponding to Saussurre's signified), and the *interpretant*. The concept of the interpretant is difficult, and it must be stressed that the Peircean interpretant is *not* the "interpreter," but can be seen, roughly, as the *proper significant effect* of the sign, a sign in the mind that is the result of the meeting with the sign.

This sign can in itself have an interpretant, which has an interpretant, and so on to generate the process that Pierce calls *unlimited semiosis*. Unlimited semiosis is only a potential, of course, since at one point the necessities of practical life demand that the interpretation stops. A mathematician could say that unlimited semiosis is a converging series, an idea with which Peirce would, in all likelihood, substantially agree.

Peirce considers three classes of signs, which he classifies depending on the relation between the sign and its object: a sign is *iconic* if it signified by virtue of its similarity with an object (as in the case of a picture of Bishop Tutu, which "means" Bishop Tutu); it is *indexical* if it stands in a causal relation with its object (as in the case of the smoke being a sign of fire, or of red dots on the skin being a sign of measles); it is *symbolic* if the relation between the sign and its object is arbitrary (as in the case of language).

This is the best known of Peirce's triadic distinctions, but his system is more complex: at the level of the representamen a sign can be a *qualisign* (a representamen made up of a quality, e.g. a color), a *sinsign* (a representamen made up of an existing physical reality, e.g. a road sign on a specific street), or a *legisign* (a representamen resting on a law, e.g. the sound of a referee in a football match). At the level of the object, the sign can be, as seen, an icon, an index, or a symbol. At the sign of the interpretant, a sign can be a *rheme* (the sign is represented as a possibility, e.g. a concept), a *dicent* (the sign is represented as a fact, e.g. a descriptive statement), or an *argument* (the sign is represented as a reason, e.g. a proposition).

These categories interact and overlap in signs.

See: Multimedia Semiotics

SHARABLE CONTENT OBJECT REFERENCE MODEL (SCORM)

Definition: The Advanced Distributed Learning (ADL) initiative introduced the Sharable Content Object Reference Model (SCORM) standard, which is intended for multimedia presentations in distance learning applications.

Distance Learning is an important application of multimedia technology. Usually, multimedia presentations contain instructional materials that can be delivered on the Internet and presented on Web browsers. In order to reuse materials and to deliver presentations on different platforms, standards are needed. The Advanced Distributed Learning (ADL) initiative (http://www.adlnet.org/) first proposed the Sharable Content Object Reference Model (SCORM) standard in 2000. Main contributors to SCORM include the IMS Global Learning Consortium, Inc. (http://www.imsglobal.org/), the Aviation Industry CBT (Computer-Based Training) Committee (AICC) (http://www.aicc.org/), the Alliance of Remote Instructional Authoring & Distribution Networks for Europe (ARIADNE) (http://www.ariadne.eu-org/), and the Institute of Electrical and Electronics Engineers (IEEE) Learning Technology Standards Committee (LTSC) (http://ltsc.ieee.org/). SCORM addresses the following four high-level requirements (http://www.adlnet.org/):

- <u>Reusability:</u> the flexibility to incorporate course materials in multiple instructions.
- <u>Interoperability:</u> the ability to take course materials developed in one location with one set of tools or platform and to use them in another location with a different set of tools or platform.
- <u>Accessibility:</u> the ability to locate and access course materials from one location and deliver them to many other locations.
- <u>Durability:</u> the ability to withstand technology changes without redesign, reconfiguration or recoding.

Reusability can be achieved by using SCORM-compliant authoring tools, which can be used to produce course materials that may be decomposed, shared, and reused among different lectures. Interoperability can be achieved by using a SCORM-compliant Learning Management System (LMS), which also includes a sequence engine to control user interactions. The SCORM 2004 (also known as SCORM 1.3) specification consists of three major parts: the Content Aggregation Model (CAM), the Run-Time Environment, and the Sequencing and Navigation.

- <u>The Content Aggregation Model (CAM):</u> Learning objects are divided into three categories (i.e., Assets, Sharable Content Objects (SCOs) and Content Organizations – these will be explained later). The contents of the learning objects are described by metadata. In addition, CAM includes a definition of how reusable learning objects can be packed, delivered, and used.
- <u>The Run-Time Environment:</u> In order to deliver learning objects to different platforms, a standard method of communication between the learning management system (LMS) and the learning objects is defined.
- <u>The Sequencing and Navigation:</u> Interactions between users (i.e., students) and the LMS are controlled and tracked by the Sequencing and Navigation definitions. This also serves as a standard for defining learner profiles, as well as a possible definition for intelligent tutoring.

The ADL initiative organizes Plugfest conferences every year. The events allow developers to exchange experiences and demonstrate newly developed tools. The SCORM specification is well-adapted by content providers and software developers of distance learning. Part of the SCORM specification (i.e., LOM) has becomes an international standard. Within a few years, I believe SCORM will be a promise of future distance learning standard.

See: Personalized Educational Hypermedia

References

1. http://www.adlnet.org/, SCORM specification, the Advanced Distributed Learning (ADL) initiative.

SIMD (SINGLE INSTRUCTION MULTIPLE DATA) PROCESSING

Definition: SIMD processing, in which single instruction is applied on multiple data, is suitable for multimedia processing, and therefore it is implemented in contemporary processors.

Single instruction multiple data (SIMD), as the name suggests, takes an operation specified in one instruction and applies it to more than one set of data elements at the same time. For example, in a traditional scalar microprocessor, an add operation would add together a single pair of operands and produce a single result. In SIMD processing, a number of independent operand pairs are added together to produce the same number of independent sums. Figure 1 illustrates traditional and SIMD processing.

The number of parallel data elements processed at the same time is dependent on the size of the elements and the capacity of the data processing resources available. Usually the capacity of the data processing resources is fixed for a given architecture.

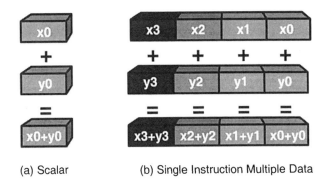

(a) Scalar   (b) Single Instruction Multiple Data

Figure 1. (a) Scalar processing, (b) SIMD processing.

Advantages of SIMD

The main advantage of SIMD is that processing multiple data elements at the same time, with a single instruction, can dramatically improve performance. For example, processing 12 data items could take 12 instructions for scalar processing, but would require only three instructions if four data elements are processed per instruction using

SIMD. While the exact increase in code speed that you observe depends on many factors, you can achieve a dramatic performance boost if SIMD techniques can be utilized. Not everything is suitable for SIMD processing, and not all parts of an application need to be SIMD accelerated to realize significant improvements.

Wireless MMX Technology

The Wireless MMX unit is an example of a SIMD coprocessor. It is a 64-bit architecture that is is an extension of the XScale microarchitecture programming model. Wireless MMX technology defines three packed data types (8-bit byte, 16-bit half word and 32-bit word) and the 64-bit double word. The elements in these packed data types may be represented as signed or unsigned fixed point integers Wireless MMX technology comprises five key functional units to implement the programmers model. Figure 2 shows the organization of the functional units within the coprocessor.

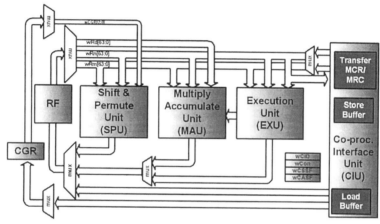

Figure 2. The organizational of the Intel's wireless MMX functional unit, which implements SIMD technology.

See: Multimedia System-on-a-Chip, Intel® XScale® Micro-architecture

References

1. N.C. Paver, B. C. Aldrich, and M. H. Khan, "Programming with Intel® Wireless MMX™ Technology: A Developer's Guide to Mobile Multimedia Applications," Hillsboro, OR, Intel Press, 2004.

SPECTRAL MODEL

Definition: Single-sensor solutions may employ a spectral model in the processing pipeline in order to take advantage of both the spatial and spectral properties of the available samples and thus eliminate color shifts and artifacts in output, single-sensor captured images [1]-[3].

The fundamental rationale behind the introduction of the spectral model is that a typical natural image exhibits significant spectral correlation among its Red-Green-Blue (RGB) color planes, as well as significant spatial correlation among its spatially neighboring pixels. Since natural color images do not have large areas exhibiting uniform image characteristics or small variations in pixels' values, modeling constraints are applied to spatial locations neighboring the pixel location selected for processing. Smoothly changing spectral image characteristics are enforced by averaging the obtained spectral quantities in the considered spatial neighborhood.

The currently used spectral models are based on the assumption of color hue or intensity constancy in localized image regions. However, these modeling assumptions often break down in high-frequency image regions. Recently proposed designs are able to overcome the limitations of the basic spectral modeling approaches, provide more degrees of freedom in modeling the spectral characteristics of the captured image, and are able to enforce the modeling assumption in both flat and high-frequency areas [1]-[3].

Since the human visual system is more sensitive to luminance information which is composed primarily of green light, most spectral models are based on a two-channel information (RG or BG) base [1],[2]. Such an approach is sufficient in color filter array (CFA) image zooming applications, however, it is of limited value in both the demosaicking and the postprocessing/enhancement phase of the single-sensor imaging pipeline [3]. To reduce processing errors, a vector model should be employed in order to utilize the complete available spectral information [3]. The vector model is a generalized spectral model which can be used to support processing of multi-dimensional data sets such as the captured image data. Through the refined tuning of its behavior, the vector spectral model controls the influence of both the directional and the magnitude characteristics of the neighboring pixels utilized during processing. New single-sensor solutions, with different design characteristics and performance, can be obtained by modifying the way the vector model is operating.

A generalized vector model can be made flexible enough to support any camera image processing operations such as demosaicking, demosaicked image postprocessing and CFA zooming. In addition, it can be used in applications such as computer graphics and color image processing to support denoising, image analysis, and color constancy algorithms. Thus, it constitutes a unique and powerful solution for the image processing pipeline [3].

See: Digital camera image processing, Demosaicking, CFA image zooming, Demosaicked image postprocessing, Color image zooming, Edge-sensing mechanism, Color image processing and enhancement.

References

1. R. Lukac and K.-N. Plataniotis, "Normalized Color-Ratio Modeling for CFA Interpolation," IEEE Transactions on Consumer Electronics, Vol. 50, No. 2, May 2004, pp. 737-745.
2. R. Lukac, K. Martin, and K.-N. Plataniotis, "Demosaicked Image Postprocessing Using Local Color Ratios," IEEE Transactions on Circuits and Systems for Video Technology, Vol. 14, No. 6, June 2004, pp. 914-920.
3. R. Lukac and K.-N. Plataniotis, "A Vector Spectral Model for Digital Camera Image Processing," IEEE Transactions on Circuit and Systems for Video Technology, submitted.

STEREOSCOPIC AND MULTI-VIEW VIDEO CODING STANDARDS

Definition: The Multiview Profile (MVP) extends the well-known hybrid coding towards exploitation of inter-view channel redundancies by implicitly defining disparity-compensated prediction.

Stereo video coding is already supported by the MPEG-2 technology, where a corresponding multi-view profile, defined in 1996, is available to transmit two video signals. The main application area of MPEG-2 multiview profile (MVP) is stereoscopic TV. The MVP extends the well-known hybrid coding towards exploitation of inter-view channel redundancies by implicitly defining disparity-compensated prediction. The main new elements are the definition of usage of the temporal scalability (TS) mode for multi-camera sequences, and the definition of acquisition parameters in the MPEG-2 syntax. The TS mode was originally developed to allow the joint encoding of a low frame rate base layer stream and an enhancement layer stream comprised of additional video frames. In the TS mode, temporal prediction of enhancement layer macro-blocks could be performed either from a base layer frame, or from the recently reconstructed enhancement layer frame. To encode stereo or multi-channel signals, frames from one camera view are defined as the base layer, and frames from the other one(s) as enhancement layer(s). Thus both disparity-compensated and motion-compensated prediction can simultaneously be used, while compatibility with monoscopic decoders is achieved, since the base layer represents a monoscopic sequence. However, there are important disadvantages: disparity vectors fields are sparse and thus the disparity-compensation is not efficient so motion-compensation is usually preferred. Furthermore, the technology is outdated and interactive applications that involve view interpolation cannot be supported.

To provide support for interactive applications, enhanced depth and/or disparity information about the scene has to be included in the bit stream, which can also be used for synthesizing virtual views from intermediate viewpoints. Experiments for encoding depth data using different video codecs by putting the depth data into the luminance channel, and simply changing the semantics of its description have been conducted by MPEG and the ATTEST IST project. Results show that this approach makes it possible to achieve extreme compression of depth data while still maintaining a good quality level for both decoded depth and any generated novel views. Furthermore, hidden (occlusion) information can be included in the form of additional MPEG-4 Video Object Planes (VOPs) or, preferably, Layered Depth Images, which are defined in a new part of MPEG-4 called Animation Framework eXtension (AFX).

Another useful tool for storing such information are the Multiple Auxiliary Components (MAC), defined by MPEG-4, where grayscale shape is generalized to include further information, besides describing the transparency of the video object. MACs are defined for a video object plane (VOP) on a pixel-by-pixel basis, and contain additional data related to the video object, such as disparity, depth, and additional texture. Up to three auxiliary components (including the grayscale or alpha shape) are possible. Only a limited number of types and combinations are defined and identified by a 4-bit integer so far, but more applications are possible by selection of a USER DEFINED type or by definition of new types. All the auxiliary components can be encoded by the shape coding tools and usually have the same shape and resolution as the texture of the video object.

See: Coding of stereoscopic and 3D images and video

References

1. A. Smolic, C. Fehn, K. Müller, and D. McCutchen. MPEG 3DAV – Video-Based Rendering for Interactive TV Applications, "Proceedings of 10th Dortmunder Fernsehseminar, Dortmund, Germany, September 2003.
2. C. Fehn, E. Cooke, O. Schreer, and P. Kauff, "3D Analysis and Image-Based Rendering for Immersive TV Applications," Signal Processing: Image Communication Journal, Special Issue on Image Processing Techniques for Virtual Environments and 3D Imaging, Vol. 17, No. 9, pp. 705-715, October 2002.

STREAMING MULTIMEDIA AND ITS APPLICATIONS IN EDUCATION

Definition: State-of-the-art streaming media-based educational systems are required to blend various types of media technologies and different types of Web-based communications technologies including email, chat, instant messaging, audio and videoconferencing, bulletin boards, discussion forums, newsgroups, white boarding, groupware (shared workplaces), and Web sites for collaborative learning.

Streaming technology

Streaming is a term used to describe the transmission of various media objects (files) from media servers to multiple users over satellites, across broadband networks, across the Internet or on corporate intranets. Streaming is a special way of sending multimedia files so that playback begins as the first data packets arrive – there are no lengthy download waits before the user(s) can view the requested multimedia content. Fast growing streaming technology differs from the well-known downloading of multimedia files in that streamed files are not entirely copied to the client computer [1]. In accordance with *AccuStream imedia research*, in 2004 alone, about 10 billion video streams served, 79 % were at broadband (100 kbps and above) rates, with an average length of view of 30 minutes per unique user per month per site.

Multimedia technology

Multimedia is a term used to describe simultaneous use of several different media to deliver information to users. As the information is presented in various digital formats, multimedia enhances user (learner) experience and makes it easier and faster to grasp information (learning content) [2]. These days, the most popular types of educational media and corresponding digital formats are 1) Web-based text (PDF, DOC, XLS, HTML, XML, PPT formats), 2) Web-based graphics, drawings, paintings, pictures, photos (JPEG,

BMP, GIF, VML, SVG formats), 3) audio, sound, music (MP3, Real Audio, WMA, AVI formats), 4) video, films, movies (AVI, MPEG, MOV, QT, RV, WMV, clips), 5) animation (animated GIF, dynamic HTML, Flash, Director Shockwave, etc.), 6) virtual reality, virtual worlds, 3D animation (VRML format), 7) software simulation and programming files (VB, C++, Java, PHP, etc.), and 8) programming or scripting files (JavaScript, VBScript, etc.) [2, 3].

Streaming media-based systems for education and training

State-of-the-art streaming media-based educational systems are required to blend 5-10 various types of media technologies and 5-7 different types of web-based communications technologies such as 1) email, 2) chat, IRC, 3) instant messaging, 4) audio- and video-conferencing, 5) bulletin boards, discussion forums, newsgroups, 6) white boarding (application and document sharing), 7) groupware (shared workplaces), and 8) web sites for collaborative learning.

A combination of rich media and communication strongly supports the *learning-by-doing* paradigm of learning; it leads to the highest possible (up to 90-95%) retention rate for students and learners [3] while *learning-by-saying-and-writing* technology provides about 70-75% retention rate, *learning-by-hearing-and-seeing* - 40-70%, *learning-by-seeing* – 40-50%, and, *learning-by-reading* technology – only 20-40% retention rate.

See: Personalized Educational Hypermedia

References

1. E. Menin, "Streaming Media Handbook," Upper Saddle River: Pearson Education, 2003.
2. W. Horton, "Designing Web-Based Training," Wiley Computer Publishing, 2000.
3. V. Uskov and A. Uskov, "Blending Streaming Multimedia and Communication Technology in Advanced Web-Based Education," International Journal on Advanced Technology for Learning, Vol. 1, No. 1, 2004, pp. 54-66.

T

TELECONFERENCING

Shervin Shirmohammadi
University of Ottawa, Canada

Jauvane C. de Oliveira
National Laboratory for Scientific Computation, Petrópolis, RJ, Brazil

Definition: *Teleconferencing is an aggregation of audio conferencing, video conferencing, and data conferencing, and includes multiple participants in a live real-time session.*

Introduction

Teleconferencing (a.k.a. Multimedia Conference Services [4]) consists of a live real-time session between multiple participants with the ability to hear and see each other as well as share data and applications. Alternatively, teleconferencing can be thought of as an aggregation of *audio conferencing, video conferencing*, and *data conferencing* (or application sharing). Although a subject of interest for many years, teleconferencing has recently grabbed a lot of attention due to current economic and social trends, which emphasize the need for rich media communication between geographically-distributed people. Economic incentives include cutting traveling costs, as well as reducing security risks, and increasing worker availability, whereas social incentives are caused by the higher expectations from technology and experience of ordinary users of today.

Figure 1 shows a sample teleconferencing session in the JETS 2000 system [1]. The participants in this session can see and hear each other, in addition to being able to do whiteboarding and application sharing. It should be noted that teleconferencing is, by nature, a *live* and therefore *real-time* multimedia application. Offline communication paradigms such as blogs, chat boards, and email are not considered to be part of teleconferencing.

Services and Requirements

A typical multimedia teleconferencing system should provide the following services:

- audio conferencing
- video conferencing

- data conferencing
- control and signaling

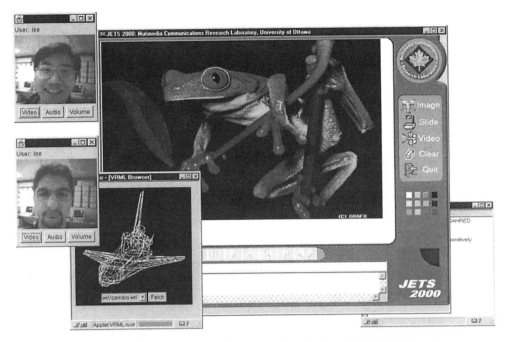

Figure 1. A Teleconferencing session running in the JETS 2000 system.

Since these services are provided in a live environment, communication lag and deficiencies such as delay, jitter, packet loss, and lack of sufficient bandwidth adversely affects the execution of the teleconferencing session. This is particularly significant in networks that don't guarantee quality of service, such as the Internet.

Audio and video are medium which are continuous by nature. As such, they both suffer from network lag. However, it is a well-known fact that, from a human perception point of view, audio is affected more adversely than video in the presence of network lag. For example, if a given video frame is delayed, one can simply repeat the previous frame until the new one arrives. This causes some "unnaturalness" in the video, but it is acceptable for all practical purposes if the repeat duration is not too long. For audio streaming; however, if audio samples are delayed, they are either replaced by undesirable silence, which become especially irritating when happening in the middle of a word, or they are replaced by the last samples available until new ones arrive, which causes noise. In both cases, the flow of audio not only becomes unnatural, but also the conversation becomes incomprehensible. Under less than desirable network conditions, participants in teleconferencing do experience such problems. In order to mitigate this undesirable phenomenon, it is common to buffer a given amount of audio and video so that there is something available for playback in the event that delays occur. Naturally this buffering introduces further delay and needs to be limited, especially in the context of a live session. To accommodate the transmission of audio and video over the network, protocols such as the RTP (Real-time Transport Protocol) [2] are used.

Teleconferencing Standards

In any field, standards are needed for compatibility: allowing products and services offered by different vendors to interoperate. Teleconferencing is no exception. In fact, the need for standards in teleconferencing is most crucial due to the large number of network operators, product vendors, and service providers.

The International Telecommunications Union – Telecommunications Standardization Sector (ITU-T) [2] has created a large set of recommendations that deal with teleconferencing, encompassing audio, video, data, and signaling requirements. The ITU-T F.702 recommendation describes what is known as Multimedia Conference Services [4]. It defines the terminology used in multimedia conferencing, as well as a description of the service with a functional model, configuration, and roles of participants, terminal aspects, applications, and additional services. There is a set of recommendations which are typically umbrella standards, each containing a number of other recommendations specifically for audio, video, data, and signaling. The most widely-used of such umbrella standards for teleconferencing on the Internet is the ITU-T H.323 [19].

ITU-T H.323 – Packet-based multimedia communications systems

The H.323 standard provides a foundation for real-time audio, video and/or data communications across packet-based networks, such as the Internet. Support for audio is mandatory, while data and video are optional [19]. By complying with the H.323 recommendation, multimedia products and applications from multiple vendors can interoperate, allowing users to communicate with ensured compatibility. H.323 is specifically designed for multimedia communications services over Packet Based Networks (PBN) which may not provide a guaranteed Quality of Service (QoS), such as the Internet.

The standard is quite broad in its scope. It encompasses stand-alone devices, embedded devices, point-to-point, and multipoint conferences. It also covers issues such as multimedia management, bandwidth management, and interoperation with various terminal types.

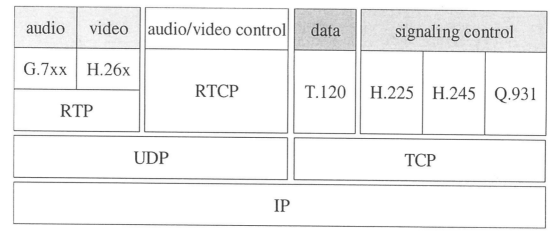

Figure 2. An example configuration of ITU-T H.323.

As an umbrella standard, H.323 specifies other standards for audio, video, data, and signaling. Figure 2 shows an example of an H.323 recommendation compliant system, illustrating audio, video, data, and signaling, and their relation with ITU-T standards and the TCP/IP protocol stack.

The specific components are briefly discussed next.

Call signaling and control

Call signaling and control is concerned mostly with setting up, maintaining, and taking down connections between teleconferencing parties. In addition, the recommendations define a *Gateway*: an optional element that provides many services, mainly used for translating between H.323 conferencing endpoints and other terminal types. This includes translation between transmission formats (H.225.0 to H.221) and between communications procedures (H.245 to H.242 [12]). The Gateway also translates between audio and video codecs and performs call setup and clearing on both the packet-based and the switched-circuit network side. Some of the relevant standards for signaling and control are:

- H.225.0 – Call signaling protocols and media stream packetization for packet-based multimedia communication systems [10].

- H.235 – Security and encryption for H-series (H.323 and other H.245-based) multimedia terminals [11].

- H.245 – Control protocol for multimedia communication [13].

- Q.931 – ISDN user-network interface layer 3 specification for basic call control [22].

- H.450.1 – Generic functional protocol for the support of supplementary services in H.323 [21].

Audio

Audio signals transmitted over the network are digitized and, most of the time, compressed. H.323 supports a number of compression algorithms but only one is mandatory: H.323 terminals must support the G.711 recommendation [5] for speech coding, which is basically uncompressed 8-bit PCM signal at 8KHz in either A-Law or μ-Law format, leading to bitrates of 56 or 64kbps. Support for other ITU-T audio recommendations and compressions is optional, and is implementation specific depending on the required speech quality, bit rate, computational power, and delay. Provisions for asymmetric operation of audio codecs have also been made; i.e., it is possible to send audio using one codec but receive audio using another codec. If the G.723.1 [7] audio compression standard is provided, the terminal must be able to encode and decode at both the 5.3 kbps and the 6.3 kbps modes. If a terminal is audio only, it should also support the ITU-T G.729 recommendation [9]. Note that if a terminals is known to be on a low-bandwidth network (<64kbps), it does not need to disclose capability to receive G.711 audio since it won't practically be able to do so. The relevant H.323 audio codecs are:

- G.711 – Pulse Code Modulation (PCM) of voice frequencies [5].

- G.722 – 7 kHz audio-coding within 64 kbit/s [6].

- G.723.1 – Dual rate speech coder for multimedia communications transmitting at 5.3 and 6.3 kbit/s [7].

- G.728 – Coding of speech at 16 kbit/s using low-delay code excited linear prediction [8].

- G.729 – Coding of speech at 8 kbit/s using conjugate-structure algebraic-code-excited linear-prediction (CS-ACELP) [9].

Video

Video support in H.323 is optional. However, if a terminal is to support video, it must at the very least support the H.261 [14] codec at the QCIF frame format. Support for other H.261 modes or the H.263 [15] codec is optional. During the initial setup, a specific video data rate is selected during the capability exchange. This rate should not be violated throughout the duration of the session. The H.261 standard uses communication channels that are multiples of 64 kbps, known as p×64, where p ∈ {1, 2, 3, ... 30]. From a video encoding perspective, there are no Bidirectional or 'B' frames in H.261. Instead, it uses Intra or 'I' frames which are fully and independently encoded, and Predicted or 'P' frames which code the difference between the frame and its previous frame by using motion estimation.

Compared to H.261, H.263 uses 1/2 pixel motion-estimation for better picture quality, and a Huffman coding table that is optimized specifically for low bit rate transmissions. H.263 defines more picture modes than H.261, as seen in Table 1. In addition, H.263 introduces the PB frames, which consist of a P frame interpolated with a Bi-directional or 'B' frame: a frame that depends not only on a previous frame but also on a forthcoming frame. Similar to a P frame, a B frame uses motion estimation to reduce the amount of information to carry. See the related article on "Video Compression and Coding Techniques" and "Motion Estimation" for further details.

Data Conferencing

The ITU-T has a set of standards for data conferencing and application sharing. The ITU-T T.120 recommendation [23] summarizes the relationships amongst a set of protocols for data conferencing, providing real-time communication between two or more entities in a conference. Applications specified as part of the T.120 family include application sharing, electronic whiteboarding, file exchange, and chat.

Table 1. ITU-T standard frame formats for H.261 and H.263.

Picture Format	Frame Size	H.261	H.263
SQCIF	128x96	not specified*	required
QCIF	176x144	Required	required
CIF	352x288	Optional	optional
4CIF	704x576	N/A	optional
16CIF	1408x1152	N/A	optional

* There is an indication that SQCIF frame format may be supported by H.261 by using padding bits to make it fit into a QCIF frame, which is fully supported by H.261. Such padding bits will have a high-compression rate, which will lead to few extra bits in the bitstream.

Data conferencing is an optional capability in multimedia conferences. When supported, data conferencing enables collaboration through applications such as whiteboards, application sharing, and file transfer. The list below summarizes the related recommendations in the T.120 family set forth herein:

- T.120 – Data protocols for multimedia conferencing [23].

- T.121 – Generic application template [24]: It defines the generic application template (GAT), specifying guidelines for building application protocols and facilities that manage the control of the resources used by the application. T.121 is a mandatory standard for products that support T.120.

- T.122 – Multipoint communication service - Service definition [25]: It defines the multipoint services allowing one or more participants to send data. The actual mechanism for transporting the data is defined by T.125, T.122 and T.125 together constitute the T.120 multipoint communication services (MCS).

- T.123 – Network-specific data protocol stacks for multimedia conferencing [26]: It defines the sequencing and transporting of the data and its flow control across the network.

- T.124 – Generic Conference Control [27]: It defines the generic conference control (GCC) for initiating and maintaining multipoint data conferences. The lists of conference participants, their applications, and the latest conference information is kept here.

- T.125 – Multipoint communication service protocol specification [28]: It defines how data is actually transmitted. One can think of T.125 as the implementation of T.122 services, among other things.

- T.126 – Multipoint still image and annotation protocol [29]: It defines how the whiteboard application sends and receives data. Both compressed and uncompressed form for viewing and updating are supported.

- T.127 – Multipoint binary file transfer protocol [30]: It defines how files are transferred, sometimes simultaneously, among users. Similar to T.126, it supports both compressed and uncompressed forms.

- T.128 – Multipoint application sharing [31]: It defines the program sharing protocol; i.e., how participants can share programs that are running locally.

Other Standards

H.320 Narrow-band visual telephone systems and terminal equipment (March 2004) [16] supports videoconferencing over ISDN. This protocol has a long and successful history. Sometimes considered a 'legacy' protocol, private industry still relies heavily on this protocol, and it provides an important bridge to the PSTN.

H.321 Adaptation of H.320 visual telephone terminals to B-ISDN environments (Feb 98) [17] provides support for videoconferencing over ATM. A number of successful systems have been built upon this technology, though the general scarce deployment of ATM limits the overall reach of these systems.

H.322 Visual telephone systems and terminal equipment for local area networks which provide a guaranteed quality of service (Mar 96) [18] used over LANs that guarantee bandwidth, such as ISO-Ethernet.

H.324 Terminal for low bit-rate multimedia communication (Mar 2002) [20] provides support for low bandwidth videoconferencing over PSTN. This protocol enjoys success particularly in Asian cellular markets.

Tools

There are many teleconferencing tools currently available. Some of the most popular commercial tools are Microsoft's NetMeeting [33], CU-SeeMe [35], ICUII [36], and Isabel developed at the Universidad Politécnica de Madrid [34]. In terms of open-source solutions, OpenH323 [32] is a widely used platform that implements the H.323 standard.

Recording a Teleconference Session

The ability to record a teleconferencing session is an important requirement for many applications. In many cases, it is necessary to play back the events that took place in a session. For example, when a participant misses a teleconferencing meeting, he/she can play back exactly what happened in the meeting, if the session was recorded. This includes conversations and discussions among participants, as well as applications and documents that were shared. Ideally, this recording should be done in a transparent way; i.e., user applications need not be modified for this recording to take place. One approach to achieve this would be for the "recorder" module to join the session as a regular client and observe what is taking place and record it. This is also referred to as non-intrusive recording. The J-VCR system is an example of a non-intrusive teleconferencing recording tool [37].

See: Video Conferencing, Audio Conferencing, Data Conferencing, Recording Teleconference Sessions

References

1. S. Shirmohammadi, J.C. Oliveira, and N.D. Georganas, "Applet-Based Telecollaboration: A Network-Centric Approach," IEEE Multimedia, Vol. 5, No. 2, April-June 1998, pp. 64-73.
2. H. Schulzrinne, S. Casner, R. Frederick, and V. Jacobson, "RTP: A Transport Protocol for Real-Time Applications," IETF RFC 1889, January 1996.
3. International Telecommunication Union, Telecommunication Standardization Sector http://www.itu.int/ITU-T.
4. International Telecommunication Union, Telecommunication Standardization Sector F.702 Recommendation – Multimedia Conference Services, July 1996.
5. International Telecommunication Union, Telecommunication Standardization Sector G.711 Recommendation – Pulse code modulation (PCM) of voice frequencies, November 1988.
6. International Telecommunication Union, Telecommunication Standardization Sector G.722 Recommendation – 7 kHz audio-coding within 64 kbit/s, November 1988.
7. International Telecommunication Union, Telecommunication Standardization Sector G.723.1 Recommendation – Dual rate speech coder for multimedia communications transmitting at 5.3 and 6.3 kbit/s, March 1996.
8. International Telecommunication Union, Telecommunication Standardization Sector G.728 Recommendation – Coding of speech at 16 kbit/s using low-delay code excited linear prediction, September 1992.
9. International Telecommunication Union, Telecommunication Standardization Sector G.729 Recommendation – Coding of speech at 8 kbit/s using conjugate-structure algebraic-code-excited linear-prediction (CS-ACELP), March 1996.
10. International Telecommunication Union, Telecommunication Standardization Sector H.225.0 Recommendation – Call signaling protocols and media stream packetization for packet-based multimedia communication systems, July 2003.
11. International Telecommunication Union, Telecommunication Standardization Sector H.235 Recommendation – Security and encryption for H-series (H.323 and other H.245-based) multimedia terminals, August 2003.
12. International Telecommunication Union, Telecommunication Standardization Sector H.242 Recommendation – System for establishing communication between audiovisual terminals using digital channels up to 2 Mbit/s, March 2004.
13. International Telecommunication Union, Telecommunication Standardization Sector H.245 Recommendation – Control protocol for multimedia communication, January 2005.

14. International Telecommunication Union, Telecommunication Standardization Sector H.261 Recommendation – Video codec for audiovisual services at p x 64 kbit/s, March 1993.

15. International Telecommunication Union, Telecommunication Standardization Sector H.263 Recommendation – Video coding for low bit rate communication, January 2005.

16. International Telecommunication Union, Telecommunication Standardization Sector H.320 Recommendation – Narrow-band visual telephone systems and terminal equipment, March 2004.

17. International Telecommunication Union, Telecommunication Standardization Sector H.321 Recommendation – Adaptation of H.320 visual telephone terminals to B-ISDN environments, February 1998.

18. International Telecommunication Union, Telecommunication Standardization Sector H.322 Recommendation – Visual telephone systems and terminal equipment for local area networks which provide a guaranteed quality of service, March 1996.

19. International Telecommunication Union, Telecommunication Standardization Sector H.323 Recommendation – Packet-based multimedia communications systems, July 2003.

20. International Telecommunication Union, Telecommunication Standardization Sector H.324 Recommendation – Terminal for low bit-rate multimedia communication, March 2002.

21. International Telecommunication Union, Telecommunication Standardization Sector H.450.1 Recommendation – Generic functional protocol for the support of supplementary services in H.323, February 1998.

22. International Telecommunication Union, Telecommunication Standardization Sector Q.931 Recommendation – ISDN user-network interface layer 3 specification for basic call control, May 1998.

23. International Telecommunication Union, Telecommunication Standardization Sector T.120 Recommendation – Data protocols for multimedia conferencing, July 1996.

24. International Telecommunication Union, Telecommunication Standardization Sector T.121 Recommendation – July 1996.

25. International Telecommunication Union, Telecommunication Standardization Sector T.122 Recommendation – Multipoint communication service - Service definition, February 1998.

26. International Telecommunication Union, Telecommunication Standardization Sector T.123 Recommendation – Network-specific data protocol stacks for multimedia conferencing, May 1999.

27. International Telecommunication Union, Telecommunication Standardization Sector T.124 Recommendation – Generic Conference Control, February 1998.

28. International Telecommunication Union, Telecommunication Standardization Sector T.125 Recommendation – Multipoint communication service protocol specification, February 1998.

29. International Telecommunication Union, Telecommunication Standardization Sector T.126 Recommendation – Multipoint still image and annotation protocol, July 1997.

30. International Telecommunication Union, Telecommunication Standardization Sector T.127 Recommendation – Multipoint binary file transfer protocol, August 1995.

31. International Telecommunication Union, Telecommunication Standardization Sector T.128 Recommendation – Multipoint application sharing, February 1998.

32. http://www.openh323.org/

33. http://www.microsoft.com/netmeeting/
34. http://isabel.dit.upm.es/
35. http://www.cuseeme.com/
36. http://www.icuii.com/
37. S. Shirmohammadi, L.Ding, and N.D. Georganas, "An Approach for Recording Multimedia Collaborative Sessions: Design and Implementation," Journal of Multimedia Tools and Applications, Vol. 19, No. 2, 2003, pp. 135-154.

TELE-HAPTICS

Xiaojun Shen and Shervin Shirmohammadi
University of Ottawa, Canada

Definition: *Tele-haptics refers to transmission of computer generated tactile sensations over the network.*

Introduction

Multimedia and Information technology is reaching limits in terms of what can be done in multimedia applications with only sight and sound. The next critical step is to bring the sense of "touch" over network connections, which is known as *tele-haptics*. *Haptics*, a term which was derived from the Greek verb "haptesthai" meaning "to touch", introduces the sense of touch and force in human-computer interaction. Haptics enable the human operator to manipulate objects in the environment in a natural and effective way, enhance the sensation of "presence", and provide information such as stiffness and texture of objects, which cannot be described completely with visual or audio feedback only. The technology has already been explored in contexts as diverse as modeling & animation, geophysical analysis, dentistry training, virtual museums, assembly planning, mine design, surgical simulation, design evaluation, control of scientific instruments, and robotic simulation. But its true potential in these areas has not yet been achieved, and its application to all aspects of dexterous training, for example is still untapped. Haptic devices typically consist of microcontrollers that use input information from sensors, and control effectors to create human sensations as outputs. Sensors range from pressure, temperature and kinesthetic sensing devices, to biofeedback equipment. Haptic effectors, evoking precise perceivable sensations, range from small motors, fans, heating elements, or vibrators; to micro-voltage electrodes which gently stimulate areas of the skin (creating subtle, localized, "tingling" sensations). Some Haptic devices are shown in Figure 1.

Compared with visual and audio displays, haptic displays are more difficult to build since the haptic system not only senses the physical world but also affects it. In contrast, we can not change the object while listening or just looking at it except in a magical world. In the haptic device world, tactile haptic devices provide sense of sensing the temperature and pressure, grasping, and feeling the surface textures in details of an object, while force haptic devices provide users with the sense of general shape, coarse texture and the position of an object. Apparently, tactile haptic device is more difficult to create than that of kinesthetic. Due to technical problems, currently there is no single haptic device that could combine these two sensations together although we cannot separate them in the real life.

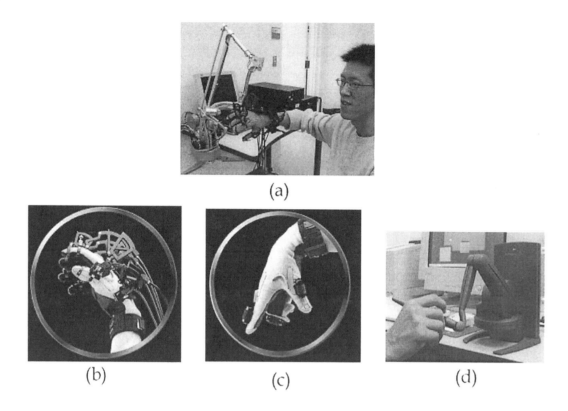

Figure 1. Some Haptic Devices: a) Immersion's CyberForce™ b) Immersion's CyberGrasp™ c) Immersion's CyberTouch™ d) SensAble's PHANToM® Desktop.

Tele-haptics can be defined as the use of haptics in a network context; it is the science of transmitting computer generated tactile sensations over networks, between physically distant users. Applications for haptics are broad, and tele-haptics in no way constrains that potential. For every single-user desktop application of haptics technology, a tele-haptics equivalent introduces, at the very least, a richer collaborative experience. A desktop modeling package can extend to collaborative modeling or design review; a dexterous task trainer can extend to remote teaching and assessment; a surgical simulator can be coupled directly to a surgical robot.

Much of the academic research and development on tele-haptics in recent years has attempted to ease the construction of virtual environments providing increased immersion through multi-sensory feedback. These environments that support collaborative touch in virtual environments are termed *Collaborative Haptic Audio Visual Environments* (C-HAVE) (Figure 2), where participants may have different kinds of haptic devices, such as the Sensable's PHANToM [1], the MPB Freedom6S Hand Controller [2], FCS Robotics' HapticMASTER [3], or Immersion's CyberGrasp [4]; or they can just be passive observers. Some of the participants in the virtual world may only provide virtual objects as a service to the remaining users. Adding haptics to a conventional *Collaborative*

Virtual Environment (CVE) creates additional demand for frequent position sampling, collision detection/response, and fast update. It is also reasonable to assume that in CVEs, there may be a heterogeneous assortment of haptics devices with which users interact with the system.

User scenarios for C-HAVE evolve from haptic VE applications. Collaboration may involve independent or dependent manipulation of virtual objects, or tele-mentoring. Independent manipulation of virtual objects allows multiple participants to haptically interact with separate objects. Each object is "owned" by a single participant. While other participants may feel the owner's manipulation of an object, in a similar fashion to a virtual audience watching virtual actors in a conventional CVE, where the owner does not receive haptic feedback from those other participants. This is termed *unilateral tele-haptics*. Dependent manipulation introduces *bilateral tele-haptics*, whereby multiple participants haptically interact with identical or coupled objects. Here, each participant feels the other's manipulation of the environment, but that sensation is indirectly perceived through the environmental modification. *Tele-mentoring* allows direct coupling of haptic devices over a network. Tele-mentoring is an educational technique that involves real-time guidance of a less experienced trainee through a procedure in which he or she has limited experience. A typical example of this is the education of surgeons, whereby a trainee can feel an expert's guiding hand. Independent manipulation of virtual environments involves augmentation of a client station and may be viewed as a simple integration of conventional CVEs with conventional hapto-visual VEs. Both application families are typically implemented upon none or soft real time operating systems. By contrast, dependent manipulation and tele-mentoring impose more stringent requirements and, like tele-robotics, demand hard real time guarantees. Since Tele-Haptics are a networked extension of Haptics, let us start by having a more detailed look at Haptics and their applications.

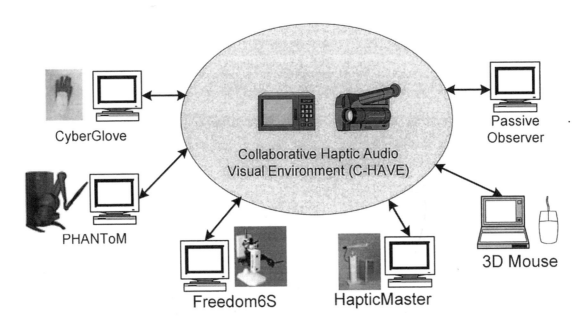

Figure 2. C-HAVE: Collaborative haptic audio visual environment.

Haptics Applications

Haptics is the study about the simulation of the touch modality and the related sensory feedback. Haptics applications are often termed "hapto-visual" or "hapto-visual-acoustic applications", in addition to the more generic "multi-sensory" applications.

Generally there are two kinds of sensory information related with human touch: *kinesthetic* and *tactile*. Kinesthetic is the human's perception on the relative movements among body parts and is determined by the velocity of movement of the links, therefore the touched object can be reconstructed in the mind by knowing the position of the corresponding links. Tactile is the sense of touch that comes from some sensitive nerve sensors on the surface of skin such as information about pressure and temperature. Haptic perception of touch involves both kinds of sensations.

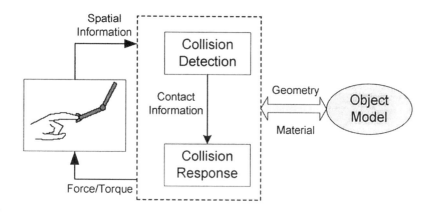

Figure 3. Haptic rendering.

Haptic Rendering

Haptic rendering is the process of converting haptic interface spatial information (position/orientation) to net force and torque feedback (some haptic devices may only generate force feedback to the users). Two major tasks in haptic rendering paradigms are *collision detection* and *collision response* (Figure 3). Collision detection is to detect collisions between the end point of the generic probe and the objects in the scene, while collision response is to respond to the detection of collision in terms of how the forces reflected to the user are computed.

Stable Haptic Interaction

A haptic device links a human operator with a virtual environment together where the operator feels the objects in the virtual scene with the sense of touch. There is physical energy flowing to and from the operator. Since in the haptic interaction, the physical haptic device generates force feedback, instability of system can damage the hardware or hurt the operator physically. For example, the Haptic MASTER from FCS Robotics can easily generate a few hundred Newton's force in less than one second which is enough to hurt a person seriously. Instability also destroys the illusion of a real object immediately. Furthermore, the instabilities degrade transparency in haptic simulation. A transparent haptic interface should be able to emulate any environment, from free space to infinitely stiff obstacles.

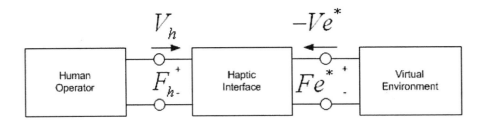

Figure 4. Haptic simulation diagram.

Many researchers have studied the stability issues in haptic simulation in different ways. In a haptic simulation, there are at least three components: human operator, a haptic interface, and a computer model of the virtual environment. Figure 4 shows their relationship using the two port network model. The star superscript indicates the variable is discrete. Typically the haptic simulation can be classified into two categories: impedance control and admittance control. Impedance control means "measure position and display force" while admittance control means "measure force and display motion or position". All these three components affect the stability of the system.

From the perspective of control theory, Minsky et. al. [11] derived an expression for the guaranteed stable haptic interaction using the impedance control theory and then modified it with the experimental results. The impedance here is used to describe a generalized relationship between force and motion of the haptic device. They noted a critical tradeoff between sampling rate, virtual wall stiffness, and device viscosity and analyzed the role of the human operator in stability concern. In the experiment, they tried to simulate a virtual wall with stiffness K and viscosity B. The derived equation for a guaranteed stability is given as follows:

$$B+b > \frac{KT}{2} ,$$

where T is sampling time and b is the device viscosity. The results shows that the rate to sample the haptic spatial information and output the force to haptic device is the most crucial factor that affects the highest stiffness can be achieved while maintain a stable system. At the same time, the device viscosity plays a role in the stability issue: the higher the device viscosity, the higher stiffness can be achieved. So it is possible to make the system stable by adding extra viscosity, or by reducing the stiffness of the simulated hard surface. But the human will feel resistance and sluggishness even in free space if the viscosity is too high.

Architecture of Haptics Applications

Multiple tasks, such as haptic sensing/actuation and visual updates must be accomplished in a synchronized manner in haptic applications. It becomes commonplace to separate tasks into computational threads or processes, to accommodate different update rates, distribute computation load and optimize computation. Conventionally, multithreading and multiprocessing software architectures (Figure 5 (a)) are applied to develop effective multimodal VEs and the optimal usage of the CPU capabilities. However, an important but little discussed consequence of the conventional architectures is that it makes the operating system an inherent component of the applications, with operating system scheduling algorithms limiting the application's quality of service. The application may request a theoretical rate of force display but it is the scheduler that determines the actual rate. This scheduler is itself a complex algorithm, particularly when considered in terms of its interactions with the other services provided by the operating system.

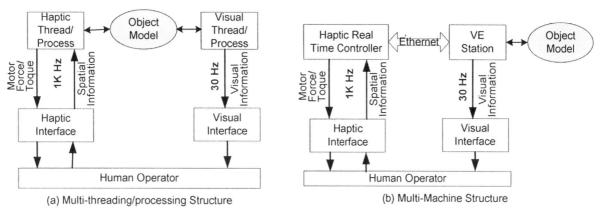

(a) Multi-threading/processing Structure   (b) Multi-Machine Structure

Figure 5. Architectures for haptics applications.

A multi-machine solution for haptic application was addressed in [5,6] as shown in Figure 5 (b). The multi-machine architecture is comprised of three parts: haptic device, Haptic Real Time Controller (HRTC) and Virtual Environment (VE) graphics station. HRTC communicates with its VE station through a local Ethernet connection. HRTC relies on hard real time operating systems (e.g. QNX Neutrino, VxWorks or Windows CE) to guarantee the stability of the control loop. The separation of functionalities of haptic and graphic rendering makes this architecture easier to extend to existing applications. Unlike conventional multithreading or multiprocessing approaches for haptics, this multi-machine model solution applies a hard real-time operating system for haptic control, while applying a mainstream OS such as Win2K or WinXP for the application and graphics.

Tele-Haptics – Networked Haptics

The concept of networking haptics is referred to as "tele-haptics" and occurs when haptic devices are located at remote locations over a communications network. Sometimes referred to as *e-touch*, tele-haptics is based on the bilateral transmission of spatial information such that either end of the communication can both sense and/or impart forces. One of the stumbling blocks to enabling real-time control of haptic devices over a network is network lag: delay, jitter, and packet loss. Haptics can actually cause greater time delay issues due to instability. In other words, the mechanical devices used to impart the sense of touch could vibrate and become dangerous. For example, with Internet time delays as little as 100msec, it is possible for on-line simulated training participants to be essentially involved in two totally different scenarios. In the case where a transcontinental latency exists, there will be a mismatch between the two participant's computers due to network time delays. If this were to be used for mission-critical simulations for pilots, for example, the effects render the training process useless.

There are, however, solutions to mitigating network lag issues [8]. These solutions, typically implemented over the transport layer (UDP), consist of communication techniques that quickly synchronize both ends in the presence of packet loss [9], or reduce the jitter by short-term buffering [8]. Another type of solution, which deals with the problem from a human-computer interaction point of view as opposed to a networking point of view, uses "decorators": visual cues that inform the user about the presence of network lag, allowing him/her to intuitively adjust to the situation accordingly [10]. Another concept that has been around for many years is *dead reckoning*. This concept has proven somewhat useful in the past, but is very susceptible to noise and becomes ineffective as time delay becomes large. Given that telehaptics is very sensitive to time delay, more advanced techniques need to be adopted to enable telehaptic applications to operate in a real-time environment, such as the Handshake [12] method of time delay compensation. This method utilizes advanced intelligent predictive modeling techniques for real time human-in-the-loop interaction. It effectively overcomes network instability issues and provides superior tracking performance as compared to dead reckoning techniques to allow a user to interact in real-time with his/her environment.

Generic Architecture for C-HAVE
Tele-haptic platforms rely on hard real time operating systems to guarantee the stability of the control loop and to minimize the delays in the network stack. As described below, the Haptic Real Time Controller compensates for network latency, so increased or unreliable latency in the network stack provided by the host operating system will either increase the complexity of the latency compensation algorithms or decrease the effective separation of tele-haptic collaborators.

A node in a C-HAVE environment with a haptic device is comprised of three parts: haptic device, HRTC, and Virtual Environment (VE) graphics station, as illustrated in Figure 6. The HRTC controls the haptic device through a device driver. A local HRTC is linked with remote HRTC(s) through a haptic channel (1 in Figure 6) and communicates with its VE station through a local channel (2 in Figure 6). The VE graphics stations are interconnected over CVE Middleware such as HLA/RTI (3 in Figure 6).

Tele-Haptics Platform – Haptic Real Time Controller
The Haptic Real Time Controller (HRTC), shown in Figure 7, in a C-HAVE system provides a modular and flexible platform to allow real time control of a haptic device or application device at one node of a C-HAVE network by a haptic device or application hardware at another node of C-HAVE, which is referred to as client/server mode. It is not limited to a client-server configuration, but is modular enough to support multiple clients or other network configurations.

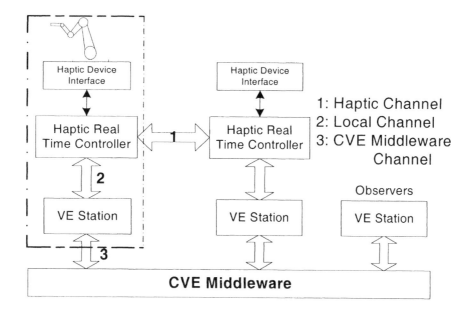

Figure 6. Generic architecture for C-HAVE.

To enable this technology, it is required that the clocks on both nodes be synchronized closely, have precise sampling periods and have the ability to perform complex control computations so that desired performance can be achieved at the client end. An important component of the HRTC is the use of hardware/software solutions to accomplish this synchronization and precision in timing. In order to enable real time control and data exchange, the software of the HRTC runs on a modular and robust real time operating system.

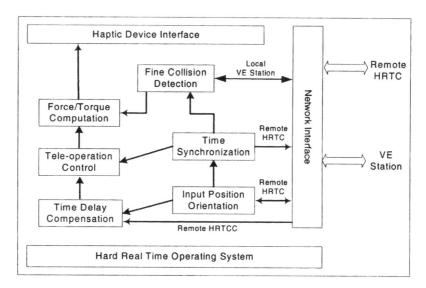

Figure 7. Tele-haptics platform - Haptic real time controller.

The time-varying network delay degrades the performance of many network applications, and can cause instability in applications involving bilateral control of haptic devices. HRTC includes sophisticated algorithms to compensate for the time-varying network delays. In essence, if the compensation were perfect, the time delays would be transparent to the system. The HRTC allows the time delay compensation to vary between full delay compensation which gives higher performance but may introduce more noise and overshoot, to partial delay compensation, to no compensation which results in low performance and instability. The time delay compensation in the HRTC does not require a mathematic model of environment, and is robust to uncertainties due to the human-in-the-loop situation.

See: Haptics, E-touch, Haptic Devices.

References

1. SensAble Technologies, http://www.sensable.com/.
2. MPB technologies, http://www.mpb-technologies.ca/.
3. FCS Control System, http://www.fcs-cs.com/.
4. Immersion Corporation, http://www.immersion.com/.
5. X. Shen, F. Bogsanyi, L. Ni, and N. D. Georganas, "A Heterogeneous Scalable Architecture for Collaborative Haptics Environments," Proceedings of the IEEE Workshop on Haptic, Audio and Visual Environments and their Applications (IEEE HAVE '03), Ottawa, Canada, September 2003, pp.113-118.
6. X. Shen, J. Zhou, A. El Saddik, and N. D. Georganas , "Architecture and Evaluation of Tele-Haptic Environments", Proceedings of the IEEE International Symposium on Distributed Simulation and Real Time Applications (IEEE DS-RT '04), Budapest, Hungary, October 2004, pp. 53-60.
7. M.A. Srinivasan and C. Basdogan, "Haptics in Virtual Environments: Taxonomy, Research Status, and Challenges (PDF)," Computers and Graphics, (Special issue on "Haptic Displays in Virtual Environments"), Vol. 21, No. 4, pp. 393-404.
8. S. Shirmohammadi, N.H. Woo, and S. Alavi, "Network Lag Mitigation Methods in Collaborative Distributed Simulations," Proceedings of the International Symposium on Collaborative Technologies and Systems (CTS '05), Saint Louis, U.S.A, May 2005.
9. S. Shirmohammadi and N.D. Georganas, "An End-to-End Communication Architecture for Collaborative Virtual Environments," Computer Networks Journal, Vol. 35, No. 2-3, February 2001, pp. 351-367.
10. S. Shirmohammadi and N.H. Woo, "Evaluating Decorators for Haptic Collaboration over Internet," Proceedings of the IEEE Workshop on Haptic Audio Visual Environments and their Applications (IEEE HAVE '04), Ottawa, Canada, October 2004, pp. 105-110.
11. M. Minsky, M. Ouh-Young, O. Steele, F. P. Brooks, and M. Behensky, "Feeling and Seeing Issues in Force Display," Computer Graphics, Vol. 24, No. 2, pp. 235-243, 1990.
12. HandShake VR Inc., http://www.handshakeVR.com.

TELE-OPERATION

Definition: The objective of tele-operation is to allow the user to interact with and operate equipment and devices in a remote location without actually being in that location.

Tele-operation can be thought of as a special case of telepresence. The objective of tele-operation is to allow the user, referred to as the "operator", to interact with and operate equipment and devices in a remote location without actually being in that location. The term itself literally illustrates two layers of implications: the users are virtually "operating" at the remote site, and that the operation is "tele" i.e. distant. The implications lead to two essential components in such systems: *location* and *communication*. Locations indicate the locations in which the users are virtually operating. Standard locations vary from conventional VR to augmented reality (AR) and to real world environments. The interactivity between host and remote locations is accomplished via networking and multimedia communications. It is generally accepted that there are three independent aspects of presence which contribute to achieving a sense of remote telepresence [1]:

- o The extent of the sensory information: it is necessary to provide the operator with the same level of sensory information that they would receive if they were actually present at the remote site.
- o Control of sensors: it must be possible to move the sensing devices around the environment as if the operator was at the remote site.
- o The ability to modify the remote site and actively interact with it.

See: Telepresence, Virtual and Augmented Reality

References

1. J. Pretlove and R. Asbery, "Get a head in virtual reality," Control of Remotely Operated Systems: Teleassistance and Telepresence, IEE Colloquium on 12 May 1995, pp. 8/1 – 8/5.

TELEPRESENCE

Xiaojun Shen and Shervin Shirmohammadi
University of Ottawa, Canada

Definition: Telepresence, also called virtual presence, is a technique to create a sense of physical presence at a remote location using necessary multimedia such as sound, vision, and touch.

Introduction

The concept of *Telepresence* may come from science fiction since science fiction writers have described conceptual versions of virtual reality (VR) and telepresence for decades [1]. The term "telepresence" was coined by Marvin Minsky in 1980 in reference to teleoperation systems for manipulating of remote physical objects [2]. According to Witmer and Singer "(Tele)presence is defined as the subjective experience of being in one place or environment, even when one is physically situated in another" [3]. Telepresence, also called *virtual presence*, is basically a technique to create a sense of physical presence at a remote location using necessary multimedia such as sound, vision, and touch. This is a networked paradigm by nature, and multimedia communications is used for the transport of information between the user and the remote site. The sense of presence is achieved by generating sensory stimulus so that the operator has an illusion of being present at a location distant from the location of physical presence. Unlike conventional concept of VR that is defined as a new medium to experience presence in a virtual space, telepresence emphasizes the interaction between people and remote site and enables people who are immersed in telepresence systems to act and receive input as if they were at the remote site. Its examples cover applications from the fields of telemedicine to remote surveillance, entertainment, education and other applications in situations where humans are exposed to hazardous and hostile environments. Both telephone and video-conferencing allow for limited types of telepresence since people's voice or video can be there without the person being physically there, while some forms of VR may enable a greater range of interactions. Telepresence systems that incorporate successful force-feedback components can be extremely helpful for a variety of applications [4], for example, space operations such as Robonaut [5], the robotic astronaut that is now in development. With the benefits of telepresence system, Robonaut can be deployed in difficult or hazardous situations with the replacement of an astronaut, while its operator, safely housed on a nearby spaceship or even on the earth, controls its actions in a fluid, intuitive fashion. Figure 1 demonstrates the concept of remotely controlling Robonaut's operations.

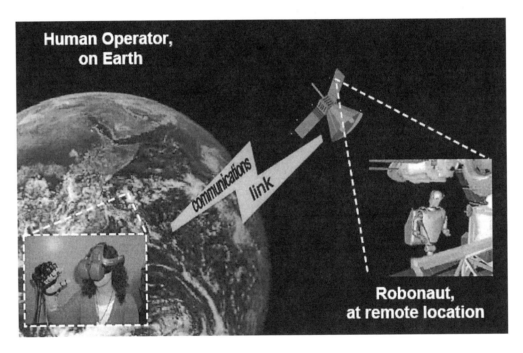

Figure 1. Example of telepresence control of robonaut.

Enabling Technology for Telepresence

The term "tele-presence" literally illustrates two layers of implications: people are virtually *present* at the remote site, and that presence is "tele" i.e. distant. The implications lead to two essential components in telepresence systems: telepresent *location* and *communication*. Telepresent locations indicate the locations in which the users are virtually present. Standard locations vary from conventional VR to augmented reality (AR) and to real world environments. The interactivity between host and remote locations is accomplished via network link. It is generally accepted that there are three independent aspects of presence which contribute to achieving a sense of remote telepresence [6]:

- o The extent of the sensory information. It is necessary to provide the operator with the same level of sensory information that they would receive if they were actually present at the remote site.
- o Control of sensors. It must be possible to move the sensing devices around the environment as if the operator was at the remote site.
- o The ability to modify the remote site and actively interact with it.

To achieve the ultimate sense of presence at a remote site requires the full combination of all these aspects and is essentially what most telepresence systems are attempting to create. The telepresence aspect of the teleoperator is to provide sensory feedback to the operator in such a way that the feeling of sensory presence is conveyed. A high degree of sensory presence is required when the operational tasks are wide ranging, complex and uncertain, for instance, in hazardous or difficult environments.

Telepresent Location Technology
Telepresence enables people physically located in their host location to behave and receive stimuli as though at a remote site. The technology used in host location is similar to what is applied in conventional VR and AR applications. The difference is that, in VR and AR applications, users are immersed in a computer synthesized environment (VR) or a combination of a real location and supplemental objects or information (AR), whereas, in telepresence, users are immersed in a remote real world. Multimedia sensory feedback is required to achieve this, which takes multiple modalities including haptic/tactile, sound, vision or even olfactory.

A visually coupled system utilizes a display system such as a Head- Mounted Display (HMD). These systems are worn over the eyes of the user and generally only give the impression that the user is immersed within the environment displayed in the images. HMDs enable a higher degree of user immersion compared with standard monitors or television displays. Haptic interfaces bring more and more realism to telepresence. Olfactory displays could also be used but practical commercial systems have yet to be developed.

Control is a key element of telepresence operations to create vivid awareness. By tracking the operators head position with a sensor, the remote camera system can be controlled in such a way that the head motion is replicated in the remote environment. The effect of this relationship between the operator and the remote mechanical system is to further enhance telepresence and to allow the operator to concentrate on the task itself instead of how to achieve it.

Most of the equipments deployed at remote locations focus on acquisition of the surroundings' information, modification of the remote site and interaction with it.

Typically, these equipments include: pan/tilt monoscopic and stereoscopic camera platforms, other sensor platforms including microphones and touch/force feedback sensors, slave manipulators and grippers, and mobility providers such as wheeled or tracked vehicles. Mostly, the approach of capturing/compressing video/sound in real time is in demand due to the bandwidth limitation of telecommunication link.

Readers are referred to two other chapters in this book for further information: Virtual and Augmented Reality, and Tele-Haptics.

Telecommunications Link
Although any available telecommunication links may be used in a telepresence system, specific systems dictated different demands on network configurations, such as bandwidth requirements, and the sensitivity to network impairments (latency, jitter and packet loss). For instance, in a telepresence system enhanced with haptic interface, the standard implementation requires that haptic information (force/kinematic data) to be transferred over communication link between home and remote locations. Since network latency adds phase lag to the signal, this lag limits the effective bandwidth of closed haptic control loop and may result in an unstable haptic display. Such instability poses a safety threat because of the relatively large force-generating capability of the hardware. Significant research results have been achieved in teleoperation domain to deal with varied network delays [7, 8, 9].

Telepresence Applications
The flexibility of telepresence system allows a myriad of applications. The following is a selection of some of the current telepresence systems, both completed and under investigation. Each can be fully realized with the latest technology, and most can operate, albeit at a reduced service level, over the existing network.

Telemedicine
Telemedicine is the delivery of healthcare services, where distance is a critical factor. For example, in a battlefield scenario, the first hour after a soldier has been injured is critical. Telepresence could be used to transport the "presence" of the medical doctor, surgeon and consultant to hospital operating rooms or the scenes of battlefield to assist paramedics. This would facilitate the more effective use of an increasingly limited resource - the medical specialist. The armed forces have an obvious interest since the combination of telepresence, teleoperation, and tele-robotics can potentially save the lives of battle casualties by allowing them prompt attention in mobile operating theatres by remote surgeons, as illustrated in Figure 2.

Hazardous and Hostile Environments
Many other applications in situations where humans are exposed to hazardous situations are readily recognized as suitable candidates for telepresence. Mining, bomb disposal, military operations, rescue of victims from fire, toxic atmospheres, or even hostage situations, are some examples. Remote controlled robotic devices are being used to detect and remove bombs and land mines. By providing the operator the ability to feel what the robot is feeling, the detection/removal task can be done more efficiently and safely.

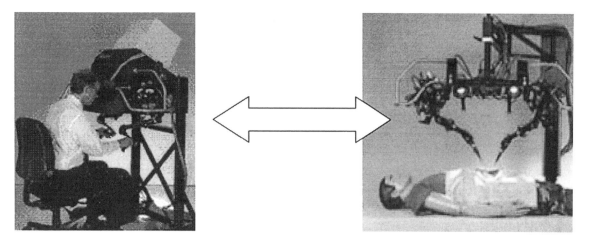

Figure 2. Telepresence surgery application (courtesy of SRI International).

Entertainment

Telepresence systems could be incorporated into theme or nature parks to allow observers to travel through coral reefs, explore underground caves, or in amusement parks the elderly or infirm could experience the thrill of live roller coaster rides without the associated risks. Figure 3 shows an example of a telepresence musical performance with musicians at two remote sites: Stockholm's KTH Royal Institute of Technology in Sweden and Stanford in the United States.

Figure 3. Connected performance between two difference spaces.

Remote Surveillance

Security forces throughout the world are increasingly resorting to video recording as a means of crime certification and prevention. Telepresence is one of the logical developments in this trend, with each security officer linked visually and orally at all times to headquarter. Sensor platforms operating autonomously in robotic mode could monitor sensitive areas. They could use software algorithms that would identify, for example, intruders. They would then proceed to track these intruders while sending an alert to a human operator requesting attention. The operator would be wearing a HMD helmet and become telepresent at the remote location and take over control of the sensor platform. This would then allow the operator to investigate more.

Teleconferencing

Teleconferencing literally means "conference at a distance", where multiple geographically dispersed users have a meeting of some sort across a telecommunications link. It is one of the uses that the integral display on the desk could be put to, producing a life size head-and-shoulder image of the remote user. The large size of the screen ensures that peripheral vision is substantially filled, thus creating the illusion of "being there". The high definition of the display allows it to be multi-tasked during teleconferencing as the main viewer and a computer monitor. By using an infra red light pen, the screen can also function as an electronic white board, allowing multiple participants to interact in the same media-space in real time. People sitting at desks thousands of miles apart can thus come together to realize a real time working environment that closely mimics reality.

See: Virtual Presence, Tele-operation.

References

1. W. Gibson, "Neuromancer," ISBN: 0441569595, Publisher: Ace Books, 1984.
2. M. Minsky, "Telepresence," Omni, pp. 45-51, 1980.
3. B.G. Witmer and M.J. Singer, "Measuring Presence in Virtual Environments: A Presence Questionnaire," Presence: Teleoperators and Virtual Environments, Vol. 7, No. 3, 1998, pp. 225-240.
4. A. Fisch, C. Mavroidis, J. Melli-Huber, and Y.Bar-Cohen, "Haptic Devices for Virtual Reality, Telepresence, and Human-Assistive Robotics," Invited Chapter in Biologically-Inspired Intelligent Robots, Eds. Y. Bar-Cohen and C. Breazeal, SPIE Press, 2003.
5. Robonaut, http://vesuvius.jsc.nasa.gov/er_er/html/robonaut/robonaut.html.
6. J. Pretlove and R. Asbery, "Get a head in virtual reality," Control of Remotely Operated Systems: Teleassistance and Telepresence, IEE Colloquium on 12 May 1995 pp. 8/1 - 8/5.
7. R. Anderson and M. Spong "Bilateral Control of Teleoperators with Time Delay" IEEE Transactions on Automatic Control, 1989, Vol. 34, No. 5, pp. 494-501.
8. N. Hogan, "On the Stability of Manipulators Performing Contact Tasks," IEEE Journal of Robotics and Automation, 1988, Vol. 4, No. 6, pp. 677-686.
9. S. Shirmohammadi, N.H. Woo, and S. Alavi, "Network Lag Mitigation Methods in Collaborative Distributed Simulations," Proceedings of the International Symposium on Collaborative Technologies and Systems (CTS '05), Saint Louis, U.S.A, May 2005.

THRESHOLD SCHEMES WITH MINIMUM PIXEL EXPANSION

Definition: In visual secret sharing schemes, attempts have been made to restrict the pixel expansion while images with high contrast are produced.

Although results obtained via a (k, n)-visual secret sharing (VSS) scheme can be easily revealed by a human observer without any computations, the size of shares is usually much larger compared to the size of the original input image. By encrypting the secret pixel into $m_1 m_2$ blocks of share pixels, the expansion is determined by the so-called expansion factor $m_1 m_2$ which denotes the number of columns of the $n \times m_1 m_2$ basis matrices. In the recent past, attempts have been made to restrict the pixel expansion while images with high contrast are produced. The designer most often has to trade pixel expansion constraints to the recovered image quality and/or the order of (k, n)-threshold schemes [1]-[3].

A probabilistic VSS scheme which offers no pixel expansion ($m_1 m_2 = 1$) which can be regarded as a VSS scheme with the minimum pixel expansion is briefly reviewed in the sequence. The reconstruction of the secret image is probabilistic. In a deterministic scheme, any given secret pixel is encrypted into $m_1 m_2$ subpixels. Hence the reconstructed image is $m_1 m_2$ times larger in size compared to the original binary input. To obtain no pixel expansion, each secret pixel is reconstructed with a single pixel in the probabilistic scheme. The binary secret pixel is correctly reconstructed with a given probability. However the quality of the reconstructed binary image depends on how large the image areas of pixels showing the same binary value are.

A probabilistic VSS scheme can be constructed using the two sets, white set P_1 and black set P_0, each consisting of $n \times 1$ matrices, respectively. When sharing a white (or black) pixel, the dealer first randomly chooses one $n \times 1$ column matrix in P_1 (or P_0), and then randomly selects one row of this column matrix to a relative shadow. The chosen matrix defines the pixel color in every one of the n shadows. A probabilistic VSS scheme is considered valid if the contrast and security conditions are met [2].

An image secret sharing (ISS) scheme in [3] can be viewed as an alternative to minimal pixel expansion based VSS schemes. The scheme is a $(2, 2)$-ISS solution suitable for cost-effective encryption of the natural images. It encrypts the decomposed 'black' bit of the original secret pixel into a black (or white) bit in each of the two shares. To differentiate between the 'black' and 'white' bits of the original secret pixels, the decomposed 'white' bits are encrypted into black and white (or white and black) pixels in the corresponding shares. Such an approach satisfies the essential perfect reconstruction property and can serve as the private-key cryptosystem.

See: Image secret sharing, Visual cryptography, Private-key cryptosystem.

References

1. P.-A. Eisen and D.-R. Stinson, "Threshold visual cryptography schemes with specified whiteness levels of reconstructed pixels," Designs, Codes and Cryptography, Vol. 25, No. 1, January 2002, pp. 15-61.
2. C.-N. Yang, "New Visual Secret Sharing Schemes Using Probabilistic Method," Pattern Recognition Letters, Vol. 25, Issue 4, 2004, pp. 481-494.
3. R. Lukac and K.-N. Plataniotis, "A New Encryption Scheme for Color Images," Computing and Informatics, submitted.

TRENDS IN MULTIMEDIA E-COMMERCE

Definition: *Trends in multimedia e-commerce will always be a function of market factors and the cultural landscape. As such, several surprising and lucrative trends have dominated land-line and wireless multimedia e-commerce in recent times.*

Ringtone E-Commerce

Ringtones are the sounds that are activated on cell phone when incoming calls arrive. In early cell phones tones were limited to a small set of just nine. Today's cell phone have the capability to play *monophonic* (a single voice), *polyphonic*, and *sampled* (e.g. clips of actual recordings) ringtones. Initially a sort of "geek sub-culture" activity, ringtone e-commerce broke-out in 2003 as service providers and 3rd party communications providers established e-commerce sites for ringtone download. Some experts estimate that consumers put down near $2 billion worldwide in that year alone for tones [1]. Ringtone e-commerce revenue generally gets split between many business entities. Some of these entities are: the wireless provider, the music label, publishers, and the 3rd party technology middlemen who provide [1]. Validating the fact that ringtone e-commerce has come of age is the news that Billboard magazine now charts the 20 top-selling ringtones in its "Hot Ringtones" chart.

Other ringtone-related trends are currently in the pipeline. One is the trend towards the insertion of humorous "samples" into conversations (e.g. the voice of a celebrity impersonator). Another newer trend for 2005 is the combination of pleasing images to go along with a ringtone. For example, a pretty image such as a sunset of landscape pops up on the phones LCD screen simultaneously with the ring. Such clips and graphics will enable a similar download economy.

Audio and Music

Although music download e-commerce was happening before Apple introduced its *iPOD* line of mp3 players in 2001, Apple's chic devices, marketing approach, and easy to use online (legal) music download site called *iTunes* are widely seen as sea-change events. Over 10 million iPODS have been sold since 2001 and while 2003 saw about 20 million legal song-downloads, 2004 saw 200 million. Research firms believe that 2004's $330 million market for online music will double in 2005. While iTunes gets most press, there are many other ways to legally acquire audio and music online including: Napster, Real, download.com, eMusic, Walmart.com, mp3.com, and Amazon.com. Such stores replace the 'first generation' of illegal file sharing systems which allowed users to trade high-quality versions of songs online at no cost. Illegal file sharing ultimately led to the Recording Industry Association of America's (RIAA) much-publicized lawsuits with individual uploaders. RIAA has thus far targeted principle sources (e.g. those users with more than 1000 songs on their hard drives) rather than casual users; however, their efforts are aimed to deter future abusers of copyrighted media.

See: Online Multimedia E-Commerce

References

1. M. Maier, The Changing Ringtone Economy, in Business 2.0, http://www.business2.com, Oct. 2004.

U

UNIVERSAL MULTIMEDIA ACCESS

Definition: *Universal multimedia access refers to access to multimedia content over wired and wireless networks on a range of devices with varying capabilities.*

Recent technology advances have made possible access to digital multimedia content over wired and wireless networks on a range of devices with varying capabilities such as mobile phones, personal computers, and digital video recorders. This Universal Multimedia Access (UMA), enabled by new technologies and standards, poses new challenges and requires new solutions. Content delivery services to resource constrained devices such as mobile phones are limited due to the mismatch between the resources required to play the content and the device capabilities.

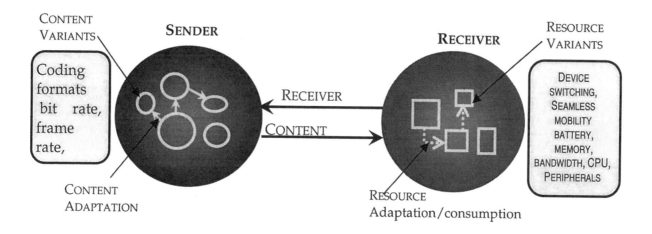

Figure 1. Pervasive media delivery environment.

Figure 1 shows the key elements of a pervasive media delivery environment. The capabilities of the receivers in such an environment vary, requiring a server that can satisfy receivers with different capability sets. The capabilities of these devices would also change with the available battery, concurrently running applications, and available resources such as memory, bandwidth, and peripherals. As the available resources on a device change, the capability of the devices to process/playback content also changes. The resource variants shown in Figure 1 represent the same device with changing capabilities. As the capabilities of a device change, the device cannot continue to play the same content. The content now has to be adapted to meet the resource requirements or the session has to be terminated. The content available at a sender may be adapted dynamically to meet the changing resource capabilities or a discrete number of content variants could be created offline to serve the receivers. The primary goal of content adaptation is to maximize the end user's quality of experience given the resource constraints at the receiver and the sender.

Content Adaptation

The mismatch between the content and resources required to play the contest is bridged using adaptation techniques. The adaptation techniques can either adapt the content to match the receiver capabilities or adapt the resources to match the content. Resource adaptation typically takes the form of resource acquisition. The content adaptation problem has two aspects 1) determining what information to send and 2) how to encode that information efficiently for transmission. Determining the right information to be sent based on user preferences and available resources uses summarization techniques that strive to maintain semantic equivalence with minimal amount of information [1]. Once the appropriate content has been determined, a suitable compression technique is selected and the content is transcoded to match the receiver capabilities [2].

Resource Adaptation

Another approach to UMA is through resource acquisition. A receiver acquires additional resources to bridge the mismatch with the content, primarily by collaborating with other devices in its environment and thus creating a virtual device. This virtual device approach to receiver adaptation was reported in [3]. The availability of Bluetooth and the upcoming short range ultra wideband communications make the virtual device a possibility. The virtual device concept works well in home and office environments with access to a number of peripherals. The key issue here is security: how can trust be established in a peripheral device.

Standardization

The UMA is also supported by the international standardization activities. The MPEG committee, under its MPEG-21 activity, has standardized tools for digital item adaptation (DIA) [4]. Digital item is a generic term for digital information that is exchanged between devices. The standard specifies tools for describing the digital items and adaptation alternatives when adaptation is necessary. The TV anytime forum has also released a series of specification to enable pervasive audio visual services [5]. The W3C has developed a standard to describe device capabilities and user preferences called Composite Capabilities/Preferences Profile (CC/PP) [6]. The CC/PP descriptions can be used during session setup to understand the receiver preferences and capabilities. These CC/PP descriptions can drive the content and resource adaptation necessary to make the content delivery possible.

References

1. L. He, E. Sanocki, A. Gupta, and J. Grudin, "Auto-Summarization of Audio-Video Presentations," Proceedings of the Seventh ACM International Conference on Multimedia (Part 1), pp. 489-498.

2. J. Xin, C.-W. Lin, and M.-T. Sun, "Digital video transcoding," Proceedings of the IEEE, Vol. 93, Issue 1, January 2005, pp. 84- 97.

3. R. Y. Fu et. al, "A framework for device capability on demand and virtual device user experience," IBM Journal of Research and Development, Vol. 48, No. 5/6, 2004, pp. 635-648.

4. ISO/IEC JTC 1/SC 29, "Information technology -- Multimedia framework (MPEG-21) -- Part 7: Digital Item Adaptation," ISO/IEC 21000-7:2004.

5. www.tv-anytime.org

6. G. Klyne, et. al., "Composite Capability/Preference Profiles (CC/PP): Structure and Vocabularies," W3C Recommendation, http://www.w3.org/TR/CCPP-struct-vocab/, 2004.

USER MODELING IN MPEG-7

Definition: *User modeling refers to building a profile of the user's preferences for consumption and usage. In MPEG-7, two tools are specifically implemented for user interaction, which are the User Preferences DS and the User History DS.*

Just as we have to model the content to describe the rich multi faceted detail stored both semantically and structurally [1], we must also model the user in a similar fashion, building a profile of the user's preferences for consumption and usage. The requirements are different but the concept remains similar, model the user by capturing the many multi faceted perspectives of the user that combine to describe the mental and corporeal needs of the user. The mental needs are the user's interests and needs for specific information; the corporeal is how, when and where they would like to view that information. The main difference between content modeling and user modeling is that the former is temporally static after creation and the latter evolves continuously over time.

As the user evolves their preferences for information, usage environment and demographic data change as well [2]. The user model must also evolve with the changing user or the model will stagnate. Demographic data does not change a great deal over time and can be adjusted manually. The user's preferences for information and to a lesser extent the usage environment data change at a much greater rate and to update this manually would be impractical. Automatic methods that track and log the user's interaction can do this without any explicit effort from the user. Although the extraction methods can be proprietary or technology specific the logging of the interactions must be MPEG-7 compliant.

Defined in MPEG-7 MDS are two tools that have been specifically implemented for user interaction, namely the User Preferences DS and the User History DS [3]. The User Preferences DS contains all the tools to describe the user both mentally and corporeally by being able to state the preferences for information contained in other tools within MPEG-7 as well the usage environment of the user. The user model consists of three separate components; preferences for content (e.g. movies, books, etc), demographic information (e.g. language, gender, etc) and usage environment (i.e. location, time, etc).

The User History DS is the MPEG-7 logging tool for user interactions; it logs the interaction with the user in terms of content viewed, the interaction with the content and where and when interactions took place. The User History DS is then analyzed and used to update the user model, keeping it current to a user's changing needs. User Preferences DS and the User History DS tools can be customized to include or exclude features of the user to provide a granular detail of the user's preferences and consumption requirements. This provides the same amount of rich and perceptively textured description of the user as you would have for content but with the additional functionality of evolving the model as the users needs change.

See: **Multimedia Content Modeling and Personalization**

References

1. I. E. G. Richardson, "H.264 and MPEG-4 Video Compression: Video Coding for Next-generation Multimedia," John Wiley, New York, 2005.
2. B.L. Tseng, C.-Y. Lin, and J.R. Smith, "Using MPEG-7 and MPEG-21 for Personalizing Video," IEEE Multimedia, Vol. 11, No. 4, October 2004, pp. 42-53.
3. H. Kosch, "Distributed multimedia database technologies supported by MPEG-7 and MPEG-21," CRC Press, Boca Raton, Florida, 2003.

V

VALENCE-DRIVEN CONQUEST

Definition: *Alliez's VD (Valence-Driven Conquest) [1] reduces the number of triangles by checking the degree of the tip vertex.*

It removes the tip vertices with valence more than 3 and tags the remaining vertices. Because the decimation follows a systematic traversal, the decompression can reverse it and reconstruct the meshes. The connectivity can be compressed to 3.7 bits per vertex and the geometry encoding takes 12 bits per vertex. The geometric data contains the error vector between the predicted and the real vertex positions. However, the selection of the vertices to be removed at each batch is only based on the connectivity, and it thus produces less accurate intermediate models than CPM [2].

The transformations at compression for Valence-driven conquest are "vertex removal" and "retriangulation". A degree-d "patch" is a set of faces incident to valence-d vertex. This valence-d vertex is the "tip-vertex" of this patch. Figure 1 shows how a degree-5 tip-vertex V is removed, and then how the patch is retriangulated and tagged with "+" and "-" signs. The inverse transformations at decompression are "patch discovery" and "vertex insertion". The decoder uses the received degree information and the current tags to discover the border of the patch and insert the new vertex.

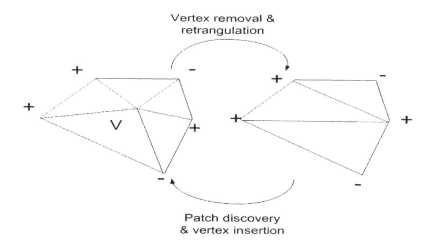

Figure 1. Valence-driven vertex removal and retriangulation.

See: Middleware for streaming 3D meshes

References

1. P. Alliez and M. Desbrun, "Progressive compression for lossless transmission of triangle meshes," Proceedings of SIGGRAPH 01.
2. J. Rossignac, "Handbook of Discrete and Computational Geometry," CRC Press, Chapter 54.

VC-1 VIDEO COMPRESSION

Definition: VC-1 is a video codec developed for broadcast interlaced video as well as progressive video by Microsoft.

VC-1 is derived from Microsoft's proprietary WMV-9 but awaits SMPTE ratification. VC-1 is pure video compression technology, and is expected to be deployed as key engines in satellite TV, IP set-tops and high-definition DVD recorders.

Simple and Main Profiles for VC-1 Video

The Simple and Main Profiles (SP/MP) of VC-1 are supposed to be the same as those of WMV-9 in progressive compression, respectively. However, there is no Advanced Profile (AP) in WMV-9 to compare with VC-1 AP. VC-1 AP mainly focuses on interlaced video compression technology. And, the interlace tools cannot be compared directly in both standards. Even the starting point is different -- the input format is YUV4:1:1 for WMV-9, but is YUV4:2:0 for VC-1. Note that only Field-based prediction and Frame-based prediction are selectively applied in each MB in the interlace tool of WMV-9. This tool is applied when the INTERLACE flag is turned on in the Sequence header.

Advanced Profile for VC-1 Video

The number of B frames is not fixed between two references in VC-1, while it is a constant value that can be found in the Sequence header in WMV-9. New distance value comes into the Picture Structure at Entry- point Layer with REFDIST_FLAG. REFDIST data indicates the number of frames between the current frame and reference one. Progressive-Picture/ Frame-Picture/ Field-Picture can be mixed in a video. It is the encoder job to construct each picture with a FCM (Frame Coding Mode). The maximum number of references is 2 for P Field-Picture. The references are specified in Picture layer. If both 2 references are selected, the selection of reference information is described in MB level and Block level. The number of references is always 4 for B Field-Picture -- no Picture layer selection is needed. So, the selection of reference is always in MB level and Block level. Note that one of reference fields for bottom field in a B frame is its top field itself. P Field-Picture has 2 MC modes (1MV with 16x16, 4MV with 8x8). B Field-Picture has 3 MC modes (1MV with 16x16 in forward or backward modes, 2MV with 16x16 in interpolative or direct modes, 4MV with 8x8 only in forward or backward modes). P Frame-Picture has 4 MC modes (1MV Frame-based prediction with 16x16, 4MV Frame-based prediction with 8x8, 2MV Field-based prediction with 16x8 (each field), 4MV Field-based prediction with 8x8 (each field 16x8 divided to left/right 8x8)). B Frame-Picture has 4 MC modes (1MV Frame-based prediction with 16x16 in forward or backward modes, 2MV Frame-based prediction with 16x16 in interpolative or direct modes, 2MV Field-based prediction with 16x8 (each field) in forward or backward modes, 4MV Field-based prediction with 16x8 (each field) in interpolative or direct modes). Once residual data is obtained after motion-estimation in encoders, transform is applied on it. In Intra MBs or Intra Blocks, transform is applied on original data. There are 2 transforms – Frame-transform and Field-transform. Frame-transform is to apply the transform on Frame-Picture data without any reordering, while Field-transform is to apply the transform on Frame-Picture data with sorting top/ bottom field data. Note that this option is only available in Frame-Pictures. Encoders decide about which transform mode is applied in each MB. In the case of Intra MBs, the mode determined is written in FIELDTX. In the Inter MBs, however, the mode is written in MBMODE. Transform block size can change adaptively, while size of motion compensation is among 16x16/ 16x8/ 8x8 in VC-1. There are 4 transform sizes as are in WMV-9 – 8x8, 4x8, 8x4 and 4x4.

The same two techniques are used in VC-1 to reduce blocky effect around transform boundary – Overlapped Transform (OLT) smoothing and In Loop deblocking Filtering (ILF). One important difference in OLT technique between WMV-9 and VC-1 is to have the control even on MB level in I frame with CONDOVER and OVERFLAGS. The 128 level-shift is done on all the Intra MBs and Intra Blocks in VC-1, while the level-shift is performed only on Intra MBs and Intra Blocks that undergo OLT in WMV-9. In interlaced video, the OLT smoothing is applied only for vertical direction in Frame-Pictures, while it is performed for both horizontal and vertical directions in Field-Pictures. Note that horizontal edge filtering might require top and bottom fields together as inputs in Frame-Pictures – this would make potential output filtered data blurry. That is why only vertical direction edge is asked to be OLT-filtered for Frame-Pictures in the VC-1 standard. On the other hand, ILF is to filter both horizontal and vertical directions in Field-Pictures of interlaced video. In Frame-Pictures of interlaced video, however, horizontal and vertical ILFs are performed differently. – ILF in vertical edges is the same as that of Field-Pictures, while ILF in horizontal edges is performed based on Field-based ILF filtering. In other words, only the same polarity data are considered in ILF filtering.

VC-1 Video Specific Semantics and Syntax

There are 6 levels of headers inVC-1 video bitstream syntax – Sequence, Entry-point, Picture, Slice, MB and Block. AP has explicit Sequence header, but SP/MP don't have any Sequence header in VC-1. The data necessary in Sequence header should be provided by external means. Sequence header contains basic parameters such as profile/ level, interlace, loop filter, max_coded_width, max_coded_height, and some other global parameters. This includes display related metadata and HRD parameters. Entry-point header is present only in AP. It is used to signal random access point and control parameter changes in the decoding. Examples include broken_link, closed_entry, refdist_flag, loopfilter, overlap, coded_width, coded_height, and other global parameters until the next Entry-point header. Picture header contains information about FCM/ TFF/ RFF/ RNDCTRL/ PQindex/ LumScale1-2 /LumShift1-2/ CONDOVER/ BFRACTION, etc. FCM is present only if the INTERACE has the value 1, and it indicates whether the frame is coded as progressive/ Field-Picture/ Field-Frame. TFF and RFF are present as Top Field First and Repeat First Field flags respectively if PULLDOWN and INTERLACE are set to 1. RNDCTRL is used to indicate the type of rounding used for current frame. In P Field-Pictures, 2 intensity compensation parameters (LumScale and LumShift) are needed for top field and bottom field, respectively. CONDOVER is present only in I pictures only when OVERLAP is on and PQUANT is less than or equal to 8. Slice header provides information about SLICE_ADDR/ PIC_HEADER_FLAG. Slice Address is from 1 to 511, where the row address of the first MB in the slice is binary encoded. The picture header information is repeated in the slice header if the PIC_HEADER_FLAG is set to 1. MB header has MBMODE/ OVERFLAGMB/ MVMODEBIT/ SKIPMBBIT/ CBPCY/ MQDIFF/ ABSMQ/ MVDATA/ BLKMVDATA/ HYBRIDPRED/ BMV1/ BMV2/ MBVTYPE, etc. MBMODE indicates whether Intra/ Inter(1MV)/ Inter(4MV)/ CBP/ MV data are present. OVERFLAGMB is present when CONDOVER has the binary value 11. OVERFLAGS indicates whether to perform OLT within the block and neighboring blocks. Other data can similarly be interpreted as those in WMV-9.

See: Video Coding Techniques and Standards

References

1. S. Sinivassan, P. Hsu, T Holcomb, K. Mukerjee, S. Regunathan, B. Lin, J. Liang, M.-C. Lee, and J. Ribas-Corbera, "WMV-9: Overview and Applications," Signal Processing Image Communication, October 2004, pp. 851-875.

VECTOR EDGE DETECTORS

Definition: *Scalar (monochrome) edge detection may not be sufficient for certain applications since no edges will be detected in gray value images when neighboring objects have different hues but equal intensities; in these cases vector edge detectors must be applied.*

Psychological research on the characteristics of the human visual system reveals that color plays a significant role in the perception of edges or boundaries between two surfaces [1]-[3]. Scalar (monochrome) edge detection may not be sufficient for certain applications since no edges will be detected in gray value images when neighboring objects have different hues but equal intensities. Objects with such boundaries are treated as one big object in the scene. Since the capability to distinguishing between different objects is crucial for applications such as object recognition, image segmentation, image coding, and robot vision, the additional boundary information provided by color is of paramount importance.

It is well-known that the color image is represented as the two-dimensional array of three-component vectors [1]. Thus, the color edge can be defined as a significant discontinuity in the vector field representing the color image function [3]. Following the major performance issues in color edge detection such as the ability to extract edges accurately, robustness to noise, and the computational efficiency, most popular color edge detectors are those based on vector order-statistics [1]-[3].

Edge detectors based on order statistics operate by detecting local minimum and maximum in the color image function and combining them in an appropriate way in order to produce the corresponding edge map. Since there is no unique way to define ranks for multichannel (vector) signals, such as color images and cDNA microarray images, the reduced ordering scheme is commonly used to achieve the ranked sequence $\mathbf{x}_{(1)}, \mathbf{x}_{(2)}, ..., \mathbf{x}_{(N)}$ of the color vectors $\mathbf{x}_1, \mathbf{x}_2, ..., \mathbf{x}_N$ inside the processing window. Based on these two extreme vector order-statistics $\mathbf{x}_{(1)}$ (lowest ranked vector) and $\mathbf{x}_{(N)}$ (uppermost ranked vector), the vector range detector detects edges through the comparison of the threshold and the Euclidean distance value between $\mathbf{x}_{(1)}$ and $\mathbf{x}_{(N)}$. The output of such an operator used in a uniform area, where all vectors inside the processing window are characterized by a similar magnitude and/or the direction, is small. However, in high-frequency regions, where $\mathbf{x}_{(N)}$ is usually located at the one side of an edge, whereas $\mathbf{x}_{(1)}$ is included in the set of vectors occupying spatial positions on other side of the edge, the response of the vector range detector is a large value.

Due to the utilization of the distance between the lowest and upper-most ranked vector, the vector range operator is rather sensitive to noise. More robust color edge detectors are obtained using linear combinations of the lowest ranked vector samples. This is mainly due to the fact that: i) the lowest ranks are associated with the most similar vectors in the population of the color vectors, and ii) upper ranks usually correspond to the outlying samples. The minimum over the magnitudes of these linear combinations defines the edge detector's output. Different coefficients in the linear combinations result in a multitude of edge detectors which vary significantly in terms of performance and/or complexity [1]-[3].

See: Color image filtering and enhancement, Edge detection, Scalar edge detectors, Distance and similarity measures, Multichannel data ordering schemes.

References

1. R. Lukac, B. Smolka, K. Martin, K.-N. Plataniotis, and A.-N. Venetsanopulos, "Vector Filtering for Color Imaging," IEEE Signal Processing Magazine, Vol. 22, No. 1, January 2005, pp. 74-86.
2. R. Lukac, K.-N. Plataniotis, A.-N. Venetsanopoulos, R. Bieda, and B. Smolka, "Color Edge Detection Techniques," In "Signaltheorie und Signalverarbeitung, Akustik und Sprachakustik, Informationstechnik," W.E.B. Universität Verlag, Dresden, Vol. 29, 2003, pp.21-47.
3. K.-N. Plataniotis and A.-N. Venetsanopoulos, "Color Image Processing and Applications," Springer Verlag, Berlin, 2000.

VIDEO AUTOMATIC ANNOTATION

Alberto Del Bimbo and Marco Bertini
Università di Firenze, Firenze, Italy

Definition: Automatic annotation of video refers to the extraction of the information about *video automatically, which can serve as the first step for different data access modalities such as browsing, searching, comparison, and categorization.*

Advances in digital video technology and the ever increasing availability of computing resources have resulted, in the last few years, in an explosion of digital video data. Moreover, the increased availability of Internet bandwidth has defined new means of video distribution, other than physical media. The major web search engines have already started to provide specific services to index, search and retrieve videos on the Internet.

Improving of video accessibility is the true challenge. In fact, access to video data requires that video content is appropriately indexed but manually annotating or tagging video is at best a laborious and economically infeasible process. Therefore, one important subject of research has been concerned with study of novel techniques to extract information about video content automatically [1]. This annotation process serves as a first step for different data access modalities such as browsing, searching, comparison and categorization.

Automatic video annotation can be carried out at different levels, from the low syntactic level, where audiovisual features are extracted up to the high semantic level where concepts are recognized. Shot detection is the most basic temporal video segmentation task, as it is intrinsically and inextricably linked to the way that video is produced. It segments a video into more manageable parts and is very often the first step in other algorithms that operate both at syntactic and semantic level. At the syntactic level, video annotation is concerned with the estimation of low and mid-level features such as motion descriptors and the derivation of compact visualization of video content, like the extraction of a representative set of frames, either independent or organized in short sequences; this visualization can be used as a substitute for the whole video for the purposes of searching, comparison and categorization and is especially useful for video browsing. At semantic level, video annotation regards the identification and recognition of meaningful entities represented in the video, like settings, text captions, people and objects, or meaningful highlights and events.

The state of the art and principal contributions in each of these subjects of investigation are discussed in the following sections.

Shot and Scene detection

Shot-change detection is the process of identifying the elementary units of video and changes in the scene content of a video sequence so that alternate representations may be derived for the purposes of browsing and retrieval, e.g. extraction of key-frames, mosaic images or further processing by other algorithms and techniques to extract information used to perform content-based indexing and classification. A common definition of shot is: "a sequence of frames that was (or appears to be) continuously captured from the same camera" ([2]). Usually this is the definition that is used for the comparison of shot detection algorithms; a shot can encompass several types of camera motions: pan, tilt and zoom, but algorithms for shot-detection may also react to changes caused by significant camera and object motion, unless a global motion-compensation is performed. Shot changes may be of different types: hard (cut), gradual (dissolve, wipe and fade) and others (special effects like push, slide, etc.).

A large body of literature has been produced on the subject of shot detection, with proposals of methods working either in the compressed or in the non compressed domain. Survey papers have reviewed and compared the most effective solutions. Boreczky et al. ([3]) compared five different algorithms: global histograms, region histograms, global histograms using twin-comparison thresholding, motion-compensated pixel difference and DCT-coefficient difference. The histograms were grayscale histograms. Dailianas et al. ([4]) compared algorithms based on histogram differencing, moment invariants, pixel-value changes and edge detection (Zabih algorithm). The histogram-based segmentation algorithms differencing methods studied were: bin-to-bin difference, weighted histogram difference, histogram difference after equalization, intersection of histograms and squared histogram difference (chi-square). Kasturi, Gargi et al. ([5]) have also recently compared histogram-based algorithms to MPEG and block-matching algorithms. The frame difference measures analyzed are: bin-to-bin difference, chi-square histogram difference, histogram intersection and average color. Three block-matching and six MPEG based methods are analyzed. The effects of different color space representation and MPEG encoders are evaluated.

Another possible partition of the video stream is the "scene". Traditionally, a scene is a continuous sequence that is temporally and spatially cohesive in the real (or represented) world — but not necessarily in the projection of the real world in the video, and may in fact be composed by several shots (e.g. a dialogue in a movie). Scene detection is a very subjective task that depends on human cultural conditioning, professional training and even intuition. But it is also strictly connected to the genre of video and its subject domain. Moreover, since it focuses on real-world actions and temporal and spatial configurations of objects and people, it requires the ability to understand the meaning of images. Due to these facts the automatic segmentation of a video into scenes ranges from very difficult to intractable, and usually is carried on using low level visual features or the knowledge of well defined patterns present in the video domain being analyzed. An approach that tries to overcome these difficulties, employing dominant color grouping and tracking to evaluate a shot correlation measure, and performing shot grouping has been presented in [2].

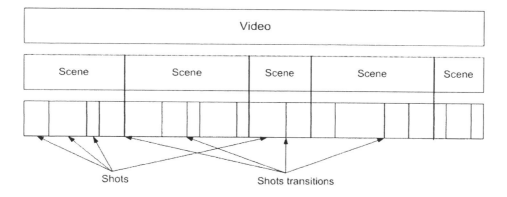

Figure 1. Shows the syntactic structure of a video stream.

Low level content annotation

Low level content annotation of videos requires setting indexes of primitives, usually extracted from the segmented parts of the video stream. These indexes may be distinguished into indexes on visual primitives, like objects and motion, indexes on audio primitives, like silence, music, words, environment or special sounds, and indexes on the meaning conveyed by primitives that can be used for video summarization. MPEG7 provides several descriptors for these indexes of primitives.

Object primitives are usually extracted from key-frames and can be used in retrieval applications for comparison with primitives extracted from a query frame. Object segmentation techniques similar to those employed in image analysis can be applied. On the other hand it is more complex for motion indexes to be extracted due to temporal dependency between video frames, which requires to study the motion of pixels between subsequent images of the sequence. Motion is induced either by camera operations and/or objects independently moving in the scene. Sometimes, the first is referred to as global motion, while the latter is called local motion. Extraction of moving objects also provides the initial step to extract semantic information on the video, useful to identify key-frames and produce condensed representations based on significant frames or video mosaics.

Most of the approaches to motion estimation use direct (gradient-based) techniques. The methods based on gradient employ the relation between spatial and temporal variations of the lightness intensity. This relation can be employed to segment images based on the speed of each point and may be considered as an approach to the more general problem of motion segmentation.

An approach commonly used when annotating video acquired from a stationary camera is to segment each image into a set of regions representing the moving objects by using a background differencing algorithm [8]. More recently, Elgammal et al. [9] have proposed background modeling using a generalization of Gaussians mixture models, where the background is assumed to be a set of N Gaussian distributions centered on the pixel values in the previous N frames. Then the average probability of each pixel's value in the N Gaussian distributions is evaluated, expressing the likelihood of belonging to the background; this approach allow us to process video streams with time varying background.

Other approaches are based on correspondence techniques. Instead of observing every point, they extract some characteristics from the image, hopefully from the "interest objects" that are supposed to stay constant in everything but the position. The search for these characteristics in two consecutive frames allows extracting a map of velocity vectors defined only for "interesting" points (see Figure 2).

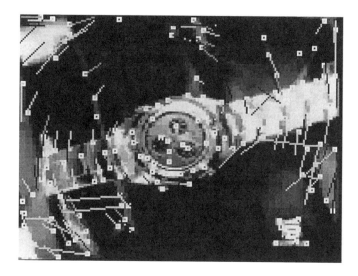

Figure 2. Feature based motion estimation.

Motion features may be employed as a cue to detect video highlights. Several authors have defined indices related to "excitement". Usually a multimodal approach that takes into account frequency of shot change, motion activity and sound energy is employed to derive these indices. Maxima of these indices, or maxima of entropy metrics based on these indices, are used to derive highlight time curves.

Typical low level audio analysis consists in audio classification of audio segments into at least four main classes: silence, music, speech and other sounds, using loudness and spectrum features. It is possible to further discriminate the sounds that belong to the fourth class in more specific sounds, usually depending on the domain, like cries, shots and explosions in movies ([6]), or whistles in sports videos.

High level content annotation

High level content annotation strives at producing semantic annotation, combining low level features, appropriate pattern recognition techniques, and usually domain knowledge. The latter is required in order to reduce the semantic gap between the observable features of the multimedia material and the interpretation that a user may have. Narrowing the application domain is the most typical approach. A good recent and comprehensive review of multimodal video annotation is provided in [7]. High level content annotation is typically concerned with detection of settings, people, text, and highlights or meaningful events. Settings are classified usually as indoor or outdoor, although finer classifications can also be obtained. Several visual features may be employed to recognize the setting of a video scene: color histograms, color coherence vectors, DCT coefficients, edge direction histograms, and edge coherence vectors, texture. Motion features are not used since settings are usually static. Typically classification of settings is performed exploiting visual information from keyframes. Special sounds or cheers can also be used to reinforce classification.

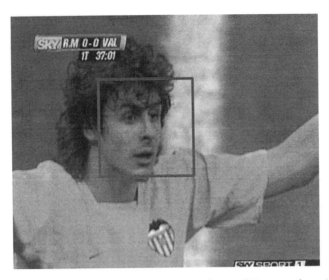

Figure 3. Face detection using the Viola and Jones algorithm.

Most of the approaches to people detection in videos deal with face detection. In general, problems arise from the large variety in locations, lighting conditions, orientation, scale and location. Most of the approaches reduce the problem of face detection to that of single frame processing. In this case you must be assured that a full view of the face is included in the frame (see Figure 3). An effective technique, recently integrated in the OpenCV library, is that proposed by Viola and Jones ([13]). Basically, the algorithm relies on a number of simple classifiers which are devoted to signal the presence of a particular feature of the object to be detected. In the case of faces, this could be the alignment of the two eyes or the symmetry in frontal views. A large number of these simple features are initially selected. Then, a complex classifier is constructed by selecting a small number of important features using AdaBoost. The method also combines increasingly more complex classifiers in a "cascade" which allows discarding quickly the background regions of the image, while spending more computation on promising object-like regions. A comprehensive survey of face detection and recognition techniques can be found in [18] and [19].

Textual information included in images or videos often contains information that otherwise is not available in other information channels, such as, for example, the name and role of an interviewed person in news videos. Video text analysis requires usually three processing steps: detection (time and space position), extraction and processing of the text image (to separate it from the background), and finally text recognition. Text may be scene text (e.g. a billboard in the background), superimposed text or closed captions. The first type of text is the most critical to be detected and processed since it may appear slanted, tilted or partially occluded; nevertheless in some cases it may be treated as superimposed captions (e.g. in commercials). The second type of text has received a lot of attention, and several approaches to perform the first two processing steps have been proposed. Typically solutions exploit the fact that text appears for several frames in the same position (see Figure 4). Some approaches use image segmentation and then connected components analysis to select regions as character candidates; constraints on text appearance and size are used [10].

Other approaches use texture as a distinctive feature. A review of these approaches is provided in [11]. Another group of algorithms relies on the fact that superimposed captions have usually a high contrast w.r.t. the background, and then search for regions composed by sharp borders o group of corners. The third type of text does not require the extraction steps, although it still requires some processing, since it may suffer from the typical phenomena that characterize spoken language, such as hesitation, ellipses, etc. Example of usage of closed captions for video abstraction was presented in [12]. Recently closed captions have been selected as a feature used by Google 's video search engine, among the others.

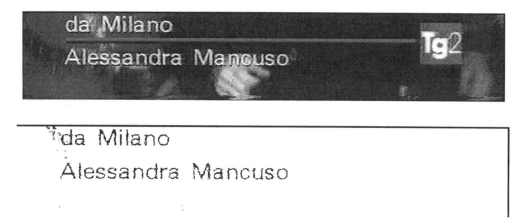

Figure 4. An example of superimposed caption extraction.
Time integration over several frames is used to enhance text appearance.

Highlight detection and recognition is dependent on the video subject domain. In the following we provide an overview of some of the most interesting solutions for highlight annotation techniques, distinguished by the domain which they have been designed for.

News videos annotation has been thoroughly analyzed by many researchers because of the well defined structure of news video, which alternates shots with anchormen and reports. After video segmentation shots are classified in one of the two classes. Approaches based on template matching may perform the classification using the spatial structure of anchorman shots, calculating mean and variance o histogram and pixel values of the areas that should belong to the anchorman or the news logo. Other approaches based on syntactic and structural matching instead use the structure of the video, identifying repeated shots that have strong similarity and low motion. Finally probabilistic methods may use HMMs trained with several clues, including feature vectors based on difference images, average frame color and audio signal. An example o this approach is presented in [21]. Semantic annotation of the news shots is performed through video OCR or speech recognition, as in the Informedia Project lead by Carnegie Mellon [14].

Due to their huge commercial appeal sports videos represent an important application domain for automatic video annotation. It is possible to identify sports videos based on detection of slow motion replays, large areas of superimposed captions, and specific camera motion. Furthermore it is possible to distinguish which type of sport is being shown by analyzing features related to the playfield, like ground color and lines. In [15] shots of sports video are classified into three classes, according to the most common scenes that are played, namely playfield, players' close-ups and crowd. A feature vector composed by edges, segments and color information is employed. Figure 5 shows the features used to distinguish the three classes. Once playfield shots have been classified it is possible to perform sport classification according to the special characteristics of the playfield. Neural networks have been employed to perform the classification.

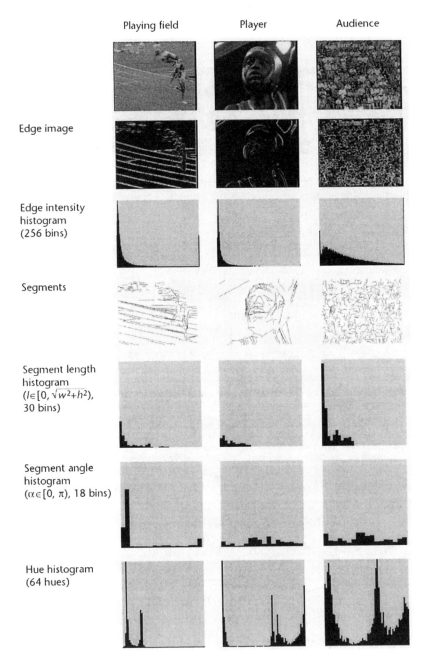

Figure 5. Edge, segment length and orientation, and hue distribution for three representative sample images. Synthetic indices derived from these distributions allow differentiation between the three classes playing field, player, and audience.

Recognition of specific highlights has been studied for different sports like soccer, tennis, basketball, volleyball, baseball, American football. Usually these methods exploit low and mid level audio and visual cues, such as the detection of referee's whistle, excited speech, crowd cheering, color and edge related features, playfield zone identification, players and ball tracking, motion indexes, etc. and relate them to a-priori domain knowledge of the sport or to knowledge of production rules. In the first case sport rules and the spatio-temporal evolution of typical actions are used. In the second case special production rules employed by directors (like the use of slow motion replays) are exploited. An example of the first approach has been presented in [16] where each highlight is modeled with a Finite State Machine: key events, defined in terms of estimated visual cues (camera motion, playfield zone framed, and players' position), determine the transition from one state to the following. Highlight models are checked against the current observations, using a model checking algorithm.

An example of the second approach has been presented in [17] where highlight detection in soccer video is performed using both shot sequence analysis and shot visual cues. It is assumed that the presence of highlights can be inferred from the occurrence of one or several slow motion shots and from the presence of shots where the referee and/or the goal box is framed.

Feature films are even less structured than sports videos, thus highlight detection is much more general. Movie genre classification, based on four visual features (shot length, color variance, motion, lighting key) extracted from movie previews has been presented in [20]. Dialogue scenes may be detected using audio analysis, face detection and localization. Alternatively similar and temporally close shots are analyzed, exploiting the fact that in many movies dialogues are obtained following the shot-reverse-shot technique. Similarity may be valuated using only visual features or adding also audio features, like the classification of audio segments into silence, speech, music and miscellaneous sound. The detection of patterns allows classifying the scene as dialogue, action or other story units. Other classifications for movie scenes are those of "violent" and "sex" scenes; this is usually done taking into account both visual and audio. Violent scenes can be detected by checking the presence of blood colored regions, high shot change rate and high motion activity ([22]). The abrupt change in audio energy can also be used as an additional feature.

References

1. N. Dimitrova, H.-J. Zhang, B. Shahraray, I. Sezan, T. Huang, and A. Zakhor. "Applications of videocontent analysis and retrieval," IEEE Multimedia Magazine, Vol. 12, No. 3, July 2002.
2. T. Lin and H.J. Zhang, "Automatic video scene extraction by shot grouping," Proceedings of the 15th International Conference on Pattern Recognition. Vol. 4, September 2000, pp. 39-42, 2000.
3. J.S. Boreczky and L.A. Rowe, "Comparison of video shot boundary detection techniques," Proceedings of the IS&T/SPIE Conference Storage and Retrieval for Image and Video Databases IV, Vol. SPIE 2670, 1996, pp. 170-179.

4. A. Dailianas, R.B. Allen, and P. England, "Comparison of automatic video segmentation algorithms," Proceedings of the Integration Issues in Large Commercial Media Delivery Systems, Vol. SPIE 2615, October 1995, pp. 2-16.

5. U. Gargi, R. Kasturi, and S. H. Strayer. "Performance characterization of video-shot-change detection methods," IEEE Transactions on Circuits and Systems for Video Technology, Vol. 10, No. 3, February 2000.

6. S. Pfeiffer, S. Fischer, and W. Effelsberg, "Automatic Audio Content Analysis," Proceedings of the ACM Multimedia 96, pp. 21-30, 1996.

7. C.G.M. Snoek and M. Worring. "Multimodal video indexing: a review of the state-of-the-art," Multimedia Tools and Applications, Vol. 25, No. 1, pp. 5-35, January 2005.

8. S.S. Intille, J.W. Davis, and A.F. Bobick, "Real Time Closed World Tracking," Proceedings of the IEEE Conference on Computer Vision and Pattern Recognition, pp. 697-703, 1997.

9. A. Elgammal, D. Harwood, and L.S. Davis, "Non Parametric Model for Background Subtraction," Proceedings of the 7th IEEE International Conference on Computer Vision, Kerkyra, Greece, September 1999.

10. T. Sato, T. Kanade, E. Hughes, and M. Smith. "Video OCR for Digital News Archives," Proceedings of the IEEE Workshop on Content–Based Access of Image and Video Databases (CAIVD'98), Bombay, India, January 1998.

11. R. Lienhart, "Video OCR: A survey and practitioner's guide," In A. Rosenfeld, D. Doermann, and D. DeMenthon, Editors, Video Mining, pp. 155–183, Kluwer Academic Publishers, 2003.

12. L. Agnihotri, K.V. Devara, T. McGee, and N. Dimitrova, "Summarization of video programs based on closed captions," Proceedings of the SPIE, Vol. 4315, pp. 599-607, Storage and Retrieval for Media Databases, 2001.

13. P. Viola and M. Jones, "Rapid object detection using a boosted cascade of simple features," Proceedings of the Computer Vision and Pattern Recognition (CVPR'01), 2001.

14. A. Hauptmann, D. Ng, R. Baron, M-Y Chen, M. Christel, S. Duygulu, C. Huang, W-H. Lin, H. Wactlar, N. Moraveji, N. Papernick, C.G.M. Snoek, G. Tzanetakis, J. Yang, R. Yan, and R. Jin, "Informedia at TRECVID 2003: Analyzing and Searching Broadcast News Video," Proceedings of TREC 2003, Gaithersburg, MD, November 2003.

15. J. Assfalg, M. Bertini, C. Colombo, and A. Del Bimbo, "Semantic Annotation of Sports Videos," IEEE Multimedia, Vol. 9 No. 2, pp. 52-60, April/June 2002.

16. J. Assfalg, M. Bertini, C. Colombo, A. Del Bimbo, and W. Nunziati, "Semantic annotation of soccer videos: automatic highlights identification," Computer Vision and Image Understanding, Vol. 92, Issue 2-3, pp. 285-305, November/December 2003.

17. A. Ekin, A.M. Tekalp, and R. Mehrotra, "Automatic soccer video analysis and summarization," IEEE Transactions on Image Processing, Vol. 12, No. 7, pp. 796-807, July 2003.

18. M.H. Yang, D.J. Kriegman, and N. Ahuja, "Detecting faces in images: A survey," IEEE Transactions on Pattern Analysis and Machine, Vol. 24, No. 1, pp. 34-58, January 2002.

19. W. Zhao, R. Chellappa, P.J. Phillips, and A. Rosenfeld, "Face recognition: a literature survey," ACM Computing Surveys, Vol. 35, No. 4, pp. 309-459, December 2003.

20. Z. Rasheed, Y. Sheikh, and M. Shah, "On the Use of Computable Features for Film Classification," IEEE Transactions on Circuits and Systems for Video, Vol. 15, No. 1, pp. 52-64, January 2005.
21. S. Eickeler and S. Muller, "Content-based video indexing of TV broadcast news using Hidden Markov Models," Proceedings of the IEEE International Conference on Acoustics, Speech, and Signal Processing, ICASSP '99, Vol. 6, pp. 2997-3000, March 1999.
22. B. Lehane, N. O'Connor, and N. Murphy, "Action Sequence Detection in Motion Pictures," Proceedings of the European Workshop on the Integration of Knowledge, Semantics and Digital Media Technology, London, U.K., November 2004.

VIDEO-BASED FACE RECOGNITION

Definition: Video-based face recognition in image sequences has gained increased interest based primarily on the idea expressed by psychophysical studies that motion helps humans recognize faces, especially when spatial image quality is low.

Although face recognition has been an active research topic for decades, the traditional recognition algorithms are all based on static images. However, during the last years face recognition in image sequences has gained increased interest based primarily on the idea expressed by psychophysical studies that motion helps humans recognize faces, especially when spatial image quality is low.

Video-based face recognition systems consist of three modules: a detection module, a tracking module and a recognition module. Given a frame of a video sequence, the detection module locates face candidates, while the tracking module finds the exact position of facial features in the current frame based on an estimate of face or feature locations in the previous frame(s). The recognition module identifies or verifies the face, integrating information from previous frames [1].

In the detection module, motion and/or skin color information may be used for segmenting the face from the background and locate candidate face regions. Face detection techniques similar to those applied for still images are then employed to find the exact location of faces in the current frame, thus initiating face and facial feature tracking. Face tracking techniques include head tracking, where the head is viewed as a rigid object performing translations and rotations, facial feature tracking, where facial features deformations due to facial expressions or speech are viewed as non-rigid transformations limited by the head anatomy, and methods tracking head and features [1]. Face and facial feature tracking is sometimes used to reconstruct the 3D shape of the face, which is subsequently used for enhancing face recognition.

The main problem of video-based face recognition is low quality of images in video sequences, while the unquestionable advantage is the abundance of information. This enables the selection of the frames that will be used for recognition and the reuse of recognition information obtained in precedent frames. Also, temporal continuity allows tracking of facial features, which can help in compensating pose or expression variations, while motion, gait and other features may enhance the performance of face recognition. Moreover, the simultaneous comprehensive exploitation of spatiotemporal cues results in increased tracking and identification accuracy [1]. Video-based techniques are ideal for surveillance or facility monitoring applications.

Figure 1. Example of face and facial features tracking in Erik image sequence.

See: Face Recognition

References

1. W. Zhao, R. Chellappa, A. Rosenfeld, and P. J. Phillips, "Face recognition: A literature survey," ACM Computing Surveys, Vol. 35, No. 4, December 2003, pp. 399-459.

VIDEO CODING TECHNIQUES AND STANDARDS

Jae-Beom Lee
Intel Corporation, Portland, USA

Hari Kalva
Florida Atlantic University, Boca Raton, USA

Definition: *Video coding techniques and standards are based on a set of principles that reduce the redundancy in digital video.*

Introduction

Digital video has become main stream and is being used in a wide range of applications including DVD, digital TV, HDTV, video telephony, and teleconferencing. These digital video applications are feasible because of the advances in computing and communication technologies as well as efficient video compression algorithms. The rapid deployment and adoption of these technologies was possible primarily because of standardization and the economies of scale brought about by competition and standardization. Most of the video compression standards are based on a set of principles that reduce the redundancy in digital video.

Digital video is essentially a sequence of pictures displayed overtime. Each picture of a digital video sequence is a 2D projection of the 3D world. Digital video thus is captured as a series of digital pictures or sampled in space and time from an analog video signal. A frame of digital video or a picture can be seen as a 2D array of pixels. Each pixel value represents the color and intensity values of a specific spatial location at a specific time. The Red-Green-Blue (RGB) color space is typically used to capture and display digital pictures. Each pixel is thus represented by one R, G, and B components. The 2D array of pixels that constitutes a picture is actually three 2D arrays with one array for each of the RGB components. A resolution of 8 bits per component is usually sufficient for typical consumer applications.

The need for compression

Consider a digital video sequence at a standard definition TV picture resolution of 720x480 and a frame rate of 30 frames per second (FPS). If a picture is represented using the RGB color space with 8 bits per component or 3 bytes per pixel, size of each frame is 720x480x3 bytes. The disk space required to store one second of video is 720x480x3x30 = 31.1 MB. A one hour video would thus require 112 GB. To deliver video over wired and/or wireless networks, bandwidth required is 31.1x8 = 249 Mbps. In addition to these extremely high storage and bandwidth requirements, using uncompressed video will add significant cost to the hardware and systems that process digital video. Digital video compression is thus necessary even with exponentially increasing bandwidth and storage capacities.

Fortunately, digital video has significant redundancies and eliminating or reducing those redundancies results in compression. Video compression can be lossy or loss less. Loss less video compression reproduces identical video after de-compression. We primarily consider lossy compression that yields perceptually equivalent, but not identical video compared to the uncompressed source. Video compression is typically achieved by exploiting four types of redundancies: 1) perceptual, 2) temporal, 3) spatial, and 4) statistical redundancies.

Perceptual Redundancies

Perceptual redundancies refer to the details of a picture that a human eye cannot perceive. Anything that a human eye cannot perceive can be discarded without affecting the quality of a picture. The human visual system affects how both spatial and temporal details in a video sequence are perceived. A brief overview of the human visual system gives us an understanding of how perceptual redundancies can be exploited.

The Human Visual System

The structure of the human eye is shown in Figure 1.

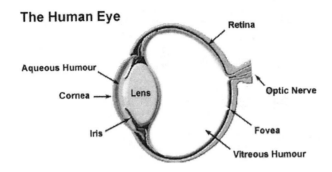

Figure 1. Structure of the human eye.

The human visual system responds when the incoming light is focused on the retina. The photoreceptors in the eye are sensitive to the visible spectrum and generate a stimulation that results in perception. The retina has two types of photo receptors 1) rods and 2) cones. Human eye has about 110 million rods and about 7 million cones. The rods and cones respond differently to the incident light. Rods are sensitive to the variations in intensity (lightness and darkness) and cones are sensitive to color. Rods function well under low illumination and cones function under well-lit conditions. There are three types of cones, Red, Green, Blue each sensitive to the different bands of the visible spectrum. About 64% of the cones are red, 32% green, and about 4% blue. The cones, however, are not uniformly distributed on the retina. The fovea, the central area of the retina, has more green cones than reds and blues resulting in different sensitivity to different bands of the visual spectrum. This makes the human eye more sensitive to the mid spectrum; i.e., the incoming blues and reds have to be brighter than greens and yellows to give a perception of *equal brightness*. Because of the large number of rods, the human eye is more sensitive to variations in intensity than variation in color.

The RGB color space does not closely match the human visual perception. The YCbCr color space (also known as YUV), where Y gives the average brightness of a picture and Cb and Cr give the chrominance components, matches the human visual perception better. The YCbCr representation thus allows exploiting the characteristics of the visual perception better.

Sensitivity to Temporal Frequencies

The eye retains the sensation of a displayed picture for a brief period time after the picture has been removed. This property is called persistence of vision. Human visual persistence is about 1/16 of a second under normal lighting conditions and decreases as brightness increases. Persistence property can be exploited to display video sequence as a set of pictures displayed at a constant rate greater than the persistence of vision. For example, movies are shown at 24 frames per second and require very low brightness levels inside the movie theater. The TV, on the other hand, is much brighter and requires a higher display rate. The sensitivity of the eye to the frame rate also depends on the content itself. High motion content will be more annoying to the viewer at lower frame rates as the eye does not perceive a continuous motion. The persistence property can be exploited to select a frame rate for video display just enough to ensure a perception of continuous motion in a video sequence.

Sensitivity to Spatial Frequencies

Spatial frequencies refer to the changes in levels in a picture. The sensitivity of the eye drops as spatial frequencies increase; i.e., as the spatial frequencies increase, the ability of the eye to discriminate between the changing levels decreases. The eye can resolve color and detail only to a certain extent. Any detail that cannot be resolved is averaged. This property of the eye is called spatial integration. This property of the eye can be exploited to remove or reduce higher frequencies without affecting the perceived quality.

The human visual perception thus allows exploitation of spatial, temporal, and perceptual redundancies.

Video Source Format

The input to video compression algorithms typically uses the YCbCr color space as this representation lends itself better to exploiting the redundancies of the human visual system. The RGB primaries captured by an acquisition device such as a camera are converted into the YCbCr format. Figure 2 shows the luma and chroma sampling for the YCbCr formats. The YCbCr 4:4:4 format has four Cb and four Cr pixels for every 2x2 block of Y pixels, the YCbCr 4:2:2 format has two Cb and two Cr pixels for every 2x2 block of Y pixels, and the YCbCr 4:2:0 format has one Cb and one Cr pixels for every 2x2 block of Y pixels. All the three formats have the Y component at the full picture resolution. The difference in the formats is that the YCbCr 4:2:2 and YCbCr 4:2:0 formats have the chroma components at a reduced resolution. The human eye cannot perceive the difference when chroma is sub sampled. In fact, even the YCbCr 4:2:0 format with chroma ¼ of the luma resolution is sufficient to please the human eye. The YCbCr 4:2:0 format is the predominantly used format and is used in applications such as DVD, digital TVs, and HDTVs. The YCbCr 4:2:2 is typically used for studio quality applications and YCbCr 4:4:4 is hardly used. The use of YCbCr 4:2:0 instead of the RGB color space represents a 50% reduction in image size and is a direct result of exploiting the perceptual redundancies of the human visual system.

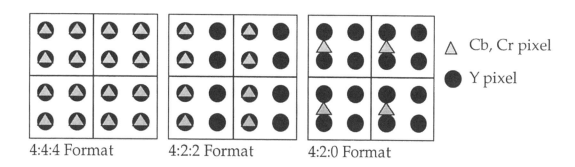

4:4:4 Format   4:2:2 Format   4:2:0 Format

Figure 2. Video source formats.

Exploiting Temporal Redundancies

Since a video is essentially a sequence of pictures sampled at a discrete frame rate, two successive frames in a video sequence look largely similar. Figure 3 shows two successive pictures in a video. The extent of similarity between two successive frames depends on how closely they are sampled (frame interval) and the motion of the objects in the scene. If the frame rate is 30 frames per second, two successive frames of a news anchor video are likely to be very similar. On the other hand, a video of car racing is likely to have substantial differences between the frames. Exploiting the temporal redundancies accounts for majority of the compression gains in video encoding.

Since two successive frames are similar, taking the difference between the two frames results in a smaller amount of data to be encoded. In general, the video coding technique that uses the data from a previously coded frame to predict the current frame is called predictive coding technique. The computation of the prediction is the key to efficient video compression. The simplest form of predictive coding is frame difference coding, where, the previous frame is used as a prediction. The difference between the current frame and the predicted frame is then encoded. The frame difference prediction begins to fail as the object motion in a video sequence increases resulting in a loss of correlation between collocated pixels in two successive frames.

Object motion is common in video and even a small motion of 1 to 2 pixels can lead to loss of correlation between corresponding pixels in successive frames. Motion compensation is used in video compression to reduce the correlation lost due to object motion. The object motion in the real world is complex but for the purpose of video compression, a simple translational motion is assumed.

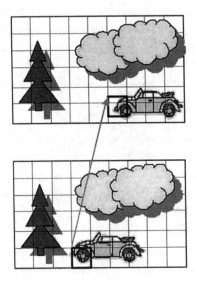

Figure 3. Successive frames in a video.

Block Based Motion Estimation

If we observe two successive frames of a video, the amount of changes within small NxN pixel regions of an image are small. Assuming a translational motion, the NxN regions can be better predicted from a previous frame by displacing the NxN region in the previous image by an amount representing the object motion. The amount of this displacement depends on relative motion between the two frames. For example, if there is a 5 pixel horizontal motion between the frames, it is likely that a small NxN region will have a better prediction if the prediction comes from an NxN block in the previous image displaced by 5 pixels. The process of finding a predicted block that minimizes the difference between the original and predicted blocks is called motion estimation and the resulting relative displacement is called a motion vector. When motion compensation is applied to the prediction, the motion vector is also coded along with the pixel differences.

Video frames are typically coded one block at a time to take advantage of the motion compensation applied to small NxN blocks. As the block size decreases, the amount of changes within a block also typically decrease and the likelihood of finding a better prediction improves. Similarly, as the block size increases, the prediction accuracy decreases. The downside to using a smaller block size is that the total number of blocks in an image increases. Since each of the blocks also has to include a motion vector to indicate the relative displacement, the amount of motion vector information increases for smaller block sizes.

The best prediction for a given block can be found if the motion of the block relative to a reference picture can be determined. Since translational motion is assumed, the estimated motion is given in terms of the relative displacement of a block in the X and Y planes. The process of forming a prediction thus requires estimating the relative motion of a given NxN block. A simple approach to estimating the motion is to consider all possible displacements in a reference picture and determine which of these displacements gives the best prediction. The best prediction will be very similar to the original block and is usually determined using a metric such the minimum sum of absolute differences (SAD) of pixels or the minimum sum of squared differences (SSD) of pixels. The SAD has lower computational complexity compared to the SSD computation and equally good in estimating the best prediction. The number of possible displacements (motion vectors) of a given block is a function of the maximum displacement allowed for motion estimation. Figure 4 shows the region of a picture used for motion estimation. If D_{max} is the maximum allowed displacement in the X and Y directions, the number of candidate displacements (motion vectors) are $(1 + 2D_{max})^2$. An NxN block requires N^2 computations for each candidate motion vector, resulting in extremely high motion estimation complexity. Complexity increases with the maximum allowed displacement. Depending on the motion activity of the source video, D_{max} can be appropriately selected to reduce the motion estimation complexity without significantly affecting the quality of the prediction. Fast motion estimation has been an active area of research and a number of efficient algorithms have been developed.

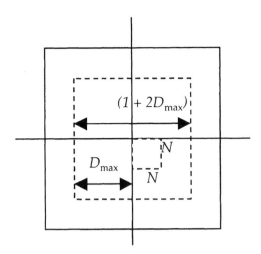

Figure 4. Motion estimation.

Exploiting Spatial Redundancies

In natural images, there exists a significant correlation between neighboring pixels. Small areas within a picture are usually similar. Redundancies exist even after motion compensation. Exploiting these redundancies will reduce the amount of information to be coded. Prediction based on neighboring pixels, called intra prediction, is also used to reduce the spatial redundancies. Transform techniques are used to reduce the spatial redundancies substantially. The spatial redundancy exploiting transforms such as the discrete cosine transform (DCT), transform an NxN picture block into NxN block of coefficients in another domain called the frequency domain. The key properties of these transforms that make them suitable for video compression are: 1) energy compaction and 2) de-correlation. When the transform is applied, the energy of an NxN pixel block is compacted into a few transformed coefficients and the correlation between the transformed coefficients is also reduced substantially. This implies significant amount of information can be recovered by using just a few coefficients. The DCT used widely in image and video coding has very good energy compaction and de-correlation properties. The transform coefficients in the frequency domain can be roughly classified into low, medium, and high spatial frequencies. Figure 5 shows the spatial frequencies of an 8x8 DCT block. Since the human visual system is not sensitive to the high spatial frequencies, the transform coefficients corresponding to the high frequencies can be discarded without affecting the perceptual quality of the reconstructed image. As the number of discarded coefficients increases, the compression increases, and the video quality decreases. The coefficient dropping is in fact exploiting the perceptual redundancies. Another way of reducing the perceptual redundancies is by quantizing the transform coefficients. The quantization process reduces the number of levels while still retaining the video quality. As with coefficient dropping, as the quantization step size increases, the compression increases, and the video quality decreases.

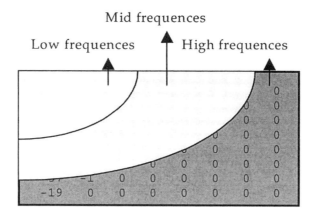

Figure 5. DCT spatial frequencies.

Exploiting Statistical Redundancies

The transform coefficients, motion vectors, and other data have to be encoded using binary codes in the last stage of video compression. The simplest way to code these values is by using fixed length codes; e.g., 16 bit words. However, these values do not have a uniform distribution and using fixed length codes is wasteful. Average code length can be reduced by assigning shorter code words to values with higher probability. Variable length coding is used to exploit these statistical redundancies and increase compression efficiency further.

Hybrid Video Coding

Video compression algorithms use a combination of the techniques presented in order to reduce redundancies and improve compression. The hybrid video compression algorithms are a hybrid of motion compensation and transform coding. Figure 6 shows the key components of a generalized hybrid video encoder. The input source video is encoded block-by-block. The first frame of video is typically encoded without motion compensation as there is no reference frame to use for motion compensation. The transform module (T) converts the spatial domain pixels into transform domain coefficients. The quantization module (Q) applies a quantizer to reduce the number of levels for transformed coefficients. The quantized coefficients are encoded using variable length coding module (VLC). The encoded block is de-quantized (Q^{-1}) and the inverse transform (T^{-1}) is applied before saving in a frame store so that the same picture data is used as a reference at the encoder and the decoder. Subsequent pictures can use motion compensation to reduce temporal redundancies. The motion estimation module (ME) uses the source frame and a reference frame from the frame store to find a motion vector that gives a best match for a source picture block. The motion compensation (MC) module uses the motion vector and obtains a predicted block from the reference picture. The difference between the original block and the predicted block, called the prediction error, is then encoded.

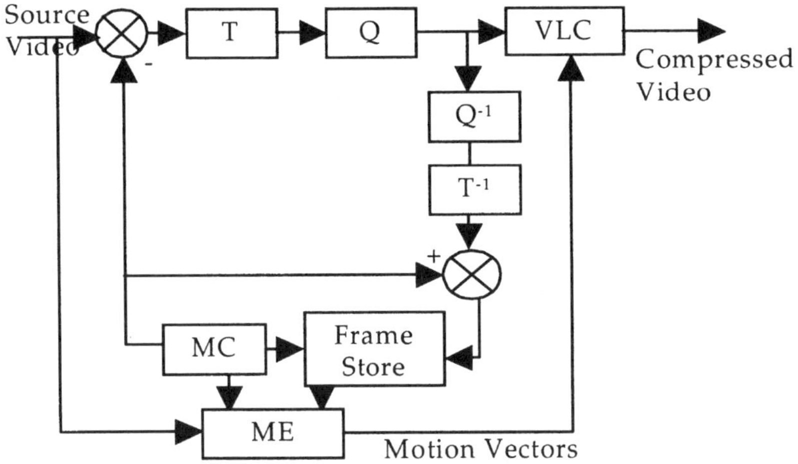

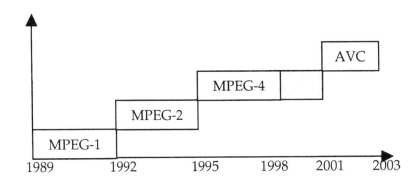

Figure 6. Hybrid video encoder.

Most of the video compression standards used today are based on the principles of hybrid video coding. The algorithms differ in the specifics of the tools used for motion estimation, transform coding, quantzation, and variable length coding. The specifics of the important video compression algorithms used today are discussed in the related short articles.

The MPEG Standardization Process

The MPEG video standards are developed by experts in video compression working under the auspice of the International Organization for Standardization (ISO). The standards activity began in 1989 with the goal of developing a standard for a video compression algorithm suitable for use in CD-ROM based applications. The committee has since standardized MPEG-1, MPEG-2, MPEG-4, and MPEG-4 AVC also known as H.264 . Figure 7 shows the timeline for standards development. The key to the success and relevance of the MPEG standards is the standardization process.

Figure 7. MPEG video standards timeline.

The MPEG process is driven by the industry with participation and contributions from the academia. The MPEG process is open and is essentially a competition among the proponents of a technology. The competing tools and technologies are experimentally evaluated and the best technology is selected for standardization. The standardization process may also combine competing proposals in developing an efficient solution. This process ensures that only the best technologies are standardized and keeps the standards relevant to the industry needs.

See: MPEG-1 Video Compression, MPEG-2 Video Compression, MPEG-4 Video Compression, H.263 Video Compression, MPEG-4 Advanced Video Compression (H.264), WMV-9 Video Compression, VC-1 Video Compression

References

1. B. Furht, "Multimedia Systems: An Overview," IEEE Multimedia, Vol. 1, pp. 47-59, 1994.
2. B. Furht, J. Greenberg, and R. Westwater, "Motion Estimation Techniques for Video Compression," Kluwer Academic Publishers, Norwell, MA, 1996.
3. D.L. Gall, "MPEG: a video compression standard for multimedia applications," Communications of the ACM, Vol. 34, pp. 46-58, 1991.
4. B.G. Haskell, A. Puri, and A.N. Netravali, "Digital Video: An introduction to MPEG-2," Chapman & Hall, Ltd, 1996.
5. M. Liou, "Overview of the P—64 kbit/s video coding standard," Communications of the ACM, Vol. 34, pp. 59-63, 1991.
6. A. N. Netravali and B. G. Haskell, "Digital Pictures – Representation, Compression and Standards," 2nd Edition, Plenum, 1995.
7. D. Marpe, H. Schwartz, and T. Weigand, "Overview of the H.264/ AVC Video Coding Standard," IEEE Transactions on Circuits and Systems for Video Technology, Vol. 13, No. 7, July 2003, pp. 560-575.
8. J. L. Mitchell, W. B. Pennebaker, C. E. Fogg, and D. J. LeGall, "MPEG video compression standard," Digital Multimedia Standards Series, Chapman and Hall, 1996, pp. 135-169.
9. F. Pereira and T. Ebrahimi, "The MPEG-4 Book," IMSC Press Series, Prentice Hall PTR, 2002.
10. W.B. Pennebaker and J.L. Mitchell, 'JPEG Still Image Data Compression Standard," Kluwer Academic Publishers, 1992.
11. K.R. Rao and P. Yip, "Discrete Cosine Transform: Algorithms, Advantages, Applications," Academic Press, 1990, ISBN0-12-580203-X.
12. I. Richardson, "H.264 and MPEG-4 Video Compression," John Wiley & Sons, 2003.

VIDEO CONFERENCING

Definition: Video conferencing allows participants in a live session to see each other; the video is transmitted over the network between users, live and in real-time.

Video conferencing is one component of teleconferencing, the others are audio conferencing, and data conferencing. Since the video must be encoded, transmitted, and decoded in real-time, special compression and transmission techniques are typically used. In a teleconferencing system that is ITU-T H.323 [1] compliant, the H.261 [2] video codec in its QCIF format must be supported. Support for other H.261 formats or the H.263 [3] codec is optional. During the initial setup, a specific video data rate is selected during the capability exchange. This rate should not be violated throughout the duration of the session. The H.261 standard uses communication channels that are multiples of 64 kbps, known as px64, where $p \in \{1, 2, 3, \ldots 30\}$. From a video encoding perspective, there are no Bidirectional or 'B' frames in H.261. Instead, it uses Intra or 'I' frames which are fully and independently encoded, and Predicted or 'P' frames which code the difference between the frame and its previous frame by using motion estimation.

Compared to H.261, H.263 uses 1/2 pixel motion-estimation for better picture quality, and a Huffman coding table that is optimized specifically for low bit rate transmissions. H.263 defines more picture modes than H.261, as seen in table 1 below. In addition, H.263 introduces the PB frames, which consist of a P frame interpolated with a Bi-directional or 'B' frame: a frame that depends not only on a previous frame but also on a forthcoming frame. Similar to a P frame, a B frame uses motion estimation to reduce the amount of information to carry. See the related article on "Video Compression and Coding Techniques" and "Motion Estimation" for further details.

Table 1. ITU-T standard frame formats for H.261 and H.263.

Picture Format	Frame Size	H.261	H.263
SQCIF	128x96	not specified*	required
QCIF	176x144	Required	required
CIF	352x288	Optional	optional
4CIF	704x576	N/A	optional
16CIF	1408x1152	N/A	optional

To transfer the live video over the network, a protocol such as the RTP (Real-time Transport Protocol) [4] is used.

See: Teleconferencing

References

1. International Telecommunication Union, Telecommunication Standardization Sector H.323 Recommendation – Packet-based multimedia communications systems, July 2003.

2. International Telecommunication Union, Telecommunication Standardization Sector H.261 Recommendation – Video codec for audiovisual services at p x 64 kbit/s, March 1993.
3. International Telecommunication Union, Telecommunication Standardization Sector H.263 Recommendation – Video coding for low bit rate communication, January 2005.
4. H. Schulzrinne, S. Casner, R. Frederick, and V. Jacobson, "RTP: A Transport Protocol for Real-Time Applications," IETF RFC 1889, January 1996.

VIDEO CONTENT ANALYSIS USING MACHINE LEARNING TOOLS

Yihong Gong
NEC Laboratories America, Cupertino, USA

Definition: Latest breakthroughs in machine learning methodologies have made it feasible to accurately detect objects and to model complex events with interrelated objects.

Introduction

The explosive growth in digital videos has sparked an urgent need for new technologies able to access and retrieve desired videos from large video archives with both efficiency and accuracy. Content-based video retrieval (CBVR) techniques developed in the past decide strive to accomplish this goal by using low level image features, such as colors, textures, shapes, motions, etc. However, as there is a huge semantic gap between data representations and real video contents, CBVR techniques generally suffer from poor video retrieval performances.

The key to strengthening video retrieval capabilities lies in higher level understanding and representation of video contents. Video content understanding based on machine learning techniques is one of the promising research directions to accomplish this goal. Machine learning techniques are superior in discovering implicit, complex knowledge from low level data sets. Latest breakthroughs in machine learning methodologies have made it feasible to accurately detect objects and to model complex events with interrelated objects. In recent years, machine learning applications have made impressive achievements in classifying video clips into predefined scene categories (i.e., indoor, outdoor, city view, landscape, etc), detecting events of interest from sports videos, etc. Compared to other approaches in the literature, machine learning-based methods often excel in detection accuracies, and in modeling complex events.

In this article, we focus on the state of the art of probabilistic data classification methods, an important subfield of machine learning, and their applications. Section 2 first provides overviews of probabilistic data classifiers by presenting two kinds of categorizations. Section 3 elaborates on the Maximum Entropy Model (MEM) which is a representative discriminative data classifier. Section 4 describes its application to baseball game highlight detections. Section 5 reveals performance evaluation results of the MEM-based system, and compares it with the system based on the Hidden Markov Model (HMM) which is a representative generative data classifier. Finally, Section 6 summarizes the paper.

Overview of Machine Learning Techniques

The tasks of scene classification, object and event detection can all be translated into a probabilistic data classification problem. Probabilistic data classification is an important sub-field of machine learning, and can be defined as the problem of classifying an example based on its feature vector into one of the predefined classes. Let x be the random variable representing feature vectors (observations) of input video clips, and y be the random variable denoting class labels. Data classifiers strive to learn a probability function $p(y \mid x)$ from a set of training examples which indicates the probability of x belonging to class y. There are many possible ways to categorize a classifier. In the remaining part of this section, we describe two kinds of categorizations which characterize various data classifiers from two different viewpoints.

Models for Simple Data Entities vs. Models for Complex Data Entities

Many data entities have simple, flat structures that do not depend on other data entities. The outcome of each coin toss, the weight of each apple, the age of each person, etc are examples of such simple data entities. In contrast, there exist complex data entities that consist of sub-entities that are strongly related one to another. For example, a beach scene is usually composed of a blue sky on top, an ocean in the middle, and a sand beach at the bottom. In other word, beach scene is a complex entity that is composed of three sub-entities with certain spatial relations. On the other hand, in TV broadcasted baseball game videos, a typical home run event usually consists of four or more shots, which starts from a pitcher's view, followed by a panning outfield and audience view in which the video camera tracks the flying ball, and ends with a global or close-up view of the player running to home base. Obviously, a home run event is a complex data entity that is composed of a unique sequence of sub-entities.

Popular data classifiers that aim to model simple data entities include Naïve Bayes [1], Gaussian Mixture Model (GMM) [2], Neural Network [3], Support Vector Machine (SVM) [4], etc. Neural Network, if the network architecture is appropriately designed for the problem at hand, has great potential to accomplish high data classification accuracies. The network design, however, usually relies heavily on the designer's experiences and craftsmanship, and the lack of uniform, practically proven design principles has certainly hampered wide applications of Neural Networks. SVM, although relatively new compared to other popular data classification models, is emerging as the new favorite because of its ease of implementation and data generalization capability. In recent years, there have been numerous research studies that report the SVM's superiority over traditional models, especially in the area of text classification.

For modeling complex data entities, popular classifiers include Bayesian Networks [1], Hidden Markov Models (HMM) [5], Maximum Entropy Models (MEM) [6], Markov Random Fields (MRF) [7], Conditional Random Field Models (CRF) [8], etc. HMM has been commonly used for speech recognition, and has become a pseudo standard for modeling sequential data. MEM and CRF are relatively new methods that are quickly gaining popularity for classifying sequential or interrelated data entities. MEM and CRF take an opposite approach to derive the conditional probability $p(y\,|\,\mathbf{x})$ compared to HMM, which is elaborated in the following subsection.

Generative Models vs. Discriminative Models

Probabilistic data classifiers typically map an input example to one of the predefined classes through a conditional probability function $p(y\,|\,\mathbf{x})$ derived from a set of training examples. In general, there are two ways of learning $p(y\,|\,\mathbf{x})$. Discriminative models strive to learning $p(y\,|\,\mathbf{x})$ directly from the training set without the attempt to modeling the observation $\mathbf{x}$. Generative models, on the other hand, computes $p(y\,|\,\mathbf{x})$ by first modeling the class-conditional probability $p(\mathbf{x}\,|\,y)$ of the observation $\mathbf{x}$, and then applying the Bayes' rule as follows:

$$p(y\,|\,\mathbf{x}) \propto p(\mathbf{x}\,|\,y)\,p(y)$$

Because $p(\mathbf{x}\,|\,y)$ can be interpreted as the probability of generating the observation $\mathbf{x}$ by class y, classifiers exploring $p(\mathbf{x}\,|\,y)$ can be viewed as modeling how the observation $\mathbf{x}$ is generated, which explains the name "generative model".

Popular generative models include Naïve Bayes, Bayesian Network, GMM, and HMM, while representative discriminative models include Neural Network, SVM, MEM and CRF. Generative models have been traditionally popular for data classification tasks because modeling $p(\mathbf{x}\,|\,y)$ is often easier than modeling $p(y\,|\,\mathbf{x})$, and there exist well-established, easy-to-implement algorithms such as the EM algorithm [2], the Baum-Welch algorithm [5], etc to efficiently estimate the model through a learning process. The ease of use, and the theoretical beauty of generative models, however, do come with a cost. Many complex data entities, such as a beach scene, a home run event, etc, need to be represented by a vector $\mathbf{x}$ of many features that depend on each other. To make the model estimation process tractable, generative models commonly assume conditional independences among all the features comprising the feature vector $\mathbf{x}$. Because this assumption is for the sake of mathematical convenience rather than the reflection of a reality, generative models often have limited performance accuracies for classifying complex data sets.

Discriminative models, on the other hand, typically make very few assumptions about the data and features, and in a sense, let the data speak for themselves. Recent research studies have shown that discriminative models outperform generative models in many applications such as natural language processing, webpage classifications, baseball highlight detections, etc.

Maximum Entropy Model

MEM is a representative discriminative model that derives the conditional probability $p(y \mid \mathbf{x})$ directly from the training data [6]. The principle of MEM is simple: model all that is known and assume nothing about what is unknown. In other words, given a collection of facts, MEM chooses a model which is consistent with all the facts, but otherwise is as uniform as possible.

To express each feature that describes the input data, MEM makes use of a feature indicator function $f_{ij}(\mathbf{x}, y)$ that is defined as follows:

$$f_{ij}(\mathbf{x}, y) = \begin{cases} 1, & \text{if feature } i \text{ is present in } \mathbf{x} \text{ and } y = j. \\ 0, & \text{otherwise.} \end{cases} \tag{1}$$

The expected value of $f_{ij}(\mathbf{x}, y)$ with respect to the empirical distribution $\tilde{p}(\mathbf{x}, y)$ is defined as:

$$\tilde{p}(f_{ij}) = \sum_{\mathbf{x}, y} \tilde{p}(\mathbf{x}, y) f_{ij}(\mathbf{x}, y) \tag{2}$$

where $\tilde{p}(\mathbf{x}, y)$ can be computed from the training data by enumerating the number of times that $(\mathbf{x}, y)$ occurs together in the training data. On the other hand, the expected value of $f_{ij}(\mathbf{x}, y)$ with respect to the model $p(y \mid \mathbf{x})$ is

$$p(f_{ij}) = \sum_{\mathbf{x}, y} \tilde{p}(\mathbf{x}) p(y \mid \mathbf{x}) f_{ij}(\mathbf{x}, y) \tag{3}$$

where $\tilde{p}(\mathbf{x})$ is the empirical distribution of $\mathbf{x}$ in the training data. With the above notations, the MEM principle can be mathematically expressed as follows:

Maximize the entropy $H(p) = -\sum_{\mathbf{x}, y} \tilde{p}(\mathbf{x}) p(y \mid \mathbf{x}) \log p(y \mid \mathbf{x})$ over all $p(y \mid \mathbf{x})$

satisfying

1. $p(f_{ij}) = \tilde{p}(f_{ij})$ for all $f_{ij}(\mathbf{x}, y)$.
2. $\sum_{y} p(y \mid \mathbf{x}) = 1.$

This is a typical constrained optimization problem that can be solved by the Lagrange Multiplier algorithm. The Lagrange function for the above problem is defined as:

$$J(p,\lambda) = H(p) + \sum_{ij} \lambda_{ij} \left(p(f_{ij}) - \tilde{p}(f_{ij}) \right) \qquad (4)$$

where λ_{ij} are the Lagrange multipliers. Fixing λ, the conditional probability $p_\lambda(y \mid \mathbf{x})$ that maximizes Eq. (4) is obtained by differentiating $J(p,\lambda)$ with respect to p and setting it to zero.

$$p_\lambda(y \mid \mathbf{x}) = \frac{1}{Z_\lambda(\mathbf{x})} \exp\left(\sum_{ij} \lambda_{ij}\, f_{ij}(\mathbf{x}, y) \right) \qquad (5)$$

where $Z_\lambda(\mathbf{x})$ is a normalizing constant determined by the constraint $\sum_y p_\lambda(y \mid \mathbf{x}) = 1.$ The dual function $\Psi(\lambda)$ of the above problem is obtained by replacing p in Eq. (4) using Eq. (5).

$$\Psi(\lambda) = -\sum_{\mathbf{x}} \tilde{p}(\mathbf{x}) \log Z_\lambda(\mathbf{x}) + \sum_{ij} \lambda_{ij}\, \tilde{p}(f_{ij}) \qquad (6)$$

The final solution $p^*(y \mid \mathbf{x})$ is defined by λ^* that maximizes the dual function Eq. (6). λ^* can be typically obtained using the Improved Iterative Scaling algorithm described in [10].

Baseball Highlight Detection Based On Maximum Entropy Model

In this section, we develop a unique MEM-based framework to perform the statistical modeling of baseball highlights [9]. Our goal is to automatically detect and classify all major baseball highlights, which include *home run, outfield hit, outfield fly, infield hit, infield out, strike out, and walk.* Traditionally, the HMM is the most common approach for modeling complex and context-sensitive data sequences. The HMM usually assumes that the features describing the input data sequence are independent of each other to make the model estimation process tractable. It also needs to first segment and classify the data sequence into a set of finite states, and then observe the state transitions during its data modeling process. In contrast, our MEM-based framework needs neither to make the independence assumption, nor to explicitly classify the data sequence into states. It not only provides potentials to improve the data classification accuracy, but also remarkably simplifies the training data creation task and the data classification process.

Baseball videos have well-defined structures and domain rules. Typically, the broadcast of a baseball game is made by a fixed number of cameras at fixed locations around the field, and each camera has a certain assignment for broadcasting the game. This TV broadcasting technique results in a few unique views that constitute most parts of baseball plays. Each category of highlights typically consists of a similar transitional pattern of these unique views. The limited number of unique views and similar patterns of view transitions for each type of highlights have made it feasible to statistically model baseball highlights. The detailed description of the MEM-based framework is provided as follows.

Multimedia Feature Extraction

We use the following 6 types of multimedia features to capture and distinguish the baseball view patterns.

1. Color distribution: A baseball field mainly consists of grass and base areas. We represent each scene shot by three keyframes: the first, the middle, and the last frames of the shot. Each keyframe is divided into 3×3 blocks, and its color distribution is composed of nine data pairs (g_i, s_i) where g_i and s_i are the percentages of green and soil colors in block i, respectively. The color distribution of the entire shot is then derived by averaging the color distributions of the three keyframes. With this feature, we can roughly figure out which part of the field the shot is displaying.

2. Edge distribution: This feature is useful for distinguishing field views from audience views. The edge distribution of a shot is computed in a manner similar to the color distribution. First, edge detection is conducted for each keyframe to obtain edge pixels. Next, the frame is divided into 3×3 blocks, and the percentages of edge pixels in the nine blocks are computed. Finally, the edge distribution of the entire shot is derived by averaging the distributions of the three keyframes of the shot.

3. Camera motion: Camera motion becomes conspicuous and intense in highlight scenes because cameras track either the ball or the players' motions to capture the entire play. We apply a simplified camera motion model [11] to estimate camera pan, tilt and zoom, which are the most commonly used camera operations in TV broadcasting.

4. Player detection: Within the playfield, we discover the areas that have non-green, non-soil colors and higher edge densities. These areas are good candidates for baseball players. Among all the candidates, false candidates and outliers can be further discovered by tracking each candidate within the scene shot because genuine candidates possess stable image features (e.g. size and color) and consistent trajectories while false candidates do not.

5. Sound Detection: Certain sounds such as cheers, applause, music, speech, and mixtures of music and speech, provide important clues for highlight detection. Our special sound detection module consists of two stages. In the training stage, we construct a model for each of the special sounds listed above using annotated training data. The mel-cepstral coefficients [13] are used as the input feature vectors of the sound models, and the Gaussian mixture model (GMM) is used to model the distributions of the input vectors. In the detection stage, we first partition the audio stream into segments each of which possesses similar acoustical profiles, and then provide each audio segment as the input to all the five sound models, which each

outputs a probability showing the likelihood of the audio segment being a particular sound. These five likelihoods will be used as part of the multimedia features in forming the feature vector of a scene shot.

6. <u>Closed Caption:</u> Informative words from closed captions often provide the most direct and abstracted clues to the detection/classification process. We extract informative words based on the mutual information metric between a word and a highlight [12]. From the training data, we have identified a list of 72 informative words for the major highlights, which include: *field, center, strike out, base, double out, score, home run,* etc. In forming the multimedia feature vector of a scene shot, we use 72 binary numbers to indicate the presence/absence of the 72 informative words.

MEM Model Construction

To cope with the asynchronous nature of different features, we set the time window of T_w seconds (T_w=5 in our implementation). For a shot $\mathbf{S}_k$ that starts at time T_{k1} and ends at time T_{k2}, we include all the image features extracted from the time interval $[T_{k1}, T_{k2}]$, and all the audio and text features detected from the interval $[T_{k1}, T_{k2} + T_w]$ to construct the multimedia feature vector of $\mathbf{S}_k$. Then, we combine the feature vectors of n (=4) consecutive shots to form an input vector $\mathbf{x}_k$ to the MEM engine. For each feature i in $\mathbf{x}_k$, we introduce an feature indicator function $f_{ij}(\mathbf{x}_k, y)$ defined by Eq. (1) (see [9] for detailed descriptions). During the training process, the MEM will iteratively adjust the weight λ_{ij} for each feature function until all the weights converge. Consequently, features i that play a dominant role in identifying the highlight j will be assigned a large weight λ_{ij} while features i that are either unimportant or unrelated to the highlight j will receive a very small or zero weight. If we know for sure that certain features i are independent of the highlight j, we can set the corresponding feature functions $f_{ij}(\mathbf{x}_k, y)$ to zero to reduce the number of parameters to be estimated. Otherwise, we can simply assume that every feature i is present in every highlight j, and let the learning process automatically determine the appropriate weight λ_{ij} for each feature function $f_{ij}(\mathbf{x}_k, y)$.

Experimental Evaluations

We collected 10 baseball videos totaling 32 hours for training and testing purposes. These games were obtained from five major TV stations in the U.S. and consist of 16 teams playing in 9 stadiums. All the games were manually labeled by three human operators who were not familiar with our baseball highlight detection/classification system. We used seven games as the training data and the remaining three games as the testing data. The labeled highlights in the testing data were used as the ground truth to evaluate the highlight detection/classification accuracy of our system.

On average, the recall and precision for highlight classification are 70.0% and 62.60%, respectively. Table 1 details the performance results for each type of highlights. The precisions for *infield hit* and *infield out* are relatively low because these two types of highlights usually have quite similar view transitional patterns which often lead to misclassifications. We missed some *home runs* due to the fact that there are not enough training samples.

Table 1. Performance comparisons between the MEM and the HMM system.

Highlights	MEM-based system		HMM-based system	
	Recall (%)	Precision (%)	Recall (%)	Precision (%)
Home run	50.0	50.0	50.0	50.0
Outfield hit	84.9	75.7	83.4	68.2
Outfield out	83.4	93.7	75.9	88.0
Infield hit	49.3	47.9	44.1	47.3
Infield out	78.5	56.3	67.5	40.8
Strike out	79.0	63.4	55.1	47.2
Walk	65.2	51.2	57.7	46.2

For performance comparisons, we implemented another baseball highlight detection system based on the Hidden Markov Model (HMM), the technique that is widely used for event detections. The HMM system uses the same set of image, audio, and text features as described in Section 4.1, and is evaluated using the same training and testing data sets as well. The training data set, however, needs to be re-labeled so that for each highlight sequence, the starting, ending points and the category of each constituent view has to be labeled as well. This training data labeling task is much more arduous and time consuming.

The HMM system consists of seven unique HMM's each of which models a particular type of highlights. For each HMM, we define the following items:

1. State *V*: is one of the seven unique views making up most parts of the baseball highlights.

2. Observation *M*: is the multimedia feature vector created for a single scene shot. It is different from the feature vector $\mathbf{x}_k$ used by the MEM-based system in that $\mathbf{x}_k$ is created by combining the feature vectors of *n* (=4) consecutive shots (see Section 4.2).

3. Observation probability p(*M*|*V*): is the probability of observing the feature vector *M* given the state *V*. We use the Bayes rule to compute p(*M*|*V*) from the training data.

4. Transition probability $p(V_{t+1}|V_t)$: is the probability that state V_t transits to state V_{t+1} at the next time instant. Given the class of highlights, the state (view) transition probability can be learned from the training data by the HMM learning algorithms.

5.   Initial state distribution π : can also be learned from the training data.

The above five items uniquely define the HMM. Given the HMM $\mathbf{H}_k$, the probability of observing the sequence $\mathbf{M} = M_1 M_2 \cdots M_T$ can be obtained as:

$$p(\mathbf{M}\,|\,\mathbf{H}_k) = \sum_{V_1 V_2 \cdots V_T} \pi(V_1)\,p(M_1\,|\,V_1)\,p(V_2\,|\,V_1)\,p(M_2\,|\,V_2)\cdots p(V_T\,|\,V_{T-1})\,p(M_T\,|\,V_T) \qquad (7)$$

where $V_1 V_2 \cdots V_T$ represents a possible state sequence. When a new video clip $\mathbf{M}_x$ (which consists of 3-5 shots depending on the HMM model) arrives, we compute the probability $p(\mathbf{M}_x\,|\,\mathbf{H}_k)$ using each HMM $\mathbf{H}_k$. If $p = \max_{\mathbf{H}_k} p(\mathbf{M}_x\,|\,\mathbf{H}_k)$ exceeds the predefined threshold, $\mathbf{M}_x$ will be classified into the highlight class $h = \arg\max_{\mathbf{H}_k} p(\mathbf{M}_x\,|\,\mathbf{H}_k)$.

For ease of comparison, we have placed the highlight classification accuracies of the HMM system shoulder by shoulder with those of the MEM system in Table 1. It is observed that the MEM produced better performance than the HMM on all highlight categories, and this advantage becomes very remarkable for the categories of *strike out* and *walk*. This difference can be explained by the fact that the HMM uses the naive bayes to calculate the observation probability $p(M\,|\,V)$, which assumes that all the features extracted from each shot are independent of each other, and the fact that the HMM is unable to handle the combined features of consecutive shots. Obviously these limitations have reduced the system's ability to model the correlations among the multimedia features as well as consecutive shots. For the highlight categories that have relatively short view transitional patterns, such as *strike out* and *walk,* the HMM might not be able to compensate for errors in the observation probabilities because less contextual information is contained within the sequence.

Summaries

In this article, we focused on the state of the art of probabilistic data classification methods and their applications. We elaborated on the MEM which is a representative discriminative data classifier, applied it to baseball highlight detections and classifications, and compared it with the HMM which is a representative generative data classifier. Because the MEM-based framework needs neither to make the feature independence assumption, nor to explicitly classify the data sequence into states, it not only provides potentials to improve the data classification accuracy, but also remarkably simplifies the training data creation task and the data classification process. Our experimental evaluations have confirmed the advantages of the MEM over the HMM in terms of highlight detection and classification accuracies. Discriminative data classifiers are becoming new favorite compared to generative data classifiers because of their superiority in data modeling abilities and classification accuracies.

References

1.   T. Mitchell, "Machine Learning," McGraw Hill, 1997.

2. R.A. Redner and H.F. Walker, "Mixture Densities, Maximum Likelihood and the EM Algorithm," SIAM Review, Vol. 26, No. 2, pp. 195-239, 1984.

3. S. Haykin, "Neural Networks," 2nd Edition, Prentice Hall, 1999.

4. N. Cristianini and J. Shawe-Taylor, "An Introduction to Support Vector Machines and Other Kernel-based Learning Methods," Cambridge University Press, 2000.

5. L.R. Rabiner, "A Tutorial on Hidden Markov Models and Selected Applications in Speech Recognition," Proceedings of the IEEE, Vol. 77, No. 2, pp. 257-286, 1989.

6. A.L. Berger, S.A. Della Pietra, and V.J. Della Pietra, "A Maximum Entropy Approach to Natural Language Processing," Computational Linguistics, Vol. 22, No. 1, March 1996.

7. S. Geman and D. Geman, "Stochastic Relaxation, Gibbs Distributions and the Bayesian Restoration of images," IEEE Transactions on PAMI, Vol. 6, No. 6, pp. 721-741, 1984.

8. J. Lafferty, A. McCallum, and F. Pereira, "Conditional Random Fields: Probabilistic Models for Segmenting and Labeling Sequence Data," Proceedings of ICML 2001, pp. 282-289.

9. Y. Gong, M. Han, W. Hua, and W. Xu, "Maximum Entropy Model-based Baseball Highlight Detection and Classification," Journal of CVIU, 96, pp. 181-199, 2004.

10. S.A. Della Pietra, V.J. Della Pietra, and J. Lafferty, "Inducing Features of Random Fields," IEEE Transactions on PAMI, 19, pp. 380-393, 1997.

11. Y.T. Tse, R.L. Baker, "Camera Zoom/Pan Estimation and Compensation for Video Compression," Image Processing Algorithms Tech. 1452 (1991) pp. 468-479.

12. X. Liu, Y. Gong, and S.H. Zhou, "Document Clustering with Cluster Refinement and Model Selection Capabilities," Proceedings of the ACM SIGIR'02, Tampere, Finland. August 2002.

13. L. Rabiner, and B.H.Juang, "Fundamentals of Speech Recognition," Prentice-Hall, 1993.

VIDEO DATABASES

C. Cesarano[1], M. Fayzullin[2], A. Picariello[1], and V.S.Subrahmanian[2]
[1]Dipartimento di Informatica e Sistemistica, Università di Napoli "Federico II", Napoli, Italy
[2]Department of Computer Science, University of Maryland, College Park, MD, USA

Definition: *Video database research falls into the following categories: video data models, video extraction, video query language, and video index structures.*

The past decade has seen explosive growth in the ability of individuals to create and/or capture digital video, leading slowly to large scale personal and corporate digital video banks. Over the last 8-10 years, there has been a tremendous amount of work on creating video databases. Video database research falls primarily into the following categories:

- ***Video data models.*** What kind of data about a video should we store?

- *Video extraction.* How should this data be automatically extracted from a video?
- *Video query language.* How should we query this data?
- *Video index structures.* How should we index this data for faster retrieval?

We discuss multiple potential answers to these four important topics.

Video data models

Throughout this paper, we will assume that a video v is divided up into a sequence $b_1,...,b_{len(v)}$ of *blocks*. The video database administrator can choose what a block is – he could, for instance, choose a block to be a single frame, or to be the set of frames between two consecutive I-frames (in the case of MPEG video) or something else. The number $len(v)$ is called the *length* of video v. If $1 \leq l \leq u \leq len(v)$, then we use the expression *block sequence* to refer to the closed interval $[l,u]$ which denotes the set of all blocks b such that $l \leq b \leq u$. Associated with any block sequence $[l,u]$ is a set of objects. These objects fall into four categories as shown in Figure 1.

- Visual Entities of Interest (Visual EOIs for short): An entity of interest is a region of interest in a block sequence (usually when identifying entities of interest, a single block, i.e. a block sequence of length one, is considered). Visual EOIs can be identified using appropriate image processing algorithms. For example, Figure 1 shows a photograph of a stork and identifies three regions of interest in the picture using active vision techniques [1]. This image may have various attributes associated with the above rectangles such as an *id*, a *color histogram*, a *texture map*, etc.

- Visual Activities of Interest (Visual AOIs): An activity of interest is a motion of interest in a video segment. For example, a dance motion is an example of an activity of interest. Likewise, a flying bird might be an activity of interest ("flight"). There are numerous techniques available in the image processing literature to extract visual AOIs. These include dancing [2], gestures [3], and many other motions [4].

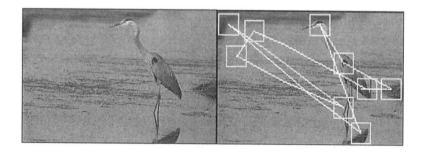

Figure 1. (a) Stork, (b) Regions of interest detected by the eye.

- Textual Entities of Interest: Many videos are *annotated* with information about the video. For example, news videos often have textual streams associated with the video stream. There are also numerous projects [5,6] that allow textual *annotations* of video - such annotations may explicitly annotate a video with objects in a block sequence or may use a text stream from which such objects can be derived. A recent commercial product to do this is IBM's AlphaWorks system where a user can annotate a video while watching it.

- Textual Activities of Interest: The main difference between Textual EOIs and Textual AOIs is that the latter pertains to activities, while the former pertains to entities. Both are textually marked up.

Any database model to store information about video content must be rich enough to store all these phenomena. Data models to store video information have been proposed based on the relational model of data [5], the object oriented data model [7] and the XML data model [8].

Video Extraction

A vast variety of image processing algorithms can be used to populate video data with visual and/or textual entities and activities of interest. From the image processing point of view, object and event detection are still considered an interesting challenge, due to significant variations in shape, color, and the high dimensionality of feature vectors used for processing [9].

In the past, template matching approaches were used extensively using a set of templates or parameterized curves. However, real objects are not always describable via a set of rigid templates – in such cases, these approaches are found to be inadequate and difficult to extend. Thus, a significant amount of domain knowledge needs to be input *a priori* [10], [11]. In more recent research, a number of learning-based techniques have been proposed [12]. Despite the diversity of approaches, there is a common underlying theme consisting of the following steps: a) provide a collection of target images containing the object class considered together with negative examples; b) transform the images into (feature) vectors using a certain representation; c) use the previous extracted features to learn a pattern recognition classifier (statistical, neural network, and so on) to separate target from non target objects.

In the area of event detection, usually we can broadly divide the proposed techniques into two parts: human action recognition and general motion-based recognition [13]. As in the preceding case, most approaches require the transformation of each frame of the image sequence into a certain feature space, and then action recognition is performed on those feature, building a 3-D model of the action and/or some measurement based temporal models [14], [15]. Motion recognition has been widely detected through the computation of basic flow fields, estimated by principal component analysis (PCA) [16] followed by robust estimation techniques or using a "motion-history image" (MHI), which represents the motion at the corresponding spatial location in an image sequence [17].

Video texts are also used to improve event detection. Technically speaking, there are two kinds of video text: texts shown in video scenes which is often called *scene text*, and the text added into the video during a post-processing phase, or *caption text* [18]: for certain kinds of video, such as sports, captions are semantically more important than scene text. In both cases, to recognize text, existing OCR (Optical Character Recognition) engine may be adopted thus transforming a binary image representation into an ASCII string result: this is used to efficiently detect objects and/or events in a video scene.

Finally, some authors propose a strategy based on a combination of different video/audio features in order to detect specific events, as suggested in [19], [20], in which "goal " detection in soccer matches has been accomplished using both visual (color histograms) and audio (RMS) features on video shots and through a simple reasoning on conjunctive simultaneous presence of several detected events.

Video Query Language

Algorithms to query video databases can and should be built on top of classical database models such as the relational calculus and the relational algebra. Picariello et. al. [21] propose an extension of the relational algebra to query videos. In their work, they assume the existence of a set of base "visual" predicates that can be implemented using image processing algorithms. Examples of visual predicates include:

- *color(rect1,rect2,dist,d)*: This predicate succeeds if the color histograms of two rectangles (sub-images of an image) are within distance *dist* of each other when using a distance metric *d*.

- *texture(rect1,rect2,dist,d)*: This predicate succeeds if the texture histograms of two rectangles (sub-images of an image) are within distance *dist* of each other when using a distance metric *d*.

- *shape(rect1,rect2,dist,d)*: This predicate succeeds if the shapes of two rectangles are within a distance *dist* of each other when using distance metric *d*.

They define selection conditions based on some *a priori* defined set of visual predicates. For example, the selection condition *O.color.blue > 200* is satisfied by objects whose "blue" field has a value over 200, while *O1.color.blue > O2.color.blue* is satisfied by pairs of objects, with the first one more "blue" than the other one. Here, *Color(rect1,rect2,10,L1)* is a visual predicate which succeeds if rectangle rect1 is within 10 units of distance of rectangle rect2 using say the well known L1 metric [22]. They then define what it means for a video block to *satisfy* a video selection condition. The analog of the relational "select" operation applied to video databases is then defined to be the set of all blocks in a video (or a set of videos) that satisfy the desired selection condition.

The *projection operation* is a little more complex. Given a video, whose blocks contain a number of different objects, projection takes as input, a specification of the objects that the user is interested in, and deletes from the input video, all objects not mentioned in the object specification list. Of course, pixels that in the original video correspond to the eliminated objects must be set to some value. In [21], authors use a *recoloring strategy* to recolor objects that are eliminated in this way.

The *Cartesian Product* operation (in terms of which join is defined) looks at two videos and is parametrized by a *merge function*. A merge function takes two frames and merges them in some way. For example, suppose f and f′ are two frames. The *"left-right split merge"* function returns a new frame with f occupying its left half and f′ occupying its right half. Likewise, the *"top-down split merge"* returns a frame with f in the top-half and f′ in the bottom half. In an "embedded split-merge", f′ is embedded in the top left corner of f. The Cartesian Product operator looks at all pairs of frames – one from each video – and orders the merge of these pairs in some order. Figure 2 below shows an example of Cartesian Product under left-right, top-down and embedded split merge.

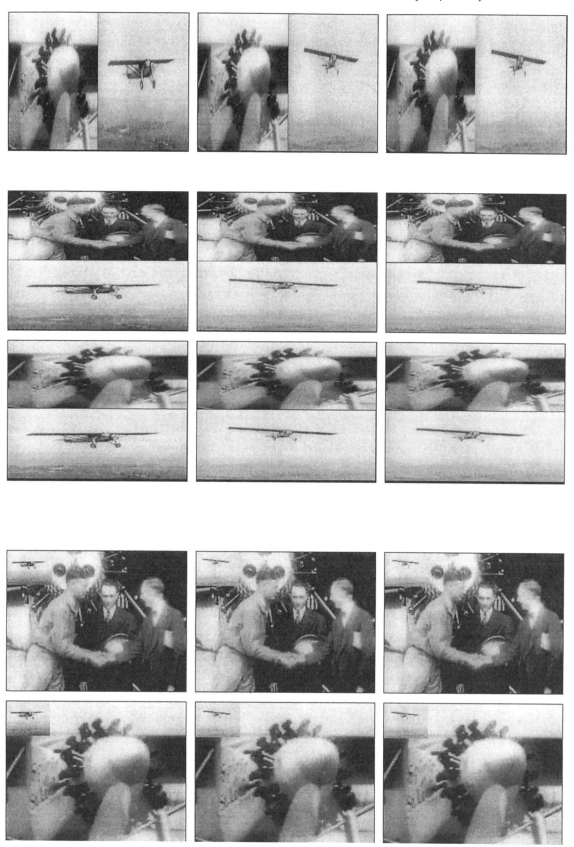

Figure 2. An example of Cartesian Product under left-right,
top-down, and embedded split merge.

The join of two videos is defined in the usual way in terms of selection and Cartesian product. In [21], a whole set of other video algebra operations has been defined.

Video Index Structures

There are numerous index structures for videos. Subrahmanian [23] describes variants of the R-tree and the segment tree to store video data. It is impossible to store video content on a frame-by-frame basis (just to fix this concept, a single 90-minute video contains 162,000 frames). There is a critical need to develop compact representations of video and of the parts in which the video may be decomposed (shots, scene). Two main data structures are used in this context: frame segment trees and R-segment trees (or RS-trees).

The basic idea behind a frame segment tree is simple. First, we construct two arrays, OBJECTARRAY and ACTIVITYARRAY. An OBJECTARRAY is an array containing, for each integer i an object oi . With each element of this array is associated an ordered linked list of pointers to nodes in the frame segment tree. For example, the linked list associated with object number 1 ($o1$) may contain a number of pointers to nodes, e.g. 15,16,19,20, representing nodes in the frame segment tree. On the other side, the ACTIVITYARRAY contains for each element i an activity ai. Also each element of this array has an ordered list of pointers to nodes in the frame segment tree.

The frame segment tree is a binary tree constructed as follows:

1. Each node in the frame segment tree represents a frame sequence $[x,y)$, starting at frame x and including all frames up to, but not including, frame y.

2. Every leaf is at level r. The leftmost leaf denotes the interval $[z_1,z_2)$ the second from the left represents the interval $[z_2, z_3)$ and so on. If N is a node with two children representing the intervals $[p_1, p_2)$, $[p_2, p_3)$, then N represents the interval $[p_1, p_3)$. Thus, the root of the segment tree represents the interval $[q_1, q_z)$ if q_z is an exponent of 2; otherwise it represents the interval $[q_1, \infty)$.

3. The number inside each node may be viewed as the address of that node.

4. The set of number placed next to a node denotes the *id* number of video objects and activities that appear in the entire frame sequence associated with that node.

The R-Segment Tree (RS-Tree) is very similar to the frame segment tree, with one major distinction. Although the concepts of OBJECTARRAY and ACTIVITYARRAY remain the same as before, instead of using a segment tree to represent the frame sequence, we take advantage of the fact that a sequence $[s, e)$ is a rectangle of length $(e-s)$ and of width 0. The rectangles are arranged in an R-tree. In this case, each R-tree node will have a special structure to specify, for each rectangle, which object or activity is associated with it. The main advantage that an RS-tree has over a frame segment tree is that it is suitable for retrieving pages from disk, since each disk access brings back a page containing not one rectangle but several proximate rectangles.

References

1. G. Boccignone, A. Chianese, V. Moscato, and A. Picariello, "Foveated Shot Detection for Video Segmentation," IEEE Transactions on Circuits and Systems for Video Technology, Vol. 15, No. 3, 2005, pp. 365- 377.

2. K.Koijima, M. Hironaga, S. Nagae, and Y. Kawamoto, "Human motion analysis using the Rhythm – a reproducing method of human motion," Journal of Geometry and Graphics, Vol. 5, No. 1, 2001, pp. 45-49.

3. L. Bretzner, I. Laptev, and T. Lindeberg, "Hand gesture recognition using multi-scale colour features, hierarchical and particle filtering", Proceedings of the fifth IEEE International Conference on Automatic Face and Gesture Recognition (FGR'02), IEEE Computer Society Press, 2002, pp. 1-6.

4. A. F. Bobick and J.W. Davis, "The recognition of human movement using temporal templates", IEEE Transactions on Pattern Analysis and Machine Intelligence, Vol. 23, No. 3, 2001 pp. 257-267.

5. S. Adali , K.S. Candan, S.-S. Chen, K. Erol, and V.S. Subrahmanian, "AVIS: Advanced Video Information Systems," ACM Multimedia Systems Journal, Vol. 4, 1996, pp. 172-186.

6. E. Hwang and V.S. Subrahmanian, "Querying Video Libraries," Journal of Visual Communication and Image Representation, Vol. 7, No. 1, 1996, pp. 44-60.

7. H. Martin and R. Lozano, "Dynamic Generation of Video Abstracts Using an Object Oriented Video DBMS," Networking and Information Systems Journal, Vol. 3, No. 1, 2000, pp. 53-75.

8. M. R. Lyu, E. Yau, and S. Sze, "A multilingual, multimodal digital video library system", JCDL '02: Proceedings of the 2nd ACM/IEEE-CS joint conference on Digital libraries, 2002, pp. 145-153.

9. T. Evgeniou, M. Pontil, C. Papageorgiou, and T. Poggio, "Image Representations and Feature Selection for Multimedia Database Search", IEEE Transactions on Knowledge and Data Engineering, Vol. 15, No. 4, 2003, pp. 911-920.

10. M. Betke and N. Makris, "Fast Object Recognition in Noisy Images Using Simulated Annealing," Proceedings of the Fifth Int. Conference Computer Vision, 1995, pp. 523- 530.

11. A. Yuille, P. Hallinan, and D. Cohen, "Feature Extraction from Faces Using Deformable Templates," Int. Journal on Computer Vision, Vol. 8, No. 2, 1992, pp. 99-111.

12. B. Moghaddam and A. Pentland, "Probabilistic Visual Learning for Object Detection," Technical Report 326, Mitmedia, 1995.

13. M. Osadchy and D. Keren, "A Rejection-Based Method for Event Detection in Video," IEEE Transactions on Circuits and Systems for Video Technology, Vol. 14, No. 4, 2004, pp. 534-541.

14. H. Sidenbladh, M.J. Black, and D.J. Fleet, "Stochastic tracking of 3D human figures using 2D image motion," Proceedings of the European Conference on Computer Vision, 2000, pp.702-718.

15. M. E. Leventon and W.T. Freeman, "Bayesian Estimation of 3-D Human Motion from image sequences," Mitsubishi Electric Research Lab, 1998, Vol. TR-98-06.

16. M.J. Black, D.J. Fleet, and Y.Yaccob, "Robustly estimative changes in image appearance," Computer Vision and Image Understanding, Vol. 78, 2000, pp.8-31.

17. A.F. Bobick and J.W. Davids, "The recognition of human movement using temporal templates," IEEE Transactions on Pattern Analysis and Machine Intelligence, Vol 23, 2001, pp.257-267.
18. M.R. Lyu, J. Song, and M. Cai, "A comprehensive method for multilingual video text detection, localization, and extraction," IEEE Transactions on Circuits and Systems for Video Technology, Vol. 15, No. 2, 2005, pp. 243- 255.
19. A. Chianese, R. Miscioscia, V. Moscato, S. Parlato, and A. Picariello, "A Fuzzy Approach to Video Scenes Detection and its Application for Soccer Matches," IEEE International Conference on Intelligent Systems Design and Applications, 2004.
20. M. Fayzullin, V.S. Subrahmanian, M. Albanese, and A. Picariello. "The Priority Curve Algorithm for Video Summarization", Proceedings of ACM MMDB 2004, pp. 28-35.
21. A. Picariello, M. L. Sapino, and V. S. Subrahmanian. "Algebraic Video Environment," in Handbook of Video Data Bases (Eds. B. Furht and O. Marques), 2003, CRC Press, pp. 457-482.
22. P. Ciaccia and M. Patella, "Searching in metric spaces with user-defined and approximate distances," ACM Transactions on Database Systems, Vol. 27, No. 4, 2002, pp. 398-437.
23. V.S. Subrahmanian, "Principles of Multimedia Database Systems," Morgan Kaufmann, 1998.

VIDEO DELIVERY OVER WIRELESS MULTI-HOP NETWORKS

Qian Zhang
Microsoft Research Asia, Beijing, China

Definition: *A wireless multi-hop network is a collection of wireless nodes that dynamically form a temporary network without an infrastructure.*

A multi-hop network is dynamically self-organized and self-configured, with the nodes in the network automatically establishing and maintaining mesh connectivity among themselves. This feature brings many advantages to multi-hop networks such as low up-front cost, easy network maintenance, robustness, and reliable service coverage. With the increase in the bandwidth of wireless channels, and in the computing power of devices, video applications are expected to become available in wireless multi-hop networks in a near future. However, limited network resource, severe interference/ contention among neighbor traffic, dynamic changing route, lack of QoS support, direct coupling between the physical layer and the upper layers, etc. pose many challenges for supporting video communication over wireless multi-hop networks.

Target at the above challenges, it is essential to improve the quality for multimedia delivery over wireless multi-hop networks from different aspects. More specifically,

- To handle the impact of channel error to compressed media, it is important to have the efficient and resilient video coding and protection solutions.

Many research works have been there trying to address the best tradeoff between error resilience and coding efficiency under different conditions. Considering wireless multi-hop network can establish more than one path between a source and a destination given their mesh topology, recently people start thinking about leveraging multi-path to further improve the efficiency. Feedback Based Reference Picture Selection (RPS), Layered Coding with Selective ARQ, and Multiple Description Coding (MDC) are three representative schemes along this direction.

- Target at dealing with the dynamic changing network condition and utilizing the uniqueness of multi-hop networks (e.g., multiple paths available due to the mesh topology), it is essential to design new network and transport protocols.

The mesh topology of multi-hop networks provides the existence of multiple routes between two endpoints which can be utilized to perform multipath streaming to better support real time multimedia applications. The two important issues need to be addressed are listed as follows. Firstly, packet losses due to different causes (i.e., congestion, channel error, and route change/break) should be differentiated so that congestion control and error control can be performed properly. Secondly, streaming protocols need to choose multiple maximally disjointed paths to achieve good streaming quality. A number of approaches including Ad Hoc TCP Friendly Rate Control (ADTFRC), Multi-flow Realtime Transport Protocol (MRTP), Robust Multipath Source Routing Protocol (RMSRP), and Ad hoc Multipath sTreaming Protocol (AMTP) are proposed to enable multimedia streaming over multiple paths in multi-hop networks.

- To provide QoS support for multimedia delivery, research studies related to link layer, including scheduling and enhanced MAC are also quite important.

Due to the existence of hidden terminal and the lack of centralized control, it is very challenge to have QoS support for multi-hop wireless networks. Several distributed scheduling algorithms, such as congestion-distortion optimized scheduling (CoDiO), opportunistic packet scheduling and auto rate (OSAR), distributed link scheduling multiple access (D-LSMA), are proposed to extend 802.11 MAC so that permit nodes to reserve periodic time slices for real-time flows. Do not change the existing 802.11 MAC, SoftMAC employs "coarse-grained" control mechanisms (e.g., distributed admission control and rate regulation) to coordinate and regulate network load and packet transmission of both RT and BE traffic among neighboring nodes in a distributed manner.

- Finally, to improve the overall wireless network performance, cross-layer approaches that jointly consider different layers, including multimedia application, routing and transport protocol, link layer scheduling, and physical layer power control are drawing great attention.

The cross-layer network design of video streaming over multi-hop wireless networks is still in its infancy. Most of the recent research considers only a subset of layers of the protocol stack. A more general framework is proposed recently, which encompasses the entire protocol stack. One thing that needs to be paid much attention is that a cross-layer approach can significantly increase the design complexity. Keeping some form of separation, while allowing layers to actively interact, appears a good compromise for enabling interaction between layers without eliminating the layering principle. Moreover, cross-layer design does not necessarily mean that all the layers should interact together. How to identify the layers, that can generate the most significant gains by interacting together present important areas of future research.

Enabling multimedia transport over wireless multi-hop networks is an exciting yet challenging task. Deeper studies are needed for each the above direction.

See: Wireless Video

References

14. S. Mao, S. Lin, S.S Panwar, Y. Wang, and E. Celebi, "Video transport over ad hoc networks: multistream coding with multipath transport," IEEE Journal on Selected Areas in Communications, Vol. 21, No. 10, December 2003.
15. K. Rojviboonchai, F. Yang, Q. Zhang, H. Aida, and W. Zhu, "AMTP: A Multipath Multimedia Streaming Protocol for Mobile Ad Hoc Networks," Proceedings of the *IEEE ICC*, 2005.
16. E. Setton, T. Yoo, X. Zhu, A. Goldsmith, and B. Girod, "Cross-layer design of ad hoc networks for real-time video streaming," IEEE Wireless Communication Magazine, 2005.

VIDEO INPAINTING

Definition: Video inpainting refers to digital video restoration and video inpainting techniques should perform spatiotemporal restoration and adapt itself to the varying structural and motion characteristics of the visual data.

Digital inpainting plays a crucial role in digital video restoration. Digital processing of archived video data, transmission over best effort networks or wireless communication channels, and aggressive coding introduce visual impairments in video sequences [1]-[3]. For example, channel fading during the wireless transmission of MPEG-coded videos can lead to packet loss which causes missed blocks in a received video. Furthermore, archived films and videos are exposed to chemical and physical elements as well as environmental conditions, which cause visual information loss and artifacts in the corresponding digital representation.

Motion video can be viewed as a three-dimensional (3-D) image signal or a time sequence of two-dimensional (2-D) images (frames) [1]. Such a visual input exhibits significant spatial and temporal correlation. Temporal restoration of motion video without spatial processing results in blurring of the structural information in the reconstructed video regardless of the motion or non-motion compensated nature of the temporal processing. On the other hand, processing each one of the video frames as still images and ignoring their temporal correlation produces strong motion artifacts. Therefore, a well designed video inpainting solution should perform spatiotemporal restoration and adapt itself to the varying structural and motion characteristics of the visual data.

In restoring archived films and videos, the presence of dirt, dust and scratches in the original medium results in speckle noise, random patches and sparkles of varying sizes and intensity [1]. In the case of transmission over best effort type of networks, dropped macroblocks create missing data patches while transmission over erasure channels, such as the Gilbert-Elliot channel may introduce random errors at the pixel level [1],[3]. The spatial position of such visual impairments varies significantly as they are application dependent. It is therefore reasonable to assume that such impairments should be modeled and localized as temporal discontinuity. Through the employed motion compensation algorithms, this discontinuity is viewed as a spatial area in the actual frame which cannot be matched to a similar area in reference frames. Thus, an artifact detection procedure should precede the inpainting technique. The detector should be able to differentiate between structural content and visual artifacts. Such design characteristics can be obtained either through the heuristic threshold(s)-based detection methods as well as model-based approaches [1]. After localizing the artifacts at the target frame, either a conventional image inpainting technique or a spatiotemporal inpainting solution can be used to fill-in the missing color, structural or textural information.

It should be noted that the utilization of an automated or semi-automated video inpainting techniques is essential for a cost-effective processing of the input. In most cases processing is performed in batch mode [2]. Therefore, the development of high-performance parallel computational platform based video restoration techniques is of paramount importance.

See: Image inpainting, Inpainting in virtual restoration of artworks, Color image filtering and enhancement.

References

17. A.-C. Kokaram, R.-D. Morros, W.-J. Fitzerald, and P.-J.-V. Rayner, "Detection of Missing Data in Image Sequences," IEEE Transactions on Image Processing, Vol. 4, No. 11, November 1995, pp. 1496-1508.
18. M. Ceccarelli and G. Laccetti, "High Performance Missing Data Detection and Interpolation for Video Compression and Restoration Applications," Proceedings of the International Parallel and Distributed Processing Symposium (IPDPS'03), April 2003, pp. 5.
19. J. Park, D.-C. Park, R.-J.-Marks, and M.-A. El-Sharkawi, "Recovery of Image Blocks Using the Method of Alternating Projections," IEEE Transactions on Image Processing, Vol. 14, No. 4, April 2005, pp. 461-474.

VIDEO OVER IP

Artur Ziviani
National Laboratory for Scientific Computing (LNCC), Petrópolis, Brazil

Marcelo Dias de Amorim
National Center for Scientific Research (CNRS/LIP6), Paris, France

Definition: *Video over IP refers to a challenging task to define standards and protocols for transmitting video over IP (Internet Protocol) networks.*

Introduction

The Internet is doubtless one of the greatest success examples ever observed in the information technology world. Its evolution can be explained by two complementary views. On the one hand, advances in communication and information technologies have allowed rapid increase in transmission capacity in both wired and wireless domains. On the other hand, users are becoming more exigent and asking to transmit larger amounts of data of multiple natures. In this context, transmitting *video* over IP networks is particularly challenging. Indeed, at the time of design of the Internet, expected data rates seen by terminals were about a few Kbps. Later, with the advent of multimedia communications, bandwidth requirements are now measured in the order of Mbps.

The Internet operates as a packet-switched network that interconnects end nodes implementing the TCP/IP protocol stack [1]. In the TCP/IP protocol stack, the network layer protocol is the Internet Protocol (IP). Under IP, each host that communicates directly with the Internet has an address assigned to it that is unique within the network. This is known as the IP address of each host. Further, each IP address is subdivided into smaller parts: a network identifier and a host identifier. The former uniquely identifies the access network to which the host is attached. The latter indicates the host within a particular network. Routers periodically exchange routing information about address identifiers of the concerned access networks. As a result of this periodic information exchange, routers are able to build routing tables that guide packet forwarding among different networks. These tables are used at each intermediate router along a path within the network to indicate the forwarding interface an IP packet (datagram) should take in order to get to its destination.

In the IP layer, if the packet size exceeds a maximum frame size of the network connected to the output interface, the packet is further divided in smaller parts in a process called fragmentation. These fragments are then forwarded by the network in separate packets toward the destination. The destination is responsible for reassembling the fragments into the original packet. Note that if a fragment is lost within the network, the destination is unable to reassemble the packet that has been fragmented and the surviving fragments are then discarded. The forwarding decision for each packet is individually taken at each intermediate node. As incoming IP packets arrive at an intermediate router, they are stored in a buffer waiting for the router to process a routing decision for each one of them to indicate their appropriate output interface. Persistent packet buffering at routers is known as network congestion. Furthermore, if a packet arrives at a router and the buffer is full, the packet is simply discarded by the router. Therefore, severe network congestion causes packet losses as buffers fill up. As a consequence of these characteristics, IP service offers no guarantees of bounded delay and limited packet loss rate. There is also no assurance that packets of a single flow will follow the same path within the network or will arrive at the destination in the same order they were originally transmitted by the source.

IP provides a connectionless best-effort service to the transport layer protocols. The main transport protocols of the TCP/IP protocol stack are the Transmission Control Protocol (TCP) and the User Datagram Protocol (UDP). TCP offers a connection-oriented and reliable service. In turn, UDP provides a connectionless best-effort service. The choice of transport protocol depends on the requirements of the adopted application. From the viewpoint of an application, UDP simply provides an extension of the service provided by IP with an additional UDP header checksum. Hence, applications using UDP see the IP service as it is. In contrast with UDP, TCP seeks to mask the network service provided by IP to the application protocols by applying connection management, congestion control, error control, and flow control mechanisms.

The Real-time Transport Protocol (RTP) [2] supports applications streaming audio and/or video with real-time constraints over the Internet. RTP is composed by a data and a control part. The data part of RTP provides functionality suited for carrying real-time content, *e.g.* the timing information required by the receiver to correctly output the received packet stream. The control part, called Real-time Transport Control Protocol (RTCP), offers control mechanisms for synchronizing different streams with timing properties prior to decoding them. RTCP also provides reports to a real-time stream source on the network Quality of Service (QoS) offered to receivers in terms of delay, jitter, and packet loss rate experienced by the received packets. These functionalities are also available to the multicast distribution of real-time streams.

The transmission of video over the Internet has received great attention from both academic and industrial communities. In this text, we summarize some of the most important topics related to video transmission over the Internet. We propose an overview of the domains by briefly addressing standards, characteristics, communication techniques, and video quality. This list is not exhaustive, but representative of the greatest advances in video transmission over the latest years.

Video Requirements

The nature of video content directly influences on the achieved compression rate of a video encoder and the resulting traffic to be transmitted. For example, at the one hand, a news video sequence usually shows a person just narrating events and, as a consequence, most of the scene is still, thus favoring video compression techniques based on motion estimation. At the other hand, an action movie is less susceptible to compression because of frequent camera movements and object displacements at the movie scenes. Furthermore, scene changes produce disruptions that result in larger coded frames. Therefore, video sequences with frequent scene changes, like music video clips, generate highly bursty network traffic.

The transmission of video sequences over the Internet imposes different requirements on video quality delivery [3, 4]. Processing, transmission, propagation, and queuing delays compose the total delay that takes a packet to be fully transmitted from the video source to its destination. The processing delay consists of the coding and packetization at the source, the packet treatment at intermediate routers, and the depacketization and decoding at the receiver. The transmission delay is a function of the packet size and transmission capacity at the links. The propagation delay is a characteristic of each communication medium. The queuing delay is unpredictable because it depends on the concurrent traffic video packets encounter at each intermediate router. Maximum delay is an important metric for interactive applications with real-time requirements, such as videoconferencing and distance collaboration. Streaming video applications also depend on packets arriving within a bounded delay for timely content reproduction. If a packet arrives too late at the receiver, the packet is considered as lost since it is useless for video playback. A solution is to transmit some packets in advance and accumulate them in a buffer before starting the video reproduction. A bounded jitter is also desirable because it reduces the buffer capacity needed at receivers to compensate these variations in delay. IP is a connectionless protocol and hence packets may follow different paths through the network. As a consequence, they may arrive at the receiver out-of-order. All these issues affect the video quality perceived at the receiver by an end user [5].

Video Compression Standards

As shown before, video data are in general greedy of network resources. In some cases, bandwidth is quite abundant and the requirements for transmitting video are not really an issue. However, the high heterogeneity of the Internet is still characterized by a large number of low-capacity terminal links. Algorithms for compressing information, and in particular video data, are highly demanded and have been the main focus of many research efforts in the latest decades [6]. In general, the idea behind compression is to assign few bits to low priority events and more bits to high priority events (the term priority is used here in its broader meaning, and can have different significations depending on the context). Two entities have contributed with the most used algorithms and standards for video compression: MPEG and ITU.

The Motion Picture Expert Group (MPEG) [7], launched in 1998, is an ISO/IEC working group that works towards standards for both audio and video digital formats and for multimedia description frameworks. The main standards for video coding released by this group include MPEG-1, MPEG-2, and MPEG-4. The MPEG-1 standard defines a series of encoding techniques for both audio and video (video is part 2 of the standard), designed for generating flows of up to 1.5 Mbps. The main goal of MPEG-1 was to address the problem of storing video in CD-ROMs, and it has become a successful format for video exchange over the Internet. However, higher rates than the 1.5 Mbps of MPEG-1 became rapidly a need. This led to the definition of MPEG-2, which defines rates from 1.5 to tens of Mbps. MPEG-2 is based on MPEG-1, but proposes a number of new techniques to address a much larger number of potential applications, including digital video storage and transmission, high-definition television (HDTV), and digital video disks (DVDs). MPEG-1 and 2 achieve good compression ratios by implementing causal and non-causal prediction. Briefly, a video flow is defined as a sequence of group of pictures (GOP), composed of three types of frames (or pictures): I, P, and B. I-frames, also called reference frames, are basically low-compressed pictures that serve as reference for the computation of P and B frames. P-frames are obtained from a past I-frame by using motion prediction, and can then be encoded with higher compression ratios. B-frames, or bidirectional frames, are based on both previous and future I and P frames within a GOP, which leads to high compression ratios. Figure 1 illustrates this hierarchical structure of GOPs.

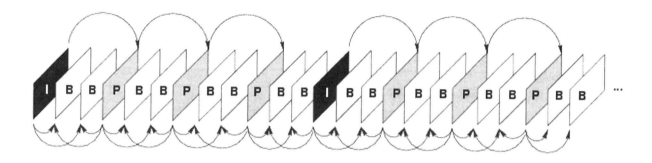

Figure 1. Example of the hierarchical structure of a GOP.

MPEG-4 part 2 (see also H.264 below) covers a gap in the objectives of the previous two standards: the need for a flexible framework that would be adaptable to the wide range of applications and the high heterogeneity found in the Internet. MPEG-4 targets the scaling from a few Kbps to moderately high bit rates (about 4 Mbps). The main innovation brought by MPEG-4 was the use of the concept of video objects, in which a scene is decomposed in a number of objects that can be treated differently one from another during the video transmission (*e.g.*, prioritization among objects).

The International Telecommunication Unit (ITU) [8], in its H series (*e.g.*, H.310, H.320, and H.324), has also addressed the problem of transmitting compressed video over the Internet. The first standard proposed by ITU is the H.261 video codec. In order to deal with a wide range of communication patterns, the H.261 standard defines a number of methods for coding and decoding video at rates of $p \times 64$ Kbps, where p varies in the range of 1 to 30. Later, three other standards have appeared: H.262, H.263, and H.264. The H.262 standard targets higher bit rates (in fact, H.262 is the result of a partnership that also led to MPEG-2), and has not been widely implemented in the H.320 series. Both H.261 and H.263 are based on the same principles, although H.263 introduces a number of improvements that lead to equivalent video quality for even half of the bandwidth. H.261 supports both QCIF (176×144 pixels) and CIF (352×288) resolutions, whereas H.263 also supports SQCIF (128×96 pixels), 4CIF (704×576 pixels), and 16CIF (1408×1152 pixels). The H.264 standard, also known as MPEG-4 part 10 or H.264/AVC, is the result of a joint work between ITU and MPEG (the partnership is called Joint Video Team - JVT), with the objective of defining a codec capable of generating, without increased complexity, good video quality at lower bit rates than previous formats (H.262, MPEG-2, MPEG-4 part 2). H.264/AVC makes use of advanced coding techniques in order to generate video for a wide range of applications, from low to high resolution and at varying bit rates (for example, DVD, broadcast, 3G mobile content) [9].

Session Setup

An important issue in multimedia communications is how sessions are set up. Session establishment applies for multimedia communications in general, and can be set up in two different ways: by announcement or by invitation. A TV program is an example of session established by announcement, whereas a videophone call is an example of session established by invitation. The Internet Engineering Task Force (IETF) [10] has proposed a set of protocols for session setup, covering description, announcement, and invitation phases. The ITU-T has also proposed a standard, H.323, but in this document we focus on the IETF's solutions.

The common protocol for session setup is the Session Description Protocol (SDP), which is used to describe the characteristics of the session to be established. In SDP, sessions are characterized by a well-defined set of descriptors in textual form, including: the name of the session, the objective, associated protocols, information about codecs, timing, among others. SDP operates in a complementary way with the protocols defined in the following. The Session Announcement Protocol (SAP) is a very simple protocol for announcing future multimedia sessions. It basically sends over a multicast session, in a periodic fashion, the description of the session defined by SDP. A bit more complicated is the Session Initiation Protocol (SIP), proposed to control multimedia sessions by invitation. The main contribution of SIP is the way it addresses corresponding nodes. In the classical telephone network, when making a call, the initiator knows exactly where the destination phone is physically located, but is neither sure that the person that will respond is the one she/he searches nor that this latter will be at the other side of the line. In SIP, the idea is to call a person and not the phone this person may be near.

Video Distribution

The way the video is transmitted from the source to the receivers has a direct impact both on the utilization of the network resources and on the quality of the video perceived at the terminals. The trivial way of sending a video to a destination is by establishing a *unicast* connection between the source and the destination. This approach is however not efficient if the same video must be sent to more than one receiver (potentially hundreds or thousands of them). Another class of communication, extensively studied in the latest years, provides interesting properties for video communication: the *multicast*. In this paradigm, data sent by the source are received by a number of destinations belonging to a multicast group. The advantage of multicasting is that the source transmits only one copy of the data to multiple receivers, instead of occupying the medium with multiple copies of the same data, thus avoiding the inefficient utilization of network resources.

Distributing video in multicast mode raises a number of technical issues [11]. End-systems in the Internet are quite heterogeneous in terms of receiving capacity. Indeed, access speeds vary from a few Kbps up to many Mbps. Thus, there is the problem of determining at which rate the source should send the video. On the one hand, if the source sets the rate to the minimum receiving capacity (in order to maximize the number of destinations able to receive the video), high-speed terminals become underutilized. On the other hand, if the source increases the transmission rate, high-speed terminals can be provided with improved video quality although slow terminals cannot be served anymore.

In order to address this problem, two techniques have been proposed so far: multiple flows and multi-layering [12, 13]. In the first one, the raw video is coded at different rates and each flow is sent over a different multicast sessions. In this way, slow terminals join multicast groups that transfer low-rate flows, whereas high-speed receivers join higher-rate multicast sessions. This solution solves the problem of satisfaction of the receivers, but leads to higher network loads; indeed, bandwidth is wasted to transmit different flows of the same video. The technique of multi-layering addresses exactly this point. This approach relies on the capacity of some coders to split the raw video in multiple layers. These layers are hierarchically organized in a base layer and one or more enhancement layers. Enhancement layers cannot be decoded without the base layer and other enhancement layers of higher priority. In this way, the base layer plus two enhancement layers result in better video quality than the configuration with the base layer and one enhancement layer. The system that adopts a multi-layer approach is similar to the one that uses multiple flows. Each layer is transmitted over a particular multicast group and receivers join as many groups as they want or are able to receive simultaneously. The multi-layering solution, although more expensive for the implementation because it needs a multi-layer codec, solves both the satisfaction and overhead problems.

More recently, some interesting solutions propose to use peer-to-peer concepts to distribute video over the Internet, for both video on demand and streaming. In the peer-to-peer communication paradigm, end-systems establish connections among them forming a logical structure called overlay network. Peer-to-peer techniques can be used for video communication in two different, not necessarily orthogonal, ways. The first one deals with the absence of central servers, and each end-system is both a server and a client. The second one, more related to the context of this text, refers to the real-time video distribution. Although native multicast, as described above, has shown to be an efficient solution for multimedia distribution, it has not been widely implemented yet. For this reason, many solutions for overlay multicast have been proposed [14]. With this solution, a logical distribution tree is established from the source to the receivers, where the receivers themselves occupy nodes of the tree. The advantage of this approach is that the load in the source's output link is dramatically reduced without requiring the implementation of native multicast.

Quality of Service (QoS)

Quality video delivery over the widely deployed IP-based networks is required by several applications, such as distance learning and collaboration, video distribution, telemedicine, video conferencing, and interactive virtual environments. Nevertheless, the best-effort model of the conventional Internet has become inadequate to deal with the very diverse requirements on network QoS of video streams. The hierarchical structure of video encoding with possible error propagation through its frames imposes a great difficulty on sending video streams over lossy networks because small packet loss rates may translate into much higher frame error rates. Besides being lost, some packets may also suffer unpredictable amounts of delay or jitter due to network congestion at intermediate routers, compromising their accomplishment of real-time constraints. All these issues related to the best-effort service of IP may seriously contribute to degrade the perceived quality of an end user at the video reproduction.

An alternative to recover from transmission errors, which can turn a frame undecodable, is to apply error concealment techniques. In the absence of a frame due to errors, error concealment may replace the lost frame by a previous one or roughly estimate it from adjacent well-received frames. Further, error concealment techniques differ on the roles the encoder and decoder play in recovering from errors. We direct the interested reader to [15] for a full review on error concealment techniques. Different QoS schemes may also be applied to the video stream in order to adapt it for transmission given the network conditions [16]. These adaptive strategies involve applying redundancy; either by using Forward Error Correction (FEC) to tolerate some losses or by using a different compression factor in the video encoding that may be achieved in changing the adopted GOP pattern. FEC schemes protect video streams against packet losses up to a certain level at the expense of data redundancy. Adopting different frame patterns allows a video stream to better adapt itself to the available transmission conditions. Within the network, unequal protection based on frame type may avoid quality degradation due to the loss of one particularly important frame and the possible propagation effect of this loss throughout the hierarchical structure of compressed video streams [17, 18]. The joint adoption of these QoS strategies may as well contribute to a better delivery quality of video streams [19]. Figure 2 shows sample visual results of the negative effects that the best-effort service of IP may impose to video sequences and how the appliance of QoS mechanisms can enhance the video delivery quality to an end user.

Summary and Outlook

An ever-increasing number of users rely on the Internet to communicate and exchange data using a wide range of applications. In particular, multimedia applications, such as those that make use of video transmissions, are on high demand. Nevertheless, the conventional best-effort model of the Internet does not necessarily meet the requirements on both network and application-level QoS imposed by video applications. In this text, we review the issues associated with transmitting video over IP, the network-layer protocol that interconnects the different networks that compose the Internet. We discuss relevant characteristics of the Internet protocols, pointing out how they impose challenges to the quality transmission of video streams in IP-based networks. We also present techniques and standards for video coding, distribution, and quality of service provision given the requirements imposed by video applications.

Currently, we witness voice over IP applications becoming really popular as the offered quality increases and users are being attracted by telephone-like quality at significantly lower costs. Video over IP has the potential to face a similar situation in the foreseeable future, given that it enables a wide range of interesting applications, including videoconferencing, video on demand, telemedicine, distance learning and collaboration, remote surveillance, and interactive virtual environments. Further developments on areas such as video adaptability to ever-changing network conditions, QoS provision and monitoring, and video distribution are essential for these video over IP applications to become a reality in the daily life of the general public.

(a)

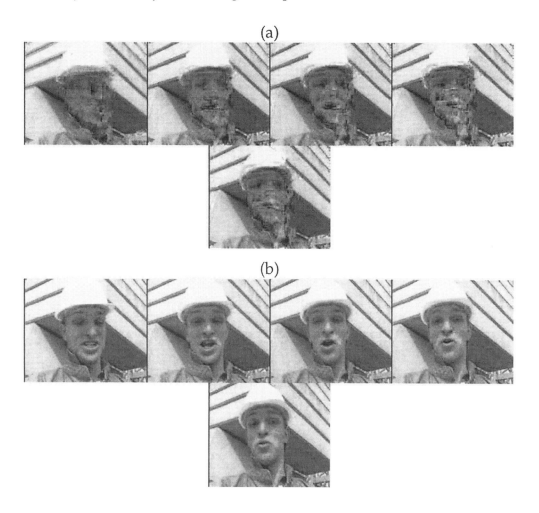

(b)

Figure 2. Sample visual results of video delivery quality using (a) best-effort and (b) QoS.

See: QoS Assessment of Video over IP, Peer-to-Peer Multicast Video.

References

1. D.E. Comer, "Internetworking with TCP/IP," Vol. 1, Prentice Hall, 1995.
2. H. Schulzrinne, S. Casner, R. Frederick, and V. Jacobson, "RTP: A transport protocol for real-time applications," IETF RFC 1889, January 1996.
3. F. Halsall, "Multimedia communications: Applications, networks, protocols, and standards," Addison-Wesley, 2001.
4. S.D. Sevetto and K. Nahrstedt, "Broadcast quality video over IP," IEEE Transactions on Multimedia, Vol. 3, No. 1, pp. 162-173, March 2001.
5. D.A. Rosenthal, "Analysis of selected variables effecting video streamed over IP," International Journal of Network Management, Vol. 14, No. 3, pp. 193-211, May 2004.
6. T. Sikora, "Trends and perspectives in image and video coding," Proceedings of the IEEE, Vol. 93, No. 1, pp. 6- 17, January 2005.

7. ISO/IEC JTC1/SC29 WG11 Moving Picture Expert Group (MPEG). http://www.chiariglione.org/mpeg/.
8. International Telecommunication Unit, Telecommunication Standardization Sector (ITU-T). http://www.itu.int.
9. G.J. Sullivan and T. Wiegand, "Video Compression - from concepts to the H.264/AVC standard," Proceedings of the IEEE, Vol. 93, No. 1, pp. 18- 31, January 2005.
10. Internet Engineering Task Force (IETF). http://www.ietf.org.
11. A. Ganjam and H. Zhang, "Internet multicast video delivery," Proceedings of the IEEE, Vol. 93, No. 1, pp. 159-170, January 2005.
12. S. McCanne, V. Jacobson, and M. Vetterli, "Receiver-driven layered multicast," ACM SIGCOMM, New York, NY, August 1996.
13. M.D. de Amorim, O.C.M.B. Duarte, and G. Pujolle, "Distinguishing video quality through differential matrices," ACM Multimedia Systems Journal, Vol. 9, No. 1, pp. 94-103, July 2003.
14. Y.-H. Chu, S.G. Rao, S. Seshan, and H. Zhang, "A case for end system multicast," IEEE Journal on Selected Areas in Communication (JSAC), Special Issue on Networking Support for Multicast, Vol. 20, No. 8, pp. 1456-1471, October 2002.
15. Y. Wang and Q.-F. Zhu, "Error control and concealment for video communication: A review," Proceedings of the IEEE, Vol. 86, No. 5, pp. 974-997, May 1998.
16. S.-F. Chang; A. Vetro, "Video adaptation: concepts, technologies, and open issues," Proceedings of the IEEE, Vol. 93, No. 1, pp. 148-158, January 2005.
17. C.-H. Ke, C.-K. Shieh, W.-S. Hwang, and A. Ziviani, "A two-marker system for improved MPEG video delivery in a DiffServ network," IEEE Communications Letters, Vol. 9, No. 4, pp. 381-383, April 2005.
18. J. Shin, J. Kim, and C.-C. J. Kuo, "Quality of service mapping mechanism for packet video in differentiated services network," IEEE Transactions on Multimedia, Vol. 3, No. 2, pp. 219-231, June 2001.
19. A. Ziviani, B.E. Wolfinger, J.F. Rezende, O.C.M.B. Duarte, and S. Fdida, "Joint adoption of QoS schemes for MPEG streams," Multimedia Tools and Applications, Vol. 26, No. 1, pp. 59-80, May 2005.

VIDEO SEARCH

Simone Santini
Universidad Autónoma de Madrd, Spain and University of California, San Diego, USA

Definition: *Video search is considered, more or less, as the next logical step from image search, but this consideration is in many aspects superficial: it shows a lack of appreciation for the peculiar characteristics of the medium and for the new class of problems that the temporal nature of video poses.*

The interest in video search has emerged in the mid- to late-90's together with the interest in other forms of search of multimedia data and, like that, has been greatly intensified by the growing number of videos available on the internet. Video search is considered, more or less, as the next logical step from image search, but this consideration is in many aspects superficial: it shows a lack of appreciation for the peculiar characteristics of the medium and for the new class of problems that the temporal nature of video poses. If, to this, one adds that image search has, to this day, failed to produce a satisfactory general purpose solution (and there are some reasons to believe that such a solution may be conceptually impossible [1], one can realize that video search is still in a very preliminary stage, quite possibly one in which its main intellectual features and cultural impact still have to be identified.

Differently from other media, there is a substantial discontinuity among the various forms of video and, correspondingly, one can expect a similar discontinuity in the methods and principles of search for different types of video. A broad distinction in organization and search principles can be made between *semiotic* and *phenœstetic* video [2].

Semiotic Video

Semiotic video is, loosely speaking, video specifically designed, constructed, or assembled to deliver a message. Produced video, from films to TV programs, commercials, or music videos are examples of semiotic video: they carry an explicit message (or multiple messages), which is encoded not only in their content, but also in the syntax of the video itself.

In other words, in addition to the information carried by the scenes represented in the video, and by the actions and situations therein depicted, one has an additional language, superimposed to it, a semiotic system whose syntax was defined, in its essential elements, by the work of Russian constructivists such as Eisenstein and Vertov in the 1920's [3]. This language is that of *montage*, based on elements such as *shots* (an uninterrupted camera take covering a certain time span), *scenes* (a collection of shots that forms a narrative unit [4]), and transitions between them.

The language of montage has extended beyond cinema through its adoption by other cultural media like TV or music videos. Its relative importance as a carrier of the semiosis of a video depends, of course, on the general characteristics of the form of expression in which it is employed, or even on the personal characteristics of the creator of a given message: we have at one extreme film directors who make a very Spartan use of montage and, at the other extreme, musical videos in which the near totality of the visual message is expressed by montage.

Montage is not the only symbolic system at work in semiotic video, although it is the most common and the easiest to detect. Specific genres of video use other means that a long use has promoted to the status of symbols in order to express certain ideas. In cartoons, for instance, characters running very fast always leave a cloud behind them, and whenever they are hit on the head, they vibrate. These messages are, to an extent, iconic (certain materials do vibrate when they are hit) but their use is now largely symbolic and is being extended especially rather crudely to other genres (such as action movies) that rely on visuals more than on dialog to describe an action: thanks to the possibilities offered by sophisticated computer techniques, the language of action movies is moving away from realism and getting closer and closer to a cartoonish symbolism.

Attempts at an automatic analysis of semiotic video have traditionally relied on the semiotic system constituted by montage, mainly due to the existence of relatively robust algorithms for the detection of cuts and of transition effects, which permit the extraction of—at least—a level of semantics without requiring the solution of the cognitive problems of image recognition. The detection of the structure of montage serves, *grosso modo*, two purposes in video search.

Firstly, it is used to break the temporal structure of the video in a spatial one in which the temporal structured is summarized, and where it can be stored and accessed as an instantaneous whole [5,6]. The break-up of the temporal structure is sometimes stored in a two-level hierarchy: shots are grouped into *scenes* (sometimes this hierarchy is referred to as a four levels one, the bottom level being represented by the individual frame, the top level by the whole film—occasionally, additional levels can be present, as in a film divided into episodes). The term *scene* used in video retrieval is only partially related to what a film director would call a scene, but it is based on the same idea of being a collection of thematically and narratively related shots [7]. The criteria for clustering shots into scenes are, to an extent, dependent on the genre of the film (what works for, say, a documentary won't probably work for a musical video). For narrative cinema, clustering criteria include color (the dominant colors are given by the background, which tend to be the same in the various shots of a scene), a statistically uniform audio, and a detection of a dialog situation (represented, e.g. by the alternance of the same faces) [8].
In some other cases, video has a structure that can constitute a priori information used to guide the segmentation process. This is true for highly structured "format" video programs, such as news [9,10]: in this cases one can start with a structure graph describing the temporal relations of the various elements of the video (anchor-person shots, stories, commercial interruptions,...) and, on one hand, create *expectations* that can be used to drive the segmentation process and, on the other hand, fill in the slots of the model with the segments detected.

The information that is associated to these fragments of video is to an extent dependent on the application that the system is expected to serve. In many cases of retrieval, a suitable set of features is extracted and is used to index the fragment; these can consist in features extracted from the whole fragment (e.g. features containing motion information [11]) or features extracted from some representative frames [12]. Representative (or "key") frames are also used to represent the fragments in the case of interactive "browsing" systems. An alternative to this is to maintain the temporal nature of video in the summarization by building *abstracts*, that is, short segments of video meant to convey the essential contents of the whole video [8].

Secondly, shots and scenes can be used as the basis for features that characterize the contents of video. This approach goes back to montage seen as a symbolic—and, therefore, conventional—semiotic system. To make but an example, typically a *cut* in a film signifies either no time discontinuity at all, or a relatively short time discontinuity, while a *dissolve* marks the passage of a certain amount of time. Conventions such as these can be used to determine important aspects of the semantics of a video. There is, here as in many other areas at the intersection of technology and creative expression, the always present risk of simplification: the use of the language of montage is highly idiosyncratic, depending on the personal language of the director, on the language of the genre in which a film is placed, and on the general convention in use at a certain time: trivialization is an ever present danger when one deals with a semiotic system as complex as video. The worst risk in this sense is that a technological trivialization will push, under the influence of marketing and of the advantages that technological complacency can have for it, towards a simplification of the film language itself.

Together with other features (the semiotic of color, for instance, is quite well known) montage has been used to create a taxonomy in advertisements [13] according to their narrative structure [14]. Similarly, montage has been used to classify video according to *genre* [15] although, in this case, the feasibility of such an operation is more doubtful given the uncertain (culturally mediated and, to an extent, subjective) definition of genres (is *The Maltese falcon* a *noir* or an action film?).

Phenœstetic video

Phenœstetic is characterized by the almost absolute absence of cultural references or expressive possibilities that rest on a shared cultural background. It is, to use an evocative albeit simplistic image, video that just happens to be. Typical examples of phenœstetic video are given by security cameras or by the increasingly common phenomenon of web cameras [16].

In this type of video, there is in general no conscious effort to express a meaning except, possibly, through the actions of the people in the video. Medium specific semiotic systems, such as montage are absent and, in most cases, the identities of the people present in the video will afford no special connotation. In a few words, phenœstetic video is a stream of undifferentiated, uninterrupted narrative, a sort of visual stream of consciousness of a particular situation.

Imposing a structure to this kind of video for the purpose of searching it is much more problematic than it is the case with semiotic video, since all the syntactic structures to which the semantic structure is anchored are absent. It would be futile, for instance, to try to infer the character of a phenœstetic video by looking at the average length of the shots or the semiotic characteristics of its color distribution, for there are no shots to be detected and colors are not purposefully selected.

One organizational principle on which search can be based is constituted by *events*. The concept of event is, of course, highly application-specific—what constitutes an event in a security environment might not constitute it for a consumer-behavioral study in a supermarket. However, once a set of *primitive* events has been selected—and the proper feature extraction algorithms and analysis procedure have been set up for their detection and placement in time—general primitives can be used to compose primitive events in complex ones [2].

With events as objects of the query process, a number of data base techniques can be used or modified to serve the needs of video search. One possibility in this sense is to use *temporal logic* for describing video sequences as well as for expressing query conditions [17], while other options are offered by the various event specification formalisms devised for event data bases [18,19]. One advantage of these formal approaches is that they provide the means to specify the intended semantics of event detection (intended here as formal semantics, e.g. denotational or operational).

Consider the detection of a composite event composed of an instance of an event A followed by an instance of an event B, and suppose that in a certain situation four primitive events are detected, placed in time as in figure below:

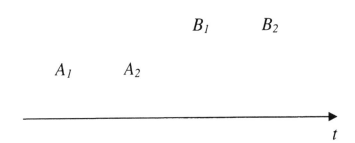

How many composite events are detected? Depending on the semantics of *follows*, one can detect just the event $\langle A_2, B_1 \rangle$, the two events $\langle A_1, B_1 \rangle$, $\langle A_2, B_2 \rangle$, the four events $\langle A_1, B_1 \rangle$, $\langle A_1, B_2 \rangle$, $\langle A_2, B_1 \rangle$, $\langle A_2, B_2 \rangle$, and so on. Several possible semantics for event detection can be defined [19,2] depending on the requirements of the application.

References

1. S. Santini, "Semantics without Annotation," in S. Handschuh and S. Staab (Eds.) "Annotation for the Semantic Web," IOS Press, 2003.
2. S. Santini, "Organizational Principles of Video Data," in B. Furht and O. Marques (Eds.) "Handbook of Video Databases," CRC Press, 2003, pp. 537—560.
3. L. Manovich, "The language of new media," Cambridge:MIT Press, 2002.
4. A. J. Greimas, « Sémantique Structurale, » Paris:Larousse, 1966.
5. A. Hampapur, R. Jain, and T. Weymouth, "Digital Video Segmentation," Proceedings of Multimedia '94, ACM Press, 1994.
6. A. Dailianas, R. Allen, and P. England, "Comparison of automatic video segmentation algorithms," Proceedings of the SPIE Vol. 2615, Integration issues in large commercial media delivery systems, Bellingham:SPIE Press, 1995.
7. M. Yeung, B. Yeo, and B. Liu, "Extracting story units from long programs for video browsing and navigation," Proceedings of IEEE Multimedia Computing and Systems, pp. 296—305, Los Alamitos:IEEE Press, 1996.
8. R. Lienhard, S. Pfeiffer, and W. Effelsberg, "Video abstracting," Communications of the ACM, Vol. 40, No. 12, December 1997.
9. D. Swanberg, C. F. Shu, and R. Jain, "Knowledge guided parsing in video databases," Proceedings of the SPIE, Vol. 1908, pp. 13—24, Bellingham:SPIE Press, 1993
10. H. J. Zhang, S. Y. Tan, S. Smoliar, and Y. Gong, "Automatic parsing and indexing of news video," Multimedia Systems, Vol. 2, No. 6, pp. 256—65, 1995.

11. N. Dimitrova and F. Golshani, "Motion recovery for video content classification," ACM Transactions on Information Systems, Vol. 13, No. 4, pp. 408—439, Oct. 1995.
12. S. Smoliar and H. J. Zhang, "Content-based video indexing and retrieval," *IEEE Multimedia*, Summer 1994.
13. C. Colombo, A. Del Bimbo, and P. Pala, "Retrieval of commercials by video semantics," *Proceedings of the IEEE International conference on pattern recognition*, pp. 572—577, Los Alamitos:IEEE Press, 1998.
14. C. R. Haas, *Pratique de la publicité*, Paris:Bordas, 1988.
15. B. T. Truong and C. Dorai, "Automatic genre identification for content-based video categorization," *Proceedings of the international conference on pattern recognition*, Los Alamitos:IEEE Press, 2000.
16. B. R. Farzin, K. Goldberg, and A. Jacobs, "A Minimalist Telerobotic Installation on the Internet," Proceedings of the *1st Workshop on Web Robots, International Conference on Robots and Intelligent Systems*, September 1998.
17. A. Del Bimbo, E. Vicario, and D. Zingoni, "Symbolic description and visual querying of image sequences using spatio-temporal logic," *IEEE Transactions on Knowledge and Data Engineering*, Vol. 7, No. 4, pp. 609—22, 1995.
18. Bhonsle, A. Gupta, S. Santini, M. Worring, and R. Jain, "Complex visual activity recognition using a temporally ordered database," *Proceedings of Visual 99: International conference on Visual Information Management Systems*, Amsterdam, June 1999.
19. S. Chakravarthy and D. Mishra, "Snoop: An Expressive Event Specification Language for Active Databases," *Data and Knowledge Engineering*, Vol. 14, No. 1, 1994.

VIDEO SUMMARIZATION

M. Albanese[1], C. Cesarano[1], M. Fayzullin[2], A. Picariello[1] and V.S. Subrahmanian [2]

[1]Dipartimento di Informatica e Sistemistica, Università di Napoli "Federico II", Napoli, Italy
[2]Department of Computer Science , University of Maryland, College Park, MD, USA

Definition: *Video summarization refers to creating a summary of a digital video, which must satisfy the following three principles: (1) the video summary must contain high priority entities and events from the video, (2) the summary itself should exhibit reasonable degrees of continuity, and (3) the summary should be free of repetition.*

The past decade has seen explosive growth in the ability of individuals to create and/or capture digital video, slowly leading to large personal and corporate digital video archives. In the corporate arena, there is a growing need for video summarization. For instance, a company that uses video technology to secure its buildings may wish to summarize the surveillance video so that only important events are included in the summary. An online education courseware seller may want to create brief summaries of educational videos that focus on the most exciting snippets of the course in question. A sports organization such as the National Basketball Association in the USA or the Fédération Internationale de Football Association (FIFA) may wish to create summaries consisting of a few game highlights so that these summaries can be shown to potential customers who would subsequently buy the whole video. Military organizations may wish to summarize airborne surveillance video so that high priority events such as missile firings or suspicious vehicle activity can be detected. Large movie databases such as the Internet Movie Database (IMDb) or movie sellers may wish to automatically create movie trailers.

In general, a summary of a video must satisfy the following three principles first enunciated by Fayzullin et al [1]. The video summary must contain high *priority* entities and events from the video. For example, a summary of a soccer game must show goals, spectacular goal attempts, as well as any other notable events such as the ejection of a player from the game, any fistfights or scuffles and so on. In addition, the summary itself should exhibit reasonable degrees of *continuity* – the summary must not look like a bunch of video segments blindly concatenated together. A third criterion is that the summary should be free of *repetition* – this can be difficult to achieve. For example, it is common in soccer videos for the same goal to be replayed several times. It is not that easy to automatically detect that the same event is being shown over and over again. These three tenets, named the CPR (Continuity, Priority and no Repetition) form the basic core of all strong video summarization methods.

The video summarization literature contains two broad classes of methods to summarize video. In the first class, that we call the *physical video property based class*, physical properties of the video stream are used to create a summary. The second class, that we call the *semantic video property class*, tries to use semantic information about the content of the video in order to determine which frames of video must be included.

Physical Video Property Based Methods

Most existing video summarization systems start with key frame extraction. In this technique, certain properties of frames are used to identify them some frames as *key* frames. For instance, one can consider frames with a large amount of motion or abrupt color changes as key frames (while avoiding frames with camera motion and special effects). The detected key frames can either be inserted into a summary as they are or used to segment the video. For example, video segmentation algorithms [2] may be used to "split" the video into homogeneous segments at key frames. One can then construct a summary by selecting a certain number of frames from each of these segments and concatenating them together.

The MoCA [3] system composes film previews by picking special events, such as zooming of actors, explosions, shots, etc. In other words, image processing algorithms are used to detect when selected objects or events occur within a video and then some of the frames in which these events occur end up in the summary. The authors propose an approach to the segmentation of video objects based on motion cues. Motion analysis is performed by estimating local spatio-temporal orientation using three-dimensional structure tensors. These estimates are integrated into an active contour model, which involves stopping an evolving curve when it reaches the spatial boundary associated with a moving object. Segmented video objects are then classified by using of the contours of its occurrences in successive video frames. The classification is performed by matching curvature features of the video object contour to a database containing preprocessed views of prototypical objects. Object recognition can be performed at different levels of abstraction.

Yahiaoui, Merialdo et al [4] propose an automatic video summarization method in which they define and identify what is the most important content in a video by means of similarities and differences between video segments. For example, consider a TV series. Different videos associated with the series will have a common part (e.g. the opening sequence) as well as various differences. The algorithms in [4] identify the common themes as well as the differences. Common parts are identified by extracting characteristic vectors from the sequence of frames - in particular, the set of analyzed features is a combination of color histograms applied to different portions of a frame. These vectors are used by a clustering procedure that produces classes of video frames with similar visual content. The frequency of occurrence of a given frame from each video within classes allows us to compute the importance of the various classes. Once video frames have been clustered, the video could be described as sets of classes of frames. A global summary is constructed with representative images of video content selected from the set of most important classes. They also suggest a new criterion to evaluate the quality of the summaries that have been created through the maximization of an objective function.

Shao et al [5] propose an approach to automatically summarize music videos based on an analysis of both video and music tracks. The audio track is separated from the visual track and is analyzed in order to evaluate linear prediction coefficients, zero crossing rates, and Mel-Frequency Cepstral Coefficients (MFCCs). Based on the features thus calculated, and using an adaptive clustering method, they groups the music frames and generate a structure describing the musical content of the video. The result of this computation is crucial for the generation of summaries that are calculated in terms of the detected structure and in terms of a domain-based music knowledge. After the summarization of the musical content, they turn the raw video sequences into a structured data set in which boundaries of all camera shots are identified and visually similar shots are grouped together. Each cluster is then represented by the shot with the longest length. A video summary is generated by collecting all the representative shots of the clusters. The final step is the alignment operation that aims to partially align the image segments in the video summary with the associated music segments. The authors evaluated the quality of the summaries through a subjective user study and compared the results with those obtained by analyzing either audio track only. The subject enrolled in the experiments rated *conciseness* and *coherence* of the summaries on a 1 to 5 scale. Conciseness pertains to the terseness of the music video summary and how much of the music video captures the essence of the music video. Coherence instead pertains to the consistency and natural drift of the segments in the music video summary. This method is primarily applicable to music videos rather than to other types of videos.

DeMenthon et al [6] represented a changing vector of frame features (such as overall macroblock luminance) with a multi-dimensional curve and applied a curve simplification algorithm to select key frames. In particular they extend the classic binary curve splitting algorithm that recursively splits a curve into curve segments until these segments can be replaced by line segments. This replacement can occur if the distance from the curve of the segment is small. They show how to adapt the classic algorithm for splitting a curve of dimension N into curve segments of any dimension between 1 and N. The frames at the edges of the segments are used as key frames at different levels of detail. While this approach works well for key frame detection, it does not consider the fact that certain events have higher priorities than others, and that continuity and repetition are important.

Ju et al [7] propose another key frame approach that chooses frames based on motion and gesture estimation. They focus on videos involving slide presentations – for example, a video showing a lecture in a computer science department would fall into this category. Assuming that a camera is focused on the speaker's slides, they estimate the global image motion between every two consecutive frames using a robust regression method. The extracted motion information is used to evaluate if a sequence of consecutive frames represents the same slide. The detected frame sequences are processed to extract key frames used to represent the slides shown during the presentation. They identify gestures in the video by computing a pixel difference between the key frames and the corresponding frames in the "stabilized" image sequence. They recognize some of these gestures (e.g. pointing towards the slides) by using a deformable contour model and analyzing the shape and the motion over the time. With a little additional inference, they can also (sometimes) zero in on the part of the slide that the speaker is referring to.

Zhou et al [8] attempt to extract and cluster features with a video so as to classify video content semantically. They use an interactive decision-tree learning method to define a set of if-then rules that can be easily applied to a set of low-level feature matching functions. In particular, the set of low level features that they can automatically extract includes motion, color and edge related features. Sample video clips from different semantic categories are used to train the classification system by means of the selected low level features. The set of rules in the decision tree is defined as a combination of appropriate features and relative thresholds that are automatically defined in the training process. They then apply their rule-based classification system to basketball videos and report on the results.

Ma et al [9] present a generic framework for video summarization based on estimated user attention. They attempt to identify how a user's attention is captured by motion, objects, audio and language. For each frame in a video, an attention value is computed, and the result for a given video is an attention curve that allows us to determine which frame or which sequence of frames is more likely to attract the user's attention. In this way, an optimal number of key frames in a video shot is determined by the number of wave crest on the attention curve. Their summary consists of the peaks of the attention curve thus created.

Semantic Video Property Class

This class of video summarization algorithms tries to perform elementary analysis of the video's semantic content and then to use this data, in conjunction with information about user content preferences, to determine exactly which frames go into the summary and which frames do not.

The Video Skimming System [17] from Carnegie Mellon finds key frames in documentaries and news-bulletins by detecting important words in the accompanying audio. The authors propose a method to extract significant audio and video information and create a "skim" video which represents a very short synopsis of the original. The goal of this work is to show the utility of integrating language and image understanding techniques for video skimming by extraction of significant information, such as specific objects, audio keywords and relevant video structure. The resulting skim video is much shorter, where compaction is as high as 20:1, and yet retains the essential content of the original segment.

In contrast to the above works, the CPR system of Fayzullin et al [1] provides a robust framework within which an application developer can specify functions that measure the continuity $c(S)$, and the degree of repetition $r(S)$ in a video summary S. The developer can also specify functions to assess the priority of each video frame $p(f)$ (or more generally, if the video is broken up into a sequence of blocks, the priority $p(b)$ of each block b). The priority of the summary $p(S)$ can then be set to the sum of the priorities of all blocks in S. The developer can assign weights to each of the three functions and create an objective function $w_1{*}c(S)+w_2{*}p(S)-w_3{*}r(S)$. Given the maximal desired size of a summary k, the system tries to find a set S of video blocks such that the size of S is less than or equal to k blocks and such that the objective function $w_1{*}c(S)+w_2{*}p(S)-w_3{*}r(S)$ is maximized.

Authors show that the problem of finding such an "optimal" summary is NP-complete and proceed to provide four algorithms. The first is an *exact* algorithm that takes exponential time but finds an S that does in fact maximize the objective function's value. Other three algorithms may not return the best S but run in polynomial time and find summaries that are often as good as the ones found by the exact algorithm.

Some examples of the continuity functions, repetition functions, and priority functions provided by Fayzullin et al [1] include:

- Continuity can be measured by summing up the numbers of common objects shared by adjacent summary blocks, divided by the total numbers of objects in adjacent blocks. Thus, the more objects are shared between adjacent summary blocks, the more continuous the summary is. To measure continuity (or, rather, discontinuity) one can also sum up color histogram differences between adjacent blocks. The lower this sum, the more continuous is the summary.

- Repetition can be computed as the ratio of the total number of objects occurring in the summary to the number of *distinct* objects. Alternatively, one can consider repetition to be inversely proportional to standard deviation of the color histogram in summary blocks. The less color changes occur in a summary, the more repetitive this summary is going to be.

- Priority of a block can be computed as the sum of user-defined priorities for objects occurring in the block or based on a set of rules that describe desired combinations of objects and events.

In a subsequent paper, Albanese et al [10] retain the core idea from [1] that the CPR criteria are important. However, they use a completely different approach to the problem of finding good summaries fast. Their *priority curve algorithm* (*PriCA* for short) completely eliminates the objective function upon which the previous algorithms were based, but captures the same intuitions in a compelling way. They leverage the following intuitions.

- Block creation. They first split the video into blocks - blocks could either be of equal sizes, or they could be obtained as a result of segmenting the video using any standard video segmentation algorithm [12,13,14,15]. The resulting segments are usually relatively small.

- Priority assignment. Each block is then assigned a *priority* based on the objects and events occurring in that block. Yet another alternative would use the audio stream and/or accompanying text associated with the video to identify the priority of each block. The priority assignment can be done automatically using object and event detection algorithms or manually, by employing a human annotator – in fact, their video summarization application uses both image processing algorithms and some manual annotation.

- Peak detection. They then plot a graph whose x axis consists of block numbers and whose y axis describes the block priorities. The peaks associated with this graph represent segments whose priorities are high. Figure 1 shows such a graph. They then identify the blocks associated with the *peaks* in this graph using a peak identification algorithm that the authors developed. Examples of such peaks are shown in Figure 1.

- Block merging. Suppose now that several different blocks are identified as peaks. If two peaks are adjacent to one another, then it is likely that the two adjacent blocks in question jointly refer to a continuous event in the video. They merge adjacent blocks on the intuition that the same or related events occur in these blocks even though the video segmentation algorithm has put them into different segments. This is because standard video segmentation algorithms use image information alone to segment and do not take semantics into account. However, it may be possible to use audio and/or accompaning text streams to identify similar video blocks without relying on visual similarity alone.

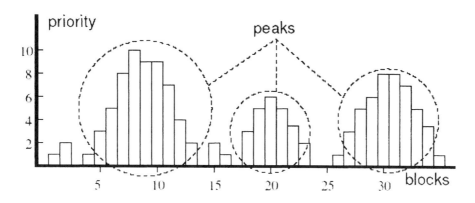

Figure 1. The peaks associated with the graph represent segments
whose priorities are high.

- **Block elimination.** The authors then run a *block elimination algorithm* which eliminates certain unworthy blocks whose priority is too low for inclusion in the summary. This is done by analyzing the distribution of block priorities, as well as the relative sizes of the blocks involved, rather than by setting an artificial threshold.

- **Block resizing.** Finally, the authors run a *block resizing algorithm* that shrinks the remaining blocks so that the final summary consists of these resized blocks adjusted to fit the desired total length.

Both the CPR and the PriCA systems provide a semi-automatic mechanism for describing and indexing video content. A preprocessing stage automatically detects shot boundaries in video streams and extracts some information about the content of each block. The user can then provide further information about those events and objects that cannot be detected and/or recognized by existing image processing and/or content analysis algorithms. In the specific implementation the authors of [1] and [10] have adapted a video segmentation algorithm from [16], based on the biological mechanisms of *visual attention*. More precisely, the shot-change detection method is related to the computation, at each time instant, of a consistency measure of the fixation sequences generated by an ideal observer looking at the video. The algorithm aims at detecting both abrupt and gradual transitions between shots using a single technique, rather than a set of dedicated methods.

Specialized image processing algorithms can then be applied in order to identify particular classes of events that occur in the blocks. In particular both the CPR and the PriCA systems have been tested on a collection of soccer matches videos and an algorithm from [11] has been used to detect a predefined set of events, namely goals, yellow cards and red cards. The algorithm takes into account both visual and audio features in order to identify the selected events. A neural network is used to analyze visual content while audio features are simply taken into account through RMS (root mean square) analysis.

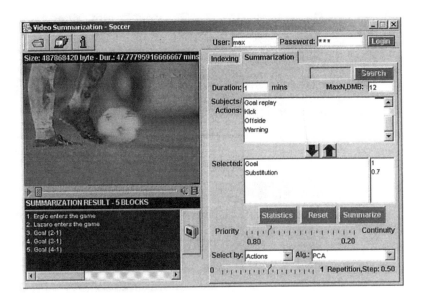

Figure 2. PCA system screen dump.

Figure 2 shows a screen dump of the PCA system, which allows to characterize video content through the above described semi-automatic process and to summarize a video using any of the four summarization algorithms in [1] and [10].

References

1. M. Fayzullin, V.S. Subrahmanian, A.Picariello, and M.L. Sapino, "The CPR Model for Summarizing Video," ACM Workshop on Multimedia Databases, 2003, pp. 2-9.
2. C.-C. Lo and S.-J. Wang, "Video segmentation using a histogram-based fuzzy c-means clustering algorithm," Proceedings of the 10th IEEE International Conference on Fuzzy Systems, December 2001, pp. 920-923.
3. R. Lienhart, S. Pfeiffer, and W. Effelsberg, "The MoCA Workbench: Support for Creativity in Movie Content Analysis," Proceedings of the IEEE Conference on Multimedia Computing and Systems, 1995, pp. 314-321.
4. I. Yahiaoui, B. Merialdo, and B. Huet, "Generating Summaries of Multi-Episode Video", IEEE International Conference on Multimedia and Expo, 2001, pp. 22-25.
5. X. Shao, C. Xu, and M.S. Kankanhalli, "Automatically Generating Summaries for Musical Video," Proceedings of the International Conference on Image Processing, 2003, Vol. 2, pp.547-500.
6. D. De Menthon, D.S. Doermann, and V. Zobla, "Video Summarization by Curve Simplification," Proceedings of ACM Multimedia, 1998, pp. 211-218.
7. S. Ju, M.Black, S. Minneman, and D. Kimber, "Summarization of Videotaped Presentations: Automatic Analysis of Motion and Gesture," IEEE Transactions on Circuits and Systems for Video Technology, Vol. 8, No. 5, 1998, pp. 686-696.

8. W. Zhou, A. Vellaikal and C.C. Jay Kuo. "Rule-Based Video Classification System for Basketball Video Indexing", Proceedings of ACM Multimedia Workshop, 2000, pp.213-216.
9. Y.P. Ma, L. Lu, H.J. Zhang, and M. Li, "A User Attention Model for Video Summarization," Proceedings of ACM Multimedia, 2002, pp.533-542.
10. M. Albanese, M. Fayzullin, A. Picariello, and V.S. Subrahmanian, "The Priority Curve Algorithm for Video Summarization," Proceedings of the ACM International Workshop on Multimedia Databases, 2004, pp. 28-35.
11. A. Chianese, R. Miscioscia, V. Moscato, S. Parlato, and A. Picariello, "A Fuzzy Approach to Video Scene Detection and its Application for Soccer Matches," Proceedings of the 4th International Conference on Intelligent Systems Design and Application, Budapest, Hungary, August 2004.
12. U. Gargi, R. Pasturi, and S.H. Strayer, "Performance Characterization of Video-Shot Change Detection Methods," IEEE Transactions on Circuits and Systems for Video Technology, Vol. 10, No. 1, 2000, pp. 1-13.
13. A. Hanjalic, "Shot-Boundary Detection: Unraveled and Resolved?" IEEE Transactions on Circuits and Systems for Video Technology, Vol. 12, 2002, pp. 90-105.
14. D. Li and H. Lu, "Model Based Video Segmentation," IEEE Transactions on Circuits and Systems for Video Technology, Vol. 5, 1995, pp. 533-544.
15. B.T. Truong, C Dorai, and S. Venkatesk, "New Enhancements to Cut, Fade and Dissolve Detection Processes in Video Segmentation," Proceedings of the 8th International Conference on Multimedia, Los Angeles, USA, November 2000, pp. 219-227.
16. G. Boccignone, A. Chianese, V. Moscato, and A. Picariello, "Foveated Shot Detection for Video Segmentation," IEEE Transactions on Circuits and Systems for Video Technology, Vol. 15, No. 3, 2005, pp. 365-377.
17. H.D. Wactlar, T. Kanade, M.A. Smith, and S.M. Stevens, "Intelligent Access to Digital Video: Informedia Project," IEEE Computer, Vol. 29, No. 5, May 1996, pp. 46-52.

VIDEO TRANSCODING

Definition: Video transcoding is the process of converting a compressed video in a given format into another compressed video bitstream.

Transcoding is necessary when a given compressed bitstream is not suitable for a video player. For example, the high bitrate video used for a digital TV broadcast cannot be used for streaming video to a mobile device. For delivery to mobile devices, we need video content that is encoded at lower bitrate and lower resolution suitable for low-resource mobile terminals. Pre-encoding video at a few discrete bitrates leads to inefficiencies as the device capabilities vary and pre-encoding video bitstreams for all possible receiver capabilities is impossible. Furthermore, the receiver capabilities such as available CPU, available battery, and available bandwidth vary during a session and a pre-encoded video stream cannot meet such dynamic needs. To make full use of the receiver capabilities and deliver video suitable for a receiver, video transcoding is necessary. A transcoder for such applications takes a high bitrate video as input and transcodes it to a lower bitrate, lower resolution, and lower complexity video suitable for a mobile terminal. The main challenges of video transcoding are: 1) complexity reduction at the transcoder, 2) complexity management at the receiver and 3) quality Vs complexity tradeoff.

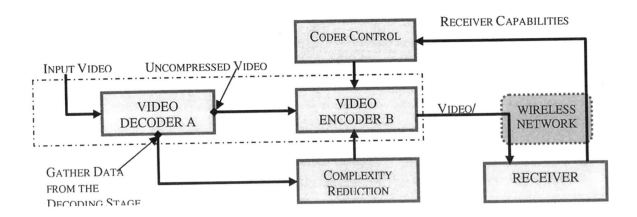

Figure 1. Video transcoder.

Video transcoding has received significant attention from the industry and academia. An overview of the issues in video transcoding was presented in [1]. Adaptation of the compressed video through bitrate reduction, sometime referred to as trans-rating, has been proposed using techniques such as dynamic rate shaping [2]. Reduced resolution transcoding is another approach to meeting receiver requirements that not only reduces the output bitrate but also the resources required at the receiver [3].

Reduced Complexity Transcoding

Figure 1 shows the general architecture of a video transcoder. A video transcoder is used to convert a compressed video bitstream in format A to a format B, where the video bitstream in format B is usually intended for a device with limited resources and capabilities. A full-complexity transcoder encompasses the full complexity of decoding the format "A bitstream" and the full complexity of encoding into a format "B bitstream." The dotted box in the figure shows a full complexity transcoder: a video decoder A followed by a video encoder B. If video formats A and B are similar or based on the same principles, the complexity of the transcoding operation can be reduced. Reduced complexity transcoders try to gather useful information during the decoding stage and reuse it in the encoding stage. Developing algorithms for reduced complexity is a challenging problem and the complexity of the transcoding algorithms depends on the video formats involved. The MPEG-2 to MPEG-4 transcoding algorithms can reuse significant amount of information because of the similarity between MPEG-2 and MPEG-4 [5]. Since the MPEG-2 and H.264 video coding algorithms are substantially different, innovative approaches have to be developed to reduce transcoding complexity [6]. Complexity reduction allows transcoding servers to server larger number of users simultaneously.

Receiver Aware Transcoding

Considering the video transcoding at a sender, a transcoder converts a given video to a format that is more suitable for playback on the receiver. A transcoder can modify the coding algorithm, resolution, frame rate, or bitrate. For a given receiver, there are a number of possible transcoding options that result in a video suitable for the receiver. Figure 2 depicts a case with five different options for the algorithm, resolution, frame rate, and bitrate. The options for the coding algorithm can be entirely different coding algorithms (MPEG-2 Vs H.264) or the same algorithm with different tools (e.g., MPEG-4 with and without error resilience). Not all of the possible combinations of options are meaningful for a given receiver. Transcoders have to determine which of the meaningful combinations meet the available receiver resources while maximizing the quality of experience for the end user. The knowledge of receiver capabilities allows a transcoder to select transcoding options that maximize the quality of the video received.

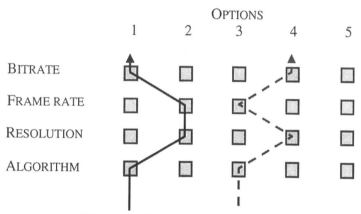

Figure 2. Video transcoding options.

Quality Vs Complexity

The quality of the transcoded video is directly related to the transcoding complexity and the decoding complexity. Producing high quality transcoded video requires significant computing resources. Similarly decoding bitstreams encoded using sophisticated algorithms requires more receiver resources. The upper bound on the required computing resources is the amount of resources required for full decoding and re-encoding and this also represents the upper bound on the achievable quality. For a given computing budget (receiver resources and capabilities), a transcoder can output bitstreams with a number of different qualities, where a bitstream quality is a function of its bitrate, frame rate, resolution, and SNR. The key challenge is making the optimal tradeoff given the playback environment and receiver capabilities. The traditional metric of peak signal to noise ratio (PSNR) is not sufficient to represent the quality of transcoded video as the quality is complex function of the playback environment, usage context, and user perception. The quality of user experience (QoE) has to be considered as a whole. The QoE of a transcoded bitstream is a function of the output bitrate, frame rate, resolution, PSNR, and the usage environment and all these factors have to be considered in quantifying the QoE.

928   V

References

1. J. Xin, C.-W. Lin, and M.-T. Sun, "Digital video transcoding," Proceedings of the IEEE, Vol. 93, Issue 1, January 2005, pp. 84- 97.
2. S. Jacobs and A. Eleftheriadis, "Streaming Video using Dynamic Rate Shaping and TCP Congestion Control," Journal of Visual Communication and Image Representation, January 1998, Vol. 9, No. 3, pp. 211-222.
3. T. Shanableh and M. Ghanbari, "Heterogeneous video transcoding to lower spatio-temporal resolutions and different encoding formats," IEEE Transactions on Multimedia, Vol. 2, No.2, June 2000.
4. A. Vetro, C. Christopoulos, and H. Sun, "Video transcoding architectures and techniques: An overview," IEEE Signal Processing Magazine, March 2003.
5. H. Kalva, A. Vetro, and H. Sun, "Performance Optimization of the MPEG-2 to MPEG-4 Video Transcoder," SPIE Conference on Microtechnologies for the New Millennium, VLSI Circuits and Systems, May 2003 (invited paper).
6. H. Kalva, B. Petljanski, and B. Furht, "Complexity Reduction Tools for MPEG-2 to H.264 Video Transcoding," WSEAS Transactions on Information Science and Applications, Vol. 2, Issue 3, March 2005, pp. 295-300.

VIDEO USAGE MINING

Sylvain Mongy, Fatma Bouali, and Chabane Djeraba
University of Lille, Lille, France

Definition: *Video usage mining refers to analysis of user behaviors in large video databases.*

Analysis of user behaviors in large video databases is an emergent problem. The growing importance of video in every day life (ex. Movie production) increases automatically the importance of video usage. To be able to cope with the abundance of available videos, users of these videos need intelligent software systems that fully utilize the rich source information hidden in user behaviors on large video data bases for retrieving and navigating through videos. In this paper, we present a framework for video usage mining to generate user profiles on a video search engine in the context of movie production. We propose a two level model based approach for modeling user behaviors on a video search engine. The first level aims at modeling and clustering user behavior on a single video sequence (intra video behavior), the second one aims at modeling and clustering user behavior on a set of video sequences (inter video behavior). Based on this representation we have developed a two phase clustering algorithm that fits these data. First results obtained from test dataset show that taking into account intra-video behavior to cluster inter-video behavior produces more meaningful results.

Introduction

With the fast development in video capture, storage and distribution technologies, digital videos are more accessible than ever. The amount of these archives is increasing at a rapid rate. To deal with it, video usage mining, which aims at analyzing user behaviors on a set of video data, is one of the key technologies to create suitable tools to help people browsing and searching the large amount of video data. Indeed, like in web mining field the extracted information will enable to improve video accesses.

In this paper, we present a framework [fig. 1] that combines intra-video usage mining and inter-video usage mining to generate user profiles on a video search engine in the context of movie production. Specifically, we have borrowed the idea of navigation history from web browsers used in web usage mining, and propose a novel approach that defines two types of log from the log data gathered on a video search engine. The first one concerns the way a user views a video sequence (play, pause, forward....) and can be called intra-video usage mining. At this level we define the "video sequence viewing" as a behavior unit. The second type of log tracks the transitions between each video sequence viewing. This part regroups requests, results and successive viewed sequences. At this higher level, like in web mining we introduce a "session" like a behavior unit.

This paper is organized as follows. In section 2, we present the related work in video usage mining. Section 3 presents our two level model based approach for modeling users' behaviors on a video search engine. Finally, section 4 describes the evaluation of the technique on some test datasets, and section 5 gives the conclusion and some future directions.

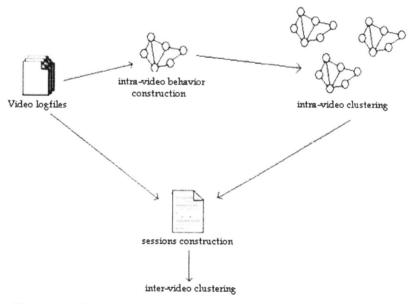

Figure 1. Overview of the video usage mining framework.

Related work

In the absence of any prior survey of video usage mining, closest related work can be classified into roughly two types: The first one concerns the analysis of user behaviors without considering the video content. These works report on statistics of user behavior and frequency counts of video access.

For example [2] analyzes the student usage of an educational multimedia system. This analysis is based on the student personality types. Indeed, the learning needs and expectations depend on the characteristics of the student type personality. To achieve this, the authors developed a program that extracts the student actions on the multimedia system and profiles what each user did each time he uses the system. These user profiles include the following statistics : number of video viewing sessions, total seconds spent viewing videos ; number of video viewing sessions that lasted more than 20 minutes, average duration of a video viewing session, average number commands per minute during video viewing sessions, forward transitions, backward transitions, forward jumps and jump ratio. While being based on the statistics collected on each type of students, they analyze how the learning multimedia system can be improved to remedy its shortcomings.

An analysis of trace data obtained from user access on videos on the web is presented in [1]. They examine properties such as how user requests vary on a day to day, and whether video accesses exhibit any temporal properties. They propose to benefit from these properties to design the multimedia systems such as web video proxy caches, and video servers. For example the analysis revealed that users preview the initial portion of a video to find out if they are interested. If they like it, they continue watching, otherwise they stop it. This pattern suggests that caching the first several minutes of video data should improve access performance.

The other type of work relates to the behavior analysis on a single video.

A framework that combines video content analysis and user log mining to generate a video summary is presented in [5]. They develop a video browsing and summarization system that is based on previous viewers browsing log to facilitate future viewers. They adopt the link analysis technique used in web mining, and propose a concept of ShotRank that measures the importance of each video shot, the user behavior is simulated with an Interest-guided Walk model, and the probability of a shot being visited is taken as an indication of the importance of that shot. The resulting ShotRank is used to organize the presentation of video shots and generate video skims.

The lack in the previous work is to correlate global behavior of the users with their behavior on each of the videos. They do not take into account actions done during a video viewing while considering navigation between video sequences. In short, these works are rather distant from our context. The navigation and research concepts in a large video data base are missing. Moreover, there are neither standards nor benchmarks on video log data.

Proposed approach

Context

One of the needs of the professional users of Companies of audio-visual sector is to be able to find existing video sequences in order to re-use them in the creation of new films. Our approach is based on the use of a well suited video search engine. Our tool [fig. 2] is a classical browser for finding video in huge databases. Researches are executed on content-based indexing. Much hidden information can be extracted from the usage and used to improve the meaningful of the videos returned by the search engine.

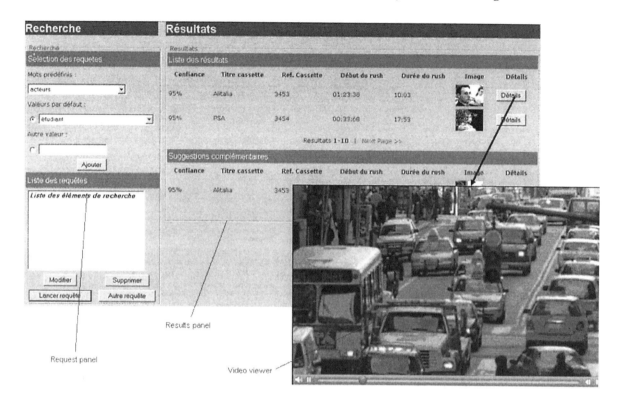

Figure 2. Our search engine tool.

To achieve this task, we first need to define what a usage of a video search engine is. Such a behavior can be divided into three parts. – 1° Request creation: the user defines its search attributes and values. – 2° Result set exploitation: founded sequences are presented to the user. They are ordered by an attribute-based confidence value. – 3° Selected sequences viewing: the user is viewing sequences he is interested in. This viewing is achieved with a video browser offering usual functions (play, pause, forward, rewind, stop, jump).

Groups of viewed sequences form sessions. They correspond to a visit of a user. They are composed of several searches and video sequences viewing.

Gathering data

All of these data are collected and written into log files. In order to create these files, we define a XML-based language. A session is gathered as followed. The first part contains the request executed and the list of video sequences returned. The second one logs the viewing of sequences.

Like web logfile, our video logfile traces the actions of users. To extract sessions, we have developed an XSLT (eXtensible Stylesheet Language Transformation) converter [8]. This converter extracts and regroups sessions from this logfile in XML format. The following part of the paper explains how we propose to model a video session.

Modeling user's behavior: a two-level-based model

From log data gathered previously, we generate two models to represent user's behavior. The first one refers to the way a user views a video sequence (play, pause, forward....). At this level we define the "video sequence viewing" as a behavior unit. The second one tracks the transitions between each video sequence viewing. This part regroups requests, results and successive viewed sequences. At this higher level, we introduce a "session" like a behavior unit. Presently our work is only based on sequences. We do not take into account the information given by the requests. This will be further upgraded.

A session is a list of viewed video sequences. The particularity and the interest of the video log data will be the ability to define importance of each sequence in each session. More than a simple weight, comparable to time comparison in web mining [4], we will here characterize several behavior types (complete viewing, overview, open-close, precise scene viewing). Based on these behaviors, viewing will be precisely defined and then we will be able to know which the use of a video was in a session.

Modeling and clustering intra video user's behavior

An intra video user's behavior is modeled by a first order non-hidden Markovian model [fig. 3]. This model represents the probability to execute an action each second of the viewing of a video. Each vertex represents one of the actions proposed to the user while a viewing. For the first version of our tool, these actions are play, pause, forward, rewind, jump, and stop. For example, the edge from play to pause means that when a user is playing a video, there is a probability of 8% that he executes a pause the next second. Its limited complexity will allow us to propose an effective clustering method of these behaviors.

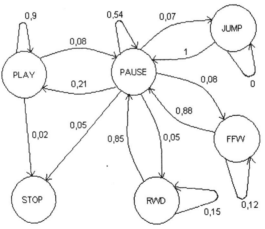

Figure 3. Video sequence viewing behavior.

We will here introduce the K-Models clustering algorithm. This technique is almost an adaptation of the well known K-Means to the use of models instead of means. We try to find K clusters in a set of viewing actions (list of the actions performed by user while viewing a video sequence) by partitioning space. Each cluster is represented by one of the models described below. The difference stays in use of probability instead of distance to associate viewings to clusters. We calculate the probability that a viewing has been generated by models. We then associate the viewing to the cluster with the highest probability.

Based on these discovered models, we create a vector of behavior for each viewing. This vector corresponds to the probabilities that the viewing has been generated by each model.

Modeling and clustering inter video user's behavior

From the initial dataset and the vector created with the intra video clustering, we construct a sequential representation of the sessions. A session is a time-ordered sequence of the viewed video. Each viewing is characterized by a couple of the unique identifier of the video and the vector of behavior connected to it. Based on this representation of sessions, we have developed a clustering algorithm that fills the following requirements: - any element belonging to a cluster has a common part with any other of the cluster. - The generality level of produced clusters relies on the definition of some parameters given by the user. These ones are presented next.

These requirements lead us to define the representation of a cluster this way: a cluster c is represented by a set of S sessions s_c of minimal length *l*. A session s is attributed to a cluster if it matches at least *p* of the *S* sessions. The session s matches s_c if s_c is a subsequence extracted from s. s_c is a subsequence of s means:

$$IsSubsequence((s_1...s_n),(s'_1,s'_m)) = \exists i \leq n/s'_1 = s_i \quad and \quad IsSubsequence((s_i...s_n),(s'_2,s'_m))$$

This way, we ensure the homogeneity of clusters and the fact that there is a common factor between any elements of a cluster. Hence, we avoid obtaining clusters composed of fully different elements, connected by a chain of next neighbors generally produced by distance-based clustering techniques [9], [10]. Parameters S, l p introduced previously are given by the analyst to allow him retrieving cluster of the required homogeneity.

The clustering algorithm itself is a classical hierarchical clustering algorithm. It starts with considering little groups of sessions as clusters and iteratively merges the two nearest clusters. The algorithm ends when the required level of homogeneity has been reached.

Results

We can point the two following points from the first experimentations. 1° regrouped sessions are homogeneous. Particularly, we are able to avoid wrong fusion. Indeed classical distance-based clustering is able to associate two completely different sessions to the same cluster. More than groups of sessions, we produce profiles that are well representing sessions which have generated them, as illustrated in Figure 4.

$$\{(12,45,28,72),(19,11,03),(81,17,60)\}$$
$$\{(12,45,72),(79,07,71),(12,17,44)\}$$

Figure 4. Example of discovered behaviors on synthetic dataset.

Figure 4 presents two generated profiles of visit. Each one is composed of sequences of video identifiers. They represent the different video that a user has viewed during a visit. We can point that the first sequences of the two profiles are quite similar. The data are not regrouped because they have a different intra-video behavior. The introduction of the intra-video behavior and its analysis in the complete process of session clustering give more precise results. We are able to differentiate groups of sessions that have explored same videos in a different manner.

Figure 5 shows that the cost of taking into account intra-video behavior by using Markovian models does not penalize too much execution time. Even if execution is longer when using them, the evolution is quite similar.

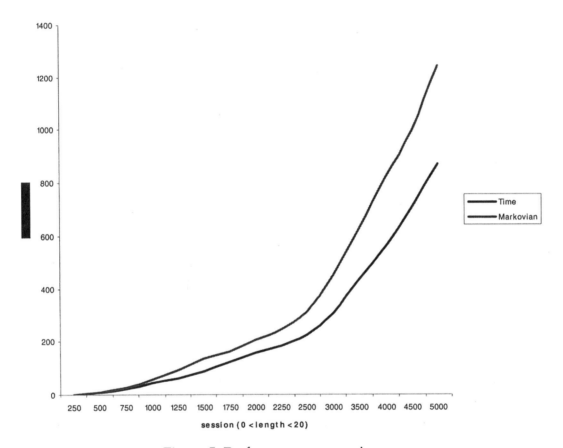

Figure 5. Performance comparison.

Future work and research

In this paper, we propose a two level model based approach for modeling user behaviors on a video search engine. The first level aims at modeling and clustering user behavior on a single video sequence (intra video behavior), the second one aims at modeling and clustering user behavior on a set of video sequences (inter video behavior). Based on this representation we have developed a two phase clustering algorithm that fits these data. First results obtained from test dataset show that taking into account intra-video behavior to cluster inter-video behavior produces more meaningful results.

The main remaining work is to validate our technique on real datasets in a context of movie production. We have to ensure that results are still interesting on huge video database explored by many users.

Another objective is to model clusters using frequent item sets instead of subsequence and compare results to measure the impact of the sequential representation.

References

1. S. Acharya, B. Smith, and P. Parnes, "Characterizing user access to videos on the World Wide Web," Proceedings of Multimedia computing and networking, 2000, CA, USA.
2. I. Cadez, D. Heckerman, C. Meek, and P. Smyth, "Visualization of Navigation Patterns on a web site using Model Based Clustering," Proceedings of the 6th ACM SIGKDD Int. Conference on Knowledge Discovery and Data Mining, pp. 280-284, Boston, Massachusetts.
20. A. I Reuther and G. Meyer, "The effect of personality type on the usage of a multimedia engineering education system," Frontiers in Education, FIE'02, 32nd Annual, Vol. 1, November 2002, pp. T3A7-T3A12.
21. W. Wang and O. R. Zaiane, "Clustering Web Sessions by Sequence Alignment," Proceedings of the 13th International Workshop on Database and Expert Systems Applications (DEXA'02), Aix-en-Provence, France.
22. B. Yu, W.-Y. Ma, K. Nahrstedt, and H-J. Zhang, "Video summarization based on user log enhanced link analysis," Proceedings of Multimedia Modeling '03, November 2003, Berkeley CA, USA.
23. B. Mobasher, H. Dai, T. Luo, M. Nakagawa, Y. Sun, and J. Wiltshire, "Discovery of Aggregate Usage Profiles for Web Personalization," Webkdd, Boston MA, USA, 2000.
24. P. Branch, G. Egan, and B. Tonkin, "Modeling interactive behavior of a video based multimedia system," Proceedings of the IEEE International Conference on Communications, 1999. Vol. 2, June 1999, pp. 978-982.
25. http://www.w3.org/Style/XSL.
26. S. Guha, R. Rastogi, and K. Shim, "CURE : An Efficient Clustering Algorithm for Large Databases," SIGMOD '98 Seattle, WA, USA.
27. S. Guha, R. Rastogi, and K. Shim, "ROCK : A Robust Clustering Algorithm for Categorical Attributes," Proceedings of the 15th Int. Conference on Data Engineering 1999, Sydney, Australia.

VIDEO WATERMARKING

Definition: Video watermarking refers to embedding watermarks in a video sequence in order to protect the video from illegal copying and identify manipulations.

A variety of robust and fragile video watermarking methods have been proposed to solve the illegal copying and proof of ownership problems as well as to identify manipulations. Although a number of broad claims have been made in the field of robustness of various digital watermarking methods, it is still difficult to handle combined or non-linear geometric transformations. The methods can be divided into techniques working on compressed or uncompressed data. In particular video watermarking is based in general on the following concepts to hide a watermark by modifying some of its characteristics:

- Spatial domain approach, also called native domain: embedding and detection are performed on spatial pixels values (luminance, chrominance, color space) or on the overall video frame characteristic,
- Feature or salient point watermarking by modifying geometric properties of the video frames,
- Frequency domain techniques where the spatial values are transformed, like DCT Discrete Cosine, FFT Fast Fourier Transform, Wavelets or fractals,
- Quantization index modulation (QIM) watermarking,
- Format specific approaches like watermarking of structure elements like Facial Animation Parameter of MPEG-4 or motion vectors.

The robust watermarking approaches usually spread the watermarking information redundant over the overall signal representation in a non-invertible manner to enforce identification or verification of ownership or to annotate the video. For example the message is spread and encoded in the 2D FFT frequencies of each video frame. In most cases prior to transforming each frame to the frequency domain, the frame data is transformed from e.g. RGB space to Weber-Fechner YCbCr space. Generically, YCbCr space consists of a luminance component Y and two color difference components Cb and Cr. The Y component contains the luminance and black & white image information, while Cb represents the difference between R and Y and Cr represents the difference between Y and B. In YCbCr space most of the frame information is in the Y component. This representation is used also during MPEG compression. The MPEG algorithm grossly removes large portions of the Cb and Cr components without damaging the frame quality. The MPEG algorithm uses compression to reduce the Y component since it has more effect on the quality of the compressed frames, which is also used in most watermarking schemes. To avoid estimation attacks the watermark signal should be adoptive designed to the overall video frame sequence characteristics by facing the problem that equal or similar watermarking pattern for each frame could allow an estimation attack based on the slide visual differences between adjacent frames, different watermarking pattern could allow an estimation attack based on the similarities between similar visual frames, see for example in [1].

Data rates are measured in bits per frame. If the watermark is embedded into the compressed domain for example MPEG video, we count the embedded data rates in bits per I, B and P frame or per GOP.

For fragile video watermarking, relevant for authenticate the data in its authenticity and integrity, a fragile watermark signal can be spread over the overall video into manipulation sensitive video elements like LSB to detect changed and manipulated regions. The watermark for authentication purposes is often designed in an invertible (reversible) manner to allow reproduction of the original, see for example an analysis of the approaches in [2]. Today we find several fragile watermarking techniques to recognize video manipulations. In the moment most fragile watermarks are very sensitive to changes and can detect most possible changes in pixel values. Only few approaches address the so-called content-fragile watermarking relevant in applications with several allowed post production editing processes. For example Mombasseri et al. in [3] addresses the recognition of video frame sequence changes with the possibility of reproduction of the original frame sequence called self-watermarking of frame-pairs.

A further idea is for example from [4] suggesting to embed a visual content feature M into the video frame with a robust watermarking method. The content-fragile watermarking approach for video authentication tries to extract the frame characteristics of human perception, called content. The approach is for example to determine the edge characteristics of the single video frame. This characteristic is transformed into a feature code for the content-fragile digital watermark. The edge characteristics of a frame give a very good reflection of each frame content, because they allow the identification of object structures and homogeneity of the video. The canny edge detector described as the most efficient edge separator is used in [4]. The author describes several strategies for generating and verification of the edge based feature codes. From the general perspective the content feature M can be embedded directly or used as a seed to generate the watermarking pattern itself.

Benchmarking of Video Watermarking

The actual available benchmarking suites mainly cover image and audio watermarking and neglect video specific aspects. In [1] we find en evaluation of video watermarking sensitivity to collusion attacks and potential solutions. [5] summarizes video specific aspects on the example of video watermarking for cinema applications like robustness to non intentional attacks such as MPEG compression, transcoding, analogue to digital and digital-to-analogue conversions, standard conversions (PAL – NTSC), change of geometry, or high probability of detection and high probability of correct extraction when the watermark is present, low false detection probability when not present, or real-time extraction for reasonable complexity both for embedding and detection.

References

1. K. Su, D. Kundur, and D. Hatzinakos, "A Novel Approach to Collusion-Resistant Video Watermarking," *Security and Watermarking of Multimedia Contents IV*, E. J. Delp and P. W. Wong, Eds., Proceedings of SPIE (Vol. 4675), San Jose, CA, January 2002.
2. St. Katzenbeisser and J. Dittmann, "Malicious Attacks on Media Authentication Schemes Based on Invertible Watermarks," Proceedings of the SPIE 2004 Conference 5306: Security, Steganography, and Watermarking of Multimedia Contents VI, 2004.
3. G. Bijan and A.E. Mobasseri, "Content-dependent video authentication by self-watermarking in color space," Proceedings of the Security and Watermarking of Multimedia Contents III, Electronic Imaging '01, San Jose January 2001, pp. 35-44.
4. J. Dittmann, "Content-fragile Watermarking for Image Authentication," In: Security and Watermarking of Multimedia Contents III, P. W. Wong and E. J. Delp III, Editors, Proceedings of SPIE Vol. 4314, pp. 175-184.
5. B. Macq, J. Dittmann, and E. Delp, "Benchmarking of Image Watermarking Algorithms for Digital Rights Management," Proceedings of the IEEE, Special Issue on: Enabling Security Technology for Digital Rights Management, pp. 971-984, Vol. 92 No. 6, June 2004.

VIRTUAL AND AUGMENTED REALITY

Xiaojun Shen and Shervin Shirmohammadi
University of Ottawa, Canada

Definition: *Virtual Reality is the technology that provides almost real and/or believable experiences in a synthetic or virtual way, while Augmented Reality enhances the real world by superimposing computer-generated information on top of it.*

Introduction

The term *Virtual Reality* (VR) was initially introduced by Jaron Lanier, founder of VPL Research in 1989. This term is a contradiction in its self, for nothing can be both real and virtual at the same time. Perhaps Real Virtuality would be a better term, because this is what new technologies have been giving. Other related terms include *Artificial Reality* (Myron Krueger, 1970s), *Cyberspace* (William Gibson, 1984), and, more recently, *Virtual Worlds* and *Virtual Environments* (1990s). Virtual Reality may be considered to have been born in the mid-1960s, based on the work of Van Sutherland from the University of Utah [1]. A paper, published in 1972 by D.L Vickers, one of Sutherland's colleagues, describes an interactive computer graphics system utilizing a head-mounted display and wand. The display, worn like a pair of eyeglasses, gives an illusion to the observer that he/she is surrounded by three-dimensional, computer-generated objects. The challenge of VR is to make those objects appear convincingly real in many aspects like appearance, behavior, and quality of interaction between the objects and the user/environment. VR is the technology that provides almost real and/or believable experiences in a virtual way. To achieve this, it uses the entire spectrum of current multimedia technologies such as image, video, sound and text, as well as newer and upcoming media such as e-touch, e-taste, and e-smell. To define the characteristics of VR, Heim [2] used the three 'I's, *immersion*, *interactivity* and *information intensity*.

- *Immersion* comes from devices that isolate the senses sufficiently to make a person feel transported to another place.

- *Interactivity* comes from the computer's lighting ability to change the scene's point of view as fast as the human organism can alter his or her physical position and perspective.

- *Information intensity* is the notion that a virtual world can offer special quality such as telepresence and artificial entities that show a certain degree of intelligent behavior.

Immersion originally depends on visual aspects implemented by 3D Computer Graphics (CG), as users need to feel that they are located in a similar-to-real world. So far users could see, hear and manipulate objects through VR. But as time goes by and technology develops, users will be able to smell, taste, touch and feel object through VR in the near future.

Interaction was meant to be a walk through in the infancy stage of VR as users could change the view not by the system but by their own operation. But in the last few years it has become very powerful not only for browsing VR but for manipulating objects and communicating with other people in real time. Interaction is the process between the user and the system or among different users and can implemented by various input and output devices.

Information intensity depends on the quantity and quality of information provided through VR for users who might have different demands. No VR can be suitable for all users. What can be offered to the different users is accuracy of objects, real-time communication, realistic simulation, interaction or a combination of all.

The applications of VR are becoming very popular in multidisciplinary fields, and the development of CG makes it more appealing by creating not only physical objects such as buildings and hair but natural phenomenon such as storms. Ever since the military and the entertainment industry developed advanced VR technology, the impact of VR has become powerful enough to attract people. Scientists use VR to visualize scientific information and architects use VR to review architectural plans for preventing fatal mistakes. Educators use VR to provide an interactive learning environment, whereas historians use VR to reconstruct historical buildings. By doing so, people can share their own ideas on the same visual information and collaborate with each other through VR.

VR systems can be categorized by intensity of immersion as *Desktop VR*, *Augmented Reality* (AR) and *Immersive VR*.

Desktop VR
Desktop VR uses a computer monitor as display to provide graphical interface for users. It is cost-effective when compared to the immersive VR as it does not require any expensive hardware and software and is also relatively easy to develop. Although they lack the immersion quality, they consist of computer-generated environments which exist in 3 dimensions (even if they are shown on a 2-D display). Figure 1a shows an example of a Desktop VR system used for industrial training [3]. In Figure 1b, the same desktop application is used but this time the user can see a stereoscopic 3D view, on a regular monitor, through the use of special software and 3D goggles. Because the worlds exist in 3 dimensions, users can freely navigate in 3 dimensions around in the worlds. Flight simulators are examples, where participants "fly" though models of real or fantasy worlds, watching the world on a 2-D screen.

Augmented Reality
Augmented Reality (AR) can be thought of as a variation of VR. In the original publication [5] which coined the term, (Computer-) Augmented Reality was introduced as the opposite of VR: instead of diving the user into a purely-synthesized informational environment, the goal of AR is to augment the real world with information handling capabilities. AR is used to describe a system, which enhances the real world by superimposing computer-generated information on top of it. VR technologies completely immerse a user inside a synthetic environment. While immersed, the user can not see the real world around him/her. In contrast, AR allows the user to see the real world, but

superimposes computer-generated information upon or composed with the real world. Therefore, AR supplements reality, rather than completely replacing it.

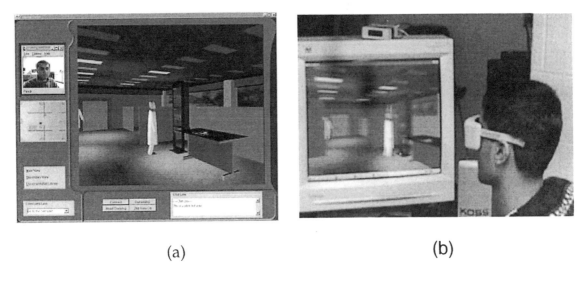

(a)   (b)

Figure 1. Desktop VR application for industrial training.

Combining 3D graphics with the real world in a 3D space is useful in that it enhances a user's perception of and interaction with the real world. In addition, the augmented information, such as annotations, speech instructions, images, videos, and 3D models, helps the user perform real world tasks. Figure 2a shows a neurosurgery planning application at the Harvard Medical School, where the internal organ of the patient is synthetically superimposed in 3D on top of the actual patient, allowing the surgeon to "see" inside the head of the patient. Figure 2b shows a wearable computer used for the implementation of AR of industry training application.

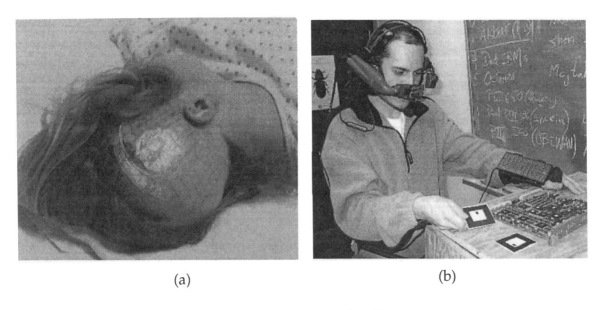

(a)   (b)

Figure 2. Augmented reality.

AR systems have been proposed as solutions in many domains, including medical, entertainment, military training, engineering design, robotics and tele-operation, and so on. For example, doctors can see virtual ultrasound images overlaid on a patient's body, giving them the equivalent of X-ray vision during a needle biopsy, while a car driver can see the infrared imagery of night vision overlaid on the road ahead. Another major domain is the assembly, maintenance, and repair of complex machinery, in which computer-generated graphics and text prompts would be developed to train and assist plant personnel during complex manipulation or equipment maintenance and repair tasks.

Although AR technology has been developed since 1993 only a few commercial products using AR appear in the market today, such as the Instructional System for the Boeing Company and the telecommunications services product for Bell Canada field-service technicians.

Immersive VR
Immersive VR, which completely immerses the user inside the computer generated world, can be achieved by using either the technologies of *Head-Mounted Display* (HMD) or multiple projections. Immersive VR with HMD uses HMD to project VR just in front of the eyes and allows users to focus on display without distraction. A magnetic sensor inside the HMD detects the users' head motion and feeds that information to the attached processor. Consequently, the user turns his or her head; the displayed graphics can reflect the changing viewpoint. The virtual world appears to respond to head movement in a familiar way and in a way which differentiates self from world. You move and the virtual world looks like it stays still. The sense of inclusion within a virtual world which this technology creates has a powerful personal impact. Figure 3a shows an HMD in action.

Immersive VR with multiple projections uses multiple projectors to create VR on a huge screen, which might be a hemispherical surface, in a room where users might ware polarized glasses to maximize the feeling of being present at the scene in standstill. The form of this immersive graphical display is known as the CAVE (stands for Computer-Aided Virtual Environment), where the immersion occurs by surrounding the body on all sides by images, rather than just the eyes. Early versions of these technologies were demonstrated at SIGGRAPH '92 in Chicago by Sun Microsystems and University of Illinois. The CAVE is essentially a five sided cube. The participant stands in the middle of cube, and images are projected onto the walls in front, above, below and on either side of the participant, utilizing full 270-degree peripheral vision. As the user travels through the virtual environment, updated images are projected onto the CAVE's walls to give the sensation of smooth motion. Figure 3b shows a CAVE at the University of Ottawa's DISCOVERLab [4].

At present, immersive VR stretches the limits of computational power, I/O design and understanding of human perception. The 3-D graphic VR worlds are usually made up of polygons. Some systems allow texture mapping of different patterns onto the polygon surfaces. The polygons may be shaded using different algorithms which create more or less realistic shadows and reflections. Displays are "laggy," with responses to motion being delayed, particularly for complicated worlds.

(a)   (b)

Figure 3. Immersive VR.

VR Graphics Rendering and Modeling

Graphics engines and displays are the cornerstone of the VR user interface. The display provides the user with a three-dimensional window into the virtual environment, and the engine generates the images for display. Traditionally, these graphics capabilities only were available on high-end graphics workstations. However, in recent years, sufficient graphics capabilities have become available on standard PCs. Add-on high-speed graphics processors are inexpensive and give PCs rendering horsepower that rivals low-to-mid-range graphics workstations. Moreover, the standard graphics API enables the development portable graphics-intensive applications.

OpenGL

OpenGL, initiated by Silicon Graphics in 1992, is an open specification for an applications program interface for defining 2D and 3D objects. With OpenGL, an application can create the same effects in any operating system using any OpenGL-adhering graphics adapter. Since its inception OpenGL has been controlled by an Architectural Review Board3 whose representatives are from the following companies: 3DLabs, Compaq, Evans & Sutherland (Accelgraphics), Hewlett-Packard, IBM, Intel, Intergraph, NVIDIA, Microsoft, and Silicon Graphics.

Most of the CG research (and implementation) broadly uses OpenGL which has become a *de facto* standard. Virtual Reality is no exception to this rule. There are many options available for hardware acceleration of OpenGL based applications. The idea is that some complex operations may be performed by specific hardware (an OpenGL accelerated video card such as those based on 3DLab's Permedia series or Mitsubishi's 3Dpro chipset for instance) instead of the CPU which is not optimized for such operations. Such acceleration allows low-end workstations to perform quite well yet at low cost.

Virtual Reality Modeling Language (VRML)

VRML 2.0, which is the latest version of the well-known VRML format, is an ISO standard (ISO/IEC 14772-1:1997). Having a huge installed base, VRML 2.0 has been designed to support easy authorability, extensibility, and capability of implementation on a wide range of systems. It defines rules and semantics for presentation of a 3D scene. Using any VRML 2.0 compliant browser, a user can simply use a mouse to navigate through a virtual world displayed on the screen. In addition, VRML provides nodes for interaction and behavior. These nodes, such as *TouchSensor* and *TimeSensor*, can be used to intercept certain user interactions or other events which then can be ROUTed to corresponding objects to perform certain operations. Moreover, more complex actions can take place using Script nodes which are used to write programs that run inside the VRML world. In addition to the Script node, VRML 2.0 specifies an External Authoring Interface (EAI) which can be used by external applications to monitor and control the VRML environment. These advanced features enable a developer to create an interactive 3D environment and bring the VRML world to life.

X3D

X3D, the successor to the VRML, is the ISO standard for representing 3D objects and scenes combining aspects of the VRML specification with the XML standard. X3D is a scalable and open software standard for defining and communicating real-time, interactive 3D content for visual effects and behavioral modeling. It can be used across hardware devices and in a broad range of applications including CAD, visual simulation, medical visualization, GIS, entertainment, educational, and multimedia presentations. X3D provides both the XML-encoding and the Scene Authoring Interface (SAI) to enable both web and non-web applications to incorporate real-time 3D data, presentations and controls into non-3D content. It improves upon VRML with new features, advanced APIs, additional data encoding formats, stricter conformance, and a componentized architecture using profiles that allows for a modular approach to supporting the standard and permits backward compatibility with legacy VRML data.

Additional features of X3D:

- Open source, so no licensing issues.
- Has been officially incorporated within the MPEG-4 multimedia standard.
- XML support makes it easy to expose 3D data to Web Services and distributed applications.
- Compatible with the next generation of graphics files - e.g. Scalable Vector Graphics [6].
- 3D objects can be manipulated in C or C++, as well as Java.

VR Haptic Interface

In an effort to bring more and more realism to the virtual world, VR developers get increasingly more creative. Devices have been invented that simulate tactile feedback and force feedback. Together these are called haptic devices. The most notable commercially available force feedback product is called Phantom, and touch feedback devices are usually some permutations of virtual gloves such as dataglove. If you are holding a virtual ball in your hand, for example, a tactile device will let you feel how smooth or rough its surface is, whereas a Phantom will let you feel how heavy it is. Gloves, by the way, are also tracking devices, because they let you feel the virtual objects you are touching (by simulating pressure and tingling sensation on your hand), at the same time feeding information about position of your fingers back to the computer. Readers are referred to the Tele-Haptics chapter in this book for further information.

Collaborative Virtual Environments

Collaborative Virtual Environments (CVE) are currently one of the most challenging VR research areas. A CVE is a shared virtual world that could radically alter the way multiple people work, learn, consume, and entertain. It adds new dimensions to the needs of human-factors, networking, synchronization, middleware, object model acquisition and representation. Take human-factors research in VR for example; it has traditionally focused on the development of natural interfaces for manipulating virtual objects and traversing virtual landscapes. Collaborative manipulation, on the other hand, requires the consideration of how participants should interact with each other in a shared space, in addition to how co-manipulated objects should behave and work together.

The main issue in a CVE, in addition to the other issues in VR, is how distributed entities share and maintain the same resources. This problem has to be solved in the framework of many hardware and software platforms, in other words, in a totally heterogeneous environment. Five important problems in implementing a CVE are listed in the sequel.

Consistency: The fundamental model presented by a CVE platform is a shared 3D space. Since all clients accessing or updating the data share the 3D graphics database, the issue of distributed consistency must be solved by any CVE to ensure the same view is presented to all participants. Since the number of participants is not fixed, and during the run time users may enter the environment after the environment has been changed from its initial state, a CVE needs to be able to provide support for latecomers and early leavers. Network lag adds an additional challenge to the consistency issue, leading to solutions where communication protocols that are both fast and timely-reliable are used [7].

Scalability: The number of possible interactions between n simultaneous users in a multi-user system is of order $O(n2)$ at any moment. Ideally network traffic should be almost constant or grow near-linearly with the number of users. Usually, not all the data in the CVE environment would be relevant to a particular user at a given time. This suggests the idea of partitioning the environment into regions (or zones, locales, auras) that may either be fixed or bound to moving avatars. Events and actions in remote zones need not be distributed and remote objects need not be visualized or might be visualized at a coarse-grain level. Most of the traffic is isolated within zones.

Ownership: A multi-user CVE world is subject to conflicts. Conflicts occur when collaborating users perform opposing actions, for example, a conflict may arise if one user tries to open a window while another user is trying to close it. These conflicts must be avoided or solved. One method to determine the attributes of objects that may be modified by certain users is to assign temporary ownership to objects. Manipulation of objects may include the change of the object's coordinate system and the change in the scene graph: users may grasp objects and take them to a different world. Operations like this are essential for applications like virtual shopping.

Persistence: Some of these applications that involve a large number of users need a large-scale, persistent collaborative virtual environment (PCVE) system that is "never-ending" or "always on". This is either because its users require that it is always running, or because it is so large or distributed that stopping the entire simulation to make changes is just not possible. There are a number of issues that should be addressed to support PDVE. Persistence would be the first feature that characterizes a PCVE system. It describes the extent to which the virtual environment exists after all participants have left the environment.

Dynamic Configuration: This property allows a PCVE system to dynamically configure itself without user interaction, enabling applications to take on new functionalities after their execution. CVEs should be modifiable at run-time by accepting the contributions of new objects and new behaviors.

Standards for Collaborative Virtual Environments

Several international standards are very likely to make a major impact on CVE technology: the Distributed Interactive Simulation (DIS) (IEEE Standard 1278.1) and the High Level Architecture (HLA) (IEEE Standard 1516). DIS is a set of communication protocols to allow the interoperability of heterogeneous and geographically dispersed simulators. Development of the DIS protocol began in 1989, jointly sponsored by the United States Army Simulation, Training and Instrumentation Command (STRICOM), ARPA and the Defense Modeling and Simulation Office (DMSO). DIS was based on SIMNET [8,9] and designed as a man in the loop simulation in which participants interact in a shared environment from geographically dispersed sites.

The successor of DIS, the High Level Architecture [10], defines a standard architecture for large-scale distributed simulations. It is a general architecture for simulation reuse and interoperability [13] developed by the US Department of Defense. The conceptualization of this High Level Architecture leads to the development of the Run-Time Infrastructure (RTI). This software implements an interface specification that represents one of the tangible products of the HLA. The HLA architecture is now an IEEE standard (No. 1516) and an OMG (Object Management Group) standard for distributed simulations and modeling.

See: Virtual Reality, Desktop Virtual Reality, Augmented Reality, Immersive Virtual Reality, Collaborative Virtual Environments, OpenGL, VRML, X3D.

References

1. I.E. Sutherland, "The Ultimate Display," Proceedings of the 1965 IFIP Congress, 2, 1965, pp. 506-508.
2. M. Heim, "Virtual Reality," Oxford University Press, New York, 1998.

946   **V**

3. J.C. Oliveira, S. Shirmohammadi, M. Cordea, E. Petriu, D. Petriu, and N.D. Georganas, "Virtual Theater for Industrial Training: A Collaborative Virtual Environment," Proceedings of the 4th World Multiconference on Circuits, Systems, Communications & Computers (CSCC 2000), Athens, Greece, July 2000, Vol. IV, pp. 294-299.

4. DISCOVER Lab, http://www.discover.uottawa.ca.

5. P. Wellner, W. Mackay, and R. Gold, Eds., "Special issue on computer augmented environments: back to the real world," Communications of the ACM, Vol. 36, Issue 7, July 1993.

6. Scalable Vector Graphics Specification , http://www.w3.org/TR/SVG/.

7. S. Shirmohammadi and N.D. Georganas, "An End-to-End Communication Architecture for Collaborative Virtual Environments," Computer Networks Journal, Vol. 35, No. 2-3, February 2001, pp. 351-367.

8. L. John et al, "Integrating SIMNET with NPSNET Using a Mix of Silicon Graphics and Sun Workstations," Naval Postgraduate School, Monterey, California, March 1992.

9. A. Pope, BBN Report No. 7102, "The SIMNET Network and Protocols," BBN Systems and Technologies, Cambridge, Massachusetts, July, 1989.

10. High Level Architecture (HLA), at http://hla.dmso.mil/hla.

11. W. R. Sherman and A. B. Craig, "Understanding Virtual Reality," Morgan Kaufmann, 2002, ISBN 1558603530.

VIRTUAL PRESENCE

Definition: Virtual presence is similar in concept to telepresence, in that it tries to give the impression to the user as if the user is present in one place or environment, even when one is physically not situated in that environment.

The difference between the two is that telepresence is a networked paradigm by nature, whereas virtual presence does not have to be networked and can run completely locally. For example, a virtual presence system can be used in a museum to recreate the Roman Coliseum, enabling the user to enter the Coliseum and to be virtually present in it. Such sites and/or locations can be created in conventional Virtual Reality or Augmented Reality. Such a system does not always require networking since there is not always a need for transmission of data between remote sites. Other than the networking requirement, virtual presence needs the other features of telepresence in order to achieve the sense of presence [1]:

  o The extent of the sensory information: it is necessary to provide the user with the same level of sensory information that they would receive if they were actually present at the site.
  o Control of sensors: it must be possible to move the sensing devices around the environment as if the user was at the site.
  o The ability to modify the site and actively interact with it.

See: Telepresence, Virtual and Augmented Reality

References

1. J. Pretlove and R. Asbery, "Get a head in virtual reality," Control of Remotely Operated Systems: Teleassistance and Telepresence, IEE Colloquium, 12 May 1995, pp. 8/1 – 8/5.

VIRTUAL REALITY

Definition: *Virtual Reality is the technology that provides almost real and/or believable experiences in a synthetic or virtual way.*

To achieve this goal, virtual reality uses the entire spectrum of current multimedia technologies such as image, video, sound and text, as well as newer and upcoming media such as e-touch, e-taste, and e-smell. To define the characteristics of VR, Heim [1] used the three 'I's, *immersion, interactivity* and *information intensity.*

- *Immersion* comes from devices that isolate the senses sufficiently to make a person feel transported to another place.
- *Interactivity* comes from the computer's lighting ability to change the scene's point of view as fast as the human organism can alter his or her physical position and perspective.
- *Information intensity* is the notion that a virtual world can offer special quality such as telepresence and artificial entities that show a certain degree of intelligent behavior.

The term *Virtual Reality* (VR) was initially introduced by Jaron Lanier, founder of VPL Research in 1989. This term is a contradiction in its self, for nothing can be both real and virtual at the same time. Perhaps Real Virtuality would be a better term, because this is what new technologies have been giving. Other related terms include *Artificial Reality* (Myron Krueger, 1970s), *Cyberspace* (William Gibson, 1984), and, more recently, *Virtual Worlds* and *Virtual Environments* (1990s). Virtual Reality may be considered to have been born in the mid-1960s, based on the work of Van Sutherland from the University of Utah [2]. A paper, published in 1972 by D.L Vickers, one of Sutherland's colleagues, describes an interactive computer graphics system utilizing a head-mounted display and wand. The display, worn like a pair of eyeglasses, gives an illusion to the observer that he/she is surrounded by three-dimensional, computer-generated objects. The challenge of VR is to make those objects appear convincingly real in many aspects like appearance, behavior, and quality of interaction between the objects and the user/environment. Figure 1 shows users interacting in a virtual reality environment.

See: Virtual and Augmented Reality

References

1. M. Heim, "Virtual Reality," Oxford University Press, New York, 1998.
2. I.E. Sutherland, "The Ultimate Display," Proceedings of the 1965 IFIP Congress, 2, 1965, pp. 506-508.

Figure 1. Users interacting in an immersive virtual reality environment.

VISION-BASED INTERACTION

Definition: *Vision-based human-computer interaction provides a wider and more expressive range of input capabilities by using computer vision techniques to process sensor data from one or more cameras in real-time, in order to reliably estimate relevant visual information about the user.*

Human-computer interaction involves information flow in both directions between computers and humans, which may be referred to as *input* (human to computer) and *output* (computer to human). Traditional computer interfaces have very limited input capabilities, typically restricted to keyboard typing and mouse manipulations (pointing, selecting, dragging, etc.). The area of *vision-based interaction* [1] seeks to provide a wider and more expressive range of input capabilities by using computer vision techniques to process sensor data from one or more cameras in real-time, in order to reliably estimate relevant visual information about the user – i.e., to use vision as a passive, non-intrusive, non-contact input modality for human-computer interaction.

In human-to-human interaction, vision is used to instantly determine a number of salient facts and features about one another such as location, identity, age, facial expression, focus of attention, posture, gestures, and general activity. These visual cues affect the content and flow of conversation, and they impart contextual information that is different from, but related to, other interaction modalities. For example, a gesture or facial expression may be intended as a signal of understanding, or the direction of gaze may disambiguate the object referred to in speech as "this" or the direction "over there." The visual channel is thus both co-expressive and complementary to other communication channels such as speech. Visual information integrated with other input modalities (including keyboard and mouse) can enable a rich user experience and a more effective and efficient interaction. Vision-based interaction may be useful in a wide range of computing scenarios in additional to standard desktop computing, especially mobile, immersive, and ubiquitous computing environments. A nice example of simple vision technology used effectively in an interactive environment was the KidsRoom project at the MIT Media Lab [2]. Another example is HandVu [3], which allows users of mobile augmented reality systems to use their hands to drive the interface, by robustly tracking hands and looking for a few known hand gestures/postures. Figure 1 shows HandVu at work.

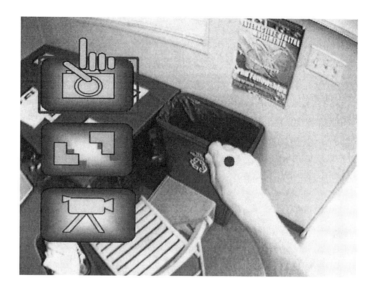

Figure 1. The HandVu system in action, providing hand-based control in a mobile augmented reality system.

In order to provide this kind of input about users, many researchers in the field of computer vision have focused on modeling, recognizing, and interpreting human behavior. Among the most studied sub-areas are face detection and location, face recognition, head and face tracking, facial expression analysis, eye gaze tracking, articulated body tracking, hand tracking, and the recognition of postures, gaits, gestures, and specific activities. Several of these have applications in areas such as security and surveillance, biometrics, and multimedia databases, as well as in human-computer interaction. Although many significant technical challenges remain, there has been notable progress in these areas during the past decade, and some commercial systems have begun to appear. In general, further research needs to improve the robustness and speed of these systems, and there needs to be a deeper understanding of how visual information is best utilized in human-computer interaction.

See: Human Computer Interactions

References

3. M. Turk and M. Kölsch, "Perceptual Interfaces," G. Medioni and S.B. Kang (Eds.), Emerging Topics in Computer Vision, Prentice Hall, 2004.
4. A. Bobick, S. Intille, J. Davis, F. Baird, C. Pinhanez, L. Campbell, Y. Ivanov, A. Schütte, and A. Wilson, "The KidsRoom: a perceptually-based interactive and immersive story environment," PRESENCE: Teleoperators and Virtual Environments, Vol. 8, No. 4, pp. 367-391, August 1999.

5. M. Kölsch, M. Turk, and T. Höllerer, "Vision-based interfaces for mobility," Proceedings of the MobiQuitous '04, 1st IEEE Intl. Conference on Mobile and Ubiquitous Systems: Networking and Services, pp. 86-94, Boston, MA, August 2004.

VISUAL CRYPTOGRAPHY

Definition: *Visual cryptography or visual secret sharing represents a group of effective schemes for image and video hading and watermarking.*

Visual cryptography (VC) or visual secret sharing (VSS) schemes [1] constitute probably the most cost-effective solution within a (k,n)-threshold framework. The VSS schemes use the frosted/transparent representation of the shares and the properties of the human visual system to force the recognition of a secret message from overlapping shares without additional computations or any knowledge of cryptographic keys [1]-[3].

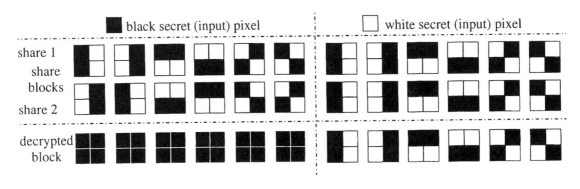

Figure 1. Visual cryptography concept demonstrated using a $(2,2)$-threshold scheme.

As it is shown in Figure 1, the conventional VSS schemes operate on a binary input. Following the encryption procedure in a (k,n)-threshold framework, the secret binary pixel is encrypted into n blocks of $m_1 \times m_2$ binary pixels. The actual share blocks are randomly generated through the column permutation of the $n \times m_1 m_2$ basis matrices. By repeating the process for all pixels of a $K_1 \times K_2$ secret (input) image, the VSS scheme produce n binary shares with dimensions of $m_1 K_1 \times m_2 K_2$ pixels. Each noise-like binary share is distributed to one of n participants. The secret image is visually revealed (Figure 2) only if any k (or more) recipients stack their shares printed as transparencies together on an overhead projector or specialized display.

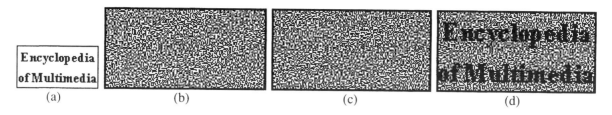

Figure 2. A $(2,2)$-VSS scheme constructed using 2×4 basis matrices with $m_1 = 2$ and $m_2 = 2$: (a) secret input image, (b,c) binary shares, (d) output image visually decrypted by stacking the share images shown in (b,c).

See: **Image secret sharing, Halftoning based VSS, Threshold schemes with minimum pixel expansion, Image watermarking using visual cryptography**

References

6. M. Naor and A. Shamir, "Visual Cryptography," Lecture Notes in Computer Science, Vol. 950, 1994, pp. 1-12.

7. P.-A. Eisen and D.-R. Stinson, "Threshold Visual Cryptography Schemes with Specified Levels of Reconstructed Pixels," Design, Codes and Cryptography, Vol. 25, No. 1, January 2002, pp. 15-61.

8. C.-N. Yang, "New Visual Secret Sharing Schemes Using Probabilistic Method," Pattern Recognition Letters, Vol. 25, No. 4, March 2004, pp. 481-494.

WATERMARKING, AUDIO

Definition: *Digital audio watermarking is a technology to embed and retrieve information into and from digital audio data.*

Audio watermarking uses common watermarking methods explained in detail in the article on Digital Watermarking. In this article, the differences to watermarking algorithms for other media types like images and video are discussed.

Raw audio data is commonly stored as PCM (Pulse code modulation) samples. Common sample sizes vary from 8 to 24 bits, sampling rates range form 8 kHz to 96 kHz. Most audio watermarking algorithms work on raw audio data. But there are others which aim at lossy compression audio formats which are commonly applied today for storage or transfer. Mp3 is the best know example for this. Some of these algorithms embed the information in some format specific information, like for example the scale factors of mp3 files. Other algorithms change the compressed files in such a way that the watermark can also be retrieved from the raw data. This is called bit stream embedding.

Common methods like LSB, pattern, statistical methods, patchwork methods, correlation of embedded noise [1] applied in image watermarking are also known for audio watermarking. In audio watermarking, individual bits are often embedded in time frames like shown in Figure 1.

But there are also approaches using specific features of audio data, like echo hiding or phase coding. Echo hiding utilizes the fact that human perception cannot perceive sounds of small energy shortly after loud sounds. An echo hiding watermarking algorithm repeats small amounts of the cover when loud sounds occur with reduced energy. The delay between sound and copy can be used to transfer information. Phase coding is based on the fact that human perception for audio phases is weak, so changes in the phase can be used for transferring information.

Audio watermarking usually addresses watermarking of sound data. But there are also solutions for watermarking musical scores and MIDI data. Musical score watermarking is more similar to watermarking of simples images or drawings due to the low complexity of the cover data. MIDI watermarking also needs to deal with a small cover files with only few possibilities of data modification. LSB watermarking methods of attack velocity codes and small timing modifications have been introduced as suitable watermarking strategies for MIDI data.

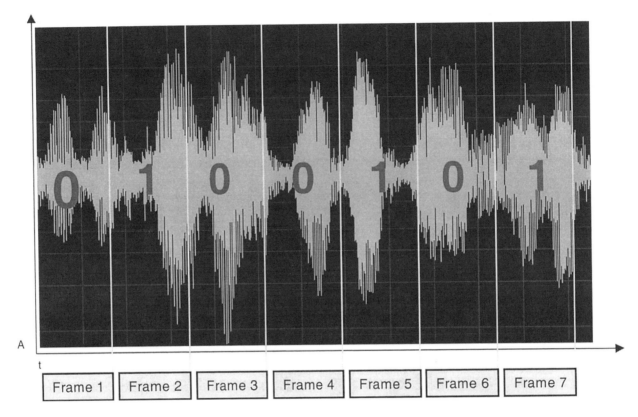

Figure 1. Audio watermarking usually embeds single bits in discreet time frames.

Challenges, attacks and benchmarking

At audio watermarking, usually two types of attacks against the watermarking robustness are important: Lossy compression and analogue transfer. Most audio files are distributed in a lossy compression format as for example mp3, wma or ogg. The watermark embedded in the audio data should survive the different compression formats and bit rates as long as an acceptable audio quality is provided. Audio often leaves the digital domain when it is consumed or used, for example in radio networks, live recordings or tape copies. Some applications require the audio watermark to stay in the audio signal and be still retrieval when transferred back into the digital domain. Current state of the art watermarking algorithms provide a good robustness against both attacks.

The growing number of attacks against watermarking systems has shown the importance of efficient and reliable benchmarking to improve the quality of existing watermarking methods. General aspects on attacks and benchmarking can be found in the article on Digital Watermarking. A wide range of image watermarking evaluation approaches and benchmarking suites have been described in the literature by neglecting audio watermarking.

With StirMark Benchmark for audio [2], a well-defined benchmark for audio watermarking robustness and security has been introduced. The benchmark contains of a set of single geometric attacks in time and frequency domain. They simulate different signal processing effects by adding or removing signals or applying filtering, common in several watermarking applications. The set of attacks allows determining robustness or fragility of a watermark embedded into the audio signal to specific single manipulations or to its arbitrary combination.

Applications

While all watermarking applications known from image and video watermarking can also be applied to audio watermarking, the protection of copyright always had an important role in audio watermarking. The best-known example for this is the Secure digital music Initiative (SDMI)) which was a group of companies planning to develop a framework for secure digital music distribution. They tried to install a framework for protected playback, storing, and distribution of digital music. SDMI participants include music content, consumer electronics, information technology, and wireless telecommunication companies. Major music labels where as well included as for example the developers of the Napster software, but complains had been raised that only a small group of participants were involved in key-problem identification and management.

References

1. B.H. Tewfik, "Digital Watermarks for Audio Signals," Proceedings of the EUSIPCO-96, VIII European Signal Processing Conference, Trieste, Italy, pp. 473-480, September, 1996.
2. M. Steinebach, F.A.P. Petitcolas, F. Raynal, J. Dittmann, C. Fontaine, C. Seibel, N. Fates, C. L. Ferri, "StirMark Benchmark: Audio watermarking attacks," Proceedings of the International Conference on Information Technology: Coding and Computing (ITCC 2001), Las Vegas, Nevada, pp. 49 - 54, April 2001.

WATERMARKING, VIDEO

Definition: Digital video watermarking is a technology to embed and retrieve information into and from digital video data.

A variety of robust and fragile video watermarking methods have been proposed to solve the illegal copying and proof of ownership problems as well as to identify manipulations. Although a number of broad claims have been made in the field of robustness of various digital watermarking methods, it is still difficult to handle combined or non-linear geometric transformations. The methods can be divided into techniques working on compressed or uncompressed data. In particular video watermarking is based in general on the following concepts to hide a watermark by modifying some of its characteristics:

- spatial domain approach, also called native domain: embedding and detection are performed on spatial pixels values (luminance, chrominance, color space) or on the overall video frame characteristic,
- feature or salient point watermarking by modifying geometric properties of the video frames,
- frequency domain techniques where the spatial values are transformed, like DCT Discrete Cosine, FFT Fast Fourier Transform, Wavelets or fractals,
- quantization index modulation (QIM) watermarking,
- format-specific approaches like watermarking of structure elements like Facial Animation Parameter of MPEG-4 or motion vectors.

The robust watermarking approaches usually spread the watermarking information redundant over the overall signal representation in a non-invertible manner to enforce identification or verification of ownership or to annotate the video. For example the message is spread and encoded in the 2D FFT frequencies of each video frame. In most cases prior to transforming each frame to the frequency domain, the frame data is transformed from e.g. RGB space to Weber-Fechner YCbCr space. Generically, YCbCr space consists of a luminance component Y and two color difference components Cb and Cr. The Y component contains the luminance and black & white image information, while Cb represents the difference between R and Y and Cr represents the difference between Y and B. In YCbCr space most of the frame information is in the Y component. This representation is used also during MPEG compression. The MPEG algorithm grossly removes large portions of the Cb and Cr components without damaging the frame quality. The MPEG algorithm uses compression to reduce the Y component since it has more effect on the quality of the compressed frames, which is also used in most watermarking schemes. To avoid estimation attacks the watermark signal should be adoptive designed to the overall video frame sequence characteristics by facing the problem that equal or similar watermarking pattern for each frame could allow an estimation attack based on the slide visual differences between adjacent frames, different watermarking pattern could allow an estimation attack based on the similarities between similar visual frames, see for example in [1].

Data rates are measured in bits per frame. If the watermark is embedded into the compressed domain for example MPEG video, we count the embedded data rates in bits per I, B and P frame or per GOP.

For fragile video watermarking, relevant for authenticate the data in its authenticity and integrity, a fragile watermark signal can be spread over the overall video into manipulation sensitive video elements like LSB to detect changed and manipulated regions. The watermark for authentication purposes is often designed in an invertible (reversible) manner to allow reproduction of the original, see for example an analysis of the approaches in [2]. Today we find several fragile watermarking techniques to recognize video manipulations. In the moment most fragile watermarks are very sensitive to changes and can detect most possible changes in pixel values. Only few approaches address the so-called content-fragile watermarking relevant in applications with several allowed post production editing processes. For example Mombasseri et al. in

[3] addresses the recognition of video frame sequence changes with the possibility of reproduction of the original frame sequence called self-watermarking of frame-pairs.

A further idea is for example from [4] suggesting to embed a visual content feature M into the video frame with a robust watermarking method. The content-fragile watermarking approach for video authentication tries to extract the frame characteristics of human perception, called content. The approach is for example to determine the edge characteristics of the single video frame. This characteristic is transformed into a feature code for the content-fragile digital watermark. The edge characteristics of a frame give a very good reflection of the frame content, because they allow the identification of object structures and homogeneity of the video. [4] use the canny edge detector described as the most efficient edge separator. The author described several strategies for generating and verification of the edge based feature codes. From the general perspective the content feature M can be embedded directly or used as a seed to generate the watermarking pattern itself.

Benchmarking of Video Watermarks

The available benchmarking suites mainly cover image and audio watermarks and neglect video specific aspects. In [1], we find an evaluation of video watermarking sensitivity to collusion attacks and potential solutions. Video specific aspects of video watermarks for cinema applications are summarized in [5]. Various features were analyzed, including robustness to non intentional attacks such as MPEG compression, transcoding, analog to digital and digital-to-analog conversions, standard conversions (PAL – NTSC), and change of geometry.

References

1. K. Su, D. Kundur, and D. Hatzinakos, "A Novel Approach to Collusion-Resistant Video Watermarking," *Security and Watermarking of Multimedia Contents IV*, E. J. Delp and P. W. Wong, Eds., Proceedings of SPIE, Vol. 4675, San Jose, California, January 2002.
2. S. Katzenbeisser and J. Dittmann, "Malicious Attacks on Media Authentication Schemes Based on Invertible Watermarks," Proceedings of SPIE Conference 5306: Security, Steganography, and Watermarking of Multimedia Contents VI, 2004.
3. B. G. Mobasseri and A. Evans, "Content-dependent video authentication by self-watermarking in color space," Proceedings of Security and Watermarking of Multimedia Contents III, Electronic Imaging '01, San Jose, January 2001, pp. 35-44.
4. J. Dittmann, *"Content-fragile Watermarking for Image Authentication,"* In Security and Watermarking of Multimedia Contents III, Ping Wah Wong, Edward J. Delp III, Editors, Proceedings of SPIE, Vol. 4314, pp. 175-184, 2001.
5. B. Macq, J. Dittmann, and E.J. Delp, *"Benchmarking of Image Watermarking Algorithms for Digital Rights Management,"* Proceedings of the IEEE, Special Issue on: Enabling Security Technology for Digital Rights Management, Vol. 92, No. 6, pp. 971-984, June 2004.

WIRELESS VIDEO

Zhihai He
University of Missouri-Columbia, Columbia, MO 65201 USA

Chang Wen Chen
Florida Institute of Technology, Melbourne, FL 32901 USA

Definition: *Wireless video refers to transporting video signals over mobile wireless links.*

Introduction

The rapid growth of mobile wireless access devices, together with the success of wireless networking technologies, has brought a new era of video communications: transporting video signals over mobile wireless links. Transport of video content over mobile wireless channels is very challenging because the mobile wireless channels are usually severely impaired due to multi-path fading, shadowing, inter-symbol interferences, and noise disturbances. Traditionally, vision has been the dominant medium through which people receive information. Visual information, coupled with intelligent vision processing, provides a rich set of important information for situational awareness and event understanding [1]. Incorporating the video capture, processing, and transmission capabilities into networked mobile devices will enable us to gather real-time visual information about the target events at large scales for situational awareness and decision making. This will create a potential impact through out the society via many important applications, including battle-space communication, video surveillance, security monitoring, environmental tracking, and smart spaces.

During the past decade, the video communication system has evolved from the conventional desktop computing and wired communication to mobile computing and wireless communication, as illustrated in Figure 1. In this scenario, the live video is captured by a camera on a portable device. The video data is compressed on-board and transmitted to remote users through wireless channels. As the communication paradigm evolves from the conventional point-to-point, wired and centralized communication to the current wireless, distributed, ad hoc, and massive communication, the system becomes more and more complex. More specifically, such massive wireless communication networks often involve a large number of heterogeneous devices, each with different on-board computation speed, energy supply, and wireless communication capability, communicating over the dynamic and often error prune wireless networks. How to characterize and manage the communication behavior of each communication devices within the network, and how to coordinate their behaviors such that each operates in a contributive fashion to maximize the overall performance of the system as a whole remain a central challenging research problem.

Over the past few decades, extensive research has been conducted on various elements of the wireless video communication networks, such as video compression [2, 3], mobile ad hoc protocol design [4], energy-aware routing [5], power management and topology control [6]. However, little research work has been done to bridge them into an integrated resource management and performance optimization framework. Developing efficient algorithms for real-time video compression and streaming over wireless networks to maximize the overall system performance under resource constraints has become one of the central research tasks in both signal processing and wireless communication research communities.

The ultimate goal in communication system design is to control and optimize the system performance under resource constraints. In mobile wireless video communication, video encoding and network communication operate under a set of resource constraints, including bandwidth, energy, and computational complexity constraints. To analyze the behavior of the mobile video communication system, manage its resources, and optimize the system performance, we need to study the intrinsic relationships between the resource constraints and the end-to-end video distortion. This study is called resource-distortion analysis. This resource-distortion analysis extends the traditional R-D analysis by considering new resource constraints. In this article, we shall analyze the major resource constraints in real-time video compression and streaming over wireless networks, and study the impact of these resource constraints on the overall system performance.

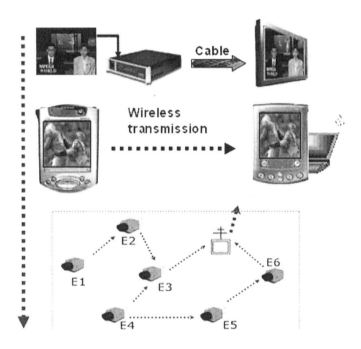

Figure 1. From desktop computing and wired communication to mobile computing and wireless communication, and furthermore to wireless sensor networks.

Rate Constraints

In traditional video communication applications, such as digital TV broadcast, and video-on-demand, video signals can be compressed offline, stored on a video server, and transmitted through the wired network to viewers upon request. In this case, the major constraint for video compression and communication is in the form of transmission bandwidth or storage space, which determines the output bit rate of video encoder [3, 7]. Therefore, the ultimate goal in this type of communication system design is to optimize the video quality under the rate constraint. To this end, rate-distortion (R-D) theories have been developed to model the relationship between the coding bit rate and signal distortion [8]. The R-D theory describes the performance limit of lossy data compression, and answers the following fundamental question: What is the minimum number of bits needed in compressing the source data at a given distortion level (or reconstruction quality).

During the last 50 years, R-D theories have been actively studied in the information theory literature, mainly focusing on performance bounds, including asymptotic analysis [8] and high rate approximation [9, 10]. It should be noted that theoretical analysis and analytical R-D performance bounds are likely to be found only for simple sources and simple encoding schemes. For complicated sources, such as 2-D images and 3-D videos, and sophisticated compression systems, such as JPEG and JPEG2000 image coding, MPEG-2, H.263, MPEG-4 [2], and H.264 [11] video encoding, this type of theoretical performance analysis is often inapplicable [12]. This is because: (1) Unlike 1-D text and acoustic data, whose compression characteristics can be easily captured by simple statistical models, such as Gaussian and Laplacian models, images and videos often exhibit very complicated source characteristics and correlation structure. The underlying scene structure of the 3-D environment, the time-varying motion patterns of scene objects, as well as the arbitrary camera movement, collectively define a very complicated source correlation structure in the video data. This type of correlation structure is often very difficult to be described by mathematical models. (2) Note that the major effort in image and video compression is to explore the spatiotemporal source correlation with various motion prediction and spatial transform techniques.

To explore the complicated source correlation structure of the video sequence, very sophisticated prediction and data representation techniques, such as multi-frame motion compensation, flexible macroblock (MB) size, intra prediction and mode decision [11], have been developed. These techniques, often seen to be ad hoc and difficult to be mathematically modeled, however have significant impact on the overall video compression performance. The difficulty in mathematical modeling of both the source characteristics and the compression system creates a significant gap between the information-theoretic R-D analysis and practices in rate control and quality optimization for video compression. To fill in this gap, over the past two decades, as more and more advanced image and video compression algorithms are being developed and finalized in international standards, a set of R-D analysis and modeling techniques algorithms for practical video compression have been developed [2, 7, 12, 13].

The analysis and estimation of R-D functions have important applications in visual coding and communication. First, with the estimated R-D functions we can adjust the quantization setting of the encoder and control the output bit rate or picture quality according to channel conditions, storage capacity, or user's requirements [2, 13]. Second, based on the estimated R-D functions, optimum bit allocation, as well as other R-D optimization procedures, can be performed to improve the efficiency of the coding algorithm and, consequently, to improve the image quality or video presentation quality [14].

Energy Constraints

In wireless video communication, video capture, compression and network streaming operate on the mobile devices with limited energy. A primary factor in determining the utility or operational lifetime of the mobile communication device is how efficiently it manages its energy consumption. The problem becomes even more critical with the power-demanding video encoding functionality integrated into the mobile computing platform [15]. Video encoding and data transmission are the two dominant power-consuming operations in wireless video communication, especially over wireless LAN, where the typical transmission distance ranges from 50m to 100m. Experimental studies show that for relative small picture sizes, such as QCIF (176×144) videos, video encoding consumes about 2/3 of the total power for video communication over Wireless LAN [15]. For pictures of higher resolutions, it is expected that the fraction of power consumption by video encoding will become even higher. From the power consumption perspective, the effect of video encoding is two-fold. First, efficient video compression significantly reduces the amount of the video data to be transmitted, which in turn saves a significant amount of energy in data transmission. Second, more efficient video compression often requires higher computational complexity and larger power consumption in computing. These two conflicting effects imply that in practical system design there is always a tradeoff among the bandwidth R, power consumption P, and video quality D. Here, the video quality is often measured by the mean square error (MSE) between the encoded picture and original one, also known as the source coding distortion. To find the best trade-off solution, we need to develop an analytic framework to model the power-rate-distortion (P-R-D) behavior of the video encoding system. To achieve flexible management of power consumption, we also need to develop a video encoding architecture which is fully scalable in power consumption.

Many algorithms have been reported in the literature to reduce the encoding computational complexity. Hardware implementation technologies have also been developed to improve the video coding speed. However, little research has been done to analyze the relationship between the encoder power consumption and its R-D performance [16].

Rate-distortion (R-D) analysis has been one of the major research focus in information theory and communication for the past few decades, from the early Shannon's source coding theorem for asymptotic R-D analysis of generic information data [8], to recent R-D modeling of modern video encoding systems [2, 7, 12, 13]. For video encoding on the mobile devices and streaming over the wireless network, it is needed to consider another dimension, the power consumption, to establish a theoretical basis for R-D analysis under energy constraints. In energy-aware video encoding, the coding distortion is not only a function of the encoding bit rate as in the traditional R-D analysis, but also a function of the power consumption P. In other words:

$$D = D(R, P) \qquad (1)$$

which describes the P-R-D behavior of the video encoding system. The P-R-D analysis answers the following question: for given bandwidth R and encoder power consumption level P, what is the minimum coding distortion one can achieve? Generally speaking, this is a theoretically difficult problem, because power consumption and R-D performance are concepts in two totally unrelated fields. However, for a specific video encoding system, for example MPEG-4 video coding [2], one can design an energy-scale video compression scheme, model its P-R-D behavior, and use this model to optimize the R-D performance under the energy constraint [16]. (See the short article.)

Encoding Complexity and Encoder Power Consumption

In embedded video compression system design, the encoder power consumption is directly related to computational complexity of the encoder. In other words, the encoder power consumption Ps is a function of the encoder complexity C_s, denoted by $P_s = \Phi(C_s)$, and this function is given by the power consumption model of the microprocessor [17]. To translate the complexity scalability into energy scalability, we need to consider the energy-scaling technologies in hardware design. To dynamically control the energy consumption of the microprocessor on the portable device, a CMOS circuits design technology, named dynamic voltage scaling (DVS), has been recently developed [18]. In CMOS circuits, the power consumption P is given by

$$P_s = V^2 \cdot f_{CLK} \cdot C_{EFF}$$

(2)

where V, f_{CLK}, and C_{EFF} are the supply voltage, clock frequency, and effective switched capacitance of the circuits [18]. Since the energy is power times time, and the time to finish an operation is inversely proportional to the clock frequency. Therefore, the energy per operation E_{op} is proportional to V. This implies that lowering the supply voltage will reduce the energy consumption of the system in a quadratic fashion. However, lowering the supply voltage also decreases the maximum achievable clock speed. More specifically, it has been observed that fCLK is approximately linearly proportional to V [18]. Therefore, we have

$$P_s \propto f_{CLK}^3 \text{ and } E_{op} \propto f_{CLK}^2$$

(3)

It can be seen that the CPU can reduce its energy consumption substantially by running more slowly. For example, according to (3), it can run at half speed and thereby use only 1/4 of the energy for the same number of operations. This is the key idea behind the DVS technology. Variable chip makers, such as Intel [17], have recently announced and sold processors with this energy-scaling feature. In conventional system design with fixed supply voltage and clock frequency, clock cycles, and hence energy, are wasted when the CPU workload is light and the processor becomes idle. Reducing the supply voltage in conjunction with the clock frequency eliminates the idle cycles and saves the energy significantly. In this work, we just use this DVS technology and the related power consumption model to translate the computational complexity into the energy consumption of the hardware.

Video Compression and Transmission under Energy Constraints

As mentioned before, the energy supply of a mobile communication device is mainly used by video compression and wireless transmission. For the power consumption in video compression and streaming, we have the following two observations. Case A: If we decrease the encoder power consumption P_s, the coding distortion D_s increases, which is due to lack of enough video processing. That is, $P_s \downarrow \Rightarrow D_s \uparrow$. Case B: Since the total power consumption P_0 is fixed, and $P_0 = P_s + P_t$, where P_t is the transmission power. If we increase P_s, then P_t decreases. This implies that less bits can be transmitted because the transmission energy is proportional the number of bits to transmit. Therefore, $P_s \uparrow \Rightarrow P_t \downarrow \Rightarrow R_s \downarrow \Rightarrow D_s \uparrow$. It can be seen that when the encoding power P_s goes too low or too high, the encoding distortion D_s will be large. This implies that there exists an optimal power P_s that minimizes the video distortion D_s. In the following, based on a simplified power consumption model for wireless transmission, we study the performance of mobile video device. More specifically, we assume the transmission power is properly chosen such that the bit error rate at the receiver side is very low and the transmission errors can be neglected. In this case, the transmission power should be given by

$$P_t = \eta(d) \cdot R_s \text{ and } \eta(d) = w + \gamma d^n \tag{4}$$

where R_s is the number of bits to be transmitted, d is the distance between the sensor node and the receiver(e.g., an AFN), and n is the path loss exponent [9, 44]. Therefore,

$$P_0 = P_s + P_t = P_s + \eta(d)R_s \tag{5}$$

and,

$$R_s = \frac{P_0 - P_s}{\eta(d)} \tag{6}$$

Since the transmission errors are negligible, we have $D_t = 0$ and $D = D_s$. According to the P-R-D model,

$$D = D_s(R_s, P_s)\big|_{R_s = \frac{P_0 - P_s}{\eta(d)}} = D_s\left(\frac{P_0 - P_s}{\eta(d)}, P_s\right), \quad 0 \le P_s \le P_0. \tag{7}$$

It can be seen that D is a function of P_s, denoted by $D(P_s)$. Using the P-R-D model, we compute the function $D(P_s)$ in (7), and plot it in Figure 2. Here, the power supply of the wireless video sensor is $P_0 = 0.3$ watts. This is a typical plot of $D(P_s)$. It can be seen that $D(P_s)$ has a minimum point, which is the minimum encoding distortion (or maximum video quality) that a mobile device can achieve, no matter how it allocates its power resource between video encoding and wireless transmission, given fixed total power supply. We call this minimum distortion as achievable minimum distortion (AMD). In Figure 3, we plot the AMD as a function of the power supply P_0. For a given power supply P_0, the AMD indicates the lower bound on the video coding distortion, or the upper bound on the video quality of a mobile video device.

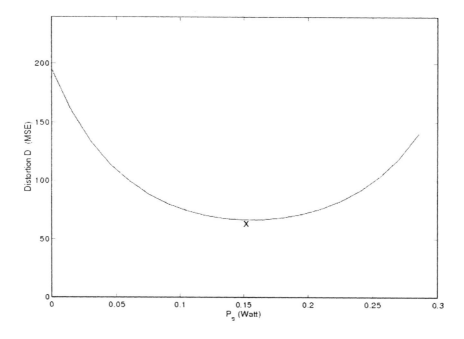

Figure 2. Plot of $D(P_s)$ in (7) and illustration of the achievable minimum distortion, given fixed total power consumption P_0.

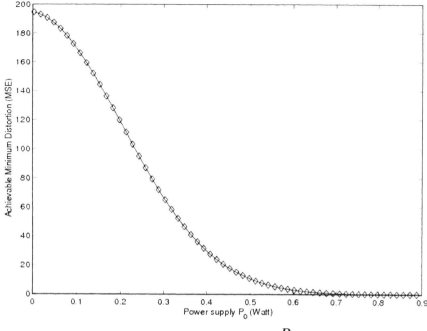

Figure 3. Plot of AMD (P_0).

It should be noted that the AMD bound in (7) is derived based on a simplified model of the mobile video device, and this bound is not tight. More specifically, first, it has not considered the transmission errors [19]. The actual video distortion should consist of both the encoding distortion caused by Quantization loss and the transmission distortion caused by transmission errors [19]. Second, the analysis assumes that the bandwidth of wireless channel is always sufficiently large. Obviously, this is not true for video transmission over the wireless channel which has a limited and time-varying bandwidth. In actual performance analysis for video compression and streaming over mobile devices, it is needed to incorporate the bandwidth constraint and the transmission distortion model [19] into the AMD analysis, and study the achievable minimum distortion in video sensing over the error-prone wireless networks. Another important problem is the mobility of video communication device. The mobility of the device poses new issues in the AMD performance analysis, because it has to deal with various characteristics of the mobile wireless channel, including time-varying path loss, shadowing, and small-scale fading.

Wireless Multi-hop Delivery, Video Adaptation, and Security Issues

Wireless video applications often involve transport over a collection of multi-hop wireless nodes to reach the destination. A multi-hop network is dynamically self-organized and self-configured, with the nodes in the network automatically establishing and maintaining mesh connectivity among themselves. This feature brings many advantages to multi-hop networks such as low up-front cost, easy network maintenance, robustness, and reliable service coverage. However, limited network resource, severe interference/ contention among neighbor traffic, dynamic changing route, lack of QoS support, direct coupling between the physical layer and the upper layers, etc. pose many challenges for supporting video communication over wireless multi-hop networks.

Another significant challenge in wireless video is to effectively deal with the heterogeneity of the wireless links and mobile devices. The needs for video adaptation have becoming more important as the advance of the wireless video has become widespread. With regard to wireless video streaming, there are generally two issues in video adaptation: rate adaptation and robustness adaptation. The objective of rate adaptation is to intelligently remove some information from the video signal itself so that end-to-end resource requirement can be reduced. A popular approach to video rate adaptation is the design of the video transcoding algorithms to bridge between two different networks. The objective of robustness adaptation is to increase the capability of the compressed video for transmission over error prone wireless links. Both error resilient source coding and error control channel coding have been used to increase the robustness.

Because wireless video rely on the wireless networks in which users communicate with each other through the open air, unauthorized users may intercept content transmissions or attackers may inject malicious content or penetrate the network and impersonate legitimate users. This intrinsic nature of wireless networks has several specific security implications. Sensitive and valuable video content must be encrypted to safeguard confidentiality and integrity of the content and prevent unauthorized consumption. A wireless device usually has limited memory and computing power. Battery capacity is also at a premium. Growth in battery capacity has already lagged far behind the increase of energy requirement in a wireless device. The security concerns mentioned above make it even worse since security processing has to take away some of the premium computing resources and battery life. To address the peculiar security problems for wireless video with significant energy constraint, we will need to design lightweight cryptographic algorithms and encryption schemes, to include security processing instructions into the embedded processors, and to integrate scalable coding and encryption with error resilience.

See: Power-Rate-Distortion Analysis for Wireless Video, Wireless Multi-hop Video Delivery, Wireless Video Adaptation, Security Issues in Wireless Video

References

1. R. Collins, A. Lipton, H. Fujiyoshi, and T. Kanade, "Algorithms for cooperative multi-sensor surveillance," *Proceedings of the IEEE*, Vol. 89, No. 10, October 2001, pp. 1456 - 1477.
3. T. Sikora, "The MPEG-4 video standard verification model," IEEE Transactions on Circuits and Systems for Video Technology, Vol. 7, pp. 19–31, February 1997.
4. Z. He and S. K. Mitra, "A Unified Rate-Distortion Analysis Framework for Transform Coding," *IEEE Transactions on Circuits and System for Video Technology*, Vol. 11, pp. 1221 -1236, December 2001.
5. C. E. Perkins, E. M. Belding-Royer, and S. R. Das, "Ad hoc on-demand distance vector (AODV) routing," *IETF Internet draft*, draft-ietfmanet-aodv-09.txt, November 2001.
6. J. Chang and L. Tassiulas, "Energy conserving routing in wireless ad hoc networks," *Proceedings INFOCOMM 2000*, Tel Aviv, Israel, pp. 22–31, March 2000.

7. J. Pan, Y. T. Hou, L. Cai, Y. Shi, and S. X. Shen, "Topology control for wireless video surveillance networks," *Proceedings of ACM Mobicom 2003*, San Diego, CA, September 2003.

8. W. Ding and B. Liu, "Rate control of MPEG video coding and recording by rate-quantization modeling," *IEEE Transactions on Circuits and Systems for Video Technology*, Vol. 6, pp. 12–20, February 1996.

9. T. M. Cover and J. A. Thomas, *Elements of Information Theory*, Wiley, 1991.

10. W. Bennett, "Spectra of quantized signals," *Bell Sys. Tech. Journal*, Vol. 27, pp. 446-472, July 1948.

11. A. Gersho, "Asymptotically optimal block quantization," *IEEE Transactions on Information Technology*, Vol. IT-23, pp. 373-380, July 1979.

12. T. Wiegand, "Text of Committee Draft of Joint Video Specification (ITU-T Rec. H.264 —ISO/IEC 14496-10 AVC)," Document JVTC167, 3rd JVT Meeting, Fairfax, Virginia, USA, 6-10 May 2002.

13. Ortega and K. Ramchandran, "Rate-distortion methods for image and video compression," *IEEE Signal Processing Magazine*, Vol. 15, No. 6, pp. 23–50, November 1998.

14. J. Ribas-Corbera and S. Lei, "Contribution to the rate control Q2 experiment: A quantizer control tool for achieving target bit rates accurately," Coding of Moving Pictures and Associated Audio MPEG96/M1812ISO/IECJTC/SC29/WG11, Sevilla, Spain, February 1997.

15. K. Ramchandran and M. Vetterli, "Rate-distortion optimal fast thresholding with complete JPEG/MPEG decoder compatibility," *IEEE Transactions on Image Processing*, Vol. 3, pp. 700–704, September 1994.

16. X. Lu, Y. Wang, and E. Erkip, "Power efficient H.263 video transmission over wireless channels," *Proceedings of the International Conference on Image Processing*, Rochester, New York, September 2002.

17. Z. He, Y. Liang, L. Chen, I. Ahmad, and D. Wu, "Power-rate-distortion analysis for wireless video communication under energy constraint," *IEEE Transactions on Circuits and System for Video Technology*, Vol. 15, No. 5, May, 2005.

18. Intel Inc, "IntelXScaleTechnology," http://www.intel.com/design/intelxscale.

19. T. Burd and R. Broderson, "Processor Design for Portable Systems," *Journal of VLSI Signal Processing*, Vol. 13, No. 2, pp. 203–222, August 1996.

20. Z. He, J. Cai, and C. W. Chen, "Joint source-channel rate-distortion analysis for adaptive mode selection and rate control in wireless video coding," *IEEE Transactions on Circuits and System on Video Technology*, Special Issue on Wireless Video, Vol. 12, pp. 511–523, June 2002.

WIRELESS VIDEO ADAPTATION

Definition: Wireless streaming requires video coding to be robust to channel impairments and adaptable to the network and diverse scenarios; wireless video adaptation deals with rate adaptation and robustness adaptation.

With the rapid growth of wireless communications and the advance of video coding techniques, wireless video streaming is expected to be widely deployed in the near future. However, due to the characteristics of wireless networks such as high error rate, limited bandwidth, time-varying channel conditions, limited battery power of wireless devices and the diversity of wireless access networks and devices, wireless video streaming faces many challenges. In particular, from the coding point of view, wireless streaming requires video coding to be robust to channel impairments and adaptable to the network and diverse scenarios. Traditional media coding standards such as MPEG-2 and MPEG-4 are not suitable any more since they are targeted to a particular range of bit rates and a particular type of applications. Therefore, the needs for video adaptation have becoming more important as the advance of the wireless video has become widespread. With regard to wireless video streaming, there are generally two issues in video adaptation: rate adaptation and robustness adaptation. These issues are further elaborated in the following.

The objective of rate adaptation is to intelligently remove some information from the video signal itself so that end-to-end resource requirement can be reduced. Generally, video rate adaptation can be implemented in three ways. The first approach is to store many non-scalable bitstreams for each video sequence. Each bitstream is coded at different formats or different spatial/temporal/SNR (signal-to-noise ratio) resolutions. When a user requests to access the video sequence, the server can send the bitstream which is closet to the user's requirements. Although this method usually costs more storage spaces in the video server and the chosen bitstream may not satisfy the user's requirement exactly, it is widely used in practical systems due to its simplicity. Recent research works have focused on the how to efficiently switch among multiple non-scalable bitstreams in order to dynamically adapt to the time-varying network conditions.

The second approach is a popular scheme based on video transcoding [21] including decreasing the spatial resolution, reducing the SNR, or down sampling the temporal frame rate through re-encoding, re-quantization, frame dropping and etc. Although transcoding is very flexible and does not require extra storage space, it needs complex extra processes and is not suitable for large-scale diverse users. The third approach is to use scalable video coding which has inherent ability to adapt video to different requirements. Scalable video coding schemes aim at encoding a video once and decode it at multiple reduced rates and resolutions to provide simple and flexible adaptability. However, since scalable video coding intends to cover a broad range of applications, the complexity of scalable video coding is typically very high, which may limit its usage on real-time wireless video applications.

The second important issue in wireless video adaptation is the robustness adaptation, for which we try to add controlled redundancy in video bitstreams for reliable transmission over wireless channels. Robust video adaptation can be generally implemented in two ways. The first approach is to build error resilience features into the coding scheme itself. Typical error resilience features for coding include the use of resynchronization markers to recover from decoding errors and intra-coded blocks to minimize error propagation. The second approach is to use the joint source-channel coding techniques which involve both source coding and channel coding to combat possible channel errors. We have seen extensive studies on FEC (forward error correction) based joint source-channel coding for robust video transmission. The common idea of most joint source-channel coding schemes is unequal error protection, i.e., the more important information is given more protection [22]. How to define and protect the important video information has been the main research focus in joint source-channel coding.

Besides the traditional low-level video adaptation, recent advance in video content analysis has introduced new space for wireless video adaptation such as semantic event based adaptation, structural-level adaptation, and video skimming [23]. For example, object-based video transcoding can be used to transmit a subset of objects for adaptive content delivery. On the other, recent advance in wireless network QoS supports has also brought in new challenges in wireless video adaptation such as cross-layer video adaptation.

See: Wireless Video

References

21. A. Vetro, C. Christopoulos, and H. Sun, "Video transcoding architectures and techniques: an overview," IEEE Signal Processing Magazine, pp. 18–29, March 2003.
22. Z. He, J. Cai, and C.W. Chen, "Joint source channel rate-distortion analysis for adaptive mode selection and rate control in wireless video coding," IEEE Transactions on Circuits and Systems for Video Technology, Vol. 12, pp. 511–523, June 2002.
23. S.-F. Chang and A. Vetro, "Video adaptation: concepts, technologies, and open issues," Proceedings of the IEEE, Vol. 93, pp. 148–158, January 2005.

WMV-9 VIDEO COMPRESSION

Definition: *Windows Media Video 9 (WMV-9) is a video codec developed by Microsoft, which is widely used for streaming media over Internet due to the popularity of MS Windows operating systems.*

Since WMV-9 is a generic coder, many algorithms/tools of it can be used for a variety of applications under different operating conditions. Originally, three profiles were defined – Simple Profile, Main Profile, and Complex Profile. However, Complex Profile was dropped unofficially. Consequently, WMV-9 more focuses on compression technology for progressive video up to Main Profile, while VC-1, a derivative of WMV-9, is developed for broadcast interlaced video as well as progressive video. Those two technologies are almost identical in important tools except the interlace tool, and VC-1 is currently under standardization by the Society of Motion Picture and Television Engineer (SMPTE).

Key Compression Tools for WMV-9 Video

Like all other MPEG standards, WMV-9 is based on motion compensated transform coding. Originally YUV4:2:0 and YUV4:1:1 were defined as input formats for progressive and interlaced video, respectively. Since interlaced video is not considered with WMV-9 anymore, 8bit YUV4:2:0 is the only input format. There is no fixed GOP structure in WMV-9. And, I, P, B, BI and Skipped P are defined as pictures/frames. Unlike MPEG standards, I (Intra) frame doesn't happen periodically. Any reference can take on I or P (Predicted) frame (except the fist frame – I). Therefore, if there is no big scene change for a lengthy period of time, there could be only P frames as references. However, the number of B frames (Bi-directionally predicted frames) between two reference frames is fixed. Maximally, there could be seven B frames. BI frames are almost identical to I frames. If there is big scene change continuously, some B frames can not capture any similarity from two reference frames. In such cases, intra mode performance might be better than prediction mode performance – BI frame compression is a good choice in such cases. Since BI is not used as a reference, frame dropping based on the ASF file format is possible under certain conditions – any reasons like lack of computation or bandwidth. The last one is Skipped P frame – if the total length of the data comprising a compressed frame is 8 bits, then this signals that the frame was coded as a non-coded P frame in an encoder. A key compression tool in WMV-9 is adaptive block size transform. Transform block size can change adaptively, while size of motion compensation is either 16x16 or 8x8 in WMV-9. Note that this is quite the opposite to that of H.264. H.264 normally uses fixed size 4x4 or 8x8 transforms with various adaptive prediction size of motion compensation. There are 4 transform sizes – 8x8, 4x8, 8x4 and 4x4. The transforms are 16 bit transform where both sums and products of two 16 bit values produce results within 16 bits – the inverse transform can be implemented in 16 bit fixed point arithmetic. Note that the transform approximates a DCT, and norms of basis function between transforms are identical to enable the same quantization scheme through various transform types [1]. There are three options for motion compensation:

1. Half-pel or quarter-pel resolution motion compensation can be used,
2. Bi-cubic or bi-linear filter can be used for the interpolation, and
3. 16x16 or 8x8 block size can be used.

These are all combined into a single motion compensation mode to be represented in the Frame level. There is a Sequence layer mode FASTUVMC for motion vector computation of Chroma components. If this is on, computed Chroma MVs are all rounded to half-pel. Thus, interpolation for quarter points is not necessary for Chroma data. Quantization is defined with two parameters, generally specified in video standards – (Qp, Dead-zone). There are two choices about Dead-zone in WMV-9 – 3Qp and 5Qp.

There are two levels where this can be described:

1. Sequence header has QUANT field for this description – 3Qp or 5Qp for entire sequence.
2. Explicit option writes in each Picture header, or Implicit option is to describe it through PQindex.

In I frames, PQAUNT is applied to entire MBs. However, DQUANT is used to adaptively describe Qp in each MB in P/B frames. There are other options to use only two Qps for an entire frame depending on either boundary MB or non-boundary MB, too. There two techniques used in WMV-9 to reduce blocky effect around transform boundary –

Overlapped Transform (OLT) smoothing and In Loop deblocking Filtering (ILF). OLT is a unique and interesting technique to reduce blocky effect based on a finely defined pre-/post-processing pair. The idea is that two forward and inverse operations are defined in such a way that original data are recovered perfectly when operations are serially applied (forward and inverse).

The forward transform is to exchange information around boundary edges in adjacent blocks. The forward operation is performed before main coding stage. Let's say one block preserves relatively good edge data, while the other block looses details of edge data. In this case, the blocky effect is so visible. In decoder side, inverse operation is required to exchange the edge data back again to original data. By doing so, good quality and bad quality edges diffuse each other. Therefore, looking of blocky effect is much lessened. On the other hand, ILF is more or less heuristic way to reduce blocky effect. Blocky pattern is considered high frequency since abrupt value changes occur around block edges.

Considering original data quality, relatively simple low pass filtering is applied about block edges in ILF. ILF is performed on reference frames I and P. Thus, the result of filtering effects quality of the next pictures that use ILFed frames as references. Entropy coding used in WMV-9 is a similar to Context-Adaptive VLC. Based on Qp, from which the original quality can be guessed, a new set of VLC tables is introduced. Such examples include Mid-rate VLC tables and High-rate VLC tables. In addition, based on MVs, another set of VLC tables is introduced. Such examples include Low-motion DC differential tables and High-motion DC differential tables.

WMV-9 Video Specific Semantics and Syntax

There are 5 levels of headers inWMV-9 video bitstream syntax – Sequence, Picture, Slice (not clearly defined in WMV-9), MB and Block. Sequence header contains basic parameters such as profile, interlace, frame rate, bit rate, loop filter, overlap filter and some other global parameters. Picture header contains information about type of picture/ BFraction/ PQindex/LumScale /LumShift/ DQUANT related/ TTMBF/ TTFRM/ DCTACMBF/ DCTACFRM, etc. BFraction data is relative temporal position of B that is factored into the computation of direct mode vectors. Note that this can be overridden with a value that has nothing to do with geometrical position. PQindex is interpreted for QS and quantizer types (3QP/5QP) in Implicit case, while quantizer types are explicitly defined in Sequence or Picture header in other cases. LumScale/LumShift are Intensity Compensation parameters. TTMBF is the flag that tells whether additional field for Transform Type is in MB level or Frame level. DCTACMBF is the flag that tells whether DCT AC Huffman table is defined in MB level or Frame level. Slice is not defined clearly in WMV-9. When STARTCODE is set in the Sequence header however, Slice header can be defined in long startcode to provide a mechanism for synchronization. MB header contains SkipMBbit/ MVmodebit (1MV/4MV option)/ MVDATA/ TTMB, etc. MVDATA tells whether the blocks are coded as Intra or Inter type. If they are coded as Inter, then MVDATA indicates MV differentials. Block layer contains all transform coefficients related data. Sub-block pattern data is included to sub-divide the block.

See: Video Coding Techniques and Standards

References

1. S. Srinivassan, P. Hsu, T Holcomb, K. Mukerjee, S. Regunathan, B. Lin, J. Liang, M.-C. Lee, and J. Ribas-Corbera, "WMV-9: Overview and Applications," Signal Processing Image Communication, October 2004, pp. 851-875.

WORKFLOW COMPUTING

Definition: Workflow Management Systems (WfMS) have been defined as "technology based systems that define, manage, and execute workflow processes through the execution of software whose order of execution is driven by a computer representation of the workflow process logic" [1].

This limits the usability of WfMS in a world where constant adaptation to new situations is necessary and where teams are increasingly mobile and distributed. Workflow management systems are typically organizationally aware because they contain an explicit representation of organizational processes. In recent years there have been considerable attempts to merge workflow, groupware, and knowledge management technologies. Industrial research labs and product teams have made significant steps forward. A WfMS can impose a rigid work environment on users, which often has a consequence. One example is among users who perform time-consuming manual "work around"; the consequence is lower efficiency and dissatisfaction with the system.

Workflow automation provides unique opportunities for enabling and tracking information flow as well as monitoring of work performance. As a consequence, WfMS enable continuous loops of sub processes such as goal setting, working, monitoring the work, measuring performance, recording and analyzing the outputs and evaluating the "productivity" of personnel. Users of WfMS often consider the controlling and monitoring possibilities as a "dark side" of these systems, which results in demotivating employees. A business process has well defined inputs and outputs and serves a meaningful purpose either inside or between organizations. Business processes and their corresponding workflows exist as logical models. When business process models are executed they have specific instances. When instantiated, the whole workflow is called a work case.

The WfMS enacts the real world business process for each process instance. A business process consists of a sequence of activities. An activity is a distinct process step and may be performed either by a human agent or by a machine. Any activity may consist of one or more tasks. A set of tasks to be worked on by a user (human agent or machine) is called work list. The work list itself is managed by the WfMS. The WfMC calls the individual task on the work list work item. To summarize, a workflow is the instantiated (enacted or executed) business process, either in whole or in parts. During enactment of a business process, documents, which are associated to tasks, are passed from one task participant to another. In most cases this passing of documents or executing applications is performed according to a set of rules. A WfMS is responsible for control and coordination such as instantiating the workflow, assigning human or non-human agents to perform activities, generating worklists for individuals, and routing tasks and their associated objects such as documents between the agents. For an in-depth analysis of

Workflow computing we refer to [2] and for a discussion of the hybrid systems integrating Workflow and Groupware Computing we refer to [3].

See: Collaborative Computing – Area Overview

References

1. Workflow Management Coalition (WfMC), Workflow Management Specification Glossary, http://www.wfmc.org.
2. D. Georgakopoulos, M. Hornick, and A. Sheth, "An Overview of Workflow Management: From Process Modeling to Workflow Automation Infrastructure," Distributed and Parallel Databases, Vol. 3, pp. 119-153, 1995.
3. S. Dustdar, "Caramba - A Process-Aware Collaboration System Supporting Ad Hoc and Collaborative Processes in Virtual Teams, Distributed and Parallel Databases," Special Issue on Teamware Technologies, Kluwer Academic Publishers, Vol. 15, No. 1, pp. 45-66, January 2004.

INDEX